WARMAN'S
Americana
& Collectibles

5TH EDITION

Edited by HARRY L. RINKER

A Price Guide Devoted to Today's
Collectibles, with Collecting Hints •
Histories • References • Clubs •
Museums • Completely Illustrated

Wallace-Homestead Book Company
Radnor, Pennsylvania

Other Volumes in the Encyclopedia of Antiques and Collectibles

Harry L. Rinker, Series Editor

Warman's Americana & Collectibles, 5th Edition,
edited by Harry L. Rinker

Warman's English & Continental Pottery & Porcelain, 2nd Edition,
by Susan and Al Bagdade

Warman's Oriental Antiques,
by Gloria and Robert Mascarelli

ISBN: 0-87069-615-7
ISSN: 0739-6457
Library of Congress Catalog Card No.: 84-643834
Manufactured in the United States of America

1 2 3 4 5 6 7 8 9 0   0 9 8 7 6 5 4 3 2 1

Additional copies of this book may be obtained from your bookstore or directly from the publisher, Wallace-Homestead Book Company, Radnor, PA 19089. Enclose $14.95 plus $2.50 for postage and handling for the 1st book, 50¢ for each additional book. Pennsylvania residents please add 90¢ state sales tax per book.

iii

Ted Hake
Hake's Americana &
Collectibles
P. O. Box 1444
York, PA 17405
(717) 848-1333
Disneyana, Political Items

Doris & Burdell Hall
B & B Antiques
P. O. Box 1501
Fairfield Bay, AR 72088
(501) 884-6571
Morton Potteries

Mrs. Mary Hamburg
20 Cedar St.
Danville, IL 61832
(217) 446-2323
Pig Collectibles

Howard Herz
P. O. Box 1000
Minden, NE 89423
*Gambling Chips, Checks,
and Tokens*

Todd Holmes
12411 Wornall Road
Kansas City, MO 64145
(816) 941-3100
*Business and Office
Equipment, Typewriters*

Tim Hughes
Hughes'
P. O. Box 3636
Williamsport, PA 17701
(717) 326-1045
*Newspapers, Headline
Editions*

Joan Hull
1376 Nevada
Huron, SD 57350
(605) 352-1685
Hull Pottery

David and Sue Irons
Irons Antiques
R. D. #4, Box 101
Northampton, PA 18067
(215) 262-9335
Irons

Ron Lieberman
The Family Album
R. D. #1, Box 42
Glen Rock, PA 17327
(717) 235-2134
Books, Limited Editions Club

Joyce Magee
7219 Auld Road
Bradford, OH 45308
(513) 447-7134
Children's Books

Wray Martin
221 Upper Paradise
Hamilton, Ontario
Canada, L9C 5C1
(416) 383-0454
Matchcovers

Richard W. Massiglia
380 Medford St.
Somerville, MA 02145
(617) 625-4067
Elephant Collectibles

Patricia McDaniel
Old Storefront Antiques
P. O. Box 357
Dublin, IN 47335
(317) 478-4809
*Drugstore Collectibles,
Veterinary Collectibles*

Nancy McMichael
P. O. Box 53132
Washington, D. C., 20009
Snowdomes

Gary L. Miller and K. M. Scotty
Mitchell
Millchell
2112 Lipscomb
Ft. Worth, TX 76110
(817) 923-3274
Electrical Appliances

Joan Collett Oates
5912 Kingsfield Dr.
W. Bloomfield, MI 48322
(313) 661-2335
Phoenix Bird Pattern

Clark Phelps
Amusement Sales
127 North Main
Midvale, UT 84047
(801) 255-4731
Punchboards

Lois Pool
The National Button Society
2733 Juno Place
Akron, OH 44313
(216) 864-3296
Buttons

Ferill J. Rice
302 Pheasant Run
Kaukauna, WI 54130
Fenton

Harry L. Rinker
P. O. Box 248
Zionsville, PA 18092
(215) 965-1122
Canal Collectibles, Puzzles

Jim and Nancy Schaut
Box 10781
Glendale, AZ 85318
(602) 878-4293
Horse Collectibles

Virginia R. Scott
275 Milledge Terrace
Athens, GA 30606
(404) 548-5966
Candlewick

George Theofiles
Miscellaneous Man
Box 1776
New Freedom, PA 17349
(717) 235-4766
Posters

John Waldsmith
Antique Graphics
P. O. Box 191
Sycamore, OH 44882
(419) 927-2930
  Bookmarks, Stereo Viewers,
  Stereographs, Viewmasters

Kathy Wojciechowski
P. O. Box 230
Peotone, IL 60468
  Nippon

Estelle Zalkin
7524 West Treasure Dr.
Miami Beach, FL 33141
(305) 864-3012
  Thimbles

INTRODUCTION

Collectibles are the things with which your parents, you, and your children have played and lived. The things that belonged to your grandparents are now *antiques*. The evolution of an object from new to desirable to collectible to antique within one's lifetime, i.e., an approximate fifty year span, is difficult for some to accept. However, it is reality.

Warman's Americana & Collectibles takes you on a nostalgic trip down memory lane. Do not get angry about the things you or your parents discarded. Be thrilled by the value of the things that were saved. Do not hesitate to buy back the things from your childhood that evoke pleasant memories. As you do, you will find that the real value of objects is not monetary, but the joy that comes from collecting, owning, and, most importantly, playing and living with them once again.

Finally, do not ever be embarrassed by what you collect. *Warman's Americana & Collectibles* is based on the premise that it is acceptable to collect anything you wish. Remember one simple fact. All of today's antiques were collectibles in the past.

WHAT IS A COLLECTIBLE?

Of the several books in the collectibles field, none offers a strong definition of the word "collectibles." The result is confusion, blurring the distinction between antiques and collectibles.

For the purpose of this book, three criteria were established to define the word "collectible." The item must have been (1) mass produced, (2) made in the twentieth century, preferably after 1945, and (3) the majority of the items in each category must sell for between a few pennies and two hundred dollars. The ideal collectible fits all three qualifications.

There is a fourth factor: attitude. I collect things relating to the American canal movement. As a result, I own a number of pieces of dark blue English Staffordshire which were made when the Erie Canal was completed in the mid–1820s. Staffordshire of this type is considered a blue chip antique, but I collect it primarily for its "canal related" value. Does this make it a collectible rather than an antique? In my eyes and mind it does.

Since collecting antiques became fashionable in the early twentieth century, there have been attempts to define certain groups of objects as "true" antiques, worthy of sophisticated collectors, and to ignore the remaining items. Most museums clearly demonstrate this attitude. Where do early twentieth century tin toys, toy soldiers, or dolls fit? We designate them as "prestige" collectibles, objects making the transition in people's minds from collectible to antique.

In reality these divisions are artificial and deserve to be broken down. Today's Star Wars items, if properly preserved, will someday be over one hundred years old. They may be a much better key to interpreting life in the twentieth century than the Knoll furniture now found on pedestals in leading museums in the United States.

In summary, your grandparents' things are antiques and your parents' objects are in transition—a few already in the antiques category, about one–third classified as prestige collectibles, and the remainder still collectibles.

INTERNATIONAL MARKET

Collectibles began to draw worldwide interest at the end of the 1980s. All of a sudden American buyers found themselves competing with buyers from Europe and Japan on their home turf. In head to head competition, the American buyers frequently lost. How can this be explained?

The most dominant portion of the 1990s collectibles market is post–World War II material. During this period, the youth of the world fell under three dominant influences—American movies, music, and television. As the children of the 1950s, 1960s, and even 1970s reach adulthood, they start buying back their childhood. Many of the things they remember and want have American associations.

America is the great motherlode of post–war collectibles. At the moment, packages and boxes of American collectibles are being sent abroad. It will not be too much longer before the volume reaches container loads.

American collectors also are expanding their horizons. They recognize that many objects within their favorite collectible category were licensed abroad. They view their collections as incomplete without such examples. Objects are obtained by either traveling abroad or by purchasing through mail or auction from foreign sources.

PRICE NOTES

Prices in the collectibles field are not as firmly established as in the antiques area. Nevertheless, we do not use ranges unless we feel they are absolutely necessary.

Our pricing is based on an object being in very good condition. If otherwise, we note this in our description. It would be ideal to suggest that mint, or unused, examples of all objects do exist. Objects from the past were used, whether they be glass, china, dolls, or toys. Because of this use, some normal wear must be expected. Furthermore, if the original box is important in establishing a price, it is assumed that the box is present with the article.

The biggest problem in the collectibles field is that an object may have more than one price. A George Eastman bubble gum card may be worth one dollar to a bubble gum card collector, but thirty-five dollars to a collector of photographic memorabilia. I saw the same card marked both ways. In preparing prices for this guide we have looked at the object within the category being considered. Hence, a "girly" matchcover sells for twenty-five to fifty cents to a matchcover collector and two to five dollars to a pin-up art collector. However, if all you can find are matchcover collectors, best take the quarter and move on.

Some collectibles do have regional interest. However, a national price consensus has formed as a result of the publication of specialized price guides, collectors' club newsletters, and magazines and newspapers. This guide also has contributed to breaking down regional pricing.

ORGANIZATION OF THE BOOK

Listings: We have attempted to make the listings descriptive enough so the specific object can be identified. Most guides limit their descriptions to one line, but not *Warman's*. We have placed emphasis on those items which are actively being sold in the marketplace. Nevertheless, some harder-to-find objects are included in order to demonstrate the market spread. A few categories in this book also appear in *Warman's Antiques and Their Prices*. The individual listings, however, seldom overlap except for a few minor instances. It is our intention to show the low to middle price range of a category in *Warman's Americana & Collectibles* and the middle to upper range in our main antiques guide, thus creating two true companion volumes for the general dealer or collector.

Collecting Hints: This section calls attention to specific hints as they relate to the category. We note where cross category collecting and nostalgia are critical in pricing. Clues are given to spotting reproductions. In most cases, we just scratch the surface. We encourage collectors to consult specialized publications.

History: Here we discuss the category, describe how the object was made, who are or were the leading manufacturers, and the variations of form and style. In many instances a chronology for the objects is established. Finally, we place the object in a social context— how it was used, for what purposes, etc.

References: A few general references are listed to encourage collectors to learn more about their objects. Included are author, title, most recent edition, publisher (if published by a small firm or individual, we have indicated "published by author"), and a date of publication.

Finding these books may present a problem. The antiques and collectibles field is blessed with a dedicated core of book dealers who stock these specialized publications. You may find them at flea markets, antiques shows, and through their advertisements in leading publications in the field. Many dealers publish annual or semi-annual catalogs. Ask to be put on their mailing lists. Books go out-of-print quickly, yet many books printed over twenty-five years ago remain the standard work in a field. Also, haunt used book dealers for collectible reference material.

Collectors' Clubs: The large number of collectors' clubs adds vitality to the collectibles field. Their publications and conventions produce knowledge which often cannot be found anywhere else. Many of these clubs are short lived; others are so strong that they have regional and local chapters.

Periodicals: In respect to the collectibles field, there are certain general monthly periodicals to which the general collector should subscribe:

Antiques & Collecting Hobbies, 1006 South Michigan Avenue, Chicago, IL 60605.
Collectors' Showcase, 7130 South Lewis, Suite 210, Tulsa, OK 74136.
The Inside Collector, P. O. Box 98, Elmont, NY 11003.

There are also a number of specialized collectible periodicals, e.g., *Antique Toy World* (P. O. Box 34509, Chicago, IL 60634). Special attention is directed toward the publications of Krause Publications, Inc., (700 East State Street, Iola, WI 54945), especially *Toy Shop*.

Although no weekly publication is devoted exclusively to collectibles, *The Antique Trader Weekly* (Box 1050, Dubuque, IA 52001) and *Antique Week* (P. O. Box 90, Knightstown, IN 46148) extensively cover the range of items listed in this book. Specialized auctions of prestige collectibles are regularly reported in depth in the *Maine Antique Digest* (Box 358, Waldoboro, ME 04572).

Museums: The best way to study a specific field is to see as many documented examples as possible. For this reason, we have listed museums where significant collections of collectibles are on display. Special attention must be directed to the Margaret Woodbury Strong Museum in Rochester, New York, and the Smithsonian Institution's Museum of American History in Washington, D.C.

Reproduction: Reproductions are a major concern, especially with any item related to advertising. Most reproductions are unmarked; the newness of their appearance is often the best clue to uncovering them. Where "Reproduction Alert" appears, a watchful eye should be kept within the entire category.

Reproductions are only one aspect of the problem; outright fakes are another. Unscrupulous manufacturers make fantasy items which never existed, e.g., Hopalong Cassidy guitar from the non–existent Jefferson Musical Toys.

RESEARCH

Collectors of the categories found in this book deserve credit for their attention to scholarship and the skill by which they have assembled their collections. This book attests to how strong and encompassing the collectibles market has become through their efforts.

We obtain our prices from many key sources—dealers, publications, auctions, collectors, and field work. The generosity with which dealers have given advice is a credit to the field. Everyone recognizes the need for a guide that is specific and has accurate prices. We study newspapers, magazines, newsletters, and other publications in the collectibles and antiques field. All of them are critical in understanding what is available in the market. Special recognition must be given to those collectors' club newsletters and magazines which discuss prices.

Our staff is constantly in the field—from Massachusetts to Florida, Pennsylvania to California. Our Board of Advisors provides regional as well as specialized information. Over one hundred specialized auctions are held annually, and their results are provided to our office. Finally, private collectors have worked closely with us, sharing their knowledge of price trends and developments unique to their specialties.

BUYER'S GUIDE, NOT SELLER'S GUIDE

Warman's Americana & Collectibles is designed to be a buyer's guide, a guide to what you would have to pay to purchase an object on the open market from a dealer or collector. **It is not a seller's guide to prices.** People frequently make this mistake and are deceiving themselves by doing so.

If you have an object in this book and wish to sell it, you should expect to receive approximately 35 to 40% of the value listed. If the object cannot be resold quickly, expect to receive even less. The truth is simple. Knowing whom to sell an object to is worth 50% or more of its value. Buyers are very specialized; dealers work for years to assemble a list of collectors who will pay top dollar for an item.

Examine your piece as objectively as possible. If it is something from your childhood, try to step back from the personal memories in evaluating its condition. As an antiques appraiser, I spend a great deal of my time telling people their treasures are not "gold," but items readily available in the marketplace.

In respect to buying and selling, a simple philosophy is that a good purchase occurs when both the buyer and seller are happy with the price. Don't look back. Hindsight has little value in the collectibles field. Given time, things tend to balance out.

WHERE TO BUY COLLECTIBLES

The collectible became standard auction house fare in the 1980s. Christie's East (219 East 67th Street, New York, NY 10021) and Sotheby's (1334 York Avenue, New York, NY 10021) conduct collectibles sales several times each year. Specialized auction firms, e.g., Lloyd Ralston Toys (447 Stratfield Road, Fairfield, CT 06432) in toys and Greenberg's (7566 Main Street, Sykesville, MD 21784) in trains, have proven the viability of the collectible as a focal point.

The major collectibles marketing thrust continues to be the mail auction, either with material on consignment or directly owned. Hake's Americana & Collectibles (P.O. Box 1444, York, PA 17405) is the leading mail auction. Hake's is being challenged by Debby and Marty Krim's New England Auction Gallery (P. O. Box 2273, Peabody, MA 01960), Smith House Toy Sales (P. O. Box 336, Eliot, ME 03903), and a host of others.

Direct sale catalogs abound. Most major categories have one or more. These dealers and many more advertise in periodicals and collectors' club newsletters. Most require an annual fee to receive their catalogs.

Of course, there is an unlimited number of flea markets, house and country auctions, church bazaars, and garage sales. However, if you are a specialized collector, you may spend days looking for something to add to your collection. If you add in your time to the cost of the object, its real cost will be much higher than the purchase price.

All of which brings us to the final source, the specialized dealer. The collectibles field is so broad that dealers do specialize. Find the dealers who handle your material and work with them to build your collection.

BOARD OF ADVISORS

Our Board of Advisors are dealers, authors, collectors and leaders of collectors' clubs from throughout the United States. All are dedicated to accuracy in description and pricing. If you wish to buy or sell an object in their field of expertise, drop them a note. Please include a stamped, self addressed envelope with all correspondence. If time or interest permits, they will respond.

We now list the names of our advisors at the end of their respective categories. Their full mailing address and often their phone numbers are in the front of this book.

COMMENTS INVITED

Warman's Americana & Collectibles is a major effort to deal with a complex field. Our readers are encouraged to send their comments and suggestions to Rinker Enterprises, P. O. Box 248, Zionsville, PA 18092.

ACKNOWLEDGMENTS

1991 has proven to be a landmark year. The publication in March of the twenty–fifth edition of *Warman's Antiques and Their Prices*, the first general price guide to reach twenty–fifth edition status, marked my tenth year as editor of this prestigious publication. In October Wallace–Homestead will publish *Price Guide To Flea Market Treasures*, by Harry Junior, my son. It is his first effort and hopefully not his last.

In February Rinker Enterprises, Inc., moved into the former Vera Cruz elementary school. Operating space increased tenfold and the staff doubled. The Warman's guides are now prepared from the largest private research and resource center for the study of antiques and collectibles in the United States.

However, the most important event of the year, as far as I am concerned, is the publication of this book. *Warman's Americana & Collectibles, Fifth Edition* means that a decade has passed since the first price guide devoted exclusively to the collectibles market was published. It has no rival. This says a great deal.

Warman's Americana & Collectibles introduced the Warman format to the trade. This format created a "user's" guide, not just a mere list of prices. The format eventually was expanded to *Warman's Antiques and Their Prices* and in the 1990s will serve as the model for a series to be known as Warman's Encyclopedia of Antiques and Collectibles.

None of the above would have been possible without YOU, the purchaser and user of this book. It is appropriate on our tenth anniversary to begin by expressing our sincere thanks for your support and encouragement. This book is what it is and contains what it does because of you.

Never, never should anyone assume that because my name is on the title page that I deserve all the credit. The heart of Rinker Enterprises, Inc., are the "Rinkettes," a staff dedicated to bringing you the most up–to–date and accurate reference and pricing information.

Ellen L. Schroy, Senior Editor, has been with me for ten years. It is high time she has her own book, and she will—a volume in the Warman's Encyclopedia of Antiques and Collectibles. Terese J. Oswald put aside a personal tragedy, the loss of her husband, to increase the scope and level of her commitment to this book. Dana M. Morykan brought a welcomed love of twentieth century collectibles to this project. A deep emersion into Country is her next assignment.

Ellen, Terese, Dana, and I would not be able to do our job without an excellent support staff. We take great delight in continuing to overwhelm Nancy M. Butt, our librarian, with assignments. Jocelyn C. Butterer deserves a medal for the amount of time she spends photocopying material for our research files. Diane Sterner checks galleys and sees that our financial picture remains bright.

Many on our Board of Advisors have been with us through all five editions. A special thank you to them. Others join us for the first time, in several cases with new category areas. We are delighted to welcome them aboard. Since no financial remuneration is provided for advisors, their willingness to provide the data is based on their desire to see that accurate information is made available about their favorite collecting category. We consider all our advisors very special people.

Supporting our efforts at Chilton Books, parent company of Wallace–Homestead and Warman, are Edna Jones and Troy Vozzella in production and a sales team directed by Neil Levin. Edna and Troy are as responsible as we for this book appearing on store shelves in October 1991. As a means of thanks, we plan to disconnect our telephones for two months following the submittal of this manuscript. As for Neil and his staff, we should warn them that we have learned first–hand what can be achieved by continual prodding. We plan to put this education to good use beginning this fall.

Finally, our best wishes to you for happy hunting and great collecting in the years ahead.

P. O. Box 248   Harry L. Rinker
Zionsville, PA 18092   Editor
                                                      October 1991

ADVERTISING

Collecting Hints: Many factors affect the price of an advertising collectible—the product and its manufacturer, the objects or persons used in the advertisement, the period and aesthetics of design, the designer and illustrator of the piece, and the form the advertisement takes. Add to this the continued use of advertising material as decorative elements in bars, restaurants, and other public places. The interior decorator purchases at a very different price level than the collector.

In truth, almost every advertising item is sought by a specialized collector in one or more collectible areas. The result is a divergence in pricing, with the price quoted to an advertising collector usually lower than that quoted to a specialized collector.

Most collectors seem to concentrate on the period prior to 1940, with special emphasis on the decades from 1880 to 1910. New collectors should examine the advertising material from the post–1940 period. Much of this material still is very inexpensive and likely to rise in value as the decorator trends associated with the 1950s through the 1970s gain in importance.

History: The earliest advertising in America is found in colonial newspapers and printed broadsides. By the mid–19th century manufacturers began to examine how a product was packaged. The box could convey a message and help identify and sell more of the product. The advent of the high speed, lithograph printing press led to regional and national magazines, resulting in new advertising markets. The lithograph press also brought the element of vivid colors into the advertising spectrum.

Simultaneously the general store branched out into specialized departments or individual stores. By 1880 advertising premiums, such as mirrors, paperweights, trade cards, etc., arrived on the scene. Premiums remained popular through the early 1960s, especially with children.

Advertising continues to respond to changing opportunities and times. The advertising character was developed in the early 1900s. By the 1950s the star endorser was established firmly as an advertising vehicle. Advertising became a big business as specialized firms, many headquartered in New York City, developed to meet manufacturers' needs.

References: Kit Barry, *The Advertising Trade Card: Information And Prices, Book I*, privately printed, 1981; Al Bergevin, *Drugstore Tins And Their Prices*, Wallace–Homestead, 1990; Al Bergevin, *Food Drink Containers And Their Prices*, Wallace–Homestead, 1978; Jim Cope, *Old Advertising*, Great American Publishing Co., 1980; M. J. Franklin, *British Biscuit Tins 1868-1939: An Aspect of Decorative Packaging*, Schiffer Publishing, 1979; Robert Jay, *The Trade Card In Nineteenth-Century America*, University of Missouri Press, 1987; Ray Klug, *Antique Advertising Encyclopedia*, Schiffer Publishing, Ltd, 1978, updated price guide; Ray Klug, *Antique Advertising Encyclopedia, First Edition*, Schiffer Publishing, Ltd, 1985; Ralph and Terry Kovel, *Kovels' Advertising Collectibles Price List*, Crown Publishers, Inc., 1986; L–W Promotions (ed.), *Antique Advertising Handbook and Price Guide*, L–W Book Sales, 1986; Murray Card (International) Ltd, *Cigarette Card Values: Murray's 1990 Guide to Cigarette & Other Trade Cards* published by authors, 1990; Joleen Robison and Kay Sellers, *Advertising Dolls: Identification and Value Guide*, Collector Books, 1980; Robert W. and Harriet Swedberg, *Vintage Advertising Series, Tins N' Bins*, Wallace–Homestead, 1985.

Collectors' Clubs: Antique Advertising Association, P.O. Box 1121, Morton Grove, IL 60053; The Ephemera Society of America, P. O. Box 37, Schoharie, NY 12157; Tin Container Collectors Association, P. O. Box 440101, Aurora, CA 80014.

Periodicals: National Association of Paper and Advertising Collectibles, *P.A.C.*, P.O. Box 500, Mt Joy, PA 17552; *PCM (Paper Collectors' Marketplace)*, P.O. Box 128, Scandinavia, WI 54977.

REPRODUCTION ALERT

Ashtray, Ernest A Brey, Quality Meats, Spinnerstown, PA, 1955, round bakelite base, $5.00.

ASHTRAY

Armstrong Tire, rubber	18.00
Chrysler Corp, 7½", brass, metal figure center, inscribed "Master Technician Service Conference/Awarded by Chrysler Corp/9 Year Award," engraved recipient's name, 1940–50	75.00
Cliff House, San Francisco, shell, litho	15.00
Fisk Tire, cast metal, boy with candle	24.00
Gallagers Honey Dew Tobacco	22.00
General Electric Motor	15.00
Howard Iron Works, metal	15.00
Kelly Heavy Duty Tire, glass, tire shape	25.00

Kentucky Colonel	8.00
LaMinerva Cigars, goddess	12.00
Luchow's Restaurant Since 1882, blue and white, stein in center	20.00
Mountain States Telephone & Telegraph, granite	85.00
Napril Laboratory, Kansas City, MO	5.00
Oakland/Pontiac	35.00
Old Judge Coffee, tin	90.00
Penn Rubber Co, tire shape	12.00
Quorum Club of Texas, 9" d	8.00
Richland Snack Bar, tin	5.00
Season's Catch, Colonial Premier Co, Chicago, baseball mitt, metal	30.00
Seiberling Tire, Market St, Williamsport, PA	18.00
Smith's General Store, Birdseye, IN, tin	4.00
Winston Cigarettes, tin	4.00
Yellow Cab, molded ceramic, 1940s cab	30.00

Candy, Goff's Atlantic City Salt Water Taffy, blue tones, woman in orange swimsuit, 8⅞ x 4⅞ x 2½", $7.50.

BOXES

Baums Horse and Stock Food, wood	125.00
Bee Soap, wood, paper label	65.00
Brach's Candy, cardboard	40.00
Bulldog Tobacco, wood, hinged lid, dog on front and back	70.00
Castile Soap, 7¼" x 3½" x 1", Oletyme Products, Indianapolis, IN, pictures castle, "Made in Accordance with the Fair Labor Standards Act of 1933," three bars	7.00
Castoria, 5¼" x 1" x 2", colorful baby head, 2 oz bottle, Purepac Corp, NY, NY	6.00
Colgate Fab, sample size, crashing sea scene	8.00
Cupples "Topseal" Jar Rings, full	3.00
DeLong Hair Pins, 3½" x 2½" x ⅝", red flowers, blue ground, includes hair pins	4.00
Diamond Union Suit	15.00
Dr Hobson's Ox Marrow Pomade, 3½" x 2" x 2", 1923, includes jar dated 1921, picture of lady on label and box	15.00

El Vampiro Bellow, 3¾" x 2¾" x ¾", bug killer, Allaire Woodard & Co, Peoria, IL, dated June 15, 1918	12.00
Fairbanks Gold Dust Washing Powder, 32" x 16" x 8", wood, paper label one end	200.00
Fairbanks Santa Claus Soap, wood, paper label one end	150.00
Fine Shoes, lithographed	50.00
Gay Times Soft Drink, children scene	20.00
Hershey's Mild and Mellow, 1¢	12.00
Hungerford's Dark Cocoa, wood	15.00
Jackson Fly Killer, display, wood	24.00
La Florita Face Powder, blue with basket of flower dec, logo, unopened, 1920s	15.00
Lenox Soap, wood, paper label	65.00
Log Cabin Syrup, shipping crate, wooden, dovetail, rope handles, cabin graphics both ends	145.00
Lydia E Pinkham's Pills for Constipation, 2½" x 1¼" x 1¼", signature on side, includes bottle and pills	10.00
Lyon Tobacco, women sorting tobacco, 1870s	95.00
Melbaline Face Powder, 3⅜" x 3⅜" x 1", lavender, gold, and purple	8.00
Nabisco, tin hinged lid	30.00
Quaker Oats, 26" x 18" x 11", wood	65.00
Parker Snuff, broken cannon on front	100.00
Reese Cigars, wood	20.00
Salome Perfumed Cigarette	20.00
Shuwhite Cream, wood	35.00
Union Biscuit	20.00
Wood's Improved Lollacapop, 3¼" l, 1¾" w, ¾" h, tin, "1 of the World's Greatest Known Antidotes for Mosquitoes, Black Flies & Gnats", picture of bugs on top	9.00

Brochure, Gold Dust, Brite Spots, yellow ground, black lettering, 3⅞ x 6", 16 pgs, $25.00.

BROCHURE

Butternut Bread, sailor boy illus 10.00
Cadillac, 1966 .... 25.00
Champion Harvesting Machine, 6 x 9",
  12 pgs, black and white illus, c1882 35.00
Cottolene, "The Evolution of an Apple
  Pie," 1898 .... 28.00
Cracker Jack, "Village Baseball Team,"
  1920s 42.00
Cushman Scooter Co, 6" x 3⅜", multi-
  color, Truckster, 24 pgs, 1955 ..... 5.00
Gentleman Beer, hunting and trapping
  manual, 1947 .... 28.00
Independent Motor Truck, Davenport,
  IA, c1920 .... 8.00
Jell–O Girl Entertains, nine O'Neill il-
  lustrations 38.00
Madame Alexander, Little Women, sto-
  rybook doll 10.00
Merry–Go–Round, Health Co, 1906, 50
  pgs 75.00
Metropolitan Life Insurance, "The Met-
  ropolitan Mother Goose," color illus-
  trations, c1920s 25.00
New England Mincemeat, "Fairie Pie,"
  pie–shaped 35.00
None Such Mincemeat, "Little Rhymes
  for Little People" 25.00
Pantasote, leather substitute, National
  Export Expo, Philladelphia, 1899 ... 40.00
Quaker Oats Nursery Rhymes 10.00
Smith and Wesson, seven shooter de-
  scription, mid 19th C 15.00
Wallpapers for Home Decor, c1930 .. 8.00
White Mountain Ice Cream, woman
  making ice cream 25.00
Woolworth, 60th Anniversary, 1939,
  multicolored merchandise photos ... 22.00

BUTTONS

A & P, green holly, red bow, c1930 ... 6.00
Bell Telephone
  7/8" d
    Blue and white rotary telephone
    dial, center inscribed "I'm For
    Automatic," issued by Auto Elec
    Co, early 1900s 18.00
    Red and white, "Soldiers and Sail-
    ors' Comfort Club," candlestick
    telephone with crossed military
    rifles, issued by Hawthorne
    Works of Western Electric, c1920 20.00
    Red, white, and blue Independent
    Telephone logo on light blue
    ground, "Central Telephone &
    Electric Co, The Up-To-Date
    Telephone Company," early
    1900s 12.00

Pinback button, The Sharples Co, Tubular Cream Separator, white ground, blue dress, red machinery, 1¼" d, $24.00.

1" d
  Blue and white, "Have You Called
  Home To-Day?," c1920 .... 10.00
  Red, white, and blue, "Federal
  Telephone," shield logo, early
  1900s 18.00
  Bell System, 1" d, blue and white,
  Bell System logo, American Tele-
  phone & Telegraph Co and As-
  sociated Companies rim inscrip-
  tion, 1920–1930s 40.00
Berry Brothers Varnishes, ⅞" d, colorful
  varnish canister on white ground,
  black rim lettering, late 1890s–early
  1900s 38.00
Black Cat Stockings, black cat, yellow
  neck bow, early 1900s 12.00
Buster Brown Bread, 1½" d, multicolor,
  red lettering on yellow rim, early
  1900s 25.00
Cattaraugus Cutlery Co, oval, Indian
  Chief, 1901–12 .... 8.00
Ceresota Flour, 1¼" d, multicolor, trademark child illus, black lettering on
  rim, 1900–1912 .... 35.00
Columbus Mutual Life Insurance Co, ⅝"
  d, blue, gold, black, and white, portrait illus of Christopher Columbus,
  1900–1912 .... 15.00
Davis Sewing Machine Co, ⅝" d, black,
  white, and red, "Davis Made," early
  1900s 15.00
Dutch Boy Paints, ⅞" d, multicolor,
  early 1900s 35.00
Dyas–Cline Sporting Goods Co, oval,
  football, c1910 .... 6.00
Frigidaire, ¹³⁄₁₆" d, red, white, and blue,

litho, "Hats Off to the New Frigidaire," 1940s 15.00

Gold Coin Stoves & Ranges, 7/8" d, black and white illus of cast iron stove on white ground, red lettering, late 1890s 28.00

Gold Dust Washing Powder, 1¼" d, multicolor, Black twins in tub of white suds, US flags, "The Best Flag, The Best Cleanser, You Can't Beat Them!", late 1890s 75.00

Gordon Hats, 7/8" d, multicolor, company logo crest, red lettering on white rim, "Do You Wear the Gordon Hat" 12.00

Hatchet Brand Canned Goods, 1¼" d, multicolor, 1897 .... 14.00

Horlick's Malted Milk, 1¼" d, multicolor, 1900–1912 .... 30.00

Hush Puppy Shoes, 1½" d, red, white, and blue, litho, "The People's Choice," 1960s–1970s 12.00

Kodak Box Camera, 7/8" d, multicolor, hand holding camera, "You Press The Button, We Do The Rest," late 1890s 40.00

Koveralls, 7/8" d, black, white, and red, two mules pulling on pair of work pants, 1907–1920 .... 15.00

Mennen's, 7/8" d, baby's face, c1915 .... 20.00

Mullen & Blueh Clothing Co, Los Angeles, CA, 1920 .... 10.00

Nabisco, "Golden Anniversary", 1¼" d, multicolor, child illus, red lettering, 1948 .... 30.00

Old Dutch Cleanser, 1¼", Dutch girl, c1930 .... 12.00

Peters Shells, celluloid, white ground . 25.00

Prudential Insurance Co, celluloid, purple lettering, Whitehead & Hoag Co 10.00

Red Seal Lye, 7/8" d, multicolor, lye canister on white ground, blue inscriptions, 1900–1912 .... 45.00

Schaeffer Pianos, 7/8" d, multicolor, brown upright piano, musical symbols, "Best in the West," 1901–1912 18.00

South Bend Watch Co, 7/8" d, multicolor, pocketwatch encased in block of ice, dark blue ground, white rim lettering, 1907–1920 .... 20.00

St Charles Evaporated Cream, 1¼", cow, c1930 .... 12.00

Star Kist Tuna, 1½" d, "Charlie for President," red, white, and blue, litho, Charlie Tuna holding top hat, 1960s 25.00

Studebaker, 7/8" d, litho, red and white, late 1930s–early 1940s 30.00

Tess and Ted School Shoes, ¾" d, multicolor, girl and boy in fancy clothes, early 1900s 40.00

Underwood Typewriter, 7/8" d, black, white, and red, typewriter illus, early 1900s 10.00

Volkswagen, 1⅜" d, blue and white,

litho, logo and "Bug Me" slogan, 1960s 15.00

William Tell Flour, 1¼" d, multicolor, 1900–1912 .... 60.00

Winchester Cartridges, 7/8" d, black, white, and red, "Always Shoot Winchester Cartridges," c1900–1912 ... 22.00

Wool Soap, 7/8" d, blue and white illus, two children comparing night shirts, ad text on back paper, late 1890s .. 20.00

Worcester Salt, 1¼" d, black and white, steam train and salt bag illus, "Sept 1904" 12.50

Zenith Radios, 7/8" d, blue, white, and orange, c1912–1920s 15.00

MIRRORS

AETNA Insurance, OK 30.00

Angelus Marshmallows, pocket 95.00

Beyerle Jeweler, Reading, PA, sepia, birthstone rim 20.00

Bruce McDonald Footwear, Montpelier, VT, tinted building scene 55.00

Central Storage, MO, 3½", colorful buildings 30.00

Copper Clad Stoves 40.00

Duffy's Malt Whiskey, pocket 45.00

Foot-Schulze-Glove, 2¾" oval, multicolored illus of rural scene, large center billboard of rubbers and arctics footwear, early 1900s 60.00

Fort Pitt Beer, metal frame 65.00

Franklin Mills Co, 2⅛", multicolored illus of Lockport, NY, factory, the "Home of Wheatlet & Franklin Flour," inscribed "All The Wheat That's Fit To Eat," early 1900s 85.00

Friend Sprayer, horse drawn foliage sprayer, c1920 .... 20.00

Good Friends Whiskey, Pilgrim and Indian shaking hands 125.00

Grapette, thermometer 40.00

Haines, 2⅛", blue and white, photo portrait of Mahlon Haines, company founder, "The Shoe Wizard," pocket, c1930s 40.00

Horlick's, pocket 55.00

Kapp's Dry Goods 15.00

Lily White Flour, two children baking . 75.00

Lodge Convention, 2¾" oval, full color illus of modern lodge building titled "Jerusalem," another building titled "Damascus," inscribed "To Rochester 1911," route passes through pyramids, tiny individuals on camels in foreground 75.00

Maryland Casualty 22.00

Missouri and Kansas Telephone Co of Bell System and American Telephone & Telegraph, 2½" l, pocket, blue and white, celluloid, early 1900s 65.00

Morton Salt, pocket 60.00

New King Snuff, 1¾ x 2¾", multicolored illus of tobacco snuff jar, inscribed "Scotch-King," bright white ground 65.00

Nutrine Candies, hand, celluloid 38.00

Pacific Coast Lumber, Seattle, 3½" l .. 16.00

Penn's Store, pocket 50.00

Queen Quality Shoes, celluloid, oval, beautiful lady 45.00

Seiver Tire & Battery, Aledo, IL, 21" x 13", 1943 calendar, Abe Lincoln ... 75.00

Shoe Worker's Union, c1910 .... 38.00

Socony Motor Gasoline 35.00

Sylvan Lake–Black Hills, photo, c1930 8.00

Texas Centennial, blue, pocket, 1936 . 45.00

The Great Majestic, The Modern Range, 2⅛" h, multicolored illus of 1900s housewife using cast iron stove 80.00

The MacCabees, pocket 45.00

Travelers Insurance Train, oval 80.00

Victor Artists, 2¼" h, black and white photo portraits of eight recording stars, c1920, minor wear to mirror silvering 65.00

Weingarten 5 cent cigars 35.00

Wheeler Publishing, Chicago, dog and cat 50.00

White Cat Union Suits, 2¾" oval, black and white, cartoon illus of white cat with black bow tie, pocket, early 1900s 70.00

Wholesale Lumber, 1¾" celluloid, Columbus, OH dealership, red design and inscription, white ground 45.00

Worth Blend Coffee, Vinnedge Co, "For Fine Hotels, Cafes & Dining Cars," pocket 55.00

MISCELLANEOUS

Badge, Kelloggs Chuck Wagon Champs, cowboy on star 10.00

Bag, paper

Black Draught Family Laxative, 4¼" x 8¼", brown, pictures people looking up at tall black and yellow box 4.00

Schoenfled Herb Tea, 4¼" x 7", red, black, and blue, pictures box of tea 5.00

Baking Tray, Calumet, 7" x 11" 10.00

Bank

Amoco 586 Oil 15.00

Rival Dog Food 10.00

Wolf's Head Oil, can shape 16.00

Banner, Federal Tires, 28 x 11", felt, early 1900s 40.00

Baseball Bat, Weatherbird Shoes 35.00

Beanie, Blue Horse School Goods, felt 10.00

Beach Bag, Maxwell House Coffee, figural, coffee can 25.00

Belt Buckle, Stroh's Beer 5.00

Bill Holder, Walker's Austex Products, wall mount 30.00

Blotter, Sunoco, bride and groom Mickey and Minnie in convertible .. 25.00

Book, Spring Song Seeds, diecut, frog shape, 14" 125.00

Bookmark

Old Gold Cigarettes, plastic 20.00

Poole Piano, celluloid 15.00

Bottle

Absorbine Jr, .47 oz introductory size, WF Young, Inc, Springfield, MA, 3¾" x 1¼" x 1¼" orig box 5.00

Add'e Mineral Oil, 10" h, 1 qt, Add'e Co, Baltimore, MD, picture of lady 15.00

Bissel's Bitters, amber, Peoria, 1868 65.00

Gold Medal Blackberry Root compound, 2 oz, S Pfeiffer, St Louis, 6" x 2⅛" x 1¼" orig box 5.00

Hydrogen Peroxide, 5" h, brown, cork stopper, aluminum cap, Columbus Wholesale Drug Co, Columbus, MS 4.00

Layman's Castor Oil, 1½ oz, 4¾" h, World Products, Spencer, IN 6.00

Snyder's Antiseptic Oil, 2 oz, 5½" h, Snyders Drug Co, Jonesboro, AR . 4.00

Teel Liquid Dentrifice, 1¼ oz, Proctor & Gamble, Cincinnati, OH, 1⅞" x 4" x 1⅞" orig box, 1945 .... 15.00

Bottle Opener

Burke's Guinness, cast iron 12.00

Coke 10.00

Coke/Sprite, boy, MIB 35.00

"Drink Dr Brown's Celery Tonic" .. 20.00

Prior Beer 8.00

White Rock 11.00

Broom Rack, Blu–Jay, holds twelve brooms 375.00

Brush, Ike Simon Clothing Store, Bradford, PA 13.00

Bucket, Heinz, wood, mincemeat, lid . 110.00

Buttonhook, Johnson & Conde Clothiers, Ballston Spa, NY 12.00

Cabinet, Fairy Dye 125.00

Cake Pan, Swansdown, angel food ... 20.00

Calendar, Franco American, miniature, 1903 .... 15.00

Can Opener, Pet Milk 10.00

Cane, wood, Osborne Farm Implements 28.00

Change pad, 8" d, felt, "Learn to Say Mi Lola" 12.00

Charm

Bull Durham, figural, bull, gold plated, c1910s 20.00

Ideal Dog Food 8.00

Chart, handwriting analysis, Folger's Coffee 10.00

Children's Book, miniature, Loeser Dept Store, set of 4 .... 22.00

Clamp, Trubyte Teeth, brass 28.00

Clipboard, Liverpool, London & Globe Insurance Co, 1936 100th Anniversary, bronze, adjustable, 9 x 6" **35.00**

Clock

B L Johnson & Co Mfg Confectioners, regulator **995.00**

G W Bishop Drugs & Jewelry, regulator **995.00**

J Stern & Son Clothiers, Baird **2,900.00**

Merrick Spool Cotton **895.00**

Mountain Dew **50.00**

Non Such Mincemeat **850.00**

Orange Crush, regulator **1,095.00**

Reed's Tonic **1,395.00**

Vermont Household Remedies **1,095.00**

Clothing Bag, 28½" x 60", wood grain color, metal hanger, pictures woman spraying clothes, giveaway from Flit moth spray **4.00**

Coal Shovel Hanger, Providence Gas Co, tin, MIB **60.00**

Coffee Cup, Mobilgas, Flying Red Horse **20.00**

Coin, Whitehead & Hoag Metal Advertising Novelties, 1¼" d, brass, emb, donkey's head and inscription on front, donkey's rear end and inscription on reverse, early 1900s **20.00**

Coloring Book Set, Bird's Eye, includes crayons, General Foods premium mailer **25.00**

Cookbook

Jell-O, box on train tracks **10.00**

Prudential, teddy bears seated at table, 1910, sgd "W Meyer" **18.00**

Counter Card, National Oats, diecut, girl carrying basket with product, c1900 .... **40.00**

Cup

Fisk Bicycle Club, tin **12.00**

National Oats, collapsible **25.00**

Patton's Sun-proof Paints, aluminum, collapsible **20.00**

Vin Fiz **7.00**

Worcester Salt **7.00**

Cutter, Ladyfinger, tin **5.00**

Date Book, Seeburg Juke Box, emb juke box cover, 1955 .... **14.00**

Demitasse Spoon, Heinz, engraved building in bowl, pickle on handle . **20.00**

Dispenser

Black Draught, 24" x 2¾" x 1⅝", porcelain, white **70.00**

T-Lax, 19½" x 1⅝" x 1¼", tin, "10¢," black and yellow **40.00**

Dispenser Rack, Magic Yeast, wall mount **120.00**

Display

Barton's Dyanshine Shoe Polish, carton, holds 12 flat, round tins **25.00**

Beech-Nut/Beechies, rack, metal, two shelf **20.00**

Calumet, cardboard, fold out **15.00**

Campbell's Soup, rack, metal, 18 x 22 x 5", 1930-40 .... **75.00**

Cosmic Diamond Rings, Santa on mica, 8 x 11" platform **40.00**

Monarch Teenie Weenie Sweet Pickles, oak keg on stand, 1920s **155.00**

Oscar Mayer Weiner Mobile, friction, Little Oscar bobs up **155.00**

Prim Genuine Briar Pipes, card, man's head at top smoking pipe, includes eight of orig twelve pipes, c1950 .... **30.00**

Red Wing Grape Juice, cardboard, bottles, two children drinking through straws **90.00**

Shelby Razor Blade, card, 9" x 12½", 20 pkgs, 1940s **18.00**

Doll

Levi, denim **32.00**

Miss Tastee Freez, 1960s **40.00**

Door Push

Cresent Flour, tin, bag of flour **85.00**

Duke's Mixture, porcelain **115.00**

Doorstop, John Deere, 10¼" w, 13" h . **45.00**

Egg Cup, NJ Bell Telephone, Lenox China **65.00**

Fan

Bissell's 'Cyco' Bearing Carpet Sweeper, folding **20.00**

Coca-Cola, 1940s **50.00**

Four Roses Whiskey **15.00**

Figure

Crayola Crayon Bear, 3", red **25.00**

Kessler, 13", chalkware, baseball player **50.00**

M&M Man, green **22.00**

Oreo Cookie, bendable **12.00**

Flipping Coin, Bull Durham **15.00**

Flyswatter, wire, 1900s **16.00**

Fork, Wesson Veg-eat-eer **18.00**

Fruit Jar, Miller's Fine Flavors, ½ gal, emb flies **48.00**

Game, Bixbys Royal Polish, cardboard, "Swarm of Bees" **40.00**

Hand, Whistle Soda Pop, 3½" x 10½", cast iron, attaches to post **295.00**

Hat, Ehler's Grade 'A' Ceylon Tea, red, white, and blue **20.00**

Honing Stone, pocket size

Cudahy's Blue Ribbon Meat Meal, pictures pig **35.00**

Goodyear Rubber Glove Co **45.00**

Inflatable Salesman, Esso, 2' h, 1950s . **95.00**

Ink Bottle, Carter's **65.00**

Inkwell, Rochester Spring Co **75.00**

Jar

Baker's Chocolate, metal lid, emb figure of lady **110.00**

DeWitt's Vaporizing Balm, 1½ oz, EC DeWitt & Co, Chicago, IL, 2⅜" x 2¼" x 2¼" orig box **8.00**

Dr Thatcher's Magic Rub, 2 oz, Allied

Drug Products Co, Chattanooga, TN, 2¼" x 2¼" x 2¼" orig box ... **5.00**

Golden Peacock Cream, 3 oz, dress tonic for hair, milk glass, lavender lid, gold label **8.00**

Horlicks, 104 oz **18.00**

Menthocol Expectorant, milk glass jar and screw on lid, "Yozo Co, Chattanooga, TN" on bottom, 3⅛" x 3⅛" x 3" orig box, 1921 .... **15.00**

National Biscuit Co, store, 1900s ... **135.00**

Ruckers–Mutton Suet Salve, 1½ oz, Allied Drug, Chattanooga, TN, 2⅞" x 1⅞" x 1⅞" orig box **5.00**

Wan–eta Cocoa, qt, amber **35.00**

Tuxedo Tobacco, 1910 stamp **95.00**

Vaseline Pomade Hair Dressing, 1¾ oz, color label, flowers, orig box, Chesebrough Mfg Co, Cons'd, NY, NY **8.00**

Jigsaw Puzzle

Gold Medal Flour, set of 3, U S Map, Presidents, and historical places, orig mailing envelope **35.00**

Tiptop Bread, set of 2, patriotic scenes **45.00**

Knife, "Apply Antiphlogistine Warm & Thick," aluminum **12.00**

Knob, Piels Beer, bakelite **55.00**

Lapel Pin, Life Boy Soap, diecut sailor **10.00**

Lard Bucket, Sunnyfield, 4 lbs **28.00**

Letter Opener

Fuller Brushman **6.50**

Pacific Mutual **25.00**

Victor Chemical Works, Chicago, baking powder materials **35.00**

Letterhead, Knox, black boy **10.00**

Lunch Box, Cracker Jack **35.00**

Lunch Pail, Pedro Tobacco **50.00**

Magazine Ad, Cream of Wheat, heavy paper, "Old King Cole with Rastus," color, 1902 .... **30.00**

Marble Bag, Weather–Bird Shoes, includes marbles **20.00**

Match Dispenser, Dr Pepper, 1930s ... **65.00**

Match Holder, Ceresota Flour **225.00**

Matchbook Cover

Ford Motor Co, Edsel **20.00**

Topps 1¢ Gum **20.00**

Matchsafe

"The Adjustment Co of NY Insurance Losses Adjusted," pocket size **25.00**

Bradley's Excel Phosphate, cast iron, orig paint **65.00**

Browning Pistol **45.00**

Dr Shoop's Coffee, tin, wall **110.00**

International Tailoring Co, 1½ x 2½", silvered brass, company logo and "King of Tailors" lion in relief and standing Indian, female figure, and symbols of commerce and industry on lid, engraved March 1, 1904 patent date **65.00**

Old Judson Whiskey **120.00**

Rochester Composite Brick Co, 1½ x 2¾", silvered brass, name and ad text on gray brick, early 1900s ... **35.00**

"Smoke Pierce's 9 Cigars" **40.00**

Measuring Glass, Borden's **25.00**

Measuring Spoon, Monibak Ground Coffee, tin **12.00**

Memo Pad, Archambault Jeweler/Watches, celluloid, cherubs and watch illus, calendar, 1889 .... **60.00**

Menu

Hotel Astor, NYC watercolor scenes, 1945 .... **7.00**

Mickey Mantle's Holiday Inn Menu, c1950 .... **75.00**

RH Macy's, large, 1937 .... **25.00**

Mixer, miniature, 6" h, emb "Woolworth," glass bottom, marked "A & J," patented 1928, assembled **27.00**

Mug

Buckeye Root Beer, pottery **45.00**

Cudahy's Rexoma, hp, German **25.00**

Mug

Dad's Root Beer, glass, barrel **30.00**

Frosty Root Beer, glass, clear, 5½", set of 6 .... **30.00**

Graf's Root Beer, ceramic **55.00**

Ovaltine, Little Orphan Annie, beetleware **40.00**

Newspaper, Buffalo Evening News, special souvenir edition, 4 x 6", space related news **8.00**

Notepad, Southern New England Telephone Co, simulated red good luck stamp on cov, black inscription, blue Bell System logo on back **20.00**

Pancake Turner, Halligan Coffee, tin .. **12.00**

Pamphlet, New Orleans Coffee, "Fairy Tales," c1899 .... **23.00**

Paper Doll, McLaughlin's Coffee, early 1900s **6.50**

Pencil Clip, Morton Salt **7.00**

Pencil Sharpener, Baker's Chocolate, figural, lady **45.00**

Photograph of Window Display, Woolworth's, licorice display, c1930 .... **25.00**

Pin

Heinz, pickle shape, composition .. **10.00**

Society Shoe, Victorian lady **25.00**

Pin Cushion, Bunny Bread, felt **12.00**

Pitcher

Kellogg's Cereal, glass **15.00**

Meredith's Diamond Club Whiskey . **45.00**

Watts Red Apple **25.00**

Plate, Adam's Stovepipe, MIB **60.00**

Playing Cards, Hearn's Dept Store, sailboat back **22.00**

Pocket Knife

King Oscar Sardines **20.00**

Purina, 3" l, red and white checkerboard design on plastic sides, black

lettering, two steel blades, Kutmaster, c1950s **25.00**
Star Brand Shoes **65.00**
Poster Book, includes Coke, Fisk, etc, black and white, some color, 1930, 110 pgs **45.00**
Pot Scraper, Babitts Cleanser **225.00**
Punch Out, Borden, train, c1950 ..... **55.00**
Radio
    Canada Dry, orig box **35.00**
    Gulden's Mustard, orig box **55.00**
    Pepperidge Farm Stuffing, orig box, unused **45.00**
    Planters Peanut Can, orig box **45.00**
Rake, Bissel Sweeper, metal, miniature **10.00**
Receipt Book, Ransom's, 1907 .... **5.00**
Rolling Pin
    Kelvinator, porcelain **85.00**
    "Use Columbus Flour," milk glass, faded red symbol and logo, wood turned handles, 17½" l **250.00**
Salt and Pepper Shakers, Heinz, miniature ketchup bottles, pr **25.00**
Scissors, "Buy CWS Goods. Cut Your Costs" **20.00**
Shoe, Thom McAnn, miniature **25.00**
Shoe Horn
    A S Beck Shoes, metal, 1940s **5.00**
    Normal Shoe Co **11.00**
Spoon
    Armour's Extract of Beef **25.00**
    Grand Union Tea Co **20.00**
    "Tums for the Tummy," ice tea **15.00**
Statue, Hercules Portland Cement, 3½" **25.00**
Stereocard, Quaker Oats **4.00**
Stick Pin
    Emerson Farm Implements, brass, 1" celluloid oval depicting bare foot on green ground, "Emerson Foot Lift Farm Implements/Emerson Mfg Co Rockford, IL" inscribed on foot, early 1900s **65.00**
    NuBlack Powder, Winchester **85.00**
    P&O Plow Co **25.00**
    Round Oak Stoves **20.00**
Story Album, Shredded Wheat **75.00**
Straight Razor, Red Devil Tobacco, adv on blade **18.00**
String Holder
    Post Toasties, round, tin front **50.00**
    Red Goose Shoes **950.00**
Tape Measure, Feeney Grocery Stores, celluloid **25.00**
Tie Clasp
    Borden, Elsie medallion, c1930 .... **35.00**
    Evinrude **18.00**
Token, Green River Whiskey **65.00**
Tumbler
    "Christmas Greetings, 1901, Olson's Big New Store," etched **45.00**
    Uneeda milk biscuit, chocolate slag glass, large size, 1900 .... **195.00**

Turtle, Spears Lumber Co, grand Rapids, MI, 3½" l, 2" w, cast iron **13.50**
Watch
    Cracker Jack, digital **35.00**
    Ford, pocket, premium **85.00**
    Kellogg's, MIB **85.00**
    Kool Aid, 1950s **125.00**
Watch Fob, Bull Dog Tobacco, celluloid, dog, "Won't Bite" **265.00**
Whisk Broom, Whiskbroom Cigars, cigar shape **30.00**
Wrapper
    Planters, 5¢ candy **15.00**
    Sunny Monday Soap **15.00**
Yardstick, Allis Chalmers **12.00**
Yo–yo, Spaulding Luxury Bread, tin ... **40.00**

Paperweight, glass, J. S. Hoskins Lumber Co, Baltimore, MD, blue lettering, white ground, $20.00.

PAPERWEIGHTS

Alan Wood Iron & Steel Co ... **25.00**
Artistic Woven Labels, Pompton Lakes, NJ, cloth under celluloid **25.00**
Bell Telephone, bell shape, cobalt blue glass **45.00**
Blgs Lumber Co, glass, compass **28.00**
Canadian National **85.00**
Crane Co, 50th Anniversary, bronze medal, 1930 .... **10.00**
E W Wagner, Commission merchant, celluloid **50.00**
Fageol Safety Coach, ⅞ x ⅞ x 2¾", lead replica of c1920s bus, inscription on both sides **20.00**
Great American Insurance **22.00**
Hamilton Felt, Miami Woolen Mills, Hamilton, OH, factory scene **10.00**
John Lovell Arms Co, Boston, glass, bust of founder **125.00**

Lehigh Foundries, cast iron, 1947 .... 10.00
Monarch 42.50
National, figural, cash register, cast
iron, orig paint 50.00
Parker Vices, figural, teddy bear, cast
iron 85.00
Purdue Foundry, Kewpie doll 25.00
Reeves Stove Co 40.00
Rogers Carriage Goods, celluloid and
iron, turtle shape 35.00
Southern Plow Co, horse–drawn plow,
decal 100.00
Superior Stove & Range Co, cast iron . 35.00
Transo Envelope Co, Chicago, IL, mirror 18.00
White Mountain Refrigerator 55.00

POSTERS

Blackberry Balsam, 25 x 38", c1800 .. 35.00
Booster Cigar, 27 x 30", black man, lady
adjusting garter, framed 175.00
Chesterfield, cardboard 18.00
Chesapeake Steamship Co, 31 x 40",
litho, 1915 .... 250.00
Florida Blossoms Minstrels, 9¼ x 42",
stamped on bottom Sept 13, 1922 .. 25.00
Granger Tobacco, 30 x 42", sea captain,
1931 .... 60.00
Hill Bros Fur Co, price list on back,
1928 .... 15.00
Kool Cigarette, 12 x 18", paper, glossy,
full color portrait of Willie the Penguin in military outfit 45.00

Sign, White House Shoes, marked "The
H. D. Beach Co, Coshocton, Ohio," 19⅜
x 9¼", $115.00.

Mandeville & Co, 17 x 20, litho, girl in
flower garden 70.00
Mission Orange Soda, 20 x 26¼", pa-
per, white "Everybody's Choice" slo-
gan, late 1940s, early 1950s 50.00
Peerless Rubber Co, 23 x 17", litho, two
scenes, framed 2,000.00
Raleigh Cigarette, 12 x 18", paper,
glossy, full color portrait, "Get War
Stamps With Your B & W Coupons"
inscription 20.00
Red Goose Shoes, Red Goose and chil-
dren outside schoolhouse, 1920 ... 275.00
Royal Baking Powder, 25 x 20", 1920s . 30.00
Schlitz Beer, horse festival 20.00
Stoctonia Flour, 19 x 14", litho, 1905 . 50.00
United States Fur Co, 20 x 14", stone
litho, 1920 .... 225.00

SIGNS

A C Speedometer for Fords, speedome-
ter and wood spoked wheels 125.00
A & P, two cats, Victorian clothes, die-
cut 110.00
Aetna Fire & Marine Ins 25.00
AK Walch's Cigar, 8" x 14", tin, red and
white 65.00
Alka Seltzer, 5 x 13", framed 60.00
Amesty Tobacco, Shaker man with
straw hat cutting plug, 1890s 750.00
Arrow Shirt, man and woman in boat,
sgd illus 375.00
Atkins Saw, reverse glass, jeweled cor-
ner 1,450.00
Austin Western, porcelain 50.00
Auto Strop Razor, tin, hand sharpening
razor 375.00
Baby Bread, baby in highchair, tin 375.00
Barker Powder, woman chased by bull,
1890 .... 450.00
Baseball Liniment A Home Run Swat,
procelain, baseball players 2,800.00
Be Cozy Under Balsam Wool, 40 x 30",
tin, snow laden house, 1920s 75.00
Bell Telephone, 7", porcelain 40.00
Blackberry Punch, 14" x 5½", card-
board, barefooted boy, bottle of
punch, bucket of blackberries 45.00
Bond Street Pipe Tobacco, paper, cutout 30.00
Borden, tin, red 55.00
Brillo Pads, hand scrubbing pot, diecut 85.00
Brown Shoes, "Baby's First Shoes,"
1901 .... 375.00
Bulletin 1¢ per Copy, double sided,
metal 30.00
Busch Ginger Ale, 12 x 26", porcelain,
c1920 .... 125.00
Butternut Bread, tin 20.00
Camels, "Don't Get Your Wind," 11 x
24", cardboard, c1920 .... 35.00
Carhartt Overalls, trainman holding oil

can, standing in front of train and round house, 1897 . . . . **4,500.00**

Cleo Cola, 13 x 29", tin, Cleopatra, 1930s **225.00**

Cliquot Club, 42 x 18, cardboard, Eskimo holding bottle, c1940 . . . . **30.00**

Coca–Cola Sold Here, Christmas bottle **145.00**

Columbus Buggy Co, buggy pulled by ostrich, driven by black boys, 1880 . . . . **8,500.00**

Cooper's Underwear, man wearing long johns **125.00**

Crown Quality Ice Cream, 20 x 28", tin, buckets of ice cream **125.00**

Dark Horse cigar, 12 x 23", paper, two race horses trotting **65.00**

Denby Cigar, tin, man with cigar **375.00**

Dental Snuff, man and woman, 1930s **85.00**

Devoe Snuff, tin, eagle and cans **110.00**

Double Orange, 24 x 25", cardboard, c1940 . . . . **125.00**

Dr Pierce's, woman wearing yellow suit on boat **265.00**

Duck Head Overalls, man wearing overalls, diecut **375.00**

Duke's Tobacco, twins wearing plaid coats with tobacco **450.00**

Duplex Corset, woman in corset, 1880 **375.00**

Dupont Paint, two painters on scaffold **225.00**

Durham Tobacco, drunk man on horse, 1890s **275.00**

Dutch Boy, 10½" x 6¾", cardboard, "Wet Paint" and "John R Laws Drug Co, Columbus, MS," black, yellow, and white **6.00**

El Wadora Cigars, 24 x 36", tin, c1930 **45.00**

Emerson Fans, articulated **175.00**

Exide Battery, 24 x 30", porcelain, c1930 . . . . **35.00**

Farmer's Union, tin **20.00**

5th Ave Playing Cards, woman holding cards, 1905 . . . . **575.00**

Fidelity Underwriters, New York Fire Insurance, 12 x 15", porcelain **45.00**

Flame Proof Wax, women ironing clothes, 1890s **875.00**

Ford Radiator, cap on radiator **150.00**

Francisco Auto Heater, 20 x 38", tin, family in 1930 Packard scene, 1930s **875.00**

Frosty Root Beer, metal, blackboard . . **45.00**

Golden Girl Cola, 33", metal, bottle cap shape **125.00**

Golden Rod Ice Cream, little girl eating **90.00**

Granger Tobacco, diecut Frank Kelly Olympic shooter with guns **95.00**

Grape Nuts, tin, framed **2,000.00**

Green's Seed Corn **60.00**

Hamm's, campfire scene, 34" w **750.00**

Heinz Soup, tin, diecut, "15¢ Bowl of Soup" **150.00**

Heinz Vinegar, woman holding pickles, orig frame **1,250.00**

Helmar Tobacco, porcelain **125.00**

Hinds Face Cream, showgirl dec, 1905 **85.00**

Hood's Tire, policeman with flag, tin . **650.00**

Howe Scale, woman on scale, 1890s . **950.00**

Howel's Root Beer, tin, emb, boy with tray **65.00**

Ideal Soap, diecut, cat scene **110.00**

International Hand Numbering Machine, 7 x 9", tin **25.00**

Iron Clad Hosiery, 10¼ x 13", cardboard, flapper girl, off–image foxing, 1920s **15.00**

Keen Kutter, 10 x 28", tin **65.00**

Kemp's Balsam for Cough, Girl with bottle, diecut **125.00**

King Midas Flour, 13 x 38", little girl . . **285.00**

Kitchen Kleanzer, cardboard, pictures can **45.00**

Klondike Cough Nuggets, prospector with 5¢ box **375.00**

Korn Krisp, doll and boxes, 1905 . . . . . **650.00**

LaCrosse Tennis Shoes, boys playing baseball **85.00**

Laddies Short Smoker, two men facing night club and fancy car scene **575.00**

Lane's Cold Tablets, woman with box . **125.00**

Lee Tires, tire scene, metal, flange **450.00**

Lime Crush, tin, lime green ground, black letters **55.00**

Lincoln Seed, metal, picture of Abe . . . **75.00**

Maple–O–Syrup, cardboard **15.00**

Mascaro Tonique for Hair, woman with bottle **185.00**

Mayer Shoe, high button shoes, flange **675.00**

Min–Lax Tonic, 16 x 20", tin, c1930 . **35.00**

Mobil gargoyle, porcelain **535.00**

Mogul Timing Gears for Cars, magician holding giant gear **75.00**

Mother's Idea Diapers, babies with doll, multicolored **225.00**

Myers Pump, tin, flange, double sided, milk maid squirts farm boy, c1900 . . **115.00**

Nehi, paper, legs, 1930s **30.00**

North Carolina Tobacco, "Our Next President's" head obscured by smoke, 1880s **550.00**

Noseman Coal, tin, Viking ship, "Tempers the North Wind" **145.00**

Nu–Grape, tin
Bottle shape **85.00**
Rect, green ground, bottle in foreground **95.00**

Nu Icy **55.00**

Old Bradbury, sewing **60.00**

Old Gold Cigarettes, 12 x 4", tin, emb, dancing box **25.00**

Oldsmobile Service, 18 x 12", porcelain, c1920 . . . . **225.00**

Oliver Plows, Knoxville, TN, plow scene, flange **275.00**

Orange Crush, tin, 1940s **125.00**

Peak Chocolates, hand holding bar, tin **475.00**

Penn Beverage Co, paper, bathing beauty, floating beverage case, framed **85.00**

Pepsi–Cola, 10 x 20", tin, "Bigger & better 5¢," 1930s **60.00**

Perfection Overalls, father and sons wearing overalls working and playing **125.00**

Peter's Ammo, retriever beside box ... **875.00**

Peters Powder, retriever puppies and wood ammonition box, diecut **875.00** **535.00**

Phillips 66, shield, porcelain **4.00**

Pittsburgh Paints, 7¼" x 9¼", cardboard, "Just Painted" and " Pittsburgh Plate Glass Co", multicolor, 1953 .. **150.00**

Pointers 5¢ Cigar, double sided ......

Pollocks Cigar, can with riverboats unloading and commerical buildings scene **175.00**

Polly Stamp, 13" w, 27" h, electric, colorful parrot, orig box, unused **85.00**

Priscilla Ware, 10 x 5¼", aluminum, 1920s, MIB **30.00** **125.00**

Quaker State Nos 961 .... **32.00**

Richardson Root Beer, 10 x 14" **850.00**

Roxbury Rye, Uncle Sam and bottle ..

Royal Typewriter, Santa Claus taking orders on typewriter, peeking family, 1920 .... **375.00**

Safe Guard Insurance Co, tin, dog guarding open safe **225.00**

Seliges Ice Cream, tin, attached thermometer **35.00**

Ship & Travel by Rail, train scene, brass **225.00**

Sky Chief Supreme, 1959 .... **50.00**

Snow King Baking Powder, 12 x 26", cardboard, c1930 .... **40.00**

Society Brand Clothes, sheik man and woman **110.00**

South Bend Fishing Tackle, man catching fish **950.00**

Spalding Plow, man plowing **375.00**

Speidel, celluloid, watch, cowboy, mountains, fence post frame **45.00**

Sprat's Dog Cakes, porcelain, strip ... **95.00**

Squirt, 11 x 27", tin, emb, 1951 .... **35.00**

Star Soap, girl on tricycle mailing letter, 1896 .... **1,450.00**

Star Shoe, farmer, carpenter, and shoes, litho **375.00**

Stevens Threshing Machine, people and thresher, 1880 ....**1,250.00**

Studebaker 1956, 17 x 11", cardboard, diecut, "Champion," self framed, ... **28.00**

1961, 18½ x 11¾", cardboard, color photo **15.00**

Sun Crest, boy with baseball bat and bottle **85.00**

Target Tobacco, 6 x 24", paper, 1931 . **10.00**

Texaco, no smoking **70.00**

Toledo Motoring School, Learn To Be

Salesman or Repairman, Model T scene **90.00**

Triangle Shirt Collar, collar inside heart **125.00**

Twenty Grand Razor Blades, tin, diecut, razor shape **125.00**

Tydol Flying A, porcelain, pump, round, five color **125.00**

Union Leader, oval, Uncle Sam smoking pipe **375.00**

Venus Pencil, wood **325.00**

Viceroy, store hours **45.00**

Virginia Slims, metal **10.00**

Washington Crisps, box with Washington on front **175.00**

Wells Fargo & Co Express, porcelain .. **90.00**

WDC Pipes, tin **95.00**

Whip Handle Cigars, buggy whip and lit cigar, tin **375.00**

White Owl, touring car with golf bags, tennis rackets and fishing gear **875.00**

Whiz Car Polish, Maxfield Parrish character **85.00**

Whiz Radiator Stop Leak, elf carrying can to touring car **275.00**

Wrigley's Chewing Gum, woman selling gum to girl **375.00**

Thermometer, A. Tvarosek Oil Co, Berwyn, IL, cardboard, black lettering, 6⅛" l, $5.00.

THERMOMETERS

Arbuckles Coffee, tin, package shape . **175.00**

Chesterfield Cigarettes, 13" **40.00**

Cobbs Creek Blended Whiskey, Drink–O–Meter, 38 x 8", c1936 .... **40.00**

Coca–Cola, bottle shape, 1952 ...... **95.00**

Doan's Pills, 6 x 24", wood, c1923 ... **115.00**

Double Cola, tin **55.00**

Dr Pepper, round **80.00**

Folger's Coffee, 9" 75.00
Frosty Rootbeer, pictures Frosty 75.00
Gaines Dog Meal, tin 75.00
Harrington's Ice Cream, 12" h, wood .   35.00
Hires Root Beer, bottle shape 65.00
Jordan's Ready–To–Eat Meats, 15",
  wood, yellow enamel paint, black
  trim, stamped red text and markings,
  c1930 . . . .   40.00
Keen Kutter 25.00
Kentucky Club Pipe Tobbacco, tin 35.00
Lincoln Laundry, 12 x 3", wood, early
  1900s 25.00
Mail Pouch, porcelain 95.00
Major Anti–Freeze, 7 x 36", wood,
  drum majorette, yellow, red, and
  black 150.00
Nesbitts's Orange 45.00
Nu–Grape, tin, bottle shape 55.00
Orange Crush, Crushie
  Tin 95.00
  Wood 135.00
Packard Automobiles 65.00
Pepsi Cola
  1965 . . . .   25.00
  1973 . . . .   35.00
Puritas Ice Cream, 12½" h, cardboard,
  c1923 . . . .   35.00
Red Seal Battery, porcelain 75.00
Royal Crown Soda 55.00
Royal Crown Cola, 25" 60.00
Salem Cigarettes 20.00
Squirt 60.00
Standard Home Heating Oils, tin, torch
  logo 35.00
Sundrop, round 65.00
Texaco, men fishing 28.00

Tin, Fisher's Mocha & Java Blend Coffee,
one pound, Fisher Bros, Cleveland, OH,
4¼" d, 5¾" h, $24.00.

Tracto Weather Station, tin, orig box . .   75.00
Universal Batteries 125.00
Westinghouse, Betty Furness 10.00

TIN

Allens Sodium Bicarbonate, Tampa
  Drug 10.00
Amurol Tooth Powder 6.00
Ann Page Cream of Tartar 7.00
Asco, 2 lb, Christmas 18.00
Baby Talcum Powder, silhouette of chil-
  dren playing 60.00
Beaver, typewriter ribbon 10.00
Blue Bird Coffee 45.00
Bond Street 8.00
Borden's Malted Milk, 5 lb 15.00
Brownie Salted Peanuts, litho, Brownie
  on both sides 125.00
Bunte Candy, 5#, gold 25.00
Butternut Coffee 14.00
Cain's Cloves 10.00
Calumet Baking Powder, sample 25.00
Campfire Marshmallows, campfire
  scene 35.00
Caroid Dental Powder 6.00
Cavalier 12.00
Choisa Ceylon Tea, 1906 . . . .   20.00
Clarion Cream of Tartar 4.50
Cocomalt 12.00
Colgate Eclat Talc 10.00
Daniel Webster, tobacco 20.00
DeLaval Cream Separator Oil 55.00
Delmonte Coffee 12.00
Doan's Pills, small, tubular 5.00
Dream Girl Talc 40.00
Droste Pastilles 10.00
Droste's Cocoa, ¼ oz, sample 50.00
Epicure Flowery Tip Orange Pekoe Tea,
  ½ lb 15.00
Forest & Stream, tobacco, fisherman,
  pocket 75.00
Frank's Cinnamon 8.50
French's Thyme 6.75
Gardenia Bouquet Talc 18.00
George Washington Instant Cofffee . . .   30.00
Giant Brand Coffee 65.00
Glendra Coffee, sample 24.00
Gold *Bond* Coffee, 1 lb 20.00
Gold Label *Baking* Powder 12.00
Good Cheer *Cigar, handled* 60.00
Goodrich Tire Repair *Outfit* 15.00
Guide Tobacco, pocket 125.00
Hodgdon's Rifle Powder 5.00
Hollingshead Neatsfoot 8.00
Honeymoon, tobacco, man in crescent,
  pocket
Hoosier Maid Mustard 8.00
Horlick's, malted milk pail, 10#, screw
  lid 125.00
Ivin's Saltines, 1 lb, round 18.00

Jolly Time Popcorn, red 18.00
Judd's Pickling Spice 7.00
Kaffee Hag Coffee, 1 lb, white, red, and
   black 22.00
Keen's Mustard, Lord Nelson, six scenes 185.00
Kentucky Club 4.00
King Cole Coffee, pictures king, key lid 18.00
Koweba Whole Cloves 8.50
Kraft Malted Milk 8.00
Kroger Bay Leaves 6.25
Little Elf Spice 6.00
Loft's Candy, ½ lb 10.00
Luzianne Coffee
   Can, red, black mammy, pry lid 50.00
   Pail, red, black mammy 75.00
MacMillan Ground Mustard 6.75
Mayfair Tea, round 12.00
Maytag Washing Machine Fuel Mixing
   Can 40.00
McCormick Bee Brand Pepper, large . . 10.00
McKessons Seidlitz Powder 10.00
Mellowmints 20.00
Mennen Shave Talc 6.00
Mentholatum, sample 12.00
Merck Powder, ducks 24.00
Merkels Tooth Powder 10.00
Monarch Cocoa, sample 25.00
Monarch Whole Mustard Seed 8.00
Monte Cristo Filmy Cut, tobacco, long 25.00
Mrs. Kline's Potato Chips 25.00
Mule Kick Pipe Cleaner, mule scene . . 12.00
National Biscuit Co, glass panel 40.00
Nestles Egyptian Henna Talc 17.00
Nutrine Candy, blue 55.00
Old Dutch Cleanser, sample, 1930s . . 38.00
Old Reliable Typewriter, beavers chew-
   ing trees 25.00
O'Neill's Vegetable Remedy 20.00
OPS "Oscar Pepper" Coffee, 1 lb 30.00
Orange Mellowmints 15.00
Packard Bulb Kit 15.00
Panama, typewriter ribbon 10.00
Petrocarbo Salve, Watkins Co, Boston,
   MA, round, red and black 20.00
Philip Morris 12.00
Planters Cashews, 4oz, 1944 . . . . 38.00
PleeZing Coffee, 1 lb, screw lid 20.00
Presto Stove Polish 6.00
Psylia Lax, Battle Creek Foods 10.00
Rawleighs Cocoa 16.00
Rawleigh's Medicated Ointment, round 15.00
Red Rose Coffee, key lid 16.00
Reed's Butterscotch Patties, 3" d, round 7.50
Regent Coffee, red checkered design,
   key lid 10.00
Rexall Band–Aid 8.00
Rexall Orderlies, tin 15.00
Royal Chef Celery Seed 5.50
Rumford Baking Powder, sample 34.00
Salada Coffee, key lid 14.00
Seacrest Oyster, boat, colorful 20.00
Shedd's Peanut Butter, pail 15.00

Tin, Tiger Chewing Tobacco, rect, 6 x 3¾ x 2¼", $60.00.

Shedds Peanut Butter, 5 lb 15.00
Sir Walter Raleigh 4.00
Skat Cleanser 6.00
Southern Rose Shortening, pail, red
   rose, bail handle 15.00
Sudan Cloves 8.00
Sultana Peanut Butter, 1 lb pail, orange 95.00
Sunset Traik Cigars 410.00
Sunshine Biscuit, US Capitol, cherry
   blossoms 65.00
Superba Tea, screw lid 12.00
Sweet Cuba, round, light green, 1 lb . . 25.00
Tannette Powder, Walgreen 8.00
Tao Tea Balls 6.00
Texaco, red star logo 20.00
Texide Water Cured Prophylactics, ¼ x
   1½ x 2", litho, multicolor illus, native
   workers extracting latex from rubber
   trees, two of three prophylactics en-
   closed, copyright 1931 . . . . 35.00
Thomas Webb Steel–Cut Coffee 12.00
Tite–Rite Dental Powder 18.00
Tryme Mace 5.50
Tuxedo 7.00
Unicy Marshmallows, 4½", tin, litho,
   red and black design, Brandle &
   Smith Co, Philadelphia, 1920–30 . . 15.00
Vantines Bath Powder, grass cloth, Ori-
   ental design, 1920s 18.00
Velvet Night Talc 24.00
Watkin's Baking Powder, 1930s 12.00
White Cap Baking Powder, ¼ lb, uno-
   pened 18.00
White House Coffee, 3" h 15.00

TRADE CARDS

Collecting Hints: Most advertising trade cards sell in the range from $1.00 to $10.00. A few command higher prices because of subject matter, artist, or scarcity. The advertised product being shown is among the most desirable features of a card. Many were made in sets, and collectors still seek to complete them today.

Cards taken from old albums should be handled with care, as there is often valuable information on the reverse side. Kit Barry's *The Advertising Trade Card* (privately printed, 1981) contains excellent information for the removal of cards from album pages.

History: These cards are small, thin cardboard pieces extolling the merits of a product and bearing the name and address of a merchant.

With the invention of lithography, colorful trade cards became a popular advertising medium in the late 19th and early 20th centuries. They were made to appeal to children, especially. Young and old alike collected and treasured them in albums and scrapbooks. Very few are dated; 1880 to 1893 were the prime years for trade cards; 1810 to 1850 cards can be found, but rarely. By 1900 trade cards were rapidly losing their popularity, perhaps due to the influx of the household magazine. By 1910 they had vanished from the American scene, except in rare instances.

Notes: The listing for trade cards is as follows: product name, description of card, copyright date if known, printer if known, and size. We have tried to focus on cards which show the product. All cards are in full color unless otherwise specified. There are thousands of cards in several hundred categories. We have tried to give a sampling to show the market range.

Bitters, Drugs, and Medicines

Bassett's Horehand Troches, diecut, bottles	**5.00**
Blair's, Henry C. Son Apothecaries, four different scenes	**8.00**

Sanford's Ginger, Potter Drug and Chemical Co, Boston, black girl with child in watermelon cradle, multicolored, Forbes, Boston, $9.50.

Burdock Blood Bitters, two bears dancing	**4.00**
Congress Bitters, Washington DC buildings	**7.00**
Dr Niemeyer's Vital Tonic, little girl, colorful	**10.00**
Kidds Cough Syrup, girl and pug dog	**5.00**

Carter's Little Liver Pills, four cats playing, adv on back, 3⅜ x 5⅛", $6.00.

Clothing

A Priesmeyer Shoes, diecut	**22.50**
Clothier & Hatter, mechanical	**45.00**
My Lady's Gloves, lady removing gloves	**4.00**
Todtman Clothier, diecut, youngster in wash tub	**10.00**
Venus Self Closing Bustle, lady attaching bustle	**4.00**

Celluloid Waterproof Collars, Cuffs, & Shirt Bosoms, 4⅝ x 3", $5.00.

Hire's Cough Cure, adv on back, Charles E. Hires Co, 3 x 5", $8.00.

Cosmetics and Perfumes

Austen's Florest Flower Cologne, cherub holding bottle 4.00
Chinese Cologne, Hartford Soldier's Memorial, brown litho on white 6.00
Espey's Fragrant Cream, lady holding fan 6.00
Hind's Honey and Cream, girl holding bottle, boy on either side, c1891 . . . 7.00
Howards Lotus Flower Cologne, lady sniffing flowers 4.00
Mennen's Borated Talcum Toilet Powder, boy popping out of can holding flag 6.00
Pozzoni's Powder, cartoon drawing . . . 4.00

Scott's Emulsion of Pure Cod Liver Oil, adv on back, Wemple & Co, NY, trimmed, 2⅝ x 5½", $6.50.

Stoddart's Peerless Liquid, lady profile **5.00**
Sweet Lullaby Bouquet, grinning man . **4.00**

Food

A & P, color litho, Ben Franklin drinking tea, 1884 . . . . **25.00**
Beeman's Pepsi Gum, hold–to light type **18.00**
Dairylea Ice Cream, 5", diecut, mechanical, boy, eyes roll, Germany **30.00**
Falstaff–Lemp, 6 x 4", double sided, brewery, white sand pouring out of beer barrel on front **95.00**
Hecker's Buckwheat, hold to light, man in moon appears eating buckwheats, 1890s **20.00**
Hires Root Beer **15.00**
Hood's Sarsaparilla, 1889 . . . . **45.00**
Huylers Chocolates rooster and baby chicks waking sleeping girl **10.00**
Libby's, calendar, 1893–94 . . . . **5.00**
Millbourne Flour, diecut, flour sack, triple fold out, color, 1894 . . . . **50.00**
Newton Brothers Pepsin Chewing Gum, figural, emb, 1887 . . . . **85.00**
Skipper Sardines, fan–out, six sections, mechanical, dinner scene **22.00**

Rising Sun Stove Polish, Morse Bros, Canton, MA, two panel; white woman chases away rival salesman, black family admires shine, multicolored, Mayer, Merkel & Ottman, NY, $8.50.

Household

Bixby & Co Shoe Polish, lady Liberty showing polished shoe **8.00**
Davol Rubber Co, celluloid, anti-colic nipple for baby bottle **15.00**
Edison Phonograph, old couple listens with amazement **6.00**
Hartshorn Shade Rollers, baby pulls down shade, mother napping in chair **4.00**

Rising Sun Stove Polish, colored, two
page litho inside 50.00
Smith's Sprinkler and Force Pump, girl,
lawn, and garden scene 5.00
Van Stan's Stratena Glue, black man lec-
turing, 1880s 32.00

Retail

Bee Tissue Paper Co, Philadelphia,
black and white 20.00
Estey Organ, figural
Boot Black Boy 10.00
Doll 4.00
Frank Miller & Son, Crown Dressing,
diecut shoe with children 10.00
Kimball, Wm S and Co, 9¾" h, diecut,
lady and bull fighter 35.00
Peerless Piano, figural, easel back 15.00
Poole Piano, diecut 5.00
St Louis Beef Canning Co, black man
running with product, 1880s 35.00

Sewing Machines

Domestic Sewing Machine Co, two children driving goat cart 5.00
Household Sewing Machine Co, little
girl talking on telephone 5.00
Standard Sewing Machine Co, spirit of
'76 scene, dated 1885 .... 6.00
Wheeler and Wilson, family watching
sewing machine delivery 4.00

Soap

Diamond Dyes, hold to light type 8.00
Larkin, Ottumwa Starch 3.00
Wool Soap 3.00
Wrigley's Soap, hold to light type, child
awakes, product appears, 1891 .... 25.00

Stoves and Ranges

Art Jewel Base Burner, girl in snow coat
and boots 4.00
Buckwater Stove Co, celluloid with
cardboard insert 15.00
Gold Medal Range, outdoor scene,
stove in center 3.00
Noble Cook Stoves, early wood stove,
happy chef 10.00

Thread

Barbour's Thread centennial, 1884 ... 25.00
Clark's, General Sheridan on horseback 4.00
Eureka, woman mending sock 3.00
J P Coates, The Champion, girl holding
rifle, wearing soldier's helmet 4.00
Merrick's Thread, hot air balloon 5.00

Willimantic Thread, litho, girl holding
parrot and cat by thread leash, 1883   15.00

Tobacco

Bull Durham, Simmons & Co, 1882 .. 20.00
Horsehead Tobacco, horse's head, plug
in mouth 8.50
Lang's Plug, barometer card 8.00
Newsboy Plug, five puppies 5.00

**Tray, Gallagher & Burton, Black Label
Rye Whiskey, gold border, 4¼", $40.00.**

TRAY

Allouez Beverages, tin, tip 68.00
Ballantine Ale 7 Beer, 12" d, litho tin,
yellow and white name, red and
black three–ring logo, blue background with scattered yellow star motifs 50.00
Banquet Ice Cream, 10½ x 15", c1930   20.00
Billy Baxter Ginger Ale, tin 35.00
Braumeister, man holding bottle and
glass 45.00
Chero–Cola 65.00
Christian Feighn–Span Breweries, lady,
1916 .... 45.00
Coca–Cola, tip, Betty, 1914 .... 90.00
Cottolene, 4¼", litho tin, full color illus,
black lady and youngster picking cot-
ton, black rim, yellow lettering,
c1920 .... 75.00
Crown Baking Powder, 10", litho 175.00
Dawson's Diamond Ale, porcelain,
playing card 125.00
Deys Dry Goods, store building 30.00
Dr. Pepper, King of Beverage 35.00
Ehret's Hellgate Brewery, pre–prohibi-
tion 95.00
Esso, Tony the Tiger 20.00
Evervess Sparkling Water, 10½ x 14" .. 35.00
Fairy Soap, tip, tin 38.00

Falls City Ice and Beverage	45.00
Ferris Brick Co, beautiful lady wearing hat, 1903	25.00
Franks' Pale Dry Ginger Ale, soda bottle illustration, 1930s	65.00
Globe Wernecke, change	85.00
Hoefler Ice Cream, oval, woman eating ice cream	200.00
Hyroller Whiskey, change	25.00
Jersey Cream, round	150.00
Kenny's Tea and Coffee, lady picking flowers	40.00
Lemon–Kola, tip	90.00
Lord Calvert Whiskey, 23"	48.00
Martha Washington Wine, Texas	95.00
Mascot Crushed Cut Tobacco	30.00
Monroe Brewing Co, king raising stein	225.00
Montrose Dairy, ice cream, Kewpie eating sundae	250.00
Nafruco Flavors, girl with horse	95.00
Old Elkhorn Rye, change	35.00
Orange Julep, bathing beauty under parasol	125.00
Parsely Salmon, change, salmon steak	40.00
Peerless Beer, oval, yellow, black, and red letters	125.00
Prudential Insruance, change, oval	18.00
Rainier Beer, 13"	110.00
Round Oak Stove, change	18.00
Ruppert Beer, Art Deco, Hans Flato	95.00
Schmidt' Valley Forge, beer, 13¼", 1930	20.00
Sheboygan Mineral Water, two black waiters	100.00
Sparks Kidney and Liver Tonic, porcelain	275.00
Stegmaier Beer, 4¼", tip	35.00
Sterling Beer, 4 x 6", change, c1930	20.00
Success Manure Spreader, rect, horses pulling wagon	1000.00
Taka Cola, tip, litho tin	75.00
Tom Moore Cigars, change	20.00
Upero Coffee, Boston, change	60.00
West End Brewing, Utica, NY, rect, two dogs at table	290.00
Williams Ice Cream, 13½" d, mother and son at table	290.00
Wrigleys' Soap, 3½" d, change	65.00

WHISTLE

Baby Ruth, Curtis Candy Co, red ground, white lettering	15.00
Blow for Harvest Bread	12.50
Dairy Queen, cone shape, plastic	15.00
Haines Shoe, trapezoid shape, plastic, black top with "Blow And Talk Of Haines The Shoe Wizard/Shoes For All," underside orange, late 1940s	20.00
Jack & Jill Gelatin, tin, litho	30.00
Millbrook Bread	10.00
New York Evening Telegraph, brass, chain	40.00

Whistle, Oscar Mayer, weiner, plastic, $7.50.

Oscar Meyer Weiner mobile	10.00
Purity Ice Cream, trapezoid shape, plastic, black top with orange name and "Penn Dairies, Inc," underside light blue, late 1940s	15.00
Royal Luncheon, tin litho, Made in Germany	12.00

ADVERTISING CHARACTERS

Collecting Hints: Concentrate on one advertising character. Three dimensional objects are more eagerly sought than two dimensional objects. Some local dairies, restaurants and other businesses developed advertising characters. This area has received little focus from collectors.

History: Advertising characters represent a sampling of those characters used in advertising from the early 20th century to the present.

Americans learned to recognize specific products by their particular advertising characters. During the first half of the 1900s, many immigrants could not read but could identify with the colorful characters. The advertising character helped to sell the product.

Some manufacturers developed similar names for products of lesser quality, like Fairee Soap versus the popular Fairy Soap. Later when trade laws were enacted, this practice was stopped. Use of trademarks had become popular by this time. The advertising character often was part of the trademark.

Trademarks and advertising characters are found on product labels, in magazines, as premiums, and on other types of advertising. Popular cartoon characters also were used to advertise products.

Some advertising characters were designed especially to promote a specific product, like Mr. Peanut and the Campbell Kids. The first time the popular Campbell Kids appeared, it was on streetcar advertising in 1906. The illustrations of Grace G. Drayton were aimed at housewives. The Campbell Kids were gradually dropped from Campbell's advertising until the television industry expanded the advertising market. In 1951, Campbell redesigned the kids and successfully reissued them. The kids were redesigned again in 1966. Other advertising characters also have enjoyed a long life, e.g., Aunt Jemima. Others, like Kayo and the Yellow Kid, have disappeared from modern advertising.

References: David Longest, *Character Toys and Collectibles*, Collector Books, 1984; David Longest, *Character Toys and Collectibles, Second Series* Collector Books, 1987; Richard D. and Barbara Reddock, *Planters Peanuts, Advertising & Collectibles*, Wallace-Homestead, 1978; Joleen Robison and Kay Sellers, *Advertising Dolls, Identification and Value Guide*, Collector Books, 1980; Dave Stivers, *The Nabisco Brands Collection of Cream of Wheat Advertising Art*, Collectors' Showcase, 1986.

Periodical: *Kids Illustrated Drayton Supplement* (K.I.D.S), 649 Bayview Drive, Akron, OH 44319.

REPRODUCTION ALERT

See: All advertising categories; Black Memorabilia; Cartoon Characters; Fast Food; Planter's Peanuts.

Campbell Kids, bib clip, silver plate, 3″ l, $5.00.

Aunt Jemima
    Booklet, 3 x 6″, 12 pgs, contains recipes, 1927 .... 8.00
    Cinnamon Shaker 18.00
    Glass, Mammy's Shanty 15.00
    Light Pull, AJ Breakfast Club 15.00
    Pinback Button, Aunt Jemima Breakfast Club, 1½ x 2¼″, tin, litho, diecut, portrait, red and white lettering 15.00
    Syrup Pitcher 25.00
Buster Brown
    Bike, merry–go–round horse, Buster Brown and Tige adv, Hollywood Jr 295.00
    Box, stockings, graphics 40.00
    Clicker, 1¼″, multicolored, c1900 .. 40.00
    Coat Hook 28.00

Jacks, orig ball, c1920 .... 10.00
Periscope, Secret Agent 20.00
Pinback Button, 1″ d, sepia, portrait illus, logo and inscription for Brown Shoe Co, St Louis on back paper, late 1890s–early 1900s ... 38.00
Plate, Buster Brown and Tige, china 55.00
Postcard, Buster and Tige, colorful, Tuck, 1906 .... 25.00
Shoehorn 40.00
Sign, 14½ x 14″, pressed board 35.00
Campbell Kids
    Baseball Bat, wood 85.00
    Case, vinyl, red 18.00
    Doll, girl, stuffed latex rubber body, soft rubber head, painted eyes, orig outfit, stamped "Campbell Kid Made By Ideal Toy Corp" on back of head 25.00
    Figure, cardboard, store advertisement 15.00
    Pennant, 17½″, felt, burnt–orange, white inscription, c1930 .... 30.00
    Plate, 7″ d, Homer Laughlin, 1935 . 25.00
    Salt and pepper shakers, F&F Mold & Die Works, pr 35.00
    Spoon, 6″ l, SP, boy on handle, c1950 12.00
Charlie Tuna
    Doll, 7″, vinyl, squeeze, painted black glasses, orange cap with raised "Charlie" letters, 1973 copyright 20.00
    Lamp 50.00
    Patch, embroidered 15.00
    Pinback Button, 1½″, litho, Charlie for President, red, white, and blue, 1960s 25.00
Dino the Dinosaur, Sinclair Oil
    Toy, inflatable, vinyl, green, brown lettering, sealed packet, c1970 ... 15.00
    Tumbler, 5″ h, green illus, "Drive with Care and Buy Sinclair," c1930 20.00
Dutch Boy
    Keychain, 2¼″ h, plastic, day glow, figural, holding brushes behind back, c1940s 30.00
    Paperweight, lead 18.00
Elsie the Cow
    Bottle
        1/2 Pint, short, Elsie on red ground, square 9.00
        Quart
            Elsie in Daisy, red ground 15.00
            "Borden's" in red, round 17.00
            Borden's Deposit bottle, orange ring on neck, square 20.00
        1½ gal, Elsies around top, "Let your grocer be your milkman" . 22.00
    Coloring Book, 1957 .... 15.00
    Game, Elsie and Her Family, 1941 Selchow & Righter Co, orig box, complete 75.00

Lamp, ceramic, Elsie holding baby . 235.00
Mug, Elsie in daisy ext., head on int.
bottom 35.00
Pail, 5½" h, tin, silvered, litho full
color portrait, wire and wood bail,
Ohio Art Co logo symbol on reverse
side, 1930–40 . . . . 40.00
Stuffed Toy, brown
1950s 45.00
1970s 35.00
1980s 25.00
Sundae Dish, 4" 17.50
Fruit Brute, General Mills Cereal, doll,
7½", soft vinyl, squeaker, brown
body, fleshtone muzzle, striped outfit,
stamped name and General Mills
trademark, c1970 . . . . 15.00
Gerber Baby
Cup, baby illus, "Babies Are Our
Business," pr 10.00
Doll, orig box, 1972 . . . . 15.00
Gold Dust Twins Washing Powder
Button, multicolored 60.00
Sign, 20 x 13", Do Your Work, orange
and black 100.00
Green Giant Sprout
Doll 22.00
Watch 30.00
Hush Puppy
Bank, figural, dog 20.00
Frisbee, 9¼" d, plastic, white day
glow, blue dog, red lettering,
1960s–1970s 12.00
Keebler Elf
Doll, 6½", soft vinyl, movable head,
stamped "1974 copyright by Kee-
bler Co" 20.00
Telephone 85.00
Wrist Watch 125.00
Kool Aid Man, bank, 5½" h, plastic,
figural, mechanical, red, yellow base,
orig instruction tag, copyright of Gen-
eral Foods, 1970–80 . . . . 20.00
Miss Sunbeam, magnet, flasher 8.00
Morris the Cat, Nine Lives Cat Food,
pinback button, 2¼", litho, Morris For
President, red, white, and blue border 10.00
Mr. Peanut
Butter Maker 30.00
Container, papier mache 175.00
Jar, 10" h, glass, emb, peanut finial . 100.00
Nut Tray, 6" l, figural, plastic, green,
matching serving spoon with figural
on handle 30.00
Nestle Quick Rabbit, cup, plastic, mul-
ticolored 7.00
Nipper, RCA Victor
Bank, 6¼", metal, orig closure 150.00
Figure, 4", chalk, emb Victor 18.00
Key Case, emb gold letters 60.00
Salt and Pepper Shakers, pr, Lenox . 35.00
Sign, cardboard, framed 20.00

**Nipper, mirror, Victor, His Master's
Voice, multicolored, 2¾ x 1¾", $90.00.**

Pillsbury Doughboy
Cookie Jar 33.00
Doll, 7" h, white vinyl, movable
head, painted blue dot eyes, 1971
copyright 25.00
Puppet 45.00
Poll Parrot
Figure, chalk 125.00
Spinner Top, metal, diecut, yellow,
red, and green, c1940s 25.00
Whistle, litho tin, oval trademark,
1930s 25.00
Red Goose
Egg Dispenser, 33" h, figural, plastic,
straw nest, c1950 . . . . 135.00
Pinback Button 7.00
Shoes, pr, boy's, orig box 20.00
Token, brass 8.00
Reddy Kilowatt
Ashtray, glass, red and white printed
design, 1950–60 . . . . 18.00
Coaster, 3½", paper, black, white,
and red, image on each, wax paper
backing, unused, set of 20 . . . . . . 15.00
Cuff Links, ¾" d, brass, clear glass
dome over multicolor face, Reddy
Kilowatt copyright 80.00
Figure, 5¼" h, plastic, diecut, white
day glow head, hands, and feet,
clear red body on black base, copy-
right 1961 . . . . 85.00
Lapel Pin 20.00
Patch, 3", fabric, woven, red stitch on
white background, blue border, silvery white inscription, c1950 . . . . 15.00
Pin, 1" h, brass, diecut, figural, red
enamel accents, 1950s 20.00
Plate, 6¼" d, metal, enamel, color
illus, light green background, inscription "Reddy Kilowatt/Servant
Of The Century" sticker marked
"Bovano," 1950s 35.00
Poster, 11 x 13½", paper, peel–off,
red, white, and blue, unused,
1960s 40.00

Smokey Bear
    Ashtray, tin, pail with chair attach-
       ment **85.00**
    Bowl, plastic, Arrowhead **9.00**
    Doll, cloth, Ideal, 1950s **60.00**
    Figurine, Aim Toothpaste premium,
       1960s **18.00**
    Salt and Pepper Shakers, figural **65.00**
    Scarf **20.00**
Snap, Crackle, Pop, Kellogg's Rice Kris-
    pies
    Figure, 4", set of 3, MIB **95.00**
    Puppet, Kelloggs premium **25.00**
    Song Book, 1937 .... **5.00**
Speedy Alka Seltzer
    Bank, 6" h, figural, rubber, painted,
       1950s–1960s **125.00**
    Lapel pin, ⅝" h, brass, enameled, die-
       cut, figural, 1950s–1960s **70.00**
    Postcard **12.00**
Tony The Tiger, Kellogg's Frosted
    Flakes, cereal bowl, 5" d, figural, hard
    plastic, white, orange plastic feet
    shape base, Kellogg's, copyright 1981 **15.00**

AKRO AGATE GLASS

Collecting Hints: Akro Agate is marked "Made in USA" and often includes a mold number. Some pieces also include a small crow in the mark. It is a thick type of glass; therefore, collectors should buy only mint pieces. The marbleized types of Akro Agate were made in many color combinations. The serious collector should be looking for unusual combinations.

History: The Akro Agate Co. was formed in 1911. Their major product was marbles. In 1914 the owners moved from near Akron, Ohio, to Clarksburg, West Virginia, where they opened a large factory. They continued to produce marbles profitably until after the Depression. In 1930, the competition in the marble business became too great, and Akro Agate Co. decided to diversify into other products.

Two of their most successful products were the floral ware lines and children's dishes, first made in 1935. The children's dishes were very popular until after World War II when metal dishes captured the market.

The Akro Agate Co. also made special containers for cosmetics firms including the Mexicali cigarette jar, which was originally filled with Pick Wick bath salts, and a special line made for the Jean Vivaudou Co., Inc. Operations continued successfully until 1948. The factory, a victim of imports, metals, and increased use of plastics, was sold to the Clarksburg Glass Co. in 1951.

Reference: Gene Florence, *The Collectors En-* cyclopedia of Akro Agate Glassware, Collector Books, 1975.

Collectors' Club: Akro Agate Art Association, P.O. Box, 758, Salem, NH 03079.

REPRODUCTION ALERT: Pieces currently reproduced are not marked "Made In USA" and are missing the mold number and crow.

Cosmetic jar, Mexicali, brown and cream, 2¾" d, 4½" h, $25.00.

Ashtray
    Ellipsoid, white and green **15.00**
    Leaf, white and orange **3.50**
    Rect, playing card, Westite, gray and
       brown marble, recessed spade ... **10.00**
    Round
       Black, two metal lions **40.00**
       Marbled, metal lion **30.00**
Basket, two handles, white, gold, and
    blue **25.00**
Bell, 5¼" h, white **40.00**
Bowl
    5¼" d, green **5.00**
    6" d, pumpkin, three toes **18.00**
    7¼" d, tab handle, cobalt **17.50**
Candlesticks, pr, 3½" h, green **25.00**
Children's Dishes
    Bowl
       Concentric Ring, blue **20.00**
       Octagonal, cereal, white **8.50**
    Creamer
       Concentric Ring, yellow **12.00**
       Interior Panel, opaque blue **25.00**
       Plain Jane, transparent green **27.50**
    Cup
       Chiquita, transparent cobalt blue . **6.50**
       Daisy, green **15.00**

Interior Panel, pumpkin 20.00
Stippled Band, dark amber 8.50
Pitcher, Stacked Disc, green 6.50
Plate
   Concentric Ring, green 4.75
   Daisy, blue 10.00
   Octagonal, yellow 3.00
   Stacked Disc & Panel, transparent
    blue 10.00
   Stippled Band, transparent green . 4.00
Saucer
   Daisy, yellow 6.00
   Interior Panel, opaque green 3.00
   Plain Jane, baked on yellow 2.00
Sugar
   Chiquita, opaque green 8.50
   Concentric Ring, yellow 10.00
Teapot
   Concentric Ring, opaque cobalt
    blue, white lid 30.00
   Interior Panel, opaque green 9.00
   Octagonal, opaque blue, white lid,
    2¾" 13.00
Tumbler
   Interior Panel, green 6.75
   Stippled Band, jade transparent op-
    tic 5.00
Water Set, Stack Disc, opaque green
  pitcher, six white tumblers, orig
  box 90.00
Children's Play Dish Set
8 pcs, Topaz, orig box 125.00
12 pcs, Concentric Rib, opaque green
  plates and cups, tan saucers 32.00
20 pcs, Plain Jane, baked on, red cups
  and bowls, yellow saucers, green
  plates, cobalt teapot and cov, creamer, and sugar 135.00
Chinese Checkers, sixty glass marbles,
  six solid colors, yellow, green, black,
  blue, red, and white, orig 4 x 6¼ x
  ½" box marked "Akro–Agate Co,
  Clarksburg, WV," c1930 .... 65.00
Cornucopia, white and orange 5.00
Demitasse Cup and Saucer, opaque yel-
  low 7.50
Flower Pot
   Banded Dart, 2½" h, aqua 6.00
   Graduated Darts, 2" h, marbleized
    white and green 8.00
   Ribbed Top, 1¾" h
    Marbleized red and white 9.75
    Opaque green 7.50
   Ribs and Flutes, 3½" h, cream 4.50
   Stacked Disk, 3" h, marbleized blue 6.50
Jar, Mexicali, cov
   Blue and white 65.00
   Green and white 40.00
   Pumpkin and white 35.00
Jardiniere, Graduated Darts, 5" h, scal-
  loped top, marbleized blue and green 12.00
Lamp, vanity, 10" h, custard, pr 50.00

Mortar and Pestle, white, hp flowers .. 12.00
Nasturium Bowl, Graduated Dart,
  pumpkin, ftd, 6" d 15.00
Planter
   Chiquita, 6" h, oval, green 3.50
   Graduated Dart, 3" h, black, scal-
    loped, emb company name and ad-
    dress 40.00
   Hexagon, opaque, green, 4½ x 2¼" 15.00
   Oval, marbleized orange 6.00
Powder Box, cov
   Colonial Lady, blue 55.00
   Concentric Ring
    Crystal 30.00
    Lime 23.00
   Spun, green marble, ftd, 3½" d 30.00
Powder Jar, Scottie dog, pink base 15.00
Vase
   4½" h, marbleized orange 6.50
   6¼" h, Westite, gray and brown mar-
    ble, tab handles 30.00

ALUMINUM, HAND WROUGHT

Collecting Hints: Some manufacturers' marks are synonymous with quality, e.g., Continental Hand Wrought Silverlook. However, some quality pieces are not marked and should not be overlooked. Check carefully for pitting, deep scratches, and missing pieces of glassware.

History: During the late 1920s the use of aluminum for purely utilitarian purposes resulted in a variety of decorative household accessories. Although manufactured by a variety of methods, the hammered aluminum with repousse patterns appears to have been the most popular and certainly was more demanding of the skill of the craftsman producing the articles.

At one time many companies were competing for the aluminum giftware market with numerous silver companies adding aluminum articles as promotional items or as a more competitive and affordable product during the depression years. Many well known and highly esteemed metal–smiths contributed their skills to the production of hammered aluminum. With the advent of mass production methods and the accompanying wider distribution of aluminum giftware, the demand began to decline, leaving only a few producers who have continued to turn out quality work by the age old and time–tested methods of metal crafting.

Reference: Dannie Woodard and Billie Wood, *Hammered Aluminum: Hand Wrought Collectibles*, published by authors, 1983; Dannie Woodard, *Revised 1990 Price List for Hammered Alu-*

minum: Hand Wrought Collectibles, Aluminum Collectors' Books, 1990.

Periodical: *The Aluminist*, P.O. Box 1346, Weatherford, TX 76086.

Ashtray, 3½", triangular shape, apple blossoms, Town/Hand Made Aluminum **3.50**

Basket

7¾", Chrysanthemum, #1088, Continental Silver Co Inc **15.00**

11", fluted edge, double handle with square knot, sailing ship, Hand Wrought by Federal S Co. **10.00**

12", flared sides, Harvest pattern, scalloped handle, Hand Forged .. **8.00**

13", flat, intaglio Wheat pattern, double strand handle, Milcraft **10.00**

Bowl

7¼", cov, wooden knob, applied leaves, Shup Laird/Argental **12.00**

10", tulip, flower ribbon handles, Rodney Kent #450 .... **20.00**

11", iris, handles, World Hand Forged **12.00**

11¼", Chrysanthemum pattern, Continental Silverlook **14.00**

Butter, cov, Buenilium **18.00**

Candleholder

2½" sq base, arrow shape, corners form feet, handle, #1020, Everlast Forged Aluminum **3.50**

6" h, beaded edge base, aluminum stem with wooden ball, Buenilum **5.00**

Candy Dish

Double, opposing rose pattern in dish, center handle with leaf pattern, Farberware **28.00**

Thick glass dish, three sections, aluminum cov, fruit pattern, pear knob, unmarked **25.00**

Casserole Holder, cov

7½", rose, beaded knob, Everlast Forged Metal **12.00**

8", twisted handles, looped finial, Buenilum **10.00**

10", footed ring, wheat and vegetables, fan shape handles and knob, baking dish, unmarked **15.00**

Cheese, cov **18.00**

Coaster

5", turtle, Wendell August Forge **3.00**

Set of 8, caddy, beaded edge, double loop finial, Buenilum **10.00**

Cocktail Shaker, straight sides, grooved Art Deco top, clear plastic knob lid, Buenilum **12.00**

Coffee Urn, stand, and warmer **60.00**

Compote, Continental Hand Wrought Silverlook, 5" h, wild rose **12.00**

Creamer and Sugar, World Hand Forged, cupped shape **8.00**

Crumb Tray, 12" with well, stamped leaf pattern, Wrought Farberware **12.00**

Desk Set, three pc, graduated sizes, Bali bamboo pattern, B 24, Forged Everlast **20.00**

Gravy Boat, Hand Forged/Everlast Metal, 7" **10.00**

Ice Bucket, cov, 11½" h, double twisted handles, plastic knob on lid, Lehman **12.00**

Ladle, Argental Cellini Craft, 14½" ... **18.00**

Lazy Susan, 18", leaf and acorns, Continental Silverlook **15.00**

Match Box Holder, Wendell August Forge **8.00**

Pitcher, Buenilum, ovoid, twisted handle **24.00**

Platter, ftd, grape leaves, tree and well **25.00**

Salad Utensils, wooden, teardrop shape aluminum dec, dogwood pattern ... **10.00**

Samovar, one gallon container with spigot, double loop finial cov, stand and cov candle holder, unmarked, Buenilum style **35.00**

Server, 11", fluted flange, stamped flowers, removable divider, cov, handles, #5010 Everlast Forged Metal **12.00**

Silent Butler, 6 x 8", oval, floral bouquet, Henry & Miller **8.00**

Tray, grapes and vine motif, Presentation College Club Golf League, 1938, marked "World Hand Forged, #105," 16 x 9¾", $5.00.

Tray

7½ x 14½", zinnia panel, spiral handle, Farber & Shlevin **18.00**

8 x 23", polo team, inscribed names, dated 4–23–38, Wendell August Forge **15.00**

10 x 16", gold anodized, chessmen, Authur Armour **15.00**

11 x 16", bird on flowering limb, N S Co. (National Silver Co) **15.00**

12 x 18", leaf and flower, fluted edge, Buenilum **17.00**

14 x 20", tulip, handles, #425, Rodney Kent **25.00**

Water Set, pitcher, eight 20 oz tumblers, applied flowers, sq knot handle on pitcher, World Hand Forged **45.00**

AMERICAN DINNERWARE

Collecting Hints: The companies who manufactured American Dinnerware made different shapes, sizes, and hundreds of patterns. Most of these dinnerware pieces are backstamped. A backstamp usually includes the company name, logo, pattern name or shape, and production numbers. Many companies changed the backstamp to promote a new line or pattern, thus creating many confusing backstamps. A collector should learn all the marks and backstamps associated with their particular area of collecting.

The majority of American dinnerware is collected by pattern or company. Remember that some companies kept the same pattern in production for several decades. Condition is the key element. Since production runs were large, do not settle for damaged pieces.

Prices for individual pieces are generally higher than when they are sold in sets. This is a phenomenon common to all dinnerware china, European or American. The reason is that many people have a basic set and are looking for filler pieces. After all, only the most avid collector will own more than a half dozen sets of china.

History: The origins of the American dinnerware industry were in East Liverpool, Ohio, an area rich in natural clay deposits. James Bennett started a factory there in 1839. Benjamin Harker assisted with financial backing and supplied raw materials. The first salesman was Issac Knowles.

By 1844, Bennett left the area and Benjamin Harker had founded the Harker Pottery Co. Many other potteries were also established. Their first products were yellow ware, named for the color assumed by the clay when fired. In 1879, white ware was developed by Harker, Knowles, and Laughlin, further establishing the dinnerware industry in the area. The development of white ware necessitated decoration and skilled people to do it.

The American dinnerware industry thrived in the 1940s, a period that saw Americans buying American made products. By the 1950s, the number of potteries decreased. The increased use of plastics and imports greatly hurt the industry. The few companies that remain have included institutional wares in their production.

References: Jo Cunningham, *The Collector's Encyclopedia of American Dinnerware*, Collector Books, 1982; Pat Dole, *Purinton Pottery*, published by author, 1985; Delleen Enge, *Franciscan Ware*, Collector Books, 1981; Winnie Keillor, *Dishes, What Else? Blue Ridge of Course!*, published by author, 1983; Lois Lehner, *Lehner's Encyclopedia of US Marks on Pottery, Porcelain & Clay*, Collector Books, 1988; Jim Martin and Bette Cooper, *Monmouth–Western Stoneware*, Wallace–Homestead, 1983; Betty Newbound, *The Gunshot Guide To Values of American Made China & Pottery*, Book 2, published by author, 1983; Betty Newbound, *Southern Potteries, Inc. Blue Ridge Dinnerware*, 3rd Edition, Collector Books, 1989; Robert H. Schneider, *Coors Rosebud Pottery*, Busche–Waugh–Henry Publications, 1984.

Collectors' Club: Blue Ridge Club, Rt. 3, Box 161, Erwin, TN 37650.

Periodicals: *The Daze*, P.O. Box 57, Otisville, MI 48463; *The New Glaze*, P. O. Box 4782, Birmingham, AL 35206; *National Blue Ridge Newsletter*, 144 Highland Drive, Route 5, Box 298, Blountville, TN 37617.

BAUER

J A Bauer established the Bauer pottery in Los Angeles, California, in 1909. Dinnerware was introduced in 1930. The firm closed in 1962.

La Linda
Carafe, chartreuse, glossy, wood handle	**20.00**
Casserole, cov, chartreuse, glossy, 1½ pint, copper frame	**25.00**
Cup, pink, matte	**5.00**
Fruit Bowl, 5¼" d, pink, matte	**7.00**
Gravy, rose	**15.00**

Plate
6½" d, pink, matte	**5.00**
9½" d, pink, matte	**13.00**
Saucer, pink, matte	**3.00**

Teapot
Four cup, light reddish brown, Aladdin	**18.00**
Eight cup, olive green, glossy pastel, Aladdin	**35.00**
Tumbler, burgundy, metal handle, glossy	**20.00**

Monterey Modern
Casserole, cov, 2 qt, chartreuse, metal frame, crazed lid	**35.00**
Cup, olive green	**12.00**

Plate
9½" d, chartreuse	**9.00**
10½" d, olive green	**15.00**

Ring
Baking Dish, cov, orange–red, 4" d .	**25.00**
Chop Plate, 12" d, yellow	**30.00**
Coffeepot, orange–red	**40.00**

Mixing Bowl
Black, #30	**35.00**
Olive Green, #12	**28.00**
Yellow, #24	**15.00**
Pitcher, 1½ qt, orange–red	**30.00**

Plate
6" d
Burgundy	**12.00**
Yellow	**8.00**

7½" d
Dark Blue	18.00
Yellow	15.00
Platter, 12" oval, red	28.00
Punch Cup, dark blue	22.00
Saucer, turquoise	3.00
Shaker, green	12.00
Tumbler, wood handle, yellow	15.00

Blue Ridge, platter, pink and blue flowers, yellow centers, green leaves, 12½" l, $10.00.

BLUE RIDGE

Blue Ridge dinnerware was produced by Southern Potteries of Erwin, Tennessee, from the late 1930s until 1956. The company used eight shapes and over 400 different patterns.

Arlington Apple, Skyline
Cup, rope handle	3.00
Plate, 9½" d	5.00
Cherry Bounce, dinner service, 45 pcs	200.00

Cherry Tree Glen
Bowl
5½" d	5.00
6¼" d	6.00
9½" d	12.00
Creamer	7.00

Plate
6" d	3.00
7½" sq	15.00
9½" d	8.00
Vegetable Bowl, 9¼" l, oval	15.00

Chintz
Bonbon	37.00
Cake Plate, maple leaf	45.00
Celery	20.00
Children's Set, complete	250.00
Creamer, pedestal	25.00

Crab Apple
Cereal Bowl, 6" d	4.00
Creamer	20.00
Plate, 8½" d, dinner	8.00

Platter, 13½" l, oval	8.00
Sugar	25.00
Vegetable Bowl, oval	10.00

French Peasant
Cake Tray, maple leaf shape	85.00
Celery	100.00
Ramekin, 5" d, red base	10.00
Salad Bowl	125.00
Salt and Pepper Shakers, pr	150.00
Vase, handle	70.00

Poinsettia
Creamer	7.50

Plate
6¼" d	3.00
9¼" d	8.00
Sugar	7.50
Quaker Apple, dinner service, service for four	130.00
Stanhome Ivy, dinner service, 69 pcs	150.00
Sunfire, dinner service, 42 pcs	200.00

COORS POTTERY

Coors Pottery was manufactured in Golden, Colorado, from 1920 to 1939.

Rosebud
Cake Plate, yellow	18.00
Cookie Jar	25.00
Cup and Saucer	7.50
Fruit Bowl, 5" d, handle	5.00
Honey Pot, cov	20.00

Plate
6" d	10.00
9½" d	12.00
Salt and Pepper Shakers, pr	18.50
Vase, 8" h, yellow	15.00

CROOKSVILLE CHINA COMPANY

The Crooksville China Company, Crooksville, Ohio, was founded in 1902 for the manufacture of artware "such as vases, flowerpots and novelties." Dinnerware soon became its stock in trade. Silhouette was one of the most popular patterns that Crooksville made. The Silhouette decal is in black on a yellow glaze ground and shows two men sitting at a table with a dog looking up at them, waiting for food.

Petit Point House
Cup and Saucer	6.00
Pie Baker	15.00
Plate, 9" d	6.00
Platter, 11" l	10.00
Soup Bowl, 7¼" d	4.00
Teapot	25.00
Utility Jar, cov	45.00
Vegetable Bowl, 9" d	7.50

Silhouette
Batter Jug, cov	45.00
Casserole, cov	28.00

Creamer	7.50
Cup	6.00
Pie Baker	18.00
Plate, dinner	8.00
Saucer	3.50
Tumbler	15.00

EDWIN M KNOWLES CHINA COMPANY

This dinnerware was manufactured in East Liverpool, Ohio, from 1900 to 1963.

Deanna

Bowl, 5¼", orange	3.50
Creamer	5.00
Cup, blue	3.50
Plate, dinner, pink	4.50
Saucer, blue	1.50
Sugar	8.50

Fruits

Batter Jug, cov	17.50
Bowl, 9" d	15.00
Casserole, cov	25.00
Creamer	10.00
Pitcher	12.50
Plate, bread and butter	12.00
Serving Plate, 11" d, handles	12.00
Sugar	5.00

Yorktown

Bowl, 6" d	3.25
Creamer	5.00
Cup	3.50
Plate	
7⅜" d	2.75
10" d	4.00
Saucer	1.50
Sugar, cov	6.00

FRANCISCAN DINNERWARE

This dinnerware has been manufactured by Gladding McBean & Co of California from 1934 to the present.

Apple

Bowl, 7½" d	25.00
Butter Dish, cov	17.50
Creamer	8.50
Cup and Saucer	14.00
Gravy	30.00
Plate	
6" d	4.00
8" d	12.00
9½" d	7.00
Salad Bowl	10.00
Salt and Pepper Shakers, pr	30.00
Sherbet, underplate	22.00
Soup Bowl	12.00
Sugar, cov	12.00
Vegetable Bowl	25.00

Autumn

Creamer	5.00
Cup	8.00
Mug	15.00
Pickle Dish, 12" l	16.00
Pitcher	
6" h	8.00
8" h	10.00
Salt Shaker, individual	8.00
Tray, three part	15.00
Vegetable, divided, tab handle	15.00

Coronado Swirl

After Dinner

Coffee Set, coffeepot, creamer, cov sugar, four cups and saucers, coral, satin	75.00
Cup and Saucer, maroon gloss	18.00
Bowl	
5¾" d, coral, satin	4.00
7½" d, coral, satin	9.00
Chop Plate, 12" d, turquoise	
Glossy	15.00
Satin	4.00
Cup, coral, satin	4.00
Gravy, underplate, turquoise, satin	18.00
Plate	
6" d, turquoise, glossy	2.00
6½" d, coral, satin	4.00
8" d, turquoise, glossy	5.00
9½" d, coral, satin	6.00
10" d, turquoise, glossy	8.00
Platter, 13" l, oval, coral, satin	17.00
Sugar, cov, coral, satin	12.00
Teapot, turquoise, satin	35.00
Vegetable Bowl, oval, yellow, satin	10.00

Desert Rose

Cup	9.50
Gravy	25.00
Plate, 8¼" d, luncheon	5.00
Saucer	6.50

Duet Rose

Baby Dish, divided	45.00
Butter Dish, cov	25.00
Casserole, cov	35.00
Chop Plate, 13" d	18.00
Creamer	6.00
Cup, green rim	2.00
Gravy, liner	15.00
Party Platter	18.00
Plate	
6" d	2.00
9" d	8.00
Platter, 15" l	16.00
Salt and Pepper Shakers, pr	12.00
Saucer	1.50
Sugar, cov	8.00
Teapot	25.00
TV Plate, indent	20.00

El Patio

Cereal Bowl, yellow gloss	5.00
Creamer, Redwood Brown	8.00
Cup, Redwood Brown	5.00

Fruit Bowl, 5", gray satin	3.50
Gravy, yellow gloss	20.00
Vegetable Bowl, divided, green gloss	15.00

Oasis

Bowl, 4¾" d	5.00
Chop Plate, 13" d	22.00
Cup	8.00
Plate, 10" d	7.00
Saucer	4.00

Starburst

Bowl, 4¾" d	7.00
Butter Dish, cov	48.00
Child's plate	50.00
Cup	5.00
Egg Cup	7.50
Plate	
6" d	3.00
8" d	4.00
Soup, flat	12.00

Tiempo, tan

Bowl, 4½" d	4.00
Cup	3.00
Plate	
5⅞" d	4.00
7¾" d	4.00
9½" d	5.00
Saucer	1.50

METLOX

Metlox Potteries was founded in Manhattan Beach, California, in 1927 and is still producing artware, novelties, and Poppytrail dinnerware.

Antique Grape

Bowl, 9½" d, divided	15.00
Cup and Saucer	6.00
Gravy, liner	15.00
Plate	
6½" d	3.00
7½" d	5.00
10½" d	6.00
Platter, oval	
12" l	15.00
14½" l	18.00
Vegetable Bowl, oval	20.00

California Ivy

Chop Plate, 13" d	25.00
Creamer	6.50
Cup	3.50
Plate	
6½" d	5.00
8" d	6.00
Salt Shaker	3.00
Saucer	1.50
Sugar	5.00

California Provincial

Bowl	
5½" d	12.00
8" d, tab handle	20.00
9¾" d	18.00
Chop Plate, 12" d	25.00

Creamer	10.00
Cruet Set	25.00
Cup	7.50
Fruit Bowl	8.00
Marmalade, cov	30.00
Plate	
6½" d, salad	8.00
7½" d, luncheon	5.00
9" d, dinner	10.00
Platter, 13½" l	25.00
Salt and Pepper Shakers, pr	20.00
Saucer	2.50
Sugar, cov	7.00
Tankard	20.00
Vegetable Bowl, divided, oblong, handles	25.00

Red Rooster

Creamer, red	7.00
Cup, red	7.00
Plate, red	
6" d	5.00
7½" d	7.00
10" d	10.00
Server, 9 x 13", three parts, red	40.00
Soup Tureen, cov, blue	75.00
Sugar, cov, red	7.00

Sculptured Daisy

Cereal Bowl, 7" d	4.00
Creamer	6.00
Cup	4.00
Fruit Bowl, 6" d	3.00
Plate	
7½" d	3.00
10½" d	5.00
Platter	
11" l	12.50
14¼" l	20.00
Saucer	2.00

PURINTON

Bernard Purinton founded Purinton Pottery in 1936 in Wellsville, Ohio. In 1941 the pottery was relocated to Shippenville, Pennsylvania. The plant ceased operations around 1959. Purinton Pottery used no decals; all wares were hand painted. William H Blair and Dorothy Purinton were the chief designers.

Apple

Bowl	6.50
Cereal Bowl	6.75
Creamer	10.00
Cup	4.00
Dutch Jug	25.00
Honey Pot	10.00
Mug	25.00
Plate, dinner, 9¼" d	12.00
Relish, divided	20.00
Salt and Pepper Shakers, pr	15.00
Sugar, cov	17.50

Fruits
    Lazy Susan, triangular can set **85.00**
    Range Top Salt and Pepper Shakers,
      pr **12.00**
Ivy
    Drip Jar **7.00**
    Teapot **20.00**

ROYAL

This dinnerware has been manufactured in Sebring, Ohio, from 1934 to the present.

Colonial Homestead
  Bowl
    6" d **2.00**
    9" d **6.00**
    10" d **7.00**
  Chop Plate **17.00**
  Cup and Saucer **3.00**
  Plate
    6¼" d **2.00**
    10" d **3.00**
  Soup, flat **3.00**
Currier & Ives, blue and white
  Ashtray **5.00**
  Bowl
    5½" d **1.75**
    6" d **6.00**
    9" d **8.00**
    10" d **10.00**
  Calendar Plate, 1977 ....   **4.00**
  Creamer **4.00**
  Cup and Saucer **3.50**
  Gravy, underplate **12.00**
  Pie Baker **7.00**
  Plate
    7" d **3.50**
    9" d **2.50**
    10" d **3.00**
  Platter **18.00**
  Soup, flat **4.00**
Memory Lane, pink and white
  Berry Bowl **4.00**
  Cake Plate, tab handle **12.00**
  Creamer and Sugar, cov **8.00**
  Cup and Saucer **3.50**
  Plate
    6" d **2.00**
    10" d **4.00**
  Soup, flat **4.00**
  Tumbler
    Old fashioned glass **4.00**
    Water, 5½" h **4.00**

STANGL

This dinnerware was manufactured in Trenton, New Jersey, from 1930 to 1978.

Antique Gold, ashtray, 9" sq **10.00**

Stangl, fruit, sandwich plate, center handle, $7.50.

Blueberry
  Cereal Bowl **4.50**
  Coffeepot **60.00**
  Cup **8.00**
  Plate, dinner **12.50**
  Saucer **4.00**
Fruits
  Dinner Service, 40 pcs **425.00**
  Teapot, individual size **12.00**
Garland
  Creamer **6.00**
  Cup and Saucer **7.50**
  Plate, dinner **8.00**
  Salad Bowl, 12" **28.00**
  Sugar **6.00**
Orchard Song
  Coffee Warmer **25.00**
  Dinner Service, service for four, 7
    serving pcs **90.00**
  Plate, 10" d **5.00**
  Server, center handle **9.00**
Thistle
  Cereal Bowl **5.00**
  Coaster **6.50**
  Creamer **13.00**
  Cup and Saucer **9.50**
  Fruit Bowl **5.00**
  Plate, 9" d **8.75**
  Sherbet **15.00**
  Sugar, cov **17.00**
Tulip, yellow
  Flower Pot
    4" d **5.00**
    5" d **7.00**
  Plate, 9¼" d **6.00**
  Platter, 12½" d, round **20.00**
White Dogwood, cup and saucer **10.00**

TAYLOR, SMITH, TAYLOR

Founded in Chester, West Virginia, in 1903, the company remained in the family's control until purchased by Anchor Hocking in 1973. The tableware division was closed in 1981. Five pastel glazes were used: Windsor Blue, Persian Cream, Sharon Pink, Surf Green, and Chatham Gray.

Autumn Harvest
Butter, cov	15.00
Casserole, cov	16.00
Cup	3.00
Plate, bread and butter	2.00
Platter	
11" l	8.00
13½" l	12.00
Salt and Pepper Shakers, pr	8.50
Saucer	1.50

Lu Ray
After Dinner	
Creamer, pink	40.00
Sugar, pink	45.00
Calendar Plate, blue	45.00
Casserole Cov, pink	38.00
Creamer, pink	5.00
Cup	
Pink	5.00
Yellow	6.50
Fruit Bowl, blue	4.00
Nut Dish, green	65.00
Plate	
6½" d	
Blue	2.00
Yellow	3.00
7¼" d, blue	4.00
9" d	
Green	5.00
Pink	5.00
Platter, oval	
11½" l, yellow	10.00
13¼" l, blue	10.00
Relish, 4 part	
Blue	75.00
Yellow	80.00
Sauce Boat, blue	20.00
Saucer, blue	1.50
Teapot, pink	50.00
Vegetable Dish, oval, gray	27.00

Vistosa
Bowl	
5¾" d, red	8.00
8½" d, two handles, green	20.00
Chop Plate, yellow	20.00
Cup and Saucer, green	15.00
Egg Cup, yellow	20.00
Pitcher, yellow	25.00
Plate	
6" d, green	3.00
7" d, cobalt blue	8.50
9" d, yellow	8.00
Salt and Pepper Shakers, pr, green	14.00
Sugar, cov, green	15.00

WATTS POTTERY

Watts Pottery was founded in 1922 for the manufacture of stoneware. In 1935 production began of kitchenware. The Crooksville, Ohio, plant was destroyed by fire in 1965 and not rebuilt.

Apple
Bowl	
#5	15.00
#8	65.00
#64	35.00
#65	45.00
Casserole, cov, #601	45.00
Creamer, adv	45.00
Mug, #121	95.00
Nesting Bowls, round, red, #07, 06, 05, and 04	125.00
Pitcher, adv	
#15	50.00
#16	60.00
#17, ice lip	235.00
Sugar, adv	85.00
Pansy	
Plate	
7" d	50.00
10" d	65.00
Starflower	
Bowl, #8, adv	30.00
Mug, barrel	100.00
Salt and Pepper Shakers, pr	100.00

AUTOGRAPHS

Collecting Hints: The condition and content of letters and documents bears significantly on value. Signatures should be crisp, clear, and located so that they do not detract from the rest of the item. Whenever possible, obtain a notarized statement of authenticity, especially for pieces over $100.

Forgeries abound. Copying machines compound the problem. Further, many signatures of political figures, especially presidents, movie stars, and sports heroes are machine or secretary signed rather than by the individual themselves. Photographic reproduction can produce a signature resembling an original. Check all signatures using a good magnifying glass or microscope.

Presentation material, something marked ''To____,'' is of less value than a non–presentation item. The presentation personalizes the piece and often restricts interest, except to someone with the same name.

There are autograph mills throughout the country run by people who write to noteworthy individuals requesting their signatures on large groups of material. They in turn sell this material on the autograph market. Buy an autograph of a living person only after the most careful consideration and examination.

Autograph items are sold using standard abbreviations denoting type and size. They are:

ADS	Autograph Document Signed
ALS	Autograph Letter Signed
AQS	Autograph Quotation Signed
CS	Card Signed
DS	Document (printed) Signed
LS	Letter Signed
PS	Photograph Signed
TLS	Typed Letter Signed
Folio	12 x 16"
4to	8 x 10"
8vo	5 x 7"
12mo	3 x 5"

History: Autograph collecting is an old established tradition, perhaps dating back to the first signed documents and letters. Early letters were few, hence, treasured by individuals in private archives. Municipalities, churches, and other institutions maintained extensive archives to document past actions.

Autograph collecting became fashionable during the 19th century. However, early collectors focused on the signatures alone, clipping off the signed portion of a letter or document. Eventually collectors realized that the entire document was valuable.

The advent of movie stars, followed by sports, rock 'n roll, and television personalities, brought autograph collecting to the popular level. Fans pursued these individuals with autograph books, programs and photographs. Everything imaginable was offered for signatures. Realizing the value of their signatures and the speculation that occurs, modern stars and heroes are less willing to sign material than in the past.

References: Mary A. Benjamin, *Autographs: A Key To Collecting*, Dover Publications, 1946/1988; Charles Hamilton, *American Autographs*, University of Oklahoma Press, 1983; Robert W. Pelton, *Collecting Autographs For Fun And Profit*, Betterway Publications, 1987; George Sanders, Helen Sanders, Ralph Roberts, *Collector's Guide To Autographs*, Wallace–Homestead, 1990; George Sanders, Helen Sanders, and Ralph Roberts, *The Price Guide to Autographs, Second Edition*, Wallace–Homestead, 1991.

Collectors' Clubs: Manuscript Society, 350 Niagara Street, Burbank, CA 91505; Universal Autograph Collectors Club, P. O. Box 6181, Washington, DC 20044–6181.

Autograph Letters Signed (ALS)
Bush, George, 41st president, 6 x 5" blue bordered personalized card, "8–14–80 Dear Bill–Just a note to

thank you for your loyal support and to wish you well. During the War I was a carrier based Navy Pilot in the Pacific. Shot Down Sept 2 1944, I was rescued by a U.S. Submarine. Hope all's well with you– George Bush," inscribed black white glossy 8 x 10" signed photo that was sent with the above ALS, penned across top area with blue ink "To Bill Dooley–a fellow vet with warm best wishes, George Bush," 6 x 5" **3,000.00**

Fromme, Lynette, member of Manson Family, attempted to kill President Ford, holograph address on back of picture post card, 1986, thanks for book, full signature **85.00**

Gluck, Alma, opera, 6 x 4" personal card, mounted on gray 12 x 16" board, book plate photo, and obituary **75.00**

Hayes, Rutherford B, 19th President, 8 x 5" lined paper **875.00**

Knobloch, WWII co–pilot, 8 x 4" plain white paper **45.00**

Izzi, Basil, WWII seaman, plain 5 x 7" paper **25.00**

Melba, Nellie, opera, personal stationery, photo, and news article about her death, 5 x 7", 3 pgs ... **85.00**

Potter, Hank, WWII navigator, 8 x 4" yellow plain paper **20.00**

Autograph Quotations Signed (AQS)
Dickinson, Anna E., suffrage leader, 4 x 3" **25.00**

Pitney, Gene, songwriter, 4 line quotation, personal blue stationery, 4 line message, 4to **55.00**

Stedman, Edmund Clarence, poet, Civil War correspondent, plain paper, Dec, 1901, five lines, 4 x 6" . **45.00**

Suyin, Han, author, 6 x 5" New Year greeting card, inscribed **45.00**

Thaxter, Cilia, author, 30 line poem, plain paper, 5 x 7" **60.00**

Cards Signed (CS)
Aaron, Hank, baseball player, 5 x 3" unlined card **5.00**

Abel, Sid, hockey player, 5 x 3" unlined card **4.00**

Bench, Johnny, baseball player, 5 x 3" unlined card **7.00**

Bryant, Paul Bear, football player, 4 x 3" unlined card **20.00**

Byrnes, Ed, actor, 8 x 10" black and white photo, 4 x 2" opening with signature, 11 x 14" black mat **15.00**

Chaplin, Charlie, actor, blue ink signature on white card, matted with magazine photo, "The Little Tramp," 11 x 16" **250.00**

Baseball, Pittsburgh Pirates, signed by all players, $95.00.

Davis, Bette, actress, 8 x 10" color photo, 4 x 2" opening with signature, 11 x 14" black mat 20.00

Diddley, Bo, musician, 5 x 3" plain white card 10.00

Hughes, Sarah T., administered oath of office to LBJ, Christmas card ... 45.00

John, Olivia Newton, musician, 5 x 3" plain white card 10.00

Jones, George, musician, 5 x 3" plain white card 5.00

Kesey, Ken, author, 5 x 3" 15.00

Kiel, Richard, actor, 9 x 7 color close–up photo as "Jaws," white card signed "Richard "Jaws" Kiel," rust colored mat, 12 x 13" 25.00

McHall, Kevin, basketball player, 5 x 3" unlined card 4.00

Rubenstein, Helena, beauty aids, post card, cancelled Paris 1933 ...... 150.00

Salk, Jonas, medicine, 5 x 3" plain white card 10.00

Schwab, C. M., industrialist, imprinted thank you card, 4 x 4" ... 35.00

Turner, Tina, musician, 4 x 3" plain white card 15.00

Williams, Esther, actress, 8 x 10" black and white photo, 4 x 2" opening with signature, 11 x 14" black mat 15.00

Zorn, Jim, football player, 5 x 3" unlined card 4.00

Document Signed (DS)

Caldwell, Erskine, author, typescript, Chapter 1, Tobacco Road, 8 x 10", 1 pg 60.00

Capote, Truman, author, news article, photo at top, black ink signature across photo, 3 x 7" 75.00

Edison, Charles, son of Thomas Edison, Nat State Bank of Newark check, 1965 .... 25.00

Fish, Hamilton, Governor NY, Bank of NY check, 1855 .... 40.00

Lennon, John (1940–80), Yoko Ono, each signed matching white album pages, approx 6 x 3" with blue ball point pen, his full signature is boldly penned across page with excellent self caricature (his face) and dated "76" beneath, Yoko signed large and clear in both English and Japanese diagonally across the page, and added 1976, mint condition 1,500.00

Thurston, Howard, magician, membership card for Society of American Magicians, 1929 .... 95.00

Van Buren, Martin (1782–1862), 8th President, 17 x 12", partly printed, 1840, as president, consul appointment to New Granada, co–signed by John Forsyth as Secretary of State, white paper wafer seal intact, left edge discoloration due to long gone frame, wrinkled left side, normal aging 800.00

First Day Covers (FDC)

Adams, Ansel and Jousuf Karsh, honoring photography 75.00

Allen, Brooke, aviation 20.00

Carr, Jerry, astronaut 12.00

Carter, Billy 25.00

Dickerson, Eric, football player, canceled Dec 9, 1984, day he broke Simpson's single season record, color photo cachet of scoring ... 30.00

Eisenhower, Mamie Doud, first lady, honoring Dwight Eisenhower, canceled, Washington, DC, May 21, 1971 .... 20.00

Jackson, Jesse, political leader, commemorating 200th Anniversary of Alexander Hamilton's birthday, canceled, NYC, Jan 11, 1957 .... 25.00

North, Oliver, honoring Bicentennial of Virginia Statehood, 1988 ...... 20.00

Thompson, Rev. James N, priest who gave Last Rites at Parkland Hospital, Dallas, honoring JFK 35.00

Trudeau, Gary, cartoonist, stamp and cachet honoring "The Great Stone Face" 25.00

Truman, Bess, First Lady 45.00

Truman, Harry S, President, honoring 150th Anniversary of Missouri statehood 125.00

Letters Signed (LS)

Hale, John P, US Attorney, lined paper, Washington, DC, 1863, 8vo . 30.00

Nutting, Wallace, painter, personal stationery, imprinted vignette of one of his works on upper center of 1st page, 1941, orig holograph envelope, 2 pgs 275.00

Seward, William H, Secretary of State, plain stationery, 1861, 12mo   **35.00**

Photograph Signed (PS)

Ashford, Evelyn, olympics, color, 4to   **12.00**

Brubeck, Dave, jazz pianist, black and white glossy, 8 x 10" **10.00**

Carey, Harry, silent cowboy, sepia, 5 x 7" **150.00**

Charo, Cuchi–Cuchi, black and white glossy, 8 x 10" **50.00**

Crosby, Bing, actor, singer, black and white matte portrait, 8 x 10" **50.00**

Denver, Bob, black and white glossy, "Gilligan," 8 x 10" **15.00**

Dern, Bruce, actor, black and white glossy, 8 x 10" **10.00**

Elway, John, football player, color, 4to **15.00**

Funicello, Annette and Frankie Avalon, black and white glossy, beach scene from "Where The Boys Are," 10 x 8" **40.00**

Ishkabibble, sepia, bust pose, wearing funny hat 4 x 5" **20.00**

Jackson, Jesse, bust pose, smiling, color, 8 x 10" **55.00**

Joel, Billy, musician, color, 8 x 10" .   **40.00**

LaBelle, Patti, musician, black and white glossy, 8 x 10" **15.00**

Walter Lantz, orig crayon and ink cartoon, framed and matted, $85.00.

Lawford, Peter, actor, sepia, 8 x 10"   **60.00**

Lombardo, Victor, bandleader, sepia portrait, 4to **20.00**

McIntyre, Joe, New Kids, color, 8 x 10" **60.00**

Meeker, Bobby, bandleader, publicity, 8 x 10" **10.00**

Montana, Joe, football player, 4to ..   **15.00**

Motley Crue, four signatures, color performance, 8 x 10" **95.00**

Nelson, Cindy, olympic skier, color, 4to **12.00**

O'Connor, Sinead, close–up, signed first name only, color, 8 x 10" **75.00**

Righteous Brothers, color, 8 x 10" ..   **55.00**

Spillane, Mickey, mystery writer, color publicity photo, Lite Beer, 5 x 7" **15.00**

Walker, Herchel, football player, color, 4to **15.00**

Typed Letters Signed (TLS)

Ferber, Edna, author, personal stationery, 1962, 4to **50.00**

Fosdick, Harry Emerson, Baptist minister and author, Union Theological Seminary stationery, 1925, 8 x 8" .   **25.00**

Galli–Curci, Amelita, opera, plain paper, 1922, 4to **75.00**

Hoover, J. Edgar, Director of FBI, FBI stationery, 1936, blue ink signature, 7 x 9" **60.00**

Hubbard, Elbert, author, Roycroft Shop stationery, 1900, 12mo **48.00**

Hughes, Charles E., Chief Justice, Supreme Court, Governor of NY, Executive Chamber stationery, gold emb seal, 1910 ....   **50.00**

Hull, Cordell, secretary of state, Dept of State stationery, 1937, 4to **50.00**

Humphrey, Hubert, vice president, Senate stationery, 1971 ....   **25.00**

MacDonald, Betty, author, personal stationery, 8vo **20.00**

McCool, Harry C, WWII navigator, plain white paper, 8 x 8" **20.00**

Mencken, H. L., editor, personal stationery, 1946, 8 x 5" **125.00**

Porter, Katherine Anne, novelist, plain stationery, 1958, 8 x 6" **85.00**

Rogers, Richard, composer, personal stationery, 1973, 7 x 9" **40.00**

Schwarzkopf, H. Norman, father of U.S. Gulf War General, founded NJ State Police, plain stationary from Tehran, Iran, September 1946 as Brigadier General, USA, fine large black ink signature at conclusion, normal aging, 6 x 7" **50.00**

Trudeau, Gary, Doonesbury stationery, 6 x 8" **45.00**

Turner, Ted, business stationery, 4to   **15.00**

AUTOMATA, MODERN

BATTERY OPERATED AND WINDUP

Collecting Hints: Prices fluctuate greatly. Many of the collectors are in Japan and dealers must allow enough margin for shipment of pieces overseas. Operating condition is a key factor. Many pieces had accessory parts; these must be present to have full value. The original box, especially if it has a label, adds 10 to 20% to the price. Also, the more elaborate the action of the automata, the higher the value.

History: Automata began as "cheap" Japanese import goods in the 1950s. They were meant for amusement only, many finding themselves located on the shelves of bars in the recreation rooms of private homes. They were marketed through 5 and 10 cent stores and outlets.

The subjects were animal—bears being favored—and humans. Most were battery operated; but some were wind–up or had remote control. Quality of pieces varies greatly, with Linemar being among the best made.

The collecting craze started in the late 1970s. In 1981 Lloyd Ralston Toys, Fairfield, Connecticut, held the first auction featuring automata. Its success established the market nationally.

References: Don Hultzman, "Battery Operated Toys," in Richard O'Brien, *Collecting Toys, No. 5: A Collector's Identification & Value Guide*, Books Americana, 1990; Brian Moran, *Battery Toys*, Schiffer Publishing Ltd, 1984.

Godzilla, wind–up, walker, sparker, yellow and green, red handle, marked "Made In Hong Kong," $25.00.

Alligator, ¾ x 5 x½" h, tin, emb, yellow, green, and red, windup, alligator bounces, jaw flaps, c1960 . . . . **30.00**

American Football Player, 5½" h, tin, plastic, and fabric, multicolor, green base, football attached to 24" l black thread, windup, made by MM/Japan, orig box **65.00**

Artist Monkey, 3½ x 3½ x 6" h, brown plush body, fabric jacket, tin face, rubber hands holding paint brush and diecut tin pallet and picture, tin base, head and arms move, windup, c1960 **30.00**

Captain Blushwell, 11" h, tin and plastic, brown plush hair, fabric clothing,

plastic "Scotch Whiskey" bottle and glass, drinks, blushes, eyes spin, battery operated, made by Yone, Japan **75.00**

Child on Tricycle, 2½ x 3½ x 4½" h, vinyl figure on litho tin tricycle, bell on back rings, feet pedal moving tricycle, windup, Marx, c1960 . . . . **25.00**

Cowboy with Lasso, 3½" h, rearing horse, tin, rubber horse tail, brown horse, red, blue, yellow, and green cowboy, marked "The King of the Rancher Mechanical Toy," made by Alps, Japan, early 1950s, orig box . . **75.00**

Crazy Clown, tin car, green, yellow, and gold, brown plastic wheels, multicolor clown, turn clowns head to start car, made by Yone, Japan, orig box . **60.00**

Dance Hawaiian, 1½ x 2½ x 6" h, yellow metal legs and feet, yellow celluloid upper body, tan hair, pink thread skirt, orig key and box marked "SSS, Made in Occupied Japan" . . . **85.00**

Elephant, 3½ x 4 x 6" h, blue plush, red felt vest, tin eyes and ears, strikes tin drum with blue rubber beater, other arm attached to metal cymbal above drum, windup, MM, Japan, c1960, orig box **30.00**

Furry Dog, 3 x 4½ x 4" h, cardboard and tin, white, gray, and brown fur covering, white felt face, yellow plastic eyes, bell on orange ribbon around neck, red boot hangs from mouth, dog bounces and shakes boot, windup, marked "Made in Japan," c1960 . . . . **40.00**

Good Time Charlie, 12" h, litho tin base, dust bin, and lamp post, figure has soft rubber face, wearing tuxedo, holding cigar and bottle, cigar lights, figure blows smoke, raises bottle, face turns red, foot wiggles, and street light blinks, battery operated, Illfelder, made in Japan, 1960–1970s **150.00**

Hippo Bank, 2½" h, tin, multicolor, hippo, with head above water, opens mouth to catch coin, made by Yone, Japan, c1960 . . . . **30.00**

Jolly Santa on Snow, 12" h, red and white plush outfit, black belt, holding cloth sack and silver bell, soft rubber face, cotton beard, brown plastic boots with wheels, battery operated, Alps, Japan, c1960, orig box **185.00**

Maynard the Counting Dog, 10" h, hard plastic body, soft rubber ears and collar, blue base, brown cord connected to back, 24 pg puzzle book, battery operated, dog barks answers to number riddles, Remco, copyright 1960 . **75.00**

Monkey, tin, flip–over, German US Zone **45.00**

Monster, one–eyed, 6" h, plastic, orange body, green feet and head, red tongue, white accents, synthetic orange hair, plastic eye, windup, walks, made by Durham Industries, Japan, late 1960s 50.00

Mother Rabbit, 10" h, gray plush body, tin face and legs, fabric skirt, pushing red, white, blue, and yellow tin carriage, tin shopping basket and plush baby holding carrot inside, tin butterfly attached by wire to carriage, battery operated, S&E, Japan 85.00

Overland Stagecoach, 7½" h, horse and coach, galloping sound, horse's legs move, battery operated, Ichida, Japan 120.00

Panda Bear, fishing, 10" h, plush, black and white, maroon pants, checkered bow tie, straw hat, tin log base, three tin fish, fishing pole, bear catches fish, growls, and removes fish from line, battery operated, Alps, Japan .. 200.00

Pango–Pango African Dancer, 6" h, litho tin, holding shield and spear, windup, made by TPS, Japan, orig box 90.00

Picnic Dog, 3 x 3 x 5½" h, yellow plush head, black ears, tin face, red plaid jacket, green felt pants, black metal base, cardboard tag around neck reads "Vacation Today," holding yellow picnic basket, windup, Yone, Japan, c1960, orig box 25.00

Rabbit, 6" h, vinyl, gray overalls, red bow tie, white gloves, holding apple, windup, made by Alps, Japan 25.00

Scottie Dog, celluloid, playing with tin shoe, windup, MIB 115.00

Smarty Pants, 2½ x 3½ x 6" h, tin boy, red fabric pants, vinyl head, arm holding baby bottle raises as he alternately lowers the back of his pants to expose his rear end, windup, Mikuni, Japan, c1960, orig box 25.00

Sparky Dog, jumps out of doghouse, voice activated, battery operated, 1930s, MIB 42.50

Teddy the Artist, 9" h, bear sitting at tin litho desk, plush face, red and yellow shirt and cap, orange plastic hands, inscribed "Teddy the Artist," battery operated, holds crayon, traces rabbit using template included with toy, Yone, Japan, orig box 215.00

Tropical Fish, 2½ x 7 x 5" h, litho tin, bright colors including orange, yellow, and blue, green plastic fins, windup, bump–and–go action, made by KO Japan, orig box, early 1960s . 80.00

Trumpet Player, resembles Louis Armstrong, 10" h, tin base, fabric jacket, shirt, and pants, tin litho shoes and hat, rubber hands and face, holding plastic trumpet, windup, walks, made by TN, marked "Made in Japan," c1950, orig box 200.00

Whistling Showboat, 7½" h, litho tin, removable hard plastic smoke stack, marked "Queen River," battery operated, bump–and–go action, riverboat whistle sound, Modern Toys, marked "Made in Japan," c1960, orig box .. 175.00

AUTUMN LEAF PATTERN

Collecting Hints: Most Autumn Leaf pieces are backstamped with two marks. Both contain the words "Halls Superior Quality" and "Mary Dunbar," the latter a Jewel Tea trademark.

History: Hall China first made Autumn Leaf pattern china in 1933 as a premium for the Jewel Tea Company. Large orders for Autumn Leaf are credited with carrying The Hall China Company through the latter years of the Depression, thus saving the company from going out of business.

Autumn Leaf remained in production until 1978. Over the years, many different pieces were added and dropped from the line. Generally, pieces with short production lives are more desirable. Other companies made matching accessories in metal, glass, and plastic and are very collectible. Also look for Jewel Tea toy trucks.

References: Harvey Duke, *Superior Quality Hall China*, ELO Books, 1977; Harvey Duke, *Hall 2*, ELO Books, 1985; Harvey Duke, *The Official Price Guide to Pottery and Porcelain*, House of Collectibles, 1989; Margaret and Kenn Whitmyer, *The Collector's Encyclopedia of Hall China*, Collector Books, 1989.

Collectors' Club: National Autumn Leaf Collector's Society, 6505 W. Cameron, Tulsa, OK 74127.

Beanpot, qt, two handles 60.00
Bowl
  Berry, 5" 4.00
  Cereal, 6½" 8.50
  Soup, 8¼" 18.00
Cake Plate 12.00

Creamer and sugar, $24.00.

Casserole, cov	45.00
Coffeepot	30.00
Cookie Jar	120.00
Creamer	6.00
Cup	7.25
Gravy Boat	15.00
Jug, ball shape	18.00
Mayonnaise, cov, underplate	40.00
Mixer Cover, plastic	20.00
Milk Pitcher	15.00
Pickle Dish, 9", oval	25.00
Plate	
Bread and Butter, 6"	5.00
Dinner, 10" d	11.25
Luncheon, 8"	8.25
Relish Dish, oval	15.00
Salt and Pepper Shaker, pr, range	12.00
Sugar, cov	10.00
Tablecloth, sq	65.00
Teapot	20.00

Tidbit Tray, 3 tiers, 11½" h, $35.00.

Tray, rect, glass, wood handles	65.00
Tumbler, 5½", frosted	14.00
Vegetable Dish, 9", cov	55.00
Water Pitcher, ice lip	15.00

AVIATION COLLECTIBLES

Collecting Hints: This field developed in the 1980s and is now firmly established. The majority of collectors focused on personalities, especially Charles Lindbergh and Amelia Earhart. New collectors are urged to look to the products of airlines, especially those items related to the pre-jet era.

History: The first airlines in the United States depended on subsidies from the government for carrying mail for most of their income. The first non-Post Office Department flight for mail carrying was in 1926 between Detroit and Chicago. By 1930 there were 38 domestic and 5 international airlines operating in the United States. A typical passenger load was ten. After World War II, four engine planes with a capacity of 100 or more passengers were introduced.

The jet age was launched in the 1950s. In 1955 Capitol Airlines used British made turboprop airliners in domestic service. In 1958 National Airlines began domestic jet passenger service. The giant Boeing 747 went into operation in 1970 as part of the Pan American fleet. The Civil Aeronautics Board, which regulates the airline industry, ended control of routes in 1982 and fares in 1983.

Major American airlines include American Airlines, Delta Air Lines, Northwest Airlines, Pan American World Airways, Trans World Airlines, and United Airlines. There are many regional lines as well; new airlines are forming as a result of deregulation.

References: Aeronautica & Air Label Collectors Club of Aerophilatelic Federation of America, *Air Transport Label Catalog*, published by club; Stan Baumwald, *Junior Crew Member Wings*, published by author; Trev Davis and Fred Chan, *Airline Playing Cards: Illustrated Reference Guide, 2nd Edition*, published by authors, 1987; Richard R. Wallin, *Commercial Aviation Collectibles: An Illustrated Price Guide*, Wallace–Homestead, 1990.

Collectors' Club: The World Airline Historical Society, 3381 Apple Tree Lane, Erlanger, KY 41018.

Periodical: *Airliners*, P.O. Box 52–1238, Miami, FL 33152–1238.

Game, Flying The United States Air Mail, Parker Bros boxed board game, 1929 copyright, 18 x 14½", $110.00.

AIRLINES

Baggage Sticker, Pan Am, blue and white, wing over globe emblem, The System of the Flying Clippers	3.50

Calendar
  Scandinavian Air Lines, 1950 ...... **8.00**
  United Air Line, 13 scenes, 1943 ... **20.00**
China, place setting, Delta, 1st class
  passenger, Wiget logo, 1969–83 ... **5.50**
Chopsticks, TWA, clear package, uno-
  pened **15.00**
Figure, three dimensional, Good Luck
  Man, United Airlines, Hawaiian, 27" **100.00**
Flatware
  National, teaspoon, 6½", National on
    handle **7.50**
  Pan Am, fork, 6½", Pan Am in globe
    on handle **6.50**
Flying Egg, United Airlines **10.00**
Glass, Eastern Airlines **10.00**
Map, Air France, world routes, early
  1940s **30.00**
Matchbook Cover, 3 x 4½", Piedmont **.50**
Mirror, KLM Airlines, illus of plane,
  brown and white **50.00**
Paperweight, Trans World Airlines,
  Framed Milestones, Man in Flight, 6
  medallions **65.00**
Pin, United Airlines, 1" w, metal, logo,
  1930–1940s **15.00**
Pinback Button, United Airlines Boeing
  247–D, ¹³⁄₁₆" litho, black and white
  illus, yellow ground **10.00**
Plate, American Airlines, 6 x 4", chain,
  marked Hall **10.00**
Playing Cards, Delta Air LInes, San Francisco on back **8.00**
Poster, TWA to Las Vegas, 28 x 40",
  1953 .... **20.00**
Punchboard, Benrus Watches, "Official
  Watch of Famous Airlines," small,
  1940 .... **10.00**
Schedule Folder, Air France, paper, 4 x
  9", opens to 9 x 20", air route map of
  Europe, fare listings, black and white
  cutaway illus of twin propeller passenger plane, photos of Golden Clip-
  per, 1930s **15.00**
Tray, beverage, Pan–Am **15.00**
Umbrella, Capital Airlines **100.00**

GENERAL

Ashtray, brass, made from shell casings **45.00**
Banner, "Welcome Trans–Atlantic Her-
  oes," 9 x 13", felt, illus of monoplane
  "Bremen" and aviators von Huene-
  feld, Fitzmaurice, and Coehl, orange
  and tan illus, yellow accents, white
  lettering, dark blue ground, April
  1928 flight **85.00**
Blotter, adv, Bond Bread, 3½ x 6¼",
  cardboard, illus and description of
  P51 North American Mustang pursuit
  plane, early 1940s **12.00**

Book
  Aeroplane Cut–outs, 9¾ x 14¾",
    Whitman, #W933, stiff paper pun-
    chout pgs, 1930 .... **75.00**
  Heroes of Aviation, Laurence La-
    Tourette Driggs, dj, 1927 .... **20.00**
Calendar Plate, 6½" d, biplane, 1912 . **35.00**
Clock, figural airplane, wood and
  metal, Sessions **40.00**
Coloring Book, Planes and Jets, Whit-
  man, 11 x 15", 1952, half neatly col-
  ored **18.00**
Comic Book, Aviation Cadets, Street &
  Smith, 1943 .... **12.00**
Employee Identification Badge, St Paul
  Airport Official, 1¾" d, yellow and
  black, c1930 .... **12.00**
Game, Aviation Air Mail, Parker Broth-
  ers, c1930s **18.00**
Helmet, leather, pilot, 1930s **35.00**
Magazine, Popular Aviation Magazine,
  Dec 1932, 68 pgs, 8½ x 11¼" **8.00**
Model
  Jap Zero, Aurora Famous Fighters of
    all Nations **35.00**
  Marine Spitfire, balsa wood, orig box,
    1962 .... **38.00**
Palm Puzzle, 3½ x 4 x 1", gold color
  tin frame, clear glass cov, litho paper
  playing surface depicting flights of
  "Lindy/Chamberlain/Byrd," three
  magnetic pellets in capsules, instruc-
  tions, "New York to Paris Aero Race,"
  and "Bar–Zim Toy Co" printed on
  bottom **70.00**
Pencil Sharpener, figural, four engine
  passenger plane, plastic, red, blade in
  base, marked "Irwin of USA," c1940 **30.00**
Pin
  Airplane shape, brass, "Jimmie Allen
    Flying Cadet/Skelly," c1934 ...... **30.00**
  Bar, silvered brass, "Captain Frank's
    Air Hawks," Post Bran Flakes pre-
    mium, c1936 .... **32.00**
  Propeller and Engine, brass, portrait
    on red ground at center, "Capt
    Hawk's Sky Patrol" **30.00**
  Wings, 1¾", brass, "Jr Birdmen of
    America," red, white, and blue
    enamel shield at center, c1930 ... **35.00**
Pinback Button
  Field Day, 1½", red, white, and blue,
    WWII era **10.00**
  Howie Wing Aviation Corps/Cadet,
    ⅞", dark blue on gold ground, club
    member button, 1930s **25.00**
  Parachute Jumps, 2¼", light blue
    photo, orange and blue inscription,
    c1930 .... **18.00**
  Welcome German Flyers, 1¼", brown
    and yellow **25.00**
Puzzle, jigsaw, Night Bombing Over

Germany, 14½ x 21", Victory Series, #315, full color, JS Publishing Corp, New York City, 1943 copyright **18.00**

Razor Blades, Take Off, airplane on store card, 12 boxes **10.00**

Replica, two propeller passenger plane, hollow white metal, nickel plated silver finish, 3¼" l, 3½" wingspan, souvenir, Hartford, CT, c1950 .... **20.00**

Sheet Music, *Come Josephine in my Flying Machine (Up She Goes!)*, 10½ x 13½", red, white, and blue cov illus, young couple in early biplane, orig loose center page, 1910 copyright **30.00**

Stamp Album, 5½ x 8", soft cov, 20 pgs, premium, issued by Tydol–Veedol service stations, copyright 1940 .... **30.00**

Tie Tac, Hughes Aircraft Co **10.00**

Toy, Rookie Pilot, wind–up, tin **210.00**

Watch Fob, 1¼", metal, silvered, emb biplane, motorcycle, and touring car, c1910 .... **35.00**

PERSONALITIES

Byrd, Richard E.

Coin, nickel, commemorative, 1¾", portrait, "First Over South Pole, Byrd Ant. Exp. 1928–1930" **18.00**

Pinback Button

Bond Bread #3, "Commander Byrd's Floyd Bennett," black, white, and blue **20.00**

Yank Junior Airplane Series, ¹³⁄₁₆" d, litho, multicolored, plane, "Fokker F32/Admiral Byrd's North Pole Plane, 1930s **20.00**

Pocket Watch, 2", silvered case, black and white dial face illus of Byrd's plane over Antarctic camp, etched image inscription "Trail Blazer/ Commemorating Byrd's Antarctic Expedition" on reverse, 1929–30 . **300.00**

Earhart, Amelia

Autograph, 3 x 2" white card, full signature **175.00**

Photograph, 7½ x 9½", black and white, supplement of Philadelphia Record, Sunday, July 11, 1937 ... **15.00**

Pinback Button, Bond Bread, #4, "Amelia Earhart's Friendship," black, white, and red **20.00**

Lindbergh, Charles

Bank, 2½ x 4 x 6½", cast aluminum, bust portrait, gold finish, N Tregor sculptor, copyright G&T 1928 .... **20.00**

Bookends, iron, bronze wash, pr ... **60.00**

Cigar Box, Lucky Lindy **45.00**

Cigar Box Label, 6½ x 7¾", Spirit of St Louis, New York and Paris sky-

lines, plane flying overhead, American Lithograph Co **15.00**

Coin, Lucky Lindbergh, 1st non–stop NY to Paris, 1927 .... **35.00**

Hand Soap **40.00**

Horn, 7" h, cardboard, noise maker, wood mouth tip, oval sepia portrait sticker, souvenir, 1927 .... **100.00**

Model, Air Force Rescue Boat, motorized, orig box, unassembled ... **48.00**

Pencil Case, litho tin, black and white photos, black "WE" inscription, Wallace Pencil Co, late 1920s ... **60.00**

Pennant, 25¾", blue felt, white portrait and "Welcome Home" inscription **50.00**

Perfume Bottle, corked **9.00**

Pinback Button

Universal Lindbergh Day, 1¼" d, black and white photo on gray silhouette of plane, red rim lettering on white ground **100.00**

Welcome Lindy, black and white photo, red, white, blue, and gold rim **65.00**

Pocket Watch, 2" d, silvered brass, illus of Lindy's plane above "New York to Paris Airplane Model" inscription, New York and Paris skyline illus on reverse **300.00**

Post Card, 3½ x 5½", black and white, luminous yellow accents, French **18.00**

Puzzle, picture on both sides, complete **25.00**

Sheet Music, Lindbergh (*The Eagle of the USA*), 9 x 12", 6 pgs, sepia photos, 1927 .... **20.00**

Tablet, 8 x 10", lined paper, black and white cov photos, Lindy and his plane, flight statistics, 1927–28 .. **32.00**

Tapestry, 19 x 56", soft colors, woven, Lindy and plane over skylines of New York and Mexico City, 1" wide fringe, blue ground **75.00**

Telephone Pad, 3 x 4", commemorative, blue and white celluloid cov depicts Lindy, his plane, Statue of Liberty, and Eiffel Tower, attaches to candlestick phone, unused, 1928–29 calendar **115.00**

Tray, commemorative, 3¼ x 5", white china, hp, Lindy's plane, US and French flags on continents, Moisy & LeRoi, dated May 21, 1927 ... **69.00**

Rickenbacker, Eddie

Autograph, 3 x 4" book plate, bust pose, casual attire **60.00**

Booklet, "Flying News," published by the American Society for Promotion of Aviation, 5 x 8", soft cov, 32 pgs, black and white photos, adv, 1930 **15.00**

Game, Rickenbacker Ace Game—
Keep Em Flying, Milton Bradley,
1945 .... **20.00**
Trout, Bobbie, pinback button, $^{13}/_{16}''$ d,
litho, black and white, "Bobbie Trout/
Woman Transport Pilot," #67 in se-
ries, 1930s **22.00**
Wright Brothers
  Calendar Plate, 1912, 8½" d **30.00**
  Pinback Button, Wright Brothers
  Home Celebration, ⅞", 1909 Day-
  ton, OH, event, full color portraits,
  green shaded ground, white text . **75.00**

AVON

**Radio, dark amber, gold cap, paper dials,
Wild Country hair lotion, 1972–73, 5″ h,
$5.00.**

Collecting Hints: Avon collectibles cover a wide range of objects, including California Perfume Company bottles, decanters, soaps, children's items, jewelry, plates, catalogs, etc. Another phase of collecting focuses on Avon Representatives and Managers' awards.

Avon products are well marked. Four main marks exist. The name of the California Perfume Company appears from 1930 to 1936. The words "Avon Products, Inc." have been used since 1937 on the trademark.

Due to the vast number of Avon collectibles, a collector should buy only items of interest. Do not ignore foreign Avon material, although it is hard to find. New items take longer to increase in value than older items. Do not change the object in any way. This destroys the value.

History: David H. McConnell founded the California Perfume Co. in 1886. He hired saleswomen, a radical concept for that time. They used a door–to–door technique to sell their first product, "Little Dot," a set of five perfumes; thus was born the "Avon Lady." By 1979 there were more than one million.

In 1929, California Perfume Co. became the Avon Company. The tiny perfume company grew into a giant corporation. Avon bottles attracted collector interest in the 1960s.

References: Bud Hastin, *Bud Hastin's Avon Bottles Collectors Encyclopedia, 12th Edition*, privately printed, 1991; Joe Weiss, *Avon 8–Western World Handbook & Price Guide to Avon Bottles*, Western World Publishers, 1987.

Collectors' Club: Western World Avon Collectors Club, P.O. Box 23785, Pleasant Hills, CA 93535.

Periodical: *Avon Times*, P.O. Box 9868, Kansas City, MO 64134.

Museums: Nicholas Avon Museum, MTD Rt. Box 71, Clifton, VA 24422.

REPRODUCTION ALERT

Note: Prices quoted are for full, mint and boxed condition.

Awards and Representatives Gifts
  Bracelet, silver, bell, ringing, 1961 . **22.00**
  Clock, travel alarm, gold label, 1977 **16.00**
  Corsage, green and gold, red holly,
  Avon seven dollar bill, 1960 ..... **20.00**
  Cup, 6½", pewter, 4A Design, 1977 **42.00**
  Earrings, 10K solid gold, diamond
  chip, MIB, 1978 .... **35.00**
  Jewelry Box, 10 x 5", brocade and
  brass, musical, 1968 .... **55.00**
  Key Chain, gold horseshoe, blue box,
  1971 .... **18.00**
  Money Clip, 10K gold filled, 4A De-
  sign, initials, 1963 .... **70.00**
  Pin, red circle, gold feather, 50th An-
  niversary, 1936 .... **50.00**
  Plate, 1978, irid crystal, Fostoria, set
  of 4 .... **35.00**
California Perfume Company
  Atomizer, glass, green paint, gold
  plated top, 1928 .... **85.00**
  Bay Rum, 8 oz, glass, green and black
  label, 1930 .... **42.00**
  Christmas Perfume, 2 oz, glass stop-
  per, 1905 .... **145.00**
  Cold Cream, 2 oz, glass, white, alu-
  minum lid, 1926 .... **48.00**
  Elite Foot Powder, paper, round, 1919 **85.00**
  Rouge, powder can, 1908 .... **50.00**
  Sachet, powder, envelopes, 1908 .. **35.00**
  Shaving Stick, nickel, 3 pcs, 1923 .. **44.00**
  Tooth Powder, glass bottle, white,
  1908 .... **105.00**
  Violet Perfume, 1 oz, gift box, 1915 **95.00**
Children's Toys
  Batman Brush, plastic, 1977 .... **6.50**
  Bumbley Bee Pin, yellow, black
  stripes, 1973 .... **5.00**
  Crayola Lip Gloss, plastic, crayon
  shape, 3 pcs, 1981 .... **4.00**

First Mate Sailor Shampoo, 8 oz, plastic, 1964 .... **14.00**

Funny Bunny Pin, perfume glace, 1973 .... **4.50**

Globe Bank, bubble bath, 10 oz, plastic, 1967 .... **15.00**

Jumpin' Jimminy, bubble bath, 8 oz, 6", 1970 .... **4.00**

Looney Lather Bubble Bath, 6 oz, 1971 .... **4.00**

Precious Lamb, baby lotion, 6 oz, plastic, white, 1976 .... **2.50**

Six Shooter, no tears shampoo, 6 oz, plastic, 1962 .... **15.00**

Snoopy Comb and Brush, 5½", 1972 **4.00**

Spinning Top, bubble bath, 4 oz, 1966 .... **8.00**

Toofie the Clown, toothbrush holder, plastic, blue and pink brushes, 1978 .... **2.00**

Windjammer After Shave, Volkswagen bottle, aqua, 4 oz, $3.50.

Men's Items

Deodorant, ½ oz, sample bottle, 1950 **24.00**

Figural

Alaskan Moose, after shave, 8 oz, glass, amber, 1974 .... **6.00**

Barber Shop Brush, cologne, 1½" oz, glass, brown, 1976 .... **4.00**

Big Whistle, after shave, 4 oz, glass, blue, 1973 .... **5.00**

Blood Hound Pipe, after shave, 5 oz, glass, tan paint, 1976 ..... **5.00**

Bugatti '27, after shave, 6½ oz, glass, black, 1975 .... **9.00**

Calculator, black, 1979 .... **5.00**

Classic Lion, after shave, 8 oz, glass, green, 1973 .... **5.00**

Dutch Pipe, cologne, 2 oz, glass, white, 1973 .... **6.00**

Ferrari '53, after shave, 2 oz, glass, amber, 1974 .... **2.00**

Fire Fighter, after shave, 6 oz, glass, red paint, 1975 .... **6.00**

Golf Cart, green, 1973 .... **4.50**

Liberty Bell, after shave, 5 oz, sprayed bronze, 1976 .... **4.00**

Longhorn Steer, after shave, 5 oz, glass, amber, 1975 .... **5.00**

Pheasant, brown, green plastic head, 1972 .... **7.50**

Piano, after shave, 4 oz, 4", glass, amber, 1972 .... **3.00**

Rainbow Trout, 1973 .... **5.00**

Smooth Going Oil Can, after shave, 1½ oz, glass, SP, 1978 .... **3.50**

Snowmobile, after shave, 4 oz, glass, blue, 1974 .... **4.50**

Spark Plug, after shave, 1½ oz, glass, white, 1975 .... **3.00**

Spirit of St Louis, silver paint, 1970 **12.00**

Stage Coach, brown **7.50**

Stein, 6 oz, glass, silver paint, 1968 **5.00**

Theodore Roosevelt, after shave, 6 oz, glass, white paint, 1975 ... **6.00**

Wild Mustang Pipe, cologne, 3 oz, glass, white paint, 1976 .... **4.00**

Hair tonic, 6 oz, glass, 1938 ...... **28.00**

Spicy Soap Set, brown, five bars, 1965 .... **20.00**

Talc, black and white can, 1959 ... **10.00**

Traveler Set, 4 oz, shaving lotion, cream, toothpaste, 1941 .... **65.00**

Windjammer Towelettes, blue and white box, 1968 .... **2.00**

Miscellaneous

Candle, turtle, glass, white and green, 1972 .... **4.00**

Christmas Plate

1975 .... **12.00**

1976 .... **12.00**

1977 .... **12.00**

1978 .... **12.00**

1979 .... **12.00**

1980 .... **12.00**

Nail Clipper, 1960 .... **6.00**

Tote, 12 x 14 x 4", nylon, tan, 1980 **6.00**

National Association Avon Collector's

Bottle, Avon lady club bottle, porcelain, blue, 1975 .... **35.00**

Mirror, convention banquet, white and red, St Louis, MO, June 1979 **9.00**

Plate, 6th in series, 1936 Avon lady, 1982 .... **30.00**

President's set, antique brush gold, six busts, 1980 .... **125.00**

Ribbon, convention banquet, blue, 1973 .... **12.00**

Women's Items

Attention, toilet water, 2 oz, purple cap, 1942 .... **45.00**

Bath Salts, ribbed glass, blue cap, 1933 .... **65.00**

Bird of Paradise, bath oil, 6 oz, plastic, blue, 1974 .... **3.00**

Cameo Brooch, gold, pink and white lady's face, 1965 .... **20.00**

Cotillion Hairspray, 7 oz, pink can, 1966 .... **5.00**

Deluxe Lipstick, carved ivory, 1970 . **4.00**

Empress Compact, green, 1971 .... **4.00**

Hand Cream, 3½ oz, glass, turquoise lid, 1945 .... 30.00

Face Powder, paper box, silver and blue, 1936 .... 20.00

Figural

Angel Song, cologne, 1 oz, frosted glass, 1979 .... 3.00

Betsy Ross, white, 1976 .... 12.00

Church Mouse Bride, milk glass base, 1978 .... 5.00

Flower Maiden, yellow paint, 1974 7.50

Golden Thimble, cologne, 2 oz, clear glass, 1972 .... 4.00

Good Fairy, cologne, 3 oz, glass, blue paint, 1978 .... 6.00

Looking Glass, hand mirror shape, 1970 .... 3.00

Magic Pumpkin Coach, cologne, 1 oz, glass, 1976 .... 4.00

Persian Pitcher, bath oil, 6 oz, glass, blue, 1974 .... 4.00

Planter, hanging, glass, green, bath crystals and rope, 1977 .... 8.00

Regal Peacock, cologne, 4 oz, glass, blue, gold cap, 1974 .... 12.00

Sea Treasure, bath oil, 5 oz, glass, gold cap, 1971 .... 10.00

Skater's Waltz, cologne, 4 oz, glass, 1979 .... 10.00

Sweet Tooth Terrier, cologne, 1 oz, glass, white, 1979 .... 4.00

Venetian Pitcher, cologne, 3 oz, plastic, blue, 1973 .... 6.00

Floral Talc Trio, 3½ oz, 1965 ...... 15.00

Foundation Lotion, 2 oz, glass, 1950 25.00

French Ribbon Sachet Pillows, satin, blue, 1978 .... 8.00

Lavender Soap, 3 pcs, 1946 .... 45.00

Mascara, paper box, blue and white feather design, 1945 .... 15.00

Nail Beauty, 1 oz, white jar and lid, 1955 .... 3.00

Pomander

American Tradition, 5 x 7", wood look frame, 1982 .... 12.00

Pampered Piglet, ceramic, 1979 .. 10.00

Parasol, wax chips, lavender, 1975 5.00

Two Turtledoves, wax, white, 1980 10.00

Pretty Peach Soap, two peach halves, seed center, 1965 .... 25.00

Rapture Perfumed Oil, ½ oz, glass, green, 1964 .... 10.00

Wishing Bath Oil, 6 oz, plastic, white, 1965 .... 15.00

Vanity Tray, 10 x 12", metal, 1980 . 10.00

BAKELITE

Collecting Hints: Bakelite often is confused with plastic. There are three key questions to help identify bakelite: 1) is it thick and in a bright,

primary color [black, green, red, or yellow]; 2) is the object from the 1920 to 1940 period; and, 3) is the object normally associated with a synthetic material?

The collecting of bakelite has reached maturity. Prices are stable. Art Deco bakelite items remain especially strong in the current market.

History: Bakelite, a substitute for hard rubber, celluloid, and similar materials, is a synthetic resinous material made from formaldehyde and phenol. It was invented by L. H. Baekeland in 1913. Bakelite was easily dyed and molded into many brightly colored objects during the Art Deco period.

Bakelite has been used as the secondary element in many household and kitchen items (especially handles), as ornamentation on clothing, and in jewelry of the Art Deco and later periods. Bakelite often imitated natural materials such as amber, tortoise shell, onyx, jet, and wood.

References: Corinne Davidov and Ginny Redington Dawes, *The Bakelite Jewelry Book,* Abbeville Press, 1988; Lyngerde Kelley and Nancy Schiffer, *Plastic Jewelry,* Schiffer Publishing, 1987; Lyndi Stewart McNulty, *Wallace-Homestead Price Guide To Plastic Collectibles,* Wallace-Homestead, 1987.

HOUSEHOLD ITEMS

Button, 1¾", black, carved, very ornate, metal shank, pr 13.00

Checkers, MIB 12.00

Compact, tortoiseshell design 20.00

Dresser Set, mirror, comb, brush, manicure accessories, yellow and orange, enamel Art Deco design 75.00

Electric Organ, toy, Magnus, marbleized brown case, gold trim 50.00

Figure

Donkey 25.00

Duck 25.00

Inkwell, 9", double, marbleized brown and yellow 80.00

Manicure Set, bakelite handles, 10 pcs and case 28.00

Mirror, rose dec 60.00

Napkin Ring, rabbit 7.00

Pen 10.00

Pencil Sharpener, Bambi 20.00

Pocket Knife, 3", shoe, Loreley 32.00

Poker Chip Set, miniature, green, yellow finial, red, butterscotch, and blue chips 100.00

Purse 125.00

Radio

Bendex, marbleized green and black 185.00

Emerson, butterscotch, 8½ x 6½ x 4" 285.00

Telephone, Art Deco, oval shape, bell and dial, Stromberg–Carlson, 1930s 75.00

Vase, red and yellow swirl, chrome base 8.00

Yarn Case, marbleized green, kittens decal 32.00

JEWELRY

Bracelet
  Link, jade green 36.00
  Marbleized, green 22.00
  Navy Blue and White 21.00
Buckle, 2 pcs, 3", green, rhinestones . 20.00
Choker, marbleized blue–green, graduated beads, knotted 14.00
Clip, butterscotch 18.00

Clip, red, brass plated metal clip, 2" l, $4.50.

Earrings, Art Deco, yellow and black circles 10.00
Necklace, links 75.00
Pin
  Penguin, black and clear 15.00
  Scottie Dog, black 25.00
Ring, marbleized green 4.00

KITCHEN

Bottle Opener, 8⅛" l, red handle 5.00
Cake Cutter, green handle 3.00
Cheese Cutter 10.00
Corkscrew, steel, yellow handle 5.00
Egg Lifter, 8" l, 2½" wire lifter, green handle 4.00
Match Safe, First National Bank, Pawtucket, RI 15.00
Mortar and Pestle, yellow and orange swirl 27.50
Potato Masher, 9½" l, yellow handle .. 4.00
Salt and Pepper Shakers, pr 35.00

MISCELLANEOUS

Helmet, fireman's 50.00
Souvenir, New York World's Fair, Trylon and Perisphere, black base, thermometer on front, gold decal, 1939 ..... 75.00

BANKS, STILL

Collecting Hints: The rarity of a still bank has much to do with determining its value. Common banks, such as tin advertising banks, have limited value. The Statue of Liberty cast iron bank by A. C. Williams sells in the hundreds of dollars. See Long and Pitman's book for a rarity scale for banks.

Banks are collected by maker, material, or subject. Subject is the most prominent, focusing on categories such as animals, food, mailboxes, safes, transportation, world's fair, etc. There is a heavy crossover in buyers from other collectible fields.

Banks are graded by condition. They should be in very good to mint condition and retain all original paint or decorative motif. Few banks are truly rare; hence, the collector should wait until he finds a bank in the condition he seeks.

History: Banks with no mechanical action are known as still banks. The first banks were made of wood, pottery, or from gourds. Redware and stoneware banks, made by America's early potters, are prized possessions of today's collector.

Still banks reached a "golden age" with the arrival of the cast iron bank. Leading manufacturing companies include Arcade Mfg. Co., J. Chein & Co., Hubley, J. & E. Stevens, and A. C. Williams. The banks often were ornately painted to enhance their appeal. During the cast iron era, some banks and other businesses used the still bank as a form of advertising.

The tin lithograph advertising bank reached its zenith between 1930 and 1955. The tin bank was an important premium, whether it be a Pabst Blue Ribbon beer can bank or a Gerber's Orange Juice bank. Most tin advertising banks resembled the packaging shape of the product.

Almost every substance has been used to make a still bank—die cast white metal, aluminum, brass, plastic, glass, etc. Many of the early glass candy containers also converted to banks once the candy was eaten. Thousands of varieties of still banks were made and hundreds of new varieties appear on the market each year.

References: Earnest and Ida Long and Jane Pitman, *Dictionary of Still Banks*, Long's Americana, 1980; Andy and Susan Moore, *Penny Bank Book, Collecting Still Banks*, Schiffer Publishing, Ltd., 1984; Hubert B. Whiting, *Old Iron Still Banks*, Forward's Color Productions, Inc., 1968, out of print.

Collectors' Club: Still Bank Collectors Club of America, 62 South Hazelwood, Newark, OH 43055.

REPRODUCTION ALERT

Advertising
  Calumet Baking Powder, 2½" d, 5" h,

cardboard canister, tin top, diecut tin figure attached to top, tips head when coin is deposited **115.00**

Dodge, 2" d, 3¼" h, tin, oil drum shape, white lettering, red ground, inscribed "Switch to Dodge and Save Money!" on back, c1930 ... **30.00**

Folger's Coffee, tin, 1920s **52.00**

Metropolitan Bank, cast iron **165.00**

Mills "High Top," 6" h, working slot machine, 10¢, Las Vegas souvenir, 1950s **65.00**

Phillips 66 premium motor oil **27.50**

Red Goose Shoes, 5" h, plastic, red, goose shape, inscribed on front base, 1940s **35.00**

Socoy Vacuum Oil Co/Cincinnati Reds, 3" d, white glass baseball shape, simulated raised stitching, Reds team symbol one side, red Pegasus logo other side, round black base, c1930 .... **65.00**

Cardboard, "My Penny Bank," book shape, emb image of teenage Penny character created by Harry Haenigsen, early 1940s **30.00**

Cast Iron
Arabian Safe **130.00**
Bank Building, turret top, 3½" **95.00**
Boy Scout, orig paint **95.00**
Camel, painted red **90.00**
Elephant
  On Tub, circus blanket, orig paint **139.00**
  Standing, howdah **70.00**
The Globe, combination, planetary globe on claw foot **99.00**
Liberty Bell, 4" h, figural, bronze finish, 1776–1926 Sesqui–centennial inscriptions on each side **75.00**
Middy Bank **85.00**
Pig, seated **60.00**
Post Office Box **40.00**
The Roller Safe **105.00**
Sears Building, Chicago World's Fair, 4½" h, painted, white, blue accents made by Arcade, 1934 .... **400.00**
Statue of Liberty, 6" **115.00**
Celluloid, 2 x 2 x 4" h, square pink and clear coin box, removable lid, 2" d portrait of Shirley Temple mounted upright on lid **280.00**
Ceramic
Darth Vader, Roman Ceramics **95.00**
ET, 6" h, glazed, figural, yellow, orange, and brown, early 1980s ... **25.00**
China
Donald Duck, standing **350.00**
Howdy Doody on Pig, 7" h, early 1950s **280.00**
Monkey, red jacket, Regal China ... **150.00**
Pig, ivory ground, pink clover and bow in relief on back **100.00**

Roy Rogers and Trigger, 7½" h, glossy glaze, inscription on base front, c1950 .... **200.00**

Composition
Baseball Player, child, 6¼" h, painted, "Pittsburgh" on uniform shirt, c1960 .... **18.00**
Black Boy, 6" h, bobbing head, red shorts, brass earrings, next to large pineapple coin receptacle, marked "Japan" **25.00**
Mickey Mouse, 5" h, alarm clock shape, "Time to Save," yellow and gold, red, white, and black image of Mickey on dial, foil sticker reads "Enesco Imports/Japan," c1960 .. **70.00**
Raggedy Ann, 6" h, painted, gold yarn hair, Japan, c1950 .... **60.00**

Glass
New York World's Fair, 6 x 6 x 4", inscribed "Watch Your Savings Grow With Esso" and "New York World's Fair 1939," Trylon and Perisphere images **50.00**
Rosco Bear, figural **10.00**

Metal
Beaky, Warner Bros **45.00**
Chevy Coupe, 7½" l, 2½" h, silver accents, black ground, black rubber tires, marked "Maryland Black," late 1940s **130.00**
Coronation Throne, 3½" h, silvered, replica English throne, profile portrait of Queen Elizabeth on backrest, inscribed "Coronation 1953," marked "Sixpenny Piece Bank" .. **25.00**
Gulliver's Travels, book shape, 1 x 3 x 4¼", key–open, simulated white leather cov, emb depiction of Twinkletoes and Gabby's horse, "The First Step" and "Zell" inscribed on spine, copyright Paramount Pictures, 1939 .... **50.00**
RCA Victor Dog, 6¼", orig closure . **250.00**

Plaster, Flower the skunk, from Bambi, 7" h, red, blue, and green airbrushed accents on black and white ground, c1940 .... **50.00**

Plastic
Fred Flintstone, 9" h, vinyl, brown base, Homecraft Products, 1973 Hanna–Barbera copyright **25.00**
Galen, 11" h, Planet of the Apes character, figural, brown base, Play Pal Plastics, copyright 1974 Apjac Productions **30.00**
Hopalong Cassidy, 4½" h, portrait bust image, bronze color, red and olive green accents, Texas bank premium, early 1950s **60.00**
Howard Johnson's Restaurants, 3½" h, restaurant replica, late 1950s .. **25.00**

McDonald's, 5¼" h, wastebasket shape, yellow lid, white bin, McDonald's logos, 1975 copyright **15.00**

Money Hungry, 6" h, spool shape, set of teeth mounted on top, inscribed "Lick Inflation/Money Talks/Put Your Money Where Your Mouth Is" around sides, Poynter Products, 1975 .... **30.00**

Penguin, 8" h, Batman character, figural from waist up, Mego, copyright National Periodical Publications **65.00**

Terrytoon character, 8½" h, gold with black and white accents, coins deposited in horn—like nose, Spec Toy, copyright Terrytoons, c1950 . **25.00**

Troll, 7" h, vinyl, blue hair, brown glass eyes, flannel outfit and hair bow, c1960 .... **50.00**

Tin, Amoco Oil Can, 2⅛" d, 2⅞" h, $5.00.

Pottery, Santa, golden brown glaze, 5", skinny, standing with bag **124.00**

Tin

Astronaut Daily Dime, 2½ x 2½ x ¾" thick, multicolor, c1960 .... **25.00**

Popeye Daily Dime Register, litho, characters pictured on sides, copyright 1956 .... **68.00**

Prince Valiant, litho, full color illus of Prince Valiant on horse, castle, King Features Syndicate, copyright 1954 .... **65.00**

Television, 1½ x 2 x 4" h, litho, brown wood design, black and white screen and accents, "Television Co of Baltimore" marked on top, c1950 .... **25.00**

Tin Can, 2¼" d, 3½" h, souvenir, litho illus, exhibit buildings, skyride, and airship, inscribed "Made by the American Can Company at a Century of Progress, Chicago, 1934" . **45.00**

World Globe, 17" h, 5" h tin litho rooster on top crows when cranked **95.00**

BARBER SHOP COLLECTIBLES

Collecting Hints: Many barber shop collectibles have a porcelain finish. If chipped or cracked, the porcelain is difficult, if not impossible, to repair. Buy barber poles and chairs in very good or better condition. A good display appearance is a key consideration.

Many old barber shops are still in business. Their back rooms often contain excellent display pieces.

History: The neighborhood barber shop was an important social and cultural institution in the 19th and first half of the 20th centuries. Men and boys gathered to gossip, exchange business news, and check current fashions. "Girlie" magazines and comic books, usually forbidden at home, were among the reading literature, as were adventure and police gazettes and other magazines.

In the 1960s the number of barber shops dropped by half in the United States. "Unisex" shops broke the traditional men-only barriers. In the 1980s several chains ran barber and hair dressing shops on a regional and national basis.

Reference: Richard Holiner, *Collecting Barber Bottles*, Collector Books, 1986; Phillip L. Krumholz, *A History of Shaving and Razors*, Ad Libs Publishing Co., 1987; Phillip L. Krumholz, *Value Guide For Barberiana & Shaving Collectibles*, Ad Libs Publishing Co, 1988.

Collectors' Clubs: National Shaving Mug Collectors' Association, 818 South Knight Avenue, Park Ridge, IL 60068; Safety Razor Collectors' Guild, P. O. Box 885, Crescent City, CA 95531.

Bench, 48" w, waiting, oak, drawer .. **300.00**

Blade Bank

Barber, bust, 4¾" h, marked "Ceramic Arts Studio, Madison, Wis" **75.00**

Treasure Chest, "Insist on Genuine Ever—Ready Blades" **15.00**

Bottle

Amethyst, enameled flowers, 7¾" .. **160.00**

Crystal, pewter top, sgd, pr **50.00**

Painted, woman on horseback, Bing Crosby estate **125.00**

Stephan's Y–5 Hair Groom, 16 oz, 9½" h, "Sold Only By Barbers," Stephen Co, Ft Lauderdale, FL ... **15.00**

Business Card, Dendy's Beauty Culture and Barber College **8.00**

Catalog, T S Simms & Co, Maker of Better Brushes, 31 pgs **30.00**

Blade Bank, "Barber's Chair For Bald Headed Men, Hair Today, Gone Tomorrow," white, black trim, rubber stopper, 5½" h, 3¼" w, $200.00.

Chair	
Oak	35.00
Walnut, carved swan head	1,100.00
Clock, Gem Safety Razors, brown	350.00
Counter Display, 11 x 13", standup, cardboard, Crescent Razor Blades, 24 pkgs of razor, quarter moon logo, Plexiglas sleeve	78.00
Dispenser, stand–up, metal, Opera double edge razor blades, 5 for 10¢, man in top hat, eleven pkgs of blades	75.00
Footstool, Koken	125.00
Hair Dying Comb, cov, metal	12.00
Hair Shaper, patent 1907	12.00
Letterhead, Madison Barbers' Supplies, c1900	10.00
Mirror	
Hand, tin, wood handle, tilts	55.00
Shaving, 15", beveled mirror, plated brass frame, marked "Apollo"	22.00
Neck Duster, 10", turned cherry handle	24.00
Photograph, 5 x 7", barber shop int.	40.00
Pole	
26" h, revolving, red, white, and blue stripes, orig case	125.00
43" l, porcelain, wall mount, milk glass globe, orig spring power, electric lights	450.00
Postcard, barber shop ext., c1900	10.00
Receipt Book, Keen Kutter, 1920s	25.00
Safety Razor Set, cased	
Ever–ready, chrome razor, purple leather case, orig box and instructions	14.00
Griffon, unused wedge blade, tin case with dark blue lettering, gold highlights	60.00
Sharpener, steel razor blades, mechanical, Kress Kross, folding crank handle, blade turns against rotating disc, flips over to sharpen other side, dated 1921	45.00
Shaving Mug	
Kern Barber Supply	50.00
Middletown Silverplate Co, soap container, brush holder, c1870	65.00
Milk Glass, double compartment, molded flowers	74.00
Occupational, carpenter tools, Limoges	150.00
Sign, metal, Member United Master Barbers of Michigan, eagle on banner, "In You We Trust"	55.00
Sterilizer, porcelain, four sections, DeWitt	65.00
Strop, Peerless Automatic, Pat 1912	12.00
Token, Gillette, King Gillette and slogan on front, razor and slogan on back	28.00
Tool Case, 9 x 6", oak, brass handle	15.00
Waste Bowl, 7½" h, cobalt blue, applied enamel and gold dec, push–up base	315.00

BARBIE

Collecting Hints: Never forget the quantities in which Barbie and related material were manufactured. Because of this, the real value rests only in material in excellent to mint condition and which has its original packaging in very good or better condition. If items show signs of heavy use, their value is probably minimal.

Collectors prefer items from the first decade of production. Learn how to distinguish a Barbie #1 doll from its successors. The Barbie market is one of subtleties. You must learn them.

Recently collectors have shifted their focus from the dolls themselves to the accessories. There have been rapid price increases in early clothing and accessories, with some of the prices bordering on speculation.

History: In 1945 Harold Matson (MATT) and Ruth and Elliott (EL) Handler founded Mattel. Initially the company made picture frames. The company became involved in the toy market when Elliott Handler began to make doll furniture from scrap material. When Harold Matson left the firm, Elliott Handler became chief designer and Ruth Handler principal marketer. In 1955 Mattel advertised its products on "The Mickey Mouse Club." The company prospered.

In 1958 Mattel patented a fashion doll. The doll was named "Barbie" and reached the toy shelves in 1959. By 1960 Barbie's popularity was assured.

Development of a boyfriend for Barbie, named Ken after the Handler's son, began in 1960. Over the years many other dolls were added to the line. Clothing, vehicles, room settings, and other accessories became an intregal part of the line.

From September 1961 through July 1972 Mattel published a Barbie magazine. At its peak the Barbie Fan Club was the second largest girls' organization, next to the Girl Scouts, in the United States.

Barbie sales are approaching the 100 million mark. Annual sales exceed five million units. Barbie is one of the most successful dolls in history.

References: Billyboy, *Barbie: Her Life and Times*, Crown Publishers, Inc., 1987; Sibyl DeWein and Joan Ashabraner, *The Collectors Encyclopedia Of Barbie Dolls and Collectibles*, Collector Books, 1977 (1988 value update); Sarah Sink Eames, *Barbie Fashion, Volume 1, 1959–1967*, Collector Books, 1990; Paris and Susan Manos, *The Wonder Of Barbie: Dolls And Accessories 1976-1986*, Collector Books, 1987; Paris and Susan Manos, *The World Of Barbie Dolls: An Illustrated Value Guide*, Collector Books, 1983 (1988 value update).

Accessories, Ken	
Baseball Cap, ball, and mitt, plastic	**3.00**
Hunting Cap, red plastic	**2.00**
Roller Skates	**2.50**
Shoes, plastic, eight pairs, copyright Mattel, 1972, unopened	**18.00**
Beauty Kit, 1961, MIB	**25.00**
Book	
Here's Barbie, 5½ x 8¼", hard cov, Random House, seven stories, copyright 1958 and 1962	**8.00**
Barbie's Fashion Success, 5½ x 8¼", hard cov, Random House, sixteen chapters, copyright 1958 and 1962	**10.00**
Clothing Outfits	
Barbie/Midge	
American Airlines Stewardess, #984, 1961	**27.50**
Ballerina, #989, 1961	**20.00**
Evening Gala, #1660, 1965	**45.00**
Sweater and Skirt, knit, red plastic shoes, miniature "Mattel Daily" newspaper, Book 4 fashion catalog, 1964 Mattel copyright, unopened pkg	**10.00**
Ken/Allan	
Graduation, black gown and mortar board	**12.50**
Rally Day, all weather coat and hat, #795	**8.00**
Shirt, white, matching blue jacket and pants, red necktie, black plastic shoes and gloves, fashion catalog, 1964 Mattel copyright, unopened pkg	**10.00**
Coloring Book, 8 x 11", Watkins-Strathmore, copyright Mattel, 1962 and 1963	**15.00**

Diary, 1 x 4 x 5½", vinyl, glossy, One Year Diary, copyright Mattel, 1961 .	**30.00**
Dictionary, *Webster's Dictionary*, 4 x 5½", glossy black vinyl cov, full color Barbie illus, 380 pgs, Standard Products copyright 1959, Mattel copyright 1963	**35.00**
Doll	
Allan, #1000, 12" h, molded red hair, painted brown eyes, blue shorts, jacket, sandals, doll stand, copyright 1960	**130.00**
Barbie, #850, 12" h, jointed, vinyl, ash-blonde bubble cut hair, red swimsuit, red high heels, wire pedestal stand, copyright 1962, orig box	**125.00**
Ken, #750, 12" h, flocked blonde hair, wire pedestal stand, Sports Shorts outfit #783, copyright 1961	**130.00**
Midge, #860, 12" h, jointed, hard plastic, soft vinyl head, rooted blonde hair, knit shirt and shorts, high heels, wire pedestal stand, copyright 1962, orig box	**120.00**
Skipper, #0950, 9" h, rooted reddish-blonde hair, painted eyes, wearing red and white playsuit, red plastic shoes, wire stand, copyright 1963	**100.00**
Doll Carrying Case	
Barbie	
Black, glossy vinyl, 6½ x 10½ x 6½" deep, black plastic handle, zipper lid, copyright 1961	**35.00**
Multicolor, vinyl, 3 x 10 x 15½", car and plane illus, black handle, "Barbie Goes Travelin'," copyright 1965	**30.00**
Barbie and Midge	
Black, vinyl, 7 x 11 x 6½", zipper lid, "Barbie and Midge Travel Pals," copyright 1963	**25.00**
Light Blue, 14 x 18 x 4" deep, vinyl, copyright 1963	**25.00**
Ken, 11 x 13 x 4" deep, vinyl, yellow/green, black handle, copyright 1962	**30.00**
Dream House, 1962	**75.00**
Game, Queen of the Prom, 18" sq board, orig box, complete, Mattel copyright 1960	**30.00**
Horse, Dallas, MIB	**30.00**
Ice Cream Shop, box	**35.00**
Lunch Box, vinyl, glossy black, thermos, King-Seely Thermos Co, copyright 1965	**80.00**
Magazine, *Mattel Barbie Magazine*, Jan-Feb 1969, 22 pgs	**15.00**
Magic Dolls, Whitman, two dolls, die-cut cardboard, glossy surface, 30-piece wardrobe, plastic base, orig box, Mattel copyright 1969	**60.00**

Paper Doll Book, *Barbie and Her Friends,* Whitman, #1981, 10 x 13", unused, 1975 .... **12.00**
Radio, earphones, uses batteries **35.00**
Radio System, AM/FM, MIB **65.00**
Record Case, 1961, MIB **20.00**
Soap, Jergens, Barbie Doll Soap Circles, MIB **30.00**
Standup Dolls, Barbie and Ken, 9" h, cardboard, diecut, cardboard carrying case, plastic bases, 40–piece wardrobe, Whitman, Mattel copyright 1962 .... **50.00**
Suitcase, 1962 Ken and Barbie **17.00**
Sunglasses, child's, orig pkg, 1978 ... **14.00**
Wristwatch, 1963 .... **48.00**

BASEBALL CARDS

Collecting Hints: Condition is a key factor. The list below is priced for cards in excellent condition, and collectors should strive only for cards in excellent to mint condition.

Concentrate on the superstars; these cards are most likely to increase in value. Buy full sets of modern cards. In this way you have the superstars of tomorrow on hand. When a player becomes a member of the Baseball Hall of Fame, his cards and other memorabilia will increase significantly.

The price of cards fluctuates rapidly; it changes on a weekly basis. Spend time studying the market before investing heavily. Finally, reproduced cards and sets have become a fact of life in this category. Novice collectors should not buy cards until they can tell the difference between the originals and reproductions.

The latest trend is the collection of rookie cards, i.e., the first year of issue for a player. This is a highly speculative category at the moment.

History: Baseball cards date from the late 19th century. By 1900 the most common cards, known as "T" cards, were those produced by tobacco companies such as American Tobacco Co., with the majority of the tobacco–related cards being produced between 1909 and 1915. By far the most popular set was "T206" issued between 1909 and 1911. During the 1920s American Caramel, National Caramel, and York Caramel candy companies issued cards identified in lists as "E" cards.

From 1933 to 1941 Goudey Gum Co. of Boston and, in 1939, Gum, Inc., were the big producers of baseball cards. Following World War II, Bowman Gum of Philadelphia (B.G.H.L.I.), the successor to Gum, Inc., lead the way. Topps, Inc. (T.C.G.) of Brooklyn, New York, followed. Topps bought Bowman in 1956 and enjoyed almost a monopoly in card production until 1981.

In 1981 Topps was challenged by Fleer of Phil-

adelphia and Donruss of Memphis. All three companies annually produce sets of cards numbering 600 cards or more.

References: James Beckett, *The Official 1990 Price Guide to Baseball Cards, Ninth Edition,* House of Collectibles, 1989; James Beckett, *Sports Americana Baseball Card Price Guide, No. 10,* Edgewater Book Co., Inc., 1988; Editors of Krause Publications, Sports, *Baseball Card Price Guide, Fourth Edition,* Krause Publications, 1990; Editors of Krause Publications, Sports, *Standard Catalog of Baseball Cards,* Krause Publications, 1990; Gene Florence, *The Standard Baseball Card Price Guide, 3rd Edition,* Collector Books, 1991; Troy Kirk, *Collector's Guide To Baseball Cards,* Wallace–Homestead, 1990.

Periodicals: The following appear on a monthly or semi–monthly basis: *Baseball Card News,* 700 E. State Street, Iola, WI 54990; Beckett Baseball Monthly, 3410 Mid Court, Suite 110, Carrolton, TX 75006; *Sports Collectors Digest,* 700 E. State Street, Iola, WI 54990.

Collectors' Clubs: There are many local card collecting clubs throughout the United States. However, there is no national organization at the present time.

REPRODUCTION ALERT: The 1952 Topps set, except for 5 cards, was reproduced in 1983 and clearly marked by Topps. In addition, a number of cards have been illegally reprinted including the following Topps cards:

1963 Peter Rose, rookie card, #537
1971 Pete Rose, #100
1971 Steve Garvey, #341
1972 Pete Rose, #559
1972 Steve Garvey, #686
1972 Rod Carew, #695
1973 Willie Mays, #100
1973 Hank Aaron, #305
1973 Mike Schmidt, rookie card, #615

Note: The listing for the cards beginning in 1948 shows the price for a complete set, common player price, and superstars. The number of cards in each set is indicated in parentheses.

PRE–BOWMAN/TOPPS PERIOD

Tobacco Insert
   T–206, white border, color
      Complete set (523) **10,000.00**
      Major League players (1–389) **15.00**
      Minor League players (390–475) . **16.00**
      Southern League players (476–523) **37.00**
Candy Companies
   E–120, American Caramels, color, 1922
      Complete set (240) **1,350.00**
      Common player (1–240) **5.00**

Goudey and Gum, Inc.
  1933, Goudey Gum, color
    Complete set (240) 7,200.00
    Common player (1–240) 15.00

**Bowman, 1951, #233, Leo Durocher,
$20.00.**

BOWMAN ERA

1948 Bowman (black and white)
  Complete set (48) 525.00
  Common player (1–36) 5.00
  Common player (37–48) 7.50
  2 Ewell Blackwell 13.50
  9 Walker Cooper 7.00
  21 Ferris Fain 9.00
  29 Joe Page 16.00
  45 Hank Sauer 16.00
1949 Bowman
  Complete set (240) 2,975.00
  Common player (1–144) 5.00
  Common player (145–240) 20.00
  6 Phil Cavarretta 18.00
  31 Dick Kokos 14.00
  36 Pee Wee Reese 50.00
  100 Gil Hodges 80.00
1950 Bowman
  Complete set (252) 1,825.00
  Common player (1–72) 10.00
  Common player (72–252) 5.00
  4 Gus Zemial 22.50
  35 Enos Slaughter 40.00
  217 Casey Stengel 50.00
  232 Al Rosen 22.50
  248 Sam Jethroe 7.50
1951 Bowman (color)
  Complete set (324) 3,850.00
  Common player (1–252) 5.00
  Common player (253–324) 15.00
  26 Phil Rizzuto 32.50
  53 Bob Lemon 22.50
  122 Joe Garagiola 50.00
  233 Leo Durocher 20.00
  314 Johnny Sain 27.50

1952 Bowman (color)
  Complete set (252) 475.00
  Common player (1–216) 1.00
  Common player (217–252) 2.00
  1 Yogi Berra 30.00
  44 Roy Campanella 85.00
  101 Mickey Mantle 600.00
  196 Stan Musial 200.00
  218 Willie Mays 400.00
1953 Bowman (black and white)
  Complete set (64) 850.00
  Common player (1–64) 10.00
  15 Johnny Mize 50.00
  27 Bob Lemon 45.00
  28 Hoyt Wilhelm 50.50
  46 Bucky Harris 25.00
1953 Bowman (color)
  Complete set (160) 1,200.00
  Common player (1–112) 10.00
  Common player (113–128) 16.00
  Common player (129–160) 12.00
  44 Berra, Bauer, Mantle 175.00
  46 Roy Campanella 110.00
  59 Mickey Mantle 500.00
  93 Rizzuto and Martin 100.00
  117 Duke Snider 250.00
  121 Yogi Berra 250.00
  146 Early Wynn 55.00
  153 Whitey Ford 175.00
1954 Bowman
  Complete set (224) 450.00
  Common player (1–128) 2.00
  Common player (129–224) 2.40
  55 Jim Delsing 3.00
  90 Roy Campanella 55.00
  132 Bob Feller 32.50
  181 Les Moss 3.50
  224 Bill Bruton 5.00
1955 Bowman (color)
  Complete set (320) 1,150.00
  Common player (1–224) 2.50
  Common player (225–320) 4.00
  22 Roy Campanella 45.00
  23 Al Kaline 50.00
  179 Hank Aaron 90.00
  202 Mickey Mantle 200.00
  242 Ernie Banks 150.00

TOPPS ERA

1951 Topps, blue backs
  Complete set (52) 625.00
  Common player (1–52) 10.00
  3 Richie Ashburn 20.00
  30 Enos Slaughter 16.00
  50 Johnny Mize 20.00
1951 Topps, red backs
  Complete set (52) 250.00
  Common player (1–52) 3.00
  1 Yogi Berra 25.00
  31 Gil Hodges 10.00
  38 Duke Snider 20.00

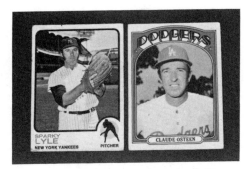

Topps: left: 1973, Sparky Lyle, $.50; right: 1972, Claude Osteen, $.50.

1952 Topps
Complete set (407)	3,800.00
Common player (1–80)	11.00
Common player (81–252)	6.00
Common player (253–310)	12.00
Common player (311–407)	25.00
1 Andy Pafko	75.00
26 Monte Irvin	50.00
33 Warren Spahn	85.00
48 Joe Page (correct)	32.50
48 Joe Page (error)	150.00
59 Robin Roberts	60.00
65 Enos Slaughter	60.00
88 Bob Feller	60.00
175 Billy Martin	150.00
191 Yogi Berra	175.00
400 Bill Dickey	250.00
407 Eddie Mathews	500.00

1953 Topps
Complete set (280)	2,800.00
Common player (1–165)	4.50
Common player (166–200)	3.50
Common player (221–280)	16.00
37 Eddie Mathews	40.00
76 Pee Wee Reese	45.00
77 Johnny Mize	27.50
82 Mickey Mantle	600.00
86 Billy Martin	45.00
147 Warren Spahn	45.00
191 Ralph Kiner	22.50
220 Satchell Paige	175.00
258 Jim Gilliam	135.00
280 Milt Bolling	50.00

1954 Topps
Complete set (250)	1,675.00
Common player (1–50)	3.50
Common player (51–75)	3.00
Common player (76–250)	3.50
3 Monte Irvin	12.50
17 Phil Rizzuto	27.50
32 Duke Snider	50.00
94 Ernie Banks	300.00
102 Gil Hodges	32.50
132 Tom Lasorda	75.00

201 Al Kaline	300.00
250 Ted Williams	150.00

1955 Topps
Complete set (210)	1,225.00
Common player (1–160)	2.50
Common player (160–210)	4.00
1 Dusty Rhodes	5.00
28 Ernie Banks	55.00
100 Monte Irvin	10.50
123 Sandy Koufax	325.00
124 Harmon Killebrew	125.00
187 Gil Hodges	475.00
194 Willie Mays	200.00
198 Yogi Berra	100.00
210 Duke Snider	100.00

1956 Topps
Complete set (340)	1,260.00
Common player (1–180)	1.50
Common player (181–260)	2.50
Common player (261–340)	3.00
10 Warren Spahn	22.50
20 Al Kaline	32.50
30 Jackie Robinson	60.00
31 Hank Aaron	80.00
79 Sandy Koufax	110.00
109 Enos Slaughter	11.00
130 Willie Mays	110.00
166 Brooklyn Dodgers	75.00
292 Luis Aparicio	50.00

1957 Topps
Complete set (407)	1,575.00
Common player (1–264)	1.25
Common player (265–352)	5.00
Common player (353–407)	1.25
1 Ted Williams	100.00
10 Willie Mays	90.00
35 Frank Robinson	100.00
76 Roberto Clemente	80.00
95 Mickey Mantle	375.00
302 Sandy Koufax	125.00
328 Brooks Robinson	175.00
407 Yankee Power Hitters, Berra, Mantle	100.00

1958 Topps
Complete set (495)	975.00
Common player (1–110)	1.25
Common player (111–440)	1.00
Common player (441–495)	.60
1 Ted Williams	100.00
5 Willie Mays	65.00
30A Hank Aaron	65.00
52A Roberto Clemente	45.00
70A Al Kaline	27.50
150 Mickey Mantle	250.00
187 Sandy Koufax	50.00

1959 Topps
Complete set (572)	975.00
Common player (1–506)	1.00
Common player (507–572)	2.50
10 Mickey Mantle	150.00
50 Willie Mays	55.00
163 Sandy Koufax	50.00

380 Hank Aaron **45.00**
514 Bob Gibson **150.00**
543 Corsair Trio **25.00**
1960 Topps
  Complete set (572) **875.00**
  Common player (1–506) .... **.75**
  Common player (507–572) **2.25**
  50 Al Kaline **13.50**
  73 Bob Gibson **16.00**
  148 Carl Yastrzemski **175.00**
  200 Willie Mays **40.00**
  250 Stan Musial **40.00**
  300 Hank Aaron **40.00**
  316 Willie McCovey **65.00**
  350 Mickey Mantle **150.00**
  564 Willie Mays, AS **40.00**
  566 Hank Aaron, AS **40.00**
1961 Topps
  Complete set (589) **1,260.00**
  Common player (1–522) .... **.50**
  Common player (523–589) **7.50**
  2 Roger Maris **50.00**
  10 Brooks Robinson **12.50**
  35 Ron Santo **6.00**
  120 Eddie Matthews **9.00**
  150 Willie Mays **40.00**
  200 Warren Spahn **11.00**
  260 Don Drysdale **9.00**
  287 Carl Yastrzemski **75.00**
  290 Stan Musial **37.50**
  417 Juan Marichal **40.00**
  475 Roger Maris **15.00**
1963 Topps
  Complete set (576) **950.00**
  Common player (1–196) **30.00**
  Common player (197–446) .... **.45**
  Common player (447–506) **2.25**
  Common player (507–576) **1.25**
  25 Al Kaline **12.00**
  54 Rookie Stars **3.75**
  108 Hoyt Wilhelm **37.50**
  115 Carl Yastrzemski **22.50**
  120 Roger Maris **22.50**
  125 Robin Roberts **4.50**
  242 Power Plus **9.00**
  340 Yogi Berra **27.50**
  360 Don Drysdale **9.00**
  412 Dodger Big Three **12.50**
  490 Willie McCovey **40.00**
  544 Rookie Stars **13.50**
1964 Topps
  Complete set (587) **600.00**
  Common player (1–370) .... **.25**
  Common player (371–522) .... **.40**
  Common player (523–587) **1.25**
  13 Hoyt Wilhelm **1.25**
  21 Yogi Berra **5.00**
  29 Lou Brock **7.50**
  50 Mickey Mantle **18.50**
  125 Pete Rose **80.00**
  146 Indians Rookies **8.00**
  225 Roger Maris **3.50**

260 Frank Robinson **4.00**
280 Juan Marichal **3.50**
342 Willie Stargell **18.00**
460 Bob Gibson **4.75**
468 Gaylord Perry **5.25**
541 Braves Rookies **15.00**
1965 Topps
  Complete set (598) **700.00**
  Common player (1–506) .... **.45**
  Common player (507–598) **1.25**
  170 Hank Aaron **6.00**
  207 Pete Rose **15.00**
  250 Willie Mays **7.25**
  300 Sandy Koufax **4.00**
  350 Mickey Mantle **10.00**
  477 Rookies **25.00**
  540 Lou Brock **4.50**
1966 Topps
  Complete set (598) **750.00**
  Common player (1–506) .... **.50**
  Common player (507–598) **3.00**
  1 Willie Mays **8.00**
  30 Pete Rose **10.00**
  50 Mickey Mantle **8.25**
  70 Carl Yastrzemski **7.50**
  126 Jim Palmer **10.00**
  500 Hank Aaron **7.50**
  550 Willie McCovey **12.00**
  598 Gaylord Perry **22.00**
1967 Topps
  Complete set (609) **825.00**
  Common player (1–533) .... **.50**
  Common player (534–609) **2.00**
  150 Mickey Mantle **8.00**
  200 Willie Mays **7.25**
  250 Hank Aaron **7.25**
  355 Carl Yastrzemski **8.00**
  400 Roberto Clemente **4.00**
  430 Pete Rose **10.00**
  569 Rookies **15.00**
  570 Maury Wills **22.00**
  581 Rookies **36.00**
  600 Brooks Robinson **35.00**
1968 Topps
  Complete set (598) **450.00**
  Common player (1–457) .... **.20**
  Common player (458–598) .... **.40**
  45 Tom Seaver **60.00**
  50 Willie Mays **22.50**
  72 Tommy John **2.00**
  150 Bob Clemente **17.50**
  247 Reds Rookies **175.00**
  257 Phil Niekro **2.50**
  363 Rod Carew, AS **4.50**
  408 Steve Carlton **15.00**
  530 Bird Belters **3.00**
1969 Topps
  Complete set (664) **425.00**
  Common player (1–218) .... **.20**
  Common player (219–327) .... **.30**
  Common player (328–512) .... **.20**
  Common player (513–664) .... **.25**

50 Bob Clemente	15.00
75 Louis Aparicio	2.50
95 Johnny Bench	60.00
100 Hank Aaron	17.50
120 Pete Rose	17.50
260 Reggie Jackson	175.00
480 Tom Seaver	40.00
485 Gaylord Perry	30.00
573 Jim Palmer	10.00

1970 Topps

Complete set (720)	325.00
Common player (1–132)	.15
Common player (133–459)	.15
Common player (460–546)	.20
Common player (547–633)	.30
Common player (634–720)	.60
10 Carl Yastrzemski	12.50
17 Hoyt Wilhelm	1.75
140 Reggie Jackson	37.50
150 Harmon Killebrew	2.50
211 Ted Williams	3.00
453 Ron Carew, AS	2.50
464 Johnny Bench, AS	4.00
470 Willie Stargell	3.25
537 Joe Morgan	3.25
539 Phillies Rookies	2.00

1971 Topps

Complete set (752)	350.00
Common player (1–523)	.20
Common player (524–643)	.35
Common player (644–752)	.70
5 Thurman Munson	10.50
14 Dave Concepcion	3.00
20 Reggie Jackson	16.00
30 Phil Niekro	1.75
55 Steve Carlton	8.00
117 Ted Simmons	4.00
264 Joe Morgan	3.00
341 Steve Garvey	37.50
525 Ernie Banks	7.50
570 Jim Palmer	6.00

1972 Topps

Complete set (787)	350.00
Common player (1–394)	.15
Common player (395–525)	.15
Common player (523–656)	.25
Common player (657–787)	.65
49 Willie Mays	9.00
79 Red Sox Rookies	30.00
100 Frank Robinson	2.50
200 Lou Brock	2.25
300 Aaron in Action	3.50
420 Steve Carlton	7.00
510 Ted Williams	3.00
595 Nolan Ryan	30.00
754 Frank Robinson Traded	11.00

1973 Topps

Complete set (660)	200.00
Common player (1–396)	.10
Common player (397l–528)	.40
Common player (529–660)	.45
1 Home Run Kings	3.75

31 Buddy Bell	2.00
160 Jim Palmer	2.75
170 Harmon Killebrew	1.75
280 Al Kaline	2.50
350 Tom Seaver	6.50
380 Johnny Bench	7.50
474 RBI Leaders	2.50

1974 Topps

Complete set (660)	150.00
Common player	.10
1 Hank Aaron	5.00
80 Tom Seaver	4.00
130 Reggie Jackson	5.50
252 Dave Parker	12.50
283 Mike Schmidt	33.50
300 Pete Rose	8.00
456 Dave Winfield	20.00

1975 Topps

Complete set (660)	225.00
Common player	.50
70 Mike Schmidt	18.00
228 George Brent	45.00
320 Pete Rose	7.50
616 Rookie Outfielders	15.00

1976 Topps

Complete set (660)	110.00
Common player	.05
230 Carl Yastrzemski	3.75
240 Pete Rose	7.50
480 Mike Schmidt	10.00
500 Reggie Jackson	4.00
599 Rookie Pitchers	5.00

1977 Topps

Complete set (660)	110.00
Common player	.08
10 Reggie Jackson	3.50
110 Steve Carlton	2.00
140 Mike Schmidt	7.00
295 Gary Carter	2.50
390 Dave Winfield	2.00
400 Steve Garvey	1.75
450 Pete Rose	4.50
476 Rookie Catchers	25.00

1978 Topps

Complete set (726)	90.00
Common player	.06
20 Pete Rose	2.00
36 Eddie Murray	17.50
40 Carl Yastrzemski	1.85
100 George Brett	2.50
120 Gary Carter	1.50
200 Reggie Jackson	2.00
350 Steve Garvey	1.50
360 Mike Schmidt	3.75

1979 Topps

Complete set (726)	60.00
Common player	.06
30 Dave Winfield	1.25
50 Steve Garvey	.60
116 Ozzie Smith	14.00
586 Bob Horner	.75

650 Pete Rose	2.25
700 Reggie Jackson	.85
1980 Topps	
Complete set (726)	60.00
Common player	.06
160 Eddie Murray	1.75
230 Dave Winfield	1.00
270 Mike Schmidt	1.00
482 Rickey Henderson	22.00
580 Nolan Ryan	2.50
1981 Topps	
Complete set (726)	60.00
Common player	.06
100 Rod Carew	.60
210 Jim Palmer	.60
261 Rickey Henderson	3.25
315 Kirk Gibson	3.50
347 Harold Baines	1.85
479 Expos Rookies	4.25
643 Lloyd Moseby	.50
1982 Topps	
Complete set (792)	56.00
Common player	.05
30 Tom Seaver	.35
70 Tim Raines	1.00
100 Mike Schmidt	.85
179 Steve Garvey	.40
346 Tom Seaver, AS	.15
383A Pascual Perez ERR	15.00
653 Angels Future Stars	1.00
668 Dale Murphy	1.00
1983 Topps	
Complete set (792)	60.00
Common player	.05
49 Willie McGee	.85
60 Johnny Bench	.35
70 Steve Carlton	.27
83 Ryne Sandberg	5.00
163 Cal Ripken	1.25
268 Storm Davis	.50
350 Robin Yount	.50
431 Gary Gaetti	2.25
482 Tony Gwynn	10.00
498 Wade Boggs	17.50
1984 Topps	
Complete set (792)	56.00
Common player	.04
8 Don Mattingly	10.00
182 Darryl Strawberry	7.50
206 Andy Van Slyke	1.25
300 Pete Rose	.60
470 Nolan Ryan	.85

BASEBALL COLLECTIBLES

Collecting Hints: Baseball memorabilia spans a wide range of items that have been produced since baseball became the national pastime over 100 years ago. This variety has made it more difficult to establish reliable values, leaving it to the collector himself to identify and determine what price to pay for any particular item he uncovers. This "value in the eye of the beholder" approach works well with the veteran collector. The novice collector should solicit the advice of a reliable dealer or advanced collector about values before investing heavily. Because of emerging interest in unique pieces, items associated with superstars such as Cobb, Ruth, and Mantle now command inordinately high prices.

Because of the unlimited variety of items available, it is virtually impossible to collect everything. Develop a collecting strategy, concentrating on particular player(s), team(s), or type of collectibles, such as Hartland Statues or Perez–Steele autographed postcards. This special emphasis allows the collector to become more familiar with the key elements affecting pricing within their area of interest, such as condition and availability, and permits him to build his collection within a prescribed budget.

History: Baseball has its beginnings in the mid–19th century and by 1900 had become the national pastime. Whether sandlot or big league, baseball was part of most every male's life until the 1950s, when leisure activities expanded in a myriad of directions.

The superstar has always been the key element in the game. Baseball greats were popular visitors at banquets, parades, and more recently at baseball autograph shows. They were subjects of extensive newspaper coverage and, with heightened radio and TV exposure, achieved true celebrity status. The impact of baseball on American life has been enormous.

References: Mark Allen Baker, *Sports Collectors Digest Baseball Autograph Handbook*, Krause Publications, 1990; James Beckett and Dennis W. Eckes, *The Sport Americana Baseball Memorabilia and Autograph Price Guide*, Edgewater Book Co, Inc., 1982; James Beckett, *The Sport Americana Price Guide To Baseball Collectibles*, Edgewater Book Co, Inc., 1988; Peter Capano, *Baseball Collectibles with Price Guide*, Schiffer Publishing, 1989; Don Raycraft and Stew Salowitz, *Collector's Guide to Baseball Memorabilia*, Collector Books, 1987.

Collectors' Club: Society for Baseball Research, P. O. Box 323, Cooperstown, NY 13326. Members receive *Baseball Research Journal*, *The SABR Bulletin* and *The National Pastime*.

Museum: Baseball Hall of Fame and Museum, Cooperstown, NY.

REPRODUCTION ALERT: Autographs and equipment.

Bank, baseball shape, 3" d, plastic, white, threaded base, threaded closure cap, issued by bank in Clairton,

PA, ten blue Pittsburgh Pirates signature, 1955–57 .... **55.00**
Baseball, autographed, 1954 Brooklyn Dodgers **600.00**
Baseball Bat
  Carl Yastrzemski, Louisville Slugger, miniature **55.00**
  St Louis Cardinals, 18" l, wood, brown symbol and name, 1950–60 **25.00**
  Willie Horton, 22", wood, Louisville Slugger, Hillerich & Bradsby logo **15.00**
Beer Can, 1979 World Champion Pirates Commemorative, 5", litho aluminum, Iron City Beer **15.00**
Book
  Big–Time Baseball, 192 pgs, Ben Olan, 1958, history text **30.00**
  The Babe Ruth Story, 96 pgs, 8½ x 11", soft cov, first edition, 1948 .. **40.00**
Cake Decoration, six painted glass figures, white uniforms with red accents, c1950s **25.00**
Cigarette Lighter, 4½", figural, china batter holding trophy, silvered metal lighter, orig box, copyright 1962 by Amico Import of Japan **50.00**
Coaster, 3½", plastic, brown, Philadelphia Phillies Trivia **7.50**
Coin, plastic
  Ken Boyer, 1959, red **10.00**
  Yogi Berra, 1954 .... **10.00**
Dart Board, metallic, Major League Baseball, orig cardboard envelope, 1950s **44.00**
Doll
  Detroit Tiger, 12", stuffed cloth, blue and white cap and uniform, "Detroit" printed on back, 1960–70 .. **20.00**
  New York Yankees, 12", stuffed, cloth, printed blue and white cap, black and white uniform, 1960–70 **15.00**

Fan, Pete Rose, "Ty–Breaker/Cobb Buster," diecut, cardboard **15.00**
Game, Play Ball, gambling tavern, counter top, 1930s **175.00**
Glass, Baltimore Orioles/World Champions 1966, 4½", clear, orange and black inscriptions and designs **25.00**
Gum Ball Machine, Play Ball, keys, 1950s **135.00**
Hartland Figure
  Mickey Mantle, 7", plastic, white uniform, blue cap, 1960s **100.00**
  Nellie Fox, 7", red and black uniform, early 1960s **200.00**
  Yogi Berra, 7", blue and white uniform, early 1960s **125.00**
Inkwell, tin, baseball mounted in center with hinged lid, white glass well, gold gilt finish, c1890 .... **125.00**
Lamp, Cubs, 4", china, white, baseball shape, black wire tripod base, 12½" parchment paper shade, c1940 .... **80.00**

Magazine, Vol. 26, No. 1, June 1921, cover art by Gerrit A. Beneker, 9½ x 11½", $25.00.

Magazine
  Babe Ruth Baseball Advice **85.00**
  Baseball Monthly, first issue, Vol 1 #1 March 1962, BRS Publishing Co, 64 pgs **30.00**
  Official Baseball Annual, No 3, Whitestone Publications, 1965 ... **25.00**
Mug, Boston "Pennant Is Ours," 5", ceramic, white, glossy, newspaper print, gold trim on edge **25.00**
Nodder
  Baltimore Orioles, 7", composition, painted, gold rounded diamond shape base, 1967–1972 .... **75.00**

Game, Peg Base Ball, Parker Bros, boxed board game, c1924, 12 x 10¾", $45.00.

Chicago White Sox, 6½" h, composition, white sq base, Chicago decal on base, 1961–62 .... **125.00**

Hank Aaron, 8", plastic, "Brewers"
name on chest, green plastic base,
c1975 .... **20.00**

Houston Colts, 6", composition,
painted, round green base, Made
in Japan marking, orig box, 1962
copyright **75.00**

Kansas City Athletics, 4½", composition, painted, white round base
with decal, 1961–62 .... **100.00**

Oakland Athletic, 6½", composition,
yellow and green uniform, gold
base with decal, copyright Sports
Specialties **35.00**

St Louis Cardinal **25.00**

Patch, Babe Ruth Champions, 3" d, flannel, emblem, stitched, Quaker Cereal
premium, c1935 .... **75.00**

Pencil
Baseball's 100th Anniversary, 5½",
wood, baseball bat shape, mechanical point, gold Hillerich & Bradsby
Co logo **15.00**

Detroit Tigers/1940 Champions, 5½",
bat shape, mechanical, brown inscription **30.00**

Yankees, 6", bat shape, wood, mechanical, black inscription, c1940 **25.00**

Pennant, felt
Baltimore Orioles, 26½", orange,
white design accented with orange
and dark gray, black lettering,
c1950 .... **40.00**

Dodger Stadium Commemorative,
27", red and blue background,
white lettering and design, grand
opening of Dodger Stadium, April
9, 1962 .... **50.00**

Little League Baseball, 12" l, blue,
white lettering and design, black
inked player's shoes, 1950–60 ... **15.00**

New York Mets, 12", black, white lettering and design, black inked player's shoes, c1962 .... **50.00**

Philadelphia Phillies, 29", red, white
design with yellow accent, c1950s **30.00**

San Francisco Giants, 12", blue,
white lettering and design, c1958 **45.00**

Washington Senators, 29", red, white
design, blue, pink, and dark gray
accents, white lettering **25.00**

Photo
Goose Goslin, 8 x 10", matte finish,
black and white, black ink signature **75.00**

Philedelphia Phillies, 9 x 11", full color
team, 1946 .... **25.00**

Pin, winner's, Dizzy Dean **15.00**

Pinback Button
Babe Ruth, "Sultan of Swat" **85.00**

Brooklyn Dodgers, 1¾", 1950s **10.00**

1983 World Series, 3½", cello, red,
white, and blue, Orioles and Phillies, Major League Baseball Players
Assn logo **15.00**

Press Pass, 1939 Chicago Cubs, 2½ x
3¾", inked Western Union employee
name, red symbol **35.00**

Program
1937 World Series, 9 x 11", 24 pgs,
New York Yankees and New York
Giants **50.00**

1940 Buffalo Bisons, 7 x 10", 16 pgs,
Offermann Stadium, Bisons and Jersey City Giants **18.00**

1945 Hagerstown Owls, 7 x 10¼",
four pgs, Owls and Wilmington,
Delaware **15.00**

1947 Chicago Cubs Game, 6 x 9",
Cubs and New York Giants at Wrigley Field **25.00**

1971 World Series, 8¼ x 10½", 72
pgs, Pittsburgh Pirates and Baltimore Orioles **25.00**

1976 Salute To Hank Aaron, 5½ x
8½", Sept 17, 1976 at Milwaukee
Co Stadium **15.00**

1983 World Series, 8¼ x 11", Philadelphia Phillies and Baltimore Orioles, 104 pgs, issued as commemorative by Major League Baseball
Promotion Corp **25.00**

Ring, Chicago Cubs, brass, glass top,
team logo inset **125.00**

Sign, Lou Gehrig Baseball Gloves **45.00**

Ticket, 1960 World Series, game 2,
Forbes Field, Pittsburgh Pirates and
New York Yankees, first floor reserved
seat **20.00**

Ticket Stub, 1945 World Series, Wrigley
Field, Chicago Cubs and Detroit Tigers **15.00**

Toy, Mickey Mantle's Backyard Baseball, 22" wood rod holds 4" d plastic
wiffle ball, yellow and black sticker
label on bat, L C Toy Division, Syracuse, 1950s **50.00**

Whiskey Bottle, Baseball's 100th Anniversary Commemorative, 10½" h,
china, Jim Beam Distilling Co, 1969 **40.00**

Wristwatch, Babe Ruth, silvered metal
case, orig silvered expansion band, 3"
d white plastic baseball shape case,
Exacta Time, c1949 .... **700.00**

Yearbook
1953 Washington Nationals, 48 pgs,
8¼ x 10½" **30.00**

1955 New York Giants, 8½ x 11", 48
pgs, Big League Book series **20.00**

1966 Dodgers, 8¼ x 11", 56 pgs, full

color illus of manager Walt Alston
on cov **30.00**

BEATLES

Collecting Hints: Beatles' collectibles date from
1964 to the present. The majority of memorabilia
items were produced from 1964–68. The most
valuable items are marked "NEMS." Most collectors are interested in mint or near mint items
only. Some items in very good condition, especially if scarce, have considerable value as well.

Each year Sotheby's holds one or two auctions
which include Beatles' memorabilia, primarily
one of a kind items such as guitars and stage
costumes. These items command high prices.
The "average" collector generally does not par-
ticipate.

History: The fascination with the Beatles began
in 1964. Soon the whole country was caught up
in Beatlemania. The members of the group included John Lennon, Paul McCartney, George
Harrison and Ringo Starr. The group broke up in
1970. After this date, the members pursued their
individual musical careers. Beatlemania took on
new life after the death of John Lennon.

References: Jeff Augsburger, Marty Eck, and Rick
Rann, *The Beatles Memorabilia Price Guide*,
Branyan Press, 1988; Barbara Fenick, *Collecting
The Beatles, An Introduction and Price Guide to
Fab Four Collectibles, Records and Memorabilia,
Volume 1* (1984) and *Volume 2* (1988), Pierian
Press; Jerry Osborne, Perry Cox, and Joe Lindsay,
*The Official Price Guide To Memorabilia of Elvis
Presley And The Beatles*, House of Collectibles,
1988.

Collectors' Club: Beatles Fan Club of Great Brit-
ain, Superstore Productions, 123 Marina, St
Leonards on Sea, East Sussex, England TN 38
OBN.

Periodicals: *Beatlefan*, P. O. Box 33515, Decatur, GA 30033; *Good Day Sunshine*, Liverpool
Productions, 397 Edgewood Avenue, New Haven, CT 06511.

REPRODUCTION ALERT: Records, picture
sleeves, and album jackets have been counter-
feited. Sound quality may be inferior. Printing on
labels and picture jackets usually is inferior to
the original. Many pieces of memorabilia also
have been reproduced, often with some change
in size, color, design, etc.

Beach Towel, 34 x 56", white cloth,
Beatles illus, facsimile signatures,
"The Beatles" and "Yeh, Yeh, Yeh"
in red and blue lettering, 1965 copy-
right by Nems **200.00**
Book, *Yellow Submarine*, punch out,

**Record case, plastic, olive green, black
figures, white handle, copyright 1966
NEMS, 8⅓" h, $85.00.**

9½ x 15", 8 pgs, glossy paper, copy-
right 1968 King Features **38.00**
Bottle Stopper, 4½" h, composition,
Ringo figural head, marked "Ringo,"
cork marked "Achatit," c1960 ..... **175.00**
Cake Decorating Set, orig box **75.00**
Charm, Twist & Shout record **5.00**
Clothes Hanger, 16 x 17", stiff diecut
cardboard attached to white plastic
hanger, George Harrison, copyright
Henderson/Hoggard Inc, King Features—Suba Films Ltd, 1968 .... **60.00**
Coloring Book, 8½ x 11", Saalfield Publishing Co, 124 pgs, copyright 1964
Nems enterprises Ltd **40.00**
Costume, Blue Meanie, orig box, no
mask **175.00**
Cup, 6½" h, plastic, transparent plastic,
color photo of Beatles playing instruments and gold facsimile signatures
on paper insert, four pink lips around
rim, copyright Nems Enterprises,
c1960 .... **52.00**
Curtains, pr, 46 x 57", fabric, black,
white, and blue illus on brown
ground, printed song titles, Beatles'
names and logo, marked "The Beatles—World Copyright NV Stoomwev-
eru Nuverheid," made in Holland,
c1960 .... **800.00**
Disk—Go—Case, 7½" d, 6¾" h, plastic,
purple/pink, holds 45 rpm records,
black illus and facsimile signatures,
Charter Industries Inc, copyright 1966
Nems Enterprises Ltd **100.00**
Doll
Set of Four, 15", vinyl, inflatable, with
musical instruments, Nems Ltd,
1966, orig pkg **125.00**

McCartney, 4½" h, molded hard plastic body, soft vinyl head, artificial hair, Remco, copyright 1964 Nems **180.00**

Fan Club Kit, Beatlemaniac **35.00**

Game, Flip Your Wig, Milton Bradley, copyright Nems Enterprises Ltd, 1964 **100.00**

Glass, 4¾" h, Ringo, portrait picture and name in black, remaining red design, marked "Nems Enterprises Ltd, Ldn," c1964 .... **110.00**

Guitar, 31" l, plastic, red back, orange and maroon front, Beatles decal, raised silver "New Beat" logo, facsimile autographs, orig box **500.00**

Gum Cards, set of 50, #116–165, third series, Topps, 1964, black and white photo and facsimile signature on each 2½ x 3½" card **40.00**

Hairbrush, 3¾" l, soft plastic, blue, photos, facsimile signatures and "The Beatle Brush" in relief, Genco, c1960s, orig unopened pkg **90.00**

Home Movie, "Ticket to Ride," 3½" plastic reel, Super 8, unopened pkg **90.00**

Keychain **15.00**

Lunch Box, Yellow Submarine, metal, King–Seely, copyright 1968 King Features Syndicate **175.00**

Mug, 4" h, glazed white ceramic, black, white, and blue photos, facsimile signatures and "The Beatles" in black, imprinted "England" on bottom, c1960 .... **150.00**

Nodder, set of four, 8" h, composition, issued by Car Mascots, Inc, 1964 .. **275.00**

Pencil Case, 3½ x 8", vinyl, blue, browntone photos, black facsimile signatures, zippered pocket, copyright 1964 by Standard Plastic Products and Beatles **95.00**

Photo Ring, plastic, set of 4 .... **35.00**

Pin

Beetle shape, 2" h, standing, gold metal, painted black jacket and shoes, red striped shirt, mink fur hair, movable head and legs, playing guitar, c1960, orig display card **60.00**

Yellow Submarine characters, set of 8, figural, 1" l, plastic metal clasps, hp, c1960 .... **65.00**

Plate, 7" d, glazed white ceramic, black, white, and blue photos, facsimile signatures, "the Beatles" in black, c1960 .... **80.00**

Pocket Disk, 4" black flexidisk record, "Hey Jude/Revolution," gray apple and Columbia logo on label, 1969, unused **200.00**

Poster, 14 x 18", pinktone photo, "The Beatles Bulletin" fan club addresses, unfolds to 18 x 28", 1969 summer issue, color band photo **23.00**

Program, concert, Chicago, Sept 5, 1964 .... **64.00**

Puzzle, "Beatles in Pepperland," 19 x 19", Sgt Pepper Band color illus, people in background, copyright 1968 King Features Syndicate, orig box .. **75.00**

Ring, ceramic **45.00**

Sheet Music, *She Loves You*, 9 x 12", 4 pgs, written by Lennon and McCartney, red and white cov design, copyright 1963 Northern Songs, London and 1964 Gil Music Corp, US . **20.00**

Stick–on Sheets, "Yellow Submarine," 9 x 12", vinyl stickers, full color, "Popstickles" line, Dal Mfg Corp, pr **30.00**

Switchplate Cover, 6 x 12", stiff cardboard, "Yellow Submarine," day glow, Blue Meanie character, inscribed "Stamp Out Fun," copyright 1968 King Features Syndicate, sealed in orig pkg **32.00**

Toy

Chubops, complete set in store display **75.00**

Ringo with Drum, Remco **55.00**

Yellow Submarine, 2 x 5 x 3", diecast metal, replica, four plastic revolving periscopes, spring operated hatches, Corgi, copyright King features and Subafilms Ltd, 1968 .... **160.00**

Wallet, 3½ x 4½", vinyl plastic, gray, folder, pinktone group photo on one side, black facsimile signatures on other side, Standard Plastic Products, copyright Rmat & Co, Ltd, London, c1964 .... **120.00**

Wig, black, Lowell Toy Mfg Co, c1960s, orig display bag **50.00**

Wrapper, 5 x 6", waxed paper, black and blue illus, yellow and red lettering, issued by Topps, c1960 .... **15.00**

BEER BOTTLES

Collecting Hints: Beer bottles often are found by digging in old dumps or wells. When found, these bottles may have become discolored and flaked. However, the key is whether the bottle remains unbroken or not. Damage to the bottle is of greater concern in pricing than the discoloration.

Concentrate on the bottles from one brewery or area. When an example is brought back to an area of its origin, it is likely to command more money then when sold outside the local region. A brewery is likely to change its bottle style several times in the course of its history. This also is true for the paper label designs found on later bottles.

The early bottles had special closures. The bottle is worth more if the closure is intact. The metal caps are not critical to the value of later bottles. However, an active collecting interest in metal caps is growing, as witnessed by dealer displays at several recent beer collector shows.

History: Breweries began in America shortly after the arrival of the first settlers. By the mid–19th century most farmsteads had a small brewery on them. Local breweries dominated the market until the arrival of Prohibition. A few larger breweries were able to adjust, but the majority closed.

When Prohibition ended, a much smaller number of local breweries renewed production. The advertising, distribution, and production costs of the 1950s and 1960s led to the closing of most local breweries and the merger of many other breweries into a few nationally oriented companies.

In the 1960s imported beers from Europe entered the American market. Some companies signed licensing agreements to produce these foreign labels in the United States. The 1980s have witnessed the growing popularity of beers brewed in Canada and Mexico.

References: Ralph and Terry Kovel, *The Kovels' Bottle List, 8th Edition,* Crown Publishers, 1987; *The Official Price Guide to Bottles Old & New, Tenth Edition,* House of Collectibles, 1986; Carlo and Dorothy Sellari, *The Standard Old Bottle Price Guide,* Collector Books, 1989.

Collectors' Club: American Breweriana Association, Inc., P. O. Box 6082, Colorado Springs, CO 80934.

Pilsner Maltcrest Brew, Pilsner Brewing Co, Inc, Bronx, NY, 12 oz, $8.50.

Embossed
Burkhardt & Brew Co, Boston, clear	**100.00**
Cumberland, MD Brew Co, amber	**7.50**
Foss–Schneider Brew Co, Cincinnati, amber	**10.00**

George W Hoxsie, Premium Beer, dark amber, early blob top	**75.00**
Hand Brew Co, Pawtucket, RI, aqua	**7.50**
Iroquois, Buffalo, Indian head, amber	**7.50**
Johann Hoff, 8", olive green, blob top	**8.00**
John Jackson Strohm, California, 7¾", light amber	**5.00**
Kessler Malt Extract, 8½", amber squat type	**8.00**
Lion Brewery LTD, 11¾", amber, crown top	**6.00**
McCormick Brewery, Boston, clear, 1897	**10.00**
National Brewing Co, Baltimore, eagle, amber, blob top	**15.00**
Oakland Bottling Co, Oakland, CA, 9", amber, blob top	**8.00**
Pittsburgh Brewing Co, 12", amber, crown top	**4.00**
Schlitz, ruby red	**12.00**
Sidney O Wagner, 11½", amber, crown top	**4.00**
William Gerst, Nashville, 11½", aqua	**7.50**
William Mulligan, Philadelphia, 9½", aqua, blob top	**5.00**

Painted Labels
Augusta Brewing Co, Augusta, GA, 7", aqua	**10.00**
Cock'N Bull Ginger Beer, 7", brown and tan, crown top	**5.00**
Geobel Beer, amber	**7.00**
James Handley Brew Co, clear, blob top	**12.50**

Paper Labels
Bohemian Lager Beer, Bodie Bottling Work, Bodie, CA, aqua, crown top	**6.00**
Grand Prize Beer, Gulf Brewing Co, 9", clear, crown top	**5.00**
Northern Brewing Co, Superior, WI .	**4.00**
Pabst Blue Ribbon Beer, Souvenir Special, 4¼", amber, metal lid, crown top	**7.00**

Stoneware
Biscombe's, 8½", brown and tan	**6.00**
Dr Earl's Premium Beer, 9½"	**32.00**
Ginger Beer Thames Ditton, Hawk's & Co, 7", inside threads	**12.00**

BEER CANS

Collecting Hints: Rusted and dented cans have little value unless they are rare. Most collectors remove the beer from the cans. Cans should be opened from the bottom to preserve the top unopened.

As beer can collecting became popular, companies issued special collectors' cans which never contained beer. Many were bought on speculation; value has been shaky.

History: Before Prohibition, beer was stored and shipped in kegs and dispensed in returnable bottles. When the Prohibition Act was repealed in 1933, only 700 of 1700 breweries resumed operation. Expanding distribution created the need for an inexpensive container that would permit beer to be stored longer and shipped safely. Cans were the answer.

The first patent for a lined can was issued to the American Can Co. on Sept. 25, 1934, for their "Keglined" process. Gotfried Kruger Brewing Co., Newark, New Jersey, was the first brewery to use the can. Pabst was the first major company to join the canned beer movement.

Continental Can Co. introduced the conetop beer can in 1935. Schlitz was the first brewery to use this type of can. The next major change in beer can design was the aluminum pop–top in 1962.

References: Editors of House of Collectibles, *The Official Price Guide To Beer Cans & Collectibles, Fourth Edition,* House of Collectibles, 1986; Thomas Toepfer, *American Beer Can Encyclopedia,* Collector Books, 1983– 84 edition.

Collectors' Club: Beer Can Collectors of America, 747 Merus Court, Fenton, MO 63026.

Note: The listings are the name, type of beer, brewery location, top identification, price. The following abbreviations are used in the listings:

CR - Crowntainer type cone top
CT - cone type
FT - flat top
PT - pull top
ML - malt liquor

7 oz.
Coors, Golden, Co, FT **6.00**

Left: Hull's Cream Ale, Hull Brewing Co, New Haven, CT, gold, black, and turquoise, $35.00; right: Schaefer Light Beer, F & M Schaefer, NYC, $30.00.

Lucky Lager, Lucky Lager, San Francisco, CA, FT **9.00**
Pabst, 5 cities, PT **1.00**
Rheingold, Rheingold, 2 cities, PT . .   **1.50**
8 oz.
Bull Dog ML, Grace, Santa Rosa, CA, FT **15.00**
Country Club, Pearl, 2 cities, PT . . .   **5.00**
Gluek's Stite ML, Gluek, Minneapolis, MN, FT **25.00**
Goebel Ale, Goebel, Detroit, MI, FT   **30.00**
National Bohemian, National, Baltimore, MD, PT **8.00**
Neuweiler, Neuweiler's, Allentown, PA, FT **15.00**
Pearl, Pearl, 2 cities, PT **2.00**
Storz–ette, (1953), Storz, Omaha, NE, FT **40.00**
University Club ML, Miller, Milwaukee, WI, FT **15.00**
10 oz.
Budweiser, Anheuser–Busch, 7 cities, PT **4.00**
Colt 45 ML, National, 4 cities, PT . .   **3.00**
Old Milwaukee (1973), Schlitz, 6 cities, PT **2.00**
11 and 12 oz.
A–1 Premium, National, Phoenix, AZ, PT **15.00**
Adler Brau, Walter, Appleton, WI, FT   **12.00**
Atlas Prager, Atlas, Chicago, IL, FT .   **55.00**
Big Apple, Waukee, Hammonton, NJ, FT **100.00**
Blackhawk, Premium, Cumberland, Cumberland, MD, FT **35.00**
Bohack Premium, Richards, Newark, NJ, PT **8.00**
Brau Haus, General, Los Angeles, CA, PT **10.00**
Brew 82, Brew 82, Cleveland, OH, FT **75.00**
Buckhorn, Hamm, 2 cities, PT **1.00**
Chippewa Pride, Leinenkugel, Chippewa Falls, WI, PT **2.00**
Croft Banquet Ale (1954), Croft, Cranston, RI, FT **85.00**
Dixie, Dixie, New Orleans, LA, PT .   **.75**
Duquesne, Duquesne, Pittsburgh, PA, FT **20.00**
El Rancho, Falstaff, San Francisco, CA, PT **3.00**
Fitger's, Fitger, Duluth, MN, FT **5.00**
Friars Ale, Drewrys, South Bend, IN, FT **25.00**
Gettelman, Gettelman, Milwaukee, WI, FT **20.00**
Gilt Edge, Bosch, Houghton, MI, PT   **15.00**
Heidelberg, Carling, Tacoma, WA, PT   **4.00**
Horlacher, Pilsner, Horlacher, Allentown, PA, FT **8.00**
International Frankenmuth Ale, International, Covington, KY, FT **25.00**

Karl's, Grace, Santa Rosa, CA, FT .. **75.00**
Kold Brau, Schoen–Edelweiss, Chi-
cago, IL, FT **35.00**
Leisy's Light, Leisy, Cleveland, OH,
FT **40.00**
Lucky Lager, Falstaff, 6 cities, PT ... **.75**
Metbrew, Metropolis, Trenton, NJ, PT **.50**
Monticello, Monticello, Norfolk, VA,
PT **50.00**
Near Beer, Goetz, St Joseph, MO, FT **5.00**
Old Milwaukee Draft, (1971), Schlitz,
8 cities, PT **1.50**
Oyster House, Pittsburgh, Pittsburgh,
PA, PT .... **.50**
Potosi, Potosi, Potosi, WI, FT **10.00**
Progress, Progress, Oklahoma City,
OK, FT **75.00**
Queens Brau, Queen City, Cumber-
land, MD, FT **45.00**
Reading, Reading, Reading, PA, PT . **1.50**
Rolling Rock, Latrobe, Latrobe, PA,
FT **12.00**
Salzburg, Schoen–Edelweiss, Chi-
cago, IL, FT **50.00**
Schlitz Light (1975), Schlitz, 6 cities,
PT .... **.75**
Stoney's, Jones, Smithon, PA, PT ... **1.00**
Texas Pride, Pearl, San Antonio, TX,
PT **1.50**
Tuborg, Carling, Baltimore, MD, PT **2.00**
Van Merritt, Van Merritt, Oconto, WI,
FT **7.00**
Walter's Light, Walter, Pueblo, CO,
PT **2.00**
Western, Cold Spring, Cold Spring,
MN, PT **1.00**
Wiedemann, Heileman, 4 cities, PT **.50**
Yusay, Pilsen, Chicago, IL, FT **20.00**
12 oz., Cone Top
Blatz Old Heidelberg Castle, Blatz,
Milwaukee, WI, CC **35.00**
Breunig's Lager, Rice Lake, Rice Lake,
WI, CT **50.00**
Champagne Velvet, Terre Haute,
Terre Haute, IN, CT **40.00**
Dawson's Pale Ale, Dawson, New
Bedford, MA, CT **40.00**
Fehr's Fehr, Louisville, KY, CR **25.00**
Ortlieb's Premium Lager, Ortlieb,
Philadelphia, PA, CT **55.00**
Stag Premium Dry, Griesedieck–
Western, 2 cities, CT **25.00**
15 and 16 oz.
Budweiser, Anheuser–Busch, 6 cities,
PT **4.00**
Eastside Old Tap, Pabst, Los Angeles,
CA, FT **15.00**
Fisher, General, 3 cities, PT .... **.75**
Land of Lakes, Pilsen, Chicago, IL, FT **20.00**
Mustang Malt Lager, Pittsburgh, Pitts-
burgh, PA, PT **25.00**
Pabst, Pabst, Milwaukee, WI, FT ... **22.00**

Piels Light, Piels, Brooklyn, NY, FT . **20.00**
Stroh's, Stroh, Detroit, MI, PT **1.50**
Weiss Bavarian, Maier, Los Angles,
CA, PT **20.00**

BELLS

Collecting Hints: The bell category is very large.
Collectors should focus on a single topic (door
bells, school bells, sleigh bells, etc.), on bells
from a single country or geographic area, or on
bells made from a single substance. Once a bell
style becomes popular, its production may last
for many decades. Only the most experienced
dealer and collector can determine age accurately.

Collecting glass bells has become very popular. Collectors should be alert for wine or cordial
glasses which have had their base removed, been
reversed, and then been converted to a bell by
the addition of a clapper. These conversions are
worth substantially less than glass forms designed
and originally made as bells.

There is an active market in limited edition
collectors' bells. Some occasionally are copies
of older models, so collectors should become
familiar with the patterns.

Develop an eye for quality. The bells of the
late 19th century show a high degree of workmanship and artistic style. Most of all, buy a bell
because you find enjoyment in it—both visually
and through its ring.

History: Bells have been used for centuries for
many different purposes. They have been traced
as far back as 2697 B.C., though at that time
they did not have any true tone. One of the oldest
bells is the "crotal," a tiny sphere with small
holes and a ball of stone or metal inside. This
type now appears as the sleigh bell, the Christmas bell or the bells on Indian dancers.

True bell making began when bronze, the mixing of tin and copper, was discovered. There are
now many types of materials from which bells
are made—almost as many materials as there are
uses for them.

Collectors' Club: American Bell Association, Rt.
1, Box 286, Natrona Heights, PA 15065.

See: Limited Editions or Collector Items.

REPRODUCTION ALERT

Animal
Cow
Brass, emb design **70.00**
Walnut, 8 x 4", hand carved **65.00**
Goat, brass, wooden clapper, leather
thong **35.00**
Sheep, cast iron, arched loop **5.00**
Turkey, brass, leather thong **42.00**

Ship bell, bronze, emb "W. Taylor, Oxford, 1847," 11" d base, $700.00.

Brass, figural handle
  Fish, 3½", engraved, marked "China," pr **18.00**
  Kewpie **35.00**
  Stork, 4½", marked "China" **15.00**
Bronze, figural
  Japanese Shrine, dark patina, God of Thunder handle, early 1800s **140.00**
  Lady, long skirt, vertical floral sprays, open fan in hand **75.00**
  Milkmaid, c1880 .... **125.00**
  Call Bell, boudoir, French, encased mother–of–pearl mollusk shells, marble base, wire depressor, late 1800s **125.00**
Chimes
  Camel, Persian, base relief decor ... **115.00**
  Saddle, Russian, pinwheels, outside clappers, c1850 .... **150.00**
Desk
  Side tap, bronze, white marble base, c1875 .... **45.00**
  Twirler type, double chime, mid 1800s **75.00**
Door, brass, Connell Patent, 1873 .... **60.00**
Glass
  Candlewick, 5" h, four bead handle **24.00**
  Cranberry, 10" h, applied clear swirl ribbed handle **125.00**
  Moser, 5¼" h, gold Arabic dome top, green cut to clear base, sgd, c1940 **35.00**
Porcelain
  Dresden–Meissen, floral decor, white cartouche, pastel ground, gold handle **50.00**
  German, figural, late 1800s
    Girl, floral spray on skirt **36.00**
    Lady, head slightly tilted **45.00**
  Japanese, bone china, figural
    Girl, pigtails **12.00**
    Lady, bonnet, basket over arm ... **18.00**

R S Prussia, hand painted, c1880
  Floral decor, smooth base **45.00**
  Rose decor, fluted base **36.00**
Shopkeeper, wall mounted, rosette, c1850 .... **35.00**
Sleigh, leather strap
  Brass, nine bells **90.00**
  Bronze, eighteen bells **100.00**
Table, figural
  Chinaman, 7½" h, upraised arms holding frame, suspended bell, gong hammer **50.00**
  St Paul, silver plated, ribbed, c1860 **25.00**
Tea, sterling silver handle, emb Art Nouveau ladies **50.00**

BICYCLES

Collecting Hints: Collectors divide bicycles into two groups—antique and classic. The antique category covers early high wheelers through safety bikes made into the 1920s and 1930s. Highly stylized bicycles from the 1930s and 1940s represent the transitional step to the classic period, beginning in the late 1940s and running through the end of the balloon tire era.

Unfortunately there are no reliable guide books for the beginning collector. A good rule is that any older bike in good condition is worth collecting.

Never pay much for a bicycle that is rusted, incomplete, or repaired with non–original parts. Replacement of leather seats or rubber handle bars does not affect value since these have a short life time.

Restoration is an accepted practice. Make certain to store an old bicycle high (hung by its frame to protect the tires) and dry (no more than 50% humidity).

Do not forget all the secondary material, e.g., advertising premiums, brochures, catalogs, posters, etc., that featured the bicycle. This material provides important historical data for research, especially for restoration.

Bicycle collectors and dealers gather each year on the last weekend in April at the Saline/Ann Arbor Swap Meet and Show.

History: In 1818 Baron Karl von Drais, a German, invented the Draisienne, a push scooter, that is viewed as the "first" bicycle. In 1839 Patrick MacMillan, a Scot, added a treadle system; a few years later Pierre Michaux, a Frenchman, revolutionized the design by adding a pedal system. The bicycle was introduced in America at the 1876 Centennial.

Early bicycles were high wheelers with a heavy iron frame and two disproportionately sized wheels with wooden rims and tires. The exaggerated front wheel was for speed, the small rear wheel for balance.

James Starley, an Englishman, is responsible for developing a bicycle with two wheels of equal size. Pedals drove the rear wheels by means of a chain and sprocket. By 1892 the wooden rim wheel was replaced by pneumatic air–filled tires to be followed by the standard rubber tire with inner tube.

1898 witnessed the development of the coaster brake. This important milestone made cycling a true family sport. Bicycling became a cult among the urban middle class. As the new century dawned, over four million Americans owned bicycles.

The automobile challenged the popularity of bicycling beginning in the 1920s. Since that time, interest in bicycling has been cyclical. Technical advances continued. The 1970s was the decade of the ten speed.

The success of American Olympiads in cycling and cycle racing, especially the Tour d'France, have kept the public's attention focused on the bicycle. However, the tremendous resurgence enjoyed by bicycling in the 1970s appears to have ended. The next craze is probably some distance in the future.

References: Frederick Alderson, *Bicycling: A History*, Praeger, 1972; A. Ritchie, *King Of The Road*, Ten Speed Press; Jim Hurd, *Introductory Guide to Collecting The Classics*, Antique/Classic Bicycle News, 1987; Jim Hurd, *1991 Bicycle Blue Book*, Antique/Classic Bicycle News, 1991.

Periodicals: *Antique/Classic Bicycle News*, P.O. Box 1049, Ann Arbor, MI 48106; *Bicycle Trader*, P. O. Box 5600, Pittsburgh, PA 15207.

Collectors' Clubs: Classic Bicycle and Whizzer Club, 35768 Simon, Fraser, MI 48026; Wheelmen, 55 Bucknell Avenue, Trenton, NJ 08619.

Museum: Schwinn History Center, Chicago.

Advertising
  Brochure, Crescent Bicycles, 1899 .   **20.00**
  Poster, Mentor Bicycles, young girls
    riding, c1890 . . . . **750.00**
  Trade Card, Clark Bicycle Co, Christmas, Santa on high wheeler, c1880   **20.00**
Badge, 1¼ x 2" link type, marked "Solid Silver" on back, enameled center front disk, hanger bar inscribed "Queens Co Course June 19–1898," pendant rim inscription "Century Medal/Survivor" and "Royal Arcanum Wheelman/New York City" .   **60.00**
Bicycle
  Beckley–Ralston, Chicago, tricycle, push pull action, wood seat and handles, spoke wheels, orig paint   **700.00**

  BF Goodrich, boy's, 26" tires, new paint, orig light, carrier, locking fork, bendix auto 2–speed **150.00**
  Comet, men's, worn orig paint, coaster brake, aluminum fenders . **85.00**
  Higgins, lady's, worn orig paint, carrier, skirt guard, truss rod, rusty rims **85.00**
  Roadmaster, girl's, cream and blue, red pinstripe, horn tank, headlight, carrier, chrome rims, orig condition **140.00**
  Walton, tandem, wood rim, block chain fixed drive, rat trap pedals, new cork grips, new polymer tires **450.00**
Catalog
  Indian Motorcycles and Bicycles, 1915 . . . . **50.00**
  Iver Johnson Bicycle & Motorcycle Supplies, 1909 . . . . **35.00**
Cereal Bowl, Bunnykin, riding bicycle, Royal Doulton **110.00**
Chain, Diamond **10.00**
Horn, Yoder, c1950 . . . . **7.00**
Lapel Stud, Corbin Bells, The Best, metal, copper finish, handlebar bell, late 1890s **30.00**
Light, Schwinn Phantom, chrome, battery operated **60.00**
Pedals, Schwinn, girl's, glass reflectors **50.00**
Pinback Button
  Damascus Bicycle, ⅞" d, multicolored, green and yellow gold Sword of Damascus, blue rim inscribed "Terre Haute Mfg Co, Dixon, IL," c1896, small tear in orig back paper **35.00**
  Topeka Wheelmen Track Association, 1¼" d, lightly tinted black and white illus, four female cyclists approaching head on, light blue center ground blending to white edges, blue rim inscription, red serial number, c1890 . . . . **60.00**
  Tried and True Pierce, 1¼" d, black and white logo, plum red ground, logo border inscribed "The Geo H Pierce Co/Makers/Buffalo, NY, USA," 1890s **50.00**
Saddle Pin, replica of bicycle seat, short stickpin soldered on back, late 1890s Mesinger, ¾ x⅞", diecut tin **30.00**
Richards Bicycle, ⅞ x 1½", silvered brass, inscription at top "Richards/Buchanan, Mich" **40.00**
Stickpin, replica of nameplate, diecut Cleveland, brightly silvered, mounted on brass backing, late 1890s **35.00**
Tribune, slightly rolled silvered brass, inscription "The Black Mfg Co, Erie, PA," late 1890s **40.00**
Tire, Schwinn, wide, white sidewalls, knobbys **15.00**
Tobacco Card, Honest Tobacco **20.00**

BIG LITTLE BOOKS

Collecting Hints: As more research is done and published on Big Little Books, the factors determining value shift. Condition always has been a key. Few examples are in pristine mint condition since the books were used heavily by the children who owned them. Each collector strives to obtain copies free from as many defects (bent edges on cover, missing spine, torn pages, mutilation with crayon or pencil, missing pages, etc.) as possible.

The main character in a book will determine price since it is a collector from another field who will vie with the Big Little Book collector for the same work. Dick Tracy, Disney characters, Buck Rogers, Flash Gordon, Charlie Chan, The Green Hornet and Tom Mix are examples. Other cowboy heroes are experiencing renewed popularity.

Until recently little attention has been directed to the artists who produced the books. Now examples by Alex Raymond and Henry Vallely command top dollar. Other desirable artists are Al Capp, Allen Dean, Alfred Andriola, and Will Gould. Personal taste still is a critical factor at this time.

Little is known as to how many copies of each book were printed. Scarcity charts have been prepared, but constantly are being revised. Books tend to hit the market in hoards, with prices fluctuating accordingly. However, the last decade has witnessed a stabilization of prices.

Larry Lowery, in the introduction to his book, has prepared an excellent section on the care and storage of Big Little Books. He also deserves credit for the detailed research which he has brought to each listing.

History: Big Little Books, although a trademark of the Whitman Publishing Co., is a term used to describe a wealth of children's books published during the 1930s and continuing to the present day. The origin of Big Little Books dates to a number of 1920s series by Whitman among which were Fairy Tales, Forest Friends and Boy Adventure.

The first Big Little Book appeared in 1933. Ten different page lengths and eight different sizes were tried by Whitman prior to the 1940s. Whitman and Saalfied Publishing Company dominated the field. However, other publishers did enter the market. Among them were Engel–Van Wiseman, Lynn Publishing Co., Goldsmith Publishing Co. and Dell Publishing Co.

Whitman also deserves attention for the various remarketing efforts it undertook with many of its titles. It contracted to provide Big Little Book premiums for Cocomalt, Kool Aid, Pan–Am Gas, Macy's, Lily–Tulip's Tarzan Ice Cream and others. Among its series names are Wee Little Books, Big Big Books, Nickel Books, Penny Books and Famous Comics.

In the 1950s television characters were introduced into Big Little Book format. Whitman Publishing became part of Western Publishing, owned by Mattel. Waldman and Son Publishing Co. under its subsidiary, Moby Books, issued their first Big Little Book– style book in 1977.

References: Larry Lowery, *Lowery's The Collector's Guide To Big Little Books and Similar Books*, privately printed, 1981; James Stuart Thomas, *The Big Little Book Price Guide*, Wallace–Homestead, 1983.

Collectors' Club: Big Little Book Collector's Club of America, P.O. Box 732, Danville, CA 94526.

Note: Books are priced in very fine condition. Cover and spine are intact with only slight bending at the corners. All pages are present; only slight discoloration of pages. Book has a crispness from cover color to inside.

No effort has been made to list the variations and premiums published by Whitman.

Abbreviations:

WBLB = Whitman Big Little Book
WBELB = Whitman Better Little Book
hc = hard cover
ms = Movie size, 4⅝ x 5¼ x ⅞"
sc = soft cover
ss = standard size, 3⅝ x 4½ x 1½"

See: Cartoon Characters, Cowboy Heroes, Disneyana and Space Adventurers.

AERONAUTICS

Air Fighters of America, WBLB, 1448, 1941, Robert Jenney, artist, Roy Snell, author, ss	**15.00**
Buzz Sawyer and Bomber 13, WBLB, 1415, 1946, Roy Crane, ss	**24.00**
Men with Wings, WBELB, 1475, 1938, Eleanor Parker, Fred MacMurray, Paramount Pictures, ss, 240 pgs, hc	**12.00**
Pat Nelson, Ace of the Test Pilots, WBLB, 1445, 1937, Dougal Lee, ss	**15.00**
Tailspin Tommy, The Dirigible Flight to the North Pole, WBLB, 1124, 1934, Hal Forest, ss	**25.00**
Thirteen Hours by Air, Lynn Publishing, L26, 1936, Wallace West, 128 pgs, 5 x 7"	**35.00**
Uncle Sam's Sky Defenders, WBLB, 1461, 1941, Erwin L Hess, artist, Peter A Wyckoff, author, ss, flip	**15.00**
Windy Wayne and His Flying Wing, WBLB, 1433, 1942, Erwin L Darwin, artist, Russell R Winterbotham, author, ss, left handed flip	**15.00**

CARTOON CHARACTERS, MOVIE

Andy Panda and the Mad Dog Mystery, WBELB, 1431, 1947, Walter Lantz Productions, ss, 288 pgs, hc 18.00

Adventures of Krazy Kat and Ignatz Mouse in Koko Land, Saalfield, Little Big Book, 1056, 1934, George Herriman, horizontal 35.00

Bugs Bunny in Risky Business, WBELB, 1440, 1948, Warner Bros Productions, ss, 288 pgs, hc 18.00

Donald Duck, Such a Life!, WBELB, 1404, 1939, Al Taliaferro, ss, 432 pgs, hc 20.00

Mickey Mouse in the Foreign Legion, WBELB, 1428, 1940, Floyd Gottfredson, ss, 432 pgs, hc 35.00

Oswald Rabbit Plays G–Man, WBLB, 1403, 1937, Eleanor Parker, Universal Pictures, ss, 240 pgs, hc 15.00

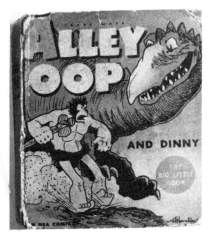

Alley Oop and Dinny, Whitman, #763, Vince T. Hamlin, author and illus, $20.00.

CARTOON CHARACTERS, NEWSPAPER

Alley Oop and Dinny, WBLB, 763, 1935, Vince T Hamlin, artist and author, ss, 384 pgs, sc 20.00

Blondie, Count Cookie in Too!, WBLB, 1430, 1947, Chic Young, ss 20.00

Dick Tracy, The Super Detective, WBELB, 1488, 1939, Chester Gould, artist and author, ss, 432 pgs, hc ... 25.00

Just Kids and the Mysterious Stranger, Saalfield, Little Big Book, 1324, 1935, Ad Carter, sc, ss 20.00

Little Orphan Annie in the Thieves' Den, WBELB, 1446, 1948, Harold Gray,

Popeye and The Jeep, Whitman, #1405, $20.00.

artist, Helen Berke, author, ss, 288 pgs, hc 20.00

Nancy and Sluggo, WBLB, 1400, 1946, Ernie Bushmiller, ss 26.00

Popeye, Saalfield, Little Big Book, 1051, 1934, Elzie Crisler Segar, horizontal 36.00

Popeye and the Quest for the Rainbird, WBLB, 1459, 1943, Bud Sagandorf, ss 28.00

Skeezix at the Military Academy, WBLB, 1408, 1938, Frank King, ss, 432 pgs, hc 12.00

Smitty in Going Native, WBLB, 1477, 1938, Walter Berndt, ss 20.00

DETECTIVE

Apple Mary and Dennie Foil the Swindlers, WBLB, 1130, 1936, Martha Orr, reprints from first Mary Worth strips, ss 24.00

Bob Stone, the Young Detective, 1432, 1937, Henry E Vallely cover, Peter K Maple, author, ss 18.00

Brenda Starr and the Masked Impostor, WBLB, 1427, 1940, Dale Messick, ss 25.00

Detective Higgins of the Racket Squad, WBELB, 1484, 1938, Herbert Anderson, Millard Thacksen, ss, hc, 432 pgs 15.00

JUNGLE

Jungle Jim, WBLB, 1138, 1936, Alex Raymond, ss 22.00

Tarzan and the Ant Men, WBLB, 1444, 1945, Rex Maxon, artist, John Coleman Burroughs, cover, Edgar Rice Burroughs, author, ss 20.00

Tarzan Twins, WBLB, 770, 1934, Edgar Rice Burroughs, ss, 432 pgs, hc 24.00

The Tiger Lady, Mabel Stark, Saalfield,

Little Big Book, 1588, 1935, Gertrude
Orr, sc **20.00**

LITERATURE

Adventures of Tom Sawyer, Saalfield,
Little Big Book, 1308, 1934, Park
Sumner, artist, Mark Twain, Charles T
Clinton, author, sc **35.00**
Great Expectations, Engel–Van Wise-
man, Inc, 8, 1934, adapted from
Charles Dickens by A J Sharick, 158
pgs, 4 x 5½" **30.00**
Little Women, WBLB, 757, 1934,
adapted from Louisa May Alcott, 160
pgs, hc, 4⅜ x 5¼ x⅞", sc spine **18.00**
Robinson Crusoe, WBLB, 719, 1934,
adapted from Daniel Defoe, 3½ x 2
x 1⅝", 360 pgs, sc **18.00**

MOVIE

Cowboy Millionaire, Saalfield, Little Big
Book, 1106, 1935, George O'Brien,
Atherton Pictures **15.00**
Jackie Cooper, Movie Star of Skippy and
Sooky, WBLB, 714, 1933, Eleanor
Packer, ss **24.00**
Laurel and Hardy, Saalfield, Little Big
Book, 1086, 1934, Charles T Clinton,
ss **28.00**
Mickey Rooney and Judy Garland and
How They Got Into the Movies,
WBELB, 1493, 1941, Henry E Vallely,
artist, Edward I Gruskin, author, ss,
432 pgs, hc **30.00**
One Night of Love, Saalfield, Little Big
Book, 1099, 1935, Charles Beahan
and Dorothy Speare, ss **16.00**
Paramount Newsreel Men with Admiral
Byrd in Little America, WBLB, 1118,
1934, photos, oversized **20.00**
Strawberry Roan, Saalfield, Little Big
Book, 1090, 1934, Ken Maynard,
Universal, Grace Mack, ss **15.00**
Union Pacific, Joel Macrea and Barbara
Stanwyck, WBELB, 1411, 1939,
Eleanor Parker, Paramount, ss **18.50**

RADIO

Calling W–1–X–Y–Z Jimmy Kean and
the Radio Spies, WBLB, 1412, 1939,
Sam Nisenson, artist, Thorp Mc-
Clusky, author, ss **18.00**
Fire Chief Ed Wynn and His Old Fire
Horse, Goldsmith Publishing, 1934,
Henry E Vallely, artist, Harold Sher-
man, author **25.00**
Mr District Attorney on the Job, WBLB,
1408, 1941, Phillips Lord's program,
ss, flip **15.00**

The Green Hornet Strikes!, WBELB,
1453, 1940, Robert R Weisman, artist, adapted from Fran Striker, ss, 432
pgs, hc **22.00**
The Shadow and the Master of Evil,
WBELB, 1443, 1941, Erwin L Hess,
artist, Maxwell Grant, author, ss, 432
pgs, hc, flip **15.00**
Uncle Don's Strange Adventures,
WBLB, 1114, 1936, Uncle Don Car-
ney, ss **15.00**

SPORTS

Brick Barton and the Winning Eleven,
Coach Bernie Bierman's, WBLB,
1480, 1938, R M Williamson, artist,
Bernie Bierman, author, ss **15.00**
Hockey Spare, Saalfield, Little Big Book,
1605, 1937, Robert A Graef, artist,
Harold M Sherman, author, ss **15.00**
Joe Palooka, The Heavyweight Boxing
Champ, WBLB, 1123, 1934, Ham
Fisher, ss **20.00**
Stan Kent, Captain, Saalfield, Little Big
Book, 1132, 1937, Louis G Schroe-
der, artist, William Heyliger, author,
ss **15.00**

WESTERN

Arizona Kid on the Bandit Trail, WBLB,
1192, 1936, Hal Arbo, artist, Peter
Maple, author, ss **18.00**
Big Chief Wahoo and the Magic Lamp,
WBLB, 1942, Elmer Woggon, Allen
Saunders, author, ss **18.00**
Buck Jones and the Two Gun Kid,
WBLB, 1404, 1937, Robert Weisman,
artist, Gaylord DuBois, author, ss ... **24.00**
Buffalo Bill Plays a Lone Hand, WBLB,
1194, 1936, Hal Arbo, artist, Buck
Wilson, author, ss **15.00**
Buckskin and Bullets, Saalfield, Little
Big Book, 1135, 1938, Luther Hittle,
artist, Ward M Stevens, ss **15.00**
Dan of the Lazy L, Saalfield, Jumbo
Book, 1160, 1939, Ralph C Hitch-
cock, artist, Mark Millis, author **15.00**
Gene Autry and the Bandits of Silver
Tip, WBELB, 1940 .... **15.00**
Kit Carson and the Mystery Riders, Saal-
field, Little Big Book, 1105, 1935,
Charles T Clinton, ss **15.00**
Lone Ranger and His Horse Silver,
WBLB, 1935, Henry Vallely, artist,
Fran Striker, author, ss **45.00**
Prairie Bill and the Covered Wagon,
WBLB, 758, 1934, Hal Arbo, artist,
G A Alkire, ss **15.00**

Red Ryder and the Circus Luck, WBLB,
1466, 1949, Fred Harman, ss **15.00**
Riders of Lone Trails, WBLB, 1425,
1937, Steve Saxton, ss, hc **17.50**

BLACK MEMORABILIA

Collecting Hints: Black memorabilia was produced in vast quantities and variations. As a result, collectors have a large field from which to choose and should concentrate on one or a combination of limited categories.

Outstanding examples or extremely derogatory designs in any given area of the field command higher prices. Certain categories, e.g., cookie jars, draw a higher concentration of collector interest resulting in higher prices. Regional pricing also is a factor.

New collectors frequently overpay for common items of little worth because they mistakenly assume all Black collectibles are rare or of great value. As in any other collecting field, misinformation and a lack of knowledge leads to these exaggerated values. The Black memorabilia collector is particularly vulnerable to this practice since so little documentation exists on the subject.

New collectors should familiarize themselves with the field by first studying the market, price trends, and existing reference material. Again, because of the limited reference material and the relative newness of the field, seeking out other collectors is especially valuable for the novice.

Black memorabilia has developed into an established collecting field primarily within the past few years and continues to grow with increased public attention and interest.

History: The term "Black memorabilia" refers to a broad range of collectibles that often overlap other collecting fields, e.g., toys, postcards, etc. It also encompasses African artifacts, items created by slaves or related to the slavery era, modern Black cultural contributions to literature, art, etc., and material associated with the Civil Rights Movement and the Black experience throughout history.

The earliest known examples of Black memorabilia include primitive African designs and tribal artifacts. Black American dates back to the arrival of African natives upon American shores.

The advent of the 1900s launched an incredible amount and variety of material depicting Blacks, most often in a derogatory and dehumanizing manner that clearly reflected the stereotypical attitude held toward the Black race during this period. The popularity of Black portrayals in this unflattering fashion flourished as the century wore on.

As the growth of the Civil Rights Movement

escalated and aroused public awareness to the Black plight, attitudes changed. Public outrage and pressure eventually put a halt to the offensive practice during the early 1950s.

Black representations still are being produced today in many forms, but no longer in the demoralizing designs of the past. These modern objects, while not as historically significant as earlier examples, will become the Black memorabilia of tomorrow.

References: Patiki Gibbs, *Black Collectibles Sold In America*, Collector Books, 1987; Patiki Gibbs and Tyson Gibbs, *The Collector's Encyclopedia of Black Dolls*, Collector Books, 1987; Douglas Congdon–Martin, *Images In Black: 150 Years of Black Collectibles*, Schiffer Publishing, 1990; Dawn Reno, *Collecting Black Americana*, Crown Publishing Co, 1986; Darrell A Smith, *Black Americana: A Personal Collection*, Black Relics, Inc., 1988; Jackie Young, *Black Collectibles: Mammy and her friends*, Schiffer Publishing, 1988.

Periodicals: *Black Ethnic Collectibles*, 1401 Asbury Court, Hyattsville, MD 20782.

Museums: Black American West Museum, Denver, CO; Black Archives Research Center and Museum, Florida A&M University, Tallahassee, FL; National Baseball Hall of Fame, Cooperstown, NY; Studio Museum, Harlem, NY; Center for African Art, New York, NY; The Jazz Hall of Fame, New York, NY; Schomburg Center for Research in Black Culture, New York, NY; John Brown Wax Museum, Harper's Ferry, WV; The Museum of African Art, Smithsonian Institution, Washington, D.C.; Robeson Archives, Howard University, Washington, D.C.

REPRODUCTION ALERT: Black memorabilia reproductions have grown during the 1980s. Many are made of easily reproducible materials which generally show signs of "newness." Collectors should beware of any given item offered in large or unlimited quantities.

Note: The following price listing is based upon items in excellent to mint condition. Major paint loss, chips, cracks, fading, tears, or other extreme signs of age warrant a considerable reduction in value, except in very rare or limited production items. Collectors should expect a certain amount of wear on susceptible surfaces.

Andirons, pr, sailor boy, cast iron **675.00**
Apron, Mammy, pecan pralines recipe,
1976 .... **23.00**
Ashtray
  Boy
    Eating watermelon slice **30.00**
    Standing under washline, peeking
    from between two pair of under-
    shorts, inscribed "Who Left This

Behind?", compartments for holding matches and cigarettes, Japan, c1930 .... **30.00**

Coon Chicken Inn **28.00**

Nat King Cole **48.00**

Natives, wearing loin cloths, inscribed "Ubangi Much?", molded china, copyright St Pierre & Patterson, 1956 .... **18.00**

Negro Face **35.00**

Three Children, on clothesline, 5" w, 3½" h, ashes, cigarettes, matches, striker, Japan **30.00**

Two children, sitting next to large handled chamber pot marked "Ashes," 5" w, 3½" h, Japan **38.00**

Bag, Plantation Coffee, cloth, pictures Negro, 1930s **4.00**

Bank

Caricature Figure, 5½" h, composition, painted, spring mounted head, two brass earrings, holding apple, Japan, 1930s **80.00**

Jolly Nigger, cast iron **275.00**

Lucky Joe **15.00**

Mammy, 6½" **55.00**

Toddler, 12", chalkware, carnival give–away **60.00**

Bell, Mammy, ceramic, souvenir **22.00**

Bell Doll, bell made of tin **50.00**

Blocks, Little Black Sambo, plastic **24.00**

Book

Little Black Sambo, 1959 .... **30.00**

Little Brown Koko, 1959 .... **30.00**

Uncle Tom's Cabin, Homewood Pub **55.00**

Bottle Stopper, Golliwog, 3" h **50.00**

Box

Adv

Coon Chicken Inn, 8 x 13", caricature bellhop, "Coon Chicken Inn" inscribed on bared teeth, "Nationally Famous Coast to Coast," c1950 .... **45.00**

Fun to Wash, washing powder, Mammy **45.00**

Eyelet, black face boy on lid **27.00**

Novelty, 3¼ x 6¼ x 1" deep, silver color lid, pair of gloves illus on sticker inscribed "One Pair Extra Fine/Undressed Black Kids," box holds a caricature of two nude children, c1930 .... **30.00**

Burned Wood Art, painted, two boys behind fence **145.00**

Cigar Box, Virginia Cheroots, 1883 ... **48.00**

Cigarette Holder, caricature, 3¼" h, bisque, painted, removable lid, outhouse shape, inscribed "One Moment Please," c1930 .... **55.00**

Cigarette and Match Holder, porter, 9½" h, brass wire figure, wood head, brass cap inscribed "Redcap," brass clips,

Messmore–Damon, New York City, late 1940s **75.00**

Coffee Tin, 1 lb, Luzianne, paper label with Mammy **45.00**

Coin, "Blackface Index," 1⅛" d, brass, emb, bellhop head above "I Bring Luck" and "Harold & Examiner Classified Ads" inscriptions, c1930 ..... **30.00**

Condiment Container, yellow plastic, spout, figural Uncle Mose handle, red, yellow, and black, c1950 ..... **45.00**

Cookbook, *Southern Cookbook*, wood cov, profile of mammy, 722 recipes . **60.00**

Cookie Jar

Black Face **300.00**

Sambo the Chef **175.00**

Crap Shooter, ceramic, boy, "Lil Joe" . **98.00**

Cup Holder, wood, Folk Art, Mammy and gray haired man **75.00**

Dancing Man, held by stick **60.00**

Doll

Aunt Jemima, oilcloth **65.00**

Boy, 5½" h, porcelain, sailor suit ... **110.00**

George Washington Carver, Hallmark **20.00**

Pickaninny, 7½" h, felt, red dress, cream petticoat, needlework borders **150.00**

Sambo, oilcloth, 9" h, stuffed, yellow felt cap, "Sambo" printed on front, c1930 .... **25.00**

Doorstop, Mammy, cast iron, black trim, 12", Hubley **425.00**

Egg Timer, boy **42.00**

Figurine

Bisque

Boy eating watermelon **45.00**

Man pushing outhouse on wheels, "My Old Country Seat" **50.00**

Two Boys, one sitting in outhouse, other looking inside, 1½ x 2 x 2" h, "Next" inscribed on base, souvenir Meadville, PA, made in Japan, c1930 .... **25.00**

Brayton Laguna–type Pottery, 12" h, young lady, hand on hip, blue and white slit skirt, bikini top **39.00**

Child, holding watermelon, 2" h, marked JM **50.00**

Girl, spotted dog, tree stumps, matches, cigarettes, 3¼" h, Japan **25.00**

Lead, man sitting on fence, eating watermelon, 1930s **55.00**

Shoeshine Man, Occupied Japan ... **30.00**

Fishing Lure, 5" l, Jock–E–Joe, novelty, MIB **42.50**

Folio, minstrel, color cov and illus, 1936 .... **28.00**

Glass, Coon Chicken Inn **27.00**

Laundry Bag, Mammy washing clothes **38.00**

Magazine, "The Negro South," 1946 . **6.00**

Map, Mammy Chicken Inn, souvenir . **35.00**

Matchbook, Coon Chicken Inn **35.00**

Game, The Game of Sambo, Parker Bros, skill type, c1920, 5⅛ x 10⅜", $100.00.

Match Holder, chalk, man with water-
melon 25.00
Medal, Martin Luther King, bronze,
1968 .... 10.00
Memo Holder
Aunt Jemima, red, yellow turban,
scarf, broom, pad 65.00
Black Chef, chalk 35.00
Menu, child's, Coon chicken Inn 65.00
Mirror, 1½" d, litho tin, pocket, carica-
ture illus, man and woman kissing,
inscribed "It's Up To You" 50.00
Mug, man shape handle 32.00
Palm Puzzle, 1⅞" d, tin frame, glass
cov, emb caricature portrait of man
with open red mouth, metal balls
form man's teeth, inscribed "Try The
Other Side," Sunshine Stoves, Fur-
nace adv, Heaters adv on reverse ... 60.00
Perfume, Golliwog 85.00
Picture, 14 x 16", "Washday Blues,"
black angel on cloud of suds, framed,
dated 1944 .... 55.00
Piebird
Mammy, holding rolling pin 55.00
Man, holding pie, flying blackbird
painted on shirt 55.00
Pinback Button
American Negro Exposition, 75th anniversary, pictures Abe Lincoln,
two red, white, and blue ribbons,
1940 .... 45.00
Aunt Jemima Breakfast Club, mint .. 10.00
Break the Noose/CORE, 1¼" d, black
and white, noose surrounding hand
inscribed "Captive Ghetto," issued
by Congress of Racial Equality ... 30.00

Gold Dust Washing Powder adv,
⅞" d, caricature of twins in washing tub, multicolor, white ground,
black rim lettering 65.00
Malcolm X/All Power to the People,
1½" d, black rim and portrait on
day glow yellow ground 12.00
Rev Dr Martin Luther King, Jr Educational Fund/Sponsored by NAACP/
1968, 1¼" d, black and white,
photo portrait 25.00
Pin Cushion, boy with pumpkin 55.00
Pipe, ceramic, bone color, Negro head 55.00
Planter, Mammy, 3 x 3 x 4" h, white
china, dark brown face and hands,
orange bandanna, multicolor dress,
brick wall illus on back, made in Japan, c1930 .... 30.00
Playing Cards, Cotton Belt Route RR,
1903, child with watermelon 60.00
Post Card, Mammy Chicken Inn 30.00
Poster, store display, "Aunt Jemima
Spice Set," 16½ x 22", paper, full
color, offers three—spice set for 50¢,
dated Nov 14, 1950 .... 100.00
Pot Holder Plaque
Boy and Girl, eating watermelon
slice, 5 x 5", plaster, painted, metal
hooks, 1930–40s 30.00
Little Black Sambo, chalkware 35.00
Mammy and Chef, 4 x 6", plaster,
embedded hooks and hanging
wire, c1930s, pr 62.00
Print, 8 x 10", "An Open Countenance,"
1896 .... 16.00
Program, "Ladies Be Seated," 5¼ x
8½", soft cov, 18 pgs, souvenir, Aunt
Jemima illus, ABC radio audience
participation show sponsored by Aunt
Jemima, issued by Quaker Oats, 1944 15.00
Puppet, hand, Floyd Patterson 45.00
Puzzle
Ball, cast metal, Negro face, "Sambo
Ball Puzzle," Enardoe, MIB 30.00
Jigsaw, Little Black Sambo 10.00
Recipe Box, plastic, red, Mammy 85.00
Reservation Card, Coon Chicken Inn .. 15.00
Salt and Pepper Shakers, pr
Aunt Jemima, F&F Mold & Die Works
3½" 40.00
5" 60.00
Baby Basket, toddler boy and girl
shakers sit in basket, marked "For-
eign," c1930 .... 25.00
Boy
Holding watermelons 65.00
Singing, gold 45.00
Sitting on commode 6.00
Luzianne, green 110.00
Mammy, red and green aprons, 1940s 26.00
Mammy and Butler, 4¾" h 75.00
Mammy and Chef, 2½" h, metal ... 55.00

Man and Woman, china, figural palm
tree holder, Japan, c1930 .... **40.00**
Negro Cook, china, 5" h **27.00**
Sheet Music
Carry Me Back to Old Virginny, color
litho of family in front of house,
1906 .... **10.00**
A Zoot Suit (For My Sunday Gal), 9 x
12", caricature of woman on front
cov, browntone photo inset of Kay
Kyser, 4 inner pgs, 1942 copyright **16.00**

Sheet Music, *It Takes A Long Tall Brown Skin Gal To Make A Preacher Lay His Bible Down,* **Marshall Walker lyrics, Will E. Skidmore music, 1917, cover design by E. H. Pfeiffer, $25.00.**

Shopping Peg Board, wood, Mammy,
"Reckon Ah Needs" **40.00**
Sign
Pepsodent, cardboard, man, 1930 .. **15.00**
Yassuh Uncle Natchel—Natural Chi-
lean Soda, 22 x 15", painted steel,
head of old man, double sided, fas-
tens right angle to wall **139.00**
Soap, boxed, Mammy and Pickaninny
on lid **25.00**
Soap Holder, 5" h, Mammy **40.00**
Soda Bottle, Mammy, 14" h **185.00**
Spice Set, ceramic **95.00**
Spoon Rest
Chef's Hat, 8¼" h, glazed ceramic,
Japan **80.00**
Mammy **75.00**
Statue, 11" h, wood, carved, bare footed
man, patched pants, wiping perspir-
ation from neck, holding primitive
tool **75.00**
String Holder, Mammy, ceramic, plaid
skirt **65.00**

Tablecloth
Dancing Mammies **85.00**
Ole Man River Theme, 48" sq, cotton
and linen, depicts 16 Negro color
graphics, green, yellow, red, and
black on white ground **90.00**
Target Game, Little Black Sambo, tin . **95.00**
Tea Set, 3 pcs, teapot, creamer, and
sugar, black face **365.00**
Thermometer
Composition child peeks around ther-
mometer **28.00**
Negro, figural, 1949 .... **24.00**
Tin, La Jean Hair Dressing, pictures Ne-
gro **5.00**
Toothpick Holder, figural, 3" h, metal,
gild finish, two boys, cotton bale, watermelons **99.00**
Valentine
4 x 5", stiff paper, diecut, late 1930s **10.00**
5½ x 6", cardboard, diecut, emb, mechanical, disk wheel, child eating
Valentine cards, dated 1924 ..... **20.00**
Vinegar and Oil Set, 5¼" h, china,
Mammy and Chef, removable heads,
neck stopper, stamped "Japan,"
c1930 .... **35.00**
Whisk Broom, 4½" h, wood handle,
painted, figural, caricature figure,
c1930 .... **25.00**

BLENKO GLASS COMPANY

Collecting Hints: Blenko glassware is unmarked but carries a paper label. The most easily identified pieces are tall, ranging from 18 to 28 inches. Colors are vibrant, and the glassware is heavy. Designs have a substantial appearance with clean modern lines and no applied decoration.

History: Blenko Glass Company, located in Milton, West Virginia, was founded in 1922 by British glassmaker, William J. Blenko. He originally made stained glass for church windows, but since 1929 has made decorative household glass and glass building slabs. Blenko provided the blown faceted glass windows for the Air Force Academy Chapel in Colorado Springs, Colorado.

Reference: Eason Eige and Rich Wilson, *Blenko Blass, 1930–1953,* Antique Publications, 1987.

Museum: The Blenko Glass Company Museum, Milton, West Virginia.

Ashtray, 8" l, freeform, amethyst **10.00**
Bowl
3" d, 4" h, amber, scalloped edge .. **10.00**
6¼" d, tangerine, turned–in edge ... **15.00**

Bookends, pr, elephant, crystal, 1980, $20.00.

6½" d, amber, scalloped edge, heavy base	15.00
Compote	
5¾" d, 6" h, red bowl shades to gold, gold stem and foot	15.00
10" d, 5½" h, amber, scalloped edge	25.00
Creamer, red, flat	18.00
Decanter	
10" h, amethyst, amethyst stopper	20.00
11½" h, crystal, pinched sides, flat stopper	18.00
15½" h, crystal, 6" h pointed stopper	25.00
Pitcher, 6½" h, crystal, bulbous, applied handle	20.00
Sand Glass, 25 minutes, 19" h, crystal, wood case	40.00
Snowman, ruby top hat	20.00
Vase	
5" h, Rosettes, cobalt blue	60.00
7" h, yellow shades to orange, pinched sides, tricorn edge	12.00
8½" h, Florette, flared, crystal	35.00
9" h, tankard shape, gold, applied handle	18.00
11" h, Crackle, green, flip	50.00
16" h, Amberina, roll top	65.00
25" h, avocado, tapered neck, scallop edge, crackled	35.00
Water Set, 10" pitcher, dark amber, random small indentation in body, six 6" tumblers, 7 pcs	65.00

BOOKMARKS

Collecting Hints: The best place to search for bookmarks is specialized paper shows. Be sure to check all related categories. Most dealers do not have a separate category for bookmarks. Instead they file them under subject headings, e.g., Insurance, Ocean Liners, World's Fairs, etc.

History: Bookmark collecting dates back to the early nineteenth century. A bookmark is any object used to mark a reader's place in a book. Bookmarks have been made in a wide variety of material including celluloid, cloth, cross—stitched needlepoint in punched paper, paper, Sterling silver, wood, and woven silk. Heavily embossed leather markers were popular between 1800 and 1860. Advertising markers appeared after 1860.

Woven silk markers are a favorite among collectors. T. Stevens of Coventry, England, manufacturer of Stevensgraphs, is among the most famous makers. Paterson, New Jersey, was the silk weaving center in the United States. John Best & Co., Phoenix Silk Manufacturing Company, and Warner Manufacturing Co. produced bookmarks. Other important United States companies that made woven silk bookmarks were J. J. Mannion of Chicago and Tilt & Son of Providence, Rhode Island.

Recently collectors have discovered the colorful folk art quality of cross—stitched bookmarks created between the 1840s and 1910s. These were a popular handcraft of young women who followed the pre—punched paper strips imprinted with a design. Plain strips were available for those wishing to design their own bookmark. Most have a religious theme, but examples have been found for birthdays, Christmas, temperance (anti—drink), and other themes. Most were attached to colorful silk ribbons.

Reference: A. W. Coysh, *Collecting Bookmarks*, Drake Publishers, 1974, out—of—print.

Periodicals: *Bookmark Collector*, 1002 West 27th Street, Erie, PA 16502; *Bookmark Quarterly*, Route 10, Box 120, Morgantown, NC 28655.

Advisor: John S. Waldsmith.

Cross—stitched, on punched paper, usually attached to silk ribbon	
Black Emancipation, 3⅞ x 1½", "Happy are we in our liberty," black couple dancing, 1860s	25.00
Diecut paper attached, 2⅝ x 7", "Ever Constant—Ever True," young girl in bouquet of flowers	5.00
Early dated examples, 1840s—70s	7.50
Extra heavy beading	11.00
Large examples, 3⅝ x 7¾" and larger	4.50
Religious, "God is Love," "Jesus, the Life, the Way," etc	3.50
Small Markers, 3¼ x ⅞" and smaller	3.00
Temperance	17.50
Paper, advertising, many are diecuts	
Biscuits, Austin Young & Co, 2 x 7", color	3.00

Stevensgraph, Centennial USA, portrait of George Washington, $75.00.

Chocolates, Apollo, Daggetts, etc, colorful	3.50
Christmas, 2 x 4½", girl behind holly leaf	3.00
Easter Crosses, 1890s–1930s, usually with silk ribbons	.75
Hoyt's German Cologne, common, colorful	1.50
LePages' Liquid Glue, diecut codfish	7.50
Mr Peanut, diecut, black and yellow	
1939 New York World's Fair logo	13.50
No World's Fair logo	11.00
Pear's Soap, 1 x 7", diecut, colorful	2.50
Pheno–Caffein Co, 2¼ x 1¼", diecut	2.50
Pianos, Cable Co, Krakamer, Winter & Co, etc	2.50
Youth's Companion, 2¾ x 6", colorful, 1902	5.50
Sterling Silver	
Ocean Grove, NJ, ¾ x 4"	67.50
Provincetown, MA, ⅝ x 1⅞", souvenir	17.50
Two Piece, opener/marker, long chain, Doskow	12.50
Wood, Mauchline Ware	
Bethlehem, NH, 1¾ x 3¾"	22.50
Pilgrim Hall, Plymouth, MA, 1 x 4¾"	8.50
Woven Silk	
Stevensgraphs, 1860s–80s	
Birthday greetings	47.50
Faith, Hope, and Charity	47.50
George Washington, 1876 Centennial	75.00
Various Paterson, NJ, and other US makers	
1876 Centennial, Warner Mfg Co	45.00

Home, Sweet Home, 2½ x 11", John Best & Co	37.50
IOOF, 2½ x 12", Best & Co, 1909	22.50
Jamestown Expo, Pioneer Mfg Co, NY, 1907	12.50
New York World's Fair, American Silk Label, 1939	18.00
Pan–American Expo, Allen Chesters, Paterson, 1901	27.50
Paris Expo, Tilt & Son, Providence, RI, 1878	32.50
Shrine Ceremonial, Warner Mfg Co, 1921	17.50
World's Columbian Expo	
JJ Mannion	62.50
John Best & Co	62.50
World's Industrial and Cotton Centennial Expo, 2¼ x 10", New Orleans, Phoenix Co, 1884–85	27.50

BOOKS—LIMITED EDITIONS CLUB

Collecting Hints: George and Helen Macy, founders of the Limited Editions Club, also owned the Heritage Press and issued popular inexpensive versions of the Limited Editions Club books under the Heritage Press imprint. These unsigned and unlimited editions usually have the same artwork and typography as the LEC books but were printed on cheaper paper and less handsomely bound.

Heritage Press Books are available in the $12.00 to $25.00 range and represent an excellent value for readers and far–sighted collectors.

History: In 1931 George and Helen Macy founded The Limited Editions Club, dedicated to the production of beautiful books and the preservation of classic works. They selected standard texts of enduring value and had them illustrated, printed, and bound by fine artists and craftsmen. Initially, distribution was limited to 1,500 subscribers. The number of subscribers increased to 2,000 after 1972.

Most copies were signed by the illustrators (including Picasso and Matisse) authors, and/or printers.

Though the quality is uneven, they are all in demand by collectors. Condition is the key. These books must be very crisp and clean with slipcases that show little wear to achieve best prices.

Advisor: Ron Lieberman.

Aristophanes, *The Frogs*, Haarlem, Holland, 1937, illus wood cuts by John Austen, octavo, top edge silver, sgd by Austen	75.00

Aristophanes, *Lysistrata, 1934, illus and sgd by Picasso* **2,000.00**

Bacon, Sir Francis, *Essays, Or Councils Civill and Morall, 1944* **100.00**

Balzac, Honore De, *Droll Stories,* Southworth Press, 1932, 3 vols, color headpieces and initials illus, octavo, deco paper boards, gilt cloth back, sgd by A. W. Dwiggins **75.00**

Balzac, Honore De, *Old Goriot,* 1948 **50.00**

Baudelaire, *Flowers of Evil,* 1940, illus by Jacob Epstein **120.00**

Baudelaire, *Les Fleurs De Mal,,* illus by Auguste Rodin **125.00**

Beckford, William, *Vathek: An Arabian Tale,* 1945 .... **50.00**

Bellamy, Edward, *Looking Backward,* 1941, illus by Elise **55.00**

Benet, Stephen, *John Brown's Body,* 1948, illus by Curry **50.00**

Bennett, Arnold, *The Old Wives' Tale,* 1941, 2 vols, illus by John Austen .. **100.00**

Boswell, James, *The Life of Samuel Johnson,* Curwen Press, 1938, 3 vols, octavo, brown cloth, leather labels . **135.00**

Bourget, *La Vengeance De La Vie,* **35.00**

Brooks, Van Wyck, *The Flowering of New England,* 1941 .... **50.00**

Buck, Pearl S., *All Men Are Brothers,* 1948, 2 vols **110.00**

Bunyan, John, *Pilgrim's Progress,* 1941 **120.00**

Burton, Richard F., *The Book of the Thousand Nights and a Night,* William Edwin Rudge, 1934, 6 vols, line illus by Valenti Angelo, octavo, paper boards, pigskin backs, sgd by Angelo **200.00**

Butler, Samuel, *Erewhon,* Pynson Printers, 1934, XXI, 229P, colored illus by Rockwell Kent, octavo, cloth, sgd by Rockwell Kent **150.00**

Butler, Samuel, *The Way of All Flesh,* Carl Purington Rollins, Yale University Press, 1936, 2 vols, illus by Robert Ward Johnson, octavo, gilt levant, sgd by Johnson **75.00**

Canis, *Le Fils Des trois Mousquetaires* . **35.00**

Carlyle, Thomas, *Sartor Resartus, The Life and Opinions of Herr Teufelsdrockh,* Oliver Simon, Curwen Press, 1931, XIX, 377P, octabo, blue gilt dec cloth, sgd by Oliver Simon **35.00**

Castillo, Diaz Del, *The Discovery and Conquest of Mexico,* 1942 .... **175.00**

Chaucer, Geoffrey, *The Canterbury Tales,* George W. Jones at the sign of the Dolphin, 1934, 2 vols, folio, dec paper boards, buckrum backed, sgd by Jones **125.00**

Chaucer, Geoffrey, *Troilus and Cressida,* 1939 .... **75.00**

Chauveau, *Ramponnot,* **35.00**

Dana, Richard Henry, *Two Years Before the Mast,* 1947 .... **60.00**

Daudet, Alphonse, *Tartarin of Tarascon,* Richard W. Ellis, The Georgian Press, 1930, 2 vols, illus by W. A. Dwiggins, 24mo, paper boards, cloth spines, sgd by Dwiggins **50.00**

De Coster, Charles, *The Glorious Adventures of Tyl Ulenspeigl* Jon, Enschede En Zonen, 1934, illus by Richard Floethe, folio, gilt dec buckrum, sgd by Floethe **60.00**

Dickens, Charles, *Great Expectations,* R. & R. Clark Ltd, 1937, illus by Gordon Ross, octavo, green cloth, sgd by Gordon Ross **95.00**

Dickinson, Emily, *The Unpublished Poems of Emily Dickinson,* **100.00**

Dumas, Alexandre, *The Black Tulip,* 1951 .... **50.00**

Emerson, Ralph Waldo, *The Essays,* John Henry Nash, 1934, folio, paper boards, sgd by Nash **75.00**

Epicurus, *The Works of Epicurus,* 1947, sgd by the book's designer Bruce Rogers **100.00**

Flaubert, *The Temptation of Saint Anthony,* 1943 .... **50.00**

Flaubert, Gustave, *Madame Bovary,* Fretz Brothers Ltd, 1938 illus by Gunter Bohmer, octavo, yellow silk cloth, sgd by Bohmer **55.00**

France, Anatole, *At the Sign of the Queen Pedauque,* 1933, illus and sgd by Sauvage **65.00**

France, Anatole, *Crainquebille,* 1949 . **45.00**

France, Anatole, *Le Chateau De Vaux Le Vicomte,* **40.00**

France, Anatole, *Penguin Island,* 1949 **45.00**

France, Anatole, *The Crime of Sylvestre Bonnard,* Marchbanks Press, 1937, illus by Sylvain Sauvage, Quarto, green dec cloth, sgd by Sauvage **75.00**

France, Anatole, *The Revolt of the Angels,* 1953 .... **50.00**

Gay, John, *The Beggar's Opera,* G. Govone, 1937, illus by Mariette Lydis, folio, blue cloth emb in gilt, sgd by Mariette Lydis **75.00**

Hamilton, Alexander et al, *The Federalist,* 1945, 2 vols **75.00**

Hawthorne, Nathaniel, *The House of the Seven Gables,* Edmund B. Thompson, 1935, illus by Valenti Angelo, octavo, boards, leather back, sgd by Angelo **85.00**

Hughes, Richard, *The Innocent Voyage,* 1944, illus and sgd by Lynd Ward .. **75.00**

Kingston, *St. George's and the Dragon,* **35.00**

Lesage, Alain-Rene, *the Adventures of Gil Blas of Santillane,* John Johnson,

1937, 2 vols, illus by John Austen, small folio, cloth, sgd by Austen ... **125.00**

Longus, *The Pastoral Loves of Daphnis and Chloe*, Porter Garnett, 1934, illus by Ruth Reeves, tall octavo, full leather with gilt medalion, sgd by Ruth Reeves **75.00**

Maccurdy, *Notebooks of Leonardo Da Vinci*, 2 vols **80.00**

Millay, Edna St. Vincent, *Conversation at Midnight*, sgd by Edna St. Vincent Millay **200.00**

Millay, Edna St. Vincent, *Huntsman. What Quarry?*, ... **165.00**

Millay, Edna St. Vincent, *Wine From These Grapes, Epitaph for the Race of Man,* **150.00**

Milton, John, *Paradise Lost and Paradise Regain'd*, John Henry Nash, 1936, lithographs by Carlotta Petrina, folio, paper boards, sgd by Carlotta Petrina **100.00**

Moncrieff, Charles Scott, *The Song of Roland*, Edmund b. Thompson, Hawthorn House, 1938, XII, 138P, tall octavo, blue deco paper boards, gilt vellum back, sgd by Valenti Angelo ... **100.00**

Montaigne, *The Essays of Montaigne*, 4 vols, illus and sgd by T. M. Cleland **125.00**

Parkman, Francis, *The Oregon Trail*, 1945, illus by Thomas Hart Benton, sgd by T. H. Benton **250.00**

Peattie, Donald Culross, *An Almanac For Moderns*, Judd & Detweiler, 1938, Wood Engraved Vignettes by Asa Cheffetz, octavo, green dec cloth, sgd by Asa Cheffetz **65.00**

Pennell, *Adventures Of An Illustrator*, . **200.00**

Plato, *The Republic*, 1944, 2 vols **100.00**

Polo, Marco, *The Travels of Marco Polo, 1271–1295*, Lester Douglas, Judd & Detweiler, Inc., 1934, 2 vols, illus by Nikolai Lapshin, octavo, sgd by N. Lapshin **75.00**

Pushkin, Alexander, *The Golden Cockerel*, 1949, illus and sgd by Edmund Dulac **140.00**

Rabelais, Francois, *Gargantua and Pantaguerl*, Southworth–Anthoensen Press, 1936, 5 vols, illus and sgd by W. A. Dwiggins, octavo, green cloth **100.00**

Reade, Charles, *The Cloister and The Hearth*, A. Colish Press, 1932, 2 vols, illus by Lynd Ward, octavo, cloth, sgd by Lynd Ward **100.00**

Rostand, Edmond, *Cyrano de Bergerac*, 1936, illus and sgd by Brissaud **50.00**

Schiller, Friedrich Von, *William Tell*, 1951 .... **35.00**

Shakespeare, *The Works*, 1939–41, 39 vols **500.00**

Shaw, George Bernard, *Back to Methu-*

selah, 1939, illus and sgd by John Farleigh **75.00**

Shelly, Mary Wollstonecraft, *Frankenstein or the Modern Prometheus*, Walpole Press, 1934, illus by Everett Henry, tall octavo, backed in leather gilt, sgd by Everett Henry **100.00**

Sheridan, R. B., *The School For Scandal A Comedy*, Oxford University Press, 1934, hand colored etchings by Rene Ben Sussan, tall octavo, dec paper over boards, sgd by Rene Ben Sussan **95.00**

Smollet, Tobias, *The Adventures of Peregrine Pickle*, John Johnson, 1936, 2 vols, illus by John Austen, folio, cloth, sgd by Austen **110.00**

Southey, Robert, *The Chronicle of The CID*, 1958, illus and sgd by Rene Ben Sussan **50.00**

Stendhal, *The Red and The Black*, illus and sgd by Rafaello Busoni **50.00**

Stephens, James, *The Crock of Gold*, 1942, illus by Robert Lawson, sgd by Robert Lawson **125.00**

Sterne, Laurence, *The Life & Opinions of Tristram Shandy Gentleman*, A. Colish, 1935, 2 vols, illus by T. M. Cleland, blue boards, sgd by T. M. Cleland **100.00**

Tolstoy, Leo, *Anna Karenina*, 1933, 2 vols, illus and sgd by Nicholas Piskariov **100.00**

Turgenev, Ivan, *Fathers and Sons*, 1951, illus and sgd by Fritz Eichenberg ... **60.00**

Virgil, *Aeneid*, 1944 .... **70.00**

Wilder, Thornton, *The Bridge of San Luis Rey*, 1962 .... **225.00**

Willke, Wendell, *One World*, 1944 ... **55.00**

Wister, Owen, *The Virginian*, 1951 ... **50.00**

BOTTLE OPENERS, FIGURAL

Collecting Hints: Condition is most important. Worn or missing paint and repainted surfaces lower value. Damaged or rusty pieces have greatly diminished value.

History: Figural bottle openers were produced expressly for removing a bottle cap from a bottle. They were made in a variety of metals, including cast iron, brass, bronze, and white metal. Cast iron, brass, and bronze openers are generally solid castings; white metal openers are usually cast in hollow blown molds.

The vast majority of figural bottle openers date from the 1950s and 1960s. Paint variation on a figure is very common.

References: Donald Bull, *A Price Guide to Beer Advertising, Openers and Corkscrews*, Donald

Bull, 1981; Michael Jordan, *Figural Bottle Openers*, available from Figural Bottle Opener Collectors.

Collectors' Clubs: Figural Bottle Opener Collectors, 13018 Clarion Road, Fort Washington, MD, 20744; Just For Openers, 63 October Lane, Trumbull, CT 06611.

Advisor: Craig Dinner.

REPRODUCTION ALERT

Donkey, white metal, painted, 3⅝" h, $25.00.

Bear, 3⅞ x 3¹/₁₆", cast iron, wall mount, head, black highlights, John Wright Co 85.00
Black Boy with green alligator
  2⅝" h, hands down, Wilton Products 145.00
  3", hand in air, green base, John Wright Co 185.00
Black Man, 4⅜ x 3¾", wall mount, smiling, red bow tie, Wilton Products 100.00
Canada Goose, head extended to ground, brown and black markings on body, green base, black neck and face with tan markings, Wilton Products . 45.00
Cathy Coed, 4⅛" h, cast iron, preppie girl holding stack of books, green base with white front, marked "L & L Favors" 400.00
Clown, 4⅛ x 4", brass, wall mount, white bow tie with red polka dots, bald head, marked "495", John Wright Co 90.00
Cowboy, drunk
  4³/₁₆" h, sign post, yellow hat, blue pants, red bandanna, yellow jacket, John Wright Co 65.00
  3⅞" h, holding green cactus, yellow hat, red bandanna, blue pants, black boots, brown jacket, John Wright Co 85.00
Dinky Dan, 3¹³/₁₆" h, cast iron, preppie boy with hands in pockets, green base, marked "Gadzik Phila" 265.00

Do Do Bird, 2¾" h, cast iron, cream, black highlights, red beak **175.00**
Drunk, Palm Tree
  4" h, bald head, orange and yellow tails, blue vest, white pants, yellow tree, green leaves, red flower on green base, Wilton Products **40.00**
  4¼" h, yellow hat, blue jacket vest, yellow pants, yellow tree, green leaves, green base, John Wright Co **35.00**
Elephant
  2 x 3", cast iron, flat, pink, black base, sitting on hind legs, trunk up, open mouth **75.00**
  3 x 2³/₁₆", brass, flat, trunk up, standing, mouth is opener, dark brown **75.00**
Freddie Frosh, 4" h, cast iron, preppie boy standing with hands in pockets, legs crossed, green base with white front, marked "L & L Favors" **310.00**
Grass Skirt Greek, 5" h, cast iron, black native girl, white sign and post, green base, marked "Gadzik Phila" **335.00**
Goat, 4¼" h, tan body with gray highlights, sitting, yellow curved horn on top of head, green base, Wilton Products **45.00**
Mademoiselle, 4½" h, cast iron, street walker by lamp post, black, flesh face, hands, and legs, yellow light, John Wright Co **22.00**
Mallard Duck, 2⅝" h, greenish, tan back, red breast, green head, yellow bead, Wilton Products **45.00**
Mexican, 2¹³/₁₆" h, taking Siesta, seated leaning on cactus, head in hands on knees, light green hat, yellow cape, red shirt, green cactus, brown pants, yellow base, Wilton Products **210.00**
Monkey, 2½" h, holding branch at left side, black with tan chest and tan face markings, brown branch, John Wright Co **135.00**
Paddy the Pledgemaster, 4" h, cast iron, preppie boy, green base with white front, marked "Gadzik Phila" **265.00**
Patty Pep, 4" h, girl with hands behind head, yellow mini skirt, blue blouse, yellow hat, emb "Women's Weekend '55" marked "L & L Favors" **425.00**
Pheasant, 2⅛" h, yellow crest, blue, red, yellow back, tail with black markings, red breast, green base, John Wright Co **165.00**
Rooster, 3⅞" h, metal, black body, red comb, orange–yellow beak and feet, green base, opener under tail, John Wright Co **65.00**
Setter, 2½" h, front left paw up, tail extended out, green base, tan dog with black patches, John Wright Co **70.00**
Squirrel, 2⅛" h, tail up, green base,

brown body, white stripe, tan tail and face, black whiskers, John Wright Co, also patented as Skunk and Grey Squirrel **125.00**
Winking Boy, 4⅛ x 4¹³⁄₁₆″, wall mount, open mouth, red lips, two white teeth top of mouth, brown hair and eye brows, right eye closed, left eye blue, Wilton Products **265.00**

BREWERIANA

Collecting Hints: Many collectors concentrate on items from one specific brewery or region. An item will bring slightly more when it is sold in its locality. Regional collector clubs and shows abound.

History: Collecting material associated with the brewing industry developed in the 1960s when many local breweries ceased production. Three areas occupy the collectors' interest—pre-Prohibition material, advertising items for use in taverns and premiums designed for individual use.

References: Donald Bull, *A Price Guide To Beer Advertising Openers And Corkscrews*, privately printed, 1981; Donald Bull, Manfred Friedrich, and Robert Gottschalk, *American Breweries*, Bullworks, 1984; Keith Osborne and Brian Pipe, *The International Book of Beer Labels, Mats, & Coasters*, Chartwell Books, 1979.

Collectors' Clubs: American Breweriana Association, P. O. Box 6082, Colorado Springs, CO 80934; Eastern Coast Breweriana Association, 312 Hamilton Blvd, Piscataway, NJ 08850; National Association of Breweriana, Advertising, 2343 Mat–tu–Wee Lane, Wauwatoca, WI 53226.

REPRODUCTION ALERT: Advertising trays have been heavily reproduced.

Ashtray, O'Keefe's Old Vienna Beer, 6″ d **5.00**
Bar Display
  Blatz Beer Tavern, full dimensional, 10″ h, 3 1/4″ d base, plastic figure, tin beer can torso, holding pennant inscribed "Blatz," 1959 copyright **75.00**
  Duquesne Pilsner, figure, composition–like, 9 1/2″ h, bellboy uniform, blue "Have a Duke!" inscription, issued by Duquesne Brewing Co, Pittsburgh, c1950s **60.00**
Baseball Score Counter, adv, Pfatt's Lager, Massachusetts Breweries Co of Boston, 2 1/4 x 2 3/4″, celluloid, die-cut, catcher's mitt shape, tan, c1915 **50.00**
Beer Bung Plunger, iron and brass **40.00**
Belt Buckle, Coors **10.00**
Blotter, Schlitz **4.00**

Advertising sign, Silver Top Beer, Duquesne Brewing Co, cardboard, 15¼″ h, $7.50.

Booklet, 1894 Pabst Brewery, *Ominous Secrets*, 50 pgs **125.00**
Bottle, 10 1/2″ h, redware, brown Albany glaze **15.00**
Bottle Opener, Harvard Brewing Co, Lowell, MA, 3 1/2″ **15.00**
Calendar, Pabst Extract, woman with parasol, 1913 .... **85.00**
Charm, Budweiser, 1876–1976, commemorative, wood **12.00**
Clay Pipe Holder, Frank Jones Brewing Co, tin **45.00**
Clock
  Griesedieck Bros Beer, cash register **90.00**
  Pabst Beer, statue, bar and bartender, clock and light **150.00**
Coaster, Ruppert Beer **5.00**
Corkscrew, Dick's Brewery **6.00**
Dictionary, pocket, Schlitz 1897 Milwaukee, 200 pgs **100.00**
Display, Falstaff Beer, cardboard and plastic, emb figure **45.00**
Flashlight, Schlitz, bottle shape, 1970 . **8.00**
Foam Scraper
  Grand Prize, celluloid **12.50**
  Piel Bros, metal two dwarfs holding keg **30.00**
Glass
  Bull Frog Beer, etched, Chicago **65.00**
  Gettleman Brewing **35.00**
Handbook, 4 1/4 x 8″, hard cov, 268 pgs, HS Rich & Co, 1902 ...... **60.00**
Handkerchief, Coors, 20″ sq **4.50**
Keg Tap, Rock Island Brewing Co, wood handle **18.00**

Matchsafe, Schlitz 55.00
Medal, Beer Brewmasters Convention,
   1907 .... 12.00
Mug
   Budweiser, Clydesdales, 50th Anni-
     versary, 1983, Ceramarte 70.00
   Coors Golden Beer, pottery, yellow . 25.00
   Falstaff Beer, glass, emb trademark, 7"
     h 25.00
   Leisy Brewery, desert scene, Peoria . 65.00
   Minneapolis Brewing Co 65.00
   Tubory Blue Horn 9.00
Pin
   Pabst Safe Driver Award, 1 1/4" sq,
     metal, enameled and silvered, red,
     white, and blue, c1950s 18.00
   We Want Prosperity, 7/8" h, brass and
     enamel, beer mug, foamy head .. 30.00
Pinback Button
   Budweiser, 3" d, litho, color illus,
     beer can above slogan "Our Can–
     To–Date," blue lettering, c1970s . 12.00
   Emil Sicks Select Beer, 1 1/2" d, red
     number six on yellow ground,
     black lettering, gold trim, c1930s . 20.00
Pitcher, Atlas Beer 150.00
Plaque, Rolling Rock, three race horses 15.00
Plate, Grain Belt Beer, emb brass 15.00
Playing Cards, Pabst Blue Ribbon Beer,
   boxed, blonde female in uniform
   serving beer, complete, c1950s 18.00
Post Card, Budweiser Beer, fold out,
   Clydesdales and wagon, 1950s 16.00
Poster
   Miller Beer, Keep On Rocking, Mich-
     igan, 25 x 34" 25.00
   Silver Spring Brewery, stone litho, 24"
     sq, matted, 1915 .... 35.00
Print, Yuengling Breweries, four scenes,
   plant buildings, 26 x 35", 1940s ... 150.00
Recipe Book, Indianapolis Brewing Co,
   1912 .... 22.00
Salt and Pepper Shakers, pr, Fort Pitt
   Beer, 3" h, figural, miniature, amber
   brown glass, bottle shape, silvered tin
   removable caps, issued by Fort Pitt
   Brewing Co, Pittsburgh, c1950s ... 15.00
Shopping Bag, Iroquois Indian Head
   Beer & Ale 5.00
Sign
   Ballantine Ale, emb 15.00
   Billy Beer, sgd Billy Carter, 21 x 27" 20.00
   Carlsburg Beer, celluloid 10.00
   Carta Blanca Beer, metal 17.50
   Chihuahua Beer, picture of train,
     metal 20.00
   E & O Beer, 9 1/4 x 11 1/4", metal . 55.00
   High Life Brewery, 16 x 14", tin litho 40.00
   Old Milwaukee, reverse painted
     glass, green bottles 75.00
Statue, plaster, Hanley's Ale, bull dog,
   17 1/2" 40.00

Stein
   Garden City Brewery, Chicago, crys-
     tal, inlaid lid 275.00
   Wurzburger Hofbray Seit, emb, metal
     top and front, 6" 20.00
Swizzle Stick Holder, Ballantine, cobalt 45.00

Suds scraper, Say Hanley's For Ale, plastic, red, gold lettering, 8¾" l, $24.00.

Tap Knob
   Dick's Beer 35.00
   Kruegar Beer, 3 1/2" 15.00
Thermometer
   Piels Beer 20.00
   Stegmaier Beer, metal frame, 9" d .. 45.00
Toy, squeaker, beer drinker, papier
   mache face, Germany 80.00
Tray, Serving
   Fehr's Famous FXL Beer 400.00
   Harvard Beer 45.00
   Iroquois, Indian head 90.00
   McSorley's, 10 1/2 x 13 1/2", litho tin,
     full color portrait by Walter Beach
     Humphrey, 1935 copyright Fidelio
     Brewery, tan lettering on brown rim 100.00
   Pickwick Ale, horse drawn wagon .. 42.00
   Superior, Indian maiden 50.00
   Trommer's Beer 25.00
   Walter Brewing, brass, factory scene 275.00
   Yuengling, blonde girl, glass of beer 65.00
Tray, tip
   Harvard Beer 35.00
   Lily Beverage, Rock Island Brewing . 49.00
   Muehlbachs Pilsner Beer 55.00
   Superior Beer, Indian maiden 45.00
Tumbler, Falstaff Beer 5.00
Yearbook, US Brewers Assoc, liquor and
   prohibition information, 1915 ...... 50.00

BRITISH ROYALTY COMMEMORATIVES

Collecting Hints: Some collectors choose one monarch around whom to build their collections. Others choose only pieces for special occasions, such as coronations, jubilees, marriages, investitures, births, or memorials. Another approach is to specialize in only one form, e.g., thimbles, mugs, beakers, teapots, spoons, etc.

   Since most early pieces were used in the home for eating and drinking, it is especially difficult to find older commemoratives in good condition. Wear from use and age often shows through fading and loss of colors and transfers. Porous pottery pieces lend themselves to crazing inside and out from age and shrinkage.

Serious collectors seek the older and rarer pieces, while keeping up–to–date with examples from the modern events. Crown shaped teapots, etched and cut crystal, hand and machine woven tapestries, and jewelry are just a few of the things that link old and new collecting.

History: British commemorative china was first produced rather crudely in design and form. These were basically cheaper and more available pieces of Delft, stoneware, and slipware. With John Brook's invention of transfer printing in the mid–18th century, British commemorative wares bore a closer likeness to the reigning monarch.

King George IV's coronation was the first royal occasion for which children received municipal gifts. Some towns presented medals, while others gave plates with commemorative inscriptions. China commemorative pieces were produced by the thousands for Queen Victoria's 1887 and 1897 jubilees. It was not until 1902 that the presentation of municipal gifts became widespread; the practice is continued today. Thousands of children received mugs with the official coronation design of Queen Elizabeth II in celebration of her 1953 coronation.

Through the years, improved production techniques combined with finer artistic design have enhanced the overall appearance of British Royalty commemoratives. Aynsley, Minton, Paragon, Royal Doulton, Shelley, Wedgwood, and other leading manufacturers have produced outstanding limited and unlimited edition items. Artists such as Clarice Cliff, Dame Laura Knight, and Professor Richard Guyatt have designed special pieces.

Some British Royalty commemoratives are easily recognized by the portraits of the monarchs they honor. Often these portraits are surrounded by decorations such as flags, the national flowers (roses, thistles, daffodils, and shamrocks), ribbons with commemorative messages or lions and unicorns. Cyphers and crowns also are popular decorations. Royal residences such as Windsor Castle, Balmoral and Highgrove House may also appear. Town mottos or crests were added to individualize municipal gifts for earlier coronations. Advertisers often linked their products to royal events.

Other British Royalty commemoratives are not easy to recognize. Many do not have portraits of monarchs on them, although there might be a silhouette profile. Other characteristics include crowns, dragons, royal coats of arms, national flowers, swords, sceptres, dates, messages and cyphers of the monarch. Earlier pieces sometimes bear crude likenesses of early monarchs. Timely

verses or couplets may be inscribed, e.g., "God Save The King," "Long Live The Queen."

A listing of outstanding achievements or inventions during a monarch's reign may appear on jubilee or memorial pieces. Some newer items list the order of succession to the throne, previous holders of a title, and family trees.

References: M. H. Davey and D. J. Mannion, *Fifty Years Of Royal Commemorative China 1887–1937*, Dayman Publications, 1988; Peter Johnson, *Royal Memorabilia; A Phillips Collectors Guide*, Dunestyle Publishing, Ltd., 1988; John May, *Victoria Remembered, A Royal History 1817–1861*, Heinemann, London, 1983; John and Jennifer May, *Commemorative Pottery 1780–1900, A Guide for Collectors*, Charles Scribner's Sons, 1972; Josephine Jackson, *Fired For Royalty*, Heaton Moor, 1977; David Rogers, *Coronation Souvenirs and Commemoratives*, Latimer New Dimensions, Ltd., 1975; Sussex Commemorative Ware Centre, *200 Commemoratives*, Metra Print Enterprises, 1979; Geoffrey Warren, *Royal Souvenirs*, Orbis, 1977; Audrey B. Zeder, *British Royal Commemoratives*, Wallace– Homestead, 1986.

Advisors: Doug Flynn and Al Bolton.

Queen Elizabeth II, February 6, 1952, to present
Coronation, June 2, 1953

Beaker, 4" h, sepia portrait color dec, Royal Doulton	**45.00**
Bowl, 9¾" d, color portrait surrounded by emb gold, hp dec, wide gold border, gold overlay on cobalt blue outside, gold foot, Aynsley bone china	**900.00**
Box	
5" h, cov, orb shape, purple and gold crown finial, hp color dec, Wedgwood & Co Ltd	**90.00**
5¼" h, cov, orb shape, emb gold, deep red background, white int., Limited Edition 50, Minton	**875.00**
Bust, 5½" h, coronation and 1953 Bermuda visit, white, light blue glazed base with gold trim, Foley bone china	**90.00**
Cup and Saucer	
Color flowers, pale green border with gold overlay, Paragon bone china	**55.00**
Lion and unicorn, royal arms on cup, color national flowers on saucer, partial hp, Stanley bone china	**80.00**
Sepia portrait, color dec, gold trim, Tuscan bone china	**60.00**
Sepia portrait, color dec, blue	

Queen Elizabeth, biscuit tin, Queen Elizabeth and Prince Phillip, Huntley & Palmer's Biscuits, Reading & London, England, 7" d, $18.50.

emb border, gold trim, Clarice Cliff design, Newport pottery ... 35.00

Jug
4½" h, black on white dec and bust portrait, mask spout, wreathed cypher and crown on reverse, Royal Worcester bone china 100.00
5¼" h, musical, raised tinted portraits, plays "Here's a Health Unto Her Majesty," color bands and gold trim, Crown Devon 140.00

Mug
3" h
Color dec, partially hp, black and white pictures of Westminster Abbey & Windsor Castle, Hammersley bone china 80.00
Sepia portraits of Queen with young Charles and Anne, Salisbury bone china 70.00
3½" h, sepia portrait, color and gold dec, "E" handle, Royal Doulton bone china 90.00
4" h, color dec with lion, unicorn, crown, and cypher, Eric Ravilious, Wedgwood 160.00

Plate
7" d, black and white portrait, color dec, gold overlay design around border, Victoria Pottery   30.00
8¾" d, sepia portrait, color and gold dec, gold emb rim with gold overlay on deep red border, Coalport bone china 120.00

9" d, sepia portrait, color dec with emb rim and gold trim, Weatherby 45.00
10½" d, large color portrait framed in emb gold, gold overlay on deep red border with emb gold rim, Aynsley bone china 350.00

Teapot
5½" h, profile white jasperware portraits on royal blue background, Wedgwood 250.00
6" h, sepia portrait, color dec, gold bands and trim, cypher and crown, Rita 100.00

Tin
5½" h, color portraits, cypher, arms, red background, Rowntree 20.00
6" h, tea caddy with color portraits, gold dec on red background, Bilsland Brothers Bakery 35.00
7" d, color portrait of Queen in State Coach, red and gold crowns 25.00

Silver Jubilee, 1977
Box
1¾" sq, raised floral design with silver highlights, Crown Staffordshire bone china 20.00
4¾ x 3¼", pr, heart shape, cov, white profile portraits and dec on royal blue background, jasperware, Wedgwood 110.00

Paperweight, 1¾" h, 3" d, Millefiore crown inside, hexagonal, full lead crystal, Lim Ed 1500, Whitefriars 395.00

Plate
10½" d, profile portrait with silver and color dec, Lim Ed 1500, Paragon bone china .. 100.00
10¾" d, lion, unicorn, coat of arms, blue, beige, and maroon dec, Royal Tuscan bone china   45.00

40th Wedding Anniversary, November 20, 1987
Model, 1¼" h, 3¼" l, miniature Rolls Royce, ruby red, beige, and black, diecast by Liedo (London) Ltd 40.00
Mug, 3" h, color portrait and flowers, slightly waisted shape, Coalport bone china 45.00

Prince Charles' Investiture as Prince of Wales, July 1, 1969
Plate
9¾" d, gold and bronze profile portrait, gold overlay on cobalt blue border, Falcon Ware Pottery ... 70.00

10½" d, color Caernavon Castle scene with Prince of Wales' feathers, Royal Worcester bone china **150.00**

Spoon, 6" l, raised Prince of Wales' feathers in bowl, dragon atop handle holds shield of four lions, SS, J D Beardmore & Co, Ltd **195.00**

Prince Charles and Lady Diana Spencer, Royal Wedding, July 29, 1981

Bust, 4½" h, white glaze, gold lettering and trim, Lim Ed 250, Coalport bone china **100.00**

Dish
3¾" d, raised portraits and prince of Wales' feathers, names and dates around border, SS **115.00**

6" d, black and white profile portraits, color dec, Wedgwood Queensware **25.00**

Jardiniere, 5¾" h, 6½" d, sepia portraits, color dec, green band around top, pottery **50.00**

Jug
6¼" h, milk jug shape, dark brown profiles, color and gold dec, A E Rodda, Cornwall **65.00**

7" h, sepia portraits, color dec and flowers, Mason's **45.00**

Kneeler, 3 x 15 x 10½", needlepoint, color dec stitched on medium blue background, color national flowers, Prince of Wales' feathers, coat of arms, initials, and date **150.00**

Knife, 3¼" l, sepia portraits in gold frames, color flowers, mother-of-pearl on reverse, two blades **25.00**

Lamp Base, 8½" h, sepia portraits, color dec, molded Prince of Wales' feathers at top, Derek Fowler Studio Ltd **110.00**

Mug
3½" h, color portraits within heart, color dec **30.00**

3¾" h, sepia portraits, feathers, gold trim, Royal Overhouse Pottery **25.00**

Plate
8" d, black and white portraits, color dec, wedding bells around border, gold trim, bone china England **30.00**

9½" d, brown tone portraits and dec, emb floral border, English Ironstone Tableware Ltd **60.00**

10¼" d, gold silhouette portraits on cobalt blue background, fretwork border, St Paul's Dome above portraits, Lim Ed 2500, Bing & Grondahl **125.00**

10¾" d, royal residences around border with doves, wedding

bells, and crowns, coat of arms, Lim Ed 5000, Caverswall bone china **75.00**

Teapot, 5¼" h, sepia portraits, color dec, Prince of Wales' feathers, flowers, ribbons, Price Kensington **65.00**

Tray, 6 x 3¼", white applied profiles and dec on pale blue jasperware, Wedgwood **60.00**

Prince William of Wales, born June 21, 1982

Bell, 3¼" h, color picture of Windsor Castle, flowers, gold ring handle, Aynsley bone china **25.00**

Loving Cup, 3¼" h, color and gold dec, gold lion handles, Paragon bone china **110.00**

Money Box, 4¼" h, book shape, colorful Bunnykins design, Royal Doulton **40.00**

Mug
2⅞" h, gold on white dec, Richard Guyatt Design, Wedgwood bone china **55.00**

3½" h, color design by children of Hornsea Primary School, Hornsea Pottery **35.00**

Plate
8¼" d, color dec, cherubs, full name, gold trim, Lim Ed 500, Royal Crown Derby **190.00**

10½" d, color portrait and dec, gold overlay on border, Lim Ed 1500, Crown Staffordshire **110.00**

Thimble, first birthday, color portrait, gold trim, Finsbury bone china . . . **10.00**

Prince Henry of Wales, born September 15, 1984

Bootee, 1¾" h, 2¾" l, color portrait with Princess of Wales, Coronet bone china **20.00**

Box, cov, 4" d, color picture of Balmoral Castle, Aynsley bone china **35.00**

Loving Cup, miniature, 1¼" h, 2¼" w, roses, color and gold dec, Royal Crown Derby bone china **80.00**

Mug, 3½" h, color dec, gold trim, Lim Ed 1000, Caverswall bone china . **50.00**

Plate, 8½" d, color flowers and gold trim, Royal Albert bone china **30.00**

Prince Andrew and Miss Sarah Ferguson, Royal Wedding, July 23, 1986

Bell, 4" h, blue silhouettes with gold dec, Royal Worcester bone china . **40.00**

Egg Cups, caricature, white pottery, pr **55.00**

Jigsaw Puzzle in tin, color portraits and dec, Waddingtons **45.00**

Loving Cup, 2⅞" h, color portraits in wedding attire, gold trim, Fenton bone china **60.00**

Mug
   3½" h, Corgis in shades of gray and black, pink background, Kiln Craft Pottery **30.00**
   3¾" h, color portraits, gold trim, Colclough bone china **25.00**
   4" h, conferment of Dukedom of York, black silhouette portraits, black, gold, and blue dec, designed by Richard Guyatt, Lim Ed 1000, Wedgwood **200.00**
Plate
   7" d, white profile portraits on light blue jasperware, Wedgwood ... **40.00**
   8" d, color portraits and dec, gold trim, Johson Ceramics bone china **24.00**
   8¼" d, color portraits and dec, light blue emb border, Royal Albert bone china **45.00**
Tray, 12" d, metal, large color portrait, blue printing and trim on white background **20.00**
Princess Beatrice, born August 8, 1988
Decanter, 8" h, color and gold dec, white background, gold stopper, Wade's Porcelain **115.00**
Mug
   2⅞" h, gold on white design by Richard Guyatt, Lim Ed 2000, Wedgwood bone china **75.00**
   3" h, burnished gold profile portraits, gold on white dec, Lim Ed 2500, Coalport bone china **70.00**
King George VI and Queen Elizabeth, December 10, 1936 to February 6, 1952
Coronation, May 12, 1937
Card Receiver, 7¼ x 4", cypher and "1937" in well, crown handles, ftd, SS **165.00**
Cuff Links, raised profile portraits, names and "1937" on each link, bronze **45.00**
Cup and Saucer, sepia portraits, small portrait of Princess Elizabeth on cup and saucer, bone china **40.00**
Loving Cup, 3¼" h, sepia portraits, color dec, gold handles and trim, cypher and crown, pottery **75.00**
Mug
   3" h, color dec, gold lion handle and trim, Paragon bone china **125.00**
   3¾" h, black and white portraits on light blue background, color dec, crown and flag, Royal Doulton bone china ... **65.00**
   4" h, sepia Marcus Adams family portrait, emb design around sides, Royal Albert bone china **80.00**
Plaque, 4¾" d, brass mounted on

King George VI, coronation, tumbler, 4⅜" h, $40.00.

wood, profile relief portraits and commemoration **50.00**
Plate
   9½" d, amber pressed glass with gold backed profile portraits and national flowers **55.00**
   9¾" d, hp dec by Charlotte Rhead, orange sq with black and gold highlights, Crown Ducal **80.00**
Teapot, 5" h, sepia portraits, color dec, blue trim, Norbury Pottery **100.00**
Queen Elizabeth, The Queen Mother, 80th Birthday, August 4, 1980
Mug
   3½" h, sepia portrait, color and gold dec, Spode bone china ... **75.00**
   3¾" h, color portrait, crown and flowers, Crown Staffordshire bone china **70.00**
Plate, 10½" d, 85th birthday, 1985, color portrait and dec, gold rim, Lim Ed 2000, Coalport bone china **100.00**
Tin, 90th birthday, 1990, color portrait, Glamis Castle, coat of arms, Walkers **30.00**
King Edward VIII, January 20, 1936, abdicated December 10, 1936 Coronation scheduled for May 12, 1937. Coronation items are not rare since most were in stores prior to the abdication.
Bowl, 9¾" d, pressed glass, profile portrait in well **70.00**
Cookie jar, 9" h, caravan shape, sepia portraits, color dec, rattan handle, Parrott and Co **200.00**
Cup and Saucer, color portrait and dec, St George slaying dragon, cy-

King Edward VIII, mug, black and white portraits, birth, marriage, death dates, purple and gold decoration, Wilton Dorincourt, $50.00.

pher and "1937," Royal Doulton bone china **80.00**

Door Knocker, 4¼ x 2", accession, crown at top, profile head and shoulders of King, "Edward VIII" and "1936," brass **125.00**

Fabric, 36 x 52", color portrait, coronation scene, procession, Buckingham Palace, Westminster Abbey, cotton chintz **45.00**

Loving Cup, 4½" h, 7" w, brown tone portrait, color dec, color flowers inside and reverse, thick gold bands around top edge and base, Shelley bone china **600.00**

Mug, 4" h, sepia portrait, color dec, empire shields, flowers on handle, gold rim, Aynsley bone china **75.00**

Plate, 8¾" d, medium blue profile portrait and dec, blue rim, Copeland Spode **145.00**

Tin, 9¼ x 7½", color portrait as Prince of Wales with gold feathers, war ships inside lid **50.00**

King George V and Queen Mary, May 6, 1910 to January 20, 1936
  Coronation, June 26, 1911
    Beaker, 3¾" h, black and white portraits with small portrait of Edward, Prince of Wales, color dec and rim gilding, bone china ... **70.00**
    Box, heart shape, cov, color dec, gilding flowers, coat of arms, Aynsley bone china **90.00**
    Egg Cups, color portrait of King on one, Queen on other, their names beneath portraits, bone china, pr **65.00**

Mug 3" h, enamel on tin, color portraits and dec, brown rim **80.00**
Silver Jubilee, 1935
  Mug, 4¼" h, color portraits and dec, King alone on reverse, gold trim **50.00**
  Tea Strainer, 5¾" l, 2¼" d, "G 1935 M" formed by holes in bowl, crown at top of handle, SS **175.00**
Marriage, 1863
  Plate, 7¼" d, brown tone portraits and ribbons, marriage date, made for William Whiteley by Doultons, bone china **190.00**
King Edward VII and Queen Alexandra, January 22, 1901 to May 6, 1910. Coronation originally scheduled for June 26, 1902, but postponed because of the King's appendicitis attack. It took place on August 9, 1902. Items with the earlier date are far more common.
  Cup and Saucer, color portraits and floral dec, gold trim, "Irthington Parish" beneath portraits, Bisto bone china **85.00**
  Dish, 6¾ x 6", color dec partially hp, gold trim and emb design, Foley bone china **65.00**
  Figure, 12¼" h, pr, Staffordshire, names on front of base **700.00**
  Mug, 2¾" h, lithophane, King Edward VII's likeness seen in base when held to light, color cypher, crown date, bone china **90.00**
  Plate, 7" d, blue crown, initials and "MCMII," floral background, Royal Copenhagen bone china **190.00**
  Tape Measure, 1¼" d, brown sepia photo of young Edward, Prince of Wales, c1863 .... **75.00**
  Teapot, 5 x 7", color portrait and dec, emb floral band and swirl handle, bone china **160.00**
  Tin, color portraits on lid, Prince of Wales and Prince Edward of Wales on ends, Coronation and outside Westminster Abbey scenes on sides **60.00**
Queen Victoria and Prince Albert, June 20, 1837 to January 22, 1901
  Coronation, June 28, 1838
    Plate 7" d, Swansea transfer portrait in blue, coronation, birth, and proclamation dates, emb floral border 1,200.00
  Marriage, February 10, 1840
    Plate, 7⅜" d, hexagonal, black and white portraits, color dec, emb border **350.00**
  Golden Jubilee, 1887
    Mug, 4" h, black portrait and dec on blue background, Foley **150.00**

Plate, 10½" d, large blue profile portrait of young queen in center, decorative border, Royal Worcester **115.00**

Diamond Jubilee, 1897

Beaker, 4" h, white raised profile portrait on lime green background, beige trim, Copeland late Spode **170.00**

Dish, 4" d, color crown and cypher, gold rim, W H Goss bone china **60.00**

Plate 8" d, color portrait, dec, servicemen, ships, angels, bone china **180.00**

Tin, 2 x 3¼ x 3", color portraits, young Queen on horseback on lid, young and mature portraits, ships, trains on sides **95.00**

In Memoriam, 1901

Beaker, 3¾" h, color portrait, purple dec, birth, accession, coronation, death dates, gold rim, Royal Doulton bone china **295.00**

King William IV and Queen Adelaide, June 26, 1830 to June 20, 1837

Coronation, September 8, 1831

Jug

5" h, purple transfer of King on front, coronation scene on reverse, Staffordshire Ironstone . **800.00**

7½" h, purple transfer of King and Queen, floral dec **700.00**

Mug, 2½" h, "Her Most Gracious Majesty Queen Adelaide" above portrait on front, coronation scene on reverse, dark red dec **1,400.00**

King George IV and Queen Caroline, January 29, 1820 to January 26, 1830

Cup and Saucer, "Long Live Queen Caroline" below black profile portrait, coat of arms opposite handle, pink luster trim **300.00**

Coronation, July 19, 1821

Plate

8½" d, color dec and emb, molded inscription "King George IV," below color profile portrait, attributed to the Portobello Factory at Edinburgh **1,500.00**

8⅞" d, black crown and national flowers, commemoration on ribbons reads "George IV Crown'd July 19, 1821," made by Hartley Greens and Co, Leeds, for the Leeds Parish Church School Dinner **1,650.00**

In Memoriam, 1830

Jug

6¾" h, 7½" w, black portrait and floral dec, birth, accession,

proclamation and death dates **1,000.00**

8¾" h, 8" w, angels and flowers in relief, profile portrait of King under spout, lion handle, light beige unglazed **1,300.00**

King George III and Queen Charlotte, October 25, 1760 to January 29, 1820

In Memoriam, bowl, 9¾" d, full length portrait of king in robes with young child, "I hope the time will come when every poor child in my dominions will be able to read the Bible" appears under the transfer, blue and white flowers around wide border **1,200.00**

Wax bust profile portrait, 2¾ x 2", framed, colors include pink, white, gray, tan, and burgundy **600.00**

BUBBLE GUM CARDS, NON–SPORT

Collecting Hints: Don't buy individual cards; buy full sets. The price of a set is below the sum of individual cards. By collecting sets you do lose some of the fun of trading cards, nevertheless, cards from this vintage are sold by sets. Any set should contain a sample of the wrapper plus any stickers that belong to the set.

Because of the availability of these cards, make certain the sets you buy are in mint condition. You can buy boxes of gum packages. With Topps you are 100% certain you will get at least one full set from a box. Donruss and Fleer average 85%.

Collectors should store cards in plastic sleeves. Place the wrapper first and then the cards in numerical order.

History: The birthplace of the modern bubble gum (trading) card is the tobacco insert cards of the late 19th century. From 1885 to 1894 there were over 500 sets issued, with only about 25 devoted to sports. Trading cards lost their popularity in the decade following World War I. However, in 1933 "Indian Gum" issued a product containing a stick of bubble gum and a card in a waxed paper package. A revolution had begun.

Goudey Gum and National Chicle controlled the market until the arrival of Gum, Inc., in 1936. Gum, Inc., issued The Lone Ranger and Superman sets in 1940. From 1943 to 1947 the market in cards was again quiet. In 1948 Bowman entered the picture. A year later Topps Chewing Gum produced some non–sports cards. A war between Bowman and Topps ensued until 1956 when Topps bought Bowman.

Although Topps enjoyed a dominant position

in the baseball card market, it had continual rivals in the non–sports field. Frank Fleer Company, Leaf Brands, and Philadelphia Chewing Gum provided competition in the 1960s. Fleer and Donruss Chewing Gum provide the modern day assault.

References: Christopher Benjamin and Dennis W. Eckes, *The Sport Americana Price Guide To The Non–Sport Cards, 1930–1960*, (1991) and *Number 3, Part Two*, (1988) Edgewater Book Company.

Periodicals: *The Non–Sport Report* (Catalog from The Card Coach, but loaded with articles), P.O. Box 128, Plover, WI 54467; *The Non–Sport Update*, c/o Christopher Benjamin, 9 Davis Street, St. Augustine, FL 32095; *The Wrapper*, 1903 Ronzheimer Ave., St. Charles, IL 60174.

DONRUSS

1961, Idiot Cards, 66 cards	**25.00**
1965	
Disneyland, 66 cards	**50.00**
King Kong	
Complete set, 55 cards	**70.00**
Wrapper	**25.00**
1966, Marvel Super Heroes, 66 cards	**50.00**
1973, Osmonds, 66 cards	**30.00**
1978, Kiss	
Series 1, 66 cards	**4.00**
Series 2, 66 cards	**4.50**
1982, Dark Crystal, 78 cards	**6.00**
1983	
Dukes of Hazzard, 44 cards	**4.50**
Magnum P I, 66 cards	**4.50**

FLEER

1960, Casper, 66 cards	**60.00**
1965, Three Stooges, 66 cards	**65.00**
1970, Believe It Or Not, 84 cards	**30.00**

LEAF

1961, Spook Stories, 144 cards	**90.00**
1965, What's My Job?	
Complete set, 72 cards	**50.00**
Sticker	**1.00**
Wrapper	**15.00**

PHILADELPHIA CHEWING GUM CO

1965, War Bulletin, 88 cards	**60.00**
1968	
Dark Shadows, pink, 66 cards	**60.00**
Robert F. Kennedy,	
Complete set, 55 cards	**37.50**
Wrapper	**6.50**
1969, Dark Shadows, green, 66 cards	**60.00**

Topps, Look 'N See, (R 714–16), 135 cards, top left: #24, Phineas T. Barnum, $.50; top right: #26, George W. Carver, $.75; bottom left: #30, Charles A. Lindbergh, $1.50; bottom right: #25, George Eastman, $.50.

TOPPS

1962	
Casey & Kildare, 110 cards	**90.00**
Mars Attacks, 55 cards	**400.00**
1963	
Flag Midgee, 99 cards	**35.00**
Flags Of The World, 77 cards	**25.00**
1964	
Beatles, 165 cards	**135.00**
Beatles Diary, 60 cards	**50.00**
1965	
Battle, 66 cards	**75.00**
Gilligan's Island, 55 cards	**125.00**
1966	
Batman, series B, 44 cards	**40.00**
Batman Riddler Back, 38 cards	**42.50**
Comic Book Foldees, 44 cards	**50.00**
Lost In Space	
Complete set, 55 cards	**115.00**
Wrapper	**25.00**
Man From UNCLE, 55 cards	**40.00**
Superman, 66 cards	**50.00**
1968	
Laugh–In, 77 cards	**90.00**
Mod Squad, 55 cards	**40.00**
1973	
Creature Feature, You'll Die Laughing, 128 cards	**40.00**

Kung Fu, 60 cards **15.00**
1975, Good Times, 55 cards and 21
   stickers **12.00**
1976
   Happy Days, series A, 44 cards and
     11 stickers **12.00**
   Hysterical History
     Complete set, 66 cards **20.00**
     Stickers, complete set, 66 stickers   **7.00**
1978, Close Encounters, 66 cards and
   11 stickers **5.00**
1979
   Black Hole, 88 cards and 22 stickers   **7.00**
   Incredible Hulk, 88 cards and 22
     stickers **7.00**
1980, Creature Feature, 88 cards and
   22 stickers **7.00**
1982
   Donkey Kong, 36 cards **7.00**
   Smurf Super Cards, 55 cards **6.50**

BUSINESS AND OFFICE EQUIPMENT

Collecting Hints: The most important considerations are condition and function. Mechanical novelty and clearly identifiable period styles heighten desirability.

Calculators and adding machines are the most commonly collected items. However, other types of machines are becoming more collectible because of their inherent scarcity. Other types of office equipment include: accounting machines, account registers, check writers and punches, dictating machines (wax cylinder machines), pencil sharpeners, staplers, mimeograph duplicators, autographic and key–driven cash registers, time recorders, slide rules, stenographic machines, telephones, etc.

Collectibility of office and business equipment has less to do with age than with its novelty and/or functionality. Many individuals buy them to keep at their offices or places of business as conversation pieces. Collectors are few and not very well organized. Calculator and adding machine collectors, often linked to the typewriter collecting community, are the exception.

Generally speaking, the smaller an item is, the more collectible it is. An example of the reverse are accounting machines. They are very scarce and difficult to find, yet they usually cost very little. The major cost involved is in the shipping hassle and expense to get them home. Many of these mechanical monsters weigh over 200 pounds.

History: The enormous growth in large business enterprises in the latter half of the 19th Century demanded increased efficiency in office operations. The old methods of record generation and organization were not sufficient to keep up with the explosion of industrial and commercial activity of the late 1800s and early 1900s. The tremendous mechanical inventiveness of many individuals resulted in a large number of, and sometimes unique, mechanical devices which offered, to a greater or lesser degree, increased efficiency and profitability.

Most office machines fall within two categories—financial record keeping and communication.

The duplicator was one of the earliest types of office equipment. It took on a number of forms, the first recognizable one being the simple letter press. A recently penned letter, its ink still wet, would be sandwiched with a number of thin absorbent sheets of paper and pressed. Copies were poor, but easier than the labor intensive hand copying. Thomas Edison's invention of the Mimeograph in the 1870s coupled with skilled marketing by A. B. Dick made the Mimeograph a common sight in nearly every turn–of–the–century office.

Calculating machines have been a part of some offices since the 1830s through the use of Thomas Arithmometers or their variations. They were not particularly suitable for high volume and high speed addition. Truly practical and useful adding machines and calculators were not perfected until late in the 19th Century. Early successful machines included Dorr E. Felt's Comptometer, Burrough's adding machines, and the numerous variations of the Baldwin–Ohdner type rotary calculators.

Checkpunches were the earliest mechanical attempts to limit the losses inflicted upon businesses through altered checks. The early machines actually punched figures in the paper check to show the true amount. They were quite slow and tedious to operate. Checkwriters in which the amount on the check was printed and the ink permanently imbedded into the paper fibers by the use of a perforating wheel or gear was the next natural evolutionary step. These machines became very popular after 1920. Next to the typewriter, the smaller checkwriters have more variations based on style than most other office equipment. Perhaps this had to do with the fact that these were generally kept on (or in) the boss's desk.

References: William Aspray, *Computing Before Computers*, 1989; *The Business Machines and Equipment Digest 1927*, Chicago, 1927; NCR, *Celebrating the Future, 1884–1984*, published by company, 1984; Michael R. Williams, *A History of Computing Technology*, Prentice Hall, 1985.

Collectors' Club: Internationales Forum Historische Burowelt e.w. (IFHB), P. O. Box 50 11 68, D–5000 Koln 50, Germany.

Museums: The Computer Museum, Boston, MA; Henry Ford Museum, Dearborn, MI; National Office Equipment Historical Museum, Kansas City, KS; Smithsonian Institution, National Museum of American History, Division of Engineering & Industry, Washington, DC.

Advisor: Todd Holmes.

See: Telephones and Typewriters.

Note: Prices are for machines with excellent original finishes and in working order.

Accounting and Related Machines

Dalton bookkeeping machine	100.00
McCaskey account register	40.00
Moon Hopkins/Burroughs accounting machine	350.00
Remington Model 23 bookkeeping machine	350.00
Sundstrand bookkeeping machine	20.00
Underwood bookkeeping machine	400.00

Adding Machines and Calculators

Addometer	10.00
American Adding machine	25.00
Brunsviga calculator	100.00
Burroughs adding machine	15.00
F & E Comptometer	20.00
Golden Gem adding machine	80.00
Lightning calculator	15.00
Star adding machine	15.00
Victor adding machine	10.00
Any small "card" adding machine with stylus	5-10.00

Checkpunches and Checkwriters

F & E	
Lightning Checkwriter Model 500	20.00
Series 600 Checkwriter	50.00
Instant Checkwriter	20.00
S & P Checkwriter	100.00
SafeGuard Checkwriter	20.00
Todd Protectograph Checkwriter	25.00

Dictating Machines, Wax Cylinder machines

Dictaphone	
Type A Model 10 dicatating machine	50.00
Type B Model 10 transcribing machine	50.00
Type S Shaving machine	50.00
Type S Shaving machine, wood stand	75.00
Ediphone	
Dictating machine	40.00
Shaving machine	40.00
Transcribing machine	40.00
Typease typewriter attachment	15.00

Duplicators and Mimeographs

A. B. Dick	
Edison Mimeoscope	300.00
Edison Model 1	175.00
Edison Model 75	20.00
Gem notecard duplicator	10.00
Rotary Neostyle 8–F duplicator	40.00

BUTTONS

Collecting Hints: Buttons are collected, and generally mounted, according to age, material, and subject matter. The National Button Society, founded in 1939, has designated 1918 as the dividing line between old and modern buttons. Shanks and backmarks are important keys in determining the age of buttons. Modern glass buttons are becoming very popular with collectors.

Buttons generally are mounted on trays or cards in artistic designs. A uniform series of circles helps outline the buttons presented. The majority of the collectors mount their buttons by the material of which the button is made, e.g., fabric, metals, glass, enamels, pearl, ceramic, etc. All buttons are classified into four divisions: Old (prior to 1918), Modern, Uniform, and Specialized. Within these divisions buttons are subdivided into sections (metals being one) and then into specialized categories (such as tin, pewter, gold, brass, copper, etc.). The National Button Society maintains a Classification Committee that annually reviews and updates the competition glossary and classification.

Competition is held within states and on a national level. Almost all states have an organized State Button Society that holds shows in spring and fall.

History: Buttons are objects used to hold articles of clothing in place. Little is known of the use of buttons prior to the 12th Century. In the 18th century buttons were worn basically by men as status symbols and a sign of wealth. During the peak of this period it was not unusual to find complete sets of 24 buttons on one coat.

Americans always have been fashion conscious and used buttons as a form of decoration. Brass buttons were made as early as 1750 by Casper Wister of Philadelphia. The Shaker colony at New Lebanon, New York, has records of button production in 1789.

Buttons, like many other objects, became ornate and very decorative during the Victorian era. Some Victorian buttons included subject matter taken from fairy tales, heroes, nursery rhymes, literature, and nature. Buttons of the late 19th century tend to feature two piece construction. Today brass, steel, and copper of the early buttons has been replaced by wood, leather, plastic, and glass.

References: There are a large number of button books; most are privately printed. Some examples are: Diana Epstein, *A Collector's Guide To Buttons*; Viviane Ertell, *The Colorful World of Buttons*; Elizabeth Hughes and Marion Lester, *The Big Book of Buttons*, 1983; Don Van Court, *The Railroad Button Book, Transportation Buttons, Volume One—Railroads*, published by author, 1987.

Collectors' Club: National Button Society, 2733 Juno Place, Akron, OH 44313.

Museum: Copper Union Museum for the Art of Decoration, New York, NY.

Advisor: Lois Pool.

REPRODUCTION ALERT Reproductions of buttons, e.g., the White House button made from the original die, do exist. Be careful.

Aluminum
  Stencils, copied from china stencils
    1930–40 .... .75 to 1.25
  Decorated with pearl, brass back ... 20.00
  Two pc chased buttons .... .50
Brass
  Engraved, one pc brass button, painted metallic pigment butterfly design 7.00
  St Cecilia at the Organ, stamped brass on painted metal background, steel back, wire shank 45.00
  Madonna and Child, copied from Raphael's Sistine Madonna 25.00
  Lion of Lucerne, copied from Lucerne monument, stamped brass, common 3.50

Night Watch, The Company of Captain Frans Banning Cocq and Lieutenant Willian Von Ruytenburch, copied from orig Rembrandt painting, sterling silver, $100.00.

Philadelphia's 1876 Bicentennial Exposition, Main Building, stamped brass 12.50
Perry at the North Pole, one pc stamped brass 20.00
Oriental Wedding, one pc, steel trim 10.00
Celluloid
  Bubble tops, pictorial designs 4.00
  Oval wafer type, incised design of lady golfer 5.00
  Perforated stick–up type 2.00
Ceramic
  Modern jasperware, mfg M L Bennett 8.00
  Norwalk Pottery, various sizes 2.00
  Ruskin Pottery, small size 2.00
China
  Calico, 1" 45.00
  Calico, small size, two color 5.00
  Calico, small size, three hole 4.00
  Calico, small sizes, many patterns .25 to 6.00
Enamel
  Little Miss Muffett, painted enamel, faceted steel border 35.00
  Who'll Buy My Lavender, small size 10.00
  Gold Enamel 2.00
  Cuff buttons, basse–taille enamel, 1930 period 4.00
Glass
  Black Glass
    Irid, luster, pictorial designs ... .40 to 5.00
    Madame Chrysantheme, various sizes 8.00
    Pierrot and Pierrette, large size ... 10.00
    Pressed, medium size 1.00
    Swirlback, goldstone overlay trim 1.00
  Clear and Colored Glass
    Kaleidoscopes, transparent glass of various shapes backed by colored foil on a metal plate 8.00
    Realistic leaf shape 65.00
    Water Mill custard glass, metal shank 21.00
  Moonglow, modern moonglows
    Paste trim .... .75
    Sew thrus 1.50
Horn
  D'Artagnan, scarce 35.00
  Two hole, sew–thru, pictorial designs 1.50
Ivoroid
  Small size with ivoroid mounted in metal, plentiful .... .50
  The White Owl In the Belfrey Sits .. 5.00
Military
  Infantry Officer, 1821–51 .... 5.00
  State Seal Buttons, US Militia, brass .... 1.00 to 3.00
  US Marines, 1820–30, one pc, gilt brass 30.00
Pants Buttons, 1920 thru 1930, metal, horn, bone, rubber, composition .25 to 2.50
Paperweight
  Charles Kazium, hunter with dog ... 75.00

John Gooderham, millefiori, signed
"J" **20.00**
Winfield Rutter, rose **10.00**
Pearl
  Abalone, grape design, small **2.00**
  Cameo carved, lily of the valley, medium size **10.00**
  Green snail, two hole, sew–thru, engraved birds and nest **6.00**
Pewter
  Bright Cut, small size, assorted designs .... **.50 to 4.00**
  Hard white, 1800–30 .... **5.00 to 8.00**
  Tinted, Ugly Duckling, bright cut ... **5.00**
Railroad, two pc, brass, nickel or gilt
  finish .... **1.00 to 4.00**
Rubber
  Goodyear Ptd, hard rubber, backmarks, pictorial design determine
  value .... **.50 to 15.00**
  Novelty Rubber Co, New York,
  Goodyear's patent 1849–51 is
  scarce **12.00**
Satsuma
  Iris, large size, blue back **40.00**
  Japanese Noblewomen **30.00**
Silver
  Cherub with a goat, British, 1889 .. **30.00**
  Fortuna, London, 1900 .... **35.00**
  Huntsman and horse, BM, Chester,
  1889 .... **30.00**
Tombac Buttons, 1760 to 1800
  Engraved design, flat, beveled rim,
  cone shank **15.00**
  Sporting designs, cone shank, engraved **75.00**
  Star design, medium **5.00**

CALENDARS

Collecting Hints: Value increases if all monthly pages are attached. Most calendars are bought by collectors interested in the subject on the calendar as opposed to the calendar itself.

History: Calendars were a popular advertising giveaway in the late 19th century and first five decades of the 20th. Recently, a calendar craze has swept bookstores throughout America. These topic-oriented calendars contain little or no advertising.

Additional Listing: Pin-up Art.

REPRODUCTION ALERT

1890, Ivory Soap **65.00**
1899, Clarks ONT **12.50**
1901, Colgate, miniature, flower **15.00**
1902, Fertilizer Co, litho, scene **20.00**
1903, Grecian Maidens, Raphael Tuck **18.00**

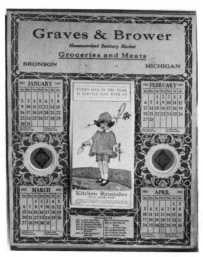

1927, Graves & Brower, Bronson, MI, shopping list style, $25.00.

1905
  Christian Herald, diecut, four panel,
  Victorian girls and birds **98.00**
  Grand Union Tea Co, 29 x 10", diecut, color, litho, four sections for
  seasons **90.00**
1906, Youths Companion Minutemen . **65.00**
1908, Metropolitan Life Insurance Co,
  mother and daughter in oval center . **60.00**
1909, leather **90.00**
1910, Chinese Student Alliance, rope
  hanger **6.00**
1915, Cosgroves Detective Agency,
  moose hunting scene **10.00**
1916, University of Wisconsin, Madison, tinted Bascom Hall photo on
  cover, 6 x 8" university building photo
  on each month **100.00**
1919, Woodrow Wilson **10.00**
1924, Pompeian Co, beautiful lady and
  man **16.00**
1926, Calgary Brewing **175.00**
1927, Wrigley's Gum, desk style, elf in
  Mother Goose scene, three unopened
  samples of gum attached **40.00**
1929, "Absence Makes the Heart Grow
  Fonder," two Indian maidens, canoe,
  moonlight **45.00**
1930, De Laval Separator Co, sgd Norman Price, "Story of John & Mary,"
  orig mailer **150.00**
1933, Keen Kutter, different products
  each month **85.00**
1935, Central's Gold Standard Footwear **15.00**
1937, C & N W, 12 x 24" **18.00**
1941, New York World's Fair, 6 x 8"
  wall plaque, Trylon and Perisphere il-

lus, foil border, inscribed "New York World's Fair 1940," thermometer ... 75.00

1942, Chesapeake & Ohio Railway, "Peake, Chessie's Old Man, Joins the Service," complete pad with cover, 15¾ x 27" 90.00

1945, Double Cola 110.00

1948
  Esquire, Ladies of the Harem, 12 sheet 15.00
  Squirt, pin–up girls 37.00

1950, Wandering Brook Farm, outdoor scene, children and animals 9.00

1955
  Marilyn Monroe, 8 x 14", cardboard, full color photo, Golden Dreams pose, red ground, Dec sheet 125.00
  Miss Sylvania Electric, pin–up girl, no pad, Elvgren 48.00

1959
  Paul Webb 35.00
  Playboy 35.00

1965, Jayne Mansfield, 9 x 14", cardboard, full color glossy photo, wearing gold gown with white polka dots, 12 sheet 85.00

1969, Elvgren Curly Horse Ranch, cowgirl 46.00

Perpetual Calendar
  Bell System, 1½" sq, aluminum, gold color, blue and white logo on disk wheel on back, black accented calendar on front, 1965–1992 ..... 12.50
  Ford Motors, 1½" sq, brass, diecut, revolving disk, Ford logo, name and location of Brooklyn agency, black accents, 1953–1980 .... 20.00
  IBM, 1½" sq, aluminum, diecut, red, white, and blue disk wheel, 1963 US Savings Bonds promotion on front, calendar on back, 1963–1990 .... 12.00
  Massachusetts Mutual, 1½" d, aluminum, diecut, 1951 100th Year Anniversary inscription with red accents on revolving disk wheel on front, calendar on back, 1950–1977 .... 15.00
  Texaco, 1¾" d, metal, diecut, keychain tag, black Texaco logo and 1902–1952 50th Year Anniversary inscription on front, revolving disk wheel on reverse, 1952–1979 ... 10.00

CAMERAS

Collecting Hints: The camera market seems to fluctuate weekly. However, the long range average price for any camera is steady. The Leica market no longer is in an upward movement, but

interest in unusual cameras, e. g., subminiatures and stereo cameras, is growing.

Leather covered cameras should have all the leather. Some wear does not detract from the value.

Folding cameras should have the bellows in good condition. Black bellows should be light tight. Colored bellows matching colored cameras need not be light tight. Having a matching bellow adds to the value of a colored camera.

History: A German monk, Johann Zahn, is credited with creating in the early 1800s the first fully portable wood box camera with a movable lens, an adjustable aperture, and a mirror to project the image. Zahn could view his image, but had no film on which to record it. In 1826 Joseph Nicephore Niepce produced the first photographic plate. Louise Jacques Mande Daguerre joined Niepce in his efforts. Peter Von Voigtlander of Vienna developed the quality lens needed. The photography industry was born.

The Germans were the initial leaders in camera manufacture. By the late 19th century the English and French had a strong market position. America's strength would begin around 1900. America's strongest contributions have come in the development of films and the Polaroid camera, invented by Dr. Land and marketed in late 1948.

George Eastman revolutionized the photography industry in 1888 when his simple box camera was introduced. It was small, 3¼ x 3¾ x 6½", and was modeled after earlier European examples. The camera had a magazine and could take 100 pictures without being reloaded. The pictures were 2½" in diameter. Many later models built upon the success of Kodak No. 1. Kodak's first folding camera was Model No. 4; the Brownie arrived in 1900.

Prior to World War II Japan made the Konica and Minolta. After the war Japan made a strong commitment to the camera market. The Japanese have introduced many technical changes into the camera, including solar power.

References: Jim and Joan McKeown, *Price Guide To Antique And Classic Still Cameras, 1989–1990*, published by authors, 1990; Jason Schneider, *Jason Schneider On Camera Collecting*, Wallace–Homestead, 1985; Douglas St. Denny, *The Jessop International Blue Book 1990–1991*, Jessop House, 1990.

Periodical: *Camera Shopper*, One Magnolia Hill, West Hartford, CT 06117.

Collectors' Clubs: American Society of Camera Collectors, 4918 Alcove Ave., North Hollywood, CA 91670; National Stereoscopic Association, P.O. Box 14801, Columbus, OH 43214; Leica Historical Soc. of America, 7611 Dornoch Lane, Dallas, TX 94116; Nikon Historical Society, P.O. Box 3213, Munster, IN 46321; Photographic Historical Society, P. O. Box 9563, Rochester, NY 14604.

Museums: International Museum of Photography, George Eastman House, 900 East Avenue, Rochester, NY 14607.

Revere Stero Camera, Model 33, 35 mm, F35, $150.00.

Adams & Co (London, England)
Idento, 3¼ x 4¼", folding, f5.3 lens, c1908 .... 175.00
Adox Kamerawerk (Wiesbaden, Germany)
L'Aiglon, meniscus lens, single speed shutter, 12 x 14mm on special roll film, c1934 .... 130.00
Aires Camera Industry Co (Japan)
Air King Camera Radio, tube-type radio and plastic 120 roll film camera, brown lizard skin covering .. 165.00
Ansco (Binghamton, NY), merged with Agfa in 1928
Billy, Igestar 105mm f8.8 lens 15.00
Karat, 35mm, folding, c1937 ...... 30.00
Official Boy Scout Memo Camera .. 175.00
Rediflex 10.00
Readyset Royal, No 1, folding, Antar lens, c1926 .... 90.00
Bell & Howell Inc (Chicago, IL)
Stereo Colorist, 35mm, Rodenstock Trinar f3.5 lens, c1952 .... 145.00
Bolsey Corp of America (New York, NY)
Model B compact camera, 35mm, c1947 .... 30.00
Canon, Inc (Tokyo, Japan)
Canonex, leaf shutter, fixed lens, c1963 .... 75.00
Ciro Cameras Inc (Delaware, OH)
35 rangefinder for 35 mm film, 1949 15.00
Ciroflex, Model A, twin lens reflex, 1940s 20.00

Eastman Kodak (Rochester, NY)
Anniversary Box Camera, tan box, given away to mark the 50th anniversary of Eastman Kodak Co in 1930 .... 25.00
Falcon, box, 101 roll film, rotary shutter, 1897– 1899 .... 65.00
Instamatic, 314, lever wind, light meter, uses flash cubes, 1968–71 ... 10.00
Pony, 135, Kodak Anaston f4.5 lens, 1950–54 .... 10.00
Retina, Stuttgart type No. 126, 35mm, viewfinder, Kodak Ektar 5cm f3.5 lens 50.00
Vest Pocket Series III, 127 roll film, 1926–1934 .... 40.00
Graflex, The Folmer & Schwing Mfg. Co (NY)
Graflex, No 1A, Kodak Anastigmat f4.5 lens, 116 roll film, 1909–1925 175.00
The Press Graflex, Bausch & Lomb Zeiss Tessar Series Ic No 16 f4.5 lens, c1908 .... 400.00
Ihagee Kamerawerk (Dresden, Germany)
Exakta B, 127 roll film, Zeiss Tessar 75mm f3.5 lens, 1936–1945 ..... 175.00
Exakta VX, 35mm, Tessar 50mm f2.8 lens, c1955 .... 100.00
Ultrix Auto, folding, Schneider Xenar 70mm f4.5 lens, c1934 .... 45.00
Mick-A-Matic, 126 cartridge, shape of Mickey Mouse's head, meniscus lens in nose, 1969 .... 80.00
Minolta (Chiyoda Kogaku Seiko Co, Ltd, Osaka, Japan)
Konan 16 Automat, Rokkor 25mm f3.5 lens, c1952 .... 125.00
Minolta 35, Model II, 35mm, c1954 90.00
Nikon Inc. (Nippon Kogaku K.K., Tokyo, Japan)
Nikon S, 35mm, Nikkor 50mm f2 coated lens, 1950–1954 .... 400.00
Nikkorex Zoom–8, 8mm movie camera, f1.8 lens, zooms 8 to 32mm, manual zoom 25.00
Perry Mason & Co (Boston, MA)
Harvard Camera, tin box, meniscus lens, c1890, premium giveaway .. 150.00
Scovill Mfg Co (American Optical Co, NY)
American Optical Revolving Back Camera, front focus, Daisy dry plate holder, c1888 .... 200.00
American Optical View Camera, brass fittings and lens, c1883 .... 170.00
Klondike, meniscus lens, rotary shutter, c1898 .... 50.00
Universal Camera Corp (New York City, NY)
Minute 16, 16mm subminiature, meniscus lens, c1950 .... 85.00

Roamer 63, folding **15.00**
Voigtlander & Son (Braunschweig, Germany)
    Bessa, 75mm f3.5 lens, folding **40.00**
    Vag, folding plate camera, c1920 . . **45.00**
    Vito, 35mm, folding, c1950 . . . . **30.00**
Wm. R. Whittaker Co, Ltd (Los Angeles, CA)
    Whittaker Micro-16, subminiature, meniscus lens, c1950 . . . . **80.00**
Zeiss, Carl, Optical Co (Dresden, Germany; merged with Contessa-Nettel, Ernemann, Goerz, Ica to form Zeiss-Ikon in 1926
    Contar II, sonnar 50mm f2 lens, 1936–42 . . . . **125.00**
    Maximar B, folding plate camera, 1940s **80.00**

CANAL COLLECTIBLES

Collecting Hints: Concentrate on one state or one specific canal. Look not only for canal material, but for the canal motif on non–canal items.

Beware of people trying to pass off tools and lanterns as having a canal origin. Ship boatyards used exactly the same tools as the canal boatyards. Insist on a good provenance for any canal item and check out the family name in the canal records.

Canal buffs are extremely well organized. Try to make contact early in your collecting interest with individuals working on the same topics as you. Many collectors own more than one example of an item and will gladly sell the duplicate to a new collector.

History: The American canal era has its origins in the 18th century with projects in New England, along the Potomac, and Louisiana. George Washington was intensely interested in canals and was a shareholder in several canal companies.

The building of the Erie and Champlain canals in New York launched canal mania. From 1825 to 1840 hundreds of canal projects were begun. States such as Pennsylvania and Ohio actually had more miles of canals than New York.

While the railroads contributed to the demise of the canals, it was the high maintenance costs, repair due to floods, and economic depressions which finally closed many of the canals.

A number of canals continued into the twentieth century. Modern canals include the Chesapeake and Delaware Canal and the Erie Barge Canal.

References: James Lee, *Tales The Boatmen Told*, Canal Press, 1977; William J. McKelvey, *Champlain To Chesapeake: A Canal Era Pictorial Cruise*, Canal Press, 1978; Harry L. Rinker, "The Old Raging Erie . . . There Have Been Several Changes": *A Postcard History Of The Erie And Other New York State Canals (1895 to 1915)*, Canal Captain's Press, 1984; Harry L. Rinker, *The Schuylkill Canal: A Photographic History*, Canal Captain's Press, 1991.

Collectors' Clubs: American Canal Society, R.R. 1, Box 87–T, Savannah, TN 38372; Canal Society of Ohio, 550 Copley Road, Akron, OH 44320; Pennsylvania Canal Society, c/o Canal Museum, P. O. Box 877, Easton, PA 18042.

Museums: Canal Museum, Hugh Moore Park, Easton, PA; Chesapeake and Delaware Canal Museum, Chesapeake City, DE; Erie Canal Museum, Syracuse, NY.

Advisor: Harry L. Rinker.

Ticket, passage, 1840s, blank, 10⅝" x 4³⁄₁₆", $25.00.

Ashtray, 5" d, Pennsbury Pottery, shows Lehigh Canal boat at dock, camelback bridge in background, advertising premium from "The Sloebury National Bank of New Hope, Pa.," green, gray, and brown, light brown ground **20.00**
Autograph, letter, ALS, J. H. Perkins, July 10, 1821, to Wm Meredith of Philadelphia, letter of introduction for Col. Baldwin, an early canal engineer, 7¾ x 9¾" **75.00**
Bank Note, Broken
    Maryland, Chesapeake & Ohio Canal Company, $20, issued in Frederick, MD, September 9, 1840, central vignette of godess sitting on cargo on wharf with sailing ship in background flanked by vignettes of Washington and DeWitt Clinton, engraved by Danforth, Underwood & Co., New York **30.00**
    New York, Chemung Canal Bank, $10, issued in Elmira, New York, September 1, 1840, central vignette of god pouring water from vessel with lock combine in background, engraved by Rawdon, Wright, Hatch & Co., New York **50.00**
    Pennsylvania, Tide Water Canal, $2, issued in Baltimore, MD, on May 1, 1840, vignette in upper right of wharf scene, vertical vignette of

canalboat pulled by mules on left, engraved by Drapper, Toppen & Co., Philadelphia and New York . **75.00**

Book

Adams, Samuel Hopkins, *Canal Town*, a romantic novel about a young doctor set in Palmyra, New York, in the 1820s, Peoples Book Club Edition, published by Consolidated Book Publishers, Chicago, 1944, 471 pgs, hardcover, dust jacket **7.50**

Colden, Cadwallader D., *Memoir, Prepared at the Request of a Committee of the Common Council of The City of New York and Presented to the Mayor of the City, at the Celebration of the Completion of the New York Canals*, printed by order of the Corporation of New York by W. A. Davis, 1825, 410 pgs, hardcover (Note: Worth significantly less if any plates missing) **500.00**

Harlow, Alvin F., *Old Towpaths: The Story of the American Canal Era*, D. Appleton and Company, 1926, 401 pgs, hardcover (Note: Has been reprinted) **50.00**

Lee, James, *The Morris Canal: A Photographic History*, first edition, Canal Press, 1973, 128 pgs, hardcover, dust jacket **40.00**

Broadside, Genesee Valley Packet Boat Arrangements, May 1851, lists two lines of packet boats and time schedule, primarily text, two small boat cuts at top, 11¼ x 16½" **350.00**

Bubble Gum Card, U. S. Presidents, Collector Series, Bowman, No. 23, James A. Garfield, shows Garfield as mule driver in background, 2½ x 3¾", multicolored **2.50**

Conch Shell, used as boatman's horn, detailed family history **40.00**

Hat Box, wall paper, 20½" x 14½" x 12¾", "Grand Canal," blue background, mule with driver aboard pulls boat from lock and across cut stone aqueduct, buildings in background (Also known in pink and yellow grounds) **500.00**

Letterhead, Office of Baltimore and Susquehanna Steam Co., 1872, cut of steamboat in upper left corner beneath which is "For Havre de Grace and Port Deposite And Tide Water Canal," 7⅝ x 9¹¹⁄₁₆" **15.00**

Lottery Ticket

New Hampshire, Amoskeag Canal, Tenth Class, No. 556, "entitle the bearer to receive the prize that may be drawn against its number, agree-

ably to an Act of the General Court of New–Hampshire, passed Dec. 30, 1799," sgd "E. Robinson" ... **50.00**

Washington City [D.C.], Lottery No. 1, for cutting a canal through the City of Washington to the Eastern Branch Harbor **75.00**

Mortgage, Canalboat, *A. R. Penfield of Oswego*, June 24, 1874, 7⅞ x 12½", copy filed with New York State Canal Department **10.00**

Patent Model

#120,264, J. S. Godfrey, October 24, 1871, "Propulsion of Vessels," metal model, c13 x 4 x 2¾", water enters through vents in front of canalboat and is expelled from rear .. **200.00**

#136,982, Thomas W. Edgar, March 3, 1873, "Means for Snubbing Canal Boats", wood model, c12½ x 4¼ x 3½", wood arm released by chain thrusts out from side of canalboat to rub against lock walls and stop movement **300.00**

Pinback

¾", "Lockport, NY," black and white photograph of flight of five locks on Erie Canal, made by Whitehead and Hoag, c1900–20 .... **15.00**

1¼", Pennsylvania Boatmen's Reunion, Rolling Green Park, August 1929, black and white photograph of Pennsylvania Main Line canalboat crossing aqueduct **20.00**

4", "Erie Canal: 1817–1967/New York State Council on the Arts," black and white nude woman sitting on rock, maker unknown **7.50**

Postcard

Chesapeake And Ohio Canal, "National Highway Between Hancock And Hagerstown, Maryland," published by The Neff Novelty Co., Cumberland, MD, photo copyright by Giblert, 1920, shows biplane flying over canal with line of cars on road along side canal, multicolored **2.50**

Delaware and Hudson Canal, "D & H Canal, Ellenville, NY," Porter Photo, shows canalboat with wash hanging on deck, canalboat tied up on berm in right background, black and white, canceled August 10, 1906 .... **4.00**

James River and Kanawha, "Richmond, Va. General View, James River and Canal from Hollywood," published by the Hugh G. Leighton Co, Portland, ME, No. 25684, printed in Germany, canceled March 28, 1908, canal to left, railroad tracks on towpath, Richmond in background, multicolored 5.00

Morris Canal, New Jersey, "Plane No. 7 - Washington, N.J.," published by Jenkins & Meeker, No. 5059, printed by George Miller and Company, Scranton, PA, plane on right, cradle at bottom, hand tinted photograph 7.50

Ohio and Erie Canal, "Sunset on the Canal, Cleveland, O.," published by the American Postcard and Publishing Company, Cleveland, Ohio, No. 2135, printed in Germany, canalboat tied up along berm, multicolored 4.00

Print

"Erie Canal near Ellenville, NY," c35½ x 13", based on painting by E. L. Henry, hand colored, scene on Delaware and Hudson Canal, framed 250.00

"View On The Erie Canal Near Little Falls," 11½" x 9½", W. H. Bartlett/J. T. Willmore, London, 1838, hand colored 40.00

Ribbon, silk, 7⅛" l, blue ground, black letters, "Celebration/Canal Centennial/October 19th/1792–1892/Music Hall/Buffalo," center vignette of canalboat passing under railroad viaduct, train on top of viaduct 50.00

Staffordshire, American Historical

Godwin, Thomas, plate, 9¼", brown transfer, "Schuykill Water Works," American View series, shows outlet lock of Schuylkill Navigation in lower right of view 85.00

Jackson, Job and John, plate, 10½", red, "View Of The Canal, Little Falls, Mohawk River," long stemmed roses border 125.00

Unknown Maker

Child's cup, 2⅜" high, 2½" bottom diameter, "View Of The Aqueduct Bridge At Little Falls" (same view as on Canal Views series pieces, see David and Linda Arman's *Historical Staffordshire: An Illustrated Check–List, First Supplement*, published by author, 1977), white ground, red band around top and red band accent line on handle 300.00

Plate, 8⅜" d, Erie Canal Inscription series, DeWitt Clinton Eulogy, "Late Governor" version, dark blue 400.00

Enoch Wood & Son, Pitcher, 6¼" h, "Erie Canal Aqueduct Bridge At Rochester/View Of The Aqueduct Bridge at Little Falls," dark blue .. 850.00

Stock Certificates

Delaware, Chesapeake & Delaware Canal Company, Capital Stock, issued June 5, 1913, to Henry Meyer for 15 shares, vignette of deep cut, covered bridge, and trestle bridge, 10⅛" x 7¼", impressed seal of company, canceled 35.00

New Jersey, Morris Canal And Banking Company

Capital $4,100,000 Bond, issued January 1, 1836 to Messr. Brooks Brothers & Co., 1,000 Pounds Sterling, numerous vignettes, three unit series on each side consisting of boat going up incline plane above and below which is Greek god head in profile, eight coupons still attached, sgd by Lous McLane, 10⅜" x 13" 500.00

Consolidated Stock, issued June 9, 1857, to D. M. Robinson for 5 shares, center vignette of canal lock combine flanked by two gods pouring water from vessels, side vignette (upper left) of boat going up incline plane, engraved by Latimer Bros. & Seymour, 9½" x 5⅝", stamp canceled 50.00

New York, New York State 5 per cent Stock, "Be it Known, That the People of the State of New–York are indebted to the Pesident, Managers and Company of the Delaware and Hudson Canal Company, or their order, in the summ of one thousand Dollars. . .", Albany, March 16, 1827, no vignettes, 9¾" x 7⅜", canceled 75.00

Pennsylvania, "This is to Certify, That Jacob Erion is entitled to one Share of "The Cordorus Navigation Company. . .," York, December 1, 1829, seal of company, 7¼" x 3¼" 40.00

CANDLEWICK

Collecting Hints: Select pieces without chips, cracks, or scratches. Learn the characteristics, shapes, and types of Imperial pieces made. Many items have been made that are similar to Candlewick and are often mixed with or labeled Candlewick at shops and shows. Learn to identify "look alikes." Be ware and Beware!

History: Candlewick, Imperial Glass Corp.'s No. 400 pattern, introduced in 1936, was made continuously until October 1982 when Imperial declared bankruptcy. In 1984 Imperial was sold to Lancaster–Colony Corp and Consolidated Stores

International, Inc. Imperial's assets including inventory, molds, buildings, and equipment were liquidated in 1985.

The buildings and site were purchased by Anna Maroon of Maroon Enterprises, Bridgeport, Ohio. At present, the site is being developed as a tourist attraction with sales shops, a glass–making shop, and plans for a museum.

Imperial's Candlewick molds were bought by various groups, companies, and individuals. Approximately 200 molds were purchased by Mirror Images, Lansing, Michigan. Eighteen small molds were bought by Boyd Crystal Art Glass, Cambridge, Ohio. At present, the location of some Candlewick molds is unknown.

Anna Maroon Enterprises, Bridgeport, Ohio, purchased the building and lands belonging to the Imperial Glass Corporation in 1985. The planned tourist attraction never developed.

Candlewick is characterized by the crystal–drop beading used around the edge of many pieces; around the foot of tumblers, shakers, and other items; in the stems of glasses, compotes, cake and cheese stands; on the handles of cups, pitchers, bowls, and serving pieces; on stoppers and finials; and on the handles of ladles, forks, and spoons. The beading is small on some pieces, while on others it is larger and heavier.

A large variety of pieces were produced in the Candlewick pattern. Over 650 items and sets are known. Shapes include round, oval, oblong, heart, and square. Imperial added or discontinued items according to popularity and demand. The largest assortment of pieces and sets were made during the late 1940s and early 1950s.

Candlewick was produced mostly in crystal. Viennese Blue (pale blue, 1937–38), Ritz Blue (cobalt, 1938–41), and Ruby Red (red, 1937–41) were made. Other colors that have been found include amber, black, emerald green, lavender, pink, and light yellow. From 1977 to 1980, four items of 3400 Candlewick stemware were made in solid color Ultra Blue, Nut Brown, Verde Green, and Sunshine Yellow. Solid black stemware was made on an experimental basis at the same time.

Other decorations on Candlewick include silver overlay, gold encrustations, cuttings, etchings, and hand–painted designs. Pieces have been found with fired–on gold, red, blue, and green beading. Other companies encased Candlewick pieces in silver, chrome, brass, and wood.

References: Virginia R. Scott, *The Collector's Guide to Imperial Candlewick, 2nd Edition*, privately printed, (available from the author), 1987; Mary M. Wetzel, *Candlewick, The Jewel of Imperial*, 2nd Edition, 1986.

Periodical: The National Candlewick Collector Newsletter, 275 Milledge Terrace, Athens, GA 30606.

Museum: Bellaire Museum, Bellaire, OH 43906.

Advisor: Virginia R. Scott.

REPRODUCTION ALERT: Six inch baskets in pink and Alexandrite and a pink four piece child's set (consisting of a demitasse cup and saucer, 6" plate, and 5" nappy) have been made by Viking Glass Co., New Martinsville, Ohio, for Mirror Images, Lansing, Michigan. In 1987 Viking made clear plates, bowls, cups, saucers, large and small flat–base sugars and creamers (400/30 and 400/122), and 6½" trays (400/29) for Mirror Images. These pieces have ground bottoms and are somewhat heavier than original Candlewick pieces. They are not marked.

Light green Candlewick items have recently appeared. The origin of these items is not presently known.

Boyd Crystal Art Glass, Cambridge, Ohio, has used Candlewick molds to make items in various slag and clear colors. All Boyd molds have been marked with a B in a diamond trademark.

In late 1990 Dalzell–Viking Corporation, New Martinsville, WV, began making a five piece place setting (6" plate, 8½" plate, 10" dinner plate, cup and saucer) in Crystal, Black, Cobalt, Evergreen, and Ruby Red. Retail price is $75 to $95 a place setting. The 1991 Dalzell–Viking Price List also includes a 5" and 6" two handled bowl, 7" and 8" two handled tray, and 10" five part relish dish in Crystal. These new pieces are quite heavy when compared to period Candlewick, have ground bottoms, and are etched "Dalzell" on the center base rim.

Ashtray	
4¼" oblong, large beads, 400/134/l,	**5.00**
6" round, large beads, 400/150	
Cobalt blue	**10.00**
Crystal	**6.00**
Lavender	**12.00**
Pink	**8.00**
Ashtray Set, nested, 4", 5", 6", three piece	
Crystal, 400/450	**17.50**
Blue, yellow, and pink, 400/550 ...	**26.50**
Red, white, and blue, patriotic, 400/550	**125.00**
Atomizer	
400/96 shaker with atomizer top made by De Vilbiss, amethyst, green, aqua, yellow, or amber ...	**95.00**
400/167 shaker bottoms, aqua and amethyst	**95.00**
400/247 shaker bottoms, aqua and amethyst	**95.00**
Banana Stand, 11" plate, 2 sides turned up, 4–bead stem, 400/103E	**500.00**
Basket, applied handle	
6½", turned up sides, 400/40/0	**27.50**
11", 400/73/0	**95.00**
Bonbon, 6", beaded edge, heart shaped,	

curved over center handle, 400/51T
Crystal 22.50
Light blue, ... 35.00
Ruby red with crystal handle 95.00
Bowl, beaded edge
  8½", two handles, 400/72B 16.00
  9", square crimped, 4 ball toes, 400/
  72SC
    Black 125.00
    Crystal 30.00
    Light blue 55.00
    Red 125.00
  10½", 400/75 .... 30.00
  11", float, cupped edge, 400/92F ... 35.00
  14", belled, large beads on sides, 400/
  104B 55.00
Buffet Set
  400/92D, 14" plate, 2 pcs 50.00
  400/166B, 5½" cheese compote,
  plain stem 50.00
  400/9266B 50.00

Butter Dish, 400/144, $25.00.

Butter Dish, cov
  California, 6¾" x 4", 400/276
    Beaded top, c1960 .... 85.00
    Plain top, c1951 .... 95.00
  Rect,¼ lb, graduated beads on cov,
  400/161 .... 23.00
  Round, 5½", 2–bead finial, 400/144 25.00
Cake Stand/Plate
  10", domed foot, wedge marked
  plate, 400/67D 55.00
  11", 3–bead stem, 400/103D 57.50
  14", round, birthday cake plate, 72
  candle holes, 400/160 .... 250.00
Candleholder
  3½"
    Domed foot, small beads, round
    handle, 400/81 .... 20.00
    Rolled saucer, small beads, 400/
    79R 10.50
  5", round bowl with beaded or fluted
  insert vase, 400/40CV 55.00
  5½", ftd, three sections arched beads
  on stem, 400/224 .... 35.00
  6½", 3–bead stem
  400/175 .... 50.00

400/1752, prisms 70.00
9", oval beaded base, three candle
cups, 400/115 .... 50.00
Candy Dish, cov
  5½", box, 2–bead finial, 400/59 ... 25.00
  6½", round bowl, sq cov, 2–bead finial, 400/245 .... 75.00
  7", 2–bead finial, three partitions,
  400/110 .... 45.00
Celery Tray, 13½", oval, 2 curved open
handles, 400/105 .... 27.50
Cheese and Cracker Set, 400/151
  cheese compote, 400/145D 11½"
  handled plate, 2 pc set 400/145 .... 50.00
Cheese, Toast or Butter Plate, 7¾" with
  cupped edge, domed cov, bubble
  knob, 400/123 .... 95.00
Cigarette Set, frosted crystal, 6½" 1776/
  eagle ashtray, 3" cigarette jar, small
  beads, 2 pc set 65.00
Clock, 4", beaded edge 100.00
Coaster, 3½" d, round, spoon rest, 400/
226 .... 10.00
Cocktail Set, 6" plate, 2½" off–center
  indent, 400/39; 1–bead cocktail
  glass; set, 400/97 .... 25.00
Compote, beaded edge, ftd
  5", 3 sections, arched beads in stem,
  400/220 .... 35.00
  8", 4 bead stem, 400/48F 65.00
  9"
    Domed foot, large bead stem,
    ribbed, 400/67B 75.00
    Flat foot, plain or crimped beaded
    edge, 400/67B 65.00
Condiment Set
  Jam Set, two 400/89 cov marmalade
  jars, 3–bead ladles, 400/159 oval
  tray; 5 pc set 400/1589 .... 75.00
  Oil and Vinegar Set, two 400/164 and
  400/166 cruets, beaded foot, 400/
  29 7" kidney shaped tray; 3 pc set
  400/2946 .... 85.00
Console Set, bowl and pr candleholders
  12" float bowl, 92F, cupped edge, 2–
  light candleholders, 400/100; set
  400/920F 75.00
  13" mushroom bowl, 400/92L on
  400/127B 7½" base, 6" ftd urn candleholders, 400/129R; set 400/136 120.00
Cordial Bottle, 15 oz, beaded foot, handle, 3–bead stopper, 400/82
  Crystal 125.00
  Crystal with red stopper and base,
  400/82 .... 250.00
Creamer and Sugar Set, ftd, beaded foot,
  plain handles, c1937, 400/31
  Crystal 35.00
  Light blue 55.00
Cup and Saucer
  After Dinner, small, slender, 4½"
  beaded saucer, set 400/77 .... 18.50

Cruet, 400/70, $45.00.

Coffee, slender, beaded handle, 400/
37, saucer, 400/35, set 400/37 ... **10.00**
Tea, round, beaded handle, 400/35,
beaded saucer, 400/35, set 400/35 **9.50**
Deviled Egg Tray, 11½", twelve inden-
tations, heart shaped center handle,
400/154 .... **80.00**
Dresser Set, 4 pcs, round mirrored tray,
400/151, powder jar, beaded base,
3–bead cov; two round perfume bottles, beaded base, 4–bead stoppers,
made for I Rice Co, 1940s **150.00**
Epergne Set, 9" ftd crimped bowl, 1–
bead stem, 400/196, 7¾" 2–bead peg
vase, set 400/196 .... **145.00**
Jelly, 6", divided, beaded edge, 400/52 **15.00**
Lamp, hurricane, 3½" saucer candleholder, 400/79R, 9" chimney
400/79, 2 pc set **50.00**
400/79, 3 pc set, including 400/152
Candlewick adapter, 400/152R ... **70.00**
Lemon Tray, 5½" plate, center handle
of 3 sections of arched beads, large
bead on top, 400/221 .... **25.00**
Marmalade Jar, round, beaded edge
cover, 2–bead finial, 400/89 .... **25.00**
Marmalade Ladle, 4¾", small bowl, 3–
bead handle, 400/130 .... **6.00**
Marmalade Set, 400/19 old fashion tumbler, beaded notched cov, 2–bead finial, 400/130 ladle, set, 400/1989 .. **35.00**
Mayonnaise Set, 7" beaded plate, 400/
23D, 5" heart shaped bowl, 400/49/
1, 3–bead ladle, 400/165, set, 400/
49 .... **30.00**
Mint Tray, 9", heart shaped center handle, 400/149 .... **25.00**
Mirror, domed beaded glass base, brass
holder and frame, 2 sided mirror flips
on hinges, maker unknown **65.00**

Mustard Jar, beaded foot, notched
beaded cover, 2–bead finial, 3½"
glass spoon, shell bowl, fleur–de–lis
handle, 3 pc set, 400/156 .... **30.00**
Nappy, 6", beaded edge, 400/3F **9.50**
Pastry Tray, 11½", beaded plate, heart
shaped center handle, 400/68D **30.00**
Pitcher
Manhattan, beaded foot, plain handle, 400/18
40 oz **110.00**
80 oz **145.00**
Water, 80 oz, beaded question–mark
handle, ice lip **95.00**
Plate, beaded edge
6", bread and butter, 400/1D **6.00**
8½", salad–dessert, 400/5D **8.00**
9", luncheon, 400/7D **12.00**
10", 2 handles, crimped, 400/72C .. **25.00**
10½" dinner, 400/10D **22.50**
12", 2 open handles, 400/145D **30.00**
Punch Set
11 pcs, cov family punch jar, domed
beaded foot, notched 2–bead cov,
400/139, small 400/139 ladle,
eight 400/77 demi–cups, 400/139/
77 set **225.00**
15 pcs, 6 quart, 400/20 bowl, 400/
128B base, 400/91 ladle, twelve
400/37 cups, question–mark handle **250.00**
Relish and Dressing Set, 10½" d, round
4 part relish, 400/112, 400/89 cov jar
fits center well, long ladle 3–beads,
c1941, 4 pcs **75.00**
Relish Dish, beaded edge
6½", 2 part, 2 tab handles, 400/54 . **10.00**
8½", oval, pickle–celery, 400/57 ... **15.00**
10½"
2 part, 2 tab handles, 400/256 ... **22.00**
3 part, 2 tab handles, also called
"Butter 'n Jam", (center holds
stick of butter), 400/262 .... **45.00**
12", rect, 3 sections one side, long
section on other, tab handle each
end, 400/215 .... **50.00**
Salad Set, 10½" beaded bowl, 400/75B,
13" cupped edge plate, 400/75V, fork
and spoon set, 400/75, 400/75 set .. **65.00**
Salt and Pepper Shakers, pr, beaded foot
Bulbous, 9 beads, plastic tops,
c1941, 400/96 .... **15.00**
Individual, chrome tops, 400/109 .. **10.00**
Round
400/96, 8 beads, chrome tops ... **10.00**
400/116, 1–bead stem, plastic or
metal tops, c1941 .... **60.00**
400/190, trumpet foot, chrome tops **32.50**
Sauce Boat Set, oval handled gravy
boat, 9" oval plate with indent, 400/
169 .... **85.00**

Stemware
  400/190 Line, bell shaped bowl, hollow trumpet shaped stems, beaded around foot, crystal
    Cocktail, 4 oz 16.50
    Goblet, 10 oz 16.50
    Seafood Icer 35.00
    Sherbet, 5 oz 12.50
    Wine, 5 oz 17.50
  3400 Line, flared bell top
    Four graduated beads in stem, crystal
      Cordial, 1 oz 25.00
      Goblet, 9 oz 15.00
      Sherbet–champagne, tall, 5 oz . 12.50
      Wine, 4 oz 20.00
    One bead stem, crystal
      Parfait 30.00
      Sherbet, 5 oz, low 10.50
      Tumbler, 12 oz, iced drink 15.00
    Ruby red bowls, crystal foot, any 3400 piece 90.00
    Solid colors, verde green, ultra blue, sunshine yellow, nut brown, made 1977–90, goblet, iced tea, sherbet, wine, each .. 35.00
Tid–Bit Server, two tier, 7½" and 10½" plates joined with metal rod, round handle at top, 400/2701
  Crystal 50.00
  Emerald green 450.00
Tid–Bit Set, nested, heart shaped, 4½", 5½", 6½", beaded edges, 400/750, 3 pcs 30.00
Torte Plate, 17", beaded edge, flat or cupped edge, 400/20V 40.00
Tumbler
  400/18, domed beaded foot, rounded top
    Dessert, 6 oz 25.00
    Iced tea, 12 oz 22.50
    Water, 9 oz 20.00
  400/19, beaded base, straight sides
    Iced tea, 12 oz 12.00
    Juice, 5 oz 8.00
    Old-fashioned, 7 oz 15.00
    Sherbet, 5 oz, low 8.00
    Water, 10 oz 10.00
Vase
  3¾", bud, beaded foot, ball, crimped top, 400/25 .... 20.00
  5¼", bud, beaded foot, tapered large beads, crimped top, 400/107 .... 25.00
  7", rolled beaded top, solid glass arched handles with small bead edging, flat foot, 400/87R 35.00
  8"
    Crimped beaded top, graduated beads down sides, 400/87C ... 22.50
    Fan shape, beaded top, solid glass arched handles with small bead edging, flat foot, 400/87F 25.00

8½", bud, beaded foot, ball
  Narrowed top slants, applied handle, 400/227 .... 85.00
  Trumpet shape top, crimped, 400/28C 35.00

CANDY CONTAINERS

Collecting Hints: Candy containers with original paint, candy and closures command a high premium, but be aware of reproduced parts and repainting. The closure is a critical part of each container; its loss detracts significantly from the value.

Small figural perfumes and other miniatures often are sold as candy containers. Study all reference books available and talk with other collectors before entering the market. Be aware of reproductions.

History: One of the first candy containers was manufactured in 1876 by Croft, Wilbur and Co., confectioners. They filled a small glass Liberty Bell with candy and sold it at the 1876 Centennial Exposition in Philadelphia.

Jeannette, Pennsylvania, was a center for the packaging of candy in containers. Principal firms included Victory Glass, J. H. Millstein, T. H. Stough, and J. C. Crosetti. Earlier manufacturers were West Bros. of Grapeville, Pennsylvania, L. E. Smith of Mt. Pleasant, Pennsylvania, and Cambridge Glass of Cambridge, Ohio.

Containers were produced in shapes that would appeal to children and usually sold for ten cents. Candy containers remained popular until the 1960s when they became too expensive to mass produce.

References: Eikelberner and Agadjanian, *American Glass Candy Containers* (out–of–print); Jennie Long, *An Album of Candy Containers*, published by author, 1978; Robert Matthews, *Antiquers of Glass Candy Containers*, published by author, 1970; Mary Louise Stanley, *A Century of Glass Toys*, published by author, n.d.

Collectors' Club: Candy Containers Collectors of America, Box 184, Lucerne Mines, PA 15754.

REPRODUCTION ALERT

Bisque
  Pumpkin Man, 3" h 35.00
  Witch, holding vegetables, 5½" h .. 40.00
Cardboard, mica coated
  House, Japan, c1940 .... 18.00
  Sled, Santa, Japan, 1920s–30s 30.00
  Snowman, 9" h, wooden carrot nose, German 45.00
Chenille, boot, 4" h, Japan 36.00
China, hat, Dresden, German 42.00
Composition
  Bug, 8½", sitting up, smiling, black

Airplane, Army Bomber, clear glass, $25.00.

top hat and glasses, red umbrella,
German 125.00
Duck, lady, 7", pink bonnet, purple
int., German 85.00
Egg, emerging chick, 4½ x 5", aqua,
bead eyes, German 135.00
Hen, 3½", white, sitting on box, two
colored eggs, wood base, German 100.00
Santa, twist off arm 95.00
Turkey, 4½" h, metal legs, black
body, red and white tail feathers,
c1930s 80.00
Cotton
Santa, body separates, Occupied Ja-
pan 89.00
Three Chicks and Mother Hen on lid,
2½ x 3½" 65.00
Crepe Paper, pumpkin man, Schrafft's
Candy, 10" h 85.00
Foil, cornucopia, 6" h, celluloid Santa
head 28.00
Glass
Airplane, Spirit of St Louis 165.00
Alarm Clock 180.00
Basket, hanging 30.00
Bathtub 300.00
Bell, Liberty Bell Candy Container .. 85.00
Bird Cage 90.00
Boat, Model Cruiser 15.00
Boot, Santa Claus 8.00
Bureau 175.00
Bus, Chicago 200.00
Cannon, Rapid Fire Gun 225.00
Cap, military style 15.00
Charlie Chaplin, Borgfeldt 125.00
Chicken on Basket 55.00
Clown 10.00
Condiment Set, 1906 .... 60.00
Dog
Little Doggie in the Window 15.00
Pup, tin top and hat 8.00
Scottie Dog, head up 20.00
With Umbrella 15.00

Duck on Basket 85.00
Elephant, GOP 150.00
Fire Engine, #11 .... 10.00
Fire Wagon 85.00
Girl, two geese 20.00
Golf Club 40.00
Gun
Cambridge Automatic 80.00
Indian Head Revolver 65.00
Square Butt Revolver 20.00
Hat
Brim 60.00
Uncle Sam's 50.00
Horn, trumpet 140.00
House 150.00
Jack–O–Lantern 155.00
Jeep 15.00
Kettle, three ftd 45.00
Kewpie, by barrel 90.00
Lantern, pat 1904 .... 25.00
Locomotive, #999 .... 95.00
Mail Box 125.00
Milk Bottle 30.00
Motor Boat 8.00
Mug, drum 40.00
Opera Glass, plain panels 100.00
Owl 125.00
Phonograph, glass horn 250.00
Pipe, fancy bowl 50.00
Powder Horn 40.00
Rabbit, seated
Eating carrot 25.00
Painted, 4½" h, green, orange ac-
cents, green tin base, early 1900s 125.00
Rolling Pin 180.00
Santa Claus, chimney 100.00
Snowman 5.00
Station Wagon 38.00
Suitcase
Milk Glass 50.00
Tin Closure, wire handle 70.00
Tank, man in turret 20.00
Telephone, Victory Glass Co, souve-
nir of Jeanette, PA 47.50
Top, winder 85.00
Truck, round top 75.00
Turkey, dressed 90.00
Village, bungalow 95.00
Watch 350.00
Wheelbarrow 75.00
Windmill, Dutch 100.00
Yacht 12.00
Net Bag, Santa, 7" h, celluloid face and
hands, Japan 80.00
Paper, painted
Irish Hat, shamrock decal, 2" h 35.00
Snowman, 4½" h, German 45.00
Witch's Hat, 3½" h, German 20.00
Papier Mache
Apple, singing, 3¾" h 185.00
Bear, white, riding brown rabbit,
wood, cloth, glass eyes, 8½" h ... 175.00

Black Cat

Face on Pumpkin, 2½" h	**75.00**
Sitting on Pumpkin, 4½" h, German	**65.00**

Chinaman, sitting on log, 4" h, German ... **245.00**
Dalmatian Pup, 11" h ... **30.00**
Devil, 3¾" h ... **90.00**
Donkey, glass eyes, blanket, 5" h, German ... **215.00**
Duck, dressed, German ... **58.00**
Father Christmas, white, glitter dec, 11" h ... **85.00**
Fish, 5" h ... **90.00**
Gentleman, top hat and tails, neck on spring, 8" h, German ... **100.00**
Hen, German ... **125.00**
Jack-O-Lantern ... **45.00**
Pear, German ... **68.00**
Pig, German ... **98.00**

Rabbit

Sitting, glass eyes, German	**52.00**
Walking, German	**68.00**

Reindeer, glass eyes, metal antlers, 8" h, German ... **185.00**
Skull 2¼" h, German ... **75.00**
St Patrick's, girl on box, German ... **88.00**
Turkey, German ... **68.00**
Valentine Heart, 5" h, German ... **42.00**
Washington in Boat, German ... **145.00**
Witch, standing, holding broom 3" h, Japan ... **45.00**

Plaster

Bird, in uniform, 4" h, German	**40.00**
Turkey, 4" h, German	**25.00**

Tin

Bank, litho, glass insert	**30.00**
Boat, submarine, tin bottom and superstructure, glass hull	**275.00**
Church, litho, glass insert	**25.00**
Fire Station, 1914	**40.00**
Football	**15.00**
Heart Shape, holly design, 5" d	**15.00**
School House, litho, glass insert	**18.00**

CANDY MOLDS

Collecting Hints: Insist on molds in very good or mint condition. The candy shop had to carefully clean molds to insure good impressions each time. Molds with rust or signs of wear rapidly lose value.

History: The chocolate or candy shops of Europe and America used molds to make elaborate chocolate candy items for holiday and other festive occasions. The heyday for these items was 1880 to 1940. Mass production, competition, and the high cost of labor and supplies brought an end to local candy shops.

The makers of chocolate molds are often difficult to determine. Unlike pewter ice cream molds, makers marks were not always on the mold or were covered by frames. Eppelsheimer & Co. of New York marked many of their molds, either with their name or a design resembling a child's toy shop with "Trade Mark" and "NY."

Many chocolate molds were imported from Germany and Holland and are marked with the country of origin and, in some cases, the mold maker's name.

References: Ray Broekel, *The Chocolate Chronicles*, Wallace-Homestead, 1985; Eleanore Bunn, *Metal Molds*, Collector Books, 1981, out of print; Judene Divone, *Anton Reiche Chocolate Mould Reprint Catalog*, Oakton Hills Publications, 1983.

Museum: Wilbur's Americana Candy Museum, Lititz, PA.

REPRODUCTION ALERT

Clown and dancer, pewter, Anton Reichet, Dresden, #17515 and #17514, each $30.00.

CHOCOLATE MOLD

Clamp Type, no hinge, two pieces
Acorn	**35.00**
Ballerina	**50.00**
Basket, 6½ x 9"	**70.00**
Bear Against Tree Trunk, 6½"	**25.00**
Boy, 5½"	**38.00**
Cat, sleek, 6½", metal	**45.00**
Chicken, tin	**20.00**
Christmas Stocking, 8", marked "59 + 4271, Larrosh, SchwGmund"	**100.00**
Corn, ear, 6½"	**45.00**
Cowboy, lasso	**45.00**
Donkey, 7", wire clamps, marked "15919, Vormenfabriek, Tillburg, Holland"	**30.00**
Egg, 3½ x 2½", pewter	**25.00**
Elephant, circus	**90.00**
Fish	**90.00**
Frog, 5"	**25.00**
Heart, 9 x 9"	**60.00**
Indian, 7½", copper, German	**30.00**
Jack O'Lantern, wire clamp	**32.00**
Jenny Lind, 3 pcs	**70.00**

Pencil, 8½"	25.00
Polar Bear, 4½ x 2½"	30.00
Poodle in hat	100.00
Rabbit, 7", girl, marked "273"	45.00
Rooster, 9"	30.00
Rose	20.00
Santa Claus, 8"	55.00
Snowman, 4", top hat	45.00
Turkey, pewter	35.00
Witch on Broom, 6"	25.00
Yule Log	70.00

Tray Type

Christmas Scene, 4½ x 8"	28.00
Hershey Candy, metal	5.00

Rabbit

5 x 7½", flat, landscape, pulling cart, sign reads "5 miles to go"	22.00
8 x 10", flat, 8 lollipop molds	50.00

HARD CANDY

Clamp type, 2 pieces

Deer, 3½ x 5"	35.00
Dog, 4 x 8", marked "17"	50.00

MAPLE SUGAR

Clamp type, 2 pieces

Dog's head, tin	60.00
Fish, tin	25.00
Heart, carved wood	65.00
Rabbit, carved wood	45.00
Rooster, three, 2 x 5", barley sugar	20.00

CARNIVAL CHALKWARE

Collecting Hints: Most chalkware pieces appear worn, either because of age or inexpensive production techniques. These factors do not affect the value, provided the piece is whole and has no repairs. Some pieces are decorated with sparkley silver. This does not add to the authenticity or value of the piece. Carnival chalkware in bank form is considered part of this category.

History: Carnival chalkware, cheerfully painted plaster of paris figures, was manufactured as a cheap, decorative art form. Doll and novelty companies mass produced and sold chalkware for as little as a dollar a dozen. Many independents, mostly immigrants, molded chalkware figures in their garages. They sold directly to carnival booth owners.

Some pieces are marked and dated; most are not. The soft nature of chalkware means it is easily chipped or broken.

Carnival chalkware was marketed for a nominal price at dime stores. However, its prime popularity was as a prize at games of chance located along carnival midways. Concessionaires, e.g.,

breaking a balloon with a dart, awarded small prizes, called a "build up." As you won, you accumulated the smaller prizes and finally traded them for a larger prize, often a piece of chalkware.

Chalkware ranges in size from three to twenty-four inches. Most pieces were three dimensional. However, some had flat backs, ranging from a plaque format to a half thick figure. Colors depended upon the taste of each individual decorator.

A wide variety of animal, character, and personality figures were made in chalkware. You can find Betty Boop, Sally Rand, Mae West, Shirley Temple, Charlie McCarthy, W. C. Fields, Mickey Mouse, etc. However, you will not find these names on the figures or in the advertising literature of the company who made them. Shirley Temple was the "Smile Doll" and Mae West was the "Mae Doll." Most character dolls were bootlegged, made without permission.

Although some carnival chalkware was made before the 1920s, its peak popularity was in the 1930s and 40s. The use of chalkware prizes declined in the late 1950s and reached its demise in the 1960s.

References: Thomas G. Morris, *The Carnival Chalk Prize*, Prize Publishers, 1985; Ted Sroufer, *Midway Mania*, L-W, Inc., 1985.

Alice the Goon, 10", c1940	60.00
Baby, 9½ x 10½", 1910–25	90.00
Bell Hop, 14¼", 1936	32.00
Betty Boop, 14½", 1930–40	185.00
Buddy Lee, 13½", 1920–30	65.00
Bugs Bunny, 9¼", flat back, c1940	38.00
Cat, 10", bank, c1940	10.00
Chipmunk, 5½", 1945–50	4.00
Circus Horse, 10", c1930	18.00
Clown, 8¾", 1930–40	25.00

Dog

Collie, 12"	8.00
Rin Tin Tin, 19"	50.00

Horse, black spots, yellow, red, and green dec, $35.00.

Terrier, 8", black and white, rhinestone eyes, c1940	10.00
Dopey, 6", c1937	42.00
Drum Majorette, 15" h	18.00
Elephant, bank, c1930	12.00
Felix the Cat, 12½"	75.00
Ferdinand the Bull, 8½", c1940	20.00
Gigolo, string holder	28.00
Girl, reading, 12 x 8½", 1920–25	70.00
Gorilla, 6¼", c1940	8.00
Kewpie, 12"	75.00
King Kong, 13¼", 1930–40	25.00
Lady and Dog, 11¼", full ruffled skirt, floral trim, c1935	12.00
Lamb, 7", flat back, marked "Rosemead Novelty Co," c1940	5.00
Lamp	
Horse, 13", 1940–50	80.00
Lighthouse, 15½", 1935–45	50.00
Little Red Riding Hood, 14", marked "Connie Mamat," 1930–40	28.00
Lone Ranger, 15" h, 3½ x 4½" base, multicolored, glitter on front, c1940s	80.00
Maggie, Bringing Up Father, 12"	45.00
Man, wearing derby hat, 10¼", 1930–40	38.00
Mexican Girl, 14½", 1925	80.00
Miss America, 15", wearing bathing suit, c1940	20.00
Monkey, bank, 12¼", 1940–50	18.00
Nude, 13"	12.00
Owl, bank, 16", 1945–50	25.00
Parrot, 13½", 1935–45	25.00
Paul Revere, 14½", 1935–45	20.00
Pirate Girl, 10¾", 1936	48.00
Porky Pig, 11", 1940–50	32.00
Sailor Girl, 9", c1940	10.00
Ship, 10", flat back, c1940	5.00
Snuffy Smith, 9¼", 1934–45	50.00
Soldier Boy, 9", c1940	10.00
Squirrel, 12", eating corn, c1940	7.50
Superman, 16", glitter dec	30.00
Vase, 11¾", 1930–40	22.00
Wimpy, 18", c1940	32.00
Windmill, 6¼", 1935–40	4.00

CARTES DE VISITE AND CABINET CARDS

Collecting Hints: The vast majority of card photographs were personal portraits and have little collecting value. Most collectors prefer photographs of uncommon subjects, e.g., animals, famous people, circus performers, military, occupational, sports, etc.

The earlier Cartes de Visite are more desirable. The photographer's imprint or logo on a card does add some value. Photographs in excellent condition with no fading, spotting, soiling, or tears bring the highest prices.

History: Cartes de Visite, or calling card, photographs were patented in France in 1854, flourished from 1857 to 1910, and survived into the 1920s. The most common Cartes de Visite was a 2¼ x 3¾" head and shoulders portrait printed on albumen paper and mounted on a card 2½ x 4". Multi–lens cameras were used by the photographer to produce four to eight exposures on a single glass negative plate. A contact print was made from this which would yield four to eight identical photographs on one piece of photographic paper. The photographs would be cut apart and mounted on cards. These cards were put in albums or simply handed out when visiting, similar to today's business cards.

In 1866 the Cabinet Card was introduced in England and shortly thereafter in the United States. It was produced similar to Cartes de Visite, but could utilize several styles of photographic processes. A Cabinet Card measured 4 x 5" and was mounted on a card 4½ x 6½". Portraits in cabinet size were more appealing because of the larger facial detail and the fact that images could be retouched. By the 1880s the Cabinet Card was as popular as the Cartes de Visite and by the 1890s was produced almost exclusively. Cabinet Cards flourished until shortly after the turn of the century.

References: William C. Darrah, *Cartes de Visite in Nineteenth Century Photography*, William C. Darrah, 1981; George Gilbert, *Collecting Photographica*, Hawthorne Books, Inc., 1976; B. E. C. Howarth–Loomes, *Victorian Photography: An Introduction for Collectors and Connoisseurs*, St. Martin's Press, Inc., 1974; O. Henry Mace, *Collector's Guide to Early Photographs*, Wallace–Homestead, 1990; Lou W. McCulloch, *Card Photographs, A Guide To Their History and Value*, Schiffer Publishing, 1981.

Periodicals: *The Photographic Historian*, Box B, Granby, MA 01033; *Photograph Collector*, 127 East 59th Street, New York, NY 10022.

Collectors' Clubs: American Photographical Historical Society, 520 West 44th Street, New York, NY 10036; Photographic Historical Society of New England, Inc., P. O. Box 189, West Newton Station, Boston, MA 02165; Western Photographic Collectors Association, P. O. Box 4294, Whittier, CA 90607.

Museums: International Museum of Photography, George Eastman House, Rochester, NY; Smithsonian Institution, Washington, D.C.; University of Texas at Austin, Austin, TX

REPRODUCTION ALERT: Excellent reproductions of Lincoln as well as other Civil War era figures on Cartes de Visite and Cabinet Cards have been made.

Note: Prices listed are for cards in excellent condition. Cards with soiling, staining, tears, or copy photographs are worth about half the prices listed. The categories on the list are for the most common or collectible types; other collecting categories do exist. CDV = Cartes de Visite. CC = Cabinet Card.

Children playing cards, H.C. Moore, Gill's Art Building, Springfield, MA, $8.50.

	CDV	CC
Animals		
Cat	9.00	8.00
Chicken	15.00	12.50
Dog	5.00	5.00
Horse	5.00	5.00
Wild Animal	10.00	8.00
Autographs on CDV or CC (add)		
Actor or Actress	100%	100%
Famous People	100%	100%
Lincoln	500.00+	500.00+
Presidents	50.00+	50.00+
Blacks	10.00	10.00
Boats		
Canoe	4.00	3.00
Paddle Wheeler	25.00	20.00
Rowboat	4.00	3.00
Children		
Cute portraits	1.50	1.00
With animal	7.00	6.00
With doll, must show doll's detail	10.00	10.00
With toy—drum, boat, gun, wagon, etc.	8.00	6.00
Circus Performers and Freaks		
Dwarfs	12.00	12.00
Fat people	12.00	12.00
Giants	12.00	12.00
Midgets	12.00	12.00
Siamese Twins	15.00	15.00
Snake Lady	15.00	15.00
Strongmen	20.00	20.00
Tattooed People	15.00	25.00
Tom Thumb		
Anthony	10.00	10.00
Brady	10.00	10.00
Others	12.00	12.00

	CDV	CC
Costumes, Native Dress		
Chinese or Japanese	7.00	5.00
Egyptian or Indian	6.00	4.00
Other	5.00	3.00
Engravings, Copies		
Anthony or Brady		
Paintings, famous	1.00	1.00
Religious	1.00	1.00
Statues	1.00	1.00
Unknown photographers		
Paintings, famous	.50	.50
Religious	.50	.50
Statues	.50	.50
World's Fairs and Expositions	8.00	8.00
Gambling, Drinking, Smoking		
Drinkers, glasses and bottles	1.00	1.00
Gamblers, with cards	12.00	12.00
Smokers, with cigars or cigarettes	1.00	1.00
Locomotive, clear, close view	35.00	30.00
Medical/Dental		
Doctor with instruments	15.00	15.00
Operating on patient	25.00	25.00
Military		
Civil War, battle ground scene	35.00	—
Civil War Soldiers, Union (Confederate add 30%)		
Armed, carbine	25.00	—
Armed, pistol or knife in belt	35.00	—
Armed, sword	15.00	—
Brady, Gardner or Gurney	10.00	—
Holding knife or pistol in front	45.00	—
Unarmed portrait	6.00	—
Civil War Officer or General, Union (Confederate add 30%)		
Brady, Gardner or Gurney	18.00	—
Custer by Brady or Gardner	175.00	175.00
Grant, by Brady or Gurney	35.00	35.00
Sherman or Sheridan by Brady	25.00	25.00
Foreign Soldiers		
Armed, carbine	10.00	8.00
Armed, sword	5.00	4.00
In uniform	8.00	3.00

	CDV	CC
Indian Wars		
Armed, carbine . . .	18.00	15.00
Armed, sword.	8.00	6.00
Soldier	4.00	3.00
Nudes, Risque		
Female, frontal view .	25.00	25.00
Male.	35.00	35.00
Objects		
Clocks	7.00	6.00
Flowers	2.00	2.00
Furniture	7.00	6.00
Still Life	3.00	2.00
Occupational		
Factories		
Exterior	8.00	6.00
Interior.	12.00	12.00
Workers, interior . .	15.00	13.00
Firemen, Policemen in		
uniform	8.00	7.00
Musician, instrument.	7.00	6.00
Workers		
In work clothes . . .	1.00	1.00
With tools	10.00	10.00
Outdoor, U.S. Subjects		
Building, single	7.00	6.00
Church.	2.00	2.00
Disaster or flood dam-		
age.	10.00	10.00
House	3.00	3.00
Scenic view	5.00	4.00
School	2.00	2.00
Streets		
Busy with people. .	12.00	10.00
Quiet	9.00	8.00
Western, people. . .	18.00	15.00
Town	9.00	8.00
People, Famous		
Actresses, Actors		
Anthony, Brady,		
Falk, Gutekunst,		
Mora or Sarony	6.00	6.00
Unknown Photog-		
raphers.	4.00	4.00
Artists.	15.00	12.00

Robert Todd Lincoln, C.M. Bell photographer, Washington, DC, $5.00.

	CDV	CC
Burnhardt, Sarah	20.00	20.00
Composers	15.00	12.00
Grant, by Anthony or		
Brady	35.00	30.00
Langtry, Lillie	20.00	20.00
Lincoln, by Anthony,		
Brady or Gardner. .	150.00	150.00
Lincoln, engraving or		
copy.	10.00	10.00
Painters	15.00	12.00
Presidents, by An-		
thony, Brady or		
Gurney	25.00	20.00
Political Figures	10.00	8.00
State Political Figures	5.00	5.00
Writers.	15.00	12.00
Photographers, Famous		
Anthony.	3.00	3.00
Bierstadt	1.00	1.00
Bogardus.	1.00	1.00
Brady	6.00	6.00
Fredericks	1.00	1.00
Gardner.	3.00	3.00
Gurney	3.00	3.00
Gutekunst	1.00	1.00
Hawes, J. J.	6.00	6.00
Sarony	1.00	1.00
Whipple	1.00	1.00
Wing	1.00	1.00
Photographers, Women,		
cards stamped with		
name or studio. . . .	1.00	1.00

Outdoor scene, farm, horses, 6³⁄₈ x 4¹⁄₄″, $6.50.

	CDV	CC
Photographic		
Cards, interesting ad on back..........	1.00	1.00
Person, camera as prop...........	15.00	12.00
Person, stereoscope..	8.00	8.00
Photographer with camera..........	150.00	150.00
Photograph Gallery		
Exterior	30.00	25.00
Interior, cameras ..	50.00	50.00
Traveling Photograph Studio	60.00	60.00
Portraits		
1 person	.10	.10
2 or 3 people	.15	.15
4 or 5 people	.50	.50
6 or more people....	1.00	1.00
Foreign portraits.....	.10	.10
Hand tinted portraits.	3.00	3.00
Twins..............	1.00	1.00
Triplets.............	1.00	1.00
Uglies	1.00	1.00
Post Mortem		
Memorial card, photo............	6.00	5.00
Memorial card, no photo............	—	1.00
Revenue Stamp On Back, common subject only	1.00	1.00
Sports		
Baseball		
Amateur, player or team..........	20.00	15.00
Professional, player or team		
Individuals	30.00	25.00
With Equipment...	45.00	40.00
Bikers		
High wheel bike ..	15.00	24.00
Portrait..........	8.00	8.00
Fisherman, rod......	7.00	6.00
Hunter, rifle	8.00	7.00
Mountain Climber...	3.00	3.00
Skaters		
Ice skater, portrait .	5.00	4.00
Roller skater, portrait............	5.00	4.00
Wedding, bride & groom	3.00	3.00
Western, west of Mississippi River		
Cowboys		
Armed	35.00	35.00
Typical western wear...........	20.00	15.00
Indians		
Armed	50.00	45.00
Full dress........	35.00	30.00

	CDV	CC
Geronimo	65.00	65.00
Group	45.00	40.00
Sitting Bull	65.00	65.00

CARTOON CHARACTERS

Collecting Hints: A vast majority of collectible categories yield an object related to a cartoon character. Cartoon characters appeared in advertising, books, comics, movies, television, and as a theme in thousands of products designed for children.

Concentrate on one character or the characters from a single strip. Most collectors tend to focus on a cartoon character that was part of their childhood. Another method is to focus on the work of a single artist. Several artists produced more than one cartoon character.

The most popular cartoon characters of the early period are Barney Google, Betty Boop, Dick Tracy, Gasoline Alley, Li'l Abner, Little Orphan Annie, and Popeye. The movie cartoons produced Bugs Bunny, Felix the Cat, Mighty Mouse, Porky Pig, and a wealth of Disney characters. The popular modern cartoon characters include Garfield, Peanuts and Snoopy.

History: The first daily comic strip was Bud Fisher's Mutt and Jeff which appeared in 1907. By the 1920s the Sunday comics became an American institution. One of the leading syndicators was Captain Joseph Patterson of the News–Tribune. Patterson, who partially conceived and named "Moon Mullins" and "Little Orphan Annie," worked with Chester Gould to develop "Dick Tracy" in the early 1930s.

Walt Disney and others pioneered the movie cartoon, both in short and full length form. Disney and Warner Brothers characters dominated the 1940 to 1960 period. With the advent of television the cartoon characters of Hanna–Barbera, e.g., the Flintstones, added a third major force. Independent studios produced cartoon characters for television and characters multiplied rapidly. By the 1970s the trend was to produce strips with human characters, rather than the animated animals of the earlier period.

A successful cartoon character created many spin–offs. Comic books, paperback books, and earlier Big Little Books followed quickly. Games, dolls, room furnishings, and other materials which appeal to children are also marketed. The secondary market products may produce more income for the cartoonist than the drawings themselves.

References: Maurice Horn and Richard Marshall (eds.), *World Encyclopedia of Comics*, Chelsea House Publications; David Longest, *Character Toys and Collectibles, First Series*, (1984) and *Second Series*, (1987), Collector Books; Freddi Margolin and Andrea Podley, *The Official Price Guide To Peanuts Collectibles*, House of Collectibles, 1990.

Museum: The Museum of Cartoon Art, Port Chester, NY.

See: Disneyana and index for specific character.

Abie The Agent, pinback button, 1¼" d, black and dark pink, white ground, "Abie, 908552, New York Evening Journal," back paper refers to contest run by newspaper 15.00
Archie, pinback button, 1½" d, blue, white, and orange, "Member Archie Club," 1950s 16.00
Barney Google
  Book, *Barney Google and Spark Plug*, published by Cupples & Leon, 1925 copyright, #3 of series, black and white comic strip reprints, 10 x 10", cardboard cov, 48 pgs 75.00
  Card, member, "Brotherhood of Billy Goats," 2¾ x 4¼", buff color, black ink, text and "Bernard Google" facsimile signature on front, text, password, and image of billy goat in tuxedo and hooded mask on reverse, Chicago Herald and Examiner premium, c1920 . . . . 30.00
  Game, Barney Google an' Snuffy Smith, Milton Bradley, boxed board game, 16 x 16" playing board, complete, 1963 . . . . 38.00
  Paperweight 40.00
  Sheet Music, Barney and Spark Plug on cov, 1923 . . . . 22.50
  Toy, Spark Plug, ¼" thick, 5" l, 4" h, jigsawed plywood, painted yellow, green, and black, red accents, wooden wheels, sgd "DeBeck," 1925 copyright 165.00
Beanie and Cecil
  Bubble Bath Kit, Disguise Cecil, 8" h vinyl figural bubble bath container, orig box with nine disguises, Bob Clampett copyright, 1949–50 . . . . 75.00
  Doll, Mattel Toy
    Beanie, 17" h, talking, cloth, molded soft vinyl head, hands, and sneakers, red sweatshirt, aqua corduroy pants, pull string, orig Mattel tag, 1949 Bob Clampett copyright 100.00
    Cecil, 24" l plush, lime green body, blue felt tail fin, back fins, and eyelashes, red mouth and

tongue, plastic eyes and nose, orig Mattel tag, 1950 Bob Clampett copyright 75.00
  Game, target, tin 60.00
  Guitar, animated, 14" h, plastic, black, litho paper scene, music crank, Bob Clampett picture trademark, Mattel copyright, 1961 . . . . 80.00
  Handbag, vinyl 100.00
Betty Boop
  Charm, 1", celluloid, tinted colors, brass loop at top, 1930s 30.00
  Figure
    Bisque, 3¼" h, musical, painted, holding accordion, "Fleischer Studios" and "Made In Japan" inscribed on back 130.00
    Celluloid, 3" h, hollow, movable arms, holding white hoop, fleshtone, green dress, gold, black, and red accents, c1930 . . . . 130.00
    Marble 12.50
  Pin, figural, silvered brass, enameled, dark red dress, sq disk with oranges and "Florida" suspended from link at wrist, 1930s 80.00
  Valentine, 3½ x 4½", mechanical, stiff diecut paper, movable feather in hair moves eyes and changes message from "Don't Keep Me Waiting For Your Love, Valentine," to "Or I'll Start Looking Around, Valentine," 1940 . . . . 30.00
Bill Bounce, pinback button, 1¼" d, multicolored, Billy flanked by polar bear holding blue umbrella, man in white apron holding lunch pail, Denslow character, c1910 . . . . 100.00
Blondie
  Book, *Blondie & Dagwood's Snapshot Clue*, text and cartoons, 1934 . . . . 45.00
  Coloring Book, Whitman #1121–15, 8½ x 11", 92 pgs, art by Chic Young, 1950 . . . . 15.00
  Cook Book, dj 35.00
  Cookie Cutters, boxed, 1948, MIB . . 125.00
  Greeting Card, 5 x 6", birthday, multicolored, Dagwood carrying large greeting card on front, int. Dagwood doing dishes, red ribbon dish towel attached, Hallmark, 1939 copyright 12.50
  Paint Box, tin, 1946 . . . . 24.00
  Pencil, Dagwood, 1929 . . . . 10.00
  Presto Slate 20.00
  Puzzle, Jaymar, orig package, set of three 35.00
  Valentine, 3 x 4", diecut stiff paper, Alexander and Daisy, c1940 . . . . . 8.00
Bringing Up Father
  Figure, set of three, Jiggs, Maggie, and daughter, 4" h, bisque, multicol-

ored, each inscribed "King Features copyright/Made in Japan" and mold number, orig box, 1934 copyright **175.00**

Mirror, pocket, 2 x 3", black and white, paper covered illus of Jiggs leaning on fence, adv Casey's Tool Works factory, balloon caption reads "So Does Mine But I Don't Advertise It On Every Fence," c1930 .... **70.00**

Pinback Button, ¾" d, red and black, white ground, Jiggs, Joplin Globe, c1930 .... **15.00**

Salt and Pepper Shakers, pr, 2½" h, china, multicolored Maggie and Jiggs, orange and black holder, marked "Made in Japan," c1930 . **70.00**

Bugs Bunny

Alarm Clock, talking **20.00**

Doll, 10" h, plush, molded soft rubber face, 1¾" d litho pinback button inscribed "What's Up Doc?" c1950 **100.00**

Figure, 7¼" h, glazed china, hollow, light gray, white, and pink, brown base, name inscribed on front, Warner Bros copyright, c1940 ... **110.00**

Film Card, Tru–Vue, #T–54, "TV Trouble," full color, Bugs, Porky, and Petunia, 1959 copyright, unopened **15.00**

Planter, 3 x 6 x 7½" h, china, glossy white, gray, and pink, figural, holding wheelbarrow, name and Warner Bros Cartoon copyright on back, late 1940s **80.00**

Casper the Friendly Ghost

Bank, plastic **35.00**

Doll, 15" h, talking, white terrycloth, stuffed, molded hard plastic face, pull cord at neck **75.00**

Buster Brown's Circus, rubber stamp set, orig box with 17 stamps, 4¾ x 5¾ x 1⅛", $75.00.

Game, Jumping Beans, orig box, 1959 .... **30.00**

Soaky Container, Wendy, 10" h, hard plastic, red and yellow, c1960 ... **15.00**

Dennis The Menace, book, Hank Ketcham, *Baby Sitter's Guide by Dennis The Menace*, Henry Holt & Co Publishers, 1954, 6 x 9", hardcover, illus by Bob Harman **10.00**

Dick Tracy

Badge

Detective Club **75.00**

Secret Service Patrol **25.00**

Big Little Book

Dick Tracy And His G–Men, Whitman Better Little Book, #1439, 1936 .... **25.00**

Dick Tracy In Chains Of Crime, Whitman, #1185, 1935 .... **25.00**

Camera **35.00**

Card Game, complete, 1934 .... **50.00**

Cards, set of 24, #121–144, 2½ x 2⅞", full color pictures, descriptions on back, Dick Tracy Caramels, issued by Walter H Johnson Candy Co, Chicago **60.00**

Crimestoppers Club Kit, MIB **80.00**

Lunch Box **100.00**

Model, Aurora, MIB **125.00**

Pin, 2" l, Dick Tracy Air Detective, brass, wings, airplane center, 1938 **65.00**

Pinback Button, 1¼" d, Dick Tracy Detective, illus of Tracy pointing gun, sgd "Chester Gould" **30.00**

Puppet, hand

Bonny Braids, 10" h, soft molded vinyl plastic head, hands, and feet, flannel pajama outfit, baby blanket, orig tag, c1953 .... **60.00**

Dick Tracy, dated 1961 .... **45.00**

Shield, brass, black and red accents, late 1930s

Dick Tracy Crime Stoppers **35.00**

Dick Tracy Detective Club **30.00**

Salt and Pepper Shakers, pr, Dick Tracy and Junior, 2½" h, plaster, painted, c1940 .... **30.00**

Tab, brass, black and red accents, Dick Tracy Detective Club premium, 1942 .... **60.00**

Wrist Radio Set, 2–Way Electronic, hard plastic, connecting cord, signal buttons, orig box with diecut display lid, Remco, c1951 .... **100.00**

Favorite Funnies, printing set, large version, includes Dick Tracy, Little Orphan Annie, orig box **50.00**

Felix The Cat

Advertising Brochure, Eastman Kodak Co, Kodatoy film projector and theater, black, white, and red Felix,

5¼ x 8¼" opens to 10½ x 16½", late 1920–30s **55.00**

Figure, 2½" h, iron, painted, name on chest, inscribed "Sullivan," 1920–30s **175.00**

Pencil Case, ½ x 5 x 8½", textured cardboard, brass snap, black and white illus, red ground, American Pencil Co, 1934 .... **60.00**

Flintstones

Ashtray, Fred and Wilma, 1961 .... **65.00**

Bank

  Dino, 8¼" h, glazed china, white ground, blue, yellow, and black accents, brown golf bag, 1961 Hanna–Barbera copyright **115.00**

  Fred, plastic, 1971 .... **20.00**

Costume, Fred, vinyl plastic molded mask, one pc cover–all costume, Ben Cooper, 1973 Hanna–Barbera copyright **25.00**

Film Card, Tru–Vue, #T–58, Sea Monster, Pebbles and Bam–Bam, 1964 Hanna–Barbera copyright, unopened **15.00**

Gun and Holster, miniature, Wilma, 5¼ x 9½" display card, leather holster, metal cap gun, diaper pin, issued by Harvell–Kilgore, Dy–De Mite Set, unopened, 1960s **40.00**

Lamp, Fred, other Flintstone characters printed on shade, 1961 ...... **110.00**

Puzzle

  Frame Tray, 1960 .... **15.00**

  Jigsaw, Whitman, 14 x 18", Fred and Wilma on floating Dino, 1962 Hanna–Barbera copyright, orig box **8.00**

Soaky Container, Bam–Bam **12.00**

Toy, roller, 1½" h, Wilma, plastic, red, c1960 .... **8.00**

Trash Can **40.00**

Foxy Grandpa, pipe, 5½" l, clay, Foxy Grandpa holding fishing pole, two boys pulling on line, inscribed "Pipe River, Germany," early 1900s **65.00**

The Gumps

Calendar, Andy Gump, 1913 ...... **65.00**

Pinback Button, ⅞" d, For President Andy Gump, 1930s **21.00**

Happy Hooligan

Bank, pottery, dated 1920 .... **175.00**

Charm, 1½" h, Alphonse, white metal, blue metallic tint, flat back, early 1900s **25.00**

Henry, valentine **12.00**

Huckleberry Hound

Bank, 9¾" h, hard plastic, tan and black, red ground, neck inscribed "Knickerbocker, Canada," c1960 . **25.00**

Cuff Links Set, pr of cuff links and tie clip, mint on card, 1959 .... **25.00**

Pencil Sharpener, mint on card **35.00**

Pin, Huckleberry Hound for President, 1960 .... **22.00**

Jetsons, Colorforms, vinyl stick–ons, black and white jet–age airport board, instruction leaflet, 1963 Colorforms and Hanna–Barbera copyrights, orig box, complete **35.00**

Katzenjammer Kids

Mask, Fritz, molded **24.00**

Ring, The Captain, plastic, figural, gold, white, and blue accents, late 1940s **30.00**

Li'l Abner

Bank

  Daisy May **145.00**

  Shmoo, 7" h, hard plastic, blue, black accents, inscribed "Li'l–Abner–Sez, Woo the Shmoo, with Lucky Money/Make Your Future Bright and Sunny!" on back, orig diecut money bag shape card, Gould & Co 1948 copyright **65.00**

Clock, wall, Shmoo, 4 x 6" diecut plastic, key wind, metal mechanism case and hanging plate, blue hands and pendulum, red numerals, Lux Clock Mfg Co, late 1940s **80.00**

Coloring Book, Saalfield, #209, 8 x 11", 80 pgs, copyright 1941 ..... **30.00**

Figure

  Chalkware, Mammy Yokum, 7" h, dated 1968 .... **16.00**

  Vinyl, Shmoo, inflated, black and white, Banguard Corp, United Features Syndicate copyright, late 1940s **60.00**

Pinback Button, ¾" d, litho, red, white, blue, and black, Sweet Shmoo, late 1940s **20.00**

Ring, brass, adjustable, raised image of Shmoo on top, two small Shmoos on side bands, late 1940s **35.00**

Toy, litho tin wind–up, multicolored, Li'l Abner And His Dogpatch Band, Unique Art, orig 6 x 9 x 8½" box **550.00**

Little Lulu

Clothespin Set, mint on card **85.00**

Little Golden Book, #203 .... **12.00**

Little King, Otto Soglow artist

Figure, 1½ x 1½ x 2½" h, composition and wood, red and white robe, yellow crown, name on base, 1944 King Features Syndicate **150.00**

Poster, 18 x 26", full color, Little King on roller skates, queen, son, and court in foreground, Simon & Schuster 1933 copyright **75.00**

Mighty Mouse

Game, Playhouse Rescue, unused, 1956 .... **50.00**

Slide Rule, orig box **30.00**
Swim Ring, inflatable, orig package,
1950s **65.00**

Moon Mullins

Bake Set, Pillsbury, eight unpunched
cards, orig box, complete **60.00**
Figure, 5" h, wood, jointed, Moon,
orig box **120.00**
Nodder, bisque, Mayo **60.00**
Salt and Pepper Shakers, pr, Moon
Mullins and Kayo **20.00**
Toothbrush Holder, 5" h, bisque, Un-
cle Willy and Emmy **118.00**

Mr Magoo, toy, crazy car, Mr Magoo
driving **275.00**

Mutt and Jeff, sheet music, 1916 . . . . .   **17.50**

Peanuts

Bank, Snoopy, glass **14.00**
Clock, Snoopy chasing butterfly, 1958   **37.00**
Lunch Box, Snoopy's doghouse **28.00**
Nodder, Linus **30.00**
Wrist Watch, Snoopy, pilot on dog-
house, 1965 . . . .   **45.00**

Pogo

Book, Walt Kelly, *The Pogo Peek–A–*
Book, Simon & Schuster, 1955, 6½
x 10¾", soft cov, first printing, 92
pgs **35.00**
Figures, set of six, vinyl plastic, Pogo
and swamp friends, movable heads
and arms, 1969 Walt Kelly copy-
right inscribed with name on base   **90.00**
Pinback Button, 1¾" d, Pogo for
Pres!, black and white, light blue
ground, LBJ caricature as see, hear,
and smell no evil monkeys **30.00**

Popeye

Advertising, tab, 2½" d, diecut card-
board, Popeye in white and blue
sailor suit, red ground, white lettering 'I Yam Strong For Sunshine Po-
peye Cookies'' **65.00**
Book, linen–like, King Features Syn-
dicate **175.00**
Chalk, orig box **22.00**
Charm, celluloid **15.00**
Figure, 6" h, chalk, Popeye the
Thinker, 1929 . . . .   **95.00**
Funny Face Maker, King Features Syn-
dicate **150.00**
Handkerchief, 8½" sq, multicolored,
Popeye giving bouquet to Olive in
center, corner pictures of Popeye
and Olive, mid 1930s **30.00**
Paint Set, Milton Bradley, five 4 x 4¾"
picture sheets, 18 water color tablets mounted on inset board, orig
box, 1934 copyright **125.00**
Palm Puzzle, ½ x 3½ x 5" h, dark
blue metal frame, clear glass cov,
illus of Popeye, The Juggler, Bar

Zim Toy Co, New York, 1929 copy-
right **35.00**
Pen, 5" l, yellow, Popeye and Olive   **95.00**
Pencil, 10½" l, mechanical, by Eagle,
marked ''King Features Syndicate''   **35.00**
Pinback Button, Popeye center, rim
inscribed ''I Yam Strong for King
Comics,'' late 1930s **30.00**
Pipe, battery operated, King Features
Syndicate, mint on card **110.00**
Play Money, Thimble Theatre, 2 x
4½", full color, cartoon currency,
1933 . . . .   **15.00**
Playing Cards, 1938 . . . .   **30.00**
Puppet, push button, orig box, Po-
peye and Olive Oyl, 1940s, pr . . .   **85.00**
Sand Pail, 8" h, tin litho, Popeye Under The Sea, continuous full color
illus, copyright 1933 T Cohn Inc .   **40.00**
Toy
Pop–Up, spinach can, head pops
up **95.00**
Squeak, Olive Oyl, King Features
Syndicate **120.00**
Strength, ''Pow'er Strength Test,'' 9
x 15" colorful cardboard diecut
figure, strength test piece
mounted in center, hitting plate,
wooden mallet, wooden can of
spinach, metal bell, plastic peg
scorer, HG Toys, c1960, uno-
pened **65.00**
Walkaway, Popeye and Wimpy,
orig box **45.00**

Porky Pig, soaky container, 9½" h,
molded vinyl plastic body, hard plastic removable head, pink and blue,
c1960 . . . .   **18.00**

Rocky and Bullwinkle

Coloring Book, Bullwinkle's How To
Have Fun Outdoors Without Get-
ting Clobbered, unused **20.00**
Doll, plush body, molded soft vinyl
plastic head
13" h, Rocky, green felt aviator's
cap, Ideal tag, 1960s **65.00**
15½" h, Bullwinkle, felt hands, red
and yellow fabric outfit, ''B'' on
chest, 1961 Terry Toons copy-
right **65.00**

Skeezix, nodder, 3" **45.00**

Skippy, pinback button, black on white
ground, 1930s
⅞" d, PL Crosby copyright **35.00**
1⅛" d, Skippy Blade **40.00**

Snuffy Smith, doll, 17" h, stuffed, felt,
amber eyes, black hat, orange shirt,
green pants and suspender, movable
head, c1930 . . . .   **130.00**

Winnie Winkle The Breadwinner, cigar
box, 2½ x 5½ x 9¼", litho paper on
wood, full color picture of Winnie

and MM Branner signature on lid, blue and white banner inscription inside lid with picture of Winnie, c1930 **30.00**

Woody Woodpecker

Alarm Clock, 1½ x 4½", metal, ivory enamel, wind–up, animated, Woody's Cafe, color dial with tree cafe, Woody stands in opening of tree, rocks back and forth as clock runs, Columbia Time Products, c1959 .... **120.00**

Christmas Card, 11 x 15½", semi–gloss paper, Walter Lantz Studios, Woody in center, surrounded by other Lantz characters, greeting on bottom, Lantz fascimile signature, Woody copyright symbol, c1950 . **75.00**

Coloring Set, orig box, 1958 .... **30.00**

Game, Travel with Woody Woodpecker, Cadaco–Ellis, 1956 Lantz copyright orig box **80.00**

Yellow Kid

Bookmark, 2½ x 6¼", diecut cardboard, issued by "A No. 1 Candy Company," full color, yellow ground, illus of Yellow Kid depicted as chocolate candy surrounded by other candies, late 1890s **60.00**

Pinback Button, "I hate to take medicine!" **28.00**

Post Card, Buster Brown, Tige, and Yellow Kid, "Over The Bounding Main," 1903 .... **45.00**

1942, Christmas **38.00**
1946, Spring & Summer, 994 pgs .. **30.00**
1969, Fall & Winter, 1436 pgs **11.00**

Sears
1941–42, Fall & Winter, 1280 pgs .. **35.00**
1944–45, Fall & Winter, 902 pgs ... **32.00**

Spiegel
1937 .... **55.00**
1944, Fall & Winter, 630 pgs **32.00**

Victor Record, 1927, $18.50.

CATALOGS

Collecting Hints: The price of an old catalog is affected by the condition, data, type of material advertised, and location of advertiser.

History: Catalogs are used as excellent research sources. The complete manufacturing line of a given item is often described, along with prices, styles, colors, etc. Old catalogs provide a good way to date objects.

Many old catalogs are reprinted for use by collectors as an aid to identification of their specialities, such as Imperial and The Cambridge Glass Co.

Reference: Don Fredgant, *American Trade Catalogs.* Collector Books, 1984.

MAIL ORDER

L. L. Bean, 1940 .... **25.00**
Macy's, 1908, 448 pgs, 15 pgs toys .. **85.00**
Montgomery Ward
1881, Fall & Winter **500.00**
1913, Men's, Women's, Children's Fashions, 224 pgs **55.00**

TRADE

A & P Premiums, 1910, 63 pgs **15.00**
American Chair Manufacturers 'Tropique' Rattan, 1940s, 16 pgs **17.00**
Atlas Portland Cement, Concrete Country Residences, c1900, 168 pgs **85.00**
Bazar Patterns, 1875, 16 pgs **20.00**
Betz, Frank S, medical supplies, 1931, 298 pgs **25.00**
Butterick, 1885, 31 pgs **25.00**
Carl Forslund Custom–Built Quaint American Furniture, 1949, 64 pgs, Drummer's Sample Furniture, Westmoreland milk glass **25.00**
Charles Broadway Rouss, NY, 1912, general wholesale **50.00**
Collis Motor Co Instruction Book & Repair Parts **35.00**
Colt, 1941 .... **20.00**
Doll Catalogue, 1962, 62 pgs **24.00**
Doyles, M. L., Fashion Guide **45.00**
Edison & Music, 1920, phonograph cabinets **38.00**
Elmira Arms Sporting Goods, 1931, 180 pgs **30.00**

Frost and Adams Catalog of Artists & Architects Supplies, 1914 .... 25.00
Goerz Cameras, 1913 .... 15.00
Greenlee Tools, Mortising, Boring, 1927, 68 pgs 10.00
Harris Homes, Chicago, 1923 .... 35.00
Higgenbothen Perlstone Hardware, Dallas, TX, 1939 .... 35.00
Homan Manufacturing, 1911, 55 pgs, 10¼ x 13½", electro–plated hollow ware, toilet ware, novelties, etc 85.00
Ideal Toy, 1950s, 8 pgs, 5 x 7", full color 15.00
Indian Art Palace, 36 pgs 15.00
Isaac Walker, 101, Peoria, IL, 1943 ... 25.00
Jacobson Architectural Ornaments, hard cover, 1915, 183 pgs 35.00
Keuffel & Essex Co, NY, drawing materials, mathematical and surveying instruments, 1915 .... 38.00
Dorrect–Way Store Displays, 1938 ... 15.00
Leacock Sports Supply, 1925 .... 25.00
Liggett & Meyers Premiums, 1912, 39 pgs 15.00
Lipscomb Co, Hardware, 1913 .... 50.00
Lufkin Precision Tools, #7 .... 22.00
Majestic Stove, 1913 .... 40.00
March Of Toys, 1952, 32 pgs, 8 x 10½" 25.00
Marshall Field Holiday Goods, Fancy Goods, Notions, 1888–89, 210 pgs, 9½ x 12½", hardcover, toiletry, cutlery, photo albums, etc 165.00
May–Stern's, Toy Sale, 1950s, 32 pgs, 8 x 10" 25.00
Merry–Go–Round, Health Co, 50 pgs, 1906 .... 75.00
National Modern Welded Pipe, 1928, 87 pgs 12.00
Newcomb–Macklin Manufacturers, c1910, 55 pgs, 14¼ x 10¾", picture frames, moldings, mirrors 50.00
Northland Electrical and Radio Supplies, 1932, 136 pgs 12.00
Pincus Jewelers, 1912 .... 25.00
John Pritzlaff House Furnishings Goods, 1910, 202 pgs, 10¼ x 12", coffee mills, scales, refrigerators 40.00
Punwani Bro, 1940, 16 pgs, illus 15.00
Remington Fire Arms, 1908–09, 64 pgs, 9⅛ x 8", illus and prices 200.00
Reynold's Watch Makers' Supplies, 1933 .... 30.00
Riverside Tires 5.00
Schwarz, FAO, 1949, 82 pgs, Christmas scene on cov, 9 x 12" 50.00
Scott's Standard Postage Stamp Catalog, 1938, 1,300 pgs 10.00
Shelly Seamless Tubes, 1920, 71 pgs . 10.00
Shure Winner, 1907, 588 pgs, toys, dolls, novelties 60.00
Specialty Engineering Co Zephyr Bodies, 1930s, beverage trucks, pictures Coca–Cola and other soft drink trucks 125.00

Spencer Fireworks Co, 1940s 20.00
Spencer Microscopes, 1930, 108 pgs . 32.00
Stanley Tool Guide, 1935 .... 25.00
Starrett Tools 20.00
Strong Aluminum, Alloys, Allco, 1928, 60 pgs, hardcover 10.00
Studebaker Champion, 1941, 8 pgs, 10¼ x 15½" 15.00
Thresher and Tractor Supply, 1926 ... 7.50
US Ammunition, 1929, pocket size ... 30.00
US Leather Good Co, Gifts of Leather, Fall 1922–23 Winter, Chicago, jewelry, toilet seats, etc 20.00
Waterford Irish Crystal, 1924 .... 20.00
Wheel Goods Catalogue, 1965, pedal cars, etc 30.00

CAT COLLECTIBLES

Collecting Hints: Cat related material can be found in almost all collecting categories. Advertising items, dolls, figurines, folk art, jewelry, needlework, plates, postcards, and stamps are just a few of them. Because of the popularity of cats, modern objects d'feline constantly are appearing on the market. However, as cat collectors become more experienced, their interests are more with antique rather than newer items.

The cat collector competes with collectors from other areas. Chessie, the C & O Railroad cat, is collected by railroad and advertising buffs. Felix is a favorite of toy and cartoon character enthusiasts.

Because cat collectors are attracted to all cat items, all breeds, and realistic or abstract depictions, they tend to buy too many items. It is best to specialize. Money and display space extend only so far; time for research is limited. Three of the most popular new areas of cat collecting are cat cards, calendars, and stickers.

Throughout the 1980s cats grew in popularity as the pet of choice. Along with this also grew the love of collecting cat items. The new and newer (secondary) market, tomorrow's collectibles, has grown by leaps and bounds. Some cat pieces bought ten years ago are showing considerable price increases. As true antique cats become rare and costly buy what you can, but also concentrate on quality, limited editions, and original pieces in the current market.

History: Cats always have been on a roller coaster ride between peaks of favoritism and valleys of superstition. In ancient Egypt cats were deified. Cats were feared by Europeans in the Middle Ages. Customs and rituals bore down brutally on felines. Cats became associated with witchcraft, resulting in tales and superstitions which linger to the present. This lack of popularity is why antique cat items are scarce.

Cats appear in TV programs, movies, cartoons, and many advertising ads in addition to those for cat food. Garfield remains popular; Felix has made a come back; and a new feline, Motley, is emerging. Objects associated with these modern cartoon cats are tomorrow's collectibles.

References: Bruce Johnson, *American Catalogue: The Cat in American Folk Art*, Avon Books, 1976; Alice Muncaster and Ellen Yanow; *The Cat Made Me Buy It*, Crown, 1984; Alice L. Muncaster and Ellen Yanow Sawyer, *The Cat Sold It!*, Crown, 1986; Silvester and Mobbs, *The Cat Fancier: A Guide To Catland Postcards*, Longman Group, 1982.

Collectors' Club: Cat Collectors, 31311 Blair Drive, Warren, MI 48092.

Museum: The Metropolitan Museum of Art, New York, NY; British Museum, London, England; The Cat Museum, Basel, Switzerland.

Advisor: Marilyn Dipboye.

REPRODUCTION ALERT

Art
  Painting
    10½ x 12½", oil on canvas, kitten in grass looking at butterfly, ornate frame **215.00**
    12 x 10", oil on silk, two white kittens with pink bows, sgd La Forat, 21 x 17" frame **10.00**
    16 x 13", oil on canvas, two kittens watching grasshopper, sgd R Heuel **350.00**

Advertising, pocket mirror, White Cat Union Suits, Cooper Underwear Co, Kenosha, WI, black ground, white letters, Parisan Novelty Co, Chicago, 2¾" h, $25.00.

    28 x 20", oil on canvas, titled "Child with Kitten," sgd Paolo Chiglia, Italian, 19th C **300.00**
  Print
    6½ x 10¼", girl with flashlight shining on litter of kittens, black wood frame **18.00**
    8 x 10", titled "Happiness," Gary Patterson, 1981 .... **7.50**
Ashtray
  Ball shape, black cat, open mouth, #109, Shafford **17.00**
  Black cat face, bow, 4" d, #16 Shafford, 1953 .... **20.00**
Bookends, pr
  Brass, Cheshire cats, c1930 .... **135.00**
  Pottery, blue cats on bases, Rookwood, c1923 .... **200.00**
Bottle
  Glass, clear, titled "Smiley," cat, painted facial features, blue bow . **48.00**
  Katz Philharmonic Cat, conductor dressed, 1970 .... **50.00**
  Majolica, figural, wearing clothing, cork stopper, incised #7216, 7" h, c1900 .... **144.00**
  Whiskey
    Ezra Brooks
      Gray and Dark Gray Cat, 14¾" h, 1969 .... **35.00**
      Reddish Brown Cat, blue ball on base, 1975 .... **30.00**
      Tan and Brown Cat, 14¾" h, 1969 .... **30.00**
    Jim Beam
      Black Cat, Regal China **50.00**
      Gold Cat, Regal China **75.00**
      Three different breeds, 1967, Regal China **18.00**
Candy Container, figural, glass, emb "Felix" on chest, 4¾" h, orig paper label, Germany on back **1,115.00**
Child's Flatware
  Fork, cat chasing rat, SP **18.00**
  Fork and Spoon, Puss 'N' Boots, SP, Regal **25.00**
Cookie Jars
  Brush, stylized Siamese **320.00**
  Majolica, pirate cat **600.00**
  McCoy, two kittens in basket, 1950s **675.00**
  Shawnee, Puss 'N' Boots, gold trim, floral decals **150.00**
  Unmarked, figural, black and white cat, laying, head lid, 11" l, 6½" h, 1985 .... **48.00**
Decanter, 8½" h, black cat with green eyes, white whiskers, red polka dots and trim, six matching shot glasses . **49.00**
Egg Cup, 3" h, black cat, Japan paper label **19.00**

Figure

   3" h, sewertile, folky cat, Staffordshire   **85.00**

   3" l, ceramic, white, kitten on brown
     shoe, Japan **9.00**

   7½" w, 3½" h, 6½" d, white porce-
     lain, laying, long haired, model
     #SR111, c1920 . . . .   **150.00**

   Royal Doulton, white persian, #2539   **150.00**

Game, Tom and Jerry, 1962 . . . .   **15.00**

Indian souvenir beadwork, heart with hump, five dangles, silver, pink, white, green, gold, lilac, and blue beads, $95.00.

Jam and Marmalade Set, black cats,
   #880, Shafford paper label **35.00**

Match Striker, 8" w, 6½" d, 5½" h, figural, majolica, two love cats, seated,
   creamy gold with gray overshot **135.00**

Measuring Cup, set of 4, black cat face   **45.00**

Movie Reel, Felix the Cat, talking, orig
   pkg, unused, 1960 . . . .   **35.00**

Mug, 4", emb black cat face, full figured
   cat handle, Shafford, Japan **28.00**

Music Box, tin litho, Felix the Cat, Made
   in France **80.00**

Needlework

   Crib Sheet, embroidered kittens fish-
     ing, 1930s **26.00**

   Tapestry, 20 x 40", rayon and cotton,
     cats and kittens, Made in Lebanon   **50.00**

   Wall Hanging, titled "Attention Chat
     Lunatique," playful cat border, 7½
     x 9½", framed, dated 1986 . . . . . .   **25.00**

Nodder, Felix the Cat **20.00**

Paper Cups, Felix the Cat, wrapper,
   1960s **20.00**

Plate

   ABC, tin, kitten playing in center, red
     and yellow, 4½" d **55.00**

   Chessie, 7" d, hammered aluminum,
     Wendell August **150.00**

Child's, Hey Diddle Diddle, 1880s .   **45.00**

Limoge, painted, cats with knocked
   over jar, gold trim, sgd Brahi,
   c1900 . . . .   **225.00**

Puppet, Top Cat, Hanna Barbera . . . .   **.1,500.00**

Puzzle

   Felix the Cat, 1949 . . . .   **30.00**

   Kitten with toppled vase of flowers,
     wood, 14 x 10½", sgd Victor
     Becker, 1930s **45.00**

Postcard, Christmas and New Year greetings, multicolored, yellow thread fringe, $5.00.

Salt and Pepper Shaker, pr

   Bavarian cat, orange **32.00**

   Black Cat

     2½" h, teapot shaped, black cats,
       Japan label **18.50**

     3¾" h, sleek sitting black cats, red
       collars, "Kasuga Ware Japan"
       paper label **15.00**

   Black cat salt, fish bowl pepper, base
     marked "Japan" **18.50**

   Cat

     Eating from one half bowl, two
       parts of bowl fit together, ce-
       ramic, Japan **25.00**

     Heads, one wearing green plaid
       cap, white ceramic, marked
       "Holt Howard 1958" **16.00**

     Sitting, white ceramic, blue bows,
       marked "Holt Howard 1958" . .   **12.00**

   Floral cat on pillow **15.00**

   Kittens on butter churns, ceramic,
     Twin Winton **45.00**

   Puss 'N' Boots, gold trim, orig paper
     label, Shawnee **45.00**

Sheet Music, Felix the Cat, music by
   Pete Wendling and Max Kortlander,
   Sam Fox Pub, copyright 1928 . . . . . .   **25.00**

Teaspoon, Salem Witch, SS **115.00**

Thermometer, bisque, figural, tabby,
   7½" h, Bradly Japan label **22.00**

Toy
Squeak, celluloid, head sticking out
of barrel, 4½" h **39.00**
Wind—up
Cat with ball, tail flips cat, Marx . **50.00**
Figaro, tin litho **165.00**

CELLULOID ITEMS

Collecting Hints: There are few collectors of celluloid per se. Most celluloid is sought because it relates to another collecting field.

It was possible to place a printed message on a celluloid surface. For this reason celluloid was a popular medium for the advertising giveaways of the 1880 to 1900 period. Old celluloid is quite brittle and can be easily broken. It must be handled carefully. Collectors should be aware of celluloid's flammable tendencies.

History: Celluloid is the trade name for a thin, tough, flammable material made of cellulose nitrate and camphor. It was invented just prior to 1870 and was used mainly in making toilet articles. It also was an inexpensive material for jewelry, figurines, vases, etc. Celluloid frequently was made to simulate more expensive materials, e.g., amber, bone, ivory, and tortoise shell.

Celluloid became a popular medium for the toy industry of the 1920s and 30s. Character toys included Charlie Chaplin and Charlie McCarthy. The advent of bakelite and plastic brought an end to celluloid items.

Bride and Groom, 1920s, pr **60.00**
Brush and Comb Set, pink, hp, flowers,
orig box, 1920s **40.00**
Buddha, 4" h, solid **12.00**
Card Holder, black base, two Mickey
Mouse figures, paper sticker reads
"Walt Disney Enterprises Ltd/Japan,"
930s **90.00**
Charm, pig in green overalls, pink cap,
holding gray trowel, brass loop, Japan, early 1930s **28.00**
Christmas Light, Kewpie **40.00**
Cigar Bowl, football player, Tampa, FL,
marked "Occupied Japan" **25.00**
Clip, 1½" d, multicolored, mounted on
steel spring clip, cherries and leaves,
white ground, blue lettering, "JF
Cherry Company," marked "Whitehead & Hoag, Made in England," on
back, early 1900s **50.00**
Disk, 3" d, mechanical, calculates cost
of gasoline ranging from 34¢ to 44¢
per gallon, American Art Works,
c1940 .... **25.00**
Dresser Set, 11 pcs, ivory, orig case .. **85.00**

Figure, 1⅞" h, Black youngster, running,
upraised arms, black base, marked
"Patent Japan," c1930 .... **40.00**
Flipper, ¾", adv, diecut, hanger pin,
early 1900s
Old Dutch Cleanser, multicolored,
cleanser can shape **20.00**
Red Cross Stoves & Ranges, company
logo shape, red and white, black
and white text on back **18.00**
San Marto Coffee, elf head shape,
black and white text **20.00**
Ink Blotter Pad, adv, India—Down Bedding, 3¼ x 7¾", cardboard pad, celluloid cov, Indian lady, c1910 ..... **75.00**

Manicure Set, traveling, 8 pcs, leather case, $125.00.

Mirror
2¼" d, Cream Dove Peanut Butter,
multicolored, boy wearing straw
hat, black lettering, white rim, early
1900s **75.00**
2¾" l, oval, Statue of Liberty,
multicolored, bronze color statue,
white ground, early 1900s **30.00**
Nail File, folding, figural, lady's leg,
painted high heel and garter **35.00**
Note Hook, 2¾", Breakfast Cheer Coffee, inserted rigid wire, full color illus
of coffee container, green ground,
early 1900s **60.00**
Note Pad, 1½ x 2½", black and white,
Provident Life and Trust Co, Philadelphia, Detroit office, illus of Detroit
office building, early 1900s **10.00**
Paperweight, celluloid over metal,
Maryland Casualty Co, company logo
and text, black, white, gold, and red,
c1920 .... **18.00**

Pen, adv, Travelers, brown 10.00
Pencil Clip, ¾" d, brown and white
photo, Larry Doby, metal clip, c1949   8.00
Pencil Sharpener, 2½" h, figural, Mickey
Mouse, black, white, and red, 1930s   75.00
Pocket Knife, marbled celluloid sides,
Trylon and Perisphere, inscribed
"New York World's Fair 1939, Impe-
rial" 70.00
Powder Box, ivory 12.00
Rattle, Mickey Mouse head, white rub-
ber handle, silver metal bells for arms,
red ears, 1930s 125.00
Ruler, adv
G Felsenthal & Sons, Chicago, 1 x 6",
list of celluloid novelties on back,
early 1900s 22.50
Western Union, 7¼" l, diecut, silver
and blue logo on each side of handle, telegraph and cable rates on
back, 1905 patent 20.00
Snooker Score Counter, adv, Ullman &
Co Whiskies, two notched wheels,
Whitehead & Hoag, c1905 . . . . 60.00
Stamp Case, 1½ x 2½", red and white
cov design, Aetna Life Insurance Co,
Hartford, CT, 1907 calendar attached   12.00
Tape Measure, adv, round, 1920–30s
General Electric Refrigerators, black
and white beehive refrigerator illus,
dark blue ground, orange rim, text
for Lima, OH dealer on back 15.00
Sears, Roebuck and Co, white letter-
ing, black ground, blue, green, and
red border and monogram, floral
design on back 12.50
Toy
Airship, 1½ x 2¼ x 5½", hollow, red,
blue, wood wheels, pull string, US
Star Co logo on tail fin, 1930s . . . 100.00
Coney Island Cop, 8½" h, hollow,
pink uniform, white gloves, "Stop"
inscribed on palm of bobbing hand,
sand filled, marked "Japan," c1930 125.00
Cowboy, on horse, wind–up 45.00
Hawaiian Dancer, wind–up, yellow
and black tin legs and feet, black
celluloid upper body, dark green
dress, grass skirt, celluloid feather
and flower in hair, marked "Made
In Japan," orig box 100.00
Rabbit, pushing cart, wind–up, 1950s 100.00
Typist Aid, 1¾ x 3¼", diecut, Remington Self Starting Typewriter, four different size openings to place over
copy to make neat erasures, illus of
typist at Remington typewriter, red
and black lettering, blank back, early
1900s 18.00
Watch Fob, adv, Alumina Soapalite, cel-
luloid lion's head center 65.00

CHILDREN'S BOOKS

Collecting Hints: Most collectors look for books
by a certain author or illustrator. Others are interested in books from a certain time period such
as the 19th century. Accumulating the complete
run of a series such as Tom Swift, Nancy Drew,
or the Hardy Boys is of interest to some collectors. Subject categories are popular too, and include ethnic books, mechanical books, first editions, award winning books, certain kinds of
animals, rag books, Big Little Books, and those
with photographic illustrations.

A good way to learn about children's books is
to go to libraries and museums where special
children's collections have been developed.
Books on various aspects of children's literature
are a necessity. You also should read a general
book on book collecting to provide you with
background information. Significant bits of information can be found on the title page and verso
of the title page of a book. This information is
especially important in determining the edition
of a book. You eventually will want to own a
few reference books most closely associated with
your collection.

Although children's books can be found at all
the usual places where antiques and collectibles
are for sale, also seek out book and paper shows.
Get to know dealers who specialize in children's
books; ask to receive their lists or catalogs. Some
dealers offer to locate certain books for you. Most
used and out-of-print book stores have a section
with children's books. If your author or illustrator
is still actively writing or illustrating, a regular
book store may carry his most recent book.

Things to be considered when purchasing
books are the presence of a dust jacket or box,
condition of the book, the edition, quality of
illustrations and binding, and the prominence of
the author or illustrator. Books should be exam-
ined very carefully to make sure that all pages
and illustrations are present. Missing pages will
reduce the value of the book. Try to buy books
in the best condition you can afford. Even if your
budget is limited, you can still find very nice
inexpensive children's books if you keep looking.

History: William Caxton, a printer in England, is
considered to have been the first publisher of
children's books. Among his early publications
was *Aesop's Fables* printed in 1484. Other very
early books include John Cotton's *Spiritual Milk
for Boston Babes* in 1646, *Orbis Pictis* translated
from the Latin about 1657, and *The New England
Primer* in 1691.

Children's classics had their beginning with
Robinson Crusoe in 1719, *Gulliver's Travels* in
1726, and Perrault's *Tales of Mother Goose*
translated into English in 1729. The well known
A Visit from St. Nicholas by Clement C. Moore

appeared in 1823. Some of the best known children's works were published between 1840 and 1900. A few are Lear's *Book of Nonsense*, Andersen's and Grimm's *Fairy Tales*, *Alice in Wonderland*, *Hans Brinker*, *Little Women*, *Tom Sawyer*, *Treasure Island*, *Heidi*, *A Child's Garden of Verses*, and *Little Black Sambo*.

Series books for boys and girls began around the turn of the century. The Stratemeyer Syndicate, established about 1906, became especially well known for their series, such as Tom Swift, The Bobbsey Twins, Nancy Drew, Hardy Boys, and many others.

Following the turn of the century, informational books such as Van Loon's *The Story of Mankind* were published. This book received the first Newbery Medal in 1922. This award, given for the year's most distinguished literature for children, was established to honor John Newbery, an English publisher of children's books. Biographies and poetry also became popular.

The most extensive development, however, has been with picture books. Photography and new technologies for reproducing illustrations have made picture book publishing a major part of the children's book field. The Caldecott Medal, given for the most distinguished picture book published in the United States, was established in 1938. The award, which honors Randolph Caldecott, an English illustrator from the 1800s, was first given in 1938 to Dorothy Lathrop for *Animals of the Bible*.

During the late 1800s, novelty children's books appeared. Lothar Meggendorfer, Ernest Nister, and Raphael Tuck were the most well known publishers of these fascinating pop-up and mechanical or movable books. The popularity of this type of book has continued to the present. Some of the early movable books are being reproduced especially by Intervisual Communication, Inc., of California.

Books that tie in with children's television programs, e.g., Sesame Street, and toys, e.g., Cabbage Patch dolls, have become prominent. Modern merchandising methods include multimedia packaging of various combinations of books, toys, puzzles, cassette tapes, videos, etc. There are even books which unfold and become a costume to be worn by children.

References: Barbara Bader, *American Picture Books From Noah's Ark To The Beast Within*, Macmillan, 1976; E. Lee Baumgarten, *Price List for Children's and Illustrated Books for the Years 1880–1940, Sorted by Artist*, published by author, 1990; E. Lee Baumgarten, *Price List for Children's and Illustrated Books for the Years 1880–1940, Sorted by Author*, published by author, 1990; Margery Fisher, *Who's Who In Children's Books: A Treasury of the Familiar Characters of Childhood*, Holt, Rinehart and Winston, 1975; Virginia Haviland, *Children's Literature, A Guide To Reference Sources*, Library of Congress, 1966, first supplement 1972, second supplement 1977, third supplement 1982; Bettina Hurlimann, *Three Centuries Of Children's Books In Europe*, tr. and ed. by Brian W. Alderson, World, 1968; Cornelia L. Meigs, ed., *A Critical History of Children's Literature*, Macmillan, 1969, 2nd ed.

Periodicals: *Book Source Monthly*, P. O. Box 567, Cazenova, NY 13035; *Martha's KidLit Newsletter*, P. O. Box 1488, Ames, IA 50010.

Collectors' Clubs: (Membership fees are not given because of the large number of listings and the frequency of change).

Louisa May Alcott Memorial Assoc., P. O. Box 343, Concord, MA 01742; Horatio Alger Society, 4907 Allison Drive, Lansing, MI 48910; International Wizard of Oz Club (L. Frank Baum), Box 95, Kinderhook, IL 62345; Thorton W. Burgess Society, Inc., P. O. Box 45, Dept. B, East Sandwich, MA 02537; Burroughs Bibliophiles (Edgar Rice Burroughs), P. O. Box 588, Wytheville, VA 24382; Lewis Carroll Society of North America, 617 Rockford Road, Silver Spring, MD 20902; Dickens Society, Dept. of English, University of Southern California, Los Angeles, CA 90089; Fantasy Association, P. O. Box 24560, Los Angeles, CA 90024; Kate Greenaway Society, 10 Felton Avenue, Ridley Park, PA 19078; Happyhours Brotherhood, 87 School Street, Fall River, MA 02770; Uncle Remus Museum (Joel Chandler Harris), P. O. Box 184, Eatonton, GA 31024; Kipling Society (Rudyard Kipling), c/o Dr. Enamul Karim, Dept. of English, Rockford College; Rockford, IL 61108; Melville Society (Herman Melville), c/o Donald Yannella, Dept. of English, Glassboro State College, Glassboro, NJ 08028; Mystery and Detective Series Review, P. O. Box 3488, Tucson, AZ 85722; Mythopoeil Society, P. O. Box 4671, Whittier, CA 90607; National Fantasy Fan Federation, c/o Sally A. Syrjala, P. O. Box 149, Centerville, MA 02632; New York C. S. Lewis Society, c/o Jerry L. Daniel, 419 Springfield Ave., Westfield NJ 07092; Series Book Collector Society, c/o Jack Brahce, 5270 Moceri Ln, Grand Blanc, MI 48439; Stowe-Day Foundation (Harriet Beecher Stowe), 77 Forest St., Hartford, CT 06105; American Hobbit Association (J. R. R. Tolkien), 2436 Meadow Drive, N., Wilmette, IL 60091; American Tolkien Society, P. O. Box 277, Union Lake, MI 48085; Tolkien Fellowships, c/o Bill Spicer, 329 N. Avenue 66, Los Angeles, CA 90042; Mark Twain Boyhood Home Association, 208 Hill Street, Hannibal, MO 63401; Mark Twain Memorial, Nook Farm, 351 Farmington Ave., Hartford, CT 06105; Mark Twain Research Foundation, Perry, MO 63462; Mark Twain Society, c/o George Daneluk, Jersey City State College, 2039 Kennedy Memorial Blvd., Jersey City, NJ 07035; Yellowback Library, 811 Boulder Ave., Des Moines, IA 50315.

Libraries and Museums: Many of the clubs maintain museums. *Subject Collections* by Lee Ash (ed.) contains a list of public and academic libraries which have children's book collections. Large collections can be found at: Florida State University, Tallahassee, FL; Free Library of Philadelphia, Philadelphia PA; Library of Congress, Washington, DC; Pierpont Morgan Library, New York, NY; Toronto Public Library, Toronto, Ontario, Canada; University of Minnesota, Walter Library, Minneapolis, MN; University of South Florida, Tampa, FL.

Advisor: Joyce Magee.

Notes: Prices are based on first editions with a dust jacket (dj) and in very good condition. The absence of a dust jacket, later printings and a condition less than "very good" are all factors that lessen the value of a book.

Autographed copies and those that come in a special box are additional factors that will increase the value. Books that have been award winners, e.g., Newbery, Caldecott, etc., generally are higher in value. Un-paged.

Reprints: A number of replicas of antique originals are now appearing on the market, with most being done by Evergreen Press and Merrimack. A new "Children's Classics" series offers reprints of books illustrated by Jessie Willcox Smith, Edmund Dulac, Frederick Richardson and possibly others.

Alger, Horatio, *Ben's Nugget*, John C. Winston, 1882, 275 pgs	7.50
Anderson, Hans Christian, *The Nightingale*, Nancy Ekholm Burkert, illus, Harper & Row, 1965, 33 pgs, 1st ed, dj	25.00
Anglund, Joan Walsh, *A Friend is Someone Who Likes You*, Harcourt, Brace & World, 1958, 1st ed	12.00
Appleton, Victor, *Tom Swift and His Great Searchlight*, Grosset & Dunlap, 1912, 214 pgs	8.00
Bannerman, Helen, *Little Black Sambo*, Gustaf Tenggren, illus, Simon & Schuster, 1948, 1st ed, Little Golden	30.00
Beard, Patten, *Twilight Tales*, Ruth Caroline Eger, illus, Rand McNally, 1929, 66 pgs	14.00
Blyton, Enid, *Just Time for a Story*, Grace Lodge, illus, MacMillan, 1948, 144 pgs	10.00
Blos, Joan W., *A Gathering of Days*, Scribners, 1979, 145 pgs, 1st ed, dj, 1980 Newbery Medal	20.00
Boston, Lucy M., *The Stones of Green Know*, Peter Boston, illus, Atheneum, 1976, 117 pgs, 1st ed, dj	16.00
Brooks, Walter, *Freddy the Cowboy*, Kurt Wiese, illus Knopf, 233 pgs, 1st ed, dj	20.00
Brown, Margaret Wise, *The Golden Egg Book*, Leonard Weisgard, illus Simon & Schuster, 1947, 1st ed	13.00
Browning, Robert, *Pied Piper of Hamelin*, Roger Duroisin, illus, Grosset & Dunlap, 1936, 1st ed, dj	17.00
Burgess, Thornton W., *The Adventures of Grandfather Frog*, Harrison Cady, illus, Little, Brown, 1944, 96 pgs, dj	20.00
Calhoun, Frances Boyd, *Miss Minerva and William Green Hill*, Reilly & Britton, 1909, 212 pgs	11.00
Carroll, Lewis, *Alice's Adventures in Wonderland*, A. E. Jackson, illus, Garden City, 216 pgs	45.00
Castleman, Jarry, *Frank in the Mountains*, John C. Winsto, 1896, 277 pgs	6.00
Chadwick, Lester, *Baseball Joe Club Owner*, Cupples & Leon, 1926, 244 pgs	12.00
Chapman, Allen, *Ralph and the Missing Mail Pouch*, Grosset & Dunlap, 1924, 242 pgs, dj	8.00
Clyne, Geraldine, *The Jolly Jump–ups Number Book*, McLoughlin, 1950, 6 pop ups	35.00
Collodi, C., *Pinocchio*, Maria L. Kirk, illus, Lippincott, 1914, 234 pgs, 1st ed	32.00
Dahl, Ronald, *Charlie and the Great Glass Elevator*, Knopf, 163 pgs, 1st ed, dj	16.00
Daniels, Leslie N, *Jack Armstrong the All–American Boy and the Ivory Tower Treasure*, Whitman, 1937, 424 pp, Big Little Book, illus, Henry E. Vallely, #1435	16.00
De Angeli, Marquerite, *Ted and Nina Have a Happy Rainy Day*, Doubleday, 1936, 1st ed, dj	27.00
De Jong, Meindert, *The Wheel on the School*, Maurice Sendak, illus, Harper, 1954, 298 pgs, 1st ed, dj	30.00
Deming, Richard, *Dragnet*, Whitman, 1957, 282 pgs, (Whitman TV series)	3.00
Dickey, James, *Tucky the Hunter*, Marie Angel, illus, Crown, 1978, 48 pgs, dj	15.00
Disney, Walt *Mickey Mouse Takes A Vacation*, Franklin Watts, 1976, puppet book	15.00
Through the Picture Frame, Simon & Schuster, 1st ed, Little Golden	40.00
Dixon, Franklin W., *Following the Sun Shadow*, Grosset & Dunlap, 1932, 215 pgs, dj, (Ted Scott Series)	5.00
DuBois, William Pene, *The Forbidden Forest*, Harper & Row, 1978, 56 pgs, 1st ed, dj	17.00
Emberley, Ed, *London Bridge is Falling Down*, Little, Brown, 1967, 32 pgs, 1st ed, dj	20.00
Ernest, Edward, *The Animated Circus*	

Book, Julian Wehr, Animateons, Saalfield, 1943 . . . . **35.00**

Farquharson, Martha, *Elsie Dinsmore,* Dodd, Mead, 1896, 342 pgs, 25 yr ed **4.00**

Fitzhugh, Percy Keese, *Tom Slade in the North Woods,* Howard L. Hastings, illus, Grosset & Dunlap, 244 pgs, dj **6.00**

Frees, Harry Whittier, *Circus Day at Catnip Center,* Manning, 1932, wraps . . **12.00**

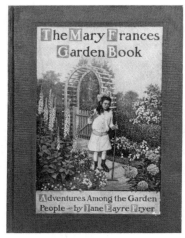

Jane Eayre Fryer, *The Mary Frances Garden Book Adventures Among The Garden People,* illus by Wm. F. Zwirner, John C. Winston Co., publisher, Philadelphia, 1916, 7 x 9½ x 1½", 377 pgs, $50.00.

Garis, Howard R., *Uncle Wiggily's Fortune,* Elmer Rache, illus, Platt & Munic, 1942, 186 pgs **8.00**

Gaspard, Helen, *Doctor Dan the Bandage Man,* Corrine Malver, illus, Simon & Schuster, 1950, Little Golden
With original bandages **15.00**
Without original bandages **5.00**

Graham, Lynda, *Pinky Marie,* Ann Kirn, illus, Saalfield, 1939, wraps **22.00**

Gray, William, *Dick and Jane,* Scott, Foresman, 1930, 40 pgs, wraps **17.00**

Gruelle, Johnny
Beloved Belindy, Johnny Gruelle, 1926 . . . . **60.00**
Wooden Willie Donohue, Volland, 1927 . . . . **50.00**

Haviland, Virginia, *Favorite Fairy Tales Told in Italy,* Evaline Hess, illus, Little, Brown, 1965, 90 pgs, 1st ed, dj **15.00**

Heisenfelt, Kathryn, *Jane Withers and the Swamp Wizard,* Whitman, 1944, 242 pgs, dj **20.00**

Hoban, Russell, *Emmet Otter's Jug–Band Christmas,* Lillian Hoban, illus, Parents Magazine Press, 1971, 41 pgs, 1st ed **10.00**

Hope, Laura Lee
Six Little Bunkers, 1918 . . . . **12.00**
Two Bunny Brown, c1920, dj **8.00**

Jenks, Tudor, *The Century World's Fair Book for Boys and Girls,* Century, 1893, 245 pgs **15.00**

Keene, Carolyn, *The Clue in the Crumbling Wall,* Grosset & Dunlap, 1945, 217 pgs, dj, (Nancy Drew Series) . . . **8.00**

Kenny, Kathryn, *Trixie Belden and the Mystery at the Emerald,* Whitman, 1965, 254 pgs **2.00**

Lenski, Lois, *Coal Camp Girl,* Lippincott, 1959, 173 pgs, 1st ed, dj **25.00**

Lindman, Maj., *Flicka, Ricka, Dicka and the Girl Next Door,* Whitman, 1938, 1st ed, dj **25.00**

Little Boy Blue, Dean's Rag Book, 1905 Ragbook **22.00**

Mack, Nila, *Let's Pretend,* Whitman, 1948, 68 pgs **15.00**

Maybee, Bette Lou, *Barbie's Fashion Success,* Random House, 1962, 188 pgs **10.00**

Mitchell, Lebbeus, *Bobby in Search of a Birthday,* Joseph Pierre Nuyttons, illus, Volland, 1916, 64 pgs, 1st ed . . **30.00**

Montgomery, Frances Trego, *Billy Whiskers Stowaway,* David Jadwyn, illus, Saalfield, 1930, 146 pgs **12.00**

Montgomery, L. M., *Anne of the Island,* Page, 1915, 326 pgs, 1st ed **15.00**

Nelson, Faith, *Randolph the Bear Who Said No,* Nedda Walker, illus, Wonder Book, 1946 . . . . **2.00**

Newman, Isidora, *The Legend of the Tulip and Other Fairy Flowers,* Willy Pogany, illus, Whitman, 1926 . . . . **9.00**

Norton, Mary, *The Borrowers Afield,* Beth and Joe Drush, illus, Harecourt, 1955, 193 pgs, 1st ed, dj **35.00**

O'Day, Dean, *Shirley Temple Story Book,* Corrine and Bill Bailey, illus, Saalfield, 1935, 106 pgs, dj **28.00**

Pansy, (Isabell Alden), *Four Girls at Chautauqua,* D. Lothrop, 1876, 474 pgs **21.00**

Pease, Howard, *The Mystery on Telegraph Hill,* Doubleday, 1961, 216 pgs, 1st ed, dj **12.00**

Perkins, Lucy Fitch, *The French Twins,* Houghton, Mifflin, 1918, 201 pgs, 1st ed **12.00**

Petersham, Maud & Miska, *The Story Book of Trains,* Winston, 1935, dj . . **8.00**

Piper, Watty, *Children of Other Lands,* Lucille W. and H. C. Holling, illus, Platt & Munk, 1933 . . . . **18.00**

Rae, John, *Grasshopper Green and the Meadow Mice*, Algonquin, 1922 ... **18.00**

Richards, Mel, *Peter Rabbit the Magician*, Manufactured for Jewel Tea Co, 1942, spiral in box, contains six magic tricks with wand **35.00**

Rip Van Winkle, McLoughlin, linen ... **30.00**

Schurr, Cathleen, *The Shy Little Kitten*, Gus Tenggren, illus, Simon & Schuster, 1946, #23, 42 pgs, 1st ed, Little Golden **27.00**

Seredy, Kate, *Lazy Tinka*, Viking, 1962, 57 pgs, 1st ed, dj **22.00**

Sidney, Margaret, *The Five Little Peppers at School*, Lothrop, 1903, 453 pgs .. **8.00**

Louis Slobodkin, *Dinny and Danny* $15.00.

Sutton, Margaret, *The Secret of the Barred Window*, Pelagie Doane, illus, Grosset & Dunlap, 1943, 207 pgs, dj, (Judy Bolton) **6.00**

Taylor, Elizabeth, *Nibbles & Me*, Duell, Sloan & Pearce, 1946, 77 pgs, dj .. **20.00**

Thorndyke, Helen Louise, *Honey Bunch: Her First Days on the Farm*, Grosset & Dunlap, 1923, 182 pgs .. **3.00**

Tousey, Sanford, *Airplane Andy*, Doubleday, Doran, 1942, 43 pgs **8.00**

Upham, Elizabeth, *Little Brown Bear and His Friends*, Marjorie Hartwell, illus, Platt & Munk, 1952 .... **14.00**

Vandegriff, Peggy, *Dy–Dee Dolls Days*, Rand McNally, 1937 .... **15.00**

Webster, Frank V., *The Boy Scouts of Flenox*, Cupples & Leon, 1915, 212 pgs **4.00**

Wells, Helen, *Cherry Ames Island Nurse*, Grosset & Dunlap, 1960, 184 pgs, dj **6.00**

West, Jerry, *The Happy Hollisters and the Ice Carnival*, Doubleday, 1958, 180 pgs, dj **3.00**

Wilde, Oscar, *The Happy Prunie and Other Fairy Tales*, Spencer Baird Nichols, illus, Frederick A. Stoker, 1913, 204 pgs, 1st ed **225.00**

Willson, Dixie, *Once Upon A Monday*, Erick Berry, illus, Volland, 1931, 39 pgs **26.00**

Winfield, Arthur M., *The Rover Boys on the River*, Grosset & Dunlap, 1905, 254 pgs **9.00**

Wirt, Mildred, *The Brownie Scouts at Snow Valley*, Cupples & Levin, 1949, 204 pgs, dj **4.00**

Wright, Dare, *Edith & Big Bad Bill*, Random House, 1968, 1st ed **15.00**

CHILDREN'S DISHES

Collecting Hints: Children's dishes were played with, so a bit of wear is to be expected. Avoid rusty metal dishes. Also avoid broken glass dishes.

History: Dishes for children to play with have been popular from Victorian times to the present. Many glass companies made small child–size sets in the same patterns as large table sets. Many young girls delighted in using a set just like mother's.

During the period when Depression glass was popular, the manufacturers also made child–size pieces to complement the full size lines. These child–size dishes were used for tea parties, doll parties, and many other happy occasions.

Child–size dishes are found in aluminum, tin, china, and glass.

References: Doris Anderson Lechler, *Children's Glass Dishes, China and Furniture*, Collector Books, 1983; Doris Anderson Lechler, *Children's Glass Dishes, China, Furniture, Volume II* Collector Books, 1986; Doris Lechler, *English Toy China*, Antique Publications, 1989; Doris Lechler, *Toy Glass*, Antique Publications, 1989; Lorraine May Punchard, *Child's Play*, published by author, 1982; Margaret and Kenn Whitmyer, *Children's Dishes*, Collector Books, 1984.

See: Akro Agate.

Akro Agate, tea set, marbleized orange, 10 pcs, orig box marked "Akro Mill America" **200.00**

Aluminum, tea set, nursery rhyme dec, 15 pcs **22.00**

China

    Cake Plate, Willow Ware, open handles **20.00**

    Casserole, cov, Willow Ware, 4¾" . **25.00**

Akro Agate, tea set, The Little American Maid, No. 3000, topaz, $250.00.

Cereal Bowl
Children with pumpkin 12.00
Rabbit with basket and flowers,
  Salem China 12.00
Cup and Saucer, Willow Ware 10.00
Creamer
Phoenix Bird 20.00
Willow Ware 9.00
Dinner Service, white, floral sprays,
six plates, two cov tureens, serving
plate, ftd compote 90.00
Gravy Boat, Willow Ware 25.00
Plate
American Modern, pink 95.00
Children on rocking horse 10.00
Girl with lamb and flowers 10.00
Luray, pastel 4.00
Willow Ware
  3¼" 6.00
  4½" 8.50
Platter, Willow Ware, 4¼" 14.00
Soup Set, 6 x 3½" tureen, cov, underplate, ladle, six 4½" bowls, blue
acorn dec, Staffordshire marks . . . 130.00
Tea Set
13 pcs, PA Dutch design, West Ger-
  many, MIB 40.00
15 pcs, dressed cats, Germany . . . 165.00
16 pcs, Nippon, rabbits on sleds,
  rising sun mark 150.00
17 pcs
Bavarian, teapot, creamer, sugar,
  six cups and saucers, vivid circus scene, luster trim, marked
  "Bavaria" 125.00
Little Hostess, four cups and sau-
  cers, plates, teapot, creamer
  and sugar, MIB 100.00

23 pcs, Moss Rose, orig box 75.00
Cutlery, 2¼" l, knife, fork, spoon,
wooden handles, marked "Ger-
many," MIB 12.00
Depression Glass
Creamer
Cherry Blossom, delphite 35.00
Doric & Pansy, teal 28.00
Laurel, custard, red trim 32.00
Cup
Cherry Blossom
  Delphite 20.00
  Pink 18.00
Moderntone, pink 6.00
Plate
Cherry Blossom, delphite 10.00
Doric & Pansy
  Pink 5.00
  Teal 10.00
Laurel, custard, red trim 12.00
Moderntone
  Black 8.00
  Pink 7.00
Saucer
Cherry Blossom, delphite 12.00
Laurel, Scotty Dog decal 12.50
Moderntone
  Black 3.50
  Pink 3.00
Sugar
Cherry Blossom, delphite 35.00
Doric & Pansy, pink 21.50
Laurel, decorated rim 30.00
Tea Set, 14 pcs
Cherry Blossom, pink 220.00
Doric & Pansy, pink, MIB 200.00
Moderntone, pastels, MIB 80.00
Graniteware
Bowl, blue and white swirls 40.00
Coffeepot, white 60.00
Cup and Saucer, blue 30.00
Pie Plate, 5" d, gray 8.50
Plate, 2½", green and white swirls . . 8.50
Teacup and Saucer, white, gold bor-
der, green leaf dec, marked "Eng-
land" 18.00
Pattern Glass
Berry Bowl
Flute 7.50
Lacy Daisy, mint green 18.00
Butter Dish
Liberty Bell 150.00
Wild Rose, milk glass 60.00
Cake Stand, Hawaiian Lei 35.00
Candlesticks, pr, Star, Cambridge
Glass, light blue 25.00
Creamer
Cloud Band, milk glass 48.00
Drum 40.00
Lamb 65.00
Pert 55.00
Goblet, Vine, cobalt blue 60.00

Pitcher, Oval Star, Northwood, gold trim	40.00
Plate, Wee Branches	48.00
Punch Bowl, Whirligig	28.00
Punch Cup, Wild Rose, milk glass	20.00
Sauce, Flute	6.50
Spooner	
Horizontal Threads	18.00
Menagerie, amber, fish	100.00
Wild Rose, milk glass	16.00
Sugar, cov	
Balder, green	115.00
Sawtooth	22.00
Table Set, butter dish, creamer, and sugar	
Colonial, Cambridge	100.00
Flattened Diamond, milk glass	95.00
Hobnail with Thumbprint Base	275.00
Tumbler	
Hobnail, 2" h, milk glass	18.00
Patee Cross	10.00
Tin	
Cup, saucer, plate, and tray, Little Red Riding Hood	24.00
Dinner Set, white rabbit dec, light blue ground, 18 pcs	30.00
Play Set, cooking utensils, pots, pans, teapot, wooden knobs, 12 pcs, MIB	18.00
Tea Set	
8 pcs, Ohio Art, Snow White, orig box	125.00
11 pcs, elephants	35.00
25 pcs, Raggedy Ann and Andy	25.00
Yellow Ware, mixing bowl, 4½" d, pink and blue bands	12.00

CHRISTMAS ITEMS

Collecting Hints: Beware of reproduction ornaments. New reproductions are usually brighter in color and have shiny paint. Older ornaments should show some signs of handling. It is common to find tops replaced on ornaments.

History: Early Christmas decorations and ornaments were handmade. In 1865 the Pennsylvania Dutch brought the first glass ornaments to America. By 1870, glass ornaments were being sold in major cities. By the turn of the century, the demand created a cottage industry in European countries. Several towns in Germany and Czechoslovakia produced lovely ornaments, which were imported by F. W. Woolworth, Sears, etc., who found a ready market.

References: Robert Brenner, *Christmas Past,* Shiffer Publishing, Inc., 1986; Maggie Rogers and Peter Hallinan, *The Santa Claus Picture Book,* E. P. Dutton, Inc., 1984; Maggie Rogers and Judith Hawkins, *The Glass Christmas Ornament, Old &*
New, Timber Press, 1977; Nancy Schiffer, *Christmas Ornaments: A Festive Study,* Schiffer Publishing, Ltd, 1984.

Periodicals: *Golden Glow of Christmas Past,* P.O. Box 14808, Chicago, IL 60614; *Hearts of Holly, The Holiday Collectors Newsletter,* P.O. Box 105, Amherst, NH 03031; *Ornament Collector,* R.R. #1, Canton, Il 61520.

Museums: Many museums prepare special Christmas exhibits.

Additional Listings: Santa Claus.

REPRODUCTION ALERT

CHRISTMAS VILLAGE/GARDEN

Animals	
Set of 6, Auburn Rubber Co	25.00
Chicken, 1½" h, composition, metal feet	6.50
Cow	
3½" h, celluloid	10.00
4" h, composition, wooden legs, Germany	25.00
Duck, celluloid, metal legs	10.00
Goat, 3" h, celluloid	8.00
Horse, 4", composition, wooden legs, Germany	38.00
Lamb, 1½" h, standing in grass, plaster, Germany	5.00
Ram, 3½", celluloid	7.50
Sheep, 5", composition, wool covering, wooden legs, paper collar with bell, Germany	55.00
Stork, celluloid body and legs	10.00
Fence	
Clothespin and wood, homemade	40.00
Wire, green, four interlocking sections	45.00
Wooden, green and red, folding, 3"	30.00
Houses	
Cardboard house, cellophane windows, bisque Santa on porch, 4", Japan	10.00
Church, 3½ x 6¼ x 10" h, cardboard, grainy texture, white, red cellophane windows, gold trim	56.00
Church, musical, carolers, brush trees, Japan	50.00
Paper village, "Peaceful Valley Farm Set," Pan Confection Factory, Chicago, 1923	48.00
House, cardboard, Japan	8.00
Wood, 18" sq, 4" h, red and green, gate	105.00
Wood, 24 x 39 x 5½" h, white pickets, green trim, gate	225.00
Wood train station, 12", tan and black, homemade	32.00
People	
Couple, park bench, Barclay	20.00

Skater, Barclay **10.00**
Sled rider, Barclay **15.00**

Puzzle, Dissected A.B.C., J. Ottmann Litho Co, red, yellow, and white puzzle pcs, c1910, 11½ x 10", $35.00.

NON TREE–RELATED ITEMS

Advertising Trade Card
"Old Lion Coffee Trade Card," child and Christmas wreath around shoulders **7.00**
"The White–King of all sewing machines," child in winter outfit holding snowball, c1889 .... **8.00**
Bank, chalkware, Santa climbing down chimney **55.00**
Book
Christmas Book, Christmas Cut Out Series, Charles Graham and Co .. **10.00**
Christmas Greetings, Holiday Publishing Co, 1906 .... **6.50**
Miracle on 34th St, Valentine Davies, Harcourt, Brace and Co, 1947 ... **10.00**
Night Before Christmas or A Visit from St Nicholas McLaughlin Bros, 1896 ...... **20.00**
Book, *The Christmas Surprise*, Grosset & Dunlap, six pop–up scenes, ten stories, 1950 .... **25.00**
Button
⅞", "Health to All," National Tuberculosis Assoc, Santa, Association symbol on his hat **7.00**
1¼", "Shop in Pottsville," Santa, white ground **15.00**
1⅜", "Santa's Guest, North Pole, N.Y.," Santa, house, and reindeer, green ground **3.00**
Candleholder, figural, Santa **10.00**
Candy Box, cardboard, string handle, fireplace and stocking scene, 3 x 5", c1940–50 .... **5.00**

Candy Canes, chenille, 5 to 8" h, set of 5 .... **12.00**
Candy Container
Santa
On skis, 4¼" **18.00**
Wearing black stove pipe hat, papier mache **65.00**
Snowman, 7½", papier mache, red hat **12.00**
Church, wind–up, musical, mica cov wood, plays "Silent Night," 1930 .. **25.00**
Figure
Choir Boy, 3½" h, hard plastic **4.50**
Reindeer
2" h, art glass, silvered, pink antlers, lying down **32.00**
3" h, celluloid, brown **7.50**
4", hard plastic **4.00**
Santa Claus riding on skis, bag of toys **15.00**
Snowman, 8" h, hard plastic, electric light insert **7.00**
Greeting Cards
"At Christmas time may Peace o'er shadow you," sgd Prang, flowers, white fringe **15.00**
Children and dog playing in the snow, Tuck, Raphael, 4 x 2" **6.00**
"Merry Christmas and a Happy New Year," children playing in a toy room **5.00**
"Same Old Line, Merry Christmas," four stockings hanging on a string across card, 1926 .... **5.00**
"The Compliments of the Season," young couple talking over fence, paper lace trim **7.50**
"Wishing you a Happy Christmas," child with sled and a doll, sgd Prang **12.00**
Jewelry, pin, 2", Christmas tree, multicolor rhinestones, Eisenberg ... **65.00**
Lamp, glass, metal, holder in base, wire handle
Four sided **25.00**
Six sided, collapsible **25.00**
Lantern, Snowman, glass, metal handle and base, 1950 .... **25.00**
Matchbook, 3¼ x 4¼", adv, matches have Christmas dec **15.00**
Nativity Scene, cardboard
Boxed set, Dennison **10.00**
Fold out, standing emb, marked Germany, 4½ x 5½" **12.00**
Postcards
"A Merry Christmas," toy soldiers, cannons **3.00**
"Christmas Wishes," Children in sled pulled by two rabbits, Germany .. **4.00**
Reflectors
Foil, bright colors, set of 6 .... **3.00**
Metal, jeweled, set of 6 .... **3.00**
Sleigh, Hubley, 19C **125.00**

Serving Tray, Coca–Cola, Santa, 1972   35.00
Stereograph Card, Keystone View Co,
   children, Santa peeping at each other
   thru keyhole, 1899 ....   10.00
Stocking
   Red flannel, stenciled Santa and
    sleigh 5.00
   White flannel, red toe, bell trimmed
    top 7.00
Toy, wind–up, reindeer, metal, rubber
   antlers, orig box, Japan 30.00
Wreath
   10" d, chenille, candle 15.00
   10½" d, red chenille, red and silver
    foil poinsettia at bottom 18.00

**Ornament, violin, blue, silver, and white,
4¾" l, $25.00.**

TREE–RELATED ITEMS

Icicles, clear plastic, tree hooks, on orig
   card, set of 6 ....   2.00
Light Bulbs
   Bubble, Noma 3.00
   Figural, Milk Glass
    Aviator, shrimp color, 2½" 20.00
    Baby, red stockings 20.00
    Birdcage 15.00
    Clown, red and yellow 20.00
    Clown, red on white ball 25.00
    Dick Tracy 40.00
    Dog, Sandy 40.00
    Dog, yellow, polo player 20.00
Light Sets, Strings
   Noma bubble lights, box, 1950s ...   19.00
   Noma, eight different figural bulbs,
    box 100.00

Ornaments
   Beaded, double cross, Czechoslova-
    kia 15.00
   Cardboard, two sided, twelve letters
    of Alphabet, Germany, orig pkg ..   10.00
   Chromolithograph, tinsel
    Bell, red and green 10.00
    Little girl sleeping 15.00
    Young couple, arms linked 20.00
   Glass
    Pine Cone, 3½" 12.00
    Santa, hp, Polish, orig box, set of 6   18.00
    Zeppelin, US flag, spun glass tail,
     1920s 85.00
   Reindeer, 3", cast metal, German,
    1930s 25.00
   Tree, 16", white, bottle brush, tiny
    ball trimmings, tin wind–up base,
    plays White Christmas 35.00
Tree
   Brush
    1½", green, red base 1.25
    3", green, red base 3.00
    5"
     Green, decorated, red base 10.00
     Green, red base 5.00
     Red, decorated, red base 10.00
    9", green, red base 12.50
   Feather Tree
    9", white, sparse, sq base 85.00
    12", green, candle clips, round
     base 100.00
Tree Stand, cast iron, three legs, black,
   bolted to hinged wood box 30.00
Tree Topper
   Angel, 4" h, hard plastic, white and
    silver 4.50
   Star
    Krystal, lighted, orig box 6.00
    Noma, metal, five candle bulbs ..   24.00
Tree Trim, foil rope, 72" l, red, silver,
   and green 5.00
Tree with lights, brush, metal base, bat-
   tery operated 15.00

CIGAR COLLECTIBLES

Collecting Hints: Concentrate on one geographical region or company. Cigar box labels usually
are found in large concentrations. Check on
availability before paying high prices.

History: Tobacco was one of the first export
products of the American colonies. By 1750
smoking began to become socially acceptable
for males. The cigar reached its zenith from 1880
to 1930 when it was the boardroom and after
dinner symbol for the withdrawal of males to
privacy and conversation.

   Cigar companies were quick to recognize national political, sports and popular heroes. They

encouraged them to use cigars and placed their faces on promotional material.

The lithograph printing press brought color and popularity to labels, seals and bands. Many have memories of a cigar band ring given by a grandfather or family friend. The popularity of the cigarette in the 1940s reduced the cigar to second place in the tobacco field. Today, cigar related material is minimal due to the smaller number of companies making cigars.

Reference: Tony Hyman, *Handbook of American Cigar Boxes,* Arnet Art Museum, 1979.

Collectors' Club: International Seal, Label and Cigar Band Society, 8915 E. Bellevue Street, Tucson, AZ 85715.

Museum: Arnet Collection, New York Public Library, New York, NY.

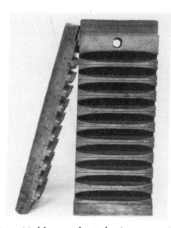

Cigar Mold, wood, maker's name, ten mold, 11¾ x 4½ x 2½", $25.00.

Advertising
Hatchet, Tom Moore Cigar	**28.00**
Trade Card, Dude Cigars, Simmons & Co, 1882	**20.00**

Box
Campaign De Luxe, 9 x 9½ x 2½", stiff cardboard, photos of FDR and Wilkie, inscribed "1940 Campaign De Luxe/All Tobacco—No Paper Binder/Roosevelt or Wilkie for President/Hand Made"	**75.00**
Harvester 5¢ Cigar, horse and coins label int.	**35.00**
Horseshoe Curve, train dec on top, label int.	**35.00**
Swanr & Co, Tampa, two drawers	**65.00**
Change Receiver, Don Digo Cigars, glass	**32.00**

Cutter
Indian on motorcycle	**90.00**
Trick Lock Cigar Cutter, 1930s	**20.00**
Cutter and Matchbox Cover Combination, 1 x 1½" metal spring cutter, hanging loop, 1903 pat date, 1½ x 1⅛ x 1¾" aluminum matchbox cov, emb "Floral Leaves Breath Perfume/Compressed Violets Recherche"	**40.00**
Dish, 5¼", cigar band	**8.00**
Holder and Case, Meerschaum, dog dec	**50.00**
Humidor, Colt	**150.00**
Key Chain, Muriel Cigars	**10.00**

Label
Las Vegas Cigars, cigar crate	**5.00**
Spirit of St Louis, cigar box, semi—glossy paper, American Lithographic Co, 1927	**15.00**
Lighter, brass, counter model	**65.00**

Matchbook Holder, adv
Muriel Cigars, blued metal, 1⅛ x 1⅝" multicolored celluloid insert, trademark "Muriel" portrait, hinged, snap closure, c1920	**65.00**
San Felice, 1½ x 2¼", blued metal, 1½" oval multicolored celluloid insert, inscribed "For Gentlemen of Good Taste," man in wicker chair reading newspaper and smoking cigar, lady's face in puff of smoke, hinged, c1920	**70.00**
Match Safe, Union—Made Cigars, 1½ x 2¾", silvered brass, celluloid cov, light blue Union Cigar label facsimile, black on white ground, issued by Cigar Makers Union #97, Boston, early 1900s	**85.00**
Mirror, pocket, 2⅛", Union Made Cigars, celluloid, light blue Union Cigar label facsimile, tan, black lettering, early 1900s	**60.00**
Mold, 20 cigars, wood, Miller, Dubrul & Peters	**32.00**

Note Pad, adv, 2½ x 4½", celluloid cov, hinged
Civil Rights Havana Cigars, signing of Magna Carter illus, pencil holder and string, 1890s	**20.00**
Francie Wilson Havana Cigars, black and white portrait, cigar text inside cov, early 1900s	**15.00**
Piercer, 3" l, silvered brass, black and white celluloid wrapper band inscribed "Winchester County Bar Association/Annual Dinner 1915," plunger	**35.00**
Pin, enameled, Tampa—Cuba Cigar Co	**45.00**
Sign, 9 x 11", Cyclone Twister/Five Cents/Cigar/Five Cents, stiff cardboard, 1928 copyright	**40.00**
Tin, Muriel 5¢ Cigar	**17.50**
Trimmer, pelican, figural	**40.00**

Watch Fob, 1¾", United Cigar Makers League, blue and white, metal strap loop, early 1900s **65.00**

CIGARETTE ITEMS

Collecting Hints: Don't overlook the advertising which appeared in the national magazines of the 1940s to 1960s. The number of star and public heroes endorsing cigarettes is large. Modern promotional material for brands such as Marlboro and Salem has been issued in large numbers, and much has been put aside by collectors. Most collectors tend to concentrate on the pre–1950 period.

History: Although the cigarette industry dates back to the late 19th century, it was the decades of the 1930s and 1940s that saw cigarettes become the dominant tobacco product. The cigarette industry launched massive advertising and promotional campaigns. Radio was one of the principal advertising vehicles. In the 1950s, television became the dominant advertising medium.

The Surgeon General's Report, which warned of the danger of cigarette smoking, led to restrictions on advertising and limited the places where cigarettes could be smoked. The industry reacted with a new advertising approach aimed at females and people in the 20 to 40 year age bracket. The need to continue the strong positive public image for cigarette smoking still leads to more and more cigarette related items entering the collectibles marketplace.

Reference: Murray Cards International, Ltd., *Cigarette Card Values: Murray's 1990 Guide To Cigarette & Other Trade Cards*, 1990.

Collectors' Clubs: Cigarette Pack Collectors Association, 61 Searle Street, Georgetown, MA 01833; International Seal, Label & Cigar Band Society, 8915 East Bellevue St, Tuscon, AZ 85715.

Ashtray, Griswold **38.00**
Box, lead glass, hinged lid **35.00**
Case
  Chrome, Indian chief profile **15.00**
  Copper, golf clubs finial, Chase **35.00**
  Lady's, black, white, and ivory, 1940 **45.00**
  Sterling silver, maroon bakelite, sgd "Dandy" **65.00**
Case and Lighter Combination
  Elgin, silver, gold deer, Magic Action Lite–O–Matic, orig box **40.00**
  Mother–of–pearl, rhinestone butterflies on lid **50.00**
Cigarette Carton, Chesterfield, Christmas, multicolored litho, service men,

Santa, happy crowd at train station going home for holidays, mint **10.00**
Holder
  Bone
    14K gold trim **28.00**
    Trumpet shape, gold bowl **38.00**
  Gutta percha, gold band **28.00**
Lighter
  Advertising
    Capital Brand, bottle shape, dated 1912 .... **90.00**
    Chesterfield **15.00**
    Hamms Beer **30.00**
    Hastings Piston Ring, 3" l, metal tube, removable black cap, red, yellow, and black trademark figure, yellow ground, 1940s **15.00**
    Road America, 1956 .... **6.00**
    Royal Crown Cola, brass, bottle shape **10.00**
    Skelly Oil, 3" l, brass, tube, removable red cap, red logo and inscription on white ground, c1940 **18.00**
  Figural
    Airplane, chrome **80.00**
    Elephant, Ronson, non–mechanical, striker **95.00**
    Horse, 5", enameled, comic **65.00**
    Ronson, pencil lighter **75.00**
    Zipp, mechanical, floating fishing lure **25.00**
Matchbox
  Hunting scene, silver plated **35.00**
  Lithophane **175.00**
Matchbox Cover, sterling **9.00**
Matchsafe
  Advertising
    Admiral Dewey, head on side **84.00**
    Red Top Dye, gutta percha, 2 pc . **75.00**
  Book, figural, stamps on side, matches on other **75.00**
  Dragon, ½ x 1½ x 3" h, brass, figural, hinged head, c1890 .... **135.00**
  Fighting Lion and Snake, silvered metal, raised depiction of each side, marked "Silveroin," early 1900s **75.00**
Poster, L & M, Gunsmoke testimonial . **65.00**
Radio, Benson & Hedges, battery, MIB **20.00**
Record, L & M Cigarettes, Christmas, Liggett & Meyers Tobacco Co giveaways, shows L & M TV quartet in Santa suits, orig carton holder **10.00**
Tamper, brass, two sided, lady holding flagon and glass **25.00**
Thermometer
  Camel **45.00**
  L & M **45.00**
Tin
  Bond Street, pocket **16.00**
  Bugler, pocket **14.00**
  Camel 100's, round **45.00**

Tin, Lucky Strike, American Tobacco Co, green ground, $10.00.

Camel 50's, flat	32.00
Edgeworth Sample	35.00
Edgeworth Tobacco, curved side, knob lid	25.00
Globe, sample	425.00
Lucky Strike 100's, round	44.00
Mi–Dia Tobacco	52.00
Old Colony Tobacco, cylindrical, ashtray top	48.00
Old Squire VP Tobacco	95.00
Phillip Morris 50's, round	38.00
Queen Pocket Tobacco	75.00
Short Bowl of Roses	125.00
Sterling Tobacco	60.00
Tom Keene Tobacco	60.00
Twin Oaks, pocket	62.00
US Marines, pocket tobacco	125.00
Tobacco Cutter, Reynold's, Brown Mule	50.00

CLICKERS

Collecting Hints: Clickers with pictures are more desirable than clickers with just printing. Value is reduced by scratches in the paint and rust. Some companies issued several variations of a single design—be alert for them in your collecting.

History: Clickers were a popular advertising medium for products and services including plumbing supplies, political aspirants, soft drinks, hotels, beer and whiskey. The most commonly found clickers are those which were given to children in shoe stores. Brands include Buster Brown, Poll Parrot, and Red Goose. Many shoe store clickers have advertising whistle mates.

Clickers were not confined to advertising. They were a popular holiday item, especially at Halloween. Impressed animal forms also provided a style for clickers.

The vast majority of clickers were made of tin. The older and rarer clickers were made of celluloid.

Frog, marked "Life Of The Party Products," Kirchhof, Newark, NJ, 3" l, $7.50.

ADVERTISING

Chesterfield Filters, tin, red, white, and black	10.00
Crackin' Good Cookies and Crackers	6.00
Ellis Beef Stew	10.00
Hasting's Bread, celluloid	8.00
Humpty Dumpty Shoes, tin, litho, full color illus, c1930	30.00
New and True Coffee	5.00
Peters Weatherbird Shoes, ¾ x 1¾", tin, litho, multicolor, 1930s	25.00
Phoenix Socks, tin, litho, red, white, and blue	8.00
Quaker State Motor Oil, tin, litho, green design, white background, 1930s	15.00
Real Kill, white, orange, and black, "Mamma Get...Real Kill"	10.00
Red Goose Shoes, ¾ x 1¾", tin, litho, red goose, yellow lettering and ground, 1930s	22.50
Smith's Ice Cream	20.00
Twinkle Shoes, green, black print	10.00

NON–ADVERTISING

Black Man, litho, 1930s, marked "Germany"	12.00
Bug Snapper, round, ladybug, green ground, 1946	7.00
Christmas, tin, litho, Santa and fireplace scene	25.00
Felix, 1¾", metal, black and white, brown ground, "Do You Really Mean All You Say Felix?" slogan	50.00
Halloween, tin, orange, black, and white, 1930s	12.00
Mickey Mouse, tin, litho, playing banjo, green background, 1930s	40.00
Nixon, "Click with Dick," tin	25.00
Rooster Weathervane, tin, litho	5.00
SG, Mysto–Snapper, tin, litho, red, white, and blue	50.00

Soldier, tin, litho, movable arms, 1930s,
    marked "Made in Germany" **50.00**

CLOCKS

Collecting Hints: Many clocks of the twentieth
century were reproductions of earlier styles.
Therefore, dating should be checked by patent
dates on the mechanism, maker's label, and construction techniques.

The principal buyers for the advertising and
figural clocks are not the clock collectors, but
the specialist with whose area of interest the
clock overlaps. For example, the Pluto alarm
clock is of far greater importance to a Disneyana
collector than to most clock collectors.

Condition is critical. Rust and non–working
condition detract heavily from the price.

History: The clock always has served a dual
function: decorative and utilitarian. Beginning in
the late 19th century the clock became an important advertising vehicle, a tradition still continuing today. As character and personality became part of the American scene, the clock was
a logical target, whether an alarm or wall model.
The novelty clock, especially figural, was common in the 1930 to 1960 period.

In the 1970s the popularity of digital wrist
watches and clocks led to less emphasis on the
clock as a promotional item.

References: Howard S. Brenner, *Identification
and Value Guide To Collecting Comic Character
Clocks and Watches,* Books Americana, 1987;
Alan and Rita Shenton, *The Price Guide To Col-
lectible Clocks, 1840–1940,* Antique Collectors'
Club.

Collectors' Club: National Association of Watch
and Clock Collectors, Inc., P.O. Box 33, Columbia, PA 17512.

Museum: Museum of National Association of
Watch and Clock Collectors, Columbia, PA.

Additional Listings: See *Warman's Antiques and
Their Prices.*

Advertising
    Blatz Barrel Drummer, electric **50.00**
    Double Cola **25.00**
    Four Roses Whiskey, emb numbers,
        c1940 .... **65.00**
    Hollow Tile Fire Proofing, Henry
        Maurer & Son, nickel case, sgd
        dial, German, 1940 .... **35.00**
    Monarch Foods, lion **45.00**
    Pennzoil **30.00**
    Proctor & Gamble, Electric Time,
        c1920 .... **90.00**
    Purina Poultry Chow, alarm, metal
        case, red, white, and blue illus on
        dial, 1930s **55.00**

Royal Crown Cola **65.00**
Warren Telephone Co, Ashland, MA,
    oak case **80.00**
Wise Potato Chips, owl shape, elec-
    tric **75.00**
Alarm, spinning wheel, Lux **50.00**
Apollo XI, animated, ivory case, red,
    white, and blue diecut, gold numer-
    als, marked "Lux Clock Mfg Co" ... **115.00**
Character
    Beatles, alarm, plastic, silver, silver
        with black illus, silver metal bells
        and feet, orig box, copyright 1988
        Apple Corps Ltd **50.00**
    Donald Duck, electric, Phinney–
        Walker, Germany **22.00**
    ET, head raised, finger & chest light
        up when alarm sounds, battery op-
        erated **120.00**
    Hamm Bear, wristwatch shape **40.00**
    Lester Maddox, alarm, plastic, red,
        white, and blue, Maddox riding bi-
        cycle seated backwards, "Wake Up
        America" on dial, black "Best
        Wishes To Betty From Lester Mad-
        dox" autograph, c1970 .... **110.00**
    Mickey Mouse, alarm, head moves to
        tick off seconds, orig box, Bayard,
        late 1960s **200.00**
    Peter Max, 9" d, cardboard, day–glo
        hands, abstract lines, circles, and
        shapes design, white painted metal
        box on back, copyright Peter Max,
        marked "General Electric," late
        1960s **75.00**
    Popeye and Swee'Pea, alarm, ivory
        enameled steel case, color illus on
        dial, Smiths, c1968 .... **100.00**
    Roy Rogers, Ingraham **100.00**
    Sesame Street, Cookie Monster, radio **15.00**

**Refrigerator, white metal, GE label, War-
ren Telechron Co, Ashland, MA, electric,
8½" h, $185.00.**

Snow White, alarm, Bayard/Blanche
Niege, Made in France **75.00**
Trix the Rabbit, alarm, c1960 . . . . . .   **18.00**
Wee Tiny Tim, Westclox, 1927 . . . .   **20.00**
Figural
Car, brass, Waltham **45.00**
Pentagon, table, celluloid, New Ha-
ven **18.00**
Ship, walnut hull, chrome plated sails
and riggings, lighted portholes,
United Clock Co, 1955 . . . .   **90.00**
Kitchen
Pottery, bluebirds on sides, ivory bor-
der **50.00**
Tin, Dutch children on face, electric   **24.00**
Mantel
Chelsea, fruitwood case, c1910 . . . .   **80.00**
Ship's wheel, wood and chrome,
electric, Sessions **65.00**
Wall
Felix the Cat, red, tail moves **25.00**
Spiro Agnew, 9" d, red, white, and
blue dial, battery operated, c1972   **30.00**

CLOTHING AND CLOTHING ACCESSORIES

Collecting Hints: Vintage clothing should be clean and in good repair. Designer labels and original boxes can add to the value.

Collecting vintage clothing appears to have reached a plateau. Although there are still dedicated collectors, the category is no longer attracting a rash of new collectors annually.

History: Clothing is collected and studied as a reference source in learning about fashion, construction and types of materials used.

References: Maryanne Dolan, *Vintage Clothing, 1880–1960, Second Edition*, Books Americana, 1988; Evelyn Haertig, *Antique Combs & Purses*, Gallery Press, 1983; Richard Holiner, *Antique Purses, Second Edition*, Collector Books, 1987; Tina Irick–Nauer, *The First Price Guide to Antique and Vintage Clothes*, E. P. Dutton, 1983; Sheila Malouff, *Collectible Clothing With Prices*, Wallace Homestead, 1983; Terry McCormick, *The Consumer's Guide To Vintage Clothing*, Dembner Books, 1987; Diane McGee, *A Passion For Fashion*, Simmons–Boardman Books, Inc, 1987.

Periodical: *Vintage Clothing Newsletter*, P.O. Box 1422, Corvallis, OR 97339.

Collectors' Club: The Costume Society of America, P. O. Box 761, Englishtown, NJ 07726.

Museums: Metropolitan Museum of Art, New York, NY; Costume and Textile Department of the Los Angeles County Museum of Art, Los Angeles, CA; Philadelphia Museum of Art, Philadelphia, PA.

Nightgown, cotton, white, c1870, $40.00.

CLOTHING

Bed Jacket, taffeta, watered, aquamar-
ine, bands of Valenciennes lace **125.00**
Blouse
Cotton, white, c1940 . . . .   **12.00**
Silk, beige, print, high neck, leg of
mutton sleeves **35.00**
Bush Jacket, cotton, white, bellow
pockets, full belt, unused, 1940s . . .   **15.00**
Camisole
Cotton, white, crocheted yoke **40.00**
Silk, pink, lace trim **24.00**
Cape
Beaded, black lace, Victorian **150.00**
Fur, blue fox **65.00**
Opera, blue, 1920s **95.00**
Wool, pearl gray, triangular shape,
tassel hung hood, narrow steel gray
braid trim, c1910 . . . .   **55.00**
Coat
Evening, silk and velvet, ermine trim   **125.00**
Fur
Mink, full length **200.00**
Raccoon, full length, c1930 . . . . .   **125.00**
Opera, full length, black, rabbit trim   **125.00**
Dress
Baby, cotton, tucked, eyelet trimmed
yoke, sleeves, skirt, 3½" open
work, scalloped hem, 38" l **20.00**
Child's, satin, black, white lace trim,
early 1900s, size 10–12 . . . .   **24.00**
Day
Cotton, polished, black, miniature
dots, ruffled bodice, leg of mut-
ton sleeves **95.00**

Lawn, white with print edge, Cluny lace bodice, net and ruffled sleeves **75.00**
Linen, white, lace trim, c1912 ... **85.00**
Work, cotton, gray, white stripe, high waist, buttons down front, long sleeves, black and white scallop trim, shell buttons **35.00**
Evening Gown
Chiffon, aquamarine over green, narrow silver braid trim, c1910 ..... **75.00**
Crepe, black, beaded, c1920 ...... **80.00**
Dotted Swiss, white, matching voile jacket, white and red chiffon flower center **125.00**
Moire, purple scoop neck, gathered front, full hip ruffle, c1940 ...... **85.00**
Organdy, peach, c1930 .... **45.00**
Satin, gold, beaded **150.00**
Velvet, dark brown, draped, weighted neckline, short sleeves **85.00**
Voile, salmon and white flowers, Hawaiian style, V neck, ¾ length sleeves, five foot train with ruffle . **60.00**
Jacket
Brocade front, pleated, brown, large mother–of–pearl buckle **50.00**
Crochet, lace, white, Irish, puffed sleeves **225.00**
Sequins, net, gold, long sleeves, c1935 .... **275.00**
Velvet, black, crushed, white silk lining, c1920 .... **50.00**
Knickers, wool, black **40.00**
Mourning Outfit, black, 5 pcs **200.00**
Nightgown, cotton, white, leg of mutton sleeves, high collar, handmade eyelet lace trim **285.00**
Petticoat
Bustle back, lace trimmed ruffles, size 8–10 .... **50.00**
Muslin, white, deep laced edge flounce, 24" waist **18.00**
Shirt, moleskin, German Army NATO . **12.00**
Skirt and top, homespun, black lace bodice and cuffs, high neck **125.00**
Slip, cotton
Full, crocheted, tucked **35.00**
Half, string waist, lace bottom **35.00**
Swimsuit, wool, orig tags and box, Jantzen, dated 1931 .... **65.00**

CLOTHING ACCESSORIES

Apron
Cotton, dainty **5.00**
Silk, white, lace dec, embroidered "Souvenir of France" **15.00**
Belt, 1" w, jet beads **40.00**
Bonnet, silk, hand crocheted lace, handmade **35.00**

Handbag, lucite, marked "Florida Handbags," $30.00.

Collar
Lace, MIB **45.00**
Satin, black, five panel, 1" jet beads **65.00**
Cuffs, pr, crochet, white **8.00**
Eyeglass case, mesh, silver **20.00**
Gloves, pr
Cotton **4.00**
Leather **5.00**
Handkerchief, lace trim, point de gaze, oak leaves, floral motif **40.00**
Hat
Cloche, flapper type, brown velvet . **15.00**
Derby, black **18.00**
Head Band, flapper's, rhinestones **25.00**
Muff, black **25.00**
Necktie, silk, Sak's Fifth Ave **20.00**
Parasol, satin, peach, crystal tip, wooden handles **75.00**
Purse
Crocheted, Victorian **40.00**
Enameled
Art Deco, 6½ x 3½", black and blue, Whiting Davis **95.00**
Mesh, Whiting Davis **50.00**
Leather, hand tooled, suede lined, 1920s **25.00**
Marcasite, framed **35.00**
Mesh
Aqua/gold **58.00**
Silver frame, blue mesh lining, blue metal inlay, silver chain, 4 x 5" **60.00**
Velvet, black, drawstring, beading, horsehair, chenille tassel on bottom **185.00**
Scarf, silk, hand embroidered **45.00**
Shawl
Lace, black, flowers, scalloped hem, 112" w, 54" l, Victorian **36.00**
Silk, paisley, 72" sq, knotted fringe . **65.00**
Shoes
Baby, leather, high top, 1930s **20.00**
Spike heel, 1950s **9.00**
Spats, pr **18.00**
Stockings, silk, rhinestone design at ankle, WWII **24.00**

Walking Stick
  Bisque head, figural **30.00**
  Snakeskin covered, brown **145.00**

COCA—COLA ITEMS

Collecting Hints: Most Coca—Cola items were produced in large quantity; the company was a leader in sales and promotional materials. Don't ignore the large amount of Coca—Cola material in languages other than English. Remember, "Coke" has a world—wide market.

History: The originator of Coca—Cola was John Pemberton, a pharmacist from Atlanta, Georgia. In 1886, Dr. Pemberton introduced a patent medicine to relieve headaches, stomach disorders, and other minor maladies. Unfortunately, his failing health and meager finances forced him to sell his interest.

In 1888, Asa G. Candler became the sole owner of Coca—Cola. Candler improved the formula, increased the advertising budget, and widened the distribution. Accidentally, a patient was given a dose of the syrup mixed with carbonated water instead of the usual still water. The result was a tastier, more refreshing drink.

As sales increased in the 1890s, Candler recognized that the product was more suitable for the soft drink market and began advertising it as such. From these beginnings a myriad of advertising items have been issued to invite all to "Drink Coca— Cola."

Dates of interest: "Coke" was first used in advertising in 1941. The distinctive shaped bottle was registered as a trademark on April 12, 1960.

References: Shelly and Helen Goldstein, *Coca—Cola Collectibles*, (four volumes, plus index), published by authors, 1970s; Deborah Goldstein Hill, Wallace—Homestead *Price Guide To Coca—Cola Collectibles*, Wallace—Homestead, 1984, 1991 value update; Allan Petretti, *Petretti's Coca—Cola Collectibles Price Guide, 5th Edition* Nostalgia Publications, Inc., 1991; Al Wilson, *Collectors Guide to Coca—Cola Items, Volume I*, Revised L—W Book Sales, 1985; Al Wilson, *Collectors Guide To Coca—Cola Items, Volume II*, L—W Book Sales, 1987.

Collectors' Clubs: The Coca—Cola Collectors Club International, P.O. Box 546, Holmdel, NJ 07733; The Cola Clan, 2084 Continental Drive, N. E., Atlanta, GA 30345.

Museum: Schmidt's Coca—Cola Museum, Elizabethtown, KY.

REPRODUCTION ALERT, especially in the area of Coca—Cola trays.

Ashtray, metal, red, 1961 . . . . **3.00**
Bank, tin, vending machine **100.00**
Banner, 18 x 54", 1941, mint **175.00**

Blotter, Season's Greetings, Haddon Sunblom, artist, 12½ x 10½", $5.00.

Baseball Bat, wood, "Knoxall," "Drink
  Coca—Cola in Bottles," 1930s **225.00**
Beach Chair, child's, aluminum frame,
  cloth cover **85.00**
Billhead
  1905, 3¾ x 8½", logo and Coke bottle, Waycross, GA **48.00**
  1923, 8½ x 7", logo, Augusta, GA . **30.00**
Blotter, with paper label bottle, 1913 . **39.00**
Bottle, perfume, 1930s **35.00**
Bottle Holder, 1950s **8.00**
Bottle Opener, brass, 1910 . . . . **40.00**
Brochure, Pause For Living, 1957 . . . . **5.00**
Calendar
  1942, framed glass, pull down pad . **225.00**
  1959, birds **12.00**
  1985 . . . . **7.00**
Carrier, ballpark vendor, holds twenty
  bottles **135.00**
Clock
  Fishtail, lighted **135.00**
  Schoolhouse, wood, 1970s, MIB . . . **275.00**
Cuff Links, figural, bottle, SS, pr **85.00**
Display Bottle
  1930 . . . . **285.00**
  1968 . . . . **100.00**
Frisbee, plastic, MIB **20.00**
Game
  Chinese Checkers, wood board, marbles **55.00**
  Tic—Tac—Toe, MIB **80.00**
Glass, 6 oz, orig box, set of 12 . . . . . . **125.00**
Hat, truck driver's, 1930s **100.00**
Jug, 1 gal, syrup, empty **15.00**
Letterhead, 2½" logo at top, red and
  green printing, 1903 . . . . **90.00**
Lunch Tote, vinyl, 1950s **25.00**
Magazine Tear Sheet, 1906, couple
  toasting with Coca—Cola **8.00**
Matchbook
  1950 . . . . **2.50**
  1970 . . . . **1.50**
Menu Board, tin, 1960 . . . . **24.00**

Playing Cards, 1943, $45.00.

Mirror, pocket, celluloid	125.00
Pencil Case, "Coca–Cola Pure Drink of Natural Flavors," two unused pencils, ruler, "School Size Blotter," used eraser, blotter, wood pen, all "Coca–Cola," complete	55.00
Perfume Bottle, 1930s	35.00
Pill Container, 2½", bottle shape, brass lined	2.00
Playing Cards	
Hund & Eger	65.00
WW II, enemy aircraft on card	60.00
Postcard, business reply, "Fashion Books," 1912	15.00
Radio	
Cassette	149.00
Coke Vendo Vending Machine, 1970, MIB	250.00
Ruler, Coca–Cola	5.00
Sign	
Arrow, 10 x 30", 1951, with bottle	125.00
Bottle, 3", diecut	250.00
Christmas bottle, 36" h, yellow background	375.00
Paper, 11 x 22", window, 1952	75.00
Plastic, 16" d, round, hanging, light up, 1950s	175.00
Porcelain	
Bottle, 36"	300.00
Fountain service	225.00
Tin, 10 x 28", 1931	150.00
Tablet, "Drink Coca–Cola," orig pencil	8.00
Ticket, 3¾ x 5½", salesman's delivery	30.00
Thermometer	
1939, girl silhouette	125.00
1950s, tin, flat bottle	95.00
Toy, fountain dispenser	25.00
Tray	
1912, tip	325.00
1938, Summer Girl	95.00
1941, ice skater	50.00
1942, Roadster Girls	95.00
Vending Machine, Vendo 44, orig	2,000.00
Wallet, leather	35.00

COMIC BOOKS

Collecting Hints: Remember, age does *not* determine value! Prices fluctuate according to supply and demand in the marketplace. Collectors

should always buy comic books in the best possible condition. While archival restoration is available, it's frequently costly and may involve a certain amount of risk.

Comic books should be stored in an upright position away from sunlight, dampness, and insect infestations. Avoid stacking comic books because the weight of the uppermost books may cause acid and oils to migrate. This results in stains on the covers of books near the bottom of the stack which are difficult or impossible to remove.

Golden Age (1939–1950s) Marvel and D.C. first issues and key appearances continue to gain in popularity as do more current favorites like Marvel's "X–Men" and D.C.'s "The New Teen Titans."

History: Who would ever believe that a cheap, disposable product sold in the 1890s would be responsible for the multi–million dollar industry composed of comic books and their spin– offs today? That 2¢ item was none other than the Sunday newspaper. Improved printing techniques helped 1890s newspaper publishers change from a weekly format to a daily one that included a full page of comics. The rotary printing press allowed the use of color in the "funnies." Comics were soon reprinted as advertising promotions by companies such as Proctor & Gamble and movie theaters.

It wasn't long until reprint books like these promotional giveaways were selling in candy and stationery stores for 10¢ each. They appeared in various formats and sizes, many with odd shapes and cardboard covers. Others were printed on newsprint and resembled comic books sold today.

Comics printed prior to 1938 have value today only as historical artifacts or intellectual curiosities.

From 1939 to 1950 comic book publishers regaled readers with humor, adventure, western, and mystery tales. Super–heroes such as "Batman," "Superman," and "Captain America" first appeared in books during this era. This was the "Golden Age" of comics, a time for expansion and growth.

Unfortunately, the bubble burst in the spring of 1954 when Fredric Wertham published his book, *Seduction of the Innocent.* That book pointed a guilt–laden finger at the comic industry for corrupting youth, causing juvenile delinquency, and undermining American values. This book forced many publishers out of business, while others fought to establish a "comics code" to assure parents that their comics were compliant with morality and decency censures upheld by the code authority.

Thus, the Silver Age of comics is marked by a declining number of publishers due to the public uproar surrounding Wertham's book and the increased production costs of an inflationary economy.

The period starting with 1960 and continuing to the present has been marked by a revitalizing surge of interest in comic books. Starting with Marvel's introduction of "The Fantastic Four" and "The Amazing Spiderman," the market has increased to the extent that many new publishers are now rubbing elbows with the giants and the competition is keen!

Part of the reason for this upswing must be credited to that same inflationary economy that spelled disaster for publishers in the '50s. This time, however, people are buying valuable comics as a hedge against inflation. Even young people are aware of the market potential. Today's piggy bank investors may well be tomorrow's Wall Street tycoons.

References: Stephen Becker, *Comic Art In America*, Simon And Schuster, Inc., 1959; Pierre Couperie and Maurice C. Horn, *A History of the Comic Strip*, Crown Publishers, Inc. 1968; Hubert H. Crawford, *Crawford's Encyclopedia of Comic Books*, Jonathan David Publishers, Inc., 1978; Les Daniels, *COMIX, A History of Comic Books in America*, Bonanza Books, 1971; Ernst and Mary Gerber (compilers), *Photo–Journal Guide To Comics, Volume One (A–J)* and *Volume 2 (K–Z)*, Gerber Publishing Co., 1990; John Hagenberger, *Collector's Guide To Comic Books*, Wallace–Homestead, 1990; Maurice Horn (ed.), *World Encyclopedia of Comics*, Chelsea House; D. W. Howard, *Investing In Comics*, The World of Yesterday, 1988; Robert M. Overstreet, *The Official Comic Book Price Guide, No. 21* House of Collectibles, 1991; Jerry Robinson, *The Comics, An Illustrated History of Comic Strip Art*, G. P. Putnam's Sons, 1974.

Periodicals: *Comic Buyers Guide*, 700 State Street, Iola, WI 54990; *Comics Values Monthly*, Attic Books, P.O. Box 38, South Salem, NY 10590.

Museum: Museum of Cartoon Art, Rye, NY.

REPRODUCTION ALERT: Publishers frequently reprint popular stories, even complete books, so the buyer must pay strict attention to the title, not just the portion printed in outsized letters on the front cover. If there's ever any doubt, look inside at the fine print on the bottom of the inside cover or first page. The correct title will be printed there in capital letters.

Buyers also should pay attention to the size of the comic they purchase. Many customers have been misled by unscrupulous dealers recently. The comics offered are exact replicas of expensive Golden Age D.C. titles, which would normally sell for thousands of dollars. The seller offers the large, 10 by 13½", copy of Superman #1 in mint condition for ten to a hundred dollars. The novice collector jumps at the chance since he knows this book sells for thousands on the open market. When the buyer gets his "find" home and checks the value, he discovers that he's paid way too much for the treasury sized "Famous First Edition" comic printed in the mid-seventies by D.C. These comics originally sold for one dollar each and are exact reprints except for the size. Several came with outer covers which announced the fact that they were reprints, but it didn't take long for dishonest dealers to remove these and sell the remaining portion for greatly inflated prices.

Notes: Just like advertising, comic books affect and reflect the culture which nurtures them. Large letters, bright colors, and "pulse–pounding" action seem to hype this product. Many would say comics are as American as mom's apple pie since good almost always triumphs over evil. Yet there's truly something for every taste in the vast array of comics available today. There are underground (adult situation) comics, foreign comics, educational comics, and comics intended to promote the sale of products or services.

The following listing concentrates on "mainstream" American comics published between 1938 and 1985. Prices may vary from region to region due to excessive demand in some areas. Prices given are for comic books in fine condition; that is, these comics are like new in most respects, but may show a little wear. Comics should be complete; no pages or chunks cut out.

Classic Comics

Classics Illustrated started with #35. All first editions carry an advertisement for the next issue (except #168 and #169) on the inside covers. All titles have been reprinted and reprints are worth only about 10–25% of first edition values. Prices listed here are for first edition titles only.

Arabian Nights, #8	15.00
Corsican Brothers, The, #2	20.00
Deerslayer, The, #12	2.00
Don Quixote, #10	2.75
Frankenstein, #6	4.00
Hamlet, #2	1.00
Last of the Mohicans, The, #4	12.00
Oliver Twist, #17	1.25
Robinson Crusoe, #10	2.50
Sherlock Holmes, #2	35.00
Uncle Tom's Cabin, #15	36.00
Crime	
All True Crime, #27	7.50
Crime and Punishment, #10	4.00
Crime Clinic, #11	10.00
Crime Fighters, #12	3.00
Crime Must Stop, #1	50.00
Crime Reporter, #2	65.00
Crime Smashers, #2	20.00
Crime Suspenstories, #16	40.00

Gangsters Can't Win, #8 .... 6.50
Funny Animals
  Billy Bunny's Christmas Frolics, #1 . 6.50
  Bugs Bunny, #30 .... 1.50
  Cosmo Cat, #1 .... 10.00
  Felix the Cat, #6 .... 5.00
  Funny Stuff, #10 .... 10.00
  Howard the Duck, #2 .... 1.00
  Jing Pals, #2 .... 4.00
  Looney Tunes & Merrie Melodies
    Comics, #55 .... 6.00
  New Funnies, #85 .... 18.00
  Nutty Comics, #1 .... 10.00
  Peter Panda, #3 .... 8.00
  Porky Pig, #25 .... 1.50
  Super Rabbit, #6 .... 12.00
Horror
  Adventures Into Terror, #3 .... 8.00
  Alarming Tales, #5 .... 7.50
  Beyond, The, #25 .... 5.50
  Chamber of Chills, #9 .... 8.00
  Haunt of Fear, #21 .... 20.00
  House of Mystery, #10 .... 15.00
  Spellbound, #32 .... 9.25
  Tales of Suspense, #44 .... 18.00
  Tales of Terror, #1 .... 1.50
  Terror Illustrated, #1 .... 18.00
  The Thing, #5 .... 17.50
  Unknown World, #1 .... 20.00
Jungle
  Jann of the Jungle, #17 .... 12.00
  Jumbo, #149 .... 10.00
  Jungle Adventures, #3 .... 1.50
  Jungle Girl, #1 .... 90.00
  Jungle Jo, #4 .... 18.00
  Jungle Thrills, #16 .... 20.00
  Korak, Son of Tarzan, #15 .... 1.25
  Sheena, Queen of the Jungle, #4 ... 30.00
  Tarzan, Lord of the Jungle, #1 ..... 4.00
  Tegra Jungle Empress, 1948, #1 ... 25.00
  White Princess of the Jungle, #5 ... 20.00
  Zegra Jungle Empress, #3 .... 20.00
Juvenile
  Adventures for Boys, #1 .... 2.50
  Adventures of the Big Boy, The, #50 1.00
  Archie's Girls Betty & Veronica, #100 4.00
  Barbie & Ken, #5 .... 10.00
  Flintstones & Pebbles, The, #2 ..... 1.50
  Jughead's Fantasy, #3 .... 10.00
  Katy Keene, #45 .... 12.00
  Kiddie Kapers, #1 .... 4.00
  Little Lotta, #7 .... 12.00
  Little Lulu, #40 .... 12.00
  Mighty Atom, #6 .... 4.00
  Raggedy Ann and Andy, #5 .... 60.00
  Teenage Mutant Ninja Turtles, #1,
    2nd printing 12.50
Newspaper Reprints
  Beetle Bailey, #5 .... 2.50
  Brenda Starr, #14 .... 50.00
  Comics Revue, #4 .... 5.00
  Flash Gordon, #4 .... 40.00

Wonder Woman, D.C. National Comics,
#124, fine condition, $4.50.

Peanuts, #4 .... 5.00
Number 1's
  Amazing Spiderman 350.00
  Fantastic Four 500.00
  Incredible Hulk, The 180.00
  Justice League of America 170.00
  Little Archie 60.00
  Strange Adventures 150.00
  Tales of the Unexpected 50.00
  Torchy 210.00
  Warlord 8.00
Radio/TV/Movie Related
  Abbott and Costello, #1 .... 24.00
  Adventures of Alan Ladd, The, #2 .. 25.00
  Adventures of Jerry Lewis, #92 .... 1.50
  Bewitched, #8 .... 3.50
  Big Valley, The, #1 .... 5.00
  Cheyenne, #25 .... 4.25
  Famous Stars, #5 .... 15.00
  Get Smart, #5 .... 4.50
  Gomer Pyle, #2 .... 2.00
  Jackie Gleason & the Honeymooners,
    #2 .... 32.00
  Jimmy Durante, #20 .... 18.00
  My Favorite Martian, #2 .... 4.00
  Star Trek, #2 .... 15.00
  Stoney Burke, #2 .... 3.00
Romance
  All Love, #26 .... 3.00
  Best Love, #35 .... 5.00
  Boy Meets Girl, #3 .... 1.35
  Brides Romances, #23 .... 2.00
  Career Girl Romances, #32 ...... 2.25
  Cinderella Love, #7 .... 4.50
  Glamorous Romances, #90 ...... 2.00
  Love Letters, #2 .... 16.00
  Secret Hearts, #40 .... 3.50

True Love Pictorial, #7 .... 15.00

Science Fiction
Attack on Planet Mars, (1951) 90.00
Doctor Solar, Man of the Atom, #10 1.50
Earth Man on Venus, (1951) 170.00
Incredible Science Fiction, #31 .... 50.00
Strange Adventures, #60 .... 5.00
Strange Planets, #16 .... 4.00
Strange Worlds, #20 .... 10.00
Tom Corbett Space Cadet, #2 ..... 10.00
UFO & Outer Space, #14 .... .50
Unknown Worlds of Science Fiction,
#3 .... 1.00
Weird Science, #11 .... 35.00

Sports
Amazing Willie Mays, The, (1954) . 45.00
Baseball Heroes, (1952) 40.00
Baseball Thrills, #10 .... 20.00
Famous Plays of Jackie Robinson, #6 20.00
Sport Thrills, #11 .... 10.00

Super Heroes
Amazing Man, #22 .... 75.00
Amazing Spiderman, #40 .... 72.00
Aquaman, #3 .... 8.00
Captain America, (1968), #100 .... 35.00
Captain Flash, #1 .... 20.00
Flash Gordon, #3 .... 30.00
Human Torch (1954), #38 .... 35.00
Iron Man, #68 .... 1.00
Metamorpho, #10 .... 2.50
Submariner Comics, #14 .... 85.00
Super Heroes, #4 .... 2.00
Tales of the Legion, #314 .... .50

Three Dimensional
Alien Worlds, #1 .... 2.00
E C Classics, #1 .... 60.00
Three Stooges (1953), #3 .... 35.00
Tor (Oct, Nov 1953) 25.00
True 3–D, #1 .... 15.00

Walt Disney
Chip 'n Dale, #6 .... .50
Disneyland Birthday Party, #1 ..... 7.50
Donald Duck, #57 .... 2.50
Mickey Mouse, #93 .... 1.50
Peter Pan, #2 .... 3.00
Picnic Party, #8 .... 15.00
Pluto, #429 .... 3.25
Silly Symphonies, #6 .... 12.00
Sleeping Beauty, #1 .... 15.00
Three Caballeros, #71 .... 145.00
Walt Disney Showcase, #30 .... 1.00
Zorro, #13 .... 4.50

War
Air War Stories, #2 .... 1.50
American Air Forces, #2 .... 4.50
Battle Squadron, #1 .... 4.50
Blazing Combat, #1 .... 12.00
Fightin' Marines, #15 .... 4.75
GI Joe, A Real American Hero, #2 . 4.25
GI War Brides, #1 .... 3.00
Military Comics, #32 .... 55.00
Our Army at War, #5 .... 18.00

Soldiers of Fortune, #11 .... 4.00
Star Spangled War Stories, #101 ... 8.50
Tell It to the Marines, #3 .... 8.00
This is War, #8 .... 4.00
War at Sea, #22 .... 1.50
War Stories, #5 .... 11.50
War Victory Adventures, #2 .... 20.00

Western
All American Western, #111 ...... 15.00
Annie Oakley & Tagg, #7 .... 8.00
Billy the Kid Adventure Magazine, #9 6.00
Black Rider Rides Again, #1 .... 12.00
Bob Colt, #3 .... 15.00
Bronco Bill, #5 .... 5.00
Clay Cody, Gunslinger, #1 .... 3.00
Gabby Hayes Western, #15 .... 8.00
Gunfighters, EC Comics, 1948, #15 35.00
Gunsmoke, #10 .... 6.00
Hopalong Cassidy, #50 .... 12.00
Lobo, #2 .... 1.50
Roy Rogers Comics, (1948), #10 ... 15.00
Tom Mix Western, #35 .... 10.00
Two Gun Western, #14 .... 5.00

COMPACTS

Collecting Hints: Only mirrors that are broken should be removed and replaced in a vintage compact. Do not replace a mirror that is discolored, flawed, or in need of resilvering. The original mirror enhances the value of the compact.

Never apply a sticker directly to the surface of a compact. The acids from the glue may discolor or irreparably damage the finish, especially an enamel finish.

If a compact comes in the original box or pouch, do not destroy or discard it. The value of the compact is increased if it has its original presentation box.

History: In the first quarter of the 20th century attitudes regarding cosmetics changed drastically. The use of make–up during the day was no longer looked upon with disdain. As women became "liberated" and more and more of them entered the business world the use of cosmetics became a routine and necessary part of a woman's grooming. Portable containers for cosmetics became a necessity.

Compacts were made in a myriad of shapes, styles, combinations and motifs, all reflecting the mood of the times. Every conceivable natural or man–made medium was used in the manufacture of compacts. Commemorative, premium, souvenir, patriotic, figural, combination compacts, Art Deco, and enamel compacts are a few examples of the compacts that were made in the United States and abroad. Compacts combined with cigarette cases, music boxes, watches, hatpins, canes, lighters, etc. also were very popular.

Compacts were made and used until the late

1950s when women opted for the "Au Natural" look. Compacts manufactured prior to that time are considered vintage compacts.

Some vintage compacts were exquisitely crafted, often enameled or encrusted with precious or synthetic jewels. These compacts were considered a form of jewelry or fashion accessory. The intricate and exacting workmanship of some vintage compacts would be virtually impossible to duplicate today.

Reference: Roselyn Gerson, *Ladies' Compacts of the 19th and 20th Centuries*, Wallace–Homestead, 1989.

Collectors' Club: The Compact Collectors Club, P. O. Box Letter S, Lynbrook, NY 11563.

Periodical: The Powder Puff Newsletter, P. O. Box Letter S, Lynbrook, NY 11563.

Advisor: Roselyn Gerson.

Sterling silver, octagonal compact with mesh vanity bag, finger ring chain, $400.00

Arden, Elizabeth, watch shape, MIB ..	**30.00**
Coty, Jingle Bells, goldtone	**60.00**
Dunhill, Clearview, leather, brown, windshield–wiper, designed to resemble book	**80.00**
Elgin, American	
Heart shape, military wings on front, "To Mother from Wally, 1943," MIB	**65.00**
Square	
Enameled flowers	**30.00**
GA state flag and flower on lid ...	**30.00**
Fuller, plastic, sleeve for comb on lid .	**40.00**
Harmony of Boston, box shape, tan, snap closing	**50.00**

Hudnut, Richard, marbleized blue plastic vanity case, SP engraved lid, powder and rouge compartments, orig fitted presentation box	**80.00**
K & K, brass color, basket shape, engine tolled, dice enclosed in plastic dome lid, emb swinging handle	**120.00**
Lady Vanity, blue leather, oval, snap closing	**40.00**
Lazell, goldtone, powder and rouge compartments, patented July 18, 1922	**60.00**
Lin–Bren, leather, round compact centered on outer lid of rect cigarette case, US Patent No 2,471,963	**150.00**
Mireve, black enamel, powder compartment, sliding lipstick and perfume bottle, France	**75.00**
Mondaine, green leather, miniature portrait of woman within gold tooled border on lid, mirror, powder, rouge, and lipstick compartments, carrying cord	**100.00**
Ronson, goldtone, brown enamel, combination compact and cigarette case, Art Deco metal design on lid	**100.00**
Stratton, enamel, goldtone, oblong, scalloped, multicolored, lipstick on lid	**60.00**
Volupte, Lucky Purse, goldtone, satin finish, outer flap reveals rouge	**80.00**
Unknown Maker	
Art Deco	
Chrome, Empire State Building on lid	**35.00**
Miniature, resembles hand mirror, rhinestone on lid, int. and ext. mirrors	**50.00**
Art Nouveau, half moon shape, silvered, enameled, multicolored swirls on lid, goldtone int., powder, rouge, and lipstick compartments, link carrying chain	**150.00**
Crystal Lucite, sq, polished metal cut–out of man taking siesta next to cactus	**60.00**
Damascene, (inlaid with gold and silver), view of Mt Fuji capped in silver on black matte–finish lid, hinged, fitted presentation box ...	**150.00**
Damask, multicolored, wallet–type closure, plastic ring on lid, France	**40.00**
Enameled	
Round, Eastern Star, jeweled	**30.00**
Square, blue, Scottie dog transfer on lid, powder compartment, metal mirror conceals rouge compartment	**40.00**
Gilded Metal, round, emb, miniature, multicolored intaglio dec lid set with blue stones and pearls, France	**125.00**
Goldtone	
Black enamel, USN insignia in gilt	

heart on lid, powder and rouge compartment 80.00

Champleve Enamel, painted ivory disc on lid, Italy 50.00

Heart shape, purple orchid inlaid in black plastic on lid 50.00

Silvered metal, lavender cloisonne enamel inset on lid, powder, rouge, and lipstick compartments, carrying chain 20.00

Leather
Book, titled "Raquel" 25.00

Oblong, black, vanity box, mirror, comb, powder, rouge, and lipstick containers, lower half opens for personal articles, lock and key 125.00

Square, tooled, gold, Venice canal scene on lid 40.00

Lizard, horseshoe shape, light brown, purse motif, Argentina 60.00

Mother–of–pearl, stylized, checkerboard, designed as book 50.00

Nickel finish, engine turned, combination compact, cigarette case and lighter, raised giraffe and palm trees on lid 90.00

Petit–point, round, resembles hand mirror, filigree handle, int. and ext. mirrors, Austria 60.00

Plastic, simulated tortoise shell, oval, raised grape and leaf design on lid, SS catches 60.00

Silvered Metal
Black enamel, combination vanity case and watch, powder, and rouge compartments 100.00

Gilt, sq, state of AK on lid 20.00

Miniature, hand mirror shape, petit–point on lid, France 40.00

Square, navy blue and white, nautical motif on lid, powder and rouge compartments 40.00

Suede, black, bird and gilt flowers on lid, powder, lipstick, and cigarette compartments, Argentina 100.00

Suede and brass, black, bolster shape, l'd conceals compact 125.00

Venine, sq, blue plastic, goldtone filigree lid, powder, and rouge compartments 60.00

Vitoge, polished goldtone, sq, compact and lipstick case, four leaf clovers, protective carrying case 60.00

Volupte, Oval Sophisticase, silver emb gilt lid, center band slides to reveal powder and utility compartments, tassel pulls out to reveal lipstick, black faille carrying case 150.00

Zell, goldtone, engraved, basket motif, pink and green flowers, emb rigid handle 80.00

COOKBOOKS

Collecting Hints: Look for books in good, clean condition. Watch for special interesting notes in margins.

History: Among the earliest Americana cookbooks are The Frugal Housewife; or, Complete Woman Cook by Susanna Carter, published in Philadelphia in 1796, and American Cookery by Amelia Simmons, published in Hartford, Connecticut in 1796. Cookbooks of this era are crudely written, for most cooks could not read well and measuring devices were not yet refined.

Other types of collectible cookbooks include those used as premiums or advertisements. This type is much less expensive than the rare 18th century books.

References: Bob Allen, A Guide To Collecting Cookbooks and Advertising Cookbooks, Collector Books, 1990; Linda J. Dickinson, Price Guide To Cookbooks and Recipe Leaflets, Collector Books, 1990.

Collectors' Club: Cook Book Collectors Club of America, P.O. Box 56, St. James, MD 65559.

Kate Smith's 55 Favorite Ann Pillsbury Cake Recipes, $7.50; The Heinz Salad Book, $5.00; Chiquita Bananas Recipe Book, $6.00; Betty Crocker's Softasilk Special Occasion Cakes, $6.50, late 1940s–early 1950s.

Amana Recipes, 1948, orig dust jacket   10.00

American Woman's Home, Catharine E Beecher, Harriet Beecher Stowe, 1869 .... 75.00

Army Food & Messing, 1942 .... 15.00

Baker's Chocolate, 1904 .... 20.00

Best From Midwest Kitchens, 1946 ...   5.00

Betty Crocker Picture Cook Book, 1950, 1st edition, orig dust jacket 30.00

Brides Book, 1934, soft cover 12.00

Cake Baking Made Easy With Airy Fairy   5.00

Calumet, Kewpie cov, c1920 .... 15.00

Campbell Soup Kids, 64 pgs 30.00

Ceresota, c1930 .... 15.00

Chicago Daily News, 1930s 9.00

Clapper Girl	12.00
Congressional Club, Bicentennial, 1976, 714 pgs	9.00
Cookies & More Cookies, L Sumption, 1938	5.00
Cooking For 2, J Hill, 1938	5.00
Every Step In Canning, G Gray, 1920, wear to orig dust jacket	5.00
General Foods, 1932, 1st edition	10.00
Gourmet In Low Calorie Kitchen	8.50
Healthy Cooking, Mrs E Kellogg, Kellogg Food, Co, soft brown cov	7.00
KC Baking Powder	12.00
Lowney's Cook Book, M Howard, 1907, 1st edition	25.00
Midwestern Jr League, 1976, 1st edition, tear in dust jacket	8.00
Mother Hubbard Flour	35.00
Mrs Peterson Simplified Cook 1924	14.00
New Congregational Church Cook Book, LaGrange, IL, 1935	9.00
New Orleans Creole Recipes, 1957	8.00
Old Warsaw, 1958, worn dust jacket	12.00
Pepperidge Farm, M Rudkin, 1st edition, orig dust jacket	24.00
Pillsbury	
A Book For A Cook, 1905	35.00
Bake Off, annual booklet	
1st year	65.00
5th year	7.00
15th year	5.00
Practical Housekeeping, 1884	15.00
Rector, 1928, ragged dust jacket	9.00
Rumford Complete, 1926	10.00
Savannah Cookbook, 1933	12.50
Sunset Kitchen Cabinet Recipes, 1944, dust jacket	6.00
Teddy Bear Baking School, Fleischmann, 1906	25.00
The New Cookery, autographed by author, 1922	20.00
Thousand Ways To Please A Husband, 1917	25.00
US Navy, 1944	12.00
Vincent Price Treasury Great Recipes, 1965, 1st edition, brown padded cov, ribbon markers	35.00
What Cooks At Stillmeadow, G Taber, 1st edition, dust jacket	35.00
White House Cookbook	
1894, white, silver cover, some wear and stains	75.00
1911	25.00
Woman's Favorite Cookbook, 1907	15.00
Yul Brynner Cook Book, 1983, 1st edition, orig dust jacket	18.00

COOKIE CUTTERS

Collecting Hints: Cookie cutters exist in abundance throughout the United States. The early cutters were handmade, and the tradition and skill survives to the present time. By the late 19th century, cutters also were manufactured and sold for a few pennies through mail order houses and in general stores.

A collector should develop a collection theme—shape, broad general approach, or cutters for use. In buying old or used cutters, carefully examine the cutters which now are available new. Many cutters identical to "old" cutters still are made. Learn which old cutters were handcrafted and which were machine made. When uncertain about whether a cutter is old and valued for its age, ask "What would I pay for it new?" This method helps to eliminate wild purchases and disappointments when a cutter is misjudged.

There are many tinsmiths working today who will duplicate any cutter, often using old techniques to make it. Cutters can be aged. Sellers often misrepresent the age of cutters out of ignorance, rather than an obvious attempt to deceive.

History: Late in the 19th century, factories began producing cookie cutters resembling the handcrafted cutters of an earlier period. It was soon obvious that making uniform backs of relatively thin material speeded up the process and cut costs. Many unusual cutters were patented during this period; advertising cutters also were made.

The 1869 Dover Stamping Company catalog is the first documented record of a manufactured cookie cutter. The cutter pictured in the catalog is well developed, far beyond a "beginning" status. Manufactured cutters probably were made before the 1869 date.

Two innovations in the 1925–1950 period were the use of aluminum and plastic. Since 1965, two events occurred which influenced the cookie cutter collecting field. The first is an influx of younger people into the collecting field through the interest in crafts. The second is the Hallmark cutters in their varied plastic tones which renewed interest in cutter use.

Reference: Phyllis S. Wetherill, *Art in the Kitchen: Cookie Cutters and Cookie Molds,* Schiffer Publishing, Ltd, 1985.

Collectors' Club: Cookie Collector's Club, 1167 Teal Road, S. W., Dellroy, OH 44620.

GERMAN CUTTERS

Cutters may or may not be marked "Germany" depending on whether they are imported, brought by travelers, or part of a set. Cutters usually are outline or outline with brace. Some are made of flimsy metal ¼" deep.

Bear (5¾" w) and duck (6" h), made in Nazareth, PA, pc of depression glass for eye, handles, each $125.00.

Dog, unusual detail, outline with damaged handle 3.00
Elephant, outline, 1½ x 1¾", thin plastic, found in yellow, blue, red, green, or lavender .... .25
Geometric Design, flatback, 4 round points, 4 sharp points 12.00
Santa
  2 x 5", with tree, flatback 10.00
  5¾ x 3¾", with bag, outline and heavy brace 15.00
  8½ x 4½", with tree, flatback 15.00

HANDCRAFTED

Early, tin, outline

Flatback, orig made without handle
  Cross and Anchor, 5 x 3½" 20.00
  Strong Man, 2½ x 3", flexing muscles 50.00
Irregular base, handle, cutters have excellent design and are in good condition
  Bird, perched, 4½ x 2" 15.00
  Dog, 2 x 3" 35.00
  Duck, small, 3½ x 2¾", complex design, bent handle 28.00
  Pig, 4½ x 2¾" 8.00
  Rooster, 4½" square, primitive design, spot soldering 55.00
  Woman, 6½ x 3½", primitive 28.00

Indeterminate Age

Arrowhead, 6 x 4¾", regular back, outline, handle, primitive design, made c1970 but aged 3.00
Dog, flatback, 5½ x 3¼", entire back soldered to 1½" deep outline to make solid one piece cutter 25.00
Dove, 5¾ x 3½", outline, flatback, handle 10.00
Fish, flatback, unusual design 5.00

Pumpkin, outline, flatback, handle ... 6.00
Rooster, flatback 5.00

Modern

Foose, sgd, distelfink with heart, 6½ x 14", outline, flatback, insert and handle 15.00
Little Fox Factory, cutters are handcrafted by members of the Fox family, orig box marked "Cookie Cutters, Bucyrus Mother of Twin Club, Handcrafted in Bucyrus, OH, The Bratwurst Capital of America," heavy ¾" deep metal, five primitive outline shapes—angel, filled stocking, 5—pointed star, map of Ohio, snowman 25.00
Kelly, P, flower with leaves, 2½ x 4", flatback, serrated frame available new 15.00
Rhoads, bird with spread wings, 7½ x 4½", outline, flatback, handle, primitive design, tin hemmed at margins 5.00
Roberts, sgd, 2 birds facing each other, 5½ x 4" outline, irregular back, handle 10.00
Smith, H, sgd and dated 1969, hat, 3 x 1¼", flatback, made for Penn Alps . 4.00

MANUFACTURED

Aluminum

Appeared in the 1920s. Most of the original designs still are made today, although silverstone shares a place with coppertone and greentone. Only a few designs were made for a short period.

Animal, card party, and geometric shapes with wooden or colored metal handles, usually red or green, colored or non—colored handle 1.00
Calmut Baking Powder
  Large 4.00
  Medium 3.00
Cutters with "self" handles are made by cutting parallel line in the center of the cutter and pushing outward, available at most hardware and notion stores for about .25 .... .20
Elephant and Santa shapes, originally made with depression for paper picture
  With complete picture 2.00
  Without picture 1.00
Gingerbread Boy 1.00
Minnie Mouse 10.00
Pillsbury Comic Ghost 4.00
Santa With Pack 6.00
Scottie
  Green wooden handle 6.00
  Red wooden handle 4.00

Metal

Usually made of tin.

Early, 20th Century
  Advertising, c1910–25
    Davis Animal Cutters, heavy, simple design, shapes of cat, goose, horse and rabbit, set of four, MIB   **20.00**
    Janes Furniture Company, Westbridge, Aurora (many local businesses used identical round cutters) **6.00**
  Identifiable or Signed
    Fagley Junior Bridge Set, orig box, cutters not marked, box not interesting **8.00**
    Fagley Noah's Ark Set, orig box, nine cutters, not marked but identifiable by sharp joining point, set, MIB . .   **15.00**
    Fries (name legible, often fades), approx twenty varieties **5.00**
    Kraemer, approx twenty varieties . . .   **5.00**
  Manufactured or Handcrafted, outline with inside design, flatback, handle, often these cutters are in poor condition with center design partially or totally missing
    Bird, pierced star, flatback **20.00**
    Camel, pierced star, flatback **25.00**
    Diamond, diamond and tulip inside, star perforation **7.50**
    Diamond, tiny tulip design in center, plastic coated **5.00**
    Doughnut, marked "Made In Canada" **10.00**
    Heart **8.50**
    Lion, pierced star **25.00**
    Star, six points **8.00**
    Sugar Cookie **6.00**
    Turkey **20.00**
  Mid to Modern 20th Century
    Outline, cutters differ in strength of metal used and in depth of metal, deep cutters often called "cake cutters;" cutters in original sets usually are priced far less than the same cutters sold individually
    Animal designs, heavy, 1" deep, simple, designs—cat, horse and rabbit **3.00**
    Astronaut, sgd "1776–1976, The Moon, 7–20–69, Pat. Pend.," MIB **5.00**
    Cake Cutters, bridge shapes, circle or star **1.50**
    Christmas Cookie Cutter Set, Novelty Manufacturing Company, tin metal, six cutters, MIB **3.00**
    Outline, handle or brace; large cutters in shapes of Christmas tree; gingerbread boy, or Santa can be pur-

chased new for approx $2.00; cutters in any shape, including all states, can be purchased from handcrafters new for $2.00 and up
    Bird, 4½" sq, sgd "Wilton–Korea," 1974 . . . .   **4.00**
    Cracker cutter with prongs, 2½" d, 4" h, wooden handles, possibly c1900 . . . .   **15.00**
    Owl, 7½ x 3 x 1½", brace, thin metal, made by Fox Run **4.00**
    Pear, elongated, 1½ x 5" **10.00**
    Shield, 2 x 1½" **5.00**

Plastic

Plastic cutters were made first in the 1940s; because of a scarcity of plastic during the Korean conflict, cutters often were made in odd colors or marbleized from the remains of plastic used for other purposes.

Angel, 3" sq, ¼" plastic margin around cutter, outline, red plastic, available new . . . .   **.25**
Camel, 3½ x 3", outline, colors white, yellow or green, Hutzler, available new . . . .   **.25**
Elephant, 3¼ x 2¼", outline, flatback, handle, orange plastic, Lone Toy Tree, available new . . . .   **.50**
Hallmark, Peanuts Christmas Set, four cutters, outline, flatback, handle, MIB   **15.00**
KO Biscuit and Cookie Cutter, outline, flatback, handle, varied colors and slight differences in design, sgd with orig tag **5.00**
Pig, 2¼ x 1¼"
  Green, outline, Wilton **1.00**
  Red or yellow, flatback . . . .   **.50**
Robin Hood set, clear, named and signed "Robin Hood Flour," colors green, blue and orange, eight cutters, handles, set **25.00**

SPECIAL TYPES

Donut Cutter, retractable center hole, cuts circles or donuts in plain or scalloped edge
  Condition, good **15.00**
  Condition, center hole missing **5.00**
Rolling Cutters
  5", all metal, makes round cookies, not signed **6.00**
  6", green wooden handle, cuts donut shapes **10.00**

COOKIE JARS

Collecting Hints: Cookie jars are subject to chips and paint flaking. Collectors should concentrate on jars which have their original lid and are in very good or better condition.

Learn to identify makers' marks and codes. Do not fail to include some of the contemporary manufacturers in your collection.

Above all, ignore the prices and hype associated with the cookie jars sold at the Andy Warhol sale in 1988. Neither is realistic.

History: Cookie jars, colorful and often whimsical, are one of the fastest growing categories in the collectibles field. Many cookie jars have been made by more than one company and as a result can be found with different marks. This resulted from mergers or splits by manufacturers, e.g., Brush–McCoy which is now Nelson McCoy. Molds also were traded and sold among companies.

Cookie jars often were redesigned to reflect newer tastes. Hence, the same jar may be found in several different style variations.

References: Harold Nichols, *McCoy Cookie Jars: From The First To The Latest,* Nichols Publishing, 1987; Fred and Joyce Roerig, *Collector's Encyclopedia of Cookie Jars,* Collector Books, 1990; Ermagene Westfall, *An Illustrated Value Guide To Cookie Jars,* Collector Books, 1983.

Abingdon

Clock	69.00
Humpty Dumpty	125.00
Porky Pig	125.00
Three Bears	75.00

American Bisque

Bear with Golf Hat	65.00
Blackboard Clown	125.00
Bull and Cow Turnabout	80.00
Cat on beehive	35.00
Churn	12.00
Collegiate Owl	60.00
Cookie Truck	50.00
Donkey with milk wagon	55.00
Granny	125.00
Lady Pig, dotted dress	55.00
Panda Bear, blue bow	48.00
Pig in Polk	60.00
Pig with Shamrocks	60.00
Puppy	65.00
Rabbit, hand in pocket	60.00
Ring for Cookies	13.00
Schoolhouse	20.00
Yarn Doll	55.00
Yogi Bear, felt tag	225.00

Avon, bear	35.00
Bellmont, lion with hat	60.00

Brush–McCoy

Cinderella's Pumpkin	150.00
Davy Crockett	175.00
Panda	225.00
Peter	185.00
Squirrel on Log	50.00

California Originals

Big Bird, #976	52.00
Goofy, cylinder	65.00
Santa	70.00

Cardinal, French Chef head	85.00
Chein, tin, Walt Disney	50.00
Enesco, lady pig	25.00
Fredericksburg Art Pottery, marked	

FAPCO

Chicken	40.00
Dutch Mill	38.00
Hen, brown, chick on back	35.00
Pink Dove	40.00

Hall, Eva Zeisel, pink and gold	75.00
Hoan, Donald Duck	30.00

Hull

Apple	9.00
Red Riding Hood, closed basket	125.00

Lefton, Santa Claus	50.00
Maddux, Queen of Knaves	95.00

McCoy

Apple, yellow	25.00
Astronauts	295.00
Baa Baa Blacksheep	65.00
Barn	150.00
Barrel	12.00
Basket of Eggs	40.00
Bear, green cap	38.00
Boy on Baseball	125.00
Boy on Football	125.00
Cabin	45.00
Cat on yellow coal bucket	150.00
Chiffonier	45.00
Chipmunk	125.00
Circus Horse	125.00
Coffee Grinder	25.00
Coffeepot, blue	35.00
Cookie Barrel	20.00
Cookie Kettle Gypsy Pot	25.00
Cookie Wagon	95.00
Cookstove, black or white	35.00
Cow	80.00
Cylinder with Fruit	15.00
Dog with letter	45.00
Donkey with Milk Wagon	55.00
Double Penguin, white	60.00
Eggs on Basket	25.00
Fireplace	65.00
Fortune Cookies	45.00
French Chef	55.00
Frontier Family	45.00
Globe, repainted	175.00
Grandma's Cookies	18.00
Granny	55.00
Honey Bear	45.00
Indian	210.00
Jack–O–Lantern	600.00
Leprechaun	350.00

Little Red Bean Pot	25.00
Log Cabin	60.00
Lollipops	40.00
Oaken Bucket	24.00
Owl, brown	45.00
Picnic Basket	40.00
Poppy Trail, squirrel on pinecone	75.00
Railroad Lantern	48.00
Smiley Face	25.00
Stoplight	65.00
Stove, black	22.00
Strawberry	40.00
Tepee	200.00
Thinking Puppy	18.00
Touring Car	48.00
Turkey	185.00
WC Fields	185.00
Wishing Well	25.00

Metlox

Bear	45.00
Duck	65.00
Gourd	30.00
Parrot	79.00

Morton Pottery Co, poodle, white ground, red dec, $25.00.

Pearl China, Chef	375.00

Pottery Guild

Boy with Skirt	65.00
Elsie the Cow	125.00
Little Red Riding Hood	90.00

Red Wing

Cattail, brown	95.00
Chef, yellow	50.00
Dutch Children	48.00
Dutch Girl, yellow	45.00
Gingerbread Boy	20.00
Monk, yellow	45.00

Regal China

Barn	130.00
Chef	200.00
Goldilocks	200.00
Quaker Oats	125.00

Robbinson Ramsbottom

Chef with Dish of Eggs	65.00
Cow Jumped Over The Moon	150.00

Shawnee

Clown, ball and seal	150.00
Dutch Boy, scarf, flowers, gold trim "Happy" in gold across stomach, orig label	125.00
Dutch Girl, #1026	98.00
Owl	50.00
Smiley Pig, tulips, dark back	70.00
Winnie The Pooh, large honey pot	80.00

Twin Winton, collegiate owl	30.00

Unknown Manufacturers

Black Cat	35.00
Boy with Churn	120.00
Cookie Monster	40.00
Elsie the Cow	65.00
Keebler Tree House	50.00
Rabbit in Basket	50.00
R2D2	85.00
Smiley Pig, red scarf	60.00
Snoopy	150.00
Star Wars	85.00
Witch	50.00

Vandor

Fred Flintstone	55.00
Howdy Doody	150.00

Walt Disney

Donald Duck	125.00
Mickey, leather ears, orig box	300.00
Tigger	125.00

Turnabout

Mickey/Minnie	110.00
Donald Duck/Jose Careoca	110.00

COWBOY HEROES

Collecting Hints: Cowboy hero material was collected and saved in great numbers. Don't get fooled into thinking an object is rare until you have checked carefully. Tom Mix material remains the most desirable, followed closely by Hopalong Cassidy, Roy Rogers, and Gene Autry memorabilia. Material associated with the western stars of the silent era and early talking films still has not achieved its full potential as a collectible.

History: The era when the cowboy and longhorn cattle dominated the Great Western Plains was short, lasting only from the end of the Civil War to the late 1880s. Dime store novelists romanticized this period and created a love affair in America's heart for the Golden West.

Motion pictures saw the cowboy as a prime entertainment feature. William S. Hart developed the character of the cowboy hero—often in love with his horse more than the girl. He was followed by Tom Mix, Ken Maynard, Tim McCoy, and Buck Jones. The "B" movie, the second feature of a double bill, was often of the cowboy genre.

In 1935 William Boyd starred in the first of the

Hopalong Cassidy films. Gene Autry, "a singing cowboy," gained popularity over the airwaves of the West and Midwest. By the late 1930s, Autry's Melody Ranch was a national institution on the air as well as the screen. Roy Rogers replaced Autry as the featured cowboy at Republic Pictures in the mid–1940s. Although the Lone Ranger first appeared on the airwaves in 1933, he did not enter the movie medium until 1938.

The early years of television enhanced the careers of the big three—Autry, Boyd, and Rogers. The appearance of the Lone Ranger in shows made specifically for television strengthened the key role held by the cowboy hero. "Gunsmoke," "Wagon Train," "Rawhide," "The Rifleman," "Paladin," and "Bonanza" were just a few of the shows that followed.

By the early 1970s the cowboy hero had fallen from grace, relegated to reruns or specials. In early 1983 The Library of Congress in Washington conducted a major show on the "Cowboy Hero," perhaps a true indication that he is now a part of past history.

References: Theodore L. Hake and Robert D. Cauler, *Six Gun Heroes: A Price Guide To Movie Cowboy Collectibles*, Wallace-Homestead, 1976; Robert Heide and John Gilman, *Box–Office Buckaroos*, Abbeville Press, 1989; Lee J. Felbinger, *The Lone Ranger Pictorial Scrapbook*, published by author, 1988; David Rothel, *The Gene Autry Book*, Empire Publishing Co, 1988; David Rothel, *The Roy Rogers Book*, Empire Publishing Company, 1987; Richard West, *Television Westerns: Major and Minor Series, 1946–1978*, McFarland & Company, 1987.

Museums: Gene Autry Western Heritage Museum, Los Angeles, CA; National Cowboy Hall of Fame and Western Heroes, Oklahoma City, OK; Roy Rogers Museum, Victorville, CA.

GENE AUTRY

Album, four–record, unused, 1947 . . .	**95.00**
Badge, 1¼" d, celluloid, "Official Gene Autry Club," portrait center, black, white, and bright orange, c1940 . . .	**65.00**
Book	
Gene Autry in Special Ranger Rule, Better Little Book, Whitman, #1456, 1945	**30.00**
Gene Autry Goes to the Circus, 5½ x 6½", hard cov, Whitman, Tell–A–Tale series, 28 pgs, 1950	**20.00**
Punch Out, unused, 1941	**160.00**
Boots, rubber, orig box	**155.00**
Bread Label, bread loaf end wrapper, 2¾" sq, diecut corners, full color photo scene, series #5, #6–8, early 1950s, set of three	**54.00**
Cap Pistol, 7½", metal, silvered, ivory	

Hopalong Cassidy clothes hamper, metal, red, cream, white, and black, $100.00.

plastic grips, rearing horse, marked "BH," inscribed "Gene Autry"	**90.00**
Coloring Books, Whitman, unused	
6¾ x 7½", #2953, 40 pgs, 1957 . . .	**14.00**
11 x 15", 48 pgs, 1949	**30.00**
Comic Book, "Gene Autry Comics," Vol 1, #20, Dell, Oct 1948	**18.00**
Guitar, 36" l, adult size, pressed wood, metal tuning keys, wire strings, black and brown, red and white western scene, facsimile Autry signature, "Melody Ranch" signpost on tuning head, 1940–50s	**175.00**
Lobby Card, "Red River Valley," 11 x 14", full color, action scene	**17.00**
Photo, 8 x 10", black and white, glossy, sgd "To Elizabeth from Gene Autry" in black ink, 1939	**125.00**
Pinback Button, 1¼" d, black and white photo, dark blue ground, "Gene Autry's Brand/Sunbeam Bread," c1950	**35.00**
Poster, 24 x 30", stiff paper, sgd "Best Wishes, Gene Autry" at center, portraits and film scenes, Pat Buttram and Smiley Burnette, inscribed "America's Favorite Cowboy/GENE AUTRY" at bottom, #191 from limited edition series, certificate of authenticity from The Art Merchant, Hollywood, copyright 1982	**100.00**
Program, "The Gene Autry Show," 8½ x 11", 8 pgs, traveling show souvenir, c1950	**32.00**
Puzzle, frame tray, 11½ x 15", Whitman, copyright 1953	**25.00**
Record	
The Chisolm Trail/The Big Corral, 78	

rpm, Playtime label, Columbia Records, early 1950s, orig sleeve . **14.00**

Rudolph the Red–Nosed Reindeer/ Tinker Town Santa Claus, 45 rpm, Cricket label, Pickwick Sales Corp, early 1950s, orig cov **8.00**

Ring, Dell Comics **95.00**

Sheet Music, *No Letter Today*, 9 x 12", blue and white cov photo, copyright 1943 .... **12.00**

Song Folio, De Luxe Edition, 9 x 12", soft cov, 96 pgs, 88 songs and ballads, 1938 .... **32.00**

Tablet, 8 x 10", lined paper, full color illus of Gene and Champion and facsimile signature on cov, inscribed "Gene Autry/Columbia Pictures," c1950, unused **22.50**

Wrist Watch, animated, 1¼", silvered metal case, color portrait on dial face, Autry holding sixgun, arm rocks as watch runs, inscribed "Gene Autry Watch" on face and "Always Your Pal/Gene Autry" on face and back, tan tooled leather straps, New Haven Watch Co, c1951 .... **315.00**

HOPALONG CASSIDY

Ad, Christmas, framed, 1953 .... **42.00**

Belt, 2" w, 30" l, leather, black, silver "Hopalong" between metal rivets and stars on center back, early 1950s ... **35.00**

Birthday Card, photo pinback button insert **35.00**

Board Game, MIB, 1950 .... **55.00**

Bowl **30.00**

Camera, 3 x 4 x 5", box type, metal, black, illus of Hoppy on Topper on title plate, Galter Products of Chicago, 1940 William Boyd copyright **90.00**

Can, popcorn, 5" h, 2¾" d, litho tin, bright colors, portrait **30.00**

Card

Fan, 3½ x 5½", color portrait, facsimile signature, blank back, early 1950 .... **25.00**

Serial Club, unpunched, includes badge **15.00**

Carton

Ice Cream, 4½" h, cardboard canister, black, white, and blue **12.00**

Milk, waxed cardboard, 5½ x 11½", red, white, and blue **12.00**

Chinese Checkers **100.00**

Coloring Book

1938 .... **50.00**

1950 .... **35.00**

Coloring Kit, color picture of Hoppy, orig box **30.00**

Comic Book, Vol 5, #29, Fawcett, March 1949 .... **55.00**

Display, Butter–Nut bread loaf **75.00**

Doll, 22" h, cloth, stuffed, molded vinyl child's face stitched to fabric head, removable black felt hat, yellow hat band inscribed "Hopalong Cassidy," plush hair and chaps, early 1950s .. **190.00**

Flashlight, Siren Lite, 7" l, metal, silvered siren cap, litho scene around side, red lettering, inscribed "Hong Kong British Empire" on cap, 1940–50s **80.00**

Glass, milk glass, 5" h, of Hoppy and message in black, raised "Hoppy" on bottom, early 1950s **25.00**

Greeting Card, birthday, 4½ x 5½", paper, portrait, opens horizontally, "Official Hopalong Cassidy Cards" inscribed on back, Buzza Cardozo, Hollywood, orig envelope, early 1950s **27.50**

Hair Trainer **45.00**

Hanger, wood, jigsawed, "Hoppy's Bunkhouse Clothes Corral," three wood pegs, inscriptions stamped in black, Northland Milk, premium ... **100.00**

Knife and Scabbard, miniature, ¾ x 5" l, black vinyl belt loop sheath, inscribed "Hopalong Cassidy," 4" l knife, single blade, white plastic handle, marked "USA," early 1950s ... **60.00**

Lunch Box, thermos, cloud label, 1950s **110.00**

Mug, 3" h, white china, color Hoppy illus, early 1950s **70.00**

Party Plates, cardboard, multicolor Hoppy on Topper, white ground, orig cellophane shrink wrap, unopened, set of 6 .... **20.00**

Pen, ball point, 6" l, black plastic, silvered metal, 3–D plastic portrait, western symbols, rope script "Hopalong Cassidy," Parker Pen Co, c1950 **70.00**

Pencil Sharpener, 1¾ x 2½", flat, image of Hoppy on Topper, black and white, dark blue ground, sharpener mounted on reverse **30.00**

Pillow, Hoppy on Topper, fringed, satin slipcase, 1950s **75.00**

Pillow Cover, 16 x 17", satin, 2" gold brocade and fringe border, head and shoulder Hoppy portrait, six shooter, cactus, Bar–20 Ranch symbol, facsimile signature, unused **60.00**

Pin, Bulldogger Savings **22.00**

Pistol, 8" l **35.00**

Playing Cards, "Hopalong Canasta," Hoppy and Topper portraits on backs, Pacific Playing Card Co, copyright 1950, pr **85.00**

Pocket Knife, colorful **65.00**

Poster **12.00**

Puzzle, MIB, set of 3 .... **55.00**

Radio, red, Arvin **125.00**

Record Album, Square Dance Hold Up,
pictures, two records **75.00**
Scrap Book, large size **125.00**
Shirt and Pants, play outfit **145.00**
Snow Dome **50.00**
Tab, litho tin, "Burry's Hopalong Cassidy Cookies" inscription and "Hoppy's Secret Code" on back, early 1950s
   Hopalong Cassidy, rope border, Hoppy portrait center **65.00**
   Topper, horse's head in horseshoe illus **45.00**
Thermos **40.00**
Tie Slide, steer head **10.00**
Transfer, iron–on, 2½ x 10", tissue, brown, "Hopalong Cassidy/Deputy," early 1950s **10.00**
TV Book, mechanical
   Hoppy and Danny, 1950, mint **55.00**
   Hoppy and Lucky at Copper Gulch, 1950, mint **75.00**
Utensils, 7½" l knife, 6" l fork and spoon, stainless steel, Hoppy on handle, vertical stem, lettering, early 1950s **65.00**
Wood Burning Set, orig box **195.00**
Wrapper, gum card **45.00**
Wrist Watch, 1" d, chrome case, silver dial face, red numerals and hands, black and white depiction of Hoppy, black lettering, engraved "Good Luck From Hoppy" on back, US Time ... **140.00**
Writing Tablet **25.00**

DAVY CROCKETT

Bank, figural, copper **40.00**
Belt, colorful, metal buckle, compass, powder horn, mint on orig card **65.00**
Belt Buckle, 1½ x 3", silvered metal, rounded, raised border, inscription, Old Betsy rifle, leather belt, brown, simulated alligator texture **32.00**
Bow and Arrow Set, 46" strung wood bow, seven feathered wood arrows, paper target sheet, orig box and sleeve with name and portrait illus, Rollin Wilson Co, mid 1950s **45.00**
Bowl, 6½ d, china, white, brown Alamo battle scene **50.00**
Box, Davy Crockett Cookies, 2 x 4½ x 8" cardboard, diecut, figural, covered wagon drawn by oxen, portrait illus, Dutch Maid, Federal Sweets & Biscuit Co, Clifton, NJ, 1952 ...... **80.00**
Clock, pendulum, MIB **125.00**
Coloring Book, 8½ x 11", Whitman, 128 pgs, cut out coonskin cap back cov, 1955 .... **30.00**

Compass Watch **35.00**
Cookie Jar, Brush **125.00**
Flashlight, ¼ x 1¼ x 3¼" h, metal case, painted, removable red cap, brown and red Crockett illus, cream color ground, fringed fabric carrying strap, Bantam Lite Inc, mid 1950s **45.00**
Glass
   5" h, frosted white, dark brown portrait illus both sides, Ritchey's Milk, mid 1950s **35.00**
   5¼" h, clear, two printed scenes, yellow, dark brown, and green, "Davy Crockett 1786–1836," mid 1950s **18.00**
Gun, 10½" l, plastic, flintlock, brown, silver accents, "Davy Crockett" in gold lettering on side, raised pirate and ship on handle, c1955 .... **30.00**
ID Bracelet, Davy Crockett Club, metal, silvered finish, expandable, raised gold color Crockett holding rifle illus on cov, hinged, photo frames inside, two black and white photos included, red, white, blue, and brown Crockett illus on inside lid, Drema Mfg Co, 22 West 19th St, NY, orig display case and charter member card, mid 1950s **85.00**
Lamp, figural, copper **85.00**
Lunch Box, steel, full color illus, silver gray ground, green trim, American Thermos, 1955–56 .... **90.00**
Mug, pottery, figural, young Davy, gun handle **15.00**
Outfit, compass, belt, powder horn, orig pkg, mint **85.00**
Pinback Button, 1¼" d, black lettering and Crockett illus, yellow ground, white metal horse head in horseshoe hanger, 1950s **15.00**
Pirate Pistol **35.00**
Planter, souvenir, 3½ x 6 x 5" h, china, figural, young Davy, bear, tree stump, "Davy Crockett Birthplace/Limestone, Tenn," inscribed in gold on back of stump, c1950 .... **25.00**
Plate, 9½", china, white, brown name and illus, Oxford China Co, mid 1950s **50.00**
Puzzle, frame tray, 10 x 12½", aerial view of fort being attacked by Indians, black and white photo of Parker in upper left corner, c1955 .... **15.00**
Ring **15.00**
Sand Pail, 8" h, litho tin, colorful scenes on red ground, Ohio Art, copyright 1955 .... **60.00**
Sheet Music, *Ballad of Davy Crockett*, Fess Parker cov, Disney **20.00**
Stamp Book, 8½ x 11", Simon & Schuster, 32 pgs, 48 color photo stamps, 1955 .... **35.00**
Thermos 8½" h, steel, plastic cap, full

color illus around sides, American Thermos, c1955–56 .... **40.00**
Tie, mounted on orig card **15.00**
Wagon **40.00**
Wall Plaque Kit, "Tap–N–Lace," three plaques, green vinyl cord, wood awl, hammer, unused, Handicraft Creators Inc, mid 1950s **37.50**
Wallet, vinyl plastic, black western illus on red and cream ground, ID card, mid 1950s **20.00**
Wrist Watch, green **145.00**

LONE RANGER

Badge
Lone Ranger, brass, red and blue Lone Ranger illus on front, two ⅜" l brass brad tabs on back attach badge to lasso, late 1930s **160.00**
Lone Ranger Chief Scout **50.00**
Lone Ranger Deputy, shield shape, brass, secret compartment on back, premium, 1949 .... **30.00**
Lone Ranger/Silver's Lucky Horseshoe, large size, brass, blue and red, premium, c1938 .... **65.00**
Silver's Lucky Horseshoe, small size, brass, blue and red, premium, c1930 .... **40.00**
Blotter, colorful, Bond Bread **10.00**
Book
The Lone Ranger, Little Golden Book, 6½ x 8", stiff cov, Simon & Schuster, 24 pgs, copyright 1956 ...... **11.00**
The Lone Ranger Rides North, 5½ x 7½", hard cov, dj, Grosset & Dunlap, 214 pgs, copyright 1946 .... **18.00**
Card
Lone Ranger US Savings Bond Peace Patrol, membership, picture of Moore, unused **20.00**
Silver Cup Bread, premium, 3½ x 5½", black and white picture, red "Hi Yo, Silver," and red and white title block for WXYZ on front, Silver Cup Bread adv on reverse, late 1930s **60.00**
Flashlight **75.00**
Game, Legend of the Lone Ranger **10.00**
Hairbrush, orig box **85.00**
Holster
Lone Ranger, molded black rubber, textured design, silvered brass buckle, "Lone Ranger" inscription on holster, metal cap gun, 11" l, glossy black, white pistol grips, "Fanner 50" and Mattel logo on each side, late 1950s **40.00**
Tonto **40.00**
Magazine, Golden West, Lone Ranger on cov **10.00**

Map, Frontier Town, four sections, set **135.00**
Mask, half face, 3½ x 6½", black fabric, molded, starched, elastic head string, 1950s **25.00**
Model Kit, Tonto, #183, plastic, brown, eight page comic book, instructions, backdrop mural, Aurora Products Corp, copyright 1974, unopened ... **32.00**
Outfit, Lone Ranger Official Outfit, two black enameled steel clicker pistols, black pebble grained stiff cardboard holster, silver accents on guns and holster, 16 x 16 x 21" triangular neckerchief with black, red, and white print, orig box, Feinberg–Henry Co, copyright 1938 .... **130.00**
Paint Book, 1940 .... **40.00**
Palm Puzzle, ½ x 3½ x 5" w, litho tin frame, red and white checkerboard design, full color Lone Ranger scene, four small metal balls fit in holes on illus, clear glass cov, #5, "Guarding Gold Panners" series, c1940 ...... **25.00**
Pedometer, 2¾", black, white, and red center dial, "Official Lone Ranger Pedometer," aluminum rim, black back, premium, 1948 .... **35.00**
Pen, Silver Bullet Secret Code Ball Point, mint on card, 1950s **75.00**
Pencil Box **125.00**
Photo Card, 3½ x 5½", Clayton Moore, black and white, glossy, facsimile Lone Ranger signature, 1956–57 ... **35.00**
Pin, 1", silvered brass, "Silver Cup Lone Ranger Safety Scout," premium, 1935 **60.00**
Pinback Button, "Lone Ranger Silver Bullet Award," 2¼" d, celluloid, red, white, and blue, bullet in center, red inscription on silver ribbon, purple ribbon, issued by Lone Ranger Family Restaurants, c1970 .... **25.00**
Pistol, 9" l, brown marbleized grips ... **35.00**
Playset, Lone Ranger Old West Playset, plastic figures and fort, tepee, Multiple Toymakers, copyright 1974, orig sealed box **40.00**
Pocket Knife, 3" l, single blade, combination screw driver/opener, white illus and inscription on red plastic grips, late 1930s **70.00**
Press Kit, "The Lone Ranger," 1950s .. **70.00**
Record Set, boxed **75.00**
Ring
Flashlight, premium, 1948 .... **80.00**
Saddle, filmstrip **75.00**
Sheet Music, Hi Yo Silver, The Lone Ranger's Song, 1938 .... **80.00**
Story Record, 78 rpm, orig picture sleeves, #6 .... **30.00**
Target Game, gun and stand, Morton Salt premium, copyright 1938, orig box **120.00**

Tin, first aid 35.00
Token, "The Lone Ranger Seventeenth
Anniversary 1933–1950," 1¼", sil-
vered brass, Lone Ranger and Tonto
on reverse, inscribed "The Lone
Ranger Lucky Piece," premium 30.00
Toothbrush Holder, LR & Co, 1938 . . . 135.00
Wind–up, Roy spinning lasso, mounted
on rearing Silver, Marx logo, copy-
right 1938 . . . . 300.00

**Tom Mix, pinback button, Ralston
Straight Shooters, Mike Shaw, black on
white ground, red checkerboard, 1" d,
$15.00.**

TOM MIX

Badge
　Secret Code 125.00
　Wrangler, brass, Tom Mix head and
　shoulders above red, blue, and
　gold foil checkerboard inset, "Tom
　Mix Ralston Straight Shooter," TM
　initial logo, 1938 . . . . 80.00
Bar Pin, red and white checkerboard
　fabric, white plastic day glow hor-
　seshoe hanger, "Tom Mix Sharp-
　shooters Award," premium, c1945 . . 100.00
Belt, 1" w, plastic, day glow, checker-
　board and western motifs, brass buc-
　kle with secret compartment, raised
　Tom image, Ralston premium, c1946 95.00
Book
　The Fabulous Tom Mix, Olive Stokes
　Mix, Eric Heath assistant, 6 x 8½",
　hard cov, dj, Prentice–Hall, 178
　pgs, copyright 1957 . . . . 15.00
　the Range War, Big Little Book 30.00
Bracelet, ID, silvered brass, pair of
　sixguns and initial "B" on oval disk,
　Ralston address and serial number on
　reverse, chain link, premium 35.00
Cereal Bowl, 2½" h, 5½" d, china,
　white, Tom on Tony illus and inscrip-
　tion "Hot Ralston Cereal For Straight

Shooters" repeated around rim,
checkerboard and T–M Bar Ranch
symbol int., Ralston Purina copyright
1982 . . . . 35.00
Chaps and Vest, suede, brown and tan,
　red trim, yellow and red stars, flannel
　lined, facsimile signatures, portrait
　patch, Ralston premium, mid 1930s 160.00
Comic Book, #3, Jan 1941, Ralston pre-
　mium 60.00
Compass, Straight Shooter, Ralston . . . 65.00
Cowboy Boots, orig box, 1930s 350.00
Dixie Lid, ice cream cup lid, 2¼" d,
　brown and white, photo, "Miracle Ri-
　der" rim inscription, 1935 . . . . 25.00
Exhibit Card 20.00
Film, 16 mm, used with toy projector . 35.00
Gun, 9" l, wood, painted, black, opens
　at top, moving cylinder, facsimile sig-
　nature, ranch brand symbol, and
　"Ralston Straight Shooters" on grip,
　premium, c1933 . . . . 150.00
Manual, *Life of Tom Mix,* 5 x 7", 24 pgs,
　revised first edition, Ralston premium,
　orig envelope, 1933 . . . . 75.00
Marble 25.00
Model Kit, Flying Model Airplane, 11"
　l, 14" upper wing span, 5" propeller,
　biplane, balsa wood, pre–cut, paper
　stickers, premium, 1937 . . . . 120.00
Movie Viewer, 6½" h, cardboard, me-
　chanical, diecut opening, axle rods at
　top and bottom for winding black and
　white paper films, "Rustler's
　Roundup" film included, Ralston pre-
　mium, 1930–35 . . . . 200.00
Patch, 3" sq, cloth, red checkerboard
　design, T–M Bar Ranch symbol in
　blue at center, Ralston premium,
　1933 . . . . 70.00
Picture Frame, 1½ x 3 x 4½" h, silvered
　brass, checkerboard design, name
　and ranch symbol on front, photo of
　Tom and Tony, Ralston premium,
　c1938 . . . . 50.00
Pinback Button, "Tom Mix Circus," 1¾"
　d, black and white portrait, black
　ground, white lettering souvenir,
　1930s 60.00
Pocket Knife, 3" l, single blade, white
　pearlized grips, black and red check-
　erboard logo, 1939 . . . . 75.00
Post Card, 3½ x 5½", photo, brown,
　inscribed with name and film title
　"Desert Love," c1920 . . . . 19.00
Postal Telegraph Signal Set, Ralston . . . 75.00
Poster, safety 30.00
Ring
　Look–in, brass, inscribed "Boston"
　on side over picture of Tom and
　sixgun, TM brand on top, small
　hole reveals black and white pic-

ture of Tom and Tony with inscription "To My Straight Shooter Pal, Tom Mix" 160.00
Signet, brass bands, logo and crossed sixguns on side, raised letter "N" on black ground, 1937 .... 150.00
Tiger Eye 90.00
Record, Original Radio Broadcasts, Vol 1, 33⅓ rpm, commemorative, first two episodes of "The Mystery of the Vanishing Village," Ralston premium, orig album cov, c1982–83 .... 18.00
Rocket Parachute, 8½" l balsa and cardboard rocket, paper parachute holds diecast metal figure, red and white Ralston checkerboard design on rocket, orig mailing box and instructions, c1933 .... 145.00
Scarf 70.00
Sheet Music, *The Old Spinning Wheel*, Straight Shooters cov photo, copyright 1933 .... 30.00
Spinner, silvered brass, red lettering, "Ralston Wheat Cereal" on handle, "Good Luck–TM" message on spinning disk, premium, 1933 .... 65.00
Spurs, aluminum, glow in the dark rowel wheels, ranch brand symbol on fork, Ralston premium, c1947 ..... 145.00
Statue, Tony, plaster 35.00
Telescope and Bird Call Combination, 3½" l, bullet shape, plastic, "Magic Tone Bird Call," premium, c1950 .. 80.00
Tobacco Card, 1½ x 2", cigarette pack insert, black and white photo, #350, series D, Orami Cigarettes, Germany, c1930 .... 10.00
Watch Fob 45.00
Wrist Watch, 1⅜" metal case, gold color, full color dial face illus, clear plastic crystal, figural arms holding pistols, marked "The Original/Registered Model," Swiss made, simulated alligator leather bands, story book included, Ralston revival premium, 1982–83 .... 70.00

ROY ROGERS

Archery Set, adult size, 4½' hickory bow, four 22" l brass tipped cedar arrows, 16" black arrow quiver, leather arm guard and finger protector, 16" unused paper target, orig box, Ben Pearson, Inc, Pine Bluff, AK, mid 1950s 80.00
Badge, brass, "Roy Rogers Deputy Sheriff," emb Roy and Trigger in center, door on reverse opens to reveal signaling reflective disk, built-in red plastic whistle, Quaker premium, early 1950s 90.00

Roy Rogers, children's book, *Roy Rogers and The Sure 'Nough Cowpoke*, authorized edition, Tell-A-Tale Books, Whitman Publishing, 1952 copyright, red ground, yellow and green letters, 6⅝" sq, $5.00.

Bank
  Boot 25.00
  Horseshoe, metal and plastic, wall mount, Roy Rogers and Trigger Savings Bank 85.00
Bedspread, 77 x 102", chenille, tan, red and brown lettering, multicolor steer skull, branding iron, and rearing horse with cowboy throwing lasso illus, green piping, c1950 .... 100.00
Binoculars, MIB 60.00
Book, *Roy Rogers on the Trail of the Zeros*, 5½ x 8", hard cov, Whitman, #1501:49, 282 pgs, 1954 .... 28.00
Boots, MIB 160.00
Box Camera, Roy on Trigger 45.00
Camera, orig box 85.00
Canister, Quaker Oats, 7¼" h, 4" d, cardboard cylinder, litho paper label, adv for branding iron ring premium, c1948 .... 75.00
Card, Roy Rogers Riders Club, 2½ x 4⅛", stiff paper, buff color, black and white Roy and Trigger photo surrounded by red lasso design, facsimile signature, nine rules for club members on reverse, 1948–50 .... 30.00
Chaps 55.00
Charm, plastic, black, black and white glossy photo inset, Roy and Dale, c1950 .... 10.00
Charm Bracelet, 6" l, silver link, four black and white photos in clear plastic disks, Roy in one disk, other stars in remaining disks, c1950 .... 60.00

Clock, 1½ x 4 x 4¼", wind–up, animated, enameled metal case, ivory color, brass frame, clear plexiglas crystal, western desert scene illus on dial face, black and white rope design numerals, diecut Roy and Trigger figure rocks as clock runs, E Ingraham Co, c1951 .... **300.00**

Coloring Book, Trigger and Bullet, 6½ x 7½", Whitman, #2958, 1959 .... **24.00**

Comic Book, Roy Rogers Comics, Vol 1, #17, Dell Publishing Co, file copy issue, May 1949 .... **80.00**

Figure, Hartland
Bullet, Roy's dog, orig tags, MIB ... **125.00**
Roy and Trigger, mint on card **120.00**

Flashlight, Signal Siren, Rogers and Trigger **35.00**

Game, Horseshoes, orig box **100.00**

Gun, "Roy Rogers' Cookies," 4½ x 8", cardboard, folder, make popping noise, premium, mid 1950s **60.00**

Harmonica, Roy Rogers' Riders, 4½" l, white plastic, silvered metal, "Good Luck" and "King of the Cowboys" on engraved plates, 1950s **38.00**

Holster, studded, cartridge belt **65.00**

Jewelry Set, Dale Evans **28.00**

Lamp, Roy and Trigger, 8" h, plaster, facsimile signatures **250.00**

Lantern, 7½" h, litho metal, replica ranch lantern, red, blue, and yellow design, horseshoe handles, wire bail, hanging loop, clear plastic globe, battery operated, mid 1950s **90.00**

Lunch Box
Roy, eight scenes, green band **85.00**
Trigger **45.00**

Lunch Pail, Double R Bar Ranch **95.00**

Mug, china **65.00**

Neckerchief, 5½ x 35", gold synthetic, Roy portrait printed on ends, rope script name, 1950 .... **55.00**

Outfit
Dale Evans, cowgirl, box **75.00**
Roy Rogers, shirt and vest, child's, khaki long sleeved shirt, "Roy Rogers Frontier Wear" label, made by Rob Roy, stitched floral design, tan leather vest, red leather pockets and straps, silver metal rosettes, "Sheplers" tag, mid 1950s **40.00**

Paint Book, 11 x 15", Whitman, #1158, 48 pgs, copyright 1948, unused **60.00**

Paint By Number Set, MIB **65.00**

Picture, Sears Roebuck Christmas giveaway **25.00**

Pinback Button
Photo, 2¾" d **22.50**
"Roy's Boots" **18.00**
Roy's Brand **18.00**

Pistol, miniature, 2¾" **22.50**

Plate, china, Roy Rogers Rodeo, unsigned **25.00**

Play Set
Roy Rogers Fix–It Chuckwagon and Jeep, plastic, Ideal Toys, orig box, mid 1950s **125.00**
Roy Rogers Rodeo Ranch **100.00**

Playing Cards **55.00**

Pocket Knife, 3½", steel, two blade, plastic strips, black and white illus, c1950 .... **75.00**

Poster, 27 x 41", "Spoilers of the Plains," full color, 1951 Republic picture **80.00**

Pup Tent, cloth, Hettrick Mfg Co **45.00**

Puzzle
Jigsaw, 15 x 21", family picture, Roy, Dale, and Dusty, Whitman, orig box, mid 1950s **26.00**
Frame Tray, 4 x 5", cardboard, Roy holding puppies, 1952 Frontiers Inc copyright, unpunched **20.00**

Raincoat, child's, knee length, vinyl, fabric lining, yellow, black trim and designs, fringe, mid 1950s **100.00**

Record, 78 rpm, Golden Record, inspirational, Roy singing The Lord's Prayer one side, Dale singing Ave Maria on other, orig cov, mid 1950s **30.00**

Record Player, litho **150.00**

Saddle **550.00**

Scarf **100.00**

Slippers, boot style, black wool felt, white felt fringe, sole edges, and spur rowel, yellow, red, black, and white ink stamped Roy and Trigger illus on sides, "Pledge to Parent" sheet included, orig box, mid 1950s **175.00**

Star, tin, silver finish, "Roy Rogers/Deputy," 1950s **35.00**

Tee Shirt, Roy Rogers **35.00**

Thermos, Double R Bar Ranch, 8½" h, litho metal, red plastic cap, mid 1950s **35.00**

Tie, yellow **75.00**

Tie Clip, 2¾" l, metal, gold color, six shooter, Double R Bar Ranch symbol on grips, fires caps, 3" l thin leather holster, c1950 .... **60.00**

Token **17.50**

Toothbrush, orig pkg **30.00**

Toy
Pull, musical, 20" l, 6" h, wood horse and wagon, litho paper sides, painted steel wheels, Roy, Bullet, and Trigger symbols, NN HIII Brass Co, c1950 .... **100.00**
Push, 34" l, wood figure of Bullet and head of Trigger at either end of wood rod joined at center by metal coupling, red steel wheels and bells at Bullet end, fabric strap reins, full

color litho paper illus on both sides, Hill Toys and Bells, NN Hill Brass Co, mid 1950s **175.00**
Telephone **40.00**
Van, litho metal, 15½" l, cab and detachable trailer van, black rubber wheels, Marx, mid 1950s **60.00**
Transfer Sheet, iron–on, 10 x 12", white tissue, cowgirl on rearing horse, desert scene in background, "Dale Evans" in rope script, mid 1950s **42.00**
View–Master Reel **15.00**
Wrist Watch
  Dale Evans **135.00**
  Roy Rogers, green ground **175.00**

CHARACTERS, OTHER

Annie Oakley, suspenders, child's charcoal gray elastic fabric, red, yellow, and white names and western motifs of Annie and Tagg, silver six shooter grips, orig display card with Gail Davis and Jimmy Hawkins illus, 1952–65, unused **28.00**
Cisco Kid
  Gun, 7¼" l, cardboard, folder, black, white, and blue illus both sides, metal "cricket" inside, inscribed "Listen to the Cisco Kid," early 1950s **30.00**
  Picture Card, 3½ x 5½", stiff paper, black and white photo, glossy, facsimile signature, red and white Wards Tip–Top Bread ad on reverse, early 1950s **18.00**
  Program, 8½ x 11", stiff paper folder, glossy, souvenir, "Cisco Kid Rodeo," dated mid July, Wrigley Field, Chicago, early 1950s **23.00**
  Puzzle, frame tray, 10¼ x 11½", jigsaw, Duncan Renaldo and Diablo portrait illus, Saalfield, copyright Doubleday & Co, 1951 .... **35.00**
  Tab, litho tin, red, white, and blue, Pancho in bright green hat, "Pancho/Weber's Bread/Cisco Kid," 1950s **20.00**
Wyatt Earp
  Big Little Book, *Hugh O'Brian TV's Wyatt Earp*, Whitman, #1644, 276 pgs, from TV Series, 1958 .... **14.00**
  Cap Gun, holster, and badge, orig card **125.00**
  Color and Stencil Set, Hugh O'Brian, MIB **135.00**
Ranger Joe
  Mug, 3" h, white glass, blue inscription and illus, early 1950s **14.00**
  Ranch Money, 2½ x 4¾", "One Buck," Ranger Joe Cereal premium, dated 1952 .... **25.00**

Red Ryder
  Belt Buckle, 2" sq, silvered brass, cowboy on bronc, name spelled twice in rope script, 1940s **35.00**
  Flashlight, 7" l, metal, litho illus by Fred Harman, copyright 1949 .... **70.00**
  Gloves, child's, black, white gauntlet, black title and illus, fringed, early 1940s **40.00**
  Molding and Coloring Kit, four soft rubber molds, plaster, orig box with Fred Harman art, Bersted's Hobby Crafts, late 1940s **70.00**
  Pop Gun, double barrel, Daisy, 1950s **75.00**
  Rodeomatic Radio Decoder, 3", paper, disk wheels, red, white, and blue, brass cotter pin, c1942 .... **55.00**
Rifleman, book, color photo cov shows Connors with rifle and Crawford, hard cov, Whitman **10.00**
Rin Tin Tin
  Canteen, "Official Rin Tin Tin 101st Cavalry," 7" h, textured plastic, brown, black cap, brown vinyl carrying strap, raised inscription, Nabisco premium, orig box, copyright Screen Gems Inc, 1957 .... **70.00**
  Doll, 9" h, plush, stuffed, gray and white, rubber face, inset brown glass eyes **62.00**
  Game, The Adventures of Rin Tin Tin, Transogram, 1955 .... **20.00**
  Paint By Number Kit, four 9¼ x 12" preprinted illus sheets, water color tablets, orig box, Transogram, 1956 **60.00**
  Palm Puzzle, 1¼" d, tin disk, clear plastic cov, three small balls fit in holes, boy in cavalry uniform yelling "Go, Rinty/Rusty," Nabisco premium, c1956 .... **12.50**
  Play Set, Rin Tin Tin at Fort Apache, #3627, 2½" h plastic figures sealed in orig bags, blue cavalrymen, assorted colored Indians, cream colored Rip Masters, Rusty, and Rin Tin Tin, tin fort, Marx, 1950s, orig box, unused **450.00**
  Punch Out Card, totem poles, plastic, emb, full color, Nabisco premium, late 1950s, set of 3 .... **30.00**
  Ring, brass, raised portrait, hinged lid reveals two ink pads, c1930 ..... **85.00**
  View–Master Reel, "Vanishing Guns," "Indian Ambush," and "High Danger," orig cov envelope, copyright 1955 .... **35.00**
Sky King
  Photo, autographed, 7 x 9", glossy, black and white, Kirby Grant, blue ink, "For Cheryl/Sky King," c1950 **65.00**
  String Tie, brown, silver tips, silvered brass tie slide with longhorn steer

illus, orig photo cover sheet and mailing envelope, Peter Pan Peanut Butter premium, c1950 .... **70.00**

Straight Arrow

Bandanna **75.00**

Card, War Drum Signals, 3½ x 7½", folder, black and white, 1949–50 **25.00**

Finger Puppets, cardboard, 7½" sq sheet, unpunched, script card, "The Stage Raider," Nabisco Shredded Wheat premium, c1955 ..... **40.00**

Ring, brass, portrait, Nabisco premium, 1950 .... **50.00**

Wild Bill Hickock

Card, Breakfast Game Score Card, 8 x 10", Kellogg's, cereal boxes and messages by Guy Madison and Andy Devine on front, check–off cards on reverse, mid 1950s **25.00**

Cavalry Game, 1950s **15.00**

Gun and Holster Set, box **150.00**

Pinback Button, ⅞" d, brown photo, light pink ground, "Wild Bill Hickock," 1950s **20.00**

PERSONALITIES

Benson, Bobby, pinback button, 1¼" d, blue lettering and rope design on yellow ground, "Bobby Benson/Special Captain," 1930s **30.00**

Buffalo Bill Cody

Figurine, 6" h, syroco–like composition and wood, "Buffalo Bill" and 1941 maker's copyright inscribed on 1½" sq base **65.00**

Photo Card, 4¼ x 6½", cardboard, black and white, facsimile signature, 1890–1900 .... **60.00**

Pinback Button

1¼", sepia photo, gold finish white metal Rough Riders–style hat suspended from bar on back of button, back paper marked "Stacy Photographer, Brooklyn," early 1900s **40.00**

1⅜", litho, black, white, tan, and dark red, Cody on horse behind buffalo, #1 of Van Brode America Series, biography on back paper, c1950 .... **20.00**

Spill Holder, 5½" h, figural, white metal, gold finish, hollow, 1¼" d x 1" deep receptacle in crown of hat for holding wood spills, souvenir, late 1890s **100.00**

Gray, Gene, pinback button, 1¼" d, blue illus and lettering, white ground, Gray on horse, "Gene Gray/Silver King of Cowboys," 1930s **25.00**

Jones, Buck

Badge, "Buck Jones Club," brass, black and red, c1930 .... **30.00**

Big Big Book, *Buck Jones and the Night Riders*, 7½ x 9½", hard cov, Whitman, #4069, 316 pgs, Hal Arbo, illustrator story by Gaylord DuBois, 1937 .... **90.00**

Guitar, adult size, 37" l, pressed wood, illus and "Good Luck/Buck Jones & Silver" on face, made by Gibson for Sears, Roebuck & Co, c1930 .... **130.00**

Manual, *Buck Jones Rangers–Cowboys Collection*, #1, 1932 ...... **65.00**

Maynard, Ken

Cigar Band, 1 x 3", diecut, emb paper, red, gold, and black design, black and white photo, 1930s ... **20.00**

Movie Card, 14 x 22", cardboard, window, red, white, blue, flesh, and brown design for 1933 Universal western film **50.00**

Pinback Button, ⅞" d, black portrait and lettering, white ground, "Ken Maynard Club/First National Pictures," 1930s **15.00**

McCoy, Tim

Big Little Book, *The Prescott Kid*, starring Tim McCoy, #1152, Columbia Pictures, adapted by Eleanor Packer, 1935, 4⅝ x 5¼", 160 pgs, hard cov, soft spine **22.50**

Pinback Button, ⅞" d, litho, blue portrait and lettering, white ground, "Tim McCoy's Vigilantes," 1930s **25.00**

Wayne, John

Mug, china, 3¼" h, issued for 1974 movie McQ, blue, gray, black, and yellow design, black "Good Luck" signature, stamped "Ketchum Originals" on bottom **30.00**

Tablet, 5½ x 9", color photo and facsimile signature on cov, c1950 ... **30.00**

CRACKER JACK

Collecting Hints: Most collectors concentrate on the pre-plastic era. Toys in the original packaging are very rare. One possibility for specializing is toys from a given decade, for example in World War II soldiers, tanks, artillery pieces and other war related items.

Many prizes are marked "Cracker Jack" or carry a picture of the Sailor Boy and Bingo, his dog. Unmarked prizes can be confused with gumball machine novelties or prizes from Checkers, a rival firm.

History: F.W. Rueckheim, a popcorn store owner in Chicago, introduced a mixture of popcorn, peanuts, and molasses at the World's Columbian Exposition in 1893. Three years later the name "Cracker Jack" was applied to it. It gained popularity quickly and by 1908 appeared in the lyrics of *Take Me Out To The Ball Game*.

In 1910 Rueckheim included coupons on the box which could be redeemed for prizes. In 1912 prizes appeared in the box itself. The early prizes were made of paper, tin, lead, wood and porcelain. Plastic was introduced in 1948.

The Borden Company's Cracker Jack prize collection numbers over 10,000 examples; but this is not all of them. Knowledge continues to expand as more examples are found in bottoms of drawers, old jewelry boxes and attics.

Today's items are largely paper, the plastic magnifying glass being one exception. The company buys toys in lots of 25 million and keeps hundreds of prizes in circulation at one time. Borden's annual production is about 400 million boxes.

Reference: Alex Jaramillo, *Cracker Jack Prizes*, Abbeville Press, 1989.

Truck, tin, red and black, 1⅜" l, $60.00.

Baseball Card, Jack in baseball uniform, 1915	**17.50**
Bird, plastic, green, c1950	**7.00**
Boat, 1 x 2½", wood, orig 3 x 4" mailing box, c1930	**50.00**
Booklet	
Angelus Recipes, 4 x 6", black and white, 14 pgs	**15.00**
Cracker Jack Riddles, 2¾ x 5", paper, Rueckheim Bros & Eckstein, 40 pgs, black and white Jack and his dog illus	**25.00**
Bookmark, 2¾" h, litho tin, brown terrier, c1930s	**18.00**
Box, Jack and Bingo, 1919	**48.00**
Card, 2 x 3½", stiff paper, diecut, mechanical, color, child eating Cracker Jack, movable jaws, ears, and eyes, early 1900s	**85.00**
Clicker, aluminum	**15.00**
Corn Popper, 14" handle, c1930	**60.00**
Decoder, Jack the Sailor	**22.00**

Delivery Van, prize, ¾" h, tin, Cracker Jack ad one side, Angelus Marshmallow adv other side, c1920s	**50.00**
Doll, stuffed cloth, sailor's outfit, Vogue Dolls, copyright 1980, orig pkg, unopened	**25.00**
Figurine, stand–up, diecut, litho tin	
Moon Mullins	**20.00**
Smitty, 1⅓" h, 1930s	**45.00**
Fish, plastic, yellow, c1950	**5.00**
Flasher, 1¼", cardboard, inscription on back, c1960	**5.00**
Fortune Wheel, 1¾", litho tin, red, white, and blue, alphabet letters, diecut opening	**35.00**
Frog, 2 x 2¼", cardboard, diecut, "Spread Me Open and See Me Jump"	**15.00**
Game	
Checkers, premium, orig envelope	**15.00**
Toy Surprise Game, Milton Bradley, 1976, complete	**28.00**
Hat, paper, "Me For Cracker Jack," red, white, and blue design, early 1900s	**65.00**
Lapel Stud, "CJ Air Corps," metal, white	**40.00**
Mask, 8½ x 10", "Cracker Jack" on front, c1960	**15.00**
Pencil, wood	**15.00**
Pinback Button, 1¼" d, lady, multicolored, black hair, pink ribbon, green ground, red and white "Cracker Jack 5¢/Candied Popcorn & Roasted Peanuts" on back paper, copyright 1910	**60.00**
Plate, 1¾" d, tin, silvered, c1930s	**35.00**
Post Card, 3 x 5½", multicolored, bears on Statue of Liberty, Cracker Jack box replaces torch, Rueckheim Bros & Eckstein, copyright 1907	**35.00**
Puzzle, 2½ x 5", c1930	**5.00**
Puzzle Book, 2½ x 4", four pgs, series one, color memory retention puzzles, Angelus Marshmallow ad on back cov, copyright 1917	**80.00**
Rocker, ⅜", metal, litho, red, white, and blue	**20.00**
Rocket Ship, 1½", plastic, green, c1950	**10.00**
Sign, 7 x 11", cardboard, c1930	**45.00**
Sled, prize, 2" l, silvered tin, marked, c1930s	**35.00**
Squeaker, 2½ x 3½", cardboard, accordion shape	**35.00**
Stationery, envelope, red and blue box	**6.00**
Tape Measure, 1½", Angelus Marshmallow design, c1930	**40.00**
Toy	
Car, metal	**45.00**
Top, 1½", litho tin, red, white, and blue, "Always on Top," c1930s	**28.00**
Train Set, 2 pcs	**22.00**
Wheelbarrow, prize, 2¼" l, silvered tin, marked	**32.00**
Whistle, ½ x 2", tin, silvered, single reed, c1930s	**30.00**

CREDIT COINS AND CARDS

Collecting Hints: Specialization is the key to successful collecting. Plan a collection that can be completed. Completeness tends to increase a collection's value.

When collecting charge coins, stay away from rusted or damaged pieces. Inferior pieces attract little interest unless rare.

Metal charge plates have little collector interest. They should remain affordable for years which means they'll probably not advance in value.

Most interest is in credit cards. Scarce and rare cards, when they can be located, are still affordable. National credit cards are eagerly sought. American Express is the most popular.

Paper and laminated paper credit cards are highly desirable. When it comes to collecting these, don't concern yourself with condition. Go ahead and acquire any you find. They're so difficult to locate that it could take years to find another specimen. Some are so rare that they might be unique!

Plastic credit cards issued before 1970 are scarce. Occasionally, you'll find a mint condition card. Generally, you'll have to settle for used. Plastic cards issued after 1980 should be collected in mint condition.

The best collecting hint is, collect what you like. You'll provide yourself with years of enjoyment and that's the best investment you'll ever make!

History: Charge coins, the first credit pieces, started being issued in the 1890s. Charge coins are approximately the size of a quarter or half dollar. Because of their size, they were often carried with change. This is why they were commonly referred to as coins.

Charge coins come in various shapes, sizes and materials. Most are square, round or oval. Some are in the shapes of shirts, socks or hats. They're made from various materials such as fiber, German silver, celluloid, steel and copper. The issuing store has its name, monogram or initials on the coin. Each coin has a customer identification number. Charge coins were still in use as late as 1959.

Metal charge plates were in use from the 1930s to the 1950s. These plates look like military dog tags. The front of the plate contains the customer's name, address and account number. The back has a piece of cardboard that carries the store's name and customer's signature space.

Paper credit cards were in use in the early 1930s. They were easily damaged, so some companies began laminating them with clear plastic in the 1940s. Laminated cards were issued until

the 1950s. In the late 1950s plastic cards replaced the laminated cards.

References: Greg Tunks, *Credit Card Collecting Bonanza*, published by author, 1986.

Periodical: *Credit Card Collector*, 150 Hohldale, Houston, TX 77022.

CHARGE COINS

Boggs and Buhl, Pittsburgh, PA, oval, white metal, knight's helmet between backward and regular B	**15.00**
Conrad's, Boston, MA, irregular round, golden plating, picture of store	**25.00**
Dives, Pomeroy & Stewart, Reading Pottsville, PA, rect, white metal, initials D F & S, thistles	**12.00**
George B Evans, Philadelphia, PA, diamond shape, white metal, drugs and gifts	**15.00**
Gilchrist, Boston, MA, golden shield, G Co	**17.50**
Gimble Brothers	
Philadelphia, PA, rect, white metal, lion holding shield, GB initials, finder mailing instructions on back	**14.00**
New York City, oval, white metal, GB in circle at top, New York at bottom	**18.00**
Lit Brothers, Philadelphia, PA, irregular oval, white metal, LB, date of issue	**20.00**
C F Massey, Rochester, MN, octagonal, white metal, ornate interlocking C F M	**15.00**
Neill, Philadelphia, PA, sq, white metal, Neill script	**12.50**
Plotkin Brothers, Boston, MA, rect, white metal, lion head over shield containing PB	**17.50**
Pocohontas Pioneer Garage, Philadelphia, PA, oval, white metal, high relief indian profile	**17.50**
R H Stearns, Boston, MA, oval, white metal, interlocking R H S Co	**15.00**
John Wanamaker, Philadelphia, PA, irregular oval, German silver, JW, fleur-de-lis, ornamental border, 1890s	**40.00**
R H White, Boston, MA, pear shape, white metal, interlocking R H W Co script	**20.00**

CREDIT CARDS

American Airlines, March 1986	**6.00**
American Express	
1958, red printing, purplish blue ground, paper	**500.00**
1968, violet, centurion on upper left	**100.00**
1970, green, "The Money Card"	**25.00**
1972, gold, "The Executive Money Card," card appears to change colors when rotated	**50.00**

ARCO, 1976, Atlantic Richfield Company 4.00

AT&T, phone card, plastic 3.00

Bank Americard, account number in tan area
Magnetic stripe 15.00
Without magnetic stripe 7.50

Bell System Credit Card, 1964, high gloss paperboard, place to hold dime 15.00

Bloomingdale's, brown on white, tan border 10.00

Carte Blanche
1973, gold, blue on gold 40.00
1977, blue on white, gold border .. 7.50

Champlin, 1967, "A great name in the Great Plains," gas pump island drawing 12.00

Chevron National Credit Card, 1967, attendants servicing car 20.00

Choice, 1984 .... 4.00

Diners Club
Booklet, April 30, 1956, 126 pgs, Hertz ad in back with drawing of '55 Ford, blank memo pgs bound inside to record charge transactions 175.00
Colored blocks, 1967, blue top 45.00
Red top, expires Nov 30, 1962 .... 55.00
Gray ground, Citicorp 12.50
Silver and blue logo, white ground . 6.00

Eastern, October 1984 .... 7.50

Esso, 1966, "Happy Motoring," waving attendant 15.00

Fina, early 1970s, lare blue Fina 5.00

Frederick's of Hollywood, "Fabulous Hollywood Fashions" 17.50

General Tire, December 31, 1953, paperboard, lightly soiled, calendar on back 25.00

Gimbels, black on brown, New York and all branch stores 4.00

Goodyear, drawing of blimp 7.50

Gulf Travel Card, land, sea, air, car, boat, and plane drawing 10.00

Hilton Hotels
1955, paperboard 35.00
1958, paperboard, large size, high glass finish 45.00

Hotel McLure, 1951–52, paperboard . 25.00

Hotels Statler, 1952, paperboard 45.00

Illinois Bankcharge, red, white, and blue shield 15.00

International Credit Card, 1960, sailing ship logo 30.00

Jordan Marsh Co, blue on white, store drawing, good in Boston, Framingham, Malden, and Peabody ... 20.00

Korvettes, personal charge plate 3.00

Lit Brothers, blue and white stripes ... 10.00

Levy's, paperboard, c1950s or early 60s, tan with brown top, Tucson, Douglans, and Warren 22.50

Lord & Taylor, flower on front 6.00

Macy's, red star, "It's smart to be thrifty" 5.00

Marshall Field & Company, green and white 5.00

Mastercard
Pre-hologram 3.00
Pre-hologram, cardholder photograph on back 6.00
Pre-hologram, gold card 6.00

Mastercharge
Early 1970s, cardholder photograph on back 60.00
Magnetic stripe 7.50

Midwest Bank Card, Charge–It, Harris Bank, 05/67, blue top 22.50

Mobil, Pegasus on Mobil sing on front upper left 10.00

Montgomery Ward, yellow and white, national charg-all card 7.50

Neiman Marcus, commemorative credit card, 75th anniversary 15.00

Pan Am Take Off Card, 1970 .... 10.00

Penneys, black on blue, "always first quality" 8.00

Phillips 66, non-expiring, "passport to everywhere" 12.00

Playboy Club International
Gold, Jan 1979 .... 6.00
Membership Card, Feb 1986 .... 5.00

Saks Fifth Avenue, paper, charge account indentification card 30.00

Sears, Sears in box 8.00

Shannon's Furniture, 1939, Tulsa, OK, black on blue, paper, store drawing 12.00

Sinclair, 1971, motoring credit, waving green dinosaur 6.00

Skelly, ladies credit card, two gloved hands holding Skelly symbol 20.00

Spur, 10/70 .... 12.00

Standard Oil, 1972, red and blue map of United States 15.00

Sunoco, custom blended gasoline pump drawing 7.50

Texaco Travel Card, car, boat, and plane drawings 5.00

The Texas Company (Texaco), 1957, tan and white, paper 60.00

TWA, 1974, getaway card, swim suited couple holding hands 10.00

Uni-Card, 1970s 10.00

Vickers Refining Co, lifetime courtesy card, crown over V logo 17.50

Visa
Atlanta Falcons, 4/89 .... 15.00
Pre-hologram 2.50

Wallachs, undated, high gloss paperboard 25.00

John Wanamaker, metal charge plate, carrying case 17.50

Woolco, orange on white 10.00

DAIRY ITEMS

Collecting Hints: Concentrate on the material associated with one specific dairy, region or national firm. Much of the material available relates to advertising such as blotters, brochures, postcards, and trade cards.

Collectors of dairy items compete with many other groups. Milk bottle collectors try to supplement their collection with these "go–withs." Farm item collectors concentrate on cream separator materials and other farm related items. Ice cream collectors seek cartons and other materials. Finally, home decorators like the milk cans and other large, showy objects.

History: There were hundreds of small dairies and creameries scattered throughout the United States during the late 19th and mid-20th centuries. Many issued a variety of material to promote their products.

Eventually regional cooperatives expanded the marketing regions, and many smaller dairies closed. Companies such as Borden distributed products on a national level. Borden created the advertising character of "Elsie, the Borden Cow" to help sell its products. Additional consolidation of firms has occurred, encouraged in part by state milk marketing boards and Federal subsidies.

Reference: John Tutton, *Udder Delight*, published by author.

Periodical: *The Milk Route*, 4 Ox Bow Road, Westport, CT 06880.

Museums: The Farmers Museum, Cooperstown, NY; Southwest Dairy Museum, Arlington, TX; Billings Farm Museum, Woodstock, VT.

Notes: A milk bottle cap refers to a plug type cap placed on a bottle by the dairy in a bottling room. A milk bottle cover was made of either metal or glass and often contained dairy advertising. It was used to cover the bottle after the paper cap was removed. A milk bottle cap pick was used to remove the plug type milk bottle caps. A milk bottle cap opener had the same function but was used to remove a different style cap found on more modern bottles, known as the DACRO type.

See: Milk Bottles.

Advertising Trade Card, T.W. Decker & Sons, little girl swinging on the moon, discussion of Decker's new plant at Pawling, NY, and listing of New York city depots on back 12.00

Bank, Rutter Bros Dairy Products, dairy truck, plastic, white, red decal, c1960 40.00

Blotter, Universal Super Strength Milk Bottles, picture of plant in Parkersburg, WV, address of NE representa-

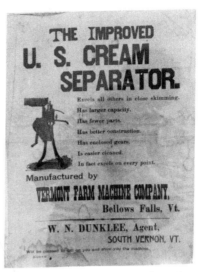

Advertising Poster, US Cream Separator, Vermont Farm Machine Co, Bellows Falls, VT, W. N. Dunklee, Agent, 12¼ x 17", $35.00.

tive in Hartford, CT, white and orange lettering, white ground 7.00

Booklet

Borden's, Streamline Your Figure, 5¼ x 7", 32 pgs, 1942 .... 8.00

Jones Milk Co, color litho, giveaway, 1935 .... 18.00

Bucket, Sunny Field Lard, 4 lbs 28.00

Butter Box, Bossie's Best Brand Butter, four color picture of a Jersey cow, Aberdeen Creamery Co., folded 5.00

Calendar, Broad View Farm, pure milk from our accredited herd, Rochester, NH, little girl climbs steps of house and reaches for a giant bottle of Broad View Farm's milk, tear sheet for each month with saying about milk, dated 1927 .... 12.00

Clock, Garst Bros Dairy, double globe 125.00

Cream Separator

Dilution Gravity, tin, blue, three wood legs 35.00

Junior #33, table top type, royal blue 145.00

Cream Siphon, Marvel, aluminum, fits in bottle and siphons cream into a cream pitcher or other vessel 6.00

Cream Top Spoon, Fritchett Bros. Dairy, Pat. Applied For 12.00

Creamer

Anthony's Cream 13.00

Freeman's Dairy, glass 20.00

Rosebud Dairy 9.00

Doilies, Carver Ice Cream, linen–like, emb, Christmas, 1920s, pkg of 12 .. 10.00

Fan, girl in highchair who has spilled
milk from her cup on front, "Compliments of Lebel's Dairy, 145 E. Hollis
Street, Nashua, NH" on back 10.00
Measuring Cup, Pyrex, 8 oz., Lenkerbrook Farms, Inc., glass, red markings   5.00
Milk Bottle

Borden Weiland, emb, round, qt ...   20.00
Gail Borden, amber, 1½ gal 22.00
VM&I Co, emb, amber, qt 50.00

Milk Bottle Cap

Davol Anti Germ, rubber, fits over lip
of milk bottle to keep out dirt, orig
container 7.00
Deerfoot Farms, Southborough, MA   5.00
Grade A Raw Milk, red and white ..   .25
Heber Springs Dairy, Heber Springs,
AR .... .10
Kents Dairy Farms, Vitamin D, Olean,
NY .... .10
Parker Goat Dairy, Raw Milk, picture
of goat 1.25

Milk Bottle Cap Opener, Brock Hall
Dairy Products, Purity Protected
Dacro Sealed Milk on back 5.00
Milk Bottle Cap Pick

Borden Select Milk 5.00
Sheffield Farms Company, Inc 5.00

Milk Bottle Carrier, metal, wire handle,
holds 6 round quarts 10.00
Milk Box, wood, has dairy name, holds
4 to 6 quarts 7.00
Milk Can, plain 10.00
Mug, Elsie in daisy on outside, Elsie
head on inside bottom 35.00
Pencil, Rutters Dairy, York and Hanover,
PA, wood, unsharpened 3.00
Pin, Dairyman's Assn, Western Ontario,
1906 .... 50.00
Playing Cards, Quality Dairy, Q motif
on each card, complete deck 8.00
Postcard

Ebert Ice Cream Company, factory
pictured 5.00
Elsie, Elmer, and Beauregard, traveling representatives of Borden's family of fine foods, shows characters
in traveling bedroom, explanation
of bedroom furnishings on back,
color 3.00

Printer's Dies, to print milk bottle caps,
dairy name, town, and state 4.00
Punch Out Train, Borden, 1950s 80.00
Puzzle, jigsaw, cardboard, 18 x 11",
Borden's milk wagon and milkman,
middle piece shaped like milk bottle,
1928 .... 100.00
Ruler

Breyer Ice Cream, colorful 15.00
Bryant & Chapman Dairy, Hartford,
CT, wood, 6" 3.00

Sewing Kit, Borden's Mitchell Dairy,

picture of Elsie on cover, slogan
"Milk's Good Anytime, Better Still
Make It Borden's" 7.00
Sign

Borden, tin, red 55.00
Meiers Ice Cream, porcelain 65.00

Tape Measure, "Cass Dairy Farm, Inc.,
Jersey & Ayshire Milk, For Service
Call 820 W Athol, MA" on front,
"You Can Whip Our Cream But You
Can't Beat Our Milk, Try Our Cream"
on back, celluloid container 28.00
Thermometer

Primrose Dairy Products 60.00
Sealtest Milk, carton 75.00

Tie Clasp, Elsie medallion, c1930 .... 35.00
Token, plastic, Muskalonge View Dairy,
Fremont, OH, good for one quart of
homogenized milk 4.00
Tray, DeLaval, tip 85.00

DEGENHART GLASS

Collecting Hints: Degenhart pressed glass novelties are collected by mold (Forget–Me–Not
toothpick holders or all Degenhart toothpick
holders), by individual colors (Rubina or Bloody
Mary), or by group colors (opaque, iridescent,
crystal, or slag).

Correct color identification is the key to full
enjoyment of collecting Degenhart glass. Because of the slight variations in the hundreds of
colors produced at the Degenhart Crystal Art
Glass factory from 1947 to 1978, it is important
for beginning collectors to acquire the eye for
distinguishing Degenhart colors, particularly the
green and blue variations. A knowledgeable collector or dealer should be sought for guidance.
Side by side color comparison is extremely helpful.

Later glass produced by the factory can be
distinguished by the trademark of a "D" in a
heart or only a "D" on certain molds where
space prohibited the full mark. Use of this mark
began around 1972 and by late 1977 most of the
molds had been marked. Prior to this time,
c1947–1972, no glass was marked with the exception of the owl, and occasionally other pieces
that were identified by hand stamping a block
letter "D" to the object as it came out of the
mold. This hand stamping was started and continued during the period 1967 to 1972.

Collecting unmarked Degenhart glass made
from 1947 to c1970 poses no problem once a
collector becomes familiar with molds and colors
being worked during that period. Some of the
most sought after colors such as Amethyst &
White Slag, Amethyst Carnival, and Custard Slag
are unmarked, yet are the most desirable. Keep
in mind that some colors such as Custard (opaque
yellow), Heliotrope (opaque purple), and Tomato

(opaque orange red) were repeated and can be found marked and unmarked depending on production date.

History: John (1884–1964) and Elizabeth (1889–1978) Degenhart operated the Crystal Art Glass factory of Cambridge, Ohio, from 1947 to 1978. The factory specialized in reproducing pressed glass novelties and paperweights. Over 50 molds were worked by this factory including ten toothpick holders, five salts, and six animal covered dishes of various sizes.

When the factory ceased operation, many of the molds were purchased by Boyd Crystal Art Glass, Cambridge, OH. Boyd has issued pieces in many new colors. All are marked with a "B" in a diamond.

Reference: Gene Florence, *Degenhart Glass and Paperweights: A Collector's Guide To Colors And Values*, Degenhart Paperweight and Glass Museum, 1982.

Collectors' Club: "The Friends of Degenhart," Degenhart Paperweight and Glass Museum, Inc., P. O. Box 186, Cambridge, OH 43725.

Museum: The Degenhart Paperweight and Glass Museum, Inc., Cambridge, OH. The museum covers all types of Ohio valley glass.

REPRODUCTION ALERT: Although most of the Degenhart molds were reproductions themselves, there are contemporary pieces that can be confusing such as Kanawha's bird salt and bow slipper; L. G. Wright's mini–slipper, daisy & button salt, and 5" robin covered dish; and many other contemporary American pieces. The 3" bird salt and mini–pitcher also are made by an unknown glassmaker in Taiwan.

Animal Dish, covered
  Hen
    3", intro 1967, marked 1973, Mint
      Green **20.00**

Pooch, intro 1976, marked 1976, Buttercup, $25.00.

5", intro 1971, marked 1972, Bittersweet	**65.00**
Lamb, intro 1961, marked 1972, Cobalt	**40.00**
Robin, intro 1960, marked 1972, Fawn	**55.00**
Turkey, intro 1971, marked 1972	
Amber	**35.00**
Tomato	**100.00**
Bicentennial Bell, intro 1974, marked 1974, Ivorene	**12.00**
Boot	
Daisy & Button, high, intro 1952, marked 1972, Peach Blo	**25.00**
Skate, intro 1961, marked 1972, Sapphire Dark	**30.00**
Texas, intro 1974, marked 1974	
Baby Green	**15.00**
Peach (clear)	**12.00**
Candy Dish, cov, Wildflower pattern, intro 1971, marked 1972	
Apple Green	**30.00**
Twilight Blue	**25.00**
Child's Mug, Stork & Peacock pattern, intro 1971, marked 1972	
Baby Green	**20.00**
Smokey Heather	**25.00**
Coaster, intro 1974, marked 1975	
Crystal	**8.00**
Shamrock	**6.00**
Creamer and Sugar	
Daisy & Button, intro 1970, marked 1972, Cambridge Pink	**75.00**
Texas, intro 1962, marked 1972	
Cobalt Carnival	**125.00**
Pine Green	**45.00**
Cup Plate	
Heart & Lyre, intro 1965, marked c1977	
Aqua	**10.00**
Mulberry	**15.00**
Seal Of Ohio, intro 1971, marked c1977, Opalescent	**15.00**
Hat, Daisy & Button pattern, intro 1974, marked 1972	
Crown Tuscan	**20.00**
Milk Blue	**12.00**
Jewel Box, Heart, intro 1964, marked 1972	
Blue Jay	**25.00**
Heliotrope	**35.00**
Owl, intro 1967, marked 1967, over 200 colors made	
Canary	**35.00**
Crown Tuscan	**40.00**
Ivory, Light	**30.00**
Misty Green	**40.00**
Nile Green Opal	**45.00**
Shell	**40.00**
Paperweight	
Crystal Art Glass, Zack & Bernard	

Boyd, Rollin Braden, Gus Theret
and William Degenhart
Hand painted plate weight 75.00
Marble 150.00
Multicolored 75.00
Red Flower 65.00
Single–colored window weight ... 200.00
Paperweight by John or Charles De-
genhart
Morning Glories 80.00
Name weight 35.00
Star Flower 70.00
Pitcher, Mini, intro 1973, marked 1973,
Jade 20.00
Pooch, intro 1976, marked 1976, ap-
proximately 110 colors made
Canary 15.00
Heatherbloom 30.00
Mauve 12.00
Smokey Blue 12.00

**Portrait Plate, Elizabeth Degenhart, blue,
5½" d, $65.00.**

Portrait Plate, Degenhart, intro 1974,
marked 1974, Crystal 35.00
Priscilla, intro 1976, marked 1976, only
40 colors made
Amber 75.00
Daffodil 100.00
Periwinkle 75.00
Salt
Bird, 1½", intro 1966, marked 1972
Amber 12.00
Orchid 15.00
Daisy & Button, intro 1970, marked
1972
Amberina 15.00
Rose Marie 12.00
Pottie, intro 1971, marked 1972
Chocolate Creme Slag 15.00
Milk White 10.00
Star & Dew Drop, intro 1952, marked
1972

Forest Green 12.00
Lemon Opal 20.00
Salt and Pepper Shakers, pr, Bird, intro
1958, marked 1973
Baby Green 35.00
Ruby 50.00
Slipper
Daisy & Button or Bow
Blue Marble Slag 25.00
Taffeta 20.00
Kat, intro 1947, marked 1972
Frosty Jade 25.00
Sapphire 15.00
Miniature, intro 1965, marked 1972
Emerald Green 12.00
Vaseline 15.00
Tomahawk, intro 1947, marked c1975,
Custard Maverick 55.00
Toothpick Holder
Baby or Tramp Shoe, intro 1962,
marked 1972
Gold 8.00
Lemon Custard 20.00
Pigeon Blood 25.00
Basket, intro 1963, marked c1974
Milk White 20.00
Sparrow Slag 15.00
Beaded Oval, intro 1967, marked
1972
Bittersweet 30.00
Tomato 45.00
Bird, intro 1959, marked 1972
Dichromatic 30.00
Persimmon 15.00
Colonial Drape & Heart, intro 1961,
marked 1972
Amethyst, Light 12.00
Ruby 20.00
Daisy & Button, intro 1970, marked
1972
Apple Green 15.00
Fawn 12.00
Peach Blo 15.00
Elephant Head, intro c1957, marked
1972
Amber 20.00
Jade 50.00
Forget–me–not, intro 1965, marked
1972, made in over 150 colors
April Green #1 .... 15.00
Bloody Mary #2 .... 40.00
Cambridge Pink 25.00
Grape 15.00
Zach Boyd Slag 40.00
Gypsy Pot, intro 1962, marked 1972
Bittersweet 30.00
Blue Fire 15.00
Elizabeth's Lime Ice 25.00
Red 30.00
Tray, Hand, intro 1949, marked c1975
Bittersweet 15.00
Taffeta 12.00

Wine
  Buzz Saw, intro 1967, marked 1973
    Honey Amber **15.00**
    Pistachio **20.00**
    Taffeta **40.00**
  Daisy & Button, intro 1969, marked
    1972, Sunset **20.00**

DEPRESSION GLASS

Collecting Hint: Many collectors specialize in one pattern; others collect by a particular color. Prices listed are for pieces in mint condition—no chips, scratches, etc.

History: Depression glass is glassware made during the period 1920–1940. It was an inexpensive machine–made glass, produced by several different glass companies.

  The colors varied from company to company. The number of items made for each pattern also varied. Like pattern glass, Depression glass pattern names are sometimes confusing; therefore, a collector should learn all names for their particular pattern.

References: Gene Florence, *The Collector's Encyclopedia of Depression Glass, Tenth Edition*, Collector Books, 1992; Gene Florence, *Elegant Glassware of the Depression Era, Fourth Edition*, Collector Books, 1990; Gene Florence, *Very Rare Glassware of the Depression Years, First Series* (1987) and *Second Series* (1990), Collector Books; Carl F. Luckey and Mary Burris, *An Identification & Value Guide To Depression Era Glassware, Second Edition*, Books Americana, 1984; Mark Schliesmann, *Price Survey, Second Edition*, Park Avenue Publications, Ltd, 1984; Hazel Marie Weatherman, *1984 Supplement & Price Trends for Colored Glassware of the Depression Era, Book 1*, published by author, 1984.

Periodical: *The Daze*, Box 57, Ottisville, MI 48463.

Collectors' Club: National Depression Glass Association, Inc., P. O. Box 11123, Springfield, MO 65808.

REPRODUCTION ALERT: Because of recent interest in collecting Depression glass, many reproductions are surfacing. Most reproductions are made in colors not originally made. They are sometimes made in the original molds and often marked. However, several patterns have been reproduced in original colors but the molds are slightly different. Thorough knowledge of patterns, colors and markings is very important.

  Send a self addressed stamped business envelope to *The Daze* and request a copy of their glass reproduction list. It is one of the best bargains in the collectibles field.

AURORA

Hazel Atlas Company, late 1930s. Made in cobalt blue and pink.

	Cobalt Blue	Pink		Cobalt Blue	Pink
Bowl			Cup	10.00	10.00
4½", deep	7.50	7.50	Plate, 6½"	5.00	5.50
5", cereal	11.00	10.00	Saucer	2.50	2.50
Creamer, 4½"	21.00	24.00	Tumbler, 4¾", 10 oz	22.00	20.00

BUBBLE

"Bull's Eye," "Provincial," Anchor Hocking Glass Company, 1934–65. Made in crystal, dark green, light blue, pink, and red.

	Crystal	Dark Green	Light Blue	Pink	Red
Bowl					
4", berry, small	2.25	4.00	6.00	—	—
4½", fruit	4.00	5.00	8.00	—	—
4½", nappy, handle	8.50	4.50	6.50	—	—
5¼", cereal	5.00	7.25	8.00	—	—
7¾", soup, flat	—	—	9.00	—	—
8⅜", berry, master	6.00	20.00	12.00	8.00	5.00
9", flanged	—	—	40.00	—	—
Candlesticks, pr	17.00	20.00	—	—	—

Bubble, creamer and sugar, light blue, each $25.00.

Moonstone, berry set, 9½" d master bowl, $9.50; four 5½" serving bowls, each $7.00.

	Crystal	Dark Green	Light Blue	Pink	Red
Creamer	7.50	10.00	25.00	—	—
Cup	2.00	4.50	3.25	27.50	—
Lamp	30.00	—	—	—	—
Pitcher, 64 oz, ice lip	—	—	—	—	37.50
Plate					
6¾", bread and butter	1.00	1.50	3.00	—	—
9⅜", dinner	2.25	6.00	6.00	—	6.00
9⅜", grill	3.00	6.75	8.50	—	—
Platter, 12"	—	—	12.00	—	—
Saucer	1.50	1.50	2.00	17.50	1.50
Sugar	7.50	10.00	25.00	—	—
Tidbit	—	—	—	—	18.00
Tumbler					
6 oz, juice	8.50	—	—	—	6.00
9 oz, water	10.00	4.75	—	—	5.75
12 oz, iced tea	—	—	—	—	6.00
16 oz, lemonade	12.50	—	—	—	15.00

CAMEO

"Ballerina or Dancing Girl," Hocking Glass Co., 1930–1934. Made in crystal, green, pink, yellow.

	Crystal	Green	Pink	Yellow
Bowl				
4¼", sauce	4.50	45.00	—	—
5½", cereal	4.00	18.00	—	22.00
7¼", salad	—	35.00	—	—
8¼", master berry	—	20.00	—	35.00
10", veg. oval	—	20.00	—	35.00
11", console, 3 legs	—	55.00	22.00	—
Butter Dish, cov	—	130.00	—	635.00
Cake Plate, 10", 3 legs	—	16.00	—	—
Candlestick, 4"	—	34.00	—	—
Candy Dish, cov, 4"	—	60.00	365.00	50.00
Compote, 5"	—	15.00	—	—
Cookie Jar	—	45.00	—	—
Creamer	—	28.00	—	25.00
Cup and Saucer	—	15.00	—	8.50
Decanter, stopper, 10"	—	80.00	—	—
Goblet				
3½", wine	—	70.00	—	—
4", champagne	—	32.00	—	—
6", water	—	35.00	95.00	—
Ice Bucket	—	90.00	375.00	175.00

	Crystal	Green	Pink	Yellow
Mayonnaise, ftd	—	35.00	—	—
Pitcher				
5¾", 20 oz milk	—	130.00	170.00	—
6", 36 oz, juice	—	30.00	—	—
8½", water	200.00	30.00	—	—
Plate				
6", sherbet	2.00	4.25	46.00	10.00
7", salad	3.50	6.50	24.00	4.50
8", luncheon	4.00	9.00	25.00	7.50
9", dinner	—	14.00	38.00	9.00
10", sandwich	—	16.00	32.00	—
10½", grill	—	32.00	—	7.00
Platter	—	20.00	30.00	40.00
Salt Shaker	—	22.50	—	—
Sherbet	—	14.00	25.00	15.00
Sugar	—	28.00	10.00	10.00
Tumbler				
3 oz, juice, ftd	—	36.25	—	—
9 oz, water	—	20.00	—	18.00
11 oz	—	18.00	—	—
Vase	—	20.00	—	—

FLORAL & DIAMOND BAND

U.S. Glass Company, late 1920s. Made in green and pink. Iridescent pieces known as Mayflower in Carnival Glass.

	Green	Pink		Green	Pink
Bowl			Pitcher, 8", 42 oz	70.00	65.00
4½", berry, small	5.00	4.50	Plate, 8", luncheon	12.00	10.00
5¾", nappy, handle	7.00	6.75	Sherbet	4.00	3.75
8", berry, master	10.00	9.00	Sugar		
Butter Dish, cov	90.00	85.00	5¼", regular	8.00	7.75
Compote, 5½"	10.00	8.00	Small	6.50	6.00
Creamer			Tumbler		
4¾", large	10.00	10.00	4", water	20.00	15.00
Small	7.00	6.50	5", iced tea	15.00	14.00

HOLIDAY

"Buttons & Bows," Jeannette Glass Co., 1947–1949. Made in pink and a limited number of pieces in iridescent.

	Pink		Pink
Bowl		Plate	
5⅛", berry	7.00	6", sherbet	3.00
7¾", flat soup	29.90	9", dinner	12.00
8½", master berry	14.00	13¾", chop	50.00
Butter Dish, cov	35.00	Platter	8.00
Cake Plate	55.00	Saucer	2.50
Candlesticks, pr	50.00	Sherbet	5.00
Cup and Saucer	8.00	Sugar, cov	12.00
Creamer	6.50	Tumbler	
Pitcher		4", flat, 10 oz	16.00
4¾", milk	45.75	4", footed	24.50
6¾"	27.50	Vegetable, oval	14.00

HOMESPUN

"Fine Rib," Jeannette Glass Company, 1939–40. Made in crystal and pink.

	Crystal	Pink		Crystal	Pink
Ashtray/Coaster	5.00	5.00	Plate		
Bowl			6", sherbet	2.00	2.00
4½", berry, small, closed			9¼", dinner	8.50	8.50
handles	4.00	4.00	Platter, 13"	8.00	8.00
5", cereal	7.00	7.00	Tumbler		
8¼", berry, master	7.50	8.00	4", 5 oz, ftd	6.00	7.00
Butter Dish, cov	40.00	40.00	4", 9 oz, water	7.00	8.00
Creamer, ftd	6.50	6.50	5¼", 13 oz, iced tea ...	12.00	12.00
Cup	4.00	4.50	6¼", 9 oz, ftd	12.00	12.00
Pitcher, 96 oz	30.00	30.00	6½", 15 oz, ftd	14.00	14.00

MODERNTONE

"Wedding Band," Hazel Atlas Glass Co., 1934–1942. Made in amethyst, cobalt blue, crystal, pink, platonite with fired on colors. Pink was made in very limited pieces.

	Amethyst	Cobalt Blue	Platonite
Ashtray	—	175.00	—
Bowls			
4¾", cream soup	7.00	8.00	—
5"			
Berry	9.00	12.50	1.00
Nut, ruffled	15.00	25.00	2.00
6½", cereal	30.00	2.50	2.50
7½", flat soup	28.00	30.00	3.00
8¾", master berry	22.00	50.00	10.00
Butter Dish, cov	—	55.00	—
Creamer	8.50	5.00	4.00
Cup	7.50	8.00	3.00
Plates			
5¾", sherbet	5.50	5.00	1.25
6¾", salad	3.25	9.00	2.00

Moderntone, salt and pepper shakers, pr, amethyst, $18.00.

Swirl, sherbet, ultramarine, $8.50.

	Amethyst	Cobalt Blue	Platonite
7¾", luncheon	3.50	7.50	3.00
8⅞", dinner	9.00	12.50	5.00
10½", sandwich	35.00	30.00	6.50
Platter, 12"	40.00	40.00	7.50
Saucer	2.50	4.00	1.25
Salt and Pepper Shakers, pr	18.00	32.00	12.00
Sherbet	7.00	10.00	3.00
Sugar	8.50	12.00	5.00
Tumblers			
5 oz., juice	—	7.00	3.00
9 oz., water	—	14.00	6.00
Whiskey	10.00	8.00	3.50

MOONSTONE

Anchor Hocking Glass Corp., 1941–1946. Made in crystal with opalescent hobnails.

	Crystal		Crystal
Bon, Bon, heart shape	6.50	Goblet, 10 oz, water	15.00
Bowl		Plate	
5½"		6¼", sherbet	3.50
Berry	7.00	8", luncheon	5.50
Dessert, crimped	4.50	10", dinner	13.50
6½", fruit, crimped, handle	5.00	Puff Box, cov	12.00
7¾", flat soup	7.50	Relish	
9½", crimped	9.75	Divided	7.00
Candlesticks, pr	14.00	Cloverleaf shape	9.50
Candy Dish	14.00	Salt and Pepper Shakers, pr	45.00
Cigarette Box, cov	18.00	Saucer	3.00
Cologne Bottle, stopper	7.50	Sugar, ftd	6.00
Creamer	6.00	Tumbler, ftd	14.00
Cup	5.00	Vase, 5½"	9.00

No. 610

"Pyramid," Indiana Glass Company, 1926–32. Made in crystal, green, pink, and yellow.

	Crystal	Green	Pink	Yellow
Bowl				
4¾", berry	12.00	14.00	12.00	24.00
8½", master berry	18.00	20.00	18.00	40.00
9½", oval	22.00	24.00	25.00	42.50
9½", pickle	24.00	24.00	25.00	45.00
Creamer	16.00	16.00	16.50	25.00
Ice Tub	60.00	70.00	65.00	175.00
Pitcher	150.00	165.00	150.00	350.00
Relish Tray, 4 part	30.00	45.00	32.00	50.00
Sugar	16.50	18.50	16.00	25.00
Tray	16.00	20.00	16.00	40.00
Tumbler				
8 oz, ftd	15.00	25.00	15.00	40.00
11 oz, ftd	32.00	42.50	32.00	—

Ring, juice tumbler, 3½" h, $5.00.

Windsor, pitcher, pink, 6¾", $18.50.

OVIDE

Hazel Atlas Glass Co., 1930–1935. Made in black, green, platonite with fired colors or white.

	Black	Green Platonite White		Black	Green Platonite White
Bowl			8", luncheon	7.50	4.00
4¾", berry	6.50	2.50	9", dinner	9.50	12.00
5½", cereal	7.00	—	Platter, 11"	15.00	—
8", master berry	14.00	—	Salt and Pepper Shakers, pr	20.00	8.00
Candy Dish, cov	25.00	15.00	Saucer	2.00	1.50
Creamer	6.00	3.00	Sherbet	6.50	3.00
Cup	5.00	2.00	Sugar	6.00	4.00
Plate					
6", sherbet	4.00	2.50			

PINEAPPLE AND FLORAL

"No. 618," Indiana Glass Company, 1932–37. Made in amber, crystal, and red.

	Amber	Crystal	Red
Ashtray	17.50	15.00	18.00
Bowl			
4¾", berry, small	22.00	45.00	25.00
5", soup, cream	16.00	14.00	15.00
6", cereal	18.50	27.00	20.00
7", salad	9.00	3.50	9.00
10", vegetable, oval	15.00	18.00	15.00
Compote	7.00	5.00	7.00
Creamer	7.00	6.50	7.50
Cup	5.00	5.00	5.00
Plate			
6", bread and butter	5.00	2.50	5.00
8⅜", salad	8.50	7.50	8.00
9⅜, dinner	12.00	10.00	12.00
11½", indentation	22.00	20.00	22.00
Platter, 11"	14.00	12.00	14.00
Relish, 11½", divided	18.00	15.00	18.50

	Amber	Crystal	Red
Sherbet	14.00	18.00	14.00
Sugar	7.00	6.50	7.00
Tumbler			
4¼", flat	25.00	22.50	25.00
5", 12 oz	—	28.00	—
Vase, cone shape	—	25.00	—

RING

"Banded Rings," Hocking Glass Company, 1927–33. Made in crystal, crystal with rings of pink, red, blue, orange, yellow, black and silver, and green. Limited production in pink, blue and red.

	Crystal	Crystal Dec	Green
Bowl			
5", berry, small	2.00	3.25	3.00
7", soup, flat	6.25	8.00	8.00
8", berry, master	4.50	7.00	6.50
Cocktail Shaker	8.00	15.00	14.00
Creamer, ftd	4.00	5.50	5.00
Cup	2.00	3.00	2.50
Decanter	17.00	25.00	25.00
Goblet, 9 oz	5.00	10.00	10.00
Ice Tub	10.00	18.00	15.00
Pitcher			
8", 60 oz	10.00	12.00	10.00
8½", 80 oz	12.00	20.00	18.00
Plate			
6", off center ring	1.50	3.75	3.50
6¼", sherbet	1.25	1.50	1.25
8", luncheon	1.75	3.00	2.00
Salt and Pepper, 3"	35.00	45.00	50.00
Sandwich Server	10.00	22.00	22.00
Saucer	1.75	2.00	2.00
Sherbet	4.25	6.00	6.00
Sugar, ftd	3.25	3.50	3.50
Tumbler			
3½", 5 oz	2.50	5.00	4.50
3½", ftd cocktail	4.00	4.75	4.50
4¼", 9 oz	3.50	4.50	5.00
5⅛", 12 oz	4.00	6.25	6.00
5½", ftd, water	3.25	4.75	4.50
6½", ftd, iced tea	5.00	9.00	8.50
Whiskey	3.50	5.00	5.00

ROSEMARY

"Dutch Rose," Federal Glass Company, 1935–37. Made in amber, green, and pink.

	Amber	Green	Pink
Bowl			
5", berry	4.00	5.00	6.50
5¼", soup, cream	14.00	16.00	15.00
6", cereal	10.00	12.50	12.50
10", vegetable, oval	14.00	18.00	15.00
Creamer, ftd	8.00	12.00	12.00
Cup	4.00	7.50	4.50

Plate	Amber	Green	Pink
6¾", salad	6.00	8.00	6.50
9", dinner	8.00	12.00	12.00
9½", grill	6.00	10.00	10.00
Platter, 12"	15.00	18.00	16.50
Saucer	2.00	3.00	2.00
Sugar, ftd	8.00	12.00	8.00
Tumbler, 4¼", 9 oz	18.00	20.00	24.00

ROUND ROBIN

Manufacturer unknown, early 1930s. Made in green and iridescent.

	Green	Irid		Green	Irid
Bowl, 4", berry	3.50	4.00	8", luncheon	4.00	4.50
Creamer, ftd	5.00	6.00	12", sandwich	5.00	6.00
Cup, ftd	3.50	4.50	Saucer	1.50	2.00
Domino Tray	20.00	—	Sherbet	3.50	4.00
Plate			Sugar	4.50	5.00
6", sherbet	2.00	2.00			

STRAWBERRY

U.S. Glass Co., early 1930s. Made in crystal, green and pink.

	Crystal	Green	Pink
Bowl			
4", berry	5.00	6.00	6.50
6¼", 2" deep	8.00	10.00	10.50
7½", master berry	12.00	14.00	15.00
Butter Dish, cov	100.00	115.00	120.00
Compote, 5¼", ftd	12.00	13.00	10.50
Olive Dish, 5", one handle	7.00	9.00	9.50
Pickle Dish, 8¼", oval	7.50	9.50	9.00
Pitcher, 7¾"	160.00	130.00	135.00
Plate			
6", sherbet	4.00	5.00	6.00
7½", salad	7.00	9.00	8.50
Sherbet	6.00	9.00	7.00
Sugar	18.00	32.50	30.00
Tumbler, 9 oz	16.00	25.00	25.00

SWIRL

"Petal Swirl," Jeannette Glass Co., 1937–38. Made in delphite, pink, and ultramarine.

	Delphite	Pink	Ultramarine
Ashtray	—	5.00	7.50
Bowl			
5¾", cereal	6.75	8.00	10.00
9", salad	10.00	12.00	20.00
10½", console, ftd	—	12.50	14.00
Butter Dish	—	150.00	150.00
Candlesticks, pr			
Double branch	—	20.00	20.00
Single branch	75.00	—	—

	Delphite	Pink	Ultramarine
Candy Dish	—	65.00	95.00
Covered	—	6.50	8.00
Open, 3 legs	—	5.00	6.00
Coaster, 1 × 3¼"	9.50	9.50	10.00
Creamer, ftd	5.00	4.00	8.00
Cup	—	—	850.00
Pitcher, 48 oz, ftd			
Plate			
6½", sherbet........................	3.00	2.00	—
7¼", salad	—	3.50	7.00
8", luncheon	4.00	3.75	7.00
9¼", dinner	7.50	6.50	13.00
10½", dinner	10.00	—	9.50
12½", sandwich	—	7.50	—
Platter, 12"	20.00	—	—
Salt and Pepper Shakers, pr	—	—	24.00
Saucer	2.00	1.50	4.00
Sherbet	—	4.50	8.50
Soup, tab handle	—	—	14.00
Sugar, ftd	9.50	8.00	10.00
Tumbler			
4", 9 oz	—	8.00	25.00
4⅝", 9 oz	—	7.50	—
4¾", 12 oz	—	8.00	35.00
Vase, ftd			
6½"	—	—	12.00
8½"	—	—	14.00

VICTORY

Diamond Glassware Company, 1929–32. Made in amber, green, and pink. Limited production in black and cobalt blue.

	Amber	Green	Pink
Bonbon, 7"	9.00	9.00	9.00
Bowl			
6½", cereal	8.00	8.25	7.50
8½", soup, flat	10.00	10.00	10.00
9", vegetable, oval	25.00	20.00	20.00
12", console	28.00	20.00	20.00
Candlesticks, pr, 3"	25.00	15.00	15.00
Cheese & Cracker Set	—	20.00	22.50
Compote, 6", h	10.00	9.50	9.50
Creamer	10.00	9.00	9.00
Cup	6.00	5.00	5.00
Goblet, 5", 7 oz	18.00	12.00	12.00
Gravy Boat, underplate	115.00	115.00	110.00
Mayonnaise Set, underplate, ladle	35.00	28.00	28.00
Plate			
6", bread & butter	4.00	3.50	3.50
7", salad	5.00	3.50	3.50
8", luncheon	5.00	4.00	4.00
9", dinner	12.00	10.00	10.00
Platter, 12"	20.00	15.00	15.00
Sandwich Server	35.00	20.00	24.00
Saucer	4.00	3.50	3.50
Sherbet	10.00	8.00	7.50
Sugar	12.00	12.00	12.00

WINDSOR

"Windsor Diamond," Jeannette Glass Co., 1936–46. Made in crystal, green and pink; limited production in amberina and delphite.

	Crystal	Green	Pink
Ashtray, 5¾"	15.00	35.00	35.00
Bowl			
4¾", berry	2.50	7.00	5.00
5", cream soup	4.50	20.00	15.00
5½", cereal	7.00	15.00	12.00
7⅛", console, 3 legs	6.00	—	17.50
8", two handles	8.00	14.00	25.00
8½", master berry	4.50	12.00	10.00
9½", vegetable oval	5.00	17.50	12.00
12½", fruit, console	20.00	—	75.00
Butter Dish, cov	22.50	70.00	37.50
Cake Plate			
10¾", ftd	8.00	12.00	15.00
13½", thick	8.00	12.00	13.00
Candlesticks, 3", pr	15.00	—	65.00
Candy Jar, cov	8.00	—	20.00
Coaster, 3¼"	5.00	12.50	8.00
Compote	5.00	12.00	10.00
Creamer	3.00	8.00	7.50
Cup	2.50	7.00	6.00
Pitcher			
4½", 16 oz	20.00	—	80.00
5", 20 oz	6.00	—	—
6¾", 52 oz	11.00	40.00	18.50
Plates			
6", sherbet	1.50	3.50	2.50
7", salad	3.00	13.50	9.50
9", dinner	3.50	13.50	9.50
10¼", sandwich, handled	4.00	10.00	9.00
13⅝", chop	7.50	30.00	30.00
15½", serving	10.00	—	—
Platter, 11½", oval	4.50	12.00	10.00
Relish, 11½", divided	9.50	—	175.00
Salt and Pepper Shakers, pr	12.50	40.00	30.00
Saucer	1.50	3.00	2.50
Sherbet	3.00	12.50	6.75
Sugar, cov	4.50	22.00	17.50
Tray, 4⅛" × 9"	12.50	35.00	75.00
Tumbler			
3¼"	6.00	25.00	15.00
5"	7.50	37.50	20.00

DIONNE QUINTUPLETS

Collecting Hints: Almost all the doll companies in the 1930s released dolls resembling the Quints. The only "genuine" Dionne Quintuplet dolls are the Madame Alexander dolls dating from 1935 to 1939. They realized the highest prices.

History: The Dionne Quintuplets were born on May 28, 1934, on a small farm between Corbeil and Callander, Ontario, Canada. The five baby girls weighed a total of 10 lbs, 1¼ ozs. They were delivered by Dr. Dafoe and two midwives. They were named Yvonne, Annette, Cecile, Emilie, and Marie.

When they were just two days old, their father, Oliva Dionne, and the parish priest signed a contract to exhibit the babies at the Chicago

World's Fair. The Canadian government passed "An Act For the Protection Of the Dionne Quintuplets" to prevent this. The girls became special wards of King George V.

A special house, the Dafoe Hospital, was built for them across the road from their place of birth. It had one–way glass through which visitors could view the children. People came by the thousands during the mid to late '30s. In this nursery they were attended by Dr. Dafoe and a staff of professionals. Newspapers gave daily reports and photographs of their progress. Souvenirs of every type were sold including rocks, called "Fertility Stones," from the farm which brought between 50¢ and $1.00.

Emilie died in a convent in August of 1954 and Marie died February 27, 1970. Yvonne, Annette, and Cecile remain alive today.

Reference: John Axe, *The Collectible Dionne Quintuplets*, Hobby House Press, 1977.

Collectors' Club: Dionne Quint Collectors, P.O. Box 2527, Woburn, MA 01888.

Fan, cardboard, multicolored, copyright 1936, NEA Service, Inc., St Paul, MN, #17000, advertisement for The Stonington Furniture Co on back, $15.00.

Advertisement, pictures quintuplets, Palmolive soap, 1936	25.00
Blotter celluloid cov, quints on toy designed for five, c1935	20.00
Book, *The Dionne Quintuplets Growing Up*, 8½ x 11", brown and white cov, 1935	40.00
Bowl	
Aluminum	35.00
China, cereal, 5½" d, Marie in high chair, c1935	18.00
Calendar	
1936, Watch Us Grow, photos and stories	18.00
1942	30.00
Coloring Book, 10 x 15", The Dionne Quintuplets Pictures To Paint, Merill, 1940	20.00
Doll, 7½", mohair wig, painted brown eyes, Madame Alexander, 1936	225.00
Fan	
8 x 9", diecut cardboard, wood handle, Elvgren illus celebrating fifth birthday	8.00
8½", cardboard, wooden handle, picture of quints and ducks at stream, adv for Howard M Davies Funeral Chapel on reverse	25.00
Handkerchief, 8½" sq, black, white, and blue portraits, red ground	30.00
Magazine Cover	
Look, Oct 11, 1938, Dr Dafoe	5.00
Woman's World, Feb, 1937	10.00
Paper Doll Book	
Annette, 9½ x 10½", 1936 Whitman, unpunched doll, four orig uncut pgs	100.00
Let's Play House with the Dionne Quints," uncut, #4	49.00
Photo, tinted, damaged frame, 1935	20.00
Picture, titled "The Darling Dionnes," holding dolls, framed	48.00
Pin	
Cecile	17.50
Marie	17.50
Poster, 14 x 32", "Today The Dionne Quints Had Quaker Oats," 1935	60.00
Puzzle, ball, steel, glass top, place quints in buggy	35.00
Sign, 11 x 16", cardboard, Quints with tea set	60.00
Spoons	
Set of five	125.00
Yvonne	12.00
Thermometer, 3⅞ x 6", cardboard, multicolored, Cupp's Dairy adv	25.00

DIRIGIBLES

Collecting Hints: All areas of dirigible material remain stable. Focus on one specific topic, e.g., material about one airship, models and toys, postcards, etc. The field is very broad, and a collector might exhaust his funds trying to be comprehensive. The most common collecting focus is material relating to specific flights.

History: The terms *airship* and *dirigible* are synonymous. Dirigible (Latin for directable) means steerable and can apply to a bicycle. Dirigible evolved through usage into a word for *airship*.

There are three types of dirigibles: (1) *Rigid* - a zeppelin, e.g., HINDENBURG, GRAF, SHEN-ANDOAH, (2) *Non–Rigid* - a blimp, e.g., GOODYEAR BLIMPS and Navy blimps, and (3) *Semi–Rigid* - non–rigid with a keel, e.g., NORGE AND ITALIA. Note: Hot air balloons, barrage balloons, hydrogen balloons, etc., are not dirigibles. They are not directable. They go where the wind takes them. Prior to 1900 only non-rigid and semi–rigid dirigibles existed.

Zeppelins dated from 1900 to 1940, the last being the LZ130 sister ship to the HINDEN-BURG. The GRAF ZEPPELIN was the most successful zeppelin, flying between 1928 and 1940. The HINDENBURG was the most famous zeppelin, due to the spectacular fire that led to its demise in 1937. Its flying dates were 1936 to 1937.

America never used its four zeppelins for passenger travel. They were strictly military. The Naval Air Station at Lakehurst, New Jersey, where the well–known zeppelins docked, has remained open to this day. However, its name has been changed to the Naval Air Engineering Center. None of its present operations include lighter–than–air vehicles, except for an occasional blimp. The famous Hangar #1 has been refurbished, but the base is currently off limits to the general public. The last Navy blimp flew from Lakehurst in 1962.

References: Walter Curley, *The Graf Zeppelin's Flights to South America*, Spellman Museum, 1970; Arthur Falk, *Hindenburg Crash Mail*, Clear Color Litho, 1976; Sieger, *Zeppelin Post Katalog*, Wurttemberg, 1981, in German.

Collectors' Club: Zeppelin Collectors Club, P. O. Box A3843, Chicago, IL 60690.

Advisor: Arthur R. Bink.

REPRODUCTION ALERT

Akron Zeppelin Items, the following articles all contain the inscription, "duralumin used in the airship *Akron*" (they were NOT made of parts of the *Akron*, but of the same alloy)

Ashtray

3" x 5", rect, shield	20.00
4½" d, no shield, rim inscription	15.00
5" sq, shield	20.00
Bank, shaped like zeppelin hangar at Akron, OH	115.00

Bookmark

Elongated, shield on top	25.00
Heart shape, shield in center	25.00
Bottle Opener	35.00
Comb, inscription on back	35.00
Letter Opener	30.00

Cut–Out, *Graf Zeppelin* over New York skyline, Statue of Liberty, G Schwax artist, shipped by first air freight from Germany to USA on *Graf Zeppelin* 1929, 8⁵⁄₁₆" w, **$145.00**.

Money Clip, also called napkin holder	25.00
Pen knife, illus of zeppelin, hangar, 1931	65.00
Picture Frame, *Akron* photo, 20¼ x 26"	265.00

Watch Fob

Shield type, leather strap	20.00
Triangular, hangar and zeppelin, keychain	10.00

Bank

Cast iron, *Graf Zeppelin* or *Akron*, 6¾"	115.00
Porcelain, Goodyear blimp, 8½" on pedestal	48.00
Candy Container, glass, *Los Angeles*, two varieties	140.00

Flight Cover

Hindenburg: these range from $20.00 for the first North American flight (1936) to several thousand dollars for the last flight crash–covers (1937); see the Sieger Zeppelin Post Catalog of flight covers (in German, 384 pages) for price information on the hundreds of flights which zeppelins flew.

U.S.S. Akron: these common envelopes, mailed on the Akron were mistakenly listed in the American Air Mail Society book at $75.00 (erroneous decimal point placement). These are the only 2 mail–carrying flights of this airship

Coast to Coast US Trip, May 1932	7.50
Tactical Training Flight from Lakehurst, August 1932	7.50
Flyer, New Jersey Central Railroad, To see The *Graf Zeppelin*, October 14, 1928, blue and white, paper, 5 x 14"	25.00

Light Bulb, Christmas tree type, zeppelin 12.00

Lighter, round, brass, French, dirigible on one side, early aeroplane on the other, 1⅝" d 75.00

Lobby Card, movie "The Hindenburg", 1975, set of 8 .... 30.00

Medal, silver, 1 oz, round, Franklin Mint, History of Flight, modern

First Electric Powered Airship, Krebs/Renard, 1884 .... 15.00

First Navigable Airship, Giffard, 1852 15.00

First Von Zeppelin Dirigible, 1900 .. 15.00

Graf Zeppelin Circles the Globe, 1929 .... 15.00

Mirror, 75th Anniversary, first successful zeppelin flight, 1901–1976, blue back 18.00

Mold

Candy

3", pencil shaped zeppelin, sheet metal 75.00

7¼", early pencil shaped zeppelin, sheet metal, marked "Germany" 145.00

10", zeppelin, marked "Los Angeles," sheet metal 110.00

12 x 15", twelve half zeppelins, turn over multiple cavity type, pewter 200.00

Ice Cream, pewter

4", tailless airship with basket gondola 135.00

6", *Graf Zeppelin* style 120.00

Movie, *Hindenburg*, 8 mm, 200 feet reel of airship and wreck 30.00

Needle Book, several types 12.00

Newspaper, orig, complete, day after *Hindenburg* crash, May 7, 1939, many, various news syndicates 15.00

Pen Knife, brass, zeppelin above lake on one side, Count Von Zeppelin portrait on the other 90.00

Pennant

Graf Zeppelin 60.00

Hindenburg 60.00

Los Angeles zeppelin 60.00

Photo, elongated style, marked Clements, Hildebrandt, or Picot (Note: Similar photos without mechanical signatures, less 25%)

6 x 18" of the *Los Angeles, Shenandoah,* 28.00

12 x 54" of the above, various airships, hangars 50.00

Plate, Cathedral of the Air, Lakehurst, NJ, showing a blimp, Balfour Ceramic, ivory, black, gold ring, 9½" . 30.00

Playing Cards, Airship No 909, Standard Playing Card Company, Chicago, orig box, 1894 date 40.00

Puzzle, "The Hindenburg", movie poster, 15½" x 18" 20.00

Rug, Century of Progress, Chicago, with zeppelin and blimp over the Fairgrounds, 40" x 24" 60.00

Sheet Music

Come Take a Trip in My Airship ... 18.00

Take Me Up with You Dearie 18.00

The Aeronaut's Flight 18.00

The Hindenburg 18.00

The R–100 (in Canada) 18.00

Wreck of the Shenandoah 18.00

Skin of Blimp, diecut into shape of blimp, "Souvenir From U.S. Naval Air Station, Lakehurst, NJ" 4.00

Toy, zeppelin

Cast iron

NAVY on sides, many colors, 4½" 50.00

ZEP on sides, red letters and star, silver ground, metal or rubber/wooden hub wheels, 5" 55.00

Champion, cast iron, two wheels, 6", silver 95.00

Erector Set, A.C. Gilbert, 53" 600.00

Marx, sheet metal wind–ups, at least five different styles, with orig boxes, 6" 150.00

Metalcraft, construction kit

18", numerous colors 135.00

27½", silver 165.00

Steelcraft, welded type, 25½", silver, decals 175.00

Strauss, aluminum, orig box

9½" 200.00

16" 425.00

Tootsietoy, diecast, two pulleys on top 55.00

Watch, pocket, white dial or black dial, "Zep" on front, "Trail Blazers" on back, *Graf Zeppelin* over Magellan's ship, 1929 .... 175.00

DISNEYANA

Collecting Hints: The products from the 1930s command the most attention. Animated celluloids range in value from $100 to tens of thousands of dollars depending on subject and complexity of the scene. Disneyana is a popular subject, and items tend to be priced on the high side.

Make condition a key element in your purchase. An incomplete toy or game should sell for 40 to 50% less than one in mint condition.

History: Walt Disney and the creations of the famous Disney studio hold a place of fondness and enchantment in the hearts of Americans and people throughout the world. The release of "Steamboat Willie" in 1928 heralded an entertainment empire.

Walt and his brother, Roy, showed shrewd business acumen. From the beginning they licensed the reproduction of Disney characters in products ranging from wrist watches to clothing.

The market in Disneyana has been established by a few determined dealers and auction houses. Hake's Americana and Collectibles has specialized in Disney material for over a decade. Sotheby's Collector Carousel auctions and Lloyd Ralston Toys auctions have continued the trend.

Walt Disney characters are popular throughout the world. Belgium is a leading producer of Disneyana along with England, France, and Japan. The Disney characters often take on the regional characteristics of the host country; don't be surprised to find a strange looking Mickey Mouse or Donald Duck. Disney has opened a new theme park in Japan; it will produce a wealth of new Disney collectibles.

References: Marcia Blitz, *Donald Duck*, Harmony Books, 1979; Robert Heide and John Gilman, *Cartoon Collectibles*, Doubleday & Co., Inc., 1984; Bevis Hillier, *Walt Disney's Mickey Mouse Memorabilia*, Harry Abrams, 1986; Leonard Maltin, *The Disney Films*, Crown Publishers, 1973; Richard Schickel, *The Disney Version: The Life, Times, Art and Commerce of Walt Disney*, Avon Books, 1968; Michael Stern, *Stern's Guide to Disney Collectibles*, First Series (1989) and Second Series 1990, Collector Books; Tom Tumbusch, *Tomart's Illustrated Disneyana Catalog and Price Guide*, Volume 1 (1985), Volume 2 (1985), Volume 3 (1985), Volume 4 (1987), Tomart Publications; Tom Tumbusch, *Tomart's Illustrated Disneyana Catalog and Price Guide, Condensed Edition*, Tomart Publications, 1989.

Archives: Walt Disney Archives, 500 South Buena Vista Street, Burbank, CA 91521.

Collectors' Club: National Fantasy Club For Disneyana Collectors, P. O. Box 19212, Irvine, CA 92713.

Periodicals: *Mouse Club Newsletter*, 2056 Cirone Way, San Jose, CA 95124; *Storyboard Magazine For Disneyana Collectors*, 2512 Artesia Blvd, Redondo Beach, CA 90278.

Advisor: Ted Hake.

Alice in Wonderland
  Figurine, 6" h, china, 1960 signature
    style Disney copyright under base   **18.00**
  Sheet Music, *In A World Of My Own*,
    9 x 12", white, blue, yellow, and
    green cov, copyright 1949 . . . .   **20.00**
Bambi
  Lamp, 12" h, open upright storybook,
    paper label inscribed with text,
    plastic Bambi and Thumper figures
    in front, Dolly Toy Co, c1950 . . .   **55.00**
  Pin, plastic, Bambi and pine trees
    above "Disneyland/Walt Disney
    Productions," red plastic heart sus-

pended below, marked "Germany," late 1950s **20.00**
  Planter, Thumper **45.00**
  Record, *Ballad of Davy Crockett*, Peter Pan Peanut Butter premium, orig picture sleeve showing Fess Parker, 1950s **25.00**
Cinderella
  Bank **30.00**
  Little Golden Book, *Cinderella's Friends*, first edition, 1950 . . . .   **20.00**
  Sheet Music, *So This Is Love*, 9 x 12", white and pink cov, copyright 1949   **20.00**
  Soaky Bottle, 10½" h, light blue dress, swivel arms, mid 1960s **15.00**

Bank, Donald Duck, plastic, 9¼" h, $38.00.

Donald Duck
  Bank, 6" h
    Ceramic, white, raised hand, painted black, blue, yellow, and red, c1940s **65.00**
    Composition, painted, orig tag inscribed "Walt Disney's Donald Duck," c1960s **35.00**
  Book
    Donald Duck in Disneyland, Little Golden Book, copyright 1955 and 1960 . . . .   **12.50**
    Donald Duck Sees Stars, Better Little Book, #1422, Whitman **60.00**
  Bookend, 7", chalkware, carrying school books **19.00**
  Bottle, soda, quart, 10" h, clear glass, two large and two small heads emb each side, inscribed "Donald Duck/Not To Be Refilled/Trademark Copyright/Walt Disney Productions," bottom marked "One Pint 8 Fl Oz," early 1960s **35.00**
  Cookie Jar, marked "Walt Disney Co by Hoan Ltd" **50.00**

Doll, Dancing Donald, 16" h, hard plastic, white vinyl hands, fabric outfit, hinged legs, Hasbro, c1970   10.00

Figure
  Bisque, 3¼" h, long–billed, holding small gold horn, 1930s 30.00
  Celluloid, 3" h, movable feet and arms, red jacket, blue bow tie, green hat, Walt Disney around one side of body, "Japan" marked on foot, c1950s 65.00
  Plywood, 4 x 6", diecut, painted, fits in groove on base, purple fabric bow tie, early 1950s 30.00

Greeting Card, Easter, 4 x 6", diecut, light brown flocked body, Hallmark, 1942 ....   25.00
Lamp, figural 45.00
Puppet, orig box, Gund 55.00
Roly–Poly, 6" d, 11" h, vinyl, figural, black, white, yellow, and blue, chimes, c1970 ....   15.00
Salt and Pepper Shakers, pr, pottery, figural, "Souv Grand Island Neb," 1930s 33.00
Toy, pull, 9" h, wood, movable arms, clicking sound, colorful paper labels, Fisher Price, c1950 ....   85.00
Wrist Watch, color illus, white ground, figural arms and hands, white flocked straps, Bradley, c1960 ....   70.00

Dumbo
  Figure, 5½" h, ceramic, seated, wearing yellow bonnet, Shaw 60.00
  Novelty, ¾" l, plastic, dark green, figural Dumbo, copyright symbol in ear, c1940s 12.50
  Pinback Button, 1¼", black, white, and red, picture of Dumbo, gasoline company premium, "Walt Disney's Dumbo D–X," c1941 ......   30.00
  Pitcher, 8" h, ceramic, pink and blue, white ground, Leeds China, "Walt Disney/Dumbo/2 Qt Jug" stamped under base, 1947 ....   85.00

Goofy
  Figure, 6" h, vinyl, day glow pink, Disney and Marx copyrights, 1971   12.50
  Flasher Button, 2⅜" d, I'm Goofy About Disneyland, red and white logo on back, c1960s 16.00
  Pin, 1", brass, enameled, multicolor, 1970s 10.00
  Valentine, 3 x 5", full color, movable arm holding net, copyright 1939 .   28.00

Mickey Mouse
  Astray, figural, Mickey and Minnie, 4 x 4 x 5", plaster, black, silver, red, and green, carnival giveaway, 1930s 100.00
  Ball, 2¼" d, rubber, baseball design,

Book, *Mickey Mouse In Giantland*, David McKay Company, 1934, Philadelphia, hard cover, 45 pgs, $35.00.

  black Mickey illus, red ground, Seiberling, c1930s 110.00
  Balloon, 5 x 3½", dark green rubber, head and ear shape, face on one side, figure on other, Oak Brand, 1930s 75.00
  Bank, 6" h, ceramic, white glaze, painted, 1940s 45.00
  Belt Buckle, man's, Sun Rubber Co, 1937 ....   45.00
  Book
    Mickey Never Fails, 6 x 8½", hardcover, school reader, DC Heath, Boston, 104 pgs, copyright 1939   30.00
    Mickey Mouse Flies the Christmas Mail, Mickey Mouse Club Book, first edition, published by Simon & Schuster, 1956 ....   18.00
  Bottle Warmer 24.00
  Car, Mickey Mouse Fire Dept, 2½ x 6½ x 4", dark red, white wheels, Mickey driving, Donald on back, Sun Rubber Co, 1940s 50.00
  Card
    Bubble Gum, #23, #24, #26, and #29, set of 4 ....   30.00
    Recipe, 3¼ x 5", paper, multicolor, from Recipe Scrapbook, recipes and Weber Baking Co adv on back, set of 4 ....   35.00
    Yarn Sewing, 4 x 6", stiff cardboard, "Big Chief Mickey Mouse and "Mickey Mouse Has a Party," issued by Marx Brothers, Boston .   30.00
  Charm
    Brass, Mickey Mouse Club, ¾",

red, white, and black, copyright
on reverse, c1960 .... 12.00
Celluloid, Mickey with guitar,
black and red, white ground, Japan, 1930s 25.00
Christmas Tree Lights, Noma, Walt
Disney Enterprises, MIB 295.00
Colorform Theatre, Mickey and Minnie puppet forms, Walt Disney Productions, MIB 55.00
Coloring Book, 1931 .... 75.00
Cookie Jar, turn–about, Mickey and
Minnie 110.00
Figure, 2½" h, composition, spring
arms and legs, bouncing, hangs
from elastic thread 60.00
Fire Truck, Sun Rubber 75.00
Flag Holder, 3¼" h, cast iron, figural,
holding pole, red paint, John
Wright Foundry, c1970s 20.00
Game
Coming Home, 16" sq gameboard,
Mickey in center, various characters on corners, paper label on
back, Marx Brothers, Boston ... 100.00
Spin—Win, 10 x 10 x 1½", metal,
black, white, red, and yellow,
various character illus, Northwestern Products, St Louis,
c1950 .... 40.00
3–D Rickety Bridge, 1972 .... 15.00
Kaleidoscope 68.00
Lamp, electric, 7" h, 5" d, round,
metal, beige, three Mickey decals
around sides, Soren–Manegold,
Chicago 85.00
Lunch Box, Disney World On Ice,
Mickey and Minnie, thermos 20.00
Paint Set, tin, Mickey and Donald,
1950s 40.00
Pinback Button
⅞", black and white, orange
ground, Mickey illus, "Mickey
Mouse Spingle–Bell–Chicko–K,"
1930s 135.00
1¼"
Eat Freihofer's Perfect Loaf/Member/Mickey Mouse Globetrotters," celluloid, red, white,
and black, orig back paper,
late 1930s 30.00
Mickey Mouse, red, white, and
black, Mickey illus, mid 1930s 110.00
Plaque, 6 x 7½", set of 4, full color,
Donald, Mickey, Bambi, and Pluto,
tin hanger on back, late 1940s ... 100.00
Puppet, punch out and put together,
Donald Duck bread premium, unpunched, 1950s 15.00
Radio, Mickey Mouse Sing Along .. 45.00
Record, Mickey and the Beanstalk, 78
rpm 28.00

Riding Toy, Hoppity Sun Products,
Tally Industries 100.00
Ring, silvered brass, adjustable, diecut, high relief, Mickey head, silver, black ears, red accents, late
1950s 30.00
Salt and Pepper Shakers, pr, pottery,
figural, 1930s 31.00
Sand Pail, 6" h, litho tin, swivel handle, Mickey leading parade, buildings outline background, Ohio Art,
marked "Walt Disney Enterprises" 100.00
Scissors, child's, 2 x 3", silver metal,
red handles, litho tin diecut of
Mickey mounted on one side,
marked "WD Ent" 90.00
Shoe Brush 25.00
Spoon, 5½" l, SP, Mickey and name
on handle, marked "William Rogers Mfg Co," Post Toasties premium 15.00
Toy, squeeze, rubber, Dell 50.00
Valentine, 2½ x 5½" diecut, movable
arms, 1939 copyright 12.50
Wall Pocket, 3 x 5 x 2", china, color
illus, Mickey playing horn and Minnie walking with umbrella, inscribed "Mickey Mouse Corp By
Walt E Disney/Made in Japan" ... 185.00
Wrist Watch, rect, black, white, red,
and yellow illus on silver dial, red
numbers, red plastic straps, Ingersoll, late 1940s 160.00
Minnie Mouse
Doll, cloth, pie eyes, 20" h 45.00
Figure
Glass, 5" h, frosted, pale pink,
standing, holding pocketbook,
marked "Walt Disney Productions" on base, c1960s 30.00
Paper, 11" h, linen texture, diecut,
stitched edge, tan, black, and red
printing, stuffed, copyright 1937
Walt Disney Ent 235.00
Fork, 4¾" l, "My Minnie Mouse" inscribed on handle, imp Mickey on
end, marked "AHB & Co Stainless
Nickel" on back 40.00
Puppet, 10" h, felt and fabric, soft rubber head, red bow on neck, orig
tag, Gund, 1950s 35.00
Miscellaneous
Disneyland
Locket, brass, heart shape, raised
castle on front, pink and blue accents, late 1950s 24.00
Map, 1970s 12.00
Postcard, 1970s 20.00
Fantasia, salt and pepper shakers, pr,
3¼" h, ceramic, oriental mushrooms, tan, marked "Disney copyright 1941/Vernon Kilns USA" 125.00
Ferdinand the Bull, hair bows, pr,

Game, Walt Disney's Donald Duck Party Game For Young Folks, Parker Bros, 1938, 19¼ x 9¾ x 1¾", $45.00.

pink fabric, brass centers and clips, orig card with full color illus, printed verse and 1938 copyright, unused 60.00

Jungle Book, doll, vulture, 5" h, felt and fabric, black yarn hair, 1966 copyright tag 40.00

Mickey Mouse Club
Hat, Mouseketeer, Mickey ears ... 35.00
Pin, 3" 25.00
View–Master Reel, Mouseketeers, three reels, #865 A, B, and C, copyright 1956 .... 25.00

101 Dalmatians, pencil case, 5 x 10 x 2", dark blue, full color paper label, copyright 1960 .... 12.50

Pollyanna, Golden record, 78 rpm, yellow, America the Beautiful, orig jacket shows Haley Mills, copyright 1960 .... 15.00

Three Caballeros, figure, Jose Carioca, 3" h, ceramic, full color, stamped "Walt Disney/Mexico" and "30" under base, 1940s 90.00

Three Little Pigs
Figure, wall type, wolf and pigs, plaster, painted, high relief, wire hook on back, 1930s 125.00
Handkerchief, 8½" sq, black and white illus, red ground, early 1930s 30.00
Puzzle, Three Little Pigs at Work and Play, orig box, 1940s 15.00
Walt Disney, stamp book, *Animals of Africa*, 8½ x 11", Simon & Schuster, 32 pgs, 1956 .... 30.00

Peter Pan
Book, *Walt Disney's Peter Pan and Wendy*, Little Golden Book, first edition, 1952 .... 20.00
Figurine, Tinkerbell 50.00

Pinocchio
Bank, ceramic 75.00
Figure, 10½", jointed composition head, wood body, arms, and legs, brown felt hat, painted, Ideal 100.00
Game, Walt Disney's Pinocchio–The

Merry Puppet Game, Milton Bradley, orig box, complete, 1939 .... 40.00

Glass, J Worthington Foulfellow, 4¾" h, clear, brown illus, four line verse on back 30.00

Golden Record, 78 rpm, orange, orig jacket, copyright 1972 .... 10.00

Hand Puppet, 9" h, composition head, red fabric body, white hands, marked "W Disney Ent" on back . 150.00

Marionette, 14", composition and wood, white felt collar, red bow tie, yellow shirt, purple vest and pants, plastic eyes, rubber nose grows from ½" to over 1", strings, cardboard, hand control, 1950s 200.00

Model Kit, Jolly Roger Pirate Ship, unassembled, orig box inscribed "From Disneyland," 1960 copyright 30.00

Paint Book, 11 x 15", Whitman, 48 pgs, c1939 .... 60.00

Pinback Button, 1¼", blue, white ground, Walt Disney's Pinocchio/ Hi Diddle Dee Dee!," English, 1960s 20.00

Toy, wind–up, Figaro the Cat, 2½" h, litho tin, black and white, color details, red, and yellow name on back, rubber ears, Marx 135.00

Transfer, 5 x 6" clear cellophane bag, colorful diecut folder, set of characters, Tower Press, England, 1950s 35.00

Valentine, Jiminy Cricket, 3 x 5", diecut, movable arms, copyright 1939 25.00

Pluto
Badge, 2½ x 3", molded plastic, multicolor illus, man beside circus tent, flasher picture of Pluto balancing on ball, mid 1960s 25.00
Figure, 3 x 3 x 6½", glazed china, tan body, light blue collar, 1970s 20.00
Toy, friction, 2 x 4½ x 2½" h, plastic, figural, yellow body, black and red details, Marx, early 1950s 40.00

Robin Hood, toy, wind–up, Friar Tuck, 4" h, figure, soft rubber, turns in circle, c1973 .... 24.00

Scrooge McDuck, key holder, wall mount, brass, sgd 8.00

Snow White and the Seven Dwarfs
Charm, Grumpy, plastic, light green, copyright symbol, 1940s 10.00
Cup, 2" d, 2½" h, SP, raised illus, engraved initials "FMU," hallmarks under base, c1939 .... 65.00
Doll, 12", Dopey, cloth body, Gund 45.00
Figurine Set, 6½" h Snow White, 4½" h, dwarfs, bisque, dwarfs hold musical instruments, Japan 700.00
Lamp, Dopey, figural 65.00

Pin, Happy, wood, painted, 1940s . 15.00
Plaque, 5 x 5", ceramic, pastel green, tan, and blue background, gold trim, high relief figure of Happy, bird in upper right corner, imp "Ceramica/Cuernavaca/Mexico" on back, 1950s 65.00
Puppet, Dopey, Gund 22.00
Puzzle, 14 x 22", full color, Snow White, dwarfs, and forest animals, cottage background, Jaymar, orig box, 1940s 30.00
Safety Blocks, set of 16, wood, alphabet letters and animals on four sides, raised character images and name on two sides, orig box, marked "by Special Permission of Walt Disney Enterprises," c1939 . 75.00
Salt and Pepper Shakers, pr, Doc, 2½" h, ceramic, figural, multicolor, marked "Foreign" on bottom, c1939 .... 25.00
Soap, figural, Doc, 3½" h, tan, red accents, Kirk, c1939 .... 25.00
Valentine, Grumpy, movable, 1930s 10.00
Zorro
Comic Book, *Walt Disney Presents Zorro*, #7, Sept 1967 .... 10.00
Costume, cape, belt, mask, orig box 69.00
Dry Cleaning Bag, cut out costume, 23 x 36", white paper, black, white red, and orange illus, dry cleaner adv and "Walt Disney Studios Presents Zorro on ABC–TV" printed on bag, c1960 .... 32.00
Little Golden Book, 1958 .... 15.00
Magic slate and game 65.00
Model, assembled, orig box, Aurora, 1966 .... 125.00
Ring, plastic, silver finish, Zorro logo on black stone, 1960s 18.00
Tie Slide, 1¼", silvered brass, black, white, and red plastic insert, c1960 30.00
TV Guide, Zorro on cov, 1958 ..... 25.00
Wrist Watch 65.00

DOG COLLECTIBLES

Collecting Hints: A collection of dog related items may be based on one particular breed. Another way to collect dog items is by items picturing a dog or even dog–shaped objects. With millions of dog owners in the United States, dog collectibles are very popular.

History: Dogs, long recognized as "Man's Best Friend," have been a part of human life since the early cavemen. The first dogs probably were used for hunting and protection against the wilder animals. After man learned that dogs could be trained to provide useful services, many types of dogs were bred and trained for specific purposes. Over 100 breeds of dogs have evolved from the first dog which roamed the earth over 15 million years ago. Today, dogs are still hunters, protectors, herders, and are trained to see and hear for people.

Man has continued to domesticate the dog, developing today's popular breeds. The American Kennel Club has divided the breeds into seven classifications: herding, hounds, sporting, non–sporting, terriers, toy breeds, and working dogs.

In 1859 in Newcastle, England, the first modern dog show was held. People enjoyed this show and many others were started. The breeding of prize dogs became important. The bloodlines of important dogs were established and recorded. Today, the dogs with the largest pedigrees command the highest prices.

As the dog's popularity grew, so did its appearance on objects. They became popular in literature, paintings and other art forms.

Museum: The Dog Museum of America, Jarville House, 1721 South Mason Road, St. Louis, MO.

Advisor: Jocelyn C. Butterer.

Advertising, Paul's Market, Saylorsburg, PA, diecut, red roof and porch, green door and grass, card holder, 7½ x 10", $15.00.

Advertising
Bank, Hush Puppies Shoes, figural, Basset Hound 25.00
Display, RCA Nipper, stuffed toy, 30", c1940 .... 175.00
Plate, Fergus Falls, MN, St Bernard . 20.00
Record Duster, RCA Nipper 50.00
Salt and Pepper Shakers, pr, RCA Nipper 20.00

Sign, Old Boston Beer, cardboard, dog pictured, 23 x 23" 25.00
Stickpin, Avery Bulldogs 35.00
Trade Card, A & P Store, Pug dog in basket, 1885 .... 25.00
Wagon, child's, Greyhound logo on sides, c1940 .... 125.00
Bank
 Dog on tub, cast iron 55.00
 German Shepard, cast iron 38.00
Blotter, Scottie, carved Jadite 18.00
Book, *Dogs, Ruff and Smooth*, Lucy Darson drawings, c1940 .... 22.00
Bookends, pr
 Setter, on point, black, cast iron, 4½ x 7½", c1920 .... 95.00
 Sailor Boy and his Dog, Frankart ... 95.00
Book Mark, Scottie and Spaniel, tin ... 25.00
Boot Scraper, Dachshund, cast iron ... 125.00
Candy Container, glass eyes, orig paint
 Collie, 7" 95.00
 Setter, 8" 100.00
Charm, Ideal dog, metal 10.00
Chimney Piece, two dogs, blue and white, on oval base, 6¼", Copeland 425.00
Cigarette Lighter, Spaniel, figural, Japan 12.00
Cookie Jar
 Dog, brown, marked "McCoy" 40.00
 Doggie in Basket 25.00
Doorstop
 Borzoi, original paint 125.00
 Boston Terrier, full bodied, old black and white paint, cast iron, red leather collar, 10" 95.00
 Cocker Spaniel, silhouette, some relief detailing, bronze, worn green patina, 17 x 11¼" 150.00
 German Shepard, full bodied, old red paint over black, cast iron, 12½" . 175.00
 Pointer, full bodied, left leg raised, old black and white paint, 15¼" . 300.00
 St Bernard, wearing keg 145.00
 Terrier, full bodied, old worn black and white re–paint, 9¼" 125.00
 Wire Haired Terrier, with bushes, orig paint, c1929 .... 115.00
Feeding Dish, emb "Dog," yellowware 8.00
Figure
 Collie, carnival chalkware, 12" 8.00
 Newfoundland, white clay, black glaze, laying on pillow, 8" 250.00
 Pointer, carved wood, leatherized cloth ears, original black and white paint, 3", mfg by J W Akin 75.00
 Scotties, pressed wood, pr 18.00
 Spaniel
  Sewer Pipe, 7½", rect base 450.00
  Staffordshire
   5¼", copper luster and white, pr 300.00
   7½", red and white, pr 330.00
 Whippet
  China, Morton Studios, c1940 ... 80.00

Figurine, Bulldog, tan and brown, red collar, incised "Germany 2777," 5" h, $45.00.

 Parian, polychrome paint, seated on cushion, 4¼" 45.00
Hitching Post, seated Spaniel, ring in neck, traces of old paint, cast iron, 11½" 925.00
Inkwell, two seated Whippets, sanded coats, tree, old polychrome paint, 5½" 250.00
Lamp, black poodles, pr 45.00
Mug, German Shorthaired Pointer head 18.00
Napkin Ring, figural, silver plated
 Dog chasing cat on top of ring 295.00
 Dog pulling sled 250.00
Painting, oil on canvas
 Boston Terrier, seated, unframed, 18 x 14" 185.00
 St Bernard, head study, gilt frame, 23½ x 21½" 75.00
Paperweight
 French Bull Dog, orig paint, 3 x 2½" 70.00
 Scottie, old black paint, cast iron, 3" 40.00
Pencil Sharpener, dog in chair 15.00
Pen Holder, Whippet, Staffordshire ... 125.00
Pin, lady with dog, Art Deco styling .. 38.00
Planter
 Bird Dog, marked "McCoy" 65.00
 Cocker Spaniel, holds green basket, marked "Royal Copley" 12.00
 Terrier, 6" 15.00
Print, Hunting Dog Puppies, sliding down board from porch, E H Osthaus, 9" x 12" 78.00
Puppet, shaggy dog, Gund, 10" 20.00
Rug, hooked, stylized dog, brown, olive on blue ground, 24" x 38" 200.00
Spoon, baby, Scottie dog shape 6.00
Stuffed Toy
 Cocker Spaniel, Steiff, button in ear, 4½" 30.00

Collie, Steiff, laying down, tag only,
9" **68.00**
Puppy, Steiff, button in ear, brown
plush, glass eyes, swivel neck,
working squeek **95.00**
Scottie Dog, black plush, 17", Ger-
many, c1945 .... **45.00**
Tape Measure, figural
Black Scottie **25.00**
Plaid dog **15.00**
Tobacco Jar, Pug **75.00**
Toy, wind–up, dog shaking shoe, white
flannel cover, glass eyes, ribbon trim **20.00**
Walking Stick, figural handle
Bull Dog, glass eyes, silver overlay
trim, silver ferrile, marked "Al-
pacca," 37½" **275.00**
Bull Dog, carved ivory handle, glass
eyes, ivory tip, 36¼" **250.00**
Sleeping dog, sterling silver handle,
Art Nouveau style, horn tip, 35½" **210.00**
Wall Pocket, Scottie, marked "Japan" . **27.00**

DOLL HOUSE FURNISHINGS

Collecting Hints: Doll house furnishings are children's toys. Some wear may be expected. It is
possible to find entire room sets in original boxes.
These sets will command a higher price.

History: Doll house furnishings are the tiny articles of furniture and accessories used to outfit
a doll house. They may be made of many types
of materials, from fine handmade wooden pieces
to molded plastic. Furnishings were played with
by children to decorate and redecorate their favorite doll house. Several toy manufacturers,
such as Tootsietoy, Petite Princess, and Renwal,
made doll house furnishings.

Doll houses and doll house furnishings have
undergone a current craze and are highly collectible. Many artists and craftsmen devote hours to
making scale furniture and accessories. This type
of artist–oriented doll house furnishings is not
included in this listing. It does, however, affect
the market by offering the buyer a choice of an
old piece versus a present day handmade piece.

References: Flora Gill Jacobs, *Doll Houses in
America: Historic Preservation in Miniature,*
Charles Schribner's Sons; Constance Eileen King,
Dolls and Dolls Houses, Hamlyn; Von Wilckens,
Mansions in Miniature, Tuttle.

Periodicals: Miniature Collector, 12 Queen Anne
Place, Marion, OH 43306; Nutshell News, Clifton House, Clifton, VA 22024.

Collectors' Clubs: International Guild Miniature
Artisans, P. O. Box 842, Summit, NJ 07901; Na-

tional Association of Miniature Enthusiasts, 351
Oak Place, Suite E, Brea, CA 92621.

Museums: Kansas City Doll House Museum,
Kansas City, MO; Margaret Woodbury Strong
Museum, Rochester, NY; Mildred Mahoney Ju-
bilee Doll House Museum, Fort Erie, Canada;
Toy Museum of Atlanta, Atlanta, GA; Washing-
ton Dolls' House and Toy Museum, Washington,
DC.

**9 pc set, piano, table and chairs, corner
cupboard, and desk, maroon plastic, Jay-
don, orig box, $15.00.**

Ashtray, standing, Renwal **2.00**
Bathinette, Renwal **15.00**
Bath Tub, metal, Tootsie Toy **12.00**
Bathroom Scale, Renwal **3.00**
Bathroom Set, 3 pcs, bath tub, toilet and
sink, white, Plasco **12.00**
Bed
Petite Princess, plastic **10.00**
Strombecker, wood, twin size **5.00**
Superior, plastic, red, double **3.00**
Tootsie Toy, twin, 1¼ x 3¼" **8.00**
Bedroom Set
3 pcs, 1" scale, Victorian, walnut, 5"
highback bed, three drawer chest,
mirror, and washstand **120.00**
4 pcs
Plastic, bed, vanity, wardrobe, and
mirror, c1930 .... **45.00**
Wooden, 1" scale, 6½" bed, chest
of drawers, nightstand, and lamp
table **100.00**
Chair
Arm, metal, Tootsie Toy **15.00**
Hitchcock, reed seat **25.00**
Ladderback **25.00**
Occasional, Petite Princess, aqua vel-
veteen **8.00**

Straight
- German, wood, fabric seat, carved floral back 10.00
- Plasco, ivory 4.00
- Renwal, brown 5.00

Wing
- Needlepoint, flame stitch 18.00
- Petite Princess, red brocade 15.00
- Strombecker 5.00

Chest of Drawers
- Petite Princess 15.00
- Renwal 6.00
- Strombecker, wood, painted white .. 10.00

China Cabinet, curved front, Isinglass door, 4" 25.00

Corner Cupboard, 8", maple, Tynee Toy 25.00

Cradle
- Plasco, pink 5.00
- Wood, blue, floral decor 10.00

Desk, stenciled top, bentwood chair .. 95.00

Dining Room Set
- 4 pcs, mahogany, 3½ x 5" table, 6" hutch, sewing cabinet, and braided rug, German 55.00
- 5 pcs, plastic, table, four chairs, c1945, MIB 8.00
- 6 pcs, cardboard, hand made, table, three chairs, corner cupboard, and buffet 125.00
- 8 pcs, Tootsie Toy, metal, 2½" pedestal table, four matching fiddleback chairs, 2½" gilt, maroon radio, and two floor lamps 60.00

Dollhouse Doll
- 2"
  - Baby, bisque, blonde human hair, orig organdy dress, matching quilt, Angel Baby #58, Eunice Tuttle 170.00
- 3", bisque
  - Baby, bent limbs, painted features, made in Occupied Japan 15.00
  - Child, German, one pc, molded, curly hair, painted facial features 50.00
  - Flapper, bisque, molded hair, orig costume, Germany, c1920 ..... 65.00
- 6", bisque
  - Lady, solid domed shoulderhead, blue eyes, orig muslin body, mohair wig 175.00
  - Young Girl, swivel head, marked "Karen #9, Eunice P. Tuttle," c1960 .... 150.00

Fainting Couch, Petite Princess, green brocade 18.00

High Chair, cast iron 25.00

Hutch
- Petite Princess 45.00
- Renwal, brown 5.00

Ice Box, metal, glass block of ice 125.00

Kitchen Set, 7 pcs, 1" scale, chestnut wood, colonial style, cupboard, table, four chairs 50.00

Kitchen Stove, 4", silver plated gas, two burners, gilded daisy on oven door, signed "505 Champion" 30.00

Lamp
- Floor, Renwal 4.00
- Table, Petite Princess 4.00

Living Room Set, 5 pcs, Sheraton style, 5" striped sofa, wing chair, drop leaf table, and stool 50.00

Mirror, cheval, 4½" oval, walnut frame, pedestal base 40.00

Piano, bench, and metronome, MIB, Petite Princess 25.00

Potty Chair, cast iron 25.00

Radio, floor model, Renwal 6.00

Refrigerator, Superior, plastic, ivory ... 2.00

Rocking Chair
- Cast Iron 20.00
- Victorian, walnut, 4", spindle back . 40.00

Rug
- Braided, oval, shades of rose, red, white 20.00
- Polar Bear, 10½ x 6½", white fur, open mouth, tiny teeth, royal purple velvet lining 25.00
- Tobacco Rug, cotton, Oriental rug style, fringed 2.50

Sofa
- Metal, Tootsie Toy 12.00
- Plastic, Superior, red, 3 molded cushions 8.00

Study Set, 7 pcs, wooden, grandfather clock, console table, candlestand, two lyre back side chairs, and two brass candlesticks, Exacto 25.00

Table
- Cast iron, 3¾ x 6½" top, 3" h, red, Arcade 10.00
- Maple, 4" d, pedestal base, removable marble top 25.00

Tea Cart, Tootsie Toy, metal 15.00

Vacuum Cleaner, Renwal 8.00

Washstand, metal, Tootsie Toy 8.00

Woodburning Stove 10.00

Wringer Washer, Renwal 12.00

DOLLS

Collecting Hints: The most important criteria in buying dolls are sentiment and condition. The value of a particular doll increases if it is a childhood favorite or family heirloom.

When pricing a doll, condition is the most important aspect. Excellent condition means that the doll has all original parts.

The wig should not be soiled or restyled. The surface of the skin must be free of marks and blemishes. Original sleep eyes must be free moving. All mechanical parts should be operational.

Original clothing means original dress, under-clothes, shoes, and socks in excellent and clean condition, preferably with original tags and labels.

A doll that is mint in the original box is listed as "MIB." Many modern collectible doll prices depend on the original box. Mattel's original Barbie doll, for example, is valued over $1,000 MIB. However, without the original box, the doll is worth much less. Another pricing consideration is appeal. Only a collector knows how important and valuable a particular doll is to her collection.

Modern and 20th century dolls are highly collectible. They offer many appealing features to collectors, one of which is price. A collector of modern dolls need not spend thousands of dollars. This type of doll collecting fits into the average person's budget.

Another feature is the size of dolls which enables collectors to artfully display them. Many dolls are made of materials easily cleaned and maintained. An attractive appeal of modern dolls is that they are easily available at flea markets, garage sales, swap meets, etc.

History: The history of modern doll manufacturers is long and varied. Competitors used similar procedures, molds, and ideas. When Effanbee was successful with the Patsy dolls, Horsman soon followed with a Patsy look–alike named Dorothy. Vogue's Ginny doll was imitated by Cosmopolitan's Ginger. Some manufacturers reused molds and changed sizes and names to produce dolls which were similar for many years.

Dolls have always been popular with Americans. The early Patsy dolls with their own wardrobes were a success in the 1930s and 1940s. During the 1950s Vogue's Ginny Doll was very successful in generating the sales of dolls, clothes, and accessories. The next decade of children enjoyed Mattel's Barbie. Collectors will determine what the collectible dolls of the 1970s and 1980s will be. Doll collecting has become a major hobby.

References: Johana Gast Anderton, *More Twentieth Century Dolls From Bisque to Vinyl, Volume A–H, Volume I–Z, Revised Edition,* Wallace–Homestead, 1974; John Axe, *The Encyclopedia of Celebrity Dolls,* Hobbie House Press, Inc. 1983; Julie Collier, *Official Identification and Price Guide to Antique and Modern Dolls, Fourth Edition,* House of Collectibles, 1989; Jan Foulke, *10th Blue Book Dolls & Values,* Hobby House Press, Inc., 1991; R. Lane Herron, *Herron's Price Guide to Dolls,* Wallace–Homestead, 1989; Jeanne Du Chateau Niswonger, *That Doll, Ginny,* Cody Publications, 1978; Susan Paris and Carol Manos, *Barbie Dolls,* Collector Books, 1982; Susan Paris and Carol Manos, *The World of Barbie Dolls,* Collector Books, 1983; Patricia R. Smith, *Modern Collector's Dolls, Editions 1, 2, 3, 4, 5,* Collector Books, 1973, 1975, 1976, 1979, 1984;

Marjorie Victoria Sturges Uhl, *Madame Alexander, Ladies of Fashion,* Collector Books, 1982.

Periodicals: *Celebrity Doll Journal,* 6 Court Place, Puyallup, WA 98372; *Contemporary Doll Magazine,* Scott Publications, 30595 W. 8 Mile Road, Livonia, MI 48152; *Costume Quarterly for Doll Collectors,* 38 Middlesex Drive, St Louis, MO 63144; *Doll Artisan,* Doll Artisan Guild, 35 Main Street, Oneonta, NY 13820; *Doll Reader,* Hobby House Press, Inc, 900 Frederick St, Cumberland, MD 21502; *Doll Times,* 218 West Woodin, Dallas, TX 75224; *Dolls, The Collector's Magazine,* 1910 Bisque Lane, P. O. Box 1972, Marion, OH 43305; *National Doll World,* 306 East Parr Road, Bernie, IN 46711; *United Collectors,* Master Key To The World of Dolls, P.O. Box 1160, Chatsworth, GA 30705.

Collectors' Clubs: Ginny Doll Club, 305 West Beacon Road, Lakeland, FL 33803; United Federation of Doll Clubs, P. O. Box 14146, Parkville, MO 64152.

Museums: Margaret Woodbury Strong Museum, Rochester, NY; Museum of Collectible Dolls, Lakeland, FL; Yesteryears Museum, Sandwich, MA.

Note: All prices listed here are for dolls in excellent condition and original clothes, unless otherwise noted.

AMERICAN CHARACTER DOLL COMPANY

The American Character Doll Company was founded in 1918 and made high quality dolls. When the company was liquidated in 1968, many molds were purchased by the Ideal Toy Co. American Character Dolls are marked with the full company name, "Amer. Char." or "Amer. Char." in a circle. Early composition dolls were marked "Petite."

8", Betsy McCall, plastic, jointed, swivel neck, brown saran wig, orig nylon chemise, shoes, and socks, MIB	185.00
8½", Teeny Weeny Tiny Tears, all vinyl, rooted blonde hair, orig clothing, 1964	24.00
10½", Tiny Toodles, vinyl, molded, painted hair, 1958	25.00
11½", Darlin' Dollface, vinyl, rooted hair, 1965	30.00
15"	
Baby Tiny Tears, hard plastic head, rubber body, molded hair, orig clothes, mark: Pat. No. 2675644 Amer. Character, 1950	90.00
Infant Toodles, heavy vinyl, car bed and orig comic book, c1959	225.00
16" Sally, composition swivel head and	

limbs, cloth body, orig plaid dress, 1935 .... **100.00**

17", Margaret–Rose, vinyl head, arms, and legs, plastic body, rooted blonde hair **48.00**

18", Little Love, composition head and limbs, cloth body, brown human hair wig, 1942 .... **60.00**

19", Butterball, vinyl, rooted ash blonde hair, MIB, 1961 .... **50.00**

21", Graduate, one piece vinyl body, orig cap and gown, 1960 .... **50.00**

28", Debutante Walker, composition, mohair wig, crier mechanism, walker, 1939 .... **135.00**

ARRANBEE

This company was founded in 1922. Arranbee's finest dolls were made in hard plastic. One of Arranbee's most popular dolls was Nancy, and later Nanette. The company was sold to Vogue Dolls Inc. in 1959. Marks used by this company include "Arranbee," "R & B," and "Made in USA."

8", Baby Marie, vinyl head and limbs, plastic body, molded hair, made for Kresges Stores, 1963 .... **15.00**

10"

Miss Cody, vinyl head, hard plastic body, rooted brown hair, walker, 1950 .... **30.00**

Oriental Baby, composition, multicolored taffeta outfit, braid trim **48.00**

11", Littlest Angel, vinyl head, hard plastic body, jointed shoulders, hips and knees, rooted dark brown hair; mark: R & B, 1959 .... **36.00**

14", Nanette, vinyl, orig skating dress, MIB, 1953 .... **40.00**

17"

Baby Donna, hard plastic head, cloth body, latex arms and legs, molded hair, 1949 .... **45.00**

Gloria Jean, vivid blue eyes, movie promotion for "A Little Bit of Heaven," 1940 .... **125.00**

18", hard plastic head and five piece body, blonde mohair wig, blue sleep eyes, MIB, c1950 .... **85.00**

19"

Judy, hard plastic, nylon blonde wig, braids, metal knob to wind hair back into head, open mouth; mark: 210 on head, Pat. 2,537,598 on body, c1951 .... **70.00**

Nancy, composition, fully jointed, mohair wig, open mouth **125.00**

Rosie, composition swivel head on shoulderplate, cloth body, molded hair, 1935 .... **80.00**

21", So Big, composition head and limbs, cloth body, 1936 .... **55.00**

Cameo, Scootles, composition, orig outfit, 12½" h, $385.00.

CAMEO DOLL PRODUCTS COMPANY

The Cameo Doll Products Company was founded in 1922. The original owner was Joseph L. Kallus. The most well known doll made by this company was the Kewpie designed by Rose O'Neill. The company was sold in 1970 to Strombecker. However, Mr. Kallus retained some company molds and is reissuing dolls like Miss Peeps under the name of Cameo Exclusive Products.

10", Margie, composition head, wood body, molded hair, painted eyes, orig dress and box, c1930 .... **275.00**

12"

Kewpie, composition, one piece head and body, jointed arms, painted features, flowered sunsuit, c1940 . **120.00**

Scootles, composition head and five piece chubby body, bold molded and painted hair, pink flowered dress and bonnet, c1930 .... **275.00**

17", Little Annie Rooney, composition head and jointed body, pale blonde hair, large painted brown eyes, watermelon smile, 1926 .... **250.00**

19", Miss Peeps, vinyl, brown skin, inset eyes; mark: Cameo on head, Cameo Doll Products/Strombecker Corp on tag, 1973 .... **32.00**

24", Plum, vinyl head, one piece latex body, molded hair, two squeakers; mark: Cameo on neck, Plum, De-

signed and Copyrighted by JLK on
box, 1952 .... **65.00**

DELUXE READING, DELUXE TOPPER, TOPPER CORPORATION, TOPPER TOYS

Deluxe Toy Creations are all names used by
Deluxe Toys. This company specialized in dolls
that can do things. The company went out of
business in 1972.

6", Dawn & Friends
Series of vinyl, jointed at neck, shoulders, waist, and hips, posable legs,
rooted hair; mark: Copyright 1970/
Topper Corp/Hong Kong on lower
back, additional mark on head
Angie, black hair, brown eyes;
mark: 51/D10 .... **12.00**
Dawn, blonde hair, blue eyes;
mark: 343/S11A **15.00**
Modeling Agency Series, vinyl,
jointed waists, snapping knees,
rooted hair, painted eyes, fashion
costumes, portfolios
Dinah, blonde hair, blue eyes;
mark: K10 .... **12.00**
Maureen, brown hair, brown eyes;
mark: H11C **12.00**
6½", Boy Friends Series
Gary, molded black hair, blue eyes . **11.50**
Ron, molded blonde hair, blue eyes **11.00**
Van, negro, molded black hair, brown
eyes **12.00**
18", Baby Catch A Ball, vinyl head,
plastic body, jointed wrists, rooted
blonde hair, stationary eyes, battery
operated to throw a ball; mark: PB2/
28/Deluxe Topper/1969 on head ... **25.00**
21", Susie Homemaker, vinyl head and
arms, plastic body and legs, jointed
hips and knees, rooted dark blonde
hair, open mouth, five painted teeth,
dimples; mark: 2/K26/Deluxe Read-
ing/1966 .... **36.00**

EEGEE DOLL MFG COMPANY

The owner and founder of this company was
E. G. Goldberger. He began his company in
1917, marking his dolls "E. G." Other marks
used by the company include E. Goldberger and
Eegee.

10½", Schoolgirl, stuffed vinyl head,
hard plastic body, jointed knees,
walker, orig jumper and blouse, 1957 **18.00**
11", Tina, vinyl head, hard plastic body,
rooted blonde hair, closed mouth,
jointed knees, walker; mark: S on
head, 1959 .... **12.00**

14"
Playpen Baby, vinyl head, plastic
body, rooted blonde hair, nurser;
mark: 13/14AA/Eegee Co, 1968 .. **12.00**
Sleepy, vinyl head and limbs, plastic
body, molded and painted hair,
asleep; mark: Eegee/1967 .... **25.00**
15", Gemette, vinyl head and arms,
plastic body, rooted brown hair,
molded adult hands, closed mouth;
mark: Eegee 1963/11 on back **15.00**
16"
Chikie, composition, bent right arm,
molded hair, tin sleep eyes, open
mouth, three upper teeth, orig tag
reads "Chikie. Another Eegee
Doll," picture of little girl feeding
baby chicks **75.00**
Newborn Baby Doll, vinyl head and
limbs, cloth body; mark: Eegee Co/
173, 1963 .... **20.00**
Rose Red Flowerkin, plastic and vinyl; mark: 8/F2/Eegee on head,
Goldberger Doll/Mfg Co, Inc/Pat
Pend on back, 1963 .... **25.00**
17", Buster, vinyl head and arms, plastic
body and legs, molded hair; mark:
1959/Eegee **22.00**
18", Posi Playmate, vinyl head, foam
body, glove hands, rooted white hair;
mark: 18LT/1/Eegee Co on head,
1969 .... **12.50**

Effanbee, Pun'kin, all plastic, brunette,
gingham dress, orig wrist tag, 1966, 11½"
h, $25.00.

EFFANBEE DOLL CORPORATION

The Effanbee Doll Corporation was founded in
1912 by Bernard E. Fleischaker and Hugo Baum
Its most successful line was the Patsy doll and it,

many variations. Patsy was such a success that a whole wardrobe was designed and sold well. This was the first marketing of a doll and her wardrobe.

Effanbee experimented with materials as well as molds. Rubber was first used in 1930; the use of hard plastic began in 1949. Today vinyl has replaced composition. Effanbee is still in business.

6½", Wee Patsy, composition, one piece head and body, jointed arms and legs, painted hair and eyes, orig blue dotted Swiss dress, c1932 .... **100.00**
7½", Baby Tinette, composition, solid domed head, five piece body, molded, painted brown baby hair, orig checkered playsuit and bonnet; mark: Effanbee on head, Effanbee Baby Tinyette on torso **132.00**
8", Fluffy, fully jointed vinyl, brown skin, molded and painted hair, closed mouth; mark: Copyright Fluffy/Effanbee, c1955 .... **45.00**
9", Patsyette, composition, five piece body, molded and painted brown bobbed hair, bangs, painted features, closed mouth, orig pink organdy dotted Swiss dress; mark: Effanbee Patsyette Doll **125.00**
10", Patsy Baby, all composition, molded and painted hair, redressed; mark: FB20, c1932 .... **135.00**
11"
Dy–Dee Baby, hard plastic head, rubber applied ears, molded hair, open mouth, nurser, 1950 .... **80.00**
Half Pints, boy and girl, fully jointed vinyl, rooted blonde hair, closed grin; mark: 10ME/Effanbee/19 copyright in circle 66, pr **75.00**
Mickey, all vinyl, molded football helmet, painted features; mark: Effanbee/10 on head, Effanbee/8 on back, 1956 .... **42.00**
Miss Black America, Wonderful World of Effanbee Doll Series, vinyl socket head and five piece body, black saran wig, brown sleep eyes, MIB, c1975 .... **75.00**
12"
My Fair Baby, all vinyl, molded hair, open mouth, nurser, right index finger crosses behind thumb; mark: Effanbee 1964 .... **35.00**
Little Red Riding Hood, set of wolf, grandma, and Little Red Riding Hood, Patsy type, all composition, painted features **325.00**
12½", Candy Kid, composition, dressed, 1946 .... **165.00**
13", Skippy, composition swivel head,

cloth body, composition hands and legs with molded socks and shoes, molded hair, painted side glancing eyes, orig military type suite, c1929 **245.00**
14", Catherine, composition, bent right arm, molded hair, red Patsy–type bob, painted eyes, orig clothes, 1927 **132.00**
Suzanne, composition, mohair wig, closed mouth, magnetic hands, orig outfit **160.00**
14½", Patricia, composition head and five piece body, light brown human hair wig in bangs and braids, brown sleep eyes, cotton flowered dress and pinafore, c1932 .... **100.00**
15"
Peaches, vinyl head and limbs, cloth body, rooted blonde hair, dimples; mark: Effanbee 1965 .... **35.00**
Twinkie, all vinyl, molded hair, open mouth, nurser; mark: Effanbee 1959 .... **45.00**
16"
Baby Grumpy, negro, composition head, cloth body, dressed **165.00**
Patsy Joan, composition head and five piece body, molded painted hair, green sleep eyes, red organdy dress, orig box **400.00**
Tommy Tucker, composition head and limbs, cloth body, molded and painted hair, blue sleep eyes, orig costume, c1940 .... **200.00**
18"
Ann Shirley, composition, drum majorette **175.00**
Sugar Baby, composition head and limbs, cloth body, molded red hair, Effanbee gold heart bracelet **85.00**
Sweetie Pie, composition head and limbs, cloth body, brown flirty eyes **100.00**
19"
Honey Walker, hard plastic swivel head, hard plastic walker body, blonde synthetic wig, blue sleep eyes, MIB, c1950 .... **250.00**
Patsy–Ann, composition socket head and five piece body, molded and painted hair, blue sleep eyes, white flowered print dress, c1928 ...... **75.00**
19½", Alyssia, vinyl head, plastic body, all fingers separate, rooted pigtails, closed mouth, walker, orig red velvet dress, white trim **150.00**
20", Mary Ann, composition head and five piece body, light brown human hair wig, open mouth with six teeth, orig pink dimity dress and shoes, orig blue metal trunk with wardrobe, c1936 .... **225.00**
21", Dy–Dee Baby, plastic swivel head, jointed soft vinyl body, brown syn-

thetic wig, blue sleep eyes, MIB, c1935 .... **200.00**

25", Bubbles, composition, straight legs **300.00**

27"

Formal Honey, all composition, blonde wig, orig clothes; mark: Effanbee on head; tag: I am Honey, An Effanbee Durable Doll, 1949 . **165.00**

Lovums, composition swivel head, cloth body, composition limbs, painted hair, blue tin sleep eyes, redressed, c1930 .... **100.00**

30", Patsy Mae, composition head and limbs, cloth body, light brown mohair wig in long curls, green sleep eyes, closed mouth, orig organdy dress, c1932 .... **325.00**

HORSMAN DOLLS COMPANY, INC.

The Horsman Dolls Company, Inc was founded in 1865 by E I Horsman, who began by importing dolls. Soon after the founding, Horsman produced bisque dolls. It was the first company to produce the Campbell Kids. They invented Fairy Skin in 1946, Miracle Hair in 1952, and Super Flex in 1954. The Horsman process for synthetic rubber and early vinyl has always been of high quality.

12", Tynie Baby, solid dome bisque head, cloth body, composition arms, blue sleep eyes, redressed, c1924 .. **500.00**

12½", Campbell Kid, composition head, cloth body, composition limbs, molded and painted head, red and white polka dot dress, c1910 ...... **225.00**

16", Baby Dimples, composition head and limbs, soft cloth body, molded and painted hair, blue tin sleep eyes, redressed, c1930 .... **150.00**

IDEAL TOY CORPORATION

The Ideal Toy Corp was formed in 1902 by Morris Michtom to produce his teddy bear. In 1915 the company had become a leader in the doll industry by introducing the first sleep eyes. In 1939, Ideal developed magic skin. It was the first company to use plastic. Some of their most popular lines include Shirley Temple, Betsy Wetsy and Toni dolls.

12"

Betsy Wetsy

Composition head, rubber body, jointed at neck, shoulders, and hips, drinks and wets; mark: IDEAL **65.00**

Hard plastic head, rubber body .. **50.00**

Hard plastic head, vinyl body **40.00**

Cinnamon, plastic, vinyl, rooted red

hair, hair grow feather; mark: 1971/ Ideal Toy Corp GH–12–H 183/ Hong Kong **35.00**

Snoozie, baby boy, composition head and limbs, cloth body, c1933 .. **125.00**

13", Shirley Temple, composition socket head and five piece jointed body, blonde mohair wig, hazel sleep eyes, orig dress, c1935 .... **350.00**

13½", Baby Coos, hard plastic head, rubber body, molded and painted light brown hair, blue sleep eyes, open/closed mouth, MIB, c1950 ... **150.00**

14"

Judy Garland Teen Doll, all composition, dark auburn human hair wig, open mouth, six teeth, 1941 **100.00**

Mary Hartline, P–90 line, blonde wig, orig red outfit, white boots, baton **85.00**

15"

Pebbles, vinyl head and limbs, plastic body, rooted blonde hair, posable head; mark: Hanna Barbera Prod/ Ideal Toy Corp/FS–16–J–I on head **40.00**

Sparkle Plenty, hard plastic head, one piece latex body, yellow yarn hair; mark: Made in USA/Pat No 2252077, 1947 .... **55.00**

Toni, plastic socket head and five piece jointed body, blonde nylon wig, green sleep eyes, orig clothes, c1948 .... **110.00**

16"

Betsy Wetsy, composition head, five piece rubber jointed body, molded hair, blue sleep eyes, redressed, c1937 .... **50.00**

Magic Skin Doll, vinyl head and limbs, oil cloth cov body, crier, 1946 .... **48.00**

Velvet, vinyl head, plastic body and legs, frosted blonde hair, hair grow feature; mark: 1969/Ideal Toy Corp **18.00**

17", Saucy Walker, hard plastic swivel head and jointed walker body, orig blonde synthetic wig, blue sleep eyes, MIB, c1951 .... **150.00**

18"

Shirley Temple, composition, jointed at neck, arms, and legs, blonde mohair wig in deep ringlets, green sleep eyes, blue polka dot dress, orig blue satin wrist bows, c1930 **400.00**

Walking Sleeping Doll, composition head and limbs, cloth body, painted tin sleep eyes, orig clothes, c1915 .... **90.00**

19", Miss Revlon, vinyl head, hard plastic body, high heel feet, rooted light brown hair, blue sleep eyes, orig tagged clothing, c1955 .... **90.00**

20", Curity Nurse, composition swivel

head and five piece jointed body, blonde mohair wig, blue sleep eyes, orig nurse uniform and cap, MIB, c1940 .... **265.00**

21"
Sara Lee, Negro, vinyl, detailed features, sprayed hair, sleep eyes, orig organdy and waffle pique dress, MIB, 1952 .... **275.00**
Shirley Temple Baby, composition swivel head on shoulder plate, cloth body, composition limbs, mohair curly wig, hazel sleep eyes, open mouth, five teeth, orig pink dress and bonnet, c1935 .... **625.00**

23", Tickletoes, hard plastic head, latex arms and legs, cloth body, open mouth, two upper teeth, felt tongue, dark brown wig, mama crier; mark: P200/Ideal Doll on head, 1948 .... **150.00**

25"
Deanna Durbin, composition, brown human hair wig, blue sleep eyes, open smiling mouth, pink flowered organdy dress, unplayed with condition, c1935 .... **210.00**
Toni Walker, hard plastic, nylon wig, c1953 .... **200.00**

26", Miss Ideal, vinyl, jointed, redressed **50.00**

36", Patty Playpal, vinyl head and rigid body, jointed wrists, rooted brown hair, blue sleep eyes, orig red check dress and white pinafore, c1960 ... **100.00**

KNICKERBOCKER TOY COMPANY

This currently operating toy company has made some dolls which collectors are beginning to recognize. One of their biggest doll lines centers around Holly Hobbie and her accessories.

7", Sunbonnet Doll, May, all vinyl, painted eyes; mark: K.T.C./Made in Taiwan/1975 .... **6.50**
9", Robbie Hobbie, rag, shirt, blue jeans, MIB **12.00**
15"
Sleeping Beauty, composition, dark blonde wig, 1939 .... **85.00**
Snow White, composition, bent right arm, black wig; mark: Knickerbocker Toy Co/NY on back, 1939 **95.00**
20", Burger King **8.00**
24", Hollie Hobbie **10.00**

MADAME ALEXANDER DOLL COMPANY

The Madame Alexander Doll Co was started in 1923 by Bertha Alexander. The dolls made by this company are beautifully done with exquisite costumes. They have made hundreds of dolls

Madame Alexander, Scarlett O'Hara, green print dress, $650.00.

including several series such as the International Dolls and the Americana Dolls. Marks used by this company include "Madame Alexander," "Alexander," "Alex," and many are unmarked on the body but can be identified by clothing tags. Today, Madame Alexander continues to make dolls which are very collectible. Many dolls are made in a limited time period of one year. Others are offered for several years before being discontinued.

7½", hard plastic, blue sleep eyes, closed mouth, orig clothes
Alexanderkin, blonde glued on wig, c1953 .... **375.00**
Cinderella, blonde mohair wig, Margaret face, glass slippers, c1950 .. **275.00**
Cousin Grace, blonde synthetic wig, bent knee walker, straw picture hat, c1956 .... **675.00**
Highland Fling, brunette synthetic wig, straight leg walker, c1955 ... **550.00**
Scarlett O'Hara, brunette synthetic wig, white straw hat, c1957 ..... **650.00**

8"
Americana Series
Ballerina, 1973 .... **85.00**
Betsy Ross, 1976 .... **175.00**
Billy, hard plastic, bending knee walker, brunette wig, one piece red and white suit, red tie, 1960 ..... **400.00**
International Series, hard plastic
African, 1966 .... **250.00**
Brazil, 1965 .... **100.00**
Denmark, 1970 .... **110.00**
Ecuador, 1963 .... **425.00**
Ireland, 1978 .... **65.00**
Japan, 1972 .... **175.00**
Russia, 1963 .... **100.00**
Little Genius, hard plastic swivel head, vinyl body, molded and painted hair, sleep eyes, open mouth, orig clothes, c1958 ...... **165.00**

Little Women Series
  Amy **80.00**
  Beth, 1951 .... **325.00**
  Marme, 1960 .... **125.00**
  Meg, 1960 .... **130.00**
Wendy, hard plastic, bending knee
  walker, red wig, side ponytails,
  1961 .... **175.00**
10"
  Cinderella, hard plastic, 1950 ...... **250.00**
  Cissette, hard plastic, blonde bubble
    cut wig, 1963 .... **100.00**
  Little Shaver, brown string wavy hair,
    black painted eyes, closed mouth,
    cloth stockinet body, orig tagged
    rose taffeta and pink organdy dress,
    c1968 .... **250.00**
12", Lucinda, vinyl, auburn long straight
  rooted hair, blue sleep eyes, closed
  mouth, Janie face, orig blue taffeta
  dress, straw hat, and parasol, c1969 **425.00**
13", Little Colonel, composition head
  and five piece body, Betty face, blue
  tin sleep eyes, blonde mohair wig,
  c1936 .... **225.00**
14"
  Jenny Lind, plastic head, vinyl five
    piece body, blonde hair, blue sleep
    eyes, blue flowered cotton dress,
    black vest, white apron, gray plush
    cat, orig tag, 1969 .... **375.00**
  Muffin, pink flannel head and body,
    yellow yarn wig, blue felt eyes,
    tagged pink floral print cotton
    dress, MIB, c1975 .... **85.00**
  Snow White, hard plastic, jointed,
    orig wig, blue sleep eyes, real
    lashes, orig tagged dress, c1952 .. **575.00**
15"
  McGuffy Ana, composition head and
    five piece body, blonde human hair
    wig in pigtails, brown sleep eyes,
    open mouth, teeth, plaid dress,
    c1943 .... **115.00**
  Patchity Pam, cloth, yellow yarn hair,
    blue felt eyes, orig tagged clothes,
    c1966 .... **100.00**
16", Elsie, plastic head, multi–jointed
  vinyl body, brown hair, blue sleep
  eyes, matte finish face, green and
  white polka dot blouse, green straw
  hat, orig tags, c1960 .... **175.00**
18"
  Cissy Flower Girl, plastic head,
    multi–jointed vinyl body, blonde
    hair, blue sleep eyes, yellow dress,
    minor surface soil to doll and dress,
    c1954 .... **375.00**
  Fairy Princess, composition head,
    jointed at neck, jointed arms and
    legs, orig blonde mohair wig,
    brown sleep eyes, real lashes,

closed mouth, white satin gown,
  silver slippers, c1950 .... **200.00**
Sonja Henie, composition socket
  head, five piece jointed composition body, human hair wig, blue
  sleep eyes, open mouth, orig outfit,
  c1939 .... **450.00**
20", Ballerina, hard plastic Margaret
  face, five piece body, brown hair,
  brown sleep eyes, tagged pink satin
  and net costume, c1951 .... **175.00**
21", Portrait Series, plastic head, five
  piece vinyl body, 1979, MIB
  Agatha, auburn hair **300.00**
  Goya, dark brown hair **215.00**
  Melanie, blonde hair **350.00**
22, Pinkie Baby, composition head and
  limbs, cloth body, molded hair, sleep
  eyes, rosebud mouth, white organdy
  christening gown and ruffled bonnet,
  clover wrist tag, MIB, c1937 .... **400.00**

MATTEL INC

Mattel Inc was started in 1945. The most celebrated doll they make is Barbie, which was
designed by one of the company's founders, Ruth
Handler, in 1958. Barbie Dolls are dressed in
bathing suits and sold in boxes. Her many outfits
and accessories are also marketed successfully.
Skipper, Ken, Midge, Skooter, and Francie are a
part of Barbie's extended circle of family and
friends. Mattel has sponsored several trade–programs for Barbie Dolls, the first in 1967. The
purpose was to introduce the new bendable Barbie. This trade–in drew back more than
1,250,000 dolls.

6", Todd and Tutti Sundae Treat Gift Set,
  vinyl, MIB, 1965 .... **250.00**
6"
  Buffy, vinyl head, Tutti body, freckles **36.00**
  Doug Davis Spaceman, vinyl, posa-
    ble, dark brown hair; mark: Mattel
    Inc/1967/Hong Kong on head **10.00**
  Major Mat Mason, vinyl, brown crew
    cut hair; mark: Mattel Inc/1967/
    Hong Kong **10.00**
10", Sweet 16 Barbie, vinyl, MIB, 1975 **75.00**
11"
  Baby Walk 'N Play, plastic, vinyl,
    rooted yellow hair, painted eyes,
    two upper teeth, battery operated,
    plays with yo–yo and walks; mark:
    1967 Mattel Inc/Hong Kong on
    head **12.00**
  Live Action Christie, vinyl, MIB, 1970 **85.00**
  Quick Curl Miss America, vinyl, bru-
    nette hair, MIB, 1973 .... **90.00**
11½", Barbie
  1959, #1, vinyl, blonde hair, MIB .. **950.00**
  1960, #3, vinyl, blonde hair, MIB .. **375.00**

Barbie's Family and Friends
1961, Ken, flocked hair **75.00**
1963, Midge **70.00**
1966, Francie **50.00**
1967, Casey **65.00**
1968, Julia **40.00**
1972, Skipper, Quick Curl **20.00**
16", Talking Baby Tenderlove, one piece, inset scalp, rooted white hair, painted eyes, open mouth, nurser, pull string talker; mark: 677K/1969 Mattel Inc/Mexico on head **12.00**

MOLLYE DOLLS, INTERNATIONAL DOLL COMPANY

Mollye Dolls, International Doll Co, was founded by Mollye Goldman in the 1930s, starting as a cottage industry in Philadelphia. Mollye also made finely detailed clothes for other dolls. The patent for Raggedy Ann, Andy, and Belinda faces are held by Mollye. Finely executed clothes were a standard of the Mollye Co.

8"
Little Angel, MIB **70.00**
Martha Washington, hard plastic, hand painted face, white mohair wig **50.00**
14", Judy Garland, Wizard of Oz, composition head and five piece body, dark brown wig in braids, blue tin sleep eyes, white checked skirt and blouse, c1940 .... **135.00**
15", Ginger Rogers, human hair wig, pageboy style, closed mouth **325.00**
16", Snosh, cloth, hand painted face mask **115.00**
17", Business Girl, hard plastic, blonde wig, business suit **125.00**
19", Princess Elizabeth Rose, hard plastic, vinyl, white wig, orig bridal outfit; mark: X in circle on head **275.00**
20", Mamie Eisenhower, hard plastic, vinyl, dark brown wig, orig gown, music box; mark: X in circle on head **325.00**

SUN RUBBER COMPANY

The Sun Rubber Co produced all rubber of lasiloid vinyl dolls. Many have molded features and clothes.

10"
Peter Pan, one piece, molded on clothes; mark: Peter Pan/W. Disney Prod./The Sun Rubber Co./Barberton, O. USA, 1953 .... **30.00**
So–Wee, Ruth Newton, bottle, booties, jacket, towel, and soap **45.00**
Tod–L–Lee, all vinyl, molded hair, closed mouth, painted on sunsuit,

shoes, and socks, jointed at neck; mark: Sun Rubber Co, 1956 ..... **30.00**
11", Gerber Baby, all rubber, molded, painted hair, open mouth, nurser, dimples, crossed baby legs, mark: Gerber Baby/Gerber Products Co ... **45.00**
12", Betty Bows, vinyl head, all rubber body, arms, and legs, molded hair with hole for ribbon, open mouth, nurser, crossed baby legs, mark: Betty Bows/The Sun Rubber Co, 1953 .... **45.00**
17", Sun–Dee, lasiloid vinyl, negro, nurser; mark: Sun–Dees/Sun Rubber 1956 .... **45.00**

TERRI LEE DOLLS

The founder and designer of the Terri Lee family was Mrs. Violet Lee Gradwohl of Lincoln, Nebraska. She made the first Terri Lee doll in 1948. Jerri Lee, a brother, was trademarked in 1948. Connie Lee joined the family in 1955. Mrs. Gradwohl issued lifetime guarantees for each doll, which were honored until the demise of the company in the 1960s.

8", Girl Scout, MIB **60.00**
9", Baby Linda, all vinyl, molded, painted hair, painted black eyes, 1951 .... **78.00**
9½", So Sleepy **60.00**
10", Tiny Jerri Lee, tag, aqua shirt, shorts **80.00**
15½", Terri Lee, all vinyl, "Lastic–Plastic," slightly molded hair under wig . **100.00**
16"
Gene Autry, all rigid plastic, hand painted hair, round up outfit, mark: Terri Lee/Pat. Pending **210.00**
Jerri Lee, yellow satin shirt, blue shorts, tag **115.00**
Terri Lee, white nylon dress, c1950 . **95.00**
17"
Bonnie Low, brown vinyl, five piece body, molded features, black saran curly wig; mark: Terri Lee, Pat. Pending, c1950 .... **500.00**
Cowgirl, plastic, white saran hair, painted features, orig pink fringed cowgirl costume, felt hat, c1950 . **225.00**
18", Terri Lee, tagged outfit, hard plastic, black caracul fur hair, painted features; mark: Terri Lee **125.00**
19", Connie Lee, plaster, five piece body, brunette, curly fleeced hair, curved baby legs, c1953 .... **300.00**

VOGUE DOLLS

Vogue Dolls was founded by Mrs. Jennie H Graves. She began a small doll shop which specialized in well made costumes. The original business of doll clothing led to a cottage industry which employed over 500 home sewers in 1950. This branch of the industry peaked in the late 1950s with over 800 home workers plus several hundred more at the factory. During World War II, the shortages created a market for an American doll source. Mrs. Graves created the Ginny Doll and promoted her heavily. For many years Vogue issued one hundred new outfits for Ginny alone. They continued to produce their own dolls and clothing for others. Ginny Dolls reached their heyday in the 1950s.

7½", Crib Crowd Baby, hard plastic head and five piece jointed baby body, blonde short curly wig, blue painted eyes, orig tagged yellow dotted Swiss dress and rubber pants, c1950	475.00
8", Ginny Doll, hard plastic	
1948–50, painted eyes, molded hair, mohair wig; mark: Vogue on head, Vogue Doll on back	
Cinderella	115.00
Easter Parade	100.00
Valentine	115.00
1950–53, moving eyes; mark: Vogue on head, Vogue Doll on back	
Catholic Nun	150.00
Christmas	120.00
Dutch Boy	250.00
Square Dancer	265.00
1954, walking mechanism; mark: Ginny on back, Vogue Dolls, Inc., Pat. Pend., Made in USA	
Nurse	160.00
Rainy Day	70.00
Roller Skater	85.00
School Dress	75.00
1957, bending knees	
Beach outfit	72.50
Davy Crockett	225.00
Southern Bell, striped skirt, straw hat	85.00
1963, soft vinyl head, rooted hair	
Bride	55.00
Jodphurs, felt	40.00
School Dress	45.00
10", Jill, hand painted, 1958	
Bride	48.00
Gift Set, doll, four extra outfits, wrist tag, MIB	300.00
12", Betty Jane, all composition, bent right arm, braided pigtails, red plaid woven cotton dress, white eyelet trim; tag: Vogue Dolls, Inc, 1947	85.00
22", Hug A Bye Baby, pink pajamas, MIB	45.00
25", Baby Dear	35.00

DRUGSTORE COLLECTIBLES

Collecting Hints: There are several suggestions to consider when starting a drugstore collection: (1) buy the best that you can afford (it is wise to pay a bit more for mint/near mint items if at all possible), (2) look for excellent graphics on the packaging of items, (3) do not buy anything that is rusty or damp, (4) before purchasing an item, ask the dealer to remove price tags or written prices (if this isn't possible, consider how badly you really want the item), (5) buy a variety of items (consider placing several like items together on a shelf for increased visual effect) and (6) purchase items from a variety of time periods.

History: The increasing diversity of health related occupations has also encouraged an awareness in collecting pharmaceutical material, items that appeared in old drugstores from the turn of the century through the 1950s. Products manufactured before the Pure Food and Drug Act of 1906 are eagerly sought by collectors. Patent medicines, medicinal tins, items from a specific pharmaceutical company, dental items, and shaving supplies are a few key collecting areas.

The copyright date on a package, graphics, style of lettering, or the popularity of a specific item at a particular period in history are clues to date a product. Other approaches to finding information are talking with a pharmacist who has been in the business for a number of years or checking old manufacturing directories at a regional library.

References: Al Bergevin, *Drugstore Tins & Their Prices*, Wallace–Homestead, 1990; Martin R. Lipp, *Medical Museums USA: A Travelguide*, McGraw Hill Publishing Co.

Advisor: Patricia McDaniel.

ALLERGIES

Ahists, Asthmanefrin Co, Inc, Portland, OR, for symptomatic relief in hay fever and colds, light blue, white, paper packet, 12 tablets in cellophane packet, 3¾ x 2⅓", 1950s	2.75
Anahist, Anahist Co, Inc, Yonkers, NY, relief of colds, hay fever, blue, white, cardboard box, contains one full bottle, 15 tablets, 2 x 1¼ x¾"	3.75
Coricidin "D" Liquid Decongestant, Schering Corp, Bloomfield, NJ, symptomic relief of sinus congestion, hay fever, colds, purple, white, cardboard box, contains one 4 fl oz bottle, 5¼ x 1¾ x 1¾"	4.00
Estavin, Schieflein & Co, New York, NY, instant relief from hay fever, minor	

eye irritations, tired eyes, white, dark blue cardboard box, ¼ fl oz bottle of liquid, dropper, 2¾ x ¾ x ⅝" **3.50**

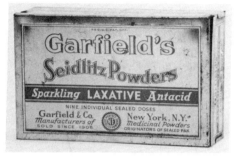

Garfield's Seidlitz Powders, Garfield & Co, New York, NY, Sparkling Laxative Antacid, nine individually sealed doses, green, gold, and blue tin, 4¾ x 3⅛ x 1¼", $50.00.

ANTACIDS

"A" Plus, Vick's Chemical Co, New York, NY, neutralizes excess acid plus relieves nervous stomach, red, blue, white paper roll, 10 tablets, 2¼ x⅝" **3.00**

Blake Soda Bicarbonate, Blake Chemical Co, Allegan, MI, tan, white, black full cardboard can, powder, 4 oz, 2½ x 1⅞" **5.00**

DeWitt's Antacid Powder, C E DeWitt & Co, Inc, Chicago, IL, light blue, black, white cardboard box, 4 oz powder, 4⅛ x 2¼ x 2¼" **4.75**

ENO, Beecham Products Inc, Clifton, NJ, cream, red, blue cardboard box, 5 x 2⅛ x 2¼", full glass 7¾" bottle of powder **8.50**

Gastrogen Tablets, Bristol Myers Co, New York, NY, light yellow, white, black cardboard box, 3⅜ x 1 x 1¼", 60 tablets **5.00**

Gold Medal Blackberry Root, Ginger, Cinnamon, Cloves, Anise Compound, The Pfeifer Co, St Louis, MO, blue, gold, cream cardboard box, contains glass bottle of syrup, an astringent carminitive and stomachic for relief of simple flatulant colic, 4⅝ x 1⅛ x 1⅛" **5.75**

Owens Pink Mixture, Charles Leich & Company, Evansville, IN, yellow, black cardboard box, full glass bottle of liquid, 1¾ oz, 4⅜ x 1¾ x 1⅛" .. **6.00**

Pfunder's Tablets, Grove Laboratories, Inc, St Louis, MO, orange, brown, green, 24 tablets, trial size, 5¾ x 2½ x 1" **5.75**

Requa's Charcoal Tablets, Requa Mfg Co, Inc, New York, NY, highly refined charcoal, black, white cardboard can, 3½ x 1⅛", 70 tablets **6.50**

Tru Blu Pep–Ti–Kao, The General Pharmaceutical Co, Cincinnati, OH, The National Antacid Powder, pink, cream, blue tin can, 4⅜ x 2½" **8.50**

APPETITE STIMULANTS

A. D. S. Special Compound, American Druggists Syndicate, Inc, New York, NY, cream, orange, blue cardboard box, full pint bottle, alcohol 17%, 9½ x 3¼ x 2¼" **10.00**

Dr Pierce's Golden Medical Discovery, Pierce's Proprietaries, Inc, Buffalo, NY, Toronto, Ontario, white, orange, blue cardboard box, full 13 fl oz, 8⅜ x 3⅜ x 2" **11.00**

Inner–Tone Tonic–Stomachic and Stimulant To The Appetite, Inner–Tone Medicine Co, Covington, KY, yellow, white, blue cardboard box, full 8 oz, 8⅜ x 3 x 1½" **9.50**

Zyrone, A Dietary Supplement, The Chattanooga Medicine Co, Chattanooga, TN, white, maroon, cardboard box, full 10 oz bottle, 8¼ x 3 x 1⅝" **7.50**

ASPIRIN

A. S. A. Compound (Acetylsalicylic Acid and Acetophenetidin Compound,) Eli Lilley & Co, Indianapolis, IN, amber pharmacy bottle, light green, red, black, partially full, 5¼ x 1⅞ x 1¼" **7.00**

Brownies, Brownie Capsule Co, Washington, IN, cream, orange, brown cardboard box, 12 capsules, 2⅛ x 1⅝ x ½" **5.00**

Ramon's Relief Compound Aspirin, Brownie Mfg Co, Distributors, Le-Rory, NY, little doctor on front, blue, white tin box, 12 tablets for 10¢, 1⅝ x 1⅛ x ¼" **5.50**

Superin, A New Relief For Pain, "superior to ordinary aspirin," Carter Products, Inc, New York, NY, maroon, white packet of 10 tablets, 2 x ⅝ x 2⅛" **5.00**

Zerbst's Grip Capsules, Zerbst Pharmacel Co, St Joseph, MO, full white, red, black cardboard box, 2 x 1½ x ⅝" . **4.50**

ASTHMA

Blosser's Cigarette's, The Blosser Cigarette Co, Daytona Beach, FL, Dr Blosser on front, red, black full cardboard box, 3¾ x 2¾ x ⅝", 1920s 8.50

Dr Kinsman's Powder, Capital Drug Co, Augusta, ME, full red tin, 3⅛ x 2½", late 1900s 18.00

Free Breath, Free Breath Products Co, Benton Harbor, MI, light blue cardboard box, empty bottle, 3¾ x 1¾ x 1" 5.00

Nyal Bronchials, Nyal Company Distributors, Detroit, MI, full, tan, cream cardboard box, 3¼ x 1½ x ¾", 1916   6.50

CONDOMS

Dean's 3 Best Tops, Dean Rubber Mfg Co, North Kansas City, MO, blue, white, three cap type condoms, 2¼ x 1⅝ x ¼" cardboard rect box 6.00

Guardian Lubricated Sealed Foil, Young's Rubber Corp, Trenton, NJ, New York, NY, cream, tan 2½" sq paper packet, professional sample .. 4.00

Sheik Rubber Prophylactics, Julius Schmid, Inc, New York, NY, horse on front of box, white, red 2¼ x 2 x ¾" cardboard box, one dozen 6.00

Trojan Naturalamb Rolled Wetskin, Young's Rubber Corp, Trenton, NJ, aqua, white 2½" sq paper envelope, foil package, professional sample ... 4.50

COUGH SYRUPS

Baron's W. O. W. (Wonder of the World,) Indianapolis, IN, red, white, black label, clear glass bottle, 3⅛ x 1", 1 fluid oz, full 5.75

Bell's Cough Syrup, Dr Bell Medicine Co, New York, NY, St Louis, MO, bell on label, white, black, clear bottle, 4¾ x 1½ x ⅝", 2 oz bottle, 1943 .. 7.00

Foley's Honey and Tar Cough Syrup, Foley & Co, Chicago, IL, beehive on label, black, yellow, 5¼ x ⅝ x ¾", clear 2 oz bottle, full 6.00

Piso's For Coughs Due To Colds, Piso Division, Pinex Co, Inc, New York, NY, green, light yellow label, dark green bottle, 6¼ x 2 x 1", 5 fluid oz, full bottle 6.75

Webster's Expectorant, The William A Webster Co, Pharmaceutical Mfgs, Memphis, TN, blue, light tan cardboard box, 5¼ x 2¼ x 1⅛" cardboard box, 3 fluid oz bottle 7.00

DENTAL ITEMS

Dent's Dental Poultice, C. S. Dent & Co, Cincinnati, OH, white back-

ground, yellow, purple, 2 x 3½ x ¼", rect cardboard 7.00

Kolynos Tooth Paste, Whitehall Pharmaceutical Co, New York, NY, 1 oz full tube toothpaste, cream colored background, 4¼ x 1 x 1" 3.50

Molafil Cavity Pellets, C E DeWitt Co, Inc, Chicago, IL, pink, white ground, 6¾ x 3⅓", rect card, full plastic container of 24 pellets 8.00

Purepac Dental Plaster, Purepac Corp, New York, NY, Chicago, IL, Los Angeles, CA, light pink rust colored, 2½ x 1¾ x 2¼" cardboard container, metal lid, 4 oz, full 5.50

Quickdental Cleaner, pink, pr of dentures in glass on front, 4¼ x 3½ x 4¼" cardboard rect box, two month's supply, glass pyrex denture bowl 12.00

Rexall Toothache Soother, Rexall Drug Co, Los Angeles, CA, Boston, MA, St Louis, MO, Toronto, Ontario, white, light blue, 2¾ x 1 x 1¼", rect cardboard box, full glass bottle, wooden applicator, two fluid drams 6.00

Squibb Tooth Powder, E R Squibb & Sons, NY, cream colored and rust, 3¾ x 3¾ x ⅞", full tin, 2½ oz 7.00

DIARRHEA

Aroban, Pitman–Moore Co, Division of the Dow Chemical Co, Indianapolis, IN, clear glass jar, tan, peach, white, 2 x 4¼" full jar, 5 oz 7.75

Rexall Dia–No, Rexall Drug Co, Los Angeles, Boston, St Louis, white, light blue, dark blue cardboard box, amber bottle, 4⅞ x 2½ x 1½", 4 fluid oz .. 6.75

DRUGSTORE GIVEAWAYS

Almanac, The Ladies Birthday, Black Draught For All The Family, Cardui For Women, Faikert Brothers Grocery Store, Nulltown, IN, women on front, gray, black booklet, 1940, 7⅝ x 5⅛", 34 pgs 6.00

Calendar, 1960, Wells, Yeager, Best Co, Prescription Drugstore, Lafayette, IN, red, black, cream, 15¼ x 9¼" 7.00

Clip, Peacock Reservoir Ends, Dean Rubber Mfg Co, North Kansas City, MO, peacock on front, yellow, green metal clip, 2¼ x 2" 75.00

Fan, Lover's Moon Hair Dressing, Booth–Davis Drugstore, Greenville, MS, black schoolteacher and two children with globe, 1940s, 9¾ x 10½" 8.50

Thermometer, Tums For The Tummy, blue, yellow, red, white, tin, 9⅛ x 4⅛" 20.00

EYE

Elastoplast Eye Occlusor, Duke Laboratories, Inc, South Norwalk, CT, aqua cardboard box, 5⅝ x 3¼ x ¾", 24 eye patches 5.00

Eyecup, unknown manufacturer
Glass, clear, ribbed sides, 2¼ x 1⅜" 5.50
Tin, 1 x 1⅜" 3.75

Ocusol Eye Lotion, The Norwich Pharmaceutical Co, Norwich, NY, blue, white, black cardboard box, blue bottle containing 4 fl oz, white plastic eyecup, 5¾ x 1⅞ x 1⅞" 7.25

FEMININE HYGIENE

Beltex Personal Belt, Beltex Corp, St Louis, MO, blue, light blue background, lady dressed in blue formal on front, 4½ x 3¾" rect cardboard box 5.00

Fibs Tampons, Kimberly–Clark Corp, Neenah, WI, gray blue 3¾ x 2¼ x 1⅜" rect cardboard box 8.00

Hygenic P.M.C. Powder, Thomas & Thompson Co, Baltimore, MD, amber glass bottle, light blue ground, dark blue lettering, 2¼ x 4" cylinder, 4 fl oz 8.00

Midol, Glenbrook Laboratories, Div of Sterling Drug, Inc, New York, NY, dark blue, white, 3 x ¼ x 1" rect tin, 12 tablets 5.00

Sanapak Sanitary Napkins, Doeskin Products, Inc, New York, NY, dark blue, white lettering, 8¼ x 2¾ x 7¼" rect cardboard box 12.00

FIRST AID

Bantex, The Modern Bandage, Bantex Co, Chicago, IL, will not adhere to the skin, allows skin to breathe, sterilized, easy to apply, red, tan, blue, white full cardboard box, 3⅝ x 2½ x ½" 4.25

Grade A Absorbent Cotton, Supreme First Aid Co, Inc, New York, NY, gray, red, white 4¼ x 1¾ x 1¾", full 6.00

Johnson & Johnson Plaster of Paris Bandage, Johnson & Johnson, New Brunswick, NJ, Chicago, IL, red, black, yellow round cardboard container, 3¼ x 2¾", full 8.00

Parke–Davis Elastic Readi–Bandages, Parke Davis & Co, Detroit, MI, cream, dark blue, light blue, red, 3½ x 1¾ x 1", full 6.00

Sanifit Vaccination Shield, Eagle Druggists Supply Co, Inc, New York, NY,

celluloid protector, ventilated, curved to fit, red, gray, 3¼ x 2½ x ⅜" full . 6.00

FOOT

Dr. Scholl's Arch Binder, The Scholl Mfg Co, Inc, Chicago, IL, arch on front of yellow, light blue cardboard box, 1936 .... 6.00

Frazex, Frazer's Solution for relief of athlete's foot, American Druggists Syndicate, Inc Distrs., New York, NY, light tan, blue cardboard box, empty bottle, 3½ x 1½ x 1", 1 oz 3.00

Jiffy Callous Plasters, Jiffy Remedies Co, Downer's Grove, IL, humorous graphics on feet on front of red, gray cardboard box, 3⅛ x 1¼ x ½" 8.00

Larkin Foot Powder, Larkin Co, Inc, Buffalo, NY, blue, white, red cardboard empty can, 3½ x 1¾" 11.00

Newton's Foot Relief, Paul D. Newton & Co., New York, NY, a scientific preparation for the relief of tired aching feet, cream, black lettering, paper label, one full cake of dry medication, 3⅝ x 1⅛ x 1", 1920's 7.50

HERBS

Black Cohosh (Cimcifuga Racemosa) Hazeltine & Perkins Druggists, Grand Rapids, MI, used for rheumatic afflictions, disorders of the female reproductive organs, strengthens the nervous system, soothes pain and relieves fever and inflammation, tan, light brown, red paper package, ¼ lb. full, 2⅞ x 1⅞ x 1¾" 5.00

Buckthron Bark (Rhammus Cathartica), Murray & Nickell Mfg Co, Chicago, IL, the bark is used for a laxative, gray, black, 1 oz, full cardboard package, 2⅛ x 2 x ¾" 4.00

Elecampane Root (Inula Helenium), Allaire & Co., Peoria, IL, the root is used for coughs and colds in bronchial tubes and lungs, also assists in loosening phlegm and relieves irritation in air passages, light yellow, green full cardboard package, 1 oz, 2⅜ x 2¼ x 1⅛" 4.00

Elm Bark (Ulmus Fulva), Humco Laboratory, Texarkana, AR–TX, the bark is used as an expectorant and diuretic, white, blue, full 1 oz cardboard package, 2½ x 2½ x 1½" 4.25

Sassafras Bark (Sassafras Albidum), Purepac Corp, New York, NY, dark blue, yellow empty tin can, 2 oz, 3½ x 2⅝ x 1¾" 6.75

INFANTS AND CHILDREN

Baby Pain–A–Lay, The Glessner Company, blue, red, white 4 x 1/3/4 x 1 1/8", application for gums, cardboard box 1 oz, 1940's **8.00**

Baby Silicare Lotion (medicated), Revlon Pharmaceutical Division, New York, NY, prevents diaper rash/heals skin irritation, white, light blue, 1 3/8 x 5 x 5/8 x 1 3/4" cardboard box, 5 1/4 oz full bottle, 1950's **10.00**

Evenflo Glass Formula Measuring Container, red lettering, clear glass, 1 qt liquid capacity **12.00**

Kooleez Sheet Crib Liner, International Latex Corp., Playtex Park, Dover, DE, 10 1/2 x 2" fluorescent lavender top, gold tube, full **7.00**

Wee–Wee Lil Squirts Travel Urinal For Both Boys and Girls, Westland Plastics, Inc., Newbury Park, CA, pale pink with child motif, 8 x 6 x 2" . . .   **8.50**

KIDNEY/URINARY

Brill's Challenge Tablets, Rectanus Drug Co., Louisville, KY, a stimulant diuretic to the kidneys, pink green full cardboard cylindrical container, 2 1/4 x 1 1/8" **4.00**

Dr. Carey's Prescription 777 Tablets, The Carey Medical Corp, Elmira, NY, Dr. Carey on front, light brown cardboard container, full bottle, 3 1/2 x 1 1/2 x 1 1/8" **8.75**

Prescription 1000 Internal, The Resce Chemical Co, Cleveland, OH, palliative (eases) in minor urethral irritation, light tan, black cardboard container, 6 1/8 x 2 3/8 x 1 1/4" contains full 4 fluid oz bottle **8.00**

Sammetto, Old Peacock Sultan Co, St Louis, MO, palatable soothing preparation to relieve irritation that results in a desire for frequent urination when caused by excess acidity of the urine, lifeguard on front of brown cardboard, cream label, 8 fluid oz, 6 1/4 x 1 3/4 x 3/4", 1940's **8.00**

LAXATIVES

Ayres Cathartic Pills, Dr. J. C. Ayer & Co., Lowell, MA, tan, cream, paper covered cardboard box with bottle of pills, 2 1/8 x 7/8 x 7", 1920's **10.00**

Green's August Flower Dyspeptic Medicine, L. M. Green, Woodbury, NJ, light brown, black paper covered full bottle 2 oz, 5 7/8 x 2 x 1 3/8", 1918 . . .   **15.00**

Indian herb Tablets, L. W. Estes Co. Inc.,

Grove's **MILD IRON** Laxative Tablets

GROVE'S
MILD IRON
Laxative Tablets
For ELDERLY PEOPLE
30¢
E.W. Grove

Grove's Mild Iron Laxative Tablets for Elderly People, E.W. Grove, Paris Medicine Co, St Louis, MO, black, red, and white cardboard box, 1930s, 2 x 1 3/8 x 1/2", $8.50

Washington, DC, Indian on front of red, black, white cardboard box, contains 120 tablets, 2 3/4 x 1 1/2 x 3/4" . . .   **9.00**

Innerclean Herbal Laxative, Innerclean Co., Los Angeles, CA, yellow, red, blue, white, full cardboard box, 3 1/3 x 2 1/4 x 1", 1924 . . . .   **8.00**

Konsyl Plantago Ovato Coating, Burton, Parsons & Co., Washington, DC, maroon, white, black full cardboard can, 3 7/8 x 2 5/8" **4.50**

Vinco Herb Tablets, "Ten Day Treatment", Vinco Herb Co, Dayton, OH, blue, cream, cardboard box six tablets, 1 1/4 x 1 1/4 x 3 1/8" **6.00**

LINIMENTS/OINTMENTS

DeWitt's Golden Liniment, E. C. DeWitt & Co, Inc, Chicago, IL, yellow, black cardboard box, full 3 3/4 oz bottle, 7 3/8 x 2 5/8 x 1 3/8" **8.00**

Great Seal Liniment, The Styron Berg Co, Newark, OH, clear full glass bottle, yellow blue, white label, 4 7/8 x 1 3/4 x 1", 3 oz **3.75**

Neat's Petro–Menta Household Antiseptic Salve, Petro–Menta Co, Louisville, KY, yellow, red cream cardboard box, full 1 1/2 oz salve, 2 1/8 x 2 1/8 x 2 1/8" . .   **4.50**

S. B. Kitche's Liniment, E. B. Wells, Coldwater, MI, clear full bottle, light tan, red, black, full one pint bottle, 7 x 2 3/8 x 2 3/8" **8.00**

Super Anahist Rub, A Development of Anahist Research Laboratories, Anahist Co, Inc, Yonkers, NY, red, white, blue tube, full 1 1/4 oz tube, 4 7/8 x 1 3/8 x 1 3/8" **6.00**

MISCELLANEOUS PHARMACEUTICAL PRODUCTS

Ban–Smoke Chewing Gum, Thompson Medical Co Inc, New York, NY, The safe effective way to help you cut down or stop smoking, yellow, black, red full cardboard box, 18 tablets, 3⅛ x 2½ x ⅝" **5.50**

Breath–O–Lator, insures pleasant breath, a project of the Bing Crosby Research Foundation, manufactured and distributed by Sigma Products Corp, New York, NY, contains breath–o–lator, the wafer and instructions are included with this wafer, green, white cardboard box, 4⅝ x 3⅛ x ¼" **15.00**

Dry Tabs, Gary Pharmaceutical Co, Chicago, IL, blue, yellow label, round plastic container, 21 tablets, helps curb bedwetting, 2 x 1" **6.00**

Little Davids, Inhibits the desire for tobacco, Little Davids, Inc, Vincennes, IN, red, green, white full cardboard box, 2½ x 2⅞ x ½" **10.00**

Mothersill's Travel Remedy, Fred T. Hopkins & Son, New York, NY, distributed by the Mothersill Remedy Co, Limited, prevents motion sickness, green, white, gold, red full cardboard box, six capsules for adults, 1⅛ x ⅞" **8.00**

N.R.G. Energy Pickups, Peppermint Flavored Dextrose, Curtiss Candy Co, label red, white, paper covered full roll, 18 tablets, 2¾ x 1" **8.25**

Serene Tranquilizing and Calming Aid, Approved Pharmaceutical Corp., Syracuse, NY, for symptomatic relief of nervous tension, black, pink, white label, full glass bottle, 24 capsules, 1⅞ x 1¼" **5.00**

S.O.S. Vermin Killer, S. Pfeiffer Mfg Co, St Louis, MO, for head lice, body and crab lice, white, red label, full bottle, 5½ x 1⅞ x ⅞" **7.50**

Stay Awake Tablets, Keep Alert, The Reese Chemical Co, Cleveland, OH, red, black, white label, full glass bottle, 25 tablets, 2¾ x 1" **5.00**

NASAL

Mistol Nose Drops, Plough, Inc, New York, NY, Memphis, TN, San Francisco, CA, white box, green, red, black lettering, 3 x 1 x 1¾" cardboard box, contains bottle with dropper, ½ fluid oz **3.75**

Nyal's Nasal Jelly, Nyal Co, Detroit, MI, to relieve the swelling and congestion of the nose in order to permit easier breathing in heads, colds, and hay fever, contains ⅝ oz tube, 4¼ x 1¼ x ¾" **5.50**

Penetro Inhaler, A Product of Plough, Inc, New York, NY, Memphis, TN, silver, red, black empty tin tube, 2⅜ x ⅝" **5.00**

Schering Nasal Solution, Schering Corp, Bloomfield, NJ, for temporary relief of nasal congestion, maroon, white full cardboard box, powder, clinical package, not for sale, 3¼ x 1 x 2", 15 cc **4.00**

Ware's Bermingham Douche, Nasal, The Walter F. Ware Co, Philadelphia, PA, nasal douche on front, light orange, black cardboard box, 4 x 1 x ½", contains one glass nasal douche **12.00**

RECTAL

Anusol Hemorrhoidal Suppositories, Warner–Chilcott Laboratories, Inc, New York, NY, gray, white, red, black cardboard rect box, 2½ x 1¾ x ½", contains one half dozen suppositories **8.00**

Directals, Hemorrhoidal Suppositories, The Norwich Pharmacal Co, Norwich, NY, light blue, white cardboard rect box, 3 x 2 x 1⅞", twelve suppositories **4.75**

Plain Dionol, tube with rectal pipe and control key, The Dionol Co, Detroit, MI, tan, dark brown, 6½ x 2 x 1½" cardboard rect box, metal rectal tube, full tube of ointment 2¼ oz **13.00**

Posistos, Improved Rectal Suppositories, McKesson & Robbins, Inc., New York, NY, Bridgeport, CT, green jar, white label, 1⅞ x 1⅞", twelve suppositories **4.75**

Rectal Medicine, The Inside Story, The Medicone Co, New York, NY, tan, red 4 x 2¾ x ⅝" rect, full professional sample packet, 1950's **5.50**

REDUCING AIDS

Estes Delicious Dietetic Mints, Butterscotch flavor, Estee Candy Co, Inc, New York, NY, butterscotch, white, black, 2⅜ x ⅝" cylinder, made without sugar or salt, full paper roll, ½ oz, 1950's **4.00**

Estee Display Cardboard Box for Estee Dietetic Mints, Estee Candy Co, Inc, New York, NY, white, black, red, 2½ x 3¼ x 2½", originally contained 20 packages **3.75**

Junex, A Dietary Supplement, Junex Products, Chicago, IL, white, maroon full cardboard box, 4⅛ x 2¾ x ⅝", contains 90 tablets, "You can be measurably thinner without a prescription diet" **4.75**

Lescal, Pennex Products Co, Inc, Pittsburgh, PA, white, red, blue, 8 oz paper label, full 8 oz can **8.75**

Metrecal Powder, chocolate flavor, Edward Dalton Co., A division of Mead, Johnson & Company, Evansville, IN, gold, maroon, full can, 3¼ x 3⅝" .. **6.75**

RHEUMATISM

Eopa Neuritis Tablets, The Eopa Co, Distributors of Eopa Remedies, San Francisco, CA, 4⅛ x 1⅛ x 1⅜", rd, tan, blue box, contains full bottle tablets **10.00**

Meritol Rheumatism Powders, American Drug & Press Association, Decorah, IA, brown, white, 4 x 3⅛ x 1⅛" full cardboard box **7.50**

Vortex Rheumatic Tablets, Bernard Laboratories, Cleveland, OH, cream, blue cardboard box, 3⅓ x 2⅛ x 1", contains 40 tablets **6.00**

SHAVING (MEN'S)

Brylcream for Smart Hair Grooming, Beecham Products Inc, Clifton, NJ, red, white, gray, 5 x 2" cylinder, dab dispenser, 4.2 oz full aerosol can ... **6.00**

Handy Grip Shaving Stick Refill, Colgate & Co., New York, NY, silver 3 x 1" empty aluminum cylinder **7.00**

Mennen Neutral Tint Shave Talc, The Mennen Co, Morristown, NJ, Toronto, Ontario, Canada, green, white, 4½ x 2 x 1¼" 4 oz full tin **8.00**

Ronson, CFL, Electric Shaver Shaving Screen, clear plastic container/thin aluminum shaving screen, 2 x ⅛ x 2" sq, contains one shaving screen **3.00**

Speedway Deluxe Double Edge Razor Blades, International Safety Razor Co, Bloomfield, NJ, 2 x 1 x ⅛", narrow thin cardboard box, contains four razors **2.75**

SKIN

Calonite Powder, Consolidated Drug Trade Products, A Division of Consolidated Royal Chemical Corp, Chicago, IL, yellow, cream cardboard box, 4¾ x 1¾ x 1¾", contains one full cardboard tube powder 1.7 oz . **8.50**

Dermassage, S. M. Edison Chemical Co, Chicago, IL, (Body Rub, Skin Treatment), nurse on front, 3 x 3⅝ x 1¼"

full glass bottle, complimentary bottle, 2 fl oz **6.00**

Linit Corn Products Sales Co, New York, NY (The Modern All Purpose Skin Powder), red, tan, blue, white, full tin can, 5½ x 1¼ x 2½", 3 oz **15.00**

Muskalene, The Great Skin Food, Frasier, Thornton & Co, Cookshire, Quebec, Canada, tan, blue, rose 2 x 2 x 2", full can salve, 4 oz **8.00**

Poison Ivy Lotion, L. Perrigo Co, Allegan, MI, blue, black gray label, clear glass jar, 6 x 2¼ x 1¼", 6 fl oz **5.00**

SLEEP

Sleep–Eze, Whitehall Laboratories, Inc, New York, NY, blue white, red cardboard box, 3⅜ x 1⅛ x 1¼", bottle containing 52 tablets **4.75**

Slumberets, Cooper Drug Co, Detroit, MI, yellow, white, blue plastic bottle, 2⅛ x 1", 12 tablets **3.00**

Twilight, The Pfeifer Co, St Louis, MO (Helps Induce Refreshing Sleep), blue, red, yellow, white cardboard box, 2¾ x 1⅛ x 1⅛", bottle containing 20 tablets **3.75**

THROAT

DeSage's Cattarah Remedy, Buffalo, NY, clear, cork stopper, emb bottle, 2¼ x 1¼ x ¾", full ½ oz, bottle of powder **6.60**

Listerine Tablets, Lambert Pharmaceutical Co, St Louis, MO, light brown box, 3¼ x 1¾ x ¾", full **8.00**

Mo–Ton Catarrah Remedy, Mo–Ton Medicine Co, Indianapolis, IN, light tan, red 3¼ x 2 x 1⅛", full cardboard box **5.00**

Thantis Lozenges, Hyson, Wescott & Dunning, Inc, Baltimore, MD, red, 2¾ x ¾ x ¾" cardboard box, one plastic cylinder contains 12 lozenges **3.50**

Thoxine, The Reece Chemical Co, Cleveland OH, dark brown, orange, tan cardboard box, 7½ x 3¼ x 1¾", 8 fl oz bottle, full **8.00**

TONICS

Cuticure Resolvent, Potter Drug & Chemical Corp, Boston, MA, clear embossed bottle, orange, black label, full 6 oz, 7¼ x 1¾" **12.00**

Piso's Healing Astringent Tonic, The Piso Co, Warren, PA, full 50 tablet wooden tube, yellow, white, red label, 2¾ x 1⅛" **13.00**

Sano–Bark Tonic Capsules, The Sano–Bark Laboratories Co, Columbus,

OH, red, white, black full cardboard box, 3 x 1¾ x ⅞" **6.50**
Wheeler's Blood Aids, The J. W. Brant Co, Albion, MI, full 50 tablet wooden tube, tan, black label, 3 x ¼" **12.00**

VITAMINS

Baravit, Schering Corp, Bloomfield, NJ, contains bassorin, Vitamin B 1, white, maroon, 4¾ x 3 x 1½" cardboard box, full, 8 oz **7.00**
Cod Liver Oil Concentrate Tablets, Modern Drugs, Inc, light tan, blue, red, green glass bottle, 3¾ x 1⅛", 50 tablets **5.25**
Dayalets Multiple Vitamins, Abbott Laboratories, North Chicago, IL, red, white, milk glass bottle, 3⅜ x 1½", full, 100 tablets **6.00**
Vi–Delta, Liquid Concentrate, Vitamins A and D, Lederle Laboratories, Inc, New York, NY, cream, blue, white, 3¾ x 2¼ x 1¼", full amber bottle, dropper, 30 cc liquid **8.00**

WOMEN (COSMETICS/NOTIONS)

Boyer Face Powder, Sun Tan Shade (Basanee) Boyer American Division, Chicago, IL, red, white full cardboard box, 3½ x 2½ x 1⅜" **5.25**
Curly Lox Hair Snaps, Manufacturer Unknown, red, green, yellow, cupid, lady on full cardboard, 5¾ x 4", 1940's **4.75**
Grip–Tite Barrette, A Solo Product, City Unknown, two red, gold metal barrettes on 4¼ x ¾" card **3.75**
Hinds Honey & Almond Fragrance Cream, Lehn and Fink Products Corp, Bloomfield, NJ, pink, cream, blue, clear glass bottle, full 6½ oz **7.00**
Tangee New Pastel Finish Face Powder, The George W. Luft Co, Inc, Distributors, New York, NY, tangerine, blue cardboard box containing 0.27 oz powder, 2½ x ½" **3.00**
Woodbury Deluxe Vanishing Facial Cream, The Andrew Jergens Co, Cincinnati, OH, flesh, rose label, milk glass jar containing full 3.8 oz **8.00**

WORM TREATMENT

Jayne's P–W Vermifuge (A recognized treatment for pin–worms) Centur–Caldwell Division of Sterling Drug, Inc, Monticello, IL, blue, pink, cardboard box containing 60 tablets, 2 x 2¾ x ⅜" **5.00**
Perrigo's Worm Syrup, L. Perrigo, Co,

W.H. Bull's Vegetable Worm Syrup, cardboard box, 1920s boy on front, 12% alcohol, full bottle of syrup, $20.00

Allegan, MI, gray, blue, white cardboard box containing bottle with 2 fl oz syrup, 5½ x 2⅛ x 1" **6.00**
Professor Field's Round Worm (Large) Powders, Byron Field & Co, Chicago, IL, black, rose cardboard box containing one dozen powders, 1⅜ x 2⅜ x ⅞" **9.00**
W. H. Bull's Vegetable Worm Syrup, W. H. Bull Medicine Co, St Louis, MO, recommended for the removal of round–worms and thread–worms, cardboard box with 1920s boy on front, contains full bottle syrup **20.00**

ELECTRICAL APPLIANCES

Collecting Hints: Small electric appliances are still readily available and can be found at estate and garage sales, flea markets, auctions, and best of all, Grandma's attic. They generally cost very little, making them attractive to collectors on a limited budget.

Most old toasters, waffle irons, and other appliances still work. Construction was simple with basic, 2–wire connections. If repairs are necessary, it usually is simple to return an appliance to good working order.

Whenever possible ask to plug in the appliance to see if it works. On "flip–flop" type toasters (the most numerous type), check to see if elements are intact around mica and not broken.

Most appliances used a standard size cord, still available at hardware stores. Some early companies did have strange plugs and their appliances will only accept cords made for that company. In such an instance, buy the appliance only if the cord accompanies it.

Do not buy an appliance that is in non–working order, in poor or rusted condition, or with missing parts unless you plan to strip it for parts. Dirt does not count. With a little care and time, most of the old appliances will clean up to a sparkling appearance. Aluminum mag wheel polish, available at auto parts stores, used with a soft rag will produce wonderful results. Also, a non–abrasive kitchen cleanser can be of great help.

As with most collectibles, the original box or instructions for any item can enhance the value and add up to 25%. Also beware of chrome, silver, and other plated articles stripped to their base metal, usually brass or copper. Devalue these by 50%.

History: The first all electric kitchen appeared at the 1893 Chicago World's Fair and included a dishwasher, that looked like a torture device, and range. Electrical appliances for the home began gaining popularity just after 1900 in the major eastern and western cosmopolitan cities. Appliances were sold door to door by their inventors. Small appliances did not gain favor in the rural areas until the late 1910s and early 1920s. However, the majority of the populace did not trust electricity.

By the 1920s, competition among electrical companies was keen; innovations in electrical appliances were many. Changes were rapid. The electric servants were here to stay. Most small appliance companies were bought by bigger companies. These, in turn, have been swallowed up by the huge conglomerates of today.

Some firsts in electrical appliances are:
1882 Patent for electric iron (H. W. Seeley [Hotpoint])
1903 Detachable cord (G. E. Iron)
1905 G. E. Toaster (Model X–2)
1905 Westinghouse toaster (Toaster Stove)
1909 Travel iron (G. E.)
1911 Electric frying pay (Westinghouse)
1912 Electric waffle iron (Westinghouse)
1917 Table Stove (Armstrong)
1918 Toaster/Percolator (Armstrong "Perc–O–Toaster")
1920 Heat indicator on waffle iron (Armstrong)
1920 Flip–flop toasters appear (everyone)
1920 Mixer on permanent base (Hobart Kitchenaid)
1920 Electric egg cooker (Hankscraft)
1923 Portable mixer (Air–O–Mix "Whip–All")
1924 Automatic iron (Westinghouse)
1924 Home malt mixer (Hamilton Beach #1)
1926 Automatic pop–up toaster (Toastmaster #1–A–1)
1926 Steam iron (Eldec)
1937 Home coffee mill (Hobart Kitchenaid)
1937 Automatic coffee maker (Farberware "Coffee Robot")

1937 Conveyance device toaster ("Toast–O–Lator")

References: Linda Campbell Franklin, *300 Years of Kitchen Collectibles, Second Edition,* Books Americana, 1984; Don Fredgant, *Electrical Collectibles, Relics of the Electrical Age,* Padre Productions, 1981; Howard Hazelcorn, *Hazelcorn's Price Guide To Old Electrical Toasters, 1908–1940,* H. J. H. Publications, no date, 1988–89 revised price list available; Greg Ivy (compiler), *Early Fans,* Kurt House, 1983; Gary Miller and K. M. Scotty Mitchell, *Price Guide To Collectible Kitchen Appliances,* Wallace–Homestead, 1991.

Collectors' Clubs: American Fan Collector Association, P. O. Box 804, South Bend, IN 46624; Electric Breakfast Club, P. O. Box 306, White Mills, PA 18473.

Advisors: Gary L. Miller, K. M. Scotty Mitchell.

BLENDERS

Berstead Drink Mixer, Eskimo Kitchen Mechanic, 1930s, Berstead Mfg Co, domed chrome motor, single shaft, lifts off metal base, receptacle for tapered ribbed glass, 12" h 30.00
Chronmaster Mixall, 1930s, Chronmaster Electric Corp, NY and Chicago, chrome and black motor, single shaft, hinged black base, orig silver stripe glass 30.00
Dorby Whipper, Model E, 1940s, chrome motor, black bakelite handle, off/on toggle, clear, measured Vidrio glass 25.00
Electromix Whipper, 1930s, Chicago, ivory, offset metal motor housing, push–down break, filler hole in lid, measured glass base, 7½" h 25.00
Gilbert Mixer, Polar Club, 1929, AC Gilbert Co, New Haven, CT, lift off gray painted metal, rear switch, blue wood handle, premium for Wesson–Snowdrift, orig box, 10" h 75.00
Hamilton Beach
　Cyclone #1, mid 1920s, heavy nickel housing, sq stand on marble base, int. push–down switch, 19" h 175.00
　Hamilton Beach Malt Machine, 1930s, chrome motor, green cast base, push–up switch, nickel cup, 18½" h 75.00
Kenmore, Sears, Roebuck & Co, Chicago
　Kenmore Hand Mixer, 1940s, small, cream colored plastic, single 4½" beater, orig box, booklet, warranty, and hanger plate 25.00
　Kenmore Whipper, 1940s, cream metal domed top, large blue bake-

lite knob, clear glass bottom, 8½"
h **15.00**
Knapp Monarch Whipper, mid 1930s,
Knapp Monarch, St Louis, MO, white
metal motor, top red plastic handle,
round milk glass base with reeded, fin
feet, white plastic beater, 9½" h **25.00**
Kwick Way, St Louis, MO, white metal
motor top over angular, clear glass
base, no switch, decal label, 7½" h **20.00**
Made–Rite Drink Mixer, 1930s, Wein-
ing Made–Rite Co, Cleveland, OH,
light weight metal, cream and green
motor, single shaft, no switch,
stamped, permanent support, no glass **20.00**
Silex Blender, 1940s, Silex Corp, NY,
sq, white cast base, push button
switch, silver foil, Art Deco label,
clear glass, four cup top has Silex
spelled out vertically on black stripe,
plastic lid **15.00**
Unmarked, whipper, late 1920–30s,
green metal motor housing, serpentine shaft, green Depression glass Vidrio cup, 7½" h **20.00**

CHAFING DISHES

American Beauty, 1910s, American
Electrical Heater Co, Detroit, MI,
three part, nickel on copper, sealed
element in base, hot water container,
separate plugs, marked "fast" and
"slow", black painted wood handles
and knob **50.00**
Manning Bowman, Meriden, CT, 1930s,
bright chrome Art Deco design,
reeded edges, two part top, hot plate
base, black bakelite knob and handles **45.00**
Universal, 1910s, Landers, Frary &
Clark, nickel on copper faceted body,
three parts, sealed element in base hot
water pan, three prong heat adjustment in base, large black wooden
handle and knob **50.00**

COFFEE MAKERS AND SETS

Coffee Robot, Farberware, 1937, SW
Farber, Brooklyn, NY
#501 set, two part coffee dripolator
#500, creamer, open sugar, and
tray, nickel chrome, walnut handles, orig booklet **75.00**
#610, round chrome two part body,
glass top, chrome lid, walnut handle, bakelite knob, screw–on cover
spout **60.00**
Manning Bowman Percolator, Manning
Bowman, Meriden, CT
Article #250, urn, late 1920s, three
part aluminum body, unique design

Coffee Maker, Royal Rochester, Model #E 610, $150.00.

prevents re–perking, front spigot,
out turned handles, clear glass insert in dome lid, 12½" h **35.00**
Cat. #32, Ser. #4–30, 1920s, 15"
percolator/urn, creamer, open
sugar, nickel chrome vertically faceted bodies, short cabriole legs on
urn, up–turned black wood han-
dles, glass knob insert **60.00**
Ser. #636, mid 1930s, graceful, tall
Art Deco design, reeded dec
around neck and base, bright
chrome, 12" h **40.00**
Porcelier Breakfast Set, 1930s, Porcelier
Mfg Co, Greensburg, PA, all porcelain
bodies, basketweave design accents,
floral transfers, silver line dec
Complete set **350.00**
Creamer and sugar, cov **30.00**
Percolator, #5007 .... **65.00**
Sandwich Grill, #5004 .... **60.00**
Toaster, #5002 .... **75.00**
Rome Electric Percolator, 1910–20s,
Rome Mfg Co, Rome, NY, coffee urn
#CEU 47, chrome, wide, flared black
wooden handles, turned feet, 14" h . **25.00**
Royal Rochester Corp, Rochester, NY
#D–30, percolator, almost white por-
celain, slight greenish luster about
shoulder and spout, spring bouquet
floral transfer, chrome lid and base,
clear glass insert **80.00**
Model E 610, coffee set, three pcs,
lusterware bodies, marked "Fraunfelter China, OH," tall vertically
faceted alternating orange luster
and white stripes, floral transfers . **150.00**
Universal, Landers, Frary & Clark, New
Britain, CT
Breakfast Set, 1930s, cream porcelain, blue and orange floral transfers

Complete Set, 5 pcs 350.00
Creamer and sugar, cov 25.00
Percolator, #E 6927 . . . . 65.00
Syrup, chrome lid 30.00
Waffle Iron, #E 6324, pierced
chrome base, porcelain insert,
front drop handle 65.00
Coffee Set, #E 9119–1, 1920s,
chrome, tall chrome handles, swirl
glass insert, octagonal body, han-
dled tray, 4 pcs 125.00
Coffee Urn, #E 9219, late 1910–20s,
sq cabriole legs, large wooden ear
handles, nickel body, oval tray, 14"
h 65.00

EGG COOKERS

Hankscraft Co, Madison, WI
Model #599, yellow china base,
large dish on top of domed chrome
that serves as knob and filler with
hole in bottom, instructions on
metal plate on bottom 25.00
Model #730, Art Deco design, ivory
china, silver trim, cooker, four egg
cups, and nickel tray, 6 pcs 50.00
Rochester, 1910s, Rochester Stamping
Co, Rochester, NY, egg shaped, four
part, chrome, small base, int. fitted
with skillet with turned black wooden
handle, six egg holder with lift out
handle, enclosed heating element . . 40.00

**Food Cooker, Eureka Portable Oven,
1930s, $80.00.**

FOOD COOKERS

EC Junior 10, Everhot, 1920s, Swartz
Baugh Mfg Co, Toledo, OH, large
chrome and black cylindrical body,
aluminum lid, Art Deco design, front
emb "Everhot," int. fitted rack, two
open semi–circular pans, one circular

lidded pan, three prong heating con-
trol, 13" h 50.00
Eureka Portable Oven, 1930s, Eureka
Vacuum Cleaner Co, Detroit, MI, Art
Deco style, cream painted body,
black edges, sides let down and contain hot plates on chrome surfaces,
fitted int. wire racks, controls across
bottom front, 15 x 13 x 19" 80.00
Hankscraft, 1920s, Hankscraft, Madi-
son, WI, green enamel pan, chrome,
detachable hinge pin lid, green lusterware china knob, chrome base,
black wooden flaring handles 50.00
Nesco Electric Casserole, early 1930s,
National Enamel & Stamping Co, Inc,
Milwaukee, WI, cream colored body,
green enamel lid, high/low control,
three prong plug, 9" d 25.00
Quality Brand, 1920s, Great Northern
Mfg Co, Chicago, IL, model #950,
cylindrical body, insulated sides and
lid, fitted int., aluminum pan lids,
brown with red stripe on body, lift out
rods, 14" h 40.00
Roaster Oven, 1940s, Westinghouse,
white metal painted body, aluminum
top with window on top, gray plastic
handle, includes lift–out gray graniteware pan, three clear glass dishes
and lids, matching stand with clock
timer and storage door 50.00

HOT PLATES

Edison–Hotpoint, 1910s, Edison Electric, New York, Chicago, and Ontario, solid iron surface, clay filled
int., very heavy, pierced legs, china
feet, copper control, china knob . . . 25.00
Thermax, 1920s, Universal, Landers,
Frary & Clark, iron top, pierced swirl
design, nickel tripod base, four
prongs to heat outer ring, inner ring
or both, special two head cord 25.00
Unmarked, 1920s, sq nickel chrome
body, slightly angled legs, no control,
9" 8.00
Volcano, 1930s, Hilco Engineering Co,
Chicago, slightly conical nickel body,
black wooden handle, slide lever on
side lifts grate 20.00
Westinghouse, 1920s, Westinghouse,
Mansfield, OH, round top, green porcelain metal top surrounding element,
hollow legs, no control, 7½" d top . 25.00

MISCELLANEOUS

Angelus–Campfire Bar–B–Q Marshmallow Toaster, 1920s, Campfire, Milwaukee, WI, 3" sq, flat topped,

pierced pyramid top pc, base stands on loop, wire legs, rubber encased feet, flat wire forks **55.00**

Coffee Grinder, Kitchen Aid, 1936, Hobart, Troy, OH, Model #A–9, first home coffee grinder, heavy cream colored cast base houses motor, course/fine adjustment on neck, clear glass jar container with screw–off top **60.00**

Flour Sifter, Miracle, introduced c1934, Miracle Products, Chicago, IL, electric, cream body, blue wooden handle at base with hold–down button, vibrates flour through wire strainer ... **35.00**

Juicer
 Sunkist, 1930s, opaque green Depression glass top, int. metal strainer, chrome body/motor housing, dark green painted cylindrical center, metal "Sunkist" plate on front ... **50.00**
 Vita–Juicer, 1930s, Kold King Dist Corp, Los Angeles, Hoek Rotor Mfg Co, Reseda, CA, heavy cream painted cast metal, three parts: base motor, container, and fitted lid, lock groove and lock down wire handle, aluminum pusher, 10" h . **35.00**

Tea Kettle, Universal, 1910s, Landers, Frary & Clark, Model #E 973, bright nickel squatty body and base in one pc, long spout, high curved black painted wood handle, vertically curved mounts **45.00**

Mixer, Hobart Kitchen Aid, Model K 4–B, 1939, mixer only, $50.00.

MIXERS

Dominion Modern Mode Mixer, 1932–33, Dominion Electrical Mfg Co, Minneapolis, MN, faceted, angular Art Deco body and base, three speed rear

lever control, runs on a.c. or d.c., two custard glass bowls and juicer, mechanism to control beater height **75.00**

General Electric, 1938, GE Corp, Ser. #10–A, upright housed motor, top speed control, three synchronized beaters in row, work light shines in bowl, two white glass bowls, black bakelite handle **40.00**

Hamilton Beach, 1930s, Hamilton Beach, Racine, WI, Model "G", cream metal, black bakelite handle, lever off–on control, mix guide in window below handle, bowl control lever, lifts off base to be portable, two white glass bowls **35.00**

Hobart Kitchen Aid, 1939, Model K 4–B, looks like today's models, but quite a bit heavier, cream body trimmed in heavy aluminum, heavy cast aluminum bowl screws to base
 Attachments, dough hook, beater, whisk, can opener, meat grinder, each **8.00**
 Mixer only **50.00**

Sunbeam Mixmaster, early 1930s, Chicago Flexible Shaft Co
 Attachments, fit most models
Bean slicer	**20.00**
Cabinet, 60½ x 24"	**175.00**
Can opener	**5.00**
Churn	**25.00**
Coffee grinder	**25.00**
Drink mixer	**15.00**
Grater, slicer shredder, three blades	**25.00**
Grinder/chopper	**8.00**
Juicer, mayonnaise maker	**8.00**
Knife sharpener	**8.00**
Pea sheller	**8.00**
Potato peeler	**20.00**
Power unit	**8.00**
Ricer	**20.00**
Silver polisher and buffer	**2.00**
 Model K, cream colored body, fold over black wooden handle, rear speed control, light green opaque Depression glass bowls, juicer, and strainer, orig booklet **65.00**

POPCORN POPPERS

Berstead, 1930s, Berstead Mfg Co, Model #302, sq, chrome, box body with circular int., Fry glass lid, large black knob on top, rod through top for stirring **45.00**

Dominion, 1920s, Dominion Electric Mfg Co, Minneapolis, MN, Style #75, one pc cylindrical nickel body, pierced band, cabriole legs, red painted wood side handles, turned knob, hand crank **25.00**

Excel, 1920s, Excel Electric Co, Muncie, IN, one pc cylindrical nickel body, metal handles form legs, lock–down levers, black wooden hand crank knob, top vent holes 25.00

Manning Bowman, early 1940s, Manning Bowman Co, Meriden, CT, Model #500, detachable, large aluminum container, chrome hotplate, floral emb glass lid, black bakelite knob, unused 15.00

Rapaport, 1920s, Rapaport Bros, Inc, Chicago, IL, sq black base, metal legs, round aluminum upper part, attached lid and red knob, chrome handle squeeze through slot in side to agitate corn, 5½" 25.00

US Mfg Corp, Decatur, IL, 1930s
  #1, all one unit, cylindrical, rounded body, painted aluminum and red, top crank, three red vertical wooden dowel legs 20.00
  #10, body and lid separate from hotplate base, top crank handle, several color combinations, (tan and brown, cream and green, and red and ivory) 15.00

White Cross, late 1910s, National Stamping & Electrical Co, Chicago, tin can base with heater and corn, wire basket fits into can, metal top with stirrer mounted through handle, side wooden handle 30.00

TOASTERS

Dominion, mid 1920s, Dominion Mfg Co, Minneapolis, MN, flip–flop type, bright chrome pierced body, green wooden handles, bakelite tab door openers, never used 30.00

Edison, mid to late 1910s, Edison Appliance Co, NY, Cat. #214–T–5, nickel open body, free swinging tab closures at top, single side knob, removable toast warming rack 45.00

General Electric, 1908, Model D–12, white porcelain base, wire body, removable wire toast rack, porcelain plug with screw in socket cord
  Complete, decorated 175.00
  Complete, plain 150.00

General Mills, early 1940s, General Mills, Minneapolis, MN, Cat #GM 5A, two slice pop–up chrome body, white dec sides, black bakelite base, a.c. or d.c., red knob, light/dark control 20.00

Heat Master, 1923–25, sq chrome body, rounded corners, end opening, two slice, manual operation, black bakelite handle and feet 30.00

Kenmore, early 1940s, Sears, Roebuck & Co, Chicago, IL, mechanical, two slice, pop–up, chrome body, rounded edges and sides, black bakelite handles, mechanical clock mechanism, light/dark control 15.00

Knapp Monarch Reverso, 1930, Cat. #505, light weight rect nickel body, rounded corners, black painted base, flip–flop doors with tab handles, no mica, wires just stretched across ... 15.00

Manning Bowman, early 1920s, Cat. #1225, open nickel body, black bakelite knobs that open toast cages that turn completely over 55.00

Miracle, late 1930s, Miracle Electric Co, Chicago, Cat. #210, slightly rounded gray enamel body, black bakelite handles, flip–flop type, unused 30.00

Montgomery Ward, mid 1930s, Montgomery Ward & Co, Chicago, IL, Model #94–KM 2298–B, flip–flop type, solid nickel chrome body, end bakelite handle, both doors open simultaneously 18.00

Steel Craft, late 1920s, open, painted green wire construction, flip–flop type, red painted wooden knobs and feet 35.00

Sunbeam, 1936, Sunbeam Corp, Chicago, IL, Art Deco design, rect, rounded corners, chrome, black bakelite base, heat indicator light on front, fitted clear "Hostess" tray 65.00

Toastmaster, Waters–Genter Co, Minneapolis, MN
  Model 1–A–1, 1927, acclaimed as first automatic pop–up, Art Deco design, chrome body, louvered sides, rounded end, manual clock timer mechanism, light/dark control from "A" to "G" and panic button 80.00
  Model 1–A–3, 1929, third model, Art Deco, chrome body, vertically scalloped sides, mechanical clock mechanism, light/dark knob 35.00

Universal, Landers, Frary & Clark, late 1920s, mechanical, clock mechanism, circular side design, nickel chrome body, end pops open and out
  Model #E 7542, single 50.00
  Model #E 7732, double 75.00

Unmarked, 1920s, nickel, pierced body, tab handles, flat warming rack top 15.00

Westinghouse, Mansfield, OH
  Toaster Stove, 1909, first toaster, flat rect body, four flat drip plates, removable cabriole legs, tray, and wire rack, orig box and paper guarantee, never used 125.00

Turnover Toaster, 1920s, Cat. #TT 3, nickel body, pierced doors and top, flat tab handles, pierced, flat warming top **15.00**

WAFFLE IRONS & SANDWICH GRILLS

Armstrong Waffle Iron, 1920, (Pat. Pend.) Model W, first waffle maker to have heat ready/thermometer light on top, round nickel body, black wooden handles, distinctive prongs, cord, 7" d **45.00**

Berstead Mfg Co, Fostoria, OH and Oaksville, Ontario, Canada
Victorian Sandwich Grill, 1920s, rect nickel body, permanent plates, flared legs, curved mounts, black turned handles, 10" l **20.00**
Waffle Iron, 1930s, low profile, rounded chrome body, little curved bakelite feet and front drop handle, top head indicator and wheat shaft dec **30.00**

Coleman Waffle Iron, early 1930s, Coleman Lamp & Stove Co, Wichita, KS, high Art Deco style, chrome, low profile, small black and white porcelain top insert of impala, black bakelite handles **45.00**

Dominion Double Waffle Iron, 1940s, Dominion Electric Corp, Mansfield, OH, rect chrome stepped body, two round waffle grills, separate temperature controls, red light heat indicator, walnut handles, top circular dec, special 2–headed cord **35.00**

Electrahot Double Waffle Iron, 1940s, Electrahot, Mansfield, OH, two 6" sets of plates mounted on oval base, dec top with heat indicators **30.00**

Excelsior Waffle Iron, 1930s, Perfection Electric Co, New Washington, OH, white porcelainized iron body, four little stamped legs, plug in front, turned painted wood handle, 6" round **20.00**

Fitzgerald Star Waffle Iron, 1920s, Fitzgerald Mfg Co, Turrington, CT, solid flared base, unique handle design locks in position for raising or carrying, 7" **35.00**

General Electric Waffle Iron, early 1940s, chrome body, ivory bakelite handles, heat control/off front lever, top dec of circle of stars surrounding stripes and leaves **35.00**

Hostess Sandwich Grill, 1930s, All Rite Co, Rushville, IN, cast aluminum body, angled at bottom to form feet,

screw off wooden handle, orig box and suggestions booklet, 5" sq **40.00**

Hotpoint Waffle Iron, 1920s, Edison, General Electric, Chicago, Ontario, round chrome body, top dec, "Automatic" below front handle, rotating cold/hot in small window on front, ivory bakelite handles, scalloped base dec **35.00**

Lady Hibbard Sandwich Grill, 1930s, Hibbard, Spencer, Bartlet & Co, Chicago, rect nickel body, cast cabriole legs, black wooden side handles, front handle swivels to form foot for top plate, enables use of both plates as grills, drip spout **18.00**

Majestic Waffle Iron/Hot Cake Griddle, 1920s, Majestic Electric Appliance Corp, San Francisco, CA, 8" round reversible plates, little pierced tower on top with bakelite cap that serves as foot for use as double grill when opened out, nickel body, brown bakelite front swing handle **45.00**

Manning Bowman
Sandwich Grill/Waffle Iron/Frying Pan, early 1920s, rect nickel body, drip tube, indented grill plates serve as frying pan, black wooden handles, two sets of plates, 10½ x 6½" **35.00**
Twin–O–Matic Waffle Iron, late 1930s, fabulous design, Art Deco, heat indicator on top with rotating knob from off to dark in numbered increments, whole chrome body flips over in brown bakelite stand, mounted on chrome base **75.00**

Sampson Waffle Iron, 1930s, Sampson United Corp, Rochester, NY, Art Deco design, chrome body, asymmetrical wing–like flared bakelite side handles, stationary front handle **40.00**

Torrid Waffle Iron, 1920s, Beardsley & Wolcott Mfg Co, Waterbury, CT, good basic design, flared base, 7½" round plate, chrome body, green up–turned handles, front knob, window on front indicates "too cold," "too hot," and "bake" **35.00**

Universal Waffle Iron, 1930s, Universal, Landers, Frary & Clark, part of larger breakfast set, large floral dec porcelain inset into chrome body, pierced round flared pedestal base with up–turned handles, fancy mounted front drop handle, light/dark adjustment . . **60.00**

Westinghouse Waffle Iron, patent date 1905–21, Westinghouse E & M Co, East Pittsburgh, PA, earliest Westinghouse waffle iron, rect chrome body, mechanical front handle, wooden

hand hold, removable cabriole legs
slip into body slots, off/on switch ...   **75.00**

ELEPHANTS

Collecting Hints: There is a vast number of elephant shaped or elephant related items. Concentrate on one type of object (toys, vases, bookends, etc.), one substance (china, wood, paper), one chronological period, or one type of elephant—African or Indian. The elephants of Africa and India do differ, a fact not widely recognized by the lay reader.

Perhaps the most popular elephant collectibles center around Jumbo and Dumbo, the Disney character who was a circus outcast and the first flying elephant. The "GOP" material is usually left to the political collector.

Because of the large number of items available, stress quality. Study the market carefully before buying. Elephant collecting is subject to phases of popularity, with its level being modest at the current time.

History: The elephant held a unique fascination to early Americans. Early specimens were shown in barns and moved at night to avoid a free look. The arrival of Jumbo in England, his subsequent purchase by P. T. Barnum, and his removal to America brought elephant mania to new heights.

American zoological parks always have had an elephant as one of their main attractions. The popularity of the circus in the early 20th century also helped draw continual attention to the elephant, through posters, setup, the parade, and center ring.

Hunting elephants was considered "big game" sport; participants included President Theodore Roosevelt. The search always was for the largest known example. It is not unexpected that it is an elephant that dominates the entrance to the Museum of Natural History of the Smithsonian Institution in Washington, D.C.

Television, through shows such as "Wild Kingdom," has destroyed some of the fascination of a first encounter with all real wild animals, the elephant included. The elephant has become so well known that it is, alas, now considered quite commonplace.

Collectors' Club: The National Elephant Collector's Society, 380 Medford Street, Somerville, MA 02145.

Advisor: Richard W. Massiglia.

ABC Plate, tin, 6" d, Jumbo in center .   **50.00**
Animal Covered Dish, standing elephant, trunk up, English, 9" l, milk glass **125.00**
Avon Product
   Packy Elephant, baby oil, shampoo, and lotion **15.00**

Pin Pals
   1973, Elphie, yellow, glace **4.00**
   1975, Pedal Pusher, blue and pink elephant on bike **3.50**
Bank, mechanical, elephant, three stars   **300.00**
Bank, still
   3¼" l, 2½" h, cast iron **60.00**
   4" l, 3" h, elephant with howdah, medium **40.00**
   4" l, 4" h, elephant on wheels **135.00**
   4¾" l, 3½" h, cast iron **95.00**
   5¼" h, cast iron, elephant on tub ..   **95.00**
   5½" l, 4" h, cast iron, GOP **125.00**
Big Little Book, *Mickey Mouse and Bobo The Elephant*, Whitman Publishing Co, Racine, WI **30.00**
Bookends, pr, models, blue matte glaze, Rookwood, 1923 ....   **165.00**
Bookmark, ivory, elephant carving **5.00**
Brush Pot, cov, 7½" h, ivory, carved elephant tusk, relief carved tigers and elephants, 19th C **800.00**

Calendar, 1941, adv ink blotter, Brown & Bigelow, St Paul, MN, drawing of elephant and monkey, entitled "Let 'Er Go," 6⅛ x 3⅜", $3.50.

Cane, carved handle, bone **35.00**
Children's Mug, china, transfer print
   Alphabet type, emb alphabet at rim, elephant and children, Staffordshire   **60.00**
   Titled "Baby Jumbo Loves His Tub," 2½" h **35.00**
Clock, wall, adv, Tetley Tea, electric, white lettering, green elephant logos   **350.00**
Cookie Cutter, 3 x 4½" l, tin, elephant with long trunk, short legs, soldered strip to backplate **60.00**
Creamer, figural, Shawnee Pottery **15.00**
Disney Collectible
   Bank, Dumbo playing drum, movable trunk, 5" h, Japan **35.00**
   Cookie Jar, Dumbo and Pluto, turn about **35.00**
   Pitcher, Dumbo the Elephant, 6" h ..   **20.00**
   Planter, 4" l, ceramic, Dumbo **10.00**
Door Stop, cast iron **40.00**
Figure
   Carved, 1" l, nephrite, diamond set

eyes, orig fitted case, Carl Faberge, St Petersburg, 1887–90 ....**3,500.00**
Glass, A H Heisey & Co, 1944–53, trunk up, orig label
    5½" l **150.00**
    6½" l **165.00**
Porcelain
    6" h, Royal Rudolstadt, late 19th C **80.00**
    6½" l, 6" h, elephant with upraised trunk, Bohemia, marked "Royal Dux," c1890 .... **75.00**
Nutcracker, cast iron **35.00**
Paperweight, clear and frosted glass, 3½" h, molded, elephant standing on circular base, chrome rim, rect modern wood base, Lalique **500.00**
Planter, figural, Niloak, Hywood Line, green matte finish **25.00**
Soda Bottle, Jumbo Soda, emb elephant, crown top, clear **8.00**
Statue, bronze, Sirio Tofanari, 31" l, deep brown patina, early 20th C . . .**2,750.00**

Toy, litho tin wind–up, Jumbo, marked "Made In US Zone, Germany," 4¼" l, 3½" h, $95.00.

Tin, peanuts, store canister **50.00**
Toy, pull
    3" l, litho tin, marked "Made In Germany" **30.00**
    10" l, Jumbo, printed wood body, movable printed legs supported on rod, 1911 .... **200.00**
Vase
    5¾" h, 8" w, cameo, carved scene of native stalking elephant, smoky green, sgd "Muller Freres," pr ... **225.00**
    12½" h, Satsuma, elephant head handles, white, brown, and gold designs, beige shaded to rose ground, Japanese, pr **175.00**
Whiskey Bottle, collector's edition
    Ezra Brooks, Asian elephant **10.00**
    Jim Beam, Political Series
        1956, elephant and donkey ashtrays, pr **35.00**

1960, elephant and donkey campaigners, pr **35.00**
1964, elephant and donkey boxers, pr **30.00**
1968, elephant and donkey clowns, pr **15.00**
1970, Agnew elephant **2,200.00**
1972
    Miami Beach, elephant and dinner plate, pr **950.00**
    San Diego, elephant **20.00**
    Washington, DC, elephant, Feb 10, 1972 .... **750.00**

FANS

Collecting Hints: Fan prices vary erratically, depending on artistry and the region in which the fan is being sold. Many collectors are overwhelmed by the auction prices realized for fans in Europe, never considering that those seemingly extraordinary values are often a reflection of equally extraordinary fans. Unfortunately, a brief catalog listing cannot always convey the differences. Most fans readily available on the American market date from the mid 1800s; earlier ones are rarer, but not always more valuable. Proximity to the point of origin is also a key consideration: Oriental fans tend to be less costly on the West Coast, while European fans are often lower priced in the East.

Some basic guidelines may help the novice:
—Loops are rarely found on fans before 1830.
—19th C artisans copied 18th C styles. True Georgian figures should have gray hair; if the wigs are white, the fan is more recent. The later fans will often have a "heavier" appearance, and anachronistic costuming.
—Empire fans were also copied. The real ones have sequins made by flattening circles of wire; a tiny line shows where the wire ends meet. Later sequins were stamped whole out of sheet metal and have no joining line.
—Ivory, bone, celluloid, and plastic may look somewhat alike. Ivory often has a subtle, textureless graining pattern and may feel smooth and buttery; bone frequently reveals channels. Look for mold marks in plastic or, if feasible, use a hot needle—if it pierces the surface, the material is plastic.
—Many leaves became damaged with wear and were replaced. These "marriage" fans can still be delightful collectibles, but beware of dating a fan merely based on one component.
—Framing a fan often causes its sticks to warp, its leaf to lose its elasticity and ability to fold. It is also difficult to tell if a fan has been sewn or glued to its backing, making its removal difficult. Thus, most collectors will

frame a fan only if there is no better way to protect it.

— If a fan needs repair and a trained conservator is not a consideration, approach the task cautiously and only with approved materials. (Armstrong's *The Book of Fans* lists sources for materials and gives directions for their use.)

— Visit museums, costume institutes, and historic societies. It is difficult to distinguish an early fan from a later copy by merely checking a book.

History: Today, people tend to think of fans as fragile, frivolous accessories wielded by women, yet the origin of the fan was no doubt highly practical. Early man may have used it to winnow his grain, shoo flies, and cool his brow. This simple tool eventually became a symbol of power: ancient lore maintains that Emperor Hsien Yuan (c2697 B.C.) used fans; the tomb of Egypt's Tutankhamen (1350 B.C.) yielded two ostrich feather fans with gold mounts. Fans also began to assume religious significance and were used to whisk flies from altars. Early Christians recognized the practicality of this and included a flabellum, or fixed fly–whisk, in their early services. Meanwhile, the Chinese and Japanese continued to use fans in their courts, often incorporating precious materials such as ivory, gold, and jade.

Until the seventh century A.D., fans were non–folding. Then, according to Japanese legend, Emperor Jen–ji noticed the logic of a bat's folded wings and applied his insight to a new fan design. Later, European traders returned from the East with samples of these wonders. By the sixteenth century sophisticated Italian women had appropriated the fans, which soon became de rigueur throughout Europe. Now primarily feminine fashion accessories, their styles changed to complement the ever–changing dress styles. Fans' popularity led to experimentation in their production and merchandising. They also became popular as a way for artists to test their skills—a fan leaf's curved, folding surface offered challenges in perspective.

World War I was the end of slower eras; the 1920s raced at a frenetic pace. The modern woman set aside her ubiquitous fan, freeing both hands to drive her roadster or carry her political banner. Fans became more an advertising tool than a fashion statement.

Fan Terminology:

Brisé—fan with no leaf, but made of rigid, overlapping sticks held together at base by a rivet and at the other end by a ribbon.

Cockade—pleated fan opening to form complete circle.

Folding fan—fan with a flexible, pleated leaf mounted on sticks.

Fontage—shape of folding fans c1890–1935, with center of leaf longer than guards.

Guard—the outermost sticks, usually the height of fan.

Leaf or mount—flexible, pleated material which unites the upper parts of a folding fan's sticks.

Lithograph—printing process invented in 1797, often subsequently hand–colored.

Loop—often "u" shaped finger holder attached to rivet at base of fan; rare before 1830.

Medallion—pictorial representation, usually circular or oval, in leaf.

Piqué–point—decorative small gold or silver points or pins set flush with surface or sticks or guards.

Rivet—pin about which sticks of a folding fan pivot.

Sticks—rigid framework of a folding fan.

Studs—exposed end of rivet, sometimes shaped as decorative paste "gem."

Washer—small disk to prevent friction between end of rivet and fan.

References: Helene Alexander, *Fans*, Batsford, 1984; Rosa Amelia Alvarado, *Entre Abanicos y Recuerdos*, Artes Graficas Senefelder, 1988; Nancy Armstrong, *A Collector's History of Fans*, Clarkson N. Potter, 1974; Nancy Armstrong, *The Book of Fans*, Mayflower Books, N.d.; Nancy Armstrong, *Fans: A Collector's Guide*, Souvenir Press, 1984; Anna G Bennett, *Fans In Fashion*, San Francisco Art Museum, 1981; Anna G Bennett, *Unfolding Beauty*, Thames and Hudson, 1988; Braintree Historical Society, *Hunt and Allen Fans*, Braintree Historical Society, 1986; Reiko Chiba, *Painted Fans of Japan*, Charles E. Tuttle Co, 1962; Debrett's Peerage, *Fans From The East*, Debrett's Peerage, Ltd, 1978; Francoise DePerthuis and Vincent Meylan, *Eventails*, Hermé, 1989; Bertha DeVere Green, *A Collector's Guide To Fans Over The Ages*, Frederick Muller Ltd, London, 1975; Tseng Yu–ho Ecke, *Poetry on the Wind*, Honolulu Academy of Arts, 1981; Neville John Irons, *Fans of Imperial China*, Kaiserreich Ltd, 1981; Neville John Irons, *Fans of Imperial Japan*, Kaiserreich Ltd, 1981; Christl Kammerel, *Der Facher*, Himmer Verlag, Munich, 1989; Susan Mayor, *A Collector's Guide To Fans*, Wellfleet Books, 1990; Susan Mayor, *Collecting Fans*, Mayflower Books, 1980; Susan Mayor, *Fans*, Vancouver Museum, 1983; Musee de la Mode et du Costome, *L'Eventail*, 1985; Audrey North, *Austrialia's Fan Heritage*, Boolarong, 1985; McIver Percival, *The Fan Book*, T Fisher Unwin Ltd, London, 1920; G. W. Woolliscroft Rhead, *The History Of The Fan*, Kegan Paul, Trench, Trubner & Co, London, 1910; Maryse Volet, *L'Imagination au Service de L'Eventail*, 1986.

Collectors' Club: FANA (Fan Association of North America), 505 Peachtree Road, Orlando, FL 32804.

Advisor: Wendy Hamilton Blue.

Note: Abbreviations:
Gdl—Guard Length
MOP—mother of pearl

Advertising, celluloid, lake motif with swans, blue tones, brass holder, figural cat holder, green fabric handle with stay, $45.00.

AMERICAN AND EUROPEAN

1760, English or French, paper leaf painted with pastoral scene of shepherdess, lover, reverses to crude landscape, 20 ivory sticks, partially painted, one with early sterling repair, clear paste stud, Gdl. 10½", open 18½" **300.00**

1845–1865, double paper leaf litho with hand–colored harem scene, reverses to small central cartouche of two women in 18th C rural costume, man bearing basket of flowers, 14 bone sticks with one early repair, flirting mirror on right guard, pierced sticks dec with silver foil, MOP washer, brass loop, orig box, Gdl. 10½", open 19" **125.00**

Mid 19th C, double paper leaf with pastoral scene of shepherds, shepherdesses in 18th C style, reverses to scene of three women, one man in 18th C costume on grounds of rural estate, 18 MOP sticks, center ones carved in relief with bucolic scene to complement leaf, red paste stud, Gdl. 10½", open 19¾" **200.00**

1860, double paper leaf with litho, painted in gouache and gilded, couples in 18th C costume walk, eat, and watch puppet show on castle grounds, reverses to three medallions of Oriental scenes amidst very ornate, stylized gold floral and architectural motifs on deep blue shiny paper, 14 japanned sticks of papier–mache, painted in oil, center sticks depict three women and two men, also in period dress, with slightly raised faces, gilt stud, loop, orig box, Gdl. 10⅞", open 20½" **140.00**

1870
Jenny Lind, named for singer who reportedly popularized style, linen "feathers" dec with silver sequins and trimmed top and sides with beige lace, 12 overlapping pierced bone sticks, Gdl. 6¾", open 13" . **55.00**

South American, probably Brazilian, round, non–folding hummingbird feather fan, edged in maribou, 10" d, 7" l turned bone handle **120.00**

1870–1890, ecru Brussels lace, flowers with center basket, mounted on 18 MOP sticks, dyed deep cream to match lace, MOP button, plain brass loop, Gdl. 10", open 18" **180.00**

1880–1900, ostrich feathers on 16 tortoise sticks, gray moire satin bow attached to tortoise loop, orig fitted case is leather base, red satin lined with shaped holder for head (bottom part of sticks), glass top, two brass latches to secure, Gdl. 9¼", feathers project past end of sticks to 15", open 24" .. **200.00**

Late 19th C
Red silk cockade in leather case with brass slide, red silk tassel on end of cord, 8" l, 1¼" w case with attached leather loop, open 9" d ... **45.00**

Vernis Martin style (named for earlier craftsman skilled in lacquer and varnish work), brisé, very ornate mythological scene painted on "leaf," Aphrodite, accompanied by seaside creatures and putti, is viewed through columns and arches, six small medallions of women's heads coifed in 18th C court style top four arches and center of fan, lower portion of sticks is painted with small medallion of pagoda, six Oriental people, reverse has center floral arrangement in urn, garlands, columns with Moorish arches, 32 ivory sticks, clear paste stud, Gdl. 7¼", open 12" .. **300.00**

1880–1890, black gauze with black lace, embroidery, 18 black wood sticks carved in sinuous shape, right guard is carved gutta percha of putti, vines, and intertwined flowers, brass floral washer, loop, black silk cord tassel, with box, Gdl. 13½", open 26" **140.00**

1890

Pale beige gauze leaf painted with six chickadees on holly branch in snow flurry, fan made by Hunt–Allen, wood sticks with discreet gold design near shoulder, shaped brass loop, Gdl. 14¾", open 28" **135.00**

Ribbon fan, clear gauze mount with tacked, looped ribbons spanning width, shading from silver at top to deep gold, ribbons form rosettes when fan is closed, stamped floral steel washer, large loop, 22 carved bone sticks, contemporary box marked "Tiffany's, Paris," Gdl. 13¾", open 24" **375.00**

1890–1910

Cabriolet, top leaf is very fine silk, center sequin–bordered medallion of 18th C musicians, side vignettes with crossed lute, recorder, smaller, lower leaf has center vignette of crossed recorders, flowers, 18 horn sticks, cut steel piqué–point, orig brocaded, padded box with store name, address, Gdl. 8¾", open 16" **160.00**

French fontage, leaf, fine white net with silver sequins and spangles, tipped with male ostrich feathers, 14 horn sticks with steel piqué–point, Gdl. 6¼", longest point, center of fan 12½", open 16" **110.00**

French fontage, neutral net with gold sequins, spangles, stamped brass floral washer, small loop, cut steel piqué–point on 14 horn sticks, sgd "Duvelleroy" with orig marked box, Gdl. 7⁵⁄₁₆", longest point, center of fan 9⁹⁄₁₆" **140.00**

White ostrich feathers on 22 horn sticks, monogram with gold crest on right guard, Gdl. 12", open 33" **280.00**

1930, Cuban, mauve cotton leaf painted in modernistic, multicolor design, 18 purple plastic sticks, brass stud, plastic loop, orig tissue paper printed with store name and location in Havana, Gdl. 8⅞", open 16" **40.00**

AMERICAN AND EUROPEAN, SOUVENIR, COMMEMORATIVE, AND ADVERTISING FANS

1867, wood brisé with yellow and orange ribbon, sgd by 36 escorts and fellow guests at dances, concerts, and socials between Dec 11, 1867 and Dec 13, 1868, 20 sticks, Gdl. 5⅝", open 9¾" **60.00**

1876, Philadelphia Centennial, paper leaf depicts eagle with US flag and dates 1776 and 1876, reverses to view of Independence Hall, stamped "Registered June 8, 1875," 30 wood sticks, Gdl. 11", open 20" **150.00**

1878, HMS Pinafore, silver paper with large beige central area printed with deck scene, crew's caps labeled "Pinafore," black washer, loop, painted black wood sticks, Gdl. 11¼", open 21" **130.00**

1893, Columbian Expo, Chicago, paper leaf, angelic herald wrapped in red and white striped skirt with starred blue sash stands on pedestal in front of large exhibit building, smaller scene with lagoons and buildings is on either side, celluloid washer, brass loop, 16 wood sticks, gilded, Gdl. 13½", open 26" **130.00**

1900, Ritz Carlton, adv, double paper leaf, front has medallions of lovers walking in lane, waiter readying private table for tete–a–tete, floral garlands, reverses to ecru background, simple brown print of flower basket, 16 wood sticks, painted white, with gold, sgd "J Duvelleroy, Paris," Gdl. 8¼", open 15" **70.00**

1904, St Louis Expo "geisha" fan, separate 3¼" Japanese woman with parasol tops each of the 22 red lacquered sticks, beneath the geishas is a thin paper leaf painted with flowers and stream, metal rivet, loop, Gdl. 9⅝", open 18" **85.00**

1925, political commemorative, cardboard handscreen, "Presidents of the United States from Washington to Coolidge," sepia tone pictures with terms of presidents around photo of US Capitol, reverse is ad for National Bank, Wampum, PA, 10⁹⁄₁₆" h **40.00**

1927, Col Charles A Lindbergh, cardboard handscreen with separate photos of Lindbergh and the Spirit of St Louis, commemorative poem "We," ad for hardware store in Warren, PA on reverse, 11¼" h, 8" w **65.00**

1930, Chromolithograph handscreen depicting suburban children and their German shepherd standing on front lawn, reverse to "Prohibition Ledger" of the Woman's Temperance Union, state of New York, 12" h **28.00**

1940, Chromolithograph handscreen of Dionne quintuplets, entitled "School Days," design is one of a series depicting important events in sisters' early lives, ad for Palmerton Sanitary Dairy, Palmerton, PA on reverse, 14¾" h 28.00

1944, tri–section fan, center shows blonde WAC, Pledge of Allegiance printed beneath her, sides pull out to show a tank and a battleship, both firing, reverse commemorates the 20th anniversary of a dance school, 7" h, 5" w closed, 10½" w open ... 15.00

Mid 20th C

Asymmetrical double paper leaf, front is ecru, painted with free flowing fashion design of woman's leg extending from long skirt, in shades of gray, taupe, black, adv "Les Bas Christian Dior," reverses to plain, pale green paper, length ranges from 8¼" on left to 13½" on right 14.00

Booker T Washington tri–section commemorative, salutes Washington for starting Tuskegee Institute and for being elected to the Hall of Fame, New York University in 1945, Smith's Grocery, Johnson, TN adv on reverse, salesman's sample, #633, 7" h, 5" w closed, 10" w open 40.00

Chromolithograph on wood stick, cartoon of man and woman advocating Alka Seltzer, reverses to graphic of product, fizzing glass, 13½" h 12.00

Cockade adv "Armour's Pork and Beans," cardboard sticks with folding paper, opens to show 20 caricatured faces of Alaska, including fisherman, Eskimo, walrus, and polar bear, 8⅜" h closed, 12½" open, 8¾" d 26.00

ORIENTAL, PACIFIC

1760, paper leaf with water colored, uncentered scene of man on horseback riding from left to right, nearing a man walking in opposite direction, stationery man with fan is between them, brass stud, wider than head of guard, 20 wooden sticks, plain except for subtle floral motif painted on top half of guards, Gdl. 11", open 18" 175.00

Mid 19th C

Chinese goosefeathers, painted orange, with red, green, and blue flowers and birds, tipped with peacock feather "eyes," brass loop, turquoise tassel with glass bead, 22 pierced bone sticks, Gdl. 9", open 21" 80.00

Mandarin or "Fan of 1000 Faces," paper leaf painted with scene of people walking, one on horseback, 24 figures, each with appliqued silk clothing and ivory face, reverse has columns of flowers with birds and insects between exposed sticks, peacock "eyes" across top, MOP washer, brass loop, white silk tassel, 16 lacquered sticks, all but guards have carved center with translucent silk inset, painted in bird or floral motif, orig silk lined fitted lacquered box, Gdl. 11", open 27" 350.00

Late 19th C

Neutral gauze mount embroidered with flowers, butterflies, dragonflies in light pastels, MOP stud, knotted silk cord, tassel, 22 sandalwood sticks carved in floral design, Gdl. 9½", open 17" 70.00

Tortoise brisé, 21 carved, pierced sticks with gold lacquerwork, center medallion depicts men seated under a tree, side floral medallions, brass stud, loop, Gdl. 8⅛", open 14½" 165.00

19th–20th C, Indonesian pierced hide screen with dancing figure, gilded accents, partial sides extend into horn handle, 12" 45.00

20th C, Balinese dancer's fan, black fabric heavily painted in gold with stylized floral motif, reverses to bright pink with gold, Gdl. 9⁹⁄₁₆", open 16" 10.00

FARM COLLECTIBLES

Collecting Hints: The country look makes farm implements and other items very popular with interior decorators. Often items are varnished or refinished to make them more appealing, but in fact this lowers their value to the serious collector.

Farm items were used heavily; collectors should look for signs of use to add individuality and authenticity to the pieces.

History: Initially farm products were made by local craftsmen—the blacksmith, wheelwright, or the farmer himself. Product designs varied greatly.

The industrial age and the "golden age" of American agriculture go hand in hand. By 1880–1900 manufacturers saw the farm market as an important source of sales. Farmers demanded quality products, capable of withstanding hard use. In the 1940s urban growth began to draw attention away from the rural areas and consolidation of farms took place. Bigger machinery was developed. Farm collectibles after 1940 have not yet achieved great popularity.

Reference: Lar Hothem, *Collecting Farm Antiques: Identification and Values*, Books Americana, 1982.

Collectors' Club: Cast Iron Seat Collectors Association, Box 14, Ionia, MO 65335.

Museum: Pennsylvania Farm Museum, Landis Valley, PA.

Ink Blotter, adv, Bird Roll Roofing, 6¼ x 3½", unused, $3.00.

Advertising Trade Card	
J I Case Steam Tractor	8.00
Moline Wagon Co, Moline, IL, couple in wagon	3.50
Almanac, International Harvester, 1913	8.00
Ashtray	
Gehl Farm Equipment	75.00
John Deere	15.00
Book	
1857 Practical Farrier for Farmers, 288 pgs	42.50
John Deere Model A Tractor Instructions and Parts List, 1936	28.00
Brochure	
International Harvester, 3 x 5½", 1910	15.00
Vulcan Plows, multicolored	5.00
Catalog	
Improved DeLaval Cream Separators, 1910	10.00
Murray Co, horse drawn vehicles, 1912, 160 pgs	65.00
Parker & Wood, Boston, 1891, 216 pgs, 6½ x 9"	75.00
Chick Feeder, tin	15.00
Clicker, Reading Bone Fertilizer Co, celluloid	8.00
Corn Husk Bag, cloth, cross and pointed rect design	650.00
Egg Basket	
Splint, 5 x 8½", wood handle	65.00
Wire, collapsible	35.00
Egg Box, 12" sq, wood, apple green wire bail	72.00
Egg Shipping Crate, Bangor, ME, 14 x 28", cardboard egg holders	25.00

Goat Yoke, single, wood, bentwood bow	50.00
Grain Cradle, 41", four fingers	60.00
Hay Fork, 65" l, metal tines	20.00
Horse Feeding Box, 13 x 17 x 8", wood	20.00
Instruction Manual	
John Deere Self Dump Rake	10.00
McCormick Grain Binder	10.00
Ledger, pocket, John Deere	
1910	10.00
1930, machinery illus	8.00
1952	5.00
Match Holder, wall, American Steel Farm Fences, tin	45.00
Mirror, Milling and Cattle Feeding, celluloid, black and white grain mill, c1900	45.00
Needle Book, Globe Fertilizer	4.00
Paperweight, Osborne Co Harvesting Machinery, glass	24.00
Pinback Button	
Ford Tractor, 1⅛", black, white, and red, c1940	5.00
Globe Feed, red, white, and blue, hen sitting on nest, inscription "Makes 'Em Lay"	5.00
Saginaw Silo, 1", oval, black, white, and red, c1900	4.00
Wilson's Certified Turkey, silver and blue, litho, c1930	3.00
Poster, Ferry's Seeds, 20½ x 27½", 1910 copyright	60.00
Print, "Battle of the Chicks," yard long, Austrian, c1902	135.00
Scoop, grain, 38", wood, hand carved	75.00
Seeder, push type	65.00
Sickle, 21", wood handle, iron blade	18.00
Sign	
Rice's Seeds, 24 x 12", paper, man with cabbage	75.00
Threshermen & Farmers Ins, 8 x 15"	25.00
Tape Measure, John Deere	25.00
Tray, tip, Bettendorf Axle Co, shows farm wagon	60.00

FARM TOYS

Collecting Hints: It is best to specialize in a single type of model, e.g., cast iron; models by one specific company; models of one type of farm machinery; or models in one size—1/16 scale being the most popular.

The tractor is the most popular vehicle. Accessories include wagons and trailers, manure spreaders, plows, disks, planters, and cultivators. Harvesting equipment also comes in model form.

History: The vast majority of farm models date from the early 1920s to the present. Manufacturers of farm equipment such as John Deere, International Harvester, Massey-Ferguson, Ford, and White Motors issued models to correspond to their full sized products. These firms contracted with America's leading toy manufacturers, such as Arcade Company, Dent, Ertl, Hubley, Killgore, and Vindex, to make the models.

The early models were cast iron, being replaced later by diecast, aluminum, and plastic. As production models were changed, so too were the toy models. Although most models are made in a scale of ¹⁄₁₆, other scales were used, e.g., ¹⁄₁₂, ¹⁄₂₀, ¹⁄₂₅, ¹⁄₃₂, and ¹⁄₅₀.

Toy manufacturers outside the United States have entered the picture. Firms such as Dinky, Corgi and Lesney produce models of American equipment as well as those of foreign manufacturers, among which are Deutz, Fiat, Leyland, and Porsche.

Limited edition models are being produced today to respond to the growing collector market. Controlled production is keeping their value high.

References: Raymond E. Crilley and Charles E. Burkholder, *International Directory of Model Farm Tractors*, Schiffer Publishing, Ltd, 1985; Dave Nolt, *Farm Toy Price Guide, 1988 Edition*, published by author, 1988; Richard Sonnek, *Dick's Farm Toy Price Guide & Checklist: Tractors and Machinery, 1886–1990*, published by author, 1990.

Periodicals: *Miniature Tractor & Implement*, 1881 Eagley Road, East Springfield, PA 16411; *The Toy Farmer*, R. R. 2, Box 5, LaMoure, ND 58458; *The Toy Tractor Times*, P. O. Box 156, Osage, IA 50461.

Collectors' Club: Ertl Replica Collectors' Club, Highways 136 and 20, Dyersville, IA 52040.

Baler, Oliver	40.00
Bulldozer	
Big Bull, yellow, Matchbox, 1979	3.50
Case, 2½", diecast, Matchbox	8.00
Caterpillar, driver, yellow, Matchbox, 1963	15.00
Cart	
Goat, 7", large ears	75.00
Horse, 7", stake sides, cast iron	30.00
Ox, 7", Kenton	35.00
Plantation, 11", tilt dump, cast iron, pressed steel, Wilkins, 1910	42.00
Caterpillar	
2", yellow, Matchbox, 1965	15.00
6", scraper, Tootsie, 1956	25.00
8½", windup, Kingsbury	175.00
Combine	
Gleaner	50.00
International Harvester, pull type, conveyor belt, 1950s	50.00
John Deere, steel, conveyor belt, scale	48.00

New Holland, zinc alloy, diecast, Ertl	30.00
Corn Picker	
John Deere, steel, Ertl	50.00
Oliver, steel, Slik	80.00
Crawler	
Allis–Chalmers, diesel, orange, rubber tracks, Product Miniature Co, 1955	130.00
McCormick–Deering, wood, model kit, Mod–AC Mfg Co	40.00
Disc	
Case, four gang, Ertl	12.00
Oliver, aluminum and steel, Slik	20.00
Drill Seeder, International Harvester, steel, Tru–Scale	20.00
Excavator, Massey–Ferguson, NZG, West Germany	18.00
Fork Lift Truck, 11", battery operated, five actions, M–T Co, 1960	25.00
Harrow, tandem disc, Ertl, 1967	10.00
Hay Rack, Arcade, 7", dump	80.00
Jeep, wood, red, 10 x 4 x 3¾", Buddy L, 1946	50.00
Loader	
Caterpillar Front End, Funho 44, 1974	5.00
International Harvestor Loader Crawler, split bucket, orange, Kidco, 1980	3.50
Log Skidder, John Deere, rear wince, front blade	20.00
Manure Spreader	
John Deere, steel, Ertl	30.00
McCormick–Deering, team of horses, Arcade	50.00
Mounted Picker, John Deere	28.50
Mower, Arcade	27.50
Plow	
Case, 4 bottom, Ertl	6.50
Horse drawn, 10¾", cast iron	65.00
John Deere, trailer, steel, Ertl–Eska	50.00
Rake Dozer, Komatsu, orange, Tomica 70B, 1980	3.50
Scraper Dozer, Komatsu, orange, Tomica, 32C, 1978	6.00
Shovel	
Loadmaster Tractor Shovel, orange, Husky 23B, 1972	6.00
Payloader Hydraulic Shovel, white, Kodco, 8105, 1978	3.50
Snowmobile, Sno–Track, red, Matchbox, 1968	6.50
Tractor	
Allis–Chalmers, lawn and garden, Ertl, 1972	12.00
Allis–Chalmers, WX, plastic	16.00
Avery, Hubley, cast iron, 1920	120.00
Case 580 Construction King, plastic, yellow, Hong Kong, 1967	125.00
David Brown, Corgi, 1977	5.00
Earth Grader, 12½", mechanical, Marx, c1950	25.00
Farmall M, cast iron, wood wheels	65.00

Ford 8–N, 5″, diecast aluminum, France, Quiralu, 1957 . . . . **75.00**
Ford 5000, Corgi, 1966 . . . . **25.00**
Fordson, 5½″, cast iron, steel wheels, Arcade **100.00**
Hatra Shovel, orange, four wheels, Matchbox, 1969 . . . . **20.00**
Highboy Climbing, 10″, tin, wind–up, Marx, c1950 . . . . **20.00**
International Harvester, Cub Cadet, lawn and garden, front end blade and trailer, 1976 . . . . **10.00**
John Deere D, cast aluminum, Old Time Toys, IL, c1960 . . . . **18.00**
Massey–Ferguson, 1150 . . . . **72.00**
McCormick–Deering, 10–20, cast aluminum, Robert Gray, IA **20.00**
Oliver 70 Row Crop, driver, rubber, Arcor **10.00**
Porsche, driver, orange, Gama, West Germany, 1958 . . . . **6.00**
Renault R–86, red, plastic, Norev, France **5.00**
Sparkling Tractor and Tractor Set, 21″, "Marbrook Farms," wind–up, Marx, c1950 . . . . **22.50**
Steam Traction Engine, miniature, represents 1925 Allchin 7–32, 1935 . . . . **36.00**
Volvo Bm 400 Tractor, red, Husky . . **6.50**
Woodhaven, wind–up, 1916 . . . . . . **25.00**
Trailer
  Calves, green, Husky, 1970 . . . . **5.00**
  Hay, blue, Matchbox, 1970 . . . . **3.50**
  Pony, two axles and ramp, tan, Matchbox, 1971 . . . . **3.00**
Truck
  Dump, 5½″, red, Tootsietoy **10.00**
  Open Bed, 4″, Auburn, 1940 . . . . . . **7.50**
  Pickup
    Ford, Buddy L, 1950 . . . . **12.00**
    Jalopy, 7″, tin, wind–up, Marx . . . **20.00**
    Model A, Hubley **20.00**
Wagon
  Cane, 11″, mule and driver, Wilkins **50.00**
  Donkey, 10½″, cast iron **36.00**
  Ford, Ertl **10.00**
  International Harvester, four wheels, steel, Tru–Scale **20.00**
  McCormick–Deering, two horses, 12½″, cast iron **30.00**
  Mule and driver, 9″, Wilkins **36.00**
  Stake, two horses, driver with reins, 15″, Kenton **100.00**

FAST FOOD MEMORABILIA

Collecting Hints: Premiums, made primarily of cardboard or plastic and of recent vintage, are

the mainstay of today's fast food collector. Other items sought are advertising signs and posters, character dolls, promotional glasses and trayliners. In fact, anything associated with a restaurant chain is collectible. The most sought after material is from McDonald's.

Collectors should concentrate only on mint items. Premiums should be unassembled or sealed in an unopened plastic bag.

Collecting fast food memorabilia has grown rapidly during the last half of the 1980s. More than ever before, the fast food chains continue to churn out an amazing array of collectibles.

History: During the period just after World War II, the only convenience restaurants were the coffee shops and diners located along America's highways or in the towns and cities. As suburbia grew, its young families created a demand for a faster and less expensive type of food service.

Ray A. Kroc responded by opening his first McDonald's drive–in restaurant in Des Plaines, Illinois, in 1955. By offering a limited menu of hamburgers, french fries, and drinks, Kroc kept his costs and prices down. This successful concept of assembly line food preparation soon was imitated, but never surpassed, by a myriad of competitors.

By the mid–1960s the race was on with franchising seen as the new economic frontier. As the competition increased, the need to develop advertising promotions was imperative. A plethora of promotional give–aways entered the scene.

Periodical: *For Here or to Go,* P.O. Box 162281, Sacramento, CA 95816.

Note: Prices are for mint condition items sealed in their original wrappers or packages and unassembled.

BIG BOY

Ashtray, glass, red and white logo **2.50**
Bank, vinyl **8.00**
Doll
  10″ h, plastic, 1974–78, name across front of shirt **2.50**
  14″, cloth, pillow type, litho, Big Boy, name on shirt **5.00**
Key Chain, red, white, and black trademark, plastic **2.00**
Nodder, 5″, papier mache head, heavy base, red and white checkered overalls **7.50**
Tee Shirt, white ground, red, white, and black trademark **6.00**

BURGER KING

Bookmark, King character, 1979 . . . . . **.75**
Calendar, Olympic Games, 1980 . . . . . **2.50**

Burger King, doll, printed cloth, red, yellow, flesh, black, and white, 16" h, $7.50.

Car, Burger King Wind Car, plastic,
1979 .... .75
Doll, Burger King 7.00
Drafting Set, plastic, blue 1.00
Eraser, pencil top, bust of King, rubber,
1979 .... .75
Glider, King Glider, styrofoam, 1978 .. 1.50
Puppet, hand, plastic, King, 1977 .... 1.50
Tablet, Burger King characters, 1979 .. 1.00
Whistle, green, plastic, pickle 1.25
Yo-Yo, Burger King Yum Yum Duncan
Yo-Yo, 1979 .... 2.50

DENNY'S

Child's Menu, games and activities,
1978 .... 2.00
Pencil, Deputy Dan 1.50
Puppet, hand, plastic, Deputy Dan,
1976 .... 1.00

HARDEE'S

Coupon, paper, roast beef sandwich
special, old style building illus ..... .25
Doll, cloth, pillow type, litho, Gilbert
Giddyup, orange cowboy outfit, 1971 8.50
Mug, plastic, Gilbert Giddyup, orange
and brown 2.00
Tumbler, multicolored illus of Smurf .. .50

HOWARD JOHNSON'S

Candy Box, salt water taffy, multicolored
.... .50
Doll, 11½", vinyl head and arms, plastic
body, girl, black painted eyes, waitress
uniform, hounds tooth check
dress, apron 12.00
Menu, ice cream cov 1.00
Soda Fountain Kit, battery operated
mixer, pencil, cups, syrup, and hats,
etc, all with HoJo logo, c1950 ..... 40.00
Swizzle Stick, plastic, HoJo logo ..... .50

KENTUCKY FRIED CHICKEN

Bank, figural, Colonel Sanders 15.00
Frisbee, plastic, red, white Colonel dec 2.25
Nodder, 7" h, Colonel, white goatee,
mustache, eyebrows, and hair, white
doublebreasted suit, marked "Kentucky
Fried Chicken" on base 12.00
Pinback Button, 1½" d, "Vote for Col
Sanders," blue and white, c1972 ... 20.00
Sand Bucket and Shovel, plastic, same
design as chicken bucket 4.00

MCDONALD'S

Box, Star Trek Meal box, six types, 1979 2.50
Button, Mayor McCheese, metal,
marked "Para Gift" 1.50
Comb, Ronald McDonald, plastic, 1980 .75
Crayons, 1½ x 4" box, red, white, and
yellow illus, orig unused crayons,
c1960 .... 1.00
Cup Holder, dark blue, orig pkg 2.50
Doll
Hamburglar 20.00
Ronald 7.00
Game, McDonald's Waste Basket
Game, 1976 .... 2.50
Hat, visor type, cloth, cloth patch on
front 1.50
Map, Ronald McDonald Map of the
Moon, 1969 .... 5.00
Music Box, restaurant shape, "Good
Times/Good Taste" theme, plays
when front door is opened, orig package
.... 17.50
Patch, cloth, 2¼ x 3½", red, white,
blue, and yellow stitching, Ronald
McDonald illus 1.50
Pin, 1984 Olympics, 1⅞" w, red, yellow,
blue, and white, brass, inscribed
"Ronald and Sam" 3.00
Pinback Button, I Support Ronald
McDonald House, children's artwork 10.00
Puppet, hand, plastic, Ronald McDonald,
red, yellow, and black,
c1977 .... 1.00
Toy, musical, 2", yellow, plastic, Hamburglar,
raised dec on one side ..... .50
Tumbler, Capt Crook 5.00
Valentine, strip of six different valentines,
1978 .... 1.50
Wallet, Capt Crook Wrist Wallet, plastic,
green, bracelet with compartment
to carry coins 1.00

PIZZA HUT

Bank, 7½", Pizza Pete, plastic 6.00
Menu, Pizza Pete and logo 2.00
Paper Napkin, logo .... .50

Puppet, hand, plastic, Pizza Pete caricature **1.00**

SAMBO

Doll, Sambo
  Cloth, 10", standing, crimson shoes,
    little red jacket, turban, holding
    closed umbrella in one hand, plate
    of felt pancakes in other, marked
    Dream Doll/R. Dakin & Co/Japan   **12.00**
  Rubber, 5", oversized head, short
    legs, marked "Copyright 1972
    Kings/Import/Spain" **5.00**
Menu, Sambo on front ....   **.75**
Placemat, paper, tiger ....   **.50**
Puppet, hand, plastic, Mother Tiger with
  spatula in hand **1.00**
Stuffed Toy, Tiger
  7", sitting on back legs, wearing chef's
    hat marked "Sambo's," fuzzy
    beard, felt facial features **10.00**
  9", knit velvet stretched over firm
    base, felt facial features, marked
    "Dream Pets/R. Dakin & Co" **5.00**

WENDY'S

Doll, cloth, 11½", Wendy **5.00**
Earrings, hamburgers **10.00**
Flying Ring, Fun Flyer, plastic, 3½" d .   **1.00**
Puppet, hand, plastic, Wendy sitting ..   **.50**

FENTON GLASS

Collecting Hints: During the past thirty years
Fenton has produced some of the most beautiful
glass ever made. Many duplicate examples made
by 19th century glass houses. Since Fenton glass
is so very difficult to find, the new collector has
turned to this reproduction glass.

Carnival glass made by Fenton after 1970 has
their logo in the glass. Milk glass made after 1973
and all Fenton glass made after 1974 is marked
with their logo.

It is advisable for the beginning collector to
understand and study Fenton glass and to purchase Fenton Glass—The Third Twenty–Five
Years so that they can identify what glass was
made from 1960 to 1980. The last ten identified
years, while not covered by this book, can be
studied, by visiting gift shops and talking to dealers.

Many collectors begin collecting with the most
recently made glass, then work their collecting
back in time. For example, Fenton first started
making Burmese in 1971. They made it almost
continuously until 1990. By beginning with
pieces in 1990, then 1989, and so on the collector will be lucky enough to put together a
collection of all Burmese pieces.

History: The Fenton Art Glass Company began
as a cutting shop in Martins Ferry, Ohio, in 1905.
In 1906 Frank L. Fenton started to build a plant
in Williamstown, West Virginia, and produced
the first piece of glass in 1907. Early production
included carnival, chocolate, custard, and
pressed plus mold blown opalescent glass. In the
1920s stretch glass, Fenton dolphins, jade green,
ruby, and art glass were added.

In the 1930s boudoir lamps, "Dancing Ladies," and various slags were produced. The
1940s saw crests of different colors being added
to each piece by hand. Hobnail, opalescent, and
two–color overlay pieces were popular items.
Handles were added to different shapes, making
the baskets they created as popular today as then.

Through the years Fenton has added beauty to
their glass by decorating it with hand painting,
acid etching, color staining, and copper wheel
cutting. Several different paper labels have been
used. In 1970 an oval raised trademark also was
adopted.

References: Shirley Griffith, A Pictorial Review
Of Fenton White Hobnail Milk Glass, published
by author, 1984; William Heacock, Fenton
Glass: The First Twenty–Five Years, O–Val Ad-
vertising Corp, 1978; William Heacock, Fenton
Glass: The Second Twenty–Five Years, O–Val
Advertising Corp, 1980.

Collectors' Club: Fenton Art Glass Collectors Of
America, Inc, P. O. Box 384, Williamstown, WV
26187.

Advisor: Ferill Jeane Rice.

**Condiment Set, Block and Star, milk glass,
$95.00.**

Animal
  Alley Cat, carnival, dark, #5177 ...   **65.00**
  Bear, Burmese, blue, reclining **50.00**
  Donkey, custard, hp daisies, #5125   **30.00**
  Duckling, satin
    Blue, hp blue roses, #5169 .....   **30.00**
    Custard, #5169 ....   **28.00**
  Frog, satin, blue, #5166 ....   **28.00**

Art Glass, Robert Barber
Egg
    Multicolored, #5008 .... **95.00**
    Pink, #5001 .... **94.00**
Vase
  7½" h
    Bittersweet, hanging heart,
      #0003 .... **210.00**
    Blue feather, #0004 .... **95.00**
  10" h, custard, hanging heart,
    #0007 .... **145.00**
  12½" h, hyacinth, feather vase,
    #0001 .... **195.00**
Ashtray
  Hobnail, blue marble, small, #3610 **30.00**
Pelican
  Crystal satin, #5178 .... **35.00**
  Jonquil yellow,#5178 .... **65.00**
Valencia
  Colonial blue, #8377 .... **25.00**
  Colonial green, #8377 .... **15.00**
Basket
  Amberina, plated, 7" deep, #1637 . **160.00**
Burmese
  Maple leaf, #7437 .... **80.00**
  Rose, 7", #7437 .... **100.00**
  Custard, hanging heart, #8939 .... **250.00**
  Dogwood on Cameo, petal blue, 5",
    #9334 .... **35.00**
Hobnail
  Blue marble, 6½", #3736 .... **24.00**
  Colonial amber, #3638 .... **25.00**
  Cranberry opalescent, 10", #3830 **120.00**
  Silver Crest, violets in snow, #8434 **45.00**
Vasa Murrhina, 11" h
  Aventurine green and blue, #6437 **95.00**
  Blue mist, #6437 .... **125.00**
  Water Lily, lime sherbet, 7", #8434 . **35.00**
Bell
  Bluebirds, hp, custard, #8267 ..... **30.00**
  Bride and Groom, crystal velvet,
    #9168 .... **20.00**
  Butterflies, hp, milk glass, #8267 .. **26.00**
  Daisy & Button, orange carnival,
    #1966 .... **30.00**
Hobnail
  Bluebells, hp, milk glass, #3667 . **25.00**
  Topaz opalescent, #3667 .... **35.00**
  Old Mill Scene, hp, custard, #7362 **40.00**
  Rosalene, Faberge, #8466 .... **30.00**
  Violets in Snow, hp, #8267 ...... **30.00**
Bicentennial
  Eagle Paperweight, chocolate, #8470 **20.00**
  Eagle Plate, chocolate **25.00**
Jefferson Compote
  Independence blue, #8476 ...... **100.00**
  Patriot red, #8476 .... **150.00**
  Lafayette Plate, Patriot red **35.00**
Stein
  Chocolate, #8446 .... **35.00**
  Independence blue, #8446 ...... **25.00**

Bonbon
  Carnival, dark, butterfly, #8230 .... **25.00**
  Hobnail, milk glass, 6", hp bluebells,
    #3926 .... **22.00**
  Rosalene, butterfly, #8230 .... **29.00**
Bowl
  Basketweave, lavender satin, #9388 **25.00**
  Curtain, Lime sherbet, #8454 ...... **40.00**
  Hexagon, #8226
    Blue satin **40.00**
    Lime sherbet **45.00**
    Rosalene **65.00**
  Persian Medallion, lime sherbet,
    #8224 .... **30.00**
  Water Lily, three toed, #8426
    Lime sherbet **40.00**
    Rosaline **65.00**
Candle Bowl, Hobnail
  Black, #3672 .... **25.00**
  Blue marble, #3872 .... **18.00**
  Colonial green, #3872 .... **10.00**
  Plum opalescent, #3771 .... **70.00**
Compote
  Flowered, footed
    Lime sherbet, #8422 .... **45.00**
    Rosalene, #8422 .... **65.00**
    Satin, blue, #8422 .... **45.00**
  Hobnail, marble, blue, #3628 ..... **10.00**
  Persian Medallion
    Lime sherbet, #8234 .... **35.00**
    Rosalene, #8234 .... **360.00**
  Plum Opalescent, 6", #3786 ...... **55.00**
Cruet, Burmese, maple leaf, #7462 .. **68.00**
Egg
  Black, white daisies **45.00**
  Carnival, dark **65.00**
  Custard, hp, violets **30.00**
Epergne
  Rose Burmese, two pc **250.00**
  Velva Rose, five pc, #7505 .... **200.00**
Fairy Light
  Currier & Ives, Crystal Velvet,
    #84009 .... **35.00**
  Heart, Rosalene, #8406 .... **75.00**
  Hobnail
    Colonial blue, #3608 .... **10.00**
    Satin, blue, #3608 .... **25.00**
  Owl
    Custard, #5108 .... **20.00**
    Lime sherbet, #5108 .... **35.00**
    Rosalene, #5108 .... **55.00**
  Santa Claus
    Lime sherbet, #5106 .... **50.00**
    Ruby, #5106 .... **55.00**
Goblet
  Empress, Colonial blue, ... **22.50**
  Thumbprint
    Colonial blue **15.00**
    Colonial pink **18.00**
Pitcher
  Burmese
    Maple Leaf, cream, #7461 ...... **65.00**

Rose, cream, #7461 .... **85.00**
Hobnail
  Milk Glass, #3762 .... **20.00**
  Powder blue, #3762 .... **45.00**
  Wild Rose, #3762 .... **65.00**
Vasa Murrhina, Blue Mist, cream ... **39.00**
Plate
  Christmas, satin, white **20.00**
  Craftsman Series, carnival
    Glass Blower **25.00**
    Tanner **30.00**
  Deer in Woods, hp, custard, #7418 **30.00**
  Mother's Day, satin, blue **20.00**
Rose Bowl
  Burmese, Rose, #7424 .... **55.00**
  Water Lily, #8429 .... **16.00**
Vase
  Bud, Plum Opalescent, 7", #3756 .. **40.00**
  Burmese, Rose, #7253 .... **85.00**
  Dolphin Handled, Velva Rose,
    c1980, #7551 .... **25.00**
  Fan, Aventurine green/blue, #6457 . **65.00**
  Jacqueline, opaline, 5"
    Pink, #9153 .... **55.00**
    Yellow, #9153 .... **48.00**
  Vasa Murrhina
    Autumn Orange, 14", #6459 .... **135.00**
    Rose Mist
      7", #6452 .... **70.00**
      8", #6456 .... **55.00**

FIESTA WARE

Collecting Hints: Buy pieces without any cracks, chips, or scratches whenever possible. Fiesta ware can be identified by bands of concentric circles.

History: Fiesta ware is colorful pottery dinnerware made by the Homer Laughlin China Company. It was designed by Frederick Read. Production started in 1936. Fiesta ware was redesigned in 1969 and discontinued in 1972. In 1986 it was reintroduced.

References: Linda D. Farmer, *The Farmer's Wife's Fiesta Inventory & Price Guide*, privately printed, 1984; Sharon and Bob Huxford, *The Collectors Encyclopedia of Fiesta with Harlequin and Riviera, Sixth Edition,* Collector Books, 1987, 1990 value update.

Ashtray
  Green **25.00**
  Red **35.00**
  Turquoise **25.00**
  Yellow **25.00**
Candlesticks, pr
  Bulbous
    Ivory **45.00**
    Turquoise **50.00**
    Yellow **40.00**

Tripod, pink, pr **85.00**
Carafe, green **85.00**
Chop Plate, 13"
  Cobalt **20.00**
  Gray **30.00**
  Ivory **17.00**
  Light Green **20.00**
  Rose **35.90**
  Yellow **20.00**
Coffeepot, cov
  Red **115.00**
  Yellow **75.00**
Compote, 12", turquoise **50.00**
Cream Soup
  Cobalt Blue, lid **35.00**
  Red **35.00**
  Turquoise **20.00**
  Yellow **30.00**
Creamer
  Cobalt, side handle **22.00**
  Red, stick handled **27.00**
  Red, individual **120.00**
Cup
  Chartreuse **25.00**
  Cobalt **18.00**
  Light Blue **12.00**
  Light Green **12.00**
  Turquoise **18.00**
  Yellow **16.00**
Deep Plate
  Light Green **20.00**
  Turquoise **20.00**
  Yellow **20.00**
Dessert Bowl, 6" d
  Cobalt Blue **25.00**
  Ivory **28.00**
  Red **35.00**
  Turquoise **20.00**
  Yellow **20.00**
Dessert Bowl, 6" d
  Cobalt Blue **25.00**
  Ivory **28.00**
  Red **35.00**
  Turquoise **18.00**
  Yellow **28.00**
Egg Cup
  Light Green **30.00**
  Turquoise **25.00**
Fruit Bowl, 4½" d
  Cobalt Blue **15.00**
  Ivory **15.00**
  Red **24.00**
  Turquoise **12.00**
  Yellow **12.00**
Gravy Boat
  Green **20.00**
  Light Blue **32.00**
  Red **50.00**
Jug, 2 pint
  Ivory **35.00**
  Light Green **39.00**
  Turquoise **39.00**

Jug, 3 pint, ivory 48.00
Juicer, cobalt 20.00
Lid, coffeepot, green 15.00
Marmalade, gold 35.00
Mug
    Forest Green 40.00
    Gray 40.00
    Red 50.00
    Rose 40.00
    Yellow 35.00
Mug, Tom and Jerry
    Ivory 28.00
    Red 55.00
    Yellow 28.00
Mustard, cov, light green 50.00
Nappy, 8½" d
    Chartreuse 30.00
    Forest Green 32.00
    Gray 32.00
    Red 32.00
    Turquoise 18.00
Pitcher
    Disc, juice, yellow 27.00
    Disc, water
        Red 75.00
        Yellow 40.00
    Ice Lip, red 95.00
Plate
    6", dessert
        Cobalt Blue 3.00
        Green 4.00
        Red 6.00
        Yellow 4.00
    9", luncheon
        Cobalt Blue 10.00
        Red 13.00
        Yellow 6.00
    10", dinner
        Gray 30.00
        Ivory 20.00
        Light Green 17.00
        Red 25.00
        Rose 30.00
        Yellow 18.00
    12", Grill
        Ivory 46.00
        Red 50.00
        Yellow 46.00
Plate
    Chartreuse 35.00
    Turquoise, oval 15.00
Refrigerator Dish, lid, Kitchen Kraft,
    round, blue 75.00
Relish Tray, light blue 18.00
Salad Bowl, individual
    Red 60.00
    Yellow 48.00
Salt and Pepper Shakers, pr
    Medium Green 45.00
    Red–orange 15.00
    Yellow 12.00

Saucer
    Chartreuse 4.00
    Cobalt Blue 2.00
    Green 1.00
    Red 2.00
    Rose 3.00
    Turquoise 3.00
    Yellow 1.00
Stack Set
    Cobalt Blue 22.00
    Green 22.00
Sugar
    Red, cov 28.00
    Yellow, individual 75.00
Syrup, yellow 125.00
Teacup
    Cobalt Blue 16.00
    Red 20.00
    Yellow 16.00

Teapot, orange, $42.50.

Teapot, red, medium 85.00
Tidbit Tray, rose 65.00
Tray, figure eight, cobalt 30.00
Tumbler
    Juice
        Green 15.00
        Rose 22.00
        Yellow 15.00
    Water
        Cobalt Blue 35.00
        Green 28.00
        Red 48.00
        Yellow 38.00
Utility Tray
    Green 16.00
    Red 25.00
Vase, red, 6½" 25.00
Vegetable Bowl, medium green 65.00

FIREHOUSE COLLECTIBLES

Collecting Hints: It was fashionable for a period of time to put a date on the back of a fireman's helmet. This date is usually the date the fire company was organized, not the date the helmet was made.

Firehouse collectibles is a very broad area of collecting. The older, scarcer collectibles, such as helmets and firemarks, command high prices. The newer collectibles, e.g., cards and badges, are more reasonably priced. This area of collecting is continually growing and expanding.

History: The volunteer fire company has played a vital role in the protection and social growth of many towns and rural areas. Paid professional firemen are usually found in large metropolitan areas. Each fire company has prided itself on equipment and uniforms. Annual conventions and parades give the individual fire companies a chance to show off their equipment. These conventions and parades have produced a wealth of firehouse related collectibles.

References: Chuck Deluca, *Firehouse Memorabilia: A Collectors Reference*, Maritime Antique Auctions, 1989; Mary Jane and James Piatti, *Firehouse Collectibles*, The Engine House, 1979.

Periodical: *The Fire Mark Circle of the Americas*, 2849 Martin Drive, Chamblee, GA 30341.

Museums: There are many museums devoted to firehouse collectibles. Large collections are housed at: Insurance Company of North America (I.N.A.) Museum, 1600 Arch St., Philadelphia, PA; Oklahoma State Fireman's Association Museum, Inc., 2716 NE 50th St., Oklahoma City, OK; and San Francisco Fire Dept. Pioneer Memorial Museum, 655 Presidio Ave., San Francisco, CA.

Alarm
Fire Station No 444 .... **80.00**
Gamewell, red, corner type **75.00**
Axe, parade type, brass blade, black
handle **150.00**
Badge
Active, Phila, 1¼ x 2", metal, rolled,
silvered, serial #1736, "VFA" in
center, early 1900s **35.00**
Eureka Fire Hose Co, NY, 1¼ x 2",
metal, bronze finish, "Compliments Of" on top linked piece, illus
of eagle and fire hoses on pendant,
early 1900s **30.00**
Vigilant JFD, 1¾", brass, emb,
c1930s **25.00**
Banner, Firemen's Parade, helmet, fire
axe, and speaking trumpet **125.00**
Bell
8" **60.00**
10", Edwards, DC transformer, 1872 **20.00**
Belt, leather, black
Columbia, We Yield To None **65.00**
Protection, red and white letters **100.00**
Book
*Our Firemen, History of New York
Fire Departments*, A E Costello,
1887, first edition **225.00**

Sheboygan Fire Dept, 1901, leather
cov **24.00**
Bucket
Galvanized Metal, "Fire Only," red . **48.00**
Leather, blue paint, gilt pin striping,
iron bail, heart shape attachments **225.00**
Card, Bowman's Firefighters, set, each
2½ x 3¾", color, series of admonishments such as "Don't Play with
Matches," "Don't Start Fire!"
No 4, Airport Crash Truck **1.75**
No 9, Ward LaFrance, three Stage
Booster **1.50**
Catalog, Darley Municipal–Fire Protection–Police Supply, c1928, 35 pgs .. **18.00**
Engine Name Plate
American Locomotive Company,
Manchester Works, Manchester,
NY **25.00**
Mack Trucks, bulldog **18.00**
Fire Extinguisher
Fyre Fyter, brass **10.00**
Miller Peerless, pump type, brass, 5
gal **25.00**
Presto Fire Extinguisher, 6", MIB,
c1940 .... **15.00**
Helmet, parade
Columbia Hose No 1, Whitestone,
NY, high eagle, 1880 .... **150.00**
Defiance Hook 7 Ladder Co, brass . **275.00**
Friendship Co No 1, leather **90.00**
Lantern
American LaFrance Dietz King **175.00**
King Fire Dept, copper bottom, Dietz **125.00**
Nozzle
Brass, 7½", Self–Propelling Nozzle
Co, patent 1922 .... **42.00**
Copper, 25½", brass fittings, BC Co . **90.00**

Sheet music, *The Midnight Fire Alarm*, written by Harry J. Lincoln, arranged by E.T. Paull, 1907 copyright, $12.00.

Patch

Flemington, NJ	**2.00**
Louisville, KY	**1.25**
Washington, DC	**1.75**

Pin, Pennsylvania State Fireman's Assn, York, 1911 . . . . **25.00**

Pinback Button, 1¾" d

Fire apparatus fighting building fire, multicolor, silvered metal rim, US flags on back, early 1900s **30.00**

Fireman rescuing infant from burning building, multicolor illus, white rim, blue lettering, dated 1898 . . . **35.00**

Postcard, Providence, RI, Fire Truck No 1, horse drawn photo **30.00**

Program, Convention 1927 . . . . **4.00**

Ribbon

Convention, "SFE Co", PA, 1895 . . . **38.00**

Somerville, NJ, parade, celluloid medallion **25.00**

Syracuse, NY, parade, Second Place **18.00**

Sheet Music, *Midnight Fire Alarm* **20.00**

Toy

Fire Engine, 12" l, red, white ladders, black rubber wheels, decals, No 301, Buddy L, 1947 . . . . **35.00**

Water Tower Truck, Keystone **325.00**

Tumbler, Union Fire Co, 1965 parade, Smokey the Bear and fire engine . . . **12.00**

FISHING COLLECTIBLES

Collecting Hints: The fishing collectibles category is rapidly expanding as the rare items are becoming more expensive and harder to locate. New categories include landing nets, minnow traps, bait boxes, advertising signs, catalogs, and fish decoys used in ice spearing. Items in original containers and in mint condition command top prices. Lures that have been painted over the original decoration or rods that have been refinished or broken have little collector value.

Early wooden plugs (before 1920), split bamboo fly rods made by the master craftsmen of that era, and reels constructed of German silver with special detail or unique mechanical features are the items most sought by advanced collectors.

The number of serious collectors is steadily increasing as indicated by the membership in the "National Fishing Lure Collectors Club" which has approximately 2,000 active members.

History: Early man caught fish with crude spears and hooks made of bone, horn, and flint. By the middle 1800s metal lures with hooks attached were produced in New York State. Later, the metal was curved and glass beads added for greater attraction. Spinners with wood–painted bodies and glass eyes appeared around 1890.

Soon after, wood plugs with glass eyes were being produced by many different makers. A large number of patents were issued in this time period covering developments of hook hangers, body styles, and devices to add movement of the plug as it was drawn through the water. The wood plug era lasted up to the mid–1930s when plugs constructed of plastic were introduced.

With the development of casting plugs, it became necessary to produce fishing reels capable of accomplishing that task with ease. Reels first appeared as a simple device to hold a fishing line. Improvements included multiplying gears, retrieving line levelers, drags, clicks, and a variety of construction materials. The range of quality in reel manufacture varied considerably. Collectors are mainly interested in reels made with quality materials and workmanship, or those exhibiting unusual features.

Early fishing rods were made of solid wood which were heavy and prone to break easily. By gluing together strips of tapered pieces of split bamboo a rod was fashioned which was light in weight and had greatly improved strength. The early split bamboo rods were round with silk wrappings to hold the bamboo strips together. With improvements in glue, fewer wrappings were needed, and rods became slim and lightweight. Rods were built in various lengths and thicknesses depending upon the type of fishing and bait used. Rod makers' names and models can usually be found on the metal parts of the handle or on the rod near the handle.

References: Jim Brown, *Fishing Reel Patents of The US, 1838–1940;* published by author; Silvo Calabi, *The Collector's Guide To Antique Fishing Tackle,* Wellfleet Press, 1989; Clyde A Harbin, *James Heddon's Sons Catalogues,* CAH Enterprises, 1977; Art and Scott Kimball, *Collecting Old Fishing Tackle,* Aardvark Publications, Inc., 1980; Art and Scott Kimball, *Early Fishing Plugs of the U. S. A.,* Aardvark Publications, Inc., 1985; Art and Scott Kimball, *The Fish Decoy,* Aardvark Publications, Inc.; Carl F. Luckey, *Old Fishing Lures and Tackle: Identification and Value Guide, Volumes I and II,* Books Americana; Albert J. Munger, *Those Old Fishing Reels,* published by author, 1982; J. L. Smith, *Antique Rods and Reels,* Gowe Printing, 1986; Richard L. Streater, *Streater's Reference Catalog of Old Fishing Lures, Volumes I and II;* Steven K. Vernon, *Antique Fishing Reels,* Stackpole Books, 1984.

Collectors' Club: National Fishing Lure Collectors Club, 3907 Wedgwood Drive, Portage, MI 49008.

Periodicals: *Antique Fishing Collectibles,* P. O. Box 627, Newtown, PA 18940; *Tackle Trader,* P. O. Box 142, Westerville, OH 43081.

Museums: National Fishing Tackle Museum, Arcadia, OK; American Fishing Tackle Mfg. Assn.

Museum, Arlington Heights, IL; Sayner Museum, Sayner, WI.

REPRODUCTION ALERT: Lures and fish decoys.

Advertising
Calendar, 14 x 18", Bristol Steel Rod
   Co, 1935 .... **55.00**
Display Sign, 18 x 24", Heddon &
   Sons Co, lures, full color **50.00**

Bait casting reel, Takapart No. 480, patent 1904–09, A.F. Meisselbach Mfg, $40.00.

Bobber (float)
  5", Panfish, hp, black, red, and white
    stripes **10.00**
  6", hand carved, painted, dull green
    and white **35.00**
Book
  *Hunting Wildlife with Camera and
    Flashlight,* George Sirjas, c1936, 2
    volumes **44.00**
  Salt Water Fishing, Van Campen Heil-
    ner, c1946, illus **18.00**
  The Standard Book of Fishing, Bruce
    Tuttle, 1956, orig box, 532 illus pgs **45.00**
  The Treasury of Angling, Larry Loller,
    1963, 251 pgs **16.00**
Catalog
  Edward vom Hofe & Co, blue cov,
    illus, 1941 .... **65.00**
  South Bend Co, color illus, rods,
    reels, and lures, 1931 .... **20.00**
Creel
  Crushed willow, 14 x 9 x 7", form fit,
    leather bound **24.00**
  Wicker, center hole in lid, early 1900 **55.00**
Decoy
  Pike, 12" l, tin fins, carved tail,
    mouth, and gills, green, white spots **85.00**
  Sucker, Randall, 6" l, cast aluminum,
    painted gold scale **40.00**
  Sunfish, 6" l, tin fins and tail, bead
    eyes, painted gills and scales,
    carved and painted body, green and
    yellow spots **45.00**

Lure (plug) wooden
  Creek Chub Co
    Giant Jointed Pikie, #800, perch
      finish, glass eyes **45.00**
    Wagtail Chub Deluxe, mullet fin-
      ish, smooth tail, glass eyes **22.00**
    Wiggler, #100, painted perch fin-
      ish, glass eyes, boxed **20.00**
  Heddon Co
    Crab Spook, #9900, natural crab
      color, bead eyes **30.00**
    Minnow
      #00, white, red and green spots,
        orig box **95.00**
      #150, green crackelback finish,
        glass eyes **55.00**
    Mouse, #4000, white body, red
      chin, glass eyes **28.00**
    Near Surface, #1700, red and
      white, multiple line tie rig **40.00**
  Miscellaneous
    Carters Bestever, 3" l, white and
      red, pressed eyes **8.00**
    J T Buel, spinner, 1:0 size, silver
      plate front, brass back **12.00**
    Keeling General Tom, black back,
      green sides, glass eyes **65.00**
    Moonlight, Pikaroom, spotted, red
      and yellow, glass eyes **45.00**
    Paw Paw, underwater minnow,
      rainbow finish, tack eyes **10.00**
  Shakespear Co
    Bass–A–Lure Jr, fancy green back
      and scale finish, glass eyes **18.00**
    Slim Jim, 4½" l, pickerel finish,
      glass eyes **32.00**
    Underwater Minnow, #44, rain-
      bow color, glass eyes **35.00**
  South Bend Co
    Pike Oreno, green scale finish,
      glass eyes, boxed **25.00**
    Underwater Minnow, #903, green
      back, silver belly, tack eyes **32.00**
Minnow Trap
  Hand made, 12 x 10 x 10", metal,
    mesh, hinged door **32.00**
  Orvis, clear glass, l gal size, emb
    name, metal hardware **65.00**
  Shakespear, pale green glass, 1 gal
    size, emb name, metal lid **85.00**
Reel
  Hendryx, raised pillar type, multiply-
    ing, fancy handle, horn knob, two
    button back plate, drag, click,
    nickel over brass **25.00**
  Meisselbach Expert, 1¾ x 3", nickel
    finish, 1886 .... **65.00**
  Pflueger Co, Akron model 1893,
    nickel finish, dual green knobs ... **20.00**
  Rochester Ideal No 1, 2⅜" d, German
    silver, 1910 .... **45.00**

Talbot Star, Kansas City, MO, German
silver, ivory handle **275.00**
E Von Hofe, Salmon, 4:0 size, dial
drag, 1879 .... **230.00**
Winona, trolling type, ¾ x 4¾", drag **42.00**
Rod, Split Bamboo Fly
Granger Special, 8' l, 3:2, green
wraps, dark colored cane, cork reel
seat, featherweight **175.00**
Hardy Deluxe, 9' l, 3:2, brown
wraps, aluminum tube, 1949 .... **135.00**
Horrocks & Ibbotson, 9' l, three
piece, two tips, maroon wraps ... **40.00**
South Bend, 9' l, three piece, two
tips, yellow wraps, orig bag **65.00**

FLAG COLLECTIBLES

Collecting Hints: Public Law 829, 77th Congress, approved December 22, 1942, describes a detailed set of rules for flag etiquette. Collectors should become familiar with this law.

The amount of material on which the American flag is portrayed is limitless. Collectors tend to focus on those items on which the flag enjoys a prominent position.

History: The Continental or Grand Union flag, consisting of 13 alternate red and white stripes with a British Union Jack in the upper left corner, was first used on January 1, 1776, on Prospect Hill near Boston. On June 14, 1777, the Continental Congress adopted a flag design similar to the Continental flag, but with the Union Jack replaced by a blue field with thirteen stars. The stars could be arranged in any fashion. Historical documentation to support the claim that Betsy Ross made the first Stars and Stripes is lacking.

On January 13, 1794, Congress voted to add two stars and two stripes to the flag in recognition of Vermont and Kentucky joining the Union. On April 18, 1818, when there were 20 states, Congress adopted a law returning to the original 13 stripes and adding a new star for each state admitted. The star would be added on the July 4th following admission. The 49th star, for Alaska, was added July 4, 1959; the 50th star, for Hawaii, was added July 4, 1960.

Reference: Boleslow and Marie–Louis D'Otrange Mastai, *The Stars and Stripes: The American Flag As Art And As History From The Birth Of The Republic To The Present,* Alfred Knopf, 1973.

Collectors' Club: North American Vexillological Association, 3 Edgehill Road, Winchester, MA 01890.

Museums: State capitals in northern states; Hardisty Flag Museum, Hardisty, Alberta, Canada; Tumbling Waters Museum of Flags, Prattville, AL.

Advisor: Richard Bitterman.

FLAGS

29 star, 7 x 10", parade flag, coarse cotton material, Great Star pattern, used during Mexican–American War, discolored **250.00**
36 star
21½ x 36", parade flag, mounted on stick, five point star design, star pattern of 6,6,6,6,6,6 .... **125.00**
25 x 22", parade flag, printed muslin **125.00**
37 star, 16 x 24", parade flag, 1867–77, muslin, all printed **95.00**
38 star
12½ x 22", coarse muslin, mounted on stick, star pattern of 6,7,6,6,7,6 **28.00**
18 x 12", triple wreath star pattern .. **75.00**

Child's parade flag, 49 stars, thin wood stick, 4 x 5¾" printed silk flag, 1959–60, Alaska, $25.00.

42 star, four flags printed on swatch, direct from flag manufacturer, uncut, were to be 11½ x 16¾" when cut up and mounted on a stick, flag makers prepared banners with 42 stars during the winter of 1889 for adoption on July 4, 1890; however, a last minute addition on July 3 of Idaho as a state made 43 stars necessary, so these banners never made it **200.00**
44 star, 3½ x 2¼", child's parade type, pattern of 8,7,7,7,7,8 and five point star **40.00**
45 star
18 x 36", cloth, two crossed flags and eagle over letters "M, W, A," (Modern Woodman of America), saying "Pur Avtre Vie" **65.00**
32 x 47", 1896–1908, printed on silk, bright colors, black heading, no grommets **110.00**
46 star, 4 x 5', 1908–12, stars sewn on, Oklahoma **95.00**
48 star
5¾ x 4½", 1912–59, printed on heavy canvas type material, used on D–Day in Infantry invasion,

men wore them under the camou-
flage net on their helmets **60.00**
9¼ x 6", "This Flag Enthusiastically
Waved To Greet President Hoover
Nov 2, 1928" printed on stripes . .   **20.00**
49 star, 4 x 5¾", 1959–60, child's pa-
rade flag, silk, wood stick, Alaska . .   **25.00**

**Game, The Flag Game, McLoughlin Bros,
card game, 1887 copyright, 8½ x 4½",
$45.00.**

FLAG RELATED

Catalog, Detra Flag Company, Catalog
#24, 6½ x 9", 1941, NY and Los
Angeles **100.00**
China and Glass
  Button
    ½" d, glass dome, flag printed in-
    side, 6 mounted on card **18.00**
    1¾" d, horse button, glass dome
    with eagle and flag **20.00**
  Magic Lantern Slide, 42 star flag,
  c1889, hand tinted, mounted in
  wood **30.00**
  Magnifying Glass, pocket, ¾ x 1¼",
  oval, Voorhees Rubber Mfg Co adv,
  American flag artwork **50.00**
  Mustache Cup and Saucer, red,
  white, and blue, "The Union For-
  ever," Civil War period **150.00**
  Plate
    10" d, Washington's Headquarters,
    Newburg, NY, 1783–1883,
    crossed flags under house, brown
    printing on cream plate **45.00**
    1904, St Louis World's Fair, Wash-
    ington, Jefferson, Lafayette, and
    Napoleon's faces, very colorful   **145.00**
  Shaving Mug, 4" h, name in gold let-
  ters
    Crossed American flag and Italian
    flag, eagle and shield **75.00**
    Eagle holding two crossed flags
    over a globe **100.00**
  Tumbler, 4" h, clear, acid etched Star
  Spangled Banner **20.00**
Fabric
  Advertising Button, Leonards Spool
  Silk, Northampton, MA, silk **20.00**

Arm Band, WWII, 48 star flag, worn
by paratrooper on D–Day invasion,
two safety pins **60.00**
Bandanna, 22 x 25", silk, flag inside
wreath of 36 stars **155.00**
Handkerchief, WWI, flags of US and
France, embroidered
  A Kiss from France . . . .̇. **8.00**
  Souvenir France 1919 . . . .   **8.00**
  To My Dear Sweetheart **8.00**
Scarf, 17 x 15", silk, Chicago 1893
Expo, panorama of Expo overlaying
American flag **100.00**
Metal
  Badge, Foresters of America, with
  red, white and blue ribbon **10.00**
  Clock, God Bless America, mantel,
  WWII vintage, small American flag
  waves back and forth as second
  hand, Howard Miller Mfg **125.00**
  Fife, 10" l, tin, red, white, and blue
  litho, marked "All American Fife" .   **15.00**
  Match Box, 1½ x 2¾", Civil War pe-
  riod, emb, picture of Stars and
  Stripes on one side, Miss Columbia
  on reverse **100.00**
  Pinback, Our Flag **6.00**
  Stickpin
    Celluloid, American flag, 48 stars,
    inscribed "S A Cook for US Sen-
    ator" **10.00**
    Metal, ⅜ x⅝", 13 stars, c1925, 2"
    long pin **10.00**
  Token, 3¾" d, "The Dix Token Coin,"
  Civil War, commemorates the order
  of General John Adams Dix, Jan 29,
  1861, "If anyone attempts to haul
  down the American flag, shoot him
  on the spot," copper–colored coin,
  picture of "The flag of our Union"
  on one side and quote on the other   **18.00**
  Toy
    Drum, 9" d, 6¾" h, emb flags, litho
    picture of Admiral Dewey, orig
    sticks, c1898 . . . .   **275.00**
    Spinner, IGA Grocery adv, red,
    white, and blue, eagle **30.00**
Paper
  Advertising Trade Card
    Hub Gore, 3½ x 6¼", Uncle Sam
    holding shoe, saying "Hub Gore
    Makers of Elastic For Shoes, It
    Was Honored at the World's Fair
    of 1893" **15.00**
    Major's Cement, 3 x 4¼", two
    American flags decorating dis-
    play of 125 lb weights holding
    suspended object, full color, adv
    "Major's Leather Cement–For
    Sale By Druggists and Crockery
    Dealers" **14.00**

Merrick's Thread, 2¼ x 4½", two infant children, one beating Civil War type drum, other waving flag, titled "Young America" ...   **10.00**
Certificate, Betsy Ross Flag Association, 1917, serial #38181, Series N, 12 x 16", C H Weisgerber painting **45.00**
Envelope
  Civil War, angry eagle with shield hanging from his mouth and ribbon that reads "Liberty or Death," 34 large stars going around all four edges; each state has its name within its own star   **27.00**
  Printed semblances of Stars and Stripes with 45 stars covering address side **27.00**
Fan, 9 x 14", hand held, Admiral Dewey, many flags, admirals, ships, lace trimmed **125.00**
Post Card, printed semblances of Stars and Stripes covering address side, picture of Wm H Taft for President, July 4, 1908, 46 stars, used **28.00**
Poster, 14 x 29", lithograph, History of Old Glory, Babbitt soap giveaway **195.00**
Print, Currier and Ives, The Star Spangled Banner, #481, 11¼ x 15½" .   **250.00**
Sheet Music
  America Forever March, E T Paull Music Co, Columbia draped in flag, shield, and eagle **45.00**
  Miss America, two step by J Edmund Barnum, lady with stars, red and white striped dress, large flowing flag **30.00**
  Stars & Stripes Forever March, John Phillip Sousa portrait in upper left hand corner, Old Glory in center, published by John Church Co ..   **30.00**
  The Triumphant Banner, E T Paull   **55.00**
Song Sheet, published by Chas Magnus, NY, 5 x 8"
  The Female Auctioneer, lady dressed in costume, waving flag   **45.00**
  The Flag With The 34 Stars, six verses and chorus, illus of soldiers marching with hand colored flag **50.00**

FOOTBALL CARDS

Collecting Hints: Condition is a key factor. Buy cards that are in very good condition, i.e., free from any creases and damaged corners. When possible strive to acquire cards in excellent to mint condition. Rob Erbe's *The American Premium Guide To Baseball Cards* (Books Americana, 1982) photographically illustrates in the introduction how to determine the condition of a card. What applies to a baseball card is equally true for a football card.

The football card market is just beginning to develop. Prices still are modest. Develop a collecting strategy, such as cards related to one year, one player, Heisman trophy winners, or one team. There are large numbers of cards available; a novice collector can be easily overwhelmed.

History: Football cards have been produced since the 1890s. However, it was not until 1933 that the first bubble gum football card appeared in the Goudey Sport Kings set. In 1935 National Chicle of Cambridge, Massachusetts, produced the first full set of gum cards devoted exclusively to football.

Both Leaf Gum of Chicago and Bowman Gum of Philadelphia produced sets of football cards in 1948. Leaf discontinued production after their 1949 issue. Bowman Gum continued until 1955.

Topps Chewing Gum entered the market in 1950 with its college stars set. Topps became a fixture in the football card market with its 1955 All–American set. From 1956 through 1963 Topps printed a card set of National Football League players, combining them with the American Football League players in 1961.

Topps produced sets with only American Football League players from 1964 to 1967. The Philadelphia Gum Company made National Football League card sets during this period. Beginning in 1968 and continuing to the present, Topps has produced sets of National Football League cards, the name adopted by the merger of the two leagues. Topps' only competition during this time came in 1970 and 1971 from Kellogg's Cereal who issued sets of football related cards.

Reference: Dr. James Beckett and Dennis W. Eckes, *The Sport Americana Football, Hockey, Basketball and Boxing Card Price Guide #5,* Edgewater Books, 1987.

Periodicals: *Current Card Prices,* P. O. Box 480, East Islip, NY 11730; *Sports Collectors Digest,* 700 E. State Street, Iola, WI 54990.

Bell Brand
  1959
    Common card **3.00**
    Sid Gilman **5.00**
  1960
    Common card **4.50**
    Gene Selawski **120.00**
Bowman Gum Company
  1948
    Common card **2.25**
    Harry Gilmer **15.00**
  1951
    Common card **1.50**
    Tom Landry **20.00**

1952
Common card
Large 1.25
Small 1.00
Tom Landry
Large 18.00
Small 13.00
1953
Common card 1.20
Frank Gifford 18.00
1955
Common card 1.00
Norm VanBrocklin 8.00
Fleer Gum Company
1960
Common card .... .35
Sammy Baugh 6.50
1961
Common card .... .30
Jim Brown 11.00
1962
Common card .... .30
George Blanda 5.50
Jack Kemp 4.75
Kellogg's Cereal
1970
Common card .... .20
Gale Sayers 1.10
1971
Common card .... .75
Bob Griese 2.00
Leaf Gum
1948
Common card 2.00
Jackie Jensen 18.00
1949
Common card 2.00
Bobby Layne 9.00
National Chicle Company 1935
Common card 7.50
Bronco Nagurski 325.00
Philadelphia Gum Company
1964
Common card .... .25
Jim Brown 18.00
1966
Common card .... .20
Fran Tarkenton 5.25
1967
Common card .... .20
Don Meredith 5.00
Topps Chewing Gum Inc
1950
Common card 2.25
Joe Paterno 20.00
1951
Common card 1.25
Bill Wade 5.00
1955
Common card 1.00
Knute Rockne 10.00

Topps, 1979, left: Dan Fouts, $.25; right:
Pat Haden, $.25.

1958
Common card .... .30
John Unitas 5.00
1960
Common card .... .30
Y A Tittle 5.00
1961
Common card .... .25
Jack Kemp 4.50
1963
Common card .... .25
Don Meredith 6.00
1964
Common card .... .25
Len Dawson 4.00
1965
Common card .... .65
Fred Biletnikoff 6.50
1966
Common card .... .20
George Blanda 5.00
1967
Common card .... .20
Joe Namath 6.00
1968
Common card .... .15
Joe Namath 7.50
1969
Common card .... .15
Brian Piccolo 13.00
1970
Common card .... .15
Bart Starr 2.25
1971
Common card .... .10
Joe Greene 3.50
1972
Common card .... .05
Terry Bradshaw 3.00
Bubba Smith 3.00
1973
Common card .... .05
Ken Anderson 3.00
Roger Staubach 3.25
1974
Common card .... .05

Fran Tarkenton	**1.50**
1975	
Common card	**.05**
Dan Fouts	**2.50**
Joe Theismann	**1.00**
1976	
Common card	**.03**
Steve Bartkowski	**1.75**
John Riggins	**.65**
1977	
Common card	**.03**
Walter Payton	**1.35**
Danny White	**1.35**
1978	
Common card	**.05**
Tony Dorsett	**3.00**
1979	
Common card	**.03**
Vince Farragamo	**.55**
1980	
Common card	**.02**
Joe Fergueson	**.30**
Dan Pastorini	**.20**
1981	
Common card	**.02**
Joe Cribbs	**.35**
Walter Payton	**.65**
1982	
Common card	**.02**
George Rodgers	**.60**

FRANKOMA POTTERY

Collecting Hints: Prior to 1954 all Frankoma pottery was made with a honey-tan colored clay from Ada, Oklahoma. Since 1954 Frankoma has used a brick red clay from Sapulpa. During the early 1970s the clay became lighter and is now pink in color.

There were a number of early marks. One most eagerly sought is the leopard pacing on the FRANKOMA name. Since the 1938 fire, all pieces have carried only the name FRANKOMA.

History: John N. Frank founded a ceramic art department at Oklahoma University in Norman and taught there for several years. In 1933 Frank established his own business and began making Oklahoma's first commercial pottery. Frankoma moved from Norman to Sapulpa, Oklahoma, in 1938.

A fire completely destroyed the new plant later the same year, but rebuilding began almost immediately. The company remained in Sapulpa and continued to grow. Frankoma is the only American pottery to be permanently exhibited at the International Ceramic Museum of Italy.

In 1983 Frankoma celebrated its fiftieth anniversary. In September 1983 a disastrous fire struck once again, destroying 97% of Frankoma's facilities. The rebuilt Frankoma Pottery reopened in July 1984. Production has been limited to 1983 production molds only. All other molds were lost in the fire.

References: Phyllis and Tom Bess, *Frankoma Treasures*, published by author, 1983; Susan N. Cox, *Collectors Guide To Frankoma Pottery, Book I* (1979), *Book II* (1982), published by author.

Ashtray	
Elephant	**65.00**
Fish	**15.00**
Batter Set, #87, 4 pcs	**75.00**
Bean Pot, cov, Plainsman, green and brown	**9.00**
Bird Feeder	**20.00**
Bookend pr	
Boots, #433	**20.00**
Bucking Bronco	**150.00**
Irish Setter	**80.00**
Bottle, 11½", morning glory blue, white int., 1979	**28.00**
Canteen, straps, new	**6.00**
Christmas Card	
1948	**75.00**
1953	**65.00**
1958	**50.00**
1965	**45.00**
1968	**35.00**
1975	**30.00**
1982	**15.00**
1984, Grace Lee & Milton Smith	**35.00**
Compote, Gracetone, #85, pine cone	**20.00**
Corn Tray	**4.00**
Cornucopia, 9½", #57	**20.00**
Decanter, orig stopper, red	
#1217, sgd "John Frank"	**77.00**
#1787, sgd "Janice Frank"	**65.00**
Dinnerware	
Bowl	
Chip and Dip	**20.00**
Divided, 7 x 13"	**8.00**
Shell, 12"	**20.00**
Gravy boat, two spouts, #6S	**6.50**
Mug	
Mustache	**7.50**
16 oz, #94M	**8.00**
Stein, #M2	**5.00**
Pitcher	
1 qt, #81	**8.00**
2 qt, #5D	**15.00**
Plate	
10", #6F	**6.00**
13", steak	**5.00**
15", chop	**25.00**
Platter, 13", Lazybones, #4P	**10.00**
Salt and Pepper Shakers, pr, #6H	**5.00**
Jewelry	
Bolo	**20.00**
Pin	**8.00**
Mask, pr, wall type, Negro, Ada clay	**100.00**

Miniature
Donkey	55.00
Jug, brass chain, set of 3	30.00
Puma	40.00
Salt and Pepper Shaker, pr, adv	20.00
Vase, #503	20.00

Mug, political
1968, elephant	55.00
1974, brown & white	35.00
1977, donkey	8.00
1984, mulberry & white	10.00

Planter
Elephant, #390	6.00
Mallard, 9½"	8.00
Turtle, #396	6.50

Plaque
Phoebe	45.00
Will Rogers	35.00

Plate
1970, Christmas	20.00
1972, Easter	15.00
1973, Annunciation	24.00
1975, Largemouth Bass, Wildlife Series	20.00
1976, Bicentennial Series	7.00
1977, Peter the Fisherman	20.00
1979, Daniel the Courageous	20.00
1985, Phoenix	15.00

Sculpture
English Setter, 5"	48.00
Gardener Boy	90.00
Indian Chief, prancing, Ada clay	80.00
Swan, 9", open tail, brown glaze	20.00

Serva—Tray, complete, stand	50.00
Tile	3.00

Toby Mug
Baseball Player, 1980	15.00
Uncle Sam, 1976	20.00

Trivet
Centennial, yellow	5.00
Five Nations or Cherokee Alphabet	20.00
Lazybones	30.00
Owl	3.00

Vase
Octagonal, 9½", red	10.00
Ringed Cylinder, 10", #72	7.00
Stove Pipe	50.00
Wagon Wheel, 6¾", mottled green	18.00

Wall Pocket, acorn	20.00

FRATERNAL ORGANIZATIONS

Collecting Hints: Fraternal items break down into three groups. The first focuses on the literature, pins and badges, and costume paraphernalia which belonged to individual members of each organization. This material can be found easily. The second group is the ornamentation and furniture used in lodge halls for ceremonial purposes. Many of these items were made locally and are highly symbolic. Folk art collectors have latched on to them and have driven prices artificially high.

The third group relates to the regional and national conventions of the fraternal organizations. Each meeting generally produces a number of specialized souvenir items. These conventions are one of the few times when public visibility is drawn to a fraternal group; hence, convention souvenirs are the most commonly found items.

Concentrate on one fraternal group. Since so much emphasis has been placed on Masonic and Shriner material, new collectors are urged to focus on one of the other organizations.

History: Benevolent and secret societies played an important part in American society from the late 18th century to the mid-20th century. Groups ranged from Eagles, Elks, Moose, and Orioles to Odd Fellows, Redmen, and Woodmen. These secret societies had lodges or meeting halls, secret ceremonies, ritualistic materials, and souvenir items from conventions and regional meetings.

Initially the societies were organized to aid members or their families in times of distress or death. They evolved from this purpose into important social clubs by the late 19th century. Women's auxiliaries were organized. In the 1950s, with the arrival of civil rights, an attack occurred on the secretiveness and often discriminatory practices of these societies. Americans had greater outlets for leisure and social life, and less need for the benevolent aspects of the groups. The fraternal movement, with the exception of the Masonic order, suffered serious membership loss. Many local chapters closed and sold their lodge halls. This has resulted in many items arriving in the antiques market.

Note: This category does not include souvenir and other items related to the many service clubs of the 20th century, such as the Lions, Rotary, etc., who replaced the focus of many of the fraternal group members. Items from these service groups are not yet viewed as collectible by the general marketplace.

Benevolent & Protective Order of Elks, B.P.O.E.

Badge
Omaha Elks Fair, 1902	20.00
Salt Lake City Elks Reunion, 1902	18.00

Book
Charles A S Vivian, biographical sketch, green and gold, hard cover	35.00
National Memorial, 1931, hardbound	30.00

Case, leather, WWII Elks Club Honorable Discharge, gold leaf logo	15.00

Badge, Foresters of America, red, white, and blue ribbon, $8.50.

Cigar Box Label, Elks Temple, emb, gold and multicolor 25.00
Cuff Links, pr, tooth, gold, raised design 125.00
Flask, 4", milk glass, tooth shape, emb 45.00
Match Holder, 2¼" h, stein type, striker, purple and brown glaze 35.00
Medal, 3¼", G L R Denver 1906, enamel, gold wash 22.00
Pillowcase, embroidered elk 15.00
Pinback Button, Elk's Helldorado Kangaroo Court, 1950s 5.00
Plate
  6¼" d, souvenir, hp, Allegheny Lodge No. 339 Elks Carnival July 10–22 1899 .... 75.00
  10" d, elk head, fancy edge, BPOE & 463, Johnson Bros, England . 45.00
Shaving Mug, 3½" h, china, elk head, vining leaves, and roses 75.00
Sign, porcelain 95.00
Stein, 4¼" h, Souvenir State Meeting, Olympia Washington, 1911, blue elk head, gold trim, printed under glaze 45.00
Tie Tack, sterling, jeweled 28.00
Tray, Elks Convention, Philadelphia, 1909, tip 45.00
Whiskey Decanter, purple, gold trim, stopper 250.00
Fraternal Order of Eagles, F.O.E.
  Shaving Mug, eagle, standing on rock, "Liberty, Truth, Justice, Equality" 15.00
  Watch Fob, bronze, "F.O.E., Liberty, Truth, Justice, Equality," 1918 .... 5.00
Improved Order of Red Men
  Grave Marker, brass, Indian at top .. 50.00

Pinback Button, gold and red ribbon, 1904 .... 45.00
Independent Order of Odd Fellows, I.O.O.F.
  Banner, 18 x 30", white silk, metallic gold braid border, wood pole at top, 19th C 75.00
  Dish, 5¾", pink luster, c1840 ...... 65.00
  Podium 20.00
  Quilt, embroidered names, logo, and insignia, feather stitched, dated Jan 24, 1908 .... 295.00
  Ribbon, Michigan, 9/25/93, red and black 25.00
  Shaving Mug, "F. L. T." in green chain links 15.00
  Trivet, 8¼" l, cast iron, insignia and heart in hand in laurel wreath 25.00
  Watch Fob, bronze, 1911 .... 10.00
Knights of Columbus
  Post Card, Knight of Columbus Hut, U S Training Station, Newport, RI, Albertype Co. Brooklyn, NY 3.50
  Shaving Mug, gold trim, black and gold lettering, blue wrapped, red, white, blue, and gold shield 50.00
  Sword, brass, ivory handle, fancy scabbard 125.00
Knights of Pythias
  Ceremonial Sword 30.00
  Watch Fob, bronze, 1906, IN 8.00
Knights of Templar
  Handkerchief, 10" sq, silk, Boston, 1895 .... 15.00
  Letter Opener, 6" l, diecut, white

Travel safety razor, Loyal Order of Moose, chrome case and razor, Ever–Ready, emblem on outside of case, $25.00.

cello, Grand Commandery Of West
Virginia for 1910 conclave in Chi-
cago souvenir 25.00
Shaving Mug, double, black
wrapped, gold trimmed shield and
emblem, T & V Limoges, France . 45.00
Souvenir Book, 1895, 160 pgs, var-
ious adv 30.00
Loyal Order of Moose
Robe, officer, velvet 120.00
Tankard Set, four mugs, 5 pcs 80.00
Watch Fob, multicolored, celluloid
center, 1912 .... 6.50
Masonic
Award, ivory, set 45.00
Book, *Mackey's Revised Encyclope-
dia of Freemasonry*, 1929, 2 vol-
umes, 1,217 pgs, illus 55.00
Bookends, pr, emblem, ornate 11.00
Certificate, engraved, Belfast, Ireland,
c1813 .... 150.00
Cup and Saucer, Concordia Lodge
#67, 1911 .... 36.00
Dish, glass, engraved 28.00
Gavel, wood, hand carved symbols . 40.00
Ice Cream Mold, 5", pewter, emblem 25.00
Medal, hanging from celluloid pin,
Sesqui, 1926 .... 15.00
Mug, enamel, three handles, Syria,
1905 .... 60.00
Paperweight, blown glass, round, em-
blems, flowers 65.00
Pin, stone 25.00
Pitcher, custard glass, Chicago, IL .. 75.00
Plate, 9½", 1903 .... 28.00
Ring, polished black onyx, 10K gold,
1896 .... 75.00
Shot Glass, 3", cut glass, decorated,
captive enclosed bottom section
holding 3 dice, emblem 150.00
Spoon, silver, Toledo 22.00
Stickpin, 32 Degree 8.00
Tape Measure, round, celluloid, fu-
neral home adv, 1917–19 .... 18.50
Tie Bar, Masonic symbol, 10K gold . 25.00
Trivet, cast brass 75.00
Wall Shelf, hand carved, folding ... 25.00
Order of Eastern Star, O. E. S.
Badge, ribbon, NYWF 15.00
Commemorative Plate, Birmingham,
AL, October 1927 .... 20.00
Cup and Saucer, emblem 10.00
Pencil, mechanical 10.00
Pin, 10K, diamond 25.00
Ring, 10K, diamond 25.00
Shrine
Champagne Glass, Syria Shrine, Pitts-
burgh, 1910 .... 50.00
Cuff Links, pr, stones 10.00
Fez Hat, felt 20.00
Lapel Pin, enameled 18.00
Letter Opener, 32nd emblem, c1920 20.00

Plate, 10½", center comic face of
bandaged, beat up Shriner, border
of camel, desert and palms 55.00
Robe, lap, Shriner's Lodge 135.00
Ring, 14K, .20 diamond, W.G. Eagle 300.00
Tie Tack, gold, jeweled 28.00
Tray, bronze, "Lu Lu Patrol of Phila,"
Rochester, NY 1911, Compliments
of J Dawson, figures, emblems,
fancy rim 60.00

FROGS

Collecting Hints: The frog is a popular theme in art work, but often enjoys a secondary rather than a primary position. As with other animal collectibles, the frog collector competes with collectors from other subject areas for the same object.

The frog has lent its name to several items from flower frog to railroad frog switches to the attachment device holding a sword scabbard to a belt. True collectors usually include an example of these in their collection.

History: A frog is a small, tailless animal with bulging eyes and long back legs. The first frogs appeared about 180 million years ago; today there are more than 2,000 species.

Throughout history frogs have been a source of superstition. One myth says frogs fall from the sky during rain.

The frog in character form has appeared in cartoons, on television and in movies. Flip the Frog is one example. The Buster Brown show featured Froggy the Gremlin. Kermit the Frog is the star of the Muppets, both on television and in the movies.

Periodical: *Flower Frog Gazette,* P. O. Box 106, Trumbull, CT 06611.

Collectors' Club: The Frog Pond, P. O. Box 193, Beech Grove, IN 46107.

Advertising trade card, Lancaster Dental Parlors, adv on back, 4¼ x 3¹/₁₆", $6.00.

Advertising Trade Card
  George B Case, Dealer in Fine Family
    Groceries **3.50**
  Lancaster Dental Parlors, 4¼ x 3¹⁄₁₆″ **6.00**
  Semon Ice Cream, 14″ l, diecut, both
    sides printed **25.00**
Ashtray, 4½″, porcelain, sitting, wide
  mouth, Japan **20.00**
Bank, Leap Frog, cast iron **145.00**
Candy Container, 3⅞″ d, frog and chick,
  oval, yellow crepe, cloth animals .. **40.00**
Candy Mold, 5″, tin **25.00**
Cane Handle, 5½″, full dimensional, sil-
  vered white metal, inset glass eyes,
  early 1900s **50.00**
Clicker, 3″, Life of Party Products, Kir-
  chhof, Newark, NJ **6.00**
Cookie Jar, marked "2645 USA" **7.00**
Figure
  Pulling shell with beetle, 2 x 4″ **22.00**
  Reclining frog wearing jacket **15.00**
  Sitting on leaf, 1″, Vienna **25.00**
Flasher, Froggie the Gremlin, television
  shape, "Buster Brown TV Theater"
  marked on bottom **15.00**

Game, Frog Pond, boxed board game, c1895–97, 18 x 10″, $45.00.

Match Safe, 2⅛″, plated metal **125.00**
Mug, 4½″, figural frog inside bottom,
  majolica **120.00**
Paperweight, figural, cast iron **30.00**
Pinback Button, Toledo Council No 10 **2.00**
Planter
  2 x 3 x 3½″, Flip the Frog, chased by
    turkey **32.00**
  3 x 3″, playing instruments near water
    lily **12.00**
Pool Fountain, 9″ h, green and black
  spots, sits on ball, hardware connec-
  tion and spray **160.00**
Stickpin, figural, bronze, wearing suit,
  c1900 .... **20.00**
Toothpick Holder
  Glass, amber, pulling snail shell **40.00**
  Porcelain, singing **24.00**
  Silverplate, pulling shell **55.00**
Toy
  Figure, 5″, Froggy the Gremlin, Sun
    Rubber **30.00**

Stuffed, Froggy, 5″, Steiff **45.00**
Wind–up, cloth over tin, glass eyes,
  Germany **50.00**

FRUIT JARS

Collecting Hints: Old canning jars can be found at flea markets, household sales, and antiques shows. Interest in fruit jars is stable.

Some collectors base their collections on a specific geographical area, others on one manufacturer or one color. Another possible way to collect fruit jars is by patent date. Over 50 different types bear a patent date of 1858. Note: The patent date does not mean the jar was made in that year.

History: An innovative Philadelphia glass maker, Thomas W. Dyott, began promoting his glass canning jars in 1829. John Landis Mason patented the screw type canning jar on November 30, 1858. The progress of the American glass industry and manufacturing processes can be studied through fruit jars. Early handmade jars show bits of local history.

Many ways were devised to close the jars securely. Lids of fruit jars can be a separate collectible, but most collectors feel it is more desirous to have a complete fruit jar. Closures can be as simple as cork or wax seal. Other closures include zinc lids, glass, wire bails, metal screw bands, and today's rubber sealed metal lids.

References: Alice M. Creswick, *The Fruit Jar Works, Volume I* and *Volume 2*, published by author; Alice M. Creswick, *Red Book No. 6: The Collector's Guide To Old Fruit Jars,* published by author, 1990; Dick Roller, *Standard Fruit Jar Reference,* published by author, 1987; Dick Roller, *Supplementary Price Guide to Standard Fruit Jar Reference,* published by author, 1987; Bill Schroeder, *1000 Fruit Jars: Priced And Illustrated,* 5th Edition, Collector Books, 1987.

Periodical: *Fruit Jar Newsletter,* 364 Gregory Avenue, West Orange, NJ 07052.

Note: Fruit Jars listed below are machine made unless otherwise noted.

Amazon Swift Seal, clear, qt, glass lid,
  wire bail **5.00**
Atlas E–Z Seal, cornflower blue, pt ... **10.00**
Ball, Masons' Patent 1858, green, qt .. **5.00**
BBGM Co, green, qt, glass lid, wire bail,
  Patent Nov 30, 1858 .... **35.00**
Bulach, green, qt, glass lid, wire clip . **3.00**
Carrolls True Seal, Star, clear, pint, glass
  lid **9.00**
Clark's Peerless, aqua, qt, glass lid ... **10.00**
Crown Cordial & Extract Co, New York,
  clear ½ pt **10.00**
Dexter, aqua, qt, glass lid, screw band **30.00**

Crown Imperial, qt, aqua, glass insert top, zinc screw band, $15.00.

Eagle, green, qt, handmade, wax seal .	75.00
Electric Fruit Jar, aqua, qt, glass lid, spherical grid shape on front	65.00
Faxon, blue, qt	8.00
Four Seasons Mason, clear, pt, zinc lid, mkd "4 Seasons Mason"	5.00
Garden Queen, qt	4.00
Gem 1908, clear, ½ gal, glass lid, screw band	8.00
Green Mountain Ga Co, green, pt, glass lid, wire bail	15.00
Hazel Atlas E–Z Seal, clear, qt, glass lid	8.00
Ivanhoe, clear, qt, metal lid, name on bottom	4.00
Johnson & Johnson, cobalt blue, qt, glass lid, emb "Johnson & Johnson/New Brunswick, NJ/USA"	40.00
Lamont Glass Co, aqua, pt, glass lid	35.00
Lustre, aqua, qt, name in script in keystone	15.00
Mason's Improved, light green, qt	15.00
Metro Easy–Pak, clear, pt	2.00
Mother Jar, aqua, qt, emb "Mother Jar/Trade Mark/R E Tonque & Bros Inc/Phila Pa"	35.00
PCG Co, aqua, qt, handmade, emb letters on bottom	18.00
Pearl, aqua, qt, handmade, emb "The Pearl"	25.00
Potter & Bodine, Philadelphia, aqua, qt, name emb in script	90.00
Protector, aqua, qt, 6 sided, name emb vertically	40.00
Quick Seal, clear, pt, name in script in oval, "Pat'd July 14 1908" emb below name	3.00
Reverse Ball, aqua, qt	5.00
Royal, aqua, qt, glass lid, emb "Royal of 1876"	80.00
Schram Automatic Sealer, aqua, qt, name emb in script	10.00
Sierra Mason Jar, clear, qt, name emb above "Made in California"	12.00

Smalley's Royal Trademar Nu–Seal, pt	**10.00**
Star Glass Co, aqua, qt, wax seal, emb "The Star Glass Co, Albany, Ind" . . .	**30.00**
Texas Mason, clear, qt	**15.00**
Victory, clear, pt, glass lid, top emb "Victory Reg'd 1925"	**5.00**
Wan–Eta Cocoa, Boston, amber, pt, zinc lid	**6.00**
White Crown Mason, milk glass, aqua, pt	**10.00**

GAMBLING CHIPS, CHECKS, AND TOKENS

Collecting Hints: Almost all the different types of casino "money" used today are collected. In the gaming industry, "checks" refers to chips with a stated value. "Chips" do not have a stated value. Their value is determined at the time of play.

Two other collectible categories are free play and drink tokens. Gaming tokens have been issued in values from 50¢ to $500.

Many collectors display chips, checks, and tokens in albums similar to those used by coin collectors.

History: Gambling chips developed as a substitute for money in the riverboat days of America's frontier. The earliest chips, made from bone or ivory, are quite rare and command high values.

In the early 1880s clay composition materials were used to manufacture chips. Most of the chips of this period do not have values, but can be found with a wide variety of designs. In the early 1920s better technology produced a high quality heat compressed chip with inlaid designs. "Checks" with stated values became popular as gambling became more established. Later club names and addresses were added. Modern chips and checks may include different shaped inlays in the center and color edge spots called "inserts." Molds with designs were impressed into the checks.

Gaming tokens were introduced in 1965 to replace silver dollars for use in slot machines and on table games.

References: *Antique Gambling Chips*, Past Pleasures, 1984; *Harvey's Guide to Collecting Gaming Checks & Chips*, High Sierra Numismatics, 1984.

Collectors' Club: Casino Chips & Gaming Tokens Collector Club, 5410 Banbury Drive, Worthington, OH 43235.

Advisor: Howard Herz.

Chips and Checks

Scrimshawed ivory chip	**35.00**

Left: Scrimshaw ivory gambling chip, $35.00; right: Inlaid clay gambling check, $3.00.

Inlaid clay check	3.00
Inlaid litho plain chip	7.50
Crest & seal check	15.00
Metal inlay check	20.00
Clay molded check	4.00
Coin inlay check	7.50
Plastic molded slug core check	5.00
CHIPCO molded check	3.00
Roulette chip	2.00

Gaming Tokens

1965–1989 $ value	2.00
1967 Sterling $5	12.00
Proofs 1965–1969	15.00

Special strikes, errors, and off metal strikes have higher values.

GAMBLING COLLECTIBLES

Collecting Hints: All the equipment used in the various banking games such as Chuck-A-Luck, Faro, Hazard, Keno, and Roulette are collected today. Cheating devices used by professional sharpers are highly sought.

A well rounded gambling collectibles display also includes old books, prints, postcards, photographs, and articles relating to the field.

History: American history reveals that gambling always has been a popular pastime for the general public, as well as a sure way to make a "quick buck" for the professional *sharper*.

In the late 18th and early 19th centuries, governmental agencies and other entities used lotteries to supplant taxes as a means to raise funds needed to construct schools, libraries, and other civic developments. Many of the state and city lotteries proved to be crooked and fixed, a fact which adds to the collecting appeal. Lottery tickets, broadsides, ads, and brochures are very ornate and display well when mounted and framed.

Most of the gambling paraphernalia was manufactured by "gambling supply houses" that were located throughout the country. They sold their equipment via catalogs. As the majority of the equipment offered was "gaffed," the catalogs never were meant to be viewed by the general public. The catalogs are sought by collectors for their information and are difficult to find.

Perhaps the most significant gambling collectibles are those relating to the American West. Many collectors of saloon and western "cowboy" items seek gambling paraphernalia traceable to the West. Equipment marked with a western manufacturer's name generally will fetch a higher price than a comparable eastern made piece.

References: *Old West Collectibles*, Great American Publishing Co.; Dale Seymour, *Antique Gambling Chips*, Past Pleasures, 1985.

CHEATING DEVICES

Book, *Tricks with Cards Complete Manual of Card Conjuring*, Professor Hoffman, 240 pgs, hardcover, gold lettering, 1st edition, 1889	25.00
Corner Rounder, lever style, solid brass, complete	750.00
Dice, weighted, black with white, always totals 12, set of three	50.00
Holdout	
Franks, Pat Nov 22, 1887	150.00
Wizard, 14", double Roulette type, carved cherry wood upper wheel with six holes, 20" lower wood wheel, controlled underneath, 1870	1,200.00

Chuck A Luck, chrome, bell rings, three wooden dice, 7½" d base, 16¼" h, $225.00.

CHUCK–A–LUCK EQUIPMENT

Dice, ⅝", celluloid, used in cage, set of three	15.00
Dice Cage, nickel plated brass	
11"h, 6" w, two celluloid dice	175.00
18½" h, 13" w, calfskin ends, 16 lbs, Mason & Co, Newark, NJ	400.00

Layout, 30½ x 9½ x ¾", vinyl, black,
yellow painted numbers, pr **75.00**

DICE

Celluloid, 1", red, white spots, round
corners, set of five, MIB **50.00**
Ivory, ⅝", pr **25.00**
Sterling Silver, ½", sq, marked "Sterling
925" **50.00**

**Dice, Card and Novelty Catalog, Hunt &
Company, Chicago, 99 pgs, c1920, 3¾ x
5⅞", $60.00.**

FARO

Cards, sq corners, Samuel Hart & Co,
New York, complete **125.00**
Casekeeper
Geo Mason & Co, Denver, CO, spade
suit, walnut, composition beads,
ace with crossed American flags .. **450.00**
George W Williams, New York, heart
suit, walnut closed box style, ivory
blue and natural colored beads,
cribbage board **425.00**
Chip Rack, 18" l, 10" w, blue–green bil-
liard cloth lined bottom **85.00**
Dealing Box, German silver, straight,
unmarked **250.00**
Layout, felt, walnut trim, George Mason
& Co, 1910 Laurence St, Denver ... **600.00**

HORSE RACE COLLECTIBLES

Bookmaker's Supply Catalog, 19 pgs,
1895, illus **35.00**
Game, Derby Day With Hurdles, Parker
Bros, boxed **12.00**
Score Card, Grand Circuit Meet, Provi-
dence, RI, 1902 .... **15.00**
Stop Watch, 2" d, long chain, Meylan **75.00**
Trade Stimulator, 3 x 10 x 8½", wood
and metal case, glass top, two
through twelve horses around out-

side, silver and black scenes, side lever spin dice **350.00**

KENO EQUIPMENT

Cards, 136, wood, covered material and
paper, H C Evans & Co, Chicago,
Keno Cards **250.00**
Hopper, walnut, blue–green billiard
cloth lined bowl, plated metal mouth,
acorn finial, three carved feet **600.00**

MISCELLANEOUS

Bingo, Cage, 9" h, metal, red celluloid
handle, eleven wood balls, 9 cards,
1941 copyright **15.00**
Book
Card Games and How to Play Them,
123 pgs, soft cov, 1900 copyright **25.00**
Gambler's Don't Gamble, Michael
MacDougall & JC Furnas, 167 pgs,
illus, 1939 .... **30.00**
Bottle, figural, slot machine shape
8 x 5", Liberty Bell, gray, 24 karat gold
dec, Ezra Brooks **25.00**
9 x 9", Barney's, red **15.00**
Card Press, 9½ x 4½ x 3", dovetailed,
holds ten decks, handle **175.00**
Catalog
H C Evans & Co, Secret Blue Book,
Gambling Supply, 1936, 72 pgs .. **75.00**
K C Card Co, Blue Book No 520
Gambling Equipment, 68 pgs **50.00**
Chromolithograph, 16 x 24", men play-
ing poker in hunting lodge, titled
"Respecters of Limits," framed, sgd
"William Eaton" **125.00**
Card Counter, plated, imitation ivory
face, black lettering **20.00**
Gambling Dirk, 9" l, mother–of–pearl,
marked "Pookes Clarke" **125.00**
Shot Glass, ribbed dec, porcelain dice
in bottom **15.00**
Sign, 11 x 30", Carlisle Whiskey adv,
titled "A Bold Bluff," dogs gambling,
silver and black background, orig
frame impressed "Carlisle Rye" **75.00**
Tintype, 2¼ x 4", two men playing cards **15.00**
Tray, 11" d, tin, red, black, and white,
martini center, card border **65.00**

POKER

Arcade Game, 10 x 15 x 6", 1¢ draw,
five play, counter top type, wood and
metal case, orig graphics, c1930 ... **400.00**
Book, The Game of Draw Poker, John
Keller, NY, 84 pgs, 1887, 4½ x 4¼" **25.00**
Chip Set
Bone, 37 rect and 39 round, geomet-
ric design, wood box **150.00**

Composition, set of 24, emb horse and jockey pattern, red, white, and blue, double sided **50.00**
Chip Holder, bakelite, pink and black, Art Deco, pressed red, white, and blue composition chips, holds four sets of 50 chips, card rack **75.00**
Chip Rack, 11½ x 4" h, revolving, wood, German silver handle, holds 400 chips and four decks of cards . .   **50.00**
Lighter, 2", poker dice set shape, marked "Old Crow The Greatest Name in Bourbon" **45.00**

ROULETTE

Ball, set of three, one metal, two composition **20.00**
Chip Rack, walnut, holds 1,500 chips   **125.00**
Game, Spear's Co, lithographed **15.00**
Layout, 40 x 19", hp, oilcloth, black and red betting areas, wood trim **150.00**
Tray, 13" d, metal, roulette wheel rim .   **45.00**
Wheel, 8" d, wood and metal, single and double zero decal, four prong spinner, cloth layout, makers stamp on bottom **50.00**

WHEEL OF FORTUNE

9½" d, table top style, yellow, black, and red numbers and designs, 12" h, black wood stand **65.00**
20", 30 numbers, cutout painted center, yellow and white, red ground, unmarked **175.00**
60", complete wheel, glass faced "Dice," mounting hardware, G Mason, Chicago **1,250.00**

GAMES

Collecting Hints: Make certain a game has all its parts. The box lid or instruction booklet usually contains a full list of all pieces. Collectors tend to specialize by theme, e.g., western, science fiction, Disney, etc. Most television games fall into the ten–five dollar range, offering the beginning collector a chance to acquire a large number of games without a big capital outlay.

Don't stack game boxes more than five deep or mix sizes. Place a piece of acid free paper between each game to prevent bleeding from inks and to minimize wear. Keep the games stored in a dry location. Extreme dryness and extreme moisture are both undesirable.

History: A board game dating from 4,000 B.C. was discovered in ruins in Upper Egypt. Board games were used throughout recorded history,

but reached popularity during the Victorian era. Most board games combine skill (from chess), luck and ability (from cards), and pure chance (from dice). By 1900 Milton Bradley, Parker Brothers, C. H. Joslin and McLoughlin were the leading manufacturers.

Monopoly was invented in 1933 and first issued by Parker Brothers in 1935. Before the advent of television, the board game was a staple in evening entertainment. Many board games from the 1930s and 1940s focused on radio personalities, e.g., Fibber McGee or The Quiz Kids.

In the late 1940s television became popular. The game industry responded. The golden age of the TV board game was from 1955 to 1968. The movies, e.g., James Bond, also led to the creation of games, but never to the extent of the television programs.

References: Avedon and Sutton–Smith, *The Study of Games*, Wiley & Son, 1971; Lee Dennis, *Warman's Antique American Games, 1840–1940, Second Edition,*, Wallace–Homestead, 1991; Walter Gibson, *Family Games America Plays*, Doubleday & Co., 1970; Jefferson Graham, *Come on Down!!!*, The TV Game Show Book, Abbeville Press, 1988; Harry L. Rinker, *Collector's Guide to Toys, Games, and Puzzles*, Wallace-Homestead, 1991.

Collectors' Club: American Game Collectors Association, 4628 Barlow Drive, Bartlesville, OK 74006.

Periodical: *Name of the Game*, P.O. Box 721, Plainville, CT 06062.

Advisor: Bob Cereghino.

Note: Prices are for games that are complete and whose boxes are in very good or better condition.

Allison
    1961, Car 54 . . . .   **100.00**
American Publishing Corp.
    1977, Gong Show **5.00**

I Dream of Jeannie, Milton Bradley, 1965, $30.00.

Athletic Products Co, Inc.
1950s, Today With Dave Garroway ... **45.00**
Frederick H. Beach
1941, Take It And Double, 2nd series ... **10.00**
Betty-B
1955, Break The Bank, 1st ed **10.00**
1956, Robin Hood **35.00**
Bilt-Rite
1956, Wild Bill Hickok **40.00**
Milton Bradley
1930s, Prisoner of Zenda **15.00**
1941–45, Bataan: The Battle Of The
Philippines **25.00**
1941–45, Bizertie Gertie **20.00**
1944, Ella Cinders, 4483 .... **35.00**
1944, Nancy and Sluggo, 4484 .... **35.00**
1946, Li'l Abner: His Game, 4166 . **22.50**
1950
Captain Video **75.00**
Hopalong Cassidy **40.00**
Howdy Doody's T.V. Game **50.00**
1955, Annie Oakley **20.00**
1955, Winchell & Mahoney Chug-
gedy Chug Game **30.00**
1956, Sgt. Preston **15.00**
1957, Name That Tune **10.00**
1958, Alfred Hitchcock Presents
Why? **10.00**
1958, Cheyenne **25.00**
1959, Rifleman **65.00**
1959, Tales of Wells Fargo **40.00**
1960, Deputy **25.00**
1960, Men Into Space **65.00**
1960, Video Village **20.00**
1960, Wagon Train **20.00**
1961, Margie **12.00**
1961, Soupy Sales Go Go Go **30.00**
1963, Patty Duke **25.00**
1964, Outer Limits **150.00**
1964, Voyage To The Bottom Of The
Sea **20.00**
1965, Eye Guess **8.00**
1965, I Dream of Jeannie **30.00**
1965, Lost In Space **75.00**
1965, PDQ **8.00**
1966, Batman **50.00**
1966, Branded **20.00**
1966, Goldfinger **20.00**
1966, Green Hornet **125.00**
1966, Ipcress File, movie **10.00**
1966, James Bond **20.00**
1967, Captain America **15.00**
1967, Personality **8.00**
1968, Barnabas Collins (with fangs) . **20.00**
1968, Flying Nun **35.00**
1968, Twiggy **20.00**
1969, Official Baseball Game **40.00**
1971, Partridge Family **10.00**
1974, Apple's Way **15.00**
1974, Emergency **1.00**
1974, Planet Of The Apes **5.00**
1974, Walton's **5.00**

1975, Baretta **5.00**
1975, Space 1999 .... **15.00**
1975, SWAT **1.00**
1977, Charlie's Angels **5.00**
1977, Family Feud, 1st ed **1.00**
1977, Starsky & Hutch **5.00**
1982, Fall Guy **1.00**
Miscellaneous
Candy Land **1.00**
Chutes and Ladders **1.00**
Easy Money **1.00**
Game Of The States **1.00**
Go To The Head Of The Class ... **1.00**
Intrique **15.00**
Park and Shop **3.00**
Pirate And Traveler **15.00**
Rack-O **1.00**
Treasure Hunt **3.00**
Uncle Wiggly **2.00**
Cardinal
1982, General Hospital **1.00**
Club Aluminum Products Company
1942, Whirling Words, wood version **30.00**
Corey Game Company
1941, You're Out, baseball game ... **20.00**
Embossing Company
1940s, Jack-Be-Nimble **8.00**
Ewing
1955, Davy Crockett **35.00**
Gardner
1956, You'll Never Get Rich (Sgt.
Bilko) **65.00**
1958, Boots and Saddles **50.00**
Gem
1965, Bewitched **40.00**
1965, Gilligan's Island **100.00**
H-G
1956, Circus Boy **50.00**
Hasbro
1959, Leave It To Beaver, three varieties, each **55.00**
1965, Munsters, three varieties, each **150.00**
1968, Dating Game, 1st ed **7.00**
1968, Laugh In **25.00**
Highlander
1955, George Goebel **20.00**
Ideal
1961, Rebel **40.00**
1962, Dr. Kildare **20.00**
1963, Combat **40.00**
1963, Godzilla **250.00**
1963, King Kong **250.00**
1963, Nurses **30.00**
1963, PT 109 .... **12.00**
1964, Addams Family **100.00**
1964, Fugitive **100.00**
1964, Twilight Zone **200.00**
1965, F Troop **60.00**
1965, Get Smart **50.00**
1965, I Spy **35.00**
1965, Man From UNCLE **20.00**
1965, 12 O'Clock High **20.00**

1966, Mission Impossible 60.00
1966, T.H.E. Cat 35.00
1966, Time Tunnel 75.00
1967, Star Trek 125.00
1975, Welcome Back Kotter 2.00
1978, Fantasy Island 3.00
1981, Dukes Of Hazzard 1.00
Leister Game Company
1945, Autographs 15.00
Lido Toy Company
1950s, Air Race Around The World . 8.00
E. S. Lowe Co., Inc.
1940s, Fox Hunt 12.50
Samuel Lowe Company
1941, Airplane Speedway Game, No.
581-11 .... 25.00
1941, Cross Country, No. 581-12,
railroad train 20.00
Lowell
1954, Beat The Clock, 1st ed 10.00
1956, I've Got A Secret 12.00
1956, $64,000 Question 15.00
1956, This Is Your Life 20.00
1958, Bat Masterson 40.00
1958, Concentration, 1st ed 10.00
1958, Gunsmoke 75.00
1959, Steve Canyon 30.00
1959, Laramie 50.00
1959, 3 Stooges 350.00
1959, Rawhide 60.00
1959, Surfside Six 60.00
1960, Peter Gunn 60.00
1960, 77 Sunset Strip 40.00
1960, Wanted: Dead Or Alive 150.00
1961, Charge Account 7.00
1961, Sea Hunt 55.00
1962, College Bowl 15.00
1963, Candid Camera 15.00
1963, Hawaiian Eye 30.00

Mattel
1963, Word For Word 6.00
1967, Gentle Ben 10.00
Memphis Plastic Enterprises, Inc.
1955, Baseball Game 30.00

Parker Brothers
1940s, Camelot 6.00
1949–50, Clue, detective game 15.00
1959, Have Gun Will Travel 40.00
1961, Number Please 9.00
1962, Mr. Ed 35.00
1966, As the World Turns 15.00
1968, Thunderbirds 60.00
1968, Under Sea World Of Jacques
Cousteau 10.00
1969, The Blondie Game 7.00
1969, Goodbye Mr. Chips, movie .. 10.00
1970, Tiny Tim 20.00
1975, Happy Days 3.00
1977, Barney Miller 3.00
1977, Laverne & Shirley 3.00
1983, Wicket The Ewok 7.00

Miscellaneous (modern production)
Children's Hour 1.00
Dig 1.00
Monopoly
Pre-1940 .... 35.00
Modern 1.00
Pit 1.00
Pollyana 5.00
Rich Uncle 1.00
Rook 1.00
Sorry 1.00
Touring 1.00
Walt Disney's Uncle Remus Game 40.00
Play Rite
1960, Johnny Unitas 50.00
Pressman
1954, Groucho TV Quiz Game 75.00
Reiss
1977, Mary Hartmann 15.00
Remco
1965, Shindig 20.00
1968, Family Affair 40.00
1968, Mod Squad 75.00
1968, That Girl 50.00
Rosebud Art Company
1940s, Jungle Hunt 20.00
Selchow & righter
1940s, Snake Eyes, black theme 25.00
1948, Huggin' The Rail 30.00
1953, The Game of Assembly Line,
No. 61 .... 20.00
1961, Straightaway 20.00
Miscellaneous (modern production)
Meet The Presidents 2.00
Mr. Ree 10.00
Parcheesi 1.00
Scrabble 2.00
Standard Toycraft
1960, Dennis The Menace 35.00
1963, Beverly Hillbillies 25.00
1963, Petticoat Junction 40.00
1964, Dick Van Dyke 50.00
1966, Gidget 30.00
Teenage Publishing Company
1957, Elvis Presley Game Of Love .. 600.00
Transogram
1955, Captain Gallant 25.00
1955, Dragnet 15.00
1955, Rin Tin-Tin 30.00
1956, Jackie Gleason, Away We Go 75.00
1957, Buccaneers 30.00
1957, Tic Tac Dough, 1st ed 10.00
1958, Gray Ghost 50.00
1958, Life And Legend of Wyatt Earp 50.00
1959, Perry Mason 25.00
1960, Its A Mad, Mad, Mad World,
Mad Magazine 10.00
1960, Johnny Ringo 40.00
1960, Philip Marlow 25.00
1961, Aquanauts 20.00
1961, Ben Casey 15.00
1961, Detectives 20.00

1961, Untouchables	50.00
1962, Game Of The Kennedys	10.00
1962, Lucy Show	25.00
1962, Route 66	75.00
1962, Virginian	45.00
1963, Burke's Law	25.00
1963, Mr. Novak	20.00
1966, Hogan's Heroes	50.00
1967, Gomer Pyle	30.00
1967, Monkees	125.00
1975, M.A.S.H.	15.00

Unknown Manufacturers

1962, Chet Huntley NBC News	20.00
1970, Spiro Agnew's American History Challenge Game	10.00
1973, Watergate Caper	10.00

Dexter Wayne

1953, Ramar Of The Jungle	25.00

Whiting

1954, Pinky Lee Runaway Frankfurters	25.00
1955, Lassie	20.00
1956, Lone Ranger	60.00

Whitman Publishing Company

1958, Zorro	25.00
1968, Dark Shadows	30.00
1981, Clash Of The Titans	7.00

GASOLINE COLLECTIBLES

Collecting Hints: There still is plenty of material in the storage area of old garages; try to find a cooperative owner. If your budget is modest, concentrate on paper ephemera, such as maps. Regionally related items will bring slightly more in their area of origin.

History: The selling of gasoline has come full circle. The general store, livery stable, and blacksmith were the first people to sell gasoline. Today the mini-market is a viable factor in gasoline sales. The gas crisis of 1973 brought the circle to a close. The gas station, whose golden era was from the 1930s to the 1960s, is beginning to disappear. The loss of the independently owned station is doubly felt because it also was the center of automobile repair.

The abolition of credit cards by ARCO marked another shift. Reduction in price for paying cash is a new marketing device. Elimination of free maps, promotional trinkets, and other advertising material already is a fact. As more and more stores in shopping centers sell oil, parts, and other related automobile products, it is doubtful whether the gasoline station will ever recover its past position.

Collectors' Clubs: Automobile License Plate Collectors Association, Box 712, Weston, WV 26452; International Petroliana Collectors Association, 2151 East Dublin–Granville Road, Suite G292, Columbus, OH 43229.

References: Scott Anderson, *Check The Oil*, Wallace-Homestead, 1986.

Periodical: *Hemmings Motor News*, Box 100, Bennington, VT 05201.

REPRODUCTION ALERT: Small advertising signs and pump globes have been extensively reproduced.

Globe, People's Choice Supply Co, 16″ d, $165.00.

Anti–Freeze Can, Standard Super, 1 gallon	15.00
Axle Grease, Texaco #5, Regal	18.00
Badge, Amoco Gasoline, Border Patrol	15.00

Bank

Phillips 66 Motor Oil, tin, 3½″	15.00
Texaco #6, MIB	45.00
Blotter, Red Crown Gasoline, 1930s	28.00

Button, pinback

Goodyear, 2½″ matte celluloid button, bright yellow, blue and white design, working thermometer, maintenance record type, c1930	20.00
Texaco, 1¼″ d, celluloid, red and green star, black letters, white ground, c1930	25.00
Tydol Gasoline, 1″ oval, red, black, and white, winged logo, bright gold celluloid ground, c1920	17.50
Calendar, White Rose Gasoline, 1933	10.00
Checkerboard Set, Standard Oil Co, adv	75.00
Clock, Cooper Cordless Tires, neon, 18″ w, orange, royal blue, and white	475.00
Crate, Conoco Aviation Gasoline, wood, paper label	125.00

Display

Autolite, case, glass front, for spark plugs	125.00
Fram Oil Filters, wall mounted	80.00
Sinclair Opaline Oil, round and flat, 1920	85.00
Vedoll Oil Guide, wall mounted, 1942–50	50.00

Gas Globe
Standard Gold Crown 235.00
Vickers, plastic 165.00
Gas Pump, glass globe, metal case
Mobil Gas 250.00
Sinclair Power X, Super Fuel 350.00
Gas Pump Sign
E–Z Serve 65.00
Good Gulf 35.00
Gulf Kerosene 58.00
Gulf No–Nox 35.00
Mobil Gas, Pegasus shield 125.00
Pure Pep 60.00
Royal 60.00
Standard Oil, crown, glass globe, one
piece, good paint 200.00
Texaco Fire Chief 55.00
Texaco Supreme 55.00
Lapel Stud, Fisk Tire, ⅝" d, emb silvered
brass, raised trademark, c1915 . . . . . 20.00
Oil Can
PA Mobilene, motor oil, 5 gallon, pat-
ent 1925 . . . . 85.00
Queen, tin, glass insert, patent 12/11/
18 . . . . 45.00
Texaco, 1927, orig spout 35.00
Padlock, gas pump, Milwaukee Tank
Works, brass 35.00
Salt and Pepper Shakers, pr, Phillips, fi-
gural gas pumps 30.00
Service Award Pin, Phillips 66, 10K
gold, 15 years, c1932 . . . . 20.00
Sign
Dodge Brothers Service Station, por-
celain, c1930, 15 x 45" 125.00
Firestone, cream, blue, and orange,
48 x 16" 65.00
Mobil Oil, projecting, gargoyle dec . 95.00
Penzoil, "Sound Your Z" oval, 32 x
22" 110.00
Standard Oil, red crown with torch . 95.00
Thermometer
Kendall Oil, round 25.00
Standard Oil, 3" x 12", tin 25.00
Tin
Duplex Outboard Motor Oil, boat . . 85.00
Shell Outboard Motor Oil, boat 35.00

GEISHA GIRL PORCELAIN

Collecting Hints Check for enamel and gold wear as well as porcelain flakes, hairlines, etc. Buy only items in good to mint condition. Become familiar with the type of items produced so you are not fooled by a "pitcher" that actually is a lidless cocoa pot, or a lidless sugar bowl which may appear to be a planter.

Check the designs on all items within a set. Be aware that a "set" contains items complementary

in size and with the same pattern executed in the same manner on all pieces. Value depends upon condition, quality, pattern, border color, and type of piece. Teapots, cups and saucers, and red bordered items are the most common.

History: Geisha Girl porcelain is a Japanese export ware whose production commenced during the last quarter of the 19th century and continued heavily until WW II. Limited quantities were produced after WW II and are called "modern" Geisha ware.

Geisha Girl porcelain features over 150 different patterns focusing on the flora and fauna, both real and mythical, and people of pre–modern Japan. The name is derived from the fact that all the wares contain lovely kimono–clad Japanese ladies as part of the pattern. It was manufactured and decorated by over 100 different establishments.

Colors and design methods vary greatly. The most common examples bear a red–orange stencil design over which artists hand painted enamels. Other examples have a different color stencil, may be wholly hand painted, or decaled. In the majority of instances, items bear a border color of red, light green, pine green, cobalt blue, greenish blue, turquoise, brown, black, or a lovely combination of several colors. Borders themselves are often further embellished with lacing, flowers, diapering, dots, or stripings of gold or contrastively colored enamels.

Although Geisha Girl was produced in an Oriental pattern, it was meant for export to the Western market. Therefore, most shapes represent those used in the West during the early days of the twentieth century. These forms include tea items, cocoa sets, luncheon sets, dresser sets, (powder jars, hair receivers, ring trees, etc.), and vases. Examples of items in children's and doll house size also exist.

Maker marks found on Geisha Girl porcelain include many of the famous Nippon trademarks, Japanese signatures (including Kutani), and post–Nippon indicators.

Reference: Elyce Litts, *The Collector's Encyclopedia of Geisha Girl Porcelain,* Collector Books, 1988.

REPRODUCTION ALERT: "Modern" Geisha ware was sold in Oriental import shops until the early 1980s. Reproduced forms, all having a red border, include bail handled tea sets, five piece dresser sets, sake sets, toothbrush holders, and ginger jars. Also produced was a children's set of demitasse cups, each having a different border color.

The chief characteristics of reproduction are very white porcelain, minimal background washes, sparse detail coloring, and no gold or occasionally very bright gold enameling. Old gold should show tarnish.

Also watch for Czechoslovakian reproductions made in the 1920s. Some will be marked with the country of origin, but others bear only a faux—Oriental mark. Generally these items are decaled or very simply hand painted. Faces of the geisha will be distinctively different than those on Japanese Geisha ware.

Toothpick holder, Parasol Modern, made in Japan, 2" h, $10.00.

BAMBOO TREE

Dark green bamboo trees are used to embellish a Processional type pattern. Borders are dark green with yellow or white enamel lines.

Cup and Saucer, tea, Torii, Made in Japan	7.00
Plate	
6"	5.00
7", chrysanthemum shape	12.00
Teapot, Japan	10.00
Tea Set, cov pot, creamer, sugar, six cups and saucers, lemon plate, 16 pcs, Japan	100.00

BAMBOO TRELLIS

Three ladies standing and kneeling at water's edge; behind them is a large trellis made of bamboo and overgrown with peonies.

Bowl, 7½", light apple green, gold, ftd	35.00
Cocoa Set, pot, six cups and saucers, fluted, cobalt blue, lattice work backdrop, reserve pattern, 13 pcs, Kutani and C O N Nippon	225.00
Mug, 4", red, gold buds, Japan	18.00
Mustard Pot, blue, scalloped	25.00
Plate, 6½", blue—green, gold buds, sparse decoration	8.00
Vase, 8½", basket, green handle, brown footrim	75.00

BIRD CAGE

Lady and child are featured in a garden. The lady holds a small bird cage.

Cup and Saucer, tea, red—orange, floral frame int	12.00
Plate, 6", red—orange, gold	8.00
Roll Tray, red—orange, gold lines and curves, sgd Yana Giku	35.00
Tete—a—tete, pot, two cups and saucers, red—orange, floral frame int	38.00

IKEBANA IN RICKSHAW

Flower arranger wearing floral headdress is kneeling in presentation of a large ikebana (flower arrangement) in a basket perched atop a rickshaw.

Bowl	
7½", three ftd, six lobed, scalloped edge, cobalt blue, gold	30.00
8", yellow, ftd	40.00
Lunch Set, teapot, sugar, creamer, six cups and saucers, six scalloped cake plates, six scalloped table plates, cobalt blue, gold, 27 pcs	250.00
Plate, 7¼", cobalt blue, gold, swirl fluted scalloped edge	18.00
Salt and Pepper Shaker, grass green, pr	15.00
Teapot, cobalt blue, gold	35.00

LONG—STEMMED PEONY

The title is a takeoff of the "long—stemmed rose," but aptly describes the unique feature of this pattern. A young boy carries the flower and is accompanied on his walk by two ladies, one with a parasol.

Creamer	
Bulbous, raised footrim, orange and gold	14.00
Slender, fluted, blue and gold, Made in Japan	9.00
Eggcup, orange	5.00
Hair Receiver, large, wavy, red—orange, lid and side pattern, Japan	30.00
Hatpin Holder, hourglass shape, ribbed, cobalt blue and gold, Made in Japan	35.00
Mustard Jar, red	15.00

PORCH

Japanese dwellings were traditionally situated on stilts with walls of sliding doors which, when slid open during the day, created a porch overlooking the gardens. A number of women are depicted against such a backdrop in a scene known to date from the Nippon but also found on modern productions.

Berry Set, master, five individuals, scalloped edge, red and gold, 6 pcs **35.00**
Celery Set, small rect master, five salts, red–orange and gold, 5 pcs, Torii Nippon **35.00**
Creamer
    Cobalt blue and gold, Torii Nippon . **20.00**
    Red–orange, modern **5.00**
Cup and Saucer
    After dinner, dark green, Made in Japan **10.00**
    Tea
      Cobalt blue, two streams of gold lacing, gold stripe handle, scalloped, 't't' mark **14.00**
      Red–orange, modern **8.00**
Dresser Set, rect tray, powder jar, hair receiver, red, modern, 3 pcs **25.00**
Nut Bowl, master, cobalt blue, Torii Nippon **25.00**

GLASS COLLECTIBLES, MODERN

Collecting Hints: For the past several years, modern glass collectibles have been a source of speculation among collectors. Some new glass now is selling below initial retail as overstocked dealers are trying to unload. All this actually has resulted in a stabilization of prices. Prices now are constant from dealer to dealer as can be seen in the advertising of *Glass Review*, a magazine for collectors of both old and new glass.

The first issue in a series often brings the highest price. Collectors are urged to concentrate on assembling full sets of one figure. Focusing on a single color is difficult because of the large variances in color and different companies' interpretation of the same color.

Several series have been left off the price list since the companies did not press their promised amount. They stopped midway or just barely into the series. This practice, while cost effective, is deceptive to the collector.

History: The popularity of limited edition plates, the success of Degenhart Crystal Art Glass and a renewed interest in old glass forms in the 1960s and 1970s led several companies to produce modern glass collectibles. Leading firms include Boyd's Crystal Art Glass Company, Fenton, Vi Hunter, Mosser, Pisello Art Glass, and Summit Art Glass Company.

The modern glass collectible is organized into four categories—limited edition series, limited edition single items, collectible company colors, and series.

The limited edition series usually has between 12 and 18 colors issued of a single pattern. The new colors appear monthly or bimonthly. The form generally is new.

The limited edition single item, often utilizing an early mold from an existing company, is issued in a color not previously used and in limited numbers from 100 to 1,000.

Collectible company colors are open stock. However, many smaller companies may make a limited amount of a color, e.g., shadings and slags. Once the color is used, it is not prepared again. Hence, some of these figurines have become collectible.

The recent closing of several glass factories, e.g., Imperial, Seneca, Tiffin, and Westmoreland, has resulted in the sale of their molds and a new collectible category within modern glass collectibles: reissues.

In the 1950s the Imperial Glass Company acquired over 10,000 molds when the Heisey and Cambridge glass factories closed. They used very few of these molds in production over the next thirty years. When Imperial Glass Company closed in early 1985, these molds, as well as their own, were sold. The Heisey Collectors of America, Inc., purchased 4,000 original Heisey molds, all except for sixty Old Williamsburg patterns. The Cambridge and Imperial molds were scattered to Michigan, Ohio, Pennsylvania, Texas, West Virginia, and Germany.

In late 1984 the Westmoreland Glass Company started selling their 20,000 molds, many from the mid-1880s. Collectors are concerned about repressings. *The Glass Review* issues a monthly update of who is acquiring the molds and what reissues are being made.

The big trend is miniatures. Several glass producers are offering miniature versions of their larger items or beginning a new item in miniature size.

Periodical: *Glass Review,* P. O. Box 7188, Redlands, CA 92373.

LIMITED EDITION SERIES

Items produced in limited amounts in a series. Usually not more than 1,000 per color for 12 to 16 variations. To distinguish between each collectible figurine a name is given each color. In some instances a name actually is molded into each figurine and changed each time the new color is issued.

Edna Barnes
    5", orange juice reamer. Made at Mosser from original Imperial Glass mold. A 2½" miniature version of the same in a series of 12. Each marked with Barnes logo: "B".
    Custard
      2½" **5.75**
      5" **9.25**
    Green Carnival
      2½" **6.50**

5" 10.00
Harvest Swirl
2½" 5.75
5" 9.25
Guernsey Glass
Rocky, rocking horse. A reproduction
of a 1915 Cambridge candy con-
tainer, 4¼" l, 3" h, 12 issues. Each
marked "B" in a triangle.
Carousel Slag 12.00
Holly Berry 10.00
Blue Boy 12.00
Hi–O–Silver 12.00
Rocky Jr, 2⅛" miniature of the above
Purple Carnival 6.00
Bob Henry
Bimbah, solid elephant, 4 x 4". Issued
July 1980 in Autumn Amber color,
24 issues. Molds now retired and
on display at the Historical Mu-
seum, Ft Wayne, IN. Approxi-
mately 1,000 of each color was
made, each signed "R. H." in a
cloverleaf and dated.
Autumn Amber 35.00
Petunia 50.00
Petunia, carnival 65.00
Lilac 18.00
Snowy Pine 18.00
Vi Hunter
Jenny, 4¼", doll, 12 per year plus
bell. First issued January 1979, in
Cornflower Blue Slag. Beginning in
1983 only 4 per year will be issued
as a series and marked "1983." All
dolls in 1979, 1980, 1981, and
1982, are marked with an "H."
Also beginning in 1983 these dolls
will be marketed in an open edition
and not a part of the limited edition
series; they will be marked "Open
Edition."
1979, set of 12, plus bell 500.00
1980, set of 12, plus bell 200.00
1981, set of 12 .... 150.00
Jenny Bell. Each Christmas a bell is
issued.
1979, No. 1, Cobalt Carnival 30.00
1980, No. 2, Pearl Carnival 25.00
1981, No. 3, Samurai Red 20.00
1982, No. 4, Mistletoe Slag 18.00
Josh, 4½", boy doll. Pairs with Jenny.
Introduced 1981 in colors to match
Jenny.
First issue 18.00
1981, set of 12, plus bell 400.00
1982, set of 12, plus bell 300.00
Mirror Images
Venus Rising, 6½", Cambridge mold
of a lady flower frog (reworked for
solid base). Series of 12, each color
available solid or frosted, each

marked "IG–81." First issued in
Midnight Magic in early 1981.
Midnight Magic 42.00
Pink Pixie 24.00
Sunmaid Frosted 24.00
Irish Lass 24.00
Empress Jade 24.00
Mosser. This company has produced
three limited edition clown figurines.
The third clown was released in 1983.
Other collectible color items from this
company listed under the "Collectible
Company Colors."
Balloon Clown, 3½", sitting, holding
balloons, 16 issues. Each individu-
ally named on back of clown. In-
troduced January 1981, with Arty.
Note that the names begin with the
first letter of the alphabet and con-
tinue through the letter O. A special
"dealer clown" with handpainted
balloons was made and sent to se-
lected dealers prior to the series
start. These are highly sought after.
Dealer Clown 225.00
Arty 100.00
Bags 20.00
Cleo 20.00
Daisy 20.00
Eros 20.00
Flip 10.00
Gabby–Maxi 10.00
McGoo 10.00
Niki 10.00
Orie 10.00
Set of 16 .... 300.00
Barrel Clown, 3½", sitting on a barrel.
Issued January 1982 with "Poko,"
12 issues in a continuation of the
alphabet P through Z, the last one
marked "The End."
Poko 12.00
Quinn 10.00
Rufus 10.00
Pee Gee Glass
Mouse Lovers, 3", boy and girl
mouse, 12 issues, "PG" logo.
Mellow Yellow 12.00
True Blue 11.00
Purple Passion 11.00
White Delight 11.00
Tickled Pink 11.00
Wild Cherry 11.00
Pisello Art Glass
Flipper, 3½ x 2½", miniature, cov-
ered dolphin. Based on Greentown
dolphin. Introduced late 1982.
Chocolate 12.00
Marigold Carnival 12.00
Vaseline Canary 12.00
Red Carnival 14.00

Summit Art Glass Company
  Melanie, 5¼", doll. Copied from Cambridge figurine, two 12 doll series plus a Mother's Day bell. First issued August 1980, in "Tom's Surprise." Mold destroyed June 10, 1983, after 24 dolls and 2 bells were pressed.

Green Swirl	15.00
Autumn Glow	15.00
Dream Spinners	15.00
Canyon Whisper	15.00
Set of 24 dolls, plus 2 bells	300.00

  Oscar, 4½" l, 2½" h, sitting lion. First issued June 1981, in Seastorm Rainbow. Mold will be destroyed after 12 issues.

Snowsparkle	12.00
Harvest Gold	12.00
Paradise Orchid	12.00
Golden Goddess	12.00

  Clown Elephant, 4¾", elephant figurine. Reproduction of Cambridge candy container. 12 issues, each with a name on the back. Introduced December 1982, in Jimmy.

Jimmy, Ringling Red	16.00
Tommy, Calliope	16.00
Billy, Emmett's Favorite	16.00

COLLECTIBLE COMPANY COLORS

Large glass companies have many molds and the amount of glass made is not limited. Smaller companies don't actually limit the amount of glass run, but certain items become "limited" because a given color will not be repeated.

Boyd's Crystal Art Glass Company. Trademark on all items "B" in a diamond.
  Debbie Duck, introduced July 21, 1981

Mardi Gras	6.00
Furr Green	6.00
Cobalt	6.00
Snow	5.00
English Yew	5.00

  Ducklings, introduced Sept 15, 1981

Mardi Gras	3.00
Furr Green	3.00
Crown Tuscan	2.50
Golden Delight	2.50
Light Rose	2.50

  Joey, leaping pony, introduced March 1980

Lavender	12.00
Chocolate	30.00
Persimmon	25.00
Candy Swirl	15.00
Zack Slag	12.00

Furr Green	10.00
Sandpiper	8.00

  Louise, doll, introduced Sept 1979

Lemon Ice	100.00
Ice Blue	25.00
Apricot	20.00
Firefly	15.00
Flame	15.00
English Yew	12.00
Golden Delight	10.00

  Skippy, sitting dog

Crown Tuscan	10.00
Golden Delight	8.00
Pippin Green	7.50
Light Rose	8.00

Mosser Glass Company. Trademark is the letter "M".
  Bear, solid, sitting

Autumn Amber	40.00
Chablis	30.00
Violet D'Orr	24.00
Tawny	10.00

  Cat, 3", sitting

Heirloom Pink	6.00
Flame	6.00
Chocolate	6.00
Cloud 9	6.00

GOLF COLLECTIBLES

Collecting Hints: Condition is very important as collectors grow in sophistication and knowledge. The more modern the item, the better the condition should be.

It is extremely rare to find a club or ball made before 1800, and any equipment made before 1850 is scarce. There were few books, with a couple of very rare exceptions, published before 1857. Few pieces of equipment made after 1895 are rare.

Some items, such as scorecards, ball markers, golf pencils, and bag tags are so common that their value is negligible.

Most American clubs and other items manufactured after 1895 are rather common. Some modern equipment, 1950–65, is in demand, but primarily for actual play rather than collection or display.

The very old material is found in Scotland and England, unless brought to this country early in this century. Christie's, Sotheby's, and Phillips' hold several major auctions of golf collectibles each year in London, Edinburgh, and Chester. Golf collectible sales often coincide with the British Open Championship each July. The English market is more established, but the American market is growing rapidly. Auctions of golf items and memorabilia now are held in the United States.

The prices of golf clubs escalated tremendously in the 1970s, but have stabilized in more recent years. The prices of golf books, which for many years remained static, have risen dramatically in the 1980s. Art prints, drawings, etchings, etc. have remained static, but pottery, china, glass, and other secondary items, especially Royal Doulton, have attracted premium prices.

History: Golf has been played in Scotland since the 15th century. Until 1850 it was a game played by gentry, with a few exceptions. With the introduction of the cheaper and more durable "guttie" ball in 1848, the game became more popular and spread to England and other countries, especially where Scottish emigrants settled.

There are documents indicating golf was played in America before the Revolution. The great popularity of golf began about 1890 in both England and the United States.

References: Henderson & Stark, *Golf In The Making*; Pat Kennedy, *Golf Club Trademarks*, privately printed; John M. and Morton W. Olman, *Encyclopedia of Golf Collectibles: A Collector's Identification and Value Guide*, Books Americana, 1985; Janet Seagle, *The Club Makers*, United States Golf Association; Shirley & Jerry Sprung, *Decorative Golf Collectibles*, Glentiques, Ltd., Inc., 1991; Tom Wishon, *Golf Club Identification and Price Guide*.

Collectors' Club: Golf Collectors' Society, P. O. Box 491, Shawnee Mission, KS 66202.

Museums: Ralph Miller Memorial Library, City of Industry, CA; United States Golf Association, "Golf House," Far Hills, NJ; World Golf Hall of Fame, Pinehurst, NC.

BOOKS

Anderson, John, *The American Annual Golf Guide*, 1924	40.00
Baeert, Raymond, *The Adventures of Monsieur Depont: Golf Champion*	225.00
Bateman, H. M., *Adventures at Golf*, 1st ed	155.00
Bauchope, C. Robertson (ed.), *The Golfing Annual*, Vol. 1	335.00
Beldam, *Great Golfers at a Glance*	155.00
Braid, James, *Advanced Golf*, 10th ed	14.00
Brown, J. L., *Golf at Glen Falls*	170.00
Christie, A., *The Boomerang Clue*	12.50
Clark, Robert, *Royal and Ancient Game*, 3rd ed, 1899	210.00
Collett, Glenna, *Ladies in the Rough*	50.00
Darwin, B., *Green Memories*, 1928	280.00
Duncan, G., *Golf for Women*	25.00
Golfers Gallery by Old Masters, A, portfolio of colored illus	425.00
Guldahl, Ralph, *Groove Your Golf*	15.00
Haultain, *The Mystery of Golf*, 2nd ed., 1912	70.00
Helme, E., *Family Golf,*	25.00
Hones, Ernest, *Swinging into Golf*	10.00

Hoyle's Games, 1790 ed	165.00
Hunter, Robert, *The Links*, NY, 1926	275.00
Jerome, *The Golf Club Mystery*	10.00
Jones, T. J. Jr., *Down the Fairway*	30.00
Martin, H. B.	
Pictorial Golf	10.00
What's Wrong with your Game	25.00
Martin, John S., *The Curious History of the Golf Ball*, 1968	155.00
Nelson, Byron, *Winning Golf*, 1947	7.50
Rice, G. & C. Briggs, *The Duffers' Handbook of Golf*, NY, 1926	115.00
Snead, Sam, *Quick Way to Better Golf*, 1937	50.00
Steel, C., *The Golf Course Mystery*	10.00
Travis, W. J., *Practical Golf*, NY, 1902	35.00
Vaile, P. A.	
Modern Golf	20.00
The Soul of Golf	20.00
Wodehouse, P. G.	
Golf Without Tears	25.00
The Clicking of Cuthbert	17.50

EQUIPMENT

Bag	
Busey Patent Caddy, mahogany, ash pipod, birch handle, canvas and leather ball pocket, club tube	280.00
Osmond Patent Caddy, ashwood, leather handles, straps, canvas club tube and ball pocket	260.00
Ball	
Bramble ball	
Haskell, patent, 1899	45.00
Spring Vale Hawk	22.00
Chemico Bob, yellow dot	35.00
Feather ball, J. Gourlay, early 19th C, maker's name	1,000.00
Glexite, Phantom, six orig wrappers	45.00
Gutty	
Hand hammered	180.00
Two mesh—marked	60.00
Lynx, rubber core	15.00
Sq Dimple	
DSO Colonel, 29 weight	60.00
North British, practice, box of 12	110.00
Club (Note: w/s—wood shaft; s/s—steel shaft)	
Iron	
Burke juvenile mashie, w/s	22.00
Hagen Iron—man sand wedge, w/s	120.00
George Nicol niblic, anti-shank, w/s	40.00
Six smooth face, w/s	25.00
Spalding F—4, c1922, w/s	10.00
Tom Stewart lofter, smooth face, w/s	45.00
Urquehart patent adjustable club, w/s	260.00
Wilson wedge, Staff model, c1959, s/s	36.00

Putter
A. Patrick, long nose, scared head,
w/s **140.00**
Forgan, scared–head, long–nose,
shaft stamped **100.00**
Mills, "L" model, aluminum head **37.50**
R. Simpson, socket head, c1900,
w/s **85.00**
Schenectady, w/s **50.00**
Spalding "Schnectady," aluminum
head **100.00**
Tommy Armour IMG Ironmaster,
s/s **85.00**
Wood
Auchterlonie scared–head brassie,
w/s **30.00**
Ben Sayers spoon, scared–head,
w/s **40.00**
C.S. Butchart, scared–head driver,
shaft stamped **35.00**
Davie Anderson scared–head
driver, w/s **65.00**
McGregor Tourney 693W driver,
c1953, s/s **115.00**
Tom Morris, scared head, bulger
and brassie, horn insert, stamped
"T. Morris, St. Andrews" **120.00**
Willie Dunn, long–nose grassed
driver, stained beech head, horn
insert **1,700.00**

Bottle opener and corkscrew, sterling silver, marked "Blackington & Co," 4¹⁄₁₆", $275.00.

MISCELLANEOUS

Cigarette Box, hammered pewter, surmounted by mesh gutty ball and two
clubs **35.00**
Cigarette Card
Cope's, 50 in set **60.00**
Player Cigarettes, 25 in set **40.00**
Wills, "Famous Golfers" **50.00**
Cigarette Case, silver, enameled Edwardian golfer scene **280.00**
Doorstop, golfer putting, green cap, red
shoes, coat, and knickers, 6½ x 8" . **65.00**
Game
Arnold Palmer, Indoor Course, ... **35.00**
Spin–Golf, Chad Valley, boxed **45.00**
Hatpin, set, 2 pcs, ball and club, 12" l,
silver **110.00**

Magazine, *Golf Digest*, 12 issues
1963 .... **12.00**
1967 .... **5.00**
Medal
Amateur Championship, British **910.00**
Royal Aberdeen, weekly handicap,
1937 .... **125.00**
Mug, Royal Bradwell **15.00**
Plate
Rabbits golfing, Royal Doulton Bunnykins **40.00**
Teddy bear playing golf, bear caddie,
6" d, c1920 .... **70.00**
Post Card
Gibson, set of 5, c1905 .... **20.00**
Rules of Golf, 9 in set, Crombie **30.00**
St. Andrews, 24 sepia views, c1900 **143.00**
Punchbowl, "Every dog has his day,"
Crombie–type golfers **700.00**
Salt and Pepper Shaker, pr, "gutty" type
golf balls **30.00**
Teapot, ball and flag cov, brown club
handle **30.00**
Teaspoon, silver, set of 6 .... **45.00**
Tile, Delft, golfer playing to a stake, pr **25.00**
Toast Rack, electroplate, four divisions
created by crossed clubs **80.00**
Trophy, silver, three handles, golf club
stem, bakelite plinth **45.00**
Walking Stick, bronze head in form of
"Jigger" **26.00**
Watch, mesh golf ball shape, Swiss ... **110.00**
Whiskey Decanter, Limited Edition
Greater Greensboro Open, Jim Beam,
1980 .... **25.00**
Hawiian Open, 1972 .... **17.50**
Yearbook, *USGA*
1931 .... **25.00**
1940 .... **17.50**

PRINTS, DRAWINGS, ETC.

Cartoon
"Golf Amenities," A T Smith, orig
Punch, India ink **225.00**
"Spy," Mure Fergusson, Vanity Fair . **50.00**
Painting
"The Golfing Lassie," unknown, oil
on board **175.00**
Winter scene showing golfers playing
to the mark, 17th C Dutch School,
oil on relaid canvas **2,750.00**
Photograph, Harry Vardon, sgd, 1929 . **200.00**
Print
Aldin, Cecil, "North Berwick: Perfection and the Redan," sgd by artist **1,000.00**
Paton, Frank, "Royal and Ancient, St.
Andrews, 1798," etching, vignettes
in margin, sgd by artist **225.00**
Sadler, Dendy, "The First Tee," etching, colored **30.00**

Sketch, black chalk, Ridgewell
  Bobby Jones **40.00**
  Gene Sarazen **35.00**

GOLLIWOGG AND DUTCH DOLLS

Collecting Hints: Study the Upton books to learn to identify the Golliwogg figure and the Dutch dolls. England is a prime source for Golliwogg material. Black collectors often will acquire Golliwogg material for their collections.

The illustrations in the Upton books have value separately. Often books are destroyed so that individual prints can be sold for framing.

History: The first volume featuring the Golliwogg and the five Dutch Dolls (Meg, Weg, Peg, Sarah Jane, and Midget) was published in 1898 by Longman, Green Co., of London, New York, and Bombay. The text and illustration were by Florence K. Upton; Bertha Upton wrote the verses. The first book contained 31 color illustrations.

The Golliwogg was adopted as an advertising character by Robertson's, a manufacturer of jams and jellies. The Golliwogg's popularity also led to a number of toy related items being issued.

Band, 3" h, plaster, EE Robertson's jam
  adv, 8 pcs **100.00**
Bank, still
  Aluminum **75.00**
  Cast Iron **200.00**
Biscuit Tin, Jacob's Biscuits, 3¾" d,
  octagonal shape, golliwogg with toy
  soldiers **60.00**
Book, titles include: *Adventures Of Two Dutch Dolls And A Golliwogg, Golliwogg At The Sea–Side, Golliwogg In Holland, Golliwogg In War, Golliwogg's Air–Ship, Golliwogg's "Auto–Go–Cart," Golliwogg's Bicycle Club, Golliwogg's Circus, Golliwogg's Desert Island, Golliwogg's Fox–Hunt, Golliwogg's Polar Adventures, Golliwogg In The African Jungle,* and *Golliwogg's Christmas;* books measure 11⅜ x 8⅝", 64 pgs
  Mint Condition **150.00**
  Excellent Condition **125.00**
  Very Good Condition **100.00**
  Fair Condition **50.00**
Book, *The Three Golliwoggs*, Enid Blyton, 1969 .... **12.00**
Doll
  Paper, 2" h, Robertson's Golden Shred Marmalade adv, same themes as pins **1.00**
  Rag, 10, 16, and 18" **15.00**
Figure, 2½" h, plaster, electrified, Robertson's Jam adv **500.00**

Book, *The Golliwogg At The Sea–Side,* Florence K. Upton, verses by Bertha Upton, 1898 copyright, 11 x 8¾", $100.00.

Pin, 1⅜", enamel on brass, promotion for Robertson's Golden Shred Marmalade, themes include: Accordion Player, Bag Piper, Boy Scout, Boxer, Cricket Player, Field Hockey Player, Golfer, Guitarist, Ice Skater, Lacrosse Player, Rugby Player, Saxaphonist, Soccer Player, Tennis Player, Trainman with stop sign, Trombonist and Violinist **15.00**
Plate
  China, Robertson & Son, made by Barratts, Staffordshire, c1904
    7" **70.00**
    9" **70.00**
  White enamel, 10", "The Golliwogg's Joy Ride" **40.00**
Playing Card, each with illus from various Upton books, Thomas DeLaRue & Co, Ltd, London **75.00**
Sugar Bowl, 3" d, china **50.00**
Toy, rubber, squeak, 6¼" h, black face, jacket and shoes, white shirt and gloves, red tie and pants, marked "Combey, made in England, 1546" . **25.00**

GONDER POTTERY

Collecting Hints: Learn to identify the Gonder glazes and forms. Once you do, you will have no trouble identifying the pieces. Since production is recent, many examples still can be found in basements and at garage sales. Dealers have been buying Gonder pieces and placing them in storage in anticipation of a future rise in prices.

History: Lawton Gonder purchased the Zane Pottery of Zanesville, Ohio, in 1941. Previously Gonder had worked for the Ohio Pottery, American Encaustic Tiling, Cherry Art Tile, and Florence Pottery. He was a consultant for Fraunfelter

China and Standard Tile. Gonder renamed the Zane Pottery the Gonder Ceramic Arts, Inc.

Gonder's pottery was high priced for its time. Besides a mingled color glaze, the pottery made a flambe glaze, a gold crackle glaze, and a line of old Chinese crackle reproduction pottery. Many shapes followed the Rum Rill patterns from the Florence Pottery.

Almost all Gonder Pottery is marked. Some had paper labels, but the majority had one of the following impressed marks: "GONDER CERAMIC ART," "Gonder/Original" in script, "Gonder" in script, "GONDER/U.S.A.," "Gonder (script)/U.S.A.," and "GONDER" in a semicircle.

The company expanded in 1946, opening the Elgee pottery which made lamp bases. The plant burned in 1954. A brief expansion occurred at the main plant, but production ceased in 1957.

Reference: Ralph and Terry Kovel, *The Kovel's Collector's Guide To American Art Pottery*, Crown Publishers, 1974.

Periodical: *The New Glaze*, P. O. Box 4782, Birmingham, AL 35206.

Collectors' Club: American Art Pottery Association, 9825 Upton Circle, Bloomington, MN 55431.

Candleholders, pr, turquoise ext., pink coral int., $18.00.

Bowl
6½" blue and pink, ribbed	7.50
7", blue and brown, swirl	14.00

Cornucopia
6", gray, pink int.	10.00
7½", brown and pink, leafy, scrolled	12.00
8½", blue, pink int.	8.00

Ewer
6", gray, pink int.	15.00
9", matte finish, green, marked "Gonder USA 434"	20.00

Figurine
Collie, 9", gray	14.00
Horse's Head, 13", bluish–green	35.00
Oriental Coolie 8", pink and green glaze	17.50
Panther, 18¼", jade green	90.00
Pitcher, 7", blue and wine, high pointed handle and spout	10.00

Planter
Gray, pink int.	8.00

Madonna, mottled pink and gray	**12.50**

Swan
6", blue, pink int.	**10.00**
7", shaded blue, pink int.	**12.00**
Teapot, brown, yellow drip	**15.00**

Vase
6", mottled green, twisted	**10.00**
7", gray and pink, fan	**12.50**
8", lavender and pink, flower shape	**15.00**
9", mottled brown, urn shape	**20.00**
11", blue, petal and leaf	**22.50**
Sea Horse	**14.00**

GOOFUS GLASS

Collecting Hints: Original paint is important. If a piece is peeling, the price is lowered by 50%.

Although Goofus glass does not respond well to cleaning with detergents, it can be restored by using a fine metal polish. Test a small area with a cotton swab before starting.

History: Goofus glass also is known as Mexican Ware, Hooligan glass, and Pickle glass. It is a pressed glass with relief or impressed designs, the back or face of which was painted. The design areas often are in red and green with the ground in metallic gold or bronze. The favorite design motif is some form of flower. The period of popularity of Goofus glass was from 1890 to 1920.

Goofus glass was used as a premium at carnivals, similar to carnival glass. It also was sold in local general and department stores. Goofus glass came in many forms—bowls, compotes, jars, jewel boxes, lamps, pickle jars, plates, powder jars, and vases. Several carnival patterns and forms have been found with Goofus decoration including Nasturtium plates, bowls, and lamp bases, Peacock Fantail lamp and vase, Beaded Oval bowl, and Grape Wheel plate. Goofus decoration also appeared on some pieces of opalescent glass.

Several companies made Goofus glass: Crescent Glass Company, Wellsburg, West Virginia; Imperial Glass Corporation, Bellaire, Ohio; LaBelle Glass Works, Bridgeport, Ohio; and Northwood Glass Co., Indiana, Pennsylvania, Wheeling, West Virginia, and Bridgeport, Ohio. Northwood marks include "N," "N" in one circle, "N" in two circles, and one or two circles without the "N."

Goofus glass lost its popularity when people found the paint tarnished or scaled off after repeated washings and wear. No record of its manufacture has been found after 1920.

Reference: Carolyn McKinley, *Goofus Glass*, Collector Books, 1984.

Ashtray, red rose dec, emb adv	**8.00**

Bowl

4½", red roses, gold trim **15.00**
5½", La Belle Rose design, sq **30.00**
7", iris, gold and red **25.00**
9", roses, gold and red, crimped rim **20.00**
9½", strawberries **40.00**
10", dahlias, scalloped **50.00**
10½", water lily **50.00**
Bon Bon Dish, 4" d, strawberry, gold,
red, and green **35.00**
Candy Dish, 8½" d, figure eight design,
serrated rim, dome footed **55.00**
Coaster, 3", floral, red dec, gold ground **10.00**
Compote, 4" d, grape and cable **30.00**
Decanter, basketweave, single rose,
rose emb stopper **45.00**
Dresser Tray, 6", Cabbage Rose, red
roses, gold foliage **28.00**
Fairy Lamp, roses, green, uses a candle **25.00**
Flask, zig zag design, milk glass, gold
paint, metal screw top **45.00**
Jewel Box, gold, single rose **45.00**
Mug, Cabbage Rose, gold ground **30.00**
Nappy, gold on gold **10.00**
Perfume Bottle, 3½" h, pink tulips **15.00**
Pin Dish, 6½", oval, red and black flo-
rals **15.00**

**Plate, adv, Old Rose Distilling Co, Chi-
cago, 8¼" d, $60.00.**

Plate

6", rose and lattice **18.00**
7¾", red carnations, gold ground ... **18.00**
8", red poppies, gold ground **25.00**
8½", Gibson cameo, red and gold .. **40.00**
11"
Dahlia, red and gold **35.00**
Roses, deep red and gold, scalloped rim **22.00**
Powder Box, 3", puffy rose, red and gold **35.00**
Salt Shaker, poppy blossom, silver, red
poppy **35.00**
Toothpick Holder, red rose and foliage,
gold ground **20.00**
Tumbler, 8", rose pattern, red and gold **20.00**

Vase

6½", grape and rose, crackle glass,
red and gold **10.00**
7¼", grape dec **25.00**
9", bird sitting on grape vine, red and
gold on satin glass **15.00**

GRANITEWARE

Collecting Hints: Old graniteware is heavier than
new graniteware. Pieces with cast iron handles
date from 1870 to 1890; wood handles date from
1900 to 1910. Other dating clues are seams,
wood knobs, and tin lids.

History: Graniteware is the name commonly
given to iron or steel kitchenware covered with
enamel coating.

The first graniteware was made in Germany in
the 1830s. It was not produced in the United
States until the 1860s. At the start of World War
I, when European manufacturers turned to the
making of war weapons, American producers
took over the market.

Colors commonly marketed were white and
gray. Each company made their own special col-
or, including shades of blue, green, brown, violet, cream, and red. Graniteware still is manufactured with the earliest pieces in greatest
demand among collectors.

References: Helen Greguire, *The Collector's Encyclopedia of Graniteware: Colors, Shapes & Values,* Collector Books, 1990; Vernagene Vogel-
zang and Evelyn Welch, *Graniteware, Collectors'
Guide With Prices, Volume 1* (1981), and *Volume
2* (1986), Wallace–Homestead.

Collectors' Club: National Graniteware Society,
4818 Reamer Road, Center Point, IA 52213.

Bathtub, baby, blue **6.00**
Berry Picking Pot, gray, handle **30.00**
Bowl
7", gray **20.00**
12" d, 6" h **20.00**
Bread Box, sq, gray, "Bread" **25.00**
Bundt Pan, gray mottled **25.00**
Cake Pan, 10 x 14", gray **8.50**
Coffee Biggin, cobalt and enamel **145.00**
Camp Mug, brown, Elite Austria **42.00**
Coffee Boiler
Blue and white swirl **100.00**
Brown, white int. **25.00**
Coffee Pot
Blue and white swirl, 10" **110.00**
Gray, gooseneck spout **30.00**
Colander
Blue and white swirl **35.00**
Brown and white swirl **65.00**
Cooking Pot, 2½ gal, gray **48.00**

Cup, blue and white speckled, rust spots 12.00
Dipper
  Blue and white 35.00
  Red and white 10.00
Drain Basket, brown swirl, bail handle 20.00
Egg Cup, rooster shape, gray 8.00
Food Mold, Turk's Head, turquoise and
  white swirl 200.00
Foot Tub, 16 x 19", gray mottle, rolled
  edges 56.00

Coffeepot, gray, $85.00.

Fruit Jar Funnel, gray and white, strap
  handle 22.00
Funnel, 8½", gray 18.00
Kettle, gray, bulbous, ear handle 12.00
Ladle, blue and white swirl 85.00
Loaf Pan, 7 x 12", gray mottled 10.00
Measure
  Blue and white swirl, pint 225.00
  Gray, 1 cup 48.00
Melon Mold, gray, ribbed, tin bottom
  with ring, marked "Extra Agate," #50 70.00
Milk Bowl, small 8.00
Milk Pitcher, blue 40.00
Mold, white, oval, scalloped, 4½ x 6" 85.00
Muffin Pan, gray, six holes 12.00
Mush Mug, brown and white swirl ... 68.00
Pie Baker, gray 8.00
Pie Pan
  Cobalt blue and white swirl 30.00
  Gray 10.00
Pitcher, 7", gray 25.00
Plate, child's, nursery rhyme 30.00
Platter, white, blue edge 24.00
Potty, gray, "Poopy Prize, 1935" 75.00
Pudding Pan, cobalt and white swirl .. 16.00
Roaster
  Cobalt blue and white swirl, tray in-
    side 90.00
  Gray 18.00
  Red, large 50.00
Scoop, sq, gray 78.00

Skillet
  Blue–green and white swirl 135.00
  Red 45.00
Soap Dish, cobalt blue swirl, hanging . 110.00
Soap Holder, blue speckled, insert, wall
  mount 30.00
Stew Pan, red and white swirl, tin lid . 40.00
Tray, 17¾", blue 45.00
Tube Pan, blue and white swirl 185.00
Wash Basin, large, handled, turquoise
  swirl 85.00
Washboard, blue 78.00

HALL CHINA

Collecting Hints: Hall China Company named many of their patterns, but some of these pattern names are being gradually changed by dealers to other names. A good example of this is the Silhouette pattern; the common name is Taverne. Dealers have also devised nicknames for shapes like J–sunshine and sani–grid.

Due to its high quality, most Hall China pieces are still in wonderful condition. There is no reason to pay full price for imperfect pieces.

History: Hall China Company was born out of the dissolution of the East Liverpool Potteries Company. Robert Hall, a partner in the merger, died within months of forming the new company. Robert T. Hall, his son, took over.

At first, the company produced the same semi–porcelain dinnerware and toiletware that was being made at the other potteries in East Liverpool, Ohio. Robert T. Hall began to experiment in an attempt to duplicate an ancient Chinese one–fire process that would produce a non–crazing vitrified china, with body and glaze being fired at the same time. He succeeded in 1911. Hall has been made that way ever since.

Hall's basic products are institutional ware (hotel and restaurant) to the trade only. However, they also have produced many retail and premium lines, e.g. Autumn Leaf for Jewel Tea and Blue Bouquet for the Standard Coffee Co. of New Orleans. A popular line is the gold–decorated teapots that were introduced for retail sale in 1920. In 1931 kitchenware was introduced, soon followed by dinnerware. These lines were decorated in both solid colors and decals for retail and premium sales.

Hall is still producing china at its plant in East Liverpool, Ohio.

References: Harvey Duke, *Superior Quality Hall China,* ELO Books, 1977; Harvey Duke, *Hall 2,* ELO Books, 1985; Harvey Duke, *The Official Price Guide to Pottery and Porcelain,* House of Collectibles, 1989; Margaret and Kenn Whitmyer, *The Collector's Encyclopedia of Hall China,* Collector Books, 1989.

Periodical: Hall China Connection, P.O. Box 401, Pollock Pines, CA 95726.

Note: Hall has been reissuing many of its products in its new Americana retail line for several years now. They are all decorated in solid colors. If you are a new collector and are unsure if an item is new or old, you may want to buy only the items with decal or gold decorations, as these pieces have not been reissued and there is no intention of doing so. Because of this reissue, prices have dropped slightly on a few solid–colored items.

See: Autumn Leaf.

PATTERNS

CAMEO ROSE. Pattern made exclusively for the Jewel Tea Company, early 1950s through the early 1970s.

Bowl, 5¼"	2.00
Butter Dish, quarter pound	28.00
Casserole	25.00
Cream Soup, 6"	7.00
Creamer	5.00
Cup	4.00
Gravy	12.00
Pickle Dish, 9"	9.00
Plate	
6½"	2.00
8"	2.50
10"	4.00
Saucer	1.00
Sugar, cov	12.00
Teapot, six cups	35.00
Tidbit Tray	28.00
Vegetable, oval	10.00

HEATHER ROSE. E–style dinnerware pattern sold during the 1940s.

Bowl	
5" d	3.00
6" d	3.50
Coffeepot	27.50
Creamer	3.75
Cup and Saucer	4.50
Fruit Dish	4.00
Gravy Boat, underplate	10.00
Pitcher	12.00
Plate	
6", bread and butter	1.25
10", dinner	4.00
Platter, 13½"	9.00
Salad Bowl, 9" d	10.00
Sugar, cov	7.00
Tureen, cov	18.00
Vegetable Bowl	
9", round	8.00
10½", oval	7.00

MT VERNON

Creamer, ftd	4.00
Cup	3.25
Fruit Bowl, 5¼" d	2.00
Plate	
6½" d	2.00
10" d, dinner	4.00
Platter, 13¼" l	9.50
Saucer	1.25
Soup Bowl, 8" d, flat	6.50
Sugar, cov, ftd	6.50
Vegetable Bowl, 9¼" l, oval	9.50

PEACH BLOSSOM. Exclusive decal made for the retail trade, designed by Eva Zeisel. Pieces marked "Hallcraft."

Butter Dish	9.00
Creamer	4.50
Gravy Basket, orig ladle	20.00
Jug, large	35.00
Ladle	5.00
Plate, 7"	2.50
Salt Shaker	5.00
Sugar, cov	7.50
Teapot	40.00

POPPY AND WHEAT. Elusive decal made for Macy's, about 1930. Made in kitchenware items only.

Baker	15.00
Bean Pot	50.00
Bowl Set, 3 pcs	30.00
Canister	60.00
Casserole, cov	25.00
Creamer	7.00
Custard	5.00
Pitcher	35.00
Salt and Pepper Shakers, pr	25.00
Sugar, cov	10.00
Tea Tile, 6"	30.00
Teapot	45.00

RED POPPY. Premium for Grand Union Tea Company. Produced from mid 1930s until mid 1950s.

Baker, French, fluted	15.00
Bowl	
5½", fruit	4.25
9", salad	10.00
Cake Plate	16.00
Cake Server	65.00
Casserole, cov	20.00
Cereal Bowl, 6"	7.00
Coffeepot	10.00
Creamer	7.50
Cup	4.00
Drip Jar, cov	12.00
Jug	18.00
Mixing Bowl, set of 3	35.00

Mustard, 3 pcs	45.00
Pitcher	18.50
Plate, 9", dinner	6.00
Salt and Pepper Shakers, pr	20.00
Saucer	2.00
Souffle Dish	14.00
Sugar	8.00
Teapot, Aladdin	50.00
Vegetable Bowl, 9⅛" round	14.00

ROSE PARADE

Bean Pot	35.00
Casserole	25.00
Drip, cov	16.00
Salad Bowl	16.00

SILHOUETTE. Premium for the Cook Coffee Company and also the Standard Coffee Company in the 1930s and 1940s.

Baker, French	14.00
Bean Pot	50.00
Bowl, 7⅞"	20.00
Coffeepot	30.00
Cookie Jar	50.00
Jug	24.00
Mug	32.00
Pretzel Jar	75.00
Salt Shaker, red handle	8.00

SPRINGTIME. Premium for Standard Tea Co. Limited Production.

Bowl, 5½"	5.00
Butter Dish	9.00
Cake Plate	12.00
Creamer	5.00
Cup	3.00
Fruit Dish	2.00
Gravy	8.00
Jug, 6"	25.00
Plate	
6⅛"	1.00
9"	4.50
Platter	7.00
Saucer	1.00
Sugar, cov	6.00
Vegetable, oval	6.00

TAVERNE

Coffeepot, china drip	110.00
Letover, rect	20.00
Mug	30.00
Tea Tile, 6", round	90.00

WILDFIRE. Premium for Great American Tea Co. Produced in 1950s.

Bowl	
5½"	5.00
6"	6.00
9"	9.25

Cup and Saucer	8.00
Egg Cup	30.00
Gravy Boat	15.00
Pie Baker	15.00
Plate, 9"	7.00
Platter, 11"	10.00
Shaker, handled, "S"	10.00
Soup Bowl	10.00

Teapot, Aladdin, blue, gold, flame finial, orig infusor, 3 pcs, $40.00.

TEAPOTS

Aladdin, maroon swag	30.00
Apple, sky blue and gold	225.00
Autumn, Aladdin	35.00
Baltimore	
Emerald	35.00
Maroon, gold label	42.00
Bird Cage, canary, gold trim	40.00
Boston, chartreuse, gold trim, eight cups	26.00
Cleveland, yellow, gold trim, six cups	45.00
Crest	20.00
Daffodil, gold trim, cosy	25.00
Gold Label, two cups, yellow, allover gold flowers, French shape, round	25.00
French Ivory, gold trim, six cups	18.00
McCormick, turquoise, infuser	17.50
Nautilus, six cup, yellow, gold trim	65.00
New York, cobalt, gold trim, six cups	35.00
Parade, canary	18.00
Philadelphia, turquoise, gold trim, six cups	18.00
Polka Dot, windshield, ivory gold label	25.00
Saf Handle, six cup, cobalt	65.00
Twin Spout, ivory	35.00

HARKER POTTERY

Collecting Hints: In 1965 Harker China had the capacity to produce 25 million pieces of dinnerware each year. Hence, there is a great deal of Harker material available at garage sales and flea markets. Many patterns also were kept in production for decades.

Between 1935 and 1955 the Harker Company organized Columbia Chinaware, a sales organization used to market Harker products in small towns across the country. The line included enamel ware, glass and aluminum products. One pattern of Columbia Chinaware was "Autumn Leaf," eagerly sought by Autumn Leaf collectors.

Collectors should focus on Harker patterns by famous designers. Among these are Russel Wright's White Clover and George Bauer's Cameoware. Many patterns will be found with different color grounds. Other patterns were designed to have mass appeal. Colonial Lady was popular at "dish nites" at the movies or other businesses.

Shapes and forms did change through the decades. An interesting collection might focus on one object, e.g., a sugar or creamer, collected in a variety of patterns from different historical periods. Watch for unusual pieces. The Countryside pattern features a rolling pin, scoop and cake server.

History: The Harker Company began in 1840 when Benjamin Harker, an English slater turned farmer in East Liverpool, Ohio, built a kiln and began making yellow ware products from clay deposits on his land. The business was managed by members of the Harker family until the Civil War when David Boyce, a brother–in– law, took over the operation. Although a Harker resumed management after the war, members of the Boyce family assumed key roles within the firm; David G. Boyce, a grandson of David, served as president.

In 1879 the first whiteware products were introduced. A disastrous flood in 1884 caused severe financial problems which the company overcame. In 1931 the company moved to Chester, West Virginia, to escape the flooding problems. In 1945 Harker introduced Cameoware made by the engobe process. The engobe or layered effect was achieved by placing a copper mask over the bisque and sand blasting to leave the design imprint. The white rose pattern on blue ground was marketed as "White Rose Carv–Kraft" in Montgomery Ward stores.

The Harker Company used a large variety of backstamps and names. Hotoven cookingware featured a scroll, draped over pots, with a kiln design at top. Columbia Chinaware had a circular stamp with the Statue of Liberty.

Harker made a Rockingham ware line in the 1960s. The hound handled pitcher and mugs were included. The Jeannette Glass Company purchased the Harker Company and the plant was closed in March, 1972. Ohio Stoneware, Inc., utilized the plant building until it was destroyed by fire in 1975.

References: Jo Cunningham, *The Collector's Encyclopedia Of American Dinnerware*, Collector Books, 1982; Betty Newbound, *The Gunshot Guide To Values Of American Made China & Pottery, Book 2*, published by author, 1983.

Periodicals: *The Daze*, P.O. Box 57, Otisville, MI 48463; *The New Glaze*, P.O. Box 4782, Birmingham, AL 35206.

See: Russel Wright.

Plate, Cameoware, blue and white, bear and balloon dec, 7⅜" d, $15.00.

Amy	
Baker, 9"	12.00
Bean Pot, individual	2.50
Bowl, 5½"	3.50
Creamer	3.50
Plate	
7½", salad	4.00
9", dinner	6.00
Rolling Pin	55.00
Sugar	3.50
Teapot	30.00
Cameoware	
Bowl, 7", pink	9.50
Cake Server	12.00
Casserole, cov	15.00
Child's	
Bowl, chrome trim	12.00
Feeding Dish	30.00
Cup and Saucer	8.50
Pie Baker	10.00
Pitcher, cov	15.00
Plate	
7⅛", luncheon	5.00
10", dinner	5.00
Sugar, cov	5.50
Chesterton, cake set, teal green, 10 pcs	25.00
Modern Tulip	
Bowl, 9½"	7.00
Cake Server, brown	12.00
Jar, cov, oval, Bake Right, modern age shape	30.00
Pie Baker	8.00
Platter, 14"	7.00
Salad Fork	12.00
Pate Sur Pate	
Clock, 8½" d, plate	38.00
Creamer, green	2.50

Platter, 13", gray	5.75
Salt and Pepper Shakers, pr, gray	6.00

Petit Point II

Bowl, 8¾"	8.50
Cake Plate	4.00
Cake Server	7.00
Casserole, cov, 7" d	25.00
Coffeepot	20.00
Cup and Saucer	5.00
Pie Baker	9.00
Plate, 8½"	4.50
Spoon	7.50
Sugar, cov	6.00

Red Apple

Bowl, 9", berry	15.00
Cake Server	12.50
Mixing Bowl, 10"	15.00
Tea Tile	20.00
Teapot	28.00

Rockingham, cider set, pitcher and six mugs, dog handle, brown glaze	115.00

Ruffled Tulip

Batter Jug	20.00
Bowl, cov	12.00
Pie Baker	17.50
Pie Server	15.00
Spoon	15.00
Utility Tray	20.00

HATPINS

Collecting Hints: Shanks of hatpins come in varying lengths. A group of hatpins in a decorative hatpin holder makes a nice accent. Purchase hatpins with straight shanks and solid mountings. Hatpins should be free of rust or tarnish and chips or flakes.

History: Hatpins were popular from 1850 through the 1920s. The main purpose of a hatpin was to hold a lady's hat to her head. When the style of fashion included large brimmed hats and long, thick hair, the hatpin was a necessity. As with other necessities, designers soon began to decorate and embellish hatpins with stylish designs, semi-precious stones and metals. Subjects of commonly found hatpins range from commemorative, insects and sporting events to florals.

Some hatpins were used as extensions of a lady's costume and had ends coordinated to the lady's outfit. Other hatpins were designed by the milliner to become an integral part of the hat design. Hatpins also served another purpose for well dressed ladies. These long shafted pins were valuable weapons when threatened and often were used to keep an overzealous suitor in his proper place.

Reference: Lillian Baker, *Hatpins & Hatpin Holders*, Collector Books, 1983 (1988 Value Update).

Collectors' Club: International Club For Collectors of Hatpins and Hatpin Holders, 15237 Chanera Avenue, Gardena, California, 90249.

Museum: Los Angeles Art Museum, Costume Department, Los Angeles, CA.

Art Deco, brass, each $15.00.

Abalone, claw mounted, 6" steel shank	8.00
Amethyst, rhinestones	29.00

Brass

2½" head, amethyst accents, c1910	35.00
3" head, Art Nouveau, four panel head, c1910	50.00

Enamel

Bow shape, pearl center	45.00
Fan shape, Art Deco, 1" head	28.00
Gilt on brass, simulated topaz, girl, flowers	60.00
Pansy	50.00

Carnival Glass

Peacock, oval	22.00
Strawberry, green	42.00
Zig–Zag, purple	48.00
Gold metal, monogram E	8.00
Goldstone, cube, 9½" steel shank	18.00
Ivory, elephant, carved	85.00
Jade, button, 14k gold setting, 11" shank	25.00
Jet, imitation, polished	18.00
Mercury Glass, Art Deco, sliding shank	70.00
Molded Glass, scarab, red, 11" shank	30.00
Mosaic, 1¼" head, double frame, granular trim, c1875	80.00
Mother–of–Pearl, snake motif, ruby head, gold top, American	175.00
Oriental Pearl	55.00

Peacock Eye Glass

Ball, 8" steel shank	30.00
Butterfly, rhinestone accents, 9½" steel shank	75.00

Porcelain

Ball, ceramic transfer, hp accents, gold overlay, c1895	110.00
Button, blue and white, 11" shank	16.00
Cottage and stream scene	55.00
Floral, surrounded by rhinestones	20.00
Portrait	65.00

Quartz, tear shape stone, gold plated
   setting **35.00**
Rhinestone
   Butterfly, figural, blue body **30.00**
   Triangle shape, open center **28.00**
Satsuma
   Birds among blossoms, 8¾" shank .. **100.00**
   Dragon, 1" round head, 8¼" shank . **110.00**
Shell, clam, 2" head, wire mounted on
   shank **10.00**
Sterling Silver
   Cherub, ¾" round head **48.00**
   Chinese Water Lily, Art Nouveau ... **85.00**
   Coral Cabochon, 1" head, Art Nou-
     veau **80.00**
   Dutch Shoe, c1900 .... **30.00**
   Florals, portrait **50.00**
   Four Leaf Clover, MOP inlay **50.00**
   Maple Leaf **20.00**
   Tennis Racket **10.00**
   Woman, flowing hair, c1900 ...... **40.00**
Tortoise Shell
   Butterfly, carved **85.00**
   Pear shape **100.00**
Venetian Glass Beads **10.00**
Wood, elongated oval, polished **15.00**

HOLIDAY COLLECTIBLES

Collecting Hints: The most common holiday item is the postcard. Collectors tend to specialize in one holiday. Christmas, Halloween, and Easter are the most desirable. New collectors still can find bargains especially in the Thanksgiving and Valentine's Day collectibles.

Holiday items change annually. Manufacturers must constantly appeal to the same buyer.

History: Holidays are an important part of American life. Many, such as Christmas, St. Patrick's Day, Easter, and Halloween have both religious and secular overtones. National holidays such as the Fourth of July and Thanksgiving are part of one's yearly planning. There are regional holidays. Fastnacht day in Pennsylvania–German country is just one example.

Some holidays are the creation of the merchandising industry, e.g., Valentine's Day, Mother's Day, Father's Day, etc. The two leading forces in the perpetuation of holiday gift giving are the card industry and the floral industry. Through slick promotional campaigns they constantly create new occasions for which to give their products. Other marketing aspects follow quickly.

Holiday collectibles also keep pace with popular trends. Peanuts is now being challenged by Strawberry Shortcake, the Smurfs, and Star Wars.

References: L–W Book Sales (pub.), *Favors & Novelties: Wholesale Trade List No. 26, 1924–1925,* price list available; Margaret Schiffer, *Holidays Toys and Decorations,* Schiffer Publishing Ltd., 1985.

Newsletters: *Hearts to Holly: The Holiday Collectors Newsletter,* P. O. Box 105, Amherst, NH 03031; *Trick or Treat Trader,* P. O. Box 1058, Derry, NH 03038.

Halloween, tambourine, metal, orange ground, black cat face, marked "T. Conn Inc., Made in USA," 7¼" d, $10.00.

Easter
Basket, reed, 6" h, pink, handle, Germany **20.00**
Candy Container
   Cardboard, rect, basket shape, two cardboard chicks on each end, marked "Ertel Bros Wmspt, PA" **18.00**
   Duck, papier mache
     3⅓" h, pink **12.00**
     6" h, "Spring," glass eyes, Germany **48.00**
   Egg
     5" l, papier mache, cov, Easter print paper
       Germany **30.00**
       West Germany **15.00**
     Tin, 6" l, litho, rabbits and chicks, marked "Colmar, USA" **22.00**
   Rabbit
     5" h, brown, sitting, papier mache, glass eyes, wooden forelegs, head separates from body, 1920s, Germany **40.00**
     11" h, brown, sitting, papier mache, glass eyes, opening in base, 1940s, U.S.A. **22.00**
     15 " h, standing, wearing yellow overalls, papier mache, paper eyes, opening in base, USA . **20.00**
   Chick
     4" h, cotton batting wire legs, glass eyes **60.00**

5½" h, composition, dressed in red
coat, marked "Germany" 38.00

Egg

Celluloid, 5" l, purple, Japan 32.00
Glass, 2½" l, painted lake scene,
dated 1897 .... 15.00

Postcard

Celluloid egg, pink background,
boxed 15.00
"Easter Greetings," baby busting
out of egg 2.50
"Easter Greetings," two rabbits kissing, children watching, 1910 .. 2.00
"Kind Easter Wishes," two boys riding white rabbits 2.00
"To Wish You A Happy Easter,"
chicks pecking out of package,
Tuck 2.50

Rabbit

Celluloid, 3" h, floppy ears, sitting,
radish in mouth, Japan 30.00
Composition, 5" h, sitting, Germany 18.00
Cotton batting, 2½" h, holding carrot, green tucksheer 85.00
Metal, white, marked Germany, set
of 4 .... 45.00
Roly Poly, 4½" h, celluloid, dressed
in purple, standing on ball, Japan 25.00
Straw stuffed, 9" h, wooden head 60.00
Tin, 5½" h, litho, on wheels, USA 25.00
Wind–up, celluloid rabbit pulling
rabbit and swan, metal green
sleigh with bell, marked "Occupied Japan" 45.00

Fourth of July

Bunting, red, white, and blue muslin,
23" w, various lengths, per yard .. 5.00
Candy Box, red, white, and blue,
shield shape, 2¼ x 2½" 10.00
Flag, 10" h, wooden stick, 48 stars . 2.00
Pencil, lead, red, white, and blue paper 3.00

Postcard

"4th of July," spelled out in red fire-
crackers, Germany 2.00
"The Glorious Fourth," large flag,
1911 .... 2.00

Halloween

Black Cat

Candy Container, 8" h, papier
mache, cut out eyes and mouth,
wire bail, Germany 58.00
Cardboard, flat, 9" h, moveable
legs and tail, Beistle Co. USA .. 12.00
Clicker, tin, litho, orange and black,
frog shape, marked "T. Cohn,
USA" 7.00

Fan

Fold–out, wooden stick, witch riding broom, black and orange,
1920s, marked "Germany" 10.00

Paper, litho, wooden handle, two
black cats, arched backs, marked
"D.R.G.M. Germany" 15.00
Ghost, 9½" h, cardboard, stand–up,
USA 15.00

Hat

Cardboard and crepe paper, black
and orange, 4" h, Germany 10.00
Crepe paper, orange and black,
gold and black band 15.00

Horn

Cardboard, black and orange, cat,
witch, and moon figures, 9" h,
USA 7.00
Paper, orange and black, wooden
mouthpiece, Germany 5.00
Wooden, black and orange, cat
face, 4" h, marked "Czecho–Sla-
vakia" 18.00

Mask

Boy, papier mache, painted face,
cloth ties 35.00
Clown, cloth, painted face 7.00
Devil, cloth, red, bells on ears ... 18.00
Elephant, cloth, black and grey .. 5.00
Face, wire mesh, painted, cloth ties 65.00

Noisemaker

Bell, tin, litho, frying pan shape,
wooden clangers, orange and
black, marked "J. Chein" 15.00
Rattle, tin, litho, pumpkins, marked
"T Cohn, USA" ....

Postcard

"Halloween," witch dancing with
pumpkin man, cat, 1908, Tuck 5.50
"Halloween," children bobbing for
apples, 1908, Tuck 5.50
Witch reading cards, brew by table,
Germany 5.00

Pumpkin

Candy Container, papier mache,
cut–out eyes and mouth, wire
handle
4" h 35.00
5½" h 45.00
7" h 65.00
Figure, head, composition, wearing
yellow shirt and pointed hat, 3"
h, Germany 25.00
Lantern, candleholder in base, papier mache, paper eyes and
mouth, wire handle, 4" h, 1910,
Germany 60.00
Stickpin, head with pointed hat,
composition, Japan 5.00

Skeleton

Pressed cardboard, jointed arms
and legs, 30½" h, marked "Germany" 50.00
Skull, bisque, sitting on book, 3½"
h, marked "Japan" 15.00
Tambourine, tin, litho, orange and

black, marked "T Cohn, Inc"

Cat face **10.00**

Witch face **10.00**

Witch, flat cardboard

Pressed, head, 12" h, marked "Germany" **35.00**

Stand–up, 10" h, USA **15.00**

Labor Day, button, 1½", "Labor Day, Justice For All," pat date 1911 ..... **5.00**

Memorial Day

Postcard

"A grateful land remembers all her promises today," children carrying garlands, Tuck **2.50**

"On Memorial Day," "Hail Columbia," musical score, angel flying with flag, 1908 .... **4.00**

Print, "On Memorial Day," widow and children dropping garlands over father's portrait, Supplement to Grit, May 29, 1904 .... **15.00**

President's Day

Axe, 7" h wooden handle, "I cannot tell a lie" painted on blade **10.00**

Candy Container

Hat, tricornered, black, cardboard, cloth cherries **30.00**

Tree stump, papier mache, composition cherries, 7" h, Germany **75.00**

Postcard

"Lincoln Centennial Souvenir," Lincoln and slaves, 1909 ...... **3.00**

Lincoln statue, surrounded by flags, Tuck **2.50**

"Three cheers for George Washington," children waving flag beneath Washington's portrait, 1909 .... **1.75**

"Washington, The Father of his Country," 1912 .... **2.00**

St. Patrick's Day

Candy Container

Irish girl holding harp, standing on box, 4½" h, marked "Germany" **32.00**

Potato, papier mache, green paper shamrock, 4" l **45.00**

Top hat, green, cardboard, bisque pipe, cloth shamrock, 3" h, Germany **25.00**

Figure, Leprechaun, celluloid, holding pig, 7" h, Japan **28.00**

Nodder, Irish boy, bisque, 3" h, marked "Germany" **35.00**

Pipe, clay, marked "Germany" **10.00**

Postcard

"Erin go Bragh," scenes of Ireland background **3.00**

"St. Patrick was a Gentleman," Irish boy standing on a chair singing **3.50**

Shamrock

Diecut, printed in Germany, set of 8 .... **2.50**

Wire wrapped, green silk floss, small bisque hat attached, 2½" l **5.00**

Sheet Music, "Sing Me A Song of Ireland," New York Publishing House, 1905 .... **10.00**

Shillelagh, wooden **12.00**

Thanksgiving

Candy Container

3" h, bisque turkey standing on cardboard container **35.00**

5" h, papier mache, folded tail, metal legs and feet, Germany .. **38.00**

5½" h, turkey, papier mache, fan tail, metal legs and feet, glass eyes, Germany **45.00**

8" h, turkey, pale orange, opening in base, marked "Atco Co., USA" **22.00**

Favor Set, turkey, two 5" h, six 2½" h, metal legs and feet, green cardboard base, Germany **65.00**

Figure, turkey, composition

2½" h, fan tail, metal legs and feet, marked "Germany" **15.00**

4½" h, green base, Japan **8.00**

Fold–out, turkey, cardboard, tissue paper base, 8¾" h, USA **12.00**

Postcard

"A Joyous Thanksgiving," boy carving pumpkin, 1913 .... **4.00**

"May glad Thanksgiving crown your days and years," woman holding Turkey, 1912 .... **2.50**

"Thanksgiving Greetings," children playing with white turkeys, 1909 **2.50**

"Wishing You a Happy Thanksgiving," turkey standing on a flag, 1910 .... **2.00**

Valentine's Day

Greeting Card

Diecut girl, emb, silver and gold paper lace, inside greeting, 9" h **15.00**

"For My Valentine," boy and girl picking flowers, inside greeting, 4" h, Whitney, USA **1.50**

"Good Wishes For You," two children framed, diecut lace, emb background, inside greeting, 6" h **8.00**

"I'd Make a Bird of a Valentine," parrot, stand–up, 5" h, Germany **4.00**

"I'd love to paint you my Valentine," boy painting a girl's portrait, fold–out, stand–up, 6" h, USA **3.00**

"Loving Greetings," diecut girl and boy sitting on chaise, emb background, fold–out, stand–up, 9" h, Germany **15.00**

"To My Sweetheart," cupid holding package, fold—out, red tissue paper, stand—up, 5" h, USA **7.00**

"To My Sweetheart," two cupids, fold—out, tissue paper, 8" h, USA **7.50**

"To My Valentine," boy and girl holding flowers, blue diecut background, fold—out, stand—up, 6" h, Germany **8.00**

"To My Valentine," boy playing a mandolin, fold—out, stand—up, diecut background, 6" h, Germany **8.00**

"To My Valentine," little ballerina, fold—out, cut—out, 6" h, Germany **5.00**

"To My Valentine," girl holding flowers, fold—out skirt, tissue paper, stand—up, 6¾", Germany .. **5.00**

"To My Valentine," girl holding envelope, red and pink fold—out, tissue paper, stand—up, 9" h, Germany **12.00**

"True to Thee," diecut flowers and girls, blue windmill background, fold—out, stand—up, 5¾", Tuck . **10.00**

"Valentine's Greetings," two girls, diecut, Germany **7.00**

Postcard

"Love's Greeting," boy and girl, 1922, sgd "Ellen H. Clapsaddle" **5.00**

"St. Valentine's Greetings," girl and boy, sgd "Ellen H. Clapsaddle" **5.00**

"To My Sweet Valentine," woman greeting three cupids, sepia tones **1.50**

"To My Valentine," Gibson girl on swing, gilded background **2.00**

"To My Valentine with Love," portrait of a young girl, emb background **2.00**

"Valentine Greetings," Gibson girl framed by heart, 1916 .... **2.00**

HOMER LAUGHLIN

Collecting Hints: The original trademark from 1871 to 1890 merely identified the products as "Laughlin Brothers." The next trademark featured the American eagle astride the prostrate British lion. The third marking featured a monogram of "HLC" which has appeared, with slight variations, on all dinnerware since about 1900. The 1900 trademark contained a number which identified month, year and plant at which the product was made. Letter codes were used in later periods.

So much attention has been placed on Fiesta that other interesting patterns have not achieved the popularity which they deserve. Prices still are moderate. Some of the patterns from the 1930 to

1940 period have contemporary designs that are highly artistic.

Virginia Rose is a shape, not a pattern name. Several different decals can be found, with delicate pink flowers the most common.

History: Homer Laughlin and his brother, Shakespeare, built two pottery kilns in East Liverpool, Ohio, in 1871. Shakespeare withdrew in 1879, leaving Homer to operate the business alone. Laughlin became one of the first firms to produce American—made whiteware. In 1896, William Wills and a Pittsburgh group led by Marcus Aaron bought the Laughlin firm.

Expansion followed. Two new plants were built in Laughlin Station, Ohio. In 1906, the first plant (#4) was built in Newall, West Virginia. In 1923 plant #6 was built at Newall and featured a continuous tunnel kiln. Similar kilns were added at the other plants. Other advances included spray glazing and mechanical jiggering.

In the 1930 to 1960 period several new dinnerware lines were added, including the Wells Art Glaze line. Ovenserve and Kitchen Kraft were the cooking ware lines. The colored glaze lines of Fiesta, Harlequin and Rhythm captured major market shares. In 1959 a translucent table china line was introduced. Today, the annual manufacturing capacity is over 45 million pieces.

References: Jo Cunningham, *The Collector's Encyclopedia of American Dinnerware*, Collector Books, 1982; Betty Newbound, *The Gunshot Guide To Values Of American Made China & Pottery, Book 2*, published by author, 1983.

Periodicals: *The Daze*, P.O. Box 57, Otisville, MI 48463; *The New Glaze*, P.O. Box 4782, Birmingham, AL 35206.

REPRODUCTION ALERT. Harlequin and Fiesta lines were reissued in 1978 and marked accordingly.

See: Fiesta.

Amberstone

Chop Plate, 12" d **15.00**

Cup and Saucer **7.00**

Dessert Bowl **3.00**

Plate

Bread and butter **2.00**

Dinner **6.00**

Brittany

Creamer, red **3.00**

Cup, red **2.00**

Plate, 7", red **2.00**

Saucer, red .... **.50**

Sugar, cov, red **5.00**

Casualstone

Cup and Saucer **6.00**

Dessert Bowl **4.00**

Plate, bread and butter **2.00**

Fortune, plate, 6½" d **1.25**

Harlequin
  After Dinner Cup and Saucer
    Aqua 22.00
    Rose 24.00
    Yellow 23.00
  Ashtray, spruce 46.00
  Bowl, 6½" d
    Blue 6.00
    Red 7.00
  Cream Soup, maroon 18.00
  Creamer, turquoise 5.50
  Cup and Saucer
    Dark Green 8.00
    Rose 8.00
    Turquoise 6.00
    Yellow 5.00
  Egg Cup, double, yellow 10.00
  Gravy Boat, yellow 8.00
  Platter, 11½" d, yellow 7.00
  Relish, aqua, yellow, mauve, red, and
    rose inserts 200.00
  Salad Bowl, individual, turquoise ... 14.00
  Spoon Rest, aqua 145.00
  Tumbler
    Maroon 37.00
    Red 27.00
    Spruce 35.00
Organdy, breakfast set, pastel lime, 10
  pcs 40.00
Ovenserve
  Bowl, 8½", flared, emb, green 12.00
  Pie Plate, 10½" d, yellow and red
    flowers, green and black leaves .. 15.00
Priscilla
  Bowl, mixing 20.00
  Cake Plate 5.00
  Casserole, cov 24.00
  Creamer 7.00
  Cup 5.00
  Gravy 6.00
  Gravy Underplate 5.00
  Pie Baker 9.00
  Plate
    8" 3.00
    9" 3.00
  Platter, 13½" 10.00
  Saucer 2.00
  Soup, flat 3.50
  Sugar, cov 12.00
  Vegetable, cov 18.00
Rhythm, Dogwood
  Bowl, 8½", yellow 8.50
  Creamer, dark green 5.00
  Cup and Saucer 12.00
  Fruit Bowl 8.00
  Plate
    Dinner 9.00
    Salad 6.00
  Serving Bowl, 9" d 16.00
Rhythm Rose
  Bowl, 5" 2.00

Plate
  6" d 1.25
  7" d 2.25
  9" d 3.00
Soup 4.00

Gravy Boat, Rhythm, red, gold, green, and black dec, 9" l, $9.00.

Riviera
  Batter Jug Set, ivory syrup, green cov
    jug, yellow platter 225.00
  Butter, cov, ½ lb, cobalt 150.00
  Cup, green 9.00
  Juice Jug, red 65.00
  Juice Pitcher, mauve 145.00
  Juice Tumbler
    Aqua 40.00
    Green 40.00
    Ivory 50.00
    Mauve 40.00
    Yellow 40.00
  Mug, ivory 110.00
  Starter Set, ivory, yellow, mauve, and
    green, four cups and saucers, des-
    sert bowls, 9" plates, 6" plates, orig
    box 175.00
  Sugar, cov, green 12.00
Virginia Rose
  Bowl
    5" 1.00
    6" 2.00
  Butter Dish 40.00
  Cake Plate 14.00
  Creamer 4.00
  Cup 3.00
  Egg Cup 12.00
  Gravy Boat 6.50
  Pitcher, milk 25.00
  Plate
    6" 1.50
    9" 3.00
  Platter 6.00
  Salt and Pepper Shakers, pr 10.00
  Saucer .... .50
  Sugar, cov 10.00
  Syrup 6.00
  Tureen, cov 28.00

HORSE COLLECTIBLES

Collecting Hints: Horses have influenced American life for centuries. As a result, the horse has been memorialized in nearly every media possible, thus creating a wide variety of equine–related memorabilia, much of which is still affordable.

There is almost no category of collecting that does not include a horse collectible. Advertising featuring horses abounds—from early buggy and farm equipment ads to current advertising featuring the Budweiser Clydesdales. China and pottery items often had a horse on them. In fact, one of the most popular Western collectibles in the 1990s is dinnerware featuring a cowboy motif.

Individuals who remember the TV cowboy movies are fascinated with them. TV cowboy materials from the 1950s are very popular. Horse–oriented books and magazines along with posters from rodeos and circuses are in demand.

Tack, from beautifully handcrafted parade saddles to the simple mochilla carried by the pony express rider, is sought after. Decorative items, especially figurines, attract collectors. Old rodeo programs, horse show trophies, state fair ribbons, Kentucky Derby glasses, soft plush toys, and advertising signs are a few additional categories.

Most horse enthusiasts, overwhelmed by the sheer volume of material available to them, choose to specialize in one particular field. For example, a sports fan may collect memorabilia of the various Olympic Equestrian Teams.

Carousel figures continue to escalate in price, with the larger, more ornate outer row horses by well–known artists such as Loof, Illions or Carmel, selling in the $20,000 to $50,000 range. Lesser figures sell in the $5,000 to $8,000 range. These prices relate only to carousel horses in fine or better condition.

History: Since the earliest days of our nation's history, horses have played a vital role in American growth and lifestyle. Even our language reflects our love and respect for the horse. If we make intelligent decisions, we are credited for having "horse sense." Children having a great, rowdy time are told to "cut out the horseplay".

The English colonists brought the horse with them to the New World for transportation, plowing, and even as food. One's social status was determined by the number and quality of his horses. (Remember the condescending term "one horse town"?)

As the country became more civilized, people could afford an occasional day of rest. It became a day to show off your horses. Organized horse races and shows evolved from the casual Sunday afternoon gatherings when one person challenged another to see who had the better animal.

Gradually, due to the manufacture of affordable motor cars, the need for a horse died out. Today's equines are generally pampered family pets, living a life that a hard–working draft animal of the 1800s could only dream about.

Reference: Jim and Nancy Schaut, *Horsin' Around: A Price Guide To Horse Collectibles*, L–W Books, 1990.

Museums: US Calvary Museum, Ft. Bliss, TX; Carriage Museum, Stony Brook, NY; National Cowgirl Hall of Fame, Hereford, TX.

Advisors: Jim and Nancy Schaut.

See: Western Americana.

Bank, metal horse and wagon, numbered commemorative of South Dakota Statehood Centennial, 1989, Ertl, $40.00.

HORSE EQUIPMENT & RELATED ITEMS

Bells, 7' l leather strap, worn, over 40 nickel bells, all same size, tug hook	**200.00**
Bit, silver, emb, marked "Garcia, Elko, NV" inside cheek piece	**50.00**
Bridle, braided rawhide strips, near mint, c1950	**75.00**
Brush, leather back, stamped "US," patent date 1860s, Herbert Brush Mfg .	**60.00**
Catalog, James Bailey Co, Portland, ME, 1912 edition, carriage & sleigh trimmings	**50.00**
Collar, draft horse, leather covered wood, brass trim	**60.00**
Curry Comb, tin back, leather handle, early 1900s	**20.00**
Harness Decoration, brass, love birds in center, stamped "Peerless, England"	**45.00**
Hobbles, chain and leather, sideline type	**75.00**
Hoof pick, bone handle, patent date 1855, Wastenholm, Germany	**40.00**
Ice Delivery Wagon, wood needs restoring, original sign on side	**950.00**
Lasso, rawhide, 1890s	**200.00**
Mane & Tail Comb, "Oliver Slant Tooth", 1940s	**15.00**
Popcorn Wagon, Creators, good orig condition	**3,500.00**

Saddle
McClelland type, large fenders for leg
protection, early 1900s 450.00
Rocky Mountain crosstree type, pack
saddle, weathered wood supports 75.00
Sidesaddle, tapestry seat, unknown
maker, pre–1920s 400.00
Shaft Bells, three, graduated, iron strap 45.00
Spurs, Humanitarian type, stamped "US
Army," early 1900s 75.00
Stirrups, stamped "CSA", brass, pr 500.00
Wagon Seat, wood, no padding, re-
painted bright red, springs 50.00
Watering Trough, 2 x 6', hollowed log,
tin lined 85.00

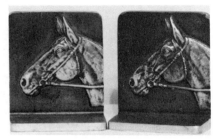

Bookends, pr, aluminum, sgd by noted thoroughbred artist Bruce Cox, $100.00.

HORSE THEME ITEMS

Bank, still, Ertl
Horse, prancing, cast iron, Dent,
1910–30 .... 85.00
Horse & Wagon, metal, commemo-
rative, J C Penny Stores 100th An-
niversary 35.00
Blanket, western theme, cowboys &
horses on brown wool, c1950 ..... 40.00
Book, *The Black Stallion*, Walter Farley,
first edition, dj 15.00
Bookends, cast aluminum, sgd Bruce
Cox, pr 100.00

Clock, brass colored, United of Brooklyn, NY, c1950, $95.00.

Calendar, 1935, Lone Ranger & Silver
illus 75.00
Carousel Horse, outside row, Charles
Carmel, c1915, near mint 33,000.00
Catalog, D F Mangels Co, Carousel
Works, Coney Island, NY, 28 pgs,
1928 edition 200.00
Cookie Jar, sitting horse, American Bis-
que 50.00
Decanter, Appaloosa, Jim Beam, Regal
China, 1974 .... 25.00
Doorstop, racehorse, Virginia Metal-
crafters, 1949 .... 125.00
Figure
Breyer, dapple gray Percheron, glossy
finish, early plastic model 50.00
Hagen Renaker, miniature donkey,
ceramic, 2" h, 1986 .... 10.00
Heisey Glass, Clydesdale, amber... 1,500.00
Kaiser, foals, standing neck to neck,
bisque, white, #16, Germany ... 125.00
Summit Art Glass, horse, blue 25.00
Vernon Kilns, unicorn, ceramic,
black, from Disney movie "Fanta-
sia" 200.00
Wade, England, miniature pony, ce-
ramic, Tom Smith artist 15.00
Fruit Crate Label, Diamond S, Califor-
nia, pears 7.00
Game, Jeu de Course, horse racing,
France, 1895 .... 500.00

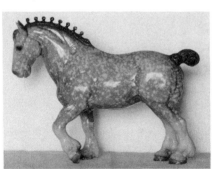

Model, plastic, Breyer, Percheron, glossy finish, $50.00.

Glass, Kentucky Derby, 1950 .... 85.00
Hobby Horse, Tom Mix, wood,
wheeled platform 350.00
Insignia, Pony Express Rider, uniform
emblem, US Post Office, pre–1971 . 15.00
Lapel Pin, US Olympic Equestrian
Team, 1988 .... 5.00
Magazine, *Saddle and Bridle*, 1931 ... 5.00
Mug, donkey, figural, red, 1976 Dem-
ocratic Party Convention souvenir,
Frankoma 35.00
Paperweight, donkey, #6241, sgd
Louise Abel, Rockwood Potteries ... 125.00

Plate, Hopalong Cassidy and Topper, W
S George Co 50.00
Post Card, linen, humorous, cowboy
bathing while horse looks on, Lon
Megargee 5.00
Poster, Kendall's Spavin Cure, litho . . .   400.00
Puzzle, Wild Horses, Jig of the Week
puzzle #5, 1933 . . . .   25.00
Reverse Painting on Glass, 5 x 8", Indi-
ans on horseback attacking stage-
coach 40.00
Salt & Pepper Shakers, mules, figural,
lifelike, pr 15.00
Sheet Music, *Dan Patch March,* cov
photo 50.00
Sign, Texas Punch, adv, tin, cowboy on
horseback 125.00
Snowdome, Lone Ranger & Silver, The
Last Roundup, glass dome, bakelite
base 90.00
Stuffed Toy, mule, "One of the Twenty
Mule Team" collar inscription, Bor-
axo promotion, 1980s 15.00

**Whiskey Bottle, Jim Beam, Regal China,
The Appaloosa, 1974, $25.00.**

Toy
Hobby Horse, #18, wood & tin,
litho, Gibbs Toy Co 125.00
Horace Horsecollar, wood pull toy,
two metal wheels, ringing bell,
N H Hill Brass Co, 1936 . . . .   225.00
Tray, adv, Coca Cola, horseback riders,
roadster 35.00
Windmill Weight, 17" h, bob tail horse,
Dempster, Beatrice, NE 225.00

HULL POTTERY

Collecting Hints: Hull Pottery has distinctive
markings on the bottom of its vases that help the
collector identify them immediately. Early stoneware pottery has an "H." The famous matte
pieces, a favorite of most collectors, contain pat-

tern numbers. For example, Camelia pieces are
marked with numbers in the 100's, Iris pieces
have 400 numbers, and Wildflower numbers
with a W— preceding their number. Most of
Hull's vases are also marked with their height in
inches, making determining their value much
easier. Items made after 1950 are marked with
"hull" or "Hull" in large script writing and are
usually glossy.

History: In 1905 Addis E. Hull purchased the
Acme Pottery Co. in Crooksville, Ohio. In 1917
A. E. Hull Pottery Co. began to make a line of
art pottery for florists and gift shops. The company also made novelties, kitchenware, and
stoneware. During the Depression, the company's largest production was tiles.

In 1950 the factory was destroyed by a flood
and fire. By 1952 it was back in production,
operating with the Hull Pottery Company name.
At this time Hull added its newer glossy finish
pottery plus developed Regal and Floraline as
trade names for pieces sold in flower shops.
Hull's brown House 'n Garden line of kitchenware and dinnerware achieved great popularity
and was the main line of pottery being produced
prior to the plant closing its doors in 1986.

Hull's Little Red Riding Hood kitchenware was
manufactured between 1943 and 1957 and is a
favorite of collectors, including many who do
not collect other Hull items.

Hull collectors are beginning to seriously collect the glossy ware and kitchen items. Since the
plant has closed, all Hull pieces have become
desirable.

References: Joan Gray Hull, *Hull: The Heavenly
Pottery,* published by author, 1990; Brenda Rob-
erts, *The Collectors Encyclopedia of Hull Pottery,*
Collector Books, 1980; Mark E. Supnick, *Col-
lecting Hull Pottery's "Little Red Riding Hood":
A Pictorial Reference And Price Guide,* L–W
Book Sales, 1989.

Advisor: Joan Hull.

PRE-1950 PATTERNS

Bow Knot
B-1-5½", pitcher 95.00
B-5-6½", cornucopia 95.00
B-10-10¼", vase 350.00
B-25-6½", basket 225.00
Dogwood (Wild Rose)
503-8½", vase 75.00
510-10½", vase 135.00
517-4¾", vase 45.00
Iris (Narcissus)
401-8", pitcher 125.00
407-7", vase 75.00
414-10½", vase 165.00
Jack-in-the-Pulpit (Calla Lily)
501-33-6", vase 55.00

510-33-8", vase **90.00**
590-33-13", console bowl **150.00**
Little Red Riding Hood
    Mustard jar, spoon, 5½" **200.00**
    Salt and Pepper, 5½" **85.00**
    Spice Jar **300.00**
Magnolia (Pink Gloss)
    H-23, console bowl **65.00**
    H-24, candleholders **50.00**
Magnolia
    1-8½", vase **60.00**
    6-12", double cornucopia **85.00**
    13-4¾", vase **30.00**
    17-12½", winged vase **125.00**

Vase, pink ground, stylized rope handles, yellow stylized wicker base, red and purple flowers, high gloss, 10¾", $35.00.

Open Rose (Camelia)
    102-8½", vase **75.00**
    110, 111, 112, tea set **250.00**
    120-6¼", vase **45.00**
    139-10½", lamp vase **200.00**
Orchid
    302-4¾" **45.00**
    303-6½" **60.00**
    307-8" **95.00**
    308-10" **225.00**
Poppy
    602-6½", planter **100.00**
    605-4¾", vase **95.00**
    610-13", pitcher **450.00**
Rosella
    R-2-5", vase **25.00**
    R-6-6½" **40.00**
    R-13-8½", cornucopia **50.00**
Stoneware
    39, H, 8", vase **40.00**
    536, H, jardiniere **70.00**
Thistle, 52-6½" **65.00**
Tile (Hull Cushion)
    Plain **20.00**
    Designed **50.00**

Tulip (Sueno)
    100-33-6½", vase **55.00**
    102-33-6", basket **125.00**
    117-30-5", jardiniere **50.00**
Waterlily
    L-3-5½", pitcher **40.00**
    L-11-9½", vase **85.00**
    L-24-8½", jardiniere **150.00**
Wildflower
    W-9-8½", vase **65.00**
    W-15-10½", fan vase **85.00**
    W-19-13½", pitcher **250.00**
    52-5½" **75.00**
    65-7", low basket **350.00**
    71-12", vase **175.00**
Woodland (Matte)
    W-4-6½", vase **45.00**
    W-13-7½", shell wall pocket **60.00**
    W-17-7½", suspended vase **115.00**

POST-1950 PATTERNS

Blossom Flite
    T-4-8½", basket **60.00**
    T-7-10½", vase **50.00**
    T-14,15,16, tea set **125.00**
Butterfly
    B-6-5½", candy dish **35.00**
    B-9-9", vase **40.00**
    B-24-25", Lavabo set **90.00**
Capri
    C-47-5¼" x 8", round flower bowl .. **35.00**
    C-81, twin swan planter **65.00**
Continental
    C-53-8½", vase **35.00**
    C-54-12½", vase **50.00**
Ebbtide
    E-2-7", twin fish vase **45.00**
    E-11-16½", basket **135.00**
Figural Planters
    24, Madonna planter **25.00**
    62, 12", deer planter **45.00**
    98, 10", unicorn base **35.00**
Parchment & Pine
    S-4-10", vase **70.00**
    S-11-10½", scroll planter **40.00**
Serenade (Birds)
    S-2-6", pitcher **25.00**
    S-11-10½", vase **65.00**
Sunglow (Kitchenware)
    54, salt and pepper **20.00**
    81, pitcher wall pocket **40.00**
    91, 6½", vase **30.00**
Tokay/Tuscany
    1-6½", cornucopia **25.00**
    8-10, vase **75.00**
    15-12", basket **95.00**
Tropicania, 56-13½", pitcher **275.00**
Woodland
    W-3-5½", pitcher **35.00**
    W-8-7½", vase **35.00**
    W-10-11", cornucopia **40.00**

HUMMEL ITEMS

Collecting Hints: A key to Hummel figures is the mark. Collectors are advised to get the early marks whenever possible. Since production runs were large, almost all figurines, no matter what the mark, exist in large numbers.

Prices fluctuate a great deal. Dealers often run ads showing discounts on the modern pieces in antiques newspapers, such as *The Antique Trader*. The slightest damage to a piece lowers the value significantly.

Before World War II and for a few years after, the Goebel Company made objects, such as vases, for export. These often had the early mark. Prices are modest for these items because few collectors concentrate on them. The Hummel books do not list them. This aspect of the Goebel Company offers the chance for an excellent research project.

History: Hummel items are the original creations of the German artist, Berta Hummel. Born in 1909 in Massing, Bavaria, to a family where the arts were a part of everyday living, her talents were encouraged by her parents and formal educators from early childhood. At the age of 18, she was enrolled in the Academy of Fine Arts in Munich to further her mastery of drawing and the palette.

She entered the Convent of Siessen and became Sister Maria Innocentia in 1934. In this Franciscan cloister, she continued drawing and painting images of her childhood friends.

In 1935, W. Goebel Co. in Rodental, Germany, conceived the idea of reproducing Sister Berta's sketches into 3–dimensional bisque figurines. John Schmid discovered the German-made figurines. The Schmid Brothers of Randolph, Massachusetts, introduced the figurines to America and became Goebel's U.S. distributor.

In 1967, Goebel began distributing Hummel items in the U.S. and a controversy developed between the two companies involving the Hummel family and the convent. Law suits and counter suits ensued. The German courts finally effected a compromise. The convent held legal rights to all works produced by Sister Berta from 1934 until her death in 1964 and licensed Goebel to reproduce these works. Schmid was to deal directly with the Hummel family for permission to reproduce any pre–convent art work.

All authentic Hummels bear both the signature M.I. Hummel and a Goebel trademark. Various trademarks were used to identify the year of production. The Crown Mark (CM) was used in 1935, Full Bee (FB) 1940–1959; Small Stylized Bee (SSE) 1960–1972; Large Stylized Bee (LSB) 1960–19 3; Three Line Mark (3L) 1964–1972; Last Bee Mark (LB) 1972–1980, Missing Bee Mark (MB) 1979–1991. In 1991, a new Crown Mark was introduced which includes the restored name of Germany as a single country.

References: John F. Hotchkiss, *Hummel Art II,* Wallace–Homestead, 1981; John F. Hotchkiss, *Hotchkiss' Handbook To Hummel Art with Current Prices,* Wallace–Homestead, 1982; Carl F. Luckey, *Luckey's Hummel Figurines & Plates, 7th Edition,* Books Americana, 1987; Lawrence L. Wonsch, *Hummel Copycats with Values,* Wallace–Homestead, 1987.

Collectors' Clubs: Goebel Collectors' Club, 105 White Plains Road, Tarrytown, NY 10591; Hummel Collectors Club, P.O. Box 257, Yardley, PA 19067.

Museum: Goebel Museum, Tarrytown, NY.

Chicken Licken, #385/1871, last bee mark, $100.00.

Annual Plate
1971, Heavenly Angel, 264, 3L	800.00
1973, Globe Trotter, 266, LBM	200.00
1974, Goose Girl, 267, LBM	115.00
1975, Ride Into Christmas, 268, LBM	115.00
1976, Apple Tree Girl, 269, LBM	90.00
1977, Apple Tree Boy 270, LBM	125.00
1978, Happy Pastime, 271, LBM	115.00
1980, School Girl, 273, MB	100.00

Ashtray
Happy Pastime, 62, 3L	95.00
Let's Sing, 114, LBM	68.00
Singing Lesson, 34, MB	80.00

Bell
1979, Farewell, 701, LBM	80.00
1980, Thoughtful, 702, MB	85.00
1981, In Tune, 703, MB	85.00
1983, Knit One, 705, MB	90.00

Bookends
Apple Tree Girl & Apple Tree Boy, 252 A & B, LBM	180.00
Farm Boy & Goose Girl, 60 A & B, MB	220.00
Good Friends & She Loves Me, She Loves Me Not, 251 A & B, SSB	225.00

Candleholder

Angelic Sleep, 25, SSB	**135.00**
Begging His Share, 9, 3L	**115.00**
Boy With Horse, 117, SSB	**42.50**
Girl With Fir Tree, 116, CM	**125.00**
Joyous News, 27/1, FB	**325.00**
Joyous News, Angel with Trumpet, 1/40/0, FB	**65.00**
Little Band, 388, MB	**132.00**
Silent Night, 54, LBM	**105.00**

Candy Box

Chick Girl, 111/57, jar style, 3L	**105.00**
Happy Pastime, 111/69, jar style, LBM	**95.00**
Let's Sing, 111/110, bowl style, SSB	**325.00**

Figurine

Accordion Boy, 185, MB	**72.00**
Angel Duet, 261, MB	**88.00**
Angel With Lute, 238/A, LBM	**24.00**
Apple Tree Girl, 141/3/0, FB	**140.00**
Apple Tree Boy, 142/3/0, LBM	**55.00**
Autumn Harvest, 355, MB	**88.00**
Baker, 128, SSB	**95.00**
Barnyard Hero, 195/2/0, SSB	**110.00**
Bird Duet, 169, 3L	**80.00**
Birthday Serenade, 218/2/0, LBM	**80.00**
Boy With Accordion, 390, LBM	**34.00**
Carnival, 328, LBM	**85.00**
Celestial Musician, 188/0, MB	**80.00**
Chick Girl, 57/0, 3L	**85.00**
Chichen–Licken, 385, 3L	**300.00**
Chimney Sweep, 12/2/0, FB	**60.00**
Christmas Song, 343, MB	**90.00**
Close Harmony, 336, MB	**125.00**
Coquettes, 179, MB	**105.00**
Crossroads, 331, MB	**185.00**
Culprits, 56/A, LBM	**110.00**
Farewell, 65, MB	**110.00**
Farm Boy, 66, SSB	**165.00**
Feeding Time, 199/0, MB	**88.00**
Gay Adventure, 356, LBM	**80.00**
Girl with Nosegay, 239/A, 3L	**40.00**
Girl With Sheet of Music, 389, 3L	**40.00**
Globe Trotter, 79, 3L	**85.00**
Going to Grandma's, 52/0, MB	**100.00**
Good Hunting, 307, LBM	**100.00**
Goose Girl, 47/3/0, FB	**140.00**
Happy Pastime, 69, CB	**325.00**
Heavenly Angel, 21/0, SSB	**65.00**
Home From Market, 198/12/0, LBM	**58.00**
In Tune, 414, MB	**120.00**
It's Cold, 421, MB	**80.00**
Joyful, 53, SSB	**75.00**
Just Resting, 112/3/0, LBM	**68.00**
Kiss Me, 311, LBM	**100.00**
Knitting Lesson, 256, MB	**220.00**
Latest News, 184, SSB	**180.00**
Letter to Santa Claus, 340, MB	**137.00**
Little Drummer, 240, FB	**125.00**
Little Gabriel, 32/0, CM	**275.00**
Little Gardener, 74, SSB	**85.00**
Little Goat Herder, 200/10, 3L	**95.00**
Little Helper, 73, LBM	**60.00**
Little Hiker, 16/2/0, CM	**145.00**
Little Scholar, 80, FB	**180.00**
Little Sweeper, 171, MB	**55.00**
Lost Sheep, 68/2/0, FB	**135.00**
Lost Stocking, 374, LBM	**68.00**
March Winds, 43, FB	**125.00**
Meditation, 13/2/0, SSB	**85.00**
Merry Wanderer, 11/2/0, FB	**135.00**
Mischief Maker, 342, LBM	**115.00**
On Holiday, 350, MB	**90.00**
Out of Danger, 56/B, FB	**250.00**
Playmates, 58/0, FB	**160.00**
Postman, 119, 3L	**110.00**
Ride into Christmas, 396/2/0, MB	**100.00**
She Loves Me, She Loves Me Not, 174, CM	**350.00**
Signs of Spring, 203/2/0, LBM	**75.00**
Singing Lesson, 63, SSB	**85.00**
Soldier Boy, 332, 3L	**90.00**
Stitch in Time, 255, 3L	**115.00**
Stormy Weather, 71, MB	**200.00**
Surprise, 94/3/0, FB	**160.00**
Sweet Music, 186, 3L	**95.00**
Thoughtful, 415, MB	**110.00**
To Market, 49/3/0, SSB	**130.00**
Trumpet Boy, 97, MB	**55.00**
Village Boy, 51/3/0, 3L	**50.00**
Volunteers, 50/2,/0, SSB	**165.00**
Wash Day, 321, SSB	**275.00**
Wayside Harmony, 111/3/0, MB	**63.00**
Which Hand, 258, LBM	**68.00**

Font

Angel Duet, 146, LBM	**24.00**
Angel Shrine, 147, FB	**82.00**
Child With Flowers, 36/0, SSB	**32.50**
Child Jesus, 26/0, MB	**17.50**
Guardian Angel, 248/0, 3L	**40.00**
Holy Family, 246, SSB	**62.00**
Madonna and Child, 243, FB	**125.00**
White Angel, 75, CM	**125.00**
Worship, 164, 3L	**35.00**

Lamp Base

Apple Tree Girl, 229, 3L	**192.00**
Birthday Serenade, 234, MB	**210.00**
Culprits, 44/A, MB	**205.00**
Just Resting, 225/1, MB	**180.00**
She Loves Me, She Loves Me Not, 227, SSB	**225.00**
To Market, 223, LBM	**245.00**
Wayside Harmony, 224/1, MB	**180.00**

Music Box, Little Band, 392/M, MB | **204.00**

Nativity Set Pieces

Angel Serenade, 260/E, 3L	**80.00**
Cow, lying, 260/M, LBM	**90.00**
Donkey, standing, 260/L, MB	**66.00**
Flying Angel, 366, color, 3L	**68.00**
Infant Jesus, 260/C, 3L	**70.00**
Joseph, 214/B, white, FB	**175.00**
King, kneeling 260/P, MB	**273.00**
Lamb, 214/0, color, SSB	**14.00**
Madonna, 260/A, MB	**290.00**

Moorish King, standing, 214/L, white, 3L	**118.00**
Sheep, standing with lamb, 260/H, 3L	**65.00**
Shepherd, kneeling, 214/G, color, SSB	**78.00**
Virgin Mary, 214/A, white, LBM	**55.00**
Wood Stable	**55.00**

Wall Plaque

Ba–Bee–Ring, 30 A & B, LBM	**95.00**
Flitting Butterfly, 139, SSB	**125.00**
Madonna, 48/0, 3L	**65.00**
Merry Wanderer, 92, LBM	**75.00**
Standing Boy, 168, MB	**80.00**
The Mail Is Here, 140, 3L	**162.00**
Vacation Time, 125, LBM	**105.00**

Wall Vase

Boy, 360/B, LBM	**68.00**
Boy & Girl, 360/A, MB	**63.00**
Girl, 360/C, LBM	**68.00**

INSULATORS

Collecting Hints: Learn the shapes of the insulators and the abbreviations which appear on them. Some commonly found abbreviations are: "B" (Brookfield), "B & O" (Baltimore and Ohio), "EC&M Co SF" (Electrical Construction and Maintenance Company of San Francisco), "ER" (Erie Railroad), "WGM Co" (Western Glass Manufacturing Company), and "WUT Co" (Western Union Telegraph Company).

The majority of the insulators are priced below $50.00. However, there are examples of threaded and threadless insulators which have exceeded $2,000. There has been little movement in the price of glass insulators for the past years. The top insulators in each category are:

Threaded

CD 139, Combination Safety/Pat. Applied for, aqua **2,500.00**
CD 180, Liquid Insulator/blank, ice aqua **2,500.00**
CD 138–9, Patent Applied for/blank, aqua **2,400.00**
CD 176, Lower wire ridge, Whitall Tatum Co. No. 12 made in U.S.A./lower wire ridge, Patent No. 1708038, straw **2,300.00**
CD 181, no name and no embossing **2,200.00**

Threadless

CD 731, no name and no embossing, white milk glass **3,000.00**
CD 739, no name and no embossing, similar to jade green milk glass **3,000.00**
CD 737, Leffert's/blank, green **2,500.00**
CD 790, no name and no embossing, known as Tea Pot, aqua **2,200.00**
CD 788, no name and no embossing, known as slash top **2,200.00**
The six Fry Glass insulators are not counted in this survey. They are not common threadless in-

sulators because they were made only between 1844 and 1865.

History: The invention of the telegraph in 1832 created the need for a glass or ceramic insulator. The first patent was given to Ezra Cornell in 1844. The principal manufacturing era was from 1850 to the mid–1900s. Leading companies include Armstrong (1938–69), Brookfield (1865–1922), California (1912–16), Gayner (1920–22), Hemingray (1871–1919), Lynchburg (1923–25), Maydwell (1935–40), McLaughlin (1923–25), and Whitall Tatum (1920–38).

Initially, insulators were threadless. Shortly after the Civil War, L. A. Cauvet received a patent for a threaded insulator. Drip points prevented water from laying on the insulator and causing a short. The double skirt kept moisture from the peg or pin.

There are about five hundred different styles of glass insulators. Each different style insulator has been given a "CD" (consolidated design) number which are found in N. R. Woodward's *The Glass Insulator In America*. Colors and names of the makers and all lettering found on the same style insulator have nothing to do with the CD number. Only the style of the insulator is the key to the numbering.

References: Bob Alexander, *Threaded Glass Insulator Price Guide...For The Year 1988*, A. B. Publishing Co., 1988; Gary G. Cranfill and Greg A. Kareofelas, *The Glass Insulator: A Comprehensive Reference*, published by author, 1973, separate price list; Michael G. Guthrie, *A Handbook For The Recognition & Identification Of Fake, Altered, and Repaired Insulators*, published by author, 1988; Paul Keating (ed.), *Milholland's Suggested Insulator Price Guide*, published by author, 1986; John and Carol McDougald, *Insulators—A History and Guide to North American Pintype Insulators*, Vols 1 and 2, published by authors, 1990; John and Carol McDougald, *1991 Price Guide for Insulators*, published by authors, 1991.

Collectors' Club: National Insulator Association, 5 Brownstone Road, East Granby, CT 06026.

Periodical: *Crown Jewels of the Wire*, P.O. Box 1003, St. Charles, IL 60174.

Museums: Big Thicket Museum, Saratoga, TX; Edison Plaza Museum, Beaumont, TX.

Note: The information on the front of the insulator is first, followed by a slash, followed by the information on the back of the insulator.

THREADED INSULATORS

CD 102
Brookfield/New York
Aqua, clear, green **5.00**

Hemingray #60, aqua, 5" h, $5.00.

Purple	15.00
California/blank, blue	15.00
CD 104, Brookfield/New York, aqua	5.00
CD 113, Hemingray 12/Made in USA	
Aqua	4.00
Emerald Green	12.00
Green	6.00
CD 133, Hemingray, opalescent	30.00
CD 145	
Brookfield/New York	
Aqua	5.00
Light Green	7.00
California/blank	
Burgundy	25.00
Green–Light Purple	15.00
Purple	20.00
Sage Green	5.00
CD 154	
Gayner/#44	
Aqua	8.00
Green	10.00
Lynchburg/#44	5.00
Maydwell 42/USA	
Clear	4.00
Pale Green	6.00
Whitehall Tatum #1/Made in USA,	
aqua	5.00
CD 160	
Hemingray 14/Made in USA	
Aqua	5.00
Clear	6.00
Dark Smoke	10.00
CD 162	
Brookfield/New York	
Aqua	5.00
Green	7.00
Ice Blue	7.00
Purple	35.00
California/blank	
Blue	8.00
Green	10.00
Peach	30.00
Purple	12.00
Smoke	7.00

Gayner/38–20, aqua	5.00
Hemingray 20/Made in USA	
Amber	125.00
Blue	8.00
Ice Blue	10.00
McLaughlin/#20	
Aqua	5.00
Light Blue	7.00
Lime Green	10.00
CD 164, McLaughlin, emerald green	10.00
CD 168	
Hemingray Made in USA/D510	
Carnival	20.00
Clear	4.00
Green	7.00
Ice Blue	6.00
Whitehall Tatum Co #11/Made in USA	
Ice Blue	15.00
Light Aqua	20.00
Light Green	30.00
CD 257, Hemingray, carnival	30.00

THREADLESS INSULATORS

CD 718, no name and no embossing	
Aqua	200.00
Black Glass	350.00
Emerald Green	300.00
Olive Green	300.00

IRONS

Collecting Hints: Heavy rusting, pitting, and missing parts detract from an iron's value. As a collector becomes more advanced, he may accept some of these defects on a rare and unusual iron. However, the beginning collector is urged to concentrate on irons in very good to excellent condition.

European, Oriental, and other foreign irons are desirable, since many unusual types come from these areas and some models were prototypes for later American–made irons.

History: Ironing devices have been in use for many centuries, with early references dating from 1100. Irons from the Medieval, Renaissance, and early industrial era can be found in Europe, but are rare. Fine brass engraved irons and hand-wrought irons dominated the period prior to 1850.

After 1850 the iron began a series of rapid evolutionary changes. New models were patented monthly. The housewife and tailor sought the latest improvement to keep "up–to–date."

The irons of the 1850 to 1910 period were heated in four ways: (1) a hot metal slug was inserted into the body, (2) a burning solid, such as coal or charcoal, was placed in the body, (3) a liquid or gas, such as alcohol, gasoline, or natural gas, was fed from an external tank and burned in the body, and (4) conduction heating, usually by drawing heat from a stove top.

Irons from the 1850 to 1910 period are plentiful and varied. Many models and novelty irons still have not been documented by collectors. Electric irons have not yet found favor among most iron collectors.

References: Esther S. Berney, *A Collectors Guide To Pressing Irons And Trivets*, Crown Publishers, Inc., 1977; A. H. Glissman, *The Evolution Of The Sad Iron*, privately printed, 1970; Brian Jewell, *Smoothing Irons: A History And Collectors Guide*, Wallace–Homestead, 1977; Judy (author) and Frank (illustrator) Politzer, *Early Tuesday Morning: More Little Irons and Trivets*, published by author, 1986; Judy and Frank Politzer, *Tuesday's Children*, published by author, 1977; Ted and V. Swanson, *The Swanson Collection*, published by author.

Collectors' Clubs: Friends of Ancient Smoothing Irons, Box 215, Carlsbad CA 92008; Midwest Sad Iron Collectors Club, 500 Adventureland Drive, Altoona, IA 50009.

Museums: Henry Ford Museum, Dearborn, MI; Shelburne Museum, Shelburne, VT; Sturbridge Village, Sturbridge, MA.

Advisors: David and Sue Irons.

REPRODUCTION ALERT: The most often reproduced irons are the miniatures, especially the swan's neck and flat irons. Reproductions of some large European varieties are available, but poor construction, use of thin metals, and the unusually fine condition easily identifies them as new.

Note: The irons listed are American made unless otherwise noted.

Charcoal
    Chinese, open bronze pan, carved
      ivory, jade handle, Glissman Fig. 6 **100.00**

Alcohol, Laundry Maid, Sears, Roebuck & Co, $35.00.

Colebrookdale Iron Co, Boyertown, PA, #4, tall spout with face damper, 7" l **125.00**
Ellipse, 1903, diminished spout, Berney #133A **100.00**
European High Base, rainbow handle, latch using man's head, rooster, etc., 6–8" l, Berney #135 (A–C) . **110.00**

Flat and Sad Irons
  English Cap Iron, Kenrick #5, 4¼" l, Politzer Fig. #173A **40.00**
  Mahoney, Troy, NY, wavy bottom, Berney #31 C **80.00**
  Mexican, wrought, expanded hollow handle, various sizes and shapes, Berney 21 A–B **50.00**
  Mrs Potts, removable wood handle, various sizes, pointed both ends, Glissman Fig. 163 .... **15.00**
  Nelson Streeter, "Sensible," various sizes, Glissman Fig. 179 .... **20.00**
  Ober, all cast, ribbed handle, various sizes, Glissman Fig. 155A **45.00**
  Soapstone, Hood's 1867, stone insulator between handle/base, Berney #28 .... **150.00**
  Weida, iron handle disengages at one end, 1870, Berney #32A–B **110.00**

Fluter
  Companion, clamp on crank style, Berney #110A **175.00**
  English Boxwood Pleater, fluted rolling pin and board, 4½ x 3" base, Berney #37A **250.00**
  Hewitt Revolving Iron, fluter attachment, Glissman Fig. 261 .... **170.00**
  Knox Machine Fluter, good Knox picture in oval recessed area, Glissman Fig. 256 .... **175.00**
  New Geneva, rocker style, Berney #88A **50.00**
  Pleating Board, wire strips on board, Glissman Fig. 237 .... **65.00**
  The Best, rocker style, Berney #98B **65.00**

Gasoline/Alcohol/Natural Gas
  Alcohol
    German, Feldmeyer, typical two rows of nine holes in base, saw grip handle, 6¾" l, Berney #144A **175.00**
    Imperial, Imperial Brass Mfg Co, 6½" l, Berney #153A **110.00**
    Monitor, cylindrical tank at front, Berney #146A **100.00**
    Sun Gas Machine Co, cylindrical tank on side, Berney #152A ... **140.00**
  Gasoline
    American Gas Machine Co, Inc, #66, light green porcelain base, 7" l **90.00**
    Montgomery Ward, pump in han-

dle, triangular tank in rear, Berney #157A **70.00**

Sun Mfg Co, ribbed body, cylindrical tank on rear, like Berney #149 .... **75.00**

Natural Gas

Clefton Plumbing & Heating Co, spout on front, Berney #166A . **120.00**

Imperial, hose coupling at rear, five holes on each side of base, Berney #174A **55.00**

The Rhythm 3754 Radiation, green porcelain body, black plastic handle, 7" l **120.00**

Miniature

Block grip handle, various sizes, Politzer Fig. 226 .... **50.00**

Cast, wire handle, 2–3" l, Politzer Fig. 84 .... **35.00**

English

Brass slug iron, trap door, Politzer Fig. 322 .... **100.00**

Goffering, all cast, wire "S", Politzer Fig. 337 .... **100.00**

Enterprise, 2½" l, solid cast, Politzer Fig. 157 .... **40.00**

French, all cast low profile base, various sizes, Politzer Fig. 196 ...... **50.00**

Swan, 2–3" l, all cast

No paint **50.00**

Original paint **150.00**

Tri bump handle, all cast, various sizes, Politzer Fig. 50 .... **40.00**

Sad iron, round back, 4½" h, 5¾" l, $18.50.

Slug

English/American, box iron, trap door on rear, various sizes and styles, Berney #12 C **90.00**

German, bullet nose, saw grip handle, various sizes and shapes, styles like Glissman Fig. 58 .... **75.00**

Speciality Irons and Accessories

Ball or Egg Iron

Hand held, Glissman Fig. 230 ... **70.00**

On stand, tripod base **175.00**

Goffering

Clamp on, all wrought, Glissman Fig. 219 .... **200.00**

Double stack, all cast, European, Glissman Fig. 207 .... **400.00**

English, brass, Queen Anne style, Glissman Fig. 211 .... **175.00**

Hat

Brim, all cast, Glissman Fig. 343A **150.00**

Wood, Tolliker, Glissman Fig. 344 **150.00**

Iron Heater

Gas type for three or more irons, Berney #290 .... **100.00**

Pyramid style, Berney #283 ..... **125.00**

Stove insert, Berney #293 .... **40.00**

Laundry Stove, flat sides on belly, supports 6–8 irons, Berney #292 .... **350.00**

Smoothing Board, all wood, carved with horse handle, Scandinavian, Glissman Fig. 27 .... **250.00**

JEWELRY, COSTUME

Collecting Hints: Two diverse factors influence price—artistic merit and personal appeal. The result is that there is a wide fluctuation in market prices. Also, the changing values of gold and silver cause prices to vary.

Jewelry prices vary regionally, depending on what is popular in a given area. Costume jewelry, since it was mass produced, should be bought in very good or mint condition. Most stones in costume jewelry are not real. Advanced collectors generally can distinguish stones and metals; novice collectors should study carefully before trusting their eyes and a ten power loop.

History: The design of jewelry closely followed costume design. Early inventions which influenced jewelry design were the pin making machine in 1832, the development of the electroplating process by the English firm of Elkington in the 1860s, and die stamping machinery.

The Art Deco and Art Nouveau eras made inexpensive costume jewelry acceptable. Mass production of tin—like pins, bracelets, rings, etc., followed. Newark (New Jersey), New York, and Philadelphia became centers for jewelry manufacturing, challenging Providence, Rhode Island, which had held the position in 1800. Coro Incorporated of Providence employed over 2,000 people in 1946.

Gold was removed from circulation in 1933, reducing the amount of gold related jewelry items. Scarcity of materials during World War II further aided the move to plastic and lesser metals. Precious stones were replaced by "gemstones" and glass imitations.

Mass produced jewelry employed the talents of many famous designers. Rapid communication of style changes through magazines and newspapers led to fads which quickly swept across the country. By the 1950s fine costume jewelry appeared on the market and received acceptance, even among the more sophisticated buyers.

References: Lillian Baker, *100 Years of Collectible Jewelry*, Collector Books, 1978 (1989 value update); Corinne Davidov and Ginny Redington Dawes, *The Bakelite Jewelry Book*, Abbeville Press, 1988; Maryanne Dolan, *Collecting Rhinestone Jewelry, Second Edition*, Books Americana, 1989; S. Sylvia Henzel, *Collectible Costume Jewelry, Second Edition*, Wallace-Homestead, 1987 (1990 value update); Lyngerde Kelley and Nancy Schiffer, *Plastic Jewelry*, Schiffer Publishing Ltd., 1987; J. L. Lynnlee, *All That Glitters*, Schiffer Publishing, Ltd., 1986; Sibylle Jargstorf, *Glass in Jewelry: Hidden Artistry in Glass*, Schiffer Publishing, 1991; Harrice Miller, *The Official Identification and Price Guide To Costume Jewelry*, House of Collectibles, 1990; Nancy N. Schiffer, *Costume Jewelry: The Fun of Collecting*, Schiffer Publishing Ltd., 1988.

Note: The following abbreviations are used:

GF—Gold filled
SS—Sterling silver
YG—Yellow gold
YGF—Yellow gold filled

Bar Pin
   Marvella **32.00**
   White Gold, 10K, filigree, center faceted amethyst **85.00**
Bracelet
   Bakelite
     Green, carved **39.00**
     Yellow and White **27.00**
   Bangle, silver plated, open work, engraved swirl design, 2 x ½" **12.00**
   Baroque Amber, Aurora Borealis, moonstones, Weiss **95.00**
   Child's, rhinestone, diamond shape . **8.50**
   Copper, hand hammered, open floral design **10.00**
   Hinged, "KJL" **24.00**
   Link, SS, ¾" charm heart with key, 7" **25.00**
   Man's, SS, ID, heavy links, unengraved name plate **25.00**
   Marcasites and yellow stones, SS, marked .935 .... **48.00**
   Pearls, gold and clear stones, marked "Regency" **33.00**
   Rhinestone
     Leru, 1½" w **30.00**
     Three strand **15.00**
   Snake, three coiled rows **65.00**
   Sterling Sorrento **25.00**

Bracelet and Earrings Set, white stones, round and rect rhinestones, Eisenberg **45.00**
Brooch
   Art Nouveau, gold filigree, five hanging cut crystal drops **35.00**
   Barclay **18.00**
   Cameo, carved, marcasite, Weiss ... **48.00**
   Eisenberg Ice **65.00**
   Mourning, gold filled, male photo .. **38.00**
   Rhinestone, blue, Regency **16.00**
   Rubies, silver, Joseff of Hollywood .. **65.00**
   Vendome **45.00**
   Yellow Gold
     10K, filigree, round, black onyx center with 5 pt diamond, two pearls **95.00**
     14K, enameled flower bouquet ... **80.00**
Brooch and Earrings Set, ice green, Eisenberg **125.00**
Chain
   14K, YG, solid rope, barrel clasp, 2 mm thick, 18" **90.00**
   SS, snake type, 15" **18.00**
   YGF, double link, 24" **35.00**
Charm
   Golf Club Bag, white metal, ⅝" **3.50**
   Girl's Head, SS **12.00**
   Horn, 14K, YG **18.00**
   Santa, metal, red enamel **28.00**
   Shark, 2" l, 14K, YG **70.00**
Choker
   Faux pearl, double strand, Miriam Haskell **85.00**
   Faux pearls and rhinestones, Trifari . **35.00**
   Mariam Haskell **30.00**
Cross
   14K, YG, fancy **25.00**
   SS, pearl in center, 1½ x 1" **20.00**
Cuff Links, pr
   Golf Motif **12.00**
   White Gold, 10K, engraved **35.00**
Dress Buckle, mother–of–pearl, plain, 1½" **5.00**
Earrings
   Baby's, 14K, YG, pierced **18.00**
   Clear Stones, coral drops, marked "Schreiner" **75.00**
   Copper, Renoir **12.00**
   Enamel on Sterling, pale blue, feather, Norway **25.00**
   Gypsy, 14K, YG, loops, deep red coral, teardrops, Victorian **65.00**
   Hatti Carnegie **16.00**
   Heart shape, 14K, YG, open work diamond **60.00**
   Hobe Shell Cameo, rhinestones, smoked crystals **45.00**
   Laguna, red bead, dangle **7.00**
   Loop, bamboo motif **85.00**
   Rhinestone
     Clear, 1½", Kramer **15.00**
     Green, 1", Weiss **18.00**

Sterling, Napier **10.00**
Turquoise, SS, Indian **18.00**
Locket
Mother–of–pearl, YGF, Navy insignia
  center, 1" **30.00**
YGF, engraved flowers, monogram,
  ¾ x 1" **25.00**
Money Clip, Golden Nugget **15.00**

Necklace and hoop earrings, frosted plastic links, lime green spacer beads, gold plated clasps, three strand necklace, $5.00.

Necklace
Aurora Borealis, three strand **26.00**
Cameo, two color, hard stone, silver
  filigree chain with jet beads,
  marked "Czech" **65.00**
Coral, 19", graduated, alternating 14K
  Etruscan granulation beads, 14K
  clasp, early 1900s **185.00**
Crystal Beads
Blue, Art Deco, two strand, gold
  and silver trim **35.00**
Pink, five stand, large pink rhinestone clasp, marked "Vendome" **75.00**
Vaseline color, faceted, graduated,
  14K gold filled fastener and
  chain, 16" **22.00**
Faux Pearls, plastic crystals, alternat-
  ing, 16½", Miriam Haskell, pat
  3,427,691 .... **85.00**
Papier Mache, fruit, 1920s **22.00**
Pearl, 17", 6mm cultured, evenly
  matched, 10K white gold clasp .. **90.00**
Rhinestone, marquise shape stone
  with cascade of round and mar-
  quise stones, SS setting **35.00**
Sterling, wide link, Danecraft **65.00**
Weiss **40.00**
Necklace and Earrings Set
Kramer **34.00**
Lisner **27.00**
Pearl and Crystal, multi–strand, neck-
  lace and ear clips, Vendome **85.00**
Plastic frosted links, lime green spacer
  beads, gold plated clasps, 13" l
  necklace, hoop earrings **5.00**
Pendant
Amethyst, 1" tear drop, YGF **35.00**
Art Nouveau, woman with swirling
  hair **25.00**

Bakelite, amber, white cameo, 2¼ x
  1¾" **60.00**
Crystal, yellow, marcasite top, SS
  chain **55.00**
Enameled, 2½ x 2½", sterling chain,
  Siam **55.00**
Marcasite, rose, 20 marcasites, SS
  chain **22.00**
Mother–of–pearl, carved horse **100.00**
Rhinestone, 1" heart, SS chain **25.00**
YGF, snake chain, fold–over pendant,
  Danecraft **25.00**
Pendant and Earrings Set, opals, en-
  cased in crystal teardrops, SS, 3 pcs **65.00**
Pin
Amethyst, SS, flower **50.00**
Art Deco, brass, Aztec design, 2 x
  1½" **8.00**
Art Nouveau, lady, butterfly wings,
  marcasite borders, 2¾", SS **110.00**
Bakelite, red, cherry, cornucopia ... **85.00**
Bow, Eisenberg **45.00**
Butterfly, enameled, marked "Robert" **12.00**
Cherries, composition, green cloth
  leaves **6.50**
Cupid, flying, carrying torch, SS, Vic-
  torian **60.00**
Elephant, Mexican silver **10.00**
Evinrude **18.00**
Fish, turquoise eye, 3", Taxco **65.00**
Flamingo, turquoise eye, SS **40.00**
Flower, multicolor rhinestones, Weiss **16.00**
Grapes, blue moonstones, Coro **18.00**
Green Holly Man, red berries, Beatrix **14.00**
Hematite **20.00**
Hollycraft **156.00**
Margot, astrological **125.00**
Mother–of–pearl, SS script "Mother" **28.00**
Mushroom, enameled, marked "Rob-
  ert" **12.00**
Shell Cameo, 1¼", 800 silver frame **65.00**
Sunburst, Los Castillos **175.00**
Pin and Earrings Set
Cameo, glass, marked "Hobe" **55.00**
Pineapple, marked "Alice Caviness" **50.00**
Plastic, hp rose, set in square white
  frame, 1⅛" pin, ¾" earrings **15.00**

Pin, wood, plastic eye, 2" l, $4.00.

Rifas	9.50
Pin and Pendant Set, faux turquoise, Southwest design, marked "Castle-cliff"	40.00
Ring	
Bakelite	
Red–orange, carved	28.00
Yellow, carved	26.00
Carnelian and Marcasite, sterling . . .	75.00
Child's, signet, 14K, YG, ornate	35.00
Lady's	
Agate, square cut, SS filigree setting	25.00
Amethyst, emerald cut, white gold filigree setting	85.00
Cameo, 14K, YG	32.00
Hematite, SS setting	40.00
Signet, 14K, YG, Victorian	55.00
Turquoise, SS, Indian	20.00
Wedding Band, 14K, YG	30.00
Man's, signet, 14K, YG, four side diamonds	90.00
Rosary, round amethyst colored stones set in dark chain	36.00
Shoe Buckle, rhinestones, clips	14.50
Stickpin, YG, 10K, topaz	50.00
Sweater Guard, plastic roses, YGF chain	5.00
Tie Clip, putter	10.00
Tuxedo Studs, mother–of–pearl on silver	20.00
Watch Pin, rhinestones, SS	15.00

JUKEBOXES

Collecting Hints: Jukebox chronology falls into four distinct periods:

In the pre–1938 period jukeboxes were constructed mainly of wood and resembled a radio or phonograph cabinet. In this period Wurlitzer jukeboxes are the most collectible, but their value usually is under $600.00.

From 1938 to 1948 the addition of plastics and animation units gave the jukebox a more gaudy appearance. These jukeboxes played 78 RPM records. Wurlitzer jukeboxes are king, with Rock–Ola the second most popular. This era contains the most valuable models, e.g., Wurlitzer models 750, 850, 950, 1015, and 1080, plus others.

The 1940–1960 era jukeboxes are collected for the "Happy Days" (named for the TV show) feeling: drive–in food, long skirts, sweater girls, and good times. These jukeboxes play 45 RPM records. They rate in value second to those of the 1938–48 period. The period is referred to as the Seeburg era. Prices usually are under $1,500.

The 1961 and newer jukeboxes often are not considered collectible because the record mechanism is not visible, thus removing one of a box's alluring qualities.

There are exceptions to these generalizations. Collectors should have a price and identification guide to help make choices. Many original and reproduction parts are available for Seeburg and Wurlitzer jukeboxes. In many cases incomplete jukeboxes can be restored. Jukeboxes that are in working order and can be maintained in that condition are the best machines to own.

Wait about three to four months after becoming interested in jukeboxes before buying a machine. Use this time to educate yourself about a machine's desirability and learn how missing components will effect its value.

History: First came the phonograph; the coin–operated phonograph followed. When electrical amplification became possible, the amplified coin–operated phonograph, known as a jukebox, evolved.

The heyday of the jukebox was the 1940s. Between 1946 and 1947 Wurlitzer produced 56,000 model 1015 jukeboxes, the largest production run of all time. The jukebox was the center of every teenage "hangout" from drugstores and restaurants to pool halls and dance parlors. They even invaded select private homes. Jukeboxes were cheaper than a live band, and, unlike radio, one could hear his or her favorite song when and as often as one wished.

Styles changed in the 1960s. Portable radios coupled with "Top 40" radio stations fulfilled the need for daily repetition of songs. Television changed evening entertainment patterns. The need for the jukebox vanished.

References: Frank Adams, *Wurlitzer Jukeboxes, 1934–1974*, AMR Publishing, 1983; Rick Botts, *A Complete Identification Guide To The Wurlitzer Jukebox*, privately printed, 1984; Rick Botts, *Jukebox Restoration Guide*, published by author, 1985; Stephan K. Loots, *The Official Victory Glass Price Guide To Antique Jukeboxes 1992*, published by author, 1992.

Periodical: *Jukebox Collector Newsletter*, 2545 SE 60th Court, Des Moines, IA 50317.

Museums: Jukeboxes have not reached the status of museum pieces. The best places to see approximately 100 or more jukeboxes in one place is at a coin–op show.

Advisor: Rick Botts.

AMI, model		
A	. . . .	900.00
B	. . . .	750.00
C	. . . .	500.00
D	. . . .	400.00
E	. . . .	500.00
Mills, model		
Empress	. . . .	1,000.00
Throne of Music	. . . .	750.00
Packard, Manhattan	. . . .	2,000.00

Rock–Ola, model

1422 ....2,000.00
1426 ....2,000.00
1428 ....1,800.00
1432 .... 700.00
1434 .... 750.00
1436 .... 750.00
1438 .... 750.00

Seeburg, model

147 .... 600.00
M100B 750.00
M100C 800.00
HF100G 810.00
HF100R 860.00
V–200 ....1,300.00

Wurlitzer, model

412 .... 750.00
600 .... 900.00
616 .... 625.00
700 ....2,000.00
750 ....4,000.00
780 ....2,500.00
800 ....2,500.00
850 ....9,500.00
950 .... 20,000.00
1015 ....6,000.00
1800 ....1,300.00
1900 ....1,000.00
2000 ....1,400.00
2300 .... 650.00

KEYS

Collecting Hints: The modern hobby of key collecting began with the publication of *Standard Guide To Key Collecting* which illustrates keys by function and describes keys by style and metal content. Most key collectors focus on a special type of key, e.g., folding keys, railroad keys, car keys, etc.

Very few, if any, American-manufactured keys can be called truly rare, although some may be currently in the very difficult stage to find. Little is known as to the quantity manufactured, how popular they were when first produced and marketed, and how many survived.

Some keys are abundant in certain areas of the country and scarce in others. Do not spend heavily just because you have never heard or seen an example before. The best advice is to seek out other collectors and join a national organization.

History: The key as a symbol has held a mystical charm since Biblical times. The Catholic Church has keys in its coat of arms. During the Middle Ages, noblemen and women carried a large collection of keys hanging from their girdles to denote their status, the more keys the higher the status.

Many kings and other royal members practiced the art of key making. Presentation keys began during the earliest years when cities were walled enclaves. When a visitor was held in high esteem by the townspeople, he would be presented with a key to the city gate. Thus, we now have the honorary "Key To The City."

When it was popular to go on a Grand Tour of Europe in the 17th to 19th centuries, keys were among the most acquired objects. Unfortunately, many of these keys were fantasies created by the inventive local hustlers. Examples are King Tut's Tomb key, the key to the house where Mary stayed in Egypt, Bastille keys, Newgate Prison keys, and Tower of London keys.

References: Don Stewart, *The Charles J. McQueen Collection, Railroad Switch Keys, United States-Canada-World*, published by author; Don Stewart, *Collectors Guide, Antique Classic Marque Car Keys, United States 1915–1970*, published by author; Don Stewart, *Collectors Guide, Yale Jail/Prison Locks & Keys, 1884–1957*, published by author; Don Stewart, *Standard Guide To Key Collecting, United States-Canada 1850–1975, Second Edition* published by author.

Collectors' Club: Key Collectors International, P. O. Box 9397, Phoenix, AZ 85068.

Museums: Lock Museum of America, Terryville, CT; Mechanics Institute, New York, NY.

Car Keys, enamel dec, each $1.50.

Cabinet, Barrel Type
  Brass, decorative bow
    1½" 3.00
    2½" 5.50
    3" 9.00
  Brass, standard bow and bit
    1½" 1.50
    2" 1.50
    3" 3.50
  Bronze, gold plated bow
    1½", decorative 8.50
    2", Art Deco design 12.00
    2½", dolphin design 12.00
  Iron, painted, 3", plastic bow, Art
    Deco design 9.50
  Nickel plated
    2¼", lyre design bow 5.50
    2½", Art Deco design bow 5.00

Steel

1½", standard bow and bit	.50
2", Art Deco design	6.00
3", standard bow and bit	.75

Casting Plate, bronze

2½"	15.00
3"	18.00
4"	22.00
6"	29.00

Car

Auburn, logo, Yale, Jr	2.00

Basco

Early, flat steel	1.50
Set, #31–54, total of 24 keys	25.00

Chrysler "Omega" keys, brass, five piece set

1933, Yale	15.00
1934, Yale	12.00
CLUM, #DB76–DB99, set of 24 keys	35.00

Dodge

Any metal, no name	.50
Brass, reverse "Caskey–Dupree" .	1.25
Nickel–Silver, reverse "Caskey–Dupree"	1.50
Dodge/Chevrolet, rear deck key	2.00
Edsel, two keys, any maker	5.00

Ford, Model "T"

Any Metal, no logo	.75

Brass, Ford logo

"B" in circle mark	2.00
C–D mark	2.00
Crown mark	8.00
Diamond mark	2.00
No mark	1.50
"V" in circle mark	12.00
Coil Switch Lever Key	2.50
Dealers Keys, set of 4	12.50

Nickel–Silver, Ford Logo

"B" in circle mark	1.75
C–D mark	1.75
Diamond mark	1.75
Ford, rear deck key	2.00
Nash logo key, Ilco #132	5.00

Omega, nickel–silver, 5 piece set, 1933 or 1934, Yale 6.50

Omega type, nickel–silver, any maker besides Yale .... .75

Packard logo key, gold plated, 50th anniversary 9.00

Studebaker

Eagle Lock Co, logo key	1.50
Yale, aluminum	1.50
Yale, Jr, logo key	1.50

Car, Special

Auto Dealer Presentation Keys

Diamond, Continental, gold	75.00
Gold Plated	1.50
Sterling Silver	12.00

Crest Key

Common Cars	1.50
Hudson, Frazer, Nash and Packard	3.00
OSCO Colt 45 Key, orig box	25.00

Door

Brass, standard bow and bit

3"	3.00
4"	5.00
5"	9.00
6"	12.00

Bronze

4", Keen Kutter bow	5.50
6", special logo bow	15.00

Steel

3", Keen Kutter bow	3.50
5", standard bow and bit	3.50

Folding, Jackknife

Bronze and Steel, bit cuts, 5"

Maker's name	18.00
No maker's name	15.00

Steel bit cuts, 5½", maker's name

Branford, MW&CO, nc	9.00
Ilco, Graham, etc	6.50

Steel, uncut, 5½"

Maker's name	6.00
No maker's name	4.00

Gate

Bronze, bit type

4"	6.00
6"	12.00

Iron, bit type

6"	4.00
8"	6.00

Hotel

Bit Type, Bronze

3", Hotel name and room number on bow	4.50
4", Tag silhouette of hotel, white metal	10.00

Bit Type, Steel, 3"

Bronze Tag	3.00
Fiber Tag, room number and name	2.25
Hotel name and room number on bow	3.75
Large Tag, oval, silhouette, bronze	9.00
Standard Tag, room number, etc, bronze	4.00

Bit Type, Steel, 4"

Bronze Tag	3.50
Large Tag, oval, hotel founder, bronze	12.00
Large Tag, rectangle, hotel name, white metal	6.50

Pin Tumbler

Large bow, hotel name and room number on bow	1.25
Plastic or Fiber tag	1.50

Jail (reproduction alert)

Bronze, bit type with cuts

4¼", open oval bow, Newell	35.00
4½", barrel type	28.00
Bronze, lever tumbler cut, 4½", Folger–Adams, oval bow with "A" ..	18.00

Nickel–Silver, pin tumbler, Yale Mogul

Cut	15.00

Uncut blank **12.00**
Spike Key, 5½"
  Bronze bow, steel bit, serial no., no
    maker's name **35.00**
  Nickel plated steel, open oval bow,
    no maker's name, no serial no.,
    bit cuts **30.00**
  Steel plated bow, serial no, Yale,
    marked **40.00**
  Steel, flat, lever tumbler, Folger–Adams
    Cut **18.00**
  Uncut blank **12.00**
Keys To The City, Presentation
  1½", gold plated, small jewel, city
    and/or recipients name **9.00**
  2", iron, brass plated, Master Lock
    Co, 1933 Worlds Fair **7.50**
  2½", white metal, "Be A Golden Key
    For Happiness" **1.50**
  6", antique bronze, any city **14.00**
  6 to 10", gold plated, name engraved
    Famous Person **32.00**
    Historical Person **75.00**
    Obscure Person **25.00**
  7", gold plated, presentation leatherette type folder **40.00**
  8", copper plated, 1933 Chicago
    Worlds Fair, Hall of Science **15.00**
  8", 22K gold plated, Cumberland, etc **24.00**
  10", Chicago Worlds Fair, copper,
    thermometer **8.50**
Pocket Door, bow folds sideways
  Bronze
    Art Deco, triangular bow **15.00**
    "T" bow, cut, knurled nut **9.00**
  Nickel Plated
    Art Deco, square bow **19.00**
    Art Nouveau, oval bow **15.00**
Pocket Door, slide stem
  Bronze, "T" bow
    Knurled nut **9.00**
    Screw **8.00**
  Steel, "T" bow, screw **10.00**
Railroad (reproduction alert)
  A&S Abilene & Southern **25.00**
  ARR Alaska Railroad **20.00**
  AT&SF Atchison Topeka & Santa Fe . **15.00**
  B&M RR Boston & Maine **20.00**
  C&O Chesapeake & Ohio **12.50**
  CM&ST P SIGNAL Chicago Milwaukee & St Paul **10.00**
  CRI & P RR Chicago Rock Island &
    Pacific **12.50**
  D&RGW RR Denver & Rio Grande
    Western **18.50**
  DT RR Detroit Terminal **18.50**
  ESS CO Eastern/Erie Steamship Co .. **19.00**
  FC NG RR Fulton County Narrow
    Gauge **85.00**
  GTW Grand Trunk Western **18.00**
  IC RR Illinois Central **10.00**

LS&MS Lake Shore & Michigan South
  Steel **15.00**
LM RR Little Miami Railroad **55.00**
MC RR Michigan Central **18.00**
MN RY Milwaukee Northern **45.00**
NP RY Northern Pacific Railway ... **18.00**
O&W RR Oregon & Washington ... **35.00**
PENN RR Pennsylvania Railroad ... **18.00**
FRISCO St Louis San Francisco **18.00**
SPCO&CS Southern Pacific **9.00**
SPTCO Southern Pacific **6.00**
TT RR Toledo Terminal Railroad ... **18.00**
UPRR Union Pacific **14.00**
VGN Virginian **30.00**
WPRR Western Pacific Railroad **12.50**

Ship, brass, factory tag, 6½" l, $12.00.

Ship, bit type
  Bronze, bit type
    Foreign ship tags **6.00**
    Ship name on bow **10.00**
  Bronze, tag, bit type, factory type tags
    2" **6.00**
    3" **9.00**
  Bronze, ship made tags, bit type, factory type tags
    2 to 3" **4.50**
    4" **5.00**
  Iron/steel, bronze tags, 3 to 4" **3.00**
  Pin Tumbler Type
    Passenger Liner Tags **9.00**
    US Army Ship Tags **8.50**
    US Coast Guard Tags **3.00**
    USN Tag **2.00**
Watch
  Brass, 1"
    Advertising type, ½ x ¾" **6.00**
    Advertising type, shield **10.00**
    Art Nouveau, loop bow **9.00**
    Plain, swivel **2.00**
  Brass/gold plated, 1", large number . **4.00**
  Brass and Steel, 1"
    Loop bow, folds **4.00**
    Swivel **2.00**
  Gold, 14K, 1", engraved **75.00**
  Gold Plated, 1"
    Advertising type **12.00**
    Decorated bow **9.00**
  Gold Plated and Silver, 1"
    Cigar Cutter accessory **25.00**
    Plain **19.00**

Jewelers Key
Brass, 6 point 18.00
Steel and Brass
5 Point 12.00
6 Point 15.00
Set, #2 to #11, brass/gold plated,
large numbers, 10 total 75.00
Sterling Silver 1″, rose on bow, etc . 35.00

KITCHEN COLLECTIBLES

Collecting Hints: Bargains still can be found, especially at flea markets and garage sales. Look to the design of appliances for statements about a given age, e.g., the Art Deco design on toasters and coffee pots of the 1910–1920 period.

The country decorating craze has caused most collectors to concentrate on the 1860–1900 period. Kitchen products of the 1900–1940 period with their enamel glazes and dependability are just coming into vogue.

History: The kitchen was a central focal point in a family's environment until frozen food, TV dinners, and microwaves freed the family to concentrate on other parts of the house during meal time. Initially, food preparation involved both the long and short term. Home canning remained popular through the early 1950s.

Many early kitchen utensils were handmade and prized by their owners. Next came a period of utilitarian products of tin and other metals. However, the housewife did not wish to work in a sterile environment, so color was added through enamel and plastic while design began to serve both an aesthetic and functional purpose.

The advent of home electricity changed the type and style of kitchen products. Many products went through fads such as the toaster, electric knife, and now the food processor. The high technology field already has made inroads into the kitchen and another revolution seems at hand.

References: Jane H. Celehar, *Kitchens and Gadgets, 1920 To 1950*, Wallace–Homestead, 1982; Linda Campbell Franklin, *300 Years Of Kitchen Collectibles*, 2nd Edition, Books Americana, 1984; Bill and Denise Harned, *Griswold Cast Collectibles: History & Values*, published by author, 1988; Mary Lou Mathews, *American Kitchen And Country Collectibles*, L–W Promotions, 1984; Kathryn McNerney, *Kitchen Antiques, 1790–1940*, Collector Books, 1991; Ellen A. Plante, *Kitchen Collectibles: An Illustrated Price Guide*, Wallace–Homestead, 1991; Frances Thompson, *Antiques From The Country Kitchen*, Wallace–Homestead, 1985.

See: Advertising, Cookbooks, Kitchen Glassware, Reamers.

Apple Peeler
Eight gears, two heart–shaped 50.00
Goodell, iron 40.00
Ashtray, skillet, Griswold #00 . . . . 22.00
Asparagus Cutter, wood, Ward's Keen
Edge 85.00
Asparagus Tongs 4.00
Baking pan, 9″, imp Rudolph the Red–
Nosed Reindeer design 15.00
Bean Dryer, rect, tin 8.00
Bean Slicer/Pea Huller, green handle,
attaches to table 25.00
Biscuit Cutter, Rumford, tin 14.00
Bowl, mixing, 10″, yellow ware, blue
bands 55.00
Bread Board, round, maple, matching
knife 45.00
Bread pan, round, 6½″ d, 2½″ deep,
stoneware, blue fireproof 50.00
Bridge Pan, Little Slam, cast iron 100.00
Broiler Tray, Griswold, aluminum, styl-
ized deer, Aristocraft Ware 30.00
Broom Holder, tin, DeLaval adv 42.00
Butter Cutter, cuts one pound into forty–
eight pats, nickel plated brass and
wire 40.00
Cabbage Cutter, maple, steel blade . . . 15.00
Cake Decorator, aluminum, tube, six
tips 9.00
Cake Mold
Santa Shape–a–Cake, instructions,
MIB 8.00
Yellowware, 10″ d, swirled center
cone 70.00
Can Opener, Peerless, patent 1902 . . . 15.00
Carpet Beater, wire, braided 20.00
Catalog
Holland–Rieger Wringer Washing
Machines, 12 pgs 8.00
Kalamazoo Stoves, 1920, 84 pgs . . . 25.00
Springfield Home Appliances, 1953,
96 pgs 6.00
Cheese Box, Jack Spratt, Marshaltown,
IA, rect, cov, wood 10.00
Cheese Grater, tin, hand held 20.00
Cherry Stoner, Enterprise, #16 . . . . 35.00
Chopper, six sided, iron handle 18.00
Cider Funnel, wood 60.00
Clothes Sprinkler, Chinaman, white and
blue 28.00
Coffee Grinder
Clamp–on, iron, LF & C 45.00
Lap, iron lid sgd "Arcade" 67.50
Table, cast iron and wood, sgd "Im-
perial" 75.00
Wall Mount, iron and glass, Crystal . 57.00
Comb Case, tin, hanging, emb, shield
and stars 20.00

Cookie Cutters, Robin Hood Flour adv,
set of 6 .... 25.00
Cookie Peel, iron, closed ring handle,
open heart shape, 18½" l, c1800 ... 350.00
Cookie Sheet
  Betty Crocker Bisquick 9.50
  Springerle 110.00
Corncob Holders, sterling, set of 12 .. 95.00
Corn Stick Pan
  Griswold
    #262 .... 85.00
    #273 .... 35.00
  Wagner Junior 28.00
  Wagnerware 28.00
Dipper, 25½" l, wrought iron 45.00
Donut Cutter
  Rumford 15.00
  Wood 32.00
Donut Master, orig box, recipes, 1940s 18.00
Dough Box, pine, 32" l, sliding lid ... 85.00
Dutch Oven, Wagner, #9 .... 45.00

Egg Basket, wire, collapsable, interlocking loop design, 9" d, $15.00.

Egg Basket, wire, folding 15.00
Egg Beater
  Bette Taptim 15.00
  Dover, cast iron, 1891 .... 20.00
  Taplin, cast iron 30.00
Egg Poacher, 3—egg, tin, stove top 25.00
Egg Separator, Rumford 30.00
Egg Skillet, Griswold, sq 25.00
Egg Timer, tin 30.00
Egg Whip, wire 12.50
Flour Sifter, child's, tin, marked "Kew-
pie" 45.00
Food Grinder, Russwin, drops open for
cleaning, 1902, #1 .... 30.00
Food Mill, tin and steel, Foley 75.0
French Fry Cutter, hand held, red han-
dles 20.00
Fruit Baller, wood handle, Germany .. 7.00
Garlic Press, wood 28.00
Grapefruit Reamer, yellow, sgd "Red
Wing" 150.00
Grater, 4 x 10", tin, Fels Napha adv .. 10.00
Griddle, Wagner, 4½", bail 125.00
Grill, Griswold, rect, #8 .... 25.00
Ice Bucket, brass, Pyrex insert 20.00

Ice Cream Dipper
  Gilchrist, wood handle 35.00
  Hamilton Beach, MIB 32.00
  Indestructo, #4 .... 23.00
  Zeroll, #12, Maumee 17.00
Ice Cream Mold, pewter, donkey 82.00
Ice Pick/Bottle Opener, Conoco 6.00
Jar Opener 12.00
Jello Mold, Phoenix glass, emb, ftd ... 8.00
Juice Extractor, Hamilton Beach, 20",
#32 .... 75.00
Ladle, mayonnaise, flat bottom, blue . 18.00
Lemon Reamer, ceramic, 2 pcs, figural 35.00
Lemon Squeezer
  Pearl, cast iron 35.00
  Williams, iron, glass insert 45.00
  Wood, turned 50.00
Match Holder, 2¾", stoneware, cone
shape, blue band 75.00
Matchsafe, cast iron, wall mounted, or-
nate, uses large box of matches 37.50
Measuring cup, Seller, clear, one cup . 20.00
Meat Grinder, Griswold, #2 .... 25.00
Meat Slicer, sterling, cast iron, #10 ... 30.00
Mold
  Griswold, lamb 85.00
  Waf–l–ette, MIB 15.00
  Wagner, lamb 85.00
Muffin Pan
  Griswold, #10 .... 40.00
  Kellogg 9.50
Noodle Roller, wood 32.00
Nutcracker
  Cast Aluminum, 11 x 8", black, squir-
  rel on leaf 20.00
  Iron, 1925 .... 10.00
Nutmeg Grater, hopper, hand crank .. 35.00
Pan, French roll type 42.00
Pastry Blender, wire and metal, wood
handle, dated 1924 .... 5.00
Pastry Crimper
  Aluminum, Just Right Pie Sealer 8.00
  Brass, black globular wood handle . 12.00
Pastry Cutter, two bladed, one wheel,
one wedge, red handle 12.00
Patty Mold Set, Griswold, #1, orig box 50.00
Pie Lifter, brass ferule, turned wood han-
dle, Shaker 50.00
Pie Tin
  Bowie Pies 5.00
  Knotts Berry Farm 6.00
Popcorn Popper, wire, green handle .. 28.00
Popover, Erie, cast iron 20.00
Potato Masher, Blue Onion 120.00
Potato Ricer, steel, red trim, 1940s ... 19.00
Pudding Mold
  Acorn, two—part 16.00
  Tin 20.00
Reamer
  Cow, 8½" 45.00
  Sunkist, jadite 60.00
Roaster, cast iron, Mi Pet 35.00

Flour Sifter, metal, painted, decal, 4⅜" d, 5⅝" h, $7.50.

Rolling Pin
Glass, clear, wood handles 55.00
Harker, Mallow 95.00
Kelvinator, porcelain 85.00
Maple, green handles 20.00
Milk Glass, wood handles, dated
1921 .... 65.00
Yellowware 200.00
Sausage Stuffer, cast iron, Enterprise,
mounted on wood bench 65.00
Sieve, 10", round, wire and tin 12.00
Skillet
Griswold
#3 .... 26.00
#6 .... 21.00
#7, large logo 23.00
#9 .... 37.50
#12, smoke ring 45.00
Martin Stove Co 15.00
Wagner
#3 .... 19.00
#4, smoke ring 21.00
#5 .... 19.00
Soap Dish, Blue Onion, drain 58.00
Soap Saver, metal 12.00
Spice Jar Set
Griffith, red metal rack, ten pcs 25.00
Hoosier, five pcs 75.00
Spoon Rest, yellowware, incised "Be-
rea, Kentucky" 45.00
String Holder
Apple, chalk 25.00
Beehive, iron, counter 65.00
Cat
Ceramic, pink yarn 28.00
Chalk 26.00
Colonial Girl 45.00
Heart, ceramic, "You'll Always have
A Pull With Me" 40.00
Hula Hula Girl 45.00
Pear, chalk 25.00
Strawberry Face 27.00
Swedish Pancake Pan, Griswold 38.00
Tea Kettle
Griswold, aluminum 15.00

Wagner
Child's, iron 40.00
5 qt 24.00
Teapot, Gladding McBeam 42.00
Tin, Advertising
Buster Brown Pickling Spice 52.00
Busy Biddy 45.00
Calumet Baking Powder, paper label 24.00
Davis Baking Powder, sample 65.00
Great American Coffee, key wind .. 18.00
Manhattan Coffee, skyline scene ... 25.00
Monarch Cocoa, hinge lid 25.00
Santa Fe Coffee, unopened 45.00
Watkins Pepper 15.00
Toast Rack, 5", SP 60.00
Vegetable Chopper, crescent blade,
wood handle 30.00
Waffle Iron
Griswold, #8 .... 110.00
Wagner, wood handle, stand, pat Feb
22, 1910 .... 90.00

KITCHEN GLASSWARE

Collecting Hints: Kitchen Glassware was made in large numbers. Although collectors do tolerate signs of use, they will not accept pieces with heavy damage. Many of the products contain applied decals; these should be in good condition. A collection can be built inexpensively by concentrating on one form such as canister sets, measuring cups, reamers, etc.

History: The Depression era brought inexpensive kitchen and table products to center stage. Hocking, Hazel Atlas, McKee, U. S. Glass, and Westmoreland were companies which led in the production of these items.

Kitchen Glassware complemented Depression Glass. Many items were produced in the same color and style. Because the glass was molded, added decorative elements included ribs, fluting, arches and thumbprint patterns. Kitchen Glassware was thick to achieve durability. The result were forms which were difficult to handle at times and often awkward aesthetically. After World War II, aluminum products began to replace Kitchen Glassware.

References: Gene Florence, *Kitchen Glassware of the Depression Years, Fourth Edition*, Collector Books, 1990; Glyndon, Shirley, *The Miracle in Grandmother's Kitchen*, privately printed, 1983.

See: Reamers.

Ashtray, blue, 3½" sq, Fire King 8.00
Batter Pitcher, transparent red 95.00
Bowl
Cobalt Blue, 8½", mixing, Hazel At-
las Glass Co 35.00
Custard, 6" 9.00

Butter Dish, opaque light blue, $30.00.

Delphite, 6"	90.00
Jadite, 4½"	10.00
Red Dot, 9½"	11.00
Tulip, 8½"	11.00
Turquoise Blue, 7"	15.00

Canister
Jadite, dark, Jeanette Glass	70.00
Red Circle, screw on lid	32.00
White, ships, 5", coffee	30.00
Casserole, cov, blue, 1 pt, Fire King	9.00
Celery, Tacoma, ruby, flat	35.00
Cereal Bowl, 5", oven blue, Fire King	11.00
Cocktail Shaker, transparent green	20.00
Cocktail Shaker Set, five shot glasses, green	35.00
Coffeepot, 2 cup drip, Silex	35.00
Cracker Jar, chocolate slag, Cherry pattern	100.00
Creamer, green, two panel	35.00
Cruet, yellow, Imperial	20.00

Drippings Jar
Jadite, Jeanette Glass Co	20.00
Tulip, Fire King	20.00
Windmill	25.00
Egg Beater Bowl, custard, McKee	22.00

Ice Bucket
Frigidaire, green, frosted	10.00
Paden City Party Line, green, hp flowers	22.00
Juice Saver, blue, Fire King	16.00
Loaf Pan, blue, Fire King	16.00
Match Holder, vaseline glass	25.00

Measuring cup
Custard glass, 4 cup	45.00
Delphite, 8 oz	85.00
Green, 1 cup, Clambroth	165.00
Jadite, 2 cup	20.00
Muffineer, hp, strawberries	45.00

Napkin Holder
Green, Serv–All, Clambroth	185.00
White, Narofold	30.00

Pie Dish, ovenproof
Cattail	25.00
Fire King, 8", blue	5.50

Reamer
Delphite, Jeanette Glass	75.00
Sunkist, yellow, Seville	35.00
Reamer Bowl, jadite	18.00

Refrigerator Dish
3½ x 5¾", cobalt blue, crisscross	95.00
4 x 4", cobalt blue, crisscross	45.00

4 x 5"
Clear, McKee	18.00
Red Dots, McKee	15.00
White, ships	15.00
4 x 8", custard, McKee	30.00
8 x 8", cobalt blue, crisscross	125.00
Round, 32 oz	35.00
Roaster, large, blue, Fire King	50.00
Rolling Pin, Harker, Rosebud	25.00

Salt and Pepper Shakers, pr
Jadite, 4½"	25.00
Lake Como	30.00
Skillet, jadite, 2–spout	20.00

Spooner
Custard Glass, Trailing Vine	55.00
Vaseline Opalescent, frosted leaves, basketweave	65.00
Sugar Shaker, transparent green	195.00

Water Bottle
Forest Green, waterfall	30.00
Green, frosted, Frigidaire	20.00
Water Dispenser, jadite, Florence 4, 91/2/2	130.00

LABELS

Collecting Hint: Damaged, trimmed or torn labels are less valuable than labels in mint condition.

History: The first fruit crate art was created by California fruit growers about 1880. The labels became very colorful and covered many subjects. Most depict the type of fruit held in the box. With the advent of cardboard boxes in the 1940s, fruit crate art ended and their labels became collectible.

References: Jerry Chicone, Jr., *Florida's Classic Crates*, privately printed, 1985; Gordon T. McClelland and Jay T. Last, *Fruit Box Labels, A Collector's Guide*, Hillcrest Press, Inc., 1983; John Salkin and Laurie Gordon, *Orange Crate Art, The Story of Labels That Launched a Golden Era*, Warner Books, 1976.

Collectors' Club: Citrus Label Society, 16633 Ventura Blvd, No. 1011, Encino, CA 91436.

Advisor: Lorie Cairns.

Apples
Bird Valley, blue crown perched on shield, orange background	2.00
Cascade, smiling boy holding partially eaten apple, blue background	.50
Flag, red flag, dark green background	1.00
Lakeview, yellow and red apples, orchard, blue background	1.00
Morjon, red apple on black triangle, yellow background	1.00

Lion, red and blue, white letters, black ground, 7 x 9″, $1.00.

Pete's Best, laughing boy, red apple, yellow background 1.00
Skookum, smiling Indian, cartoon face, red and blue apples, green background 1.00
Snow Owl, snowy owl, blue background 2.00
Webster, spider web, navy background 2.00
Yakima Chief, Indian chief wearing headdress 3.00

Asparagus
Caligras, men harvesting asparagus, horse drawn wagon 2.00
Chickie, fluffy yellow chick, bunch of green asparagus, black background 2.00
King O' Hearts, playing card, red heart on black background 1.00
Mo–Chief, asparagus bundle, scenic background, Fresno, CA 2.00
Red Rooster, crowing rooster, yellow, red, and navy background 1.00
Spring Time Magic, elves celebrating asparagus harvest 1.00
Carrot, DOE, doe's head, bunch of carrots 1.00

Broom
Auto No 6, speeding race car ...... .50
Dixie, black man seated on Bench, playing banjo 1.00
Indian Queen, Indian lady in forest, tepees .... .50
Skysweep, bi–plane, dated 1931 ... .50
Winner, lady holding torch .... .50

Butter
Hill Country Butter, yellow, black, white, stylized floral border 1.00
Wilson's Clearbrook Butter, yellow, black, white, and red, farm scene 2.00

Cherry
California Cherries, four cherries, poppies .... .25

Exposition, black bing cherries, red background .... .15
Mountain, snowy Mt Hod, red cherries, red border .... .50
San Ardo, red cherries cluster, farm scene, blue background .... .25

Cigar
Buzzer, ornate butterfly, cigar body . 3.00
J A C, tobacco leaves .... .25
La Venga, eagle, outstretched wings .50
Peg, black high to shoe 1.00
Rosa Moro, brunette lady, two lions 1.00
Traveler, fancy design, gilt, black and red .... .25

Cosmetic
Fairy Cream, emb, gilt, florals ..... .75
Mentholated Cream, floral, leaves, emb, gild .... .50
Odor Roses, rose branch, with hazel .75
Superior Bay Rum, green bay leaf, gilt border .... .50
Violet Ammonia, purple flowers, white background, York, PA ..... .75

Cranberry
Arbutus, pink arbutus flower spray, green leaves 2.00
Heather, pink and green heather spray 2.00
Rancocas, indian village, green valley, river, horses, and tepees 3.00

Firewood
Firewood, snowy night scene, cowboy on horseback 2.50
Storytime, hearth scene, pioneer family seated by fireplace, dated 1977, sgd James Dowlen 1.00

Grape
Baby Turtle, naked baby on turtle back, blue grapes, red background .50
Domingo, yellow grapes, country scene .... .50
Good Year, red, green, and yellow bunches of grapes .... .25
Mirador, ranch scene, red grapes, Uncle Sam's hat 1.00
Old Mission, Spanish Mission scene, mission bells, green grapes, 1920s .50
Pride of Dinuba, lady wearing yellow flowing gown, holding bunches of grapes, blue and red background . .50
Reliance, three kinds grapes, yellow background .... .25
Small Black, black child, grapes, red background .... .75
Valley Beauty, girl, bunch of purple grapes, two hands holding wine glasses, red background .... .50
Grapefruit, Dixie boy, black child eating half grapefruit 2.00

Lemon
Arboleda, scenic, Goleta 1.00
El Merito, lemons, blue, green, and yellow background, Santa Paula .. 1.00

Gateway, two horseback riders, redwood forest, dark blue background, Lemon Cove 2.00

Kaweah maid, Indian girl wearing turquoise beads, brown background, Lemon Cove 3.00

Lemonade, three large lemons and leaves, orchard background, Ivanhoe 1.00

Ocean Spray, glass lemonade, red roses in blue vase, Santa Paula ... 5.00

Red Ball Californian Lemons, red ball, yellow letters, black background, Los Angeles .... .50

Schooner, sailing vessel, sky background, Goleta 2.00

Sunside, two lemons and leaves, orange and brown background, Santa Paula 1.00

Vesper, people going to church, maroon background, Porterville 1.00

Orange

Altissimo, pink, aqua and blue mountains, dated 1918, Placentia 1.00

Big J, red and yellow letter J, blue seal, San Francisco 1.00

Bronco, cowboy swinging lariat, riding galloping brown horse, western desert scene, Redlands 2.00

Cambria, brown eagle, two torches, blue background, brown border, Placentia 1.00

Esperanza, pretty senorita wearing lace mantilla, holding fan, blue background, Placentia 2.00

Golden Trout, trout leaping out of water, Orange cove 25.00

Hill Choice, orchard scene, orange with leaves and blossoms, aqua background, Porterville 1.00

Lincoln, "Honest Abe" portrait, orange and leaves, riverside 2.00

Miracle, genie holding tray with three oranges, dated 1928, Placentia ... 4.00

Nimble, orchard scene, aqua background, Santa Paula 1.00

Pala Brave, Indian Chief wearing headdress, maroon background, Placentia 3.00

Royal knight, brave knight in armor on horseback, castle, yellow background, Redlands 2.00

Shamrock, shamrock in sky over orange groves, Placentia 1.00

Symbol, California poppies, maple leaf, wrapped Sunkist orange, Riverside 2.00

Pear

Blue Parrot, green and blue parrot on flowering branch .... .75

Duckwall, wood duck standing by brick wall 2.00

Lady of the Lake, lady in green gown standing by lake, holding pear ... 2.00

Maltese Cross, maltese cross, white background, gilt dec 1.00

Mopac, Modoc Indian portrait, blue background 1.00

Oh Yes–We Grow The Best, two yellow pears, blue background ..... .50

Pirate's Cove, lake and country scene .50

Round Robin, wide–eyed robin, blue background 3.00

Summit, snowy mountains, forest scene 2.00

Triton, red Neptune holding trident and apple and pear, scenic background 1.00

Westside, orchard and mountain scene, palm tree and big pear 2.00

Plum, Valley Home, purple plums, aqua background 1.00

Prune, Wellman, nude Mercury standing on world 1.00

Tomatoes

Award, farmer holding box of tomatoes, ranch background .... .25

Big Chief, Indian chief and tomatoes .25

Green Feather, green feather, black background .... .25

Sun Prince, tomato background .... .25

Texus, cowboy, lug size .... .25

Top: Bronco Buster Brand, California Vegetables, blue ground, $.50; bottom: Woo Woo Brand, pretty girl, pink letters, black ground, $.50.

Yam

Coon, raccoon holding large yam .. 3.00

Jack Rabbit, gray rabbit on red triangle, aqua background, green border 2.00

Louise Anna, two large yams, yellow and aqua background .... .50

Sunset Packers, two yams, deco look design .... .50

Treasure, pirates treasure chest, four large yams **1.00**
Vitamin, kitchen scene, mother feeding son **1.00**

LETTER OPENERS

Collecting Hints: The advertising and celluloid letter openers are the most eagerly sought. Most letter openers dating from 1940 to the present have little collector interest and value.

New collectors might focus on the openers issued from within a specific geographic region. Blanks were available that could be used to carry a local message.

History: The letter opener reflects the attributes of the period in which it was created. In the Colonial period elegant silver letter openers graced the desks of the middle and upper class. As letters became inexpensive to mail and a popular form of communication, the need for letter openers grew.

The late 19th century witnessed the popularity of the lithographed tin, advertising letter opener. They usually were given away. By the 1920s brass and other metals captured the flowing lines of the Art Nouveau and Art Deco periods. The handcraft movements, e.g., Roycroft, produced some distinctively styled letter openers during the 1910 to 1930 period.

By the early 1950s letter openers lost their individuality. Americans phoned, rather than wrote. Plastic openers of uniform design became standard. Letter openers were relegated from the desk top to the desk drawer.

Advertising
Anaconda Copper & Brass, figural, arrowhead **14.00**
Armstrong Cork Co, 6½", white cello, early 1900 .... **15.00**

Advertising, National Office Registers, cash register illus, 5¾" l, $45.00.

AS&W Co, figural, nail **12.00**
Autocar, celluloid handle, 1920s ... **15.00**
Donegal & Conoy Mutual Fire Insurance Co, 9", brass, Marietta, PA, c1920 .... **35.00**
Dupont Explosives, silver handle ... **85.00**
Fuller Brush Man, figural **16.00**
James G Wilson Blinds and Shutters, New York City, white cello, black and white illus, c1900 .... **35.00**
Mechanics Savings Bank, Manchester, NH, bronze **18.00**
National Cash Register, 5½" l, white cello, diecut, black illus, early 1900s **30.00**
Pittsburgh Steel Co **10.00**
William Hoskins Co, Office Supply, 6" l, white cello, early 1900 ..... **15.00**
Brass
Dragon, 9" **40.00**
Enamel dec, ornate **38.00**
Napoleon, head and shoulders, brass wash **35.00**
Rearing horse, cut out floral blade, 7¼" **18.00**
Bronze
Chicken foot handle **28.00**
Seagull **25.00**
Tiffany, Adams pattern, sgd **115.00**
Cast Iron, Greyhound trailer bus, 10½" **75.00**
Celluloid
Indian with pipe **20.00**
Owl, figural **18.00**
Figural, 7¾", John Philip Sousa, bronze colored metal, inscribed "Veteran Corps April 19th, 1912" **50.00**
Ivory
Elephant handle, hand carved **30.00**
Oriental maiden, carrying jar, 8" ... **50.00**
Scrimshaw, floral design, ivory **32.00**
Sterling
Dagger, Art Nouveau, ornate flowered handle **40.00**
Rooster, Art Deco **25.00**
Wood, souvenir plank, "From the Teak of H M S *Ironduke*, Admiral Jellice's Flagship, Jutland, 1916," 10" **45.00**

LIMITED EDITIONS OR COLLECTOR ITEMS

Collecting Hints: The first edition of a series usually commands a higher price. When buying a limited edition collectible be aware that the original box and/or certificates increase the value of the piece. Be alert to special discounts and sales.

History: Limited edition plate collecting began with the advent of Christmas plates issued by

Bing and Grondahl in 1895. Royal Copenhagen soon followed. During the late 1960s and early 1970s, several potteries, glass factories, and mints began to issue plates, bells, eggs, mugs, etc. which commemorated special events, people, places, holidays. For a period of time these items increased in popularity and value. But in the late 1970s, the market became flooded with many collectibles and the market declined.

There are many new issues of collector items annually. Some of these collectibles can be found listed under specific headings, such as Hummel, Norman Rockwell, etc.

References: *The Bradford Book of Collector Plates, 12th Edition,* published by Bradford Exchange, 1987; Diane Carnevale, ed., *Collectors' Information Bureau's Collectibles Market Guide & Price Index to Limited Edition Plates, Figurines, Bells, Graphics, Steins, and Dolls, Ninth Edition,* Collectors' Information Bureau, 1991; Gene Ehlert, *The Official Price Guide To Collector Plates, Fifth Edition,* House of Collectibles, 1988; Paul Stark, *Limited Edition Collectibles, Everything You May Ever Need To Know,* New Gallery Press, 1988.

Periodicals: *Collector Editions,* 170 Fifth Ave, New York, NY 10010; *Collectors Mart,* 15100 W. Kellogg, Wichita, KS 67235; *Plate World,* 9200 North Maryland Avenue, Niles, IL 60648; *Precious Moments Collector,* P. O. Box 410707, Kansas City, MO 64141.

Collectors' Clubs: Foxfire Farm (Lowell Davis) Club, 55 Pacella Park Drive, Randolph, MA 02368; M.I. Hummel Club, P. O. Box 11, Rte. 31, Pennington, NJ 08534; Lalique Society of America, 11 East 26th Street, New York, NY 10010; Lllardo Collectors Society, 43 West 57th Street, New York, NY 10019; Precious Moments Collectors' Club, 1 Enesco Plaza, Elk Grove Village, IL 60009.

Museum: Bradford Museum, Niles, IL.

BELLS

Anri, J. Ferrandiz, artist, wooden
1976, Christmas, FE	50.00
1977, Christmas	40.00
1978, Christmas	40.00
1979, Christmas	30.00
1980, The Christmas King	18.50
1981, Lighting the Way	18.50
1982, Caring	18.50
1983, Behold	18.50
1985, Nature's Dream	18.50
1987, The Wedding Bell, silver	25.00
1988, Bride Belles, Caroline	27.50
1989, Christmas Pow–Pow	25.00
1990, Indian Brave	25.00

Bing & Grondahl, Christmas
1974	180.00
1980	70.00
1981	15.00
1982	35.00
1983	45.00
1984	45.00
1985	45.00
1986	45.00
1987	48.00
1988	48.00
1989	50.00

Danbury Mint, Norman Rockwell art
1976, No Swimming	40.00
1977, Santa's Mail	40.00
1979, Grandpa's Girl	28.00

Enesco Corp, Precious Moments
1981, Prayer Changes Things	40.00
1982, Mother Sew Dear	25.00
1983, Surrounded With Joy	60.00
1984, Wishing You A Merry Christmas	40.00
1989, Your Love Is Special To Me	20.00
1990, Here Comes The Bride	25.00

Franklin Mint, 1979, Unicorn, porcelain   35.00

Gorham
1975, Sweet Song So Young	50.00
1976, Tavern Sign Painter	30.00
1977, Chilling Chore	30.00
1978, Currier & Ives	20.00
1979, Beguilling Buttercup	30.00
1980, Christmas	25.00
1981, Ski Skills	27.00
1982, Young Man's Fancy	25.00
1983, Christmas Medley	30.00
1984, Young Love	28.00
1985, Yuletide Reflections	32.50
1986, Home For The Holidays	32.50
1987, Merry Christmas Grandma	30.00
1988, The Homecoming	36.00

Hummel, see HUMMEL

Hutschenreuther, 1978, Christmas	8.00
Llardo, 1987, Christmas	30.00

Pickard
1977, The First Noel, FE	75.00
1978, O Little Town of Bethlehem	70.00
1979, Silent Night	80.00
1980, Hark! The Herald Angels Sing	80.00

Reco International
1980, I Love You, FE	20.00
1981, Sea Echoes	20.00
1982, Talk to Me	20.00
1988, Charity	15.00
1989, The Wedding	15.00

Reed and Barton
1980, Noel, musical	45.00
1981, Yuletide Holiday	15.00
1982, Little Shephard	14.00
1983, Noel, musical	45.00
1984, Noel, musical	48.00
1985, Caroller	17.50
1986, Noel, musical	25.00

River Shore
1979, Allison	48.00

1980, Katrina	45.00
1981, Spring Flowers	175.00
1982, American Gothic	50.00

Schmid

Peanuts

1976, Christmas	25.00
1977, Christmas	18.00
1978, Mother's Day	15.00
1979, A Special Letter	25.00
1980, Waiting for Santa	25.00
1981, Mission for Mom	20.00
1982, Perfect Performance	18.00
1983, Peanuts in Concert	12.00
1984, Snoopy and the Beagle Scouts	12.00
Walt Disney, 1981, Christmas	18.00

Zemsky

1978, Christmas	20.00
1979, Christmas, pewter	25.00

Towle Silversmiths, silverplated

1980, ball	17.50
1982, musical	27.50
1984, musical	25.00
1986, ball	30.00
1988, musical	35.00

Vague Shadows

1985, Hail to the Chief	18.00
1986, Westward Ho!	18.00
1987, Small Talk	18.00

Wedgwood

1979, Penguins, FE	48.00
1981, Polar Bears	40.00
1982, Moose	35.00
1983, Fur Seals	32.00
1984, Ibex	50.00
1985, Puffin	60.00
1986, Ermine	60.00

DOLLS

Enesco Imports, Precious Moments

1983, Katie Lynne, 16" h	185.00
1984, Kristy, 12"	160.00
1985, Bethany, 12"	145.00
1986, Bong Bong, 13"	165.00
1987, Angie	160.00
1989, Wishing You Cloudless Skies	115.00

Gorham

1981

Alexandria, 19" h	400.00
Christina, 16"	650.00
Melinda, 14"	285.00
Ellice, 18"	325.00

1982

Jeremy, 23"	550.00
Mlle. Monique, 12"	275.00
Mlle. Yvonne, 12"	325.00
Mr. Anton, 12"	165.00
1983, Ashley	950.00

1984

Holly, Christmas	750.00
Nicole	850.00

Summer Holly Hobbie, 12"	115.00

1985

Amanda, 19"	365.00
Ariel, 16"	175.00
Lydia, 19"	1,500.00

1986

Jessica	150.00
Meredith	225.00
Veronica, 19"	300.00

1987

Silver Bell, 17"	175.00
Valentine Lady, Jane	145.00
1988, Christa	850.00
1989, Rose	225.00

Hamilton Collection

1981, Hakata, Peony Maiden	150.00
1985, American Fashion Doll Collection, Heather	125.00
1986, Nicole	50.00
1987, Priscilla	50.00
1988, Mr Spock	75.00
1989, Scotty	75.00

Royal Doulton by Nisbet

Big Sister	225.00
Little Model	185.00
Pink Sash	145.00
Royal Baby	350.00
The Muffs	175.00
Winter	180.00

Easter Egg, Noritake, 1978, $14.00.

EGGS

Anri, 1979, Beatrix Potter	5.00
Cybis Studios, 1983, FE, 5" h, Faberge style	300.00

Ferrandiz

1978, FE	15.00
1979	12.00
1980	9.50
1981	9.00
1982	8.00
1983	18.00
Franklin Mint, 1979, porcelain	35.00

Goebel

1978, Easter	10.00
1979, Easter	8.00

1980
   Crystal **6.00**
   Easter **9.75**
1981, Easter **12.00**
1982, Easter **8.00**
1983, Easter **28.00**
Gorham, bone china, pink rose, 4¼" . **18.00**
Noritake
   1971, Easter, FE **75.00**
   1972, Easter **35.00**
   1973, Easter **18.00**
   1974, Easter **8.00**
   1975, Easter **10.00**
   1976, Easter **10.00**
   1977, Easter **12.50**
   1978, Easter **14.00**
   1979, Easter **14.00**
   1980, Easter **14.00**
   1981, Easter **15.00**
   1982, Easter **15.00**
   1983, Easter **28.50**
   1984, Easter **20.00**
Royal Bayreuth
   1975 .... **8.50**
   1976 .... **6.50**
   1977 .... **5.50**
   1979 .... **16.00**
   1980 .... **15.00**
Veneto Flair
   1975 .... **14.50**
   1976 .... **14.50**
   1977 .... **15.00**
   1983, FE, luster finish, new series .. **20.00**
Wedgwood
   1977 .... **35.00**
   1978 .... **25.00**
   1979 .... **18.00**
   1983 .... **40.00**

FIGURINES

Anri, Sarah Kay artist
   1983, Morning Chores, FE **475.00**
   1984, Flowers for You, 6" **400.00**
   1985, Afternoon Tea, 6" **295.00**
   1986, Our Puppy, 1½" **75.00**
   1987, Little Nanny, 4" **180.00**
   1988, Purrfect Day, 6" **200.00**
   1989, Garden Party, 4" **195.00**
   1990, Season's Greetings, 4" **225.00**
Burgues
   1972, Canon Wren **875.00**
   1976, Anniversary Orchid **120.00**
   1978, Young Cottontail **325.00**
   1981, Joy **85.00**
   1982, Frosty **75.00**
   1983, Oscar, cat **100.00**
   1984, Cymbidium, Pink Blush **80.00**
Cybis
   1963, Magnolia **400.00**
   1964, Rebecca **345.00**
   1967, Kitten, blue ribbon **500.00**

1968, Narcissus **500.00**
1969, Clematis with House Wren .. **315.00**
1970, Dutch Crocus **750.00**
1971, Appaloosa Colt **285.00**
1973, Goldilocks **325.00**
1974, Mary, Mary **750.00**
1975, George Washington Bust **300.00**
1976, Bunny **125.00**
1977, Tiffin **400.00**
1978, Edith **300.00**
1985, Nativity Lamb **125.00**
1986, Dapple Gray Foal **185.00**
Enesco Corp, Precious Moments
   1979, Jesus Loves Me **30.00**
   1980, Come Let Us Adore Him **90.00**
   1981, But Love Goes On Forever ... **165.00**
   1982, Cameo **30.00**
   1983, Sharing Our Season **100.00**
   1984, I Get A Kick Out of You **75.00**
   1985, Baby's First Christmas **35.00**
   1986, God Bless America **50.00**
   1987, This Is The Day The Lord Hath
     Made **35.00**
   1988, Faith Takes The Plunge **30.00**
   1989, Wishing You Roads of Happi-
     ness **50.00**
   1990, To My Favorite Fan **15.00**
Goebel
   1971, Fritz the Happy Boozer **50.00**
   1972, Bob the Bookworm **50.00**
   1973, Maid of the Mist, 14" **750.00**
   1978, Smiling Through, 5½" **75.00**
   1982, The Garden Fancier **40.00**
   1984, On The Fairway **45.00**
   1985, Gentle Breezes **45.00**
   1987, Chuck on a Pig **65.00**
   1988, Beautiful Burden **165.00**
   1989, My First Arrow **70.00**
   1990, El Burrito **60.00**
Hummel, see HUMMEL
Llardo
   1971, Elephants **475.00**
   1973, Going Fishing **90.00**
   1974, Passionate Dance **2,500.00**
   1975, Wedding **100.00**
   1977, My Baby **1,115.00**
   1978, Chrysanthemum **225.00**
   1980, Reading **175.00**
   1983, California Poppy **100.00**
   1984, Torch Bearer **125.00**
   1985, Youthful Beauty **800.00**
   1986, Ragamuffin **125.00**
   1987, Spring Bouquets **125.00**
   1989, Reflecting Clown **325.00**
River Shore
   1978, Akiku, Baby Seal, FE **145.00**
   1979, Rosecoe, red fox kit **50.00**
   1980, Lamb **48.00**
   1981, Zuela, elephant **60.00**
   1982, Kay's Doll **90.00**
Rockwell, Norman, see NORMAN
ROCKWELL

Royal Doulton
  1969, HRH Prince Charles, bust ... **400.00**
  1974, Lady Musicians, cymbals **475.00**
  1976, Fledging Bluebird **450.00**
  1977, Winter Wren **375.00**
  1982, Sweet and Twenties, Monte
    Carlo **175.00**
  Series
    Beatrix Potter
      Benjamin Bunny **25.00**
      Lady Mouse **20.00**
      Mrs. Rabbit & Bunnies **25.00**
      Old Mr. Brown **20.00**
      Peter Rabbit **25.00**
      Rebecca Puddle-duck **20.00**
    Bunnykins
      Artist **15.00**
      Autumn Days **17.00**
      Clean Sweep **14.00**
      Family Photograph **24.00**
      Grandpa's Story **17.00**
      Sleepy Time **12.00**
      Springtime **18.00**
      Tally Ho **15.00**
    Dickens
      Bumble **20.00**
      Mrs. Bardell **24.00**
      Scrooge **25.00**
    Lord of Rings, Tolkien
      Aragorn **45.00**
      Bilbo **35.00**
      Gandalf **50.00**
      Gimli **45.00**
      Gollum **35.00**
      Legolas **45.00**
Royal Orleans Porcelain, Marilyn Mon-
  roe **80.00**
Schmid
  Lowell Davis, artist
    1979, Country Road **275.00**
    1980, Two's Company **45.00**
    1981, Plum Tuckered Out **225.00**
    1982, Right Church, Wrong Pew . **80.00**
    1983, Stirring Up Trouble **165.00**
    1984, Catnapping Too **72.00**
    1985, Out of Step **45.00**

MUGS

Bing & Grondahl
  1978, FE **50.00**
  1980 .... **25.00**
Franklin Mint, 1979, Father's Day **40.00**
Gorham
  1981, Bugs Bunny **8.00**
  1981, Tom & Jerry, 4 × 4" h **9.00**
Lynell Studios, 1983, FE, Gnome Series
  Gnomelyweds **8.00**
  Mama Gnome **7.00**
  Gnome Sweet Gnome **6.50**
Royal Copenhagen
  1967, large **200.00**

Mug, John James Audubon, Cardinal, 4"
h, $5.00.

1968, large **24.00**
1972, large **24.00**
1976, large **25.00**
1979, small **28.00**
1980
  Large **65.00**
  Small **25.00**
1981
  Large **70.00**
  Small **35.00**
1983, small **30.00**
Royal Doulton, Santa, second edition . **75.00**
Schmid, Zemsky, musical, 1981, Paddington Bear **25.00**
Wedgwood
  1971, Christmas **35.00**
  1972, Christmas **30.00**
  1973, Christmas **40.00**
  1974, Christmas **30.00**
  1975, Christmas **30.00**
  1976, Christmas **30.00**
  1977, Father's Day **25.00**
  1978, Father's Day **25.00**
  1979, Christmas **25.00**
  1980, Christmas **25.00**
  1981, Christmas **35.00**
  1982, Christmas **40.00**

MUSIC BOXES

Anri
  Jemima **100.00**
  Peter Rabbit **100.00**
  Pigling **100.00**
Ferrandiz
  Angel **140.00**
  Chorale **125.00**
  Drummer **185.00**
  Flower Girl **150.00**
  Going Home **275.00**
  Letter, The **150.00**
  Proud Mother **140.00**
  Spring Arrivals **120.00**

Wanderlust **110.00**
Gorham
  Cardinal, double, 6" h, hp, sculp-
    tured, porcelain **30.00**
  Happy Birthday, animals **35.00**
  Santa & Sleigh, 6" h **20.00**
  Sesame Street, Big Bird & Snowman,
    7" h **24.00**
Schmid
  Paddington Bear
    1981, Christmas **35.00**
    1982 .... **22.00**
  Peanuts
    30th Anniversary **18.00**
    1981
      Christmas **28.00**
      Mother's Day **18.00**
    1982
      Christmas **30.00**
      Mother's Day **20.00**
  Raggedy Ann
    1980 .... **15.00**
    1981 .... **15.00**
    1982, Flying High **20.00**
Walt Disney
  1980, Christmas, FE **42.00**
  1981, Christmas **30.00**
  1982, Christmas **25.00**

ORNAMENTS

Anri
  Beatrix Potter Series
    Amiable Guinea **12.00**
    Hunca Munca **12.00**
    Jeremy Fisher **12.50**
    Mrs. Rigby **10.00**
    Pigling Bland **12.00**
    Tom Kitten **12.75**
  1982, Alpine Mother, pastel pink ... **14.00**
Danbury Mint, angel, 4" **45.00**
Davis, Lowell, R.F.D. Series, FE **15.00**
Ferrandiz
  1978, FE **22.00**
  1979 .... **15.00**
  1980 .... **15.00**
  1981 .... **18.00**
Goebel
  1978
    Santa, colorful, FE **12.00**
    Santa, white, FE **10.00**
  1982, Santa **18.00**
Gorham
  1972, Snowflake **25.00**
  1973, Snowflake **35.00**
  1979, Tiny Tim, FE **8.00**
  1980
    Santa, FE, miniature series **8.00**
    Snowflake, SP **8.00**
  1981
    Doll, Rosebud, china, 8" h **12.00**
    Santa, miniature **10.00**

Snowflake **30.00**
Toy Soldier, wooden, red jacket,
  blue hat **4.50**
Hallmark
  1974, Mary Hamilton, orig Charmer
    Design **7.50**
  1975, Betsy Clark **7.50**
  1979, Special Teacher, satin **4.50**
  1980, Baby's First Christmas **15.00**
  1981
    Candyville Express **25.00**
    Friendly Fiddler **15.00**
    St. Nicholas, tin **10.00**
  1982
    Soldier, clothespin, FE **25.00**
    Cookie Mouse **17.50**
    Cowboy Snowman **10.00**
    Jingling Teddy **12.00**
    Peeking Elf **6.50**
Haviland
  1972 .... **8.00**
  1973 .... **8.00**
  1974 .... **12.00**
  1975 .... **6.00**
  1976 .... **6.00**
  1977 .... **8.00**
  1978 .... **7.50**
  1979 .... **7.25**
  1980 .... **18.00**
  1981 .... **20.00**
  1982 .... **22.00**
International Silver, Twelve Days of
  Christmas, SS, each **25.00**
Lenox, 1982, FE, snowflake emb porcelain, 24K gold finials, date, 6" h .. **40.00**
Lunt
  1974, Trefoil **20.00**
  1980, Medallion **18.00**
Reed & Barton
  1980, Christmas Castle **28.00**
  1981
    Bringing Home The Tree, SP **15.00**
    Cross **18.00**
  1982, Little Shepherd Yuletide, SS .. **15.00**
Schmid
  Paddington Bear, 1982
    Ball **5.00**
    Figural **10.00**
  Raggedy Ann
    1976, FE **6.00**
    1977 .... **3.50**
    1978 .... **3.00**
    1979 .... **3.25**
    1980 .... **3.00**
    1982, Figural **10.00**
Walt Disney
  1974, FE **15.00**
  1975 .... **5.00**
  1976 .... **10.00**
  1977 .... **4.50**
  1978 .... **4.00**
  1979 .... **4.00**

1980	3.50
1981	3.00
1982 Figural	10.00

Towle
1971, Twelve Days of Christmas, SP
medallion .... | 250.00
1985, Poinsettia .... | 40.00
1987, White Christmas .... | 35.00
1988, Holly .... | 40.00
Wallace Silversmiths
1971, Sleigh Bell .... | 900.00
1972, Sleigh Bell .... | 350.00
1980, Snowman .... | 15.00
1983, Boy Caroler .... | 15.00
1985, Sleigh Bell .... | 45.00
1987, Candy Cane .... | 35.00

PLATES

Anri (Italy)

Christmas Plates, J Ferrandiz, 12" d
1972 Christ in the Manager .... | 230.00
1973 Christmas .... | 220.00
1974 Holy Night .... | 90.00
1975 Flight Into Egypt .... | 80.00
1976 Tree of Life .... | 60.00
1977 Girl with Flowers .... | 175.00
1978 Leading the Way .... | 165.00
1979 The Drummer .... | 170.00
1980 Rejoice .... | 150.00
1981 Spreading the Word .... | 150.00
1982 The Shepherd Family .... | 150.00
1983 Peace Attend Thee .... | 150.00
Mother's Day Plates, J Ferrandiz
1972, Mother Sewing .... | 200.00
1973, Alpine Mother & Child ...... | 150.00
1974, Mother Holding Child .... | 150.00
1975, Dove Girl .... | 150.00
1976, Mother Knitting .... | 200.00
1977, Alpine Stroll .... | 125.00
1978, The Beginning .... | 150.00
1979, All Hearts .... | 165.00
1980, Spring Arrivals .... | 160.00
1981, Harmony .... | 150.00
1982, With Love .... | 150.00

Bareuther (Germany)

Christmas Plates, Hans Mueller artist,
8" d
1967 Stiftskirche, FE .... | 90.00
1968 Kapplkirche .... | 25.00
1969 Christkindlemarkt .... | 20.00
1970 Chapel in Oberndorf .... | 18.00
1971 Toys for Sale .... | 20.00
1972 Christmas in Munich .... | 35.00
1973 Christmas Sleigh Ride .... | 20.00
1974 Church In The Black Forest ... | 20.00
1975 Snowman .... | 25.00
1976 Chapel in the Hills .... | 25.00
1977 Story Time (Christmas Story) .. | 30.00

1978 Mittenwald .... | 30.00
1979 Winter Day .... | 40.00
1980 Miltenberg .... | 38.00
1981 Walk in the Forest .... | 40.00
1982 Bad Wimpfen .... | 40.00
1983 The Night Before Christmas ... | 45.00
1984 Zeil on the River Main .... | 42.50
1985 Winter Wonderland .... | 42.50
1986 Christmas in Forchhe .... | 42.50
1987 Decorating the Tree .... | 46.50
1988 St Coloman Church .... | 80.00
1989 Sleigh Ride .... | 50.00
1990 The Old Forge in Rothenburg . | 50.00

Berlin (Germany)

Christmas Plates, various artists, 7¾" d
1970 Christmas In Bernkastel ...... | 130.00
1971 Christmas In Rothenburg On
Tauber .... | 30.00
1972 Christmas In Michelstadt ..... | 50.00
1973 Christmas In Wendelstein .... | 42.00
1974 Christmas In Bremen .... | 25.00
1975 Christmas In Dortland .... | 60.00
1976 Christmas Eve In Augsburg ... | 30.00
1977 Christmas Eve In Hamburg ... | 32.00
1978 Christmas Market At The Berlin
Cathedral .... | 55.00
1978 Christmas Eve In Greetsiel .... | 55.00
1980 Christmas Eve In Miltenberg .. | 55.00
1981 Christmas Eve In Hahnenklee . | 50.00
1982 Christmas Eve In Wasserburg . | 55.00
1983 Chapel In Oberndorf .... | 55.00
1984 Christmas in Ramsau .... | 50.00
1985 Christmas Eve in Bad Wimpfen | 55.00
1986 Christmas Eve in Gelnhaus ... | 65.00
1987 Christmas Eve in Goslar ...... | 70.00
1988 Christmas Eve in Ruhpolding . | 100.00

Bing and Grondahl (Denmark)

Christmas Plates, various artists, 7" d
1895 Behind The Frozen Window . | 3,400.00
1896 New Moon Over Snow-cov-
ered Trees .... | 1,975.00
1897 Christmas Meal Of The Spar-
rows .... | 725.00
1898 Christmas Roses And Christmas
Star .... | 700.00
1899 The Crows Enjoying Christmas | 900.00
1900 Church Bells Chiming In Christ-
mas .... | 800.00
1901 The Three Wise Men From The
East .... | 450.00
1902 Interior Of A Gothic Church .. | 285.00
1903 Happy Expectation of Children | 150.00
1904 View of Copenhagen From
Frederiksberg Hill .... | 125.00
1905 Anxiety Of The Coming Christ-
mas Night .... | 130.00
1906 Sleighing To Church On Christ-
mas Eve .... | 95.00

Bing and Grondahl, Christmas, 1915, $120.00.

1907 The Little Match Girl	125.00
1908 St. Petri Church of Copenhagen	85.00
1909 Happiness Over The Yule Tree	100.00
1910 The Old Organist	90.00
1911 First It Was Sung By Angels To Shepherds In The Fields	80.00
1912 Going To Church On Christmas Eve	80.00
1913 Bringing Home The Yule Tree	85.00
1914 Royal Castle of Amalienborg, Copenhagen	75.00
1915 Chained Dog Getting Double Meal On Christmas Eve	120.00
1916 Christmas Prayer Of The Sparrows	85.00
1917 Arrival Of The Christmas Boat	75.00
1918 Fishing Boat Returning Home For Christmas	85.00
1919 Outside The Lighted Window	80.00
1920 Hare In The Snow	70.00
1921 Pigeons In The Castle Court	55.00
1922 Star Of Bethlehem	60.00
1923 Royal Hunting Castle, The Hermitage	55.00
1924 Lighthouse In Danish Waters	65.00
1925 The Child's Christmas	70.00
1926 Churchgoers On Christmas Day	65.00
1927 Skating Couple	110.00
1928 Eskimo Looking At Village Church In Greenland	60.00
1929 Fox Outside Farm On Christmas Eve	75.00
1930 Yule Tree In Town Hall Square Of Copenhagen	85.00
1931 Arrival Of The Christmas Train	75.00
1932 Lifeboat At Work	90.00
1933 The Korsor-Nyborg Ferry	70.00
1934 Church Bell In Tower	75.00
1935 Lillebelt Bridge Connecting Funen With Jutland	65.00
1936 Royal Guard Outside Amalienborg Castle In Copenhagen	70.00
1937 Arrival Of Christmas Guests	75.00
1938 Lighting The Candles	110.00
1939 Ole Lock-Eye, The Sandman	150.00
1940 Delivering Christmas Letters	170.00
1941 Horses Enjoying Christmas Meal In Stable	345.00
1942 Danish Farm On Christmas Night	150.00
1943 The Ribe Cathedral	155.00
1944 Sorgenfri Castle	120.00
1945 The Old Water Mill	135.00
1946 Commemoration Cross In Honor Of Danish Sailors Who Lost Their Lives In World War II	85.00
1947 Dybbol Mill	70.00
1948 Watchman, Sculpture Of Town Hall, Copenhagen	80.00
1949 Landsoldaten, 19th Century Danish Soldier	70.00
1950 Kronborg Castle At Elsinore	150.00
1951 Jens Bang, New Passenger Boat Running Between Copenhagen And Aalborg	115.00
1952 Old Copenhagen Canals At Wintertime With Thorvaldsen Museum In Background	85.00
1953 Royal Boat In Greenland Waters	95.00
1954 Birthplace Of Hans Christian Andersen, With Snowman	100.00
1955 Kalundborg Church	115.00
1956 Christmas In Copenhagen	140.00
1957 Christmas Candles	155.00
1958 Santa Claus	100.00
1959 Christmas Eve	120.00
1960 Danish Village Church	180.00
1961 Winter Harmony	115.00
1962 Winter Night	80.00
1963 The Christmas Elf	120.00
1964 The Fir Tree And Hare	50.00
1965 Bringing Home The Christmas Tree	65.00
1966 Home For Christmas	50.00
1967 Sharing The Joy Of Christmas	48.00
1968 Christmas In Church	45.00
1969 Arrival Of Christmas Guests	30.00
1970 Pheasants In The Snow At Christmas	20.00
1971 Christmas At Home	20.00
1972 Christmas In Greenland	20.00
1973 Country Christmas	25.00
1974 Christmas In The Village	20.00
1975 The Old Water Mill	24.00
1976 Christmas Welcome	25.00
1977 Copenhagen Christmas	25.00
1978 A Christmas Tale	30.00
1979 White Christmas	30.00
1980 Christmas In The Woods	42.50
1981 Christmas Peace	50.00
1982 The Christmas Tree	55.00
1983 Christmas in Old Town	55.00
1984 Christmas Letter	55.00
1985 Christmas Eve at the Farmhouse	55.00

1986 Silent Night, Holy Night **55.00**
1987 The Snowman's Christmas Eve **60.00**
1988 In The Kings Garden **72.00**
1989 Christmas Anchorage **65.00**
Mother's Day Plates, Henry Thelander, artist, 6" d
1969 Dog And Puppies **400.00**
1970 Bird And Chicks **35.00**
1971 Cat And Kitten **24.00**
1972 Mare And Foal **20.00**
1973 Duck And Ducklings **20.00**
1974 Bear And Cubs **24.00**
1975 Doe And Fawns **20.00**
1976 Swan Family **22.00**
1977 Squirrel And Young **25.00**
1978 Heron **25.00**
1979 Fox And Cubs **30.00**
1980 Woodpecker And Young **35.00**
1981 Hare And Young **40.00**
1982 Lioness And Cubs **45.00**
1983 Raccoon And Young **45.00**
1984 Stork and Nestlings **40.00**
1985 Bear and Cubs **40.00**
1986 Elephant with Calf **40.00**
1987 Sheep with Lambs **42.50**
1988 Lapwing Mother with Chicks . **48.00**
1989 Cow with Calf **48.00**
1990 Hen with Chicks **50.00**

Franklin Mint (United States)

Audubon Society Birds
1972 Goldfinch **115.00**
1972 Wood Duck **110.00**
1973 Cardinal **110.00**
1973 Ruffed Grouse **120.00**
Christmas Plates, Norman Rockwell, artist, etched sterling silver, 8"
1970 Bringing Home The Tree **275.00**
1971 Under The Mistletoe **125.00**
1972 The Carolers **125.00**
1973 Trimming The Tree **100.00**
1974 Hanging The Wreath **100.00**
1975 Home For Christmas **125.00**

Goebel (Germany), see Hummel

Haviland (France)

Mother's Day (The French Collection)
1973 Breakfast **25.00**
1974 The Wash **30.00**
1975 In The Park **25.00**
1976 Market **40.00**
1977 Wash Before Dinner **35.00**
1978 Evening At Home **40.00**
1979 Happy Mother's Day **30.00**
1980 Child & His Animals **55.00**
1,001 Arabian Nights, Lillian Tellier artist
1979 Cheval Magique, Magic Horse **60.00**
1980 Aladin et Lampe **60.00**

1981 Scheherazade **55.00**
1982 Sinbad the Sailor **55.00**
The Twelve Days Of Christmas Series, Remy Hetreau, artist, 8⅜" d
1970 A Partridge In A Pear Tree, FE **115.00**
1971 Two Turtle Doves **40.00**
1972 Three French Hens **35.00**
1973 Four Calling Birds **35.00**
1974 Five Golden Rings **30.00**
1975 Six Geese A'Laying **30.00**
1976 Seven Swans A'Swimming **30.00**
1977 Eight Maids A'Milking **45.00**
1978 Nine Ladies Dancing **35.00**
1979 Ten Lords A'Leaping **40.00**
1980 Eleven Pipers Piping **50.00**
1981 Twelve Drummers Drumming . **55.00**

Haviland & Parlon (France)

Christmas Series, various artists, 10" d
1972 Madonna And Child, Raphael, FE **80.00**
1973 Madonnina, Feruzzi **95.00**
1974 Cowper Madonna And Child, Raphael **55.00**
1975 Madonna And Child, Murillo . **45.00**
1976 Madonna And Child, Botticelli **50.00**
1977 Madonna And Child, Bellini .. **40.00**
1978 Madonna And Child, Fra Filippo Lippi **65.00**
1979 Madonna Of The Eucharist, Botticelli **150.00**
Lady And The Unicorn Series, artist unknown, 10" d
1977 To My Only Desire, FE **60.00**
1978 Sight **40.00**
1979 Sound **50.00**
1980 Touch **110.00**
1981 Scent **60.00**
1982 Taste **80.00**
Tapestry Series, artist unknown, 10" d
1971 The Unicorn In Captivity **145.00**
1972 Start Of The Hunt **70.00**
1973 Chase Of The Unicorn **120.00**
1974 End Of The Hunt **120.00**
1975 The Unicorn Surrounded **75.00**
1976 The Unicorn Is Brought To The Castle **55.00**

Edwin M. Knowles (United States)

Americana Holidays Series, Don Spaulding, artist, 8½" d
1978 Fourth Of July, FE **35.00**
1979 Thanksgiving **35.00**
1980 Easter **30.00**
1981 Valentine's Day **25.00**
1982 Father's Day **35.00**
1983 Christmas **35.00**
1984 Mother's Day **20.00**
Annie Series
1983 Annie And Sandy, FE **25.00**

Knowles, Mother's Day, Reflections, 1979, $40.00.

1983 Daddy Warbucks	20.00
1983 Annie & Grace	19.00
1984 Annie and the Orphans	20.00
1985 Tomorrow	21.00
1986 Annie, Lily, and Rooster	24.00
1987 Grand Finale	24.00

Gone With The Wind Series, Raymond Kursar, artist, 8½" d
1978 Scarlett, FE	300.00
1979 Ashley	225.00
1980 Melanie	75.00
1981 Rhett	50.00
1982 Mammy Lacing Scarlett	60.00
1983 Melanie Gives Birth	85.00
1984 Scarlett's Green Dress	50.00
1985 Rhett and Bonnie	35.00
1985 Scarlett and Rhett: The Finale	30.00

Wizard Of Oz Series, James Auckland, artist, 8½" d
1977 Over The Rainbow, FE	65.00
1978 If I Only Had A Brain	30.00
1978 If I Only Had A Heart	30.00
1978 If I Were King Of The Forest	30.00
1979 Wicked Witch Of The West	35.00
1979 Follow The Yellow Brick Road	35.00
1979 Wonderful Wizard Of Oz	50.00
1980 The Grand Finale (We're Off To See The Wizard)	60.00

Lalique (France)

Annual Series, lead crystal, Marie-Claude Lalique, artist, 8½" d
1965 Deux Oiseaux (Two Birds), FE	800.00
1966 Rose de Songerie (Dream Rose)	215.00
1967 Ballet de Poisson (Fish Ballet)	200.00
1968 Gazelle Fantaisie (Gazelle Fantasy)	70.00
1969 Papillon (Butterfly)	80.00
1970 Paon (Peacock)	50.00
1971 Hibou (Owl)	60.00
1972 Coquillage (Shell)	55.00
1973 Petit Geai (Jayling)	60.00
1974 Sous d'Argent (Silver Pennies)	65.00
1975 Due de Poisson (Fish Duet)	75.00
1976 Aigle (Eagle)	100.00

Lenox (United States)

Boehm Bird Series, Edward Marshall Boehm, artist, 10½" d
1970 Wood Thrush, FE	175.00
1971 Goldfinch	65.00
1972 Mountain Bluebird	65.00
1973 Meadowlark	60.00
1974 Rufous Hummingbird	50.00
1975 American Redstart	50.00
1976 Cardinal	58.00
1977 Robins	55.00
1978 Mockingbirds	60.00
1979 Golden-Crowned Kinglets	65.00
1980 Black-Throated Blue Warblers	75.00
1981 Eastern Phoebes	100.00

Boehm Woodland Wildlife Series, Edward Marshall Boehm, artist, 10½" d
1973 Raccoons, FE	80.00
1974 Red Foxes	50.00
1975 Cottontail Rabbits	60.00
1976 Eastern Chipmunks	60.00
1977 Beaver	60.00
1978 Whitetail Deer	60.00
1979 Squirrels	75.00
1980 Bobcats	90.00
1981 Martens	100.00
1982 Otters	100.00

Llardo (Spain)

Christmas, 8" d, undisclosed artists
1971 Caroling	30.00
1972 Carolers	35.00
1973 Boy & Girl	50.00
1974 Carolers	75.00
1975 Cherubs	60.00
1976 Christ Child	50.00
1977 Nativity	70.00
1978 Caroling Child	50.00
1979 Snow Dance	80.00

Mother's Day, undisclosed artists
1971 Kiss of the Child	75.00
1972 Birds & Chicks	30.00
1973 Mother & Children	35.00
1974 Nursing Mother	135.00
1975 Mother & Child	55.00
1976 Vigil	50.00
1977 Mother & Daughter	60.00
1978 New Arrival	55.00
1979 Off to School	90.00

Reco International Corp. (United States)

Days Gone By, Sandra Kuck artist
1983 Sunday Best	55.00
1983 Amy's Magic Horse	30.00
1984 Little Anglers	30.00

1984 Little Tutor 30.00
1984 Easter at Grandma's 30.00
McClelland Children's Circus Series,
   John McClelland, artist, 9" d
1981 Tommy The Clown, FE 30.00
1982 Katie The Tightrope Walker ... 31.00
1983 Johnny The Strongman 31.00
1984 Maggie The Animal Trainer ... 29.50
McClelland's Mother Goose Series, John
   McClelland, artist, 8½" d
1979 Mary, Mary, FE 250.00
1980 Little Boy Blue 100.00
1981 Little Miss Muffet 30.00
1982 Little Jack Horner 30.00
1983 Little Bo Peep 40.00
1984 Diddle, Diddle Dumpling 30.00
1985 Mary Had A Little Lamb 42.00
1986 Jack and Jill 25.00

Reed & Barton (United States)

Christmas Series, Damascene silver,
   11" d through 1978, 8" d 1979 to
   present
1970 A Partridge In A Pear Tree, FE   200.00
1971 We Three Kings Of Orient Are   65.00
1972 Hark! The Herald Angels Sing   60.00
1973 Adoration Of The Kings 75.00
1974 The Adoration Of The Magi .. 60.00
1975 Adoration Of The Kings 65.00
1976 Morning Train 60.00
1977 Decorating The Church 60.00
1978 The General Store At Christmas
   Time 67.00
1979 Merry Old Santa Claus 65.00
1980 Gathering Christmas Greens .. 75.00
1981 The Shopkeeper At Christmas . 75.00

Rockwell, see Norman Rockwell

Rosenthal (Germany)

Christmas   Plates,   various   artists,
   8½" d
1910 Winter Peace 550.00
1911 The Three Wise Men 325.00
1912 Shooting Stars 250.00
1913 Christmas Lights 235.00
1914 Christmas Song 350.00
1915 Walking To Church 180.00
1916 Christmas During War 235.00
1917 Angel Of Peace 210.00
1918 Peace On Earth 210.00
1919 St. Christopher With The Christ
   Child 225.00
1920 The Manger In Bethlehem 325.00
1921 Christmas In The Mountains .. 200.00
1922 Advent Branch 200.00
1923 Children In The Winter Wood   200.00
1924 Deer In The Woods 200.00
1925 The Three Wise Men 200.00

1926 Christmas In The Mountains .. 175.00
1927 Station On The Way 200.00
1928 Chalet Christmas 175.00
1929 Christmas In The Alps 225.00
1930 Group Of Deer Under The Pines 225.00
1931 Path Of The Magi 225.00
1932 Christ Child 195.00
1933 Through The Night To Light .. 190.00
1934 Christmas Peace 200.00
1935 Christmas By The Sea 185.00
1936 Nürnberg Angel 185.00
1937 Berchtesgaden 195.00
1938 Christmas In The Alps 190.00
1939 Schneekoppe Mountain 195.00
1940 Marien Church In Danzig 250.00
1941 Strassburg Cathedral 250.00
1942 Marianburg Castle 300.00
1943 Winter Idyll 300.00
1944 Wood Scape 275.00
1945 Christmas Peace 400.00
1946 Christmas In An Alpine Valley   250.00
1947 The Dillingen Madonna 975.00
1948 Message To The Shepherds ... 875.00
1949 The Holy Family 185.00
1950 Christmas In The Forest 185.00
1951 Star Of Bethlehem 450.00
1952 Christmas In The Alps 190.00
1953 The Holy Light 185.00
1954 Christmas Eve 185.00
1955 Christmas In A Village 190.00
1956 Christmas In The Alps 190.00
1957 Christmas By The Sea 195.00
1958 Christmas Eve 185.00
1959 Midnight Mass 195.00
1960 Christmas In Small Village 195.00
1961 Solitary Christmas 225.00
1962 Christmas Eve 185.00
1963 Silent Night 185.00
1964 Christmas Market In Nürnberg   225.00
1965 Christmas In Munich 185.00
1966 Christmas In Ulm 250.00
1967 Christmas In Regensburg 185.00
1968 Christmas In Bremen 195.00
1969 Christmas In Rothenburg 220.00
1970 Christmas In Cologne 165.00
1971 Christmas In Garmisch 100.00
1972 Christmas Celebration In Franconia 90.00
1973 Christmas In Lubeck-Holstein . 110.00
1974 Christmas In Wurzburg 100.00
Bjorn Wiinblad (artist) Christmas Plates
   Series
1971 Maria and Child 1,250.00
1972 Caspar 550.00
1973 Melchior 450.00
1974 Balthazar 500.00
1975 The Annunciation 200.00
1976 Angel With Trumpet 200.00
1977 Adoration Of The Shepherds .. 250.00
1978 Angel With Harp 275.00
1979 Exodus From Egypt 310.00
1980 Angel With A Glockenspiel ... 360.00

1981 Christ Child Visits Temple **375.00**
1982 Christening of Christ **375.00**

Royal Copenhagen

Christmas Plates, various artists, 6" d
1908, 1909, 1910; 7" 1911 to present
1908 Madonna And Child **1,750.00**
1909 Danish Landscape **150.00**
1910 The Magi **120.00**
1911 Danish Landscape **135.00**
1912 Elderly Couple By Christmas
Tree **120.00**
1913 Spire Of Frederik's Church, Copenhagen **125.00**
1914 Sparrows In Tree At Church Of
The Holy Spirit, Copenhagen **100.00**
1915 Danish Landscape **150.00**
1916 Shepherd In The Field On
Christmas Night **85.00**
1917 Tower Of Our Savior's Church,
Copenhagen **90.00**
1918 Sheep and Shepherds **80.00**
1919 In The Park **80.00**

Royal Copenhagen, Christmas plate,
1920, Mary and Child Jesus, $75.00.

1920 Mary With The Child Jesus ... **75.00**
1921 Aabenraa Marketplace **75.00**
1922 Three Singing Angels **70.00**
1923 Danish Landscape **70.00**
1924 Christmas Star Over The Sea
And Sailing Ship **100.00**
1925 Street Scene From Christian-
shavn, Copenhagen **85.00**
1926 View of Christmas Canal, Copenhagen **75.00**
1927 Ship's Boy At The Tiller On
Christmas Night **140.00**
1928 Vicar's Family On Way To
Church **75.00**
1929 Grundtvig Church, Copenhagen **100.00**
1930 Fishing Boats On The Way To
The Harbor **80.00**
1931 Mother And Child **90.00**

1932 Frederiksberg Gardens With
Statue Of Frederik VI **90.00**
1933 The Great Belt Ferry **110.00**
1934 The Hermitage Castle **115.00**
1935 Fishing Boat Off Kronborg Castle **145.00**
1936 Roskilde Cathedral **130.00**
1937 Christmas Scene In Main Street,
Copenhagen **135.00**
1938 Round Church In Osterlars On
Bornholm **200.00**
1939 Expeditionary Ship In Pack-Ice
Of Greenland **180.00**
1940 The Good Shepherd **300.00**
1941 Danish Village Church **250.00**
1942 Bell Tower of Old Church In
Jutland **300.00**
1943 Flight Of Holy Family To Egypt **425.00**
1944 Typical Danish Winter Scene . **160.00**
1945 A Peaceful Motif **325.00**
1946 Zealand Village Church **150.00**
1947 The Good Shepherd **210.00**
1948 Nodebo Church At Christmastime **150.00**
1949 Our Lady's Cathedral, Copenhagen **165.00**
1950 Boeslunde Church, Zealand .. **175.00**
1951 Christmas Angel **300.00**
1952 Christmas In The Forest **120.00**
1953 Fredriksborg Castle **120.00**
1954 Amalienborg Palace, Copen-
hagen **150.00**
1955 Fano Girl **185.00**
1956 Rosenborg Castle, Copenhagen **160.00**
1957 The Good Shepherd **115.00**
1958 Sunshine Over Greenland **140.00**
1959 Christmas Night **120.00**
1960 The Stag **140.00**
1961 Training Ship Danmark **155.00**
1962 The Little Mermaid At Wintertime **200.00**
1963 Hojsager Mill **80.00**
1964 Fetching The Christmas Tree .. **75.00**
1965 Little Skaters **60.00**
1966 Blackbird At Christmastime ... **55.00**
1967 The Royal Oak **45.00**
1968 The Last Umiak **40.00**
1969 The Old Farmyard **35.00**
1970 Christmas Rose And Cat **95.00**
1971 Hare In Winter **80.00**
1972 In The Desert **85.00**
1973 Train Homeward Bound For
Christmas **85.00**
1974 Winter Twilight **80.00**
1975 Queen's Palace **85.00**
1976 Danish Watermill **80.00**
1977 Immervad Bridge **75.00**
1978 Greenland Scenery **80.00**
1979 Choosing The Christmas Tree . **60.00**
1980 Bringing Home The Christmas
Tree **60.00**
1981 Admiring The Christmas Tree . **55.00**

1982 Waiting For Christmas **65.00**
1983 Merry Christmas **60.00**
1984 Jingle Bells **55.00**
1985 Snowman **55.00**
1986 Wait for Me **55.00**
1987 Winter Birds **58.00**
1988 Christmas Eve in Copenhagen . **70.00**
1989 The Old Skating Pond **50.00**
1990 Christmas at Tivoli **50.00**
Mother's Day Plates, various artists,
6¼" d
1971 American Mother **125.00**
1972 Oriental Mother **60.00**
1973 Danish Mother **60.00**
1974 Greenland Mother **55.00**
1975 Bird In Nest **50.00**
1976 Mermaids **50.00**
1977 The Twins **50.00**
1978 Mother And Child **25.00**
1979 A Loving Mother **30.00**
1980 An Outing With Mother **35.00**
1981 Reunion **40.00**
1982 The Children's Hour **45.00**

Royal Doulton (Great Britain)

Beswick Christmas Series, various artists, earthenware in hand-cast bas-relief, 8" sq
1972 Christmas In England, FE **40.00**
1973 Christmas In Mexico **25.00**
1974 Christmas In Bulgaria **40.00**
1975 Christmas In Norway **54.00**
1976 Christmas In Holland **45.00**
1977 Christmas In Poland **100.00**
1978 Christmas In America **45.00**
Mother And Child Series, Edna Hibel artist, 8¼" d
1973 Colette And Child, FE **450.00**
1974 Sayuri And Child **150.00**
1975 Kristina And Child **125.00**
1976 Marilyn And Child **120.00**
1977 Lucia And Child **100.00**
1978 Kathleen And Child **95.00**
Portraits Of Innocence Series, Francisco Masseria artist, 8" d
1980 Panchito, FE **160.00**
1981 Adrien **110.00**
1982 Angelica **100.00**
1983 Juliana **145.00**
Valentine's Day Series, artists unknown, 8¼" d
1976 Victorian Boy And Girl **60.00**
1977 My Sweetest Friend **40.00**
1978 If I Loved You **40.00**
1979 My Valentine **40.00**
1980 On A Swing **40.00**
1981 Sweet Music **35.00**
1982 From My Heart **40.00**
1983 Cherub's Song **45.00**
1984 Love In Bloom **40.00**
1985 Accept These Flowers **40.00**

Schmid, Christmas, Peanuts, 1977, **$15.00.**

Schmid (Japan)

Christmas, J Malfertheiner, artist
1971 St Jakob in Groden, FE **125.00**
1972 Pipers at Alberobello **120.00**
1973 Alpine Horn **375.00**
1974 Young Man and Girl **100.00**
1975 Christmas In Ireland **90.00**
1976 Alpine Christmas **200.00**
1977 Legend of Heligenblut **125.00**
1978 Klockler Singers **175.00**
1979 Moss Gatherers **130.00**
1980 Wintry Churchgoing **165.00**
1981 Santa Claus in Tyrol **160.00**
1982 The Star Singers **160.00**
1983 Unto Us A Child Is Born **150.00**
1984 Yuletide in the Valley **150.00**
1985 Good Morning, Good Year ... **160.00**
1986 A Groeden Christmas **75.00**
1987 Down From The Alps **175.00**
Disney Christmas Series, undisclosed artists, 7½" d
1973 Sleigh Ride, FE **400.00**
1974 Decorating The Tree **175.00**
1975 Caroling **20.00**
1976 Building A Snowman **35.00**
1977 Down The Chimney **25.00**
1978 Night Before Christmas **20.00**
1979 Santa's Surprise **20.00**
1980 Sleigh Ride **30.00**
1981 Happy Holidays **18.00**
1982 Winter Games **20.00**
1987 Snow White Golden Anniversary **48.00**
1988 Mickey Mouse & Minnie Mouse 60th **50.00**
1989 Sleeping Beauty 30th Anniversary **75.00**
1990 Fantasia Relief **25.00**
Disney Mother's Day Series
1974 Flowers For Mother, FE **80.00**

1975 Snow White And The Seven
   Dwarfs **45.00**
1976 Minnie Mouse And Friends ... **20.00**
1977 Pluto's Pals **25.00**
1978 Flowers For Bambi **20.00**
1979 Happy Feet **25.00**
1980 Minnie's Surprise **20.00**
1981 Playmates **25.00**
1982 A Dream Come True **20.00**
Peanuts Christmas Series, Charles
Schulz, artist, 7½" d
1972 Snoopy Guides The Sleigh, FE **90.00**
1973 Christmas Eve At The Doghouse **120.00**
1974 Christmas Eve At The Fireplace **65.00**
1975 Woodstock, Santa Claus **15.00**
1976 Woodstock's Christmas **30.00**
1977 Deck The Doghouse **15.00**
1978 Filling The Stocking **20.00**
1979 Christmas At Hand **20.00**
1980 Waiting For Santa **50.00**
1981 A Christmas Wish **20.00**
1982 Perfect Performance **35.00**
Peanuts Mother's Day Series, Charles
Schulz, artist, 7½" d
1972 Linus, FE **50.00**
1973 Mom? **45.00**
1974 Snoopy And Woodstock On Parade **40.00**
1975 A Kiss For Lucy **38.00**
1976 Linus And Snoopy **35.00**
1977 Dear Mom **30.00**
1978 Thoughts That Count **25.00**
1979 A Special Letter **20.00**
1980 A Tribute To Mom **20.00**
1981 Mission For Mom **20.00**
1982 Which Way To Mother? **20.00**
Peanuts Valentine's Day Series, Charles
Schulz, artist, 7½" d
1977 Home Is Where The Heart Is,
   FE **25.00**
1978 Heavenly Bliss **28.00**
1979 Love Match **20.00**
1980 From Snoopy, With Love **24.00**
1981 Hearts-A-Flutter **20.00**
1982 Love Patch **18.00**
Raggedy Ann Annual Series, undisclosed artist, 7½" d
1980 The Sunshine Wagon **65.00**
1981 The Raggedy Shuffle **25.00**
1982 Flying High **20.00**
1983 Winning Streak **20.00**
1984 Rocking Rodeo **22.50**

U. S. Historical Society (United States)

Stained Glass Cathedral
1978 Canterbury **175.00**
1979 Flight into Egypt **175.00**
1980 Washington Cathedral/Ma-
   donna **160.00**
1981 The Magi **160.00**
1982 Flight Into Egypt **160.00**

1983 Shepherds at Bethlehem **150.00**
1984 The Navitity **145.00**
1985 Good Tidings of Great Joy, Boston **125.00**
1986 The Nativity from Old St. Mary's
   Church, Philadelphia **165.00**
1987 O Come, Little Children **160.00**

Wedgwood (Great Britain)

Calendar Series
1971 Victorian Almanac, FE **20.00**
1972 The Carousel **15.00**
1973 Bountiful Butterfly **14.00**
1974 Camelot **65.00**
1975 Children's Games **18.00**
1976 Robin **25.00**
1977 Tonatiuh **28.00**
1978 Samurai **32.00**
1979 Sacred Scarab **32.00**
1980 Safari **40.00**
1981 Horses **42.50**
1982 Wild West **50.00**
1983 The Age of the Reptiles **50.00**
1984 Dogs **55.00**
1985 Cats **55.00**
1986 British Birds **50.00**
1987 Water Birds **50.00**
1988 Sea Birds **50.00**
Christmas Series, jasper stoneware, 8" d
1969 Windsor Castle, FE **225.00**
1970 Christmas In Trafalgar Square . **30.00**
1971 Piccadilly Circus, London **40.00**
1972 St. Paul's Cathedral **40.00**
1973 The Tower Of London **45.00**
1974 The Houses Of Parliament **40.00**
1975 Tower Bridge **40.00**
1976 Hampton Court **46.00**
1977 Westminster Abbey **48.00**
1978 The Horse Guards **55.00**
1979 Buckingham Palace **55.00**
1980 St. James Palace **70.00**
1981 Marble Arch **75.00**
1982 Lambeth Palace **80.00**
1983 All Souls, Langham Palace ... **80.00**
1984 Constitution Hill **80.00**
1985 The Tate Gallery **80.00**
1986 The Albert Memorial **80.00**
1987 Guildhall **80.00**
Mothers Series, jasper stoneware, 6½" d
1971 Sportive Love, FE **25.00**
1972 The Sewing Lesson **20.00**
1973 The Baptism Of Achilles **20.00**
1974 Domestic Employment **30.00**
1975 Mother And Child **35.00**
1976 The Spinner **35.00**
1977 Leisure Time **30.00**
1978 Swan And Cygnets **35.00**
1979 Deer And Fawn **35.00**
1980 Birds **48.00**
1981 Mare And Foal **50.00**
1982 Cherubs With Swing **55.00**

1983 Cupid And Butterfly	55.00
1984 Musical Cupids	55.00
1985 Cupids and Doves	55.00
1986 Anemones	55.00
1987 Tiger Lily	55.00

Queen's Christmas, A Price artist

1980 Windsor Castle	30.00
1981 Trafalgar Square	25.00
1982 Piccadilly Circus	35.00
1983 St. Pauls	32.50
1984 Tower of London	35.00
1985 Palace of Westminster	35.00
1986 Tower Bridge	35.00

LITTLE GOLDEN BOOKS

Collecting Hints: Little Golden Books offer something for everybody. Collectors can pursue titles by favorite author, illustrator, or their favorite television show, film, or comic strip character. Disney titles enjoy a special place with nostalgia buffs. An increasingly popular goal is to own one copy of each title and number.

Books published in the forties, fifties, and sixties are in the most demand at this time. Books from this period were assigned individual numbers usually found on the front cover of the book except for the earliest titles where one must check the title against the numbered list on back of the book.

Although the publisher tried to adhere to a policy of one number for each title during the first thirty years, old numbers were assigned to new titles as old titles were eliminated. Also, when an earlier book was re-edited and/or re-illustrated, it was given a new number.

Most of the first thirty-six books had blue paper spines and a dust jacket. Subsequent books were issued with a golden-brown mottled spine. This was replaced in 1950 by a shiny gold spine.

Early books had 42 pages. In the late 1940s the format was gradually changed to 28 pages. Early 42 and 28 page books had no price on the cover. Later the price of 25¢ appeared on the front cover, then 29¢, followed by 39¢. In the mid-fifties the number of pages was changed to 24. In the early fifties books were produced with two lines that formed a bar across the top of the front cover. This bar was eliminated in the early sixties.

Little Golden Books can still be found at yard sales and flea markets. Other sources include friends, relatives, and charity book sales, especially if they have a separate children's table. Also attend doll, toy, and book shows. These dealers are sources for books with paper dolls, puzzles, and cut outs. Toy dealers are also a good source for Disney, television, and cowboy titles.

Look for books in good or better condition. Covers should be bright with the spine paper intact. Rubbing, ink and crayon markings, or torn pages lessen the value of the book. Pencil markings are fairly easy to remove, unless extensive. Stroke gently in one direction with an art gum eraser. Do not rub back and forth.

Within the past two years competition has increased dramatically, thus driving up prices for the most unusual and hard-to-find titles. Prices for the majority of titles are still at a reasonable level.

History: Simon & Schuster published the first Little Golden Books in September, 1942. They were conceived and created by the Artists & Writers Guild Inc., which was an arm of the Western Printing and Lithographing Company. The initial twelve, forty-two page titles, priced at 25¢ each, sold over 1.5 million books within five months of publication. By the end of WWII thirty-nine million Little Golden Books were sold.

A Disney series was begun in 1944, and Big and Giant Golden Books followed that same year. In 1949 the first Goldencraft editions were introduced. Instead of side-stapled cardboard, these books had cloth covers and were sewn so that they could hold up under school and library use. In 1958 Giant Little Golden Books were introduced, most combining three previously published titles together in one book.

1958 also marks Simon & Schuster selling Little Golden Books to Western Printing and Lithographing Company and Pocket Books. The books then appeared under the Golden Press imprint. Eventually Western bought out Pocket Books' interest in Little Golden Books. Now known as Western Publishing Company, Inc., it is the parent company of Golden Press, Inc.

In 1986 Western celebrated the one-billionth Little Golden Book by issuing special commemorative editions of some of its most popular titles, such as *Poky Little Puppy*, and *Cinderella*. In 1992 Golden Press will celebrate the 50th birthday of Little Golden Books.

Note: Prices are based on the first printing of a book in mint condition. Printing is determined by looking at the lower right hand corner of the back page. The letter found there indicates the printing of that particular title and edition. "A" is the first printing and so forth. Occasionally the letter is hidden under the spine or was placed in the upper right hand corner, so look closely. Early titles will have their printings indicated in the front of the book.

Any dust jacket, puzzles, stencils, cutouts, stamps, tissues, tape, or pages should be intact and present as issued. If not, the book suffers a drastic reduction in value—up to 80 percent less than the listed price. Books that are badly worn, incomplete, or badly torn are worth little. Sometimes they are useful as temporary fillers for gaps in a collection.

References: Dolores B. Jones, *Bibliography of the Little Golden Book*, Greenwood Press, 1987; Barbara Bader, *American Picture Books from Noah's Ark to the Beast Within*, Macmillan, 1976; Steve Santi, *Collecting Little Golden Books*, Books Americana, 1989; Rebecca Greason, *Tomart's Price Guide To Golden Book Collectibles*, Wallace–Homestead Book Company, 1991.

Advisor: Kathie Diehl.

Activity

#A2, *Circus Time,* Marion Conger, illus Tibor Gergely, c1955, with wheel **10.00**

#A6, *Trucks,* Kathryn Jackson, illus Ray Quigley, c1955, with trucks to punch–out **35.00**

#A17, *Stop and Go,* Loyta Higgins, illus Joan Walsh Anglund, c1957, with wheel **15.00**

#A34, *Little Red Riding Hood,*illus Sharon Koester, c1959, with paper dolls, uncut **45.00**

#A39, *My Little Golden Calendar for 1961,*illus Richard Scarry, c1960, soft cover **25.00**

#285, *How To Tell Time,* Jane Werner Watson, illus Eleanor Dart, c1957, with clock face and hands, "Gruen" on face **15.00**

Advertising

#129, *Tex and His Toys,* Elsa Ruth Nast, illus Corinne Malvern, c1952, with Texcell Tape **35.00**

#203, *Little Lulu and Her Magic Tricks,* written and illus Marge Henderson Buell, 1954, with orig Kleenex **50.00**

#399, *Doctor Dan at the Circus,* Pauline Wilkins, illus Katherine Sampson, c1960, with orig Johnson & Johnson Band–Aids **40.00**

#550, *The Good Humor Man,* Kathleen N. Daly, illus Tibor Gergely, c1964, about Good Humor Ice Cream **20.00**

General Interest

#8, *The Poky Little Puppy,* Janette Sebring Lowrey, illus Gustaf Tenggren, c1942, with dust jacket **45.00**

#13, *The Golden Book of Birds,* Hazel Lockwood, illus Feodor Rojankovsky, c1943, with dust jacket .. **22.00**

#23, *The Shy Little Kitten,* Cathleen Schurr, illus Gustaf Tenggren, c1946, with dust jacket **40.00**

#24, *The New House In The Forest,*

Lucy Sprague Mitchell, illus Eloise Wilkin, c1946, with dust jacket .. **45.00**

#49, *Mr. Noah and His Family,* Jane Werner, illus Alice and Martin Provensen, c1948 .... **14.00**

#57, *Little Black Sambo,* Helen Bannerman, illus Gustaf Tenggren, c1948 .... **40.00**

#67, *The Jolly Barnyard,* Annie North Bedford, illus Tibor Gergely, c1950, puzzle edition, with puzzle in back cover **60.00**

#119, *A Day at the Playground,* Miriam Schlein, illus Eloise Wilkin, c1951 .... **15.00**

#142, *Frosty the Snowman,* Annie North Bedford, illus Corinne Malvern, c1951 .... **5.00**

#149, *Indian Indian,* Charlotte Zolotow, illus Leonard Weisgard, c1952 **10.00**

#159, *The Tin Woodman of Oz,* Peter Archer, illus Harry McNaught, c1952 .... **20.00**

#169, *Rabbit and His Friends,* written and illus Richard Scarry, c1953 .. **3.00**

#174, *Bible Stories of Boys and Girls,* Jane Werner, illus Rachel Taft Dixon, c1953 .... **3.00**

#194, *The Twelve Dancing Princesses,* illus Sheilah Beckett, c1954 **6.50**

#208, *Tiger's Adventure,* William P. Gottlieb, c1954, photos **7.00**

#210, *The Kitten Who Thought He Was A Mouse,* Miriam Norton, illus Garth Williams, c1954 .... **14.00**

#215, *The Bunny Book,* Patricia Scarry, illus Richard Scarry, c1955 **6.00**

#227, *The Twins,* Ruth and Harold Shane, illus Eloise Wilkin, c1955 . **22.00**

#236, *Heroes of the Bible,* Jane Werner Watson, illus Rachel Taft Dixon and Marjorie Hartwell, c1955 .... **3.00**

#238, *5 Pennies to Spend,* Miriam Young, illus Corinne Malvern, c1955 .... **8.00**

#243, *Numbers,* Mary Reed and Edith Osswald, illus Violet LaMont, c1955 .... **2.50**

#251, *Cars,* Kathryn Jackson, illus William J Dugan, c1956 .... **5.00**

#305, *The White Bunny and His Magic Nose,* Lily Duplaix, illus Feodor Rojankovsky, c1957 ...... **12.00**

#317, *More Mother Goose Rhymes,* illus Feodor Rojankovsky, c1958 . **10.00**

#325, *Play Ball!,* Charles Spain Verral, illus Gerald McCann, c1958 . **6.00**

#418, *My Dolly and Me,* Patricia Scarry, illus Eloise Wilkin, c1960 . **20.00**

#443, *Puff the Blue Kitten,* written and illus Pierre Probst, c1961 .... **14.00**

#451, *Ten Little Animals,* Carl Memling, illus Feodor Rojankovsky, c1961 .... 4.00

#460, *My Little Golden Book of Manners*, Peggy Parish, illus Richard Scarry, c1962 .... 4.00

#569, *Little Mommy*, written and illus Sharon Kane, c1967 .... 8.00

Television, Film, Comics

#121, *Howdy Doody and Clarabell*, Edward Kean, illus Art Seiden, c1951 .... 12.00

#136, *Bugs Bunny Gets a Job*, Annie North Bedford, illus Warner Bros, c1952 .... 8.00

#223, *It's Howdy Doody Time*, Edward Kean, illus Art Seiden, c1955 18.00

#226, *Rootie Kazootie Joins the Circus*, Steve Carlin, illus Mel Crawford, c1955 .... 14.00

#234, *J. Fred Muggs*, Irwin Shapiro, illus Edwin Schmidt, c1955 ...... 10.00

#266, *Winky Dink*, Ann McGovern, illus Richard Scarry, c1956 ...... 12.00

#287, *Cleo*, Irwin Shapiro, illus Durward B. Graybill, photos, c1957 . 12.00

#290, *Circus Boy*, Irwin Shapiro, illus Joan Walsh Anglund, c1957 ..... 14.00

#356, *Steve Canyon*, written and illus Milton Caniff, c1959 .... 8.00

#360, *Party in Shariland*, Ann McGovern, illus Doris and Marion Henderson, c1959 .... 12.00

#372, *Woody Woodpecker Drawing Fun for Beginners*, Carl Buettner, illus Harvey Eisenberg and Norman McGary, c1959 .... 12.00

#378, *Ruff and Ready*, Ann McGovern, illus Harvey Eisenberg and Al White, c1959 .... 10.00

#395, *Yogi Bear*, S. Quentin Hyatt, illus M. Kawaguchi and Bob Barritt, c1960 .... 10.00

Walt Disney's Zorro And The Secret Plan, D77, 1958, $10.00.

#408, *Rocky and His Friends*, Ann McGovern, illus Ben DeNunez and Al White, c1960 .... 12.00

#432, *Dennis the Menace Waits for Santa Claus*, Carl Memling, illus Al White, Norm McGary, Bill Lorencz, c1962 .... 10.00

#450, *The Flintstones*, written and illus Mel Crawford, c1961 .... 14.00

#476, *Little Lulu*, Gina Ingoglia Weiner, illus Woody Kimbrell and Al White, c1962 .... 10.00

#483, *Mister Ed The Talking Horse*, Barbara Shook Hazen, illus Mel Crawford, c1962 .... 12.00

#500, *The Jetsons*, Carl Memling, illus Al White and Hawley Pratt, c1962 .... 18.00

#537, *Beany Goes To Sea*, Monica Hill, illus Hawley Pratt and Bill Lorencz, c1963 .... 20.00

#546, *Fireball XL5*, Barbara Shook Hazen, illus Hawley Pratt and Al White, c1964 .... 18.00

#556, *Peter Potamus*, Carl Memling, illus Hawley Pratt and Bill Lorencz, c1964 .... 9.00

Disney

#D2, *The Cold Blooded Penguin*, Robert Edmunds, illus Walt Disney Productions, c1944, with dust jacket 40.00

#D16, *Santa's Toy Shop*, adapted by Al Dempster, illus Walt Disney, c1950 .... 7.00

#D21, *Grandpa Bunny*, Jane Werner, illus Walt Disney Studios, c1951 . 14.00

#D26, *Peter Pan and the Indians*, Annie North Bedford, illus Walt Disney Studios, c1952 .... 12.00

#D48, *Robin Hood*, Annie North Bedford, illus with scenes from the film, c1955 .... 6.50

#D50, *Jiminy Cricket Fire Fighter*, Annie North Bedford, illus Samuel Armstrong, c1956 .... 14.00

#D65, *Old Yeller*, Irwin Shapiro, illus Edwin Schmidt and E. Joseph Meany, c1957 .... 7.00

#D68, *Zorro*, Charles Spain Verral, illus Walt Disney Studios, c1958 . 10.00

#D83, *Goliath II*, written and illus Bill Peet, c1959 .... 14.00

#D95, *Swiss Family Robinson*, Jean Lewis, illus Paul Granger, c1961 . 6.00

Western

#147, *Hopalong Cassidy and the Bar–20 Cowboy*, Elizabeth Beecher, illus Sahula Dycke, c1952 18.00

#213, *Dale Evans and the Lost Gold Mine*, Monica Hill, illus Mel Crawford, c1955 .... 12.00

#231, *Roy Rogers and the Mountain Lion,* Ann McGovern, illus Mel Crawford, c1955 . . . .   **12.00**
#254, *Buffalo Bill, Jr.,* Gladys Wyatt, illus H. Milton Greene, c1956 . . .   **7.00**
#263, *The Lone Ranger,* Steffi Fletcher, illus Joseph Dreany, c1956 . . . .   **15.00**
#318, *Cheyenne,* Charles Spain Verral, illus Al Schmidt, c1958 . . . . . .   **12.00**
#328, *Tales of Wells Fargo,* Leon Lazarus, illus John Leone, c1958 . . . .   **15.00**

LUNCH KITS

Collecting Hints: The thermos is an intregal part of the lunch kit. The two must be present to have full value. However, there has been a tendency in recent years to remove the thermos from the lunch box and price the two separately. The wise collector will resist this trend.

Prices on lunch kits have increased significantly in the last couple of years, largely due to publicity generated by Scott Bruce and others. Prices now appear to be stablizing as the lunch box craze of the 1980s nears its end.

The values listed reflect realistic prices for a kit with thermos, both in near mint condition. Scratches and rust detract from a metal kit's value and lower value by more than fifty percent.

History: Lunch kits date back to the 19th century when tin boxes were used by factory workers and field hands. The modern child's lunch kit, the form most sought by today's collector, began in the 1930s. Gender, Paeschke & Frey Co. of Milwaukee, Wisconsin, issued a No. 9100 Mickey Mouse lunch kit for the 1935 Christmas trade. An oval lunch kit of a streamlined train, marked "Decoware," dates from the same period.

Television brought the decorated lunch box into a golden age. Among the leading manufacturers are Aladdin Company; Landers, Frary and Clark; Ohio Art (successor to Hibbard, Spencer, Bartlett & Co.) of Bryan, Ohio; Thermos/King Seeley; and Universal.

References: Scott Bruce, *The Fifties and Sixties Lunch Box,* Chronicle Books, 1988; Scott Bruce, *The Official Price Guide To Lunch Box Collectibles, First Edition,* House of Collectibles, 1989.

Periodical: *Hot Boxing,* P.O. Box 87, Somerville, MA 02143.

Annie Oakley, 1955	**85.00**
Archies, 1969	**35.00**
Astronaut, dome	**100.00**
Atom Ant, 1966	**25.00**
Barn, open door	**95.00**
Barbie and Midge, black, vinyl, 1965 .	**45.00**
Barbie, World of, vinyl, thermos, 1971	**60.00**

Train, oval, silver and red, 8½ x 3½", $20.00.

Battle of the Planets, litho metal, plastic thermos	**35.00**
Beatles, thermos	**130.00**
Bedknobs & Broomsticks	**45.00**
Beverly Hillbillies, 1963	**59.00**
Blondie, 1969	**75.00**
Bonanza, green, thermos, 1963	**110.00**
Brady Bunch, 1970	**30.00**
Cabbage Patch Kids	**15.00**
Chuck Wagon, dome, 1958	**100.00**
Cracker Jack	**25.00**
Daniel Boone, 1955	**85.00**
Davy Crockett at Alamo, Adco, 1955 .	**95.00**
Dick Tracy, 1967	**70.00**
Disney Firefighter, dome	**100.00**
Disney School Bus	**75.00**
Disney World, thermos	**20.00**
Donnie & Marie, vinyl	**125.00**
Dukes of Hazzard, thermos	**13.00**
Dynomutt, litho metal, plastic thermos	**30.00**
Early West Pony Express	**40.00**
El Chapulin Colorado, 1979–84	**40.00**
Emergency, dome	**100.00**
Evel Knievel, 1974	**40.00**
Fall Guy, thermos	**22.00**
Flintstones, 1962	**95.00**
Flying Nun, thermos, 1961	**25.00**
Fritos	**95.00**
Gentle Ben, 1968	**40.00**
GI Joe, mid 1960s	**115.00**
Gomer Pyle, 1966	**80.00**
Gremlins	**25.00**
Grizzly Adams, dome, thermos	**75.00**
Guns of Will Sonnett, 1968	**130.00**
Gunsmoke	**75.00**
Have Gun Will Travel, 1960	**60.00**
Hee Haw	**30.00**
Hogan's Heroes, dome, 1966	**150.00**
Holly Hobbie, thermos	**15.00**
Hong Kong Phooey	**25.00**
Hopalong Cassidy, red, thermos, 1951	**150.00**

Huckleberry Hound and Friends, thermos	**165.00**
It's About Time, dome, 1967	**175.00**
Jungle Book, 1966	**39.00**
Kiss, 1977	**35.00**
Kung Fu	**35.00**
Land of the Giants	**165.00**
Lassie, thermos	**38.00**
Laugh–In Tricycle, thermos	**175.00**
Lawman, 1960s	**35.00**
Lidsville	**55.00**
Little House on the Prairie	**20.00**
Ludwig Von Drake, 1961	**100.00**
Man From UNCLE, thermos	**150.00**
Mary Poppins, 1964	**50.00**
Munsters, 1965	**60.00**
Muppet Show	**15.00**
NFL	**15.00**
Partridge Family	**75.00**
Pele	**38.00**
Pigs in Space	**15.00**
Pink Panther, vinyl	**75.00**
Police Patrol	**60.00**
Popeye, 1964	**60.00**
Popples	**12.00**
Porky Pig	**150.00**
Return of the Jedi	**15.00**
Road Runner, 1970–73	**30.00**
Robin Hood	**58.00**
Ronald McDonald Cactus Canyon, thermos	**50.00**
Roy Rogers & Dale Evans, steel thermos, American Thermos, 1953–54	**115.00**
Scooby Doo, 1973	**30.00**
See America	**30.00**
Snoopy, 1968	**25.00**
Star Trek	**40.00**
Star Wars, thermos	**38.00**
Superman	
1967	**30.00**
1978, thermos	**20.00**
Tom Corbett, thermos	**125.00**
US Mail, dome, thermos	**40.00**
Washington Redskins	**35.00**
Yellow Submarine, etched name, 1968	**125.00**

MAGAZINE COVERS AND TEAR SHEETS

Collecting Hints: A good cover should show the artist's signature, have the mailing label nonexistent or in a place that does not detract from the design element, and have edges which are crisp, but not trimmed.

When framing vintage paper use acid free mat board and tape with a water soluble glue base such as brown paper gum tape or linen tape. The tape should only be affixed to the back side of the illustration. The rule of thumb is do not do anything that can not be easily undone.

Do not hang framed vintage paper in direct sunlight which causes fading or in a highly humid area (such as a bathroom or above a kitchen sink) which causes wrinkles in both the mat and art work.

History: Magazine cover design attracted some of America's leading illustrators. Maxfield Parrish, Erte, Leyendecker, and Norman Rockwell were dominate forces in the 20th century. In the mid–1930s photographic covers gradually replaced the illustrated covers. One of the leaders in the industry was *Life*, which emphasized photojournalism.

Magazine covers are frequently collected by artist signed covers, subject matter, or historical events. Artist signed covers feature a commercially printed artist signature on the cover, or the artist is identified inside as "Cover by..." Most collected covers are in full color and show significant design elements. Black memorabilia is often reflected in magazine covers and tear sheets. It is frequently collected for the positive affect it has on African–Americans. However, sometimes it is a reflection of the times in which it was printed and may represent subjects in an unfavorable light.

Many of America's leading artists also illustrated magazine advertising. The ads made advertising characters such as the Campbell Kids, the Dutch Girl, and Snap, Crackle and Pop world famous.

References: Patricia Kery, *Great Magazine Covers of The World*, Abbeyville Press, 1982; check local libraries for books about specific illustrators such as Parrish, Rockwell, and Jessie Wilcox Smith.

Periodical: *PCM (Paper Collector's Marketplace)*, P. O. Box 127, Scandinavia, WI 54977.

Note: Prices of covers and complete magazines have remained stable the last few years, but those of tear sheets have declined as more and more magazines have glutted the market. While only a short time ago magazines were thrown away when attics and garages were cleaned, now they are offered for sale. The public has been educated by seeing many magazine tear sheets being offered for sale at flea markets and mall shows. Dealers prefer to purchase complete magazines and gleen their profit from the contents.

As more and more magazines are destroyed for the tear sheets, complete magazines rise in value as the supply decreases. If a magazine is in mint condition, it should be left intact. We do NOT encourage removing illustrations from complete magazines. Only the complete magazine can act as a tool to interpret that specific historical time period. Editorial and advertising together define the spirit of the era.

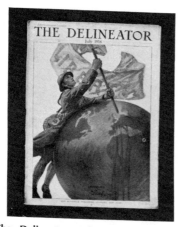

The Delineator, July 1918, Doughboy cov, $20.00.

Artist Signed

Armstrong, Rolf	15.00
Atkins, Alan	6.00
Bayer, Herbert	6.00
Benito, Edwardo	20.00
Cassandre, A M	20.00
Christy, F Earl	18.00
Coffin, Haskell	15.00
Crane, S W	8.00
Davis, Marguerite	6.00
Drayton, Grace, Campbell's Soups, color, small kids	1.75
Drayton/Weiderseim, Campbell's Soups	
Black and white	1.50
Color, large kids	6.00
Duncan, Fredrick	8.00
Eastman, Ruth	6.00
Fancher, Louis	6.00
Flagg, James Montgomery, black and white illus	5.00
Freed, Maurice	4.00
Giusti	3.00
Gunn, Archie	8.50
Hays, Mary A	6.00
Hoff, Guy	9.00
King, Hamilton	9.00
Leyendecker	6.50
Lustig	3.00
McClelland, Barclay	10.00
O'Neill, Rose	
Illus stories, other than Kewpies	3.00
Jello, quarter page	3.00
Jello, full page, full color	10.00
Kewpie pages	18.00
Parrish, Maxfield	
Jello	20.00
Story illus, headings only	3.50
Penfield, Edward	30.00
Petruccelli	8.00

Phillip Coles, color	8.00
Reid, Robert	4.00
Rockwell, Norman	
Black and white	3.00
Color	5.00
Sambrook, Russell	3.00
Sandberg, Valentine	8.00
Schulze, Otto W	2.00
Smith, Jessie Wilcox	
Early story illus	10.00
General	6.00
Stanlaws, Penny	9.00
Texidor	3.00
Vargas	
Black and white	3.00
Centerfold or pin–up	20.00
Color	6.00
Willenborg, Lee	2.00
Wilson, John F	5.00
Wireman, Henry	6.00
Wistehuff, Revere	3.00
Wood, Lawson	
Monkey images	8.00
Other images	6.00
Automobile	
Prior to 1918	
Black and white	2.00
Color	4.00
1919–1937	
Black and white	2.00
Color	3.00
1938–1941	
Black and white	4.50
Color	4.50
1942–1955	
Black and white	1.50
Color	2.50
1955–1975	
Black and white	1.00
Color	1.50
Any outstanding Art Nouveau or Art Deco Auto Ads, e.g. Cadillac produced ads with silver ink	10.00
Aviation	
Prior to 1935	
Black and white	1.50
Color	2.00
After 1935	
Black and white	1.00
Color	1.00
Named airlines with route maps	4.00
Beverage	
Beer	
Hamm's Bear	4.00
Identified brand, color	3.00
No brand	1.50
Coca–Cola	
Prior to 1925	
Black and white	2.00
Color	8.00
1925–1950	
Black and white	1.50

Color	6.00
Featuring vending machine	8.00
Santas	12.00
Santas on National Geographic	6.00
Dr Pepper, early	10.00
Orange or Tomato Juice	.75
Seven–up	2.00
Wines and Liquors	1.50

Black Memorabilia

Cereal, Aunt Jemima	5.00
Stories of black history	3.00

Camera

Prior to 1918

Black and white	2.00
Color	3.00

Fashion

Prior to 1930

Black and white	2.00
Color	4.00

After 1930

Black and white	1.00
Color	2.00
Eric, signed	3.00

Food

Candy, Lifesavers with children or animals	4.00

Cereal

Cream of Wheat	8.00
Kelloggs, children by Leyendecker	8.00
Large image of product	2.00
Dairy products, milk, cheese, ice cream	1.00

Gum

Adams Art Nouveau style	6.00
Other	1.50

Jello

Animals or children	4.00
General, color	1.50
O'Neill, signed, with Kewpies, color	18.00
Parrish, signed	25.00
Meats	1.50
Soups, Campbell Kinds	
Large images	8.00
Small images	1.00

Furniture

Black and white	1.00
Color	3.00

Household Products

Bon Ami, children	2.00
Dutch Cleanser, full page, color	
Large format	5.00
Small format	3.00
Furniture Polish, early, colorful	3.00
Others	1.00

Jewelry

Black and white	1.00
Color	1.50

Movie Stars and Famous People

Bacall, Lauren	5.00
Beatles	20.00
Bogart, Humphrey	10.00

Carson, Johnny	2.00
Chaplin, Charlie	2.00
Douglas, Kirk	2.00
Fields, W C	7.50
Garbo, Greta	5.00
Kelly, Grace	6.00
Mansfield, Jane	4.00
Marx Brothers	5.00
Monroe, Marilyn	10.00
Wayne, John	5.00
West, Mae	8.00

Toys

Bikes	3.00

Dolls

Shirley Temple	4.00
Unknown	2.00
Erector Sets	3.00
Teddy Bears	6.00
Trains, Lionel and Ives	2.50
Wagons	2.00

Train, major railroad lines

Black and white	1.00
Color	2.00
Color, route maps and large image trains	3.50

MAGAZINES

Collecting Hints: A rule of thumb for pricing general magazines without popular artist–designed covers is the more you would enjoy displaying a copy on your coffee table, the more elite the publication, and the more the advertising or editorial content relates to today's collectibles, the higher the price. *Life* magazine went into millions of homes each week, *Harper's Bazaar* and *Vogue* did not. Elite families had a greater tendency to discard last month's publication while middle–class families found the art on the *Saturday Evening Post* and *Collier's* irresistible and saved them. The greater the supply, the lower the price.

History: In the early 1700s general magazines were a major means of information for the reader. Literary magazines, such as *Harper's*, became popular in the 19th century. By 1900, the first photo–journal magazines appeared. *Life*, the prime example, was started by Henry Luce in 1932.

Magazines created for women featured "how to" articles about cooking, sewing, decorating, and child care. Many were entirely devoted to fashion and living a fashionable life, such as *Harper's Bazaar* and *Vogue*. Men's magazines were directed at masculine skills of the time, such as hunting, fishing, and woodworking, supplemented with appropriate "girlies" titles.

References: Jack Bramble, *The Playboy Collectors Guide & Price List, 5th Edition*, Budget Enterprises, 1982; Marjorie M. and Donald L.

Hinds, *Magazine Magic*, The Messenger Book Press, 1972; *Official Price Guide To Paperbacks and Magazines*, House of Collectibles, 1986.

Note: The prices for general magazines are retail prices. They may be considerably higher than what would be offered for an entire collection filling your basement or garage. Bulk prices for common magazines such as *Life*, *Collier's*, and *Saturday Evening Post* are generally from fifty cents to one dollar per issue. Dealers have to sort, protect with plastic covering, discard ones that have items clipped from the interior, or have marred covers, and make no money on those which they never sell. The end result is that a lower price is paid for magazines purchased in bulk.

Boys' Life, August, 1957, Creig Flessel cov illus, $15.00.

All Hands, Sept, 1945, Navy magazine, End of War edition, atomic photos	18.00
American, Dec, 1926, Earl C Christy cov	10.00
American Artist, April, 1960	5.00
American Golfer, Dec, 1932	10.00
American Motorist, 1916	8.50
Antiques, Oct, 1931	7.50
Art and Beauty, 1926	4.00
Atlantic Monthly, Nov, 1907, anniversary edition	18.00
Barnum & Bailey Circus, 1909, 30 pgs	20.00
Better Photo, 1913	2.50
Bonanza, Vol #1, 1965	25.00
Boys' Life, 1916, Rockwell cov	25.00
Breed's Gazette, The, April, 1885	6.50
Building Age National Builder, 1920s	5.00
Carpenter Magazine, 1916, 60 pgs	2.00
Child's Life, 1930	3.00
Children's Play Mate, Sept, 1953	5.00
Collier's, June 9, 1938	7.00
Cosmopolitan, 1907	5.00
Country Gentleman, 1914, Leyendecker cov	20.00

Delineator, 1902	20.00
Demorist Fashion, Sept, 1876	10.00
Designer, The, 1900–04, color fashion plates	20.00
Esquire, Sept, 1934	12.00
Etudes, 1940s	2.00
Farm Journal, April, 1936	1.50
Farm Mechanics, mid 1920s	8.00
Farmer's Wife Magazine, The, June, 1936	2.00
Golf Illustrated, Sept, 1934	10.00
Harvest World, 1931	2.50
Highway Traveler, Greyhound, 1936	2.50
Hobbies, August, 1942	2.00
Hollywood Dream Girl, 1955, 1st issue, 13 pgs of Marilyn Monroe photos	30.00
Home Needlework, 1910	12.00
Hounds & Hunting, 1922	4.00
Jack & Jill, 1960, Howdy Doody cov	12.00
Ladies Home Journal, 1917	4.00
Literary Digest, June 24, 1922, Norman Rockwell cov	3.00
Living Church, The, 1924	1.00
Look, Nov 17, 1964, John F Kennedy memorial issue	20.00
Mattel Barbie Magazine, Nov–Dec, 1963	5.00
McCall's, 1925	15.00
Mechanics' Arts, 1989	2.50
Motor, Jan, 1927	50.00
Motorcycling & Bicycling, 1920	25.00
Movie Star Parade, Jan, 1947	22.00
National Geographic, June, 1926	3.00
National Observer, Dec, 1968	1.00
Naturo–Post, German, health magazine, 1904	2.50
Needlecraft, 1927	3.00
New England Home, 1898	2.00
New Idea Woman's Magazine, 1902	20.00
New Yorker, 1948	2.50
Outdoor Life, 1932	4.00
Physical Culture, 1917	2.00
Pictorial Review, March, 1915	12.50
Playboy, Dec, 1962	8.00
Popular Mechanics, 1952	1.50
Popular Songs, 1930s	2.00
Prairie Farmer, Feb, 1867	4.00
Radford's American Builder, 1920s	6.00
Redbook, April, 1925	5.00
St Nicholas, 1928	7.00
Saturday Evening Post	
1922, New Year's Eve, Leyendecker cov	20.00
1923	
Pearl Harbor	10.00
Rockwell cov	25.00
1936, Springtime, Norman Rockwell	7.50
1938, Christmas, Leyendecker	5.00
1952, Norman Rockwell	4.00
Scientific American, June, 1933	3.50
Spinning Wheel, July, 1960	30.00
Sport, Stan Musial cov, 1950	30.00

Stage and Screen, 1926	**4.50**
Sunbathing for Health, Dec, 1951	**2.50**
Time	
1939	**1.00**
1940, Mickey Rooney	**10.00**
Tip Top Weekly, 1904	**9.00**
Tobacco World, 1902	**8.00**
Town and Country, July, 1948, Dali cov,	
poppy, cornflower, and wheat	**35.00**
Travel, 1915, Santa cov, Murad	**25.00**
Vogue, March, 1935	**12.00**
Wild West Weekly, 1915	**7.00**
Woman's Home Companion	
1915	**15.00**
1916	**20.00**
1917, Betty Bonnett	**25.00**
1925	**20.00**
Woman's World, Feb, 1936	**1.50**
Working Craftsman, The, winter, 1977	**4.00**
World Today, The, 1909	**4.00**
Youth's Companion, bound year, 1908	**125.00**

MARBLES

Collecting Hints: Hand—made glass marbles usually command higher prices than machine—made glass, clay, or mineral marbles. There are a few notable exceptions, e.g., machine—made comic strip marbles were made for a limited time only and are highly prized by collectors. Care must be taken in purchasing this particular type since the comic figure was stenciled on the marble. A layer of glass was to be overlaid on the stencil. However, many examples exist that were not overlaid, and the stencils rub or wear off.

Some of the rarer examples of hand—made marbles are Clambroth, Lutz, Indian Swirls, Peppermint Swirls, and Sulphides. Marble values are normally determined by their type, size, and condition. Usually, the larger the marble, the more valuable it is within each type.

A marble in mint condition is unmarred and has the best possible condition with a clear surface. It may have surface abrasions from rubbing in its original package. A marble in good condition may have a few small surface dings, scratches, and slight cloudiness. However, the core must be easily seen, and the marble must be without large chips or fractures.

History: Marbles date back to ancient Greece, Rome, Egypt, and other early civilizations. In England, Good Friday is known as "Marbles Day" because the game was considered a respectable and quiet pastime for the hallowed day.

During the American Civil War, soldiers carried marbles and a small board to play "solitaire," a game whose object is to jump the marbles until only one is left in the center of the board.

In the last few generations, school children have identified marbles as peewees, shooters, commies, and cat's eyes. A National Marbles Tournament has been held each year, beginning in 1922, in June. Wildwood, New Jersey, is its current site.

References: Paul Baumann, *Collecting Antique Marbles, Second Edition* Wallace–Homestead, 1991; Jeff Carskadden and Richard Gartley, *Chinas–Hand–Painted Marbles of the late 19th Century,* Muskingum Valley Archaeological Society, 1990; Everett Grist, *Antique Marble Price Guide, Second Edition,* Collector Books, 1988; Marble Collectors Society of America, *Identification and Price Guide,* privately printed, 1989; Mark E. Randall, *Marbles As Historical Artifacts,* Marble Collectors Society; Mark E. Randall and Dennis Webb, *Greenberg's Guide to Marbles,* Greenberg Publishing Co., 1988.

Collectors' Clubs: Marble Collectors' Unlimited, 503 West Pine, Marengo, IA 52301; Marble Collectors Society of America, P. O. Box 222, Trumbull, CT 06611; National Marble Club of America, 440 Eaton Road, Drexel Hill, PA 19026.

Museums: Corning Museum of Glass, Corning, NY; Sandwich Glass Museum, Sandwich, MA; Smithsonian Institution, Museum of Natural History, Washington, D.C.; Wheaton Village Museum, Millville, NJ.

Advisor: Stanley A. Block.

REPRODUCTION ALERT: Comic marbles are being reproduced.

Swirl, red, white, blue, and yellow swirl, 2½" d, $175.00.

AGATE

A form of chalcedony quartz with banded or irregular appearance; it is usually a translucent stone found in all shades of earth colors, the most common being tones of brown with tan to white bands. Agate can be artificially dyed.

Sizes	Mint	Good
To 7/8"	15.00	8.00
1" to 1½"	65.00	20.00
1⅝" to 1⅞"	85.00	30.00

CLAMBROTH

Milk glass marbles in a solid color having many thin outer swirl lines of a different color running from pontil mark to pontil mark.

Sizes	Mint	Good
To ⁷⁄₈"	175.00	90.00
1" to 1½"	1,200.00	400.00

CLAYS

Marbles made of clay which may or may not be colored or glazed.

Sizes	Mint	Good
To ⁷⁄₈"	.10	.05
1" to 1½"	3.00	1.00
1⅝" to 1⅞"	10.00	4.00
2" and over	15.00	5.00

COMIC

Marbles manufactured by the Peltier Glass Co. 1927 to 1934 with one of twelve comic strip character faces stamped on the marble and fired so as to be permanent.

Sizes	Mint	Good
To ⁷⁄₈"	75.00	35.00

END–OF–DAY

Usually composed of a solid multicolored inner surface coated with an outer covering of clear glass; also known as Cloud Marbles.

Sizes	Mint	Good
To ⁷⁄₈"	30.00	15.00
1" to 1½"	200.00	60.00
1⅝" to 1⅞"	250.00	100.00
2" and over	350.00	150.00

INDIAN SWIRL

Handmade, opaque black glass marble with very colorful swirls applied next to or on top of surface.

Sizes	Mint	Good
To ⁷⁄₈"	100.00	50.00
1" to 1½"	600.00	250.00

LATTICINIO CORE SWIRL

Inner part of the marble has a latticinio or lace center; usually with outer swirls of varying colors running from pontil mark to pontil mark.

Sizes	Mint	Good
To ⁷⁄₈"	10.00	4.00
1" to 1½"	75.00	25.00
1⅝" to 1⅞"	100.00	50.00
2" and over	200.00	90.00

LUTZ (BANDED)

Handmade glass marbles usually with colored swirls, some of which contain copper flecks; also called Goldstone swirls. Other types of Lutz (end of day, ribbon, and opaque banded Lutz) are worth two to three times the values shown for banded Lutz.

Sizes	Mint	Good
To ⁷⁄₈"	125.00	50.00
1" to 1½"	300.00	175.00
1⅝" to 1⅞"	600.00	250.00
2" & over	900.00	400.00

MACHINE–MADE GLASS

Glass marbles made by machines after World War I.

Sizes	Mint	Good
To ⁷⁄₈"	.05	.02
1" to 1½"	.50	.10

MICAS

Mineral silicates occurring in thin sheet and usually reflective of silvery in appearance; handmade glass marbles of various types (usually clear colored glass) having silvery flakes inside.

Sizes	Mint	Good
To ⁷⁄₈"	20.00	10.00
1" to 1½"	300.00	75.00
1⅝" to 1⅞"	600.00	400.00

OPEN CORE SWIRL

Handmade glass swirl marble with open colored bands in center of marble.

Sizes	Mint	Good
To ⁷⁄₈"	10.00	4.00
1" to 1½"	75.00	25.00
1⅝" to 1⅞"	100.00	50.00
2" and over	200.00	90.00

PEPPERMINT SWIRL

Swirl glass marble resembling peppermint stick candy, usually incorporating red, white, and blue colors.

Sizes	Mint	Good
To 7/8"	100.00	50.00

POTTERY

Earthenware as distinguished on the one hand from porcelain and stoneware, and on the other hand from brick and tile.

Sizes	Mint	Good
To 7/8"	1.00	.50
1" to 1½"	10.00	4.00

SOLID CORE SWIRL

Glass marble having a solid one–color or varicolored center looking like a piece of candy with outer swirls running from pontil mark to pontil mark.

Sizes	Mint	Good
To 7/8"	15.00	6.00
1" to 1½"	100.00	60.00
1 5/8" to 1 7/8"	200.00	110.00
2" and over	300.00	150.00

SULPHIDES

Objects made of china clay and supersilicate of potash for inserting in marbles and a variety or other glass objects, usually three dimensional; marbles are of clear glass containing a sulphide object, usually an animal figure. Antique sulphides with numbers, human figures, or colors are worth three to ten times the value shown.

Sizes	Mint	Good
1" to 1½"	150.00	100.00
1 5/8" to 1 7/8"	175.00	125.00
2" & over	250.00	150.00

MATCHCOVERS

Collecting Hints: Matchcovers generally had large production runs; very few are considered rare. Most collectors remove the matches, flatten the covers, and mount them in albums by category. They prefer the covers be unused.

Trading is the principal means of exchange among collectors, usually on a one for one basis. At flea markets and shows matchcovers frequently are seen marked for $1.00 to $5.00 for categories such as beer covers or pin–up art (girlies) covers. Actually these purchasers are best advised to join one of the collector clubs and get involved in swapping.

History: The book match was invented by Joshua Pusey, a Philadelphia lawyer, who also was a chemist in his spare time. In 1892 Pusey put 10 cardboard matches into a cover of plain white board. Two hundred were sold to the Mendelson Opera Company who, in turn, hand–printed messages on the front.

The first machine made matchbook was made by the Binghamton Match Company, Binghamton, New York, for the Piso Company of Warren, Pennsylvania. The only surviving cover is now owned by the Diamond Match Company.

Few covers survive from the late 1890s–1930s period. The modern craze for collecting matchcovers was started by a set of ten covers issued for the Century of Progress exhibit at the 1933 Chicago World's Fair.

The Golden Age of matchcovers was the mid–1940s through the early 1960s when the covers were a popular advertising medium. Principal manufacturers included Atlas Match, Brown and Bigelow, Crown Match, Diamond Match, Lion Match, Ohio Match and Universal Match.

The arrival of throw–away lighters, such as BIC, brought an end to the matchcover era. Manufacturing costs for a matchbook today can range from below a cent to seven or eight cents for a special die–cut cover. As a result, matchcovers no longer are an attractive "free" give–away item.

Because of this, many of the older, more desirable covers are seeing a marked increase in value. Collectors have also turned to the small pocket type boxes as a way of enhancing and building their collections.

References: Yosh Kashiwabara, *Matchbook Art*, Chronicle Books, 1989; Bill Retskin, *The Matchcover Collectors Resource Book and Price Guide*, published by author, 1988; H. Thomas Steele, Jim Heimann, Rod Dyer, *Close Cover Before Striking, The Golden Age of Matchbook Art*, Abbeville Press, 1987.

Periodical: *The Front Striker Bulletin*, 3417 Clayborne Avenue, Alexandria, VA 22306–1410.

Collectors' Clubs: Rathkamp Matchcover Society, 1359 Surrey Road, Vandalia, OH 43577; Trans–Canada Matchcover Club, Box 219, Caledonia, Ontario, Canada NOA–1A0. There are 33 regional clubs throughout the United States and Canada.

Advisor: Wray Martin.

SPECIAL COVERS

Air Force One	**5.00**
Apollo flights, 8 through 17, Cameo's, each	**5.00**
Charles Lindburgh, photo on front	**500.00**
Dwight D Eisenhower, 5 Star General .	**15.00**
Economy Blue Print, girlies, set of 6, 1950s	**45.00**

Billiards, $.05.

General Douglas MacArthur, I Shall Return

Box	30.00
Cover	100.00

Joe Louis and Max Schmeling championship fight, giant 25.00
President Kennedy, White House cover .. 5.00
Presidential Helicopter, "Marine One" .. 10.00
Presidential Yacht, "Patricia" 10.00
Pull for Wilkie, pullquick match 28.00
Racquel Welch, color photo, South African made 15.00
Stoeckle Select Beer, Stoeckle Brewery, giant 6.00
Washington Redskins, pictures on back, set of 20 .... 40.00

TOPICS

Americana	.05
American Ace, boxes	.12
Atlas, four color	.05
Banks	.02
Beer and Brewery	.75
Best Western	
Non Stock design	.15
Stock design	.10
Bowling Alleys	.02
Cameo's, Universal trademark	.05
Canadian, four color	.05
Casinos	.05
CCC Camps	1.00
Chinese Restaurants	.04
Christmas	.05
Classiques	.50
Coca–Cola	1.00
Colleges	.10
Contours (diecut)	.10
Conventions	.03
Country Clubs	.07
County Seats	.05
Credit Unions	.10
Crown Match	.75

Dated	.10
Diamond Quality	1.00
Easel Backs	.20
Elks	.10
Fairs	.10
Features	.50
Federal Match	.75
Foilites, Universal trademark	.05
Foreign	.05
Fraternal	.05
Full Length	.10
Giants	1.00
Girlies	
Non Stock design	.50
Stock design	.15
Group One	
Movies, old	1.00
Non–advertising, new	.03
Non–advertising, old	.50
Sports, old	2.00
Hillbillies	.05
Hilton Hotels	.15
Holiday Inns	
Non Stock design	.15
Stock design	.10
Indians	.25
Jewelites	.05
Jewels	.05
Knot Holes	.20
Matchorama's, Universal trademark	.08
Matchtones, Universal trademark	.10
Midgets	.75

Motor Hotel, $.05.

Navy Ships	.30
Odd Strikers	.25
Patriotic	.05
Pearltone	.05
Personalities	1.00
Political	1.50
Pull Quick	1.00
Radio and TV	.05
Railroads	.25
Rainbows, Universal trademark	.10
Restaurants	.02

Savings and Loan	.02
Service	
New	.05
Old	.15
Shiplines	.10
Signets, Universal trademark	.05
Small Towns	.05
Soft Drinks	.75
Souvenir	.20
Sports	
New	.15
Old	1.00
Ten Strikes	.05
Transportation	.15
Travelodges	.05
Truck Lines	.10
Trust Companies	.02
VA Hospitals	.15
Whiskey	.30
Woodgrains	.10

McCOY POTTERY

Collecting Hint: Several marks were used by the McCoy Pottery Co. Take time to learn the marks and the variations. Pieces can often be dated by the mark used.

History: The J. W. McCoy Pottery Co. was established in Roseville, Ohio, in September, 1899. The early McCoy Company produced both stoneware and some art lines, including Rosewood. In October, 1911, three potteries in the Roseville area merged, creating the Brush-McCoy Pottery Co. This company continued to produce the original McCoy lines and added several new art lines. Much of the early pottery is not marked.

In 1910, Nelson McCoy and his father, J. W. McCoy, founded the Nelson McCoy Sanitary Stoneware Co. In 1925, the McCoy family sold their interest in the Brush-McCoy Pottery Co. and started to expand and improve the Nelson McCoy Company. The new company produced stoneware, earthenware specialities and artware. Most of the pottery marked McCoy was made by the Nelson McCoy Co.

Reference: Sharon and Bob Huxford, *The Collectors Encyclopedia of McCoy Pottery,* Collector Books, 1980.

REPRODUCTION ALERT: The Nelson McCoy Pottery Co. is currently producing reproductions of their original work. This may add to the confusion about this company's products and will probably affect prices.

Ashtray	
Hands, leaf dec, yellow, 1941	6.50
Square, brown, white dappled edges, 1964	3.75
Baby Planter	
Cradle, pink	7.50

Lamb, white, blue bow	8.00
Stork, green	7.00
Bank, Happy Face	20.00
Basket, oak leaf and acorns, cream, brown highlights, 1952	15.00
Bookends, pr, jumping horses, marked "Nu–Art"	18.50
Bowl, 5 x 6½", ftd, drippy green over onyx glaze	35.00
Cat Dish	55.00
Centerpiece Bowl, blue, tulips dec, 8¾" d	7.50
Cookie Jar	
Black Cat, fish bowl	65.00
Cat, pink basket base	25.00
Chipmunk	175.00
Clown in barrel	65.00
Coffee Grinder	25.00
Coffeepot, brown top, white base	45.00
Cookie Barrel, sign	25.00
Dalmatians	250.00
Elephant	125.00
Granny, gold glasses	50.00
Log Cabin	45.00
Happy Face	25.00
Mouse	25.00
Mr & Mrs Owl	95.00
Picnic Basket	35.00
Potbelly Stove, white	30.00
Red Apple	20.00
Teapot, bronze	25.00
Timmy Tortoise	35.00
Touring Car	90.00
Wishing Well	25.00
Cornucopia	18.00
Creamer, Elsie The Cow adv	15.00
Custard Cup, light blue, beaded edge, c1953	3.00
Flower Pot, attached base	
Embossed flowers, pink glaze, 1940	5.00
Plain, matte blue glaze	4.00
Gravy, rooster on nest	55.00
Grease Jar, cov, cabbage, 1954	17.50
Jardiniere, white, applied bud, 1947	8.50
Lamp, cowboy boots	34.00
Mug, Happy Face	8.00
Pitcher, ball jug, yellow, c1950	15.00
Planter	
Blossom Time, yellow	5.00

Planter, frog, green, 8" l, $8.50.

Frog	8.50
Rabbit, ivory	7.00
Sprinkling Can, white, rose decal	6.50
Turtle	14.00
Uncle Sam	15.00
Wagon, green, yellow wheels, umbrella	55.00
Salt and Pepper Shakers, pr, cabbage, 1954	10.00
Snack Dish, three leaves, rustic glaze, 1952	8.50
Spoon Rest, penguin, 1953	15.00
Teapot, Grecian pattern	25.00
Tumble Up, blue and white spatter, 1975	4.00
Vase	
5½" h, matte green	20.00
7" h, ripple ware, green, bright pink rim trim, 1950	5.00
7½" h, mottled green, marked "Brush, #709"	18.00
8" h, pink hyacinth	13.00
9" h, light green, sq, stylized floral sculpting, 1941	8.00
10" h, light green, straight ribbed sides, 1957	6.50
Vegetable Dish, divided, brown and cream drip	8.00
Wall Pocket	
Flower, rustic glaze, 1946	10.00
Umbrella, yellow, 1955	12.50
Wash Bowl and Pitcher, white, blue trim, 1967	12.00

McKEE GLASS

Collecting Hint: McKee Glass was mass produced in most colors. Therefore, a collector should avoid chipped or damaged pieces.

History: The McKee Glass Company was established in 1843 in Pittsburgh, Pennsylvania. In 1852 they opened a factory to produce pressed glass. In 1888, the factory relocated in Jeannette, Pennsylvania, and began to produce many types of kitchenwares. The factory was among several located there to make Depression era wares. The factory continued until 1951 when it was sold to the Thatcher Manufacturing Co.

The McKee Glass Company produced many types of glass including glass window panes, tumblers, tablewares, Depression glass, milk glass, and bar and utility objects.

McKee named its colors Chalaine Blue, Custard, Seville Yellow, and Skokie Green. They preferred Skokie Green to jadite which was popular with other manufacturers at the time. McKee also made several patterns on these opaque colors, including dots of red, green, and black and red ships. A few items were decaled. Most of the canisters and shakers were lettered in black for the purpose they were made for.

References: Gene Florence, *Kitchen Glassware of the Depression Years, Third Edition,* Collector Books, 1987; Lowell Innes and Jane Shadel Spillman, *M'Kee Victorian Glass,* Dover Publications, 1981.

Bird House, gray, red roof	150.00
Bowl	
4" d, Rock Crystal, clear	15.00
9" d, Laurel, Skokie green	12.00
9½" d	
Floral Band, Skokie green, ftd	12.00
Rock Crystal, milk glass, orig label	55.00
Butter Dish, cov, one pound	
Custard, green stripe	40.00
Red Dots	75.00
White, floral dec	35.00
Cake Stand, Rock Crystal, green, low pedestal	50.00
Candlesticks, pr, Rock Crystal, clear	36.00
Canister, cov	
Custard, coffee, round	45.00
Delphite, 10 oz	90.00
Red ships, 3½" h	10.00
Seville yellow, 10 oz, round	20.00
Cheese Dome, Laurel, Skokie green	20.00

Children's dishes, opaque white, red trim, ten pcs, $65.00.

Cocktail, Rock Crystal, 4¼" h	14.50
Compote, Rock Crystal, amber, 11½" h	85.00
Cordial, Rock Crystal, 2⅞" h	22.50
Creamer, ftd, Laurel, Skokie green	9.00
Cup	
Laurel, Skokie green	6.00
Rock Crystal, clear	18.00
Egg Beater Bowl, Skokie green, pouring spout	12.00
Egg Cup, custard	14.00
Flour Shaker, custard	22.00
Goblet, Rock Crystal, 6¾" h	16.00
Grapefruit Bowl, Rock Crystal, red	45.00
Juice Tumbler, Rock Crystal, flat, 3½" h	15.00

Measuring Cup	
Custard, 2 cup	25.00
Delphite, 2 cup	165.00
Skokie green, 4 cup	35.00
Measuring Pitcher, Skokie green	30.00
Mixer Bowl, 9½" d, Magic Maid, Skokie green	10.00
Mixing Bowl, 8" d, red ships	10.00
Mug, Tom and Jerry, scroll red trim	2.00
Nappy, Seville, yellow	7.50
Pitcher, Delphite blue, two cup	45.00
Plate	
7½" d, Rock Crystal, amber	8.00
9" d, Laurel, Skokie green	8.00
Platter, 8 x 11", Laurel, Skokie green	15.00
Punch Bowl Set, Tom and Jerry, bowl, six mugs, custard	150.00
Refrigerator Dish, custard, 4 x 5", ridges on top	20.00
Saucer, Laurel, Skokie green	2.00
Sherbet	
Laurel, Skokie green	7.00
Rock Crystal	10.00
Snack tray, jadite	30.00
Sugar, ftd, Laurel, Skokie green	9.00
Tumbler, Rock Crystal	
5¼" h, flat	20.00
5½" h, ftd	20.00
Vase, 11" h, Rock Crystal, amber	75.00
Whiskey, Rock Crystal, 2½" h	15.00
Wine, Rock Crystal, 4¾" h	16.00

MILITARIA

Collecting Hints: Saving militaria may be one of the oldest collecting traditions. Militaria collectors tend to have their own special shows and view themselves outside the normal antiques channels. However, they haunt small indoor shows and flea markets in hopes of finding additional materials.

History: Wars always have been part of history. Until the mid-19th century, soldiers often had to fill their own needs, including weapons. Even in the 20th century a soldier's uniform and some of his gear is viewed as his personal property, even though issued by a military agency.

Conquering armed forces made a habit of acquiring souvenirs from their vanquished foes. They brought home their own uniforms and accessories as badges of triumph and service.

References: Ray A. Bows, *Vietnam Military Lore 1959–1973*, Bows & Sons, 1988; Robert Fisch, *Field Equipment of the Infantry 1914–1945*, Greenberg Publishing, 1989; North South Trader's *Civil War Magazine's Civil War Collectors' Price Guide*, 5th Edition, North South Trader, 1991; *Official Price Guide To Military Collectibles*, House of Collectibles, 1985; Jack H. Smith, *Military Postcards 1870–1945*, Wallace–Home-

stead Book Company, 1988; Sydney B. Vernon, *Vernon's Collector's Guide to Orders, Medals, and Decorations*, published by author, 1986.

Periodicals: *Military Collectors' News*, P. O. Box 702073, Tulsa, OK 74170; *North South Trader*, P.O. Drawer 631, Orange, VA 22960.

Collectors' Clubs: American Society of Military Insignia Collectors, 1331 Bradley Avenue, Hummelstown, PA 17036; Association of American Uniform Collectors, 446 Berkshire Road, Elyria, OH 44035; Company of Military Historians, North Main Street, Westbrook, CT 06498; Imperial German Military Collectors Association, Box 38, Keyport, NJ 07735.

Additional Listings: See World War I, World War II, and *Warman's Antiques And Their Prices* for information about firearms and swords.

REVOLUTIONARY WAR

Autograph, card signed, 3 x 1"	
Lincoln, B	60.00
Peters, Richard, dated	30.00
Shubrick, WB, title included	25.00
Trumball, Joseph	30.00
Document	
Letter, Ed Carrington, 7 x 9" stationery, Richmond, 1785, letter regarding shipment and payment of tobacco and books	145.00
Pay Voucher, CT, Jan 17, 1783, 6 x 7"	50.00
Newspaper, *The Providence Gazette And Country Journal*, April 4, 1778	75.00
Pamphlet, "An Alarm to the Legislature of the Province of New York, Occasioned by the present Policital Disturbances, in North America: Addressed to the Honourable Representatives in General Assembly Convened," printed Jan 17, 1775 in New York for James Rivington, 13 pgs	360.00
Sword, American, "Town" type, brass hilt, fluted shell guard with hunting motif, 30" broad fullered single edged blade	150.00

WAR OF 1812

Belt, sword, Civil War type dirk	135.00
Hat, leather, attached brass eagle, metallic rope twists, orig label	600.00
Newspaper, *Columbian Centinel*, June 27, 1812, proclamation of war	25.00
Sword, light cavalry officer's saber, hilt with straight cross guard, silver wire wrapped sharkskin cov back swept grip, 28½" sharply curved single edged blade, long false edge	165.00

Civil War, belt, Union infantry soldier, 1863, $150.00.

CIVIL WAR

Autograph, card signed
Butler, MC, Confederate, 3 x 2"	60.00
Denver, JW, Union, 5 x 2"	45.00
Garland, AH, Confederate, dated, 4 x 3"	60.00
Hamilton, CS, Union, dated 1863, 3 x 1"	20.00
Hilliard, Henry, Confederate, 4 x 3"	40.00

Badge, helmet, brass shield and eagle, company number in center **45.00**

Bayonet, rifled musket, blade stamped "US," socket stamped "A," orig black leather scabbard with brass tip, brown leather frog stamped "Army/US/Ord. Dept/Sub Inspector," and "R. Nece/ Philad" **175.00**

Button, brass, US eagle imprint **8.00**

Canteen, wood, cloth cov **75.00**

Daguerreotype
Confederate, 2 x 2½"	125.00
Union, 2¾ x 3¼"	85.00

Document
Appointment, Benjamin F Butler, Union general, appointment of Major John Cassels as officer in the National Asylum for Disabled Volunteer Soldiers **195.00**

Enlistment Roster, twenty–one individual full signatures with county listed, Harmony Church, Kentucky, Dec, 1862 .... **100.00**

Letter, Wm Sprague, Union BGV, 8 x 9" lined stationery, Camp Clark, July 11, 1861 .... **75.00**

Pay Voucher, partially printed, sgd J M Schofield, Union general, July 31, 1864, 17 x 11" **75.00**

Flag, US, 36 stars, 1864–67, 72 x 98" **500.00**

Hat, slouch, Confederate cavalry **650.00**

Jacket, shell, Union cavalry, complete with buttons, lining, and inspector's marks........................... **350.00**

Knife and Spoon, combination **25.00**

Mess Kit, bone handles, orig leather case **175.00**

Newspaper, The Lutheran and Mission-

ary Newspaper, July 14, 1864, USS Kearsarge sinks the USS Alabama ... **15.00**

Ribbon, 1861–65, Lincoln's head surrounded by "With Malice Toward None, With Charity For All," blue gray **90.00**

Saddle, Cavalry, McCullem type **300.00**

Saddle Bag, Allegheny Arsenal, 1864 . **275.00**

Spy Glass, 16", four sections, leather wrapped **250.00**

Stereoscope Card, "The War of the Union" **7.50**

INDIAN WAR

Belt Buckle, Naval officer, brass stamped "Horstman, Phila" **115.00**

Hat Insignia, cavalry, brass, crossed sabers, 3" w **65.00**

Sleeve Patch, US Military, wool, green maltese cross, dark blue ground **25.00**

Uniform, officer **275.00**

SPANISH AMERICAN WAR

Button, pinback, Remember The Maine, battleship scene, patent 1896 ...... **25.00**

Buckle, Anson Mills, Patent Feb 1, 1881 **25.00**

Cartridge Box, US Army **125.00**

Coat, enlisted man's, 1st sergeant stripes **145.00**

Hat Badge, infantry, brass, crossed krag rifles, 2" l **60.00**

Spy Glass, pocket, Naval, brass, round holder, brown leather grip, 16" **100.00**

Uniform, khaki, tunic and pants **40.00**

VIETNAM WAR

Ammo Box, steel, M5–20A1, dated ... **10.00**

Autograph, card signed, ER Zumwalt, first day cover **12.00**

Book, Frontline–The Commands of Wm Chase, 1975, autographed 1st edition, 228 pgs **38.00**

Helmet, US tanker, dark green fiberglass, intercom system on side **25.00**

Leaflet, South Vietnamese Propaganda, 5 x 7", dated April, 1969 .... **5.00**

Medal, Air Force Commendation, parade ribbon and lapel bar, case **20.00**

Tunic, US Army, sergeant, green, gold stripes, 5th Division red diamonds insignia **25.00**

MILK BOTTLES

Collecting Hints: Many factors influence the price—condition of the bottle, who is selling, the part of the country in which the sale is transacted, and the amount of desire a buyer has for the bottle. Every bottle does not have universal appeal. A sale of a bottle in one area does not mean that it would bring the same amount in another locale. For example, a rare Vermont pyro pint would be looked upon as only another "pint" in Texas.

A general trend indicates the growing popularity for pyroglaze (painted bottles) over embossed bottles. Pyro bottles display better at home or at shows.

History: Hervey Thatcher is recognized as the father of the glass milk bottle. By the early 1880s glass milk bottles appeared in New York and New Jersey. A. V. Whiteman had a milk bottle patent as early as 1880. Patents reveal much about early milk bottle shape and manufacture. Not all patentees were manufacturers. Many individuals engaged others to produce bottles under their patents.

The Golden Age of the glass milk bottle is 1910 to 1950. Leading manufacturers include Lamb Glass Co. (Mt. Vernon, Ohio), Liberty Glass Co. (Sapulpa, Oklahoma), Owens–Illinois Glass Co. (Toledo, Ohio), and Thatcher Glass Co. (New York).

Milk bottles can be found in the following sizes: gill (quarter pint), half pint, 10 ounces (third quart), pint, quart, half gallon (two quart), and gallon.

Paper cartons first appeared in the early 1920s and 30s and achieved popularity after 1950. The late 1950s witnessed the arrival of the plastic bottle. A few dairies still use glass bottles today, but the era has essentially ended.

References: Don Lord, *California Milks*, published by author; John Tutton, *Udder Delight*, published by author.

Periodical: The Milk Route, 4 Ox Bow Road, Westport, CT 06880.

Museums: The Farmers Museum, Cooperstown, NY; Southwest Dairy Museum, Arlington, TX; Billings Farm Museum, Woodstock, VT.

Butler Bros, clear glass, 45½" h, 2⅛" d, $2.00.

Half Pint
  Embossed, round
    Bay Point Farm, "Store Bottle 3 Cents" **22.00**
    Brookside Dairies, Inc, Waterbury, CT, "First National Stores" **18.00**
    Dairyland Creamery, Coos Bay, OR, "Pasteurized Milk and Cream" **24.00**
    Lackawanna Dairy Co, 420 Electric Avenue, Lackawanna, NY **14.00**
  Pyro–glazed, round
    Carpenters Dairy, Springvale, ME, orange **12.00**
    Hazel Dell Dairy, Salem, OR, "Grade A," blue **22.00**
    Woodworths, Grand Rapids, MI, black **12.00**
  Pyro–glazed, square, Korters Pasteurized Milk, Moscow, ID, yellow .. **16.00**
Pint
  Embossed, round
    American Oyster Co, Providence, RI, AO logo both sides **26.00**
    Chestnut Farms Dairy, Washington, DC, seal and ribbon on reverse, ribbed neck **12.00**
    Coo's Bay Ice & Cold Storage Co, Marshfield, OR **26.00**
    Our Own Dairies, Inc, Los Angeles, six point star is slug plate **18.00**
    Racy Cream Co, Knoxville, TN, bowling pin bottle **24.00**
  Pyro–glazed, tall, round
    Hunts Dairy, Skowhegan, ME, dial GR–4–2604, "Drink More Milk for Health," red **15.00**
    Litchfield Dairy Association, Litchfield, MI, "Use Litchfield Butter," black and orange **12.00**
    Mountain Lily Dairy, Alturas, CA, mountain scene illus on front, dairy farm illus on reverse, green **22.00**
    T & M Dairy, Hanover, NM, bowl of ice cream, arrow, and target illus, "T & M Ice Cream Really Hits the Spot," brown **16.00**
    Valley Dairy, Yerington, NV, phone 367, "Drink Milk for Health," maroon **26.00**
    Vons Dairy Farm, Monroe, MI, dairy farm illus, "Fresh from the Farm," red and blue **14.00**
Quart
  Embossed, cream–top, round
    Bartholomay Co, 24, Rochester, NY **16.00**
    Cheyenne Creamery, Cheyenne, WY **38.00**
    Round Top Farms, Damariscotta, ME **24.00**

Embossed, tall, round
  Blue Grass Dairy, Lawrence Gallen-
    stein, Maysville, KY 24.00
  Cheyenne Creamery Company ... 28.00
  Connors Dairy, Wilmington, DE,
    large diagonal script 34.00
  Harding Dairy, Magna, UT 32.00
  Illinois Dairy, Pasteurized, Peoria,
    IL, "this bottle property of &
    filled by" on base 18.00
  K–C Dairy Inc, Kingsport, TN,
    beaded neck 16.00
  Lone Star Creamery Company,
    Houston, TX, boy's head and
    "Honey Boy Ice Cream/Gee It's
    Good" emb on shoulder, star,
    ribbed neck 38.00
  Newfair Dairy, Honolulu, diagonal
    script, ribbed neck 75.00
Pyro–glazed, cream–top, round
  Cloverleaf Store Bottle, Blue Rib-
    bon Farms, Stockton, CA, grocer
    illus, "Buy Milk from your Care-
    ful and Courteous Grocer," red . 38.00
  Oak Park Dairy, Westbury, LI,
    phone 25, Oak Park Dairy Co
    building illus, black 28.00
  Producers Dairy, pasteurization/
    temperature scale illus, "No Sub-
    stitution for Quality," black 24.00
Pyro–glazed, tall, round
  Almhurst Dairy, Westwood 83,
    Denver, CO, cow kicking up
    heels illus, orange 32.00
  Dolly Madison Dairy Products,
    Denver, CO, Mrs Madison eating
    ice cream illus, "The Highest
    Peak of Quality," red 26.00
  Forest Dairy Co, Kansas City, MO,
    child holding bottle illus, "Yours
    for Health/They Need the Best,"
    black 28.00
  Home Owned Dairies, Inc, Salt
    Lake City, UT, child illus and
    "Building America" in shield on
    front, milkman illus on reverse,
    red 34.00
  JA Kelso & Son, Boscawen, NH,
    dairy cow illus, "Pure Ayrshire
    Milk/Clearbrook Farm," black .. 28.00
  Markwell Milk & Ice Cream, Pas-
    teurized, Sulphur, OK, house-
    wife cooking meal illus, "Every-
    thing is Better with Butter/Enrich
    your Favorite Dishes with Natu-
    ral Vitamins," orange 32.00
  Meadow Brook Milk & Cream,
    Green River, WY, phone 66J,
    dairy farm illus, maroon 16.00
  Michigan State College Creamery,
    M Circle logo on side, dairy
    products list on reverse, green . 58.00

Model Dairy, Pueblo, CO, dairy
    barn illus, "Golden Quality Ice
    Cream," green 26.00
  Modern Dairy, Fallon, NV, phone
    160W, dairy farm and cows illus
    and "Direct from Farm to You"
    on front, crossing guard illus and
    "Be Careful" on reverse, green . 42.00
  Shadow Brook Dairy, Tunkhan-
    nock, PA, dairy barn and silo il-
    lus, maroon 16.00
  Stedland Jersey Farms, Grade A
    Pasteurized Milk, Memphis, TN,
    dairy farm and milking parlor il-
    lus, "Stedland Dairy Farms," or-
    ange 26.00
War Slogan, pyro–glazed, tall, round
  Braden's Milk, "It's Pasteurized,"
    US map, stars, and Statue of Lib-
    erty illus, "America is a Great
    Place to Live, Let's Keep it that
    Way," red 55.00
  Emmett's Dairy, Central, NM, milk-
    man milking cow illus, "We're
    All Pulling for Uncle Sam/Milk
    Plays a Vital Part in Maintaining
    the Health of Our Armed Forces
    and Defense Workers," orange . 75.00
  Mullan Store Bottle, 10 Cents De-
    posit, arc welder illus, "America
    at Work/Our Army is Fighting for
    Us/Let Us Work for Them," yel-
    low 48.00
  Producers Dairy, fighter plane illus,
    stars between letters VIM, "Keep
    'Em Flying" and "V for Victory/
    M for Milk," orange 75.00
  Spokane Bottle Exchange, Inc,
    home in shield illus, "Double
    Protection for the Home/Drink
    Milk for Health & Buy War Bonds
    & Stamps," red and brown 36.00
  Valley Gold, Albuquerque's Favor-
    ite Milk, milkman delivering milk
    illus, "To Save our Freedom We
    Must Save our Materials/America
    Saves/Save this Bottle and Return
    to Dairy," red 45.00

MONSTERS

Collecting Hints: This is a category rampant with
speculative fever. Prices rise and fall rapidly depending on the momentary popularity of a figure
or family group. Study the market and its prices
carefully before becoming a participant.

Stress condition and completeness. Do not buy
any item in less than fine condition. Check carefully to make certain that all parts or elements
are present for whatever you buy.

Since the material in this category is of recent

origin, no one is certain how much has survived. Hoards are not uncommon. It is possible to find examples at garage sales. It pays to shop around before paying a high price.

While an excellent collection of two dimensional material, e.g., comic books, magazines, posters, etc., can be assembled, stress three dimensional material. Several other crazes, e.g., model kit collecting, cross over into monster collecting, thus adding to price confusion.

History: Collecting monster related material began in the late 1980s as a generation looked back nostalgically on the monster television shows of the 1960s, e.g., Addams Family, Dark Shadows, and the Munsters, and the spectacular monster and horror movies of the 1960s and 1970s. Fueling the fire was a group of Japanese collectors who were raiding the American market for material relating to Japanese monster epics featuring reptile monsters such as Godzilla.

It did not take long for collectors to seek the historic roots for their post-World War II monsters. A collecting revival started for Frankenstein, King Kong, and Mummy material. Contemporary items featuring these characters also appeared.

Reference: Ted Hake, *Hake's Guide To TV Collectibles*, Wallace–Homestead Book Company, 1990.

ADDAMS FAMILY

Bank, 3¼ x 4½ x 3¼", The Thing, plastic, black, green hand grabs coins, orig box, 1964–66 . . . . 50.00
Book, *The Addams Family*, Pyramid Books, 1965 copyright, 176 pgs 15.00
Coloring Book, 8½ x 11", Saalfield, #4595, 1965 . . . . 25.00
Figure
　Lurch, 5½", hard plastic body, soft molded vinyl head, Remco, copyright 1964 Filmways TV Productions Inc 75.00
　Morticia, 5", plastic, molded soft vinyl head, long black glossy gown, base with 1964 Filmways copyright 100.00
Game, The Addams Family, Ideal Toy, 1964, orig box 110.00
Lunch Box, 7 x 8½ x 4", litho metal, full color scenes, thermos missing, King–Seeley, 1974 copyright 25.00
Magazine, *Monster World*, #9, July 1966, Warren Publishing Co, full color family photo on front cov, 5 pg article 28.00
Playing Cards, Milton Bradley, 38 cards from orig 39, instruction card, full color photo on each 25.00
Puppet, 10", hand, Gomez, cloth body,

soft molded vinyl head, 1964 copyright Filmways TV Productions 75.00
Record, 33⅓ rpm, RCA Victor label, six orig music themes, 12¼" cardboard album with full color family photo, 1965 copyright 22.00
TV Guide, Oct 30, 1965, full color cov photo of Gomez and Morticia, four page article 28.00

DARK SHADOWS

Book, *Barnabas Collins vs. The Warlock*, Marilyn Ross, Paperback Library, 156 pgs 10.00
Comic Book, Gold Key, #5, May 1970 12.00
Game
　Barnabas Collins/Dark Shadows Game, Milton Bradley, orig box, 1969 . . . . 25.00
　Dark Shadows, Whitman, orig box, 1968 . . . . 50.00
Record, 33⅓ rpm, Philips label, sixteen orig music themes, 12¼" album, 4 pg black and white photo poster sheet, 1969 copyright 15.00

DRACULA

Bank, figural, porcelain, 1970s 45.00
Doll, 8", glow–in–the–dark eyes, removable cape, marked "copyright Mego 1974" 25.00
Film, super 8, 8mm, issued by Castle Films, box 18.00
Magazine, *Famous Monsters of Filmland*, #92, Sept 1972, Warren Publishing Co, full color cover portrait, 76 pgs 10.00
Paint Set, Dracula Oil Painting By Numbers, 12 x 16" canvas panel, 14 oil paints, one paint brush, orig box, Hasbro, marked "Made In England," copyright 1963 Universal Pictures Corp 100.00
Promotion Ad, exhibitor's trade magazine, graphic photo 225.00
Puzzle, full color illus of Dracula holding girl, Frankenstein sleeps in coffin, titled "Vampire's Nest," orig box, Jaymar, copyright 1963 Universal Pictures 28.00
Toy, Dracucycle, glows–in–the–dark, coffin shape, includes Dracula figure, haunted house winder, orig box, Ideal toys, copyright 1978 . . . . 48.00

FRANKENSTEIN

Doll, 8", glow–in–the–dark eyes and hands, Mego, copyright 1974 . . . . . . 25.00

Figure

Frankenstein, 7¾", flexible rubber, molded, elastic cord mounted in top of head, orig tag "World's Famous Super Monsters," Ahi, 1973 Universal Studio copyright 25.00

Hunchback, 4", molded plastic, orange, Marx and Universal Picture copyright, 1960s 28.00

Glass, 6½", clear, purple, black, and green illus, purple background, copyright Universal Pictures Co Inc, late 1960s 40.00

Mold Kit, Mix 'N Mold, sealed box, issued by Catalog Shoppe, West Hartford, CT, 1970s 28.00

Notebook, 10 x 11", vinyl, three ring binder, black, full color illus on front, late 1960s 50.00

Promotion Ad, exhibitor's trade magazine, graphic photos 150.00

Puzzle, 8 x 6", jigsaw, Jaymar, 1963 .. 129.00

Robot, 14", battery operated, drops pants and blushes, orig box, Galoob, 1960s 138.00

Soaky Bottle, 10", plastic, Colgate–Palmolive Co, 1960s 25.00

Toy, Frankencycle, glows–in–the–dark, skull on front, includes Frankenstein figure and haunted house winder, orig box, Ideal, copyright 1978 .... 48.00

Trash Can, 16" h, tin litho, wrap–around illus, J Chein & Co, 1970s 75.00

GODZILLA

Figure, 18" h, plastic, dark green, yellow claws, teeth, and eyes, wheeled feet, movable arms and legs, copyright 1977, Mattel 100.00

Game, Godzilla Game, 18½ x 19" playing board, orig box, Ideal, copyright 1963 .... 100.00

Model Kit, unassembled, MIB, Aurora, 1964 .... 479.00

Pinback Button, 1⅝", Godzilla Vs Megalon, litho, yellow, dark brown image, red lettering, 1970s 15.00

Puzzle, 10 x 14" assembled, 150 pcs, full color illus, HG Toys, copyright 1978 Toho Co 15.00

View Master Pack, unused, 1970s 8.00

KING KONG

Autograph, Fay Wray, 5½ x 6" page, Wray and Bruce Cabot photo and King Kong illus 50.00

Doll, 11" h, plush, black, soft rubber face, hands, and feet, zippered compartment back reveals radio, orig tag marked 1978 Amico Inc copyright, orig box 45.00

Game, King Kong, Ideal Toy, 1976, orig box 50.00

Glass, King Kong on Twin Towers 3.50

Gum Pack, 2½ x 3½", sealed, Donruss, 1965 .... 75.00

Lunch Box, 7 x 9 x 4", metal, full color illus, copyright 1977 Dino De Laurentis 15.00

Magazine

Famous Monsters of Filmland, #108, July 1974, Warren Publishing Co, 84 pgs, full color cov portrait of Kong, article from pgs 6–49 ..... 10.00

King Kong, April, 1977, Sportscene Publications 3.50

Monsters of the Movies, #1, June 1974, Magazine Management Co, 84 pgs, 10 pgs photo article on different Kong film versions 12.50

Science Fiction Illustrated, 1977, L/C Print Publications 3.00

Model, 9", assembled, unpainted, girl in right hand, Aurora, 1964 copyright 40.00

Movie Poster, 24 x 28", stiff paper, 1963 Universal Pictures 50.00

Pinback Button, Happy Anniversary Kong 1933–1983, black, white, and red 4.00

Socks, photo illus, unused, orig illus display card, 1977 .... 22.00

Toy, 8" h, plush, mechanical, walks and beats chest, opens and closes mouth, growling noise, MIB, Marx 300.00

Children's Book, The Monster Hunters, Francis Rolt-Wheeler, Lothrop, Lee & Shapard, 1916, Charles R Knight, illustrator, $20.00.

MISCELLANEOUS

Button, The Phantom, 3½", full color illus, red background, copyright Universal Pictures Co on rim, 1960s ... **25.00**

Calendar, 1966, 9 x 12", each month pictures different Don Post monster masks, unused **39.00**

Camera, Monster Sun Picture, 2½ x 4½", simulated cardboard, orig store display bag, 1960s **18.00**

Card Game, Monster Old Maid, 1964 Milton Bradley, 39 cards, instruction card, boxed **50.00**

Figure
  Cyclops, 3", plastic, Palmer, 1962 .. **52.00**
  Kraken, 15", hard plastic, green, red mouth, white eyes and teeth, movable arms, copyright 1980 Metro–Goldwyn–Mayer Inc **50.00**
  Monster–Niks, molded soft vinyl plastic, ape face, toddler's body, orig unopened plastic holder, M & W Industries, 1960s **22.00**

Game
  Korg, based on movie, Milton Bradley, 1970s **30.00**
  Phantom of the Opera, unused, Hasbro, 1963 .... **249.00**
  The Monster Squad, Milton Bradley, 1977, orig box **50.00**

Greeting Card, glossy, includes record, features Universal monsters, unused, set of 3 different cards, Buzza, 1963 **42.00**

Gum Wrapper, Spook Stories, 6 x 6¼", Leaf Gum, issued 1963–65 .... **50.00**

Lobby Card, 11 x 14", I Was A Teenage Frankenstein, 1957 American International Picture **15.00**

Lunch Box, 7 x 9 x 4", Clash of the Titans, metal, full color illus, copyright 1980 Metro–Goldwyn–Mayer . **22.00**

Magazine
  Cracked For Monsters Only, first issue, Vol #1, Nov 1965, 68 pgs .. **15.00**
  Horror of Party Beach, Warren Publishing Co, 1964, 68 pgs **15.00**
  Monsters Unlimited, #5, Non–Pareil Publishing Corp, 1965, 36 pgs ... **18.00**

Mask, Cousin Eerie, soft rubber, Eerie Magazine figure issued by Warren Publications, late 1960s **75.00**

Movie Poster
  The Lady And The Monster, 27 x 41", Morgan Litho Corp, 1944 .... **75.00**
  The Vampire, 14 x 36", full color, John Beal and Coleen Gray, 1957 United Artist Corp **25.00**

Nodder, 6", Phantom of the Opera, 1963 .... **79.00**

Pez Container, Creature, includes vending machine box, 1963 .... **89.00**

Pressbook, Creature With The Atom Brain, 12 x 16", 1955 Columbia Pictures **25.00**

Record Album, Power, 1963, cover features Creature, Mummy, and King Kong **32.00**

Soaky Bottle, 10", Creature, soft plastic body, hard plastic head, metallic green, 1960s **75.00**

Trading Card, Monster Magic Action Trading Cards, boxed set of 24 cards, full color illus, Abby Finishing Corp, 1960s **25.00**

Window Card
  The Creature Walks Among Us, 14 x 22", 1956 Universal–International, full color illus **50.00**
  The Incredible Shrinking Man, 11 x 14", 1957 Universal–International, full color scene **15.00**

MUMMY

Doll, 8", glow–in–the–dark hands and eyes, orig box, Mego **28.00**

Film Box, The Mummy's Ghost, 1960s **15.00**

Model Kit, unassembled, MIB, Aurora, 1963 .... **279.00**

Pin, 1" d, color photo, 1963 .... **10.00**

Promotion Ad, exhibitor's trade magazine, graphic photo **175.00**

Puzzle, jigsaw, 8 x 6" box, Jaymar, 1963 **129.00**

Transfer, 9 x 12", blue and red illus, 12 x 18" tee shirt shape retail card, Mani–Yack, copyright 1964 Universal Pictures **50.00**

MUNSTERS

Book
  The Last Resort, Whitman, #1567, 1966, 214 pgs **15.00**
  The Munsters and the Great Camera Caper, 5½ x 8", hard cover, Whitman, 1965, 212 pgs **15.00**

Comic Book
  Gold Key
    #4, Oct 1965 .... **18.00**
    #15, Nov 1967 .... **15.00**
  Whitman, #4, Oct 1965 .... **15.00**

Doll
  Eddie, 8½" h, vinyl plastic, movable head, arms, and legs, orig Ideal Toy tag, 1965 Ideal copyright homemade clothing **30.00**
  Herman, 20", stuffed cloth, molded soft vinyl plastic head and hands, disconnected pull cord, orig Mattel tag with 1964 copyright **75.00**
  Lily, 8½" h, vinyl plastic, movable head, arms, and legs, orig Ideal Toy

tag, 1965 Ideal copyright, orig Ideal
Toy tag **40.00**
Game
The Munsters Card Game, 9½ x 14"
playing board, 42 cards, two plastic
markers, orig box, Milton Bradley,
copyright 1964 .... **48.00**
The Munsters Masquerade Party, Hasbro 1964, orig box **100.00**
The Munsters Picnic, Hasbro 1964,
orig box with full color illus **125.00**
Gum Wrapper, Leaf, 1966, green,
black, and red design, Spook Hand
premium **50.00**
Magazine, *Citizen's Band Radio Magazine*, black and white cov photo of
Herman and Grandpa listening on
early radio shortwave unit **25.00**
Puppet, 10½", hand, Grandpa, printed
fabric, molded soft vinyl head, copyright 1966 Kayro–Vue Productions .. **75.00**
Puzzle, 11½ x 14½", frame tray, full
color illus, Whitman, #4531, 1965
copyright **28.00**
Ring, set of 4, blue plastic, green, black,
and white image changes when tilted,
Herman, Lily, Grandpa, and Eddie,
c1966 .... **28.50**
Sticker Book, 8½ x 12" Whitman, 1965 **68.00**
Thermos, 6½", litho metal, red plastic
cap, King–Seeley, 1965 copyright .. **45.00**
TV Guide, July 10, 1965, full color cov
photo of Yvonne DeCarlo and Fred
Gwynne **25.00**

WOLFMAN

Button, 3½" d, full color illus, dark blue
background, Universal Pictures copyright on rim, late 1960s **25.00**
Comic Book, Dell, 1963 .... **8.00**
Doll, 8", glow–in–the–dark hands and
eyes, gray suit, orig box, Mego, copyright 1973 .... **28.00**
Figure, 4", plastic, brown, movable
head, black hair, blue cloth pants,
1960s **18.00**
Model Kit, assembled, painted, Aurora,
1962 .... **49.00**
Soaky Bottle, 10" h, plastic, metallic
gold and brown, blue trousers, 1960s **75.00**
Swizzle Stick, 7", plastic, 4" figure on
top, unused **15.00**

MORGANTOWN GLASS WORKS

Collecting Hints: Morgantown Glass Works produced glass in a wide range of colors during the
1920s and 1930s. Some distinctive color com-

binations were red and black, yellow and black,
pink and magenta, rose and rose amber, and
color and crystal. Popular items were beverage
and liquor sets, tumblers, and stemware.

A distinctive characteristic of many stemware
pieces is a decorative insert between the bowl
and base, e.g. a smooth or faceted ball or an
open square or diamond. Other stem variations
were branched, beautifully finished columns, or
twists. Stemware often had clear bowls and colored stems or the reverse arrangement.

History: Morgantown Glass Works, Morgantown, West Virginia, was founded in the late 19th
century. By 1903 it was reorganized was named
the Economy Tumbler Company. The blown
tumbler lines were expanded to include pressed,
blown, cut, and etched patterns. Morgantown
also sold blanks to other companies for finishing.

With the introduction of color in 1924, the
name was changed to Economy Glass Company
and its wares were marketed under the "Old
Morgantown" label. In 1939 the name Morgantown Glass Works was revived. Additional reorganizations occurred after 1940. The factory, no
longer bearing the Morgantown name, closed in
the early 1980s.

Reference: *Old Morgantown, Catalogue of
Glassware, 1931,* catalog reprint available from
Old Morgantown Glass Collectors' Guild.

Collectors' Club: Old Morgantown Glass Collectors' Guild, PO Box 894, Morgantown, WV
26507.

Bowl, Connoisseur
10¼" d **15.00**
12" d, ftd, bubble stem, Stiegel green **18.00**
Candlestick
Sharon **12.00**
Steel, burgundy, 8¾" h **40.00**
Candy Jar, cov, Old English, ftd **20.00**
Champagne
Cressey cut, crystal **10.00**
Old English, ruby **12.00**
Cocktail
American Modern, Russel Wright,
seafoam, 2½" **22.00**
Rooster stem, 3½ oz **12.00**
Venetion, red **22.00**
Cordial
American Modern, Russel Wright,
seafoam, 2" h **35.00**
Spanish red, golf ball **30.00**
Goblet
American Modern, Russel Wright
Coral, 4" h **30.00**
Seafoam **30.00**
Button **15.00**
Dancing Girl, blue **48.00**
Ducal **18.50**
Ebony, octagonal **8.50**
Fairwin **18.00**

Old English, ruby	12.50
Palm Optic, pink	8.50
San Tog	15.00
Square	12.00
Virginia Etch, crystal, 7½" h, set of 6	100.00
Willow	12.00

Iced Tea Tumbler
American Modern, Russel Wright, 5" h	
Chartreuse	18.00
Seafoam	20.00
El Mexicano, amethyst	15.00

Ivy Ball
Crystal, cut dec, 4" d	15.00
Peacock Blue, golf ball, 6¾" d	65.00

Jug, Old Bristol	25.00

Juice
American Modern, Russel Wright, chartreuse, 4" h	15.00
El Mexicano, amethyst	10.00

Liquor Set, decanter, six glasses
Little King, Ritz blue	70.00
Sparta, rose	65.00

Martini Set, 9¾" h shaker, three 3" h ftd
tumblers, amethyst	30.00
Parfait, Old English	15.00

Pitcher
Connoisseur	25.00
Crinkle Amy, tankard	95.00
Crinkle Pink	95.00
Old Bristol, Ritz blue	40.00
Peacock Optic, green	25.00
Sommerset, Stiegel green	25.00

Plate
Ebony, octagonal	7.50
Palm Optic, pink	5.00
Primrose Lane, pink	7.50

Sherbet
American Modern, Russel Wright, 2½" h	
Coral	24.00
Gray	20.00
Seafoam	20.00
Button	12.00
Marilyn	8.00
Old English, red, crystal stem	8.00
Radiant Stem, cobalt, v shape stem, set of 12	265.00
Simplicity	7.50

Tumbler
American Modern, Russel Wright, seafoam, 4½" h	17.00
Crinkle Red	
4⅛" h, 7 oz	12.50
4¼" h, 11 oz	16.00
5⅛" h, 12 oz	20.00
El Mexicano, amethyst	12.00
Palm Optic, green	10.00
Pineapple Optic	6.00
Square	6.00
Zombie, 15 oz, set of 8 different colors	160.00

Vase
5⅞" h, crystal, trellis etching	18.00
6" h, green, oval	45.00

Wine
American Modern, Russel Wright, 3" h	
Coral	25.00
Gray	25.00
Seafoam	25.00
Art Moderne	12.00

Witch Ball, side opening
3½" d, crystal	30.00
6" d, crystal, ebony base	40.00

MORTON POTTERIES

Collecting Hints: The potteries of Morton, Illinois, used local clay until 1940. The clay fired out to a golden ecru color which is quite easy to recognize. After 1940 southern and eastern clays were shipped to Morton. These clays fired out white. Thus, later period wares are sharply distinguished from the earlier wares.

Few pieces were marked by the potteries. Incised and raised marks for the Morton Pottery Works, the Cliftwood Art Potteries, Inc., and the Morton Pottery Company do surface at times. The Cliftwood, Midwest, Morton Pottery Company, and American Art Pottery all used paper labels in limited amounts. Some of these have survived, and collectors do find them.

Glazes from the early period, 1877–1920, usually were Rockingham types, both mottled and solid. Yellow ware also was standard during the early period. Occasionally a dark cobalt blue was produced, but this color is rare. Colorful drip glazes and solid colors came into use after 1920.

History: Pottery was produced in Morton, Illinois, for 99 years. In 1877 six Rapp brothers, who emigrated from Germany, began the first pottery, Morton Pottery Works. Over the years sons, cousins, and nephews became involved in the production of pottery. The other Morton pottery operations were spin-offs from the original pottery and brothers. When it was taken over in 1915 by second generation Rapps, Morton Pottery Works became the Morton Earthenware Company. Work at that pottery was terminated by World War I.

The Cliftwood Art Potteries, Inc., operated from 1920 to 1940. One of the original founders of the Morton Pottery Works and his four sons organized it. They sold out in 1940, and the operation continued for four more years as the Midwest Potteries, Inc. A disastrous fire brought an end to that operation in March 1944. These two potteries produced figurines, lamps, novelties and vases.

In 1922 the Morton Pottery Company, which had the longest existence of all of the Morton's potteries, was organized by the same brothers who had operated the Morton Earthenware Company. The Morton Pottery Company specialized in beer steins, kitchenwares, and novelty items for chain stores and gift shops. They also produced some of the Vincent Price National Treasures reproductions for Sears Roebuck and Company in the mid-1960s. The Morton Pottery closed in 1976, thus ending the 99 years of pottery production in Morton.

By 1947 the brothers who had operated the Cliftwood Art Potteries, Inc., came back into the pottery business. They established the short-lived American Art Potteries. The American Art Potteries made flower bowls, lamps, planters, some unusual flower frogs, and vases. Their wares were marketed by florists and gift shops. Production at American Art Potteries was halted in 1961. Of all the wares of the Morton potteries, the products of the American Art Potteries are the most elusive.

Reference: Doris and Burdell Hall, *Morton's Potteries: 99 Years*, published by author, 1982. Doris and Burdell Hall also have written a number of articles on the Morton Potteries that have appeared in the *American Clay Exchange*, (800 Murray Drive, El Cajon, CA 92020), the most recent of which is "Morton Pottery Company Wallpockets" in the January 1988 issue.

Museum: Illinois State Museum, Springfield, IL; Morton Public Library (permanent exhibit), Morton, IL.

Advisors: Doris and Burdell Hall.

American Art Pottery, planter, bird on leaf, stump planter, blue, 6½" h, $12.00.

MORTON POTTERY WORKS AND MORTON EARTHENWARE COMPANY, 1877–1917

Baker, 1¾" h, 5½" d, brown Rockingham mottled glaze **35.00**
Coffeepot
   ¾ pt, individual, dark brown glaze .   **25.00**
   5 pt, brown Rockingham, ornate emb top and bottom **90.00**

Jar, stoneware, Albany slip glaze, marked on side, 2 gal **65.00**
Miniature
   Coffeepot, 3" h, brown glaze, 4 pcs   **75.00**
   Pitcher
     1¾" h, bulbous
       Brown glaze **20.00**
       Green glaze **25.00**
     3¼" h, cobalt blue glaze **55.00**
Mixing Bowl, 12½" d, yellowware, wide white band, narrow blue stripes top and bottom **45.00**
Pie Plate
   9" d, brown Rockingham mottled glaze **100.00**
   11" d, yellowware **80.00**
Spittoon, 15" d, scalloped dec top and bottom, brown Rockingham mottled glaze **55.00**
Teapot, 4½" h, individual, 1 cup, brown Rockingham glaze
   Acorn shape **30.00**
   Pear shape **35.00**

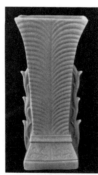

Cliftwood, vase, rect, simulated palm frond dec, matte turquoise, 14" h, $30.00.

CLIFTWOOD ART POTTERIES, INC., 1920–1940

Beer Set, pitcher and six steins, barrel shape, yellow **100.00**
Bookend, pr, 6 x 5 x 3½", elephant, blue mulberry drip glaze **85.00**
Candlestick, pr, 11" h, chocolate drip glaze, sq base **50.00**
Clock, 7" h, octagonal shape, two inkwells and pen tray in base, chocolate drip glaze **140.00**
Compote, 6" h, 8½" d, four dolphins support bowl, old rose glaze **75.00**
Creamer, 4" h, 3" d, chocolate drip glaze **35.00**
Figurine
   Cat, 4½" l, 1½" w, reclining, cobalt blue glaze **25.00**

Elephant on log, 6½" h, oriental jar
on back, chocolate drip glaze **60.00**
Flower Insert
Turtle #1, 4" l, blue–mulberry drip
glaze **12.00**
Turtle #2, 5½" l, dark green glaze . **12.00**
Lamp
7½" h, owl on log, yellow **35.00**
12" h, donut shape, clock base, blue–
mulberry drip glaze **125.00**
20" h, art deco, three bulb fixtures,
blue, gray drip glaze **50.00**
Wine Decanter, 6½" h, spherical,
molded swirl design, mottled green
glaze, matching stopper **25.00**

MIDWEST POTTERIES, INC., 1940–1944

Figurine
Bear, 6 x 10", brown spray glaze ... **30.00**
Cowboy on bronco, 7½" h, black,
gold dec **25.00**
Deer, 12½" h, art deco, antlers, head
faces tail, brown, green spray glaze **25.00**
Dog, 6 x 4", cocker spaniel, black
gloss glaze **25.00**
Female Dancer, 8½" h, art deco,
white, gold dec **25.00**
Goose, 5¾" h, long neck, white, yellow dec **8.00**
Hen, 7" h, rooster, 8" h, white, gold
painted combs, pr **35.00**
Heron, 12" h, stylized, blue, green,
yellow spray glaze **22.00**
Parrot on Stump, 4½" h, blue, yellow,
brown spray glaze on white **12.00**
Roadrunner, 8" h, stylized, white,
gold dec **12.00**
Stallion, 10¾" h, rearing on hind legs,
gold **25.00**
Flower Bowl
4", sq, basket weave, lime green
white overspray **10.00**
7½" h, two orbs, nude figure, plati-
num **35.00**
10" d, 5½" h, circular, brown, yellow
drip glaze, 2 pcs **16.00**
11" d, 2½" deep, flat, matt turquoise **15.00**
Mask, wall type, 18th C English male
busts, white
5 x 3¼", front view
Pouting, mustache, goatee **16.00**
Smiling, curly hair **16.00**
5 x 4½", right side view, braided hair,
bangs **20.00**
5¾ x 4¾", left side view, bald,
bearded **22.00**
Miniature
Bird, 2" h, blue **5.00**
Camel, 2½" h, brown, yellow spray
glaze **7.00**

Goose, 2" h, white, gold dec **6.00**
Rabbit, pr, 2½" h, kissing, blue, gold
dec **20.00**
Sailboat, 2" h, light blue **6.00**
Swan, 2½" h, matt white **5.00**

Morton Pottery Company, vase, woodland glaze, green and brown spatter on
yellow ware, spherical, 32″ d, 10½″ h,
$200.00.

MORTON POTTERY COMPANY, 1922–1976

Miniature
Bear, 2½" h, brown **10.00**
Deer with antlers, 5" h, white **7.50**
Elephant
Trumpeting, 2½" h, green **6.50**
Trunk over head, gray **6.50**
Kangaroo, 2½" h, burgundy **6.50**
Squirrel, 2½" h, brown **6.50**
Swordfish, 5" h, yellow **7.50**
Wren on stump, 7" h, natural colors **8.50**
Pie Bird, 5" h, white, multicolored
wings and back **22.00**
Pie Duckling, 5" h, white, pink base and
wings **25.00**
Planters
Art Deco, female bust, broad brim
hat, matt white, 7½" h **30.00**
Cowboy and Cactus, 7" h, natural col-
ors **12.00**

Morton Pottery Works, beer stein, yellow
ware, blue slip stripes, $10.00.

Mother Earth Line, natural colors
Apple 3.00
Banana 3.00
Orange 3.00
Pineapple 5.00
Plum 3.00
Rabbit, 9½" h
Female with umbrella, pink blouse,
egg planter 12.00
Male with top hat, blue vest, egg
planter 12.00
Shoe House Variations, 9½" h, yellow
Bank, cold paint red roof 20.00
Lamp, cold paint red roof 25.00
Planter, green glazed roof 18.00
Wall Plaque, green glazed roof 12.00
Vase
4½" h, hand, V for Victory bud, white 8.00
6" h
Bud, bulbous, long neck, multicol-
or 6.00
Grecian urn, handled, pink 12.00
8½" h, cornucopia on shell base, blue 14.00
20" h, cylinder, emb crane and bam-
boo dec, white 20.00

Morton Pottery Company, wall pockets, gardener, one with hoe, other with watering can, ringed pot in front, each $10.00.

Wall Pocket
6½" h, teapot, white, red apple dec,
red finial 12.00
7½" h, Mary Quite Contrary, red
dress, blue apron 10.00
8½" h, parrot on bunch of grapes,
natural colors 18.00
8¾" h, violin, two musical notes,
white, hp dec, pr 20.00
10" h, harp, white, hp underglaze floral dec 14.00
Woodland Glaze Items, yellowware,
brown and green spatter over transparent glaze
Coffee Server, 8 cup 85.00
Milk Jug, 4½" h, adv 80.00
Pie Plate, 9" d 100.00
Salt and Pepper Shakers, pr, 5" h ... 110.00
Teapot, 4 cup 65.00

American Art Pottery, vase, pitcher shape, white, rust spackling, 14" h, $20.00.

AMERICAN ART POTTERIES, 1947– 1961

Bowl
5" d, 3" h, inverted umbrella shape,
gold bisque, bronze spatter 10.00
10 x 4 x 2", octagonal, elongated,
green, yellow int. 8.00
Compote, 10" d, 6" h, ftd, dark green
bisque, high gloss spatter 15.00
Dinnerware
Creamer and Sugar, 3" h, stylized
flowers, blue, peach spray glaze . 18.00
Demitasse Cup and Saucer, 3" h, stylized flower on cup, flat blossom on
saucer, gray, pink spray glaze 14.00
Sugar, 3" h, bulbous, handled, blue,
gray spray glaze 10.00
Doll Parts, miniature, 1¼" h head, hp
features, yellow hair, 1½" arms and
legs 40.00
Lamp, TV
7 x 10", conch shell, purple, pink
spray glaze 18.00
9 x 12", horse and colt, running, gray,
mauve spray glaze 30.00
12 x 10", leopard, crouched on tree
limb, black, gray spray glaze 25.00
14 x 6", panther, slinking position,
black spray glaze 20.00
Planter
5" h, 5½" l, fish, purple, pink spray
glaze 14.00
6" h, cowboy boot, blue, pink spray
glaze 12.00
7" h, log, applied squirrel figure, gray
spray glaze 15.00
9½" h, quail, natural color spray
glaze 22.00
Vase
6½" h, pitcher shape, mauve spray
glaze, gold dec 18.00

8" h, bud, blue, pink spray glaze ... **8.00**
10½" h, cornucopia, gold, white int. **10.00**
12½" h, bulbous, blue, encircled by
molded pink blossoms **30.00**
Wall Pocket, 5" h, tree stump, applied
woodpecker, brown spray glaze **12.00**

MOVIE MEMORABILIA

Collecting Hints: Collectors tend to focus on blockbuster hits, with "Gone With The Wind" and "Casablanca" among the market leaders. The cartoon image, especially Disney material, also is very popular.

Much of the material is two dimensional. Collectors have just begun to look for three dimensional objects, although the majority of these are star and personality, rather than movie related.

The market went crazy in the mid–1970s when people sought to speculate in movie memorabilia. A self disciplining has taken place with prices falling in the 1980s. The area was compounded further by the large number of reproductions, many made in Europe, which flooded the market.

History: The golden age of movie memorabilia was the 1930s and 1940s. The star system had reached its zenith and studios spent elaborate sums promoting their major stars. Initially, movie studios and their public relation firms tightly controlled the distribution of material such as press books, scripts, preview flyers, costumes, props, etc. Copyright has expired on many of these items, and reproductions abound.

The current interest in Hollywood memorabilia can be traced to the pop art craze of the 1960s. Film festivals increased the desire for decorative film–related materials. Collecting movie posters was "hot."

Piracy always has plagued Hollywood and is responsible for the release of many items into the market. Today the home video presents new challenges to the industry.

References: Tony Fusco, *The Official Identification and Price Guide To Posters,* House of Collectibles, 1990; John Hegenberger, *Collector's Guide To Treasures from the Silver Screen,* Wallace–Homestead Book Company, 1991; Leslie Halliwell, *The Filmgoers's Companion,* Avon, 1978; Ephraim Katz, *The Film Encyclopedia,* Perigee Books, 1979; Leonard Maltin (ed.), *TV Movies and Videos Guide,* New American Library, 1987; John R. Warren, *Warren's Movie Poster Price Guide,* Overstreet Publications, 1986; Dian Zillner, *Hollywood Collectibles,* Schiffer Publishing, 1991.

Periodicals: *Big Reel,* Route 3, P. O. Box 83, Madison, NC 27025; *Classic Images,* P. O. Box 4079, Davenport, IA 52808; *Movie Collectors' World,* P. O. Box 309, Fraser, MI 48026; *Nos-*talgia World,* P. O. Box 231, New Haven, CT 06473.

Collectors' Club: Studio Collectors Club, P. O. Box 1566, Apple Valley, CA 92307.

See: Cartoon Characters, Disneyana, Movie Personalities, and Posters.

Wizard of Oz, sheet music, EY Harburg lyrics, Harold Arlen music, 1939, Leo Frist, NYC publisher, $10.00.

Almanac, *1941–42 International Motion Picture Almanac,* 6½ x 9¼", 1026 pgs, Quigley Publishing Co, 1946–47 .... **25.00**
Book
Adventures of Robin Hood, 8½ x 11", 36 pgs, complete story and black and white film scenes Conklin, Publishing Co, 1938 copyright ... **75.00**
Gone With The Wind, motion picture edition **50.00**
Screen Personalities, 9 x 12", hard cov, 110 pgs, biography picture book, Grosset & Dunlap, 1933 copyright **40.00**
The Sea Hawk, 8 x 11", story and black and white film scenes, Whitman, 1940 .... **65.00**
Brooch, *Gone With The Wind* **65.00**
Doll, *Wizard of Oz,* Dorothy, 8" h, jointed **35.00**
Folder, *Gone with the Wind,* 8½ x 10½", tinted sepia portrait illus, text biography, and production statistics, "will not be shown anywhere except at advanced prices, at least until 1941" marked on back, Loew's Theatre imprint **75.00**

Glass

The Creature, 6½", clear, green illus, Universal Pictures Co Inc copyright, late 1960s **38.00**

The Wizard of Oz, pr, 5" h, clear, weighted bottom, Dorothy with pink design and white inscription, other with Scarecrow with white design and light orange inscription, S & Co, 1950s **25.00**

Handbill, *Spellbound,* 8 x 11", 4 pgs . **20.00**

Lobby Card

*M*A*S*H,* Donald Sutherland photo **5.00**

The Long Gray Line, 11 x 14", 1955 Columbia Picture, set of 8 .... **25.00**

Lunch Box, *Planet of the Apes,* 7 x 9 x 4", metal, emb, full color illus, copyright 1974 20th Century Fox **50.00**

Paint by Number Set, *Phantom of the Opera,* Hasbro, orig box, copyright 1963 Universal Pictures Corp **200.00**

Pinback Button

The Red Ace, stars Marie Walcamp, serial, 1920s **24.00**

The Wizard of Oz, blue "Coming Soon! MGM's The Wizard of Oz" inscription **95.00**

Playing Card, *Star Trek the Wrath Of Khan,* complete deck, full color photo on each card, orig box **7.50**

Poster

Blood Feast **135.00**

Crack in the World **20.00**

Destination Inner Space **18.00**

First Men in the Moon **45.00**

Hasty Heart, 13 x 30", Warner Bros, 1949 .... **25.00**

Horrors of the Black Museum, 27 x 41", black and white illus, English, 1959 .... **50.00**

Jungle Drums of Africa, 27 x 41", features Clayton Moore, 1952 ...... **30.00**

Marooned **8.00**

Not As A Stranger, 27 x 41", 1955 United Artist film **25.00**

Sands of Iwo Jima, 14 x 36", paper, features John Wayne, John Agar, and Adela Mara **50.00**

Space Master X–7 .... **50.00**

Spike Jones And His City Slickers, 27 x 41", color images, 1954 Universal–International **48.00**

Terror in the Haunted House **50.00**

The Alligator People **40.00**

The Day the Earth Caught Fire **12.00**

The Earth Dies Screaming **15.00**

The Space Children **65.00**

The Unearthly **50.00**

They Came From Beyond Space **12.00**

Zombies of Mora Tau **55.00**

Press Book

Donovan's Reef, John Wayne, 1963 **7.00**

The Court Jester, Danny Kaye, 1956, 22 pgs **8.00**

The Girl Of The Golden West, Jeanette MacDonald, Nelson Eddy, 14 x 20", c1938 .... **15.00**

Program

Beau Geste, 9 x 12", illus, 1926 .... **25.00**

Captain January, Shirley Temple **40.00**

Dubarry Was A Lady, Betty Grable .. **20.00**

Gone With The Wind, 6¼ x 9½", buff paper, brown illus, 1939 .... **50.00**

Jungle Drums of Africa, 27 x 41", 1952 Republic 12–chapter film serial **25.00**

MacBeth, 9 x 12", 16 pgs, includes film scenes and photos and biography pages of Orson Welles and stage production, 1949 .... **25.00**

O Mistress Mine, Fontanne and Lunt, 1946 .... **20.00**

The Great Dictator, Chaplin **24.00**

The Last Outpost, Cary Grant, 1935 **20.00**

The Littlest Rebel, Shirley Temple ... **40.00**

The Ten Commandments, 9 x 12", illus, 1923 .... **25.00**

Promotion Ads, exhibitor's trade magazine, graphic photos

Allegheny Uprising, 1939 John Wayne **35.00**

Dracula's Daughter **75.00**

Mysterious Island **10.00**

Pirates of the High Seas, Buster Crabbe serial **10.00**

The Crimson Trail, Buck Jones feature **10.00**

Scarf, 27 x 23", *Little Women,* MGM, 1949, silk, pictures Elizabeth Taylor, Margaret O'Brien, June Allyson, Janet Leigh, and movie scenes **125.00**

Script

El Cid, Charlton Heston, Sophia Loren, 1960, 169 pgs **60.00**

Jesse James, Tyrone Power, Henry Fonda, Randolph Scott, 1938, 182 pgs, studio copy **40.00**

Sheet Music

Casablanca, As Time Goes By, 9 x 12", 8 pgs, 1931 copyright **50.00**

Thin Man, Smoke Dreams, 9¼ x 12¼", William Powell and Myrna Loy pictures on cov, 1936 .... **15.00**

Sticker Book, *My Fair Lady,* 8½ x 11", 1965, Ottenheimer Inc **5.00**

Window Card

Around the World Under the Sea ... **10.00**

Fantastic Voyage **20.00**

For Me And My Gal, 14 x 22", 1942 MGM **100.00**

Journey To The Far Side of the Sun . **8.00**

The Errand Boy, 14 x 22", 1961 copyright, Paramount **30.00**

The Green Slime **12.00**

The Lost Continent **7.00**

Wild, Wild Planet **9.00**
Umbrella, *The Wizard of Oz* **32.00**

MOVIE PERSONALITIES

Collecting Hints: Focus on one star. Today, the four most popular stars are Humphrey Bogart, Clark Gable, Jean Harlow, and Marilyn Monroe. Many of the stars of the silent era are being overlooked by the modern collector. Nostalgia appears to be a key to the star on which a person focuses.

Remember that stars have big support staffs. Not all autograph items were or are signed by the star directly. Signatures should be checked carefully against a known original.

Many stars had fan clubs and the fans tended to hold on to the materials they assembled. The collector should be prepared to hunt and do research. A great deal of material rests in private hands.

History: The star system and Hollywood are synonymous. The studios spent elaborate sums of money promoting their stars. Chaplin, Valentino, and Pickford gave way to Garbo and Gable.

The movie magazine was a key vehicle in the promotion. *Motion Picture, Movie Weekly, Motion Picture World,* and *Photoplay,* are just a few examples of this genre. *Photoplay* was the most sensational.

The film star had no private life and individual cults grew up around many of them. By the 1970s the star system of the 1930s and 1940s had lost its luster. The popularity of stars is much shorter lived today.

References: Tony Fusco, *The Official Identification and Price Guide To Posters,* House of Collectibles, 1990; John Hegenberger, *Collector's Guide to Treasures from the Silver Screen,* Wallace Homestead, 1991; Leslie Halliwell, *The Filmgoer's Companion,* Avon, 1978; Ephraim Katz, *The Film Encyclopedia,* Perigee Books, 1979; Leonard Maltin (ed.), *TV Movies and Video Guide,* New American Library, 1987; John R. Warren, *Warren's Movie Poster Price Guide,* Overstreet Publications, 1986; Dian Zillner, *Hollywood Collectibles,* Schiffer Publishing, 1991.

Periodicals: *Big Reel,* Route 3, P. O. Box 83, Madison, NC 27025; *Classic Images,* P. O. Box 4077, Davenport, IA 52808; *Movie Collectors' World,* P. O. Box 309, Fraser, MI 48026; *Nostalgia World,* P. O. Box 231, New Haven, CT 06473.

Collectors' Club: Studio Collectors Club, P. O. Box 1566, Apple Valley, CA 92307.

See: Autographs, Magazines, Movie Memorabilia, and Posters.

Game, Polly Pickles The Great Movie Game, A Burlesque, Queen of the Movies, Parker Brothers, $50.00.

Bogart, Humphrey, sheet music, *Someday, I'll Meet You Again,* 4 pgs, words and music, black and white photo with Michele Morgan on pink montage background, 1944 copyright ... **23.00**
Chan, Charlie
  Autograph, photo, Sidney Toler, matted **175.00**
  Card game, Sidney Toler graphic on box, complete, 1939 .... **30.00**
  Game, The Great Charlie Chan Detective Mystery Game, Milton Bradley, 1937 .... **125.00**
Chaplin, Charlie
  Book, *The Charlie Chaplin Book,* 6½ x 12½", Samuel Gabriel Sons, 1916 copyright **40.00**
  Figure, 8", leather, stuffed, natural tan, inked black portrait image, c1920 .... **48.00**
  Mirror, 1¾ x 2¾", pocket, celluloid, black and white photo, Hartsook Photo inscription, 1920s **100.00**
  Puppet, paper, diecut, jointed, full color, marked "Germany," c1920 **35.00**
Coogan, Jackie
  Muffler, 6 x 42", striped, orig box with Coogan wearing muffler around neck, late 1920s, early 1930s **25.00**
Crosby, Bing
  Coloring Book **35.00**
  Stationery, 7¼ x 10½", blue letterhead, thank you message, dated Aug 14, 1934 .... **48.00**
Davis, Bette, paper doll, Merrill #4816, includes 40 pcs clothing, 1942 .... **35.00**
Diller, Phyllis, pin, jeweled, photo, autographed, matted, from "Traveling Saleslady" **35.00**
Fairbanks, Douglas Sr, tablet, 6 x 9", white cov, marked "Picture Land Stars—Douglas Fairbanks," c1920 ... **15.00**
Fields, WC
  Cookie Jar, 11" h, figural, ceramic,

marked "USA" and "153" on bottom 25.00

Doll, Centennial, Effanbee, MIB, 1980 .... 100.00

Figurine, 7", bisque, "Made in Taiwan" sticker on bottom 28.00

Garbo, Greta, puzzle, black and white portrait, boxed, 1920–30 .... 50.00

Garland, Judy, photo, Dorothy and Good Queen, twenty Munchkin autographs 75.00

Grable, Betty, paper doll, Merrill, #1558, three dolls, includes 65 pcs clothing, 1951 .... 45.00

Hayworth, Rita, paper doll book, 10¾ x 12½", Saalfield #1529, full color portrait illus of Hayworth wearing Carmen dress, unused 100.00

Heston, Charlton, autograph, 8 x 10", black and white photo, bold black ink signature, mid 1950s 25.00

Hope, Bob, coloring book, 11 x 14", Saalfield, unused 16.50

Lamarr, Hedy, paper doll, Saalfield, #2600, 1951 .... 28.00

Laurel and Hardy
  Coloring Fun Kit, Transogram, Larry Harmon Pictures Corp copyright, 1962, unused 25.00
  Game, Transogram, 1962 copyright 40.00
  Mask, pr, paper, caricature face, uncut, c1966 .... 25.00
  Planter, 4¼" h, china, caricature portraits, marked "Japan" 100.00
  Puppet, 11", Oliver Hardy, fabric body, soft vinyl head, orig attached tag, Knickerbocker Toys copyright 1966 .... 25.00
  Salt and Pepper Shaker, pr, china, 4" h Laurel, 3" h Hardy, includes 4" white tray, Beswick of England ... 100.00

Leigh, Vivien
  Perfume, Scarlett O'Hara Perfume, figural, glass vial extends under skirt to removable wood head 100.00
  Photo, 5½ x 7", sepia matte, orig mailing envelope 15.00

Lewis, Jerry
  Movie Card, 14 x 22", The Errand Boy, full color photo, red and blue lettering, white background, 1961 copyright 25.00
  Puppet, 9" h, hand, fabric, soft vinyl head, c1950 .... 50.00

MacDonald, Jeanette
  Coloring Book, Jeanette MacDonald Costume parade, 10¼ x 15", Merril Book, 1941 .... 18.00
  Portrait, 8 x 10", autographed, funeral announcement 65.00

Mitchum, Robert, photo, 5 x 7", black and white, low gloss, bold blue ink

"To Lila, Thank You, Bob Mitchum" signature 50.00

Monroe, Marilyn
  Magazine, Life, 1959 .... 35.00
  Tray, tip, 4⅛" d, litho metal, full color photo, red ground, mahogany rim, 1950s 38.00

Pickford, Mary, photograph, color frame, autographed 12.00

Rooney, Mickey, paint book, 10 x 15", Merrill, 1940 .... 40.00

Tin, Gloria Swanson, Art Deco styling, marked "Beautebox/Canco," 7½" d, $65.00.

Swanson, Gloria, magazine cover, Quick, 1950 .... 20.00

Taylor, Elizabeth, photo, 7¾ x 10", black and white, blue ink signature "Best Wishes Elizabeth Taylor Warner," 8–20–79 date on bottom margin 25.00

Three Stooges
  Colorforms Set, MIB, 1959 .... 200.00
  Coloring Set, 18 7 x 9" sheets, ten unsharpened colored pencils, plastic sharpener, orig package, Colorforms Toy, 1959 .... 200.00
  Flicker Ring, Curly, 1950s 9.00

Valentino, Rudolph
  Figure, Swiss metal, jointed, riding outfit, high boots, SABA 300.00
  Sheet Music, Respectfully Dedicated to Rudolph Valentino, 9 x 12", brown and white, 1932 .... 22.00

Wayne, John
  Exhibit Card, 3½ x 5½", blue tone photo, 1940s 10.00
  Magazine, Look, Oct 6, 1942, full color front cover photo, three pg movie review 24.00
  Tablet, 5½ x 9", color photo cov, 1950s 23.00

West, Mae

Photo, 9 x 12", black and white, simulated black and white frame, Lux Soap premium, mid 1930s, "Belle Of The Nineties" title on reverse . **25.00**

Statue, 15", chalk plaster, painted, 1930–40 .... **60.00**

MOXIE

Collecting Hints: A general rule is the older the Moxie item, the higher the price. Due to the vagaries of the Moxie Company's various managements, some recent items have acquired value. A large, 16 page, multicolored brochure published in 1929 by the soon defunct Moxie Company of America is one example. The short lived New Moxie venture made New Moxie bottles scarce. "The Great New Taste" debacle of the late 1960s was not successful. Its dimpled bottles are unknown to many Moxie collectors.

Moxie items, especially those associated with Ted Williams, have risen dramatically in value. Baseball collectors are constantly outbidding Moxie collectors for the Williams' advertising items for Moxie and for Ted's Root Beer items. Lately, Moxie has been marketed in other soda–pop bottles, even beer bottles. For more information write Don Wortham, 179 Orchard Drive, Pittsburgh, PA 15235.

History: At the height of its popularity, 1920 to 1940, Moxie was distributed in approximately 36 states and even outsold Coca–Cola in many. It became so popular that the word "moxie," meaning nervy, became part of the American language.

Moxie is the oldest continuously produced soft drink in the United States, celebrating its 100th anniversary in 1984. It originated as Moxie Nerve Food, a nostrum concocted by Dr. Augustin Thompson from Union, Maine. It was first produced in Lowell, Massachusetts.

Moxie's fame is due in large part to the promotion efforts of Frank Morton Archer, an intrepid entrepreneur armed with charisma, wizardry, and a magnificent imagination. With a genius for showmanship and prophesying profits galore, Archer uncorked an advertising phenomenon by blazing a trail with eye catching advertising vehicles and new benchmarks in unabashed barnstorming.

Bottle wagons were replaced by horseless carriages. Some folks called cars "Moxies," since the first automobile they saw had MOXIE lettered on its side. Next, Archer mounted a saddled, dummy pony in the sidecar of a motorcycle and put his TNT Cowboy Outfit on the road. He followed with an even more amazing machine—a dummy horse mounted on an automobile chassis driven from the horse's saddle.

Scarcely an event occurred in the first half of the 20th century which Archer did not exploit for Moxie. It was not by accident that the well remembered Uncle Sam poster, "I Want You For The U. S. Army," closely resembled another that already was familiar to the public—a steely–eyed Moxie man pointing at his viewers and commanding them to "Drink Moxie."

Moxie continues today, remaining especially popular in the New England area. A mountain of memorabilia surrounds the Moxie legend, much of which its aficionados claim are superior to Coke's both in quality and investment potential.

There are many firms which attempted to play upon the Moxie name. During the late 1920s the Moxie Company published a 64–page pamphlet entitled *This Book About Substitution* which contained "A Little History of Many Big Cases." Among the names imitative of Moxie were: Proxie, Hoxie, Noxie, Noxie Nerve Tonic, Nox-all, Nerv–E–Za, Non–Tox, Appetizer, Visner, Puro, Nickletone, Neurene, Nerve Food (East India, Excelsior, Imperial, Standard), Miller, Manola, Modox, Rixie, Toxie, two Canadian Moxies and several others. Since only a limited amount of each spurious product was produced and many imitative bottles destroyed "whether full or empty" by court order, those which remain are eagerly sought by collectors.

References: Q. David Bowers, *The Moxie Encyclopedia*, Vestal Press, 1985; Frank N. Potter, *The Book of Moxie*, Collector Books, 1987; Frank N. Potter, *The Moxie Mystique—The Word, The Drink, The Collectible,* published by author, 1981.

Museums: Clark's Trading Post, North Woodstock, NH; Mathews Museum of Main Heritage, Union, ME.

REPRODUCTION ALERT: Modern Moxie items are being produced and sold by Kennebec Fruit Company, 2 Main Street, Lisbon Falls, ME 04252.

Advertising, thermometer, litho tin, 12 x 9³⁄₁₆", $750.00.

Ashtray, ceramic, white, Moxie man,
three notches 25.00
Belt Buckle, bronze finish 17.50
Book
The TNT Cowboy, Archer, 1919, pur-
ple cover, 81 pgs 125.00
This Book About Substitution Law,
1919, Vol I 100.00
Bottle
Diet Moxie, emb neck, paper label . 15.00
Foxy Moxie, green, dumbbell shape,
fox label, 1950s 50.00
Moxie
10 oz, clear, dimpled, ACL
"Moxie," 1960s 30.00
26 oz, green tint, emb high shoul-
der 7.50
Moxie Nerve Food, emb "Lowell,
Mass," clear 22.50
New Moxie, ACL, 7 oz 10.00
Pureoxia, green 10.00
Bottle Case, wood
Moxie, "It's Always A Pleasure,"
holds 12 bottles 20.00
Moxie Nerve Food, twelve bottles, no
hand holes 35.00
Wheels or runners, wheelbarrows,
carts, sleds 50.00
Bottle Carrying Bag, paper
Kid Moxie, 6 bottle, 7 oz 7.00
Moxie/Pureoxia, 3 bottle, 26 oz, red
semicircles 6.50
Bottle Hangers, paper and cardboard
Attached Moxie shoulder patch 5.00
Bottle Cap drawing, 6 for 37¢ 2.00
Crown upper left, 10 oz bottle, king
size 6.00
The 3 Moxie–teers, 3 bottle, 7 oz .. 6.00
Bottle Opener
Moxie/Pureoxia, wire, straight handle 2.50
Moxieland, red, slide–out 15.00
Bowl
Cereal 20.00
Soup 25.00
Bumper Sticker
I've Got Moxie, red and orange, black
lettering 5.00
What this Country Needs Is Plenty of
Moxie 2.00
Butter Dish, cov 60.00
Calendar, 1962, Old Fashion Moxie .. 5.00
Clicker, marked "Mfg by Whitehead &
Hoag Co" 50.00
Clock
Mantel, Moxie man 275.00
Pendulum, wall, banjo shape 500.00
Plastic, lighted, round 17.50
Clothing
Cap, historic, Moxie Festivals 10.00
Mitten, pr 8.00
Scarf 10.00
Sweatshirt 18.00

T shirt, historic, Moxie Festivals 15.00
Cuff Links, pr 25.00
Cup and Saucer 20.00
Egg Cup, large 50.00
Glass
Flared top, red band 12.50
Frosted label, syrup line 17.50

Hat, fabric, $8.50.

Ice Pick and Opener, "Moxie 5¢ The
Best Drink in the World" 44.00
Lap Board, Moxie/Pureoxia 10.00
Mirror, purse size, Zodiac signs 8.00
Mug, ceramic 20.00
Napkin, boy and dog 20.00
Novelty, Hitchy Koo, carved head 250.00
Pendant, SS 100.00
Pinback Button
Moxie man, pointing 25.00
Uncle Sam's hat 35.00
Pitcher, small 65.00
Plate
Dinner 25.00
Luncheon 25.00
Platter 35.00
Playing Cards, Moxie man 6.50
Post Card, two children with cutouts
and sign 27.50
Poster
Bathing Beauty, white swimsuit, pa-
per 150.00
Bottle, cardboard, diecut 20.00
Drink Moxie, 21 x 35", squarecut,
cardboard, corrugated 7.50
Let's Get Acquainted, six–pack 5¢,
squarecut, cardboard 9.00
Moxie League, baseball offer, paper 20.00
Record
Moxie song, Gennet, sung by Arthur
Fields, 10", 78 rpm, 1921 .... 50.00
Radio Spots, Kasper–Gordon, 12",
World War II 75.00
Serving Tray, Moxie Centennial, 1984 . 35.00
Sheet Music, Moxie Song, one–step,
1921 .... 10.00
Sign
Drink Moxie 100%, octagonal, diecut 75.00
Pureoxia, squarecut, red oval on rec-
tangle 75.00
Yes! We Sell Moxie, Moxie Nerve
Food, diecut, round, "X" 200.00

Sugar, cov	**60.00**
Tape	
Cassette, Moxie Monarch NuGrape Co	**25.00**
Open Reel, Mad about Moxie, jingles, 1967	**25.00**
Thermometer	
New England's Own Soft Drink, white	**7.50**
Remember Those Days, metal, round, orange	**20.00**
Ya Gotta Have Moxie, yellow, kid boxer	**25.00**
Tip Tray, girl's face	**100.00**
Tray	
Boy's face, glass	**325.00**
Our Idol, Moxie man	**175.00**

MUSIC BOXES

Collecting Hints: Any figurine or box–shaped object has the potential for insertion of a music box. The following list of music boxes deals with objects in which the music box is secondary to the piece. Antique music boxes are covered in *Warman's Antiques And Their Prices.*

Collectors often tend to focus on one tune, trying to collect all the variety of ways it is used. Others concentrate on a musical toy form, such as dolls or teddy bears. A popular item is the musical jewel box, prevalent during the 1880 to 1930 period.

History: The insertion of a small music box into toys and other products dates back to the 18th century. Initially these were limited to the children of the aristocracy; but the mass production of music boxes in the late 19th century made them available to everyone.

The music box toy enjoyed greater popularity in Europe than in America. Some of the finest examples are of European craftsmanship. After World War II there was an influx of cheap music box toys from the Far East. The popularity of the musical toy suffered as people reacted negatively to these inferior products.

Reference: *The Official Price Guide To Music Collectibles, Sixth Edition,* House of Collectibles, 1986.

Collectors' Club: Musical Box Society International, R. D. #3, Box 205, Morgantown, IN 46160.

Museums: Bellms Car and Music of Yesterday, Sarasota, FL; Lockwood Matthews Mansion, Norwalk, CT.

Ballerina, 9", bisque, glass eyes, cylinder base, French	**300.00**
Bank, plastic, Gorham	
Acrobat, 7½", green	**18.00**
Cyclist, 7½", red	**18.00**

Waiting For Santa, Norman Rockwell Museum, 7½ x 5½ x 5¼", $50.00.

Barrel organ, 5½", Ohio Art	**5.00**
Bear, hand carved	**65.00**
Bird, figural, ceramic	
Cardinal, 6½"	**18.00**
Dove, 6¼"	**15.00**
Owl, 6"	**20.00**
Box	
1¼ x 4¼ x 3½", Thoren's cylinder, grained wood case plays Bicycle Built for Two	**45.00**
2½", Santa, white, plays Jingle Bells	**8.00**
2½", snowman and lady, red, plays Frosty the Snowman	**8.00**
2½ x 3½ x 6½", leather, porcelain plaque painting of five mallards on cov	**70.00**
3 x 3 x 5", Manivelle, three tunes, litho on cov, children feeding swan, tune sheet on bottom, Swiss	**80.00**
Children on Merry Go Round, 7¾", wood, figures move, plays Around the World in 80 Days	**22.00**
Children on See Saw, 7", wood, figures move in time to music	**20.00**
Christmas Tree Stand, revolving, Germany	**65.00**
Church, 4 x 6", tin, hand crank, Germany	**125.00**
Cigar holder, 15", wood and brass	**75.00**
Clown, 5½", plastic, dome Gorham	**18.00**
Coffee Grinder shape, 3"	**30.00**
Dog, 12", Nipper, ceramic	**45.00**
Doll	
Drum Major, 15", blue uniform, plays Cecile	**100.00**
Sammy Kay, 11", composition, sways	**65.00**
Dove, figural, ceramic	**18.00**

Easter Egg, tin	15.00
Kitten with ball, 5½", ceramic	18.00
Lamp, night, 6½", merry–go–round, c1950	30.00
Man, leaning against lamp post, cast iron, plays How Dry I Am, New York City souvenir	18.00
Merry–Go–Round, three horses and riders, 1904	45.00
Mess Cart, two horses, tin, painted	30.00
Phonograph, 5¾ x 3¼ x 3¼", miniature, upright, wind-up, Swiss	78.00

Powder Box

3½ x 4¼", metal, silver, litho cov, c1940	25.00
4½", enamel, floral, c1950	38.00

Snowball, glass, wood base

Frosty the Snowman, 5", red base	10.00
Mr and Mrs Santa, 5", green base	10.00
Santa and Rudolph, 5", green base	10.00
Statue, Elvis Presley on music box base, plays Love Me Tender	60.00
Stein, 5", porcelain, diamond dec	35.00

Toy

Bear, hand carved, spin with hand	65.00
Chimp, jolly	35.00
Clock, Hickory Dickory, Mattel, 1952	28.00
Ferris Wheel, moving, cardboard, c1940, MIB	18.00
Santa Claus, 14", head moves	35.00
Three Little Pigs, Jaymar	48.00

NAPKIN RINGS

Collecting Hints: Concentrate on napkin rings of unusual design or shape. This is one collectible which still can be used on a daily basis. However, check for the proper cleaning and care methods for the type of material you have. Many celluloid items have been ruined by storage in too dry an area or by washing in too hot water.

An engraved initial or other personalizing mark detracts, rather than adds value to a napkin ring. Many collectors and dealers have these marks removed professionally if it will not harm the ring.

History: Napkin rings enjoyed a prominent role on the American dinnertable during most of the 19th and early 20th centuries. Figural napkin rings were used in the upper class households. However, a vast majority of people used the simple napkin ring.

The shape does not mean that the decorative motif could not be elegant. Engraving, relief designs, and carving turned the simple ring into works of art. When cast metal and molded plastic became popular, shaped rings, especially for children, were introduced.

The arrival of inexpensive paper products, fast and frozen foods, and the quickened pace of American society reduced American's concern for elegant daily dining. The napkin ring has almost disappeared from the dining table.

Akro Agate, green and white swirl	6.00
Bakelite, hexagonal, red, yellow, and green, orig box, set of 6	24.00
Bisque, 2 x 3", cat, marked "Japan"	20.00
Brass, 1⅛", emb leaf, dog, and dragon design	15.00
Bronze, bulldog, right paw raised, glass eyes, hammered ring	50.00

Celluloid

Round, grape motif, emb dec	10.00
Scottie Dog	15.00
Child's, nursery rhyme figures, SS	25.00
Cloisonne, multicolored dec, set of 6	100.00

Cut Glass

Brilliant cutting	75.00
Harvard pattern	75.00
Hobstar and bow tie fans	85.00
Thistle pattern	45.00
Gilt Metal, Detroit souvenir	18.00

Ivory, carved

Dragon, black eyes	50.00
Fish and birds, 2"	45.00
Milk Glass, triangular	30.00

Nippon

Figural, owl on tree stump, 4" h, Wreath mark	375.00
Florals, glossy finish, rising sun mark	55.00
Multicolored jewels, heavy gold dec, turquoise ground, maple leaf mark	65.00

Noritake

Art Deco, orig box, pr	75.00
Floral, butterfly	15.00
Onion Meissen	25.00
Papier Mache, green	2.50

Pattern Glass

Diamond Point, 1" w	18.00
Hobstar and Fan	35.00
Pewter, dragon	20.00
Pot Metal, Brownie, Palmer Cox	35.00
R S Germany, green, pink roses, white snowballs	45.00
Sabino, birds, opal	45.00

Scrimshaw, carved ivory

Floral dec	45.00
Stalking lion	50.00

Shell

Band, encrusted with tiny shells	12.00
Souvenir, Atlantic City, 1895	28.00

Silver Plate

Bow shape	25.00
Cat, glass eyes, Victorian	100.00
Dog in house, Meriden	65.00
Fox chasing bird	75.00
Kangaroo, 1¾ x 2¼"	50.00
Rabbit	45.00
Two boys holding ring on backs	125.00

Sterling Silver

Art Nouveau design, 1½"	30.00

Sterling silver, monogrammed, hall-marked "SSMC," 1⅝" d, $35.00.

Flowers and leaves, engraved and dated	25.00
Kitten and ring, rect base, Reed and Barton	60.00
Knight standing beside ring, round base, Babcock & Co	40.00
Monogrammed, 1⅜"	35.00
Wood, hand carved, leaves	15.00

NEW MARTINSVILLE VIKING

Collecting Hints: New Martinsville glass predating 1935 appears in a wide variety of colors. Later glass was only made in crystal, blue, ruby, and pink.

Look for cocktail, beverage, liquor, vanity, smoking and console sets. Amusing figures of barnyard and sea animals, dogs, and bears were produced. Both Rainbow Art Glass and Viking glass are handmade and have a paper label. Rainbow Art Glass pieces are beautifully colored and the animal figures are more abstract in design than New Martinsville. Viking makes plain, colored, cut and etched tableware, novelties, gift items. Viking began making black glass in 1979.

History: The New Martinsville Glass Manufacturing Company, founded in 1901, took its name from its West Virginia location. Early products were opal glass decorative ware and utilitarian items. Later productions were pressed crystal tableware with flashed-on ruby or gold decorations. In the 1920s innovative color and designs made vanity, liquor, and smoker sets popular. Dinner sets in patterns such as Radiance, Moondrops, and Dancing Girl, as well as new colors, cuttings and etchings were produced. The '40s brought black glass formed into perfume bottles, bowls with swan handles and flower bowls. In 1944 the company was sold and reorganized as the Viking Glass Company.

The Rainbow Art Glass Company, Huntington, West Virginia, was established in 1942 by Henry Manus, a Dutch immigrant. This company produced small, hand fashioned animals and decorative ware of opal, spatter, cased and crackle glass. Rainbow Art Glass also decorated for other companies. In the early 1970s, Viking acquired Rainbow Art Glass Company and continued the production of the small animals.

Reference: Hazel Marie Weatherman, *Colored Glassware of the Depression Era, Book 2,* Glassworks, Inc., 1982.

Salt and pepper shakers, pr, Muranese, 3½" h, $48.00.

Animal		
	Elephant	75.00
	Polar Bear	45.00
	Rooster, large	80.00
	Squirrel	45.00
	Swan	
	5¼", cobalt blue	32.00
	10", crystal body, ruby neck	65.00
Ashtray		
	Fish, 4"	10.00
	Skillet, 5"	12.00
Basket, crystal, sq, 14"		25.00
Bicentennial Plate		15.00
Bonbon, Janice, crystal		18.50
Bookends, pr, crystal		
	Nautilus Shell	35.00
	Police Dog	55.00
	Starfish	50.00
	Wolfhound	55.00
Bowl, Radiance, 13" d, ruby		65.00
Butter Dish, Radiance, crystal, sterling silver overlay		100.00
Candlesticks, pr, Hostmaster, cobalt blue, sterling silver trim, 8½" h		35.00
Candy Dish, cov, orange, pedestal, orig Viking label, 8" h		8.50
Cheese and Cracker Set, Prelude		85.00
Compote, Radiance, crystal, sterling base, 11"		70.00
Creamer and Sugar, Janice, light blue		65.00
Cup and Saucer, Hostmaster, ruby		12.00

Decanter, Moondrops, pink, 10" h	25.00
Goblet	
Hostmaster, cobalt blue, 6¼"	20.00
Mt Vernon, cobalt blue	18.50
Prelude, crystal, etched	22.00
Ice Bucket, Janice, forest green	40.00
Iced Tea Tumbler, Prelude	10.00
Luncheon Set, Janice, blue, twelve	
luncheon plates, cups, and saucers,	
two serving plates	245.00
Perfume, triangle, green frosted, silver	
trimmed dauber	40.00
Powder Jar	
Cinderella Coach, crystal	25.00
Diamond, three toes, frosted, laven-	
der celluloid lid	11.00
Triangle, green frosted	15.00
Plate	
Florentine, 9" d	12.00
Meadow Wreath, 11" d	15.00
Moondrops, 9½" d, pink	10.00
Punch Bowl, Radiance, crystal, 14" d .	115.00
Relish, Radiance, amber, 5 x 8¼"	20.00
Salt and Pepper Shakers, pr, Radiance,	
amber	48.00
Sugar, cov, Florentine	12.00
Tumbler	
Hostmaster, cobalt blue	8.50
Moondrops, ruby	12.00
Vase	
Cornucopia, crystal, 6" h	20.00
Morning Dove, 9" h	42.00
Radiance, 10" h	
Amber, etched	55.00
Ruby	65.00

NEWSPAPERS, HEADLINE EDITIONS

Collecting Hints: All newspapers must be complete with a minimal amount of chipping and cracking. The post–1880 newsprint is made of wood pulp and deteriorates quickly without proper care. Pre–1880 newsprint was composed of cotton and rag fiber and has survived much better than its wood pulp counterpart.

Front pages only of 20th century newspapers command about 60% of the value for the entire issue, since the primary use for these papers is display. Pre–20th century issues are collectible only if complete, as banner headlines were rarely used. These papers tend to run between four and eight pages.

Major city issues are preferable, although any newspaper providing a dramatic headline is collectible. Banner headlines, those extending completely across the paper, are most desirable. Also desirable are those from the city in which the event happened and command a substantial premium over the prices listed. Complete series col-

lections carry a premium as well, such as all 20th century election reports, etc.

Twentieth century newspapers are easily stored. Issues should be placed flat in polyethylene bags, or acid free folders that are slightly larger than the paper, and kept from high humidity and direct sunlight.

Although not as commonly found, newspapers from the 17th through the 19th century are highly collectible, particularly those from the Revolutionary War, War of 1812, Civil War, and those reporting Indian and "desperado" events.

Two of the most commonly reprinted papers are the *Ulster County Gazette,* of January 4, 1800, dealing with Washington's death and the *N.Y. Herald,* of April 15, 1865, dealing with Lincoln's death. If you have either of these papers, chances are you have a reprint.

History: America's first successful newspaper was *The Boston Newsletter,* founded in 1704. The newspaper industry grew rapidly, experiencing its golden age in the early 20th century. Within the last decade many great evening papers have ceased publication, and many local papers have been purchased by the large chains.

Collecting headline edition newspapers has become popular during the last twenty years, largely because of the decorative value of the headlines. Also, individuals like to collect newspapers related to the great events which they have witnessed or which have been romanticized through the movies, television, and other media, especially those reporting events, the Old West, and the gangster era.

Reference: Harold Evans, *Front Page History,* Salem House, 1984; Robert F. Karolevitz, *From Quill To Computer: The Story of America's Community Newspapers,* National Newspaper Foundation, 1985.

Periodical: *PCM (Paper Collector's Marketplace),* P.O. Box 127, Scandinavia, WI 54977.

Advisor: Tim Hughes.

Note: The listing concentrates on newspapers of the 20th century. The date given is the date of the event itself. The newspaper coverage usually appeared the following day.

1865, April 15, Lincoln Assassinated ..	375.00
1869, May 9, Transcontinental Railroad	
Completed	80.00
1886, September 4, Geronimo Surren-	
ders	85.00
1886, October 28, Statue Of Liberty	
Dedicated	55.00
1898, February 15, The Maine Is Sunk	50.00
1898, front page, Spanish–American	
war battle reports	10.00
1901, September 6, McKinley Is Shot .	45.00
1901, September 14, McKinley Dies ..	40.00
1903, December 17, Wright Bros Fly .	255.00

1906, April 18, San Francisco Earthquake **60.00**
1912, April 15, Titanic Sunk **185.00**
1914, August 15, Panama Canal Opened **20.00**
1915, May 7, Lusitania Sunk **130.00**
1917, March 5, Woodrow Wilson Inaugurated **15.00**
1917–18, front page, World War II reports **8.00**
1918, November 11, Armistice Signed **65.00**
1919, June 28, Peace Treaty Signed .. **25.00**
1920, August 26, 19th Amendment Ratified (women vote) **25.00**
1921, July 14, Sacco & Vanzette Convicted **10.00**
1922, August 2, Alexander Graham Bell Dies **8.00**
1927, May 21, Lindbergh Flies The Atlantic **40.00**
1929, February 14, St Valentine's Day Massacre **80.00**
1929, October 28, Stock Market Crash **70.00**
1932, March 1, Lindbergh Baby Kidnapped **20.00**
1932, November 8, Franklin Roosevelt Elected **18.00**
1933, January 5, Calvin Coolidge Dies **15.00**
1933, December 5, Prohibition Repealed **27.00**
1934, May 23, Bonnie & Clyde Killed **85.00**
1934, July 22, Dillinger Shot & Killed . **45.00**
1937, May 6, Hindenberg Crashes ... **50.00**
1941, June 21, Hitler Wars On Russia **14.00**
1941, December 7, Japan Attacks Pearl Harbor **45.00**
1941, December 11, U S Declares War On Italy & Germany **20.00**
1942–45, major World War II headline **8.00**
1945, May 7, War In Europe Ends **27.00**
1945, August 6, First Atomic Bomb Dropped In Japan **27.00**
1945, August 14, Japan Surrenders—War Over **28.00**
1948, November 3, "Dewey Defeats Truman," Chicago Tribune Error Headline **650.00**
1953, July 26, Truce Signed Ending The Korean War **15.00**
1955, April 18, Albert Einstein dies ... **10.00**
1955, May 17, Court Bans School Segregation **15.00**
1958, June 30, Alaska Joins The Union **20.00**
1959, March 12, Hawaii Joins The Union **22.00**
1963, November 22, Kennedy Assassinated **27.00**
1968, April 5, Martin Luther King Slain **18.00**
1969, July 20, Man Walks On The Moon **23.00**
1977, August 16, Elvis Presley Dies ... **12.00**
1986, January 28, Challenger Explodes **5.00**

Man Walks On Moon, July 21, 1969, New York Times, $23.00.

1989, November 10, Berlin Wall Falls **5.00**
1991, January 16, War In The Gulf Begins **5.00**
1991, February 28, Gulf Cease Fire Declared **5.00**

NILOAK POTTERY

Collecting Hints: Mission Ware pottery is characterized by swirling layers of browns, blues, reds and cream. Very few pieces are glazed on both the outside and inside. Usually only the interior is glazed.

History: Niloak Pottery was made near Benton, Arkansas. Charles Dean Hyten, the founder of this pottery, experimented with the native clay and tried to preserve the natural colors. By 1911 he had perfected a method that produced this effect. The result was the popular Mission Ware. The wares were marked Niloak, which is Kaolin, the type of fine porcelain clay used, spelled backwards.

After a devasting fire the pottery was rebuilt and named Eagle Pottery. This factory included the space to add a novelty pottery line which was introduced in 1929. This line continued until 1934 and usually bears the name Hywood-Niloak. After 1934 the name Hywood was dropped from the mark. Mr. Hyten left the pottery in 1941. In 1946 the operation closed.

Ashtray
    Hat, figural, blue **7.50**
    Round, Mission Ware **40.00**
Bowl, 8 x 3", chocolate brown, tan, and turquoise swirls, Mission Ware **60.00**
Candlestick, 9" h, Mission Ware **125.00**
Cornucopia
    3", light pink **5.00**
    7", light blue **6.50**
Creamer and Sugar, rose glaze, Hywood line **24.00**

Planter, wishing well, dusty rose, 7¼" h, $12.00.

Figure

Canoe, 7½", white matte	30.00
Frog	20.00
Polar Bear, white matte	35.00
Paperweight, rabbit, orig paper label	30.00

Pitcher

3¼", yellow	12.00
7", dark green glaze	14.00

Planter

Bear, 3", tan	18.00
Camel, 3"	22.00
Cannon, 3", blue	15.00
Deer, 8", pink and blue, matte	30.00
Duck, 5", pink and blue	18.00
Elephant, 6", white	20.00
Fox, 4", red	20.00
Frog, 4", seated on lily pad	35.00
Kangaroo, 5", white, brown accents	10.00
Log, 7", white	15.00
Parrot, 5", white, orange accents	12.00
Policeman and Donkey, 5", blue	25.00
Rabbit, 3", green	12.00
Squirrel, 6", light blue shading to tan	25.00
Swallow, 2", green	8.50
Swan, 3", light brown	10.00
Wishing Well, 7¼", dusty rose	12.00
Toothpick Holder, Mission Ware	35.00

Vase

4" h, Mission Ware, red, cream, and brown	36.00
6" h, bud, leaf, Hywood line, blue glaze	18.00
7" h, maroon, handles	15.00
7½" h, bud, Mission Ware	85.00
8" h	
Aqua–green glaze, Hywood line, orig paper label	18.00
Gray shaded to pink ground, four flowers	28.00
8¼" h, swirl, Mission Ware	95.00
9¼" h, swirl, Mission Ware	100.00

Wall Pocket, 6" h, Mission Ware, brown, blue, and tan **75.00**

NIPPON CHINA, 1891–1921

Collecting Hints: Examine each item carefully. Try not to purchase items with chips, cracks, hairlines, spiderwebs, or that have been restored. The condition of each item, in relationship to selling price, should be taken into consideration.

Also try to avoid buying sets which are incomplete. No matter what people say, you do not easily find the lid which is missing from your humidor, the cup and saucer to complete your chocolate set or the creamer to match your sugar bowl. Know what constitutes a complete set.

Beginning collectors should try to purchase only Nippon marked items. Learn the difference between the authentic marks and the reproduction marks. There are unmarked pieces from the Nippon era, but the purchase of these items should be put off until the collector has a commanding knowledge of Nippon.

History: Nippon, Japanese hand painted porcelain, was made for export between the years 1891 and 1921.

In October 1891, the McKinley Tariff Act was passed by Congress, proclaiming that "All articles of foreign manufacture, be stamped, branded, or labeled, and all packages containing such or their imported articles, shall, respectively, be marked, stamped, branded, or labeled in legible English words, so as to indicate the country of their origin; and unless so marked, stamped, branded, or labeled they shall not be admitted to entry."

The Japanese chose to use "Nippon," which is the English equivalent of Japan, as their marking.

The McKinley Tariff Act also set rules and regulations on the marking system, stating that "all articles of foreign manufacture which are capable of being marked without injury shall be marked with the country of origin in legible English words and marking shall be nearly indelible and permanent as the nature of the article will permit." Paper labels were accepted. In the case of small articles shipped together, only the inside and outside packages were marked with the country of origin.

In 1921 the Government reversed its position and decided that "Nippon" was no longer in compliance with the law. "After examination into the history and derivation of the word 'Nippon' and its treatment by lexicographers of recognized standing, the department is constrained to the conclusion that 'Nippon' is a Japanese word, the English equivalent of which is 'Japan,' and the weight of authority does not support the earlier view that the word has become incorporated into the English language." All Japanese items now had to be marked "Japan," thus ending the Nippon era.

Nippon marks were applied by two methods—an under the glaze decal sticker or direct imprinting.

There are over 221 recorded Nippon backstamps or marks known to collectors today. The three most readily found and widely recognized are the "M" in Wreath, Maple Leaf, and Rising Sun marks.

The majority of all marks are found in three color variations: green, blue, and magenta. The color of the mark indicates the quality of the porcelain used: green denotes first grade quality of porcelain; blue denotes second grade; and magenta denotes third grade.

References: Gene Loendorf, *Nippon Hand Painted China*, McGrew Color Graphics, 1975; Joan Van Patten, *The Collector's Encyclopedia Of Nippon Porcelain, Series One*, Collector Books, 1979; Joan Van Patten, *The Collector's Encyclopedia Of Nippon Porcelain, Series Two*, Collector Books, 1982; Joan Van Patten, *The Collector's Encyclopedia of Nippon Porcelain, Series Three*, Collector Book, 1985.

Collectors' Clubs: Great Lakes Nippon Collectors Club, Rt. 2, Box 81, Peotone, IL 60468; International Nippon Collectors Club, P.O. Box 88, Jericho, NY 11753; Long Island Nippon Collectors Club, P.O. Box 88, Jericho, NY 11753; New England Nippon Collectors Club, 22 Mill Pond, North Andover, MA 01845.

Advisor: Kathy Wojciechowski.

REPRODUCTION ALERT: Most so-called Nippon reproductions do not even resemble the Nippon era wares, but there is a "Nippon" backstamp found on them, thus fooling many collectors and dealers.

The pattern most often found and on the biggest variety of pieces is "Wildflower." These items have a bisque finish, outside edges are highlighted with gold, and pink to lavender flower blossoms are used as the decoration. All wares in this pattern are marked with a bogus hourglass in a wreath mark.

The "Green Mist" pattern items are reminiscent of Limoges pieces in shape, have a bisque finish, a light to medium green background, pink flowers, and gold trim. The mark found on these pieces is similar to the familiar Nippon rising sun mark except that the rays are connected rather than open as in the genuine mark.

The "Antique Rose" pattern is one of the newest patterns being reproduced. This can be found in a variety of shapes and bears the bogus maple leaf mark, which is almost a duplicate of the genuine mark except that it is much larger in size.

Most reproduction Nippon wares are manufactured in Japan and have a "Nippon" mark of some type under the glaze and a small paper label on the bottom saying "Made in Japan." Dealers buy wholesale from the importing firms. First, they discard the shipping boxes, then the paper label, resulting in a genuine marked "Nippon" item for the market.

Berry set, master 9" bowl, six 5⅛" bowls, handpainted blue mark, $18.00.

Ashtray, 5" l, attached matchbox holder, white, hp flowers	75.00
Basket	
4" l, pale blue tiny flowers outlined in gold, gold handle, rising sun mark	48.00
6½", Tree of Life design, center handle, green M in wreath mark	55.00
7" l, bisque, scenic, lake, trees, and cottage, beaded handle, wreath mark	75.00
Berry Set, master 10" d berry bowl, five matching small bowls, scenic of lake, trees, and boat, sunset colors, crown mark	65.00
Bowl	
6½" d, cream ground, bunches of purple violets, wreath mark	48.00
7" d, three open handles, two large pink peonies in center, cobalt trim, gold overlay design, wreath mark	45.00
8½", sq, Oriental floral dec	50.00
Cake Set, serving plate and six matching smaller plates, pink floral on ivory ground, brown trim with blue beading, rising sun mark	125.00
Calling Card Tray, 7¾ x 6", mythical dragon and bird, blue maple leaf mark	50.00
Candlesticks, 8", Dutch woman chasing child, bunnies and chicks on borders, pr	150.00
Candy Dish, scalloped edge, twisted handle, pink roses, gold trim	50.00
Celery Dish	
12" l, Indian in native boat, leaf mark	50.00

13" l, white ground, gold overlay designs, wreath mark **65.00**

Cheese and Cracker Dish, two tiers, pink and gold roses **65.00**

Child's Feeding Dish

7" d, children, birds, and animals, rising sun mark **75.00**

8" d, child playing with dog, rising sun mark **70.00**

Chocolate Pot, 9½" h, melon ribbed, cream ground, groups of red and pink roses **75.00**

Cigarette Box, 4½" l, farm scene on lid, floral dec on base, wreath mark **175.00**

Compote, jelly, underplate, blue and yellow ground, overall rose dec **75.00**

Condiment Set, 4½" d tray, salt and pepper shakers and mustard jar, white ground, top band of tiny pink and mauve flowers, Crown mark **50.00**

Cracker Jar, 4½ x 8½", squatty, bisque finish, large green and white floral design, gold handles and trim, wreath mark **115.00**

Creamer and Sugar, white ground, top and bottom bands of yellow flowers, TEOH mark **50.00**

Cup and Saucer

Bisque, scenic, cottage and forest, Shinzo mark **36.00**

Gold overlay design, gold beading, forest green ground, pedestal base cup, maple leaf mark **85.00**

Dish

4¾" sq, bisque, scenic, cottage and trees, lavender and blue, wreath mark **25.00**

7" h, ftd, large red roses, gold tracings, cobalt and gold trim, wreath mark **65.00**

8 x 5½", gaudy floral, mauve, green, and gold design with roses, open pierced handles, unmarked **45.00**

Doll, bisque

4½", painted on clothes, policeman uniform, incised mark **135.00**

6" h, movable arms, painted on green dress, brown hair, scarf, incised mark **120.00**

Dresser Set, tray, powder box, hair receiver, and pin tray, white ground with bands of pink and blue flowers, green foliage, rising sun mark **125.00**

Egg Cup, child's, children playing, green M in wreath mark **35.00**

Hair Receiver

4½", sq, tiny top and bottom bands of lavender violets, wreath mark . **45.00**

5", black ground, yellow and red roses, blue maple leaf mark **60.00**

Hatpin Holder, 3½" h, white ground,

top and bottom bands of light and dark pink roses, gold trim **55.00**

Inkwell, 2¾" w, scenic, man on camel, wreath mark **125.00**

Jam Jar, floral dec, gold trim **48.00**

Mayonnaise Set, ftd bowl, underplate, ladle, cream ground, orange poppies outlined in gold, R. C. mark, 3 pcs . **100.00**

Mug, 4¾" h, light green and lavender ground, center Christmas deer, bunches of holly under deer's neck, heavy moriage trim, wreath mark ... **125.00**

Mustard Jar, bisque, scenic, sailing ships, shades of orange, brown beaded rim, wreath mark **60.00**

Napkin Ring, turquoise ground, multicolored jewels, heavy gold dec, maple leaf mark **65.00**

Nappy

5" sq, green roses, overall gold lacing, beading, blue maple leaf mark ... **25.00**

7", pink and green, heavy gold lacing, blue maple leaf mark **35.00**

Pin Box, 2" d, Geisha girls and pagodas, Royal Nishiki mark **50.00**

Pincushion, bisque, doll shape, movable arms, pale green satin dress, blue bow molded into hair, incised "Nippon" **175.00**

Pitcher, 5", milk, scalloped shape, cobalt, large red flowers, elaborate gold overall design **130.00**

Plaque

9", large multicolored roses, leaves outlined in black, heavy gold border **150.00**

10", river and forest scene, wreath mark **175.00**

Plate

7", bisque, scenic, cottage, TEOH mark **30.00**

7½", pale green, hp orange poppies, green foliage, gold trim, green M in wreath mark **48.00**

9", heavy red florals, wreath mark .. **65.00**

9¼", handled, white, hp scenic landscape, gold and black, gold trim, green M in wreath mark **32.00**

Powder Box, cov, 5½", hunt scene ... **100.00**

Ramekin, band of colorful bunches of grapes and grape leaves, maple leaf mark **35.00**

Reamer, pitcher, gold and floral trim, rising sun mark **125.00**

Relish Dish, 7¾", center handle, white and pink roses dec **36.00**

Ring Tree, gold, beading, green M in wreath mark **45.00**

Salt and Pepper Shakers, pr, white ground, top band of pastel florals, rising sun mark **35.00**

Shaving Mug, white ground, red and green floral, rising sun mark **45.00**
Spoonholder, 7¾" w, yellow florals, black and green leaves **35.00**
Stamp Box, geometric black stripes, inside tray with two compartments, wreath mark **85.00**
Sugar Shaker, wild rose floral pattern, gold dec handle, cobalt and gold tracings trim, wreath mark **75.00**
Tea Set, teapot, creamer, and sugar, white ground, large flying blue birds, gold handles, finials, and rims, wreath mark **100.00**
Tea Strainer, white ground, wide cobalt bands, heavy pink and red roses, gold trim, wreath mark **55.00**
Tea Tile, 5¼" d, large windmill, cottage, and lake, shades of brown, wreath mark **70.00**
Teapot, bisque, scenic, cottage, lake, and trees, earth tones, TEOH mark . **50.00**
Toothpick Holder, 2½", fruit and floral dec, rising sun mark **65.00**
Tray, 9½ x 6¾", cream, hp orange poppies, blue rising sun mark **48.00**
Vase
  6", handled, scenic cartouche front, overall beading, sgd **100.00**
  6¼", bisque and glossy finish, blue ground, floral, pink and burgundy roses, outlined in gold, wreath mark **60.00**
  8½", large clipper ship, earth tones, wide jeweled and enameled top and bottom bands, gold loop handles, wreath mark **200.00**
  9¼", shaded ground, woodland and water scene, gold handles, green M in wreath mark **150.00**
  12", serpentine handle, scenic, English countryside and lake, black top and bottom **175.00**
Wall Pocket, 6", molded dog, floral dec **95.00**

NORITAKE AZALEA CHINA

Collecting Hints: There are several backstamps on the Azalea pattern of Noritake China. The approximate dates are:

Prior to 1921: Blue rising sun, printed "Hand painted NIPPON"
1921–1923: Green wreath with M, printed "Noritake, Hand painted, Made in Japan"
1923–1930s: Green wreath with M, printed "Noritake, Hand painted, Made in Japan 19322"
1925–1930s: Red wreath with M, printed "Noritake, Hand painted, Made in Japan 19322"
1935–1940: Red azalea sprig, printed "Noritake Azalea Patt., Hand painted, Japan No. 19322/252622"

Most of the saucers and underplates do not have a backstamp, except those stamped "Azalea 19322/252622."

Most collectors assemble sets and are not concerned with specific marks. Those concentrating on specific marks, particularly the NIPPON one, may pay more. There presently are individuals who offer replacement service.

History: The Azalea pattern of Noritake China, made of fine china, was produced first in the early 1900s. Each piece was hand painted. The individuality of each artist makes it almost impossible to find two pieces with identical painting.

In the early 1900s the Larkin Company of Buffalo, New York, sold many household items to the American public through their catalog (similar to the Sears, Roebuck catalog). In the 1924 Larkin catalog a basic, Azalea pattern, serving set was advertised. The set included the larger coffee cups with the blue rising sun backstamp.

Two forces came together in the 1920s to make the Azalea pattern of Noritake China one of the most popular household patterns in this century. First, the Larkin Company initiated their "Larkin Plan," in which housewives could sign up to become "Larkin Secretaries." Each Larkin Secretary formed a small neighborhood group of five or more women who would buy Larkin products for their homes. The Larkin Secretary earned premiums based on the volume of sales she obtained. Household items, including Azalea china, could then be purchased either for cash or premiums.

Second, many households in the 1920s could not afford a complete set of fine china in a single purchase. The Larkin Club Plan enabled them to obtain items in the Azalea pattern one or a few at a time.

Over the years, and to provide more enticements, additional pieces, such as the nut/fruit shell shaped bowl, candy jar, and child's tea set were added. Glassware, originally classified as crystal, was introduced in the 1930s but was not well received.

It became somewhat of a status symbol to "own a set of Azalea." The Azalea pattern china advertisement in the 1931 Larkin catalog claimed, "Our Most Popular China."

Some Azalea pieces were advertised for sale in the Larkin catalogs for 19 consecutive years, while others were advertised for only 4 or 5 years. These latter pieces are more scarce, and more sought after by collectors, resulting in a faster appreciation in value.

The ultimate goals of most serious collectors are the child's tea set, which we believe was advertised in only two Larkin Fall catalogs, and the so-called salesmen's samples, which were never advertised for sale.

The Larkin Company ceased operations as a distributor in 1945. Due to the quality and popularity of the Azalea pattern, this beautiful china remains cherished and highly collectible.

Reference: Larkin catalogs from 1916 through 1941.

Note: The Larkin catalog numbers are given in parentheses behind each listing. If arranged numerically, you will notice gaps in the numbering. For example, numbers 41 through 53 are missing. The "Scenic" pattern, presently called "Tree in the Meadow," of Noritake China also was popular during this same time period. Many of the missing Azalea numbers were assigned to the Scenic pattern.

Teapot, #400, marked "Handpainted, Japan," 5½" h, $425.00

CHINA

#2, cup and saucer	14.00
#3, mayonnaise set, regular, 3 pcs	25.00
#4, plate, tea, 7½"	7.50
#7, creamer and sugar, cov	30.00
#8, plate, bread and butter, 6¼"	8.00
#9, sauce dish	8.00
#10, cake plate, 9¾"	25.00
#12, salad bowl, round, 10"	28.00
#13, plate, dinner, 9¾"	18.00
#14, condiment set, 5 pcs	35.00
#15, teapot, regular	75.00
#16, casserole, cov, regular	60.00
#17, platter, 14"	40.00
#18, relish, oval, 8½"	12.50
#39, refreshment set, 2 pcs	35.00
#40, gravy boat	28.00
#54, butter tub, insert	25.00
#56, platter, 12"	40.00
#97, syrup pitcher, underplate	70.00
#98, plate, breakfast, 8½"	15.00
#99, bread tray, 12"	35.00

#100, milk jug	150.00
#101, vegetable bowl, oval, 10½"	30.00
#119, relish, four sections, 10"	100.00
#120, egg cup	32.00
#121, lemon plate	12.00
#123, creamer and sugar, open	65.00
#124, bouillon cup and saucer, 5¼"	15.00
#125, jam jar set, 3 pcs	115.00
#126, salt and pepper shakers, pr, 2½"	10.00
#169, tile, 6"	30.00
#170, compote	60.00
#172, vegetable bowl, oval, 9½ x 6¾"	32.00
#182, coffeepot	450.00
#183, demitasse cup and saucer	110.00
#184, bonbon dish, 6¼"	35.00
#185, grapefruit bowl, 4½"	100.00
#186, platter, 16"	300.00
#187, vase, fan, ftd	120.00
#189, spoon holder, 8"	65.00
#190, cruet bottle	170.00
#191, mustard jar	45.00
#192, toothpick holder	75.00
#193, basket	120.00
#194, relish, oval, 7¼"	45.00
#253, child's set, 15 pcs	1,500.00
#310, bowl, deep	42.00
#311, platter, 10¼"	150.00
#312, butter chip, 3¼"	65.00
#313, tobacco jar, cov	500.00
#314, cheese dish, cov, 6¼"	85.00
#315, plate, sq, 7⅝"	40.00
#338, plate, grill, 10¼"	120.00
#372, casserole, cov, gold finial	400.00
#400, teapot, gold finial	425.00
#401, creamer and sugar, lid, gold finial	100.00
#439, bowl, divided	225.00
#444, celery dish, 10"	240.00
#452, vase, bulbous	900.00
#453, mayonnaise set, scalloped, 3 pcs	400.00

GLASSWARE, HAND PAINTED

#11, fruit bowl, 8½"	40.00
#111, cheese and cracker set, 2 pcs	50.00
#112, tray, 10"	40.00
#113, compote, 10"	48.00
#114, candlestick holders, pr	32.00
#124, cake plate, 10½"	38.00

NUTCRACKERS

Collecting Hints: The most popular modern nutcrackers are the military and civilian figures which are made in Germany. These are collected primarily for show and not for practical use.

Nutcracker design responded to each decorating phase through the 1950s. The figural nutcrackers of the Art Deco and Art Nouveau periods are much in demand. Concentrating on 19th century models results in a display of cast iron ingenuity. These nutcrackers were largely utilitarian and meant to be used.

Several cast iron animal models have been reproduced. Signs of heavy use is one method to tell an older model.

History: Nuts keep well for long periods, up to two years, and have served as a dessert or additive to cakes, pies, bread, etc., since the colonial period. Americans most favorite nuts are walnuts, chestnuts, pecans, and almonds.

The first nutcrackers were crude hammers or a club device. The challenge was to find a cracker that would crack the shell but leave the nut intact. By the mid-19th century cast iron nutcrackers in animal shapes appeared. Usually the nut was placed in the jaw section of the animal and the tail pressed as the lever to crack the nut.

The 19th and early 20th century patent records abound with nutcracker inventions. In 1916 a lever-operated cracker which could be clamped to the table was patented as the Home Nut Cracker, St. Louis, Missouri. Perhaps one of the most durable designs was patented on January 28, 1889, and sold as the Quakenbush plated model. This hand model was plain at the top where the grip teeth were located and had twist-style handles on the lower half of each arm with the arms ending in an acorn finial.

Parrot, cast iron, painted, green, red, and gold, 10" l, $30.00.

Alligator, cast iron, 6" l	25.00
Bear, wood, figural, glass eyes	100.00
Bird, wood, figural, curved neck, long tail, worn finish	100.00
Cat, brass, figural, 4½"	40.00
Chicken head, wood, glass eyes, 1850s, 7"	90.00
Dickens, brass, figural	40.00
Dog, cast iron, figural, bronzed	45.00
Dragon, brass, figural	50.00
Elephant, cast iron, figural, painted	145.00
Fish, brass, figural, 5"	35.00
Jester, brass, figural	75.00
Lady's legs, brass, figural	35.00
Lion, brass, figural head	35.00
Man's head, wood, figural, carved mustache	115.00

Monkey, wood, figural, painted eyes	80.00
Parrot, cast iron, figural	30.00
Pliers type, silver plate, orig picks, c1909	35.00
Rooster, brass, figural	40.00
Squirrel, cast iron, figural,	48.00
Table top, cast iron, Home, screw mechanism, long lever, 1915 patent	25.00
Toy Soldier, wood, figural, red, black, and white paint, furry beard, German	75.00
Twist and screw type, cast iron, nickel plated, palm size, 5"	15.00
Wolf, cast metal, 1920 patent	60.00

OCCUPIED JAPAN

Collecting Hints: Buyers should be aware that a rubber stamp can be used to mark "Occupied Japan" on the base of objects. Finger nail polish remover can be used to test a mark. An original mark will remain since it is under the glaze; fake marks will disappear. This procedure should not be used on unglazed pieces. Your eye is your best key to identifying a bad mark on an unglazed item.

Damaged pieces have little value unless the piece is extremely rare. Focus on quality pieces which are made well and nicely decorated. There are many inferior examples.

History: At the end of World War II, the Japanese economy was devastated. To secure needed hard currency, the Japanese pottery industry produced thousands of figurines and other knick knacks for export. From the beginning of American occupation until April 28, 1952, these objects were marked "Japan," "Made in Japan," "Occupied Japan," and "Made in Occupied Japan." Only pieces marked with the last two designations are of strong interest to Occupied Japan collectors. The first two marks also were used at other time periods.

The variety of products is endless—ashtrays, dinnerware, lamps, planters, souvenir items, toys, vases, etc. Initially it was the figurines which attracted the largest number of collectors; today many collectors focus on non–figurine material.

References: Gene Florence, *The Collector's Encyclopedia Of Occupied Japan Collectibles*, *1st Series* (1976), *2nd Series* (1979), *3rd Series* (1987), and *4th Series* (1990), Collector Books.

Collectors' Clubs: Occupied Japan Collectors Club, 18309 Faysmith Ave., Torrance, CA 90504; O. J. Club, 29 Freeborn Street, Newport, RI 02840.

Ashtray	
Brown Elephant	15.00
Square, 4", porcelain, green floral	12.00
Baby Bootie, 4", bisque, white	10.00

Bell, Dutch girl, 4½" 10.00
Bookends, colonial couple, pr 15.00
Box, 2¼", heart shape, floral dec cov,
    gold trim 10.00
Candelabra, 6", bisque, lotus, double . 30.00
Candlestick, 3½", colonial lady 15.00
Cane, bamboo 20.00
Canister Set 75.00
Celery Tray, 8½", rect, fan shaped han-
    dles 8.00
Child's Dishes, Blue Willow two place
    settings 35.00
Christmas Ornament, star shape 10.00
Cigarette Box
    Floral, blue and white 10.00
    Floral and Scroll, 3¾ x 4 x 5",
        multicolor, gold dec 12.00
Cigarette Lighter
    Cornucopia, metal 15.00
    Donkey 18.00
    Pencil 12.00
Coffeepot, lid, blue and ivory plaid,
    green apples, white dots 8.00
Cologne Bottle, glass, pink 18.00
Compote, candy, metal 5.00
Cuckoo Clock 100.00
Demitasse Cup and Saucer
    Flamingoes, pink 23.00
    Floral, pink and lavender 8.00
    Swirl pattern, cobalt blue and white 10.00
Doll
    Celluloid, kewpie–type, blue suit ... 25.00
    Composition, 3" h, blue dress, red
        shoes 28.00
Fan
    Bamboo, mother–of–pearl, silk tassel 25.00
    Paper, folding, striped, red, white,
        and blue 5.00
Figure
    Baker's Man 35.00
    Ballerina, lace skirt, bisque 22.50
    Bird, 7¼" h 35.00
    Black figures, outhouse 60.00
    Boy, 4" h, playing violin, seated 12.50
    Coach, 8¼" h, two horses 75.00
    Colonial Girl, 6¼" h, holding skirt .. 18.00
    Colonial Man and Woman, 7½" h, pr 45.00
    Dog, 4", brown 15.00
    Flamingo, marked Lefton 35.00
    Frog, 3½" 4.50
    Indian, turban, 6" h, pr 35.00
    Lady, 6⅛" h, Moriyama 25.00
    Man and Woman, wood, carved, pr 45.00
    Musicians, pr 75.00
    Oriental Girl, 10" h, gold trim 28.00
    Shoeshine Boy 60.00
    Skier 30.00
    Squaw, 5" h 12.00
    Swan, 3¾" h, wings spread 10.00
    Three Monkeys, ceramastone 24.00
Fish, celluloid 12.00
Fish Bowl Ornament, 3 pc 25.00

Ice Bucket, tongs, black, floral pattern 25.00
Incense Burner, cov, blue floral, gold
    trim, 3 pcs 35.00
Jar, cov, strawberry shape 10.00
Jewelry Box
    Metal, twelve drawers 12.00
    Wood 10.00
Lamp, 11" h, bisque, Colonial couple . 55.00
Lobster Dish, cov 17.00
Mask, Halloween, paper 12.00
Match Safe, bisque, Andrea 45.00
Mug, 4", brown, purple grapes 10.00
Nut Dish, 6", metal, floral border 5.00
Pencil Holder, cat shape 4.00
Pin Cushion, tin, red velvet top, mirror
    inside lid 20.00
Pin Tray, metal, souvenir, NY City 4.00
Pitcher, 4½" h, windmill motif 17.50
Planter
    Dog, 2½" h 8.00
    Donkey, pulling wagon, 4¾" l 10.00
    Lamb 6.00
    Stork, 7½" 35.00
    Zebra 6.00
Plaque, flying duck 15.00
Plate
    Maple Leaf, white and gold 8.00
    Portrait, cupid, two maidens 125.00
Platter, 14", oval, Blue Willow 18.00
Pocket Mirror 12.00
Reamer, 3¾" h, 2 pcs, strawberry shape,
    red, green leaves and handle 65.00
Reindeer, celluloid, white, pink accents 12.00
Rice Bowl, 6", porcelain, emb dragon 25.00
Salt and Pepper Shakers, pr
    Angelfish 15.00
    Gondola, 5½" l, 3 pc, shakers form
        cab, hull base, hp, floral dec, MK 23.00
    Red Squirrels 15.00
    Tomato 6.00
Shamrock, 1½", paper and wire 1.00
Shelf Sitter, musicians, seated, pr 40.00

Toby, ceramic, black hat, yellow coat,
green vest, brown pants, marked, 3" h,
$12.00.

Tape Measure, pig, celluloid, pink ...	**15.00**
Teapot, lid	
Brown	**10.00**
Floral, 6½" h, brown ground	**22.00**
Tomato	**45.00**
Tea Set	
Doll size, porcelain, hp, cream lustre, nine pcs, MIB	**55.00**
Hand painted, teapot, two handle sugar, creamer, 1945, 3 pcs	**55.00**
Toby Mug	
Indian	**35.00**
Man, 2½" h, black hat, blue collar .	**15.00**
Uncle Sam	**25.00**
Toby Pitcher, parson, 7½" h	**70.00**
Toothpick Holder, donkey, pulling cart	**4.00**
Toy	
Clever Bear, windup, orig box	**75.00**
Convertible Car, driver	**95.00**
Ice Cream Vendor, 4" h, litho tin cart, celluloid boy, windup, 1930s	**100.00**
Ragtime Band, boxed	**45.00**
Sancho Panza, sitting on donkey, 6" h, celluloid, windup, orig box, 1940s	**185.00**
Seal, windup, orig box	**65.00**
Sedan, blue	**75.00**
Tray, 5 x 3", metal, souvenir, Chicago	**6.00**
Vase	
Cat	**4.00**
Cherub, playing tuba, bud, 3¾" h ..	**14.00**
Lamb	**4.00**
Landscape scene, 4½" h	**12.00**
Snake Charmer	**25.00**
Wall Pocket, 5½ x 4", flying goose ...	**25.00**

OCEAN LINER COLLECTIBLES

Collecting Hints: Don't concentrate only on ships of American registry. Many collectors do favor material from only one liner or ship line. Objects associated with ships involved in disasters, such as the *Titanic*, often command higher prices.

History: Transoceanic travel falls into two distinct periods—the era of the great Clipper ships and the era of the diesel powered ocean liners. The latter craft reached their "Golden Age" in the period between 1900 and 1940.

An ocean liner was a city unto itself. Many had their own printing rooms to produce a wealth of daily memorabilia. Companies such as Cunard, Holland-America, and others encouraged passengers to acquire souvenirs with the company logo and ship name. Word-of-mouth was a principal form of advertising.

Certain ships acquired a unique mystique. The *Queen Elizabeth*, *Queen Mary*, and *United States* became symbols of elegance and style. Today the cruise ship dominates the world of the ocean liner.

Collectors' Clubs: Steamship Historical Society of America, Inc., 345 Blackstone Boulevard, Hall Building, Providence, RI 02906; Titanic Historical Society, P. O. Box 53, Indian Orchard, MA 01151-0053.

Ashtray, M/V Freeport, black ground, white decal, 8 x 3½", $7.50.

Ashtray	
Matson Lines, plastic, flag shape, green, center circle with red "M" on white ground	**25.00**
Princess, glass, Swedish	**10.00**
Baggage Tag, *Canadian Pacific*, engraved vessel, c1930	**3.00**
Bill of Lading, *SS Illinois*, Philadelphia, 1874	**22.00**
Book	
Rigby's Book of Model Ships, punch–out, 1953 copyright, unused	**50.00**
Wreck of the Titanic, Everett, 320 pgs	**30.00**
Booklet, White Star Line, sailing list, 1933	**38.00**
Brochure, *Empress of Japan*, Transatlantic sailings, 1930–31	**8.00**
Card, White Star Line, *Georgic* ship illus and log abstract on reverse, 1933 ..	**20.00**
Creamer, New England Steamship Co .	**35.00**
Key Chain, *Carnival*, lucite case, ship photo	**2.50**
Magazine, *Canadian Pacific Princess*, travel type, 16 pgs	**3.50**
Letterhead, *Empress of Australia I*, Round the World Cruise, 1929–30 .	**2.00**
Log, Lykes Bros 1938 Ripley SS, New Orleans to Calcutta	**8.00**
Matchbook Cover, Holland-American Lines	**1.75**
Menu	
Holland–American, 1963	**5.00**
Johnson Line	**10.00**
Matson Line	**7.00**
SS City of Omaha, Christmas 1940 .	**5.00**
SS France, final voyage	**10.00**
SS Oakwood, American Export Lines, Christmas, 1939	**5.00**
SS United States, 8½ x 11", Aug 25, 1952, full color cov illus, red, white, and blue cord binding	**8.00**

USS Maryland, 5½ x 8½", Christmas day, 1927 .... **10.00**

Mirror

American Line, celluloid, ship illus . **25.00**

Augustus, steamship, pocket, emb .. **52.00**

Passenger List

Aquitaina, 1937 .... **15.00**

SS Leviathan, 1924 .... **15.00**

Transylvania II, Anchor Line, June 22, 1938 .... **18.00**

Pennant, 27" l, *Caribe,* felt, blue, white ship **3.00**

Photograph

Carnival, aerial view, color **1.50**

Duchess of Bedford, black and white **4.00**

Pictorial Layout, *Mauretania,* 33 x 32", cruise ship, diagrams and pictures .. **30.00**

Playing Cards, American President Lines, plastic, color ship on each card, double deck, orig case **27.50**

Poster

Queen Elizabeth II, 24 x 36", ship leaving skyline for Europe titled "For Once In Your Life, Live," post war gray hull **22.00**

SS Washington, 25 x30", 1933 ..... **150.00**

Radio Message Form, Cunard White Star Line, transmits to and from *RMS Queen Mary,* 8½ x 9½" folder, unused **7.50**

Sign, *Costa Line,* plastic, "Please do not Disturb" **2.00**

Stereo Card, ship *Texas,* 1898 .... **20.00**

Stock Certificate, Cunard Steam Ship Co, Ltd **7.50**

Ticket Folio, Cunard Line, c1928 ..... **50.00**

Tin

Bremen, coffee, *Bremen* at sea on front panel, 1930s **50.00**

Queen Mary, candy, full color *Queen Mary* illus on lid, 1930s **40.00**

Toothpick Holder, Swedish–American Line **15.00**

History: Owls have existed on earth for over sixty million years. They have been used as a decorative motif since before Christ. An owl was used with Athena on an ancient Greek coin.

Every culture has superstitions surrounding the owl. Some believe the owl represents good luck, others view it as an evil omen. The owl has remained a popular theme in Halloween material.

Of course, the owl's wisdom is often attached to scholarly pursuits. Expanding this theme, the National Park Service uses "Woodsey" to "Give A Hoot, Don't Pollute."

References: Allan W. Eckert and Karl E. Karalus, *The Owls Of North America,* Doubleday & Company, Inc. 1974; Faith Medlin, *Centuries Of Owls In Art And The Written Word,* Silvermine Publishers Incorporated, 1967; Heimo Mikkola, *Owls Of Europe,* Buteo Books, 1983; Jozefa Stuart, *The Magic Of Owls,* Walker Publishing Co., Inc., 1977; Krystyna Weinstein, *Owls, Owls: Fantastical Fowls,* Buteo Books, 1985.

Periodical: *The Owl's Nest,* Howards Alphanumeric, P. O. Box 5491, Fresno, CA 93755.

Collectors' Club: Russell's Owl Collector's Club, P. O. Box 1292, Bandon, OR 97411.

REPRODUCTION ALERT: Recently, reproduction fruit crate labels with an owl motif have been seen at several antiques and collectibles dealers who wholesale to dealers. These labels are appearing at flea markets and in shops where they are being passed as originals.

The Westmoreland molds have been sold to several different manufacturers. The owl sitting on two books is being reissued with the original "W" still on top of the books. The three owl plate mold also was sold. As of fall 1987, no reproductions have been spotted.

The Imperial owl molds have also found new owners. Again, no reproductions have been seen, but chances are good they will appear in the near future.

OWL COLLECTIBLES

Collecting Hints: If you collect the "creature of the night" or the "wise old owl," any page of this book might conceivably contain an owl-related object since the owl theme can be found in hundreds of collectible categories. A sampling of these categories includes advertising trade cards, books, buttons, postcards, etc. But, don't confine yourself to these categories. Let your imagination be your guide.

Don't confine yourself just to old or antique owls. Owl figurines, owl themes on limited edition collectors' plates, and handcrafted items from modern artisans are plentiful. There are many examples available in every price range.

Salt and pepper shakers, pr, metal, yellow eyes, 3" h, 2¼" w, $75.00.

Ashtray, 5½" w, tricorn, Nippon, green mark **165.00**

Bank

    Brass, glass eyes **65.00**

    Tin, 2 x 2½", child size, owl pictured on side **50.00**

Book

    Lavine, Sigmund, *Wonders Of The Owl*, Dodd, Mead & Co, NY, 1971 **1.50**

    Rome, Clair, *An Owl Came To Stay*, Crown Pub, NY, 1980 .... **3.25**

    Sparks and Soper, *Owls: Their Natural & Unnatural History*, Taplinger Pub, NY, 1970 .... **5.75**

Bookends, pr, brass, Frankart **35.00**

Calendar Plate, owl on open book, 1912, Berlin, NE **25.00**

Calling Card Tray, 8½ x 7", quadruple plate, emb music staff and "Should Owl's Acquaintance Be Forgot," two owls sitting on back of tray **85.00**

Candy Container, glass, owl on branch **50.00**

Clock

    China, wind–up, eyes move, 1970s, Shanghai **20.00**

    Metal, 2" dial, 1–day, Bentley, German **25.00**

    Wood, 6½" h, hand carved **110.00**

Cookie Jar, 11" h, cream, one winking eye, Shawnee **45.00**

Drugstore Tin, 4¼" d, 3" h, Theatrical Cold Cream, Owl Drug Co, orange ground, black print **24.50**

Fairy Lamp, double faced figure, 3⅜" d, 4⅛" h, pyramid size, frosted cranberry glass, lavender enameled eyes, Clarke base **200.00**

Figure

    3" h, Fenton, carnival glass **20.00**

    4" h, Mosser, carnival glass **18.00**

    5½" h, milk glass, glass eyes, souvenir of Hot Springs, SD **100.00**

    11" h, soapstone, horned owl, red–brown, Italian **24.00**

Inkwell, 8 x 4", brass, glass inset, hinged lid, pen tray, 2" owl figure **75.00**

Jelly Jar, cov, milk glass **95.00**

Jewelry, pin, blue, green, and gold enamel, amber eyes with rhinestone eye disks, pearl tail feathers **12.50**

Mask, papier mache, c1915 .... **90.00**

Match Holder

    2½" h, dark green, Wetzel Glass Co **5.00**

    8" h, 2" w, metal, hanging type **18.00**

Medal

    Bronze, Natural History Society of Montreal, 1¾", cast, owl with branch in beak **20.00**

    Metal, white, 2¼", 1890 Leeds International Exhibition, bust of Queen Victoria on one side **25.00**

Mustard Jar, milk glass, 5" h, screw top, glass insert, Atterbury, orig lid **150.00**

Napkin Ring, owl sitting on stump, Nippon **225.00**

Nightlight, figural, Noritake, sgd **425.00**

Paperweight, cast iron, owl family, two babies, plus baby in papa's arms ... **35.00**

Pitcher, yellow shading to orange, Kanawha Glass Co, 5" h, $9.00.

Pitcher

    8" h, 6" d top, pressed glass, figural **110.00**

    9½" h, semi–vitreous china. cov, Edwin M Knowles China Co **37.50**

Plate, milk glass

    6" d, three owl heads, fluted open work edge, gold paint **50.00**

    7½" d, Owl Lovers **40.00**

Ring Tree, 3¼" d, 4" h, shallow brown dish, blue lining, brown and tan owl perched on back, marked "Doulton Stoneware" **325.00**

Sheet Music

    Beautiful Ohio, owl on cover **3.50**

    The Pansy and the Owl **4.50**

    The Wise Old Owl **3.50**

Soda Bottle, blob top, 9½" h, Owl Drug Co, teal green, two wing, San Francisco **48.00**

Spillholder, wood, hand carved, owl on tree branch, red glass eyes **32.50**

Thermometer, 6" h, plaster body **75.00**

Tobacco Jar, 6¾" h, octagonal, Nippon, green mark **375.00**

Toothpick Holder **22.00**

Valentine, 15" l, girl and boy riding balloon, owl sitting on moon above, "Nobody's looking but the owl and the moon!" **8.00**

Vase

    5¾ x 3½ x 2¾", Phoenix Glass, white ground, green foliage, two coral owls on each side **90.00**

7", moriage owl, two handles, Nippon, blue maple leaf mark **235.00**
8¼", Knifewood, Weller **145.00**
12½", ruffled rim, two handles, 4 feet, marked on bottom "Royal Nishiki Nippon Hand Painted" **350.00**
Watch Fob, owl, chain made of braided human hair **125.00**
Whiskey Shot Glass, clear, Owl Drug Co, one wing **15.00**

PADEN CITY

Collecting Hints: All Paden City glass was hand-made and unmarked. The early glassware was of non–descript quality, but in the early 1930s quality improved dramatically. The cuttings were unpolished "gray cuttings," sometimes mistaken for etchings.

Paden City is noted for its colors: opal (opaque white), ebony, mulberry, Cheriglo (delicate pink), yellow, dark green (forest), crystal, amber, primrose (reddish–amber), blue, rose, and the ever popular red. No free–blown or opalescent glass was produced. Quantities of blanks were sold to decorating companies for gold and silver overlay and for etching.

History: Paden City Glass Manufacturing Co. was founded in 1916 in Paden City, West Virginia. David Fisher, formerly of the New Martinsville Glass Manufacturing Co., operated the company until his death in 1933 when his son, Samuel, became president. The additional financial burden placed on the company by the acquisition of American Glass Co. in 1949 forced Paden City to close in 1951.

Reference: Jerry Barnett, *Paden City The Color Company,* published by author, 1978.

Bowl
  Largo, 11¼" d, ruby, handled **25.00**
  Orchid, 8¾" d, cobalt blue **30.00**
  Sunset, amber, 9" d, ftd, wide etching **35.00**
Cake Stand
  Ardith, yellow, cherry etch, 11½" d, ftd **60.00**
  Black Forest, 11" d, low **60.00**
  Crow's Foot, 12" d, ruby **75.00**
Candlesticks, pr
  Callente, orange **20.00**
  Cheriglo, low **24.00**
  Garret, 8½" h, black **30.00**
Candy, cov
  Ardith etching, topaz **24.00**
  Crow's Foot, crystal, gold encrusted flowers **18.00**
  Gazebo, crystal, three part **35.00**
Champagne, Popeye & Olive, ruby ... **10.00**
Cheese and Cracker Server
  Glades, cobalt blue **45.00**

Candy Dish, amethyst, etched, dots and floral vine dec, stepped domed lid, button finial, 6⅝" h, $60.00.

SS Dreamship, blue, 12" d plate **60.00**
Cocktail Set, Hotcha Glade etch, frosted ice bucket, four ftd glasses **50.00**
Compote
  Ardith, yellow, cherry etch **55.00**
  Black Forest, 7½" d, green **55.00**
  Crow's Foot, 5" d, yellow, sq **20.00**
  Party Line, Marie cutting, 4½" d, pink, ftd, orig spoon **45.00**
Console Bowl, Ardith, yellow, 12" d .. **40.00**
Console Set, Largo, crystal, sterling trim **35.00**
Cordial, Cupid **12.00**
Creamer
  Cupid, ftd **25.00**
  Orchid, green **15.00**
Cup, Penny Line, amethyst **6.00**
Decanter, stopper, Ardith, oval, 5¾" w **95.00**
Figurine, pheasant
  Blue, shaded, 14" l **125.00**
  Crystal **55.00**
Gravy Boat and Underplate, pink, gold encrusted trim **40.00**
Goblet
  Cupid **15.00**
  Penny Line **8.00**
Ice Tub, 6" d, Nora Bird **45.00**
Mayonnaise, Secrets, crystal, 2 pc **15.00**
Pitcher, Popeye & Olive, green **25.00**
Plate
  Black Forest, 7½" d **50.00**
  Callente
    10½" d, orange **7.00**
    13" d, orange **11.00**
  Crow's Foot, amber, 9" d **9.00**
  Cupid, 10" d, green **15.00**
  Largo, 12" d, crystal, sterling trim .. **15.00**
  Penny Line, 7½" d, amethyst **5.00**

Wotta Line, 8" d, ruby	7.00
Reamer, amber, shaker type, gold trim	48.00
Relish, three part, Sunset, amber	20.00
Salt and Pepper Shakers, pr, Callente, cobalt blue	5.00

Sandwich Tray

Amy, chrome handles	20.00
Swan handle, crystal	30.00

Sherbet

Peacock Reverse	25.00
Penny Line, amethyst	5.00

Sugar, cov

Peacock Reverse, yellow, 2¾" h	40.00
Wotta Line, ruby	8.00

Tray

Gothic Garden, 9½" l, yellow, sq center	45.00
Popeye & Olive, 10½" l, green	8.00

Tumbler

Nora Bird, 4" h	25.00
Peacock Reverse, ruby	35.00

Penny Line, amethyst

3½" h, flat	6.50
5¼" h, flat	8.00

Vase

Black Forest, 6½" h, pink	45.00
Cupid, 8¼" h, pink	50.00
Orchid, 10" h, yellow	35.00
Peacock & Wild Rose, black	48.00
Utopia, green, 10½" h	125.00
Whiskey Glass, Penny Line, 2 oz, ruby	7.50

PADLOCKS

Collecting Hints: Padlocks must be more than just old and scarce to attract collector interest. They also must have some kind of appeal, e.g., historical, elaborate design, or intricate mechanism. Desirable padlocks are embossed in raised letters with the name or initial of a defunct company or railroad, a logo, an event (such as an exposition), or shapes such as a heart, figure, floral motif, or scroll design. Other desirable types include unique construction, unusual size, intricate and trick mechanism, or those made and used during the early days of old companies.

The name or initial of a manufacturer is usually just stamped on a lock. This adds to value, especially if the lock is not embossed with other identification. A lock made by a small company in the 1850s can be worth many times more than a similar lock made by a large, prolific manufacturer. There always are exceptions. For example, "Smokies" do not have much value no matter how old or scarce.

The difference in value between types of padlocks is inexplicable. The round "Lever Push Key" locks can be valued at several times more than other locks with identical embossments. Locks classified as "Story" are worth many times more than similar locks classified as "Warded."

Regardless of the value of unmarked locks, collectors are challenged by the task of identifying them. Old hardware and lock catalogs help. A comprehensive book on United States lock companies, their padlocks, and padlock construction remains to be published.

Some collectors specialize in just one type of padlock (combination, logo, etc.) or a specific manufacturer. The reason is the breadth of the field and the wealth of locks made by the 200–plus manufacturers. The Eagle Lock Co., for example, made about 400 types and variations between 1880 and 1930. The most competitive collecting is in the embossed brass locks from defunct short line railroads or the very early locks from larger railroads.

Collectors will not knowingly buy padlocks if they are repaired, cracked, corrosion pitted, damaged internally, or appreciably dented. A rare lock at a greatly reduced price can be an exception. An original key increases the value of a padlock, but other keys have no value to most collectors.

Most collectors prefer American manufactured padlocks.

History: Padlocks of all shapes and sizes were made in Europe and Asia from the 1600s. The mass production of identifiable padlocks was pioneered in the United States in the mid–1800s. Almost all padlock mechanisms were adapted from earlier door and safe lock patents.

Over 200 United States padlock manufacturers have been identified. Six of the most prolific are:

Adams & Westlake, 1857– , "Adlake" trademark started c1900, made railroad locks.

Eagle Lock Co., 1833–1976, a general line of padlocks from 1880, with padlock patent dates from 1867.

Mallory, Wheeler & Co., 1865–1910, partnership history started in 1834, predominate manufacturer of wrought iron lever (smokies) padlock.

Miller Lock Co. (D. K. Miller from 1870 to c1880, Miller Lock Co. to 1930), general line of padlocks.

Star Lock Works, 1836–1926, largest manufacturer of Scandinavian padlocks.

Yale & Towne Mfg. Co., 1884– , (Yale Lock Mfg. Co. from 1868 to 1884), started c1840 by Linus Yale, Sr., as the "Yale Lock Shop," started making padlocks c1875.

Railroad, express, and logo locks are identified with the names of the companies that bought and used them. A series of odd and heart–shaped cast-iron padlocks produced from about 1880 to 1900 with various decorative or figural embossments are called "Story Locks."

Thousands of companies had locks custom made with their names to create logo locks. Logo locks are not to be confused with locks that are embossed with the names of jobbers. This applies particularly to the round six lever push key locks. If "6–Lever" is included with the name, it is not a logo lock. Since 1827 there have been over 10,000 railroad companies in the United States, not counting trolleys and interurbans. Most of these companies used at least two types of locks; some used dozens of types.

Padlock Types: Padlocks are categorized primarily according to tradition or use: Story, Railroad, etc. The secondary listing theme is according to the type of construction. For example: if a brass lever lock is marked with a railroad name, it is called a railroad lock. Scandinavian locks have always been called "Scandinavians." "Story" locks became a common usage term in the 1970s. In the 1880s they were listed in various ways.

Reference: Franklin M. Arnall, *The Padlock Collector, Illustrations and Prices of 1,800 Padlocks of the Last 100 Years, Fifth Edition,* The Collector, 1988.

Collectors' Club: American Lock Collectors Association, 36076 Grennada, Livonia, MI 48154.

Museum: Lock Museum of America, Terryville, CT.

Advisor: Franklin M. Arnall.

REPRODUCTION ALERT: Beware of brass story locks, locks from the Middle East, railroad switch locks from Taiwan, and switch lock keys from the US Midwest. Early story locks should be embossed cast-iron. However, beware. There are excellent iron reproductions of the skull and crossbones story lock.

Screw key, trick, iron lever, and brass lever locks are being imported from the Middle East. The Taiwan switch locks are rougher and lighter in color than the old brass ones. The crudely cast new switch keys are obvious. The high quality counterfeits are expertly stamped with various railroad initials, tumbled to simulate wear, and aged with acid. They can be detected only by an expert.

Authentic railroad, express, and logo locks will have only one user name or set of initials. The size and shape will be like other locks that were in common use at the time, except for a few modified locks made for the US government.

All components of an old lock must have exactly the same color and finish. The front, back, or drop of an old lock can be expertly replaced with a reproduced part embossed with the name or initials of a railroad, express company, or other user.

Note: The prices shown are for padlocks in original condition and without keys.

Brass Lever, emb "O.V.B," $75.00.

Combination

Barrett Keyless, brass and steel, 3" h	10.00
Brass lettered dials, 1¾" w	50.00
Dot Lock, brass, 3¼" h	30.00
E Gornicec Lock Mfg Co, brass 3" h	75.00
Kultur Patent, 4 dials, 4⅜" h	100.00
Miller Lock Co, steel, 3⅛" h	8.00
Rochester, brass, round case, 2½" h	100.00
Slaymaker, laminated steel, 2⅞" h ..	10.00
Steel case, brass dial, 2¾" h	3.00
Sutton Lock Co, brass, 3" h	175.00

Commemorative

AYPEX, Alaska Yukon Pacific Exposition, 1909 Seattle, emb, steel, 3⅛" h	350.00
Dan Patch, horseshoe emb on back, iron, 2" h	125.00
Man riding a buffalo, 1901 Pan–American Exposition, emb, brass .	85.00

Lever, brass

Automatic, round, emb, 2⅛" d	10.00
Corbin, emb, 3" h	8.00
Detroit Brass Works, shackle both ends, 6¼ x 2¼"	120.00
Leader, emb, 2" h	4.00
Mercury, emb, 2¾" h	20.00
SB Co, emb, long shackle, 3" h	35.00
Tooker & Reeves, patent, 5¼" h	450.00
W Bohannon, heart shape	
1¼" h	5.00
3⅜" h	15.00
4½" h	125.00
Yale, Y & T, rect, emb	
1½" to 2" w	3.00
3" w	65.00

Lever, iron and steel

Browns Patent, heart shape, iron, 3" h	25.00
Eagle, emb, steel	
2" h	2.00
2¾" h	5.00
4⅜" h	35.00
Gold Seal, emb, steel, 2⅞" h	5.00
Heart shape, iron, 3¼" h, several manufacturers	10.00
King Korn, emb, steel, 2⅞" h	15.00
Lloyd, iron, 5¾" h	300.00
Rugby, emb, steel, 3" h	10.00

UL Co of NY, Universal Changeable Lever, iron, 3⅝" h, 2⅛" w 250.00

Yale & Towne, lion head emb on front, steel, 3" h 65.00

Lever Push Key

Champion Six Lever, emb, brass, 2¼" d 4.00

Diamond Six Lever, emb, brass 2¼" d 25.00

Empire Six Lever, emb, brass, 2¼" d 10.00

JHW Co, heart shape, brass, 1¼" h . 25.00

Miller, Six Secure Levers, iron and brass, 3½" h 2.00

SB Co, crank, emb, brass, long shackle, 3¼" h 35.00

SB Co Eight Lever, emb, brass, 2⅜" d 125.00

Lever, wrought iron (Shield, Smoke House, Smokies)

DM & Co, brass drop, 3½" h 8.00

Flower emb on brass drop, 3⅞" h .. 30.00

HB & Co, brass drop, 3½" h 12.00

M & W Co, false lower keyhole, brass drop on keyhole, 3⅞" h 35.00

WW & Co, brass drop, 3½" h 5.00

Logo

Bell System, Best 10.00

BIR, Yale 15.00

Sun Pipeline Co, emb, Yale 30.00

US Customs, American Seal Lock Co 300.00

US Forest Service, pine tree, emb, Yale 85.00

USN, Chicago Lock Co 5.00

West Baking Co, lever push key type 150.00

Pin Tumbler

Bell, #62 .... 35.00

Corbin, brass case

1½ to 2" w 1.00

3" w 60.00

Keyhole in front 25.00

Corbin, steel case 4.00

RE Co, sq, brass case 110.00

Segal, iron case 4¼" h 40.00

WB, brass 4.00

Yale

Brass case, emb 1.00

Iron case, brass panels, round ... 5.00

Railroad, G P and Signal

C & EI, brass, pin tumbler 8.00

I C RR, emb, lever push key 80.00

I C RR Commun Dept, emb, brass lever 10.00

L & N, Yale, emb, pin tumbler 20.00

P & R, emb, lever push key 125.00

So Ry Signal, emb, brass lever 50.00

Union Pacific CS–21, Roadway and Bridge, emb, brass lever 35.00

Woman's Toilet, Missouri Pacific lines, steel 40.00

Railroad, Switch, Brass Lever

CP RR of CA, stamped on back 110.00

D & RG RR, stamped on shackle ... 75.00

Erie RR, emb in panel 100.00

Wrought iron lever, shield, smoke house, emb brass drop, $12.00.

Illinois Traction System, emb in panel **125.00**

LV RR, emb in panel 175.00

MK & T RY, emb in panel 200.00

NE RR, emb on back 450.00

N & W RY Co, emb on back 35.00

Penna Co, emb in panel 80.00

STL & SF RY, stamped on back 40.00

TRRA, stamped on shackle 20.00

Union Pacific, emb in panel 40.00

UP USY Co, stamped on shackle ... 20.00

Railroad, Switch, Steel

AT & SF RY and other common railroads 4.00

CRI & P RY, A & W, laminated shackle 35.00

NC & STL, Yale, figure eight lock .. 20.00

Scandinavian

Corbin, emb, brass, 2½" h 70.00

JHW Climax, iron, 4" h 40.00

McWilliams, iron, 3⅝" h 65.00

R & E Co, iron, 2⅞" h 30.00

Star emb on bottom, iron

2¾" h 18.00

4½" h, short shackle 75.00

5¼" h, long shackle 110.00

Six Lever and Eight Lever

Electric Eight Lever, steel 20.00

Mammoth Eight Lever, steel 10.00

Quality Six Lever, Simmons, steel .. 4.00

Samson Eight Lever, brass 15.00

Steel State Six Lever, steel 4.00

Railroad, C & O Ry Co, lever push key type, $225.00.

Story, emb, cast iron
Cupid and bird emb on front, round
case **300.00**
Floral and scroll, shield or heart shape
2⅜" h **90.00**
3⅛" h **150.00**
Flowers emb on front, round case,
2⅝" h **150.00**
Skull and Crossbones, emb, floral
back **175.00**
Warded
Floral and scroll, rect case, emb, iron
or brass **12.00**
Old Glory, emb, brass case **4.00**
Samson, emb, round iron case **8.00**
Twiskee Lock & Mfg Co **40.00**
W emb on front, brass case **10.00**
Winchester, brass case with panels . **100.00**

PAPERBACK BOOKS

Collecting Hints: For collecting or investment purposes, books should be in fine or better condition because many titles are common in lesser condition as well as being less desirable. Unique items, such as paperbacks in dust jackets or in boxes, often are more valuable and desirable.

Most collections are assembled around one or more unifying themes. Some common themes are: author (Edgar Rice Burroughs, Dashiell Hammett, Louis L'Amour, Raymond Chandler, Zane Grey, William Irish, Cornell Woolrich, etc.); fictional genre (mysteries, science fiction, westerns, etc.); publisher (early Avon, Dell and Popular Library are most popular); cover artist (Frank Frazetta, R. C. M. Heade, Rudolph Belarski, Roy Krenkel, Vaughn Bode, etc.); and books with uniquely appealing graphic design (Dell mapbacks and Ace double novels).

Because large quantities of paperbacks still turn up, many collectors are cautious as they assemble their collections. Books in the highest condition grades remain uncommon. Many current dealers try to charge upper level prices for books in lesser condition, arguing that top condition is just too scarce. This argument is not valid, just self–serving.

History: Paperback volumes have existed since the 15th century. Mass–market paperback books, most popular with collectors, date from the post 1938 period. The number of mass market publishers in the 1938–50 period was much greater than today. These books exist in a variety of formats, from the standard size paperback and its shorter predecessor to odd sizes like 64 page short novels for 10¢ and 5¼" x 7½" volumes known as digests. Some books came in a dust jacket; some were boxed.

The "golden" period for paperback books was from 1939 to the late 1950s, a period generally characterized by a lurid and colorful graphic style of cover art and title lettering not unlike that of the pulp magazines. Many early paperback publishers had been or were publishers of pulps and merely moved their graphic style and many of their authors to paperbacks.

References: Kenneth Davis, *Two–Bit Culture: The Paperbacking of America,* Houghton Mifflin, 1984; Kevin Hancer, *Hancer's Price Guide to Paperback Books, Third Edition,* Wallace–Homestead, 1990; Piet Schreuders, *Paperbacks USA, A Graphic History, 1939–1959,* Blue Dolphin, 1981; Jon Warren, *The Official Price Guide to Paperbacks,* House of Collectibles, 1991.

Periodicals: *Paperback Market,* 5813 York Avenue, Edina, MN 55410.

Museum: University of Minnesota's Hess Collection of Popular Literature, Minneapolis, MN.

Note: The prices given are for books in fine condition. Divide by 3 to get the price for books in good condition; increase price by 50% for books in near mint condition.

Adventure
Anderson, Paul, *Golden Slaves,*
Avon, T–388 .... **3.00**
Burroughs, Edgar Rice, *Tarzan and
the Lost Empire,* Ace, F–169 ..... **3.60**
Chidsey, Donald Barr, *Panama Passage,* Perma Book, P–248 .... **1.75**
Fox, Gardner F., *Woman of Kali,* Gold
Medal, 438 .... **2.75**
Horner, Lance, *Rogue Roman,* Gold
Medal, T1978, cov by Frazetta ... **1.75**
Raddall, Thomas, *Roger Sudden,* Harlequin, 141 .... **4.50**
Siegel, Jerry, *High Camp Superheroes,*
Belmont, B50–695, comic book reprints from the co–creator of Superman **3.50**
Biography
Cellinie, Benvenuto, *The Autobiography of Cellini,* Bonie Book **3.20**
Martin and Miller, *The Story of Walt
Disney,* Dell, D–266 .... **3.00**
Thomas, T. T., *I, James Dean,* Popular
Library, W–400 .... **2.40**
Wright, W., *Life and Loves of Lana
Turner,* Wisdom House, 104 ..... **1.50**
Combat
Bartlett and Lay, *Twelve O'Clock
High,* Bantam, 743 .... **2.40**
Boyington, Gregory, *Baa Baa Black
Sheep,* Dell, F–88 .... **1.50**
Busch, Harold, *U–Boats at War,* Ballantine, 120 .... **3.00**
Grove, Walt, *The Wings of Eagles,*
Gold Medal, 649, tie–in with John
Wayne movie **3.60**
Tiempo, E. K., *Cry Slaughter,* Avon,
T–179 .... **1.75**

Uris, Leon, *Battle Cry*, Bantam, F–
1996 .... **1.50**

Erotica/Esoterica

Bingham, Carson, *The Gang Girls*,
Monarch, 372 .... **4.00**

Drago, Sinclair, *Women to Love*,
Novel Library, 16 .... **4.00**

Farmer, Philip Jose, *Fire and the
Night*, Regency, 118 .... **4.00**

Leem, Hannah, *Yaller Gal*, Handi–
Book, 84 .... **2.40**

Swados, Felice, *House of Fury*, Avon,
298 .... **12.00**

Thayer, Tiffany, *One Man Show*,
Avon, 327 .... **6.00**

Van Vechten, Harold, *Nigger Heaven*,
Avon, 314 .... **10.00**

Whitney, Hallan, *Backwoods Shack*,
Carnival, 943, Whitney is a pseudonym for Harry Whittington **2.40**

Woodford, Jack, *The Abortive Hussy*,
Avon, 146 .... **2.40**

Horror

Avallane, Michael, *The Coffin Things*,
Lancer, 74– 942 .... **3.20**

Bradbury, Ray, *The Autumn People*,
Ballantine, EC, comic reprints with
Frazetta cov **4.00**

Davenport, Basil (ed.), *Tales to be
Told in the Dark*, Ballantine, 380 . **2.40**

Finney, Jack, *The Body Snatchers*,
Dell, 42 .... **5.20**

Lovecraft, H. P., *Weird Shadow over
Innmouth*, Bart house, 4 .... **18.00**

Stoker, Bram, *Dracula*, Perma Book,
M–4088, tie–in with Christopher
Lee movie **4.00**

Humor

Addams, Charles, *Nightcrawlers*,
Pocket Book, 1964 .... **2.40**

Capp, Al, *L'il Abner*, Ballantine,
350K, tie–in with movie **2.40**

Cavanaugh and Weir, *Dell Book of
Jokes*, Dell, 89 .... **21.00**

Gaines, William (ed.), *The Brothers
Mad*, Ballantine, 267K **4.00**

Hatlo, Jimmy, *They'll Do It Every
Time*, Avon, 366 .... **3.60**

Kurtzman, Harvey, *Help!*, Gold
Medal, K–1485 .... **1.75**

Links, Marty, *Bobby Sox*, Popular Library, 678 .... **2.00**

Mystery

Adams, Cleve, *And Sudden Death*,
Prize Mystery, 5 .... **4.00**

Barry, Joe, *The Third Degree*, Prize
Mystery, 12 .... **4.00**

Bliss, Tip, *The Broadway Butterfly
Murders*, Checkerbook, 2 .... **15.00**

Carr, J. D., *The Four False Weapons*,
Berkley, G–91 .... **2.40**

Carter, Nick, *Death has Green Eyes*,
Vital Book, 3 .... **4.00**

Irish, William, *Bluebeard's Seventh
Wife*, Popular Library, 473 .... **6.00**

Lyon, Dana, *I'll Be Glad When You're
Dead*, Quick Reader, 132 .... **2.00**

Woolrich, Cornell, *The Black Curtain*,
Dell, 208 .... **4.20**

Non–fiction

Blackstone, Harry, *Blackstone's Tricks
Anyone Can Do* , Permabook, 15 **7.50**

Disney, Walt, *Our Friend the Atom*,
Dell, LB–117 .... **1.50**

Galus, Henry, *Unwed Mothers*, Monarch, 524, Robert Maguire cov ... **2.00**

Hershfield, Harry, *Book of Jokes*,
Avon, 65 .... **6.00**

Hynd, Alan, *We are the Public Ene-
mies*, Gold Medal, 101 .... **4.00**

Sinclair, Gordon, *Bright Path to Adventure*, Harlequin, 288 .... **3.60**

Vagts, Alfred, *Hitler's Second Army*,
Penguin, S–214 .... **2.40**

Romance

Baldwin, Faith, *Men Are Such Fools*,
Dell, 138 .... **2.40**

Bronte, Emily, *Wuthering Heights*,
Quick Reader, 122 .... **4.50**

Christian, Paula, *Edge of Twilight*,
Crest, 267 .... **3.60**

Edmonds, Walter, *The Wedding Journey*, Dell, 10¢, 6 .... **3.60**

Gaddis, Peggy, *Dr. Prescott's Secret*,
Beacon, B–302 .... **1.50**

Science Fiction

Campbell, John W., *Who Goes
There?*, Dell, D–150 .... **3.00**

Heinlein, Robert A., *Beyond this Horizon*, Signet, 1891 .... **2.00**

Hubbard, L. Ron, *Return to Tomorrow*, Ace, S–66 .... **5.00**

Kline, Otis Adelbert, *Maza of the
Moon*, Ace, F–321, Frazetta cov . **3.60**

Lafferty, R. A., *Space Chantey*, Ace
H–56, Vaughn Bode cov **2.40**

Orwell, George, *Animal Farm*, Signet, 1289 .... **4.00**

Silverberg, Robert, *Regan's Planet*,
Pyramid, F–986 .... **1.75**

Sports

DiMaggio, Joe, *Lucky to Be a Yankee*,
Bantam, 506 .... **2.40**

Robinson, Ray (ed.), *Baseball Stars of
1961*, Pyramid, G–605 .... **1.50**

Scholz, Jackson, *Fighting Coach*,
Comet, 25 .... **1.50**

Stern, Bill, *Bill Stern's Favorite Boxing
Stories*, Pocket Books, 416 ...... **2.40**

Western

Brackett, Leigh, *Rio Bravo*, Bantam,
1893, tie–in with John Wayne
movie **5.20**

Fisher, Clay, *War Bonnet*, Ballantine,
11 .... **2.00**
Grey, Zane, *Nevada*, Bantam, 3 .... **2.40**
L'amour, Louis, *Hondo*, Gold Medal,
347, tie–in with John Wayne movie **4.00**
Lehman, Paul Evan, *Range Justice*,
Star Books, 8 .... **1.40**
Robertson, Frank C., *Red Rustlers*,
Readers Choice Library, 24 ...... **1.75**
Sperry, Armstrong, *Wagons West-
ward*, Comet, 1 .... **1.50**
Striker, Fran, *The Lone Ranger and the
Secret of Thunder Mountain*, Ban-
tam, 14 .... **27.50**

PAPER DOLLS

Collecting Hints: Most paper dolls are collected
in uncut books, sheets, or boxed sets. Cut sets
are priced at 50% of an uncut set providing all
dolls, clothing, and accessories are present.

Many paper doll books have been reprinted.
An identical reprint is just slightly lower in value.
If the dolls have been redrawn, the price is re-
duced significantly.

Barbara Ferguson's *The Paper Doll* has an excellent section on the care and storage of paper
dolls.

History: The origin of the paper doll rests with
the jumping jacks (pantins) of Europe. By the
19th century famous dancers, opera stars, Jenny
Lind, and many general subjects were available
in boxed or die–cut sheet form. Raphael Tuck in
England began to produce ornate dolls in series
form in the 1880s.

The advertising industry turned to paper dolls
to sell products. Early magazines, such as *Ladies'
Home Journal, Good Housekeeping,* and *Mc-
Call's,* used paper doll inserts. Children's publications, like *Jack and Jill,* picked up the practice.

The paper doll books first appeared in the
1920s. The cardboard covered books made paper dolls available to the mass market. Leading
companies were Lowe, Merrill, Saalfield, and
Whitman. The 1940s saw the advent of the celebrity paper doll books. Celebrities were drawn
from screen and radio, followed later by television personalities. A few comic characters, such
as Brenda Starr, also made it to paper doll fame.

The growth of television in the 1950s saw a
reduction in the number of paper doll books
produced. The modern books are either politi-
cally or celebrity oriented.

References: Marian B. Howard, *Those Fascinating Paper Dolls: An Illustrated Handbook For
Collectors,* Dover, 1981; Martha K. Krebs, *Advertising Paper Dolls: A Guide For Collectors,*
two volumes, privately printed, 1975; Mary
Young, *A Collector's Guide To Paper Dolls: Saalfield, Lowe, and Merrill,* Collector Books, 1980;

Mary Young, *A Collector's Guide To Paper Dolls,
Second Series,* Collector Books, 1984; Mary
Young, *A Collector's Guide To Magazine Paper
Dolls: An Identification & Value Guide,* Collector
Books, 1990.

Collectors' Club: United Federation of Doll
Clubs, P. O. Box 14146, Parkville, MO 64152.

Periodicals: *Celebrity Doll Journal,* 6 Court
Place, Puyallup, WA 98372; *Doll Reader,* Hobby
House Press Inc, 900 Frederick St, Cumberland,
MD 21502; *Midwest Paper Dolls & Toys Quar-
terly,* P.O. Box 131, Galesburg, KS 66740; *Paper
Doll News,* P.O. Box 807, Vivian, LA 71082;
Original Doll Artist Guild, Paper Doll Haven,
Box 507, Sharpee, FL 32959.

Museums: Children's Museum, Indianapolis, IN;
Detroit Children's Museum, Detroit, MI; Kent
State University Library, Kent, OH; Museum of
the City of New York, New York, NY; Newark
Museum, Newark, NJ; The Margaret Woodbury
Strong Museum, Rochester, NY.

Notes: Prices are based on uncut, mint, original
paper dolls in book or uncut sheet form. It is not
unusual for two different titles to have the same
number in a single company.

Grown–Up Paper Dolls, Merrill #3408,
1936, uncut, $35.00.

BOOKS

Abbott, Lowe's jobber trade name
1804, Patti Page, 1958 .... **35.00**
1805, Janet Leigh, 1958 .... **50.00**
Artcraft, division of Saalfield
4283, Nanny And The Professor,
1970–71 .... **10.00**

4413, Kewpie–Kin Paper Dolls, 1967   **40.00**
Bonnie Book
  2731, Rosemary Clooney, 1958 ....   **55.00**
  2734, Patti Page, 1958 ....   **50.00**
Lowe
  1040, King Of Swing And Queen Of
    Song, 1942 ....   **12.00**
  1074, Harry The Soldier, 1941 .....   **8.00**
  1242, Cinderella Steps Out, 1948 ..   **10.00**
Merrill
  1561, The Little Family And Their Lit-
    tle House, 1949 ....   **12.00**
  1564, Baby Sister and Baby Brother
    Dolls **5.00**
  2564, Lindy–Lou 'N' Cindy–Sue,
    1954 ....   **8.00**
  3426, Baby Sandy, 1941 ....   **40.00**
  3492, Sonja Henie, 1940 ....   **75.00**
Reuben H Lilja & Co, 904, Miss Silver
  Screen, 1946 ....   **15.00**
Saalfield
  1510, Baby Sparkle Plenty, 1948 ...   **50.00**
  1519, Henry & Henrietta Paper Dolls
    for Tiny Tots, 1938, unused **50.00**
  1715, Shirley Temple Standing Dolls,
    1935 ....   **50.00**
  2097, Comics Paper Doll Cut–Out
    Book, 1935
  2216, The Princess Paper Doll Book,
    1939 ....   **55.00**
  2335, Children Of America, 1941 ..   **10.00**
  2358, Little Miss America, 15 un-
    punched dolls, uncut clothes **50.00**
  2427, Mary Martin, 1942 ....   **45.00**
  2721, Wedding Party, 1951 ....   **10.00**
  2738, Paper Doll Patsy And Her Pals,
    1954 ....   **10.00**
  2760, Majorette Paper Dolls, 1957 .   **6.00**
  4213, Nanny And The Professor,
    1970 ....   **5.00**
  4310, Eve Arden, 1953 ....   **25.00**
  4447, Shari Lewis, 1958 ....   **15.00**
  5112, Tuesday Weld, orig box, un-
    used, 1960 ....   **50.00**
Stephens Co, 165, Playhouse dolls,
  1949 ....   **15.00**
Whitman
  960, Movie Starlets, five punchout
    dolls, 6 pgs clothing **100.00**
  996, Baby Sand, 18″ doll, 5 pgs par-
    tial cut clothing **25.00**
  1176:15, Queen Holden's Nursery
    School Dolls, 1953 ....   **40.00**
  1952, Doris Day, 1956 ....   **50.00**
  1953, Ava Gardner, one of two 9″
    dolls, some neatly cut clothing, rest
    uncut **15.00**
  1955, Grace Kelly, 9¼″ cut dolls, 8
    pgs uncut clothing **30.00**
  1958, Happy Bride, 1967 ....   **15.00**
  1967, Thumbelina, 1969 ....   **25.00**
  1970, Lydia, 1977 ....   **25.00**

  1978:69, Sabrina and the Archies,
    1971 copyright Archie Music Corp,
    unused **25.00**
  1979, Lennon Sisters, 1957 ....   **45.00**
  2086, Vera Miles, 1957 ....   **75.00**
  2089, Carol Linley, 1960, auto-
    graphed **55.00**
  2090, Sports Time, 1952 ....   **15.00**

UNCUT SHEETS

Jack & Jill
  January 1951, Folk Festival, Philadel-
    phia's Mummers, drawn by Janet
    Smalley **5.00**
  May 1941, Lieutenant Greene, JG,
    drawn by Tina Lee **10.00**
  September 1953, Journey Friends,
    Stewardess and Pilot, drawn by
    Ann Eshner **5.00**
Ladies Home Journal, February 1921,
  Johnny Funny Bunny And The Tad-
  pole Baby, drawn by Harrison Cady   **10.00**
McCalls, Betsy McCall and Sandy
  McCall, 1958–1960 issues **15.00**

PATRIOTIC COLLECTIBLES

Collecting Hints: Concentrate on one symbol, e.g., the eagle, flag, Statue of Liberty, Uncle Sam, etc. Remember that the symbol is not always the principal character on items. Don't miss examples with the symbol in a secondary role.

Colored material is more desirable than non-colored material. Much of the material is two dimensional, e.g., posters and signs. Seek three dimensional objects to add balance to a collection.

Much of the patriotic material focuses around our national holidays, especially the Fourth of July. Other critical holidays include Flag Day, Labor Day, Memorial Day, and Veterans' Day.

Finally, look to the foreign market. Our symbols are used abroad, both positively and negatively. One novel collection would be how Uncle Sam is portrayed on the posters and other materials from communist countries.

History: Patriotic symbols developed along with the American nation. The American eagle, among the greatest of our nation's symbols, was chosen for the American seal. As a result, the eagle has appeared on countless objects since that time.

Uncle Sam arrived on the American scene in the mid-19th century. He was firmly established by the Civil War. Uncle Sam did have female counterparts—Columbia and the Goddess of Liberty. He often appeared together with one or both of them on advertising trade cards, buttons, posters, textiles, etc.

Uncle Sam achieved his modern appearance largely through the drawings of Thomas Nast in *Harper's Weekly* and James Montgomery Flagg's famous World War I recruiting poster, "I Want You." Perhaps the leading promoter of the Uncle Sam image was the American toy industry. The American Centennial in 1876 and Bicentennial in 1976 also helped. A surge of Uncle Sam related toys occurred in the 1930s led by American Flyer's cheap version of an earlier lithographed tin, flatsided Uncle Sam bicycle string toy.

See: Flag Collectibles.

**Stamp box, spread wing American eagle, sterling silver, Foster and Bailey, 1 x 1⅛",
$85.00.**

Eagle
   Advertising Tray, Ruppert Beer–Ale, maroon ground, orange and white letters, white eagle 20.00
   Badge
      1" multicolored, eagle and lettering on celluloid inset, 1½" brass rim, brass frame hanger bar, "33rd Annual Meeting, New Orleans, 1914 of the Association of Railway Telegraph Superintendents"   30.00
      1½ x 3½", brass, links, eagle sitting on miner's pan, lower part with miner's burro, Fraternal Order of Eagles, Denver, 1905 .... 12.00
   Campaign Button, Bryan, silver eagle hanger at top, 1896 .... 18.00
   Charm, black and white porcelain, brass hanger, "Barnes White Flier Club," c1890 .... 50.00
   Medal, 1½" d, bronze pendant, "Chicago Daily News Patriotism Medal," spread eagle in center holding shield, crossed flags on bar engraved with name, red, white, and blue ribbon, orig velvet lined box, 1900 .... 25.00
   Pin, 1 x 1¼", copper colored metal,

WSS Medal of Honor, issued by US War Savings Service, young boy and girl, WSS torch and eagle in center 10.00
Pinback Button
   1¼", multicolored, cartoon type, "Now Will You Be Good," eagle carrying Spaniard in beak 40.00
   1¾", black and white, "Victory Celebration/Official Souvenir" 88th Division, WWI 18.00
Poster, 28 x 41", "The Navy Is Calling–Enlist Now," L N Britton, huge American eagle, shield on chest, towering over Naval crew 200.00
Sheet Music, Charles Lindbergh, *The Eagle of the USA* 15.00
Stickpin, 2¼", brass, "Huguenots," 225th anniversary of landing, New Rochelle, NY, 1913 .... 12.00
Stud, ⅞", multicolored, metal stud back, enrollment type, "US Boys Working Reserve" and "Enrolled" 3.50

Flags and Shields
   Advertising
      Mirror, 2", "The Peoples Store, Stylish Clothes, Kingston, NY," red, white, and blue stars and stripes ground, letters in shield shape . 25.00
      Paper Clip, 1½" red, white, and blue celluloid, steel spring clip, center inscription in shield "The Grand Rapids Furniture Record," 1922 .... 10.00
      Paperweight, 6" d, Flor De Moss, Kraus & Co, Inc Successors, litho, monogram with shield in center, black letters, gold trim . 30.00
      Pin, celluloid, flag shape, multicolored, The Grand Andes/The Best Ranges Made, made by Whitehead & Hoag 5.00
      Pinback Button
         1", R–S Motorcycle, red, white, blue, and gold shield, white ground, Reading Standard Co 18.00
         1¼" d, Ohio Funeral Directors, multicolored, flag edged in yellow, white ground, black letters, 1898 .... 5.00
         1¾", multicolored, "National Cycle," eagle and shield, 1900 8.00
   Flag, 46 stars, red, white, and blue silk, issued when Oklahoma became a state, 7 x 9" 15.00
   Pin, brass, Pearl Harbor, double, tiny brass link chain, blue enamel "Dec 7, 1941" on upper piece, ½" red, white, and blue enamel shield ... 20.00
   Pinback Button
      ⅞", Trolley Union, red, white, blue, and green, Boston Car-

men's Union Division 589, March 1918 .... **3.50**

1¼"

Stars and Stripes Forever! red, white, and blue, WWII **10.00**

Welcome Home Reception, full color, seven Allied flags and US shield, 1919 .... **12.00**

Liberty Bell

Advertising

Mirror, 4" d, celluloid, "Wm F Murphy's Sons Company Blank Book and Loose Leaf Manufacturers, Stationers, Printers, Die Stampers, Lithographers, 1820–1920," full color illus of headquarters, founder, and Liberty Bell **35.00**

Sign, 29½ x 34", litho tin, Dr Bell's Pine Tar Honey, yellow and black **35.00**

Jar, 6 x 6½", clear glass, emb "Liberty Cherries Jar 1776–1976," metal lid with flag and black letters **8.00**

Pin

¼ x⅜", blue enameled brass, die-cut, "Local and Long Distance Telephone," Bell Telephone, c1920 .... **7.50**

1¾", brass plated white metal, red, white, and blue accents on eagle, movable bell **20.00**

Presidential

Advertising trade cards, 2¾ x 4½", black and white

Adams, John Quincy, Allentown, PA, clothing store adv on back . **5.00**

Harrison, William Henry, Allentown, PA, clothing store adv on back **5.00**

Washington to Harrison, adv on back, complete set **15.00**

Washington to Van Buren, adv for Schaefer Bros Groceries, Rochester, NY, on back, complete set **20.00**

Clock, metal, black and white portraits of presidents from Washington to LBJ, names and dates of office, center blue and white White House image, wall, electric, by Spartus, c1964 .... **40.00**

Statue of Liberty

Book, *Liberty Enlightening the World*, c1890, hardbound, blue cover, center fold out of station **15.00**

Figure, American committee model .**2,300.00**

Lamp, 16" h, bronzed, c1930 ...... **175.00**

Pinback Button

1", red, white, and blue, "Liberty Button," Sept, 1918 .... **10.00**

1¼", aqua–yellow, "Welcome Home 77th Division," WWI ... **8.00**

Poster, 27 x 41", "New York–The

Wonder City of the World–New York Central Lines," Adolph Treidler, statue illuminated from below at night, panorama of night time city scene in background, c1930 . **350.00**

Watch, commemorative, 1986, quartz, orig box and papers **50.00**

New York City Chapter, DAR, revolving calendar, Louis Prang, 1896, red, white, and blue ribbon, $95.00.

Uncle Sam

Advertising

Sign

Sherwin Williams, Uncle Sam and clerk **20.00**

Use Jaxon Soap, 4½" w, 8" h, Uncle Sam leaning on fence, jackknife in hand, whittling on stick, easel back **50.00**

Trade Card

Brooks Oil Co, Cleveland, OH, Bunker Hill Harness Oil **6.00**

Emmert Proprietary Co, Uncle Sam Harness Oil **5.00**

Frank Millers Blacking, Uncle Sam shaving with straight razor, using polished boot as mirror, eagle looking at reflection on other boot **25.00**

Bank, 6¼", sheet metal, "Uncle Sam's Register Bank," red enamel, gold and black labels **40.00**

Christmas Ornament, Uncle Sam in stocking **35.00**

Dish, cov, 6⅝" l, milk glass, Uncle Sam on battleship, c1900 .... **50.00**

Mailbox Holder, 75½" h, wood, cut–out, red, black, and white paint, folk art type, 20th C **60.00**

Paper Doll, Uncle Sam's Little Helpers Paper Dolls, Ann Kovach, 1943 **15.00**

Pin, 2¼", figural, brass, red, white, and blue clothing, "US" backpack, rifle over shoulder, c1898 .... **50.00**

Pinback Button, 1¼", multicolored, cartoon, "The Yanko Spanko War," Uncle Sam using a paddle on Spaniard **45.00**
Post Card, Uncle Sam sporting pr of Taft campaign buttons on lapels, 1908 copyright **35.00**
Poster
    10 x 11", trolley car, full color Uncle Sam, "First Call–I Need You In The Navy This Minute!" James Montgomery Flagg **275.00**
    26 x 38", "Defend Your Country, Enlist Now in The Army," Uncle Sam pulling up his sleeves **100.00**
    21 x 31", "Save Seed Corn Now, An Alarming Shortage Exists," Uncle Sam with arm around farmer, 1918 .... **115.00**
Sheet Music, 9 x 12", *Any Bonds Today*, 6 pgs, Uncle Sam on cover, theme song of the National Defense program, copyright 1941 .... **15.00**
Stickpin, ¼ x½", brass, emb, profile, 1¾" brass stickpin **18.00**
Watch Fob
    Always A Winner, Uncle Sam standing by globe **35.00**
    Chicago Stockyard Co **30.00**
Window Sticker, 2¾ x 4", miniature of Flagg's classic poster, Uncle Sam pointing finger, "I Want You" **40.00**
George Washington, lottery ticket, black and white, illus of George, woman, three workers with raised hands holding three different two digit numbers, inscribed "Mechanics Art Union," c1800, 2 x 5" **20.00**

PENNSBURY POTTERY

Collecting Hints: Concentrate on one pattern or type. Since the pieces were hand carved, aesthetic quality differs from piece to piece. Look for pieces with a strong design sense and a high quality of execution.

Buy only clearly marked pieces. Look for decorator and designer initials that can be easily identified.

Pennsbury collectors are concentrated in the Middle Atlantic states. Many of the company's commemorative and novelty pieces relate to businesses and events in this region, thus commanding their highest price within that region.

History: Henry and Lee Below established Pennsbury Pottery, named for its close proximity to William Penn's estate "Pennsbury," three miles west of Morrisville, Pennsylvania, in 1950.

Henry, a ceramic engineer and mold maker, and Lee, a designer and modeler, had previously worked for Stangl Pottery in Trenton, New Jersey. Many of Pennsbury's forms, motifs, and manufacturing techniques have Stangl roots. A line of birds similar to those produced by Stangl were among the earliest Pennsbury products. The carved design technique is also Stangl in origin. The high bas-relief mold technique did not originate at Stangl.

Pennsbury products are easily identified by their brown wash background. The company also made pieces featuring other background colors. Do not make the mistake of assuming that a piece is not Pennsbury because it does not have a brown wash.

Pennsbury motifs are heavily nostalgia, farm, and Pennsylvania German related. Among the most popular lines were Amish, Black Rooster, Delft Toleware, Eagle, Family, Folkart, Gay Ninety, Harvest, Hex, Quartet, Red Barn, Red Rooster, Slick–Chick, and Christmas plates (1960–70). The pottery made a large number of commemorative, novelty, and special order pieces.

In the late 1950s the company had 16 employees, mostly local housewives and young girls. In 1963 employees numbered 46, the company's peak. By the late 1960s, the company had just over 20 employees. Cheap foreign imports cut deeply into the pottery's profits.

Marks differ from piece to piece depending on the person who signed the piece or the artist who sculpted the mold. The identity for some initials has still not been determined.

Henry Below died on December 21, 1959, leaving the pottery in trust to his wife and three children with instructions that it be sold upon the death of his wife. Lee Below died on December 12, 1968. In October 1970 the Pennsbury Pottery filed for bankruptcy. The contents of the company were auctioned on December 18, 1970. On May 18, 1971, a fire destroyed the pottery and support buildings.

Reference: Lucile Henzke, *Pennsbury Pottery*, Schiffer Publishing, 1990.

Look Alike Alert: The Lewis Brothers Pottery, Trenton, New Jersey, purchased fifty of the lesser Pennsbury molds. Although they were supposed to remove the Pennsbury name from the molds, some molds were overlooked. Further, two Pennsbury employees moved to Lewis Brothers when Pennsbury closed. Many pieces similar in feel and design to Pennsbury were produced. Many of Pennsbury's major lines, including the Harvest and Rooster patterns, plaques, birds, and highly unusual molds, were not reproduced.

Glen View, Langhorne, Pennsylvania, continued marketing the 1970s Angel Christmas plate with Pennsbury markings. The company continued the Christmas plate line into the 1970s utilizing the Pennsbury brown wash background. In 1975 Lenape Products, a division of Pennington, bought Glen View and continued making products with a Pennsbury feel.

Ashtray, "Such Schmootzers"	20.00
Beer and Pretzel Set, Sweet Adeline, 9 pcs	120.00
Bird Figurine, cream body, brown trim	
Hen, 11" h	225.00
Rooster, 12" h	225.00
Bread Tray, Wheat pattern	25.00
Coaster, Sweet Adeline	10.00
Creamer, Red Rooster, 4" h	30.00
Cruet, oil and vinegar, Amish, figural head stoppers, pr	110.00
Desk Basket, B & O RR	45.00
Mug	
Red Barn, 4½" h	40.00
Rooster, red	27.50
Sweet Adeline	25.00
Valentine, brick company anniversary	19.00
Pie Plate, apple tree dec	85.00
Pitcher	
Eagle, 6¼" h	50.00
Hex, 6½" h	39.00
Rooster, 6¼" h	70.00

Plaque, PA RR, 1856 Locomotive, $48.00.

Plaque	
B & O Railroad	30.00
Walking to Homestead, 6"	35.00
Plate	
Angel	20.00
Christmas, 1970 Yuletide, 1st edition, sgd	28.00
Leaf pattern, 6½" d	8.00
Mother's Day, 1971	32.00
Pretzel Bowl, Sweet Adeline	45.00
Tile, 4" sq	
Dutch Couple	25.00
Outen Light	25.00
Skunk, round	15.00
Tray, NEA Centennial, 1857–1957	10.00

PENS AND PENCILS

Collecting Hints: Any defects seriously affect the price downward. Defects include scratches, cracks, dents, warping, missing parts, bent levers, sprung clips, nib damage, and mechanical damage. Engraved initials or names do not detract seriously from the price.

History: The steel pen point or nib was invented by Samuel Harrison in 1780. It was not commercially produced in quantity until the 1880s when Richard Esterbrook entered the field. The holders became increasingly elaborate. Mother-of-pearl, gold, Sterling silver, and other fine materials were used to fashion holders of distinction. Many of these pens can be found intact with their velvet lined presentation cases.

Lewis Waterman invented the fountain pen in the 1880s. Three other leading pioneers in the field were Parker, Sheaffer (first lever filling action, 1913), and Wahl–Eversharp.

The mechanical pencil was patented in 1822 by Sampson Mordan. The original slide–type action developed into the spiral mechanical pencil. Wahl–Eversharp was responsible for the automatic "clic" or repeater type pencil which is used on ball points today.

The flexible nib that enabled the writer to individualize his penmanship came to an end when Reynolds introduced the ball point pen in October, 1945.

References: Glen Bowen, *Collectible Fountain Pens*, L–W Book Sales, 1986 (Revised); Cliff Lawrence, *Fountain Pens: History, Repair & Current Values, Second Edition*, Pen Fancier's Club, 1985.

Periodical: *Pen World*, World Publications, 2240 Northpark Drive, Kingwood, TX 77339.

Collectors' Clubs: American Pencil Collectors Society, 603 East 105th Street, Kansas City, MO 64131; Pen Fancier's Club, 1169 Overcash Drive, Dunedin, FL 33528.

Advisor: Dick Bitterman.

Conklin	
Crescent Fill, #3 nib, g.f., filigree, MIB	400.00
Cushion Point, pen, silver–pink stripes, g.f. trim, NOZAK filler, 1945	65.00
Duragraph, black hard rubber, large size, long cap	175.00
Endura	
Desk set, black marble base, two pens, 7¾" l, side lever fill, double narrow gold color bands, marked "Patent Nov 17, 1925" on pen barrel, black–brown overlay color	185.00

Pen

　　Medium size, black, gold **90.00**
　　Oversize, red, hard rubber, orig
　　　price sticker **195.00**
　　Model 20, pen, 5⁵⁄₁₆" l, #2 Conklin
　　　point–nib, black crescent filler
　　　#20, gold clip, narrow gold band
　　　on cap, patent date May 28, 1918
　　　stamped on clip, 1918 .... **70.00**
　　Model 25P, pen, ladies filigree cap
　　　ribbon, black, crescent filler, 1923 **80.00**
　　Model 30, pen, black hard rubber,
　　　1903 .... **80.00**
Dunn, pen, black, red barrel, gold
　　plated trim, 1920 .... **35.00**

Epenco, pen, black case, gold plated
　　trim **20.00**
Eversharp
　　C A model, ball point pen, black, g.f.
　　　cap, 1946 .... **55.00**
　　Doric
　　　Desk pen, gold seal green marble
　　　　cov, lever fill, large adjustable
　　　　nib, 1935 .... **100.00**
　　　Pen, ladies, Eversharp Gold Seal,
　　　　green marble color, 14 carat
　　　　point, twelve sided cap and bar-
　　　　rel, 1931 .... **130.00**
　　Pencil, green marbleized base, upper
　　　half gold color metal cap, first of
　　　the repeater pencil, 1936 .... **45.00**
　　Skyline model, "Gift Of A Lifetime,"
　　　14K, small dent in cap **165.00**

Laughlin, pen, silver overlay case, eye-
　　dropper filled, 1905 .... **200.00**

Marvel, black chased hard rubber, eye-
　　dropper filled, 1906 .... **70.00**
Moore
　　Desk Set, gray and black marble base,
　　　black pen, 12 carat NIB, side lever
　　　fill **80.00**
　　Fingertip Set, black, matching pencil,
　　　box, and instructions, continuous
　　　feed **80.00**
　　Pen, rose color, fancy band around
　　　cap, warranted nib, side lever filler **75.00**
　　Pen and Pencil Combo, black and
　　　gray, red marble **225.00**
　　Ribbon Pen, ladies, black, three nar-
　　　row gold bands on cap, lever filler,
　　　patent nib #2 .... **95.00**

Onoto, Ink Pencil Stylographic pen,
　　black chased hard rubber, eyedrop-
　　per, 1924 .... **37.50**
Parker
　　Duofold
　　　Centennial Model, black, MIB ... **175.00**
　　　Deluxe, pen and pencil set, black
　　　　and pearl, three narrow gold col-
　　　　or bands on cap, push button fill,
　　　　1929 .... **625.00**

Deluxe Junior, green, pearl, g.f.
　　trim, barrel discolored **70.00**
English, black, aerometric filler, g.f.
　　trim, minor wear **30.00**
Ladies, streamline, yellow, triple
　　g.f. band trim on cap, 1929 ... **175.00**
Senior Model
　　Flashing Black, 1923 .... **220.00**
　　Lapis blue, streamline, MIB **325.00**
Streamline, burgundy and black,
　　double narrow band on cap,
　　1932 .... **170.00**
Vacumatic, gray–black, arrow clip,
　　arrow design engraved on nib,
　　silver color clip and band on cap,
　　oversized model **110.00**
Vacumatic Maxima, brown, pearl,
　　g.f. trim **195.00**
Lucky Curve
　　Pen, push button filler, 1917 ..... **175.00**
　　Ring Pen, black hard rubber, g.f.
　　　trim, 1921 .... **195.00**
Model 48, pen, ring top, g.f. barrel
　　and cap, button filled, 1915 ..... **220.00**
Model 78M, ladies pencil, 1927
　　fuchsia color, gold color cap and
　　tip, orig sold for $3 .... **125.00**
#42, pen, g.f. metal mounted, 1927 **115.00**
#51, first model with aluminum
　　jewel, lusterloy cap, g.f. band,
　　metal filler **100.00**

**Sheaffer's, pen and pencil set, White Dot
Triumph, 14K point, $90.00.**

Sheaffer
　　Crest Set, black, yellow g.f. caps, side
　　　lever fill, mint condition **80.00**
　　Lifetime, flat end
　　　Large, black, pearl tip **190.00**
　　　Oversize, humped clip, g.f. trim . **50.00**
　　PFM–II, maroon, palladium silver
　　　nib, snorkel filler, mint condition . **110.00**
　　PFM–III, set, green, g.f. trim, 14K nib,
　　　MIB **220.00**
　　Sheaffer Clip, #3, self filling nib,
　　　early g.f. overlay, excellent condi-
　　　tion **150.00**
　　Streamline, standard size, dark green,
　　　g.f. band, very good condition ... **85.00**
　　Valiant Set, maroon, g.f. trim, touch-
　　　down filler, mint condition **40.00**

Security, pen, check protector, red hard rubber, g.f. trim, 1923 . . . . **70.00**

Swan (made by Mabie, Todd & Co, NY and London)

Pen, Eternal Model, black, g.f. trim, marked "44 E.T.N., Model 4," nib marked "14 K" **55.00**

Pen, hard rubber, red marbleized, lever fill, double gold band on cap, marked "Eternal" **60.00**

Pen, red ripple, band at top and bottom of cap, marked "Model 54 Eternal" on barrel, nib marked "14 K" **70.00**

Wahl

Ribbon pen, ladies, double narrow band on cap, 14 carat #2 nib, lever fill, 1928 . . . . **65.00**

Tempoint No 305A, pen, g.f. metal mounted, eyedropper, 1919 . . . . . **125.00**

Wahl–Eversharp

Chevron pattern, g.f., ladies model, MIB **60.00**

Equapoise Pen, slim, pearl and black, g.f. trim, #2 manifold nib **85.00**

Gold Seal, ladies ribbon top, streamlined, bronze, g.f. trim, lever fill . **45.00**

Greek Key, oversize, pen and pencil set, rosewood **395.00**

Signature Set, #2, green, ink stained barrel, black emblem on cap, g.f. trim **100.00**

Waterman, L. E.

#14, black chased, hard rubber, two chased g.f. bands, near mint **115.00**

#52, ripple, g.f. trim, very good condition **55.00**

#52V, ladies, ring, new condition, orig price tag, near mint **40.00**

#55, ripple, g.f. trim, unmarked nib **95.00**

#72, black chased, hard rubber, faded nickel clip, eyedropper filled, good condition **40.00**

#452½, ladies set, sterling filigree, MIB **80.00**

#0552, Gothic pattern, g.f. overlay, nib marked "Canada" **150.00**

#0646, black chased, hard rubber, safety, double g.f. bands, good condition **220.00**

PHOENIX BIRD CHINA

Collecting Hints: Phoenix Bird pattern has over 450 different shapes and sizes. The quality found in the execution of design, shades of blue, and shape of the ware itself also varies. All these factors must be considered in pricing. The maker's mark tends to add value; over 100 marks have been cataloged.

The more one studies Phoenix Bird china, the more one recognizes the variances. Collectors are urged to travel with a notebook in which is listed the shape, pattern, backstamp, dimensions, and conditions of the pieces owned. If the head of the phoenix is on a forward slant and its head feathers point upwards, also on somewhat of a slant, the rest of the motif will be well executed. If this is combined with a piece having an oversized border, the collector has found a "superior piece." Generally these superior pieces are marked with a flower with a "T" inside, but not always. The one rule about Phoenix Bird is that there always is an exception to the rule.

Don't buy Phoenix Bird unseen. Insist on a drawing of the piece, but most preferably a photograph. Photographs can be deceiving so ask for the dimensions as well. Xeroxing a plate is helpful for a buyer's identification of Phoenix Bird China or any of the similar Phoenix patterns.

History: The manufacture of Phoenix Bird pattern china began in the late 19th century. The ware was heavily imported into the United States during the 1920s to the 1940s. The Phoenix Bird pattern shows a bird facing back over its left wing, spots on its chest and wings that spread upward. The vast majority of the ware was of the transfer print variety. Blue and white was the dominant color. Pieces also can be found in green (celadon), but are quite rare. Coveted are the few hand painted pieces in blue which are signed with six Japanese characters on the underside and which always have the heart border.

Some of the transfer pieces also have a heart like border and are referred to as HO–O for identification. Many of these early pieces are not marked. The majority of Phoenix bird has the traditional border called the cloud and mountain (c/m) and sometimes has "Nippon" backstamped when of the 1891–1921 era.

Phoenix Bird pattern china primarily was sold through Woolworth's 5 & 10 Cent stores. It could also be ordered from the wholesale catalogs of Butler Brothers and the Charles William stores, the latter also retailing it as its New York City store. All the pieces offered were only the most basic shapes. Phoenix Bird also was carried by A. A. Vantine Co., NY, exported by Morimura Brothers, Japan.

A Phoenix Bird breakfast set could be acquired by selling a certain number of subscriptions to *Needlecraft* magazine. Ward's Grocery Catalog and A. J. Kasper Importers, Chicago, offered a Phoenix Bird cup and saucer as a premium for purchasing a particular brand of tea or coffee.

Once known as "Blue Howo Bird China," the Phoenix Bird pattern is the most sought after of several variations of the HO–O bird series. Other variations are:

Firebird—one of several less common patterns, flowing tail dragging downward; majority are hand painted, marked with six oriental characters.

Flying Dragon—all over pattern comes in blue and white as well as green and white; always has six characters underneath; bird's wings are fatter and rounder; in place of flower there is a pinwheel-like design.

Flying Turkey—blue and white with heart border, head always facing forward; no spots on chest; and left wing, as one faces design, only half showing; majority are transfer printed, a larger minority than Phoenix Bird are hand painted, mark is six oriental characters.

Howo—in some cases the pattern's name is on the underside along with "Noritake," other times it is not; phoenix shows no feet, flower is more peony like.

Twin Phoenix—made by Noritake, but not always marked; pattern is only on outer–edge, rest is white; two birds face one another in pairs.

During the 1920s and 1930s an overwhelming number of potteries put their trademarks on the pieces. A majority have "Made in Japan," an M/wreath (concave M), crossed stems with a convex "M," or a flower with a "T" inside and "Japan" underneath. The last mark shows up on some of the more uniquely shaped pieces and pieces of highest quality. Most Japanese potteries were destroyed during WWII, making it difficult to trace production records. The Phoenix Bird pattern was copied by an English firm, Myott & Son, in the mid–1930s. The English examples are earthenware and not porcelain as are the Japanese pieces.

References: Joan Collett Oates, *Phoenix Bird Chinaware, Book I* (1984), *Book II* (1985), *Book III* (1986), *Book 4* (1989), published by author.

Collectors' Club: Phoenix Bird Collectors of America, 5912 Kingsfield, West Bloomfield, MI 48322.

Museums: Historic Cherry Hill, Albany, NY; Huntingdon County Historical Society, Huntingdon, PA; Charles A. Lindbergh Home, Little Falls, MN; Eleanor Roosevelt's Vall–Kill Cottage, Hyde Park, NY.

Advisor: Joan Collett Oates.

REPRODUCTION ALERT. Reproduction of later shapes, with the exception of cups and saucers, have been around since 1970. The reproductions are more modern in shape, have more precise designs, more brilliant blue, have a milk–white ground and rarely are backstamped, with the exception of a covered jam jar and a butter pat dish. The reproductions generally had paper stickers on them at one time. Diagonal lines within the various designs are prevalent. The all–over design is more sparse on the post 1970

pieces and does not always reach the bottom of an item as it does on earlier Phoenix Bird; the majority of pieces do not have a backstamp.

A new type of Phoenix is on the market in various forms and also is a dark blue design. It is called "T–Bird" for identification. At least one maker has been identified, Takahashi. Sometimes it is found with a group of oriental markings within a blue square.

Note: The numbering system used to identify pieces is from the four volume set of *Phoenix Bird Chinaware* by Joan Collett Oates.

Plate, 7¼" d, $10.00.

Bread and butter plate, 6" d	**6.00**
Cake tray, round, open handles, Noritake Howo pattern	**5.00**
Children's dishes	
Tea set, #4, teapot, creamer, and sugar, 3 pcs	**65.00**
Tureen, cov, oval	**65.00**
Creamer, #6, mark 16	**25.00**
Dessert plate, 7¼" d	**10.00**
Dinner plate, 9¾" d	**45.00**
Fruit bowl, 7½" d, mark 4	**40.00**
Luncheon plate, 8½" d	**18.00**
Olive dish, 7" l, mark 16	**35.00**
Relish dish, oval, Noritake Howo pattern	**45.00**
Soup dish, 7½" d	**30.00**
Teapot, #9, mark 16	**55.00**
Vegetable dish, oval, individual size	**25.00**
Wicker encased plate, 7¼" d	**35.00**

PHOTOGRAPHIC ACCESSORIES

Collecting Hints: Photographic accessories divide into five major areas: darkroom material; camera accessories including literature; photographic studio items; objects associated with camera shops, drugstores, and other places where cameras and films were sold; and items related to major camera manufacturers. There are specialized collectors for each of these subject areas.

Most photographic accessories were used. Normal wear is accepted by the collector. Beware if collecting chemical material! Make certain chemicals and film are stable. Early nitrate film often decomposes and is flammable.

Perhaps the most desirable items are those from the photographic studio. Neck braces and big portrait cameras are common. Backdrops, especially if painted, are very hard to find.

Many still usable camera accessories, e.g., lenses, have a second value as used equipment. This value may be far above the collecting value.

History: The studio photographer dominated the photographic scene until the 1890s when the box camera, developed by George Eastman in 1888, became popular. By 1900 America had gone photography mad.

Retail outlets for cameras and supplies developed quickly. Imports, with Germany as the leading supplier, were an important factor from the outset. A number of critical mergers took place among firms in the 1920s. The fiftieth anniversary of Eastman Kodak in 1930 marked its dominance of the market, especially in film and film processing. Kodak still enjoys the major market share.

Reference: James M. McKeown and Joan C. McKeown, *Price Guide To Antique and Classic Cameras, 1989–1990, Seventh Edition,* Centennial Photo Service, 1989.

Advertising, whistle, Agfa Film, black ground, red and blue box, white text, $4.00.

Advertising
  Booklet
    "Leitz Close–up and Photomicrography with the Lecia Camera," E
    Leitz, NY, 48 pgs 15.00
    "Making Titles and Editing Your
    Cine–Kodak Films," 30 pgs,
    1931 .... 20.00
  Brochure, "Kodak Medalist II," 24
    pgs, c1940 .... 20.00
  Sign, 36 x 2", enamel, metal, large
    red "Kodaks," yellow ground,
    Swiss, Kodak, c1930 .... 150.00
  Trade Card, 2 x 2¼", Heywood's
    Mammoth Photograph, Ambrotype
    Gallery, Boston, MA 15.00
  Window Display, 8 x 10", glossy,
    "Color Experts," Kodak, 1949 .... 30.00

Book
  Emanuel, W D, *Lecia Guide,* Focal
    Press, 1945/1953, 112 pgs 8.00
  Hanworth, Viscount, *Amateur Carbro
    Colour Prints,* Focal Press, London,
    1950–51, 188 pgs, third edition, dj 20.00
  Tydings, Kenneth S, *Guide to Kodak
    Retina, Retina Reflex, Signet and
    Pony,"* 1952, soft cover, 128 pgs . 8.00
Bottle, Kodak Chemicals, brown glass,
  full graphic paper label, emb "Kodak" on back, one ounce 10.00
Case
  Hasselblad 500C, soft, non–Hassy .. 15.00
  Kodak Retina Automatic 10.00
Catalog
  George Murphy Camera, 1917, 192
    pgs 25.00
  Graflex, 1937, 28 pgs 20.00
  Kodak
    1914, 64 pgs 30.00
    1924, 64 pgs 25.00
  Kodaks and Brownies, October 1938,
    36 pgs 15.00
  Korona, 1926, 52 pgs 25.00
  Leica
    1939, 97 pgs 35.00
    1955, 84 pgs 15.00
  Rochester Camera and Supply Co,
    Rochester, NY, Poco Cameras,
    1903, 44 pgs 30.00
  Schneider Lens, 1930, 20 pgs 20.00
  Voigtlander, 1930, 28 pgs 30.00
  Watson and Sons, Ltd, Camera Lenses
    and Accessories, 1937, 24 pgs ... 20.00
  Wollensak Lenses and Shutters,
    1916–17, 36 pgs 20.00
Chemical Box, Kodak, "Eastman's Kodak Developing Powders for use in
  Brownie Tank Developer," c1900 .. 8.00
Cut Film Plate Holder, Kodak, 9 x 12
  cm, for Recomar 3.00
Document
  Invoice, Horgan, Robey & Co, Boston, dated 1895, graphics with
    lens, 6 x 9" 10.00
  Billhead, EK Co to Kittell & Co, Kinderhook, NY, monthly statement,
    1914 .... 10.00
Drying Rack, 12", wood, used for negatives 12.00
Film, box
  Ansco Dollar Camera, black, 127 size 20.00
  Kodak
    Verichrome Film Pack, 9 x 12 cm,
    c1933 .... 15.00
    V118, c1935 .... 4.00
    V124, c1935 .... 5.00

Glass Plate Attachment, Blair Camera
  Co, Rochester, special back for #3
  folding hawk–eye, worn orig box ... 20.00

Lens
    Canan Serenar, 85mm f2, case, finder **100.00**
    Kodak Anastigmat, 7½", barrel **35.00**
    Voigtlander Euryscope #5, 18", brass,
       slot for waterhouse stops **100.00**
Magazine
    Audio Times, 1968–83, 158 issues . **30.00**
    Studio Light, 1917–29, 107 issues . . **200.00**
Manual, Lecia, second edition, first
    printing **35.00**
Medal, Kodak, 2¾", brass, employee
    award, obverse: high relief profile
    bust of George Eastman; reverse:
    "Presented to...in recognition...,"
    name space blank **40.00**
Original Instructions
    Eastman's No 2 Eureka Camera, 18
       pgs, c1899 . . . . **20.00**
    Kodak, #4 Folding Pocket Kodak, 56
       pgs, 1910 . . . . **15.00**
    Lecia Reflex Housing, 8 pgs, 1956 . **5.00**
Pencil Sharpener, folding plate camera,
    MIB **5.00**
Price List, EK Co, 1901, "Condensed
    Price List", 48 pgs **18.00**
Service and Parts Manual
    Graflex, 60 pgs, punched for binder,
       c1948 . . . . **15.00**
    Sound Kodascope FS–10–N, 55 pgs,
       large format, c1947 . . . . **7.00**
Shutter Curtains, K–24, curtains for ae-
    rial camera, MIB **25.00**
Tote Bag, Canon, Montreal 1976 Olym-
    pic insignia **20.00**

PIG COLLECTIBLES

Collecting Hints: Bisque and porcelain pig items from the late 19th century European potters are most widely sought by collectors. Souvenir items should have the decals in good shape; occasionally the gilding wears off from rubbing or washing.

History: Historically the pig has been an important food source in the rural economies of Europe and America. It was one of the first animals imported into the American colonies. A fatted sow was the standard gift to a rural preacher on his birthday or holiday.

As a decorative motif the pig gained prominence with the figurines and planters made in the late 19th century by English, German, and Austrian potters. These "pink" porcelain pigs with green decoration were popular souvenir or prize items at fairs or carnivals or could be purchased at five-and-dime stores.

Many pig figurines were banks. "Piggy Bank" became a standard term for the coin bank by the early 20th century. When tourist attractions began along America's sea coasts and mountain areas, many of the pig designs showed up as

souvenir items with the name of the area applied in gilded decal form.

The pig motif appeared on advertising items associated with farm products and farm life. The era of the movie cartoon introduced "Porky Pig" and Walt Disney's "Three Little Pigs."

In the late 1970s pig collectibles caught fire again. Specialty shops selling nothing but pig related items were found in the New England area. *Time* magazine devoted one and a half pages to the pig phenomena in one of its 1981 issues.

Advisor: Mary Hamburg.

See: Cartoon Characters and Disneyana.

REPRODUCTION ALERT: Reproductions of three German-style, painted bisque figurines have been spotted in the market. They are pig by outhouse, pig playing piano, and pig poking out of large purse. The porcelain is much rougher and the green is a darker shade.

Advertising Mirror, Newton Collins Short Order Restaurant, St Joe, MO, yellow and orange pastels, 2⅛" d, $40.00.

Ashtray
    Bowling, one pig bowling, one
      watching, pink and green, 5" w . . **90.00**
    Pig artist painting, pig sketch on tablet **85.00**
    Two pigs hugging, sitting in dish, bis-
      que, stamped "Made In Germany" **80.00**
    Two pigs looking into old fashioned
      camera, 4½" w **75.00**
    Two pigs looking into old fashioned
      victrola, 4½" w **75.00**
Bank, 3½" h
    "Saving His Pennies To Make
      Pounds" as caption, pink pig along
      side of bank **75.00**
    "Souvenir of Danville, IL," front of
      pink pig sticking out of bank, back
      end sticking out other end, yellow
      pouch **45.00**

Figure

Barber shop scene, caption "Little Bit Off The Top," incised "Made in Germany", 2¾" h 75.00
Caboose end, two pink pigs 70.00
Canoe, pink pig 70.00
Cart, pink pig wheeling cart with three piglets, caption "The More The Merrier" 75.00
Chef pig, standing by barrel, blue hat and jacket 85.00
Dutch Shoe, pig sitting inside 35.00
Gazebo, orange roof, two pink pigs sitting on bench, 5½" h 100.00
Heidsieck Dry Champagne cork, two pigs in front, 3" h 75.00
Jar, orange, pig along side, 2¾" h .. 50.00
Money bag, $5,000,000 on front, pink pig poking out 65.00
Organ, one pig playing organ, one along side playing banjo, caption "Home Sweet Home" 75.00
Outhouse, pig looking in, caption "Engaged," 2½" w, 4" h 60.00
Table tennis, two pink pigs playing, caption "Patience" 90.00
Train engine, pig, 4¼" l 85.00
Washtub, pig in small washtub 60.00
Windmill, pink pig sitting, orange roof 80.00
Gravy Boat, porcelain, light pink pigs swinging, 4" w, English 55.00
Inkwell, pink pig sitting on top of inkwell, 3" h 100.00
Match Safe

Cigar smoking pig ready to bowl ... 100.00
Fat pink pig in pig pen 70.00
Pink pig poking head thru fence, 4½" w 65.00
Sa?

Bucket, two pigs along side, stamped "Made in Germany," 3½" 50.00
Water trough, three little pigs around trough, 2½" 50.00

Planter, pigs and sled, 6" l, German, $200.00.

Toothpick Holder

Automobile, two pigs riding 55.00
Camera, pink pig 55.00
Pig with mug in hand leaning on fence, 3" 60.00
Three large pigs in front of water trough, 4" 60.00
Two little pigs in front of egg, 2¾" h 50.00
Vase

Red devil's arm around pink pig, sitting on log, 7¼" l 110.00
Two pigs looking out of large shoe, Germany 60.00

PINBALL MACHINES

Collecting Hints: Cosmetic condition is paramount. Graphics are complex and difficult or impossible to repair. Graphics are unique to a specific model, especially backglass and playfield plastics, making replacements scarce. Prices are given for cosmetically good, 95% or more of backglass decoration present, games in good working condition.

Some wear is expected in pinballs as a sign that the game was a good one, but bare wood detracts from overall condition. Watch for signs of loose ink on the rear of the glass. Unrestorable games with good cosmetics are valuable for restoration of other games. Discount 30 to 40% of the price for a non–working game.

Add 10% if the paper items such as score card, instruction card, and schematic are present and in good condition. It is fair to suggest that regardless of mechanical condition, a game in good cosmetic condition is worth roughly twice what the same game is worth in poor cosmetic condition.

Pinball collecting is a new hobby which is still developing. It can be started inexpensively, but requires space to maintain. The tremendous diversity of models made has prevented the market from becoming well developed. There are relatively few people restoring antique pinball machines to sell. Expect to buy games in non–working condition and learn to repair them yourself.

History: Pinball machines can trace their heritage back to the mid–1700s. However, it was not until 1931 when Gottlieb introduced "Baffle Ball" that pinball machines caught on and became a popular and commercial success. It was the Depression, and people were hungry for something novel and the opportunity to make money. Pinball machines had both. The first games were entirely mechanical, cost about twenty dollars and were produced in large numbers—25,000 to 50,000 were not uncommon.

Pinball developments include:
1932—addition of legs
1933—electric, at first using batteries
1936—addition of bumpers

1947—advent of flippers
1950—kicking rubbers
1953—score totalizers
1954—multiple players
1977—solid state electronics

The size also underwent change. The early countertops were 16 x 32 inches. Later models were free standing with the base 21 x 52 inches and the backbox 24 x 30 inches.

The total number of pinball models that have been manufactured has not yet been determined. Some suggest over 10,000 different models from 200 plus makers. After 1940 most models were produced in quantities of 500 to 2,000; occasionally games had production figures as high as 10,000. Pinball machines have always enjoyed a high attrition rate. New models made the most money and were introduced by several of the major manufacturers at the rate of one entirely new model every three weeks during the mid-1940s and 1950s. Today the rate of new model introduction has slowed to an average of four to six new games per year.

Most operators of pinballs used the older games for spare parts to repair newer models. Earning life was less than three years in most markets. Many games were warehoused or destroyed to keep them from becoming competition for the operator's newest games; they did not want older pinball machines winding up in the wrong hands. At the very least, the coin mechanisms were removed before the game was sold. Most machines that have survived have come from home basements or from operators' storage.

Most pinballs were made in Chicago. Major manufacturers were Gottlieb, Williams, and Bally. Pinballs by D. Gottlieb & Co. are the most sought after due to generally superior play and graphics, from the 1947 to mid–1970s period especially.

Pinball art is part of the popular culture and kinetic art. The strength of the pinball playfield design carried Gottlieb as the predominant maker through the 1950s and into the 1970s. During the 1960s Gottlieb's fame grew due to the animated backglasses, intended to both amuse and attract players, which featured movable units as part of the artwork. The combination of animation and availability make the 1960s machines a key target period for collectors.

The advent of solid state games in 1977, coupled with the video game boom, dramatically changed the pinball machine market. The late electromechanical games became obsolete from a commercial point of view. Initially Bally was the predominant maker, but Williams has since attained this position. Solid state game production was high as manufacturers attempted to replace all obsolete electromechanical games. A severe dent in pinball machine production was caused by the video games of the 1980s. Collectors, who are rediscovering the silver ball, are

helping the pinball machine recover some of its popularity.

References: Richard Bueschel, *Pinball I: An Illustrated Historical Guide To Pinball Machines, Volume 1,* Hoflin Publishing Ltd; Gary Flower and Bill Kurtz, *Pinball: The Lure of the Silver Ball,* published by authors; Donald Mueting and Robert Hawkins, *The Pinball Reference Guide,* Mead Co.

Periodical: *The Pinball Collectors' Quarterly,* R. D. #3, 46 Velie Road, Lagrangeville, NY 12540 has suspended publication, but back issues are available for $20.00 postpaid; *Pinball Trader,* P. O. Box 440922, Brentwood; MO 63144.

Note: Pinballs are listed by machine name and fall into various classifications: novelty with no awards, replay which awards free games, add–a–ball which awards extra balls instead of games, and bingo where players add additional coins to increase the odds of winning bingo cards played. Some payout games were made in the mid to late 1930s which paid out coins for achieving scoring objectives. After the first add–a–ball games in 1960, many game designs were issued as both replay and add–a–ball with different game names and slight play rule modifications but similar art work.

Williams, four corners, 1952, $375.00.

Bally
1933, Airway, first mechanical scoring 325.00
1947, Nudgy, electric shaker 425.00
1951, Coney Island, bingo 350.00
1963, Moon Shot, replay 275.00
1964, Mad World, captive ball 250.00
1968, Safari, replay 275.00
1968, Rock Makers, replay, unusual
     playfield 250.00

1973, Nip—It, ball grabber **225.00**
1975, Bon Voyage, replay **275.00**
1978, Lost World, electronic **350.00**
1979, Harlem Globetrotters, electronic **300.00**
1980, Xenon, electronic **425.00**

Chicago Coin
1948, Spinball, spinner action **175.00**
1974, Gin, replay **175.00**

Exhibit
1941, Big Parade, patriotic theme, classic art **450.00**
1947, Mam'selle, replay **400.00**

Genco
1937, Cargo **375.00**
1949, Black Gold, replay **325.00**

Gottlieb
1934, Relay, relay balls **275.00**
1936, Daily Races, one—ball **375.00**
1948, Buccaneer, replay, mirrored graphics **350.00**
1950, Just 21, turret shooter **325.00**
1954, Mystical Marvel, replay, double award **450.00**
1955, Duette, replay, first 2—player . **325.00**
1956, Auto Race, replay **350.00**
1961, Big Casino, replay **250.00**
1963, Gigi **375.00**
1965, Cow Poke, animation classic . **475.00**
1966, Hurdy Gurdy, add—a—ball version of Central Park **375.00**
1967, King of Dinosaurs, replay, roto **375.00**
1968, Royal Guard, replay, snap target **300.00**
1969, Spin—A—Card, replay **300.00**
1970, Aquarius, replay **325.00**
1971, Roller Coaster, replay, multi—level **325.00**
1975, Atlantis, replay **350.00**
1977, Target Alpha, multi—player ... **350.00**
1978, Close Encounters, electronic . **300.00**
1981, Black Hole, electronic, multi—level **475.00**

Mills Novelty Co, 1932, Official, push button ball lift **350.00**

Pacific Amusement, 1934, Lite—A—Line, first light up backboard **325.00**

Rock—Ola
1932, Juggle Ball, countertop, rod ball manipulator **295.00**
1935, Flash, early free play **315.00**

United
1948, Caribbean, replay **225.00**
1951, ABC, first bingo **400.00**

Williams
1948, Yanks, baseball theme, animated **300.00**
1952, Four Corners, replay **375.00**
1953, Army Navy, replay, reel scoring **300.00**
1956, Perky, replay **325.00**
1958, Gusher, disappearing bumper **375.00**
1961, Metro, replay **225.00**

1964, Palooka, add—a—ball **275.00**
1967, Touchdown, annimation **250.00**
1972, Olympic Hockey, replay **275.00**
1973, Travel Time, timed play **225.00**
1975, Triple Strike, replay **300.00**
1977, Grand Prix, replay **350.00**
1980, Firepower, electronic **450.00**
1980, Gorgar, electronic, talking ... **465.00**
1980, Black Knight, electronic, multi—level **485.00**

PIN—UP ART

Collecting Hints: Try to collect calendars intact. There is a growing practice among dealers to separate calendar pages, cut off the date information, and sell the individual sheets in hopes of making more money. Buyers are urged not to succumb to supporting this practice.

Concentrate on the work of one artist. Little research has been done on the pin—up artists so it is a wide open field. The original works of art, whether in oils or pastels, on which calendar sheets and magazine covers are based, have begun to appear on the market. High prices are being asked, but the market is not yet stabilized—beware!

Pin—up material can be found in many other collectible categories. Usually the items are referred to as "girlies" on the list. Many secondary pin—up items are not signed, but a collector can easily identify an artist's style.

History: Charles Dana Gibson created the first true pin—up girl with his creation of the Gibson Girl in the early 1900s. Other artists followed such as Howard Chandler Christy, Coles Phillips and Charles Sheldon. The film magazines of the 1920s, such as *Film Fun* and *Real Screen Fun*, developed the concept further. Their front covers featured the minimally clad beauties designed to attract a male readership.

The 1930s featured the work of cover artists Charles Sheldon, Cardwell Higgins and George Petty. Sheldon did calendar art for Brown & Bigelow as well as covers. *Esquire* began in 1933; its first Petty gatefold appeared in 1939.

The golden age of pin—up art was 1935 to 1955. The 1940s brought Alberto Vargas (the "s" was dropped at *Esquire's* request), Gillete Elvgren, Billy DeVorss, Joyce Ballantyne and Earl Moran into the picture. Pin—up girl art appeared everywhere—magazine covers, blotters, souvenir items, posters, punchboards, etc. Many other artists adopted the style.

Photographic advertising and changing American tastes ended the pin—up reign by the early 1960s.

Note: Prices have been stable for the last five years.

Blotter, 4 x 9", "Going My Way," girl standing in rubber raft while hitch hiking, sea plane overhead, sgd by Del Masters, adv Laony Motor Services, Inc, Chicago 4.50

Calendar

1942, Esquire, Varga Girl, 8½ x 12", plastic spiral binding, 12 pgs, horizontal format, verses by Phil Stack 90.00

1944, MacPherson, 9 x 14", artist sketch pad, poetry on each month, plastic spiral hanger 75.00

1945, Starlight, Earl Moran, full color blonde, nude, dark green drape, black ground 47.00

1946, Vargas, complete, orig mailing envelope, excellent condition 125.00

1947

Munson, 9 x 14", artist sketch pad, spiral plastic hanger, mint condition 75.00

Petty, 9 x 12", spiral bound, orig envelope, Fawcett Publications . 70.00

1948, unnamed artist, artist sketch pad, little poetry, pin–up boy for April 90.00

1950, Medcalf, artist sgd, adv Ditzler Paint Auto Body, blonde with Scottie dog splashing foot in ocean, 14 x 45", Dec only 55.00

1954, Petty Girl, 8¼ x 11", 12 pgs, vertical format, verses 60.00

1956, Marilyn Monroe, 8 x 14", four full color pictures 200.00

1961, Playboy Playmate, 5½ x 6½", desk, MIB 45.00

Card, 3½ x 5", c1940, set of 3

Earl Moran, red ground 22.00

Zoe Mozert, full color 18.00

Centerfold, Vargas, verse by Stack, 11 x 16", matted, 1944 .... 48.00

Christmas Card, 5½ x 8", tan, red, black, and blue, MacPherson 25.00

Cigarette Lighter, 1⅞" h, black and white photos, green and red tints .. 27.00

Date Book, Esquire 5 x 7", color cov, spiral binding, full color pin–up photos, copyright 1943, George Hurrell 40.00

Folder

Petty Girl Revue, from Dec 1941 issue of Esquire, double sided, verses, different girl in each drawing, four 3¾ x 8½" drawings, six 5 x 7⅝" drawings, one 6½ x 5½" drawing 65.00

Sally of Hollywood & Vine, cardboard, sliding insert changing from dress to underwear to nude 40.00

Hair Pin, Petty, orig 4 x 5½" yellow, red, black, and white card, 1948, artist sgd 30.00

Kit, Esquire Magazine, 1944 Vargas girl calendar, 8½ x 12", Susan Hayward

puzzle, 10 x 13", orig 10 x 14" envelope 80.00

Magazine

Marilyn Monroe Pin–Ups, 1953, 8½ x 11", 32 pgs, black and white and full color photos 70.00

Movieland Pin–Ups, Anita Ekberg, cov, 1955 .... 16.00

Match Book Cover

Petty Girl, "Its In The Bag," Martins Tavern, Chicago, late 1940s 3.00

Petty Girl, "Snug As A Bug," Martins Tavern, Chicago, late 1940s 3.00

Note Pad, 3 x 4½", pastel, 1944 calendar on back 6.00

Playing Cards, Elvgren, titled "52 American Beauties," Creative Playing Card Co, Inc, St Louis, MO, plastic coated, $35.00.

Playing Cards

Bob Elson's Petty Pipping, 52 cards, dressed as bride 45.00

Vargas Girl Drawings, 53 cards, different illus, plastic coated, mfg by Creative Playing Card Co, St Louis, green box 150.00

Poster

17 x 33", full color, woman in shorts walking wire hair terrier, c1951, Walt Otto 50.00

22 x 40", Martin Senour Paint, "If It's Worth Covering, It's Worth Martin Senour Synthol Enamel," woman removing robe to reveal sheer underwear 100.00

Print

Armstrong, Rolf, brunette in shorts like overalls, yellow blouse, 11 x 14", matted and framed 30.00

Elvgren, Thar She Blows, 8 x 10", framed 25.00

Vargas, from Esquire, Phil Stack verse, WWII, 11 x 14", matted, framed . 65.00

Punch Board Label, 3¾ x 8", Elvgren, unused 14.00

PLANTERS PEANUTS

Collecting Hints: Planters Peanuts memorabilia is easily identified by the famous Mr. Peanut trademark. Items from the 1906 to 1916 period have the "Planters Nut and Chocolate Company" logo.

Papier mache, diecut, and ceramic pieces must be in very good condition. Cast iron and tin pieces should be free of rust and dents and have good graphics and color.

History: Amedeo Obici and Mario Peruzzi organized the Planters Nut and Chocolate Company in Wilkes–Barre, Pennsylvania, in 1906. Obici had conducted a small peanut business for several years and was known locally as the "Peanut Specialist."

Early peanut sales were the Spanish salted, red skins which sold for 10¢ per pound. Soon after Obici developed the whole, white, blanched peanut, his product became the consumer's favorite.

In 1916 a young Italian boy submitted a rough version of the now famous monocled and distinguished Mr. Peanut as an entry in a contest held by Planters to develop a trademark. A wide variety of premium and promotional items were issued shortly thereafter.

Planters eventually was purchased by Standard Brands, which itself later became a division of Nabisco.

Reference: Richard D. and Barbara Reddock, *Planters Peanuts Advertising and Collectibles*, Wallace–Homestead Book Company, 1978.

Collectors' Club: Peanut Pals, 3065 Rumsey Drive, Ann Arbor, MI 48105.

REPRODUCTION ALERT

Ashtray
  Bisque, 4" 45.00
  Metal, gold, Mr Peanut in center, orig box 75.00
Box, 9" h, 8" w, cardboard, red and black, old logo on three sides 30.00
Clock, alarm 40.00
Cookie Cutter, plastic, red 22.00
Dish, 5½" d, divided, plastic, green,

center figural handle, slotted spoon, 6" l, figural handle 25.00
Glass Football, Mr Peanut illus
  Black and Tan 20.00
  Yellow, old logo 45.00
Jar
  Round, red printing 150.00
  Square, emb four sides, peanut finial 100.00
Kazoo, blue and yellow, 1970s 12.00
Keychain Figure, 2¼"l, figural, plastic, day glow, molded keychain loop, 1940s 25.00
Letter Opener, figural Mr Peanut, brass 75.00
Marble Bag, premium 30.00
Measuring Cup, Mr Peanut shape 15.00
Mug, yellow Mr Peanut, old logo 65.00
Nodder, orig box 125.00
Peanut Butter Maker, boxed, unused .. 20.00
Pencil, adv
  Mechanical, Mr Peanut floating in oil 38.00
  Plain 9.00
Pin, tin, victory, Air Force, Mr Peanut hanger, 1940s 35.00
Pinback Button, 1⅛" d, Vote for Mr Peanut, black and white figure, white ground, white lettering on red rim, 1930s 25.00
Ring, metal, adjustable, figural Mr Peanut, enameled, yellow and black, 1960s 30.00
Salt and Pepper Shakers, celluloid, figural Mr Peanut, made in USA, pr .. 18.00
Spoon, nut server, blue plastic 12.00
Swizzle Stick 5.00
Tab, figural Mr Peanut, 2" h, white plastic day glow, WWII Victory wings at top, red, white, and blue litho metal tab 30.00
Tin, Novola, 5 gal, peanut oil, Mr Peanut logo, light green and yellow Mr Peanut on orig box 95.00
Thermometer, 16" h, tin, blue and yellow 40.00
Whistle, 2½", Mr Peanut 5.00

PLASTICVILLE

Collecting Hints: Collectors most prize mint condition buildings in their original box. Do not glue any pieces together. Also make certain that all pieces, including accessories, are in the box. There are many variations within each model; some models have over six color variations. Also, additional variations can be created by mixing the wrong colors together. Check carefully before buying.

Care must be exercised in storing Plasticville. Mildew will develop on the plastic if stored in a damp environment.

Collecting Plasticville is a brand new area.

Nut Dish, plastic, brown, ftd, $15.00.

Prices are low. A collection can be assembled without a great outlay of money.

History: Bachmann Bros., Inc., began its operations in 1883 making handles for canes and walking sticks from hand carved ivory. In the late 1880s they switched to hair barrettes and similar ornaments and in 1912 to the manufacture of eyeglasses.

In 1949 the first train-related item was produced—a picket fence. A log cabin followed in 1950. Six to ten new buildings in O/S gauge were introduced each year. In 1955 an HO line was launched and in 1968, N gauge material. Bachmann carefully stores its dies so material can be reintroduced as demand necessitates.

Plasticville is marked either with the name or the letters "BB" on a banner within a circle. The snap together system used by Bachmann was patented and is unique to their products. All but the N gauge material is American made.

Plasticville was challenged briefly by Littletown; but, Bachmann acquired Unlimited Plastics Corp. of New York, its maker, in 1956.

References: Frank C. Hare, ed., *Plasticville "O" & "S" Scale: An Illustrated Price Guide*, published by author, 1981; *Plasticville: Market Price Guide*, April Publications, Inc., 1982.

Note: The same building was issued in as many as eight different number codes. The listing includes some, but not all of these numbers for each building and accessory.

Ranch house, #1603/100, $15.00.

Airport Hangar, HO Gauge, red, white, and blue, orig box, 1950s **28.00**
Barn, #BN–1, red and white, orig box, 1950s **15.00**
Barnyard Animal Set, 18 animals, orig box **18.00**
Cattle Loading Pen, #1623, flesh colored, 5 steers, 22 pcs, 1958 .... **15.00**
Church, #CC–7, white sides, gray roof, 1950 .... **4.00**
Diner, HO gauge, silver and yellow, red lettering, orig box, 1950s **30.00**
Flagpole, #FP–5, 1027, white, 1953 . **1.00**
Hardware and Pharmacy, HO gauge, black, yellow, and silver, orig box, 1950s **25.00**

House
Cape Cod, #HP–8, HP–9, 1400, 1502, 1630, white sides, royal blue roof, 7 pcs, 1950 .... **4.00**
Log Cabin, #LC–2, 1303, 1501, 1985, reddish brown, chimney, 7 pcs, 1951 .... **6.00**
Independence Hall, #PH–1, 1905, 1776, 2921, 2950, red sides, gray roof, 20 pcs, 1955 .... **18.00**
Outhouse, #SA–7, SA–9, 1050, red sides, white roof, 1950 .... **1.50**
Playground Equipment, #1406, 1982, yellow accessories, pool, 15 pcs, 1957 .... **15.00**
Post Office, #PO–1, 1602, gray front, tan sides, red roof, 1953 ... **15.00**
Signal Bridge, #SG–2, SG–3, black, 2 pcs, 1954 .... **2.00**
Supermarket, HO gauge, red and white, cardboard storefront inserts, orig box, 1950s **23.00**
Trellis, #GT–1, white, blue bird, 1950 **4.00**
Watchman's Shanty and Gate, #1407, 1633, 1816, 1952, 5407, brown sides, gray roof, 10 pcs, 1958 ..... **2.50**
Yard Accessories, HO Gauge, pump, barbecue, trees, bushes, benches, outhouse, orig box, 1950s **24.00**

PLAYING CARDS

Collecting Hints: Always purchase complete decks in very good condition. Do research to identify the exact number of cards needed. An American straight deck has 52 cards and usually a joker; pinochle requires 48 cards; tarot decks use 78. In addition to decks, uncut sheets and single cards, if very early, are sought by collectors.

Many collectors focus on topics. Examples are politics, trains, World's Fairs, animals, airlines, advertising, etc. Most collectors of travel-souvenir cards prefer a photographic scene on the face.

The most valuable playing card decks are unusual either in respect to publisher, size, shape, or subject. Prices for decks of late 19th and 20th centuries cards remain modest.

History: The first use of playing cards dates to 12th century China. By 1400 playing cards were in use throughout Europe. French cards were known specifically for their ornate designs. The first American cards were published by Jazaniah Ford, Milton, Massachusetts, in the late 1700s. United States innovations include upper corner indexes, classic joker, standard size, and slick finish for shuffling. Bicycle Brand was introduced in 1885 by the U.S. Playing Card Company of Cincinnati.

Card designs have been drawn or printed in every conceivable size and on a variety of surfaces. Miniature playing cards appealed to children. Novelty decks came in round, crooked, and die-cut shapes. Numerous card games, beside the standard four suit deck, were created for adults and children.

References: Gene Hockman, *Encyclopedia of American Playing Cards*, several parts, privately printed, 1976 to present; Sylvia Mann, *Collecting Playing Cards*, Crown, 1966; Roger Tilley, *Playing Cards*, Octopus, London, 1973.

Periodical: *Playing Card World*, 188 Sheen Lane, East Sheen, London SW148LF England.

Collectors' Clubs: Chicago Playing Card Collectors, Inc., 1559 West Platt Blvd., Chicago, IL 60620; Playing Card Collectors Assn., Inc., 3621 Douglas Avenue, Racine, WI 53404.

Note: We have organized our list by both topic and country. Although concentrating heavily on cards by American manufacturers, some foreign makers are included.

Souvenir, Canadian, published by Canadian Pacific Railroad News Service, Consolidated Lithographing & Manufacturing Co, Montreal, Canada, $40.00.

COUNTRY

Austria
  Classic, Piatnik, 1955, 53 cards 16.00
  La Provence, Piatnik, 1960, 53 cards 22.00
Belgium, Joyaux De Belgique "Sieradan Van Belgie," Royal Belgian Coat of Arms, 54 cards 20.00
England
  Coronation King Edward VII, 1902, his picture on back, 53 cards, orig box 80.00
  Prince of Wales National Relief Fund, World War I, De La Rue, 1914, MIB 30.00
France
  Bataille De Nancy, Grimaud, 500th Anniversary, Grimaud, 1977, 54 cards 12.00
  The Parlou Sibyl, Grimaud, 1968, 3 x 4½", 52 cards 20.00
  Holland/America, orig box 25.00
Italy
  Cucci, Maseghini, c1969, 2 x 3⅝", 40 cards complete, orig box 20.00

World Bridge, Modiano, 1953, 54 cards 28.00
Oriental
  Fujitsu, Nintendo, Japan, 1973, 2½ x 3¹⁵/₁₆", orig box 30.00
  Victoria, British Hong Kong, 54 cards, MIB 12.00
United States
  Braille, USPC, 54 cards, special case 20.00
  A Dougherty Triplicate Cards, #18, 1876, 53 cards, MIB 42.00
  W C Fields, 1971, pictures of Fields with famous sayings, 53 cards, pamphlet "16 Proven Ways to Cheat at Cards" 30.00
  Maxfield Parrish, limited edition of 1,000 .... 15.00
  Politicards, Politicards Corp, 1971, caricatures of political persons, 54 cards, MIB 25.00
  World War II 4.00

TOPIC

Advertising
  Bluebird Bus System, 1947 .... 22.00
  Buster Brown and Tige, USPC, miniature, 1908, 52 cards 35.00
  Coca–Cola, 1943 .... 65.00
  Coors Beer, complete deck, sealed . 3.00
  Edison Mazda Lamps, logo at top, reproduction of Parrish "Reveries," 1926 copyright 25.00
  Fleet Wing Gasoline, c1910 .... 18.00
  Gatorade 1.50
  Hard–Q–Port Cut Plug (119), 53 cards, c1890 .... 70.00
  Hearn's Dept Store, sailboat back .. 22.00
  Jack Daniels 4.00
  Kiwi Bacon Co, John Dickinson Co, Wellington, New Zealand, 53 cards, orig box 10.00
  Marantz Superscope, comic case, double deck 12.00
  Nestle's Chocolate, assorted candy bars pictured 10.00
  Peter's Meats 8.00
  River Whiskey, green backs 40.00
Games and Fortune Telling
  Gypsy Witch, fortune telling cards .. 10.00
  Military Fortune Tellers, Loring, 1917, 56 cards, MIB 35.00
  Nile Fortune Cards, boxed, c1900 .. 45.00
  Poker Taurino, Mexican, complete deck, Spanish inscription on box, c1950 .... 12.00
  Prof A F Sewards Fortune Telling Cards, Standard PC Co, c1900, 52 cards, MIB 35.00
  Squadron Insignia Card Game, 17 pairs of duplicated cards and single

"Enemy" titled card, orig box, All–
Fair, mid 1940s **75.00**
Teuila Fortune Telling Cards, USPC,
1923, 45 cards **30.00**
Whirlaway, race horse, two complete
decks and joker cards, orig box,
early 1940s, Fanfare **30.00**
Souvenir
Brown & Bigalow's 50th anniversary **4.00**
Magna Carta, Congress, c1950 ..... **6.00**
Niagara, orig box **10.00**
Presenting the Dionne Quintuplets,
pictures of quints in gold ovals, 52
cards, MIB **55.00**
The Vista Dome, complete deck,
1950–60 .... **15.00**
Tarot
Grand Tarot Belline, J M Simon,
1966, 2¹⁵⁄₁₆ x 6¼", gold edges, orig
black and gold box, manual in
French, 78 cards **60.00**
Tarot Arista, Grimaud, 2⁵⁄₁₆ x 4⁷⁄₁₆",
French, 78 cards, orig box **15.00**
The New Tarot, Hurley & Horler, 2nd
edition, 1974, 2½ x 3½", 78 cards,
MIB **12.00**
Transportation
Airline, complete deck **2.50**
Burlington Northern **4.50**
Delta **2.00**
Golden West Along Southern Pacific
Lines (SR16), 52 cards, MIB **35.00**
Eastern/Ryder, MIB **5.00**
New York Central Railroad, orig box **10.00**
Ozark Airlines, 1984 World's Fair,
sealed deck **2.00**
Republic, "Thank You" on back, MIB **15.00**
Southern Pacific Railroad, gold edges,
red and black train passing a mis-
sion, 53 cards, MIB **25.00**
World's Fairs and Exposition
Brussells World's Fair, 1958, 54
cards, orig box **20.00**
Columbian Exposition, Clark, blue
back, landing of Columbus, 1892,
52 cards **65.00**
New York World's Fair, complete
deck, orig box, complimentary gift
from Markwell Staplers **25.00**
Pan American Exposition, 1901, color
design, orig box **35.00**

POCKET KNIVES

Collecting Hints: The pocket knife collector has
to compete with other collectors such as advertising, character collectors, and period collectors.
The pocket knife with a celluloid handle and
advertising underneath dates back to the 1880s.
Celluloid handled knives are considered much

more desirable than the plastic handled models.
Collectors also tend to shy away from purely
souvenir related knives.

History: Pocket knife collecting falls into two
major categories. There are collectors who concentrate on the utilitarian and functional knives
from firms such as Alcas, Case, Colonial, Ka-Bar,
Queen, Remington, Schrade, and Winchester.
The second group deals with advertising, character, and other knives, which, while meant to
be used, were sold with a secondary function in
mind. These knives were made by companies
such as Aerial Cutlery Co., Canton Cutlery Co.,
Golden Rule Cutlery Co., Imperial Knife Company, and Novelty Cutlery Co.
The larger manufacturing firms also made advertising, character, and figural knives. Some
knives were giveaways or sold for a small premium, but most were sold in general stores and
souvenir shops.

References: James F. Parker, *The Official Price
Guide To Collector Knives, Ninth Edition,* House
of Collectibles, 1987; Jim Sargent, *Sargent's
American Premium Guide To Pocket Knives:
Identification and Values,* Books Americana,
1986; Ron Stewart and Roy Ritchie, *The Standard
Knife Collector's Guide,* Collector Books, 1986.

Periodical: *Knife World,* P. O. Box 3395, Knoxville, TN 37917.

Collectors' Clubs: American Blade Collectors, P.
O. Box 22007, Chattanooga, TN 37422; The
National Knife Collectors Association, P. O. Box
21070, Chattanooga, TN 37421.

Museum: National Knife Museum, Chattanooga,
TN.

REPRODUCTION ALERT: Advertising knives,
especially Coca-Cola, have been heavily reproduced.

Note: See *Warman's Antiques and Their Prices*
for a list of knife prices for major manufacturers.

Advertising
Anheuser–Busch **45.00**
Champion Spark Plugs **30.00**

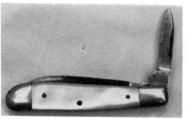

**Mother-of-pearl, two blades, marked
"AW Wadsworth & Son, Germany," 2⅝"
l, $20.00.**

Columbia Clay Co, SC, 2⅞"	**70.00**
Fernet Branka, Italian wine company	**35.00**
House Hasson Hardware Co, 3⅛" . .	**22.00**
Purina, 3⅜", checkerboard	**200.00**
Say It With Flowers, 5¼", white cel-luloid	**45.00**
Schrade Cutlery Co, NY, marine pearl	**60.00**
Swift's Canned Foods, 5", ivory cel-luloid	**145.00**
The Franklin Fire, Philadelphia 1829–1929, 3", metal	**75.00**
Art Nouveau, 6", sterling silver, ferrule MOP blade	**22.00**
Bartender's, 3", marine pearl	**22.00**

Character

Hopalong Cassidy	
Black, white, name engraved on back, miniature	**50.00**
Blue, riding Topper, belt loop	**40.00**
Dick Tracy, red and white, celluloid	**40.00**
Jimmy Allen, silver wings	**65.00**
Roy Rogers, 3¼", chain, black and white	**32.00**
Tom Mix and Tony, blue and white .	**40.00**
Dog Grooming, 3¾", Airedale head . .	**200.00**

Figural

Fish, 2¾", silver, W.B. Kero Co, maker, Curby Pat. 1885	**100.00**
Letter Opener, 4", pearl, 9" handle .	**300.00**
World's Fair, NY Administration Hall of Communications, full color picture under clear plastic	**20.00**

POLICE COLLECTIBLES

Collecting Hints: Police collectibles are primarily collected by people employed in law enforcement areas. Collectors often base their collection on badges or material from a specific locality. As a result, prices are regionalized, e.g., a California collector is more interested in California material than items from another state.

Condition is critical. Badges were worn everyday so a minimum of wear is expected.

The emphasis on police shows on television has attracted many non–law enforcement people to the field of police collectibles.

History: The first American colonists appointed someone from among their midst to maintain and enforce the laws of the land. The local sheriff was an important social and political position.

The mid–nineteenth century witnessed the development of two important trends: the growth of the professional police force in cities and the romanticizing of the western lawman. Arthur Conan Doyle's Sherlock Holmes novels popularized the modernization of police methods. Magazines, such as the *Police Gazette*, kept the public's attention focused on the sensationalism of police work.

The Gangster era of the 1920s and 1930s and the arrival of the "G–Men," glamorized by Hollywood movies, kept police work in the limelight. Finally, television capitalized on the public's enthusiam for police drama through shows such as Dragnet, The Untouchables, Starsky and Hutch, and Hill Street Blues.

Reference: George E. Virgines, *Badges of Law and Order*, Cochran Publishing Co., 1987.

Collector's Club: Police Insignia Collectors Association, Inc., 35 Pierson Street, Bloomfield, NJ 07003.

REPRODUCTION ALERT, especially police badges.

Badge, DL & W RR Co, railway police, nickel plated brass, c1920, $90.00.

Badge	
Illinois State Police, Corporal	**60.00**
New Mexico, Deputy Sheriff, made from US silver dollar, hand carved, c1967	**150.00**
Belt Buckle, NYC, brass	**75.00**
Call Box, Chicago Police, cast aluminum, c1920	**120.00**
Club, San Francisco Police, mahogany, carved handle, cord and tassel, c1900	**75.00**
Handcuffs, key, c1900	**70.00**
Magazine Cover	
Harper's Weekly, March 27, 1897 . .	**40.00**
Saturday Evening Post, Norman Rockwell painting, Nov 4, 1939	**8.00**
Nodder, policeman, marked "Japan" .	**18.00**
Painting, 22 x 11", wood board, old time policeman	**100.00**
Paperweight, plastic, souvenir of Los Angeles	**8.00**
Patch, Baltimore Police, cloth	**3.00**
Pocket Watch, Boston Police, engraved badge, silver, Waltham, c1800	**485.00**
Postcard, policeman on horse, The Texas Ranger	**4.00**
Plate, Texas Ranger Anniversary, 1973, SS	**120.00**

Shaving Mug, blue uniform, badge, and
   nightstick **675.00**
Sheet Music, Police Parade March,
   c1917 .... **22.00**
Statue
   Old Time Policeman, 8", ceramic,
      color **48.00**
   Present Day Policeman, 12" **38.00**
   Sheriff, 5½", pewter sculpture, c1975 **100.00**
Suspenders, slide adjusters marked "Po-
   lice," club engraving **22.00**
Toy
   Motorcycle, policeman on top, rub-
      ber **8.00**
   Patrol Car, Number 79, litho tin,
      spring mechanism, red and yellow,
      Cragston, c1950 .... **25.00**

POLITICAL AND CAMPAIGN ITEMS

Collecting Hints: Items selling below $100 move
frequently enough to establish firm prices. Items
above that price fluctuate according to supply
and demand. Many individuals now recognize
the value of political items, acquiring them and
holding them for future sale. As a result, modern
material has a relatively low market value.

The pioneering work in the identification of
political materials has been done by Theodore L.
Hake, whose books are listed below. Two books
have greatly assisted in the identification and
cataloging of campaign materials, especially for
the earlier period: Herbert R. Collins's *Threads
of History* and Edmund B. Sullivan's *American
Political Badges and Medalets 1789–1892.*

History: Since 1800 the American presidency
always has been a contest between two or more
candidates. Initially, souvenirs were issued to
celebrate victories. Items issued during a campaign to show support for a candidate were actively distributed in the William Henry Harrison
election of 1840.

Campaign items cover a wide variety of materials—buttons, bandannas, tokens, license
plates, etc. The only limiting factor has been the
promoter's imagination. The advent of television
campaigning has reduced the emphasis on individual items. Modern campaigns do not seem to
have the variety of materials which were issued
earlier.

Modern collectors should be aware of Kennedy material. Much has been reproduced and
many items were issued after his death. Knowledgeable collectors also keep in touch with Presidential libraries to find out what types of souvenir items they are offering for sale. The
collector should concentrate on the items from
the time of the actual campaigns.

References: Herbert R. Collins, *Threads of His-
tory,* Smithsonian Institute Press, 1979; Richard
Friz, *The Official Guide To Political Memorabi-
lia, First Edition,* House of Collectibles, 1988;
Theodore L. Hake, *Encyclopedia of Political But-
tons, United States, 1896–1972,* Americana &
Collectibles Press, 1985; Theodore L. Hake, *Po-
litical Buttons, Book II, 1920–1976,* Americana
& Collectibles Press, 1977; Theodore L. Hake,
Political Buttons, Book III, 1789–1916, Ameri-
cana & Collectibles Press, 1978; Theodore L.
Hake, *1991 Revised Prices For The Encyclopedia
Of Political Buttons,* Americana & Collectibles
Press, 1991; Edmund B. Sullivan, *American Po-
litical Badges and Medalets, 1789–1892,* Quar-
terman Publications, Inc., 1981.

For information about the Americana & Collectibles Press, write to: Americana & Collectibles Press, P.O. Box 1444, York, PA 17405.

Periodicals: *The Political Bandwagon,* P.O. Box
348, Leola, PA 17540; *The Political Collector
Newspaper,* P.O. Box 5171, York, PA 17405.

Collectors' Club: American Political Items Collectors, P. O. Box 340339, San Antonio, TX
78234.

Museums: Museum of American Political Life,
Hartford, CT; Smithsonian Museum, Washington, DC.

Advisor: Ted Hake.

Abraham Lincoln, 1860, 1864
   Cigar Box, wood, tan, black and
      white paper edge strips, black,
      white, gold, and gray label, "Old
      Abe Cigars, Honest/True/Merit/
      Quality," c1900, 6 x 8½ x 2½" .. **20.00**
   Print, photographic portrait, color
      tinting, green–gold background,
      name, birth and death dates, cap-
      tion "Art Supplement to The Phila-
      delphia Press, Feb 9, 1896," wood
      frame, 12 x 16" **65.00**
   Token, ¾", portrait on front sur-
      rounded by stars and 1864, reverse
      with eagle and slogan "Lincoln and
      Union," German silver, bright silver
      luster **100.00**
Ulysses S Grant, 1868, 1872
   Portrait Plate, 8½" d, glazed china,
      black and white portrait, brown
      border of foliage, flags, and eagle,
      inscription "1869/1877 Ulysses S
      Grant/General," marked "Made in
      Germany" **40.00**
   Tobacco Card, Blackwells Durham,
      multicolored, 3 x 4", portrait of Til-
      den and verse, opens to reveal por-
      trait of Grant with verse about ac-
      cepting nomination, company logo
      on back, 1876 .... **40.00**

James A Garfield, 1880

Plate, pressed glass, 11½" d, center portrait, floral border, inscription "We Mourn Our National's Loss," birth date, date of shooting, death date, 1881 .... **35.00**

Poster, 21½ x 28", black and white, names below, text identifying Republican candidates for Pres and VP, 1881–1885, slogan "Morgan's Sapolio," some darkening, browning, and minor damage **125.00**

James G Blaine, 1884

Ballot, "For President...Blaine/Vor Vice President...Logan/The Republican Ticket," lists NH presidential electors and other state candidates, jugate portraits, 6 x 13" **40.00**

Cigar Box, "James G Blaine/The Greatest Statesman of Them All," red, green, black, and white edge trim, large full color end labels, early 1900s, 5½ x 9 x 3" **35.00**

Ribbon, 2½ x 9", black portrait, white ground, red and blue stripes, inscribed "Blaine Reception Committee/Detroit Oct 14, 1884" **50.00**

Grover Cleveland, 1884, 1888, 1892

Bandanna, 16½" sq, black and white center portrait, red, white, and blue striped border, minor fading and damage **60.00**

Lapel Stud, red, white and blue, fabric covered, American flag center, 1884 .... **20.00**

Ribbon, 2¼ x 4", black and white portrait, bright red, white, and blue flag, gold eagle design, facsimile signature at bottom **80.00**

William McKinley, badge, 1896, Hake #3222, $75.00.

Benjamin Harrison, 1888, 1892

Badge, "Harrison/Reid Our Choice," silvered brass, black incised letters and design, pr of bright red, white, and blue fabric flags on back, 1892, 2½ x 3" **110.00**

Lapel Stud, ivory colored celluloid disk, black portrait, c1892 .... **35.00**

Ribbon, jugate, woven silk, bright red, white, and blue designs and lettering, facsimile signatures under portraits of Harrison and Reid, 1892, 2 x 6" **100.00**

William McKinley, 1896 and 1900

Jugate, 1¾", black and white portraits of McKinley and T Roosevelt, bright gold ground, large red, white, and blue bow **55.00**

Lapel Stud

"McKinley/Hobart," sepia photo, names above **15.00**

"McKinley–Protection '96," brass, diecut, ⅞" l, Napoleon's hat shape **25.00**

Ribbon, "McKinley and Hobart, Sound Money and Protection," black letters and portrait, bright yellow, 1896, 2½ x 5½" **25.00**

Stickpin, goldbug, emb brass shell, 1¾" stickpin, 1896 .... **30.00**

Tray, litho tin, oval, color portrait, green ground, facsimile signature, minor wear and paint nicks, c1900, 13 x 16" **100.00**

William Jennings Bryan, 1896, 1900, and 1908

Medal, 1¼" brass, Taft's portrait on one side with 1908 and slogan "I'll Toss You," other side with Bryan and "I'll Match You" **20.00**

Watch Fob, Bryan and Kern, enamel, eagles and flags center, orig strap . **35.00**

Theodore Roosevelt, 1904 and 1912

Jugate, Roosevelt and Fairbanks, brownish–white portraits **20.00**

Lapel Stud, ¾", brass, on back of rearing horse, small red, white, and blue fraternal enamel symbol and letters "P.O.S. of A." **30.00**

Post Card

"Teddy in Africa," caricature shaking hands with baboon, 1909 copyright, 3½ x 5½", unused .. **35.00**

"TR/Coming Home/Glad Tidings," multicolored, figures of Uncle Sam, GOP Elephant, and Taft dancing on dock, 1910 .... **35.00**

Tobacco Tag, "Square Deal Chewing Tobacco," silvered tin, sq, red sq at center, reverse with two pointed prongs **10.00**

Token, 1¼" d, aluminum, portrait on

front, reverse "26th President/New
York/Republican," birth and death
dates, c1930 .... 5.00
Watch Fob, "Roosevelt Fairbanks/
1904 Washington," rect, brass, orig
leather strap, black lettering, orig
luster 35.00
Alton B Parker, 1904, pinback button,
"Alton B Parker," black and white,
red, white, blue, and gold rim 25.00
William Howard Taft, 1908 and 1912
Jugate, Taft and Sherman, brown and
white, 1908 Geo Prince copyright 15.00
Pinback Button, ⅜", "For President
Wm H Taft," gray and white 15.00
Post Card, "Hello Bill!," multicol-
ored, opossum dressed as Uncle
Sam, 8 line verse, unused 20.00
Woodrow Wilson, 1912 and 1916
Necktie, Wilson/Marshall, black fab-
ric, 1½" w, 47" l, white embroi-
dered names, red, white, and blue
flag 50.00
Spoon, "Wilson, In God We Trust,"
silver plate, portrait handle with ea-
gle, c1916, 6" l 20.00
Charles Evans Hughes, 1916, pinback
button, "For President Charles E
Hughes," black and white 15.00
Warren G Harding, 1920 Pinback But-
ton, "Harding & Coolidge," red,
white, and blue litho 10.00
James M Cox, 1920, pinback button,
"Cox/Roosevelt," red, white, and
blue, dark blue ground 45.00
Calvin Coolidge, 1924
Bell, brass, Ring for Coolidge 25.00
Fan, 9 x 15", cardboard, wood han-
dle, black letters "We Will Help To
Keep Cool–idge," imprinted "Mif-
flin County Women's Coolidge
Club Lewistown, Pennsylvania
1924" 40.00
Pinback Button
"Coolidge and Courage," bright
red, white, and blue 25.00
"Coolidge and Dawes," red, white,
and blue, names on elephant's
blanket 18.50
"Coolidge–Dawes Full Dinner
Pail," red, white, and blue 20.00
"Coolidge For President/H.L. Davis
For Governor," ⅞", black and
white 60.00
Pitcher, 4½ x 6 x 6", dark blue and
white, illus of Coolidge's home,
marked "The Adams Souvenir Se-
ries/Made In England" 35.00
Herbert Hoover, 1928 and 1932
Bar Pin, brass, red, white, and blue
enamel 12.00
Flue Cover, "Hoover For President,"

litho tin, white portrait, dark blue
ground, 8" d 35.00
Pinback Button
"For President Herbert Hoover/For
Vice–President Charles Curtis,"
red, white, and blue litho, 2¼" d 160.00
"Hoover and Curtis," red, white,
and blue, PA keystone symbol,
GOP elephant, celluloid 12.00
Alfred E Smith, 1928
Flue Cover, "For President Al Smith,"
litho tin, portrait, name, light blue
and cream, 8" d 40.00
Key Chain, silvered brass ring, black
enamel donkey's head 35.00

**Franklin Roosevelt, fan, cardboard, litho,
adv for Boyd School, Washington, DC on
back, 7½ x 10½", $20.00.**

Franklin D Roosevelt, 1932, 1936,
1940, and 1944
Automobile Attachment, diecut tin,
gold colored donkey and name reflect headlights, marked "Luma-
syne Inc, Wash, DC," minor dents
and wear, 7 x 8" 55.00
Bust
"NRA/We Do Our Part/FD Roosevelt," white metal, dark gold finish, dark blue eagle, red and
white lettering, minor loss to finish, 2½ x 2½ x 6" 75.00
"Roosevelt/Century of Progress,"
white metal, dark bronze finish,
finely detailed, 2¾" h 40.00
Cigar Band, black, white, red, and
gold, "Franklin D Roosevelt Hand
Made," c1933, 3" l 10.00
Diecut, "Roosevelt/Schricker," red,
white, and blue litho tin, loop pin
at top 20.00
Flag, miniature, "Again With Roose-

velt," red, white, and blue fabric, mounted on straight pin **15.00**

Pinback Button

"Re–Elect Our President Franklin D Roosevelt," black and white, 3½" d, c1940 .... **30.00**

"Roosevelt/Four More Lucky Years," red, white, and blue, horseshoe design **8.00**

"Three Good Terms Deserves Another," blue letters, white ground **10.00**

Sheet Music, *Nation's Prayer For The President/Dedicated To Franklin D Roosevelt*, black and white, 1933 copyright, 9½ x 12½" **15.00**

Thermometer, plaque, bright gold ground, black NRA symbol, portrait, and inscription "Together We Cannot Fail," issued by NH casket distributor, brass frame, chain at top for hanging, damaged thermometer, 4 x 6" **35.00**

Token, brass

"Elect Roosevelt/Make This Token and 5¢ Good For A Beer," opposite side "Vote For Roosevelt And Repeal" **10.00**

"Lucky Tillicum/Re–Build With Roosevelt," portrait on front, airship flying over US Capitol on back **8.00**

Alfred Landon, 1936, pinback button, "Landon/Knox/G.O.P.," bright yellow, dark brown ground, celluloid .. **10.00**

Wendell L Willkie, 1940

Jewelry, pin, red, white, and blue enameled white metal, 2 x 3½", ribbon like design, ten inset rhinestones and center Willkie button . **35.00**

License Plate, 4 x 13½", orange, gold letters outlined in dark blue, blue edge **20.00**

Pinback Button

"New Deal Waste Basket," black and white cartoon illus **25.00**

"Up On America/Win With Willkie," red, white, and blue, 2⅜" l, Phila Badge back paper . **80.00**

"Willkie Square Deal," red, white, and blue litho **15.00**

Sticker, diecut foil, 3½ x 6", silver, blue, and red, inscribed "Willkie/The Hope of America" **10.00**

Thimble **15.00**

Thomas E Dewey, 1944 and 1948

Arm Band, "Dewey/Bricker, Liberty Belle," light blue felt strip, bright yellow image and lettering, 4 x 15" **25.00**

Campaign Booklet, portrait on cov, black and white photos and information about Dewey, Bricker, and PA candidates, 24 pgs, 2½ x 4" .. **6.00**

Pennant, "Thomas Dewey For President," white letters, bright red felt, yellow felt streamers, 4 x 11" **15.00**

Ribbon, "Elect Dewey and Warren/Vote Republican," black letters, silvery white fabric ribbon, 2 x 6" .. **20.00**

Tie, "Dewey In '48," white image, dark brown fabric, orig tags inscribed "Rembrandt Paints Another Crosley Creation," 2½ x 8" **35.00**

Harry S Truman, 1948

Autograph, signed magazine photo, 5 x 8", black ink "Kind regards from Harry Truman 7/11/64" **175.00**

Book, *Out Of The Jaws Of Victory/ The Astounding Election of 1948*, Jules Abels, Henry Holt Publisher, 1959, 336 pgs, review copy with orig press release and review card, slight wear to dust jacket, 6 x 8½" **12.00**

Fan, Philadelphia Evening Bulletin Newspaper, Democratic National Convention, Decker cartoon on one side, "Welcome Delegates" on other, 1948 .... **28.00**

Magazine, Time, Man Of The Year issue, Dec 31, 1945, Artzybasheff cover artist **20.00**

Pinback Button

"Forward With President Truman/ No Retreat," red, white, and blue **35.00**

"Harry S Truman," black and white, bright red, white, and blue rim **20.00**

Portrait, 3½" d, dark blue eagle, crossed red, white, and blue flags, gold wreath surrounding black and white portrait **75.00**

Program, Inaugural Ball, gold cov, blue binding cord, Jan 20, 1949, National Guard Armory, portraits of Pres and Mrs Truman, Margaret, and Barkley, 8½ x 11" **35.00**

Dwight D Eisenhower, 1952 and 1956

Autograph, signed photo, 5 x 7" sepia, seated at desk, uniform, blue ink fountain pen signature, matted, wood frame **400.00**

Bandanna, "Win With Ike For President," blue and white image, bright red ground, 26" sq **60.00**

Matchbook, Inaugural, portraits, unused, 1953 .... **10.00**

Necktie, shiny rust colored fabric, 3½ x 10" image of bright yellow lightning bolt leading into US Capitol building, tan and white photo of Ike in military uniform, pink air brushed building and graduate's hat, orig label "Famous Stetson Cravat Slip Stitch Construction" .. **35.00**

Pen, 5" l, brass, black and white plas-

tic, slogan "For The Love Of Ike—Vote Republican" **15.00**
Pennant, 11 x 29", dark brown felt, white illus and lettering "Eisenhower—Nixon Inauguration," white Capitol building with blue, yellow, and green shading, 1953 .... **20.00**
Pinback Button
  "Ike and Dick, Sure To Click," black and white slogan, 3½" d, 1952 .... **30.00**
  "Make The White House The Dwight House," blue letters, yellow ground **8.00**
Adlai E Stevenson, 1952 and 1956
  Pinback Button
    "Adlai Is Okay," red, white, and blue litho **12.00**
    "Stevenson 1960," hopeful button, blue star, gold lettering **10.00**
  Tie Tac, "Adlai" in diecut letters, brass finished metal **20.00**
John F Kennedy, 1960
  Bandanna, 31" sq, rayon type fabric, full color portrait, white ground, red, white, and blue flag border, 1965 copyright tag **15.00**
  Button, 1¾", inauguration, black and white, 7" blue ribbon, gold lettering and presidential seal **35.00**
  Campaign Hat, 11 x 13 x 4", white plastic, red, white, and blue striped paper strip with black lettering "Kennedy for President," stars with state abbreviations, 1960 .... **25.00**
  Coloring Book, "JFK Coloring Book," black ground, brown, blue, and white letters, illus of Kennedy, family, personalities, drawings by Mort Drucker, 24 pgs, 10 x 13", unused **20.00**
  Magazine, Time, Election Extra, 1960, 16 pgs, photos and summary of election **12.00**
  Pinback Button
    "Kennedy/Johnson," red, white, and blue celluloid **20.00**
    "Kennedy/Liberal/Row C," black and green letters, white ground **25.00**
  Pitcher, "Mrs John F Kennedy," white china, full color photo, gold accents, 2¾" h **20.00**
  Plate, "President and Mrs John F Kennedy," white china, full color portraits, gold edge band, 7" d **15.00**
  Tie Clip, silvered brass, black and white flashing disk, portrait plus slogan "The Man For The 60s" .. **25.00**
Richard M Nixon, 1960, 1968, and 1972
  Autographed first day cov, both Nixon and Ford signatures **195.00**
  Coloring Book, 1973, titled "Water-

gate Coloring Book/Join The Fun/Color The Facts," 8 x 11", 48 pgs **15.00**
Christmas Card, full color photo of family, first name facsimile signatures, orig envelope postmarked 1967, New York return address, 4 x 6" **30.00**
Figure, vinyl, 3–dimensional, thin plastic cord goes to suction cup, multicolored, giving "V" sign with both hands, mint in orig plastic bag, c1972, 4" h **20.00**
Pinback Button
  "Democrats for Nixon Lodge," red, white, and blue **7.00**
  "Dick Nixon For President," red, white, and blue litho, 1960 .... **10.00**
  "Member National Nixon Lodge Club," black and gold **12.00**
  "Nixon/Nunn," white and orange **10.00**

Johnson-Humphrey, jugate, red, white, blue, and black, 1¼" d, $2.00.

Lyndon B Johnson, 1964
  Autograph, Lady Bird Johnson, 3 x 5" card **15.00**
  Bottle Stopper, three dimensional, composition, 4" h **35.00**
  Magazine, Time, Election Extra, 1964, 16 pgs, photos and summary of election **8.00**
  Pinback Button
    "All The Way With LBJ," red, white, and blue **5.00**
    "Educators for Johnson Humphrey," red, white, and blue ... **5.00**
    Inauguration, 6" d, full color portrait, red, white, and blue rim .. **10.00**
    "Republicans for Johnson," white letters, dark blue ground **4.00**
Barry M Goldwater, 1964
  Book, A Texan Looks At Lyndon/A Study In Illegitimate Power, J Evetts Haley, 256 pgs, paperback, "Issued by Citizens For Goldwater Tacoma,

WA'' stamped on title page, 4½ x 6" **12.00**

Pinback Button

"Americans For Goldwater," blue letters, yellow ground **10.00**

"Goldwater Miller GOP Party 1964," red, white, and blue ... **5.00**

Poster, "A Choice...Not An Echo," 14 x 21", red, white, and blue **15.00**

Soda, "Gold Water," 5" h metal can, metallic green, gold, and white, caption "The Right Drink For The Conservative Taste," unopened, orig contents, 1964 .... **35.00**

Hubert H Humphrey, 1968

Pinback Button

"Button Collectors for Humphrey/ Muskie," red, white, and blue . **12.00**

"Humphrey," blue and white, 1972 hopeful campaign **5.00**

"Justice For All/Humphrey–Muskie in 1968," red, white, and blue . **8.00**

Tab, 2", blue, green, red, white, and black, "Labor for Humphrey" **3.00**

George McGovern, 1972

Bandanna, "McGovern For President/ Come Home America," silk like fabric, red and blue, white ground, large US image, campaign slogans, 1972, 31" sq **35.00**

Comb, plastic, blue, smiling face ... **4.00**

Jugate, McGovern/Schriver, black, white, and blue, 1972 .... **8.00**

Pinback Button

"McGovern for A New America," black, white, and red, outline of US Capitol **10.00**

"North Carolina's One Of A Million/McGovern," white letters, dark pink ground **3.00**

Gerald R Ford, 1976

Autographed first day cover **55.00**

Pinback Button

"For President 1976 Ford," black and white, bright red, white, and blue rim **8.00**

"Ford Dole," blue and white **3.00**

James E Carter, 1976

License Plate, "Jimmy Carter/A New Beginning" plastic, white, red, blue, and green, shows Alamo, Plains, DC, Phila, George Washington, Liberty Bell, and Carter like caricatures, 6 x 12" **15.00**

Pinback Button

"Carter Mondale 76," black and white, green logan **3.00**

"Labor Supports Carter/Mondale/ Brotherhood Of Railway & Airline Clerks," white letters, green litho **5.00**

Toy, "Amy At The White House Play-

set," boxed set by The Toy Factory, cardboard punchouts of family, White House, limousine, rose garden, 10 x 18 x 1", orig shrink wrap **20.00**

Walter Mondale, 1976

Campaign Give–Away, 6" sq white ceramic tile, orig box, clear plastic cov, three newspaper front pages illus, "Thanks For All Your Help In Making This Possible, Fritz & Joan" **15.00**

Pinback Button, "Mondale/Ferraro," red, white, and blue litho **5.00**

Geraldine A Ferraro, 1984

Autograph, paperback book, *Official Proceedings of the 1984 Democratic National Convention*, large black signature on cov **35.00**

Pinback Button, "Ferraro for VP," white letters, light blue ground ... **6.00**

Ronald Reagan, 1980 and 1984

Autograph

Campaign brochure, 4 x 9" folded, blue ball point signature **150.00**

Photo, black felt tip pen inscription, "Very Best Wishes, Ronald Reagan," minor frame damage, 8 x 10" **125.00**

Button, Reagan/Bush, '84, flashing red lights, musical, 2¼" d red, white and blue button, 3½ x 6" colorful orig card, clear plastic cov, battery operated, pr **20.00**

Menu, White House, navy blue stiff cardboard folder, full color presidential seal, blue fabric cord, light blue menu sheet **10.00**

Mug, 5" h, white ceramic, blue portraits of Reagan and Bush, red letters, inscribed "Republican National Convention August 20–23, 1984" **12.00**

Pinback Button

"Jobs Not War/Stop Reagan's Cuts/ YSA," blue, orange, white, and gray, Young Socialists Alliance . **8.00**

"Vote Reagan For President In 1980," black and white ground, red and blue slogans **5.00**

George Bush, 1980, 1984, 1988

Cigars, Bubble Gum, "Bush/Dukakis Presidential Favorites," red, white, and blue boxes, 24 cigars, Philadelphia Chewing Gum Corp, c1988, full, unopened box, 5½ x 6½ x 1½", pr **20.00**

Golf Ball, full color decal of vice presidential seal, white ball, orig blue box with gold facsimile signature, Wilson **35.00**

Dan Quayle, 1988, autograph

3 x 5" card, Marilyn Quayle **10.00**

Vice president, card **65.00**

POST CARDS

Collecting Hints: Concentrate on one subject area, publisher, or illustrator. Collect cards in mint condition, when possible.

The more common the holiday, the larger the city, the more popular the tourist attraction, the easier it will be to find postcards about these subjects because of the millions of cards that still remain in these categories. The smaller runs of "real" photo postcards are the most desirable of the scenic cards. Photographic cards of families and individuals, unless they show occupations, unusual toys, dolls, or teddy bears have little value.

Stamps and cancellation marks may affect the value of cards, but rarely. Consult a philatelic guide.

Post cards fall into two main categories: view cards and topics. View cards are easiest to sell in their local geographic region. European view cards, while very interesting, are difficult to sell in America.

It must be stressed that age alone does not determine price. A birthday postcard from 1918 may sell for only ten cents, while a political campaign card from the 1950s may bring ten dollars. Every collectible is governed by supply and demand.

Although the most popular collecting period is 1898–1918, the increasing costs of postcards from this era have turned collectors' interest to postcards from the 1920s, 1930s, and 1940s. The main interest in the 1920–1930 period is cards with an Art Deco motif. The cards collected from the 1940s are "linens" which feature a textured "linen–like" paper surface.

Cards from the 1950–1970 period are called chromes because of their shiny surface paper. Advertising postcards from this chrome era are rapidly gaining popularity while still selling for under $3.00.

History: The golden age of postcards dates from 1898 to 1918. While there are cards printed earlier, they are collected for their postal history. Postcards prior to 1898 are called "pioneer" cards.

European publishers, especially in England and Germany, produced the vast majority of cards during the golden age. The major postcard publishers are Raphael Tuck (England), Paul Finkenrath of Berlin (PFB–German), and Whitney, Detroit Publishing Co., and John Winsch (United States). However, many American publishers had their stock produced in Europe, hence, "Made in Bavaria" imprints. While some Tuck cards are high priced, many are still available in the "ten cent" boxes.

Styles changed rapidly, and manufacturers responded to every need. The linen postcard which gained popularity in the 1940s was quickly replaced by the chrome cards of the post–1950 period.

References: Many of the best books are out–of–print. However, they are available through libraries. Ask your library to utilize the inter–library loan system.

Diane Allmen, *The Official Price Guide to Postcards*, House of Collectibles, 1990; Frederic and Mary Megson, *American Advertising Postcards—Set and Series: 1890–1920*, published by authors, 1985; Cynthia Rubin and Morgan Williams, *Larger Than Life; The American Tall–Tale Postcard, 1905–1915*, Abbeville Press, 1990; Dorothy B. Ryan, *Picture Postcards In The United States, 1893–1918*, Clarkson N. Potter, 1982, paperback edition; Jack H. Smith, *Postcard Companion: The Collector's Reference*, Wallace–Homestead Book Company, 1989; Jane Wood, *The Collector's Guide To Post Cards*, L–W Promotions, 1984, 1987 values updated.

Periodicals: *Barr's Postcard News*, 70 S. 6th Street, Lansing, IA 52151; *Postcard Collector*, Joe Jones Publishing, P. O. Box 337, Iola, WI 54945.

Special Note: An up–to–date listing of books about and featuring postcards can be obtained from Gotham Book Mart & Gallery, Inc., 41 West 47th Street, New York, NY 10036.

Collectors' Clubs: *Barr's Postcard News* and the *Postcard Collector* publish lists of over fifty regional clubs in the United States and Canada.

Note: The following prices are for cards in excellent to mint condition—no sign of edgewear, no creases, not trimmed, no writing on the picture side of the card, no tears, and no dirt. Each defect would reduce the price given by 10%.

Comics, Three Blind Mice, $25.00.

ADVERTISING

American Motor Co, Brockton, MA, motorcycles **8.00**

American Soda Fountain Co, smiling
   sphinx 25.00
Appleton, William, Florist 2.00
Ballard's Obelisk Flour 4.00
Berry Brothers Varnishes 4.50
Conkey's Poultry Remedies 3.00
Chrysler Corp, Detroit, MI, 1942 ..... 10.00
Curtis Publishing Co, Phila 3.50
Diamond Expansion Bolt Co, Garwood,
   NJ 4.00
Elgin Watch Co 3.50
Estey Pipe Organ Co, Brattleboro, VT . 5.00
Fox Visible Typewriter 7.50
Fralinger's Candy Co, Atlantic City, NJ,
   nursery rhyme 8.00
Genesse Brewing Co, Rochester, NY,
   linen 5.00
Grand Union Tea Co 5.00
Hartley's Jam Works 2.00
Hill's Nursery 4.25
Hotel Astor, NY 3.50
Independent Wall Paper Co, int. 2.50
Iowa Seed Co 2.00
Johnson's Corn Flour 8.50
Kalamazoo Savings Bank, Kalamazoo,
   MI 3.00
Kugler's Restaurants 2.00
Lash's Bitters 4.00
Luray Caverns, Luray, VA 2.00
Mandell Bros, Chicago, Dept Store ... 2.50
Mother's Magazine, David C Cook ... 4.00
National Press, Lovers' Edition 4.00
New York Life Insurance, NY 2.00
Ohio Dairy Co 5.00
Old Town Canoe Co, Old Town, ME . 6.00
Pacific Mail Steamship Co 2.50
Pratt Food Co, Phila 3.75
Quaker Oats Co, Chicago, movie star . 3.00
Rainier Beer, Seatle 3.00
Rogers Brothers Silverplate 3.00
Santesa Grape Fruit 2.00
Sloppy Joe's Bar, Havana, Cuba, pho-
   tographic 3.00
Sugar Creek Creamery 2.00
Tip Top Baking Goods, Tip Top Boy .. 3.00
Troy Detachable Collars 3.25
Uhlen Baby Carriages 3.75
United Cigar Stores 2.00
Vaughan, H. G., San Francisco photog-
   rapher 2.00
Walker House, Toronto 3.00
Wilson's Supply Co, Long Island 5.00
Wrigley's Chewing Gum 2.00
Zimmerman's Hungarian Restaurant,
   NY, int 2.75

ARTIST SIGNED

Attwell, Mabel Lucie
   Early by Tuck 8.00
   Regular 5.00
Basch, Arpad, Art Nouveau 85.00

Artist signed, F. Earl Christy, "Roses Are Always In Season," $24.00.

Bertiglia, children 9.00
Boileau, Philip
   By Reinthal Neiman 15.00
   Tuck publishing 75.00
Bompard 15.00
Boulanger, Maurice, cats 12.00
Brill, Ginks 6.00
Browne, Tom
   American baseball series 9.00
   English comics 3.50
Brundage, Frances
   Children 12.00
   Early chromolithographic 30.00
Brunelleschi, Art Nouveau 150.00
Busi, Art Deco 15.00
Caldecott
   Early 5.00
   1974 reprints .... .25
Carmichael, comic 3.00
Carr, Gene 6.00
Chiostri, Art Deco 40.00
Christy, Howard Chandler 10.00
Clappsaddle, Ellen
   Children 9.00
   Floral, bells, non-children 3.00
   Mechanicals, Halloween 85.00
   Suffrage 55.00
Corbella, Art Deco 15.00
Corbett, Bertha, sunbonnets 12.00
Curtis, E, children 3.00
Daniell, Eva, Art Nouveau 100.00
Drayton/Weiderseim, Grace, children . 30.00
Dwig 5.00
Fidler, Alice Luella, women 6.00
Fisher, Harrison 10.00
Gassaway, K, children 8.00
Gibson, Charles Dana 5.00
Golay, Mary 2.00
Greiner, M.
   Blacks 8.00
   Children 3.50
   Molly and her Teddy Bear 8.00

Griggs, H.B.	9.00
Gunn, Archie	3.50
Gutmann, Bessie Pease	17.50
Humphrey, Maud, signed	55.00
Innes, John	5.00
Johnson, children	6.00
Kirchner, Raphael	
First period	125.00
Second period	65.00
Third period	40.00
Klein, Catherine	
Alphabet	15.00
Alphabet letters X,Y,Z	25.00
Floral	3.00
Kohloer, Mela, early	85.00
Mauzan, Art Deco	15.00
May, Phil, British	8.00
McCay, Winsor, Little Nemo	20.00
Mucha, Alphonse	
Art Nouveau, months of the year	125.00
Art Nouveau, Slavic period	60.00
Women, full card design	500.00
O'Neill, Rose	
Black, from Puck	75.00
Kewpies	30.00
Suffrage	120.00
Opper, Frederick	6.00
Outcault	
Buster Brown calendars	12.00
Yellow Kid calendars	55.00
Parkinson, Ethel, children	6.00
Patella, women	25.00
Payne, Harry	22.00
Phillips, Coles	15.00
Price, Mary Evans, (M.E.P.)	4.50
Remington, Frederic	25.00
Robinson, Robert	25.00
Rockwell, Norman, after 1918	35.00
Russell, Charles	9.00
Shinn, Cobb	4.00
Smith, Jessie Wilcox	15.00
Studdy, Bonzo Dog	10.00
Tam, Jean	15.00

Thiele, Arthur	
Blacks, large faces	25.00
Blacks, on bikes	35.00
Cats, in action	15.00
Cats, large head	8.00
Twelvetrees, Charles, comic children	4.00
Underwood, Clarence	7.00
Upton, Florence, Golliwoggs, Tuck	35.00
Wain, Louis	
Cats	40.00
Paper dolls	200.00
Wall, Bernhardt, sunbonnets	15.00
Wood, Lawson	6.00

EXPOSITION

Alaska-Yukon-Pacific	6.00
California Midwinter	195.00
Cotton States Exposition	125.00
Hudson-Fulton	7.50
Jamestown	4.50
Jamestown Bears, mechanical, 144 designs on one card	300.00
Lewis and Clark Exposition	8.00
Pan American	
Black and white	4.50
Color	9.50
Panama-California	4.50
Panama-Pacific	
General	8.00
Mitchell Publishing	2.00
Portland Rose Festival	3.50
Portola Festival	
Poster advertising	15.00
Views	1.50
Priest of Pallas	8.50
Saint Louis 1904 Exposition	
Eggshell paper	6.00
H-T-L (Inside Inn)	95.00
Hold-to-lights	35.00
Silver background	7.50
Trans-Mississippi	
Advertising	100.00
Officials	55.00
World Columbian Exposition 1893	
Official	15.00
Preofficials	75.00

GREETINGS

April Fools	
Comic	1.50
French with Fish	5.00
Birthday floral	.10
Christmas, no Santas	.50
Christmas, Santa	
German, highly embossed	20.00
Installment, unused	100.00
Red suits	6.00
Suits other than red	12.00
Easter	
Animals, dressed	3.50

Blacks, artist signed, Arthur Thiele, $25.00

Chick or rabbits	1.50
Children dressed as animals	4.50
Crosses	.50
Fourth of July	
No children	1.50
Uncle Sam or children	4.50
Ground Hog Day	
Early large image	150.00
After 1930	18.00
Halloween	
Children	3.50
Children, extremely colorful	7.50
Plain	2.00
Labor Day	
Lounsbury	185.00
Nash	85.00
Leap Year	4.50
Mother's Day, early	4.00
New Years	
Bells, no children	.50
Children or Father Time	2.50
Saint Patrick's Day	
Children	4.50
No children	1.00
Thanksgiving	
Children	3.50
No children	1.00
Valentines	
Children, women	3.50
Hearts, comics no children	.50

Novelty, artist signed, Arthur Thiele, $15.00.

PATRIOTIC

Decoration Day	7.50
Lincoln	4.50
Patriotic Songs	3.00
Uncle Sam	6.00
Washington	3.50
World War II vintage, linens	1.00

PHOTOGRAPHIC

Children under Christmas trees	3.50

Children with animals or toys	4.50
Christmas trees	2.00
Circus Performers, close-up	8.00
Exaggerations	
Conrad, after 1935	6.00
Martin	8.50
Main Streets	
Added trains or trolleys	20.00
Large Cities	4.00
Small towns	9.00
Unidentified	.50
People on Paper Moons	3.00
Railroad Depots, with Trains, identified	20.00
Shop Exteriors, identified location	6.00
Shop Interiors	
Clear images of products	15.00
Workers: barbers, blacksmiths, etc	20.00
Unidentified familys	.50

POLITICAL AND SOCIAL HISTORY

Billy Possum	8.00
Blacks	8.00
Campaigns	
1900	75.00
1904	45.00
Indians, named	6.00
Jewish, comic	8.00
McKinley's death	6.00
Prohibition	6.00
Roosevelt's African Tour	3.00
Russo-Japanese War	6.00
Suffrage	
Cargill publisher, number 111 only	100.00
General	15.00
Parades	15.00
Taft, cartoons	10.00
Wilson	6.00

PUBLISHERS

Detroit	
Indians	8.00
Views	1.50
PFB	
Children	8.00
Comic	6.00
Santas	20.00
Paul Finkenrath/Berlin (PFB), greetings	1.50
Tuck Publishing	
Children, unsigned	4.50
Greetings	1.00
Views	1.00
Whitney	
Children	4.50
Nibble Nicks, Santas	12.00
Winsch Publishing	
Greetings	1.50
Halloween by S. L. Schmucker	65.00
Santas	15.00
Valentines by Schmucker	35.00

RARE AND UNUSUAL

Boileau, Tuck	75.00
Coke Advertising, Hamilton King	350.00
DuPont Dirigible	65.00
Frog-in-the-Throat, oversized	50.00
Greenaway, Kate, signed	350.00
Hold-to-lights, other than buildings	30.00
Installment, Uncle Sam	85.00
Kewpie ice cream advertising post cards, spell Victory	90.00
Kewpies by Gross Publishing Co	125.00
Mechanicals	65.00
PFB, mechanical Punch and Judy	75.00
Paper Dolls, Tuck	90.00
Santa Claus	
Black-faced	90.00
Hold-to-light	100.00
Silks	
Applied, Santas and state bells	35.00
Woven	65.00
Tuck Scouts, Harry Payne	100.00
Warner Corset, Mucha	300.00
Waverly Cycle, Mucha	4,800.00
Wiener Werkstatte, Kokoschka	1,500.00

POSTERS

Collecting Hints: Posters are collected either for their subject and historical value, e.g. movie, railroad, minstrel, etc., or for their aesthetic appeal. Modern art historians have recognized the poster as one of the most creative art forms of our times.

Often a popular film would be re–released several times over a period of years. Most re–releases can be identified by looking at the lower right corner in the white border area. A re–release will usually be indicated with an ''R'' and a diagonal slash mark with the year of the newest release. Therefore, a ''R/47'' would indicate a 1947 issue.

History: The poster was an extremely effective and critical means of mass communication, especially in the period before 1920. Enormous quantities were produced, helped in part by the propaganda role played by posters in World War I.

Print runs of two million were not unknown. Posters were not meant to be saved. Once they served their purpose, they tended to be destroyed. The paradox of high production and low survival is one of the fascinating aspects of poster history.

The posters of the late 19th century and early 20th century represent the pinnacle of American lithography printing. The advertising posters of firms such as Strobridge or Courier are true classics. Philadelphia was one center for the poster industry.

Europe pioneered in posters with high artistic and aesthetic content. Many major artists of the 20th century designed posters. Poster art still plays a key role throughout Europe today.

References: John Barnicoat, *A Concise History of Posters*, Harry Abrams, Inc., 1976; Tony Fusco, *The Official Identification and Price Guide To Posters*, House of Collectibles, 1990; Walton Rawls, *Wake Up, America!: World War I and the American Poster*, Abbeville Press, 1988; Stephen Rebello and Richard Allen, *Reel Art: Great Posters From The Golden Age of the Silver Screen*, Abbeville Press, 1988; George Theofiles, *American Posters of World War I: A Price and Collector's Guide*, Dafram House Publishers, Inc.

Collectors' Club: Poster Society, Inc., P.O. Box 43171, Montclair, NJ 07043.

Advisor: George Theofiles.

REPRODUCTION ALERT: Some of the posters by A. M. Cassandre have been reproduced in France.

ADVERTISING

Alaga Syrup, 20 x 10", Willie Mays, color or photo offset, c1950	50.00
Ann Fulton YWCA—The Chintz Room—A Quiet Restaurant—Men Are Welcome, 22 x 28", c1914	135.00
Buckwheat Flour, 19 x 10", flour bag shape	25.00
Eat More Fruit For Health & Vitality, 20 x 15", pin–up girl and baskets of fruits, English, c1938	80.00
Fatima Turkish Cigarettes, 14 x 17", harem girl's face, yellow, red, and green ground, c1910	125.00
Grand Parisi Champagne, 11 x 15", Art Deco litho, c1925	100.00
Henry Clay Habana, 19 x 25", c1903, Clay in center, plant, banded cigars, and boxes surround	425.00
Pacific Paints, 47 x 62", Charles Verneau, sailors rowing out to steamship, c1900	135.00
San–Tox Pine Balsam, 35 x 19", stone litho, early 20th C, linen backing	50.00
Swing With Sinclair, 44 x 28", red car, blue ground, c1938	85.00
Take Some Home—Independent Brewing Co of Pittsburgh, 21 x 11", Maynard Williamson, 1910	85.00
The Rose Tea Rooms—Regent Street, London, 20 x 29", Misti, c1900, linen backing	275.00
Wrigley's Gum–Pioneer Women Helped Build Our Great Country, 28 x 11", Otis Shepard, 1943	115.00
Won't Wrinkle Ever! Van Heusen Cen-	

tury Shirts, 23 x 17", Ronald Reagan modeling shirt, 1953 .... **45.00**

CAUSES

American Field Service, Nuyttens, 20 x 30", 1917, man in French helmet leads way for transport under flare lit sky, light and dark blues **275.00**
Be Ready! Keep Him Smiling, United War Work, anonymous, 21 x 11", smiling Doughboy **95.00**
Cleveland–Many Peoples One Language, Board of Education, JH Donahey, 11 x 18", 1917, appeal in six languages, gives locations where classes are held **175.00**
Hey Fellows! Your Money Brings The Book We Need, JE Sheridan, 20 x 30", 1918, Doughboy holds book high while sailor reads at his side, vivid orange background **75.00**
1919 War Chest–Minneapolis, J Almars, 54 x 40", lists agencies to be financed by campaign **175.00**
The Comforter, Gordon Grant, 18 x 24", Red Cross nurse comforts refugee, pinks, blue, red, and brown **125.00**

MOVIES

One Sheet, 27 x 41"
Alaska, Monogram, 1944, Ken Taylor, John Carradine, Margaret Lindsay, orange, blue, and black litho of stars, dance scene in front of mountain setting **100.00**
Black Swan, Fox, 1942, Tyrone Power, Maureen O'Hara, mounted on linen **400.00**
Crazy Knights, Monogram, 1944, Three Stooges, Shemp Howard, Billy Gilbert, Maxie Rosenbloom . **125.00**
Flying High, MGM, 1931, Pat O'Brien, Bert Lahr, Tooker litho .. **150.00**
Great Plane Robbery, Columbia, 1940, Jack Holt **75.00**
Haunted House, Monogram, 1940, Jackie Moran, Marcia Mae Jones . **75.00**
Laurel & Hardy In The Big Noise, Fox, 1944, Tooker litho **300.00**
One New York Night, MGM, 1935, Franchot Tone, Una Merkel **110.00**
Paleface, Paramount, 1948, Bob Hope, Jane Russell **100.00**
Rookie Cop, RKO, 1939, Ace the Wonder Dog, Tim Holt **100.00**
Song of Love, MGM, 1947, Katherine Hepburn, Paul Henreid **75.00**
Sweet Rosie O'Grady, Fox, 1943, Betty Grable, Robert Young, Adolphe Menjou **150.00**

Up The River, Fox, 1938, Preston Foster, Tony Martin **100.00**
Three Sheets, 41 x 81"
Arizona Wildcat, Fox, 1937, Jane Withers, Tooker litho **175.00**
Courtship of Andy Hardy, MGM, 1942, Mickey Rooney, Tooker litho **110.00**
Guilty, Monogram, 1944, Bonita Granville, Don Castle **125.00**
Phantom of 42nd Street, PRC, 1945, Dave O'Brien, Kay Aldridge **100.00**
Wintertime, Fox, 1943, Sonja Henie, Cesar Romero, Carole Landis, Woody Herman and orchestra, Tooker litho **225.00**

SPORTS

British Empire & Commonwealth Games, Perth, Western Australia, 25 x 40", panorama of city, 1962 ..... **150.00**
Fidass Sporting Goods, 29 x 52", F Romoli, Italian soccer player, 1946 ..... **300.00**
Grays of Cambridge, 24 x 39", Affiches Marci, large tennis racket bounces "The Light Blue Tennis Ball" toward viewer, c1947 .... **225.00**
High Diver, 27 x 29", Arthur Albrecht & Co, swimming exhibition, c1910 ... **325.00**
Let's Go Skiing–Use The New Haven RR Snow Trains, 14 x 22", Sascha Maurer, c1937 .... **125.00**
Munich Olympics 1972–Fencing, 33 x 46", Gaebele, posted at Olympics .. **125.00**
Ninth International Students' Games Paris 1947, 30 x 46", P Colin **350.00**
Philadelphia Sunday Press, 16 x 22", red haired female tennis player, c1896 . **125.00**
Samson Kina, 20 x 30", Goffart, Brussels, chromolithograph of two boxers, c1910 .... **275.00**
The Saturday Evening Post 100th Year of Baseball, 22 x 28", Norman Rockwell, 1939 .... **175.00**
Winter Sports–National and State Parks, 27 x 40", D Waugh, high style Art Deco couple in ski attire, c1935 ... **225.00**

THEATER

A Royal Rogue Starring Jefferson De Angelis & Company, 40 x 80", Metropolitan Printing, c1900 .... **175.00**
Blue Jeans, 40 x 30", Enquirer Co, c1905 .... **200.00**
Charles A Gardner In His New Comedy–The Prize Winner, 42 x 80", Greve Litho Co, Milwaukee, c1900 . **175.00**
Child Slaves of New York, 20 x 30", Strobridge Litho, 1903 .... **165.00**
La Glu, 26 x 35", Robert DuPont, 1910 **175.00**

Lena Horne: The Lady and Her Music, 14 x 22", c1980 .... **35.00**

Life's Shop Window, 40 x 80", Ritchey Litho, c1900 .... **210.00**

Madam Butterfly—A Grand Opera by Giacomo Puccini, 28 x 42", Enquirer Litho Co, c1900 .... **175.00**

Nip and Tuck, Detectives Out Of The Window Into The Water, 28 x 21", J M Jones Co, Chicago, c1880 ...... **225.00**

Patterson's New York Opera Co—In The Queen's Handkerchief, 13 x 28", Currier Co, Buffalo, c1885 .... **250.00**

Penelope, 27 x 35½", George Rochegross **150.00**

Rosemarie, 40 x 90", English, c1948 .. **200.00**

Salsbury's Troubadours—Nelly McHenry, 20 x 30", Strobridge, c1880 . **225.00**

TRANSPORTATION

Air France—Afrique Du Nord, 24 x 39", Villemot, c1947 .... **175.00**

Automobile Club Show Old Deer Park, London, 20 x 30", c1905 .... **600.00**

British Airways, 24 x 33", c1934 ..... **400.00**

Chicago, Milwaukee And St Paul Railway, 24 x 34", c1870 .... **250.00**

Clement Cycles and Automobiles Paris, 49 x 36", F Bombled, French army officers, c1914 .... **325.00**

Favor Cycles, 62 x 47", c1925, linen backing **350.00**

National Flying Day, 15 x 23", 1937 .. **100.00**

Nice Auto Races—12 June 1949, 25 x 39", J Ramel, 1949 .... **350.00**

Speed To Winter Playgrounds In Pullman Safety and Comfort, 19 x 27", William Welsh, 1935 .... **300.00**

SS France, A New Concept In Luxury For All, 34 x 45", Bob Peak Litho, launching, 1962 .... **225.00**

Swiss Air, 27 x 39", Herbert Leupin, c1955 .... **250.00**

Veritable Vieux Systems, 17 x 23", chromolithograph, drinkers in hot air balloon gondola, 1890 .... **175.00**

TRAVEL

American Airlines to Ireland, 30 x 40", E McKnight Kauffer, 1948 .... **200.00**

Arizona: American Airlines, 40 x 30", c1955 .... **50.00**

Berwick Upon Tweed—It's Quicker By Rail—liner, 25 x 40", Frank Mason, 1935 .... **275.00**

British Railways: Visit London In Coronation Year, 40 x 25", 1953, linen backing **150.00**

Britain In Winter, 29 x 19", Terence Cuneo **50.00**

Come to Britain for Racing, 20 x 30", Lionel Edwards, litho, c1948 ...... **65.00**

Genoa and the Italian Riviera, 27 x 39", Graffonara, 1931 .... **325.00**

Land of the Pueblos—New Mexico—Santa Fe Railway, 18 x 24", c1940 . **75.00**

Montage De France, 24 x 39", Nathan, c1947 .... **125.00**

Sunny Ryhl—The Children's Paradise, 25 x 40", Mays, c1946 .... **300.00**

Visit Tunisia, 24 x 38", Yahia, c1938 . **150.00**

WORLD WAR I

An Education For You—Join The Tanks, US Army, JP Wharton, 18 x 24", orange, black, and white **175.00**

Britishers—Enlist Today 280 Broadway, Guy Lipscombe, 27 x 40", brilliant Union Jack against deep British green borders **225.00**

Columbia Calls—Enlist In The Army, Francis A Halstead, 28 x 40", chromolithograph, Columbia with banner and sword atop globe, sky blue ground **200.00**

Enlist In The Navy, Louis Raemakers, 30 x 40", Uncle Sam as doughboy, frees woman from Kaiser Wilhelm in front of foggy image of Statue of Liberty .. **165.00**

Follow The Flag For Freedom The Navy Strikes Now, James Daugherty, 14 x 22", stylized Columbia points sword to multicolored horizon as sailor looks on, vivid colors **125.00**

Join The Quartermaster Corps, John W Sheeres, 18 x 26", 1919, smiling Uncle Sam in doughboy outfit, purple starry heavens **150.00**

USN Travel and Learn In The Navy, CB Falls, 14 x 21", c1919, woodblock style **175.00**

WORLD WAR II

Arise Americans, Your Country And Your Liberty Are In Grave Danger, McClelland Barclay, 28 x 41", 1941, sailor preparing deck gun **150.00**

Defend Your Country—Enlist Now US Army, Tom Woodburn, 21 x 11", 1940, determined Uncle Sam against red, white, and blue stars and stripes background, card stock **100.00**

Enlist Now US Marine Corps, Okinawa, As part of the 10th Army the first and sixth Marine divisions...shared in the victory in Okinawa, JR McDermitt, 29 x 40", 1945, fiery battle scene **200.00**

Flying Steel, Walter L Greene, 28 x 41", 1936, *USS Farragut*, A New Destroyer

World War II, WAAC, This Is My War Too!, $65.00.

Equipped with the Most Modern Machinery **125.00**
Freshman! Sophomores! Now You Can Stay In College And Become A Naval Officer, McClelland Barclay, 14 x 22", 1942 .... **125.00**
Good Soldier–The Wac, anonymous, 25 x 38", c1944, smiling full color WAC **150.00**
Keep 'Em Flying–Sure I'll Help! US Army Air Corps, Graves, 25 x 38", 1943 .... **150.00**
Scrap Will Help Win–Don't Mix It, anonymous, 22 x 34", 1942, Mandel Company, conservation image, red background **125.00**
Think American–Great Americans Don't Take Time Off, CR Miller, 20 x 28", 1943, male and female factory workers working lathe in front of ghostly battle scene **125.00**
Time For Action–Join The Coast Guard, anonymous, 28 x 42", silk screen of Coast Guard torpedo boat firing at Japanese fighter plane **150.00**
United Nations Fight For Freedom, Broder, 29 x 40", 1942, flags of all nations atop silvery Statue of Liberty **100.00**
What To Do In Blackouts, anonymous, 28 x 43", 1943, Civil Defense broadside **75.00**

ELVIS PRESLEY

Collecting Hints: Official Elvis Presley items are usually copyrighted and many are dated.

Learn to differentiate between items licensed during Elvis's lifetime and the wealth of "fantasy" items issued after his death. The latter are collectibles, but have nowhere near the value of the pre–1977 material.

Also accept the fact that much of the modern limited edition issues are purely speculative investments. It is best to buy them because you like them and plan to live with them for an extended period of time.

History: When Elvis Presley became a rock 'n' roll star, he became one of the first singers to have a promotion which was aimed at teenagers. The first Elvis merchandise appeared in 1956. During the following years new merchandise was added both in America and foreign countries. After his death in 1977, a vast number of new Elvis collectibles appeared.

References: Rosalind Cranor, *Elvis Collectibles,* Collector Books, 1983; Jerry Osborne, *Elvis Presley Record Guide,* O'Sullivan Woodside, 1983; Jerry Osborne, Perry Cox, and Joe Lindsay, *The Official Price Guide To Memorabilia of Elvis Presley and The Beatles,* House of Collectibles, 1988; Richard Peters, *Elvis, The Golden Anniversary Tribute,* Salem House, 1984.

Museums: Jimmy Velvet's Elvis Presley Museum, Franklin, TN; Graceland, Memphis, TN.

Book, *The Elvis Presley Story,* Hillman Books, 1960, 160 pgs, 32 black and white photo pgs **25.00**
Booklet, 4 x 6", 8 pgs, Fun In Acapulco, Paramount Pictures issue, 1963 .... **50.00**
Bracelet, 3", silver metal, stretch band, cover flips up, reveals black and white photo, marked "Hong Kong," 1960 .... **100.00**
Bust, 22" h **80.00**
Button
3", color photo portrait, blue signature, 1956 Elvis Presley Enterprises copyright **50.00**
3½", full color photo, "Sincerely Elvis," 1970s **12.00**
Calendar Card, 2¼ x 3¾", full color photo on front, calendar back, issued by RCA Victor, 1963 .... **18.00**
Catalog, Elvis RCA Victor Records, 3½ x 7", pictures, forty–five different albums and 45 rpm singles **18.00**
Charm Bracelet, metal link band, gold finish, 1956 Elvis Presley Enterprises **120.00**
Doll, 21", hard vinyl body, soft molded vinyl head, Celebrity Collection, white leather jumpsuit with gold trim, red scarf, white vinyl boots, jewelry accessories, microphone in one hand, includes authenticity certificate and 8 pg magazine, orig box, World Doll, copyright 1984 Elvis Presley Enterprises Inc **125.00**
Guitar, 31", hard plastic, brown marble body, white plastic top, braided strap,

marked "Emenee Official Elvis Presley Guitar" **400.00**
Lamp, 36", figural, bust **110.00**
Lobby Card, 11 x 14"
   Flaming Star, color illus, copyright 1960 20th Century Fox **12.50**
   Love Me Tender, 20th Century Fox, 1956 .... **22.00**
Magazine, *Country and Western Music Stars*, 8 x 11", issue #1, 2 pg article, Fawcett Publications, copyright 1958 **25.00**
Mug, plastic, multicolored, marked "Elvis the King Lives On, 1935–1977" . **5.00**
Pennant, 18", felt, red and green, center photo **12.00**
Perfume Bottle, 3½" h, glass, Teddy Bear, white plastic cap, black and white photo sticker, orig box, 1957 copyright by Elvis Presley Enterprises Inc **150.00**
Photo, 11¾", sq, full color portrait, light red background, 1960s **12.00**
Pillow, 10 x 10", cotton stuffed, blue piped trim, blue printed picture, Love Me Tender, and signature, orig tag marked "Personality Products Co Decorative Autographed Pillow" and 1956 Elvis Presley Enterprises copyright **250.00**
Pin, Fan Club **15.00**
Post Card, 3¼ x 5", two full color photos, Army uniform, marked "Holiday Greetings to You All From Elvis And The Colonel" in red **30.00**
Poster, 27 x 41", Blue Hawaii, Paramount, 1961 .... **50.00**
Record
   Hard Headed Woman/Don't Ask Me Why, 45 rpm, RCA Victor label, 1958 .... **25.00**
   King Creole, RCA Victor, black label, long play **15.00**
   Love Me Tender/Any Way You Want Me, RCA Victor label, 1956 ..... **50.00**
   Loving You, 45 rpm, includes Lonesome Cowboy, Hotdog, Mean Woman Blues, and Got A Lot O' Livin To Do, orig sleeve, 1957 ... **20.00**
Sheet Music
   Doncha' Think It's Time, 9 x 12", blue tone photo, 2 pgs, copyright 1958 Elvis Presley Music Inc **12.50**
   Hot Dog, 9 x 12", brown tone photo, 3 pgs, copyright 1957 Elvis Presley Music Inc **15.00**
   Wear Your Ring, 1958 .... **15.00**
Tab
   2" d, tin litho, blue and gold lettering, "I Love Elvis," metallic gold background, 1970s **10.00**
   2¼", tin litho, yellow, red name with blue inscription, c1970 .... **15.00**

Wallet, 3 x 4½", vinyl, red, key chain edge, color illus, marked "Elvis Presley Rock n' Roll, copyright 1956 Elvis Presley Enterprises" **350.00**

PSYCHEDELIC COLLECTIBLES

Collecting Hints: Look for psychedelic material in a wide range of areas, e.g., books, magazines, newspapers, clothing, jewelry, home decorations, music and music festivals, and television. Include as many three dimensional items as possible. When displaying your collection, keep it concentrated in one location. The psychedelic era emphasized a wild intermingling of color and design.

An excellent collection can be built focusing solely on pieces associated with the social protest movement. Collect over a wide range. A collection of just anti-war material is too limited.

History: Psychedelic collectibles are defined by period, 1960s and 1970s, and by the highly innovative use of colors and design. The roots of psychedelic art and color are many, e.g., late nineteenth century graphics, paisley fabrics, quilts and coverlets, the color reversal techniques of Joseph Alberts, American Indian art, and dancer Loie Fuller's diaphanous material which produced a light show as she moved and swirled.

It was a period without limits on design. As a result, the period was marked by eclecticism, rather than unity. Among its features was the incorporation of new technological advances, e.g, vinyl, polyester, metallic fabrics, non-woven fabric (paper), into its products. Inflatable plastic furniture was made. Everywhere the look was "far out" and informal.

Peter Max was the leading designer of the period. Few items in the late 1960s escaped his art. Although mass produced, many items fall into the scarce category.

References: Paul D. Grushkin, *The Art of Rock: Posters from Presley to Punk*, Abbeville Press, 1987; Alison Fox, *Rock & Pop—Phillips Collector's Guide*, Dunestyle Publishing/Boxtree, 1988; Joel Lobenthal, *Radial Rags: Fashions of the Sixties*, Abbeville Press, 1990; Susanne White, *Psychedelic Collectibles of the 1960s & 1970s: An Illustrated Price Guide*, Wallace–Homestead, 1990.

Bed Spread, Laugh-In, yellow, pink, blue, orange, black, green, and white, c1969 .... **65.00**
Belt, leather, fringed, wood beads, purple and cream, 1969 .... **10.00**
Book
   Man From Utopia, Rick Griffin,

printed by Calitho, San Francisco, CA, 1972 .... 20.00
Psychedelic Art, Robert E L Masters, Jean Houston, Ballance House Book, Grove Press, 1968 .... 45.00
Book Cover, 10 x 13", full color Peter Max illus, late 1960s 12.50
Boots, go–go, metallic gold, 1968 .... 40.00
Clothing
  Jacket, Nehru, blue, purple buttons, 1965–67 .... 40.00
  Mini Dress, polyester, white, black, and red, Lucite circles, c1968 ... 55.00
  Pants, cotton, red, white, and blue stars and stripes, c1969 .... 45.00
  Pantyhose, gray, red, brown, purple, and blue design, 7 x 9" retail bag, Peter Max design, full color photo of girl wearing stockings, Burlington Cameo, late 1960s 25.00
  Shirt, black and white check, Golden Fleetline, 1967–68 .... 30.00
  Sport Coat, man's, all–over white, black, tan, rust, and olive green floral, Original from Brad Whitney, California 65.00
  Vest, suede, fringed, Neiman–Marcus, 1968 .... 40.00
Concert Poster
  Family Dog, 14 x 20", Nov 11–12, 1966, Avalon Ballroom, green and purple design, white background . 50.00
  Woodstock, 18 x 24¼", Aug 15–17, 1969, art by Skolnic 200.00
Curtain, 60" l, 36" w, beaded, plastic, red, white, and blue, c1969 .... 48.00
Doll, 18" h, Chrissy, hippy outfit, Ideal Toy Corp, 1972 .... 40.00
Earrings, vinyl, daisy shape, white, pink, and green, 1968 .... 8.00
Embroidery Set, Peter Max Embroidery Set, embroidery hoop, six printed designs, thread, beads, felt shapes, picture frame, and instruction book, orig box, unused 30.00
Hat, cotton, blue, pink, orange, olive, and yellow design, marked "Made in Hong Kong," c1970 .... 35.00
Ice Bucket, 16" h, vinyl and lucite, red, orange, green, purple, white, and blue design, c1970 .... 32.00
Magazine, *Peter Max,*, Vol 1, #1, Peter–Lee Inc, 1970 .... 48.00
Movie Poster
  Psych–Out, 40 x 60", American International Pictures, white, black, and multicolored, 1968 .... 100.00
  The Wiz, 13⅞ x 23", black, white, green, blue, and purple, 1974 ... 75.00
Mug, 3¼", pottery, white, black "Peace" and symbol 12.50
Necklace, pewter, "Peace" 8.00

Necktie, cotton, orange, yellow, white, and tan tie–dye design, c1970 ..... 12.00
Newspaper, *Oracle,* San Francisco 45.00
Pillow, 12", plastic, daisy shape, clear, yellow and orange accents, marked "Made in Taiwan," c1970 .... 12.00
Place Mats, 15 x 10½", set of 4, cotton, all–over white, green, and yellow peace symbols 45.00
Poster Book, Peter Max, 11 x 16", sixteen full color posters, dated 4/3/70 25.00
Print, 18½ x 25", Check Nude, artist Lawrence, white and black, framed, 1968–70 .... 50.00
Scarf, rayon, all–over white, red, and blue peace symbols, 1971–72 ..... 38.00
Waste Can, 16" h, 9½" d, tin litho, three people on trapeze illus, rainbow and stars background, marked "Peter Max," early 1970s 100.00
Writing Paper, 7¾ x 10¾", flourescent pink, yellow, orange and green "Mod" and designs, unused, 1968–69 .... 12.00

PULP MAGAZINES

Collecting Hints: Pulps in the finest condition are the most highly prized, but even pulps in lesser condition are collectible if priced accordingly.

Pulp collections can be limited to certain themes or as unlimited and varied as a collector's interest. Many collectors specialize in certain titles (e.g., *Weird Tales*), certain genres (science fiction and horror being the most popular), special characters (Doc Savage, The Shadow, The Spider, Wu Fang, G-8, Tarzan, etc.), or special authors (H. P. Lovecraft, Robert E. Howard, Edgar Rice Burroughs, Dashiell Hammett, etc.).

A typical collecting problem for many novice collectors is the unknowledgeable dealer who, knowingly or unknowingly, prices common issues far above any retail price that could possibly be realized from a serious collector. Much of the overpricing results because the general dealer has no experience with pulps and their actual prices among collectors. New pulp collectors are advised to find an established pulp dealer early in their collecting career to avoid overpaying for the core portion of their collection.

History: The pulp magazine was the direct descendant of the dime novel and the ancestor of the paperback book, coming into popularity in the early 20th century and lasting into the early 1950s.

The early pulps were dimensionally a little smaller than the average magazine. They derived their collective name from the fact that they were printed on cheap, pulpwood paper. Most had untrimmed edges.

Pulp magazines generally were aimed at a male audience and devoted to so-called "cheap" genres such as western, mystery, science fiction, jungle adventure, sport, air war and combat, horror, and girlie themes. "Nothing was too cheap that could not be exploited," wrote the early pulp writer Frank Gruber.

A main attraction of pulp magazines is some of the most lurid and colorful cover art ever produced. These covers were created to entice the buyer. Many are totally outrageous. The covers promised (and sometimes delivered) an interior filled with excitement, adventure, and enchantment.

Pulp magazines reached their peak of general public popularity in the 1930s, the "golden age" of this collectible in most collectors' eyes.

World War II paper shortages caused the demise of many titles and several publishers. The emergence of the popular mass market paperback a few years later finished the job. After early 1953, very few pulps existed in their original format. Those that did survive changed to a handier, digest size format.

There was a considerable renewal of interest in the pulps in the 1960s. Some of the most popular characters, e.g., Doc Savage and The Shadow, were revived and reprinted in paperback form.

References: Tony Goodstone, *The Pulps*, Chelsea House, 1980; Frank Gruber, *The Pulp Jungle*, Sherbourne Press, 1967; Kenneth Jones, *The Shudder Pulps*, FAX Collectors Editions, 1975; McKinstry and Weinberg, *The Hero Pulp Index*, Opar Press, 1971; Robert Sampson, *Yesterday's Faces: Glory Figures, Vol. 1*, Bowling Green University Press, 1983; Robert Sampson, *Yesterday's Faces: Strange Days, Vol. 2*, Bowling Green University Press, 1984.

Periodicals: *Echoes*, 504 E Morris St, Seymour, TX 76380; *Golden Perils*, 5 Milliken Mills Road, Scarboro, ME 04074; *Nemisis, Inc.*, 2438 S Highland Ave, Berwyn, IL 60402; *Pulp and Paperback Market*, 5813 York Ave, Edina, MN 55410; *Pulp Collector*, 8417 Carrollton Parkway, New Carrollton, MD 20784; *Pulp Vault*, 5451 N East River Rd, #1209, Chicago, IL 60656.

Museum: The Hess Collection of Popular Literature, University of Minnesota, Minneapolis, MN.

Adventure, 8/1/35, contains part one of "The Feud at Single Shot" by Luke Short [NOTE: Luke's first published work]	6.00
All–Story, 10/12, contains "Tarzan of the Apes" by Edgar Rice Burroughs [NOTE: This is the first appearance of Tarzan and is the complete novel, not a short story version]	625.00

Smokehouse Monthly, Sept 1929, Fawcett Publications, Inc, Capt Billy Fawcett Editor, 5¼ x 7½", $20.00.

All–Story Weekly	
10/21/16	10.00
12/02/16, contains part four of "Tarzan and the Jewels of Opar" by Edgar Rice Burroughs	23.00
Amazing Stories	
1/41, contains "John Carter and the Giant of Mars by Edgar Rice Burroughs and John Coleman Burroughs	10.00
6/49	2.00
Argosy	
8/22/36, contains part one of "Don Peon" by Johnston McCulley	7.50
1/07/39, contains part one of "Synthetic Men of Mars" by Edgar Rice Burroughs	9.50
Avenger, The, 11/40	7.00
Black Mask, 9/49, contains story by Louis L'amour	4.00
Blue Book	
8/16	12.00
9/16, contains part one of "The New Stories of Tarzan" by Edgar Rice Burroughs	25.00
Detective Fiction Weekly, 8/03/40, contains story by Clayton Rawson	6.00
Detective Novel Magazine, Spring/42	4.00
Detective Short Stories, 11/42	4.50
Detective Story Magazine, 6/46	2.00
Doc Savage	
4/36, Canadian edition	10.00
7/36	20.00
Famous Fantastic Mysteries, 12/40	2.75
Fantastic Novels, 9/40	2.00
Fantastic Story Quarterly, Summer/50	2.00
Fantastic Universe, 4/56, digest size, contains story by Robert E. Howard	2.50
Future Science Fiction, #28, 1955, digest size, contains the Tarzan and Conan parody "Cornzan the Mighty" by L. Sprague de Camp	2.00

Guilty Detective Story Magazine, 3/60,
digest size 2.25
Hopalong Cassidy, Winter/51, contains
"Hopalong Cassidy and the Trail to
Seven Pines," by Louis L'amour writ-
ing under the pseudonym of Tex
Burns 25.00
Ideal Love, 3/48 .... 2.75
Imagination, 2/53, contains story by
Charles Beaumont 2.00
Lone Ranger, 10/37 .... 25.00
Masked Rider, 5/45 .... 4.50
New Western, 9/49 .... 3.50
Operator 5, Jan–Feb/38 .... 20.00
Other Worlds, 6/51, digest size 3.50
Phantom Detective, 11/39 .... 6.50
Pioneer Western, #1, 1950, contains
comic book section 7.00
Planet Stories, Summer/49 .... 3.00
Popular Western, 4/47 .... 3.50
Red Star Mystery, 6/40, contains story
by Clayton Rawson 30.00
The Shadow, 11/36 .... 24.00
Sparkling Love Stories, #1, 1950, con-
tains comic book section 7.00
Startling Stories, Summer/45 .... 2.50
Super Detective, 12/49 .... 4.50
Super Science Fiction, 4/57, digest size,
contains story by Harlan Ellison 2.50
Super Science Stories
1/41 .... 2.75
4/44 .... 3.50
Ten Story Fantasy, #1, 1951 .... 9.00
Thrilling Detective, 6/46 .... 2.50
Thrilling Western, 10/48 .... 3.50
Thrilling Wonder Stories, 4/37 .... 5.00
Weird Tales, 7/35 .... 30.00
Wonder Story Annual, #1, 1950 ..... 4.00

PUNCHBOARDS

Collecting Hints: Punchboards which are unpunched are collectible. A punched board has
little value unless it is an extremely rare design.
Like most advertising items, price is determined
by graphics and subject matter.

The majority of punchboards sell in the $8.00
to $30.00 range. The high end of the range is
represented by boards such as Golden Gate
Bridge at $85.00 and Baseball Classic at
$100.00.

History: Punchboards are self-contained games
of chance made of pressed paper containing
holes with coded tickets inside each hole. For an
agreed amount the player uses a "punch" to
extract the ticket of his or her choice. Prizes are
awarded to the winning ticket. Punch prices can
be 1¢, 2¢, 3¢, 5¢, 10¢, 20¢, 50¢, $1.00 or
more.

Not all tickets were numbered. Fruit symbols
were used extensively as well as animals. Some

punchboards had no printing at all, just colored
tickets. Other ticket themes included dice, cards,
dominoes, words, etc. One early board had
Mack Sennet bathing beauties.

Punchboards come in an endless variety of
styles. Names reflected the themes of the boards.
Barrel of Winners, Break the Bank, Baseball,
More Smokes, Lucky Lulu and Take It Off were
just a few.

At first punchboards were used to award cash.
As legal attempts to outlaw gambling arose,
prizes were switched to candy, cigars, cigarettes,
jewelry, radios, clocks, cameras, sporting goods,
toys, beer, chocolate, etc.

The golden age of punchboards was the 1920s
to the 1950s. Attention was focused on the keyed
punchboard in the film "The Flim Flam Man."
This negative publicity hurt the punchboard industry.

Museum: Amusement Sales, 127 North Main,
Midvale, UT 84047.

Advisor: Clark Phelps.

Bell Pots, slot symbols, $1.00 punch .. 30.00
Big Bills, 25¢ punch 18.00
Block Buster, 5¢ punch, double jackpot,
cash pay 18.00
Canasta, 5¢ punch, removable score
card 50.00
Cross Country Winner, seals, cash pay 20.00
Dime Joe, cash pay, 10¢ punch 15.00
Full of Tens, 25¢ punch, cash pay 15.00
Good As Gold, colorful, seals 20.00
Hi Yo Silver, 25¢ punch, cash pay with
jackpot 15.00
Joe's Special Prize, 25¢ punch, cash
board 18.00
Junior Kitty, kitten picture, cash pay .. 30.00
National Winner 20.00
Nickel Fins, 1,000 holes with seals ... 15.00
Pass–Hit & Crap, dice tickets, 50¢
punch 25.00
Pick a Cherry, cherry seals, cash pay .. 20.00
Planters Peanuts, 5¢ punch, peanut logo 30.00
Prize Pots, red head girl, 50¢ punch .. 65.00
Sports Push Cards, baseball, football,
basketball 5.00
Take It Easy, colorful, nude 50.00
Ten Big Sawbucks, 20¢ cash board ... 20.00
Worth Going For, 50¢ punch, girlie
board 20.00
Yankee Trader 20.00
Your Pick, 10¢ punch, money seals ... 30.00

PUZZLES

Collecting Hints: Choose a rationale for collecting based on your interests. Some collectors
choose puzzles for their visual appeal, some for
the challenge of putting them together, and

others for the patterns used in cutting the puzzles. Some collectors specialize according to subject matter, e.g., advertising, maps, transportation, or comic characters. Puzzles are easiest to find in the east, where historically they were most popular.

Puzzles are often difficult to date. Collectors should be aware that some puzzles, such as Milton Bradley's Smashed Up Locomotive, were produced for decades. The most popular prints were kept in inventory or reproduced as need arose, often by several different manufacturers. Thus, the date when a puzzle was made is often years later than the date or copyright on the print or box.

Collectors should avoid puzzles whose manufacturer can not be determined, unless the puzzle has specially attractive graphics or craftmanship.

Assembled puzzles can be displayed in frames, but should never be glued together. Exposure to light over long periods of time will cause fading. Dax or other plastic box frames are ideal for displays which can be changed periodically.

The market for puzzles is increasing because collectors of toys and character items usually want one or more puzzles in their collections too. Prices have especially soared for character puzzles and top quality nineteenth century children's puzzles.

The number of collectors is growing, so that prices have risen about 50 percent in the last five years. Puzzle collecting is most established in England. Prices for European children's puzzles were well defined in 1984 when Sotheby's auctioned the dazzling Hannas collection in London.

History: John Spilsbury, a London mapmaker, made the first jigsaw puzzles in the 1760s. Spilsbury "dissected" maps and sold them as educational toys. By 1850 children's jigsaw puzzles on all subjects were being made in the United States. Prominent manufacturers of the late nineteenth century include McLoughlin Brothers, Milton Bradley, and Selchow and Righter. Although the prints on very early puzzles were hand colored, color lithography was almost universal by 1870.

The early puzzles were made from solid wood or thick cardboard, with individual pieces "hand cut" one at a time with saws. Nineteenth century puzzles had few interlocking pieces, usually only on the edges. The widespread use of plywood and better saws after World War I led to more complex puzzle designs with all the pieces interlocking. Thinner cardboard puzzles, with all the pieces stamped out at once by steel dies, were introduced around 1890. Gradually these die–cut puzzles supplanted the hand–cut puzzles.

Puzzles for adults, more than 75 pieces, are a product of the twentieth century. Their introduction in 1908 unleashed a craze lasting several years. Puzzles were even more popular in the depression years of 1932–35 when many unemployed people had time to both cut up puzzles and put them back together. This period saw the emergence of many small–scale craftspeople who cut puzzles for local markets.

Some makers, such as Par (1932–1974), specialized in high quality custom designed wood puzzles for celebrities. Few makers of the more expensive hand–cut puzzles survived after World War II. Today there are only a handful of craftspeople still cutting puzzles in the United States. Among the post World War II die–cut puzzles, Springbok, now owned by Hallmark, is the premier domestic manufacturer.

References: Linda Hannas, *The English Jigsaw Puzzle, 1760–1890,* Wayland, 1972, out–of–print; Linda Hannas, *The Jigsaw Book,* Dial Press, 1981; Harry L. Rinker, *Collector's Guide To Toys, Games, and Puzzles,* Wallace–Homestead Book Company, 1991; Francene and Louis Sabin, *The One, The Only, The Original Jigsaw Puzzle Book,* Henry Regnery Co., Chicago, 1977, out–of–print; Anne D. Williams, *Jigsaw Puzzles: An Illustrated History and Price Guide,* Wallace–Homestead Book Company, 1990.

Collectors' Club: American Game Collectors Association, 4628 Barlow Drive, Bartlesville, OK 74006.

Museums: Most toy and game museums include some jigsaw puzzles in their collections. The Dairy Barn (P. O. Box 747, Athens, OH 45701) mounts an exhibit of antique and collectible puzzles in conjunction with the National Jigsaw Puzzle Championships held every other year.

Advisor: Harry L. Rinker.

Price Notes: Prices quoted refer to puzzles in very good condition, with the original box, and with *no* missing pieces. If pieces are missing, prices are generally 25 to 50 percent lower, although a very rare puzzle may still be well worth collecting even with missing pieces. A missing box should subtract about 25 percent from the price.

The only way to be sure of condition is to see the puzzle assembled. Unassembled puzzles should be priced cheaper, since graphics, condition and completeness can not be easily determined.

Twentieth century die–cut cardboard puzzles are quite inexpensive, usually in the 50¢ to $4.00 range. These puzzles are usually non descript, e.g., autumn woods, storms at sea, etc.

Handcut wooden puzzles for adults are more costly, generally $12.00 to $65.00. Price depends on subject matter, number of pieces, and quality of cut. Nineteenth century children's puzzles command the highest prices, often $50.00 to $500.00. They are still less expensive than many contemporary children's games of the same period.

Note: Dimensions listed give width first, then height.

Eat Famous Biscuits, Little Tommy Tucker, $35.00.

CHILDREN/JUVENILE PUZZLES

Pre–1915

Milton Bradley Company, Smashed Up Locomotive, 9 x 7", wood box **250.00**
E. I. Horsman, New York, NY, Prize Mother Goose Pictures Dissected ... **75.00**
Seymour Lyman, New York, Tally Ho Puzzle, 30 sliced pcs, 28½ x 13¼", box lithography of stage coach crash **250.00**
J. Ottmann Lithography Company, Dissected Circus, sliced pcs, 18½ x 12¾" **75.00**
McLoughlin Brothers, New York, NY
  Locomotive Picture Puzzle, puzzle pictures engine at station, 24¾ x 18", 1887 .... **225.00**
  The Young Blue Jackets, set of two, United States Cruiser *Columbia*, 18 pcs, 10" x 6", and United States Cruiser *San Francisco*, 15 pcs, 9 x 6½", box lithography shows three sailors around naval gun **150.00**
Peter G. Thomson, Cincinnati, OH, "The Blow Up Steam Boat, *Queen City* going up Ohio River," sliced format, 28 pcs, 16¼ x 12¼", box with guide picture **275.00**

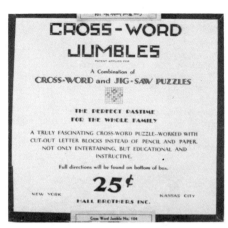

Cross-Word Jumbles, Hall Brothers, Inc., $20.00.

1915–1945

Milton Bradley Co., 4341, Wee Willie Winkie, double sided puzzle, 30 pcs, 7¼ x 10", one guide picture on box **20.00**
Consolidated Paper Box Co., Big 4 Circus Puzzles Jig–Saw Type, three puzzle set, Set No. 1, each puzzle approx 9⅜ x 7¼" **15.00**
E. E. Fairchild Corporation, All–Fair Puzzle, No. 680, Children of American History Picture Puzzle, two puzzle set, Series 3, each puzzle 9½ x 6¾" **8.00**
Ideal Book Builders, No. 416, Building Fun, pop–out pcs, five cards each with two pictures, 1912, 1914, and 1916 copyright dates **12.00**
Madmar Quality Company, Utica, NY, Madmar Dissected Map Puzzle, Junior Series, No. 773, California, guide picture on box **25.00**
Parker Brothers, Robber Kitten Picture Puzzles, set of two, 15 pcs each, 10¼ x 7¼", box with guide picture for robber kitten **40.00**
Saalfield Publishing Co.
  No. 567, Kitty–Cat Picture Puzzle Box, six puzzle set, Fern Biesel Peat illus, each puzzle approx 7⅞ x 9⅞", guide picture for one puzzle on box lid **45.00**
  No. 910, Just Kids Picture Puzzles, four puzzle set, each puzzle approx 9¾ x 8", guide picture for one of puzzles on front of box **40.00**
Squarecut Puzzle Co., New York City, Movie Squarecut Puzzle, "Keeper of the Flame," more than 500 pcs, 22 x

16¾", two sections, small guide picture on box 60.00

Whitman Publishing Company, No. 3932, Edgar Bergen's Charlie Mc-Carthy Picture Puzzles, two puzzle set, approx 7¼ x 10", 1938 copyright ... 35.00

Wylder Picture Puzzles, "There was an old woman who lived in a shoe...," 25 pcs, 7½ x 5¾", guide picture on box 8.00

Post–1945

Milton Bradley
  4318, Dr. Kildare Jigsaw Puzzle, No. 2, "We are going to call him Jimmy," over 600 pieces, includes 14 x 12" color portrait for framing, guide picture on box, 1962 copyright 17.50
  4691–1, James Bond 007 Jigsaw Puzzle, Thunderball, No. 1, "Spectre's Surprise," over 600 pcs, approx 24 x 14", portion of puzzle pictured on box cover 25.00

Consolidated Paper Box Company, No. 41, 2 Perfect Jig Saw Type Interlocking Children's Puzzles, No. 5, boy stopping girl from crossing street and boy and grandfather in rowboat (Hintermeister illus), each puzzle 7⅛ x 9¼", box shows boy and girl waving puzzle boxes 7.50

E. E. Fairchild, Weird–Ohs Picture Puzzle, 1652, Freddy Flameout: The Way Out Jet Jockey, one of series of four, 108 pcs, approx 15 x 10½", guide picture on box 15.00

HG Toys, No. 465–02, Happy Days Featuring "The Fonz," 150 pcs, approx 14 x 10", guide photograph on box 5.00

Jaymar
  Bedtime Story Picture Puzzle, "Puss In Boots," guide picture on box .. 5.00
  No. 2060, Mr. I. Magination, 414 pcs, 19¼ x 14", 1951 copyright, guide picture on box 15.00

National Biscuit Company, Straight Arrow Indian Jig Saw, series of 12, "Straight Arrow with Packy and Fury, To the Rescue," 9 x 7", envelope with glassine window, 1949 copyright ... 16.00

Sifo Company, St. Paul, MN, Sammy Sun - tells the Days and Months, frame tray clock with months and numbers in outer circle and days of week in inner circle, central sun ... 10.00

Whitman
  Series 302, Authorized Jr. Jigsaw Puzzle, Hugh O'Brian As Wyatt Earp, 63 pcs, guide picture on box 15.00

2991, Little Golden Picture Puzzle, Tottle, 6⅛ x 7½", guide picture on box, 1946 copyright 10.00

Frame Trays

Built Rite, Sta–N–Place Inlaid Puzzle
  No. 1129, Blondie, Dagwood and children rush out door while Blondie watches, 13½ x 10⅝", early 1960s 15.00
  No. 1229, Jungle Jim, chimp rubs Jungle Jim's hair, 10¾ x 13½", 1956 copyright 20.00

Milton Bradley, Sons of Hercules, No. 4572-X8, Hercules stops Roman two–horse chariot, 43 pcs, 14¼ x 10⅛", 1966 copyright 20.00

E. E. Fairchild Corporation, 1600-2, Little Roquefort and Percy Puss, A Terry–Toon Puzzle, Percy holds Roquefort in hand, 11 x 8½" 8.00

Jaymar Specialty Company
  Rudolph the Red-Nose Reindeer, Rudolph leads sled, 11 x 14", 1950 copyright 15.00
  Walt Disney's 101 Dalmatians, couple and maid admiring new born puppy, 12¾ x 9¾" 12.00

National Fire Protection Association, Boston, MA, "A Clean House Seldom Burns!," Sparky sweeping up basement, 8½ x 10½" 15.00

Saalfield
  Artcraft, 7042, Diver Dan, Dan in bottom of sea surrounded by three fish, mermaid in background, 10½ x 14", 1957 copyright 20.00
  Authorized Edition, "Would You Believe?", Don Adams in Get Smart, Adams lighting match around boxes of TNT, 10½ x 14", 1965 copyright 30.00

Whitman Publishing Company
  2628, Little Beaver Picture Puzzle, drawing of Little Beaver fishing, 11⅜ x 14⅞", 1954 copyright 15.00
  2975, Walt Disney Cinderella Picture Puzzle, Cinderella carrying wood to kitchen stove, 14⅞ x 11½", 1950 copyright, wrapper with guide picture on front with puzzle piece lines and unmarked picture on back suitable for framing 17.50
  4420, Walt Disney's Fantasyland, Donald and Mickey on aerial ride, 11¼ x 14½", 1957 copyright 15.00
  4427, Tales of Wells Fargo, photograph of hero drawing gun as he enters saloon, 11¼ x 14½", 1958 copyright 17.50
  4427, Wagon Train, drawing of wa-

gon master and scout hunting buffalo, 11⅜ x 14½", 1961 copyright **12.50**

4454, Walt Disney's Babes In Toyland, couple sharing drink, large Queen of Hearts card in background, 11¼ x 14⅜", 1961 copyright **12.00**

4457, Hanna–Barbera Top Cat, Top Cat sits in trash can sipping milk from bottle on porch while policeman looks on, 11⅜ x 14⅜", 1961 copyright **15.00**

McKeeson's Products, $17.00.

ADULT PUZZLES

Hand Cut

A–1 Puzzle Club, Impressionist Landscape by August Renoir (untitled, 1882 painting), woman strolling along road of tree–shaded landscape, 24 x 20", 600 pcs, c1910 .... **55.00**

Bliss, R. W., Wallaston, MA, The Arab Raiding Party, A. D. Schreyer print of armed horsemen riding at dusk, 12 x 9", 153 pcs, black and orange box, early 20thC **25.00**

Milton Bradley Co., Premier Jigsaw Puzzles

168 pcs, Port of Heart's Desire, 1920s kneeling mother holding daughter, 8 x 10", original box **20.00**

500 pcs, Why the Guests Were Late, country scene of snowbound coach being rescued, Talbert Wright artist, 19 x 12", 37 figural pcs, original box **50.00**

Fretts, Alden L., The Yankee Cut-ups, Home Memories, English thatched roof cottage and garden scene,

Thompson illus., 23 x 16", 676 pcs, 24 figural pcs, c1930s **35.00**

Gleason, H. A., Cheerio Jig Saw Puzzles, Mine's the Largest, 1940s style pin–up girl with ten gallon hat, Holt Armstrong illus., 16 x 12", 326 pcs, 7 figural pcs, original box **30.00**

Glencraft/Glendex, Fishing Pier, harbor scene of New England fishing boats, 22 x 15", 720 pcs, c1960s **35.00**

Hanks Puzzle Shop, Conway, NH, A Colonial Sweetheart, portrait of Dutch colonial woman with vase of flowers, J. Van Vredand artist, 16 x 20", 538 pcs, original box **50.00**

Hassett, Waman S., Pine Tree Puzzle, In Old Kentucky, Daniel Boone–style deerslayer sighting his prey, 12 x 16", 410 pcs, original box **25.00**

Hodges, William, Mt. Desert, ME, Acadia National Park, photograph of ocean surf on rocky Maine coast, 11 x 8", 334 pcs, original box, c1970s . **20.00**

Houser, Glad, The Rug Merchant, Near Eastern woman displaying rug to elderly gentleman buyer, Balesio Roman Tivol artist, 8 x 6", 100 pcs, original box, c1920 .... **15.00**

Kingsbridge by Atlantic, The Arrival (A Hunting Morn), hunters pause in Tudor town, L. Cury Cox artist, 15 x 11", 400 pcs, original box, 1960s **20.00**

Leisure Hour Puzzle Co., Paul Revere's Ride, F. M. Stone artist, 16 x 19", 589 pcs, original box **35.00**

Macy's Jigsaw Puzzle, On a Canal in Venice, canalboat at sunset in Venice, 10 x 12", 253 pcs, wooden slice–top box, 1930s **30.00**

Madmar, Interlox Puzzle, Spoils of War, Prussian officers enjoying leisurely evening of music and relaxation in European parlor, 20 x 16", 755 pcs, original box **50.00**

Miller's Pharmacy, cut for Fessenden's Library, Venetian Revelers, harbor scene at sunset, Moran artist, 13 x 10", 251 pcs, c1930s **30.00**

Parker Brothers, Pastime Picture Puzzle

183 pcs, Master of the House, H. M. Brett portrait of family with infant at table, 13 x 9", 19 figural pcs, c1920s **20.00**

200 pcs, Chess Players, drawing room scene of gentlemen at game table, 14 x 10", 17 figural pcs, original box, late 1930s **25.00**

350 pcs, A Shady Pathway, lake country scene with shepherd and sheep, 17 x 11", 36 figural pcs, original box, dated March 28, 1931 ..... **30.00**

482 pcs, Coolidge's Birthplace, misty

landscape of President's farm amidst fields and mountains, 21 x 16", 48 figural pcs, original box, dated January 28, 1932 . . . . **55.00**

523 pcs, Landscape with Mountains (untitled), American western scene of fertile valley with sandstone butts and snow–capped mountains in background, 23 x 16", 60 figural pcs, c1930s **35.00**

1,305 pcs, Mediterranean Harbor (untitled), scene of young couple watching sunset and return of sailboats to mooring in small Mediterranean village, 37 x 29", 148 figural pcs, original box **75.00**

Picture Puzzle Exchange, Boston, The First Note of the Bell, colonial Philadelphia scene of christening of Liberty Bell, 14 x 10", 196 pcs, original box, 1916 . . . . **30.00**

Pixie Picture Puzzle, Melrose, MA, Halting at the Inn, huntsmen enjoying quaff outside Tudor Tavern, 10 x 8", 175 pcs, original box **25.00**

Shenandoah Community Workers (Virginia), Audubon Bird Picture Puzzles, set of 3 : Chickadee (Allen Brooks artist), Scarlet Tanager (R. Bruce Hersfall artist), and Belted Kingfisher (R. Bruce Hersfall artist), each print shows male and female of species and is encased in its own tray, each puzzle 6 x 8", approx 30 pcs per puzzle, late 1930s, original box **45.00**

Straus, Joseph K.

282 pcs, White Clipper, three–masted square rigger under full sail, 16 x 12", D. Sherring artist, original box, 1940s **20.00**

482 pcs, Guardians of Liberty, World War II scene of battleship and planes passing Statue of Liberty, T. J. Slaughter artist, 16 x 20", 482 pcs, original box, mid–1940s **25.00**

Tuck's Famous Zig–Zag Picture Puzzle, English, The Band of the Household Cavalry Passing the King at Buckingham Palace, 13 x 9", 150 pcs, 17 figural pcs, original box **25.00**

Unknown cutters

64 pcs, Wing and Wing (untitled), lead sloop sailing with the wind, 9 x 10", c1940s **10.00**

80 pcs, The Birth of Our Country, Ben Franklin in colonial heartside scene, Hy Hintermeister artist, 13 x 9", c1920 . . . . **20.00**

101 pcs, The Heart of Nature, landscape scene of stream coursing through mountainous countryside, 7 x 9", dated March 12, 1933 . . . **20.00**

200 pieces, Old Glory Forever, John Van Arsdale's exploit at Fort George, November 25, 1783, Clyde G. DeLand artist, 14 x 10" . **25.00**

296 pcs, Hallowed Moment, European scene of flower vendor pausing to honor a remembered soul, 16 x 12", dated February 3, 1933 **45.00**

300 pcs, Dined Well But Not Wisely, English, Pears' print of English "diners" discovering a buddy who has had one too many, 12 x 18", c1910 **45.00**

323 pcs, My Little Girl, elderly host introducing marriageable–age daughter to young huntsman, 14 x 10" **30.00**

495 pcs, Sulgrave Manor, The Ancestral Home of George Washington, 20 x 16" **30.00**

Victory Artistic Wood Jigsaw Puzzle, English

300 pcs, Mountain Retreat, color photograph of couple with goats in Alpine scene, 14 x 12", figural pcs, original box, post–1950 . . . . **20.00**

500 pcs, Calvi, Mediterranean harbor scene, M. Buzle, artist, 20" x 15", original box **35.00**

West, W. Frank, Newport, RI, Picture Puzzles, In a Japanese Store, 1920s print of two American women perusing wares at Japanese bazaar, Ethel Pennewill Brown illus, 11 x 9", 130 pcs, original box, c1930s **25.00**

Die Cut

American News Company, Miss America Puzzle Series, No. 4 of four known, "In Blossom Time," over 300 pcs, 13¼ x 10", 1933 . . . . **15.00**

Ballyhoo Magazine, Ballyhoo, "No Nudes is Bad Nudes," 333 pcs, 10½ x 15½", 1930s, cardboard box **30.00**

Milton Bradley

The Dover Jig Picture Puzzle, No. 4728, "The Circus," over 300 pcs, 1930s, guide picture on box **10.00**

Piccadilly Jig Picture Puzzle, No. 81, "On the Loire," over 200 pcs, 1930s, box with blue and white ground **5.00**

J. R. Brundage, Empire Jig Picture Puzzle, "A Canadian Landscape," over 400 pcs, box features sketch of Empire State building **4.00**

Consolidated Paper Box

Big Star, No. 1010, "School Patrol," over 250 pcs, approx 10 x 13½," late 1930s, guide picture on blue tone box **2.00**

Big 10 Perfect Picture Puzzle, No.

1010, "Millstream in Winter," over 250 pcs, approx 13½ x 10", late 1930s, box **1.00**

Perfect Picture Puzzle, "Mountain Warfare," over 375 pcs, approx 19½ x 15½", c1943, eight stars on box **12.50**

Perfect Picture Puzzle, No. 25, "Dawn's Early Light No. 305," over 375 pcs, approx 15½ x 19½", small guide picture on box with puzzle pieces theme, orange ground **6.00**

Perfect Picture Puzzle, No. 2016, "No. 211 Cool and Silence," over 450 pcs, small guide picture on box **3.00**

Perfect Picture Puzzle, No. 250-29, "Proof Positive," boy photographing dog holding fishing float, over 375 pcs, approx 19½ x 15½", c1950s **2.00**

Dell Publishing Co., All–American Picture Puzzle, No. 2, "Wings in the Night", aerial combat over enemy harbor, approx 280 pieces, 1942, guide picture on box **15.00**

Einson–Freeman, Every Week Jig–Saw Puzzle Series No. 17, "Abraham Lincoln," Ray Morgan illus, 10⅝ x 14½", box **12.00**

E. E. Fairchild Corporation, No. 647, Finesse Picture Puzzle, "Gypsy Love Call," over 250 pcs, approx 11 x 14", guide picture on box **6.00**

Gebhart Folding Box Co., Dayton, OH, Wonder Picture Puzzle, "The Cascade," over 300 pcs, box **5.00**

Harter Publishing Company, Cleveland, OH, No. H–131, Series III, No. 4, "Fishin' and Wishin'," over 200 pcs, approx 15 x 11", green tone box ... **2.00**

Jaymar Specialty Company, Hobby Jig Saws, "Grizzly Bear," over 300 pcs, approx 14 x 22", small guide picture on box, green ground in treasure chest motif **3.00**

Lutz & Sheinkman, Merry Mood Jig Saw (Type) Puzzle, "After the Hunt" by R. Jlinek, over 400 pcs, approx 18½ x 14½", 1930s, box measures 4⅜ x 10⅜ x 2⅜" **12.00**

Movie Cut–Ups, Peabody, MA, Movie Cut-Up No. 7, "Bitter Tea of General Yen," over 225 pcs, 9⅞ x 13⅛", box **25.00**

J. Pressman & Co., Inc., Victory Picture Puzzle, No. 20, "Flying Fortresses Bombing Enemy Base," over 375 pieces, approx. 19¼ x 15¼", c1945, guide picture on box **15.00**

Regent Specialties, Inc., De Luxe Picture Puzzle, "Snow Capped Peaks," approx 400 pieces, approx 20 x 16", 1930s, box measures 4¾ x 9¾ x 2½" **10.00**

The Reynolds & Reynolds Co., Dayton, OH, The American Individual Pictured Puzzle, "19B A Bit of French Tapestry," over 350 pcs, orange tone box **3.00**

A. Schoenhut Co., Philadelphia, PA, "Schoenhut" Picture Puzzle, "Let's Go," over 200 pcs, 10 x 22", box .. **6.00**

Simkins Paper Box Mfg. Co., Philadelphia, PA, Simco Jig Puzzle, "The Landing," over 300 pieces, approx 16 x 12", box marked "Par 4 Hours" .. **5.00**

Tichnor Brothers, Inc., Cambridge, MA, See American First, No. 39, "Natural Bridge, Va.," over 300 pcs, box **5.00**

University Distributing Company, Jig of the Week Puzzle, No. 23, "Hunters," 13⅛ x 10⅛", insert, box **10.00**

Upson Company, Tuco Picture Puzzle "Quietude," over 200 pcs, approx 16 x 12", gold stripes on red ground box **4.00**

"The Last Roundup," over 300 pcs, approx 20 x 16", horizontal maroon bands across box lid, guide picture covers approx one–half lid **6.00**

Viking Manufacturing Company, Picture Puzzle Weekly

Series A–4, "Lions at Sunset", 13⅞ x 10", box **10.00**

Series D–1, "The Olde Kentucky Home", Blacks surround banjo player, white woman listens in background, 14½ x 10⅝", box ... **17.50**

Whitman Publishing Co., Guild Picture Puzzle, No. 2900, Series RR, "Millpond," 304 pcs, approx 18 x 15½", guide picture on box **1.50**

ADVERTISING PUZZLES

Burgess Battery Co., "Sparkalong Burgess," young cowboy jumps wooden fence riding animal that is part horse and part zebra, 5⅞ x 4", glassine envelope rubber stamped with distributor **12.00**

Campfire or Angelus Marshmallows, No. 1 in series of four, "Fishing Boats," boats tied up at wharf, 48 pcs, 9¾ x 6¾", paper envelope **10.00**

Chevrolet, boxed set of 2 puzzles, "Superior Chevrolet Utility Coupe" and "Superior Chevrolet 5 Passenger Touring," 12 pcs each puzzle, each puzzle 6½ x 4½", box with picture of Superior Chevrolet 5–Passenger Sedan, 1923–24 .... **150.00**

Cocomalt, R. B. Davis Co., "The Windmill Jig–Saw Puzzle", windmill and harbor at low tide, 65 pcs, 10 x 6½", paper envelope **10.00**

Baby Ruth, Curtiss Candy Company, Chicago, $20.00.

Curtis Candy Company, "Singing in the Rain" Jig Saw Puzzle, double sided, front shows boy and girl under umbrella, reverse shows one cent candies produced by Curtis, 5⅝ x 7½", paper envelope 20.00

Dearborn Truck Company, Chicago, IL, "For Every Job the Dearborn Truck," shows stake body truck, 30 pieces, 10½ x 7", paper envelope 40.00

Green Spring Dairy, Baltimore, MD, shows processing machinery in dairy, 10¾ x 9", envelope missing 20.00

Heinz 57 Varieties, shows children playing store with all 57 products displayed on shelf, 10⅛ x 12", paper envelope 30.00

Jack and Jill Jell, Special Offer, 5 Boxes of Jack & Jill Jell and a 100 piece The Fisher Bros. Co. Picture Puzzle, No. 17, "Modern Beauty," two 1930s beauties, 10¼ x 8", paper envelope 15.00

Lambert Pharmacal Co., Listerine, three children in bathroom gargling with Listerine, dog taking part, Frances Tipton Hunter illus., 13¾ x 10¾", paper envelope, premium from radio show Phillips Lord, The Country Doctor 25.00

R. J. Mrizek Co., makers of Mrizek's Bohemian Rye Bread, Chicago, "Washington's Childhood Home," 7 x 8⅝", paper envelope 12.00

Pacific Coast Borax Co., "Hauling 20 Mule Team Borax Out Of Death Valley," 20 mule head figural pieces, 10¾ x 8¼", 1933, paper envelope with newsprint cartoon insert 20.00

Penick & Ford, Vermont Maid Syrup, 2 Jig–saw Puzzles, "Home" and "Ready For The Pasture," 49 pcs per puzzle, each puzzle 7⅜ x 9¼", green letter on paper envelope, envelope notes "New Series" 17.50

Pennzoil, winter scene of snowball fight behind freezing snowman, 16 pcs, line cut, 5¾ x 8", paper envelope .. 8.00

Phillips Petroleum Company, double sided puzzle, Alaska and Hawaii, central map of each state surrounded by scenes from state, 15 x 11", 1973, can 8.00

Plee–Zing Palm Oil Soap, Free Jig–Saw Puzzle with 4 Bars, ocean liner entering New York harbor, 9⅞ x 7¾", paper envelope 16.00

RCA Victor, "All that the Victrola gives to others it will give to you," seated couple in front of record player surrounded by miniature musicians, folk singers, and opera singers, RCA logo in lower right, 8⅞ x 8", dated 1932, paper envelope 50.00

Richfield Golden Gasoline/Richlube Motor Oil, "Goofy Golf" Jig–Saw Puzzle, No. 2 in a series of six, "In Hawaii—And How!," 49 pcs, 7 x 9", paper envelope, front of envelope contains golf lesson by Alex Morrison 30.00

Shultz's Pretzels, Hanover, PA, winter scene featuring stone arch bridge, adv. information printed on puzzle, 3 x 6", paper envelope 10.00

Swift & Company, "Milking Time at a Brookfield Dairy Farm," central scene of dancing cows above information oval on "Brooksie" the famous white cow and her pals, pieces within puzzle spell out "SWIFT & CO.," 12 x 12", box 45.00

Sunshine Lone Star Sugar Wafers, child pushing wheelbarrow filled with children, 40 pcs, 9¼ x 7", Twelvetrees illus., 1932, paper envelope with guide picture 25.00

MULTIPURPOSE PUZZLES

Cadco-Ellis, Jingo: The Jigsaw Bingo Game, the first player to fit 5 piece vertically, horizontally, or diagonally into his Jingo Board wins the round, 1941, box measures 13¼ x 10 x 1" . 35.00

Einson-Freeman Lithograph Co., "Mystery–Jig" Puzzle, No. 2 in series of four, "By Whose Hand," approx. 300 pcs, 19⅞ x 14", booklet enclosed, 1933 cardboard box 25.00

Janus Games, Inc., The Janus Mystery Jigsaw Puzzle, No. 1 of four, "The Case of the Snoring Skinflint" by Henry Slesar, over 500 pcs, approx 22 x 15", 1973, story on back of cardboard box 12.00

Oxford Specialty Co., Boston, MA, "Budge:Sports," die cut cardboard,

17 x 17", cardboard box contains instructions for four players to race to assemble their quarters first **22.50**

Picture Puzzle Post Card, U. S. 616, Roxbury, Mass., Statue of Joseph Warren, 18 pcs, perforated, 3½ x 5½", mailing envelope **8.00**

Volland, birthday card, B–101, "Happy Birthday–and I'm Not Telling," verse beneath semi-circle with home, bird, and tree branch motif, 6 x 5", envelope **10.00**

Whitman, Sound A Round Talking Puzzle Master Unit, durable frame holds talking record and sturdy large piece puzzle, self adjusting magic tone arm, hard cover story book, "Choo–Choo at the Zoo," box measures 15½ x 11 x 2¼" **15.00**

RADIO CHARACTERS AND PERSONALITIES

Collecting Hints: Many items associated with radio characters and personalities were offered as premiums. This category focuses mostly on the non–premium items. Radio premiums have their own separate listing elsewhere in this book.

Don't overlook the vast amount of material related to the radio shows themselves. This can include scripts, props, and a wealth of publicity material. Collecting autographed photographs was popular, and many appear on the market. Books, especially Big Little Books and similar types, featured many radio related characters and stories.

Radio characters and personalities found their way into movies and television. Serious collectors do differentiate the products which spun off from these other two areas.

History: The radio show was a dominant force in American life from the 1920s to the early 1950s. Amos and Andy began in 1929, The Shadow in 1930, and Chandu the Magician in 1932. Although many of the characters were fictional, the individuals who portrayed them became public idols. A number of figures achieved fame on their own—Eddie Cantor, Don McNeill of The Breakfast Club, George Burns and Gracie Allen, Arthur Godfrey, and Jack Benny.

Sponsors and manufacturers were quick to capitalize on the fame of the radio characters and personalities. Premiums were offered as part of the shows themes. However, merchandising did not stop with premiums. Many non–premium materials such as bubble gum cards, figurines, games, publicity photographs, dolls, etc., were issued. Magazine advertisements often featured radio personalities.

Reference: Tom Tumbusch, *Tomart's Price Guide to Radio Premium and Cereal Box Collectibles,* Wallace–Homestead, 1991.

See: Big Little Books, Comic Books, Radio Premiums, Super Heroes.

Horace Heidt, advertising tin, Tum's Pot-O-Gold, 2¼" l, $18.50.

Jimmie Allen
Model, 19" l, 24", wingspan, thunderbolt, orig box, unassembled, 1930s **100.00**
Pocketknife, 3¼" l, plastic simulated wood grips, pair raised wings marked "Jimmie Allen" one side, two blades, 1930s **285.00**
Wings, 1⅞" wide, brass, Flying Cadet, logo, c1934 . . . . **15.00**

Amos and Andy
Ashtray, 5 x 5 x 8", plaster, standing either side of barrel, inscribed "Ise Regusted," 1930s **90.00**
Booklet, All About Amos 'n Andy, 128 pgs, photos, scripts, 1929 . . . . **50.00**
Card Party, two score pads, eight tallies, complete, orig box, M Davis Co copyright 1938 . . . . **70.00**
Cut Outs, cardboard, 1930s **140.00**
Game, Acrobat Ring and Disk, 1930s **95.00**
Postcard, Atlantic City **10.00**
Sheet Music, *Three Little Words,* 1930 **25.00**

Jack Armstrong, pedometer, silver trim **35.00**
Bobby Benson, cereal bowl **10.00**

Jack Benny
Program, Jack Benny Show, 9 x 12", 12 pgs, black and white photos, Phil Harris signature, Lucky Strike Cigarettes sponsor, late 1930s **22.00**
Record Set, 78 rpm, comedy sketches, orig cov, Top Ten Records, copyright 1947, set of four records **45.00**

Blondie, handkerchief, 8½ x 9", linen, white, blue, red, green, black, and yellow, 1940s **15.00**

Eddie Cantor, poster, 11½ x 19", paper, movie and radio show adv, New Pebeco Tooth Paste, 1935–36 . . . . **70.00**

Chandu the Magician
Photograph, 8½ x 11", autographed "Chandu, Gayne Whitman" **12.00**

Pinback Button, celluloid, white ground, browntone portrait, brown lettering, Chandu Magicians Club, 1930s **180.00**

Mitzi Green, pinback button, 1¼" d, photo, "I'm on the Air, Mitzi Green, in Happy Landings/Ward's Soft Bun Bread, WKAN, Tues & Thurs, 6:00 pm," white rim lettering, 1930s **5.00**

Lone Wolf Tribe
Pin, arrowhead **10.00**
Watch Fob, tribe **25.00**

Lum and Abner, malt maker, Horlick .. **25.00**

Charlie McCarthy
Bank, still, composition **57.50**
Doll, ventriloquist **120.00**
Dollar Bills, Mazuma, pkg of 20 ... **25.00**
Game
Bingo **27.50**
Topper, 1938 .... **30.00**
Greeting Card, get well, talking **20.00**
Pencil Sharpener, figural, plastic, die-cut, color decal, 1930s **68.00**
Radio, 6" h, plastic, ivory color, electric, figural Charlie, Majestic, c1940 .... **800.00**
Record, *Lessons in Ventriloquism,* 33⅓ rpm, Edgar and Charlie, wrapped, mint **25.00**
Spoon, SP, Duchess **15.00**
Wrapper, Bergen's Better Bubble Gum **6.00**

Fibber McGee, The Merry Game Of Fibber McGee And The Wistful Vista Mystery, Milton Bradley, 1940, $20.00.

Fibber McGee and Molly, game
The Amazing Adventures of Fibber McGee story and instruction book, 32 pgs, cards, scoring disks, orig box, Milton Bradley, 1936 .... **35.00**
Wistful Vista Mystery Game, complete **20.00**

Orphan Annie
Big Little Book, *Little Orphan Annie and Sandy,* Whitman, #716, 1933 **25.00**
Glass, The Sunday Funnies, 5½" h,

clear, continuous illus, Annie, Sandy, Daddy Warbucks, Asp, and Punjab, copyright 1976 .... **12.50**
Manual, ROA Secret Society, 6 x 8¾", 12 pgs, paper, color illus, 1936 .. **50.00**
Mug, 50 Year Anniversary, 5" h, plastic, white, red lid, 1932 and 1982 Annie and Sandy illus, Ovaltine premium, 1982 .... **15.00**
Ring, ROA secret message, silvered brass, club symbols, 1937 .... **65.00**
Slide Whistle, 5" l open size, brass, diecut, figural Annie head top, 1941 .... **70.00**

Professor Quiz, Radio Game, complete, orig mailer, 1939 .... **25.00**

Seckatary Hawkins
Pinback Button, ⅞" d, blue and white, club member, c1932 ..... **14.00**
Spinner, silvered brass, red accents, spinning checkerboard design, Fair and Square, c1932 .... **18.00**

Sergeant Preston
Coloring Book, 8½ x 11½", Whitman, 32 pgs, unused, 1943 ..... **20.00**
Coloring set, orig box **50.00**
Comic Book, miniature, 1956 ...... **20.00**
Gold Ore Detector **95.00**
Man of Yukon Territory, 7½ x 9½", color, c1955 .... **26.00**
Pedometer, 2½" l, polished aluminum, facsimile signature, Preston and Yukon King illus, 1952–54 .. **75.00**

The Shadow
Ink Stamp, wood and rubber, "Member, The Shadow Club" stamp, mid 1930s **175.00**
Lapel Stud, ¾" d, silvered brass, The Shadow Club, mid 1930s **85.00**

Skippy, pinback button, ⅞" d, Skippy Skinners Secret Society, PL Crosby copyright 1932 .... **15.00**

Kate Smith, pinback button, 2¼" d, black and red lettering, white ground, photo illus, "Kate Smith's Philadelphia A & P Party/Nov 4, 1935/Hello Everybody" **25.00**

Special Investigator, book, *Is It A Fraud,* 5 x 7½", 40 pgs, soft cov, orig mailing envelope, Mutual Network, Commercial Credit Corp copyright 1947 .... **15.00**

Dick Tracy
Badge, 2½", brass, diecut, emb, Dick Tracy Secret Service Patrol/Captain, 1938 .... **170.00**
Flashlight, 3" l, metal and plastic, dark red and white, black Tracy illus, Dick Tracy Secret Service, 1939 .... **80.00**
Pinback Button, 1⅜" d, white, dark blue, and gold, Member Dick Tracy Secret Service Patrol, 1938 ...... **24.00**

Uncle Don, pinback button, 7/8" d, red, black, and white, Uncle Don eating ice cream at WOR microphone, "Uncle Don's Ice Cream Club/Borden's"   23.00

RADIO PREMIUMS

Collecting Hints: Most collections are centered around one or two specific personalities or radio programs.

History: Radio premiums are nostalgic reminders of childhood memories of radio shows. Sponsors of shows frequently used their products to promote the collection of premiums, such as saving box tops to exchange for gifts tied in with the program or personality.

References: Tom Tumbusch, *Tomart's Price Guide to Radio Premium and Cereal Box Collectibles,* Wallace–Homestead, 1991.

REPRODUCTION ALERT

See: Radio Characters and Personalities.

Amos 'N' Andy, map, Webber City, 15 x 20", cartoon illus, orig cover letter and mailing envelope, Pepsodent Toothpaste, 1935 ....   60.00
Bachelor's Children, book, 5 x 7¼", hard cov, 26 pgs, photos and stories, Old Dutch Cleanser, 1939 ....   15.00
Buck Rogers
   Helmet, child's size, stiff paper, multicolored, Cocomalt, c1933 ..   175.00
   Photo, 7½ x 10", glossy, Buck and Wilma, cov letter, facsimile signatures, Cocomalt, c1934 ....   80.00
Captain Midnight
   Magic Blackout Lite–Ups Kit, 5 x 8" folder, luminous paper sheets, orig mailer and instructions, Ovaltine, 1941–42 ....   175.00
   Manual, Secret Squadron, 6 x 8½", 8 pgs, color illus, Ovaltine, 1946 ..   100.00
   Photo, Chuck Ramsey, 6 x 7½", black and white, matte, white facsimile signature, Captain Midnight's ward, Skelly Oil, c1939 ....   65.00
   Pictures, set of three 100.00
   Shake–Up Mug, 5" h, plastic, orange, blue lid, raised portrait, "Remember Your Secret Squadron Pledge," Ovaltine, c1947 ....   90.00
   Stamp Album, 5 x 6¾", stiff paper, 8 pgs, 16 stamps, Skelly Oil, c1939   35.00
   Transfer, iron–on, 4" d, Captain Midnight's Secret Squadron, orig envelope, Ovaltine, c1948 ....   110.00
Chandu, Ball and Vase Trick, 2½" h red wood vase, black wood ball, orig instruction sheet and mailing box, illus

letter from Chandu, Beech–Nut, 1930s 75.00
Counter–Spy, certificate, Counter–Spy Junior Agents Club, 6 x 8½", paper, Pepsi–Cola, c1950 ....   25.00
Lone Ranger,
   Badge, star shape, 1½" h, two–tone brass, "A Republic Serial/The Lone Ranger," 1938 ....   70.00
   Ring, brass bands, plastic six–gun, sparking, 1947 ....   75.00
Lum And Abner, family almanac, 6 x 9", 34 pgs, orig mailing envelope, Horlick's Malted Milk, 1936 ....   40.00
Charlie McCarthy, game, Radio Party, orig mailing envelope, complete, 1938 ....   35.00
Tom Mix
   Arrowhead, Ralston Straight Shooters Signal Arrowhead, 2½ x 3½", lucite, clear, whistle, siren, and magnifying lens, 1949 ....   70.00
   Bracelet, ID, silvered brass chain, disk, two six–guns, letter "J," Ralston address and serial number, 1947 ....   50.00
   Catalog, premiums, folder, paper, 8¼ x 10¼" 25.00
   Decoder, brass, revolving six–guns, 1941 ....   85.00

Orphan Annie, Beetle Ware mug, Ovaltine, 3" h, $65.00.

Orphan Annie
   Catalog Folder, 4 x 7¼", Ovaltine, orig mailing envelope, c1935 ....   150.00
   Handbook, Secret Guard, 3¾ x 8½", paper sheet, decoder, clicker, orig mailing envelope, Quaker Puffed Wheat Sparkies and Rice Sparkies, 1941 ....   90.00
   Manual, Secret Society, 6 x 9", 8 pgs, password, signs, and signals, Ovaltine, 1938 ....   60.00

Mug, 3" h, white ceramic, Annie and
Sandy illus, Ovaltine, 1932 ...... **65.00**
Puzzle, Tucker County Horse Race, 9
x 12½", orig instruction sheet and
mailing box, Ovaltine, c1933 .... **70.00**
Shake–Up Mug, 5" h, Beetleware,
brown, orange lid, decal, Ovaltine,
1937 .... **60.00**
Sheet Music, *Little Orphan Annie's
Song*, 8¾ x 11¼", 4 pgs, black and
white, Harold Gray illus cov, Ovaltine, 1931 .... **24.00**
Sun Watch, metal, silver and brass
colored, compass and sundial
front, Egyptian symbols back, Ovaltine, 1938 .... **50.00**
Talking Stationery, 12 sheets and envelopes, 4 pg folder, orig mailer,
Ovaltine, 1937 .... **100.00**
Sergeant Preston
Flashlight, 3" l, plastic, black, red and
green color disks, facsimile signa-
ture, "Challenge of the Yukon"
copyright 1949 .... **25.00**
Photo **35.00**
Melvin Purvis
Badge, 1½" h, two–toned brass, black
and red enamel, "Roving Operative
Melvin Purvis Junior G–Man
Corps," 1936 .... **25.00**
Ring, brass, adjustable, eagle and
shield design, 1936 .... **30.00**
The Shadow
Matchbook Cover, 1½ x 4" open size,
black and red silhouette illus, skeleton holding dagger, diecut portrait
flap inside, Pawtucket, RI sponsor,
1940s **30.00**
Ring, alligator, plastic, white day
glow, black plastic insert, Carey
Salt, 1947 .... **575.00**
Superman, ring, Superman Crusader,
silvered brass, 1938–40 .... **160.00**
Tarzan, badge, 1½", brass, red and
black enamel accents, blue rim, "Tar-
zan Radio Club/Drink More Milk,"
early 1930s **250.00**
Those We Love, photo book, 6 x 7½",
soft cov, 32 pgs, titled "The Friends
We've Made," orig mailing envelope,
Ponds Extract **20.00**
Dick Tracy, ring, litho tin, Post Raisin
Brand, copyright 1948 .... **25.00**
Wheatenaville Sketches, newspaper,
birth announcement issue, 10½ x
16", 12 pgs, Vol 3, #1, Special Stork
Edition, orig mailing envelope,
Wheatena, 1934 .... **18.00**
Don Winslow
Badge, ¾", silvered brass, Squadron
of Peace/Ensign, 1939 .... **30.00**
Bank, "Uncle Don's Ernest Saver

Club," 2¼" h, oval, paper label,
photo and cartoon illus, Greenwich
Savings Bank, New York City,
1930s **35.00**

RADIOS

Collecting Hints: Radio collectors divide into
three groups: those who collect because of nostalgia, those interested in history and/or acquiring
radios that represent periods prior to or after
World War II, and collectors of personality and
figural radios. Most collectors find broadcasting,
and therefore broadcast receivers, their primary
interest.

The significant divisions of broadcast receivers
that are represented in a small collection are:
—Crystal sets and battery powered receivers
of the early 1920s
—Rectangular electric table models of the
late 1920s
—Cathedrals, tombstones, and consoles of
the Thirties
—Midget plastic portables and wood cabinet
table models built before and after World
War II
—Shaped Bakelite and other plastic cased
radios
—Personality and figural radios beginning in
the 1930s and extending into the 1960s.
Because the emphasis for nostalgia seems to
fall on the decade of the Thirties, the cathedral
style, socket powered radios, e.g., the Philco
series, have become sought after items. Recently
the younger set has exhibited a very strong nostalgia interest in the plastic cabinet radios built
between 1945 and 1960.

The underlying force that values a radio to a
traditional collector, and consequently sets the
price in the market, is rarity. Very rare radios
usually go directly to major collectors, seldom
appearing in the general market. Wireless equipment and radios used commercially before World
War I are considered rare and are not listed here.

With the newer radio collector, the controlling
force is novelty with the outside appearance the
primary feature. The radio must play; but, shape,
color, decoration, and condition of the case far
outweigh the internal workings of the set in determining desirability and consequently the
price. Enclosures that represent things or figures
e.g., Mickey Mouse, command premium prices.

The prices of 1920s radio sets have been stabilized by collectors' demands. Typical prices
are listed. The values of Thirties' radios fall into
two ranges. Cathedrals bring an average of $100
to $150 with Philco and Atwater Kent on the
high end, and names like Airline and Stewart
Warner on the low end. Consoles bring substantially lower prices, seldom reaching $100 except

for very ornate models, such as the Victrola Hyperion or Orchestrion and the Atwater Kent Model 812.

The squarish table models of the later Thirties and the midget sets of the late 1930s and 1940s recently have attracted the attention of nostalgia buffs and new collectors. Generally their demand in the face of supply keeps their price low, holding below $75. An exception to this rule is based on decoration. Columns, figurework, and dramatic changes in texture add interest and raise the potential prices. A radio with columns outlining the dial or the speaker opening can command $150. Another exception to this is the novelty radio. Treasure chest barrels, mirrored cases, and specialty items bring prices as high as $500.

The value of a radio is directly related to its condition. The critical factors are appearance and operability. The prices listed are for sets of average to good condition and based upon an electrically complete receiver that operates when powered.

Minor scratches are to be expected as is alligatoring of the surface finish. Gouges, cracks, and delaminated surfaces will cut the price by 50%. However, the penalty for a crack or broken place for plastic closures is severe. A Catalin radio with a blue case might bring $400–$600 in good condition, but with a visible crack the price drops to $30.

If parts, tubes, or components are missing or if major repairs must be made in order for the set to work, the price again must be reduced by as much as 50%. A particular radio that is unrestored, in excellent or mint condition, and playing satisfactorily can command an increase of 30 to 50% over the prices listed below.

In addition to radios, many collectors specialize in a facet of the general radio art such as loudspeakers, tubes, microphones, memorabilia, or brand names. As a result, auxiliary and related radio items are becoming collectibles along with radios themselves.

History: The art and science of radio as a communication medium is barely ninety years old. Marconi was the first to assemble and employ the transmission and reception instruments that permitted electric message–sending without the use of direct connections. The early name for radio was "Wireless," and the first application was in 1898 as a means of controlling ships. Early wireless equipment is not generally considered a collectible since its historic value makes it important for museum display.

Between 1905 and the end of World War I many technical advances, including the invention of the vacuum tube by DeForest, resulted in an extensive communication art and a very strong amateur interest in the strange new technology. The receiving equipment from that period is considered highly desirable by collectors and historians but is rarely available outside the main body of early radio and wireless collectors.

By 1920, radio technology offered the means to talk to large numbers of people simultaneously and bring music from concert halls directly into living rooms. The result was the development of a new art that changed the American way of life during the 1920s. The world became familiar in the average listener's home.

Radio receivers changed substantially in the decade of the Twenties, going from black boxes with many knobs and dials and powered from expensive and messy batteries, to styled furniture, simple to use, and operated from the house current that had become the standard source of energy for service in the home. During the Twenties radios grew more complicated and powerful as well as more ornate. Consoles appeared, loudspeakers were incorporated into them, and sound fidelity joined distance as criteria for quality.

In the early 1930s demand changed. The large expensive console gave way to small but effective table models. The era of the "cathedral" and the "tombstone" began. By the end of the Thirties, the midget radio had become popular. Quality of sound was replaced by reduction of price and most homes had more than one radio.

Shortly after World War II the miniature tubes developed for the military were applied to domestic radios. The result was further reduction in size with a substantial improvement in quality. The advent of FM also speeded the development. Plastic technology made possible the production of attractive cases in many styles and colors.

The other post-WWII development that drastically changed the radio receiver was the invention of the transistor. A whole new family of radio sets that could be carried in the shirt pocket became popular. As they became less and less expensive, their popularity grew rapidly. Consequently, they were throwaways when they stopped working. Today they are not easy to find in good condition and are quite collectible.

References: Robert F. Breed, *Collecting Transistor Novelty Radios: A Value Guide*, L–W Books, 1990; Marty and Sue Bunis, *Collector's Guide To Antique Radios*, Collector Books, 1991; Philip Collins, *Radios: The Golden Age*, Chronicle Books, 1987; Alan Douglas, *Radio Manufacturers of the 1920's, Volume I* (1980) and *Volume 2* (1989), The Vestal Press, Inc.; Robert Grinder and George Fathauer, *Radio Collector's Director and Price Guide,*, Ironwood Press, 1986; David and Betty Johnson, *Guide To Old Radios–Pointers, Pictures, and Prices*, Wallace–Homestead, 1989; Michael Lawlor, *Lawlor's Radio Values: Catalin, Character Mirrored, Novelty, Plastic*, Bare Bones Press, 1991; John Sideli, *Classic Plastic Radios of the 1930s and 1940s: A Collector's Guide To Catalin Radios*, E. P. Dutton, 1990.

Periodicals: *Antique Radio Classified*, 9511 Sunrise Blvd., Cleveland, OH 44133; *Radio Age*, 636 Cambridge Road, Augusta, GA 30909; *Sight, Sound, Style*, P.O. Box 2224, South Hackensack, NJ 07606.

Collectors' Clubs: Antique Radio Club of America, 81 Steeplechase Road, Devon, PA 19333; Antique Wireless Association, 17 Sheridan Street, Auburn, NY, 13021.

Museums: Antique Wireless Museum (AWA), East Bloomfield, NY; Caperton's Radio Museum, Louisville, KY; Muchow's Historical Radio Museum, Elgin, IL; Museum of Wonderful Wireless, Minneapolis, MN; New England Museum of Wireless and Steam, East Greenwich, RI; Voice of the Twenties, Orient, NY.

Admiral
Model 33, 35, 37, battery, portable .	40.00
Plastic, portable, brown	35.00
Tilt tuner console	90.00

Advertising
Atlas Car Battery	40.00
Pet Milk	40.00
Schlitz Beer	25.00
Stroh's Beer	25.00
Winston Cigarettes	30.00

Airline, AC–DC, table model, Pre–WWII ... 35.00

Arvin
Plastic, table model, brown	30.00
Rhythm series, table and console model	55.00

Atwater Kent
Model 10, instruments on board, five tubes	150.00
Model 12, instruments on board, six tubes	260.00
Model 20, mahogany case, three dials	40.00
Model 30, mahogany case, single dial	40.00
Model 40, metal cabinet, electric ..	25.00
Model 46, table, green metal case, 1929	115.00
Model 55, electric, set in Kiel table .	75.00
Model 70, 80, 90 Series, console style	30.00
Model 80, 90 Series, table	80.00
Console style, three digit numbers ..	40.00

Bulova, clock radio ... 100.00

Catalin and other phenolic case radios
A partial list of manufacturers includes Addison, Air–King, Bendix, Crosley, De Wald, Emerson, Fada, General Electric, Garod, Kadette, Motorola, RCA, Sentinel, Sonors, Sparton, Stewart–Warner, Zenith. The prices for these radios are almost independent of brand name but depend directly on the color.
Black	30.00
Blue	200.00
Brown	25.00
Green	175.00
Red	95.00
Yellow	100.00

Crosely
Bandbox	60.00
Cathedral	40.00
Harko or Ace V	55.00
Pup	120.00
Travette and Companion	45.00
Trirdyne, flat cabinet	80.00
4–29	70.00
IV	65.00
VI	75.00
X	115.00
516, table model	35.00
66T	30.00

DeForest
D–10, coil	175.00
Everyman, crystal	120.00

Emerson
Mickey Mouse	125.00
Model U Series	40.00
Plastic, AC/DC, table set	30.00

ERLA, clock radio ... 40.00

Federal
Crystal Set	110.00
58	180.00
59	225.00
110	125.00

Freed Eiseman
Electric Set	45.00
NR5, 6, and 7	75.00

Freshman Masterpiece ... 35.00

General Electric
Clock radio, plastic	25.00
K and J Series, table model	50.00
Model L	50.00

Grebe
CR Series, set	150.00
Electric, set	45.00
Syncrophase	75.00

International Kadette
International	40.00
Junior	50.00
36, 87	30.00

Majestic, Pre–WWII
Console	50.00
Table model	45.00

Mohawk, battery operated ... 40.00

Motorola
Plastic, portable, brown	30.00
Table model	30.00

Neutrowound ... 60.00

Novelty, figural
Globe, cracked, working condition .	35.00
Microphone	145.00
Snoopy's doghouse	55.00

Paragon
RA 10, DA amplifier	350.00
RD5	185.00

Phenolic cases (see Catalin)

Philco
Cathedrals, up to Model 90	60.00

Clock radio	35.00
Console	40.00
Model 116	80.00
Table models after 1932	20.00
Transistor, pocket	15.00

Philmore, crystal set

Early	40.00
Modern	10.00
Poley, cabinet for Atwater Kent	275.00

Radiola

I	145.00
II	150.00
V or VI	140.00
X, Regenoflex, WD11 tube	155.00
17 and 18	30.00
24 and 26	100.00
25 and 28	75.00
33, speaker	40.00
60	60.00

RCA

Cathedral, electric	50.00
Console	40.00
Table model, post–WWII	20.00
Radicon, clock radio	85.00
Regency, TR–4, transistor	35.00
Tom Thumb, model TT–600	40.00

Western Electric

3B	290.00
4D	280.00

Westinghouse

Aeriola

Amplifier	90.00
Junior, crystal set	90.00
Senior	80.00
RADA or RC	90.00

Zenith, trans oceanic wave magnet, $65.00.

Zenith

Cathedral	60.00
Console	45.00
Midget, transistor	15.00
Model 5–G-n401D, portable, gray, handle, 1949	25.00

RAILROAD ITEMS

Collecting Hints: Most collectors concentrate on one railroad as opposed to one type of object. Railroad material always brings a higher price in the area from which it originated. Local collectors tend to concentrate on local railroads. Material from railroads which operated for only a short time realizes the highest prices. Nostalgia also influences the collector.

There are many local railroad clubs. Railroad buffs tend to have their own specialized swap meets and exhibitions. A large one is held in Gaithersburg, Maryland, in the fall each year.

History: It was a canal company, the Delaware and Hudson, which used the first steam locomotive in America. The Stourbridge Lion moved coal from the mines to the canal wharfs. Just as America was entering its great canal era in 1825, the railroad was gaining a foothold. William Strickland recommended to the Commonwealth of Pennsylvania that they not build canals, but concentrate on the railroad. His advice went unheeded.

By the 1840s the railroad was established. Numerous private companies, many in business for only a short time, were organized.

The Civil War demonstrated the effectiveness of the railroad. Immediately following the war the transcontinental railroad was completed, and entrepreneurs such as Gould and Vanderbilt constructed financial empires built on railroads. Mergers created huge systems. The golden age of the railroad extended from the 1880s to the 1940s.

After 1950 the railroads suffered from poor management, a bloated labor force, lack of maintenance, and competition from other forms of transportation. The 1970s saw the federal government enter the picture through Conrail and Amtrak. Thousands of miles of track were abandoned. Many railroads failed or were merged. Today the system still is fighting for survival.

References: Stanley L. Baker, *Railroad Collectibles: An Illustrated Value Guide, Fourth Edition,* Collector Books, 1990; Phil Bollhagen, *The Pictorial Value Guide To Railroad Playing Cards,* published by author, 1987; Arthur Dominy and Rudolph A. Morgenfruh, *Silver At Your Service,* published by authors, 1987; Richard Luckin, *Dining On Rails,* published by author, 1983, out–of–print.

Periodicals: *Key, Lock and Lantern,* P.O. Box 15, Spencerport, NY 14559; *U. S. Rail News,* P. O. Box 7007, Huntingdon Woods, MI 48070.

Collectors' Clubs: Railroad Enthusiasts, 456 Main Street, West Townsend, MA 01474; Railroadiana Collectors Association, 795 Aspen Drive, Buffalo Grove, IL 60089; Railway and

Locomotive Historical Society, 3363 Riviera West Drive, Kelseyville, CA 95451.

Museums: Baltimore and Ohio Railroad, Baltimore, MD; Museum of Transportation, Boston, MA; New York Museum of Transportation, Albany, NY; California State Railroad Museum, Sacramento, CA.

Ashtray
 B & O RR, Lafayette **30.00**
 Chesapeake & Ohio, Chessie cat, 4" **50.00**
Badge, CRI & P RY, Special Police, six point star **195.00**
Baggage Sticker
 Milwaukee Road, "Hiawatha," 3½" d, streamlined Hiawatha steam locomotive, multicolored **5.00**
 Santa Fe, "El Capitan," 3" d, Sante Fe logo, red, yellow, black, and white **4.50**
Bell, steam locomotive, bronze, 17" d, yoke and cradle **700.00**
Blotter, Soo Line, unused, 1920s **1.75**
Book
 History of Burlington Route, Overton, NY, 1st edition, 1965 .... **30.00**
 History of Pennsylvania RR, 1846–1946 .... **65.00**
 The Official Guide of Railways & Steam Navigation Lines of the United States, Puerto Rico, Canada, Mexico & Cuba, includes timetables of "Railroading in Central America," 1929 .... **100.00**
Booklets and Brochures
 Canadian Pacific, "Montreal Viewbook," 1915 .... **8.00**
 Erie, "The Erie Limited," 8½ x 11", June, 1929, three large panels, nine int. views, four ext. views of equipment, blue and white cov **15.00**
 Lehigh Valley, "Claremont–The Great Terminal of the World's Great Port," 7 x 10", c1920, data and bird's eye view of Jersey City facility **18.00**

China, Northern Pacific, soup bowl, marked "Ivory, Lamberton, Scammel," 9" d, $25.00.

Northern Pacific RR, 1913 .... **30.00**
Oregon and Idaho Railroad, locomotive on cov **20.00**
Pacific RR, "Wayside Notes on Sunset Route" **8.00**
Salt Lake Route, "Southern California Mid–Winter Excursion," four panels, Feb, 1913 .... **8.00**
Boxcar Seal, lead, set of 4 .... **15.00**
Calendar
 CNW RR, 1949 .... **35.00**
 GN RR, 1934, Reiss painting **50.00**
 Missouri Pacific, wall type, perpetual, litho, tin, streamliner **175.00**
 Pennsylvania RR, pocket, colorful train, mountain scene **8.00**
 UP RR
  c1960 .... **10.00**
  c1970 .... **7.50**
  c1980 .... **5.00**
Catalog, Pullman Coach Co, 1920 .... **16.00**
China
 Bouillon Cup
  CM St P **30.00**
  Pennsylvania Railway **35.00**
 Butter Pat
  B & O, Centenary, Shenango backstamp **45.00**
  Santa Fe RR, blue and white **35.00**
 Cup and Saucer, Olympian **125.00**
 Demitasse Cup and Saucer, Chesapeake & Ohio, silhouette of gazebo, Syracuse backstamp **60.00**
 Hot Food Cov, 6", B & O RR **100.00**
 Milk Pitcher
  B & O RR **90.00**
  New York Central, train on blue border, 1831, Buffalo China ... **85.00**
 Plate
  B & O, Centenary, 6¾", Lambeton backstamp **60.00**
  Baltimore & Ohio RR, blue and white, engine border, Harpers Ferry center **80.00**
 Platter
  B & O RR, 11 x 8", gold capitol dome **75.00**
  New York Central, 7½ x 11¾" ... **38.00**
 Soup Bowl, 8¾", B & O RR **90.00**
Cigar Box, Northwestern RR **29.00**
Cigarette Lighter
 Canadian National Railways **10.00**
 Frisco **22.00**
 Pennsylvania **18.00**
Clock, Seth Thomas, #2 Regulator, oak case, orig **850.00**
Conductor's Hat, PRR **60.00**
Handbook, NYC RR, rules, 1951 ..... **4.50**
Hat Badge, Wabash Railway, brakeman **50.00**
Inkwell, Pennsylvania RR, emb, glass . **125.00**
Kerosene Can, GNRY
 1 gal **11.00**
 5 gal **8.00**

Lamp
  Caboose, D & GR **40.00**
  Carbide, German **60.00**
Lantern
  B & O, Adams & Westlake, hand,
    clear cast 5⅜" globe **65.00**
  Belt Railroad, hand type **45.00**
  C M St P & P, red globe, unfired ... **65.00**
  Chicago, Milwaukee, & St Paul,
    switch, emb metal, 5½" globe ... **60.00**
  D & H RR, Adlake Kero, red Fresnal
    3¼" globe **25.00**
  D SS & A, amber globe **90.00**
  GNRY, Adams & Westlake, Adlake
    Reliable, 5⅜" clear globe, "Safety
    Always" **175.00**
  MK & T RR, bell bottom, etched globe **120.00**
  Missouri Kansas Texas, amber globe,
    etching **60.00**
  PRR, Keystone Casey, hand, 1903,
    clear cast 5⅜" globe, cleaned to
    metal, keystone logo **35.00**
  Rock Island, clear globe **50.00**
  Southern, Armspear Manufacturing,
    hand, clear cast 5⅜" globe **75.00**
Letter Opener, Pacific Railroad, brass . **40.00**
Linens
  Headrest Cover
    Norfolk & Western, tan, red name **10.00**
    Seaboard Coast Lines, gold, light
      blue letters, train illus **10.00**
  Napkin
    Pennsylvania Railroad **12.00**
    Rock Island Lines, logo in center . **10.00**
    Seaboard Railway, linen, pr **50.00**
  Tablecloth
    B & O, 40" sq, train in center,
      "Linking the Great Train with the
      Nation" **40.00**
    Frisco Railway, 36" sq, white,
      Frisco emblem, white on white **30.00**
    Union Pacific, pink, bridge table
      size **25.00**
  Towel
    Illinois Central, dated "64," white,
      red letters **10.00**
    Penn Central **4.50**
    Pullman, white and blue **8.00**
Lock, steel, emb "CR RR" **125.00**
Magazine, Saturday Evening Post, May
  8, 1943, "A Night on Troop Train,"
  Norman Rockwell illus, 2 pgs of
  sketches **50.00**
Map
  United States, Canada, Indian terri-
    tories, 1855, tinted, 21½ x 31½" . **175.00**
  Wisconsin, linen, routes of 41 rail-
    roads, 1898 .... **135.00**
Match Holder, Burlington Zephyr, stain-
  less steel **22.00**
Matchbook, gift pack
  Delaware/Hudson **10.00**

Magazine, Don't Miss It, Thos. W. Jackson Pub. Co., 1908 copyright, revised 1940, 5⅜ x 7⅞", $15.00.

Union Pacific **15.00**
Soo Line **12.00**
Matchsafe, Union Pacific, aluminum,
  emb **56.00**
Meal Ticket, Santa Fe, 1920 .... **4.00**
Menu
  Canadian Pacific Railroad, 1928 ... **6.00**
  Frisco, dinner, 6 x 9¼", color cov .. **6.50**
  Great Northern, 1944 .... **12.50**
  Lehigh Valley, A la Carte Breakfast,
    c1950, logo in lower corner **3.75**
  Sante Fe, Super Chief, luncheon,
    folder, 1971, unused **4.25**
Meter, Chicago trolley, brass, orig bell **200.00**
Milk Bottle, Missouri Pacific, half pint **10.00**
Model, steam engine and tender, in-
  scribed "Model of the Hudson type
  locomotive used in the 20th Century–
  service built by American Locomotive
  Co for New York Central Lines," sgd
  Van Gytenbeck Sales Co Inc, New
  York, 1928 .... **185.00**
Notebook, Missouri Pacific **16.00**
Paperweight, Missouri Pacific RR **55.00**
Pass
  Atchison, Topeka & Sante Fe **3.50**
  Erie RR **8.00**
  Erie RR Veteran Assoc **12.00**
  Pennsylvania RR **10.00**
Pin, 25 Year Rutland Service **16.00**
Playing Cards
  C & O RR, Peake Chessie's "Old
    Man" **5.00**
  Chicago, Milwaukee & St Paul, 53
    scenic views, orig box, 1919 .... **40.00**
  New York, New Haven & Hartford
    RR, orig wrapper and box **65.00**
  Southern Pacific **20.00**

Postcard
  Depot, interior view **1.50**
  Freedom Train, 6¼ x 8", full color
  "Spirit of 1776" steamliner engine,
  General Electric logo, American
  Heritage Foundation, 1949 copy-
  right, unused **10.00**
  Train Wreck, c1900 .... **1.50**
Posters and Signs
  Chicago Aurora & Elgin RR, "Bad Or-
  der" placard, 3½ x 8", stiff card .. **1.50**
  New York Central, poster/handbill,
  "State Fair—Syracuse—Sept 7 to Sept
  12, 1931," includes fare chart from
  numerous stations on upstate
  branch lines, old NYC oval herald
  with speeding locomotive at bot-
  tom **6.00**
  Old Colony Line to Cottage City, Oak
  Bluffs, Martha's Vineyard & Nan-
  tucket, wall poster, map of line and
  connections, c1880, 18 x 28" **30.00**
  Railway Express Agency, depot ext.,
  yellow letters, black porcelainized
  steel, 11½ x 72" **150.00**
Schedule, Southern Pacific RR, 1927 . **7.50**
Service Pin, Pennsylvania, locomotive
  illus **18.00**
Silver Flatware and Holloware
  Caster Set, Chicago, Burlington, and
  Quincy, three bottles, California
  Zephyr route, SP frame **150.00**
  Coffeepot
    PRR, individual, International Sil-
    ver Co, 10 oz **85.00**
    Union Pacific, hinged cov, wing fi-
    nial, Challenger pattern, marked
    "International Silver Co, 32 oz" **250.00**
  Creamer, Wabash, 2 oz, backstamped
    International Silver **45.00**
  Creamer and Sugar, Atchison, Topeka
    & Santa Fe, SP, bottom stamped
    "Fred Harvey, Gorham Mfg Co" . **60.00**
  Crumb Scraper, Louisville/Nashville
    RR **45.00**
  Dish Cover, Rock Island Lines, SP,
    1927 .... **120.00**
  Fork
    Dinner, Southern Pacific, Broad-
    way pattern **8.50**
    Oyster, NYC, Century pattern, un-
    derside marked "NYC" **10.00**
    Pickle, Rock Island Lines, 5¼" ... **5.00**
  Knife
    Bread and Butter, ACL, Zephyr pat-
    tern, handle marked "ACL" **8.00**
    Dinner, New York Central **10.00**
  Spoon
    Iced Tea, MP Lines, Century pattern **18.00**
    Soup, Frisco, Art Nouveau style .. **25.00**

Sugar Bowl, cov, Burlington Railroad,
  silver, double handles, Reed & Bar-
  ton **75.00**
Sugar Tongs, Southern RR **26.00**
Teapot, Union Pacific, SP, marked
  "Reed & Barton" **40.00**
Tray, oval, 8", International 1936,
  backstamped **25.00**
Vase, GM & O, bud, 7", backstamped
  International Silver **75.00**
Stocks and Bonds
  Buffalo and Susquehanna Railroad,
  100 shares preferred, engraved bor-
  ders in orange—rust, vignette of
  steam locomotive hauling coal
  train, issued and canceled **20.00**
  Erie RR Co, stock certificate, 1950s . **8.00**
  Erie—Lackawanna Railroad Co, stock
  certificate, 1960s **6.00**
  Gulf Mobile & Northern, stock certif-
  icate, train vignette, issued **7.50**
  New Haven & Northampton, $5,000
  bond, engraved vignette of speed-
  ing steam locomotive pulling pas-
  senger train, unissued **12.00**
Survey Lithograph, Pacific RR, 1855 .. **17.50**
Switch Key
  Chicago & Northwestern **13.00**
  Illinois Valley & Northern **55.00**
  Michigan Central **25.00**
  Monon **12.00**
  Pere marquette **30.00**
  San Antonio & Arkansas Pass **24.00**
Tape Measure, N & W RR, 50 ft **23.00**
Ticket Punch **15.00**
Timetable
  Chesapeake & Ohio, 1957 .... **5.00**
  Great Northern RR, 1896 .... **40.00**
  Illinois Central, 1961 .... **5.00**
  New York Central, 1959 .... **6.00**
  Rutland, 1957 .... **5.00**
  Santa Fe, 1962 .... **5.00**
  Southern Pacific, 1948 .... **10.00**
  Union Pacific, 1963 .... **6.00**
Token
  B & O, brass, 1927 .... **20.00**
  C & O, "Good for Sanitary Cup,"
  brass **14.00**
  Union Pacific, 1934 .... **5.00**
Tool, raises coach window, hinged ... **75.00**
Uniform, brakeman's, C & O, coat,
  pants, vest, and hat **450.00**
Wax Seal, mushroom shape top, marked
  "S Jackson, Conductor" **45.00**
Whistle
  Peanut, C & O RR, brass **40.00**
  Steam, brass
    3" **110.00**
    10" I valve **100.00**

RAZORS

Collecting Hints: A major revolution has occurred in razor collecting in the 1980s. At the beginning of the decade almost all collectors focused on the straight razor. By the late–1980s the collecting of safety razors and their related material as well as electric shavers achieved a popularity that, by the 1990s, should equal or exceed that of the straight razor collectors.

Many straight razor collectors focus on the products of a single manufacturer. Value is increased by certain names, e.g., H. Boker, Case, M. Price, Joseph Rogers, Simmons Hardware, Will & Finck, Winchester, and George Wostenholm. The ornateness of the handle and blade pattern also influences value. The fancier the handle or more intricately etched the blade, the higher the price. Rarest handle materials are pearl, stag, Sterling silver, pressed horn, and carved ivory. Rarest blades are those with scenes etched across the entire front.

Initially safety razor collectors are focusing on those razors that were packaged in elaborately lithographed tins during the 1890 to 1915 period. Since a safety razor involves several items, i.e., razor, blades, case or tin, instructions, etc., completeness is a critical factor. Support items such as blade banks, boxes, and sharpeners also attract collectors. Many safety razors from the early period already exceed $50. As a result, new collectors are seeking safety razors from the 1920s through the 1950s because a comprehensive collection can still be assembled at a modest price.

When buying an electric shaver, make certain that it is complete and in working order. Many were sold originally with cleaning kits, most of which have been lost.

History: Razors date back several thousand years. Early man used sharpened stones. The Egyptians, Greeks, and Romans had metal razors.

Straight razors made prior to 1800 generally were crudely stamped WARRENTED or CAST STEEL with the maker's mark on the tang. Until 1870 almost all razors for the American market were manufactured in Sheffield, England. Most blades were wedge shaped; many were etched with slogans or scenes. Handles were made of natural materials—various horns, tortoise shell, bone, ivory, stag, silver and pearl. All razors were handmade.

After 1870 most straight razors were machine made with hollow ground blades and synthetic handle materials. Razors of this period usually were manufactured in Germany (Solingen) or in American cutlery factories. Hundreds of molded celluloid handle patterns were produced, such as nude women, eagles, deer, boats, windmill scenes, etc.

By 1900 the safety razor was challenging the straight razor for popularity among the shaving community. A wealth of safety razor patents were issued in the first decade of the 20th century. World War I insured the dominance of the safety razor as American troops abroad made it their preferred shaving method.

By the 1930s the first electric shavers appeared. However, electric shavers did not achieve universal acceptance until the 1950s.

References: Robert A. Doyle, *Straight Razor Collecting*, Collector Books, 1980, out-of-print; Phillip L. Krumholz, *Value Guide For Barberiana & Shaving Collectibles*, Ad Libs Publishing Co., 1988.

Collectors' Club: Safety Razor Collectors' Guild, P. O. Box 885, Crescent City, CA 95531.

Star, Kampee, NY, patent 1900, built in strop, 4" l, 2" w, $35.00.

Blade Bank
Ever–Ready, 2 x 1½ x 1", tin, treasure chest shape, orange, black, and gold lettering **20.00**
Gem Blades, 2" h, tin, book shape, gold, red, and black **15.00**
Listerine Shaving Cream Co, 3" h, porcelain, frog shape **18.00**
Blade Box and Case
Herbert Robinson & Co, coffin shape box, black celluloid handles, etched blades **25.00**
Marlin, red, white, and blue **12.00**
Star, tin, dark green, Kampfe's stropping device illus, one blade, American Can Co **25.00**
Yankee, red, white, and blue American shield, gold and black lettering, red scroll **50.00**
Blade Sharpener
Blade Master, Abercrombie & Fitch Co **15.00**
Everkeen Magnetic, instructions, boxed **12.00**

Kriss Kross, stropper style, pr **12.50**
Rotello, oak case, removable handles **25.00**
Electric Shaver
Schick, black bakelite, stamped
"Model S," orig case and cord ... **20.00**
Vibro Shave, Art Deco style, blades,
instructions, boxed **35.00**
Safety Razor
Men's
Devine, ivory handle, double edge,
blade guard, leather covered
wood case, includes "The De-
vine Caretaker Chicago, USA"
adv sharpener **75.00**
Ever–Ready, red and black box,
cardboard blade holders **20.00**
Gem Junior Bar, leather covered
wood case, four blades
Gem Cutlery Co, New York, patent
1901 .... **20.00**
Gem Minute Man, metal, wall
mount type, blade holder **25.00**
Gillette, travel set, gold plated razor, blade holder, and two powder tins, emb leather covered
wood case **50.00**
Griffon, orig wrapped instructions,
brown and black tin, patents date
to 1901 .... **75.00**
Keen Kutter, NRA stamped boxes,
instructions, set of 5, unused .. **50.00**
Maktor, triangular head, blades, instruction sheet, orig box **50.00**
Mappin & Webb, ivory handles,
"NULLI SECUNDUS" etched
blades, 7–day set, emb leather
case **100.00**
Mohican, instructions, orig Mohican stamped blade, orig tin **100.00**
Segal, gold plated, blades, instructions, boxed **15.00**
7 O'Clock, orig green tin and
blades **50.00**
Sextoblade Razor Style B, ivory
handle, blade guard, leather
bound wood case, emb days of
the week tag, W Weck & Son,
Inc, NY **50.00**
Stahly, wind–up type, vibrates as it
shaves, plastic case **15.00**
Star Razor, interchangeable pieces,
dates up to 1901 on head of razor, Kampfe, New York, orig tin **60.00**
Torrey No 3, orig green and yellow
tin with gold and black lettering,
Made by JR Torrey Razor Co,
Worcester, Mass, USA, c1905 . **75.00**
Wilkinson Sword Company, plated,
7–day set, razor fitted in holder
over leather strop, blades engraved day of the week, blue vel-
vet/satin lined chrome case **50.00**

Winchester, instructions, orig box **50.00**
Yankee, fancy engraved head, 2½
x 1¼" orig red, white, and blue
tin **75.00**
Women's
Curvfit, instructions, orig blue and
gold box **5.00**
Kewtie Cosmetic Razor, celluloid
handle and case, light blue **25.00**
Laurel, Ladies Boudoir, purple tin,
cardboard box, instructions **25.00**
Schermack, round head, boxed .. **10.00**
Straight Razor
Crown & Sword, etched Crown &
Sword Manufactory scene blade,
clear horn handle, German silver
ends, dated "1873–1898" **25.00**
Dixon Cutlery Co, ivory and raised
bark and pine cone pattern handle,
Germany **15.00**
Garland Cutlery Co, etched "The Im-
proved Eagle Razor Blade," spread
American eagle, black handle **10.00**
Korn, George W, Art Nouveau style,
black **25.00**
Scott, James T, ivory handle, inlaid
engraved metal scene **20.00**
Stewart & Co, tortoiseshell handle, in-
laid German silver shield, semi–
wedge shape blade, c1815 ...... **100.00**
Torrey Razor Co, ear of corn pattern
handle, plain blade **35.00**
Wade & Butcher, Sheffield, semi–
wedge blade, bone handle, spread
American eagle, "E. Pluribus
Unum" banner **60.00**

REAMERS

Collecting Hints: Reamers seldom are found in
mint condition. Cone and rim nicks are usually
acceptable, but cracked pieces bring considerably less. Ceramic figurals and U. S. made glass
are collected more than any other category.

Reamer collecting first became popular with
the advent of the Depression Glass collector in
the mid–1960s. Reamer collecting can be an
endless hobby. It may be impossible to assemble
one of every example made. One–of–a–kind
samples do exist; they never were put into mass
production.

History: Devices for getting the juice from citrus
fruit have been around almost as long as the fruit
itself. These devices range in materials from
wood to glass and from nickel plated and Sterling
silver to fine china.

Many different kinds of mechanical reamers
were devised before the first glass one was
pressed around 1885. Very few reamers have
been designed since 1940 when frozen juice en-

tered the market. Modern day ceramists are making clown and teapot shaped reamers.

References: Gene Florence, *Kitchen Glassware of the Depression Years, Fourth Edition,* Collector Books, 1990; Mary Walker, *Reamers—200 Years,* Muski Publishers, 1980, separate price guide; Mary Walker, *The Second Book, More Reamers—200 Years,* Muski Publishers, 1983.

Collectors' Club: National Reamer Collectors Association, Rt. #1, Box 200, Grantsburg, WI 54840.

REPRODUCTION ALERT. Reproduced reamers include:

An old 5" Imperial Glass Co. reamer, originally made in clear glass, was reproduced for Edna Barnes in dark amethyst. 1,500 were made. The reproduction is marked "IG" and "81."

Mrs. Barnes has reproduced several old 4½" Jenkins Glass Co. reamers in limited editions. The reproductions are also made in a 2¼" size. All Jenkins copies are marked with a "B" in a circle.

Note: The first book on reamers, now out–of–print, was written by Ken and Linda Ricketts in 1974. Their numbering system was continued by Mary Walker in *Reamers—200 Years.* The Ricketts–Walker numbers will be found in the china and metal sections. The numbers in parentheses in the glass section are from Gene Florence's *Kitchen Glassware of the Depression Years.*

China, face, yellow spatter, black trim, blue eyes, pink nose, teal handle, green leaves, No. F-46, 5" h, 4¼" d, $35.00.

CHINA AND CERAMIC

Bavaria, 4" h, orange shape, yellow, green leaves and handle, white top, 2 pc (L–7)	**18.00**
Czechoslovakia, 3¾" h, orange lustre, pink flowers, green leaves, 2 pc (E–48)	**30.00**
Japan	
Baby's Orange, 4½", blue on white (B–4)	**28.00**
Clown, 7½" h, pale green and white, orange hands and feet (C–40)	**40.00**
Duck, 2¾" h, various color combinations, 2 pc (F–12)	**30.00**
Good Morning, 8½" pitcher, set of cups, modern, 2 pc (P–25)	**18.00**
Pear, 4½ x 5", yellow and orange, green leaves, 3 pc (L–39)	**32.00**
Saucer style, 4½" d, flat, loop handle, yellow, green leaves (D–40)	**22.00**
Nippon, 3¼" h, hp, white, floral, 2 pc	**75.00**
United States	
Hall China, large, flat, lettuce green, marked "Hall," 1 pc	**155.00**
Red Wing, 6¾" h, pedestal type, yellow, 1 pc (A–7)	**75.00**

GLASS

Cambridge, Seville yellow, grapefruit (145–4–1)	**275.00**
Federal, green transparent, pointed cone, tab handle (135–3–4)	**28.00**
Fenton, clear, elephant dec, two handles (131–7–5)	**95.00**
Fry	
Canary Vaseline, tab handle (133–3–2)	**60.00**
Pearl Opalescent (133–3–1)	**22.00**
Hazel Atlas	
Cobalt Blue, tab handle, small (138–4–3)	**225.00**
Pink, tab handle, large (138–4–4)	**26.00**
White Opaque, blue dec, 2 cup set (137–3–3)	**57.50**
Hocking, green	
Circle Pitcher, reamer top (139–1–1)	**55.00**
Clambroth, tab handle (193–3–3)	**88.00**
Indiana, amber, handle opposite spout (135–4–1)	**200.00**
Jeannette	
Jadite, dark, small (143–3–1)	**40.00**
Pink, Hex Optic, bucket reamer (143–1–1)	**55.00**
MacBeth–Evans, clambroth (142–3–2)	**375.00**
McKee	
Chalaine Blue, emb Sunkist (146–3–3)	**185.00**
Delphite, small (147–5–4)	**345.00**
Vaseline Green, emb Sunkist (146–5–4)	**38.00**
US Glass	
Green, four cup pitcher set (151–1–2)	**75.00**
Light Pink, two cup pitcher set (151–2–1)	**35.00**
Westmoreland, baby	
Crystal, 2 pc (131–1–2)	**95.00**
Pink, 2 pc (131–1–1)	**195.00**

METAL

Gem Squeezer, aluminum, crank handle, table model, 2 pc (M–100)	**10.00**

Knapps Orange Juicer, aluminum, hinged, crank handle, hand held (M–86) **10.00**

Kwicky Juicer, aluminum, pan style, Quam–Nichols Co (M–97) **8.00**

Lemon–Lime Roto Squeezer, 6¾" l, scissor type (M–73) **5.00**

Pearl, cast iron, wood insert, long handled (M–27) **18.00**

Presto Juicer, porcelain, metal stand (M–112) **60.00**

Sealed Sweet, mechanical, clamps to table, tilt model (M–120) **40.00**

Yankee–Lidon, iron, cast aluminum parts, long handled (M–62) **20.00**

RECORDS

Collecting Hints: Collectors tend to focus on one particular area of the music field, e.g., jazz, the big bands, rock 'n' roll, or on one artist. Purchase records with original dust jackets and covers whenever possible.

Also check the records carefully for scratches. If the record cannot be played, it is worthless.

Proper storage of records is critical to maintaining their value. Keep stacks small. It is best to store them vertically. Place acid free paper between the albums to prevent bleeding of ink from one cover to the next.

History: The first records were cylinders produced by Thomas Edison in 1877 and played on a phonograph of his design. Edison received a patent in 1878, but soon dropped the project in order to perfect the light bulb.

Alexander Graham Bell, Edison's friend, was excited about the phonograph and developed the graphaphone which was marketed successfully by 1889. Early phonographs and graphaphones had hand cranks which wound the mechanism and kept the cylinders moving.

About 1900 Emile Berliner developed a phonograph which used a flat disc, similar to today's records. The United States Gramophone Company marketed his design in 1901. The company eventually became RCA Victor. By 1910 discs were more popular than cylinders.

The record industry continued to develop as progress was made in the preservation of sound and the increased quality of sound. The initial size of 78 rpm records was replaced by 45 rpm, then 33⅓ rpm, and finally, compact discs.

References: L. R. Docks, *1915–1965 American Premium Record Guide, Third Edition,* Books Americana, 1986; Jerry Osborne, *The Official Price Guide Movie/TV Soundtracks and Original Cast Albums,* House of Collectibles, 1991; Jerry Osborne, *The Official Price Guide To Records, Ninth Edition,* House of Collectibles, 1990; Neal Umphred, *Goldmine's Price Guide To Collectible Record Albums,* Krause Publications, 1989.

Periodicals: *Discoveries,* P. O. Box 255, Port Townsend, WA 98368; *Goldmine,* 700 E. State Street, Iola, WI 54990.

Note: Prices are for first pressings in original dust jackets or albums.

Additional Listings: Elvis Presley and Rock 'N' Roll.

Big Bands
Gus Arnheim & His Orchestra

If I Can't Have You, Okeh, 41037	**6.00**
Love In The Moonlight, Victor, 24235	**7.00**
The Image Of You, Brunswick, 7900	**8.00**

Les Brown, Decca

Lazy River, 1323	**7.00**
Ramona, 1296	**8.00**
Swamp Fire, Decca, 1231	**10.00**

Benny Carter

Blue Lou, Okeh, 41567	**18.00**
Devil's Holiday, Columbia, 2898–D	**18.00**
Everybody Shuffle, Vocalion, 2870	**12.50**

Count Basie & His Orchestra

Exactly Like You, Decca, 1252 ...	**10.00**
Louisiana, Columbia, 35448	**5.00**
The Blues I Like To Hear, Decca, 2284	**8.00**

Bob Crosby & His Orchestra, Decca

And Then Some, 502	**7.00**
On Treasure Island, 614	**6.00**
What's The Name Of That Song?, 727	**8.00**

Tommy Dorsey, Okeh

It's Right Here For You, 41178 ...	**12.00**
You Can't Cheat A Cheater, 41422	**12.00**

Duke Ellington

Black and Tan Fantasy, Okeh, 40955	**15.00**
Cotton Club Stomp, Victor, 38079	**25.00**
Creole Rhapsody, Brunswick, 6093	**10.00**
Ebony Rhapsody, Victor, 24622 ..	**10.00**
Got Everything But You, Victor, 21703	**18.00**
Sam And Delilah, Victor, 23036 .	**15.00**
Tishomingo Blues, Brunswick, 3987	**12.50**

Billie Holiday, Vocalion

Under A Blue Jungle Moon, 4786	**8.00**
When A Woman Loves A Man, 4029	**10.00**

Benny Goodman

Ain'tcha Glad?, Columbia, 2835–D	**22.00**
King Porter, Victor, 25090	**6.00**
Overnight, Melotone, 12024	**15.00**
Riffin' The Scotch, Columbia, 2687–D	**20.00**
We Can Live On Love, Melotone, 12120	**20.00**

Glen Miller
  Solo Hop, Columbia, 3058–D ... **35.00**
  Sweet Stranger, Brunswick, 8041 . **10.00**
  Wistful And Blue, Decca, 1284 .. **10.00**
Mills Brothers, Brunswick
  Doin' The New Low–Down, 6517 **12.00**
  Smoke Rings, 6225 .... **8.00**
Rudy Vallee
  Me Minus You, Columbia, 2715–D **8.00**
  Nasty Man, Victor, 24581 .... **8.00**
  Right Out Of Heaven, Harmony,
    724–H **10.00**
Thomas "Fats" Waller
  Birmingham Blues, Okeh, 4757 .. **25.00**
  I'm Crazy 'Bout My Baby, Colum-
    bia **30.00**
  Stompin' The Bug, Victor, 20655 . **24.50**
Country/Western
  Aiken Country String Band, Okeh
    Charleston Rag, 45219 .... **12.00**
    Harrisburg Itch, 45294 .... **10.00**
  Allen Brothers
    Chattanooga Mama, Victor, 23567 **40.00**
    Daddy Park Your Car, Vocalion,
      02853 .... **15.00**
    It Can't Be Done, Bluebird, 5533 . **15.00**
    Pile Drivin' Papa, Victor, 23578 .. **45.00**
    Salty Dog Blues, Columbia,
      15175–D **25.00**
    Triple Blues, Bluebird, 5104 ..... **12.00**
    Unlucky Man, Victor, 23623 .... **30.00**
  Gene Autry
    Cowboy Yodel, Gennett, 7243 ... **75.00**
    Dust Pan Blues, Champion, 16119 **32.50**
    That's How I Got My Start, Supe-
      rior, 2681 .... **50.00**
  Boone County Entertainers, Supertone
    Arkansas Traveler, 9163 .... **7.00**
    Something Wrong With My Gal,
      9182 .... **10.00**
  Carter Family
    Broken Hearted Lover, Vocalion,
      02990 .... **18.00**
    Carter's Blues, Victor, 23716 .... **32.00**
    Keep On The Sunny Side, Bluebird,
      5006 .... **6.00**
    My Native Home, Decca, 5241 .. **10.00**
    On The Rock, Victor, 23513 ..... **25.00**
  Delmore Brothers, Bluebird
    Big Ball In Texas, 7560 .... **8.00**
    Hey! Hey! I'm Memphis Bound,
      5857 .... **10.00**
    Lonesome Yodel Blues, 5299 .... **12.50**
  East Texas Serenaders
    Combination Rag, Columbia,
      15229–D **5.00**
    Ozark Rag, Brunswick, 538 ..... **10.00**
  Johnny Horton, Abbott
    Candy Jones, 100 .... **8.00**
    Smokey Joe's Barbeque, 106 ..... **12.00**
  Kessinger Brothers, Brunswick
    Arkansas Traveler, 247 .... **8.50**

    Little Brown Jug, 468 .... **8.50**
    Midnight Serenade Waltz, 352 ... **10.00**
    Ragtime Annie, 540 .... **12.00**
  Bradley Kincaid
    Old Coon Dog, Brunswick, 485 .. **10.00**
    The Cowboy's Dream, Decca,
      5048 .... **8.00**
    The Fatal Wedding, Gennett, 6363 **20.00**
    The Old Wooden Bucket, Bluebird,
      5201 .... **5.00**
  Lone Star Rangers
    Farm Relief Song, Paramount, 3202 **8.00**
    The Train That Never Arrived,
      Broadway, 8142 .... **10.00**
Movie and TV Soundtracks
  Advance To The Rear, Columbia,
    1964 .... **25.00**
  Auntie Mame, Warner Bros, 1958 .. **50.00**
  Avengers, 1966 .... **45.00**
  Barbarella, Dyno Voice, 1968 ..... **22.00**
  Big Chill, Motown, 1983 .... **8.50**
  Blue Hawaii, RCA Victor, 1961 .... **35.00**
  Bye Bye Birdie, Columbia, 1960 ... **25.00**
  Cactus Flower, Bell, 1970 .... **12.00**
  Camelot, orig cast, Columbia, 1960 **22.00**
  Car Wash, MCA, 1978 .... **8.00**
  Cocoon, Polydor, 1985 .... **8.00**
  Damn Yankees, orig cast, RCA Victor,
    1955 .... **25.00**
  Dragnet, RCA Victor, 1953 .... **55.00**
  East Of Eden, Columbia, 1957 ..... **30.00**
  Fitzwilly, United Artists, 1968 ...... **18.00**
  Footloose, Columbia, 1983 .... **8.00**
  Fun In Acapulco, RCA Victor, 1963 **45.00**
  Guess Who's Coming To Dinner, Col-
    gems, 1968 .... **18.00**
  Gypsy, orig cast, Columbia, 1959 .. **12.00**
  Hair, RCA Victor, 1967 .... **8.00**
  Hamlet, orig cast, Columbia, 1964 . **18.00**
  Hawaii Five–O, Capitol, 1969 ..... **15.00**
  It's A Mad, Mad, Mad, Mad World,
    United Artists, 1963 .... **18.00**
  Ivanhoe, MGM, 1952 .... **26.00**
  Jamaica, RCA Victor, 1957 .... **25.00**
  King Solomon's Mines, Restless, 1985 **8.00**
  Lady Sings The Blues, Motown, 1972 **10.00**
  Lawrence Of Arabia, Colpix, 1962 . **38.00**
  Let's Make Love, Columbia, 1960 .. **20.00**
  Macbeth, studio cast, RCA Victor,
    1953 .... **45.00**
  Magnificent Seven, United Artist,
    1960 .... **18.00**
  Mary Poppins, Sidewalk, 1968 ..... **10.00**
  Miami Vice, MCA, 1985 .... **8.00**
  Night Shift, Warner Bros, 1982 ..... **10.00**
  No Way To Treat A Lady, Dot, 1968 **8.00**
  Oh Calcutta, Aidart, 1969 .... **12.00**
  Oklahoma, orig cast, Decca, 1943 . **12.50**
  Patton, 20th Century Fox, 1970 .... **10.00**
  Pennies From Heaven, Warner Bros,
    1981 .... **12.50**
  Pink Panther, RCA Victor, 1964 .... **12.50**

Psycho II, MCA, 1983	8.00
Ragtime, Electra, 1981	8.50
Rocky, United Artists, 1976	10.00
Rosemary's Baby, Dot, 1968	25.00
Scarface, MCA, 1984	10.00
Some Like It Hot, United Artists, 1959	25.00
Summer of '42, Warner Bros, 1971 .	10.00
Taste Of Honey, studio cast, Atlantic, 1960	20.00
Three Days of the Condor, Capitol, 1975	22.00
To Kill A Mockingbird, Ava, 1962 . .	30.00
What's New Pussycat?, United Artists, 1965	15.00

Rock N' Roll

Paul Anka

Diana, ABC Paramount	15.00
My Heart Sings, ABC Paramount, 296	12.00

Beach Boys

Surfin', Candix, 301	50.00
The Beach Boys Today, DU, 2269	25.00

Beatles

All You Need Is Love, Capitol, 5964	18.00
Please Please Me, Vee Jay, 498	75.00

Big Bopper, Chantilly Lace, Mercury,

71343	30.00

Ray Charles, Atlantic

Genius, 1312	12.50
What'd I Say, 8029	12.00
Chubby Checker, The Class, Parkway, 804	55.00

Bobby Darin

Dealer In Dreams, Decca, 30225	10.00
Queen Of The Hop, Atco, 6127 .	18.00
Rock Island Line, Decca, 29983 .	10.00
Splish Splash, Atco, 6117	22.00

Bo Diddley

Bo Diddley, Chess, 1431	30.00
Have Guitar Will Travel, Chess, 2974	18.00
Say! (Boss Man), Checker, 878 . . .	8.00

The Drifters

Bip Bam, Atlantic, 1043	5.00
The World Is Changing, Crown, 108	45.00
Duprees, Have You Heard, Coed, 906	40.00

The Everly Brothers, Cadence

Bird Dog, 1350	25.00
Everly Hits, 3062	12.00
Wake Up Little Susie, 1337	18.00

Bill Haley and The Comets

Crazy Man Crazy, Essex, 321	15.00
Green Tree Boogie, Holiday, 108 .	80.00
Rock The Joint, Essex, 303	12.00
Shake, Rattle And Roll, Decca, 2168	10.00

Buddy Holly, Coral

Listen To Me, 81169	20.00
Peggy Sue Got Married, 81191 . . .	15.00

Jerry Lee Lewis, Sun

Great Balls Of Fire, 281	20.00
Whole Lot Of Shakin' Going On, 267	7.00
Muddy Waters, Loving Man, Chess, 1585	10.00

Ricky Nelson

Stood Up, Imperial, 5483	12.00
Teenager's Romance, Verve, 10047	10.00

Orioles, Jubilee

At Night, 5025	90.00
Gettin' Tired Tired Tired, 5084 . . .	40.00
When You're Not Around, 5071 .	60.00

Platters

I'll Cry When You're Gone, Federal, 12164	30.00
The Flying Platters, Mercury, 20298	12.00

Supremes

Just For You And I, Ace, 534	12.00
Meet The Supremes, Motown, 606	30.00
Tonight, Old Town, 1024	35.00
Mel Tillis, Teen Age Wedding, Columbia, 41115	8.00

Ritchie Valens, Del–Fi

Ritchie Valens, PR–1	12.00
His Greatest Hits, 1225	25.00

Wanderers

Everybody's Somebody's Fool, Kent, 356	12.00
Thinking Of You, Onyx, 518	15.00

Slim Whitman, Imperial

My Love Is Growing Stale, 8134 .	12.00
Restless Heart, 8189	10.00

RED WING POTTERY

Collecting Hints: Red Wing Pottery can be found with various marks and paper labels. Some of the marks include a red wing which is stamped on, a raised "Red Wing U.S.A. #___", and an impressed "Red Wing U.S.A. #___". Paper labels were used as early as 1930. Pieces with paper labels easily lost their only mark.

Many manufacturers used the same mold patterns. Study the references to become familiar with the Red Wing forms.

History: The category of Red Wing Pottery covers several potteries which started in Red Wing, Minnesota. The first pottery, named Red Wing Stoneware Company, was started in 1868 by David Hallem. The primary product of this company was stoneware. The mark used by this company was a red wing stamped under the glaze. The Minnesota Stoneware Company was started in 1883. The North Star Stoneware Company opened a factory in the same area in 1892 and went out of business in 1896. The mark used by this company included a raised star and the words Red Wing.

The Red Wing Stoneware Company and the Minnesota Stoneware Company merged in 1892.

The new company was called the Red Wing Union Stoneware Company. The new company made stoneware until 1920 when it introduced a line of pottery.

In 1936 the name of the company was changed to Red Wing Potteries Incorporated. They continued to make pottery until the 1940s. During the 1930s they introduced several lines of dinnerware. These patterns were all hand painted, very popular, and sold through department stores, Sears, and gift stamp centers. The production of dinnerware declined in the 1950s. The company began producing hotel and restaurant china in the early 1960s. The plant was closed in 1967.

References: Dan and Gail DePasquale and Larry Peterson, *Red Wing Collectibles*, Collector Books, 1985, 1988 value update; Gary and Bonnie Tefft, *Red Wing Potters and Their Wares, Second Edition* Locust Enterprises, 1987; Lyndon C. Viel, *The Clay Giants: The Stoneware of Red Wing, Goodhue County, Minnesota, Book 2* (1980), *Book 3* (1987), Wallace–Homestead.

Collectors' Club: Red Wing Collectors Society, Route 3, Box 146, Monticello, MN 55362.

Ashtray, wing shape 35.00
Basket, white, semi gloss 20.00
Bookends, pr, fan and scroll, green ... 15.00
Centerpiece, 12 x 2", round, deep green, three holes on rim hold 2" white baby birds on branch, mother and father figures sit inside bowl, six pcs, orig label 65.00
Commemorative, Minn Twins 1965 World Series, double bowl 65.00
Cookie Jar
  Chef 55.00
  Monk, yellow and brown 40.00
  Rooster, green, semi gloss 30.00
Cornucopia, burgundy, high glass, leaf dec 12.00
Dinnerware
  Bobwhite
    Bowl
      5½" d 7.00
      6½" d 12.00
    Bread Tray 75.00
    Butter Dish, cov 33.00
    Casserole, cov, stand, 4 qt 65.00
    Cookie Jar 75.00
    Cup and Saucer 10.00
    Hors D'oeuvre Bird 32.00
    Lazy Susan 75.00
    Pitcher, 60 oz 28.00
    Plate
      6" d 5.00
      6½" d 7.00
      8" d 8.00
    Platter
      13¾" l 23.00

      20" l 32.00
    Relish, three part 35.00
    Salt and Pepper Shakers, pr 20.00
    Sugar, cov 20.00
    Vegetable Dish, divided 25.00
  Driftwood
    Gravy boat, blue 15.00
    Nappy, 6½" 12.00
    Salad plate 7.00
    Saucer 2.00
  Lute Song
    Coffee, cov 25.00
    Custard Cup 7.50
    Fruit bowl 7.50
    Platter, 13" l 20.00
    Sauce Dish 2.00
    Vegetable Bowl, divided 20.00
  Merrileaf
    Bread Tray 28.00
    Cup and saucer 10.00
    Gravy, cov 20.00
    Salt and pepper shakers, pr 12.00
    Vegetable, divided 15.00
  Pepe
    Cup 3.00
    Plate, 6½" d 3.00
  Plum Blossom
    Bowl, 5½" 3.00
    Cup, yellow 3.00
    Plate, 10" d 5.00
    Soup, flat 6.00
    Sugar, cov 6.00
  Random House
    Coffeepot, tall 25.00
    Cup and saucer 8.00
    Plate, 10½" d 7.00
    Relish dish, 13¼" 15.00
  Tampico
    Casserole, cov 18.00
    Creamer 4.00
    Cup and saucer 5.00
    Turtle Dove, platter, 13" l 12.00
  Two Step
    Creamer 3.00
    Plate, 10" d 4.50
Flower Block, Dolphin 25.00
Planter
  Canoe, matte ivory, brown int. 25.00
  Guitar, black, semi gloss 15.00
  Puppy, aqua, semi gloss 15.00
Spongeware
  Bowl, 7¼" d 85.00
  Lid, 6" d 75.00
Stoneware, adv
  Bean Pot 50.00
  Beater Jar 85.00
  Bowl, 8", gray stoneware, blue dec, Greek Key border, marked "Luhman & Sanders, Potsville, Iowa" . 75.00
  Jar, Kansas Druggist adv 100.00
  Teapot, yellow rooster, gold trim 65.00
  Trivet, Minnesota Centennial 60.00

Vase, paneled, scroll handles, light green, marked, 6" h, $15.00.

Vase, 6" h, fan, paneled, scroll handles,
  light green **15.00**
Wall Pocket, bird on grapevine, gray—
  green **18.00**

ROBOTS

Collecting Hints: The name for robots comes from markings on the robot or box and from the trade. Hence, some robots have more than one name. Do research to know exactly what robot you have. A leading auctioneer of robots is Lloyd Ralston Toys, Fairfield, Connecticut.

Condition is critical. Damaged lithographed tin is almost impossible to repair and repaint. Toys in mint condition in the original box are the most desirable. The price difference between a mint robot and one in very good condition may be as high as 200%.

Working condition is important, but not critical. Many robots never worked well, and larger robots stripped their gearing quickly. The rarer the robot, the less important is the question of working condition.

Finally, if you play with your robot, do not leave the batteries in the toy. If they leak or rust, the damage may destroy the value of the toy.

History: Atomic Robot Man, made in Japan between 1948 and 1949, is the grandfather of all robot toys. He is an all metal wind-up toy, less than 5" high and rather crudely made. Japanese robots of the early 1950s tended to be the friction or wind-up variety, patterned in brightly lithographed tin and made from recycled materials.

By the late 1950s robots had entered the battery-powered age. Limited quantities of early models were produced; parts from one model were used in later models with slight or no variations. The robot craze was enhanced by Hollywood's production of movies such as Destination Moon (1950) and Forbidden Planet

(1956). Robby the Robot came from this latter movie.

Many Japanese manufacturers were small and lasted only a few years. Leading firms include Horikawa Toys, Nomura Toys, and Yonezawa Toys. Cragstan was an American importer who sold Japanese-made toys under its own label. Marx and Ideal entered the picture in the 1970s. Modern robots are being imported from China and Taiwan.

The TV program Lost in Space (1965–68) inspired copies of its robot character. However, the quality of the late 1960s toys began to suffer as more and more plastic was added; robots were redesigned to reduce sharp edges as required by the United States government.

Modern robots include R2D2 and C3PO from the Star Wars epics, Twiki from NBC's Buck Rodgers, and V.I.N.CENT from Disney's "The Black Hole." Robots are firmly established in American science fiction and among collectors.

References: Teruhisa Kitahara, *Tin Toy Dreams: Robots*, Chronicle Books, 1985; Teruhisa Kitahara, *Yesterday's Toys, & Robots, Spaceships, and Monsters*, Chronicle Books, 1988; T.N. Tumbusch, *Space Adventure Collectibles*, Wallace-Homestead, 1990; Robert Maline, *The Robot Book*, Push Pin Press/Harcourt Brace, 1978; Crystal and Leland Payton, *Space Toys*, Collectors Compass, 1982; Stephen J. Sansweet, *Science Fiction Toys and Models*, Vol. 1, Starlog Press, 1980.

Note: The following abbreviations are used:
SH = Horikawa Toys
TM = K. K. Masutoku Toy Factory
TN = Nomura Toys
Y = Yonezawa Toys

Answer Game Machine, 14" h, metal,
  addition and subtraction, orig box,
  Ichida, Japan 1960s **350.00**
Atomic Robot, 6" h, litho tin, windup,
  plastic arms, Yone, Japan **200.00**
Attacking Martian
  9½" h, litho tin and plastic, battery
    operated, orig box, SH, Japan,
    1970s **150.00**
  11" h, litho tin, battery operated,
    marked "Made in Japan," 1960s . **175.00**
Captain Astro Spaceman, walking,
  windup, 6" h, litho tin and plastic,
  orig box, Mego, marked "Japan,"
  copyright 1972 .... **160.00**
Coca–Cola Cobot, remote control robot, 9" h, battery operated, orig box
  and instructions, c1979 .... **175.00**
Computer Robot, battery operated,
  boxed, Bandi, Japan **400.00**
Dux–Astroman #150, 14" h, plastic,
  battery operated, orig box and folders, West German, 1964 .... **850.00**

Dux Astroman, green plastic, clear dome, white conical head, red features, transparent green lucite over mechanism, Western Germany, orig box, 14″ h, $850.00.

Great Garloo, 18″ h, plastic, remote, tiger skin waist cloth, orig box and instruction book, Marx 350.00

Interplanetary Explorer, 7½″ h, litho tin, windup, green body, red, white, and blue accents, orange helmet, red oxygen tanks 180.00

Lost in Space Robot, 10″ h, plastic, black and silver, battery operated, orig box, 20th Century Fox Film Corp copyright 1977 .... 225.00

Martin the Martian, 10½″ h, plastic, battery operated, orig box and instructions, Yone, Japan 215.00

Mechanical Mighty Robot, 5½″ h, metallic green, windup, sparking, orig box, N, Japan 120.00

Mini–Robo Tank, 4½″ h, litho tin and plastic, battery operated, orig box, TN, marked "Made in Japan," 1960s 175.00

Monster Robot, 9½″ h, litho tin and plastic, battery operated, orig box, 1980s 75.00

Piston Head Robot, battery operated, boxed, SH, Japan 195.00

Robert the Robot, talking, boxed, Ideal 65.00

Robotrac Bulldozer, 7″ h, litho tin, battery operated, rubber treads, orig box, Linemar, 1950s 350.00

Roto Robot, battery operated, SH, Japan 145.00

Son of Garloo, 6″ h, litho tin, windup, tin and plastic, Marx 140.00

Space Dog, 4″ h, litho tin, friction, KO, Japan 75.00

Space Explorer Robot, 7″ h, litho tin, battery operated, orig box, Yone, 1960s 195.00

Sparking Robot, 6½″ h, windup, SY, Japan 75.00

Sparky Robot, windup, orig box, KO, Japan 350.00

Super Astronaut, 11″ h, litho tin, battery operated, marked "Made in Japan," 1960s 200.00

Super Robot, windup, MIB, Hiro, Japan 145.00

Talking Robot, 11″ h, tin and plastic, friction movement, battery powered talking mechanism, orig box, Cragstan 900.00

Walking Robot, 8½″ h, plastic, battery operated, orig box, marked "Made in Hong Kong," 1960–70 .... 80.00

Zeroid Robot, 5½″ h, plastic, rubber treads, gray, red, and silver, Ideal, 1968 .... 25.00

ROCK 'N' ROLL

Collecting Hints: Many rock 'n' roll collections are centered around one artist. Flea markets and thrift shops are good places to look for rock 'n' roll items. Prices range according to the singer or group. The stars who have died usually command a higher price.

Glossy 8 x 10's of singers, unautographed, are generally worth $1.00.

History: Rock music can be traced back to early rhythm and blues music. It progressed and reached its golden age in the 1950s. The current nostalgia craze of the 1950s has produced some modern rock 'n' roll which is well received. Rock 'n' roll memorabilia exists in large quantities, each singer or group having many promotional pieces made.

References: L. R. Docks, *1915–1965 American Premium Record Guide, Third Edition*, Books Americana, 1986; Alison Fox, *Rock & Pop*, Boxtree Ltd. (London), 1988; Paul Grushkin, *The Art of Rock—Posters From Presley To Punk*, Abbeville Press, 1986.

See: Beatles and Elvis Presley.

Autograph, 8 x 10″ photo, glossy, black and white

Chubby Checker, black felt tip "It Ain't Over Till It's Over, Keep It Up, Love Chubby Checker 86" 30.00

Pearl Bailey, blue felt tip pen "Love, Pearl," early 1950s 25.00

Badge, The Who, 1½″ l, guitar shape, yellow, gold lettering, mid 1980s ... 8.00

Book

James Dean, Ballantine Books, 150 pgs, biography by William Bast, paperback, 1956 .... 15.00

Woodstock 69, Scholastic Book Ser-

vices, copyright 1970, Joseph J Sia,
124 pgs 25.00
Box, gum, Monkees, 4 x 8 x 1½", held
24 bubble gum packs, Donruss, 1966
series, full color picture, yellow back-
ground, red design, diecut lid 25.00
Bracelet, gold chain link, burnished
gold disk with raised Monkees guitar
symbol, orig retail card, 1967 copy-
right 25.00
Bubble Gum Card, James Dean, #65,
Topps Gum, mid 1950s 20.00
Button
Fats Domino 20.00
Freddy and the Dreamers, 3½", black
and white photos, red and white "I
Love Freddy and the Dreamers,"
copyright Premier Talant Associates
Inc, 1960s 22.00
Herman's Hermits, 3½", five black
and white photos, red and white "I
Love Herman's Hermits," copyright
Premier Talent Associates Inc, late
1960s 15.00
James Dean, 2½", color photo 58.00
Pat Boone, 3½", blue "Swoon With
Pat Boone" inscription, white back-
ground, red rim 5.00
Rock–Ola, 3", red, white, and blue
illus, black "Rock–Ola Leads
Again," c1950 .... 15.00

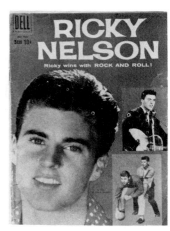

**Comic Book, Ricky Nelson, Dell Publish-
ing Co, 1958, No. 956, $4.50.**

Costume
Kiss, Gene Simmons, vinyl plastic and
black synthetic , 1978 copyright . 30.00
Monkees 25.00
Cuff Links, pr, Dick Clark, MIB 30.00
Doll
Boy George, 12", hard plastic, soft

vinyl head, hat, microphone and
posing stand, orig box, made in
China for LJN of New York 25.00
Diana Ross, 19", molded hard plastic
body, vinyl face and arms, gold glitter dress, orig box with the Supremes picture, Ideal, copyright
1969 Motown Inc 100.00
Dick Clark, 25" h, soft plush stuffed
body, hard molded vinyl head and
hands, brown pants and jacket, red
vest, plaid tie and socks, saddle
shoes, marked "Juro," 1950s 150.00
Michael Jackson, 12", hard plastic,
soft molded vinyl head, poseable,
Grammy Awards outfit, LJN, copyright 1984 MJJ Productions Inc, orig
box 45.00
Figure, display, 37½" h, Mick Jagger,
diecut, promotes 1971 Sticky Fingers
record 25.00
Flip Book, Monkees, 2½ x 3½", Peter
on motorbike, #4 from set of 16,
1967 Topps Gum 15.00
Game
Duran Duran Into The Arena, Milton
Bradley, copyright 1985 .... 15.00
Kiss on Tour, 17" sq board, full color
photos, orig box, 1978 copyright
Aucoin Management 45.00
Tiny Tim Game Of Beautiful Things,
18" board, cull color center photo,
orig box, 1970 Parker Brothers ... 50.00
Hanger, Jimmi Hendrix, cardboard,
black and white photo on each side,
marked "Manufactured Exclusively
By Sunders Enterprises/Jimmi Hendrix" 100.00
Hat
Purple People Eater, 11 x 13½", plastic, two diecut plastic pointed ears,
orig display card 50.00
Rock Around The Clock, 9" l, blue
felt, removable cardboard record
on top, marked "Manufactured by
Bing Crosby Phonocards Inc,"
c1950 .... 60.00
Jacket, tour, satin, silver/gray, yellow
and white embroidered girl and guy
dancing with black "Rock and Roll"
above, gold, black, and white, "The
Drifters On Broadway" on back, embroidered 1963, tag inside marked
"Ragtime Collection" 150.00
Magazine
Dick Clark Official American Band-
stand Yearbook, 9 x 12", 40 pgs,
color and black and white photos,
c1950 .... 25.00
Kiss Creem Special Edition, black and
white photos, 1978 Creem Magazine 25.00

Rock and Roll Songs, 8½ x 11", Vol 3 #11, Dec 1957 .... **15.00**

Marionette, Donny and Marie Osmond **50.00**

Pin, Beatles, record shape, plastic, black **22.00**

Postcard, Rolling Stones, 4½ x 6½", two, perforated, "The Rolling Stones Exile On Main Street" in red, marked "Scene 1" and "Scene 2," c1972 ... **15.00**

Poster

Doors, 24 x 36", full color, green bottom border, white Doors logo, copyright 1968 Doors Production Corp **20.00**

Fabian, "Teen Dreams," 11 x 14", full color, orig sealed bag, 1950s **25.00**

Family Dog, 14 x 20", Feb 2–4, 1968, Avalon Ballroom, full color illus .. **75.00**

Fleetwood Mac, 33 x 46", full color, Jan 1970 concert, Deutsches Museum, Munich, West Germany ... **30.00**

Grateful Dead Fan Club, 14 x 20", gold and blue, black and white photo, marked "The Golden Road To Unlimited Devotion," late 1960s **50.00**

James Gang, 14 x 22", Curtis Hixon Hall, Tampa, FL, Oct 2, 1971 ... **15.00**

Jefferson Airplane, 13 x 9", Fillmore concert, April 11–13, shiny silver Statue of Liberty illus, black background, 1960s **50.00**

Miller Blues Band, 14 x 20", Fillmore West concert, Jan 10–15, 1967, orange, blue, and red, copyright 1967 Neon Rose **50.00**

Moody Blues, 18½ x 25½", stiff paper, April 1, 1970 concert, Terrace Ballroom, Salt Lake City, UT **50.00**

Yard Birds, 14½ x 23½", red, white, and blue, Civic Auditorium, 1967 **50.00**

Program

Kiss, 1977–78 World Tour, 11 x 17" **15.00**

The Who, 8½ x 11", photo biography of each member, English concert, late 1960s **12.50**

Puzzle, 11 x 17" assembled, 200 pcs, Love Gun album scene, orig box, American Publishing Corp, 1977 copyright **15.00**

Record

Buddy Holly, 78 rpm, *Peggy Sue/ Every Day*, Coral label, 1957 .... **25.00**

Fabian Hound Dog Man, 45 rpm, includes Hound Dog Man, This Friendly World, Pretty Little Girl, I'm Grown Up, Single, Chancellor label, orig cardboard sleeve, 1950s **20.00**

Grateful Dead, fan club, 33⅓ rpm, on side marked "Robert Hunter Tales Of The Great Rum Runners, other marked "Garcia," both sides

marked "Sampler For Deadheads," orig 8 x 8" mailing envelope, copyright 1974 .... **50.00**

Ring, Official Member Monkee Ring Club, plastic, silver finish, colorful plastic flasher inset, portrait surrounded with red heart design **24.00**

Sheet Music

Bill Haley and the Comets, 9 x 11", *Green Tree Boogie*, greentone photo on front, 2 pgs music and lyrics, copyright 1955 Myers Music **20.00**

Purple People Eater, 9 x 12", purpletone photo of Sheb Wooley, 2 pgs lyrics, copyright 1958 Cordial Music Co **15.00**

The Who, *Substitute*, 8½ x 11", 2 pgs, bluetone group photo on cov, copyright 1966 Fabulous Music Ltd ... **12.50**

Sign, Brenda Lee, black and white photo, small inset color "This Is Brenda" record album photo, top marked "The Exciting Brenda Lee/ America's Newest Singing Sensation," pop-out easel **75.00**

Thermos, Monkees, 6½", metal, full color illus, copyright 1967 Rayburt Productions Inc **25.00**

Tour Book, Bob Dylan, 10 x 14", 28 pgs, c1977 .... **25.00**

Toy

Guitar, Monkees, 20", plastic, full color diecut litho paper label, 1966 copyright **75.00**

Saxophone, Spike Jones Sax–O–Fun, 7", hard plastic, marked "A Trophy Product," c1950 .... **25.00**

Wallet

Boy and girl dance around when wallet is moved back and forth, vinyl, black ext., red int., zippered pouch, mirror, comb, and nail file, 1950s **25.00**

Connie Francis, vinyl, tan, includes comb, emery board, coin holder, photo slots, and unused notepad, snap closure with attached keychain, late 1950s, early 1960s ... **25.00**

Yearbook, Dick Clark Rock 'n' Roll Yearbook, 1973 .... **20.00**

NORMAN ROCKWELL

Collecting Hints: Learn all you can about Norman Rockwell if you plan to collect his many artworks. His original artworks and illustrations have been transferred onto various types of objects by clubs and manufacturers.

History: Norman Rockwell, the famous American artist, was born on February 3, 1894. His first professional illustrations were for a children's book, *Tell Me Why Stories,* at age 18. Next he worked for *Boy's Life* magazine. Then he illustrated for the Boy Scouts and other magazines. By his death in November 1978, he had painted over 2,000 paintings.

Many of his paintings were done in oil and reproduced as magazine covers, advertisements, illustrations, calendars, and book sketches. Over 320 of these paintings became covers for the *Saturday Evening Post.*

Norman Rockwell painted everyday people in everyday situations with a little humor mixed in with the sentiment. His paintings and illustrations are well loved because of this sensitive nature. He painted people he knew and places with which he was familiar. New England landscapes are found in many of his illustrations.

Because his works are so well liked, they have been reproduced on many objects. These new collectibles should not be confused with the original artwork and illustrations. The new collectibles, however, offer Norman Rockwell illustrations to the average pocketbook and serve to keep his work alive.

References: Denis C. Jackson, *The Norman Rockwell Identification and Value Guide,* privately printed, 1985; Mary Moline, *Norman Rockwell Collectibles Value Guide, Sixth Edition,* Green Valley World, 1988.

Collectors' Club: Rockwell Society of America, 597 Saw Mill Road, Ardsley, NY 10502.

Museums: Corner House, Stockbridge, MA; Norman Rockwell Museum, Northbrook, IL.

Figure, Goin Fishin, Rockwell Museum, 1984, 6″ h, $50.00.

Bell
    Gorham
        1976, Snow Sculpture 45.00
        1980, Chilly Reception 25.00
        1982, Lovers 30.00
        1983, Christmas Medley 30.00
    Grossman, Dave
        1976, Drum For Tommy 28.00
        1979, Leapfrog 50.00
    River Shore
        1978, Garden Girl 40.00
        1981, Looking Out To Sea 85.00
Figurine
    Gorham
        After the Prom, 1980 .... 125.00
        Annual Visit 90.00
        At The Vets 50.00
        Beguiling Buttercup 60.00
        Captain 80.00
        Christmas Dancers 75.00
        Day In The Life Of A Boy 85.00
        Day In The Life Of A Girl 85.00
        Four Seasons, 1980, A Helping
            Hand, set of 4 .... 450.00
        Gay Blades 60.00
        Jolly Coachman 50.00
        Old Mill Pond 57.00

        Pride of Parenthood 60.00
        Skating 50.00
        Wet Sport 40.00
    Dave Grossman Designs, Inc
        Back To School 45.00
        Dreams Of Long Ago 110.00
        Exasperated Nanny, 1980 ...... 125.00
        Listening 100.00
        Magic Potion 100.00
        Secret 100.00
        Take Your Medicine 85.00
        Young Artist 85.00
    Lynell Studios
        Artist's Daughter, 1980 .... 75.00
        Cradle of Love 85.00
        Scotty's Stowaway 125.00
        Snow Queen, 1979 .... 85.00
    River Shore
        Grandpa's Guardian 125.00
        Looking Out To Sea 135.00
    Rockwell Museum
        Bedtime 50.00
        Bride & Groom 90.00
        Celebration 135.00
        Cobbler 50.00
        Country Doctor 35.00
        Lighthouse Keeper's Daughter 50.00
        Memories 60.00
        Mother's Helpers 85.00
        Music Lesson 40.00
        Ringing In Good Cheer 50.00
        While The Audience Waits 65.00
        Words of Wisdom 35.00
Ingot
    Franklin Mint
        1972, Spirit of Scouting, set of 12   275.00

1974, Tribute to Robert Frost, set of
12 .... **285.00**
Hamilton Mint
1975
Christmas, silver **40.00**
Saturday Evening Post Covers, set
of 12 .... **210.00**
Santa Planning A Visit, gold
plated silver **45.00**
Magazine Cover
American
1918, November **20.00**
1921, May **18.00**
American Boy
1916, December **30.00**
1917, July **30.00**
1920, April **27.50**
American Legion, 1978, July **5.00**
Boys Life
1915, August **50.00**
1927, February **45.00**
1947, February **45.00**
1957, June **42.50**
Colliers, 1919
March 1 .... **25.00**
April 19 .... **20.00**
Country Gentleman
1918, February 9 .... **50.00**
1920, May 8 .... **48.50**
1922, March 18 .... **45.00**
Family Circle
1967, December **8.00**
1968, December **7.50**
Fisk Club News, 1917, May **18.00**
Jack and Jill, 1974, December **5.00**
Literary Digest
1918, December 14 .... **30.00**
1922, April 15 .... **18.00**
Look, 1964, July 14 .... **10.00**
McCall's, 1964, December **12.00**
Parents
1939, January **10.00**
1951, May **9.00**
Red Cross, April, 1918 .... **25.00**
Saturday Evening Post
1916, June 3 .... **130.00**
1918, Sept 21 .... **85.00**
1920, Jan 17 .... **75.00**
1922, Feb 18 .... **85.00**
1945, March 21 .... **70.00**
1946, Nov 16 .... **25.00**
1950, April 29 .... **80.00**
1952, Aug 30 .... **40.00**
1955, March 12 .... **20.00**
1957, Sept 7 .... **21.50**
1960, Feb 13 .... **60.00**
1962, Jan 13 .... **12.00**
Scouting
1934, February **10.00**
1944, December **12.00**
1953, October **8.50**
TV Guide, 1970, May 16 .... **5.00**

Yankee, 1972, August **9.50**
Paperweight, River Shore **100.00**
Plate
Franklin Mint
1970, Bringing Home The Tree .. **330.00**
1971, Under The Mistletoe **175.00**
1973, Trimming The Tree **165.00**
1975, Home For Christmas **190.00**
Gorham
Boy Scout
1975, Our Heritage **60.00**
1977, The Scoutmaster **60.00**
1977, A Good Sign **35.00**
1978, Campfire Story **20.00**
Christmas Series
1974, Tiny Time **65.00**
1975, Good Deeds **64.00**
1977, Yuletide Reckoning **45.00**
1979, Santa's Helpers **20.00**
1981, Santa Plans His Visit **30.00**

Plate, The New Arrival, Norman Rockwell Museum, $40.00.

Four Seasons, Sets of 4
1971, A Boy & His Dog **400.00**
1973, Ages of Love **300.00**
1975, Me & My Pal **200.00**
1979, A Helping Hand **100.00**
1980, Dad's Boy **130.00**
1981, Old Timers **100.00**
Presidential Series
1976, John F Kennedy **55.00**
1976, Dwight D Eisenhower ... **35.00**
Grossman Designs, Dave
Annual Series, bas–relief
1979, Leapfrog **50.00**
1980, Lovers **60.00**
1981, Dreams of Long Ago **60.00**
1982, Doctor And The Doll ... **65.00**
Christmas Series, bas–relief
1980, Christmas Trio, FE **80.00**
1981, Santa's Good Boys **75.00**
1982, Faces of Christmas **75.00**
Huckleberry Finn Series
1979, The Secret **49.00**
1980, Listening **40.00**
1981, No Kings Nor Dukes **40.00**

Tom Sawyer Series
  1976, Whitewashing Fence **75.00**
  1977, First Smoke **65.00**
  1977, Take Your Medicine **50.00**
  1978, Lost In Cave **50.00**
Lynell Studios
Christmas
  1979, Snow Queen **30.00**
  1980, Surprises For All **30.00**
Mother's Day
  1980, Cradle of Love **40.00**
  1981, Mother's Blessing **30.00**
  1983, Dear Mother **25.00**
Special Issues Series
  1980, Artist's Daughter **65.00**
  1980, Poor Richard's Almanac . **45.00**
River Shore
  1979, Spring Flowers **120.00**
  1980, Looking Out To Sea **110.00**
  1982, Grandpa's Guardian **80.00**
  1982, Grandpa's Treasures **80.00**
  1982, Jennie & Tina **40.00**
Rockwell Museum
American Family Series
  1978, Happy Birthday Dear
    Mother **85.00**
  1979
    First Prom **30.00**
    Little Mother **65.00**
    Mother's Little Helpers **65.00**
    The Student **65.00**
American Family II Series
  1980, New Arrival **40.00**
  1981
    Almost Grown Up **81.00**
    At The Circus **95.00**
    Sweet Dreams **90.00**
    We Missed You, Dad **90.00**
Rockwell Society
Christmas Series
  1974, Scotty Gets His Tree **160.00**
  1975, Angel With Black Eye ... **100.00**
  1977, Toy Shop Window **50.00**
  1979, Somebody's Up There ... **30.00**
  1981, Wrapped Up In Christmas **30.00**
Heritage Series
  1977, Toy Maker **260.00**
  1978, The Cobbler **155.00**
  1980, Ship Builder **60.00**
  1982, The Tycoon **20.00**
Mother's Day Series
  1976, A Mother's Love **120.00**
  1977, Faith **75.00**
  1979, Reflections **38.00**
  1981, After The Party **25.00**
  1983, Add Two Cups **24.00**
Royal Devon
Christmas Series
  1975, Downhill Daring **49.00**
  1976, The Christmas Gift **92.00**
  1978, Puppets For Christmas ... **45.00**
  1980, Gramps Meets Gramps .. **35.00**

Mother's Day Series
  1975, Doctor And The Doll ... **85.00**
  1976, Puppy Love **83.00**
  1978, Mother's Day Off **72.00**
  1980, Mother's Treat **35.00**
Stein
  Gorham, Pensive Pals **37.50**
Rockwell Museum
  Braving The Storm **75.00**
  Fishin' Pals **75.00**
  For A Good Boy **85.00**
  The Music Lesson **90.00**

ROSE O'NEILL

Collecting Hints: Study the dolls carefully before purchasing. Remember that composition dolls were made until the 1950s; hence, every example is not one of the early ones.

Many collectors concentrate only on Kewpie items. A specialized collection might include other O'Neill designs, such as Scootles, Ragsy, Kewpie-Gal, Kewpie-Kins and Ho-Ho.

History: Rose Cecil O'Neill (1876–1944) was a famous artist, novelist, illustrator, poet, sculptress, and creator of the Kewpie doll. O'Neill's drawing "Temptation" won her a children's art prize at the age of 14 and launched her career as an illustrator.

The Kewpie first appeared in art form in the December, 1909, issue of *Ladies' Home Journal* in a piece entitled "Kewpies Christmas Frolic." The first Kewpie doll appeared in 1913. Assisting in the design of the doll was Joseph L. Kallus. Although Geo. Borgfeldt Co. controlled the production and distribution rights to Kewpie material, Kallus continued to assist in design and manufacture through his firm, the Cameo Doll Company.

Kewpie dolls and china decorated items rapidly appeared on the market. Many were manufactured in Germany. Twenty-eight German factories made products during the peak production years. Later other manufacturers joined in the effort.

O'Neill eventually moved to south west Missouri, settling at Bonniebrook near Bear Creek. She died there in 1944. In 1947 Bonniebrook burned to the ground. Production of Kewpie items did not stop at O'Neill's death. Today Kewpie material still appears as limited edition collectibles.

References: Lois Holman, *Rose O'Neill Kewpies And Other Works*, published by author, 1983; Maude M. Horine, *Memories of Rose O'Neill*, booklet, published by author; Ralph Alan McCanse, *Titans and Kewpies*, out-of-print; Rowena Godding Ruggles, *The One Rose*, out-of-print.

Collectors' Club: International Rose O'Neill Club (IROC), P.O. Box 688, Branson, MO 65616.

Museum: Shephard of the Hills Farm and Memorial Museum, near Branson, MO.

REPRODUCTION ALERT

Teapot, child's, marked "Copyrighted Rose O'Neill Wilson Kewpie Germany," lid not original, 4" h, $100.00.

Action Doll and Figurine
2", Blunderboo on sled	350.00
3¼", Farmer, large brimmed hat, bisque, "C" mark	375.00
3¾", Sweeper, attached broom and waste can, bisque, "O'Neill" on foot and "C" mark	350.00
4", Reader, "C" mark	350.00
4¾", insect on head, sitting by basket, "C" mark	500.00
5", Thinker, sgd	25.00
Baby Spoon and Fork, sterling silver, hallmarked Paye & Baker, marked "P" and "B" in equal sized hearts . .	250.00
Bell, brass	65.00
Blanket, 15 x 28", flannel, five Kewpies over center, Kewpie borders, "C" and "Rose O'Neill" marks	50.00
Candleholder, 10", cast, 4½" Kewpie at base, Kewpie trademark	175.00
Candy Container	40.00
Candy Mold, chocolate type, pewter, 6"	65.00

Carnival, plaster
Large	25.00
Small	15.00
Crumb Tray, brass	30.00

Doll, Kewpie
Cameo Dolls Products, Port Allegany, vinyl, fully jointed, orig clothes
10"	25.00
14"	60.00
16"	85.00
20"	150.00

Unidentified makers, legs together, movable arm, "O'Neill" incised bottom of foot; some still have gummed heart stickers on chest, black and white. Four different

stickers used c1913, copyright sticker on back.
4"	100.00
6"	145.00
9"	375.00
10"	600.00
Feeding Dish, 10", alphabet border . . .	150.00
Handkerchief	28.00
Ice Cream Mold, 7"	50.00

Jewelry
Charm, Ho–Ho	50.00
Pin, 2", Cameo Kewpie	50.00
Ring, S, Paye & Baker, marked "P" and "B" in equal sized hearts	125.00

Doll, bisque, small blue wings, marked "Germany," 6" h, $225.00.

Letter Opener, 7", Kewpie finial, pewter	40.00
Pin Box, 2½", Kewpie with foot in air on lid, marked "Goebel"	450.00
Plate	35.00
Poster, 1973	30.00
Recipe Book, Jello	30.00
Thimble, metal, marked "Kewpie" . . .	35.00

ROSEVILLE POTTERY

Collecting Hints: Because of the availability of pieces in Roseville's later commercial ware, the prices for this type of ware are stable and unlikely to rise rapidly.

For the popular middle period patterns, which were made during the Depression and had limited production and sale, the prices are strong. Among the most popular patterns from this middle period are Blackberry, Cherry Blossom, Falline, Ferella, Jonquil, Morning Glory, Sunflower, and Windsor. The Art Deco craze has focused on Futura, especially the more angular shaped pieces.

Pinecone in blue or brown glaze continues to have a strong following as do the earlier lines of Juvenile and Donatello.

Desirable shapes include baskets, bookends, cookie jars, ewers, tea sets, and wall pockets.

Most pieces are marked. However, during the middle period paper stickers were used. These often were removed, leaving the piece unmarked.

Roseville made over one hundred and fifty different lines or patterns. Novice collectors would benefit from reading one of the several books about Roseville and viewing the offerings of dealers who specialize in art pottery. Collections generally are organized around a specific pattern or shape.

History: In the late 1880s a group of investors purchased the J. B. Owens Pottery in Roseville, Ohio, and made utilitarian stoneware items. In 1892 the firm was incorporated and joined by George F. Young who became general manager. Four generations of Youngs controlled Roseville until the early 1950s.

A series of acquisitions began: Midland Pottery of Roseville in 1898, Clark Stoneware Plant in Zanesville (formerly used by Peters and Reed), and Muskingum Stoneware (Mosaic Tile Company) in Zanesville. In 1898 offices moved from Roseville to Zanesville.

In 1900 Roseville developed its art pottery line—Rozane. Ross Purdy designed a line to compete with Weller's Louwelsa. Rozane became a trade name to cover a large series of lines by designers such as Christian Neilson, John J. Herold, and Gazo Fudji. The art lines of hand decorated underglaze pottery were made in limited quantities after 1919.

The success of Roseville depended on its commercial lines, first developed by John J. Herald and Frederick Rhead in the first decade of the 1900s. Decorating techniques included transfers, pouncing (a method producing a pattern on the ware which could be followed), and air brush or sponging following embossed motifs. Among the lines from this early period are Dutch, Juvenile, Cameo, and Holland.

George Young retired in 1918. Frank Ferrell replaced Harry Rhead, who had replaced Frederick Rhead, as art director. Ferrell developed over 80 lines, the first being Sylvan. The economic depression of the 1930s caused Roseville to look for new product lines. Pine Cone was introduced in 1935, made for 15 years, and issued in over 75 shapes.

In the 1940s a series of high gloss glazes were tried to revive certain lines. Other changes were made to respond to the fluctuating contemporary markets. Mayfair and Wincraft date from this period. In 1952 Raymor dinnerware was produced.

None of these changes brought economic success back to Roseville. In November, 1954, Roseville was bought by the Mosaic Tile Company.

References: Sharon and Bob Huxford, *The Collectors Encyclopedia of Roseville Pottery,* Collector Books, 1976; Sharon and Bob Huxford, *The Collectors Encyclopedia of Roseville Pottery, Second Series,* Collector Books, 1980.

Collectors' Club: American Art Pottery Association, 9825 Upton Circle, Bloomington, MN 55431.

Note: For pieces in the middle and upper price range see *Warman's Antiques And Their Prices.*

Ashtray
  Pine Cone
    Blue, 4" **120.00**
    Brown **135.00**
    Snowberry, pink **45.00**
Basket
  Bittersweet, green, marked "810–10" **175.00**
  Bleeding Heart, hanging **175.00**
  Freesia
    Blue, marked "391–8" **95.00**
    Brown, marked "390–7" **75.00**
  Gardenia, 10", 609 . . . . **120.00**
  Imperial I **80.00**
  Peony, hanging **135.00**
  Snowberry, green, 10" **95.00**
  Zephyr Lily, brown **87.50**
Bowl
  Baneda, pink **180.00**
  Clematis, brown, marked "459–10" **75.00**
  Columbine, blue, #402 . . . . **75.00**
  Imperial I
    Shallow, 10" **58.00**
    Ftd **55.00**
  Mostique, 7" **38.00**
  Pine Cone, green, 4½", marked "457–7" **155.00**
  Snowberry, handle **60.00**
  Sunflower, 4" **180.00**
  Topeo, blue **145.00**
Box, Wincraft, rect, chartreuse, 4½" l . **65.00**
Candleholder
  Panel, brown, pr **48.00**
  Pine Cone, triple, green **95.00**
Candlestick, Dahlrose, 3½", pr **105.00**
Compote, Florentine **30.00**
Console Bowl
  Apple Blossom, blue, marked "331–12" **80.00**
  Baneda, green, 9" **275.00**
  Columbine, console, rose to green, marked "405–12" **95.00**
  Gardenia, console, gray, marked "627–8" **80.00**
  Iris, marked "361–8" **95.00**
  Magnolia, console, brown **95.00**

Zephyr Lily, dark blue, marked "478–12" **90.00**
Console Set, Thorn Apple, double candlestick and bowl, all one piece **140.00**
Cornucopia
   Cosmos, blue, marked "136–6" **75.00**
   Gardenia, marked "621–6" **35.00**
Creamer and Sugar, Zephyr Lily, brown **90.00**
Ewer
   Freesia, marked "19–6" **70.00**
   Silhouette, marked "717–10" **48.00**
Flower Frog, Peony, green **28.00**
Jardiniere
   Clematis, marked "667–4" **50.00**
   Corinthian, 9 x 12" **160.00**
   Donatello, 22", stand **595.00**
   Foxglove, marked "659–3" **50.00**
   Moss, pink, 4" **70.00**
   Mostique, 8" **90.00**
   Normandy, 7" **65.00**
   Pine Cone, marked "632–5" **100.00**
   Poppy **67.50**
   Snowberry, green, 4" **50.00**
   Sunflower, 4" **75.00**
   Water Lily, pink, pedestal **700.00**
Match Holder, marked "498–3" **150.00**
Mug, Bushberry, brown **50.00**
Pitcher
   Pinecone, brown, marked "485–10" **250.00**
   Tulip **65.00**
   White Rose, green and rust, 1234 .. **75.00**
Planter, hanging
   Apple Blossom **110.00**
   Silhouette, burgundy **75.00**
   Water Lily, brown **155.00**
   Zephyr Lily **115.00**
Urn
   Foxglove, marked "161–6" **75.00**
   Ivory II, Tourmaline shape, 5½" **32.00**
   Magnolia, blue, marked "446–6" .. **90.00**
   Topeo, blue, 6" **130.00**
Vase
   Apple Blossom, green, marked "388–10" **95.00**
   Baneda, pink, 4½" **160.00**
   Blackberry, beehive, 5½" **235.00**
   Bleeding Heart, blue, marked "964–6" **95.00**
   Bushberry, brown, 12½" **225.00**
   Cherry Blossom, 5" h **150.00**
   Clematis
      6", #188 .... **65.00**
      7", #105 .... **55.00**
   Dahlrose, 6" **65.00**
   Dogwood, 8" **48.00**
   Donatello, 10" **82.00**
   Foxglove, 6½" h, bulbous, side handles, flowers in relief **49.00**
   Freesia, blue, marked "124–9" **100.00**
   Fuschia
      Blue, 7", 895 .... **115.00**
      Brown, 9" **155.00**

Futura, blue, fan shape, 6" **380.00**
Imperial I, bud, marked "31–9" **75.00**
Iris, marked "917–6" **75.00**
Jonquil, 4" **70.00**
Laurel, 6½" **50.00**
Pine Cone
   Blue, marked "709–10" **260.00**
   Green, marked "839–6" **85.00**
   Tan gloss, fan shape, marked "272–6" **65.00**
Primrose, brown, marked "767–8" . **70.00**
Snowberry, blue, marked "IV–6" ... **55.00**
Thorn Apple, blue, marked "810–6" **65.00**
White Rose, blue, marked "979–6" **45.00**
Wincraft **28.00**

Wall pocket, Dahlrose, 8¼" l, $75.00.

Wall Pocket
   Clematis, brown **90.00**
   Dahlrose, 8" **115.00**
   Imperial I **75.00**
   Peony, yellow **130.00**
   Rosecraft Vintage **100.00**
   Snowberry, pink **65.00**
   Tuscany, orig sticker **110.00**
   White Rose, brown, 6½" **110.0**
Window Box
   Freesia, brown **45.00**
   Gardenia, green **45.00**
   Magnolia, brown **45.00**

SALT AND PEPPER SHAKERS

Collecting Hints: Collect only sets in very good condition. Make certain the set has the proper two pieces, and base if applicable. China shakers should show no signs of cracking. Original paint and decoration should be intact on all china and metal figures. All parts should be present, including the closure if important.

A collector will have to compete with collectors in other areas, e.g., advertising, animal groups, Blacks, and holiday collectibles. Many shakers will have souvenir labels which may have been added later to stock items. The form, not the label, is the important element.

Black figural shakers are rising in price. The same is true for advertising sets and comic and cartoon characters.

History: The Victorian era saw the advent of the elaborate glass and fine china salt and pepper shaker. The pioneering research work by Arthur Goodwin Peterson in books such as *Glass Salt Shakers: 1,000 Patterns* attracted collectors to this area. Figural and souvenir shakers, most dating from the mid-20th century and later, were looked down upon by this group.

This attitude is slowly changing. More and more people are collecting the figural and souvenir shakers, especially since prices are lower. Many of these patterns were made by Japanese firms and imported heavily after World War II.

Production of a form might continue for decades; hence, it is difficult to tell an early example from a modern one. This is one factor in keeping prices low.

References: Gideon Bosker, *Great Shakes: Salt and Pepper For All Tastes,* Abbeville Press, 1986; Melva Davern, *Collectors' Encyclopedia of Figural and Novelty Salt & Pepper Shakers, First Series* (1985), *Second Series* (1990), Collector Books, 1985; Helene Guarnaccia, *Salt & Pepper Shakers Identification and Values, Book I* (1984) and *Book II* (1989), Collector Books; Mildred and Ralph Lechner, *The World of Salt Shakers,* Collector Books, 1976; Arthur G. Peterson, *Glass Salt Shakers,* Wallace–Homestead, 1970.

Collectors' Clubs: Antique and Art Glass Salt Shaker Collectors Society, 348 N. Hamilton Street, Painted Post, NY 14807; Novelty Salt and Pepper Shakers Club, 581 Joy Road, Battle Creek, MI 49017; Salt Shaker Collectors Club, 2832 Rapidan Trail, Maitland, FL 32751.

Advisor: Bea Morgan.

Advertising, loaves of bread, Miller Bakery, Morton, IL, 1909-1959, Morton Pottery Co, orig box, $18.00.

Ceramic, Popeye and Olive Oyl, 2¾" h, Japan, prewar, pr	**78.00**
China, pr	
Bears, brown, huggies, Van Tellingen	**25.00**

Black Head, watermelon	**95.00**
Boy and Dog, huggies	**35.00**
Cats, 3½" h, white, green eyes, Goebel, P208	**29.00**
Clown, 5¼" h	**50.00**
Ducks, yellow, huggies, Van Tellingen	**20.00**
Elsie and Elmer, Borden adv, cows, 4" h, holding bowl, c1940	**50.00**
Friar Tuck, Goebel	**35.00**
Greyhound Dogs, Rosemeade	**20.00**
Kangaroos, Rosemeade	**40.00**
Laurel and Hardy, figural, tray base, Dresden, 1930s	**100.00**
Mallard Ducks, Rosemeade	**60.00**
Max and Moritz, 3½" h, Katzenjammer Kids characters Fritz and Hans, c1930	**75.00**
Nipper, adv, dog, 3" h, black and white, "His Master's Voice" and "RCA Victor" base inscriptions, Lenox, 1930s	**48.00**
Pigs, standing	**7.00**
Popeye, 2½" h, marked "Foreign," 1930s	**48.00**
Roosters, 7" h, Japan	**12.00**
Snap and Pop, Rice Krispies adv, 2½" h, Japan, 1930s	**23.00**
Trylon and Perisphere, 3" h, white, gold trim, orange and white serving tray, souvenir, 1939 New York World's Fair, Japan	**55.00**
Glass	
Art Glass, each	
Blossomtime, amethyst colored, hp, two piece top	**145.00**
Christmas Pearl, yellow ground, hp leaves, earthy colors, dated and sgd agitator	**115.00**
Tomato, yellow ground, hp pink and white rosebuds, Mt Washington	**85.00**
Wavecrest, hp, green tint, orange flowers, Kelva	**235.00**
Depression Glass, pr	
American Sweetheart, Monax	**265.00**
Delphite, round, Jeannette	**45.00**
Floragold	**40.00**
Florentine #2, yellow	**38.00**
Madrid, amber, flat	**60.00**
Moderntone, blue	**35.00**
Royal Lace, clear	**30.00**
Sharon, pink	**42.00**
Thistle, green, tray	**50.00**
Transparent Green, sq, Owens Illinois	**20.00**
Vitrock, red tulip, range, Hocking	**15.00**
Pattern Glass, each	
Aster, blue opaque, sq, pedestal, tinplate top	**55.00**
Atterbury Twin, white opaque, vertical center divider	**95.00**

Banded Fleur–De–Lis, clear, large,
US Glass Co 32.00
Beaded Bulb, green and white slag,
domed top 110.00
Chrysanthemum Sprig, pale cus-
tard, tinplate top, Northwood .. 115.00
Curlique, clear, small pedestal,
pewter top 38.00
Daisy and Button, sapphire blue,
small pedestal, moon and stars
pewter top 36.00
Dewey, green, pewter top 95.00
Earlybird, clear, bird shape, pewter
top 55.00
Everglades, blue opalescent, pew-
ter top, Northwood 115.00
Flat Flower, green opaque, Dith-
ridge 85.00
Inverted Fan and Feather, pink slag,
Northwood 485.00
John Bull and Mary, milk glass ... 125.00
Opal Ribbon, vaseline and white
stripes, short, reverse swirl, brass
top 65.00
Oval and Fan, cobalt blue and
white slag, tinplate over brass top 115.00
Polka Dot Swirl, blue opalescent,
white dots, Hobbs 85.00
Quilted Phlox, dusty blue, white
color stained, cylindrical, tall,
emb design, silverplate top 65.00
Rib Eight, pigeon blood, brass top,
Consolidated Lamp and Glass .. 95.00
Ribbed Opal, white opalescent,
brass plated top 55.00
Seashell, blue and white slag, rect,
seashells, brass top 110.00
Shrine, clear, domed tinplate top,
US Glass 68.00
Vermont, custard, hp green and
pastel florals, curved patterned
legs, brass top, US Glass 58.00
Willow Oak, amber, tinplate top,
US Glass 45.00
Plaster, Orphan Annie and Sandy, 3" h,
1940s, pr 25.00

Praying hands, ceramic, dark brown glaze, gold trim, 3½" h, $4.50.

Plastic, pr
Dog and Cat, Ken L Ration adv, F&F **15.00**
Luzianne, red, F&F **165.00**
TV set, 3" h, brown, gold accents and
legs, white viewing screen, on/off
switch raises shakers, orig box,
1950s **65.00**
Washer and Dryer, Westinghouse adv **15.00**
Wood, natives, pr **15.00**

SANTA CLAUS

Collecting Hints: The number of Santa Claus related items is endless. Collectors are advised to
concentrate on one form (postcards, toys, etc.)
or a brief time period. New collectors will find
the hard plasic 1950s Santas easily accessible
and generally at a reasonable price.

History: The idea for Santa Claus developed from
stories about St. Nicholas, who lived about 300
AD. By the 1500s, "Father Christmas" in England, "Pere Noel" in France, and "Weihnachts-
mann" in Germany were well established.

Until the 1800s Santa Claus was pictured as a
tall, thin, stately man wearing bishop's robes and
riding a white horse. Washington Irving in *Knickerbocker's History of New York*, 1809, made him
as a stout, jolly man who wore a broad brimmed
hat and huge breeches and smoked a long pipe.
The traditional Santa Claus image came from
Clement C. Moore's poem "An Account of a Visit
from St. Nicholas" (*Troy Sentinal*, NY, 1823) and
the cartoon characterizations by Thomas Nast
which appeared in *Harper's Weekly* between
1863 and 1886.

References: E. Willis Jones, *The Santa Claus
Book*, Walker, 1976; Maggie Rogers and Peter R.
Hallinan, *The Santa Claus Picture Book: An Ap-
praisal Guide*, E. P. Dutton, Inc., 1984.

Additional Listings: Christmas Items.

Advertising
Button, pinback
⅞", red, green, fleshtone, white
ground, issued 1921 by National
Tuberculosis Assn, Santa with
boy and girl at top of chimney,
inscription "Merry Christmas/
Healthy New Year" **20.00**
13/16", multicolored, Wiebolt's,
Santa greeting young girl at
Christmas tree, white ground,
blue lettering, light blue rim,
c1935 .... **22.00**
1¼", multicolored, Orr's Santa,
light green background, black
letters, 1940–50 .... **15.00**
Children's Book, adv give aways
L L Stearn's Dept Store, Williams-

port, PA, *Santa Claus Book,* color
illus, 1920s **12.50**
Snellenberg's Dept Store, Philadelphia, PA, *Snellenberg's,* Santa
and children cov, 1930s **10.00**
Display Figure, Santa head, papier
mache, hollow, Westinghouse, 30
x 42" **85.00**
Display Stand–Up, Pepsi–Cola Santa,
60" h, cardboard, one leg raised,
bottle in hand **65.00**
Game, First National Bank, Berwick,
PA, "Season's Greetings, Santa
Claus Ring Toss," 10" h **7.00**
Toy, Coca–Cola Santa, 16" h, plush,
stuffed, plastic face, holds minia-
ture "Coke" bottle, 1950 .... **75.00**
Trade Card
   Bank of Newberry, PA, 6" h, bell,
   Santa head dec **5.00**
   Dundee Smart Clothes, Allentown,
   PA, Santa, pack on back **4.00**
   First National Bank, Bloomsburg,
   PA, 7" h, Santa, pack on back,
   train at feet **4.00**
   Greenpoint Savings Bank, Brook-
   lyn, NY, Santa, pack on back .. **4.00**
   Santa Claus Soap, Santa, tree over
   shoulder, child and doll at feet,
   1899 .... **15.00**
   West Haven Savings and Loan, Ha-
   zelton, PA, 7" h, Santa, pack on
   back **4.00**
   Woolson Spice Co, Father Christ-
   mas, Santa and reindeer **12.00**
Tray, CD Kenny Coffee Co, 9½",
round **48.00**
Automata, battery operated, 9" h, Santa
sitting on metal house, ringing bell,
holding toys, Japan **40.00**
Bank
   Bisque, Father Christmas figure
      2" h, green base, marked "Japan" **12.00**
      3¼" h, marked "Japan" **20.00**
   Chalkware, 11" h, Santa in chimney,
   pack on back, 1950s **25.00**
   Metal, 6½" h, Santa sleeping in chair **30.00**
Book
   Around the World with Santa Claus,
   McLoughlin Bros, NY, 1900 ..... **25.00**
   *How Santa Filled the Christmas Stock-
   ings,* Stecher Litho Co, Rochester,
   NY, 1916 .... **12.00**
   Old Saint Nicholas, Chicago, Home-
   wood Publishing Co **15.00**
   Watching for Santa Claus, Hurst & Co,
   NY, 1912 .... **15.00**
Calendar Plate, 1909, 9¾", Santa on
sleigh, whip in hand, four reindeer . **48.00**
Candy Box, cardboard, rect, Santa face
on all sides, 1950s **7.50**

Candy Container
   Glass, 5½" h, Father Christmas in
   chimney, metal base, Victory
   Candy Co **72.00**

**Candy Container, St Nicholas, papier
mache, red coat, blue pants, 5⅜" h,
$65.00.**

Papier Mache
   4"
      Red coat **25.00**
      White coat **25.00**
   4½", red coat, large belly, USA .. **20.00**
   6", white coat, red trim, open pack,
   c1920 .... **40.00**
   9", waving, large belly, red coat,
   USA, 1940s **48.00**
Pressed Cardboard
   10" h, red coat, 1922 .... **35.00**
   10½" h, red coat, USA, 1940s ... **48.00**
Candy Dispenser, Pez type, 4" h, plastic, red and white **10.00**
Candy Mold
   Santa and sleigh, tin **30.00**
   Santa, head, flat, one piece **18.00**
Card, Greeting
   "Christmas Greetings In My House,"
   5" h, house shape, Santa with tree
   inside, 1930s **3.00**
   "Christmas Greetings," 7" h, Santa cut
   out, poem inside, 1930s **3.50**
   "Merry Christmas," 8" h, fold out,
   Santa on front, pictures to trace in-
   side, 1930s **3.00**
Card Holder, paper, fold–up Santa and
reindeer, Hallmark, 1940s **18.00**

Figure
  Cardboard
    4" h, Santa holding tree, black cardboard platform, ¼" thick **7.00**
    4½ x 3", composition face, flannel suit, celluloid deer, and mica covered sleigh, Japan **25.00**
  Celluloid
    2½" h, all red, Irwin, USA **10.00**
    4" h
      Father Christmas, red coat, Irwin, USA **22.00**
      Santa, standing, holding doll behind back, Japan **35.00**
      Santa, standing, pack on back, red, Irwin **22.00**
    4" l
      Santa, car with gifts and tree in back, Irwin **32.00**
      Santa, sleigh, one deer, Irwin, USA **22.00**
    5" h, skier, metal skis, wood and celluloid poles, Irwin, USA **28.00**
    7" l, red, white, and green sleigh, one white deer, Irwin, USA **35.00**
    8½", Father Christmas, red and white, pack over shoulders, Irwin **48.00**
    12" l, sleigh, four brown elk, brown cloth harness, Japan **48.00**
    16" l, sleigh, two deer, Japan **55.00**
  Chalk, 3" h, face, open at top, 1940s, USA **8.00**
  Chenille, 3" h, composition face, red, Japan **40.00**
  Cloth, 6½", litho, Hallmark tag **7.50**
  Composition
    3½" h, red coat, marked "Germany" **25.00**
    6½" h, skier, red cloth coat, tan pants, wood skis and poles, Japan **60.00**
    8" h, Father Christmas
      Blue pants, red flannel jacket, rabbit hair beard, basket on back, holding feather tree, 1920s, marked "Germany" . . **200.00**
      Blue pants, red cloth coat, cotton batting hands, holding eskimos, cardboard base, Japan . **50.00**
  Cotton Batting
    3" h, composition face, Japan **40.00**
    5" h, Father Christmas, composition face, 1920, Germany **85.00**
  Crepe Paper, coat, cotton batting bears, pack with toys, marked "France" **18.00**
  Homemade, 10" h, painted walnut face, red cloth coat, crepe paper boots **40.00**
  Papier Mache
    7", red coat, standing on snow, waving **20.00**

9" h, Father Christmas in chimney, white coat, USA, 1940s **48.00**
12", Father Christmas, yellow coat, 1910 . . . . **750.00**
Plastic, hard
  3", red, standing and waving **5.00**
  3½"
    Riding on motorbike, red **5.00**
    Skier, green metal skis, red and white figure, USA **13.00**
    Standing, red and white **5.00**
  4½" h
    Skier, green skis, 1950s, USA . . **7.00**
    White snowshoes, holding green tree, USA, c1950 . . . . **6.50**
  5", fur trim, red and white, rattles **7.00**
Glass Ornaments
  1½" h, red, standing **25.00**
  3" h
    Red, tree **35.00**
    Yellow, tree **38.00**
  4½" l, red Santa in yellow chimney . **48.00**
Lantern, battery operated, green metal base, 1950s, Japan
  Face **25.00**
  Standing **25.00**
Light Bulb, milk glass
  Bell, 2½" h, Santa faces, Japan **20.00**
  Father Christmas, 3½" h **25.00**
Mask, painted cloth, cotton batting beard, 1930s **15.00**
Music Box, "Jingle Bells," wood sleigh, composition Santa face, flannel body, two 10" h celluloid deer, Japan **100.00**
Nodder, 3", bisque figure, Germany . . **110.00**
Pin, wood, diecut, shellacked finish, c1940 . . . . **8.00**

Post Card, green outfit, red ground, relief decoration, $12.00.

Planter, stoneware, painted 28.00
Post Card
    "A Merry Christmas," Father Christ-
    mas, blue coat, presents, tree, Ger-
    many 6.00
    "A Merry Christmas To You," Santa
    beside donkey loaded with toys,
    1904 .... 5.00
    "Christmas Greetings," Father Christ-
    mas, putting toys through window,
    Germany 7.00
    "Christmas Greetings," Santa driving
    three wheeled motorbike, 1909 .. 10.00
    "Happy Christmas Wishes," Santa
    steering ship's wheel, Germany .. 5.00
    "Joyful Christmas," Father Christmas
    face, two children, 1913 .... 4.50
    "Loving Christmas Wishes," emb,
    Father Christmas face, surrounded
    by holly 4.00
    "May your Christmas be Merry and
    Gay," Father Christmas photo-
    graph, peeping through doorway,
    Germany 6.00
    Santa Trio, 5–7", cloth and cardboard
    bodies, paper and celluloid faces,
    1950s, Japan 45.00
Print, framed
    "Merry Old Santa Claus," Thomas
    Nast, Harper's Weekly 100.00
    "The Marriage of Santa Claus," 1928 32.00
Sticker Box, 1 x 1½ x 1½", cardboard,
    Dennison, white ground, emb Santa
    portrait on cov seal, c1925 .... 8.00
Token, 1" d, copper colored emb coin,
    detailed portrait, inscriptions "Merry
    Christmas, Santa Claus' Xmas Gift
    Store, Dives Pomeroy & Stewart,"
    c1920 .... 8.50
Toy
    Friction, 4" h, plastic, wheels in base,
    Funworld, Inc 3.50
    Jack–in–the–Box, composition Santa
    face, red cloth coat, cardboard
    chimney box, Germany 75.00
    Squeeze, 8½" h, plastic, Sani–Toy,
    Inc 5.00
    Wind–up
        5½", tin, Santa ringing bell, holding
        sign "North Pole, NY," Japan,
        1950s 38.00
        7" h, plastic and tin, ringing bell,
        holding celluloid balloons, Ja-
        pan, 1950s 48.00
        8" h, metal and plastic, red flannel
        coat, reading ABC book, flips
        pages with magnet, Japan, 1950s 50.00
        8" l, celluloid Santa and reindeer,
        metal green sled, marked "Oc-
        cupied Japan," MIB 50.00
    Whistle, Sears 15.00

SCOUTING

Collecting Hints: Nostalgia is one of the principal reasons for collecting scouting memorabilia; individuals often focus on the period when they were in the scouting movement. Other collectors select themes, e.g., handbooks, jamborees, writings by scout movement leaders, Eagle Scout material, etc. Jamboree ephemera is especially desirable.

Scouting scholars have produced a wealth of well researched material on the scouting movement. Many of these pamphlets are privately printed and can be located by contacting dealers specializing in scouting items.

Scout material enjoys popularity among collectors. The greatest price fluctuation occurs in modern material and as collectors define new specialized collecting areas.

Girl Scout material is about five to ten years behind Boy Scout material in respect to collecting interest. A collection can still be assembled for a modest investment. While Boy Scout uniforms have remained constant in design throughout time, the Girl Scout uniform changed almost every decade. This increases the number of desirable collectibles.

History: The Boy Scout movement began in America under the direction of William D. Boyce, inspired by a helping hand he received from one of Baden-Powell's English scouts when he was lost in a London fog in 1910. Other American boy organizations, such as the one organized by Dan Beard, were quickly brought into the Boy Scout movement. In 1916 the Boy Scouts received a charter from the United States Congress. Key leaders in the movement were Ernest Thompson-Seton, Dan Beard, W. D. Boyce, and James West.

A young illustrator, Norman Rockwell, received his first job as editor of Boys' Life in 1913, which began a lifelong association with the Boy Scouts.

The first international jamboree was held in England in 1920. America's first jamboree was held in 1937 in Washington, D.C. Manufacturers, quick to recognize the potential for profits, issued a wealth of Boy Scout material. Local councils and Order of the Arrow lodges have added significantly to this base, especially in the area of patches.

The Girl Scout movement began on March 12, 1912, under the direction of Juliette Gordon Low of Savannah, Georgia. The movement grew rapidly and in 1928 the Girl Scout manual suggested selling cookies as a way of raising funds. The Girl Scout movement also received wide recognition for its activities during World War II, selling over $3 million of bonds in the fourth Liberty Loan drive.

References: Mary Degenhardt and Judy Kirsch, *Girl Scout Collector's Guide,* Wallace–Homestead, 1987; William Hillcourt, *Norman Rockwell's World of Scouting,* Harry Abrams, 1977; Alburtus Hoogeveen, *Arapaho I, Council Shoulder Patches, Red & Whites, Council Patches, Jamboree Patches, Council Histories,* privately printed; Alburtus Hoogeveen, *Arapaho II, Order of the Arrow, Complete Guide To Order Of Arrow Insignia,* privately printed; J. Bryan Putman, ed., *Official Price Guide To Scouting Collectibles,* House of Collectibles, 1982; R. J. Sayers, *Identification & Value Guide To Scouting Collectibles,* Books Americana, 1984; Harry D. Thorsen, *Scouts On Stamps Of The World,* privately printed.

Privately printed pamphlets defining specialized collecting interests (contact "The Stevensons" for a price list, see Advisory Board) include: James Froehlig, *Boy Scout Fiction, Mathiews, Fitzhugh and Every Boys Library;* Kenneth Kittleberger, *Cigarette And Trade Cards Featuring Baden-Powell,* Sheldon Levy and John Adams, *United States Boy Scout (coin) Medallions;* Dr. Stephen Lomazow, *Norman Rockwell & The Boy Scouts;* D. W. Miller, *Every Boys Library Boy Scout Editions;* H. Compton Pembroke, *All Boy Scout of America Publications, 1910–1970,* 104 pgs; Max J. Silber, *Friendship Gifts;* James Stevenson, *Ernest Thompson Seton, Dan Beard, and Robert Baden-Powell;* Harry D. Thorsen, *Eagle Scout Badges;* Harry D. Thorsen, *Wood Scout Tokens.*

Collectors' Club: Scouts On Stamp Society International, 20 Cedar Lane, Cornwell, NY 12518.

Periodical: *Scout Memorabilia Magazine,* c/o The Lawrence L. Lee Scouting Museum, P. O. Box 1121, Manchester, NH 03105.

Museums: Boy Scout Museum, Murray, KY; Girl Scout National Headquarters, New York, NY; The Lawrence L. Lee Scouting Museum and Max J. Silber Scouting Library, Manchester, NH; Juliette Low National Center, 142 Bull Street, Savannah, GA; Western Scout Museum, Los Angeles; Zitelman Scout Museum, Rockford, IL.

REPRODUCTION ALERT, especially Boy Scout jamboree patches and rare Order of the Arrow patches.

BOY SCOUTS

Binoculars, leather, tan, 1920s	**80.00**
Canteen, c1930	**20.00**
Certificate, Asst Scout Master, Warren, PA, 1914, sgd by Theodore Roosevelt, framed	**100.00**
Door Hanger, 6 x 7", diecut, stiff paper, full color Liberty Bell illus, issued by	

Handbook, *Scouting For Boys,* Handbook for Boy Scouts, 1935 printing, English, $7.50.

Freedom's Foundation and Boy Scouts of America	**8.00**
Figure, 4¼" h, metal, scout shape, copper colored, black plastic base, award plate for 1951 Scouting Fair of Valley Forge Council	**25.00**
Game, The Game of Boy Scouts, 50 cards, orig box, Parker Bros, 1930s	**45.00**
Handbook	
Handbook For Boys, 23rd through 32nd edition	**10.00**
Handbook For Scoutmasters, blue cov, 1922	**15.00**
Lone Scouts of America, 4¼ x 7", 50 pgs, illus, 1915–20	**25.00**
Scoutmaster, 1923	**25.00**
Handkerchief, boy fishing, 1915	**22.00**
Ink Blotter, 4 x 9", cardboard, Scout portraits and "God And My Country" theme, unused	**5.00**
Knife, Remington	**65.00**
Magazine, *Boy's Life,* Norman Rockwell cov	**25.00**
Manual, Adventuring For Senior Scouts, first edition, 1938	**10.00**
Nail File, 4½" l, bronze color finish, diecut Liberty Bell and insignia, 1957 National Jamboree at Valley Forge details	**4.00**
Notepad, membership note and memo pad, Boy Scouts signaling illus on front cov, 1914 copyright	**15.00**
Paperweight, silver, Explorer symbol	**5.00**
Patch, 3¼", cloth, stitched, yellow, red, white, and black design, 50th Scout Anniversary Jamboree in Colorado Springs, unused	**15.00**
Plaque, 6½ x 9½", award, masonite, full color portrait, Onward For God And My Country Program, awarded by National Council of Boy Scouts, cardboard easel back	**25.00**

Pocket Watch
   Ingersol, dollar type, patented July 2,
     1916 .... **350.00**
   Westclox, 2" d, silvered brass case,
     black numerals and logo, 1950s .. **100.00**
Sign, 10 x 12", advertising uniforms,
   Scout illus, silver inscriptions, Sweet–
   Orr, 1930s **75.00**
Tie Slide
   Plastic, white, raised red Indian head,
     1951 .... **8.00**
   Wood, varnished, attached leather
     slide band on back, made during
     1957 National Jamboree **10.00**
View–Master Set, 8th World Boy Scout
   Jamboree, set of 3 full color reels, in-
   cludes booklet, orig envelope, 1955 **25.00**
Wallet, Cub Scout, 1950s **15.00**
Wrist Watch, Ingersol, patented July 2,
   1914 .... **350.00**

Merit Badges, Public Health, $8.00; Personal Health, $8.00.

GIRL SCOUTS

Book, *Juliette Lowe and The Girl Scouts*,
   Choate & Ferris, 1928 .... **10.00**
Calendar
   1953, full color cov photo, unused . **20.00**
   1954, 8½ x 10", full color photo, pen-
     ciled notes **15.00**
Certificate, guardian, 8½ x 15", wood
   grain paper, brown construction pa-
   per backing, numbered 8816 ...... **25.00**
Charter, 9 x 14¾", tan textured paper,
   dated Jan 1921, dark brown inscrip-
   tion and design, inked signatures ... **22.00**
Comic Book, Daisy Lowe of the Girl
   Scouts, 6½ x 10", 16 pgs, history text,
   full color, 1954 copyright **15.00**
Magazine, *The American Girl*, June,
   1934, 8½ x 12", 52 pgs **8.00**
Pin, 11⁄16", Fiftieth Anniversary **8.00**
Sewing Kit, Brownies, red case, 1940s **10.00**
Tray, wood, trefoil, 1940s **12.00**

SEWING ITEMS

Collecting Hints: Collectors tend to favor Sterling
silver items. However, don't overlook the material in metals, ivory, celluloid, plastic, and wood.

Some metals were plated; the plating should be
in very good condition before you buy a piece.
   Advertising and souvenir items are part of sewing history. Focusing on one of these aspects will
develop a fascinating collection. Another focus
is on a certain instrument, with tape measures
among the most common. Finally, figural items
have a high value because of their strong popularity.
   Most collectors concentrate on material from
the Victorian era. A novice collector might look
to the 20th century, especially the Art Deco and
Art Nouveau periods, to build a collection.

History: Sewing was considered an essential skill
of a young woman of the 19th century. The
wealth of early American samplers attests to the
talents of many of these young seamstresses.
   During the Victorian era a vast assortment of
practical as well as whimsical sewing devices
appeared on the market. Among the forms were
tape measures, pincushions, stilettos for punch-
work, and crochet hooks. The sewing birds attached to table tops were a standard fixture in
the parlor.
   Many early sewing tools, e.g., needleholders,
emery holders and sewing boxes, were made of
wood. However, the Sterling silver tool was considered the height of elegance. Thimbles were
the most popular. Sterling silver-handled items
included darning eggs, stilettos, and thread holders.
   In the 20th century needlecases and sewing
kits were an important advertising giveaway.
Plastic sewing materials are available, but they
have not attracted much collector interest.

References: Pamela Clabburn, *The Needlework
Dictionary,* William Morrow & Co., 1976; Joyce
Clement, *The Official Price Guide To Sewing
Collectibles,* House of Collectibles, 1987; Estelle
Zalkin, *Zalkin's Handbook of Thimbles and Sew-
ing Implements,* Warman Publishing Co., Inc.,
1988.

Museums: Fabric Hall, Historic Deerfield, Deerfield, MA; Museum of American History, Smithsonian Institution, Washington, DC; Shelburne
Museum, Shelburne, VT.

See: Thimbles.

Basket
   Shaker, 10½" d, 3" d, round, octago-
     nal base, cheese weave splint,
     c1830 .... **150.00**
   Sweet Grass, 8½" d, woven handles,
     made by Maine Indians, c1923 .. **30.00**
   Wicker, round, beaded lid **22.00**
Booklet
   1901, Singer the Universal Sewing
     Machine, diecut, Pan Am Expo .. **65.00**
   1905, construction hints, dresses of
     the time, pictures on every page . **10.00**

Advertising Trade Card, Singer Sewing Machine, titled "The First Lesson," adv on back, 5⁹⁄₁₆ × 4¹⁄₁₆", $8.50.

1930, Singer, "How to Make Children's Clothes," illus 8.00
Box, child's, two girls on cover, includes supplies and key, Victorian, c1910 .... 45.00
Button Box, round, wood shoe, boot label 22.50
Catalog, McCall's, 1940s 25.00
Charm, thimble figural, sterling, gold wash 10.00
Clamp, wood
    Painted, pin cushion, cupid decal .. 95.00
    Sycamore, pin cushion, horn embroidery hoops 85.00
Crochet Hook, metal, capped 15.00
Darner, egg, scissors inside 42.00
Emery, cat head, black 18.00
Mending Kit
    Art Deco, "Handy Pack" 10.00
    Bakelite
        Purple, German 14.00
        Red, thimble cap 16.00
    Birchwood, hp flowers, French souvenir 26.00
    Bullet Shape, Mt Royale 18.00

Needle Book, Trans-Atlantic Aeroplane, litho, $6.50.

Eastern Star 22.50
Leather Box, "Needles & Cotton/ Should Not Be Forgotten," scissors 25.00
Leather and Brass, book shape, 1923 30.00
Plastic, bee with scissors 16.00
Suede Envelope 18.00
Needle Book, Army–Navy, German ... 7.00
Needle Case
    Advertising
        Bengal Range 8.00
        Crystal Baking Powder 10.00
        Lydia Pinkham 15.00
    Felt, basket shape 12.00
    Ivory, scrimshaw, sgd 145.00
    Leather, "Needles to say..." 12.00
    Wood, beaded, Victorian 165.00
Needle Gripper, Nimble Thimble, orig pkg 20.00
Needle Sharpener
    Cat 48.00
    Strawberry 6.00
Needle Threader, adv, Prudential 8.00
Pin Cushion
    Advertising, Success Horse Drawn Manure Spreader 60.00
    Apple, figural
        Satin, 2½ x 3", red and yellow, green leaves and stem 60.00
        Silk, hp, celluloid baby head in bonnet on top, green fabric leaves 55.00
    Camel, figural 15.00
    Disc, velvet, embroidered 12.00
    Doll
        China, holding mirror, German .. 90.00
        Cloth, Black, holding pin cushion 28.00
        Composition 25.00
        Indian–made 26.00
    Doll face, bisque, blue glass eyes, blonde hair, open mouth with teeth, mounted on purple orchid, 5" h, 5½" w, orig box, German .. 85.00
    Dutch Boy, figural 10.00
    Flower, plump 12.00
    Heart, Indian beadwork 48.00
    Hitler, dated 1941 .... 45.00
    Horse and Wagon 10.00
    Orange, figural 25.00
    Reindeer Hoof, fur and velvet shoe, 1908 .... 23.00
    Revolving, tape measure in base, thimble 30.00
    Shoe, figural, metal, Dutch boy and girl dec 45.00
    Silk, blue, hair filled 6.00
    Strawberry, 3 x 5", red velvet, green felt leaves, c1870 .... 85.00
    Turtle, cast iron body 22.00
Pin Disc, adv, Prudential 4.00
Pin Holder, adv
    Cube, German 12.00
    Prudential 7.00

Punch, gauge, sterling silver, pat 1909   **60.00**
Scissors
  Embroidery, stork figural **35.00**
  Ornate handle, 9½" l, Solinger, Ger-
    many **22.50**
Scissors and Holder, sweet grass **25.00**
Sewing Bird, brass, pat 1858 .... **175.00**
Sewing Machine
  Kayanee, metal, wood dovetailed
    base, manual or battery operated,
    US Zone **55.00**
  Stitchwell, child's, cast iron **45.00**
Shuttle, wood **60.00**
Spool Cabinet, JP Coats, metal, black,
  glass slant front **95.00**
Spool Holder, souvenir, Indian head de-
  cal **18.00**
Tape Measure
  Advertising
    Hoover Vacuum **25.00**
    Lydia Pinkham, celluloid, portrait
      front, adv back **79.00**
  Chrome, brass owl front, German .. **55.00**
  Figural
    Apple, hard plastic, red, leaf pull . **18.00**
    Clock **35.00**
    Dog, tongue pull **65.00**
    Fish, celluloid **25.00**
    Indian Boy Head, celluloid **30.00**
    Little Boy, wearing clown hat, 4¼"
      h, German **18.00**
  Ivory **60.00**
Tatting Shuttle, adv, Lydia Pinkham, cel-
  luloid, portrait top, adv bottom **99.00**
Thimble Case
  Brass, walnut **20.00**
  Crocheted **5.00**
  Sweet Grass **25.00**
Thread Caddy, metal, 2 tiers **25.00**
Thread Winder, figural fish, mother-of-
  pearl **12.00**
Tin, Dr Moon's Sewing Machine Oil,
  4⅛" **5.00**

SHAWNEE POTTERY

Collecting Hints: Many Shawnee pieces came in
several color variations. Some pieces also contained both painted and decal decorations. The
available literature will indicate some, but not
all of the variations.

Not a great deal of interest is being shown in
the Shawnee art and dinnerware lines. Among
the lines are Cameo, Cheria (Petit Point), Diora,
and Touche (Liana). New collectors may wish to
concentrate in these areas.

History: The Shawnee Pottery Co. was founded
in 1937 in Zanesville, Ohio. The company acquired a 650,000 square foot plant that formerly
housed the American Encaustic Tiling Company.

There it produced as many as 100,000 pieces of
pottery per day. In 1961 the plant closed.

Shawnee limited its chief production to kitchenware, decorative art pottery, and dinnerware.
Distribution was primarily through jobbers and
chain stores.

Shawnee can be marked "Shawnee," "Shawnee U.S.A.," "USA #——," "Kenwood," or with
character names, e.g., "Pat. Smiley," "Pat. Winnie," etc.

Reference: Mark Supnick, *Collecting Shawnee
Pottery,* L-W Books, 1989.

Ashtray, oak leaf, #350 .... **8.00**
Bank, bulldog **38.00**
Bookends, geese, #4000, pr **15.00**
Bowl, cereal, 6½", Corn King, #94 ... **25.00**
Candleholders, red, white rim, #1386,
  pr **12.00**

**Cookie Jar, basket of fruit, yellow basket-
weave base, 7⅜" d, $30.00.**

Casserole, cov, Corn King, large **40.00**
Cookie Jar
  Dutch Boy, blue pants **52.00**
  Dutch Girl **100.00**
  Puss N Boots **150.00**
  Teddy Bear, 1940 .... **40.00**
  Winking Owl **115.00**
  Winnie Pig **125.00**
Creamer
  Puss N Boots **15.00**
  Smiley Pig, #86 .... **24.00**
Figurine
  Gazelle, #614 .... **20.00**
  Teddy Bear **22.00**
Jug, water, Smiley Pig **22.00**
Lamp, dog **8.00**
Pitcher
  Bo Peep, white **70.00**
  Chanticleer, #17/2/4 .... **55.00**
  Corn King, 12 oz **36.00**
  Tom the Piper's Son **35.00**
Planter
  Children, shoe, blue, #525 .... **14.00**
  Doe and Log **20.00**
  Dutch Children, well, #710 .... **12.00**

Planter, squirrel by tree stump, green and brown, imp mark, 3½" h, $9.50.

Elf, shoe, #765	10.00
Gazelle Head, black, 10"	18.00
Girl, fence, gold trim	15.00
Goose, flying, gold trim, #707	18.00
Man, pushing cart, gold trim	20.00
Rickshaw, #539	6.00
Salt and Pepper Shakers, pr	
Chanticleer Rooster, large	85.00
Corn King, 3" h	22.00
Farmer Pig, #23/1/1	14.00
Milk Cans	12.00
Mugsey	22.00
Owls, 3" h, #23/3/2	20.00
Puss N Boots	20.00
Smiley, small	25.00
Winnie, large	50.00
Sugar Bowl, clover	22.00
Sugar Shaker, white, Corn King	25.00
Teapot, Granny Anne	62.00
Vase	
Cornucopia, #865	10.00
Dove, red, #829	20.00
Gazelle and Baby, matte black, #841	60.00
Pineapple, #839	12.00
Swan, #806	10.00
Wall Pocket	
Bo Peep, #586	18.00
Jack Horner, #585	18.00
Telephone, #529	15.00

SHEET MUSIC

Collecting Hints: Center your collection around a theme—show tunes, songs of World War I, Sousa marches, Black material, songs of a certain lyricist or composer—the list is endless.

Be careful about stacking your sheets on top of one another. The ink on the covers tends to bleed. The most ideal solution is to place acid free paper between each cover and sheet.

Unfortunately, people used tape to repair tears in old sheet music. This discolors and detracts from value. Seek professional help in removing tape from rarer sheets.

During the late 1980s, mid–nineteenth century sheet music increased rapidly in value. World War I and covers featuring Blacks currently enjoy great popularity among collectors.

History: Sheet music, especially piano scores, dates to the early 19th century. The early music contains some of the finest examples of lithography. Much of this music was bound in volumes and accompanied a young lady when she was married.

Sheet music covers chronicle the social, political, and trends of any historical period. The golden age of the hand illustrated cover dates from 1885. Leading artists such as James Montgomery Flagg used their talents in the sheet music area. Cover art work was critical to helping the song sell.

Once radio and talking pictures became popular, covers featured the stars. A song sheet might be issued in dozens of different cover versions depending on who was featured. By the 1950s piano playing was no longer as popular and song sheets failed to maintain their high quality of design.

References: Debbie Dillon, *Collectors Guide To Sheet Music*, L-W Promotions, 1988; Daniel B. Priest, *American Sheet Music With Prices*, Wallace–Homestead, 1978.

Collectors' Clubs: National Sheet Music Society, 1597 Fair Park, Los Angeles, CA 90041; New York Sheet Music Society, P. O. Box 1126, East Orange, NJ 07019; Remember That Song, 5821 North 67th Ave., Suite 103–306, Glendale, AZ 85301; The Sheet Music Exchange, P. O. Box 69, Quicksburg, VA 22847.

The Banjo Pickers, Frederic Groton, 1929, Carl Fisher Inc, green on white cover, $20.00.

A Little Bird Told Me	2.00
After I Say I'm Sorry, 1926	2.00
After The War Is Over, 1917	5.00

Ah, Sweet Mystery of LIfe, 1910, Vic
Herb cover **2.00**
Among My Souvenirs, 1927 .... **2.00**
Anchors Aweigh, 1907 .... **2.00**
Angel Eyes, Nat King Cole **5.00**
Animal Crackers In My Soup, Shirley
Temple, 1935 .... **18.00**
Any Bonds Today?, Irving Berlin, 1941 **7.00**
April Showers, Al Jolson **10.00**
Army Air Corp, 1939 .... **3.00**
Ave Maria, 1935 .... **1.00**
Babes in Toyland **10.00**
Barney Google, 1923 .... **15.00**

**Barney Google Fox Trot, song by Billy
Rose and Con Conrad, Jerome H Remick
& Co publishers, $15.00.**

Beyond The Blue Horizon, 1930 ..... **6.00**
Blueberry Hill, early version **2.00**
Dixie, 1961 .... **2.00**
Down Among The Sheltering Palms,
1914 .... **5.00**
El Rancho Grande, Bing Crosby cov .. **5.00**
Father Was Crazy To Aviate, 1911 .... **18.00**
For Me And My Gal, Judy Garland ... **8.00**
Going My Way, Bing Crosby Cov, 1944 **5.00**
Gone With The Wind, c1954 .... **12.00**
Good Ship Lollipop, Shirley Temple .. **12.00**
Heartbreak Hotel, Elvis Presley, orig edi-
tion **20.00**
High and Mighty, 1954 .... **8.00**
Home Sweet Home, c1871 .... **7.00**
Huggable, Kissable You, Rudy Vallee . **5.00**
I Can't Begin To Tell You, Betty Grable,
1945 .... **5.00**
I Got Stung, Elvis Presley **20.00**
In My Harem, Irving Berlin, 1913 .... **8.00**
Irene, show tune, 1919 .... **6.00**
Ja Da, 1918 .... **5.00**
Land Of Long Ago, Charles Knight,
1912 .... **2.00**
Little Orphan Annie **15.00**
Louisiana Purchase Exposition March . **8.00**

Love Me Tender, Elvis Presley **15.00**
Mickey Mouse March, 1955 .... **17.00**
Mona Lisa, Nat King Cole **5.00**
My Buddy, Al Jolson, c1922 .... **10.00**
Oh, How I Hate To Get Up In The
Morning, Irving Berlin, 1914 .... **7.00**
Old Black Joe, 1906 .... **8.00**
One Alone, 1926 .... **2.00**
Our Little Girl, Shirley Temple **30.00**
Over The Rainbow, Judy Garland **15.00**
Paper Doll, Frank Sinatra **5.00**
Roses In The Rain, Frank Sinatra **5.00**
Say 'Au Revoir' But Not Good–Bye,
World War I **5.00**
Serenade, 1924 .... **2.00**
Smiles, World War I **3.00**
Somebody Stole My Gal **5.00**
Song Of The South, Disney, 1946 .... **10.00**
Sonny Boy, Al Jolson **5.00**
Stars And Stripes Forever, Sousa, 1897 **10.00**
Stein Song, Rudy Vallee **5.00**
Three Little Words, Amos & Andy **15.00**
Tonight, West Side Story **6.00**
Toot Toot Tootsie, Al Jolson, 1922 ... **10.00**
True Love, Grace Kelly, Frank Sinatra,
and Bing Crosby, 1955 .... **7.00**
When I Lost You, Irving Berlin, 1912 . **4.00**
When I'm With You, Shirley Temple .. **12.00**
When It's Circus Day Back Home,
c1917 .... **8.00**
When My Ship Comes Sailing Home,
1913 .... **6.00**
When The Kaiser Does The Goose Step,
World War I **15.00**
When The Moon Comes Over The
Mountain, Kate Smith, 1931 .... **5.00**
When You Wish Upon A Star, Pinocchio **15.00**
Whistle While You Work, Snow White
and the Seven Dwarfs **10.00**
White Christmas, Irving Berlin, 1924 .. **7.00**
Wild Rose **2.00**
Woody Woodpecker, 1954 .... **5.00**
You Keep Sending 'Em Over & We'll
Keep Knocking 'Em Down World War
I **10.00**
You, The Great Ziegfeld, 1936 .... **5.00**
You Oughta Be In Pictures, 1934 ..... **4.00**
You're Just In Love, 1950 .... **5.00**
You're The Cream In My Coffee, 1928 **5.00**
You Will Remember Vienna, 1930 ... **2.00**

SILVER FLATWARE

Collecting Hints: Focus on one pattern by one
maker. Several makers used the same pattern
name and a similar pattern design. Always check
the backmarks carefully; several thousand patterns were manufactured. Popularity of pattern,
not necessarily age, is the key to pricing.

A monogram on a piece will reduce its value

substantially, at least by 50%. On Sterling, monograms occasionally can be removed. This, however, is not the case with silver plate. A worn piece of silver plate virtually has no market value.

Silver flatware sold in sets often brings less than pieces sold individually. The reason is that many buyers are looking to replace pieces or add place settings to a pattern they already own. Sterling silver sets certainly retain their value better than silver plate sets. A number of dealers specializing in replacement services have evolved in past years. Many advertise in the weekly issues of *The Antique Trader.*

Flatware marked as Alaska Silver, German Silver, Lashar Silver, and Nickel Silver is not silver plated. These materials are alloys designed to imitate silver plate.

Doris Snell's *American Silverplated Flatware Patterns* contains a section on the care and cleaning of flatware. Individuals must keep in mind that plated wares have only a very thin surface over the base metal. Once removed, it cannot be easily replaced.

Finally, there is one form of silver flatware that has value with a monogram. It is the flatware used by American railroads, for which there exists a strong market among railroad buffs.

History: The silver table service became a hallmark of elegance during the Victorian era. The homes of the wealthy had Sterling silver services made by Gorham, Kirk, Tiffany, and Towle. Silver place settings became part of a young girl's hope chest and a staple wedding gift. Sterling silver consists of 925 parts silver and 75 parts copper per 1,000 parts sterling.

When electroplating became popular, silver plated flatware gave the common man a chance to imitate the wealthy. Silverplated flatware has a thin layer of silver plated by a chemical process, known as electrolysis, onto a base metal, usually britannia (an alloy of tin, antimony and copper) or white metal (an alloy of tin, copper and lead or bismuth). Leading silver plate manufacturers are Alvin, Gorham, International Silver Co. (a modern company which merged many older companies such as Holmes & Edwards, Rogers, etc.), Oneida, Reed & Barton, Wm. Rogers, and Wallace.

References: Fredna Harris Davis and Kenneth K. Deibel, *Silver Plated Flatware Patterns*, Bluebonnet Press, 1981; Tere Hagan, *Silverplated Flatware: An Identification & Value Guide, Fourth Edition*, Collector Books; Dorothy T. and H. Ivan Rainwater, *American Silverplate*, Schiffer Publishing, Ltd., 1988; Jeri Schwartz, *The Official Identification and Price Guide To Silver and Silverplate*, House of Collectibles, 1989.

Periodical: *The Magazine Silver*, P.O. Box 22217, Milwaukie, OR 97222.

Note: Mono – monogrammed.

Acorn, Jensen	
Fish knife	35.00
Pie server	125.00
Allure, Rogers, 1939, cheese knife	4.50
Blossom, Jensen, gravy ladle	125.00
Bridal Rose, Alvin	
Butter knife	25.00
Butter pick	100.00
Cream soup spoon	60.00
Dessert spoon	55.00
Dinner fork	55.00
Gumbo soup spoon, mono	38.00
Ice cream form	65.00
Sauce ladle	85.00
Sugar tongs, large	85.00
Teaspoon	20.00
Cactus, Jensen, carving set	300.00
Cambridge, Gorham	
Bouillon ladle, mono	210.00
Cracker scoop, pierced	350.00
Game knife, mono	38.00
Horseradish, gold wash	125.00
Sardine	45.00
Tongs	40.00
Canterbury, Towle, cheese spreader, mono	15.00
Chapel Bells, Alvin	
Butter knife, flat handle	13.00
Cream soup spoon	14.00
Luncheon fork	20.00
Salad fork	19.00
Teaspoon	12.00
Chatham, Durgin, berry spoon	55.00
Chippendale, Alvin, olive fork	25.00
Classique, Gorham	
Knife	22.00
Place setting, luncheon	74.00
Sugar spoon	20.00
Teaspoon	16.00
Colonial Antique, Watson, baby fork	26.00
Concord, Towle, gravy ladle	50.00
Concord, Whiting	
Butter knife, flat handle	15.00
Cold meat fork	37.00
Cream soup spoon	17.00
Dinner fork	24.00
Dinner knife	19.00
Salad fork	21.00
Soup spoon, oval	18.00
Sugar spoon	16.00
Tablespoon	34.00
Teaspoon	14.00
Contour, Towle	
Cocktail fork	20.00
Place setting	80.00
Place spoon	28.00
Sugar spoon	24.00
Teaspoon	15.00
Copenhagen, Manchester	
Butter, master, flat	22.00
Sugar spoon	20.00

Corsage, Stieff
Bonbon 34.00
Butter, master, flat 26.00
Cold meat fork 60.00
5 O'Clock teaspoon 16.00
Gravy ladle 54.00
Iced tea spoon 25.00
Pickle fork, two tines 24.00
Pie server 38.00
Place setting, luncheon, 8 pcs 87.00
Salad fork 26.00
Sugar spoon 24.00
Tablespoon 50.00
Damask Rose, Oneida, butter knife ... 13.00
Dawn Mist, Wallace, butter knife 14.00
Della Robbia, Alvin
Dinner fork 19.00
Luncheon fork 11.00
Sugar spoon 12.00
Teaspoon 11.00
DuBarry, International
Cocktail fork 30.00
Dinner fork 34.00
Dinner knife 30.00
Meat fork 85.00
Soup spoon, oval 37.00
Tablespoon, pierced 85.00
Edgewood, International, tomato server 185.00
Empress, International
Butter Spreader 10.00
Citrus spoon 12.00
Cocktail fork 8.00
Dinner fork, 7¼" 16.00
Salad fork 13.00
Sugar shell 12.00
Enchanting Orchard, Westmoreland
Luncheon fork 20.00
Luncheon knife 20.00
Teaspoon 15.00
Enchantress, International
Butter knife, flat handle 17.00
Cream soup 20.00
Gravy 26.00
Iced tea spoon 20.00
Luncheon place setting, 4 pcs 57.00
Salad serving fork 70.00
Tablespoon 40.00
Evangeline, Alvin
Cream soup 12.00
Strawberry fork 11.00
Teaspoon 10.00
Fairfax, Durgin
Butter knife, flat handle 16.00
Demitasse spoon 24.00
Sugar Spoon 24.00
Teaspoon 17.00
Tongs 20.00
Fashion Lane, Durgin
Butter knife
Hollow handle 15.00
Master, flat handle 18.00
Cocktail fork 16.00

Cream soup spoon 22.00
Demitasse spoon 13.00
Dinner knife 24.00
Iced tea spoon 21.00
Jelly spoon 20.00
Pickle fork 17.00
Soup spoon, oval 23.00
Sugar spoon 19.00
Fleetwood, Manchester
Bouillon spoon 17.00
Butter knife, flat handle 14.00
Cocktail fork 15.00
Cream soup spoon 19.00
Dinner fork 28.00
Grapefruit spoon 18.00
Ice cream fork 25.00
Luncheon fork 26.00
Pickle fork 16.00
Teaspoon 13.00
Forget Me Not, Stieff
Dinner fork 30.00
Dinner knife 35.00
Serving spoon 30.00
Teaspoon 20.00
Gainsborough, Alvin
Cream soup spoon 14.00
Sugar spoon 13.00
Teaspoon 12.00
Georgian, Towle
Chocolate spoon, gold wash 60.00
Cold meat fork, 8" 175.00
Sardine, gold wash 295.00
Sugar spoon 42.00
Tongs, tiny 52.00
Horizon, Easterling
Butter knife, master, flat handle 13.00
Cold meat fork 33.00
Cream soup spoon 15.00
Gravy ladle 36.00
Luncheon fork 20.00
Luncheon knife 17.00
Salad fork 19.00
Soup spoon, oval 16.00
Sugar spoon 14.00
Tablespoon 30.00
Teaspoon 12.00
Inaugural, State House
Butter knife, master, flat handle 12.00
Cream soup spoon 14.00
Grill fork 21.00
Grill knife 17.00
Luncheon fork 20.00
Luncheon knife 16.00
Soup spoon, oval 15.00
Sugar spoon 13.00
Teaspoon 11.00
King Albert, Whiting
Bouillon spoon 13.00
Butter, flat handle 12.00
Jelly spoon 14.00
Luncheon fork 19.00
Tablespoon 29.00

Teaspoon 11.00

King George, Gorham
Dinner knife, mono 37.00
Luncheon knife, mono 32.00
Salad fork, mono 55.00
Soup spoon, oval, mono 37.00
Steak knife, 8¼", mono 36.00

Lady Sterling, Weidlich
Bonbon 11.00
Cocktail fork 10.00

Lancaster, Gorham
Dinner fork 30.00
Place spoon 25.00
Serving spoon 40.00
Teaspoon 13.00

Lily of the Valley, Gorham
Dinner fork, 7¾" 25.00
Dinner knife, 9½" 24.00
Iced tea spoon 28.00

**Malibu, Wm. A. Rogers A1 Plus, pierced
cake server, 1934, $18.00.**

Madame Morris, Durgin, preserve
spoon 16.00
Mazarine, Dominick & Haff, claret ladle 150.00
Meadowbrook, 52 pc set 125.00
Medallion, Duhme, tablespoon 115.00
Monticello, Lunt
Dinner fork 17.00
Sugar tong 30.00
Teaspoon 15.00
Moselle, American Silver Co, 1847 Rog-
ers Bros
Cold meat fork, mono 55.00
Gravy ladle 75.00
Serving spoon, Moselle 95.00
Teaspoon 18.00
Normandie, Wallace, lemon fork 16.00
Old Maryland, Kirk–Steiff, bacon server,
engraved 87.00
Old Medici, Gorham, oyster ladle 200.00
Prelude, International
Butter knife, flat handle 13.00
Luncheon fork 18.00
Place setting 55.00
Teaspoon 12.00
Princess Patricia, Gorham
Bonbon 17.00
Bouillon 18.00
Butter knife, flat handle 14.00

Carving set, 2 pcs 47.00
Coffee spoon 12.00
Cream soup spoon 21.00
Lemon fork 15.00
Pickle fork 16.00
Salad fork 26.00
Sugar spoon 19.00
Sugar tongs 20.00
Teaspoon 13.00
Queen, Howard
Citrus spoon 25.00
Vegetable fork, large 195.00
Queen Anne, Williamsburg, Stieff
Butter knife, hollow handle 16.00
Fruit fork, 6½" 26.00
Place fork, 7¾" 30.00
Place knife, 9⅛" 22.00
Place setting 95.00
Salad fork, 6⅜" 30.00
Soup spoon, oval 36.00
Steak knife, 8¼" 20.00
Tablespoon 45.00
Teaspoon, 5⅝" 15.00
Rambler Rose, Towle
Butter knife, flat handle 13.00
Cream soup spoon 15.00
Luncheon fork 19.00
Luncheon knife 18.00
Salad fork 18.00
Sugar spoon 14.00
Tablespoon 29.00
Teaspoon 12.00
Renaissance Scroll, Reed & Barton
Butter knife, hollow handle 14.00
Cheese knife 16.00
Jelly spoon 18.00
Lemon fork 15.00
Place fork 24.00
Place knife 20.00
Salad fork 22.00
Soup spoon, oval 19.00
Sugar spoon 17.00
Teaspoon 13.00
Rococo, Dominick & Haff, cream ladle 40.00
Romantique, Alvin
Butter knife, master, flat handle 17.00
Cream soup spoon 20.00
Iced tea spoon 19.00
Luncheon fork 26.00
Pickle fork 18.00
Salad fork 23.00
Sugar spoon 18.00
Teaspoon 14.00
Royal Danish, International, cocktail
stirrer 75.00
Savannah, Reed & Barton
Tablespoon 48.00
Tablespoon, pierced 55.00
Teaspoon 12.00
Silver Wheat, Reed & Barton
Butter knife 13.00
Luncheon fork 21.00

Place fork, 7⅛"	20.00
Place knife, 9⅜"	20.00
Salad fork	17.00
Sugar spoon	15.00
Teaspoon	12.00
Silver Spray, Towle, place knife	20.00
Southern Charm, Alvin	
Butter knife, flat handle	15.00
Cream soup spoon	15.00
Sugar spoon	14.00
Teaspoon	12.00
Spanish Lace, Wallace, luncheon fork .	14.00
Star, Reed & Barton	
Fork, salad	20.00
Knife, place	18.00
Strasbourg, Gorham	
Fork, 7"	28.00
Jelly server	28.00
Knife	
8⅞"	22.00
9⅛"	24.00
Pastry server	26.00
Place setting	92.00
Salad fork	22.00
Seafood fork	16.00
Trousseau, International	
Butter knife, flat handle	
Master	15.00
Place	14.00
Gumbo soup spoon	17.00
Luncheon fork	23.00
Salad fork	22.00
Sugar spoon	16.00
Teaspoon	13.00
Valencia, International	
Butter knife, master, hollow handle .	14.00
Place fork	20.00
Place knife	16.00
Sugar spoon	15.00
Teaspoon	13.00
Venetian Scroll, Oneida	
Bonbon	20.00
Butter knife, hollow handle	10.00
Cold meat fork	39.00
Lemon fork	13.00
Olive fork	12.00
Sauce ladle	18.00
Serving spoon, pierced	39.00
Soup spoon, oval	22.00
Tablespoon	36.00
Tomato server	49.00
Virginia Carvel, Towle	
Butter knife, flat handle	12.00
Bouillon spoon	18.00
Cream soup spoon	18.00
Iced tea spoon	16.00
Knife, blunt end, 9½"	18.00
Luncheon fork, mono	18.00
Luncheon knife, mono	15.00
Pickle fork	12.00
Salad fork, mono	16.00
Tablespoon	28.00

Teaspoon, mono	12.00
Virginian, Oneida, butter knife	13.00
Winslow, Frank Smith	
Bouillon spoon	13.00
Cocktail fork	12.00
Gumbo soup spoon	15.00
Iced tea spoon	14.00
Luncheon fork	20.00
Teaspoon	11.00
Young Love, Oneida	
Bonbon	14.00
Butter knife, hollow handle	13.00
Gravy ladle	30.00
Place fork	20.00
Place knife	16.00
Salad fork	18.00
Soup spoon, oval	15.00
Teaspoon	12.00

SLOT MACHINES

Collecting Hints: Check the laws in your state. Some states permit the collecting of slot machines manufactured prior to 1941, while others permit the collecting of all machines 25 years old or older provided that they are not used for gambling. A few states prohibit the ownership of any gambling machine.

A complete slot machine is one that is in working order, has no wood missing on the case, and no cracked castings. All that is needed to restore the machine is some work on appearance. Restoration costs range from $100 to over a thousand dollars. The average restoration includes plating of all castings, refinishing the cabinet, repainting the castings to the original colors, rebuilding the mechanism, tuning up the operation of the mechanism, new reel strips, and a new award card. A quality restoration will add between $400 to $800 to the value of a machine. If buying a restored machine from a dealer, a guarantee usually is given.

Most collectors stay away from foreign machines; foreign coins are hard to find. If the machine has been converted to accept American coins, it frequently may jam or not pay off the proper amount on a winner.

Condition, rarity, and desirability are all very important in determining the value of a machine. Try to find one that is in as close to new condition as possible, as "mint original" machines are bringing the same or more money than restored machines.

History: The first three-reel slot machine was invented in 1905 by Charles Fey in San Francisco. The machine was called the Liberty Bell. One of the three known survivors can be seen at the Liberty Bell Saloon, his grandson's restaurant, in Reno, Nevada.

In 1910 the classic fruit symbols were copyrighted by Mills Novelty Company. They were immediately copied by other manufacturers. The first symbols still are popular on contemporary casino machines. The wood cabinet was replaced by cast iron in 1916. By 1922 aluminum fronts were the norm for most machines. In 1928 the jackpot was added.

The 1930s innovations included more reliable and improved mechanisms with more sophisticated coin entry and advance and slug detection systems. In the 1940s drill-proof and cheat-resistant devices were added. The 1950s brought electronic lighting and electronics.

Although the goosenecks of the 1920s and 1930s often are more intricate and rarer than the models of the 1930s and 1940s, the gimmick and more beautiful machines of this later period, such as Rolatop, Treasury, Kitty or Triplex, bring more money.

References: Jerry Ayliffe, *American Premium Guide To Jukeboxes and Slot Machines*, Books Americana, 1985; Richard Bueschel, *Illustrated Guide To 100 Collectible Slot Machines, Volume 1*, Hoflin Publishing Co., 1978, 1989 value update; Marshall Fey, *Slot Machines: A Pictorial History of the First 100 Years*, published by author, 1983; Daniel R. Mead, *Loose Change Blue Book Slot Machine Price Guide*, 1986–87 Edition, published by author, 1987.

Periodical: *Chicagoland Antique Advertising, Slot Machine & Jukebox Gazette*, and *Coin Op Newsletter* are published by Ken Durham, 909 26th Street, N.W., Washington, DC 20037; *The Coin Slot*, 4401 Zephyr Street, Wheatridge, CO 80033; *Loose Change,*, 1515 South Commerce Street, Las Vegas, NV 89102; *Slot–Box Collector*, 6560 Backlick Road, Ste. 217, Springfield, VA 22150.

Note: All machines listed are priced as if they were in "good" condition, meaning the machine is complete and working. An incomplete or non–working machine is worth only 30% to 70% of the listed price.

Machines listed are for 5¢ and 10¢. Quarter and 50¢ machines can run several hundred dollars higher. A silver dollar machine, if you are lucky enough to find one, can add $400 to $800 to the price.

Buckley
  Bones, countertop, spinning disks roll dice for craps, similar to Bally's Reliance **3,500-5,000.00**
  Criss Cross, revamp of Mills machine, escalator coin entry, fancy casting around escalator and jackpot, usually has guaranteed jackpot . **800-1,000.00**
Caille
  Cadet, circular jackpot, escalator moves from bottom up **800-1,200.00**
  Detroit Floor Wheel, upright one ree-

ler, six way play action, bettors pick color wheel will land on . **7,000-9,500.00**
Playboy, three reel, jackpot, c1936 .... **800-1,600.00**
Superior, nude woman on front, scroll–work lower casting, coin entry in center above award card **1,400-1,800.00**
Victory Mint, center pull handle, ladies pictured on both sides of handle **3,500-5,000.00**
Groetchen, Columbia, ⅔ the size of normal slot machine, club handle, small reels, coins go around in circle behind coin head **300-500.00**
Jennings
  Challenger Console, 4' h, vertical glass and horizontal glass with silk-screen design, reels seen from top of lower glass, plays two coin denominations, usually 5¢ and 25¢ **1,400-1,800.00**
  Duchess, three reel, front vendor with mints or candy displayed behind windows flanking jackpot, orig decal, c1934 .... **1,600-2,500.00**
  Export Chief, chrome finish, brass tiered triangle above jackpot **800-1,100.00**
  Four Star Chief, Indian carrying deer on front, large Indian chief above jackpot, four stars on top ... **850-1,150.00**
  Governor, tic tac toe theme, Indian head above jackpot **750-1,000.00**
  Little Duke, large coin headcasting on top of machine, classic Art Deco design, reels spin concentrically **950-1,350.00**
  Silver Moon, moon above jackpot, stars on side of jackpot **750-950.00**
  Sportsman, golf ball vendor, pay card placed at angle **1,400-2,000.00**
  Standard Chief, chrome finish, teardrop design on both sides of jackpot, flat Indian above jackpot **800-1,100.00**
  Victoria, three reel, two jackpots, fortune strips, c1932 .... **1,500-2,500.00**
  Victory Chief, wood front, eagle above jackpot, minutemen soldiers to right and left of eagle **750-950.00**
Mills
  Black Cherry, escalator, painted silver with black case, four applied cherries, bib award card front .. **850-1,000.00**
  Criss Cross, high top, orig condition, working **700.00**
  Diamond Front, escalator, ten raised diamonds around large "bib" award card **850-1,200.00**
  Futurity Bell, three reel, 5¢, 1936 .... **1,900-2,800.00**
  Lion Front, gooseneck coin entry,

Mills Special Award 7-7-7, c1940, $875.00.

large lion with mouth open around
jackpot, three rows of six circles
below reels **1,150-1,450.00**
Melon Bell, three reel, high top,
melon on front, 1948 ..... **1,200-1,800.00**
Mint Vendor, Future Play feature ...**1,200.00**
Mystery Front, three reels, 26" h,
c1932 .... **1,500-2,500.00**
Operator Bell, 23½", 5¢, three
reel **500-800.00**
Pointsettia, gooseneck coin entry,
flowers on lower casting, Liberty
bell under coin entry **800-1,100.00**
Silent Golden, three reel, Roman's
head on front, 1932 ..... **1,900-2,800.00**
Twentieth Century, 5' 5", 5¢, oak
case, nickel plated mounts, cast
paw feet **3,000-5,000**
Vest Pocket, three reel, box shape,
plain design, 1938 .... **350-550.00**
Pace
All Star Comet, rotary escalator, stars
and vertical pointed stripes on
front **850-1,150.00**
Bantam, three reel, jackpot vendor
front, appealing design ... **1,200-1,800.00**
Star, three reel, circular coin escalator, 25¢, c1948 .... **850-1,300.00**
Watling
Blue Seal, gooseneck, twin jackpot,
fancy front **900-1,100.00**
Exchange, one wheel, countertop
model, five way coin head, oak
case, c1910 .... **2,000-3,000.00**
Gumball Vender, gooseneck, ornate
casting around reels, gumball ven-
ders on each side of twin jackpot,
1¢ only **1,000-1,200.00**

Rol-a-top, rotary escalator, twin jackpot with eagle above, checkerboard **1,300-1,700.00**

L. E. SMITH GLASS COMPANY

Collecting Hints: L.E. Smith glass is hand made
and usually unmarked. Some older pieces bear
a "C" in a circle with a tiny "S." Current glass
has a paper label. The collector of older items
should especially study black and Depression
pieces. The Moon and Star pattern has been reproduced for many years. Smith glass of recent
manufacture is found in house sales, flea markets, and gift and antiques shops.

History: L. E. Smith Glass Company was founded
in 1907 in Mount Pleasant, Pennsylvania, by
Lewis E. Smith. Although Smith left the company
shortly after establishment, it still bears his name.
Early products were cooking articles and utilitarian objects such as glass percolator tops, fruit
jars, sanitary sugar bowls, and reamers.

In the 1920s, green, amber, canary, amethyst,
and blue colors were introduced along with an
extensive line of soda fountain wares. The company also made milk glass, console and dresser
sets, and the always popular fish-shaped aquar-
iums. During the 1930s, Smith became the largest producer of black glass. Popular dinner set
lines were Homestead, Melba, Do–Si–Do, By
Cracky, Romanesque, and Mount Pleasant.

L. E. Smith presently manufactures colored reproduction glass and interesting decorative objects. A factory outlet is available as well as factory tours. Contact the factory for specific times.

Reference: Hazel Marie Weatherman, *Colored
Glassware of the Depression Era 2*, Glassbooks,
Inc., 1982.

Animal
Cat, black, reclining, marked, c1930   **20.00**
Cow, black, reclining, marked, c1930   **18.00**
Dog, Scottie, black, reclining,
marked, c1930 .... **20.00**
Goose, black, reclining, marked,
c1930 .... **18.00**
Horse
Blue, rearing **35.00**
Crystal **20.00**
Green **38.00**
Rooster, black, reclining, marked,
c1930 .... **15.00**
Swan, small, white opaque **15.00**
Aquarium, 10" h, 15" l, green, King–
Fish, c1920 .... **250.00**
Ashtray, elephant, black **35.00**
Bonbon, ftd, handle
Cobalt blue **13.00**

Vase, black, molded dancing girls, made for F W Woolworth Co, 1930s, 7″ h, $15.00.

Green, #81	7.00
Bookends, pr, rearing horse	
Amber, 8″ h, c1940	42.00
Cobalt blue, 1930s	60.00
Crystal, 1930s	45.00
Bowl	
Amethyst, #77	8.00
Black, #515, 7″ d, ftd	20.00
Melba green, 10½″, ruffled	10.00
Cake Plate, Do–Si–Do, handles	12.00
Candlesticks, pr	
By Cracky, green	12.00
Mt Pleasant, black	15.00
Romanesque, pink	10.00
Casserole, 9½″ l, oval, Melba	12.00
Compote, cov, Moon n' Star, amberina	35.00
Cookie Jar, cov, black amethyst, floral	
dec	45.00
Cordial Tray, #381	
Green	9.00
Pink	9.00
Creamer	
Do–Si–Do	3.00
Homestead, pink	5.00
Moon n' Star, amberina	10.00
Cruet, Moon n' Star, ruby	30.00
Cup and Saucer	
Do–Si–Do, pink, gold trim	6.50
Melba, pink	4.50
Fairy Lamp, Moon n' Star, ruby	30.00
Fern Bowl, 3¾″ d, flower frog top,	
Greek Key rim dec, black	10.00
Flower Block, By Cracky, 3″	3.75
Flower Pot, 4″, black, silver floral dec	8.00
Goblet, water, Moon 'n Star, amberina	15.00
Mayonnaise, Kent	6.00
Mug, crystal, 12 oz	5.00
Parfait	
Homestead	5.00
Soda Shop	5.00

Planter, black amethyst, nude dancers	
on sides, marked "L. E. Smith"	**45.00**
Plate	
6″, Melba, amethyst	**4.50**
8″	
Homestead, pink	**4.50**
Mt Pleasant, pink, scalloped edge	**6.00**
9″, Homestead, grill	**5.00**
Rose Bowl, Mt Pleasant, cobalt, 3 ftd,	
rolled edges	**18.00**
Salt and Pepper Shakers, pr	
Dresden, white	**18.00**
Mt Pleasant, cobalt	**24.00**
Sherbet, Romanesque, black	**10.00**
Slipper, 2½″, Daisy and Button, amber	**4.00**
Soda Glass	
Jumbo, crystal, ribbed	**6.50**
Soda Shop	**6.00**
Sugar, cov	
Homestead	**5.50**
Kent	**6.50**
Melba	**6.00**
Moon n' Star, amberina	**12.00**
Tray, 15 x 6″, oval	
Black	**12.00**
Crystal	**10.00**
Vase	
5¾″ h, cobalt blue, stippled thumb-	
print	**7.50**
6″ h, black, #49	**13.00**
6½″ h, black, #102–4	**11.00**
7″ h, black, #433	**20.00**
7¼″ h, black, #1900	**20.00**
7½″, fan, Romanesque, black	**12.00**
7¾″ h, black, #405	**21.00**
Violet Bowl, Hobnail, white opaque ..	**7.50**
Window Box	
6¼″ l, white, Pan and dancing girls .	**9.00**
7¾″ l, black, #405	**21.00**
Wine	
Moon 'n Star, amberina	**12.00**
Ruby bowl, crystal stem	**5.00**

SNOWDOMES

Collecting Hints: Snowdomes are water-filled paperweights with figurines and/or panels inside a globe or dome, which are magnified by the water. The water contains loose particles (white snow, metallic or colored flecks, etc.) which swirl when the globe is turned upside down.

There are two distinctly different types of snowdomes. The first have round, leaded glass balls set on a base of ceramic, bakelite, or other plastic, wood or "marble." These are older and generally 3–4″ high. The second have plastic objects, in dozens of shapes ranging from simple designs such as drums, cubes, and bottles, to elaborate figurals. Production of this second type, which average 2½″ high, started in the 1950s.

Within both categories, especially the plastic,

there are many sub-groups and themes which appeal to collectors, e.g., Christmas (probably the most familiar), tourist souvenirs, Biblical scenes, Disney and other cartoon characters, commercial advertisements, fairy tales, scenic railroads, famous buildings, sailing ships, geographic regions, or one-from-each-state.

There is great variety not only in the subject of the inner image of snowdomes, but in the outer shapes as well. Collectors find it challenging to find as many of the dozens of shapes as possible.

Figurals are divided into two categories: first, the entire object is a figural, such as a house, apple, a bear, or seated cartoon character with the water ball incorporated into the design at different places, and second, a plastic figurine is placed on top of the dome. Christmas figurals alone constitute a large category. At least six different figurines of a standing Santa are known, to say nothing of the dozens of elaborate designs. Other novelty features include battery-powered flashing lights which illuminate the inner scene; salt and pepper snowdomes, perpetual calendars and banks designed in the base; and water/ring-toss games.

Many snowdomes have parts that move: a see-saw, bobbing objects attached to strings, and small objects that move back and forth on a groove in the bottom of the dome. Objects range from a ferry or bus to Elvis Presley.

The value of a particular snowdome depends on several factors, starting with the physical condition of the object itself. In dealing with glass domes it is important that the water is clear enough to see the object or is at a level which does not distort the image. Although it is possible to open and refill many of the older glass and ceramic or bakelite base styles, it is a risky procedure. Examine, also, whether the ceramic base is cracked, the condition of the label (if there is one), the condition of the figurine, and whether the paint has chipped or the colors seem faded.

The water level is not a factor in any plastic snowdome that has a plug either on the bottom of the base, or at the top of the dome. Bottle-on-its-side shapes cannot be refilled, and the domes designed by the Marx Company in the 1960s have safety plugs that cannot be removed. Safety caps on the plugs of snowdomes made for "Walt Disney Production" can be pried off with a knife point. Murky water can be drained and replaced. Clumped, dirty snow can be caught in a handkerchief, washed, and put back. While distilled water is preferred, tap water will stay clear for a year.

Of great importance is whether the front of the dome is free of streaking that may obscure the scene inside. Any cracks or holes would prevent re-filling with water.

While long-time collectors recognize common snowdomes, even new collectors can make an educated guess at scarcity by remembering a few key points. Snowdomes with a glass, ceramic, or bakelite base, single figurine, and no specific label on the base were the most common. The same figurine with a decal on the base saying "Souvenir of. . ." is more valuable as a smaller number were sold of that figurine with that particular decal. The same figurine was used for innumerable places, hence there is often no connection between the object and the place. An incongruous match-up may have value to a particular collector, but would not necessarily affect its market value. Of greater value are those snowdomes which were obviously made for a specific place or event, where the object and the decal match, e. g., the ceramic base snowdome with a bisque Trylon and Perisphere in globe, with a decal "1939 Worlds Fair."

Plastic snowdomes are also subject to the same principle of logic. "Generic" ones, without a name plaque, had the widest possible distribution.

Souvenirs of states and popular tourist attractions had a wide distribution. Since many more were made and sold their prices are lower than commemoratives or souvenirs of smaller places. SCARCITY, which can be determined by the size or popularity of a city or tourist attraction, is very important in pricing snowdomes and is a factor in the desirability of particular domes.

While mismatched figurines and decals of the glass/ceramic style should not be priced higher than logical match-ups, there are many examples of obvious mistakes in the plastic variety which are worth more than a perfect one, e. g., a dome with "Milano" printed upside down or a souvenir of a religious shrine with a "Kings Island" plaque.

The age of a plastic snowdome affects its value and can usually be determined by examining stylistic differences. It is often the style associated with a certain era that bears on its value, rather than the actual age itself. Generally, early snowdomes (1950s and 1960s) have greater detail and more sophisticated colors. Later snowdomes are less rich in detail and have a harsh, mass-produced appearance. Many early mass-produced snowdomes look as if they were hand-painted. Characters often have a "folk" quality to them. Most important, earlier snowdomes have much more specific detail. 1950s and 1960s state souvenirs have many panels inside depicting noted tourist attractions, famous citizens, and the state slogan. Later versions use only one feature. The newest mass-produced state souvenirs consist of a rainbow with a pot of gold and a glittery outline of the state's shape on a clear panel. There is no individuality.

The effects of time on snowdomes vary. A dome's physical deterioration, i. e., fading, chipping paint, even "bleaching" of the words on the plaque must be constantly evaluated by the collector. The plastic snowdomes that were introduced in the 1950s were fragile objects, easily broken, and often discarded. It is indeed a challenge to find unusual "survivors."

History: Snowdomes originated in mid–19th century Europe, particularly in France, where they evolved from the round, solid glass paperweights. By 1878 there were seven French manufacturers of snowdomes. They also were produced in what is now Germany, Austria, Poland, and Czechoslovakia, often in "cottage industries."

Snowdomes were widely popular during the Victorian era as paperweights, souvenirs, and toys. Early domes featured religious scenes and saints, tourist sites, and children and animals associated with winter or water. A variety of materials were used to create the "snow," ranging from ground porcelain and bone to rice. The figurines inside were made of carved bone, wax, porcelain, china, metal, or stone. The bases were made in a variety of shapes in many materials, including marble, wood, glass, and metal.

German companies exported their snowdomes to North America in the 1920s. The bases were blue cobalt glass and were occasionally etched with the name of a town or tourist attraction.

The first American patent was granted in 1927 to a design of a fish floating on a string among seaweed. The Novelty Pond Company of Pittsburgh was the manufacturer. Japanese companies soon copied the idea. Novelty and other American manufacturers used a black plastic base, either smooth or tiered; Japanese companies used a glazed brown ceramic base.

In addition to an enormous number of figurine designs, either painted or unpainted bisque, domes also featured Art Deco buildings, saints, and snow babies. Another design form consisted of a flat, rubberized insert showing a photograph of a tourist attraction, such as Niagara Falls or the Skyline Drive.

The Atlas Crystal Works was founded in the early 1940s to fill the void created by the unavailability of the popular glazed style which had been made in Japan. Atlas became the giant in the snowdome field, creating hundreds of different designs. Popular series included U.S. servicemen, servicewomen, and generals. Decals were added by towns and tourist attractions, creating some unusual matches, e.g., a skier from "Atlantic City."

Snowdomes also were manufactured in Italy in the late 1940s using a distinctive scalloped–shaped base covered with seashells and pebbles. The glass globe contains a flat rubberized panel with the name of the tourist attraction or Saint shown inside written on a shell on the base.

In the 1950s, the Driss Company, Chicago, Illinois, made four designs of popular characters—"Frosty the Snowman," "Rudolph the Red Nosed Reindeer in the Snow," "Davy Crockett," and "The Lone Ranger: The Last Round-Up"—with the decals on the base. The Davy Crockett and Lone Ranger domes used identical figurines, in identical poses, with different clothes and accessories. The Lone Ranger also was a ring-toss game, in which you looped his lasso over the calf's head. The Driss Company made many other "novelty" designs, such as an American flag with red, white, and blue "snow."

Progressive Products, of Union, New Jersey, created a variation of the classic snowdome in the 1940s and 1950s. They filled their glass ball with an oily liquid, either clear or yellow, and used a glittery "snow." They squared the base and widened it at the bottom, giving it a more angular, Art Deco look. In addition to their "generic" snowdomes with a single object inside, they made souvenirs with the name of a place written on the front of the base.

Their specialties, however, were awards and commercial advertisements. Many of the awards used a royal blue or red base with white trim around the bottom. One image could be adapted to many uses: a golden crown suspended in the liquid was used for a Winter Sports King, an ad for "Crown Termite Control," and a Baltimore newspaper. The same was true for a specific backdrop panel. There were three basic designs—an Art Deco city skyline, country landscape, and a Southwest Indian scene. A wide range of objects and images were placed inside the ball: trucks, ships, a Masonic symbol, faucet, a fishing boat used for seafood restaurants, and even a two-sided photo of a publishing house owner.

In the early 1950s three West German companies, using plastic, created small cubed or domed snowdomes. Koziol and Walter & Prediger, two of these companies, remain in business manufacturing hand painted domes with blizzards of white snow. Herr Koziol claims it was the "domed" view of a winter snow scene as seen through the rear window of a VW that inspired the shape. As a result of court action, Walter & Prediger gained the right to the dome shape and Koziol was restricted to the round ball shape.

The Erwin Perzy Company of Vienna, Austria, founded in 1900, creates glass snowdomes with traditional themes as Christmas and other holidays, snowmen, skiers, mountain chalets, clowns, bears, and sailboats. These have smooth black (or white) plastic bases and a red sticker that reads "Made in Austria."

The majority of plastic and glass snowdomes in the 1990s are made in the Orient. A few are produced in France and Italy. There are no American manufacturers, but rather dozens of large gift companies who design and import an array of styles, shapes, and themes. Enesco Corporation, Elk Grove Village, Illinois, is one of the largest.

Reference: Nancy McMichael, *Snowdomes,*
Abbeville Press, 1990.

Collectors' Club: Snow Biz, P.O. Box 53262,
Washington, D.C. 20009.

Advisor: Nancy McMichael.

**Advertising, left: "Crown Termite Con-
trol," 2¾" d glass ball with oily liquid, 3"
w x 4" h brown bakelite base, 1950s,
$35.00; right: "Jello," plastic dome, 3¾"
l, 2¾" w, 2½" h, 1970s, $12.00**

Advertising
  Heinz Ketchup, bottle, black lettered
    words "The Sign Of Good Eating"
    on front of white plastic dome, 2½"
    flat sides, "H & R Tomato Prod-
    ucts" printed on side of truck, oily
    liquid, 1950s 50.00
  News Post and American, printed
    gold letters on front, 5" l black plas-
    tic desk pen set, 2½" glass globe
    with figure of paperboy, oily liquid,
    1950s 60.00
  Newsweek, "No one covers the
    world like Newsweek" printed on
    red plastic base, large dome, 3½"
    l, 2½" w, 2¾" h, globe inside with
    floating plastic bars printed with
    "Newsweek" 15.00
  Nikon, camera company logo, small
    plastic dome 10.00
  Snow Tech/Larchmont Engineering,
    telephone number, man and snow-
    blowing machine, small plastic
    dome 10.00
Amusement Park
  Carowinds, 3" h, plastic dome, ski lift
    swinging from top, park scene ... 6.00
  Coney Island, glass globe, beach
    scene, shell encrusted scalloped
    shape base, marked "Made in It-
    aly," 1940s 30.00
  Great Adventure, 1½" plastic cube,
    three animals inside 5.00
  Heidi Park Soltau, Switzerland, small
    plastic dome, stage coach scene . 8.00
  Kings Dominion
    Large dome, figural lion on top .. 20.00
    Small plastic dome, Scooby Doo
     inside 6.00

Sea World, 5½" l, large bottle, dol-
    phin jumping thru hoop on a see–
    saw 6.00
The Enchanted Forest, 3" l, bottle,
    round sides, forest scene 6.00
Wildworld, plastic ball, red base,
    park scene, perpetual calendar ... 7.00
Ashtray, Empire State Building, black
    bakelite, 2¾" d glass ball, bisque fig-
    ure, tiered base, early 1940s 50.00
Award, title printed on front of flat,
    black 2½" base, 2½" glass globe, oily
    liquid
    Jiminy Cricket Award for Outstanding
     Community Chest Service–1958,
     figure of Jiminy with his award ... 80.00
    Winter Sports King, Brookfield Sau-
     sage Promotion January–1954,
     golden crown inside 55.00
Bank, coin slot on back
    Florida, beach scene, plastic ball, red
     base, flat sides, perpetual calendar 5.00
    Paris, pale blue plastic 8.00
Black, Watermelon Boy Down In New
    Orleans, gold decal on front of black
    ceramic base, heavy glass globe,
    painted figure of black boy eating wa-
    termelon, marked "Atlas Crystal
    Works, Covington, Tenn," 1940s ... 80.00
Bottle Shape
  Lying on side
    Flat side, Rhode Island, The Ocean
     State, plaque in neck, three other
     plaques and scenes 8.00
    Round, Atlanta Stadium, Atlanta,
     Georgia, two sportsmen on see–
     saw 8.00
  Upright
    Flat sides, Jamaica in neck, police-
     man inside, 5" h 9.00
    Round shape, Wales on plaque,
     woman in native costume inside,
     3" h 7.00
Boxed Set, Wild West Snow Scenes, 6
    Assorted by Marx," boxed set, small
    plastic domes, c1960, cowboy and
    Indian characters
    Sold individually 10.00
    Sold as set 100.00
Breweriana, Guinness, label on beer
    bottle and beer stein, 5" h blue plastic
    dome, int. plaque reads "Ireland,"
    1970s 15.00
Cartoon Character
  Dogpatch USA, 2⅜ x 2½ x¾", TV
    shape, plastic, brown, shows
    Mammy and Pappy Yokum, 1960s 12.00
  Flintstones, on plaque, Hanna Bar-
    bera Productions on other plaque,
    three characters in front of cave .. 15.00
  Kermit the Frog, 3½ x 3", sitting on
    brown trunk, clear dome, round

base, marked "Koziol" on bottom, 1980s **10.00**

Little Orphan Annie, 3⅝ x 2⅞ x 2¾", plastic dome, Annie and Sandy, 1970s **11.00**

Popeye, figural, seated, plastic, holds water ball between hands, Olive Oyl, Sweetpea, and Wimpy in row boat that moves, King Features Syndicate, 1950s **30.00**

Snoopy, 3¾ x 2½ x 2¾", lying on doghouse, clear sides, yellow, green, and orange base **5.00**

Ziggy, 3¾ x 3 x 4", raised letters, fuchsia base, hearts instead of snow **4.00**

Character

Davy Crockett, glass ball, decal and profile on base, marked "The Driss Co, Chicago, IL, Made in USA," late 1950s **50.00**

Elvis, singing into mike, rect shape, moves back and forth in front of Graceland mansion panel, Graceland plaque, 1970s **10.00**

Lone Ranger, round glass ball, bakelite base, green, yellow, and red, decal "Lone Ranger: The Last Round–Up" **40.00**

Marilyn Monroe, small red plastic dome, marked "Koziol" **30.00**

Christmas

Bell, clear, red church and pine trees, 1970s **7.00**

Elf, figural, red suit, green jester collar, ball in tummy, snowman, trees, and house scene, 1960s **15.00**

Fireplace, 3½ x 3¼ x 2¼", child sleeping in pajamas in hearth, Santa in sled on see–saw in dome, marked "CSA Inc, Curt S. Adler, Inc., NY, NY 10010," 1970s **15.00**

Frosty the Snowman, figural, 5½" h, standing black boots and top hat, removable broomstick, angel and deer in ball, 1960s **9.00**

Nativity Scene, 4½ x 3¼ x 3", round dome, eight panels, three dimensional figures, late 1950s **8.00**

Rudolph the Red Nosed Reindeer, green plastic base, "Rudolph the Red Nosed Reindeer in the Snow, copyright RLM" on decal, 1950s . **25.00**

Santa

Figural, 5¾ x 3½ x 1", driving sleigh, two reindeer, rect dome with elf sitting under a mushroom, 1960s **11.00**

Pivot, plastic, round dome, holding boy and girl, yellow bag of toys, marked "MCMLXVI" and "Louis Marx" **7.00**

Workshop, figural, red brick de-

sign, Mr and Mrs Claus work at workbench, rocking horse, marked "SANTA'S WORK-SHOP" on top **15.00**

Sled, 2¼ x 1¼ x 1⅝", Santa, tree with candles, and reindeer, green, brown, and orange, arch dome, orange snowflake plug, beige base, marked "Made in West Germany," 1950s **12.00**

Three snowmen, slanted eyes, red plastic base, seaweed trees, marked "Made in Japan," 1960s **8.00**

Disney

Bambi, plaque, television shape, marked "WDP," 1959 .... **25.00**

Disneyland, 2¾ x 2¼ x 2", plastic dome, Tinkerbell and castle, 1970s **10.00**

Mickey Mouse, figural, plastic, 5" h, holds 2" d ball in lap, castle scene, 1960s **30.00**

Pirates of the Caribbean, bottle shape, sq sides, three panels, "Disneyland copyright Walt Disney Productions" plaque **12.00**

Figural, left: Old Salts, plastic, 5½" h, 2¾" d water ball, 1970s, $12.00; right: Mickey Mouse, 5½" h, Disneyland in 2¾" d water ball, 1970s, $10.00.

Figural

Alligator, 5" h, ball is between hands and bent legs, two gators on see–saw, dark green, Florida plaque, 1970s **8.00**

Apple, red, green leaves, round white base, New York City plaque, 1980s **10.00**

Bird, on side of plastic ball, elongated base **15.00**

Church, steeple, 2¼ x 2¾ x 2½", plastic, altar, bride, and groom, marked "W Germany" on bottom, 1980s **15.00**

Dolphin, 4 x 2½ x 4½" dome, dolphin draped over dome, wave covered elongated base, Florida plaque, two dolphins on see–saw, 1970s **7.00**

Fish, 4 x 7", plastic, bright orange, green movable plastic fins, Florida plaque, 1970s **15.00**

Heart, red, gold letters, I Love NY, city skyline, 1980s **7.00**

Lantern, 4 x 2", movable handle on top, red frame, clear plastic on four sides, girl pulling sled, trees, 1980s **3.00**

Mermaid, 4 x 2½ x 4½" dome, mermaid draped over dome, wave covered elongated base, Weeki Wachi Spring, Florida plaque, water–skiers and boat in dome, 1970s .. **15.00**

Panda Bear, souvenir of Washington, DC **10.00**

Sea Captain, standing, 5½" h, 2½" d ball in middle, white beard, blue cap, orange shirt, movable pipe, Ocean City, Maryland plaque, sailing ships against clouds, 1970s .. **12.00**

Tiger, 3½" , two tigers in dome, "Southwick's Wild Animal Farm, Mendon, MA," 1970s **14.00**

Game, ring toss
Dolphin, 2½" h clear plastic dome, colored rings
Cape Hatteras plaque **7.00**
Florida plaque **5.00**
Without plaque **3.00**

Halloween
Cat, 6½" h, figural, black, 2¾" d orange plastic ball, witch riding broomstick **20.00**
Jack 'O Lantern, black cat, 3¾" d clear glass ball, wood base **5.00**
Owl, 5½" h, figural, brown, outstretched wing, scarecrow in 2¼" ball, orange ground **20.00**

Hotel
Hyatt at Palmetto Dunes Hilton Head, SC, 1½" plastic cube **8.00**
Kuwait International Hotel, phone and fax numbers also printed on ext. of white plastic base, 3" l, 1½" w, 2½" h **50.00**
Regency Hyatt House Atlanta Georgia, 3" h, plastic **5.00**

Indians
Family, Winchester, VA, in front of large tee pee, large plastic dome . **6.00**
Village, American, painted scene, brown bakelite base, oily liquid, late 1940s **20.00**

Moving Parts
Balloons on string, 3½ x 2¾ x 3", monkey swings on hook, four animals in cage, "Philadelphia Zoo," 1970s **10.00**
Champagne, shot, and martini glass on strings, 3¾ x 2¾ x 2¼", naked lady, painted "The Bar is Open" bar scene backdrop, "This one is

on me" plaque, "Las Vegas" on outside, 1960s **15.00**

Dice, 2⅝ x 2 x 2¼", red, float in water, blue ground, main strip in Vegas scene, 1970s **7.00**

Rocking Horse on glider, 3⅛ x 1¼ x 2⅝", toy soldier on his back, arched dome, black base, 1970s . **8.00**

Wagon, horse drawn, bottle shape, moves in and out of covered barn, large dome, "New Hampshire," 1970s **7.00**

Museum
Roy Rogers and Dale Evans Museum, Victorville, CA, plastic dome, barn scene and Trigger moves on slide, 1960s **10.00**
Salem Witch Museum, 1692, 2¾ x 2¼ x 2", small plastic dome, house and witch on broomstick, 1970s . **7.00**
The American Museum of Natural History, Hayden Planetarium, NY," 2¾ x 2¼ x 2", plastic dome, printing on back, camera and city skyline scene, 1980s **6.00**

Ocean Liner, glass ball, sq white base, *SS Independence*, blue lettering, ship in globe, Art Deco city skyline ground, oily liquid, 1940s **45.00**

Pencil Sharpener
Niagara Falls, large plastic dome, Maid of Mist moves in groove, standard pencil sharpener attached to bottom **6.00**
UFO shape, figural, pink plastic, pencil sharpener hole in side of space ship, domed top with space creatures floating in water, marked "Koziol" on bottom **10.00**

Regional
California Redwoods, large plastic dome with orange trees and deer . **6.00**
Cape Cod, MA, bottle shape, three sea captains in front of clouds, 1970s **8.00**
Florida, small plastic dome, fisherman and fish on see–saw **4.00**
Massachusetts, small dome with historic sites, 1960s **8.00**
Ohio, red bird in tree, yellow flowers, state outline on front, 1970s
Bottle shape **8.00**
Small dome **6.00**
Skyline Drive, VA, small plastic dome, two deer on see–saw **5.00**
West Virginia, large plastic dome, three dimensional bear figurine, 1960s **8.00**

Religious
Bethlehem, small plastic dome, Holy Family **10.00**
Crucifixion, 3⅝ x 2⅞ x 2¾", plastic

dome, Jesus on cross, battery operated, 1960s **15.00**
Holy Family and Atlantic City decals,
black ceramic base, glass globe,
three figures, 1940s **60.00**
Nativity Scene, small plastic dome,
1980s **3.00**
Noah's Ark, small plastic dome,
1970s **8.00**
The Resurrection, rounded dome,
Christ flanked by two sleeping soldiers, red ground, cut–out starburst
lights up, 1970s **10.00**
Salesman's sample, "Sample Sno–
Globe Tell–A–Story No. 2166–GLT"
printed in gold lettering on front, sq
black bakelite base, 2½" sides, 2½"
glass globe, office scene, clients looking at snowdome with company
name, oily liquid, 1950s **50.00**
Salt and Pepper Shakers, pr
Civil War, 3¼ x 1¼ x 2", plastic, pink
"P" with American flag, blue "S"
with Rebel flag, soldiers and cannon scene, back compartments,
1960s **14.00**
Florida's Silver Springs, 3 x 2¼ x 1",
TV shape, plastic, blue "P," pink
"S," boat on see–saw, side compartments, 1970s **12.00**
Mickey Mouse, inverted cone, clear,
cylinder in center **12.00**
Sea Shell Covered Base, glass ball sits
on scalloped shape base, cov with
pebbles and sea shells, St Anthony
figure inside, marked "Made in Italy"
on bottom **25.00**
Souvenir
Chinatown, NY, small plastic dome,
Oriental scene, 1960s **10.00**
Hearst Castle, large dome, two zebras
on see–saw in front of castle **8.00**

Hoover Dam, small plastic dome,
dice in water **8.00**
Story Land, plastic club, fairy tale
characters, 1960s **7.00**
Wisconsin Dells decal, glass globe,
tiered black plastic base, seaweed
and fish on strings inside, 1930s . **40.00**
World's Fair
1939, New York World's Fair
Administration Building, white bisque figure of building **75.00**
Trylon and Perisphere bisque figurine, brown ceramic base
With decal **60.00**
Without decal **50.00**
1964–65, New York World's Fair
Unisphere, plastic, round ball, red
sq base, perpetual calendar,
"Unisphere presented by USS
United States Steel, 1964
NYWF" **15.00**
1982, 3½ x 2 x 1¼", tall dome, Sun-
sphere **9.00**
1984, plastic dome, fair archway,
ferry moves back and forth on
groove, plaque **7.00**
World War II
Douglas MacArthur, America's Hero,
glass ball, black ceramic base, bisque bust **45.00**
General Eisenhower, glass ball, black
ceramic base, bisque bust, "General Dwight D Eisenhower, Commander in Chief, Allied Invasion
Forces" decal, marked "Atlas Crystal Works, Covington, TN, US Patents 231423/4/5," 1940s **60.00**
Plane, painted bisque figurine, red
star on wings, tail and nose markings, glass ball, black ceramic base,
marked "Atlas Crystal Works, Trenton, NJ, Patents Pending, Made in
USA," 1940s **45.00**

**Left: War Between the States, plastic
dome, 3¾" l, 2¾" w, 2½" h, 1970s, $5.00;
right: airplane, banking, painted bisque
plane, marking on wings, 2¾" d leaded
glass ball, 4" h ceramic base, 1940s,
$35.00.**

SODA BOTTLES

History: Soda bottles were made to contain soda
water and soft drinks. A beverage manufacturer
usually made his own bottles and sold them
within a limited area. Coddball stoppers and a
stopper perfected by Hutchinson were popular
with early manufacturers before the advent of
metal or screw top caps.

References: Paul & Karen Bates, *Commemorative Soda Bottles*, Soda Mart, 1988; Paul & Karen
Bates, *Embossed Soda Bottles*, Soda Mart, 1988;
Paul & Karen Bates, *Painted Label Soda Bottles*,
Soda Mart, 1988; Ralph & Terry Kovel, *The Kovels' Bottle Price List, Eight Edition*, Crown Publishers, Inc, 1987; Jim Megura, *The Official Iden-*

tification and Price Guide To Bottles, Eleventh Edition, House of Collectibles, 1991; Carlo & Dot Sellari, *The Standard Old Bottle Price Guide,* Collector Books, 1987.

Note: The books by Paul and Karen Bates are continually updated through a subscription service.

Periodical: *Antique Bottle And Glass Collector,* P. O. Box 187, East Greenville, PA 18041.

See: Coca–Cola, Moxie, and Soft Drink Collectibles.

Soda Water Works, Uniontown, PA, 7½ fluid oz, $9.50.

American Soda Works, trademark, Portland, OR, green	8.00
Arizona Bottling Works, aqua	8.00
Bartlett Bottling Works, clear	8.00
Boardman, ground pontil, blue	35.00
Boley & Co, Sacramento City, CA, cobalt	50.00
Borello Bros Co, Fresno, CA, crown top, aqua	5.00
Carbonating Apparatus Co, Buffalo, NY	15.00
Celery Cola, C under bottom, clear	5.00
City Bottling Works, Cleveland, OH, aqua	12.00
Coca Cola, Macon, GA, aqua	8.00
Concord Bottling Co, Concord, NH	8.00
Cottle Post & Co, Portland, OR, blob top, green	20.00
Deacon Brown Mfg Co, Montgomery, AL, aqua	7.50
Distilled & Aerated Water Co, Mitchell, SD	10.00
Dr Pepper, King of Beverage, Dallas Bottling Co, Dallas, TX	10.00
Empire Soda Works, Vallejo, CA, crown top	8.00
Ferber Bros, Phoebus, VA	8.00
Fleming Bros, Meadville, PA	10.00
Gaffney & Morgan, Amsterdam, NY, panel base	10.00
Great Bear Springs, Fulton, NY, round bottom	10.00

Headman, Philadelphia, PA, graphite pontil	**65.00**
Hewlett Bros, Salt Lake City, UT, aqua	**10.00**
Ingalls Bros, Portland, ME, squat type	**15.00**
Johnston & Co, Philadelphia, PA, blob top, green	**50.00**
Kroger Bros, Butte, MT, aqua	**12.00**
Lancaster Glass Works, NY, graphite pontil	**50.00**
Lyman Astley, Cheyenne, WY, aqua	**10.00**
Mason & Burns, Richmond, VA, blob top, green	**30.00**
Monroe Cider & Vinegar Co, Eureka, CA, clear	**8.00**
North Main Street Wine Co, Providence, RI, blob top, clear	**8.00**
Pepsi–Cola, Norfolk, VA, amber	**35.00**
Perry Mfg Co, Sonora, KY	**7.50**
Quinan & Studer 1888, Savannah, GA	**18.00**
Ryder, John, Mt Hollow, NJ, blob top	**15.00**
Sass & Hainer, Chicago, IL	**10.00**
Sioux Bottling Works, Watertown, SD, clear	**12.00**
Superior Soda Water, Davenport, IA, fancy shoulder, blue	**22.00**
Tampa Bottling Works, Tampa, FL, green	**8.00**
Tonopah Soda Works, Tonopah, NE, clear	**15.00**
Union Bottling Co, Wilmington, DE	**12.00**
Union Glass Work, Philadelphia, PA, graphite pontil, green	**55.00**
Virginia Fruit Juice Co, thick bottom, clear	**7.50**
Vogel Soda Water Co, St Louis, MO, squat, crown top	**8.00**
Wheeler Bros, Waukesha Soda Water Co, Waukesha, WI, slug plate, blob top, green	**10.00**

SODA FOUNTAIN AND ICE CREAM COLLECTIBLES

Collecting Hints: The ice cream collector competes with collectors in many other categories—advertising, glassware, postcards, food molds, tools, etc. Material still ranges in the twenty-five cent to $200 range.

When buying a tray, the scene is the most important element. Most trays were stock items with the store or firm's name added later. Always look for items in excellent condition.

History: From the late 1880s through the end of the 1960s the local soda fountain was the social center of small town America, especially for teenagers. The soda fountain provided a center for conversation and gossip, a haven to satisfy the mid-afternoon munchies, and a source for the most current popular magazines.

Ice cream items began to appear about 1870 and extend to the present. The oldest items are the cone shaped ice cream scoops. Beginning in the 1920s, manufacturers of ice cream began to issue premiums. These items are among those most eagerly sought by collectors.

References: Paul Dickson, *The Great American Ice Cream Book*, Galahad Books, 1972; Ray Klug, *Antique Advertising Encyclopedia*, Schiffer Publishing, Ltd, 1978; Ralph Pomeroy, *The Ice Cream Connection*, Paddington Press Ltd, 1975.

Collectors' Club: The Ice Screamers, 1042 Olde Hickory Road, Lancaster, PA 17601.

Museums: Greenfield Village, Dearborn, MI; Museum of Science and Industry, Finigan's Ice Cream Parlor, Chicago, IL; Smithsonian Institution, Washington, DC.

REPRODUCTION ALERT

ICE CREAM

Ashtray
Breyers, 90th Anniversary, 1866–
1956 .... **20.00**
Roxco Ice Cream, Rockford, IL, brass **15.00**
Book, *Theory and Practice of Ice Cream Making*, Hugo Sommer, 1938 ...... **25.00**
Booklet, Eskimo Pie, 2 pgs, premiums, 1952 .... **15.00**
Can
Abbott's Ice Cream, ½ gal, Amish girl, c1940 .... **15.00**
Graniteware, gray, 1 qt **40.00**
Carton, Batman Ice Cream, Slam–Bang Banana Marshmallow flavor, color graphics, unused, 1966 .... **52.00**
Catalog, Ice Cream Manufacturers' Equipment, 5¾ x 8¾", soft cov, 60 pgs, black and white illus, #31, Thos Mills & Bro, Inc, Philadelphia, early 1900s **65.00**
Cone Holder
Heisey, individual **50.00**
Vortex, patented 1916 .... **6.50**
Fan, Hoffman Willis Ice Cream Co, girl eating ice cream **15.00**
Freezer
Frost King, wood, galvanized metal . **40.00**
Kress, tin, patented July 23, 1912 .. **25.00**
Ice Chipper, Gilchrist, #50 .... **8.00**
Mold, pewter
Battle Ship, #1069 .... **48.00**
Bull, #223 .... **45.00**
Cannon, #273 .... **40.00**
Mars, #3251 .... **50.00**
Paper Doll, Carnation Ice Cream, 1950s **20.00**
Pinback Button
Semon Ice Cream, 1¼" d, red, white,

and gold, black lettering, "Semon Can't Make All the Ice Cream so He Makes the Best," early 1920s . **14.00**
Skippy Ice Cream, 1⅛" d, litho, red, white, and blue, 1930s **12.00**
Post Card
Bodle's Ice Cream Store, diecut **8.00**
Telling's Ice Cream **1.50**

Ice cream scoop, Erie Speciality Co, No. 10, Erie, PA, $70.00.

Scoop
Dover, brass **68.50**
Erie, round, size 8, aluminum **180.00**
Gilchrist, #30, size 8, polished **65.00**
No–Pak 31, size 5 .... **75.00**
Scoop Rite **15.00**
Sign
Crown Quality Ice Cream, tin, large wooden buckets of ice cream, lettering on side, 20 x 28" **125.00**
Jane Logan Ice Cream, tin **35.00**
Meadow Gold Ice Cream, porcelain, two sided **125.00**
Spoon, Borden's, silver plated **1.50**
Tape Measure, Cunningham's Ice Cream **15.00**
Thermometer, Harrington's Ice Cream, wood, 12" h **35.00**
Toy, truck, Sealtest Ice Cream, 3", litho tin, friction **10.00**
Trade Card
Dairylea Ice Cream, diecut, mechanical boy with cap, rolls eyes, 5" h, Germany **30.00**
Semon Ice Cream, diecut, frog, 14" l, printed both sides **25.00**
Tray
Furnace Ice Cream, girl holding serving tray, 1920s **150.00**
Hoefler Ice Cream, oval, woman eating ice cream **200.00**
Williams Ice Cream, 13½" d, mother and son at table **185.00**
Tumbler, Sealtest Ice Cream, 5¼" h, red label **10.00**
Wafer Holder
Reliance **165.00**
Tin, polished **100.00**
Watch Fob, Watson and Aven Ice Cream **45.00**

Whistle
Smith's Ice Cream, The Cream of Perfection, 4¾" **16.00**
Velvet Ice Cream, paper, 2⅛ x 3½" . **15.00**
Wrapper, Howdy Doody fudge bar, Standard Ice Cream Co **10.00**

Tip Tray, Binghamton Ice Cream Co, young lady, red kerchief, red border, "Everybody's Favorite," 6⅛ x 4⅜", $40.00.

SODA FOUNTAIN

Ashtray, Richland Snack Bar, tin **4.00**
Bin, counter, Quaker Brand Salted Peanuts, 9 x 13¾ x 4¼" **40.00**
Blackboard, Squirt, 15 x 30" **18.00**
Clock, Seven–Up, "You Like It, It Likes You," wood frame **75.00**
Dish, ice cream
Amber, banana split **12.50**
Elsie **15.00**
Display Case, countertop, Popcorn, wood and glass, hinged lid, 11 x 11" **45.00**
Display Rack
Beech–Nut Chewing Gum, 1920s .. **300.00**
Lance Candy, four shelves **15.00**
Door Pull, Drink Hire's, tin **50.00**
Fan, Goold's Orangeade, cardboard, wooden handle **15.00**
Hot Plate, commercial, Nestle's Hot Chocolate, 8" x 12" standing metal sign, red and white snowman graphics, late 1940s–early 1950s **95.00**
Jar, Borden's Malted Milk, glass label . **175.00**
Magazine Cover, *Saturday Evening Post,* young soda jerk talking to girls at counter, Norman Rockwell, Aug 22, 1953 .... **12.00**
Malt Mixer, Dairy Bar, metal, white Bakelite canister, logo **110.00**
Milk Shake Machine
Gilchrist, orig cup, c1926 .... **65.00**

Hamilton Beach, push down type .. **135.00**
Mirror, Horlicks Malted Milk, maid with cow **30.00**
Pinback Button
Hi–Hat Ice Cream Soda 10¢, 2¼" d, McCrory's, c1940 .... **15.00**
Sanderson's Drug Store, 1" d, blue and white, soda fountain glass illus, "Ice Cream Soda/Choice Cigars/ Fine Candies," 1901–12 .... **24.00**
Post Card, Gunther's Soda Fountain, Chicago **12.00**
Sign
Bowey's Hot Chocolate, black logo . **150.00**
Coca–Cola, fountain service, porcelain, diecut, shield shape **425.00**
Golden Rod Ice Cream, diecut, girl with ice cream **85.00**
Nehi, diecut, woman at marble soda fountain, sitting on wire stool, sipping through two straws, giant bottle on floor, Columbus, GA, 1920 **1,250.00**
Orange County Fountain, 24 x 18", porcelain on steel, yellow oval center, blue and white lettering, dark blue ground **100.00**
Soda Holder, metal, blue, ... **5.00**
Straw Jar, glass
Frosted Panel **225.00**
Green Panel **410.00**
Illinois, lid **450.00**
Red, metal lid, 1950s **175.00**
Syrup Dispenser Pump, Hires **135.00**
Thermomter, Hire's Root Beer, tin, bottle shape, 28½" **65.00**
Tin, Schraffts's Marshmallow Topping, 25 lbs **35.00**
Tray
Chero–Cola **65.00**
Pepsi Cola, Hits the Spot, 1940s ... **15.00**
Schuller's Ice Cream, 13 x 11", ice cream sodas and cones **200.00**

SOFT DRINK COLLECTIBLES

Collecting Hints: Coca-Cola items have dominated the field. Only recently have collectors begun concentrating on other soft drink manufacturing companies. Soft drink collectors must compete with collectors of advertising, bottles and premiums for the same material.

National brands such as Canada Dry, Dr. Pepper, and Pepsi-Cola are best known. However, regional soft drink bottling plants do exist, and their products are fertile ground for the novice collector.

History: Sarsaparilla, a name associated with soft drinks, began as a medicinal product. When carbonated water was added, it became a soft drink and was consumed for pleasure rather than medical purposes. However, sarsaparilla was only one type of ingredient added to carbonated water to produce soft drinks.

Each company had its special formula. Although Coca-Cola has a large market share, other companies provided challenges in different historical periods. Moxie was followed by Hire's which in turn gave way to Pepsi-Cola and 7-Up.

The 1950s brought soft drinks to the forefront of everyday life. Large advertising campaigns and promotional products produced a wealth of material. Regional bottling plants were strong and produced local specialities such as "Birch Beer" in eastern Pennsylvania. By 1970 most of these local plants had closed.

Many large companies had operations outside of the United States, which also produced a wealth of advertising and promotional materials. Today, the diet soda is a response to the American lifestyle of the 1980s.

Reference: Bill Vehling and Michael Hunt, *Pepsi-Cola Collectibles*, L–W Book Sales, 1986.

Collectors' Club: Pepsi-Cola Collectors Club, P. O. Box 1275, Covina, CA 91722.

See: Coca-Cola and Moxie.

Container, wax coated, Richardson Root Beer, Rochester, NY, 9¾" h, $8.00.

Badge, Dad's Root Beer, "Fastest Draw in the West" 30.00
Blackboard, Nehi, tin 75.00
Blotter, Pete & Pepsi, #709, 1930 .... 100.00
Book, adv
   Hire's Root Beer, *1940 Football Book*, schedules and rules, 40 pgs 28.00
   Hood's Sarsaparilla, palette shape, 1894 .... 30.00
Booklet, adv, Hire's Root Beer, fantasy, *The Legend of the Golden Chair*, 3½ x 5", 16 pgs, black and white illus, c1894 .... 6.00

Bottle, Pepsi, commemorative, University of Illinois, 1983 .... 5.00
Bottle Carrier, 7–Up, aluminum, twelve bottles 50.00
Bottle Opener
   Pepsi 5¢ 40.00
   7–Up, cast iron 15.00
Calendar
   Nehi, 1927, woman leaning on boat at beach 125.00
   Nu–Grape 45.00
Carrying Case, Uncle Joe's Soda, 1929 75.00
Catalog, Nehi premiums, baseball, pocket knives, watches, 1920s 22.00
Chair, wood, folding, red, "Drink Coca–Cola in Bottles," white stencil, c1923 .... 245.00
Clock
   Dr Pepper, bottle cap 60.00
   Royal Crown Cola 90.00
   Sun Crest Orange 35.00
Coupon, Hire's Root Beer, Good For One Stein or Glass, St Louis Fair ... 28.00
Dispenser, child's, 7-Up Uncola 20.00
Door Plate
   Canada Dry, bottle 45.00
   Pepsi, tin 38.00
Kaleidoscope, 2½" d, 4¾" h, cardboard canister, tin lid, Pepsi can shape, red, white, and blue, copyright 1981 ... 14.00
Match Holder, Dr Pepper 5.00
Miniature Bottle, Canada Dry, 3½", c1950 .... 5.00
Mirror, Hire's Root Beer, oval, Victorian lady with roses 80.00
Pin Tray, Dr Pepper, 3", oval, black boy eating watermelon illus 275.00
Pinback Button, Fresh Up Freddie, 7–Up adv, 1⅜" d, litho, multicolor, cartoon bird illus, 1950s 15.00
Poster, Orange Crush, 12 x 18", cardboard, woman wearing swimsuit beach 32.00
Puzzle, Hood's Sarsaparilla Rainy Day Puzzle 35.00
Radio, Pepsi, cooler shape, orig box, 1960s 320.00
Record, Pepsi–Cola, WW II serviceman's, orig envelope 20.00
Salt and Pepper Shakers, 7–Up, orig box, pr 4.00
Sign
   Dad's Root Beer 85.00
   Dr Pepper, porcelain, 10½ x 26" ... 125.00
   Dr Swift's Root Beer, diecut, girl holding drinks, asking for ride, boy in pedal car, tongue hanging out ... 375.00
   Hire's Root Beer, tin 175.00
   Nehi, paper, woman's legs, bottle, 1920s 35.00
   7–Up, diecut, grocer with bottles ... 85.00
   Squirt, tin, yellow, flange 110.00

Wonder Orange, tin, colorful	**150.00**
Thermometer	
Dr Pepper, round	**80.00**
Frosty Root Beer, Frosty illus	**75.00**
Hire's, bottle shape, diecut	**78.00**
Pepsi	
1950s, 7 x 27", with bottle cap	**65.00**
1960s, "Say Pepsi Please"	**50.00**
Sun Drop Cola	**65.00**
Token, Moxie, 1¼", aluminum, Good	
For One Drink, c1900	**15.00**
Toy Truck, Canada Dry–Special Sparkle, 4" l	**25.00**
Tray, Hire's Root Beer, boy, Just What the Doctor Ordered, 1914	**385.00**

SOLDIERS, DIMESTORE

Collecting Hints: Soldier figures are preferred over civilian figures. The most valuable figures are the ones which had short production runs, usually because they were less popular with the youthful collectors of the period.

O'Brien and Pielin use numbering systems to identify figures in their books. Newcomers should study these books, taking note of the numerous variations in style and color.

Condition, desirability and scarcity establish the price of a figure. Repainting or rust severely reduces the value.

Auction prices often mislead the beginning collector. While some rare figures have sold in the $150 to $300 range, most sell between $10 and $15.

History: Three dimensional lead, iron, and rubber soldier and civilian figures were produced in the United States by the millons before and after World War II. These figures were called "Dimestore Soldiers" because they were sold in "Five and Dime" stores of the era, the figures usually costing a nickel or dime. Although American toy soldiers can be traced back to the early 20th century, the golden age of the Dimestore Soldier was 1935 until 1942.

Four companies—Barclay, Manoil, Grey Iron and Auburn Rubber—mass produced the three–inch figures. Barclay and Manoil dominated the market, probably because their lead castings lent themselves to more realistic and imaginative poses than iron and rubber.

Barclay's early pre–war figures are identifiable by their separate glued–on and later clipped–on tin hats. When these are lost, the hole in the top of the head always identifies a Barclay.

The Manoil Company first produced soldiers, sailors, cowboys, and Indians. However, the younger buyers of the period strongly preferred military figures, perhaps emulating the newspaper headlines as World War II approached. Man-

oil's civilian figures were made in response to pacifist pressure and boycotts mounted before the war began.

Figures also were produced by such companies as All–Nu, American Alloy, American Soldier Co., Beton, Ideal, Jones, Lincoln Log, Miller, Playwood Plastics, Soljertoys, Tommy Toy, Tootsietoy, and Warren. Because of the short lived nature of these companies, numerous limited production figures command high prices, especially those of All–Nu, Jones, Tommy Toy, and Warren.

From 1942 through 1945 the wartime "scrap drives" devoured tons of the dimestore figures and the molds that produced them.

In late 1945 Barclay and Manoil introduced modernized military figures, but they never enjoyed their pre–war popularity. "Military operations" generally were phased out by the early 1950s. Similarly, the civilian figures could not compete with escalating labor costs and the competition of plastic.

References: Richard O'Brien, *Collecting Toy Soldiers: An Identification and Value Guide*, Books Americana, 1988; Don Pielin, *American Dimestore Soldier Book*, privately printed, 1983.

Periodicals: *Old Toy Soldier Newsletter*, 209 N. Lombard, Oak Park, IL 60302; *Toy Soldier Review*, 127 74th Street, North Bergen, NJ 07047.

REPRODUCTION ALERT. Some manufacturers identify the newer products; many do not.

Notes: Prices listed are for figures in original condition with at least 95% of the paint remaining. Unless otherwise noted, uniform colors are brown.

Civilian figure, Barclay, young boy, $10.00.

CIVILIAN FIGURE

Auburn Rubber
Baseball **20.00**
Football **20.00**
Barclay
Boy Scouts
    Frying eggs **28.00**
    Saluting **20.00**
    Signaling **25.00**
    With walking staff **18.00**
Civilian Figures
    Fireman
        With axe **18.00**
        With hose **20.00**
    Little girl in coat **7.00**
    Mailman **9.00**
    Minister holding hat **10.00**
    Newsboy **9.00**
    Railway porter, black **12.00**
    Redcap with bag, black **15.00**
    Train mechanic **10.00**
    Woman with dog **9.00**
Cowboys
    Cowboy
        Mounted, firing pistol **15.00**
        With lasso **10.00**
    Indian
        Kneeling with bow and arrow .. **8.00**
        Mounted, with rifle **23.00**
Winter Figures
    Man
        On sled **12.00**
        Pulling children on sled **18.00**
    Santa Claus on skis **38.00**
    Skaters **9.00**
Grey Iron
American Family Series, 2¼" h ..**3.00-20.00**
Western
    Cowboy, mounted on bucking
        bronco **20.00**
    Indian
        Mounted **17.00**
        Shielding eyes **14.00**
        With hatchet **9.00**
Manoil
Happy Farm Series
    Blacksmith
        Making horseshoes **15.00**
        With wheel **20.00**
    Darky eating watermelon **58.00**
    Farmer
        Carrying pumpkin **13.00**
        Cutting with scythe **18.00**
    Lady
        Laying wash on grass **20.00**
        With child **14.00**
        With pie **19.00**
    Man
        Chopping wood **17.00**
        Juggling barrel **30.00**
    Man and woman on bench **17.00**

Scarecow **13.00**
Watchman blowing out lantern ... **20.00**
Western
    Cowboy
        Hands raised **12.00**
        One gun raised, flat base **10.00**
    Indian with knives **12.00**

Soldier, Barclay, machine gunner, $15.00.

MILITARY FIGURE

Auburn Rubber
Bugler **8.00**
Cavalry officer **25.00**
Charging with Tommy gun **9.00**
Grenade thrower **10.00**
Machine guner, kneeling **9.00**
Marching with rifle **7.00**
Motorcycle with sidecar **28.00**
Motorcyclist **20.00**
Soldier
    Kneeling with binoculars **8.00**
    Searchlight **28.00**
    Sound detector **27.00**
Barclay, pod foot series
Post War, pot helmet
    Flagbearer **20.00**
    Machine gunner, prone **18.00**
    Standing, firing rifle **12.00**
    Tommy gunner **15.00**
Pre-World War II
    Bugler **13.00**
    Cameraman, kneeling, tin hat **18.00**
    Cavalryman **25.00**
    Chinese rifleman, tan **65.00**
    Crawling with rifle, tin hat **14.00**
    Doctor, in white, treating soldier,
        duplex **48.00**
    Drum major, tin hat **15.00**
    Drummer, tin hat **12.00**
    Flagbearer, tin helmet **12.00**
    Machine gunner, kneeling, tin hat **10.00**

Motorcyclist, in cap	18.00
Nurse, kneeling with cup, white	14.00
Parachutist, landing	15.00
Pilot, standing	9.00
Prone	
Long binoculars, tin hat	13.00
Machine gunner	13.00
Short binoculars, tin hat	55.00
Sailor	
Marching, rifle, white	9.00
Signal flags, white	18.00
Skier, in white, no skis	12.00
Sniper, rifle, prone, tin hat	14.00
Soldier	
Anti-aircraft gun	12.00
Dog, tin hat	25.00
Peeling potatoes	16.00
Standing behind searchlight	15.00
Tommy gunner, standing, tin hat	12.00
Two soldiers on raft, paddle	50.00
Grey Iron	
Cavalry officer, mounted	22.00
Doughboy	
Charging	9.00
Supporting wounded soldier	65.00
Drummer	13.00
Ethiopian Soldier	
Charging, tan	25.00
Shoulder arms, tan	22.00
Grenade thrower	14.00
Kneeling	
With binoculars	10.00
With rifle	14.00
Radio operator, kneeling, no antenna	20.00
Rifleman	
Bayoneting	15.00
Over head	16.00
Sailor, signal flags, white	15.00
Signalman, flags overhead	17.00
Ski Trooper, white	15.00
Stretcher bearer	20.00
Walking, ammunition boxes	18.00
Wounded on crutches	18.00
Manoil	
Post War, pot helmet	
Flagbearer	16.00
Kneeling	
Bazooka	17.00
Mine detector	20.00
Machine gunner, standing	16.00
Marching, rifle	13.00
Sniper, firing in air	25.00
Post War, 2½" size, mkd "U. S. A."	
Aviator, holding bomb	18.00
Bazooka	17.00
Binoculars	13.00
Flagbearer	22.00
Machine gunner, shooting upward	20.00
Marching	15.00
Sniper, kneeling	18.00
Pre-World War II	
Aviator	

Carrying bomb sight, looking up	17.00
Propeller next to head	55.00
Boxer	65.00
Cameraman, flash overhead	32.00
Camouflaged soldier in the grass, rifle	17.00
Crawling, pistol, arm outstretched	35.00
Deep Sea Diver, silver	15.00
Digging trench	27.00
Drummer, vertical drum	18.00
Flagbearer	14.00
Firefighter, "Hot Papa," gray	58.00
Gas mask, flare pistol	15.00
Lineman, telephone pole	45.00
Looking Up, searchlight	18.00
Machine Gunner, prone, white	32.00
Nurse, white, red dish	10.00
Paymaster, foot on strongbox	75.00
Sailor	
Firing deck gun, white	14.00
Signal flags, white	18.00
Seated	
At table, map	15.00
Eating with spoon	20.00
Writing letter, cigarette in mouth	52.00
Tightening large shell	22.00
Two man machine gun team	15.00
Wounded, standing, arm in sling	13.00

SOLDIERS, TOY

Collecting Hints: Consider three key factors: condition of the figures and the box, the age of the figures and the box, and the completeness of the set.

Toy soldiers were meant as playthings. However, collectors consider them an art form and pay premium prices only for excellent to mint examples. They want figures with complete paint, all moving parts, and additional parts.

The box is very important, controlling 10 to 20% of the price of a set. The style of the box is a clue to the date of the set. The same set may have been made for several decades. The older the manufacture date, the more valuable the set.

Sets have a specific number of pieces or parts. They must all be present to have full value. The number of pieces in each set, when known, is indicated in the listings below.

Beware of repainted older examples and modern reproductions. Toy soldiers still are being manufactured, both by large companies and private individuals. A contemporary collection may prove a worthwhile long-term investment, at least for the next generation.

History: The manufacture of toy soldiers began in the late 18th century by individuals such as the Hilperts of Nuremberg, Germany. The early figures were tin, pewter or composition. By the late 19th century companies in Britain (Britain, Courtenay), France (Blondel, Gerbeau and Mignot), and Switzerland (Gottschalk, Wehrli) were firmly established. Britain and Mignot dominated the market into the 20th century.

Mignot established its French stronghold by purchasing Cuperly, Blondel and Gerbeau who had united to take over Lucotte. By 1950 Mignot had 20,000 models representing soldiers from around the world.

Britain developed the hollow cast soldiers in 1893. Movable arms also were another landmark. Eventually bases were made of plastic, followed finally by the whole figure in plastic. Production ceased within the last decade.

The English toy soldier was challenged in America in the 1930 to 1950 period by the dimestore soldiers of Barclay, Manoil, and others. Nevertheless, the Britains retained a share of the market because of their high quality. The collecting of toy soldiers remains very strong in the United States.

References: Peter Johnson, *Toy Armies*, Forbes Museum, 1984; Henry I. Kurtz & Burtt R. Ehrlich, *The Art Of The Toy Soldier*, Abbeville Press, 1987; Richard O'Brien, *Collecting Toy Soldiers: An Identification And Value Guide*, Books Americana, 1988; Art Presslaff, *Hitler's Army of Toy Soldiers Featuring Elastolin, Lineol, & Tipco, 1928–40: A Price Guide*, published by author, 1987; James Opie, *Britain's Toy Soldiers, 1893–1932*, Harper & Row, 1986; John Ruddle, *Collectors Guide To Britains Model Soldiers*, Argus Books Ltd, 1980.

Periodicals: *Old Toy Soldier Newsletter*, 209 North Lombard, Oak Park, IL 60302; *Toy Soldier Review*, 127 74th Street, North Bergen, NJ 07047.

Collectors' Club: American Model Soldier Society, 1528 El Camino Real, San Carlos, CA 94070.

REPRODUCTION ALERT

Britain, Types of the Turkish Army, Turkish Infantry, $300.00.

Authenticast, Russian Infantry advancing with rifles at the ready, 2 officers carrying pistols and swords, no box, 14 .... **65.00**
Blenheim
  B2, Coldstream Guards Colors, 1812, 2 color bearers, escort of 4 privates, orig box, 6, mint, box excellent .. **115.00**

B17, Royal Marines, 1923, marching at the slope, officer, sword at carry, orig box, 6, mint, box excellent .. **75.00**
B63, Royal Company of Archers Colors, 2 color bearers, escort of 4 privates, orig box, 6, mint, box excellent **90.00**
C13, 17th Lancers, 1879, foreign service order, officer, bugler, and trooper with lance, orig box, 3, mint, box excellent **150.00**
U. S. Naval Academy Color Guard, 4 standard bearers, escort of 2 midshipmen, orig box, 6, mint, box excellent **100.00**
Britain, sets only
  7, British Soldiers, The Royal Fusiliers, City of London Regiment ... **135.00**
  24, 9th Queen's Royal Lancers, mounted on the trot, slug lances and officer, no box, 6, excellent . **130.00**
  27, Band of Line, full instrumentation and drum major, late pre–WW II set, retied in orig "Types of the World's Armies" box, 12, excellent, box good **200.00**
  31, King's Dragons, pre war **100.00**
  48, Egyptian Camel Corps, mounted on camels, detachable riders, tied in orig box, 5, mint, box excellent **80.00**
  55, Royal Marines **100.00**
  100, Empress of India's Twenty–first lancers, 1903, box excellent **225.00**
  101, Band of the Life Guard, mounted in state dress, kettle drummer and bandmaster with baton, retied in orig box, 12, excellent to mint, box excellent **450.00**
  147, Zulus of Africa, charging with spears and knobkerries, tied in orig box, 5, mint, box excellent **135.00**
  177, Austro–Hungarian Infantry of the Line, marching slope arms, orange and red kepi and trousers, 6, excellent condition **150.00**
  195, British Infantry, battle dress and steel helmets, marching at the trail, officer carrying swagger stick, orig box, 8, excellent, box excellent .. **125.00**
  201, General Staff Officers, mounted, field marshall, general officer and 2 aides–de–camp, tied in orig box, 4, mint **200.00**
  229, U. S. Cavalry Service Dress, olive uniform, bare handed swords at saddle, three brown, two black horses, 5, very good condition ... **75.00**
  1426, St John Ambulance, stretcher bearers and casualty, excellent ... **115.00**
  1470, Her Majesty's Stage Coach, 8 Windsor Greys, Queen Elizabeth II

and Prince Philip, 10, excellent, orig Historical Series box, excellent **250.00**

1519, Waterloo Highlanders, standing at attention with muskets, 9, very good condition **175.00**

2017, British Army Ski Troops, white uniforms, no box, 4, excellent . . . **350.00**

2032, Red Army Infantry, summer uniform, May Day Parade pose, rifle with fixed bayonet, both arms move, 10, very good condition . . **85.00**

2039, The Life Guards, mounted and foot sentries, tied in orig box, 6, mint, box excellent **90.00**

2092, Seaforth Highlanders, pipers, 1953, tied, box excellent **200.00**

2094, State Open Landau, drawn by 6 Windsor grays, Queen Elizabeth II and Prince Philip, tied in orig box, 13, mint **220.00**

2099, Venezuelan Military School Cadets, marching at the slope, officers and standard bearer, no box, 15, very good condition **165.00**

9144, Royal Welsh Fusiliers, marching at the slope, officer and goat mascot, orig box, 7, excellent, box good **100.00**

9216, 9th Queens Royal Lancers, black uniform, standing horses, slung lance, excellent condition . . **125.00**

9301, Royal Company of Archers, Queen's Bodyguard of Scotland, long skirted coats, cap with feather, 14 . . . . **250.00**

9307, Sovereigns Standard of The Life Guards and Escort, trumpeter in state dress, farriers and corporals of The Royal Horse Guards, orig box, 8, mint, box good **175.00**

9406, Mounted Band of the Lifeguards, state dress, musicians on horseback, gold and maroon jackets, matched, boxed set, excellent condition **550.00**

9482, U. S. Marines Color Party, 2 flagbearers, escort at shoulder arms, dress blues, excellent condition, box excellent **235.00**

Elastolin/Lineol

Flak Gunner, blue and gray uniform, kneeling with shell, very good condition **40.00**

Medic, walking, helmet, big pack with red cross **35.00**

Nurse, attending wounded, kneeling, holds foot of soldier sitting on keg, excellent condition **40.00**

Staff Officer, pointing, field glasses, aristocratic pose **35.00**

Heyde

Chicago Police, 1890s, on foot with

billy clubs, including policeman with dog, standard bearer and mounted policeman, 11, very good **220.00**

French Ambulance Unit, horse drawn ambulance, 2 horse team, rider with whip, stretcher bearers, stretchers and casualties, mounted and foot medical officers and medical orderly, orig box, 14, very good, box fair **280.00**

Hessian Infantry, 1777, marching at the slope, officers, standard bearer, four mounted dragoons, movable reins on horses, no box, 19, good **375.00**

German Infantry, WW I, attacking with fixed bayonets, officer with extended sword, no box, 11, very good **90.00**

U. S. Army World War I Pontoon Train, 4 horse drawn pontoon wagons, pontoon boats, engineer detail on foot with mounted officer, orig display box, 24, very good, box poor **470.00**

Mignot

Band of the 3rd Regiment of Dutch Grenadiers, 1812, body guard to King Louis Napoleon Bonaparte of Holland, full instrumentation, bandmaster, tied in orig box, 12, mint, box excellent **350.00**

French Ambulance, set 1512, drawn by 4 horse team, horse handler, driver with whip, orig box, excellent, box excellent **220.00**

French Cuirassiers, 1914, marching dismounted carrying swords, officer, bugler and standard bearer, orig box, 12, excellent **75.00**

French Line Infantry, 1914, marching at the slope, trumpeter, standard bearer and officer, orig box, 12, excellent, box excellent **80.00**

French Sailors, 1914, marching at the slope, blue uniforms, officer bugler and standard bearer, orig box, 12, mint to excellent, box excellent . . **175.00**

Julius Caesar's Chariot, drawn by four galloping horses, mounted on base, scenic backdrop, orig box, 6, mint, box excellent **225.00**

Prussian Grenadier, 1800, assaulting, drummer, standard bearer and officer, c1955, no box, 12, very good **130.00**

602, Circus Display Set, 4 seated musicians, standing conductor with baton, clowns, show horses, trainer with whip and others, tied in orig box, 12, mint, box excellent **200.00**

8th Bavarian Regiment, 1812, marching at the slope, blue uniforms, plumed helmets, officer, drummer, and standard bearer, tied in orig box, 12, mint, box excellent **150.00**

Militia Models

Gatling Gun Team of 3rd London Rifles, Gatling gun and gunner, 2 ammunition carriers, officer holding binoculars, orig box, 5, mint, box excellent **90.00**

The Pipes and Drums of 1st Battalion Royal Irish Rangers, limited edition, pipe major and 4 pipers, 2 snare and 2 tenor drummers, drum major, orig box, 11, mint, box excellent . **125.00**

Nostalgia

1st Gurkha Light Infantry, 1800, red and blue uniforms, marching with slung rifles, officer with sword at the carry, orig box, 8, excellent, box excellent **80.00**

Kaffrarian Rifles, 1910, gray uniforms, plumed pith helmets, marching at the trail, officer with sword at the carry, orig box, 8, mint, box excellent **125.00**

New South Wales Irish Rifles, 1900, marching at the trail, officer holding sword at the carry, orig box, 8, mint, box excellent **95.00**

New South Wales Lancers, 1900, marching carrying lances on the shoulder, khaki uniforms, trimmed in red and plumed campaign hats, officer holding swagger stick, orig box, 8, mint, box excellent **85.00**

S. A. E.

1358, Royal Horse Guards, 1945, mounted at the halt with officer, orig box, 6, mint, box excellent . . **50.00**

1761, French Cuirassiers, mounted at the walk, orig box, 6, mint, box excellent **85.00**

3310, 1st Bengal Lancers, at the halt, orig box, 6, mint, box excellent . . **115.00**

SOUVENIR & COMMEMORATIVE ITEMS

Collecting Hints: Most collectors of souvenir and commemorative china and glass collect items from a region which is particularly interesting to them—a hometown, birthplace or place of special interest such as a President's home. This results in regional variations in price, because a piece is more likely to be in demand in the area it represents.

History: Souvenir and commemorative china and glass date to the early fairs and carnivals when a small trinket was purchased to take back

home as a gift or remembrance of the event. Other types of commemorative glass include pattern and milk glass made to celebrate a particular event. Many types of souvenir glass and china originated at the world's fairs and expositions.

During the 1900s it became popular to have souvenir plates made for churches and local events such as centennials, homecomings, etc. These plates were well received because of their local interest. Collectors search for them today because they were made in a limited number. Many show how the area changed architecturally and culturally.

Reference: Bessie M. Lindsey, *American Historical Glass,* Charles E. Tuttle, 1967; Frank Stefano, Jr., *Wedgwood Old Blue Historical Plates and Other Views of the United States Produced for Jones, McDuffe & Stratton Co., Boston, Importer, A Check–List With Illustrations,* published by author, 1975.

Periodical: *Travel Collector,* P.O. Box 475, Marion, WI 54950.

Collectors' Club: Souvenir China Collectors Society, Box 562, Great Barrington, MA 01230.

Canoe, milk glass, white, red, yellow, green, and black lettering, 3⅝" l, $10.00.

Axe, 4", "Cut Out the Whiskey, Laurel Stove Detroit," Carrie Nation, 1901 . **25.00**

Bank, 6", Las Vegas, slot machine, marked "Mills High Top," 10¢ **65.00**

Book, *Guys & Dolls,* broadway/stage, 1950s **30.00**

Booklet, Yosemite Visitor's Guide, 32 color photos **8.00**

Bottle

Deadwood, SD **95.00**

Dodge City **25.00**

Bowl, Centenary M E Church, South Bonne, Terre, MO, 6", scalloped edge, blue tint **12.00**

Card Folder, Yellowstone Park, 1928 . . **5.00**

Comb, hair bun, pictures Golden Gate Bridge, wood **6.00**

Compact, Empire State Building, Art Deco **35.00**

Creamer

St James, MN **25.00**

The Flume, Franconia Notch, NH, left handed **25.00**

Creamer and Sugar, Cambridge Springs, Georgia Gem, breakfast size, custard glass 90.00
Corkscrew, Widmers Wines, Naples, NY, wood 15.00
Frying Pan, Beach, ND, glass 12.00
Fur Clip, Beckman Bros, Great Falls, MT 25.00
Hair Receiver, "Souvenir of Bev, MA," Austria 25.00
Ink Blotter, Yellowstone Park, metal ... 35.00
Invitation, Norris Locomotive Works, employees annual ball, emb, 1860s 35.00
Loving Cup, 3½" h, Oneonta, NY, ruby to clear, gold trim, two handles 45.00
Match Box, Niagara Falls, SS 100.00
Mug
　Ottawa, IL, 3", Star & Punty Band pattern, custard glass, gold trim 35.00
　Saratoga Springs, NY, 5½", frosted, weighted bottom, horses crossing finish line and spouting spring illus, 1950s 20.00
Paperweight
　Apollo II, 4", venetian glass, brass back, limited edition #1969/50,000 .... 45.00
　Old South Church, Boston, MA, 4 x 2½", glass, brown tone photo scene 18.00
Pencil Box, Alaska, snap closure, pyrography of Eskimo totem pole 13.00
Pipe and Match Holder, Hot Springs, AR, glass, cobalt blue 22.50
Pitcher
　Conneaut Lake, pressed glass 52.00
　Post Office, Kawanee, IL, 3½", brightly colored, white ground ... 15.00

Plate, milk glass, reticulated border, 5½" d, $20.00.

Plate
　City Meat Market, Leonardsville, KS, sheep 35.00
　Clark House, Lexington, MA, four sided, 5" 12.00
　Fort Duquesne, Pittsburgh, PA, La Francaise Porcelain, 1764 .... 28.00
　Ocean Pier & Fun Chase, Wildwood, NJ, 4", pierced border 8.00

Perry Centennial, 10½", 1913, Cauldon 28.00
St Lawrence Seaway, 10", green, Wedgwood 50.00
Theodore Roosevelt, Rowland and Marcellus 60.00
Ring, Yellowstone Park, brass, enameled bear 15.00
Salt and Pepper Shakers, pr, The Baker Hotel, Mineral Wells, TX, hp 18.00
Syrup Pitcher, Fisherman's Mem, Gloucester, MA, underplate 25.00
Tea Set, Niagara Falls, hp scenic transfers, Stadler 120.00
Token
　Jerome, AZ 35.00
　Pearce, AZ 65.00
　Sing Sing Prison 25.00
Toothpick Holder, Marshalltown, Iowa, ruby flashed 18.00
Tray, Gettysburg Battlefield, 1863, oval, 16½" 45.00
Tumbler
　Pearl Harbor 10.00
　Saratoga Springs, 1901, pewter 8.00
Vase
　Camp Lake View, Lake City, MN ... 12.00
　Seven Falls, Cheyenne, cobalt, cannon, elaborate handles 20.00
　Sawyer, WI 42.00

SOUVENIR & COMMEMORATIVE SPOONS

Collecting Hints: When collecting souvenir spoons be aware of several things: condition, material, subject, and any markings, dates, etc. Damaged spoons should be avoided unless they are very rare and needed to complete a collection. Some spoons have enamel crests and other decoration. This enameling should be in mint condition.

History: Souvenir spoons are mementos of special events, people, and places of interest. The peak of spoon collecting was reached in the late 1800s. During that time two important patents were issued. The first patent was issued on December 4, 1884, to Michael Gibney, a silversmith in New York who patented the first design for flatware. The other important patent was the first spoon design which commemorated a place. That patent was given to Myron H. Kinsley in 1881 for his spoon of Niagara Falls. The spoon showed the suspension bridge and was the first of many spoons to be made showing Niagara Falls.

Spoons depicting famous people soon followed with the issue of May, 1889, showing

George Washington. That was followed by the issuance of a Martha Washington spoon in October of 1889. These spoons, made by M. W. Galt of Washington, D.C., were not patented, but were trademarked in 1890.

Spoon collecting is enjoying a comeback today with many new spoons being made for souvenir and commemorative purposes.

References: Dorothy T. Rainwater and Donna H. Felger, *American Spoons, Souvenir and Historical*, Everybodys Press, Inc., 1977; Dorothy T. Rainwater and Donna H. Felger, *A Collector's Guide To Spoons Around The World*, Everybodys Press, Inc., 1976; *Sterling Silver, Silverplate, and Souvenir Spoons With Prices*, L–W Books, 1988.

Periodical: *Spoony Scoop Newsletter,* 84 Oak Avenue, Shelton, CT 06484.

Collectors' Club: American Spoon Collectors, 4922 State Line, Westwood Hills, KS 66205.

Note: Spoons listed below are sterling silver teaspoons unless otherwise noted.

New Orleans, LA, Canal Street, sterling silver, 5⅜" l, $20.00.

Anita Stewart	35.00
Art Palace, 1893 Columbian Expo	65.00
Atlantic City, NJ	28.00
Avon, figural, Indian and corn on handle	45.00
Battle Monument, Trenton, NJ	25.00
Ben Franklin, Philadelphia	40.00
Bermuda, palm trees in bowl, enameled crest on handle	40.00
Brooklyn Bridge, bridge in bowl, state seal on handle	35.00
California	25.00
Calvin Coolidge	35.00
Canada	25.00
Canadian Flag, Knights of the Garter Crest	20.00
Centralia, WA, figural handle, miner, demitasse	30.00
Charley McCarthy, SP	15.00
Chief Seattle, totem pole	22.00
Cincinnati, emb monument in bowl, twisted handle	25.50
Colorado, Seven Falls, pierced handle	25.00
Columbus, bust, plated	15.00
Columbus, OH, state capitol	30.00

Coney Island, skyline	25.00
Delmont, SD, figural wheat and leaves on handle	35.00
Denver Columbine handle	16.50
State Capitol in bowl, flower handle	35.00
Duba, Morro Castle	40.00
Eastern Star	25.00
El Camino Real, CA, cut out handle	25.00
Florida, cut out enameled oranges on handle	25.00
Fort Dearborn	12.00
Fort Sumter, emb view of St Michael's Church on handle	45.00
Fredericton, New Brunswick, spiral handle, gold wash bowl	30.00
Friendship 7, capsule orbiting earth in bowl, raised John F Kennedy portrait on handle, SP	25.00
Golden Gate, San Francisco	30.00
Gorham's Salt Lake City, woman blowing trumpet	25.00
Harriet Beecher Stowe	32.50
Huckleberry Hound, SP	8.00
Hudson River Steamboat, Rip Van Winkle handle	25.00
Indianapolis, Soldier's & Sailor's Monument	18.00
Iron Mountain, MI, flowers and leaves handle	35.00
Jackson Monument	45.00
Jamestown Expo	35.00
Joplin, Mo, full figure miner handle	60.00
Lake Worth, Palm Beach, FL	58.00
Lakewood, NJ, Cathedral Drive view in bowl, state seal on handle	30.00
Madison, WI	10.00
Marshalltown, IA, plain handle	25.00
McKinley Monument, cut–out buffalo handle	40.00
Mickey Mouse, SP	20.00
Minnehaha Falls, MN	23.00
Montreal, enameled maple leaves on handle	30.00
Mt Rainer, Seattle, WA, totem pole handle with Chief Seattle head on top	30.00
Mt Vernon	10.00
Mt Washington, Tip Top House view, 1853 on handle	25.00
New York Peace Monument, Lookout Mountain, TN, picture bowl	25.00
New York World's Fair, mines and mining, 1939	20.00
Niagara Falls, Indian head handle	30.00
Norma Sherer	35.00
Notre Dame	110.00
Old Hickory, Jackson Monument	55.00
Oroville, CA, gold dredger in bowl, state seal on handle	30.00
Palm Springs Aerial Tramway, SP, John Brown, marked "Antico"	100.00
Pittsburgh, Ft Pitt	38.00

Portland, ME, Longfellow's house, emb,
  portrait handle **60.00**
Quebec, open work handle **15.00**
Queen Elizabeth, 1953 Coronation ... **15.00**
Riviere Du Loup, entwined handle,
  marked "Canada" **35.00**
Rochester, NY **35.00**
Ryan, Rt Rev Archbishop, 25th Anni-
  versary, beaded handle **25.00**
San Antonio, TX **28.00**
San Francisco, Mission Dolores 1776,
  bear on dec handle, gold bowl **35.00**
Santa **35.00**
Saugatuck, MI **15.00**
Seattle World's Fair, 1962 .... **22.00**
Settle Memorial Church, Owensboro,
  KY **25.00**
Skagway, AK **32.00**
St Augustine, Old City Gates, emb
  bowl, emb oranges on handle **20.00**
Statue of Liberty, Tiffany **60.00**
Susan B Anthony **45.00**
Teddy Roosevelt, riding horse, full fig-
  ure handle **85.00**
Thomas Jefferson **35.00**
Toronto, Canada, enameled crest on
  handle **25.00**
Union Station, emb design in bowl ... **30.00**
Virginia, fancy bowl and handle **20.00**
Waggner, SD, enameled floral handle . **50.00**
Washington, DC
  Capitol **28.00**
  McKinley handle **26.00**
Wausau, WI, 1890 .... **50.00**
Whittier's Birthplace, Haverhill, MA,
  emb handle **18.00**
Wichita, KS Post Office **20.00**
William Penn, Independence Hall **58.00**
William Sherman **40.00**
Yacht **20.00**
Yogi Bear, SP **8.00**

SPACE ADVENTURERS AND EXPLORATION

Collecting Hints: There are four distinct eras of fictional space adventurers—Buck Rogers, Flash Gordon, the radio and television characters of the late 1940s and 1950s, and the Star Trek and Star Wars phenomenon. Condition is not as major a factor in Buck Rogers material, because of its rarity, as it is in the other three groups. Beware of dealers who break apart items and sell parts separately, especially game items.

In the early 1950s a wealth of tin, battery operated, friction, and wind-up toys, not associated with a specific Space Adventurer, were marketed in the shape of robots, space ships, and space guns. They are rapidly gaining in popularity.

The "Trekies" began holding conventions in the early 1970s. They issued many fantasy items, which must not be confused with items issued during the duration of the TV show. The fantasy items are numerous and have little value beyond the initial selling price.

The American and Russian space programs produced a wealth of souvenir and related material. Beware of astronaut signed material that may contain printed or autopen signatures.

History: In January, 1929, "Buck Rogers 2429 A.D." began its comic strip run. Buck, Wilma Deering, Dr. Huer, and Killer Kane, a villain, were the creation of Phillip Francis Nowlan and John F. Dille. The heyday of Buck Rogers material was 1933 to 1937 when products such as Cream of Wheat and Cocomalt issued Buck Rogers items as premiums.

Flash Gordon followed in the mid-1930s. Buster Crabbe gave life to the character in movie serials. Books, comics, premiums, and other merchandise enhanced the image during the 1940s.

The use of rockets at the end of World War II and the beginnings of the space research program gave reality to future space travel. Television quickly capitalized on this in the early 1950s with programs such as Captain Video and Space Patrol. Many other space heroes, such as Rocky Jones, had short-lived popularity.

Star Trek enjoyed a brief television run and became a cult fad in the early 1970s. *Star Trek: The Next Generation* already has an established corps of watchers and the first collectibles are appearing. *Star Wars* (Parts IV, V, and VI) and *ET* produced a wealth of merchandise which already is collectible.

In the 1950s, real life space pioneers and explorers replaced the fictional characters as the center of the public's attention. The entire world watched on July 12, 1969, as man first walked on the moon. Although space exploration has suffered occasional setbacks, the public remains fascinated with its findings and potential.

References: Sue Cornwell and Mike Kott, *The Official Price Guide To Star Trek and Star Wars Collectibles, Second Edition,* House of Collectibles, 1986; Chris Gentry and Sally Gibson-Downs, *An Encyclopedia of Trekkie Memorabilia: Identification and Value Guide,* Books Americana, 1988; Don and Maggie Thompson, *The Official Price Guide To Science Fiction and Fantasy Collectibles, Third Edition,* House of Collectibles, 1989; T. N. Tumbusch, *Space Adventure Collectibles,* Wallace–Homestead, 1990.

See: Robots and Space Toys.

Buck Rogers
  Atomic Pistol, 10" l, blued metal bar-
    rel, gold finish, sparking, Daisy Mfg
    Co, c1946 .... **100.00**

THE CITY BEYOND THE CLOUDS

THE GREAT MARVEL BOOKS
ROY ROCKWOOD

Book, Roy Rockwood, *The City Beyond The Clouds,* Cuppes & Leon Co, New York, 1925, $9.50.

Attack Ship, #1033, 5" l, cast metal, orig box, Tootsietoy, 1930s **420.00**
Battlecruiser, #1031, 5" l, cast metal, orig box, Tootsietoy, 1937 .... **367.00**
Big Little Book, *Buck Rogers and the Depth Men of Jupiter,* Whitman, #1169, 1935 .... **65.00**
Board Game, TransOgram, 1965 ... **98.00**
Century Destroyer, #1032, 5" l, cast metal, orig box, Tootsietoy, 1930s **434.00**
Communications Outfit, 25th Century, Remco **250.00**
Flash Blast Attack Ship, Tootsietoy, 1930s **135.00**
Kite, orig pkg **39.00**
Pencil Box, 10½" l, cardboard, action illus on dark green ground, mid 1930s **95.00**
Pictures, Magic Erasable Dots, sealed, 1950s **35.00**
Pin, brass **50.00**
Pinback Button, 1" d, club member, "Buck Rogers in the 25th Century," c1935 .... **50.00**
Puzzle, Marauder, #3 of series, Milton Bradley, orig sealed box, Universal City Studios copyright 1979 **15.00**
Rocket Pistol, 25th Century, 9½" l, metal, blued and silvered, Daisy Mfg Co, late 1934 .... **125.00**
Sonic Ray Gun, 7½" l, plastic, black, yellow, and red, orig box, Norton–Honer, 1952 .... **180.00**
Space Ship, Morton's Salt premium, umbrella girl on bomb sight, orig pkg **75.00**
Venus Duo–Destroyer, 5" l, blue and white, orig box, Tootsietoy, 1930s **120.00**

Captain Video
Playset, Superior Space Port, litho tin building, nine litho tin wall sections, gateway, space cannon, 14 plastic figures, nine ships, plastic pcs marked "Captain Video," complete **225.00**
Poster, movie **325.00**
Pressbook, 7½ x 10½", 4 pgs, glossy, black and white, "Captain Video/ Hero of Outer Space" promotion, Columbia Pictures, 1958 .... **50.00**
Rocket Tank, 1940s, MIB **40.00**
Secret Ray Gun, 3½" l, Power House candy bar premium, orig instructions **65.00**
Tom Corbett
Belt, child's, leather, black and silver, repeated "Space Cadet" and illus, leather slide attachment, mint on card, 1950s **75.00**
Book, punch–out, *Tom Corbett Space Cadet,* 10½ x 14", 6 pgs, Saalfield Publishing Co, unused, Rock Hill Productions copyright 1950 ...... **60.00**
Coloring Book **30.00**
Compass, wrist band **69.00**
Disk, plastic, red, black and white flasher, "Space Cadet Rocket Ship" **15.00**
Lunch Box, thermos **125.00**
Molding and Coloring Set, Kay Stanley's Model–Craft, 7 rubber molds, watercolor palette, paint brush, orig box, early 1950s **75.00**
Patch, 4" l, fabric, stitched Space Cadet name and symbol, Kellogg's premium **45.00**
Playset, Space Academy, Marx **250.00**
Record, Rescue in Space, 78 rpm, RCA Victor label, Little Nipper series, orig album cov, Rockhill Productions copyright 1952 .... **20.00**
Ring, "Space Cadet Dress Uniform" **15.00**
Watch, Tom Corbett Space Cadet, 1" d dial, Corbett and rocket illus, black, white, red, and yellow, red lightning bolt hands, orig illus straps, 1950s **200.00**
Flash Gordon
Big Little Book, *Flash Gordon in the Water World of Mongo,* Whitman, #1407, 1937 .... **70.00**
Compass, wrist, 1950s, mint on card **40.00**
Dixie Picture, 8 x 10", stiff paper, Buster Crabbe photo **50.00**
Poster, movie, "Flash Gordon Conquers the Universe," chapter 11, Stark Treachery, 27 x 41", black, white, and red, 1973 .... **50.00**
Record, City of Sea Caves, 6½" d, 78 rpm, cardboard, color illus, clear plastic recordings both sides,

#F301A, Record Guild of America, copyright 1948 .... **35.00**

Spaceship, 3" l, metal, diecast, blue, white accents, LJN Toys, orig pkg, copyright 1975 .... **12.00**

Space Patrol

Bubble Helmet, collar **950.00**

Catalog **175.00**

Coin, 1¼" d, plastic, metallic blue, "Terra/Interplanetary Space Patrol Credits" **12.00**

Cosmic Smoke Ray Gun, 6" l, plastic, metallic green, fires smoke puffs, early 1950s **175.00**

Dart Gun, 9½" l, plastic, red, black and white trim, logo, 1950s **85.00**

Emergency Kit, 7 x 7 x 2" plastic case, gray and white, raised lettering and illus, two slide out trays, bandages, tape, space emergency rations, space sickness pills, cosmic ray pills, complete, Regis Space Toys, early 1950s **800.00**

Handbook, *Space Patrol Handbook*, 4½ x 6", 16 pgs, black and white illus, 1950s **90.00**

Helmet, 21" d, 11" h, plastic, inflatable blue vinyl neck and shoulder protectors, window front and back, ear holes, logo decal, marked "Commander," rubber oxygen intake tubes, orig box, early 1950s . **650.00**

Lunar Fleet Base, Ralston premium, copyright 1952 .... **175.00**

Microscope **165.00**

Party Plates, 8½" sq, paper, spaceships and planets illus, sealed, 1950s, set of 6 .... **28.00**

Projector, Space Patrol Terra V, rocket shape, 5½" h, hard plastic, blue and yellow, 1950s **200.00**

Ring, 1¼" l, siren, silvered white metal, Japan, 1950s **150.00**

Script, television program #544, 8½ x 11", 16 pgs, April 10, 1952 .... **90.00**

Sheet Music **35.00**

Slides, Stori–View, cast portraits, color, copyright Space Patrol Enterprises, set of 6, 1950s **98.00**

Super Beam Signal Ray Gun, 8" l, plastic, red, white, and blue, marked "Official Space Patrol," Marx, 1950s **175.00**

Wristwatch, ⅞" d, silvered chrome, black lettering, military time, orig band, US Time, early 1950s **175.00**

Star Trek

Astrocruiser, 9" l, orig box, Remco, copyright 1967 .... **90.00**

Board Game, Hasbro, complete, 1974 .... **50.00**

Book, action toy cut out, uncut **25.00**

Bowl and Mug, plastic, "The Motion Picture," 1979 .... **20.00**

Cards, set of 88, complete, 1979 ... **35.00**

Carrying Case, 10½ x 16 x 10", vinyl, USS Enterprise flight deck, Mego Corp, copyright 1975 .... **85.00**

Costume, Mr Spock, mask, Paramount Pictures, 1975 .... **55.00**

Doll, Klingon **18.00**

Folio, Star Trek Blueprints, 12 sheets, 9 x 30", complete Enterprise layout, Ballantine Books, Franz Joseph Designs copyright 1973 .... **15.00**

Jet Disk Tracer Scope, 18" l, plastic, metallic gold, white handle, 100 plastic jet disks, orig box, Ray Line, copyright Desilu Productions 1968 **95.00**

Lunch Box **40.00**

Mobile, Enterprise, paper, orig envelope **35.00**

Photo, television series, autographed, cast, 8 x 10", glossy, black and white **100.00**

Program Book, International Convention, 1973 .... **55.00**

Starship, inflatable **25.00**

Tracer Gun, 7" l, plastic, blue and black, red jet discs, orig blister pkg, Grand Toys, Montreal, Canada, copyright 1966 .... **55.00**

Vulcan shuttle and Sled, replica, 8" l, plastic, detachable space craft, docking stand, decal sheet, orig box, Airfix, Paramount Pictures Corp copyright 1980 .... **50.00**

Star Wars

Alarm Clock, talking, MIB **75.00**

Belt, Darth Vader, boxed **20.00**

Book, pop–up **12.50**

Bottle, Star Wars Luke Skywalker Shampoo, 9" h, soft plastic body, hard plastic head, orig contents, sealed, story booklet, Omni Cosmetics Corp, Lucasfilm Ltd copyright 1981 .... **12.00**

Card Set, 2½ x 3½", color photo front, text and puzzle piece back, Topps, 66 cards, 20th Century Fox Film Corp copyright 1977 .... **15.00**

Clock, MIB **110.00**

Cookie Jar, R2D2 .... **65.00**

Costume, C–3PO, Ben Cooper, orig box, 20th Century Fox Film Corp copyright 1977 .... **25.00**

Game, Escape from Death Star, Kenner, 10th Century Fox Film Corp copyright 1977, complete **15.00**

Helmet, Darth Vader, Don Post, orig box, 1977 .... **90.00**

Model Kit **25.00**

Poster, orig movie **90.00**

Radio, R2–D2 .... **75.00**

Rebel Armored Snow Speeder Vehicle, remote operated landing gear, detachable cannon and guns, sealed orig box, Kenner, Lucasfilm Ltd copyright 1982 .... 15.00

Roller Skates, Return of the Jedi/Darth Vader, child's size 3, black, red trim, laces and wheels, Darth Vader and royal guard illus, orig box, Brookfield Athletic Shoe Co, Lucas Film Ltd copyright 1983 .... 24.00

Sigma Mug, Luke Skywalker 22.00

Sneakers, child's size 5½, Star Wars shoelaces, Darth Vader illus, orig illus box and punch–out sheet, Stride Rite, Lucasfilm Ltd copyright 1982 .... 12.00

Watch, windup, Bradley 75.00

SPACE EXPLORATION

Ashtray, Apollo 11, 3¼" d, glass, clear dark green, gold trim, official insignia, set of 4 .... 15.00

Autograph
Garriot, Owen, First Day Cover 12.00
Irwin, James, 3 x 5" card, quarter moon illus 30.00
Resnick, Judy, 3 x 5" card 85.00

Bank, replica space capsule
Metal, copper bronze finish, marked "United States" 40.00
Plastic, 4½" h, gold colored, inscribed "Authentic Replica of First US Spacecraft," "Astronaut Capsule/Project Mercury/Redstone/Atlas," and "Pioneer Astronaut Flights," Independent Bank, Orange County 25.00

Book, Conquest of the Moon, 8 x 11", soft cov, 64 pgs, Wonder Book, Apollo 11 photos and illus, 1969 ... 17.00

Calendar, 9½ x 11", spiral bound, wall hanging, commemorates Apollo 11, moon landing illus, Sept 1969 to Aug 1970 sheets, complete 15.00

Cards, educational, 3 x 6", stiff paper, NASA photos and illus, orig box, Gelles–Widmer copyright 1963, set of 48 .... 52.00

Clock, moon landing illus, Florn, Germany, dated July 20, 1969 .... 75.00

Coin, Apollo 14, official mission insignia symbol and names on front, moon landing illus on back 12.00

Coin Set, Man in Space, 8 x 10" recessed display card, space galaxy photo illus, 21 different 1" d brass coins, copyright 1969 .... 32.00

Coloring Book, Apollo/Man on the Moon, 8½ x 11", Saalfield, July 20, 1969 moon landing illus, unused ... 15.00

Decanter, commemorative, Apollo 11, ceramic, space capsule shape, 1967 35.00

Figure, John Glenn, 16½" h, stiff paper, jointed 23.00

Glass, Mercury Spacecraft/Cape Canaveral, 5½" h, clear weighted bottom, frosted light blue top, silver and orange spacecraft and galaxy illus, souvenir, early 1960s 35.00

Key Chain, coin, Freedom 7, aluminum, brass plated, raised capsule illus, dated May 5, 1961, Pledge of Allegiance, issued by AMVETS 12.50

Lunch Box, Space Shuttle Challenger, vinyl, copyright 1982 .... 65.00

Magazine, Life, 10½ x 13½", 136 pgs, recovery photo cov, 10 pg article, Alan Shepard first US space flight, black and white photos, May 12, 1961 issue 14.00

Model Kit, Edwin "Buzz" Aldrin's space walk, Aurora Plastics Corp, #409–100, orig box and instructions, complete, unassembled, c1966 .... 60.00

Paperweight, John Glenn Flight Commemorative, 2" h, solid aluminum, Friendship 7 replica, engraved "John Glenn Jr Feb 20, 1962" 50.00

Patch, "Teacher in Space," 3½ x 4", woven fabric, official Challenger Space Shuttle insignia symbol 13.00

Pennant, 7 x 17½", felt, white, red and blue illus and lettering, 3" black and white Glenn photo, commemorates Feb 20, 1962 first US orbital space flight 40.00

Photograph, autograph, Alan Shepard, 8 x 10", c1962 .... 45.00

Pinback Button
1¼" d, Lunar Contact, white lettering, aqua blue ground, c1969 .... 10.00
1¾" d, John Glenn, celluloid, black and white photo, red, white, and blue border, gold lettering on purple ribbon 28.00
2½" d, Columbia/Young, Crippen, celluloid, white ground, multicolor illus, 1981 .... 4.00
3½" d, Gordon Cooper, celluloid, commemorates 22 orbits around Earth, black and white photo, red rim, 1963 .... 20.00

Plaque, Apollo 11, 15" d, plaster, raised moon landing illus, "Small Step, Giant Leap" inscription, dated July 1969 .... 40.00

Plate, First Moon Landing, 7" d, white china, Apollo 11 lunar module illus, astronaut facsimile signatures, Crown Ducal, England 15.00

Puzzle
Astronauts of Apollo 11, Milton Brad-

ley, Aldrin, Collins, and Armstrong color portrait illus, orig sealed box, copyright 1969 .... **30.00**

Journey to the Moon, jigsaw, Life puzzle series, 13 x 20", magazine cover photo illus, orig box and 29 x 40" poster, copyright 1969 ..... **20.00**

Record, The Eagle Has Landed/First (Man on the Moon), 45 rpm, pressed one side, WLW Radio, AVCO Broadcasting Corp, orig jacket **14.00**

Ring, flasher, Michael Collins, plastic, blue **10.00**

Spoon, commemorative
Friendship 7, 6" l, silverplated, capsule bowl illus, raised John F Kennedy handle illus, vertical lettering, Wm Rogers, c1963 .... **25.00**

Moon Landing, 6¼" l, silverplated, names Armstrong, Aldrin, and Collins engraved in bowl, geometric floral design and moon landing illus handle, inscribed "Apollo 11/July 20, 1969/Man on the Moon," orig box, Holland **20.00**

Thermos, 7¼" h, litho metal, ivory plastic cap, rocket scene illus, commemorates John Glenn flight **28.00**

Tie Bar, Freedom 7, metal, gold colored, space capsule illus, unmarked, early 1960s **20.00**

Tray, moon landing, 5 x 6¾", dark clear glass, gold and white design and inscriptions, commemorative moon plaque illus **15.00**

View Master Reel Set, US Spaceport, NASA JFK Space Center, orig envelope and catalog sheet, set of 3 .... **13.00**

SPACE RELATED

Book
Andy Astronaut, 6½ x 16", hard cov, Golden Press, 24 pgs, copyright 1968 .... **12.00**

Into Space With the Astronauts, 8 x 11", soft cov, Wonder Book, 48 pgs, 1965 .... **15.00**

Man in Flight, 8 x 11", soft cov, Saalfield, 48 pgs, 1962 .... **17.00**

Bracelet, silvered metal, ¾" oval plastic inset, spaceman photo, 1950s spacesuit **18.00**

Clock, alarm, animated, steel case, glossy black enamel, orbiting spacecraft illus, digital numerals, Westclox of Scotland, 1960s **180.00**

Coin, space, Schuler's Potato Chips, 1⅜" d plastic frame, color litho paper illus insert, set of 5 .... **22.50**

Coloring Book, Rockets and Space,

Treasure Books, 65 pgs, unused, copyright 1960s **15.00**

Comic Book, "The Outer Limits," Dell, April 1963 .... **2.50**

Crayon Box, spaceship shape, cylinder, stiff litho cardboard, enameled wood nosecone, diecut porthole openings reveal multiplication tables **20.00**

Flashlight
7" l, "Space Boy Siren–Lite," red, white, blue, yellow, and green illus of spaceman holding gun, planets, rocket ships, c1950 .... **30.00**

8" l, "Captain Ray–O–Vac Rocket Ship," bright red, chrome ends, decal of spaceman with battery body soaring through space, colorful box, MIB **38.00**

Game
Moon Flight, Avon Products, complete, orig box, 1970 .... **20.00**

Operation Rescue Game, Citation Products, red, white, and blue cardboard insert gameboard and pcs, color illus on front of box, 1963 .... **40.00**

Globe, The Moon, 6" d, metal, metal base, Repogle Globes, c1969 ..... **75.00**

Key Chain, 2¼", multicolored plastic rocket, puzzle type, c1950 .... **18.00**

Lighter, space rocket shape, 5½" h, chrome colored, red, and black plastic, tabletop model, "Miners National Bank," 1950–60s **28.00**

Mask, face, diecut paper, black, white, blue, yellow, and red, cut outs for eyes, simulated ear pcs, lightning bolt design and red light at top, elastic headband, adv for Manyunk, PA store **12.00**

Mug, 6½" h, ceramic, white, green New York Times illus, July 21, 1969 "Men Walk on Moon" edition, ESB Brands Inc **20.00**

Needle Case, "Rocket," 3½ x 6", diecut cardboard, full color illus of giant needle flying through space, starry ground, planet Saturn in distance, marked "Made in Occupied Japan," orig needles, unused **15.00**

Pencil, mechanical, 3" l, red, plastic, rocketship, brass nosecone, brass key chain, c1950 .... **8.00**

Planter, space explorer, figural, 5½" d, 5" h, china, toddler wearing space uniform, white, pink and blue accents, late 1960s **24.00**

Pocket Knife, 3½" l, bright yellow plastic knife, rocketship shape, working siren whistle in nosecone, brass key chain loop, c1950 .... **35.00**

Record, The Space Story, 12" d, 33⅓ rpm, NASA Radio Presentation, 1976 **12.50**

Stamp Album, 5½ x 8¼", Science Service, Washington DC, Doubleday, 64 pgs, early 1970s **8.00**

Tin, candy container, 6" d, Riley's Toffee, litho tin, Riley Bros, Halifax, England, two children in space outfits, moonscape, c1950 .... **25.00**

SPACE TOYS

Collecting Hints: The original box is an important element in pricing, perhaps controlling 15 to 20% of the price. The artwork on the box may differ slightly from the toy inside; this is to be expected. The box also may provide the only clue to the correct name of the toy.

The early lithographed tin toys are more valuable than the later toys made of plastic. There is a great deal of speculation in modern toys, e.g., Star Wars material. Hence, the market shows great price fluctuation. Lloyd Ralston Toys, Fairfield, Connecticut, is a good barometer of the auction market.

Collect toys in very good to mint condition. Damaged and rusted lithographed tin is hard to repair. Check the battery box for damage. Don't ever leave batteries in a toy after you have played with it.

History: The Hollywood movies of the early 1950s drew attention to space travel. The launching of Sputnik and American satellites in the late 1950s and early 1960s enhanced this fascination. The advent of man in space culminating with the landing on the moon made the decade of the 1960s the golden age of space toys.

The toy industries of Japan and America responded to this interest. Lithographed tin and plastic models of astronauts, flying saucers, spacecraft and space vehicles followed quickly. Some were copies of original counterparts; most were the figments of the toy designer's imagination.

The 1970s saw a shift in emphasis from the space program and a decline in the production of science fiction-related toys. The earlier Japanese and American-made products gave way to cheaper models from China and Taiwan.

References: Teruhisa Kitahara, *Yesterday's Toys, Robots, Spaceships, and Monsters,* Chronicle Books, 1988; Crystal and Leland Payton, *Space Toys,* Collectors Compass, 1982; Stephen J. Sansweet, *Science Fiction Toys and Models,* Vol. 1, Starlog Press, 1980.

Note: Any rocket related toy, whether military or space, is included in this category. The following abbreviations are used:

SH = Horikawa Toys
TM = K. K. Masutoko Toy Factory
TN = Nomura Toys
Y = Yonezawa Toys

See: Robots and Space Adventurers and Exploration.

REPRODUCTION ALERT

Capsule, Friendship 7, litho, tin, and plastic, red and silver, pilot moves around and handles controls, marked "SH, Japan," $75.00.

Astronauts and Spacemen
Captain Astro Spaceman, windup, MIB, Mego, Japan **195.00**
Mark Apollo Astronaut, 7½" h, plastic, jointed, orange space suit, white helmet, plastic accessories, orig instructions and box, Marx .. **125.00**
Moon Explorer, MIB, Gakkentoy, Japan **425.00**
United States Spacemen, 2" h, red, white, and blue, orig pkg, Multiple Toys Makers, copyright 1969, 58 figures **40.00**
Flying Saucer
Mercury X–1 Space Saucer, battery operated, MIB, Y, Japan **195.00**
Gun
Astroray Gun, MIB, Shudo, Japan .. **75.00**
Cosmic Ray Gun, 8" l, plastic, red, blue, and amber, transparent barrel, sparking, orig box, Ranger Steel Products Corp, 1950s **28.00**
Plastic Spacegun, 5" l, plastic, black, 10 plastic missiles, unopened, 1950s **12.00**
Super Target Rocketship Gun, spaceship shape, plastic, red, three suction cup darts, 15 x 23" litho target, rocketship illus, 11 x 18" poster, orig box and instructions, Superior Toys, 1950s **90.00**
Rocket Gun Space Ranger, 3" h space ranger figure, spring loaded rocket gun, five plastic missiles, unopened, Best, 1950s **40.00**
Miscellaneous
Flashlight, rocket shape **75.00**
Matt Mason Space Probe Pak, plastic, space probe launcher, chemical de-

contamination gun, chemical tank, flare gun, binoculars, decal sheet, unopened, Mattel, copyright 1966   **60.00**

Palm Puzzle, 1¼" d, cardboard disk, plastic cov, 2 metal balls, planet and rocketship illus, Keds Shoe premium, 1950s **10.00**

Pinball Game
Electric Lunar Landing, 13 x 24", battery operated, orig box, unused, Wolverine, 1969–70 ....   **200.00**
Johnny Apollo Moon Landing, 11 x 16 x 2", rocket and moon illus, one black and nine white marbles, orig box, Marx, c1970 ...   **25.00**

Space: 1999 Chest Pack Radio, 8" h, plastic, white, transistor radio, microphone, ear plug, carrying strap, orig box, Illfelder Toy Co, ATV Licensing Ltd copyright 1976 ......   **75.00**

Satellite
Floating Satellite, battery operated, SH, Japan **185.00**
Space Satellite Flying Saucer, propeller in ring saucer, tin and copper, wood handled cord launcher, instruction sheet, Formis Mfg Co, Chattanooga, 1950s **27.50**
Sputnik, hemisphere in center, two 6" wires protrude from either side, tin Sputnik replica attached to one, red, white, blue, and yellow spaceship attached to other, globe spins, rubber disk on base, late 1950s ..   **95.00**

Spacecraft, Rockets, and Capsules
Alpha–1 Ballistic Missile and Launcher, 10" l plastic rocket and launch pad, glass oxidation storage and dilution tanks, fuel drums, oxidizer pkgs, manual, orig box, Scientific Products Co, 1960s **40.00**
Flying Jeep, 8½" l, litho tin and plastic, friction, orig box, Asahitoy, Japan **100.00**
Friendship–7, 6½" l, litho tin, friction, red, white, blue, and silver, SH Japan, 1960s **95.00**
Friendship Space Capsule, 11" l, litho tin and plastic, bump–and–go action, c1962 ....   **120.00**
Gama A–9, exploration vehicle, 10" l, battery operated, plastic, remote, marked "Made in Western Germany," orig box marked "Monsieur Tap–Tap," c1969 ....   **80.00**
Interplanetary Spaceship Atom Rocket–15, 13" h, litho tin and plastic, battery operated, orig box and instruction sheet, Yone, Japan, early 1970s **115.00**
Lunar–1 Two–Stage Moon Rocket, plastic rocket and launch pad, fuel,

oxidizer, measuring tank, pivot pin, release cord, manual, orig box, Scientific Products Co, 1960s **50.00**
Matt Mason Uni–Tread Space Hauler, 6" h, plastic, red, white, and black, battery operated, orig box, Mattel Inc copyright 1968 ....   **85.00**
Mini Apollo, 6" l, litho tin, windup, non–fall action, orig box **125.00**
Moon Car, 3 x 5 x 4", plastic, yellow, two seated astronauts, Space: 1999 sticker, Ahi, copyright 1976 ....   **45.00**
Moon Orbiter, plastic, windup, Apollo labels, gray plastic astronaut, Yone, Japan **65.00**
Moon Rocket, 9" l, litho tin, battery operated, non–fall action, orig box, Modern Toys, Japan **175.00**
NASA 905 Space Shuttle Challenger/ Flying Jet Plane, metal and plastic red, white, and blue Boeing 747, plastic black and white Challenger shuttle, suction cup fastener, orig box and insert sheet, Poty, Taiwan   **100.00**
Planet Explorer, 6" l, litho tin and plastic, battery operated, non–fall action, blue, silver, and red, orig box, Modern Toys, Japan **125.00**
Project Mercury Recovery Set, helicopter, space capsule, and astronaut, orig pkg, Marx, c1961 .....   **75.00**
Rocketship, gumball machine **200.00**
Sky Patrol, 13" l, litho tin, battery operated, bump–and–go action, orig box, TN, Japan, 1960s **600.00**
Sonicon Rocket, 14" l, litho tin, battery operated, Modern Toys, Japan   **250.00**
Spacecraft Apollo, 7½" h, litho tin and plastic, battery operated, orig box, Alps, Japan **100.00**
Spaceship X711, saucer shape, plastic, white, bump–and–go action, blinking lights, orig box, 1970s ..   **25.00**
United States Capsule, battery operated, SH, Japan **145.00**
X–07 Space Surveillant, 9" l, litho tin, battery operated, bump–and–go action, orig box, Modern Toys, Japan, c1970 ....   **90.00**

Tank
Robo Tank, battery operated, TN, Japan **215.00**
Space Tank, X–7, crank wind, MIB, marked "KO Japan" **425.00**

SPORTS COLLECTIBLES

Collecting Hints: The amount of material is unlimited. Pick a favorite sport and concentrate on it. Within the sport, narrow collecting emphasis to items associated with one league, team, individual, equipment, or chronological era. Include as much three dimensional material as possible.

Each sport has a "hall of fame." Make a point to visit it and get to know its staff. This can be an excellent source of leads for material that the museum does not want. Induction ceremonies provide an excellent opportunity to make contact with heroes of the sport as well as with other collectors.

History: Individuals have been saving sports–related equipment since the inception of sports. Some of this equipment was passed down from generation to generation for reuse. The balance occupied dark spaces in closets, attics, and basements.

In the 1980s two key trends brought collectors' attention to sports collectibles. First, decorators began using old sports items, especially in restaurant decor. Second, card collectors began to discover the thrill of owning the "real" thing. Although the principal thrust was on baseball memorabilia, by the beginning of the 1990s all sport categories were collectible, with automobile racing, boxing, football, and horse racing especially strong.

Reference: Ted Hake & Roger Steckler, *An Illustrated Price Guide to Non–Paper Sports Collectibles*, Hake's Americana & Collectibles Press, 1986.

Periodical: *Sports Collectors Digest*, 700 East State Street, Iola, WI 54990.

See: Baseball Collectibles and Golf Collectibles.

BASKETBALL

Nodder, basketball player, 7", composition, holding basketball, rounded gold base, sticker inscribed "Millersville," 1960s **22.00**
Program
  Harlem Globetrotters, 8½ x 11", 16 pgs, 1948–49 .... **25.00**
  Magicians of Basketball, Harlem Globetrotters, 8 x 10½", 30 pgs, 1965 .... **15.00**

BOATING

Pinback Button
  Annual International Yacht Competition, ⅞", white background
    Mayflower 1886 .... **8.00**
    Puritan 1885 .... **10.00**
    Vigilant 1893 .... **10.00**
    Volunteer 1887 .... **7.50**
  Devil's Lake Regatta, 1¼", blue and white, speedboat races, July, 1934 **12.00**

Outboard Regatta, 2⅛", tan, cello, black lettering, 1930s **12.00**
The Shamrock, ⅞", America's Cup competition, yacht racing, green shamrock trimmed in gold, white background **10.00**

BODY BUILDING

Book, *Joe Bonomo Exercise Training Course*, 96 pgs, photos and text instructions for spring cable exerciser, 1954 copyright **12.00**
Exerciser, Jiffy–Gym, black rubber stretch belt, molded rubber hand grips, instruction sheet, orig box, Moosehead–Whitely Co, NY, 1950s **22.00**
Photo, John Grimek, held titles of Mr American and Mr USA, 11 x 12½" glossy sheet with 8½ x 9½" photo, black and white, 1940s **15.00**
Poster, 14 x 22", York Streamlined Barbell and Body Building System, red and blue, 1950s **15.00**

BOWLING

Dispenser, marbleized plastic bowling ball, chrome push top, six glasses, figural bowler handle **60.00**
Nodder
  5", pr, boy and girl, kissing, composition, girl wearing cheerleading outfit has magnetized lips, boy has magnetized cheek, bowling ball and pins at feet, and "My Hero" decal on base, Japan, pr **35.00**
  6", composition, yellow shirt and shoes, blue trousers, holding bowling ball, mounted on wood block base, inscribed "You're Right Down My Alley" **45.00**

BOXING

Autograph, Muhammad Ali, 8½ x 11" black and white photocopy sheet, typewritten principles of Muslim statement, sgd "To Frank from Muhammad Ali 11–12–87", black ink . **50.00**
Big Little Book, *Joe Louis, The Brown Bomber*, Whitman #1105, 238 pgs, black and white photos, Gene Kessler, 1936 .... **30.00**
Book, *Jack Dempsey/The Idol of Histiana*, 1936 revised edition, Nat Fleischer, 158 pgs, inked autograph "To Bob/Best Wishes/Nat Fleischer" **25.00**
Boxing Gloves
  Jack Dempsey, brown, white vinyl trim, orig box, Everlast, c1950 ... **35.00**
  Rocky Graziano, orig box **135.00**

Bust, John Sullivan, Red Top Beer **240.00**
Charm, miniature, plastic, printed boxer's name
Eddie Zivic, yellow, lightweight con-
tender, 1933–34 .... **10.00**
Harry Greb, white, middleweight
champion, 1923–26 .... **10.00**
Ike Williams, red, lightweight cham-
pion, 1945–51 .... **8.00**
Mickey Walker, white, welterweight
champion, 1922–26 .... **10.00**
Sandy Saddler, white, featherweight
champion, 1948–49 .... **8.50**
Game, Muhammad Ali's Boxing Ring,
mechanical, Mego Corp, 1976 copy-
right Herbert Muhammad Enterprise
Inc, orig box **50.00**
Magazine, Life, Oct 23, 1970, 6 pg ar-
ticle on Muhammad Ali titled "No
More Boasting, Just The Fight" **15.00**
Pinback Button, 1¾", black and white
photo, 1940s **15.00**
Puppet, Joe Louis, Zimmerman, orig
box **225.00**
Ring, Gene Tunney, plastic, yellow, insert illus, issued by Kellogg's cereals,
1950s **12.50**
Statue, Louis Golden, Hollywood Studios, 1947 .... **350.00**
Whiskey Flask, John Sullivan **225.00**
Wrist Watch, Muhammad Ali, gold colored metal, color photo on dial, black
numerals, black inscriptions, De-
praz–Faure America Corp, c1980 .. **75.00**

FOOTBALL

Alarm Clock, windup, 6" h, helmet illus
on dial, Lafayette Watch Co, c1960 **29.00**
Bank, Pittsburgh Steelers, helmet shape,
6" h, plastic, 1970s **23.00**
Charm Bracelet, 6½" l, brass link, four
¾" charms, punter, football, NFL symbol, and Coca–Cola logo, 1970s **17.50**
Cushion, stadium, 11 x 16", vinyl,
stuffed, red, NFL team names and
mascot illus, orig tag, unused, 1950s **18.00**
Glass, 5½" h, clear, printed black and
white newspaper page design, Baltimore Sun Jan 16, 1967, Green Bay
Rips Chiefs In First Super Bowl, 35–
10 headline **12.50**
Nodder, Dallas Cowboys, 7", composition, gold base with NFL decal,
stamped "Japan," and 1962 .... **25.00**
Pennant, Boston Yanks, 28" l, felt,
green, football player illus, yellow lettering, c1950 .... **20.00**
Pin Set, NFL Super Bowl XIX, helmet
shape of each football team, NFL, and
Super Bowl, Coca–Cola part of design, displayed on black background,

wood frame, orig white corrugated
box with red, white, and blue inscription **110.00**
Program, Illinois–Notre Dame Football
game, 8 x 11", 20 pgs, Oct 9, 1937,
includes black and white photos and
roster **25.00**
Puzzle, jigsaw, Joe Namath, 16 x 20",
American Publishing Corp, copyright
1971 .... **14.00**
Yearbook, Giants, 1970 .... **10.00**

HORSE RACING

Ashtray, 5¼", china, full color thoroughbred racehorse portrait, Kentucky
Derby and Belmont Stakes winner .. **15.00**
Glass, 5¼"
1986 Kentucky Derby, clear, frosted
white panel, red roses and green
leaf accents, red and green inscriptions **10.00**
1964 Kentucky Derby/Churchill
Downs, frosted, horse head illus,
gold inscription, white lettering on
back **12.00**
Nodder, jockey, 6½", composition,
holding saddle and yellow and blue
blanket, sq base painted red, stamped
Japan 1962 .... **60.00**
Pennant, Derby Day, 18", felt, red,
white lettering, red and white design
with pink accents, 1939 .... **15.00**
Pin, Triple Crown, 1", metal, gold colored, red and white enamel accents,
crown and thoroughbred illus, winners names **8.00**
Pinback Button, Pimlico Preakness, 1¾"
d, multicolored, horse head illus,
white ground, blue lettering, 1960s . **15.00**

MARBLES

Bag, 4½ x 6", cheesecloth, red fabric
cov, drawstrings, printed black illus
and "Marble King/Glass Marbles" inscription, 1930s **24.00**
Pinback Button, 1½" d, Harrisburg Telegraph Tenth Marble Tournament, issued for 1932 tournament, 1931 winner photo, blue and white **25.00**
Tray, 4¼" d, litho tin, black and red
racehorse illus, ivory ground, spinner
bump in bottom, Missouri Brick Company giveaway, 1930s **18.00**

OLYMPICS

Book, 19 Olimpiada, 9 x 12", 302 pgs,
Spanish and American text, final 1968
Olympic results, dj **18.00**
Cent, 1980 Winter, rolled, 1½" oval,

Olympics, 1980, stickpin, $12.00.

stamped "Lake Placid, NY," pine tree, Olympic rings **8.50**

Cigarette Lighter, 1984 Winter Olympics, 2¾" h, red plastic, silvered metal, Olympic ring symbol, insignia, and "Sarajevo, Yugoslavia" in black on one side, black cartoon snowman illus other side **10.00**

Ewer, 12", ceramic, nude man stringing bow, Olympic logo **33.00**

Fan, 8 x 14" w open size, folding, paper, hp, balsa sticks, Tenth Olympic Games/1932/Los Angeles, chapel building illus, Olympic symbol, Japan **34.00**

Flask, 5½" h, white china, issued by Lufthansa Airlines, Olympic logo, "XVII Olympiade Rom 1960" inscription **15.00**

Glass, 1932 Olympics, 5½", clear, frosted white picture **50.00**

Magazine, Sports Illustrated, Nov 19, 1956 issue, Summer Olympic articles **15.00**

Manual, Olympic Edition, 3¼ x 6¼", 48 pgs, issued by Shell Petroleum, 1936 .... **15.00**

Patch, 6½" d, felt, bluish–purple background, blue, yellow, black, green, and red symbol **48.00**

Pin, 1984 Summer, 1 x 1", diecut, metal, gold colored, enameled, cartoon parrot wearing Uncle Sam hat inscribed with Olympic rings, holding Coke bottle, "Have a Coke and a Smile," copyright Olympic Committee and Coca–Cola **12.50**

Pinback Button

Olympic Champions Club, 1⅛", red, white, and blue, litho, 1932 ..... **15.00**

Olympic Team Support, 1¼", red, white, and blue, 1970s **8.00**

US Ski Team, 1", red, white, and blue, enamel, diecut, brass, 1960s **15.00**

Winter Olympics, 1⅛", diecut brass, red, blue, green, black, and white, 1980 Winter Olympics, Lake Placid **8.00**

Program

1948 Summer Olympic Trials, 8 x 10½", weight lifting trials, 20 pgs **15.00**

1952 Olympic Tryouts, July 3–5, 1952, rowing tryouts, 72 pgs **20.00**

Puzzle, 1932 Olympic Games, 10 x 13¼", Toddy Inc, 1932 copyright .. **30.00**

Stadium Cushion, 11 x 13½", 1956 Summer, red vinyl, yellow, white, and blue Olympics logo **45.00**

SWIMMING

Autograph, Gertrude Ederly, 6½ x 8" sheet, printed black and white drawing, blue ink inscription "Hold Strongly To 'Faith' in All You Do!/Best Always/Swimmingly Yours/Gertrude Trudy Ederly/New York/Successful Channel Swim/August 6, 1926/35 miles In 40½ Hrs/Cape Gris Nez to Kingdown," inked 1969 date **22.00**

Tennis, inkwell, bronze, figural player, porcelain well, 7¼ x 4½ x 5½", $280.00.

TENNIS

Pinback Button, US Open Tennis Championship, 2⅛", cello, 1975 championships **10.00**

Racket, 9 x 27", full color portrait on handle, Wilson Sporting Goods Co

Alice Marble, 1930s **20.00**

Maureen Connolly, 1950s **15.00**

STEREOGRAPHS

Collecting Hints: Value is determined by condition, subject, photographer (if famous), rarity, and age—prior to 1870 or after 1935. A revenue stamp on the back indicates a date of 1864–66, when a federal war tax was imposed. Litho printed cards have very little value.

Collect images that are of good grade or above, except for extremely rare images. Very good condition means some wear on the mount and a little dirt on the photo. Folds, marks on the photo, or badly worn mounts reduce values by at least 50%. Faded or light photos also reduce value.

Don't try to clean cards or straighten them. Cards were made curved to heighten the stereo effect, an improvement made in 1880.

With common cards it pays to shop around to get the best price. With rarer cards it pays to buy them when you see them since values are increasing annually. Dealers who are members of the National Stereoscopic Association are very protective of their reputation and offer a good starting point for the novice collector.

Use your public library to study thoroughly the subject matter you are collecting; it is a key element to assembling a meaningful collection.

History: Stereographs, also known as stereo views, stereo view cards, or stereoscope cards, were first issued in the United States on glass and paper in 1854. From the late 1850s through the 1930s, the stereograph was an important visual record of every major event, famous person, comic situation, and natural scene. It was the popular news and entertainment medium until replaced by movies, picture magazines, and radio.

The major early publishers were Anthony (1859–1873), Kilburn (1865–1907), Langeheim (1854–1861), and Weller (1861–1875). By the 1880–1910 period the market was controlled by large firms among which were Davis (Kilburn), Griffith & Griffith, International View Company, Keystone, Stereo Travel, Underwood & Underwood, Universal Photo Art, and H.C. White.

References: William C. Darrah, *Stereo Views, A History Of Stereographs in America And Their Collection,* published by author, 1964, out-of-print; William C. Darrah, *The World of Stereographs,* published by author, 1977, out-of-print. (Copies available from N. S. A. Book Service); John Waldsmith, *Stereo Views: An Illustrated History and Price Guide,* Wallace–Homestead, 1991.

Collectors' Club: National Stereoscopic Association, Box 14801, Columbus, OH 43214.

Advisor: John S. Waldsmith.

Note: Prices given are for very good condition, i.e., some wear and slight soiling. For excellent condition add 25%, and for mint perfect image and mount, double the price. Reverse the process for fair, i.e., moderate soiling, some damage to mount, minor glue marks, some foxing (brown spots) and poor folded mount, very dirty and

damage to tone or both images. Where applicable, a price range is given.

Animal
Birds, Hurst's 2nd series, #7, birds in
tree 4.00
Cat
Keystone #2314, average cat view   4-5.00
Keystone #9651, man and cat . . .   4.00
Soule, The Pickwickian Ride,
highly collectible 20.00
Dog
Kilburn #1644, "Home Protection," dog close up 6.00
U & U, the puppies singing school   4.00
Universal #3231, average dog
view 4-5.00
Farm Yard, Kilburn #739, sheep and
cows, 1870s 4.00
Horses, Schreiber & Sons, Jarvis and
sulky, early 18.00
Walrus, Keystone #V21232, Bronx
Zoo 3.00
Zoo, London Stereo Company, animals in London Zoo, each 8-10.00

Advertising, Vail's Ideal Tooth Powder, top: scene on Wisconsin River, New York state, bottom: Jacob's Ladder, Mt. Washington, NH, orange ground, each, $7.50.

Astronomy
Comet, Keystone #16645, Morehouse's 9.50
Mars, Keystone #16767T, the planet   6.00
Moon
Beer Bros. 1866, photo by Rutherford 15.00
Kilburn #2630, full moon 6.00
Soule #602, last quarter 8.00

Planetarium, Keystone #32688, Adler's Chicago **10.00**

Aviation

Air Mail Plane

Keystone #29446, at Cleveland .. **25.00**

Keystone #32372, Inaugural, Ford Tri-motor, air-rail serivece NY to LA, 7/2/29 .... **20.00**

Aviators, Keystone #26408t, 6 men who first circled earth **15.00**

Balloon, Anthony #4114, Prof. Lowe's flight from 6th Ave. in NYC **100.00**

Dirigibles and Zeppelins, Keystone #17397, Los Angeles at Lakehurst **45-50.00**

#17398, The Los Angeles **45.00**

#18000, flying over German town **5.00**

#32277, Graf Zeppelin in hanger at Lakehurst, NJ **35.00**

#32740, framework of ZRS-4, Akron **55-65.00**

#V19216, 1918, R-34 at Mineola, from WWI set, common view .. **15.00**

General View, Keystone #32785, five biplanes fly over Chicago's field museum **10.00**

Lindbergh, Keystone

#28029, in plane with wife **45.00**

#30262T, next to Spirit of St. Louis **30.00**

Plane, Keystone

#18920, Michelin bomber **15.00**

#19049, Nieuport **9.00**

#V18921, twin seat fighter **9.00**

Wright Bros., Keystone #V96103, in flight at Ft. Meyers **85.00**

Blacks

Keystone #9506, "we done all dis a' morning," picking cotton **6.00**

Kilburn #14317, boy and mule, typical, common **3.00**

Singley

#10209, "one never came up," swimmers **12.00**

#10217, "one got an upper cut," fighting **10.00**

U & U, "Cotton is King," picking .. **5.00**

U & U, Keystone, Kilburn, Whiting, etc., cheating at cards, stealing millions, infidelity, etc **10-15.00**

Whiting

#960, "there's a watermelon smiling on the vine" **10.00**

#961, "Happiest Coon" **8.00**

Cave

Keystone

#9586, man in front of Great Oregon Caves **6.00**

#33516, int. of Crystal Springs Cave, Carlsbad **5.00**

U & U, Luray Caverns, typical **8.00**

Waldack, 1866, #8 Mammoth Cave, typical early magnesium light view **15.00**

Christmas

Brownies & Santa, Universal #4679, Graves, sleigh in foreground **20.00**

Children with Tree

Griffith #16833, children's Christmas dinner **17.00**

Keystone, 1895, #987, Santa in front of fireplace **10-15.00**

Santa coming down chimney, Keystone #11434, Santa with toys .. **10-15.00**

Santa with Toys, Keystone 1898, #9445, Santa loaded with toys .. **10-15.00**

Comics

Bicycle Bum, Graves #4551–58, "Weary Willie," 4 card set **20.00**

Drinking

Kilburn 1892, #7348, "Brown just in from the club" **3.00**

R. Y. Young 1901, woman drinking, two cards, unusual subject **16.00**

U & U, 1897, man sneaks in after drinking, 2 card set **7.50**

English, boy carves roast, "The Attack," ivory mount, hand tinted .. **4.00**

Humor

Keystone #2346-7, before (cuddling) and after (reading) marriage **7.00**

U & U, 1904, "Four queens and a jack," 4 girls and a jackass **4.00**

Infidelity

Foolin–around, 1910, husband fools around with his secretary, 12 cards **45.00**

Keystone #12312–22, The French Cook **35-40.00**

U & U

Sneaking–in, 1897, caught by wife after nite on the town .. **6.00**

The French Cook, 10 card set .. **45.00**

Romance

U & U, "Going with Stream," hugging couple **6.00**

Weller #353, "Unexpected," necking **4.00**

Rumors, H. C. White, 5576-5578, quickest way to spread news: "Tell a graph, tell a phone, tell a woman," 3 card set **20.00**

Sentimental, American Stereo, #2001-2012, He goes to war; wounded; returns; reunited, etc., 12 card set **50.00**

Wedding Set, White #5510–19, getting ready, wedding, reception, alone in bedroom **40.00**

Disaster

Boston Fire, 1872, Soule, ruins **8-10.00**

Chicago Fire, 1871, Lovejoy & Foster, ruins **8-10.00**

Galveston Flood, 1900, Graves, ruins **4-6.00**

Johnstown Flood, ruins

Barker	9.00
U & U	7.00

Mill Creek Flood, 1874, popular series, house ... 4.00

Portland Fire, 1866, Soule #469, ruins ... 8.00

St. Pierre Eruption, Kilburn #14941, ruins ... 3.00

San Francisco Earthquake Scenes

Keystone #13264, Market St	5.00
U & U #8180, California St	15.00
Train Wreck, Dole	50.00

Worcester, MA, Flood, 1876, Lawrence, damage ... 5.00

Doll

Graves #4362, Sunday School Class ... 20.00

Kilburn

#15, tired of play	15.00
When will Santa come?	12.00

U & U

#6922, playing doctor	15.00
#6952, girl asleep with cat and doll	9.00

Webster & Albee #160, doll's maypole ... 20.00

Entertainer

Actress, J. Gurney & Son, 1870s, Mrs. Scott or Mrs. Roland, etc. ... 10.00

Dancers, Keystone #33959, Bali, Dutch Indies ... 2.00

Natives, Keystone #16423, Java, good costumes ... 3.00

Singer

J. Gurney & Son, Annie Cary ... 15.00

James Cremer, opera, studio pose in costume ... 12.00

Expositions, World's Peace Jubilee, 1872, coliseum, exterior, $10.00.

Exposition

NY Sanitary Fair, Anthony #1689-2864, fair view of fountain (for better view, double value) ... 15.00

1872, World Peace Jubilee, Boston, Pollock, interior view of Coliseam ... 8.00

1876, U.S. Close Up Centennial, Centennial Photo Co.

Common view of grounds and buildings ... 4-10.00

Corliss Engine ... 12.00

Monorail	**65.00**
Statue of Liberty	**85.00**

1894

California Mid-Winter, Kilburn #9474-2894, urns, etc. (for better subject, double value) ... **12.00**

Columbian Chicago, Kilburn

Most views	**4-7.00**
Ferris Wheel	**7-10.00**

1901, Pan American Buffalo, Kilburn

Most views	**4-6.00**
President McKinley	**7-9.00**

1904, Louisiana Purchase Exposition, St. Louis

Graves for Universal Photo or U & U, most views ... **4-8.00**

White #8491, Education & Manufacturing buildings ... **8.00**

Whiting #620, Missouri Fruit Exhibit ... **8-12.00**

1905, Lewis & Clark Centennial, Portland, Watson Fine Art #34, building ... **9.00**

1907, Jamestown Exposition, Keystone #14219, life saving demonstration ... **4-6.00**

1908, West Michigan State Fair, Keystone #21507 ... **12.00**

1933, Century of Progress, Chicago, Keystone #32993, Lief Ericksen Dr. ... **12-20.00**

Hunting & Fishing

Bass, Ingersoll #3159, string of bass ... **5-6.00**

Deer, Keystone #26396, hunters and kill, typical ... **4.00**

Halibut, Keystone #22520, commercial fishing ... **5.00**

Moose, Keystone #9452, 1899, typical big game kill ... **4-6.00**

Trout, Kilburn, #115, 1870, a day's catch ... **5.00**

Wildcat, Keystone #12264, man shoots sleeping wildcat ... **6.00**

Indian

Burge, J. C., Apaches bathing ... **75-125.00**

Continental Stereo Co., Pueblo eating bread ... **50-65.00**

Griffith #11873, Esquimau at St. Louis Fair ... **8.00**

Hayes, F. J.

#865, Crow burial ground	**17-25.00**
#1742, Sioux	**40-60.00**

Ingersoll #496, lithograph of Gray Eagle, typical printed Indian ... **1.00**

Jackson, Wm. H., #202, Otoe, with bow, rare ... **90-125.00**

Keystone

#23095, Chief Black Hawk	**8.00**
#23118, Indian girl, common view	**2-4.00**
#V23181, Blackfeet	**8.00**

Montgomery Ward, squaws ... **8.00**

Soule #1312, Piute squaw ... **40-60.00**

U & U
Hopi **9.00**
Wolpi **9.00**
White #12279, pueblo **12.00**
Mining
Alaska Gold Rush
Keystone
#9191, men with supplies get-
ting ready to climb the "golden
stairs" at Chilkoot Pass **9.00**
#9195, preparing to climb the
"golden stairs," common **9.00**
#21100, panning for gold **12.00**
U & U #10655, looking into glory
hole **15.00**
Universal, Graves, 1902, man
working a sluice, scarce card by
scarce publisher **40.00**
Easter, Anthony #474, working a gold
chute **45.00**
Gold Hill, Houseworth #743, city
overview **65-95.00**
Hydraulic, Houseworth #799, typical
water spraying **60-80.00**
Virginia City
Houseworth #713, street view .. **65-95.00**
Watkins
Opera House **75-95.00**
Panorama, new series **85-125.00**
Miscellaneous
Auto
Keystone #33143, employees leav-
ing Ford **1-2.00**
U & U, early auto in Los Angeles,
1903 .... **17-20.00**
Beach scenes, H.C. White, #476,
bathers, Atlantic City **5.00**
Bicycles
Kilburn #11924, women and bike **6.00**
Thorne, big two wheeler, early
1870s **35-50.00**
Circus
U & U, Chicago **20.00**
Windsor & Whipple, Olean, NY,
people with elephant **35-40.00**
Crystal Palace, yellow mount, out-
side, general view **25.00**
Firefighting
Early 1870s, unknown maker, close
view of pumpers **40.00**
Keystone #11684, action view of
pumpers **25.00**
Glass Stereos
Foreign Scenes, e.g., Fifth, etc. . **60-80.00**
United States Scenes, e.g., Niagara
Falls **50-100.00**
Groups, various, Rogers statuaries
such as "Taking the Oath," or
"Courtship in Sleepy Hollow" ... **7-9.00**
Gypsies, unknown maker, in front of
tent **15-20.00**

Hawaii, Keystone
#10156, hula girls **9.00**
#10162, Waikiki Beach **9.00**
Lighthouses
Keystone #29207, common view **4.00**
Williams, Minot Ledge Light **15-17.00**
New York City, Anthony #3938, typ-
ical street view **15-25.00**
Opium Dens
X82, 1900 .... **25.00**
Unknown Maker, two tier bed, pipe
for smoking opium **60.00**
Prisons, Pach, view of cabinets of ri-
fles **15.00**
Tinted Views
Foreign **4-6.00**
United States **5-10.00**
Tunnel, ward #808 Hoosac Tunnel,
just completed **15.00**
Toy train, Keystone P-21329, boy
playing with Lionel trains **25.00**
National Park
Death Valley, Keystone #32666, pool **9.00**
Garden of the Gods, Rodeo Mc-
Kenney, Pike's Peak **5.00**
Grand Teton, Wm. H. Jackson,
#503, average for this prized pho-
tographer **20.00**
Yellowstone
Jackson, Wm. H., #422, average
for this prized photographer ... **15.00**
Universal, nice, average peak view **4.00**
Yosemite
Keystone #4001, Nevada Falls ... **4.00**
Kilburn #9284, Bridal Veil Falls .. **4.00**
Reilly, tourists at Yosemite Falls .. **8.00**
U & U, Glacier Point **5.00**
Niagara Falls
Anthony #3731, falls **4.00**
Barker, ice bridge **2.00**
U & U
Tourists, common **2.00**
Whirlpool rapids **1.00**
White #7, tourists, 1903 .... **4.00**
Occupational
Blacksmith, Keystone #18206, many
tools in picture **4-5.00**
Cowboys, Keystone
#12465, Kansas **7.00**
#13641, Yellowstone, Montana .. **7.00**
Farming, Kilburn #1796, hay, 1870s **7.00**
Fireman
G. K. Proctor, Mid-distance hook-
ladder, horse drawn **35.00**
1870s, good view of steam pumper **45.00**
Milkman, Keystone #P-26392, hor-
sedrawn wagon **10.00**
Mill, U & U, linen factory, typical in-
dustrial view **2-3.00**
Store, Keystone #18209, grocery
store int. **15.00**

Oil
  Pennsylvania
    Detlor & Waddell, #76, burning
      tanks **12-20.00**
    Robbins #32, Triumph Hill **12-20.00**
    Keystone #20352T, shooting a well **3-4.00**
    Robbins, #88, gas well **8.00**
    Wilt Brothers, Allegheny area **8.00**
  Texas, Keystone #34864, tanks near
    Kilgore, common **6.00**
Person, Famous
  Barton, Clara, Keystone #28002,
    founder of American Red Cross . **40-60.00**
  Bryan, W. J., Keystone #15539, on
    way to hotel in NYC **25-30.00**
  Buffalo Bill, American Scenery
    #1399, on horseback in New York
    City, most common view **50.00**
  Buntline, Ned, J. Gurney, portrait **150-200.00**
  Burbank, Luther, Keystone #16746,
    with a cactus **4-6.00**
  Coolidge, President, Keystone
    #26303, President and Cabinet . **20-30.00**
    #28004, at desk, typical **15-25.00**
  Custar, General
    Lovejoy & Foster, with bear he
      killed **350-500.00**
    Taylor #2438, with his dog in
      camp **500-600.00**
  Czar of Russia, U & U, with President
    of France **10.00**
  Edison, Thomas
    Keystone, #V28007, in lab **85-100.00**
    U & U, in lab **100-125.00**
  Edison, Ford and Firestone, Keystone
    #18551 . . . . **70-75.00**
  Eisenhower, President, Keystone, at
    table with microphones, about
    1954, rare **150-250.00**
  Faraqutt, Admiral, Anthony, from
    Prominent Portrait Series **45.00**
  Ford, Henry, Keystone #28023 . . . **35-45.00**
  Gandhi, Mahatma, Keystone
    #33852, portrait **15-20.00**
  Gehrig, Lou, Keystone #32597, base-
    ball player **200-250.00**
  Grant, President, Bierstadt Bros., on
    Mount Washington **45-75.00**
  Harding, W., president, addressing
    boy scouts **15-20.00**
  Hayes, B., president, party at
    Hastings **125-150.00**
  Hoover, President, Keystone #28012,
    close portrait **30-35.00**
  Kettering, C. F., Keystone, inventor of
    auto self starter **60.00**
  Kingman, Seth, no maker, famous
    California Trapper **95-120.00**
  Lincoln, Abraham, Anthony
    Funeral, #2948 . . . . **40-65.00**
    President, #2969, scarce, highly
      prized view **800-1,200.00**

Marconi, Keystone #V11969, radio
  inventor **40.00**
McKinley, President, Keystone, Kil-
  burn, U & U, most views **4-15.00**
Morse, Samuel, J. Gurney **200-250.00**
Queen Victoria, U & U 1897, having
  breakfast with Princesses **35.00**
Rockefeller, J.D., Keystone
  #V11961, world's richest man . . . **25.00**
Rogers, Will, Keystone #32796, at
  1932 Chicago Democratic Conven-
  tion **65-75.00**
Roosevelt, Franklin D., president,
  Keystone #33535, at his desk . . . **65-75.00**
Roosevelt, Theodore, president
  Keystone, Kilburn, U & U, most
  views [at Panama Canal, Glacier
  Pt., Yosemite, etc.] **8-30.00**
  U & U, on horseback, typical
  view **12-20.00**
Ruth, Babe, Keystone #32590, base-
  ball player **200-250.00**
Sarazen, Gene, Keystone #32436,
  golfer **35.00**
Schmeling, Max, Keystone #28028,
  boxer **75.00**
Shaw, Dr. Anna, Keystone #V26151,
  suffrage leader **25.00**
Shaw, George Bernard, Keystone
  #34505, on a ship **50-60.00**
Strauss, Johann, Gurney, typical of a
  Gurney well-known person such as
  Bret Harte, Horace Greeley, etc . . **90.00**
Taft, President, U & U #10062, at
  desk **20.00**
Thomas, Lowell, Keystone #32812,
  world travel expert and newsman **40-50.00**
Twain, Mark
  Evans & Soule **300-350.00**
  U & U #8010 or White #13055,
  in bed writing **200-250.00**
Washington, Booker T., Keystone
  #V11960, with Andrew Carnegie **50-70.00**
Wirewalkers, Barker
  Belleni on wire **10.00**
  Blondin on rope **15.00**
Young, Brigham, C. W. Carter, bust
  portrait **10-15.00**
Photographer, Famous
  Brady, Anthony
    1863, Tom Thumb Wedding **30-40.00**
    #428, Captain Custer with Confed-
      erate prisoner **900.00**
    #3376, Jeff Davis Mansion **50.00**
  Houseworth, San Francisco, e.g.,
    #150, show photo studio **100-150.00**
    #429, Golden Gate **35-45.00**
  Langenheim, 1856, Trenton Falls,
    typical view, but scarce, on glass . **135.00**
  Muybridge
    #318, The Golden Gate **80.00**
    #880, Geyer Springs **35-45.00**

#1623, Indian scouts **250.00**
O'Sullivan, T.H., Anthony #826,
Men's Quarters **60.00**
Pond, C. L., #786, Mirror Lake **30.00**
Watkins, C. E.
Panoramic, #1338, from Telegraph
Hill **45-55.00**
San Francisco street scene, e.g.,
#767, panorama from Russian
Hill **55.00**
Trains, any **75-140.00**
Virginia City, NV, Panorama, new
series **90.00**
Yosemite series, #1066, Yosemite
Falls **25-30.00**
Photographica
Camera, Houseworth #1107, wet
plate camera in Yosemite **75.00**
Comic, Keystone #423, many view-
ers and cards in this comic
"mouse" routine **15.00**
Gallery, American scenery, street with
gallery sign visible **50.00**
Photo Wagon, Weitfle's Photograph
Van, close view with sign on wag-
on **75-1500.00**
Photography with stereo camera
above street, Keystone #8283,
classic collectible **65.00**
Viewing, Keystone #11917, looking
through viewer **10.00**
Railroad
American stereo, view in Penn Station **15.00**
Centennial, 1876 Monorail, World's
Fair, scarce **65.00**
Keystone
#2367, loop at Georgetown, com-
mon **5.00**
#7090, interior of Baldwin Works **8.00**
#37509, The Chief, 1930s **45.00**
Kilburn
#135, pushing car up Jacob's Lad-
der **5.00**
#432, large side view of locomo-
tive **30.00**
#779, train with engineer posed,
1870 .... **50.00**
#2941, silver ore train **5.00**
U & U
#52, train going through Pillars of
Hercules, common **7.00**
#6218, Royal Gorge, common .. **5.00**
Universal Photo Art #2876, Colum-
bian Express **20.00**
Unknown Maker, dramatic close-up
of a 1870 locomotive **75.00**
Religious
Bates, open *Bible*, St. Luke **3.00**
Keystone, Billy Sunday, evangelist .. **20.00**
Keystone, Kilburn, U & U, Holy Land,
Palestine, etc **1-2.00**
Pope, any **4-7.50**

Life of Christ, unmarked, usually set
of photos of drawings or litho-
graphed set, per set of 10-12 .... **7.00**
Shakers, Irving, view of people **50-75.00**
Risque
1820's, unmarked, typical "peek-a-
boo" **10-20.00**
Griffith #2427, two girls, arms
around each other, lightly clad ... **20.00**
Keystone, #9489, school girls retir-
ing, in nightgowns **7.00**
Nude, early, bare breast **45.00**
Nude, 1920s or 1930s **40.00**
Sets
Boxer Rebellion, U & U 1901, 72
cards, rare **150-200.00**
Bullfight, U & U, set of 15 .... **100.00**
China, Stereo Travel, set of 100, un-
usual subject **350-450.00**
Egypt, U & U set of 100 ...... **225-250.00**
France
Stereo Travel, set of 30, typical for
this publisher, popular country **70-80.00**
U & U, set of 100 .... **250-275.00**
Glacier Park, Forsyth, set of 30 . **125-150.00**
India, U & U, set of 100 .... **180-250.00**
Italy, U & U, set of 100 .... **150-175.00**
Switzerland, U & U, set of 100,
guidebook and maps **200.00**
United States, U & U, set of 100 **175-200.00**
Wild Flowers, Keystone, 100, hand
tinted **400.00**
World Tour, Keystone
Set of 200, trip from U.S. around
world and back **200-225.00**
Set of 400 .... **450-500.00**
Set of 600, trip from U.S. around
world and back **600-650.00**
Yellowstone, U & U, set of 30 ... **90-100.00**
Yosemite, U & U, set of 30 ..... **100-125.00**
Ship
Battleships
Griffith #2535, 1902, USS *Brook-
lyn* **8.00**
Universal Photo Art, USS *Raleigh*,
common **7-9.00**
Cruiser, White #7422, 1901, USS
New York **10.00**
Deck View, American Stereo, 1899,
USS *Iowa* **8.00**
Foreign, Keystone #16090, HMS *Al-
bemarie* **6.00**
Riverboat, Anthony #7567, stern-
wheeler at Cincinnati **25.00**
Sailboat, Anthony #22 or #5179,
early view **15-20.00**
Steamers
Pettit, Wilson, 1880 .... **15-20.00**
Yukon, Keystone #24704, stern
wheeler being loaded in
Alaska **330-35.00**

Steamships
Anthony #8691, *Bristol*, good average early view **15.00**
London Stereo, *Great Eastern*, early view **75.00**
Submarine, Keystone #16667, at San Diego **8.00**
Survey
Amundsen, Keystone #13327, at Antoretie Glacier, 1911 .... **7.00**
Gerlache, Keystone #13328, hunting seals at South Pole **6.00**
Hayden, Jackson #796, people view, typical **22-25.00**
Lloyd, Grand Canyon, U & U, at work on mountain, 1903 .... **25.00**
Perry, Greenland, Keystone #13325, ships **6.00**
Powell, #13, the wall, typical **10-20.00**
Wheeler, William Bell
#14, Canon de Chelle, wall, 1873 **40.00**
#15, Canon de Chelle, wall, 1872 **25.00**
Tissue, French
Balloon, close view **60-70.00**
Diablo, 1870s, devils, skeletons, etc., good shape with lots of "evil" ... **30.00**
Interior scene, 1870s, minor damage, viewable **7.50**
Interior scene, 1870s, nice stereo, pin-pricked, no tears **20.00**
Wedding, Young #7, typical US, wedding vows **10.00**

War, Civil War, Brady photographs, Virginia harbors, each, $25.00.

War
Boer, U & U, artillery firing, typical view **6.00**
Boxer Rebellion, U & U, 1901, typical view **4-7.00**
Civil War
Anthony
#3031, Dunlop Home **30.00**

#3365, Brady, Libby Prison, yellow mount **25.00**
#3406, chair in which Lincoln was shot **60.00**
Gardner #237, home of Rebel sharpshooter **45-50.00**
Taylor & Huntington
#458, Conferdate fortifications . **25.00**
#2557, pontoon boats **25.00**
#6705, powder magazine **35.00**
Russo-Japanese, U & U #4380, general view of Port Arthur, typical view **5.00**
Spanish American, U & U, typical view **5-12.00**
World War I Keystone
Set of 100 .... **225-250.00**
Set of 200 .... **300-350.00**
Set of 300 .... **400-450.00**
Whaling
Freeman, beached whales **35-50.00**
Keystone
#14768, floating whale station, common **6-8.00**
#V27198, whalers cruising, common **4-6.00**
Nickerson, beached whales **40-50.00**
Unknown maker, beached whale .. **18-30.00**

STEREO VIEWERS

Collecting Hints: Condition is the key in determining price. Undamaged wooden hood models are scarce and demand a premium price if it is bird's-eye maple. All original parts increases the value. Lots of engraving adds 20 to 30%.

Longer lenses are better than small. Lenses held in place by metal are better than shimmed in by wood.

Because "aluminum" was the same price as silver in the late 19th century, aluminum viewers often are more collectible.

History: There are many different types of stereo viewers. The familiar table viewer with an aluminum or wooden hood was the joint invention in 1860 of Oliver Wendell Holmes and Joseph Bates, a Boston photographer. This type of viewer also was made in a much scarcer pedestal model.

In hand viewers, three companies—Keystone, Griffith & Griffith, and Underwood & Underwood—produced viewers between 1899 and 1905 in the hundreds of thousands.

In the mid-1850s a combination stereo viewer and picture magnifier was developed in France and eventually made in England and the United States. The instrument was called a Graphascope. It usually consisted of three pieces and folded for storage. When set up, it had two round lenses for stereo viewing, a large round magnifying lens to view cabinet photographs and a slide, often with opaque glass, for viewing stereo glass slides. The height was adjustable.

A rotary or cabinet viewer was made from the late 1850s to about 1870. Becker is the best known maker. The standing floor models hold several hundred slides, the table models hold 50 to 100.

From the late 1860s to 1880s there were hundreds of different viewer designs. Models had folding wires, collapsible cases (Cortascope), pivoting lens to view postcards (Sears' Graphascope) and telescoping card holders. The cases also became ornate with silver, nickel and pearl trimmed in velvets and rosewood.

Reference: John Waldsmith, *Stereo Views, An Illustrated History and Price Guide,* Wallace-Homestead, 1991.

Viewer, walnut base and standard, teak top, 15¾" h, $100.00.

Hand, common maker
Aluminum hood, folding handle **95.00**
Bird's eye maple hood, folding handle **115.00**
Walnut, screw on handle, velvet hood **85.00**
Hand, unknown maker, scissor device to focus, groove and wire device to hold card **125.00**
Pedestal
Foreign, probably French, nickel and velvet **450.00**
Keystone, school and library type, black crinkle metal finish, light ... **85.00**
Sculptoscope, counter top style, penny operated **600.00**
Stand, Bates–Holmes, paper or wood hood **175.00**
Stereographascope, Sears Best, lens rotates to allow viewing of photos or post cards **100.00**
Telebinocular, binocular style, black crinkle metal finish, excellent optics, many have book box **45.00**

STOCK AND BOND CERTIFICATES

Collecting Hints: Some of the factors that affect price are (1) date [with pre-1900 more popular and pre-1850 most desirable], (2) autographs of important persons [Vanderbilt, Rockefeller, J. P. Morgan, Wells and Fargo, etc.], (3) number issued [most bonds have number issued in text], and (4) attractiveness of the vignette.

Stocks and bonds are collected for a variety of reasons, among which are the graphic illustrations and the history of romantic times in America, including gold and silver mining, railroad history, and early automobile pioneers.

History: The use of stock to raise capital and spread the risk in a business venture dates back to England. Several American colonies were founded as joint venture stock companies. The New York Stock Exchange on Wall Street in New York City traces its roots to the late eighteenth century.

Stock certificates with attractive vignettes date to the beginning of the nineteenth century. As engraving and printing techniques developed, so did the elaborateness of the stock and bond certificates. Important engraving houses emerged, among which were the American Bank Note Company and Rawdon, Wright & Hatch.

Reference: Bill Yatchman, *The Stock & Bond Collectors Price Guide,* published by author, 1985.

Periodical: *Bank Note Reporter,* 700 East State Street, Iola, WI 54990.

Collectors' Club: Bond and Share Society, 24 Broadway, New York, NY 10004.

Airline, United Air Lines, 1970s
Brown, $1000 share **6.00**
Olive, $100 share **6.00**

Stock, State of New York, Canal Department, Draper, Toppan & Co, NY, engravers, 1842, 10½ x 8", $15.00.

Automobile
Bond
Ford International Capital Corporation, 1968, $1000 bond, blue, black, and white **12.00**
General Motors Corp, green $1000 bond, vignette of streamlined car, truck, locomotive, three heads, and factory building, coupons, 1954, issued **15.00**
Stock
Ben–Hur Motor Car, 1917, issued but not cancelled
Brown certificate, car and chariot vignette **125.00**
Green certificate, globe vignette **75.00**
Continental Motors Corp, vignette of car engine, issued, orange certificate **15.00**
Thomas B Jeffery Co of California, eagle vignette, c1910
Issued and cancelled **125.00**
Unissued **10.00**
Kaiser–Frazer Corp, blue or brown certificate, 1940s, issued **6.00**
Business and Industry, Stock
Chicago Cotton Manufacturing Co, ornate design in brown in center of certificate, place for revenue stamp, factory vignette, 1870, unissued **10.00**
Gambrinus Brewing Co, vignette of king savoring a glass of beer, Columbus, OH, 1909–13, issued ... **25.00**
Fruit of the Loom Inc, script certificate for fractional share of common stock, 1938, green, black, and white **5.00**
Jantzen Knitting Mills, engraved, vignette of woman in early swim suit diving into water, 1930s, issued .. **35.00**
Northampton Brewery Corp, orange certificate, engraved, vignette featuring woman, ship, and city skyline, Pennsylvania, 1930s, issued . **15.00**
Ottaquechee Woolen Co, Vermont, 1870s, unissued **4.50**
Pabst Brewing Co, green certificate, vignette of brewery, Milwaukee, WI, 1900s
Issued and signed by Pabst as president **95.00**
Unissued **25.00**
Penn National Bank & Trust Co of Reading, gray certificate, vignette of colonial man, Pennsylvania, 1930, issued but not cancelled ... **15.00**
Pepsi–Cola United Bottlers, orange or green certificate, vignette of goddess holding world globe and Pepsi bottle in oval medallion to left of her feet, issued **10.00**

Piggly Wiggly Western States Co, orange certificate, photo vignette of early Piggly Wiggly food store, 1920s issued **7.50**
Santa Clara Valley Mill & Lumber Co, vignette of early lumber mill, California, 1873, unissued **15.00**
Sentinel Radio Corp, green or brown certificate, vignette of goddess and two radio towers, 1956, issued ... **5.00**
Waldorf System Inc, purple certificate, engraved, vignette of apple with motto in circle flanked by goddesses, issued **5.00**
Mining, stock
American Antimony Company, Utah Territory, 1883, vignette of eagle atop a bee hive, flanked by Indian village and locomotive passing through town, second vignette of young girl **75.00**
Egypt Silver Mining Company, Franklin, ME, vignette of miners working with pick and shovel, 1880s, unissued **10.00**
Fairview Golden Boulder Mining Co, brown certificate, gold nugget vignette, Nevada, 1900, unissued .. **12.00**
Plymouth Rock Mining Co, gray and white certificate, vignette of four miners working underground, Territory of New Mexico, 1880, issued **35.00**
Wee–Wee Antic Gold, Silver, and Copper Mining Company, Stockton, CA, 1863, black and white, no cancellation marks, affixed revenue stamp **250.00**
Nautical, stock, Submarine Signal Co, green certificate, vignette of ship on ocean, 1940, issued **15.00**
Railroad
Bond
Atchison, Topeka & Santa Fe RR, blue $1000 bond, two vignettes of railroad station int., issued .. **18.00**
Central New York & Western RR, green $1000 gold bond, engraved, old train vignette, very decorative border, pages of coupons, 1892, issued but not cancelled **85.00**
Lehigh Valley RR, different colors, vignette of steam locomotive in switch yard with tower and workers, issued **25.00**
Stock
Cincinnati, New Orleans & Texas Pacific RR, gray and white certificate, steam train vignette, issued
1900s **22.00**
1910s **18.00**
1920s **15.00**

1930s 13.00
Nashville, Cahattanooga & St Louis RR, bright pink certificate, vignette of old trains at railroad station, issued 10.00
New York Central RR, brown certificate, vignette of Commodore Vanderbilt, 1940s, issued 10.00
Pacific Railroad of Missouri, green certificate, vignette of train and mountains, 1875, issued but not cancelled 75.00
Rio Grande Southern RR, rust certificate, engraved, vignette of train coming out of mountain pass, signature of Otto Mears as president, Colorado, 1890s
Issued 250.00
Unissued 95.00
Tide Water and Southern RR Co, olive certificate, engraved, vignette of river boat at dock, Stockton, CA, 1910, unissued .. 28.00

Railway (Trolley)
Bond
Wisconsin Interurban System, green, orange, or brown gold bond, state seal vignette, coupons, 1917, issued but not cancelled 45.00
Broadway Surface RR, gray $1000 bond, eagle and flag vignette, New York City, 1885, issued ... 35.00
Columbus & Ninth Ave RR, brown $5000 gold bond, engraved, fancy company name, coupons, New York City, 1893, issued ... 35.00
Stock
California Street Cable RR Co, cable car vignette, punch cancelled 125.00
Fairmount Park Transportation Co, green certificate, Philadelphia, PA, 1900–02, issued 12.00
Oakland Traction Co, orange certificate, engraved, two vignettes of old trolley cars, California, 1910s, issued 25.00
Utica & Mohawk Valley Railway, engraved, street car vignette, c1900, unissued 25.00

Utility
Bond
Arlington Gas Co, $1000 bond, state seal vignette, coupons, New Jersey, 1880, issued 20.00
Consolidated Edison Co of New York, blue $1000 bond, vignette of tower with light on top with Brooklyn Bridge and New York city in background, 1949, thirty year bond, issued 7.50
Southern Bell Telephone & Tele-

graph, $1000 bond, top vignette of person speaking on phone with city and rural landscapes in background flanked by seated goddesses, center vignette of large bell, coupons, 1947, issued 15.00
Stock
General Public Utilities Corp (owner of Three Mile Island), green certificate, vignette of man and generator wheel, issued ... 3.00
Tuolumne County Water Co, California gold rush 1854–62 certificate, vignette of mining methods in use at time 75.00
Vallejo City Water Co, vignette of early Vallejo city area, California, 1868, unissued 15.00

STUFFED TOYS

Collecting Hints: The collector tends to focus on one type of animal and collects material spanning a long time period. The company with the strongest collector following is Steiff.

Collectors stress very good to mint condition. Often stuffed toys had ribbons or clothing. All accessories must be intact to command full value.

History: The stuffed toy may have originated in Germany. Margarete Steiff GmbH of Germany began making stuffed toys for export beginning in 1880. By 1903 the teddy bear had joined Steiff's line and quickly worked its way to America. The first American teddy bears were made by the Ideal Toy Corporation. Not much is known about earlier manufacturers since companies were short lived and many toys have lost their labels.

The stuffed toy has enjoyed a favorite position in the American market. Some have music boxes inserted to enhance their appeal. Carnivals used stuffed toys as prizes. Since the 1960s America has been subjected to a wealth of stuffed toys imported from Japan, Taiwan, and China. These animals often are poorly made and are not popular among serious collectors.

References: Peggy and Alan Bialosky, *The Teddy Bear Catalog*, Workman Publishing, 1984, revised edition; Kim Brewer and Carol–Lynn Rössel Waugh, *The Official Price Guide To Antique & Modern Teddy Bears*, House of Collectibles, 1990; Shirley Conway and Jean Wilson, *Steiff Teddy Bears, Dolls, and Toys with Prices*, Wallace–Homestead, 1984; Margaret Fox Mandel, *Teddy Bears And Steiff Animals*, First Series (1984), *Second Series* (1987), and *Third Series* (1990), Collector Books; Helen Sieverling, *3rd Teddy Bear & Friends Price Guide*, Hobby House

Press, 1988; Jean Wilson, *Steiff Toys Revised*, Wallace–Homestead, 1989.

Periodicals: *The Teddy Bear and Friends*, Hobby House Press, Inc., 900 Frederick Street, Cumberland, MD 21502.

Collectors' Clubs: Good Bears Of The World, P. O. Box 8236, Honolulu, Hawaii 96815; Steiff Collectors Anonymous, 1308 Park Avenue, Piqua, OH 45356.

Note: Stuffed toys dealing with advertising, cartoon, television, and other character types will be found elsewhere in the book.

Bison, 10", mohair and felt, brown, glass eyes, metal wheels, pull toy, Steiff, 1914	**400.00**
Camel	
8", tan plush, single hump, glass eyes, c1950	**65.00**
13½", Cosy, orig tags	**90.00**
Cat	
Siamese, 9", mohair, sitting, c1950	**100.00**
Tabby, Steiff	**65.00**
Tom, 5", black velvet body, mohair tail, glass eyes, sewn nose and mouth, c1960	**85.00**
Chick, Steiff	**55.00**
Deer	
9", straw stuffed, mohair	**28.00**
15", Bambi, plush, Gund, 1953	**60.00**

Dinosaur, Allsaurus, green, white felt teeth, plastic eyes, R Dankin & Co, 1980, $12.00.

Dinosaur, 14", multi–mohair, glass eyes, felt fins, 1960	**100.00**
Dog	
Beagle	
4", Steiff	**40.00**
9", plush, glass eyes	**25.00**
Collie, long and short mohair, glass eyes, sewn nose, felt mouth	**125.00**
Dalmatian, 5½", jeweled crown, red taffeta cape, Steiff, c1950	**175.00**

Laika, Steiff	**292.00**
Poodle	
10", plush, c1960	**125.00**
12", curly, gray, standing, 1960	**15.00**
Schnauzer, 11", mohair, gray, 1950s	**100.00**
Scottie, 18"	**39.00**
Duck	
7", yellow and green, felt beak	**60.00**
8", pull toy, felt and velvet, metal wheels	**275.00**
Elephant	
8", acrylic, gray and pink, Steiff, c1950	**60.00**
14½", musical, sitting, gray and white, 1960	**30.00**
Elf, 10", felt body, mohair beard, glass eyes, 1930s	**100.00**
Frog	
4", felt, orig neck tag	**45.00**
9", green, velvet top, white satin bottom, c1960	**12.00**
Giraffe, 11", gold and orange mohair, felt ears, glass eyes, 1950s	**70.00**
Grasshopper, 18", mohair, felt clothes, glass eyes, 1950s	**100.00**
Hamster, 5", mohair, gold, jointed head, glass eyes, felt paws and mouth	**48.00**
Kangaroo, 20", baby in pouch, Steiff	**475.00**
Lamb, 10", black, curly, glass eyes, embroidered features, ribbon at neck	**110.00**
Leopard Cub, 18", plush, green glass eyes, paper	**150.00**
Lion, 45", Leo, mohair, reclining, orig tag, c1955	**600.00**
Lobster, 7", felt, orange, glass eyes	**45.00**
Monkey	
Mango, Steiff	**120.00**
Mohair, 8", jointed, glass eyes, felt clothes, 1953	**90.00**
Plush, 18", brown, curly, swivel neck and bent arms, felt paws, glass inset eyes, paper label, Steiff	**75.00**
Straw stuffed, rubber face	**40.00**
Mouse	
6" l, felt, gray, red tongue	**15.00**
8", velvet, jointed, button eyes, nose, felt clothes, 1953	**125.00**
Ocelot, 6½ x 13", gold and black mohair, sewn nose and mouth, 1955	**95.00**
Owl, Wittie, small, Steiff	**165.00**
Penguin, small, Steiff	**40.00**
Pig, 6½", mohair, pink, felt mouth and tail, cord on neck	**85.00**
Polar Bear, 16", champagne plush, straw fill, movable arms and legs, long snout, black button eyes, stitch face, leather collar, c1920	**300.00**
Porcupine, mohair, brown, felt ears and feet, jointed head	**48.00**
Rabbit, 19", "Ruth the Rabbit", gold plush, standing, jointed, purple bead eyes, long lashes, sheer organdy over	

flowered print costume, cloth tag, c1934 .... 525.00

Ram, 7½" h, woolly coat, black velvet trim, glass eyes 35.00

Reindeer, mohair, Steiff 70.00

Seal
5½", mohair, Steiff 45.00
6", Floppy Robby, soft stuffing, sewn eyes, c1950 .... 65.00
10", black fur, black glass eyes 85.00

Teddy Bear
7", gold mohair, shoe button eyes, swivel head, jointed, black sewn nose and mouth 85.00
8", Cosy Orsi, Steiff 85.00
11", Bellhop, mohair, German 275.00
13", plush, dark brown, jointed hips and shoulders, felt paws, black sewn nose and mouth 25.00
14", wool fabric, jointed limbs and head, shoe button eyes 150.00
16½", mohair, gold, jointed, sewn nose and mouth, button eyes, Steiff 600.00
17", plush, brown, cream paws, plastic eyes, molded nose and mouth, tail squeaks, Ideal label 40.00
19", on wheels, removable wood rockers, orig Steiff blanket 950.00
21", mohair, brown, fully jointed, Knickerbocker 250.00
22", Roddy, mohair, jointed limbs, mechanical tail moves head, English 400.00
24", mohair, brown, fully jointed, c1925 .... 600.00

Tiger
13", Shere Kahn, Disney character, Steiff 140.00
16", mohair, reclining, orig button, Steiff 400.00

Turtle, 5", mohair body, vinyl shell, glass eyes, Steiff 65.00

Walrus, 4", mohair, plastic tusks, 1950s 50.00

Zebra
5", black and white felt, Steiff, c1950 40.00
8", mohair, black and white, 1950s . 70.00

SUPER HEROES

Collecting Hints: Concentrate on a single super hero. Because Superman, Batman, and Wonder Woman are the most popular, new collectors are advised to focus on other characters or one of the modern super heroes. Nostalgia is a principal motivation for many collectors; hence, they pay prices based on sentiment rather than true market value for some items.

Comics are a fine collectible but require careful handling and storage. An attractive display requires a three dimensional object. Novice collectors are advised to concentrate on these first before acquiring too many of the flat paper material.

History: The Super Hero and comic books go hand in hand. Superman made his debut in 1939 in the first issue of *Action Comics*, six years after Jerry Siegel and Joe Shuster conceived the idea of a man who flew. A newspaper strip, radio show, and movies followed. The Superman era produced a wealth of super heroes, among them Batman, Captain Marvel, Captain Midnight, The Green Hornet, The Green Lantern, The Shadow, and Wonder Woman.

These early heroes had extraordinary strength and/or cunning and lived normal lives as private citizens. A wealth of merchandising products surround these early super heroes. Their careers were enchanced further when television chose them as heroes for Saturday morning viewing as well as in prime time.

The Fantastic Four—Mr. Fantastic, The Human Torch, The Invisible Girl, and The Thing—introduced a new type of super hero, the mutant. Among the most famous of this later period are Captain America, Spiderman and The Hulk. Although these characters appear in comic form, the number of secondary items generated is small. Television has helped to promote a few of the characters, but the list of mutant super heroes is close to a hundred.

References: Steven H. Kimball, *Greenberg's Guide To Super Hero Toys, Volume I*, Greenberg Publishing Co., 1988; Jeff Rovin, *The Encyclopedia of Super Heroes*, Facts on File Publications, 1985.

See: Comic Books and Radio Characters and Personalities.

Better Little Book, *The Ghost Avenger Strikes,* **RR Winterbotham, author, Henry E Vallely artist, 1943, Whitman, $12.00.**

Aquaman

Board Game, Justice League of America, Hasbro, 1967 .... **180.00**

Costume, Ben Cooper, orig box, 1967 **198.00**

Puzzle, jigsaw, Whitman, 1967 .... **40.00**

Tattoo, orig wrapper, unused, 1967 . **50.00**

Batman and Robin

Bank, porcelain, figural, mint **45.00**

Batcraft, 6½" h, plastic, battery operated, bump–and–go action, orig box, Marx, National Periodical Publications copyright 1966 ..... **175.00**

Batmobile, 11½" l, metal, blue body, red accents, yellow interior, seated Batman and Robin figures, bump–and–go action, battery operated, ASC, Japan, c1966 .... **200.00**

Batplane, 10½" l, plastic, battery operated, orig box, Azrak–Hamway, copyright National Periodical Publications 1975 .... **75.00**

Buckle, 3½" l, metal, orig pkg, Morris Belt Co, National Periodical Publications copyright 1966 .... **25.00**

Cake Decoration, figures, 4" h, plastic, Batman, Robin, and 1940s bat logo, stands, unused, 1966 ...... **29.00**

Color By Number Book, 11 x 13½", Whitman, 20 illus, unused, 1966 . **25.00**

Colorforms, diecut vinyl, Batmobile and skyline illus, orig box and instructions, Colorforms toys, copyright 1976 .... **10.00**

Costume, molded plastic full face mask, blue and yellow fabric cape, Ben Cooper, orig box, National Periodical copyrights 1965 and 1966 **35.00**

Drink Mix, Punch–O, unused, 1966 **50.00**

Figure, Robin, jumping, 4" l, soft rubber, string attached to neck, Fun Things, unopened, copyright National Periodical Publications 1966 **28.00**

Game

Pinball, 10 x 21½ x 1", plastic and litho metal, orig box, Marx, National Periodical copyright 1966 **100.00**

Shooting Arcade, metal and plastic, black gun, Marx, 1966 .... **25.00**

Grenade Gun, plastic, 17" l, green, gold trim, blue plastic grenade, orig display card, Lincoln International, copyright National Periodical Publications, 1966 .... **95.00**

Jokermobile, Corgi, 3" l, diecast metal, Mettoy Co, unopened, copyright DC Comics Inc 1978 .. **23.00**

Lamp, Bat Cave, figural **75.00**

Marionette, Robin, 14" h, plastic head, fabric body, marked "Batman Characters," National Periodical Publications copyright, 1966 ..... **100.00**

Model, Batmobile, #486–98, Aurora

Plastics Corp, complete, unassembled, copyright 1966 .... **115.00**

Night Light, 2½ x 2½", figural, plastic, Snapit, copyright National Periodical Publications 1966 .... **25.00**

Paint By Number Book, 11 x 13½", Whitman, 40 illus, unused, 1966 . **20.00**

Pencil Box, gun shape, contents **20.00**

Pennant, 29" l, felt, black, white lettering, full color illus, copyright 1966 .... **25.00**

Print Putty Colorforms, orig display card **75.00**

Sponge, 5" d, blue Batman illus, yellow ground, orig pkg, copyright National Periodical Publications 1966 .... **20.00**

Stationery, bond paper, 7¼ x 10½", purple bat symbol and trim, yellow ground, purple "Bat Mail" symbol on envelopes, five sheets and envelopes, c1966 .... **18.00**

Sunglasses, Mask Specs, 7" l, plastic, Marx, orig pkg, copyright National Periodical Publications 1966 ..... **80.00**

Trash Can, 1966 .... **35.00**

Captain America

Badge, Sentinels of Liberty **330.00**

Coloring Book, Whitman, unused, 1966 .... **32.00**

Figure, 12" h, plastic, flying, Trans O Gram, orig display card, 1966 ... **52.00**

Hand Puppet, molded soft vinyl head, Imperial Toy Corp, Marvel Comics Group copyright 1978 .... **15.00**

Puzzle, boxed, jigsaw, 14 x 18", attacking zombies illus, Whitman, Marvel Comics Group copyright 1976 .... **18.00**

Transfer, iron–on, Kirby art, unused, 1960s **10.00**

Captain Marvel

Balloon Whistle, 4½", yellow and red, 1941 .... **39.00**

Book, Dime Action, *Captain Marvel and the Return of the Scorpion*, 4 x 5½", soft cov, 192 pgs, black and white illus, Fawcett Publications Inc copyright 1941 .... **65.00**

Cereal Bowl, plastic, white, "Captain Marvel/Shazam," 1973 .... **29.00**

Pencil Clip, silvered brass, cream color ground, red and blue portrait illus, "Captain Marvel/Shazam," 1940s **75.00**

Pennant **95.00**

Puzzle, envelope **25.00**

Rocket Raider, punch–out figures, Captain Marvel and missile, stand–up, cardboard, Reed, 1940 ...... **98.00**

Ski Toy, punch out, mint in package **8.50**

Transfer, iron–on, tissue paper sheets,

orig black, white, and red envelope, set of six, c1940 .... **28.00**

Captain Midnight

Better Little Book, *Captain Midnight and the Secret Squadron vs the Terror of the Orient*, Whitman, #1458, 1942 .... **50.00**

Decoder, 1¾", disk, plastic, silvered, "SQ," 1955–56 .... **175.00**

Ring

Flight Commander, eagle and shield design brass bands, wing and propeller design top, marked "Captain Midnight Super Code 3," 1940–41 .... **185.00**

Initial, wing design brass bands, "CM" and clock illus top, removable cap, ink pad, 1948 ... **225.00**

Whistle, plastic, dark blue, logo, code wheel, "Captain Midnight's SS 1947" **75.00**

The Flash

Board Game, Justice League of America, Hasbro, 1967 .... **300.00**

Figure, 3" h, plastic, hp, Ideal, 1967 **160.00**

Glass, Pepsi premium, 1973 .... **29.00**

Puzzle, jigsaw, Whitman, battle scene illus, 1967 .... **59.00**

Ring, flasher, Flash running/Flash punching villain, 1960s **20.00**

Green Hornet

Badge, 3" l, flasher **18.00**

Black Beauty Car, Corgi, 5" l, diecast metal, black, orig box, Greenway Productions Inc copyright 1966 .. **175.00**

Flasher, 7½", cardboard **30.00**

Fork and Spoon, silvered metal, vertical lettering and Hornet illus on handle, Imperial, c1966 .... **25.00**

Hummer, wood and paper, 1966 ... **6.00**

Lunch Box, King–Seely Thermos Co, Greenway Productions Inc copyright 1967 .... **100.00**

Magic Rub–Off Set, eight 8½ x 11" glossy cardboard pictures, crayons, tissues, orig box, Whitman, copyright National Periodical Publications 1966 .... **100.00**

Mug, white, color illus, 1966 ...... **35.00**

Pez, candy container, 1966 .... **300.00**

Print Putty, Colorforms, orig display card, 1966 .... **59.00**

Record, The Horn Meets The Hornet, Al Hirt, orig jacket **20.00**

Tee Shirt, Hornet logo, 1966 ...... **39.00**

Wallet, 3½ x 4½", plastic, green, Hornet and Kato illus, magic slate, wood stylus, coin holder, photo section, and black and white Kato photo inside, Mattel, copyright 1966 .... **25.00**

The Phantom

Board Game, Trans O Gram, Phantom skull ring, diecut cardboard figures, sealed, 1965 .... **240.00**

Coloring Book, Ottenheimer, unused, 1965 .... **42.00**

Costume, Collegeville, purple silk, orig box, 1956 .... **200.00**

Model Kit, Revell, unassembled, 1965 .... **190.00**

Oil Painting Set, Hasbro, orig 12 x 10" box, unused, 1965 .... **129.00**

Transfer Set, rub–on, Hasbro, orig 12 x 10" box, 1965 .... **60.00**

Spiderman

Model, Aurora the Amazing Spider–Man, orig box, American issue, unassembled, Marvel Comics Group copyright 1966 .... **175.00**

Rubber Band Gun, 7" l, plastic, orange, decal, four targets, unopened pkg, Gordy International, Marvel Comics Group copyright 1978 ... **15.00**

Watch, 1¼", metal case, gold colored, Spiderman illus dial face, navy blue straps, orig box, Swiss, Super Time Inc, Marvel Comic Group copyright, 1977 .... **110.00**

Superman

Badge, 1½", brass, diecut, enameled, holding flag inscribed "Superman/ American," c1940 .... **175.00**

Balloon, 3¼", rubber, red, black illus, copyright 1966 .... **4.00**

Bank, dime register, 2½" sq, metal, blue and red lettering, yellow ground, Superman illus, 1940s ... **80.00**

Bedspread **35.00**

Button, Superman Club of America . **50.00**

Candy Box, 6 x 2", multicolor, 1966 **12.00**

Cap, nautical, cotton twill, glossy black vinyl visor, 1960s **60.00**

Centerpiece, 10" h, stiff cardboard, diecut, red tissue paper honeycomb base, Hallmark, c1966 .... **25.00**

Disk, 2" d, plastic, blue, Clark Kent/ Superman flasher portrait center, "Happy Birthday 50 Years," DC Comics Inc copyright 1982 ...... **8.00**

Figure

Eyes light up, orig card **28.00**

Flying, orig pkg, 1965 .... **150.00**

Fork **20.00**

Glass, Superman Finds the Spaceship, 4¼" h, light blue continuous illus, pink lettering, National Periodical Publications copyright 1964 ..... **50.00**

Hand Puppet, Ideal, 1965 .... **30.00**

Krypto–Ray Gun, projector, 7" l, metal, seven filmstrips, orig box, Daisy Mfg Co, 1940s **200.00**

Marble, 1" d, white glass, red and yellow logo	**10.00**
Mug, 4" h, plastic, insulated, red and yellow Superman symbol, blue ground, white trim, Nestles' premium, DC Comics copyright 1944, c1980	**10.00**
Patch, Supermen of America, 2 x 2½", premium, 1940s	**300.00**
Pillow Case, Superman flying, saving Lois Lane illus, 1966	**39.00**
Poster, Superman at Bay, 27 x 41", chapter 14 of Columbia serial, 1948	**100.00**
Puzzle, slide tile, Roalex, orig display card, 1966	**98.00**
Record Player	**25.00**
Scrapbook, 10½ x 14½", spiral bound, black and white movie star pictures, Superman Inc copyright 1940	**100.00**
Valentine, 4½ x 5", diecut, Superman Inc copyright 1940	**28.00**
Wonder Woman	
Costume, Ben Cooper, orig box, 1976	**15.00**
Doll, Steve Trevor, 12" h, pilot uniform, orig box, Mego	**69.00**
Model Kit, Aurora, unassembled, 1965	**400.00**
Planter, ceramic, 1978	**15.00**
Tattoo, unused, 1966	**50.00**

SWANKYSWIGS

Collecting Hints: Ideally select glasses whose pattern is clear and brightly colored. Rarer patterns include Carnival, Checkerboard, and Texas Centennial. Look–alike patterns from other manufacturers include the Rooster's Head, Cherry, Diamond over Triangle, and Circus pattern. The look–alike patterns date from the 1930s to the 1950s–60s.

History: Swankyswigs are decorated glass containers that were filled with Kraft Cheese Spreads. The first Swankyswigs date from the early 1930s. Production was discontinued during the last days of World War II because the paints were needed for the war effort. Production was resumed after the war ended. Several new patterns were introduced including Posy or Cornflower No. 2 (1947), Forget–Me–Not (1948), and Tulip No. 3 (1950). The last colored pattern was Bi–Centennial Tulip (1975).

In the mid–1970s, several copycat patterns emerged including: Wildlife Series (1975) and Sportsman Series (1976), most likely Canadian varieties; Rooster's Head, Cherry, Diamond over Triangle, and Circus. Kraft Cheese Spread is still available today, but in crystal–type glass.

Swankyswigs were very popular with economy minded ladies of the Depression era and used as tumblers and juice containers. They served as perfect companions to Depression glass table services and also helped to chase away the Depression blues.

The first designs were hand applied. When the popularity of Swankyswigs increased, new and more intricate machine–made patterns were introduced. Designs were test marketed. As a result of limited distribution, designs that failed are hard to identify and find.

The lack of adequate records about Swankyswigs makes it very difficult to completely identify all patterns. Since 1979, quite a few look–alikes have appeared. Although these glasses were similar, only Kraft glasses are considered Swankyswigs.

References: M. D. Fountain, *Swankyswigs, Price Guide*, privately printed, 1979; Ian Warner, *Swankyswigs, A Pattern Guide Checklist*, Depression Glass Daze, 1982.

Advisor: M. D. Fountain.

Pricing Note: If a Swankyswig retains its original label, add $4.00 to the value of the glass. Glasses with labels or original lids are scarcer than the checkerboards.

Left: Antique Series, clock and coal bucket, black, $4.00; right: Kiddie Cups (Animal Series), pony and duck, $2.25.

Antique	
Black, coffeepot and trivets	**4.25**
Brown, coal bucket and clock	**4.00**
Orange, crib and butter churn	**2.25**
Bands, black and red	**3.00**
Bicentennial, 1938 type tulip, red, yellow or green, coin dot design, 1975	**10.00**
Bustlin Betsy	**2.25**
Carnival, Fired on Fiesta colors, dark blue, orange, yellow, and light green	**7.50**
Checkerboard, green, red, and dark blue	**25.00**
Daisies, red daisies on top row, white in middle, green leaves	**3.00**
Dots & Circles, black, blue, green, or red	**4.50**

Kiddie Cup or Animal
Black, pony and duck **2.25**
Blue, pig and bear **2.00**
Brown, deer and squirrel **2.00**
Dark Blue, pig and bear **2.25**
Green, kitten and bunny **2.00**
Orange, puppy and rooster **2.00**
Red, bird and elephant **2.00**
Modern Flowers, dark and light blue,
red, or yellow
Cornflower **3.00**
Forget–me–not **3.00**
Jonquil, yellow, green leaves **3.00**
Posy **3.00**
Tulip, dark and light blue, red, or yel-
low flowers, green leaves
No. 1, 1937, white leaves **6.00**
No. 2, 1938, six mold bands
around top **20.00**
No. 3, four molded bands around
top **3.00**
Violets, blue flowers, green leaves . .   **2.00**

Bustlin Betsy, brown, 3¾", $2.25.

Sailboat, red, green, or dark blue, racing
or sailing **20.00**
Star, black, dark blue, green, or red . .   **5.00**
Texas Centennial, cowboy, riding buck-
ing horse on one side, Texas State
Seal on other, black, dark blue, green,
and red **9.00**

TARZAN COLLECTIBLES

Collecting Hints: Correct identification of first editions has long been a problem because many people confuse the copyright date with a publication date, resulting in many reprints being improperly identified as first editions (and overpriced accordingly). Reprinted books are common, gaining in value if they have the original pictorial dust jackets.

Some collectors focus only on books, movie items, or toys. Other collectors narrow their scope only to Tarzan and not Burroughs's other material. A third group wants virtually everything associated with Burroughs, including magazines that merely mention Tarzan and any material related to the actors who played Tarzan. Peripheral items usually are not worth a great deal, but may be easily saleable.

Serious collectors tend to be very knowledgeable and want items in the best condition. The market is competitive.

The imitation Tarzan items also have an established market.

History: In 1912 Edgar Rice Burroughs (1875–1950), an American author, created one of the world's most popular and enduring characters, Tarzan. Although not a great writer, Burroughs was one of the greatest literary storytellers of all time, with a seemingly limitless imagination. His stories of heroic and fantastic adventures, whether in the jungles of Africa or on faraway planets, were incredibly popular from the very beginning of his career and spawned numerous imitations throughout the years.

Burroughs inspired many fan clubs, with perhaps more fan publications devoted to him and his career than any other author.

Following his death in 1950, his books were allowed, for the most part, to disappear from bookstore shelves even though the demand was still strong. At least one book publisher who was trying to secure print rights reported that his inquiries to the Burrough estate were not even answered.

This odd situation changed in the early 1960s when a librarian in Downey, California, tried to remove Tarzan books from the library shelves because of her mistaken belief that Tarzan and Jane never were properly married. The issue caught the attention of the media. The end result was an incredible demand for Burroughs books that was satisfied by a veritable flood of new editions, authorized or not. Between 1962 and 1963 Burroughs books accounted for almost one–thirtieth of all U. S. paperback sales, a staggering achievement.

References: Lloyd Currey, *Science Fiction and Fantasy Authors/A Bibliography Of First Printings Of Their Fiction,* G. K. Hall, 1979; Kevin Hancer, *Collector's Guide To Edgar Rice Burroughs,* Crimson Cutlass, 1985; John Harwood, *The Literature of Burroughsiana,* Cazedessus, 1963; Henry Hardy Heins, *The Golden Anniversary Bibliography Of Edgar Rice Burroughs,* Donald Grant, 1964; Irwin Porges, *Edgar Rice Burroughs: The Man Who Created Tarzan,* Brigham Young University Press, 1975.

Collectors' Clubs: The Burrough Bibliophiles, P. O. Box 588, Wytheville, VA 24382; The Jungle Club, 5813 York Avenue, Edina, MN 55410.

Museum: The University of Louisville (Belknap Campus), Louisville, KY.

Comic Book, #137, August 1963, Edgar Rice Burrough, KK Publications, $5.00.

Belt Buckle, premium, Gaylord's Ltd,
1970s **5.00**
Better Little Book
Tarzan And The Jewels of Opar,
#1495, 1940 .... **25.00**
The Son of Tarzan, #1477, Whitman,
1939 .... **28.00**
Big Little Book, *New Adventures of Tarzan,* Whitman Publishing Co, #1180,
1935 .... **50.00**
Book
Jungle Tales of Tarzan, Grosset and
Dunlap wartime reprint, dj **15.00**
King of the Jungle, 5¼ x 8", 128 pgs,
Wm E Wing, Jacobsen–Hodgkinson Corp, Burroughs copyright ... **50.00**
Return of Tarzan, Armed Services edition, paperback **25.00**
Tarzan, 9½ x 13", Big Golden Book,
Western Printing, copyright 1964
Edgar Rice Burroughs, 24 pgs **25.00**
Tarzan and a Daring Rescue, 64 pgs,
illus, Pan–Am Gasoline and Motor
Oil premium, 1938 copyright **75.00**
Tarzan and the Golden Lion, 5 x 7",
336 pgs, dj, Grosset & Dunlap,
copyright 1924 .... **28.00**
Tarzan and the Lost Empire, Dell, paperback, 1951 .... **7.50**
Tarzan of the Apes, 7 x 9", hard cover,
80 pgs, Grosset & Dunlap, 1929
Burroughs copyright **75.00**
Tarzan, Lord of the Jungle, Pinnacle,
English, c1950 .... **8.00**
The New Adventures of Tarzan, pop–
up, 8 x 9¼", 20 pgs, Blue Ribbon
Press series, Pleasure Books Inc,
1935 copyright story by Edgar Rice
Burroughs, 1935 copyright pictures
by Stephen Slesinger **150.00**

The Son of Tarzan, A L Burt reprint . **6.00**
Bookmark, 2½ x 7", stiff paper, black
and white illus, red background,
1930s **48.00**
Campaign Book, 11 x 17", four sheets **48.50**
Clicker, Japanese, 1950s **6.00**
Coloring Book, *Tarzan,* Top Sellers Ltd,
English, 1972 .... **10.00**
Comic Book
Dell, Tarzan, 7 x 10", Vol 1, #17,
Sept–Oct 1950 .... **30.00**
Gold Key, Tarzan, #134, 1962 .... **3.00**
March of Comics, #82, Sears shoe
department giveaway **15.00**
Sparkler Comics, #26 .... **8.00**
Decal, early **15.00**
Figure, set of 9, includes Tarzan, chimpanzee, serpent, gorilla, tiger, lion,
goat, zebra, and crocodile, orig 11 x
15¼" retail display card, unbroken
plastic, Aurora Plastics Corp, 1967
copyright **75.00**
Game, Tarzan To The Rescue, 18½ x
18½" gameboard, orig box, Milton
Bradley, 1977 .... **20.00**
Gum Card, Tarzan and the Crystal Vault
of Isis, complete set, numbered 1–50,
Canadian Chewing Gum Co, Ltd,
1930s **500.00**
Knife, magic, knife blade slides back
into handle, Japanese, 1950s **8.00**
Lobby Card, 11 x 14", chapter titled,
issued for Universal Pictures Corp, individually numbered, set of 10 ..... **200.00**
Magazine Ad, 8¼ x 11½", full page adv,
clipped from Apr 1932 Illustrated
Love Magazine, film scenes stars
Johnny Weissmuller, orange accented
title **15.00**
Model, 6¾" h, plastic, includes 8 page
comic book, instruction booklet, mural backdrop, Aurora, copyright 1974 **25.00**
Notebook Filler Band, 5 x 8", Tarzan
illus and Mickey Mouse Ingersoll
watch adv, 1930s **18.00**
Poster
Tarzan of the Apes, 23½ x 30", black
and white photo, Chicago American Newspaper, 1930s **50.00**
Tarzan and the Lost Safari, 27 x 41",
copyright 1957 .... **28.00**
Tarzan's Fight for Life, 1956 .... **30.00**
Pressbook, Tarzan the Ape–Man, 1981
remake with Bo Derek **8.00**
Puzzle, 8½ x 10½", full color, Screen
Book Magazine issue, orig envelope
with contest information on back ... **125.00**
Record
Tarzan in the Eyes of the Lion, 33 rpm
soundtrack for first TV episode,
MGM Leo the Lion Series **8.75**
Tarzan in the Valley of Talking Goril-

las, 78 rpm, set of 3 in album, Tarzan Records, 1950s **25.00**
Tarzan Song and Jungle Dance, Little Golden Records, 1952, pictorial sleeve **6.75**
Tablet, 5 x 8″, cover illus, Nifty Line, Birmingham Paper Co, 1920s **75.00**
Transfers, ironøn, Tarzan Paint 'N Wear Kit, set of 2, reusable, full color, orig box, Avalon, copyright 1976 .... **12.50**
View–Master Reel
#975, full color photos, includes 4 pg booklet, copyright 1950 ...... **38.00**
#976A–C, full color photos, set of 3, copyright 1955 .... **22.00**
Window Card, 14 x 22″, Tarzan the Magnificent, full color illus, copyright 1960 Solar Film Productions **20.00**

TEAPOTS

Collecting Hints: Most collectors focus on ceramic examples. Do not overlook teapots made in other materials ranging from silver and silver plate to wood.

The approach to collecting teapots is almost as unlimited as the number of teapot forms and designs. Some common approaches are country, color, design motif, and manufacturing material. One approach, albeit expensive, is to collect teapots designed by famous industrial designers.

History: The origin of the teapot has been traced back to the Chinese village of Vi–Hsing in the late sixteenth Century. The teapots, similar to ones still being produced today, were no bigger than the tiny cups previously used for drinking tea.

By the seventeenth century, the drinking of tea spread throughout the world. Every pottery and porcelain manufacturer from the Orient to Europe to the Americas produced teapots. The number and variety is unlimited. Form ranges from functional to ornately decorative and whimsical. The vast majority of teapots available in today's market date from 1870 to the present.

References: Philip Miller and Michael Berthud, *An Anthology of British Teapots* (Available from: John Ives Bookseller, 5 Normanhurst Drive, Twickenham, Middlesex, TW1 1NA, England); Garth Clark, *The Eccentric Teapot: 400 Years of Invention*, Abbeville Press, 1989.

Periodicals: *Hot Tea*, 882 South Mollison, El Cajon, CA 19020; *Tea Talk*, 419 North Larchmont Blvd., #225, Los Angeles, CA 90004.

Museums: Greater Gibson County Area Chamber of Commerce (P. O. Box 464, Trenton, TN 38382, sponsors annual Teapot Festival in May; A. Houberbocken, Inc., 230 Wells, Milwaukee, WI 53203, annual display.

Advisor: Tina M. Carter.

Reproduction Alert: Watch out for figural teapots mimicking older ones, e.g., Granny Anne, Little Old Lady, and blue and white duck. There are several modern reproductions in the Blue Willow pattern.

Bone China, blue, white, and gold, Wedgwood, c1905 .... **110.00**
China, 5″ h, floral, Victoria Carlsbad, Austria **30.00**
Cottage Ware, house, lid is roof, marked "Price Kensington, Made in England, Ye Olde Cottage" **28.00**
Dragonware, 6 cup, raised dragon and coralene dec, gold trim, marked "Made in Occupied Japan" **30.00**
Earthenware
Brown, "Simple Yet Perfect", c1905 **95.00**
Double spout, slip dec, c1890 ..... **80.00**
Figural
Bluebird, 6 cup, bright blue, Lefton China, Japan **28.00**
Cat, 6 cup, beckoning pose, black and white, green eyes and ribbon, paper label, Cortendorf Germany . **45.00**
Scottie Man, spout is nose, lid is cap, brown, yellow or green, Wade, England **40.00**
Snow White, 6″ h, lid is Snow White, body is her dress, dwarfs in relief, musical, marked "Walt Disney Productions" **50.00**
Whimsical man, spout is nose, pastel pink, blue, and yellow, marked "Japan," c1930 .... **25.00**

Hall China, maroon, gold trim, 6 cups, gold and black marks, 6¼″ h, 10½″ w, $25.00.

Ironstone, 2 cup, floral, Ellgreave, Wood & Sons, England **35.00**
Jasperware, 2 cup, blue and white, Wedgwood, c1784 .... **210.00**
Miniature, tea set, teapot, creamer and sugar, cov casserole, salt and pepper, six plates, cups and saucers, Moss Rose, Japan **85.00**
Musical, 6 cup, oval, Wales, Japan ... **8.00**

Pearl Lustre, 6 cup, oval, gold trim, Po-
land **45.00**
Pottery, brown glaze, hp flowers,
"Royal Canadian Art Pottery, Royal
Dripless, Hamilton Canada" im-
pressed in bottom **30.00**
Silver Lustre, 6 cup, hexagonal, Suth-
erland, England **60.00**
Souvenir
   2" h, tea set, teapot, cup and saucer,
   hp, California Redwoods, Chande-
   lier Drive–Thru Tree, Victoria Ce-
   ramics, Japan, c1940 . . . .   **18.00**
   3¼" h, cobalt, scene, Lewis & Clark,
   Portland, OR, no mark, 1905 . . . .   **15.00**
   4½" h, sq, gold trim, scene, US Capitol, Washington DC, Germany . .   **20.00**
   5⅞" h, teepee shape, spout is Indian,
   handle is totem pole, "Greetings
   from Canada," made by Clarice
   Cliff, Britain, c1950 . . . .   **150.00**

TV PERSONALITIES & MEMORABILIA

Collecting Hints: Collectors of television memorabilia fall into two categories. One is those
who specialize in acquiring items from a single
television series. Among these, Star Trek, Hopalong Cassidy, Howdy Doody, Roy Rogers, and
Leave It To Beaver are the most popular series.
The other category specializes in TV memorabilia
of one type such as TV Guides, model kits, films,
and cards.

There have been over 3,750 series on television since 1948. Therefore, the number of artifacts and memorabilia relating to television is
large. Especially rich in TV collectibles are the
early space shows and cowboy adventure series.
The premiums from these types are beginning to
show up at auctions and commanding high
prices; they are eagerly sought by the pop culture
collectors.

Systematic scheduling of television programs
developed a new type of publication called TV
Guide. The early guides are sought avidly. The
first schedules were regional such as *TV Today*
in Philadelphia, *TV Press* in Louisville, *Radio-
Television Life* in Los Angeles. The first national
TV Guide was published on April 3, 1953. Collectors enjoy these older magazines because they
are often good sources for early stories about stars
and their lives.

History: The late 1940s and early 1950s was the
golden age of television. The first programming
began in 1948. Experimentation with programming, vast expansion, and rapid growth marked
the period. Prime time live drama series were
very successful. Many popular stars of today first
appeared on these live dramas, such as Paul

Newman, Steve McQueen, Rod Steiger, Jack
Lemmon, and Grace Kelly. The stars signed autographs and photographs to promote the dramas. These items, plus scripts and other types of
articles have become very collectible.

After the period of live drama came to an end,
the Western assault began. In 1959 there were
26 "Western" series. Many of them were movie
and radio heroes adapted to life on television.
The Western era continued until the early 1960s
when it was replaced by the space adventure
series and science fiction.

The 1970s brought the era of situation come-
dies, including All In The Family and M*A*S*H*.
The collectibles resulting from these series are
numerous. Only time can tell what values they
will have.

References: Jefferson Graham, *Come On
Down!!!–The TV Game Show Book*, Abbeville
Press, 1988; Ted Hake, *Hake's Guide To TV
Collectibles*, Wallace–Homestead, 1990; Vin-
cent Terrace, *Encyclopedia Of Television–Series,
Pilots, And Specials, 1937-1973*, 3 volumes,
New York, Zoetrope, 1986.

Museum: Smithsonian Institution, Washington,
DC.

Addams Family
   Back Scratcher, 12" l, "Thing" hand,
   orig display card, unused, Den–
   Lei, 1960s **98.00**
   Card Game, complete, 1965 . . . .   **30.00**
   Coloring Book, 8½ x 11", Saalfield,
   #4595, 1965 . . . .   **32.00**
   Flashlight Pen, miniature, orig photo
   card, 1965 . . . .   **80.00**
   Light Bulb, Uncle Fester, lights when
   placed in mouth, orig box, unused,
   1965 . . . .   **148.00**
   Plate, ceramic, artist Chas Addams,
   Wednesday, miniature family man-
   sion bird house, occupied by vul-
   ture, 1960s **40.00**
All in the Family, Archie Bunker Card
   Game, 1972 . . . .   **25.00**
Bat Masterson, costume, Ben Cooper,
   orig box, 1958 . . . .   **50.00**
Ben Casey, MD, board game, unused .   **45.00**
Bionic Woman, bank **15.00**
Bonanza
   Ponderosa Ranch Weapons, 31" l ri-
   fle, 9" l revolver, 9½" l knife, plastic
   and metal, vinyl cartridge belt and
   holster, plastic knife sheath and
   bullets, orig unopened pkg, Marx,
   late 1960s **180.00**
   Tin Cup, Ponderosa, pictures of ranch
   and cast of show **15.00**
Bozo the Clown, record set, Circus
   Band, three records **20.00**
Buffalo Bill Jr, belt buckle **5.00**

Captain Kangaroo
Badge **15.00**
Grandfather Clock Punch–out, 17",
cardboard, diecut clock, punch–
out clock pieces, moving eyes,
mouth, and secret panel, Buster
Brown premium, Keeshan–Miller
Enterprises Corp copyright 1956 . .   **23.00**
Charlie's Angels
Pendant **15.00**
Wallet **22.00**
Cheyenne, boxed puzzles, set of three   **15.00**
Columbo, board game **25.00**
Combat!, board game **35.00**
Death Valley Days, 20 mule team
model, premium, unassembled,
sealed in orig mailer **25.00**
Ding Dong School, Spools & Corks &
Pipe Cleaners Craft Set, Miss Frances
on orig box **10.00**
Dr Kildare
Punch–Out Book, Golden Funtime,
1962 . . . .   **20.00**
Thumpy the Heart Beat stethoscope,
picture of Richard Chamberlain on
pkg **35.00**
Dragnet
Cap Gun, Detective Special, MIB . .   **65.00**
Crime Lab Set, Trans O Gram, com-
plete, 1955 . . . .   **139.00**
Water Pistols, 5" l, marked "Dragnet,"
red, yellow, and black, Empire
Plastic Corp, copyright 1953, case
of 12 . . . .   **98.00**
Fall Guy, lunch box **15.00**
Flipper, colorform set, Standard Toy-
kraft, orig box, 1966 . . . .   **52.00**
Flying Nun, flying figure with launcher,
MIB **35.00**
Get Smart, lunch box **50.00**
Groucho Marx, cocktail napkin set, se-
ries #1, "That's Me, Groucho," pa-
per, cartoon illus, orig box, 36 nap-
kins, monogram of California,
copyright 1954 . . . .   **45.00**
Gunsmoke
Arcade Card, James Arness **4.00**
Big Little Book, 1958 . . . .   **14.00**
Comic Book, 1958 . . . .   **13.00**
Gun and Holster Set, black vinyl, sil-
ver trim, 8" l gray plastic six-
shooter, black vinyl belt, orig uno-
pened pkg **45.00**
Puzzle, frame tray **10.00**
Vest, cowboy, orig pkg, 1959 . . . . . .   **35.00**
Happy Days
Lunch Box **18.00**
Puzzle, jigsaw, 1976 . . . .   **15.00**
Have Gun Will Travel, figure, Paladin
and horse, Hartland, mint on card . .   **135.00**
Howdy Doody
Cap, Hoop Head, 10" d plastic ring

**Howdy Doody's TV Game, Milton Brad-
ley, 1950s, 9¼ x 9⅝ x 1⅝", $20.00.**

mounted on top, Kagran copyright
1951–56 . . . .   **46.00**
Ceiling Shade, 11½" sq, glass, four
character portraits, Kagran copy-
right, 1951–56 . . . .   **175.00**
Disk, 1¾" d, cardboard, "Clarabell
Says..." and portrait illus front,
Wonder Bread adv back, attached
pin and string, Kagran copyright . .   **10.00**
Doll, Goldberger, MIB **35.00**
Figure
Clarabell, Bend–Me Toy, 12" h,
foam rubber over wire, orig un-
opened bag, Ben–Her Industries,
Kagran copyright, 1951–56 . . . .   **20.00**
Howdy Doody, wood, jointed,
push–up, NBC microphone **145.00**
Mittens, pr, 8" h, wool, red, Howdy
and Clarabell portrait illus **25.00**
Place Mat, set of 8 . . . .   **45.00**
Puzzle, frame tray, 11½ x 15", amuse-
ment park airplane ride illus, Whit-
man, Kagran copyright 1953 . . . . .   **24.00**
Spoon, ice cream **40.00**
Wrapper, Howdy Doody Fudge Bar,
1950s **3.00**
I Love Lucy
Doll, Ricky Jr, 1950s **250.00**
Vase, figural head, Lucille Ball **20.00**
Jackie Gleason
Aw–a–a–ay We Go Climbing Toy,
Reggie Van Gleason III, mint on
card, 1950s **95.00**
Bus Driver Uniform, includes cap,
coin changer, coins, bus tickets,
and ticket puncher, VIP, orig box,
1956 . . . .   **395.00**
Kit Carson
Record, western songs, 7", 78 rpm,
orig picture sleeve **9.00**
Saddlebag Coloring Set **75.00**
Kukla, Fran & Ollie, game **25.00**
Land of the Giants
Book, *Flight of Fear*, 5¼ x 8", Carl
Henry Rathjen, hard cov, Whitman,
#1516, 212 pgs, 1969 . . . .   **17.50**
Coloring Book, 8 x 10", Whitman,
#1138, unused, 1969 . . . .   **25.00**
Lassie, wallet, photo front, membership

card, Campbell Soup premium, orig
envelope, 1958 .... **40.00**

Laugh–In
Drawing Set, Lakeside, unused, orig
box, 1968 .... **60.00**
Notebook Binder, 1969 .... **20.00**
Trash Can, character illus **35.00**

Liberace, sheet music, *I'll Be Seeing
You*, 9 x 12", 6 pgs, bluetone photo
portrait, copyright 1938, republica-
tion c1953 .... **15.00**

Man From UNCLE
Board Game **25.00**
Card Game **25.00**
Gum Cards, complete set, 1960s ... **60.00**
Ring, Solo and Kuryakin portraits,
plastic, dark blue, 1960s **12.00**

MASH, 4077 Jeep, boxed **30.00**

Maverick
Cap Gun, 10½" l, silvered metal,
white plastic grips, crossed hor-
seshoes inset, c1960 .... **40.00**
Paint By Number Set, oil, unused,
photo of Garner on box **125.00**
Puzzle, frame tray, 11½ x 14½",
Whitman, gunfight illus, 1959 ... **22.00**

McHale's Navy
Board Game, PT 109, 1963 .... **25.00**
Model Kit, PT 73, Revell, complete,
unassembled, orig instructions and
box, Sto–Rev Co copyright 1965 . **85.00**

Mory Amsterdam, button, Yuk Apuk .. **25.00**

Mr Ed, doll, talking, Mattel **65.00**

Munsters
Book, *The Munsters and the Great
Camera Caper*, 6 x 7½", hard cov,
Whitman, #1510, 212 pgs, 1965 **15.00**
Doll, Lily, 8½" h, vinyl, movable
arms, legs, and head, gray and sil-
ver streaked hair, Mini–Monster se-
ries, Ideal copyright 1965 .... **25.00**
Lunch Box **75.00**
Ring, flasher, plastic, blue, Herman,
Lily, Grandpa, and Eddie, c1966,
set of four **50.00**
Wrapper, gum card, 6" sq, waxed pa-
per, Leaf, 1966 .... **54.00**

Our Gang, book, color, 1939 .... **35.00**

Ozzie and Harriet, candy box, Mounds,
Nelson family cartoon illus, 1957 .. **98.00**

Partridge Family, lunch box, metal thermos **40.00**

Paul Winchell, Ozwald "talking" toy,
MIB **50.00**

Perry Mason, game, Missing Suspect,
1959 .... **39.00**

Police Woman, doll, Angie Dickinson,
boxed **22.50**

Ramar of the Jungle, puzzles, boxed set
of four **65.00**

Rawhide, canteen, orig pkg **35.00**

Sea Hunt, magic slate, 1960 .... **59.00**

Sky King, teleblinker ring **90.00**

Starsky & Hutch, puzzle, jigsaw, 1976 **15.00**

Tales of Wells Fargo
Board Game, complete **40.00**
Tv projector and film set, orig unused
batteries, MIB **135.00**

Toast of the Town, ashtray, 4 x 4",
glazed ceramic, seashell shape, blue,
standing Topo Gigio nodder, composition, painted, flocked head, orig tag
and box, 1950s **100.00**

Trouble With Father, coloring book,
June and Stu Erwin, 11 x 14", Whitman, 16 pgs, unused, 1954 .... **35.00**

Wagon Train
Coloring Book, Whitman, unused,
1959 .... **30.00**
Covered Wagon, 20" l, plastic and
fabric, orig box, Louis Marx, c1960 **100.00**

Wanted: Dead or Alive, rifle, Mares Laig
replica, plastic and metal, orig card **75.00**

Winky Dink
Clay Doodle, MIB **20.00**
Pinback Button, 1⅛" d, litho, black
ground, white Winky head, yellow
star, 1950s **45.00**

TELEVISIONS

Collecting Hints: There are two distinct types of
early television sets: mechanical and electronic.
Mechanical televisions, the earliest, look nothing
like their modern counterparts. Mechanical sets
from the 1920s typically have a motorized 12"
diameter metal disc with a "glow tube" in back
and a magnifier in front. Starting in 1938 sets
used picture tubes as they do today. Generally
the earlier the set, the smaller the screen. The
easiest way to gauge the age of a television set
is by the numbers found on the channel selector.
Pre–1946 television sets will tune a maximum of
five stations, usually channels 1–5. In 1946
channels 7–13 were added, thus sets made between 1946 and 1948 will show channels 1–13
on the station selector.

In 1949, channel 1 was dropped, leaving all
1949 and newer sets with V.H.F. channels 2–13,
as we have them today. The U.H.F. band was
added in 1953, thus any set with U.H.F. capa-
bility is less than 40 years old.

Brand and model number are essential to determining a set's worth. However, physical condition of the cabinet is much more important than
the operating condition of the set.

History: There are three distinct eras of early
television. The first, the "mechanical" era, was
from 1925–32. Sets often were known as "ra-
diovisors," since they were visual attachments to
radios. Many mechanical television sets did not
have cabinets and resembled an electric fan with
a round metal disk in place of the blades. These

units were most prevalent in the New York City and Chicago areas.

Any complete mechanical set is valued in the several thousand dollar range. Manufacturers included Jenkins, Baird, Western Television, Insuline Corp. of America, Short–Wave and Television Corp., Daven, See–All, Rawls, Pioneer, Travler Radio & Television Corp., and others.

The second era was the pre–World War II era, which spanned 1938–1941. These were the first all–electronic sets and usually were combined with a multi–band radio in fancy cabinets. A favorite design of the era was the use of a "mirror in the lid" arrangement, whereby a mirror in the underside of a lift–lid reflected the picture tube, which was pointed straight up. No more than 2,000 sets were produced during the three years. They were concentrated in those areas with pre-war television stations: New York City, Albany/Schenectady/Troy, Philadelphia, Chicago, and Los Angeles. Depending on model and condition, these sets usually start at $1,000 and can range to $5,000 or more.

The final era of television started in 1946 with the resumption of post–war television production. Production rose rapidly. Few sets after 1949 have collectible value. There are some notable exceptions, e.g., the first "color wheel" sets [1951], the giant Dumont 30" screen sets [1953], and limited production or "oddball" sets.

References: Morgan E. McMahon, *A Flick of The Switch*, Vintage Radio, 1975; Harry Poster and John Sakas, *1990 Price Guide To Vintage TV's and Collectible Radios*, Sight, Sound, Style, 1990.

Periodicals: *TV Collector*, P. O. Box 188, Needham, MA 02192; *Sight, Sound, Style*, P.O. Box 2224, South Hackensack, NJ 07606.

Caution: Do not plug in a set that has been in storage for more than 30 years without an inspection by a serviceman. Components can go bad and short–circuit, causing a fire. Many early sets had no fuses for protection.

1925–1932, MECHANICAL

Daven, parts kit	500.00
Insuline Corp of American (ICA)	
Bakelite cabinet model	3,000.00
Oak box kit	1,000.00
Jenkins, Model 202	4,000.00
See–All, open frame	1,500.00
Short–Wave and Television Corporation, drum scanner	3,000.00
Western Television Corp, "Ship's wheel," cabinet type	2,000.00

1938–1941, ELECTRONIC

Andrea	
1–F–5	4,000.00

Philco, reconditioned, $300.00.

KTE–5	2,500.00
Dumont	
180	2,000.00
181	3,000.00
General Electric	
HM–171	2,500.00
HM–225	5,000.00
HM–226	3,000.00
RCA	
TRK–5, television "Attachment"	4,000.00
TT–5	3,500.00
TRK–9	3,000.00
TRK–12	2,500.00
TRK–120	4,000.00
RR–359	5,000.00
Stromberg–Carlson, 112	5,000.00

1946 AND LATER

CBS/Columbia, 12CC2, color wheel set	5,000.00
Hallicrafters, T–54	200.00
Motorola, VT–71	150.00
Philco	
Predicta	
Pole Model	500.00
Table Model	250.00
Two Piece Model	200.00
Safari	350.00
Pilot, TV–37	
Carry case	100.00
Magnifier	100.00
Set	250.00
RCA	
621TS	500.00
630TS	250.00
648PTK	250.00
721TS	200.00
8TS30	150.00
CT–100, 1st RCA Color Set	500.00

SHIRLEY TEMPLE

Collecting Hints: Dolls are made out of many materials—composition, cloth, chalk, papier mache, rubber, and vinyl. Composition dolls are the earliest. Shirley Temple's popularity received a renewed boost through television, resulting in a new series of Shirley Temple products being issued in the 1950s.

History: Shirley Jane Temple was born April 23, 1928, in Santa Monica, California. A movie scout discovered her at a dancing school. "Pie Covered Wagon" in 1932 was her screen test. During the 1930s she made twenty movies, earning as much as $75,000 per film.

Her mother supervised the licensing of over fifteen firms to make Shirley Temple products. These included dolls, glassware, china, jewelry, and soap. The first Shirley Temple dolls were made in 1934 by The Ideal Toy Company. They varied in height from 11 to 27 inches and were composition (pressed wood). Ideal made the first vinyl dolls in 1957.

References: John Axe, *The Encyclopedia of Celebrity Dolls*, Hobby House Press, Inc., 1983; Patricia R. Smith, *Shirley Temple Dolls And Collectibles, Series 1*, (1977) and *Series 2* (1979), Collector Books, 1977.

REPRODUCTION ALERT

Barrette, bow, Temple cameo	**85.00**
Book	
Dimples, 9½ x 10", 1936	**20.00**
Heidi, 1937	**22.00**
My Life & Time by Shirley Temple, 1936	**25.00**
Shirley Temple at Play, 1935	**45.00**
Shirley Temple Through the Day, 1935	**45.00**
Suzanna of the Mounties, 9½ x 10", 1939	**22.00**
Bowl, 6½", glass, blue	**35.00**
Bracelet, child's, charm, 1930s	**45.00**
Button, c1936	**50.00**
Cake Topper, Happy Birthday	**75.00**
Christmas Card, 4 x 5", Hallmark, 1935	**12.00**
Cigar Band, Spanish, 1930s	**22.00**
Clothes Hanger, cardboard, blue, 1930s	**10.00**
Clothing Tag, 3 x 5", black and white photo, endorsed by Shirley Temple, orig string cord, 1930s	**12.00**
Doll	
12", orig clothes, 1957	**95.00**
13", composition, 1935	**450.00**
16", red polka dot dress, 1972	**120.00**
19", vinyl, 1959	**250.00**
22", composition, marked "Curly Top," 1934	**600.00**
23", composition, orig clothes, pin, wig, Ideal	**750.00**

Figure	
5"	**45.00**
6½", bisque, movable arms and legs, marked "Made in Japan"	**90.00**
Gloves, leather, blue, 1930s	**38.00**
Headband, pink, cameo and name in center	**85.00**
Handkerchief, 9 x 9", "Little Colonel"	**20.00**
Lobby Card, "Adventure in Baltimore," RKO, 1949	**12.00**
Magnetic TV Theater, MIB	**125.00**
Mirror, purse size	**15.00**
Movie Still	
"Captain January," 8 x 10", 1936 ...	**15.00**
"Poor Little Rich Girl," 8 x 10", 1936	**15.00**
Paper Doll, clothes, orig box, Gabriel Co, 1958	**25.00**
Party Invitations, packet of ten, 1973 .	**4.00**
Paperweight	**40.00**
Pen, blue, name on body and clip	**85.00**
Pencil, pink	**85.00**
Pin	
Everybody Loves Me, Miss Charming, oval, black and white, doll pictured	**85.00**
Everybody Loves Me, Little Miss Movie, oval, blue and white, doll pictured	**85.00**
Sunday Referee, Shirley Temple League, round, porcelain, finger to face, copper back marked "Roden London"	**85.00**
Playing Cards, Temple in duck dress, complete deck, 1930s	**45.00**
Portrait, 8 x 10", sepia	**10.00**
Purse, 2⅞ x 4", 1958	**32.00**
Sewing Machine, Little Miss	**125.00**
Sheet Music	
Stowaway	**12.00**

Sheet Music, The Toy Trumpet, Circle Music Publications, Inc, 9⅜ x 12", $18.00.

That's What I Want For Christmas, 6
pgs, sung in Stowaway film, green-
tone photo on cov, 1935 copyright ... **25.00**
Sign, 11 x 14", cardboard, c1930 .... **60.00**
Soap, 5", figural, two in orig box **85.00**
Statue, 14½", plaster, painted, rosy ac-
cents, late 1930s **110.00**
Store Display Sign, 19 x 30", cardboard,
"Shirley Temple Loves Quaker Puffed
Wheat" **90.00**
Tablecloth, 1930s **18.00**
Tablet, writing, 5½ x 9", 1935 .... **20.00**
Tea Set, glass, pink **85.00**
Treasure Board, wipe–off back **65.00**

THIMBLES

Collecting Hints: Collectors tend to specialize in
a limited variety of thimbles, depending on what
appeals to them. Novice collectors are best advised to begin with a specialized thimble dealer
before going "bargin" hunting on their own.

Thimble collectors use the following grading
scale to determine thimble values:

Mint:	used, perfect condition
Excellent:	A slight degree of wear on the highest points, but in general, excellent condition
Fair:	Very worn from constant use, bent, or pierced by a needle
Poor:	Damaged, pierced with two or more holes, cracked, badly bent, half the design worn off, or chipped enamel

During the 19th century and earlier a lady
would take her favorite thimble to a silversmith
to have it mended if it became pierced from
constant use. As a result, mended, 19th century
thimbles commonly are found. Collectors must
decide for themselves if they wish to add this
condition of thimble to their collection.

Thimble collecting has two specialized off-
shoots—advertising and political thimbles. Old
campaign thimbles in mint condition are rare. It
is best not to try to "touch up" the paint, as this
diminishes the value. Collectors of political items
use the term "brummagem," meaning showy but
inferior and worthless, to refer to political thimbles after 1960. They consider these later thimbles as non–official campaign items.

History: Thimbles often are thought of as common household sewing tools. Many are. However, others are miniature works of art, souvenirs
of places, people, and events, or gadgets (thimbles with expanded uses such as attached thread-
ers, cutters, or magnets).

There were many thimble manufacturers in the
United States prior to 1930. Before we became

a "throw–away" society, hand sewing was a
never ending chore for the housewife. Garments
were mended and altered. When they were beyond repair, pieces were salvaged to make a
patchwork quilt. Thimble manufacturers tried to
create a new thimble to convince the home
sewer that "one was not enough."

By the early 1930s only one manufacturer of
gold and silver thimbles remained in business in
the United States, The Simons Brothers Company
of Philadelphia, which was founded by George
Washington Simons in 1839. Simons Brothers
thimbles from the 1904 St. Louis World's Fair
and the 1893 Columbian Exposition are prized
acquisitions for any collector. The Liberty Bell
thimble, in the shape of the bell, is one of the
most novel.

Today, the company, owned by Nelson Keyser,
continues to produce silver and gold thimbles.
The Simons Brothers Company designed a special thimble for Nancy Reagan as a gift for dip-
lomats' wives who visited the White House. The
thimble has a picture of the White House and
the initials "N.D.R."

Thimbles have been produced in a variety of
materials: gold, silver, steel, aluminum, brass,
china, glass, vegetable ivory, ivory, bone, celluloid, plastics, leather, hard rubber, and silk.
Common metal thimbles usually are bought by
the intended user, who makes sure the size is a
comfortable fit. Precious metal thimbles often
were received as gifts. Many of these do not show
signs of wear from constant use. This may result
from ill fit of the thimble or from it simply being
too elegant for mundane work.

During the 20th century thimbles were used
as advertising promotions. It is not unusual to
find a thimble that says, "You'll Never Get Stuck
Using Our Product" or a political promotion stating, "Sew It Up—Vote for John Doe for Senator."

References: Cecile Dreesmann, *A Thimble Full*,
Cambium, Netherlands, 1983 (printed in Dutch
and English); Helmut Greif, *Talks About Thim-
bles*, Fingerhutmuseum Creglingen, Germany,
1983 (English edition available from Dine–
American, Wilmington, DE); Edwin F. Holmes,
A History Of Thimbles, Cornwall Books, 1985;
Eleanor Johnson, *Thimbles*, Shires Publications,
England, 1982; Myrtle Lundquist, *The Book Of
A Thousand Thimbles*, Wallace–Homestead,
1970; Myrtle Lundquist, *Thimble Americana*,
Wallace–Homestead, 1981; Myrtle Lundquist,
Thimble Treasury, Wallace–Homestead, 1975;
Averil Mathis, *Antique & Collectible Thimbles
And Accessories*, Collector Books, 1986, 1989
value update; Gay Ann Rodgers, *American Silver
Thimbles*, Haggerston Press, 1989; John von
Heille, *Thimble Collectors Encyclopedia*, Wal-
lace–Homestead, 1986; Estelle Zalkin, *Zalkin's
Handbook of Thimbles & Sewing Implements*,
Warman Publishing Co., 1988.

Periodical: *Thimbletter,* 93 Walnut Hill Road, Newton Highlands, MA 02161.

Collectors' Club: Thimble Collectors International, P. O. Box 2311, Des Moines, IA 50310.

Advisor: Estelle Zalkin.

REPRODUCTION ALERT. Reproductions can be made by restrikes from an original die or cast from a mold made from an antique thimble. Many reproductions are sold as such and priced accordingly. Among the reproduced thimbles are a pre–revolution Russian enamel thimble and the Salem Witch thimble (the repro has no cap, and the seam is visible).

Silver, Mexican, $20.00.

Gold, 1900–1940
Plain band	75.00
Scenic band	100.00
Semi precious stones on band	250.00

Ivory
Modern scrimshaw	20.00
Vegetable ivory	60.00

Metal, Common
Brass with ornate band	15.00
Brass, plain band	3.00
Cast pot metal, "For a Good Girl"	2.00
Cloisonne on brass, China	10.00
Diragold, Scandinavian gold	75.00
Toledo, Spain damascene	20.00

Patented and Gadget
M T (Magic Thimble), thread cutter and needle threader	25.00
Thread cutter lip on band	15.00

Porcelain
Meissen, modern, hp, Germany	125.00
Modern collectible with transfer print design	15.00

Royal Worcester, hp
England, sgd	50.00
Powell, sgd, birds	300.00

Silver, 1900–1940
Applied wire work, Mexico	10.00
Cupid in high relief	125.00
Flowers in high relief	50.00
Paneled band	35.00
Scenic band	35.00

Souvenir and Commemorative
Applied enamel shield, silver plated
Liberty Bell, 1976 issue, silver	75.00
Statue of Liberty, silver, France	50.00

Thimble Holders
Glass, slipper	100.00
Silver, round filigree	150.00

TINSEL ART

Collecting Hints: Look for those pieces which are elaborate in design and contain different colored foil. Signed pictures often are viewed as folk art and may be priced higher.

Nineteenth century material is preferred over the nondescript 20th century examples. However, Art Deco and Art Nouveau designs of quality are sought by collectors from these fields.

History: Tinsel pictures (or paintings) were both a "cottage art" and a commercial product which enjoyed popularity from the late 19th century through the 20th century. The "painting" took two forms. The first was similar to a reverse painting on glass. A design was placed on the glass and colored foil was placed behind to accent the piece. The second form consisted of a silhouette or cutting, separate from the glass, placed over a layer of crumpled foil.

The reverse painting type was highly personalized; a mother and her children could work on tinsel pictures as a family project. This handiwork often contained presentation remarks and was artist signed and dated. The silhouette type appears to be related to the Art Deco and Art Nouveau periods and may have been a form of souvenir at carnival games and the seashore. The sameness of many designs, e.g., flamingos in a swamp–like setting, denotes its commercial production.

Flamingos, palm tree, reeds, yellow sun, black ground, 10¾ x 8¾", $70.00.

Birds, exotic, perched in bouquet of
flowers, 15¾ x 22" **250.00**
Bowl, with flowers, multicolored, black
ground, molded walnut frame, gold
liner, 26 x 36" **250.00**
Cornucopia, variety of garden blossoms,
supplemented with painted motifs,
American, 19th C, 11 x 15½" **325.00**
Family Tree, portraits of mother, father,
and ten children, surrounded by leafy
tree, 21½ x 18½" **1,000.00**
Flamingos, palm tree, reeds, yellow
sun, black ground, 10¾ x 8¾" **70.00**
Floral
10 x 12", cross–counter frame **40.00**
10¼ x 22½", wild roses, buds and
leaves **90.00**
11½ x 15½", spray of garden blossoms, 19th C **100.00**
12¾ x 17½", red and green, black
ground, curly maple frame **45.00**
Peacock, perched on garden wall, pot
of roses, flowers, white ground, made
by Jos Mollack, Providence, RI, late
19th C, 12 x 16" **300.00**
Stork, standing, floral motif, multicolored, black ground, sgd A S Kessler,
PA, 12¼ x 14¼" **150.00**

TOOTHPICK HOLDERS

Collecting Hints: Toothpick holders have been
confused with many forms—from match holders,
shot glasses, miniature spoon holders to toy table
setting, mustard pots without lids, rose or violet
bowls, individual open sugars, and vases. Use
toothpicks to test what you have. The toothpicks
should rest well in the holder with an ample
extension to allow an individual toothpick to be
selected easily. Match holders often are figural
in nature and have a striking surface on them.

The biggest danger to the collector is a salt
shaker with a ground top or a wine glass with
the stem removed. Knowing the forms of salt
shakers and wine glasses will avoid any confusion.

Among the forms, perhaps the silverplated figural toothpicks are least appreciated. They offer
the beginner a reasonable area upon which to
build an inexpensive collection.

History: Toothpick holders are small containers
used to hold toothpicks. They were an important
table accessory during the Victorian period.

Toothpick holders were made in a wide range
of material—Art glass, colored pattern glass, colored glass novelties, milk glass, china, bisque
and porcelain, crystal pressed glass, cut glass,

and silverplated figurals. Makers include both
American and European firms.

Toothpick holders were used as souvenir items
by applying decals or transfers. The same blank
may contain several different location labels.

References: William Heacock, *Encyclopedia of
Victorian Colored Pattern Glass, Book I, Toothpick Holders from A to Z,* Antique Publications,
1981; William Heacock, *1000 Toothpick Holders: A Collector's Guide,* Antique Publications,
1977; William Heacock, *Rare & Unlisted Toothpick Holders,* Antique Publications, Inc., 1984.

Collectors' Club: National Toothpick Holder
Collector's Society, P. O. Box 246, Red Arrow
Highway, Sawyer, MI 49125.

Additional Listings: See *Warman's Antiques And
Their Prices.*

**Custard glass, souvenir of Flagstaff Park,
Mauch Chunk, PA, sawtooth top, gold
trim, $48.00.**

Art Glass
Amberina, Optic Diamond Quilt, sq
polished top **75.00**
Cranberry, British Barrel, imp inverted
thumbprint, applied vaseline feet . **65.00**
Greentown Glass, Indian head, choc-
olate **175.00**
Purple Slag, boot **25.00**
Satin, Cone pattern, blue **60.00**
Bisque, boy with bottle **25.00**
Brass, "I'm From Missouri" **25.00**
China
Baby Pierrette, imp "Germany 3315",
3" h **40.00**
Bavarian, hp, florals **40.00**
Hand Painted, pink roses on yellow
and green ground, yellow pedestal
base, 2½" **35.00**
Majolica, sunflower **90.00**
Nippon, windmill scene, gold dec
and beading, 3" **20.00**
Occupied Japan, boot, floral dec,
2¾" **10.00**

R S Prussia, lily of the valley dec, three handles, white ground, blue rim shading 250.00

Royal Bayreuth
Elk's head, figural 85.00
Woman with basket, boats, sterling rim 50.00

Custard Glass
Bees–On–A–Basket 50.00
Jefferson Optic, enameled rose dec . 85.00

Glass, figural
Anvil, Windsor, amber 35.00
Beggar's Hand, frosted 30.00
Cat on cushion 45.00
Dolphin, amber 65.00
Gattling Gun, blue 35.00
Horse pulling cart, amber 75.00
Peek–a–Boo, clear 28.00

Milk Glass
Boy with Pack, blue 48.00
Button & Bulge, hp floral dec 35.00
Owl 45.00
Scrolled Shell, enamel dec 20.00
Tramp's Shoe 30.00

Opalescent Glass
Bubble Lattice, blue 75.00
Sprig, white 35.00
Stars and Stripes, clear 22.00
Swirl, blue 50.00
Wreath and Shell 100.00

Pattern Glass
Alabama, clear 50.00
Banded Portland, clear, gold 24.00
Bull's Eye and Fan, trace of gold ... 15.00
Cornell, blue 40.00
Daisy, kettle, amber 25.00
Diamond Dandy 20.00
Fancy Loop, Heisey 50.00
Iris and Meander, blue 100.00
Leaf and Star, amber, pedestal 35.00
Pennsylvania, green 38.00
Texas, clear, gold trim 50.00
US Rib, green 35.00

Ruby Stained Glass
Button Arches 25.00
Daisy and Button 28.00
Diamond Peg 25.00
Spearpoint Band 28.00
Zipper Slash 25.00

Silver Plate
Cat, arched back 45.00
Chick, half egg and wishbone 30.00
Dog
Hunting breed 125.00
Seated with bone, ornate holder, Tufts 115.00
Kate Greenaway, seated girl 100.00
Owl, seated on branch, 2" h 75.00
Porcupine, octagonal base, Wilcox . 45.00
Rabbit, beside egg 24.00
Tin, woodpecker on stump, picks toothpick up with bill, painted 35.00

TOYS

Collecting Hints: Condition is a very critical factor. Most collectors like to have examples in very fine to mint condition. The original box and any instructional sheets add to the value.

Sophisticated collectors concentrate on the tin and cast iron toys of the late 19th and early 20th centuries. However, more and more collectors are concentrating on the 1940 to 1970 period, including products from firms such as Fisher-Price.

Many toys were characterizations of cartoon, radio, and television figures. A large number of collectible fields have some form of toy spinoff. The result is that the toy collector constantly is competing with the specialized collector.

History: In America the first cast iron toys began to appear shortly after the Civil War. Leading 19th century manufacturers included Hubley, Dent, Kenton, and Schoenhut. In the first decades of the 20th century Arcade, Buddy L, Marx, and Tootsietoy joined the earlier firms. The picture became complete with the addition of firms such as Built Rite, Ideal, and Fisher Price.

In Europe, Nuremberg, Germany, was the center for the toy industry from the late 18th through the mid–20th century. In England the Britain and Lesney companies challenged the German supremacy. Lesney originated the famous matchbox toys. German manufacturers were especially skilled in the areas of toy trains and stuffed toys.

References: Linda Baker, *Modern Toys, American Toys, 1930–1980,* Collector Books, 1985, 1988 value update; Robert Carter and Eddy Rubinstein, *Yesterday's Yesteryears: Lesney "Matchbox" Models,* Haynes Publishing Group (London), 1986; Jurgen and Marianne Cieslik, *Lehmann Toys,* New Cavendish Books, 1982; Don Cranmer, *Collectors Encyclopedia, Toys–Banks,* L–W Books, 1986; Edward Force, *Corgi Toys,* Schiffer Publishing Ltd., 1984, 1991 value update; Edward Force, *Dinky Toys,* Schiffer Publishing Ltd., Edward Force, *Matchbox and Lledo Toys,* Schiffer Publishing Ltd., 1988; Edward Force, *Miniature Emergency Vehicles,* Schiffer Publishing Ltd., 1985; Richard Friz, *The Official Price Guide to Collectible Toys, 5th Edition,* House of Collectibles, 1990; Gordon Gardiner and Alistar Morris, *Illustrated Encyclopedia of Metal Toys,* Harmony House, 1984; Lillian Gottschalk, *American Toy Cars & Trucks,* Abbeville Press, 1985; Dale Kelley, *Collecting The Tin Toy Car, 1950–1970,* Schiffer Publishing, Ltd, 1984; Constance King, *Metal Toy & Automata,* Chartwell Books, 1989; Ernest & Ida Long, *Dictionary Of Toys Sold In America,* published by author, two volumes; David Longest, *Character Toys and Collectibles, First Series* (1984) and *Second Series* (1987), Collector Books; David

Longest, *Toys: Antique & Collectible*, Collector Books, 1990; Albert W. McCollough, *The Complete Book Of Buddy "L" Toys: A Greenberg Guide*, I. Greenberg Publishing Co., 1982, out-of-print; Brian Moran, *Battery Toys, The Modern Automata*, Schiffer Publishing, Ltd, 1984; John J. Murray & Bruce Fox, *Fisher–Price, 1931–1963: A Historical, Rarity, Value Guide*, Books Americana, 1987; Nigel Mynheer, *Tin Toys*, Boxtree (London), 1988; Richard O'Brien, *Collecting Toys: A Collectors Indentification and Value Guide, 5th Edition*, Books Americana, 1990; Maxine A. Pinsky, *Greenberg's Guide To Marx Toys, Volume I* (1988) and *Volume II* (1990), Greenberg Publishing Co.; David Richter, *Collectors Guide to Tootsietoys*, Collector Books, 1990; Harry L. Rinker, *Collector's Guide To Toys, Games, and Puzzle*, Wallace–Homestead, 1991; Nancy Schiffer, *Matchbox Toys*, Schiffer Publishing Ltd., 1983; Peter Viemeister, *Micro Cars*, Hamilton's, 1982; James Weiland and Dr. Edward Force, *Tootsie Toys, World's First Die Cast Models*, Motorbooks International, 1980; Blair Whitton, *The Knopf Collector's Guide To American Toys*, Alfred A. Knopf, 1984.

Periodicals: *Antique Toy World*, P. O. Box 34509, Chicago, IL 60634; *Model and Toy Collector*, 330 Merriman Road, Akron, OH, 44303; *Plastic Figure & Playset Collector*, Box 1355, La Crosse, WI 54602; *Toy Collector News*, P. O. Box 451, River Forest, IL 60305; *Toy Shop*, 700 East State Street, Iola, WI 54990; *Toy Values Monthly*, Attic Books, Inc., 19 Danbury Road, Ridgefield, CT 06877; *Wheel Goods Trader*, P. O. Box 435, Fraser, MI 48026; *U.S. Toy Collector Magazine*, P.O. Box 4244, Missoule, MT 59806; *YesterDaze Toys*, P. O. Box 57, Otisville, MI 48463.

Collectors' Clubs: American–International Matchbox, 522 Chestnut Street, Lynn, MA 01904; Antique Toy Collectors of America, Two Wall Street, New York, NY 10005; Matchbox Collectors Club, 141 West Commercial Avenue, Moonachie, NJ 07075.

Museums: American Museum of Automobile Miniatures, Andover, MA; Museum of the City of New York, New York, NY; Smithsonian Institution, Washington, DC; Margaret Woodbury Strong Museum, Rochester, NY; Toy Museum of Atlanta, Atlanta, GA.

See: Automata, Cartoon Characters, Disneyana, Dolls, Games, Paper Dolls, Radio Characters, Dimestore Soldiers, Toy Soldiers, Toy Trains and many other categories.

ARCADE

The Arcade Manufacturing Company first produced toys in 1893. In 1919, the firm began to make the yellow cabs for the Yellow Cab Com-

pany of Chicago. The exclusive advertising rights were sold to the cab company with Arcade holding the right to make toy replicas of the cabs. This idea was popular and soon was used with Buick, Ford, etc., and McCormack and International Harvester farm equipment. The company continued until 1946 when it was sold to Rockwell Manufacturing Company of Pittsburgh.

Arcade, Greyhound Bus, A Century of Progress, Chicago, 1934, painted cast iron, white and blue, green lettering, 10½" l, $225.00.

Coupe	**175.00**
Four Door Sedan, Model T, 6½" l, cast iron, nickel plated spoked wheels	**557.00**
Model A Car, 4" l, cast iron, nickel plated wheels, 1930s	**120.00**
Railplane	**175.00**
Road Roller, 5½" l, cast iron, wooden roller	**300.00**
Roadster, 4½" l, cast iron, white rubber tires, 1930s	**138.00**
Stake Truck	**175.00**
Trailer, 3½" l, two wheel	**95.00**

AUBURN RUBBER

Auburn Rubber Company was founded in 1913 in Auburn, Indiana, as the Double Fabric Tire Corp. It began making toys in 1935 with the production of toy soldiers. Production of animals and wheeled vehicles soon followed. The toy production line was purchased in 1960 by the town of Deming, New Mexico and continued there until it ceased operation in 1968. Auburn also made wheels for other toy manufacturers.

Fire Truck, 7½" l, red, yellow plastic wheels, silver accents, hood marked "Auburn F.D./Fire Department"	**12.50**
Mickey and Donald Fire Car, 6½" l	**84.00**
Mickey's Tractor, 5" l, 1940s	**92.00**
Olds 1937 Four–Door Sedan, 4½" l, red, black rubber tires	**22.50**
Police Motorcycle, 6" l, hard rubber, spoked wheels, c1948	**40.00**
Telephone Truck, 7" l, bright yellow, black plastic wheels, silver accents, 1950s	**15.00**

BANDAI

Bandai Co, one of the many toy manufacturers which began production in Japan after World War II, started with tin toys and later changed to plastic and steel. Bandai Toys are found with friction action and battery operated. They are often marked "Bandai Toys, Japan." Bandai still produces toys and is a major Japanese exporter to the U. S. and other foreign countries.

Aircraft Carrier and Helicopter, 7" l, litho tin, friction, marked "T15 Bay," orig box 122.00
Auto–Top Ferrari, 11" l, tin, battery operated, bump–and–go action, vinyl driver, orig box 460.00
Buick Century, 8" l, tin, friction, plastic steering wheel and windshields, 1958 182.00
Ford
    Fairlane 500, 8" l, tin, friction, tin steering wheel, plastic windshield, orig box, 1958 .... 363.00
    Gasoline Carrier, 9" l, tin, friction, marked "Mobilgas," flying horse logo, orig box, 1950s 227.00
    T–Bird Convertible, 8" l, tin, friction, plastic steering wheel and windshield, orig box 242.00
Isetta, #588, 6½" l, tin, friction, two tone green, tin steering wheel, opening door, orig box 390.00
Ocean Boat, 12" l, litho tin, crank, goggled driver, orig box 138.00
Plymouth Valiant, 8" l, tin, friction, plastic windshield and steering wheel, litho tin interior, engine noise, 1961 111.00
Rambler
    Sedan, tin, friction, light blue, orig box 54.50
    Station Wagon, cream colored, dark brown top, orig box 58.00
Sparkling Rocket Car, 7½" l, tin, friction, black rubber tires, plastic and tin windshield, orig box, 1950s 224.00
Vespa, scooter, 9" l, tin, friction, Vespa license plates 280.00
VW Beetle, 8" l, tin, friction, plastic steering wheel and windshield 111.00

Buddy L, steam shovel, $225.00.

BUDDY L

The Buddy L Toy Company was founded in 1921 by Fred Lundahl. It produced high quality, finely detailed toys. Many were large enough to ride on. Production changed from steel to lighter weight, smaller toys in the 1930s. A limited number of wooden toys were made during World War II. The firm still operates today.

Baggage Truck, 26½" l, yellow, red, green, and black, barrel skid, #11, 1936 .... 130.00
Medical Corps Truck, 20½" l, white, #206 .... 165.00
Sand and Gravel Truck, 1940s 185.00
Sand Loader 295.00
Squirt Gun 100.00
Steam Shovel, 27½", 1930 .... 225.00
Texaco Gas Truck, 24" l, pressed steel, plastic tires, orig box, 1950s 275.00
Wrecker, flashing light, removable wheel, orig box 225.00

Chein, ferris wheel, litho tin, windup, yellow and red, $170.00.

CHEIN

The Chein Company was in business from the 1930s through the 1950s. Most of these lithographed tin toys were sold in dimestores. Chein toys are clearly marked.

Alligator, 15" l, litho tin, windup, native holding reins riding on back, snapping jaws 175.00
Chicken, windup, marked "USA" 45.00
Clown, 8" h, litho tin, windup, spinning parasol, c1920 .... 160.00
Disney Top, 5½" d, litho tin, Walt Disney Productions, c1950 .... 77.00
Drummer, 8½" h, litho tin, windup, orig box, 1950s 125.00
Duck, litho tin, windup 20.00
Elephant on Drum, bank, litho tin, windup 90.00

Ferris Wheel, 16" h, litho tin, four cars, 1950s **235.00**

Hopping Rabbit, 5" l, litho tin, windup, wearing tuxedo and bowtie, 1930 .. **138.00**

Mechanical Turtle, 8" l, litho tin, windup, native holding reins riding on shell, orig box, #145 .... **403.00**

Monkey, "Thank–You," bank, litho tin, windup **65.00**

Motorboat, 8", litho tin, windup **30.00**

Organ, church, litho tin, cranking **150.00**

Pig Waddler, 4½" h, litho tin, windup . **75.00**

Popeye, 7" h, litho tin, windup, wearing barrel, diecut pipe, copyright 1932 . **200.00**

Roller Coaster
  Circus, 8 x 19½ x 9", litho tin, windup, red, white, and blue tin cars, yellow metal ramps, bell rings, circus scenes around sides, built–in key, 1950s **350.00**
  Disney, Mickey Mouse **105.00**

Sand Pail, 4" h, nursery rhyme characters **50.00**

Seaplane, 8½" l, litho tin, windup, pilot, spinning propellers, orig box, 1930s **287.00**

Tea Set, Mickey Mouse Disneyland, boxed **65.00**

Toy Town Helicopter, windup **95.00**

Wobbling Duck, litho tin, windup **45.00**

Wringer Washer, Three Little Pigs, 8" h, litho tin, crank, wood and tin ringer attachment, 1930s **213.00**

CORGI

Playcraft Toys introduced Corgi miniature vehicles in 1956. This popular line soon became Corgi Toys. The first cars were made on a 1:45 to 1:48 scale. Corgi cars were the first miniature cars to have clear plastic windows. Other design features included opening doors and interiors. In 1972, the scale of 1:36 was introduced. This scale was more durable for play but less desirable to collectors. Finally, the company added other types of cars and trucks, including character representations.

Austin Cambridge, 1956–61 .... **75.00**

Bedford Fire Tender, 1960–62 .... **90.00**

Chipperfield's Circus
  Animal Cage **65.00**
  International 6 x 6 Truck **95.00**

Euclid Caterpillar Tractor, 1960–64 ... **120.00**

Fordson Tractor and Plough, 1961–63 **80.00**

Heinkel Bubblecar, 1961–72 .... **40.00**

Priestman Shovel and Carrier, 1963–72 **115.00**

Standard Vanguard, mechanical, 1957–59 .... **85.00**

Ford Thunderbird Hard Top, mechanical, 1959 .... **85.00**

Toyota 2000 Car, Bond, 5" l, metal, firing missiles, orig box, 1967 .... **148.00**

Tractor and Tipping Trailer, 1959–63 . **70.00**

CRAGSTON

A Japanese firm known for their lithographed tin and cloth battery operated toys. See Automata and Space Toys for additional listings.

Ford T–Bird, 11" l, battery operated, remote control, retractable roof, orig box **259.00**

Lincoln Airport Limousine, 9" l, tin, friction, rubber tires, plastic windshield, engine noise, orig box, 1959 ...... **160.00**

Lincoln Ambulance Car, 9" l, tin, friction, rubber tires, plastic windshield, engine noise, orig box, 1959 ...... **185.00**

Plymouth Barracuda, Wild Wheels Series, 4" l, diecast metal, purplish pink, white racing stripes, orig card, copyright 1969 .... **25.00**

Teddy the Boxing Bear, 10" h, battery operated, plush Teddy, tin face **144.00**

DINKY

Dinky Toys, made by the Meccano Toy Company of England, were first created by Frank Hornby in 1933. The Dinky series of diecast cars and trucks continued until World War II precluded the use of metal for toys. In 1945, production of diecast metal toys began with the introduction of a military line, as well as new cars and trucks. Production continued in factories in England and France until competition from Corgi, Tootsietoy, and Matchbox caused a decline in sales. The Dinky line was discontinued in 1979.

Articulated Lorry, 6¼" l, diecast, six wheeler, spare tire, orig box, #409 . **70.00**

Ferrari, #234 .... **25.00**

Lincoln Zephyr Coupe, 4¼" l, diecast . **60.00**

Packard, Super 8 limo, 4¼" l, diecast, 1938 .... **50.00**

Plymouth Station Wagon, 4⅛" l, diecast, 1947 .... **35.00**

Rambler, Fire Chief, 4" l, diecast, 1958 **25.00**

ERTL

Fred Ertl, Senior founded Ertl in 1945. Blueprints obtained from companies such as John Deere and International Harvester were used as patterns, thus insuring a high level of similarity when comparing the toy with the original. Ertl produces a full line of wheeled vehicles and is recognized as the world's largest manufacturer of toy farm equipment.

Car Carrier, 22" l	75.00
Case Tractor, #2560	60.00
International Pay Hauler	50.00
Pedal Tractor, International Harvester, restored, 404C	225.00
Sports Van	40.00

FISHER PRICE

Fisher Price Toys was formed in East Aurora, NY, in 1930. The original company consisted of Irving L. Price, retired from F. W. Woolworth Co., Herman G. Fisher, who was associated with the Alderman–Fairchild Toy Co. in Churchville, NY, and Helen M. Schelle, a former toy store owner. Margaret Evans Price, wife of the company president, was the company's first artist and designer. She was formerly a writer and illustrator of children's books. The company began with sixteen designs. Herman Fisher resigned as president in 1966. In 1969 the company was acquired by the Quaker Oats Company.

Black and white rectangular logos appeared on all toys prior to 1962. The first plastic part was used after 1949.

Big Bill Pelican, 8" h, wooden, paper labels, plastic beak, feet, and cord, #794, 1961	40.00
Big Performing Circus Parade, 9" h, removable roof, #250, 1932	180.00
Bunny Drummer, wooden, yellow cart, bell, #505, 1948	40.00
Cacklin' Hen, #123	25.00
Chick Cart, #407	35.00
Circus Train, engine, two cars, engineer, trainer, clown, animals	35.00
Circus Wagon, #900	75.00
Doll House, two dolls, furniture, car, 1969	38.50
Donald Duck, 8½" h, pull toy, wooden, paper labels, movable arms, #460	110.00
Donald Duck, Huey, Louie, 12½" l, wood, #479, 1941	100.00
Dr Doodle, 10" h, #132, 1940	70.00
Elephant	75.00
Farm, #1005	43.00
Fire Engine #1	38.00
Happy Hippo	65.00
Hickory Dickory Dock, radio and clock	25.00
Horse, pull toy, #978	20.00
Huffy Puffy Train, MIB, 1955	250.00
Kris Kricket, 9" l, #678	60.00
Little Snoopy, 5" h, dog, wood and plastic, paper labels, spring mounted tail, wooden shoe, #693, late 1960s	40.00
Merry Mousewife, #662	65.00
Mickey Mouse Choo–Choo, #485	75.00
Mighty Tractor, #629	22.00
Molly Moo Moo, cow	65.00
Musical Duck, 6½" h, #795, orig box, 1952	100.00

Penguin	10.00
Pony Express, #733	70.00
Popeye, 10" l, 10½" h, riding horse, wooden, litho paper sides, orange base, yellow wheels, mechanical movement, 1929 copyright, issued 1937	180.00
Pop–Up Kritter, Pluto, wood, Walt Disney Enterprises copyright	38.00
Prancy Pony, #617	15.00
Quackie Family, #799	85.00
Roly–Poly Chime Ball, animals, musical	25.00
Running Bunny, pull toy, #722	40.00
Scotty Dog, #20	75.00
Snoopy, #181	35.00
Tailspin Tabby, pop–up critter, wood, black and yellow beads, oilcloth ears	80.00
Teddy Zilo, 11" h, metal xylophone, #752, 1946	75.00
Telephone, #747	14.00
Thumper, #533	95.00
Tip–Toe Turtle, 5½" h, wood and plastic, paper labels, #773, 1960s	20.00
Train, 4 pc, #999	60.00
Walking Duck Cart, 7" h, wood and plastic, #305, 1957	25.00
Western Town, #934	35.00
Winky–Blinky Fire Truck, #200	85.00
Woodsy–Wee Zoo, 5 animals, 10 connecting wires, orig box, #205, 1931	350.00
Woofy Wagger, 9½" h, wooden	50.00

GILBERT

The A. C. Gilbert Company was founded in 1916. Alfred Carlton Gilbert Jr was an amateur magician who began to produce magic kits under the name of Mysto Manufacturing Co. The company was located on Erector Square in New Haven, Connecticut. Alfred Carlton Gilbert III took over after his father's death. The company still produces fine quality toys and other non–toy products. It's most famous product is the Erector Set.

Bond 007	
Aston Martin Slot Car, blue, chrome bullet shield, 1965	32.00
Dragon Tank, Hydrofoil, orig pkg	35.00
Erector Set	
#3, orig box and manual, 1913	195.00
#10053, rocket launcher	50.00
Microscope Set, orig box, 1940s	20.00
Mysto–Magic Exhibition Set, 11 tricks, instruction booklet, orig box, 1938	95.00

HUBLEY

The Hubley Manufacturing Company was founded in 1894 in Lancaster, Pennsylvania, by John Hubley. The first toys were cast iron. In 1940 cast iron was phased out and replaced with lesser metals and plastic. The production of cap pistols was increased at this time. By 1952 Hubley made more cap pistols than toys. Gabriel Industries bought Hubley in 1965.

Air Compressor Truck, 7" l, metal, black rubber tires, orig box	**97.00**
Airplane, 5" l, hard plastic, retractable black rubber wheels, tail marked "US Army," wing marked "Hubley Kiddie Toy," 1950s	**17.50**
Bell Telephone Truck, 12 " l, cast metal, green, red cast iron trailer, crane, wooden telephone pole, winch, sliding roof, 1950s	**75.00**
Cap Pistol	
Colt Detective Special	**12.00**
Pal	**20.00**
Trooper	**17.00**
Corvette, diecast metal, marked "Hubley/Corvette," 1954	**75.00**
Dump Truck, 6" l, plastic, green and yellow, silver accents, rubber wheels, spring loaded bed, 1950s	**24.00**
Farm Trailer, #5	**8.00**
Gyro Plane, 4" l, cast iron, nickel propeller and piston assembly	**282.00**
Jet Plane, 5" l, diecast, single engine, retractable landing gear, red and silver, blue stars, #430, 1950s	**25.00**
Kiddie Toy Race Car, 7" l, metal, red, rubber tires, nickel plated driver, 1950s	**15.00**
Lindy Plane, 4" l, cast iron, nickel plated, rubber tires, orange, gold lettering, late 1920s	**110.00**
Model A, roadster, 3¾"	**125.00**
Model T, cast iron, movable parts	**100.00**
Mr Magoo, crazy car, tin	**295.00**
Racer #6, 4¾" l, cast iron, nickel plated driver, white rubber tires, red, 1930s	**95.00**
Railway Express, 4"	**250.00**
Tractor, plow, #500	**45.00**
Twin Engine Plane, cast iron, 4" l, nickel plated wings and propeller, orange body, wings marked "TAT NC–431," white rubber wheels, 1930s	**75.00**
WW II Bomber	**45.00**

IDEAL

The Ideal Toy Company was owned by Lewis David Christie. It was located in Bridgeport, Connecticut. Among the toys it produced were dolls, cars, trucks, and even a line of toy soldiers produced c1920 until 1929.

Automatic Car Wash, car, plastic, orig box, 1950s	**39.00**
Car, 8" l, plastic, blue, resembles Jaguar, hood lifts, silver plastic engine, 1950s	**15.00**
Evel Knievel Precision Miniature, 4½" l	

diecast metal Formula 5000 race car replica, white, orig box, copyright 1977	**18.00**
Fix–It Truck, plastic, tools, flat tire, spare, jack, 1950s	**35.00**
Flintstone Cave House, 1964	**50.00**
Jeep, 4" l, plastic, brown, star sticker, 1950s	**20.00**
Mr Machine, 1970s	**25.00**
Washing Machine, windup, MIB	**40.00**

Lehmann, Tut Tut Car, litho tin, windup, 7" l, c1910, $1,000.00.

LEHMANN

The Ernst Paul Lehmann Company was located in Brandenburg, Germany. The company began in 1881 and continues to the present. Lehmann toys are known for attractive lithography and patina. The use of clockwork and mechanical friction action was prevalent. Export to the United States was sporadic after 1933. Most Lehmann toys were sold in America through jobbers, such as Butler Bros, George Broadway Rouss, and Montgomery Ward. Many popular toys, such as the Balky Mule, were offered for over 25 years. Lehmann toys are marked "E.P.L." and/or "Lehmann".

Balky Mule	**100.00**
Bibi Top, #855, West Germany, c1955	**74.00**
Gaudi Yoyo, #800, US Zone Germany, c1952	**69.00**
Nu–Nu, #733, 5½" h, tin, windup, orig pigtail, 1913	**865.00**
Quack Quack, 8" l, litho tin, windup, mother mallard pulling basket of three ducklings, 1903	**330.00**
Rigi Cable Car, #900, 8" h, tin, replica, crank, West Germany	**100.00**
Tam Tam, top, #677, litho tin, spiral drive rod, spring, hand grasp mechanism, orig box, 1920	**413.00**
Torpedo Boat Taku, #671, 10" l, litho tin, windup, 1907	**650.00**

LINEMAR

Linemar is a subsidiary of Marx. Linemar toys are manufactured in Japan.

Air Defense Truck, 14" l, tin, friction,
   battery operated guns, orig box **185.00**
Army Plane, 3" l, litho tin, friction, red,
   white, and blue, 1960s **25.00**
Bambi, lever action **395.00**
Barney Bear, 4" h, litho tin, windup,
   brown, blue, and yellow, 1960s **35.00**
Capital Airlines Viscount, 11½" l, red,
   white, blue, and silver, battery operated, remote control, 1950s **175.00**
Clarabelle, 7" h, litho tin, remote control hand lever, copyright Kagran,
   1950s **330.00**
Coca–Cola Dispenser, 1¢, 9½" h, metal,
   bright red, battery operated, white let-
   tering, orig box **375.00**
Coco Puffs Train, windup **225.00**
Cowboy, Sheriff Pig **65.00**
Fred Flintstone on Dino, 8" l, litho tin,
   windup, vinyl Fred head **275.00**
Go–Mobile, Walt Disney's Babes in
   Toyland, 6" l, 5" h, friction, tin car
   and figure, molded vinyl head, 1961 **85.00**
Hauler and Trailer, 12 " l, friction, litho
   tin, marked "Pacific Intermountain
   Express," orig box, 1950s **95.00**
Hopping Frog, windup, orig box **35.00**
Jet, friction, red, white, gray, marked
   "USAF F–102," 1960s **18.00**
Livestock Trailer, tin, 14" **95.00**
Louie and His Dream Car, 4½" l, tin,
   friction, Disneyland roadster **500.00**
Motorcycle, tin, friction, balancing
   wheels, red, rider wearing green
   jacket, 1950s **30.00**
Pan–American Jet Airliner, 13" l, litho
   tin, battery operated, remote control,
   marked "Clipper Meteor," orig box,
   1960s **90.00**
Patsy the Pig, 4" h, litho tin, windup,
   pink, blue, and yellow, orig box,
   1960s **45.00**
Playtime Airlines, 7½" wing span, tin,
   friction, four metal propellers **134.00**
Pluto, pulling cart, 8½" l, tin, friction . **400.00**
Red Ball Express, friction **145.00**
Rudy the Rooster, 4" h, litho tin,
   windup, orange and yellow, wearing
   tuxedo, orig box, 1960s **50.00**
Service Van, RCA **35.00**
Sneezing Bear, 9" h, plush, litho tin
   base, battery operated, black and
   white, orig box, 1950s **120.00**
SP–1 Space Car, 6" l, litho tin, friction,
   engine noise, sparks, orig box, 1950s **700.00**
Super Racer, 9½" l, litho tin, friction,
   orig box, 1950s **175.00**

MARX

Louis Marx founded the Marx Toy Company in 1921, stressing quality at the lowest possible price. His popular line of toys included every type of toy except dolls. The company was sold to Quaker Oats Company, who sold it in 1976 to the European company of Dunbee–Combex–Marx.

Air Raid Warning Siren, litho tin, spark-
   ing signal pistol, blue and red, orig
   decal **80.00**
Airplane, litho tin, windup, US Army,
   sparking **325.00**
Airport, orig box, 1930s **120.00**
American Airliner, 27" **135.00**
Animal, litho tin, windup **65.00**
Army Building, tin **14.00**
Army Truck **135.00**
Auto Transport Truck, metal and plastic,
   two plastic cars, orig box, 1940s ... **179.00**
Balky Mule **100.00**
Bengal Tiger on Wheels, hard plastic,
   movable mouth **32.00**
BO Plenty **100.00**
Carousel Truck, friction **95.00**
Castle and Bridge, opening doors, stone
   wall sides, plain cardboard roadway,
   orig box missing two side panels,
   1930s **75.00**
Chris Craft Cruiser, boat, 18" l, plastic,
   windup, white, brown deck, red keel,
   1950s **78.00**
Climbing Fireman **175.00**
Coal Dump Truck, tin, automatic dump-
   ing, forward, and reverse, battery operated, MIB **125.00**
Construction Camp, tin building, construction equipment and accessories,
   orig box **110.00**
Convertible, Fix–All, hard top, 10" l,
   plastic, yellow and blue, small tools
   in trunk, orig box, 1950s **80.00**
Corn Planter, 5" l **95.00**
Corvette Sting Ray, battery operated,
   plastic, orig box, c1960 .... **150.00**
Deluxe Delivery Van, 9½" l, plastic, red
   and yellow, back doors open, orig
   box, 1950s **45.00**
Donald Duck Duet **385.00**
Drumming Major, litho tin, windup ... **120.00**
Dump Truck, 4½" l, 1930–40s **60.00**
Easter Bunny Delivery **85.00**
English Soldier Kit, 2 officers, 2 drum-
   mers, 4 guardsmen, unassembled,
   orig box, 1950s **50.00**
Farm Mower, 10" l **95.00**
Felix the Cat, red ball **185.00**
Ferdinand the Bull **135.00**
Flippo Dog **30.00**

Futuristic Car, 5" l, hard plastic, metallic
gold colored, #3, c1953 .... **60.00**
Hess Tank Trailer, 13½" l, hard plastic,
battery operated lights, rubber hose,
orig box, c1972 .... **75.00**
Gold Star Transfer Co Truck, 22" l, rear
doors open, company name on
trailer, 1950s **50.00**
Huckleberry Car, friction, MIB **310.00**
International Agent Car, 4" l, litho tin,
friction, marked "UEA United Espio-
nage Agency," copyright 1966 ..... **70.00**
Jaguar Coupe, E Type, 8" l, plastic, battery operated, red, silver accents, re-
mote control unit, orig box, England,
1960s **75.00**
Jalopy **95.00**
Jeepers, little doll creeper, windup, MIB **65.00**
Jumpin' Jeep Crazy Car, windup **150.00**
Jungle Shooting Range, orig box **49.00**
Lazy Days Farm Truck, 18" l, steel, dairy
farm illus on sides, wheels marked
"Lumar," c1960 .... **75.00**
Life Saver Dump Truck, 9" l, plastic,
red, white logo, holds 10 Life Saver
Rolls, 1950s **115.00**
Luxury Liner, tin, sparking, friction, MIB **195.00**
M–16 Assault Rifle, 32" l, plastic, 1966 **20.00**
Machine Gun, 50 caliber, 28" l, alumi-
num tripod, 1950s **48.00**
Marxie Mustard, 4" l, litho tin, friction,
soft vinyl caricature mustard bottle
driver, copyright 1969 .... **20.00**
Masterbuilder Kit, capitol, 35 miniature
presidents, MIB **95.00**
Medical Corps, ambulance **125.00**
Midget Climbing Tractor, 5" l, litho tin,
windup, red, black and yellow trim,
orig box, c1950 .... **70.00**
Midget Racer, windup, #7 .... **35.00**
Mot–O–Run 4–Lane Hi–Way Set, 1949,
MIB **345.00**
Mystery Police Cycle, windup **150.00**
Nutty Mad Car, 2 x 4 x 3", litho tin,
friction, red, various illus, soft molded
vinyl head, 1960s **52.00**
Pepsi Cola Truck, plastic, white, remov-
able litho tin body, "Drink Pepsi
Cola" decal, 1950s **95.00**
Pioneer Express Train **135.00**
Prehistoric Playset, #3398, cave, 36 di-
nosaurs, 12 cavemen, eight trees and
ferns, orig bags, box, and instruction
sheet, copyright 1971 .... **225.00**
Racer
Friction, 6" l, plastic, black, 1960s . **12.00**
Windup
5" l, tin, red, white, and black, diecut driver's head, 1930s **75.00**
6¼" l, #1 .... **120.00**
Rake and Plow **45.00**

Ramp Walker
Cat, 2½" h, plastic, black and white,
blue and white bow tie, holding red
balloon **20.00**
Santa, 3" h, plastic, carrying toy sack,
1950s **22.00**
Right–O–Way Railroad Signs, 2½" h,
plastic, black and white, orig box,
1950s, set of 12 .... **24.00**
Rock'em Sock'em Robots, yellow plastic boxing ring, two 9½" h red and
blue robot boxers, controls, score
card, orig box **65.00**
Rollover Cat **40.00**
Rollover Dog **65.00**
Rolls Royce, 5" l, litho tin, friction, dark
maroon, silver accents, orig box,
1960s **45.00**
Sand Truck, 13" l, pressed steel, red,
tilting bed, c1950 .... **50.00**
Scottie Dog, litho tin, windup **175.00**
Sheriff Sam, crazy car, windup **145.00**
Shop King Playset, MIB **65.00**
Sparkling Tank, MIB **115.00**
Station Wagon and Trailer, hard plastic,
4" l green wagon, 2" l yellow trailer,
auto–wind, orig card, 1950s **23.00**
Tank, litho tin, windup, #3 .... **65.00**
Taxi
5" l, Sky View, plastic, yellow,
windup, 1950s **23.00**
6½" l, litho tin, yellow, red accents,
black lettering, 1950s **52.00**
11" l, Yellow Cab Co, litho tin, yellow, red lettering and trim, friction,
c1950 .... **45.00**
Top Cat TV Scenes Tinykin, Snooper figure and accessories, orig box, Hanna
Barbera copyright 1961 .... **20.00**
Tri–City Express Truck **55.00**
Tricky Fire Chief Car **50.00**
Tricky Taxi, litho tin, windup **80.00**
Tricycle, 4" h, litho tin, windup, celluloid rider, bell, copyright 1964 ..... **60.00**
Twirling Ballerina, 6", litho metal,
windup **99.00**
Waldo the Weightlifter, figure, vinyl,
dark green, Nutty Mads series, copy-
right 1963 .... **15.00**
Walking Toddler Doll, female, 8½" h,
hard plastic, windup, wearing yellow
pajamas, orig box, 1950s **85.00**
Wanted/Public Enemy, pinball game,
metal and plastic, c1953 .... **18.00**

MATCHBOX

Matchbox cars were first manufactured by Lesney Products, an English company founded in
1947 by Leslie Smith and Rodney Smith. Their
first diecast cars were made in 1953 on a scale
of 1:75. The trademark "Matchbox" was regis-

tered in 1953. In 1979, Lesney Products Corp made over 5.5 million toys a week. The company was sold to Universal International in 1982.

Case Tractor, #K17	**14.00**
Construction Kit, orig box	**45.00**
Daimler Bus, double decker, #74	**8.00**
Drott Excavator, #58, MIB	**35.00**
Euclid Quarry Truck, #6, MIB	**35.00**
Greyhound Bus, #66	**8.00**
Interstate Double Freighter, #M9	**10.00**
Land Rover Fire Truck, #57, MIB	**35.00**
Trailer Caravan, #23, MIB	**35.00**
Yesteryear, first series, #2	**65.00**

MATTEL

Mattel, formed by Harold Mattson and Ruth and Elliot Handler in 1945, originated in a garage in Los Angeles. From its humble beginnings as a manufacturer of picture frames, the company evolved as a manufacturer of doll house furniture, burp guns, and eventually, the Barbie doll, its most famous product.

Agent Zero–M
Night Fighter Machine Gun, infrared scope, blue and black camouflage design, orig box, 1964 .... **159.00**
Radio Rifle, orig box, 1964 .... **129.00**
Snap Shot Camera Pistol, orig box, 1964 .... **89.00**
Egg, 7", tin, windup, plays "Here Comes Peter Cottontail," 1953 ..... **26.00**
Mickey Mouse pull string talker **18.00**
Musical Man on Flying Trapeze, plastic clown, tin litho base, crank, plays "Man on the Flying Trapeze," orig box, 1953 .... **113.00**
Outdraw the Outlaw, 18" h, outlaw figure, draws gun, orig box, 1959 .... **45.00**
XP–1960 Dream Car, 8" l, plastic, friction, 1950s **80.00**

MISCELLANEOUS COMPANIES

Alps
Anti Aircraft, 5" l, tin, windup, guns, attached revolving plane, celluloid soldier, orig box **220.00**
Mountain Cable Lift, 15" h, tin, battery operated, 25" l track, two cable cars, station house, orig box **220.00**
Princess French Poodle, 8½" h, fabric and plush, battery operated, remote control, gray and black, orig box . **75.00**
American Plastics, building bricks, 15" h illus canister, 1948 .... **42.00**
Asahitoy, pickup truck, 7" l, litho tin, battery operated, green, marked "GBC," 1960s **45.00**

Barclay, truck, 32" l, red, white rubber wheels, 1930s **28.00**
Child Guidance Products Inc, Sanitation Truck, 16" l, hard plastic, battery operated, orig box, 1970s **35.00**
Courtland
Ice Cream Truck, 6" l, litho tin, windup, marked "Ice Cream 5¢," bell, driver, built–in key, 1950s .. **85.00**
Tractor, 6" l, mechanical, black, white, red, and yellow, black rubber wheels, three dimensional tin driver, built–in key, orig box, 1950s **75.00**
Daiya
Astronaut, 6½" h, tin, crank, plastic arms **320.00**
Caterpillar, 18" l, litho tin head and tail, green plush over spring coil body, battery operated, remote control, orig box **300.00**
Cheerful Choo Choo, train, litho tin, bump–and–go action, puffing noise, orig box, Japan, 1960s **45.00**
Fukuda, drummer, 4½" h, tin, celluloid head, windup, 1930s **150.00**
H Fishlove & Co, Mr Bones Talking Skull, 2 x 3 x 2½" h, plastic, white, windup, orig box, moving jaws, clicking sound, copyright 1954 .... **20.00**
Ichiko, Musical Santa Car, 1950s style, 7½" l, litho tin, friction, orig box ... **266.00**
Irco, Cunningham Sports Car, 1950s style, 7½" l, tin, friction, orig box .. **160.00**
Kanto Toys, Lucky Trotter, 2½ x 7 x 3½", litho tin, horse pulling cart with seated boy, built–in key, orig box, 1960s **50.00**
Kay–An–Ee, sewing machine, Sewmaster, metal, 5½" h, orig box, instructions **64.00**
Kenner
Easy Bake Oven, oven and appliances, orig box, 1962 .... **39.00**
Easy Show Movie Projector, movie reels, orig box, 1966 .... **120.00**
Give–A–Show Projector, 32 slides, orig box, 1961 .... **79.00**
Kilgore
Eagle Six Shooter Cap Gun, 8" l, metal, plastic handles, raised eagle illus, disc cap type, orig box **75.00**
Rebel Scatter Gun, 14" l, metal and plastic, orig box, 1960 .... **895.00**
Kyowa Toy Co
Golden Jet Racer, 10" l, tin, friction, plastic wheels, driver, orig box ... **92.00**
Greyhound Bus, 8" l, litho tin, friction, marked "Scenicruiser Greyhound," orig box, 1970s **35.00**
Lego, No. 706 .... **19.00**
Lincoln Logs, orig box, 1923 .... **45.00**

Lindstrom
  Dancing Indian, 5½" h, tin, windup,
    holding knife and tomahawk, vi-
    brates, 1930s **70.00**
  Dancing Katrinka, 8" h, litho tin,
    windup, vibrating, 1930s **149.00**
  Sweeping Betty, 8" h, litho tin,
    windup, holding broom, vibrating,
    1930s **200.00**
Lupor, police car, friction, siren **95.00**
Marasun
  Electromobile, 8" l, tin, battery oper-
    ated, orig box **252.00**
  Emergency Wagon, Bulldog toy, 18"
    l, pressed steel, black rubber tires **79.00**
  Speed Fire Engine, 5½" l, litho tin,
    friction, molded design, fireman,
    orig box **150.00**
Metal Masters Co, bus, 7" l, blue, black
  plastic wheels, 1930s **225.00**
Metalcraft
  CW Brand Coffee Truck, 11" l,
    pressed steel, tin tires, c1930 .... **462.00**
  St Louis Truck, 11" l, pressed steel,
    tin tires, hinged rear gate, c1930 . **366.00**
Multiple Products, Fire Engine, steamer,
  8" l fire truck, detachable ladders,
  four horses and harness unit, five firemen, accessory pcs, 1960s **35.00**
Rosco Plastics, fire truck, 10" l, hard
  plastic, green, three fireman, metal
  bell, 1950s **40.00**
Sanshin, jeep, 5" l, litho tin, battery operated, steering, orig box **42.00**
Seiberling Latex Co, car, Ford, 4" l, yellow hard rubber, one white rubber
  wheel, 1930s **22.00**

Straus, Jenny The Balking Mule, litho tin, windup, fruit in cart, yellow, red, green, and black, $235.00.

Strauss
  Butterfly, 7" l wingspread, litho tin,
    windup, flapping wings, c1925 .. **85.00**
  Jenny the Balking Mule, 9" l, tin,
    windup, mule cart, clown driver,
    c1920 .... **235.00**
Structo, log truck **25.00**
Tandard Toykraft, Priscilla Crayons, orig
  tin, 1937 .... **35.00**

US Metal Toy Mfg Co, Brooklyn, US
  Champion Derby Racer, model #8,
  litho tin parts, brown plastic wheels,
  flat wood chassis, orig box **25.00**
Yamaichi, Rotary Road Sweeper, 7" l,
  tin, friction, orig box **106.00**
Yone
  Flying Elephant, 6" l, litho tin,
    windup, gyro attached to trunk,
    orig box, 1950s **91.00**
  Spin Turn Racer, 5" l, tin, windup,
    plastic tires, orig box **62.00**

MODERN TOYS

The Modern Toy Company produced action
type tin toys in Japan during the occupation.
Most of these colorful toys are marked "Modern
Toys, Occupied Japan."

Antique Car, 5½" l, litho tin, dark green,
  gold trim, 1960s **28.00**
Engine, 5½" l, litho tin, multicolor, engineer's cap activates friction mechanism, 1950s **45.00**
Patrol 95 Helicopter, 13" l, litho tin and
  plastic, detachable propellers, three–
  dimensional litho tin pilot, marked
  "Made in Japan," 1960s **45.00**
Police Car, 5½" l, litho tin, black and
  white, red beige, blue, and yellow
  detailing, orig box marked "Press Action Car," 1950s **30.00**

NYLINT

Nylint began manufacturing steel vehicles in
Rockford, Illinois in 1946.

Auto Hauler, 21 x 5" **15.00**
Deliverall, 10" l, windup, orig box,
  c1950 .... **85.00**
Dump Truck, 12½", super cab **20.00**
Ford U–Haul pickup **40.00**
Michigan Shovel, 31½" l, #22200 ... **180.00**
Scootcycle, 7" l, tin, windup, goggled
  driver, plastic windshield, orig box,
  #800 .... **500.00**
Tow Truck, 13 x 8" **15.00**

OHIO ART

The Ohio Art Company was started in 1908
by Henry S. Winzeler, in Archbold, OH. The
company produced metal picture frames. Toy
production began in 1912. In 1969, Ohio Art
purchased Emenee Industries. Ohio Art is noted
for colorful lithographed tin toys.

Crawling Indian, 9" l, litho tin, windup,
  holding hatchet **90.00**

Crawling Soldier, 9" l, litho tin, windup,
holding rifle **82.00**
Cup, saucer, plate, tin **12.00**
Donald Duck Watering Can, 3" h, litho
tin, Donald being hit by brick illus,
1938 .... **66.00**
Drum, tin, marching band illus **15.00**
Giant Ride Ferris Wheel, 17" h, litho tin,
windup, carnival midway scenes, six
plastic gondolas, plastic children, bell
noise, orig box **365.00**
Ironing Board, Sunnie Miss **25.00**
Sand Pail **6.00**
Tea Cart, doll, white rubber tires, 1930s **35.00**
Tea Set, tin
Circus motif, 30 pcs **70.00**
Geisha, 1931, MIB **175.00**
Squirrel motif, 1932, 24 pcs **60.00**
Top, circus, tin **9.00**
Wash Tub, 7" **10.00**
Washing Machine, Three Little Kittens,
sgd Fern Bisel Peat **145.00**

REMCO

Hamilton's Invaders Grenade Pistol, 12"
l, plastic, silver, orig box, 1964 .... **42.00**
Long Range Bazooka, shells, orig box,
1961 .... **59.00**
Marine Raider Long Range Mortar,
metal and plastic, shells, tripod legs,
meter gauge, orig box, 1960 ...... **129.00**
Mighty Magee, aircraft carrier, 4 x 18 x
4½", hard plastic, gray and blue,
twelve plastic planes, one truck, man-
ually operated elevator, orig instruction sheet, 1960s **50.00**
Project Yankee Doodle, 17 x 13", battery operated, launching pad, sky
dome, warning siren, missiles, orig
box, 1959 .... **143.00**

SCHUCO

Schreyer und Co, better known as the Schuco
Toy Company, was formed in Nuremburg, Germany, in 1912 by Heinrich Muller and Heinrich
Schreyer. In 1914 both owners were conscripted
into the army. Schreyer subsequently left the
company, and Muller teamed up with Adolf
Kahn. In 1936 Kahn was forced to flee Germany
and temporarily resettled in the United States.
Following World War II, Kahn and his son returned to Nuremburg and formed a branch of
Schuco Toy Co with exclusive import rights to
the United States and Canada. The company
closed in 1972.

Boy with Mug **135.00**
Clown Violinist, windup **210.00**
Columbus Ocean Liner, windup **45.00**
Combinato 4003, windup **195.00**

Dancing Girl Pig, 6", pink mohair head
and arms, fabric dress, stick legs ... **75.00**
Drummer, orig box **185.00**
Lion, key wind **85.00**
Mercedes Benz Convertible, litho tin,
windup, plastic interior, 190SL,
#2095, 1950s **90.00**
Micro Racer, 3½" l, green, gray wheels **45.00**
Monkey with Violin, windup **185.00**
Motodrill 1006, 5" l, litho tin, windup,
orig box, US Zone Germany **600.00**
Radio Car, #4012, 6" l, litho tin,
windup, West Germany **375.00**
SOS Fex III Car, 6" l, litho tin, windup,
orig box, US Zone Germany **263.00**
Submarine, battery operated, MIB **165.00**

**Sun Rubber, Hoppity Mickey Mouse,
Walt Disney Productions, 23" h, $45.00.**

SUN RUBBER

The Sun Rubber Company was located in Bar-
berton, Ohio. During the 1930s it produced a
number of character dolls and Disney items in
addition to a general line. It was forced to cease
production during World War II because of the
scarcity of rubber. Production revived after World
War II and continued through the 1950s.

Bus, streamlined, 4¼" l, 1938 .... **45.00**
Donald Duck Car, 6½" l **75.00**
Racer, 7" l, white rubber tires **165.00**
Truck, streamlined, 5½" l, dark red
cargo area, light gold cab, white rub-
ber wheels **52.00**

TONKA

In 1946 Mound Metal Crafts Inc, Mound, Minnesota, manufactured the first Tonka Toys. *Tonka*
was derived from the firm's proximity to the
banks of Lake Minnetonka. The company intro-

duced a full line of trucks in 1949. In 1956 it changed its name to Tonka Toys.

AAA Wrecker 65.00
Car Hauler 40.00
Fire Truck, 17½" l, 1950s 75.00
Livestock Trailer, 8½" l 28.00
Pickup Truck, 12½" l, sign on door
   "Gambles, Need Help," 1950s 38.00

Tootsietoy, battleship, silver, red guns, conning tower, and tip of smoke stakes, blue airplane, $9.00.

TOOTSIETOY

The first Tootsietoys were made in 1911, although the name was not registered until 1924, and it was not until after 1930 that the name appeared on the toys. Tootsie was an early manufacturer of prizes for Cracker Jack. Tootsie produced copies of real vehicles beginning in 1914 and continued until World War II. After the war, cars were made as toys rather than models.

Andy Gump Car, 2½" l, white metal,
   diecast, painted, rocking action 185.00
Automobile, 3" l, resembles MG, dark
   red, silver grille and headlights 25.00
Blimp, USN Los Angeles, 1930s 175.00
Bluebird 1 Daytona Racer, 3¾" l, white
   rubber wheels, 1930s 35.00
Buick Y Experimental Roadster, 4" l,
   light green, silver trim, 1940s 30.00
Cadillac Four–Door Sedan, 6" l, gray
   and silver, black rubber wheels,
   c1954 .... 15.00
Cannon, Civil War, 1950s 30.00
Car Carrier, International, 1940s 85.00
Chevrolet
   Corvette, metallic copper color, black
      plastic wheels, 1955 style 25.00
   Roadster, #6201 .... 85.00
Chrysler Thunderbolt Experimental
   Roadster, 6" l, bright red, silver trim,
   1940s 53.00
Civil War Figures, wagon, caisson, two
   horses, orig card, 1950s 14.00
Fiat 20.00
Fire Department Set, 6" l 1947 Mack
   pumper, ladder and hose attach-
   ments, 9" l 1947 Mack fire trailer, 4"

l 1950 Pontiac fire chief sedan, 4" l
1950 Chevy panel truck ambulance,
   fire hat and shovel, orig box, 1950s   181.00
Fire Truck
   Aerial Hook and Ladder, 9" l, red,
      silver accents, two–piece ladder,
      orig box 80.00
   Pumper, 6" l, diecast, red, silver ac-
      cents, three ladders, two rubber
      hoses, orig box, 1950s 85.00
Ford
   LTD, 1969 .... 20.00
   Thunderbird, dark blue, black rubber
      wheels, c1955 .... 18.00
Grand Coupe, 4" l, orange body, brown
   running board and fenders, six tires,
   1933–35 .... 45.00
Greyhound Bus, 6" l, silver and blue,
   Greyhound Lines logo, 1950s 70.00
Kaiser Sedan, 6" l, dark blue, silver trim,
   marked "K," 1947 .... 40.00
Le Sabre Experimental Roadster, 5½" l,
   blue, silver accents, 1951 .... 25.00
Oil Tanker, 9" l, red, silver accents, orig
   box, 1950s 65.00
Plane, tri–motor 85.00
RC Cola Truck 12.00
Service Station Set, #5710, 5" l car lift,
   5" l gas station island, 1955 Ford,
   1956 Ford oiltanker, 1954 MG roads-
   ter, 1954 Ford wagon, 1949 Ford
   pickup, orig box 140.00
Shell Truck 35.00
Sohio–Giro Plane, 4" l, light green, yellow propeller, 12 pg instruction book-
   let, issued by Standard Oil Co, copyright 1931 .... 100.00
Standard Oil Truck 35.00
Wagon, child's, 4" l, red, silver grille,
   streamlined front 22.50
Yellow Cab, #4629 .... 85.00
Zephyr Train, midget, MIB 95.00

UNIQUE ART CO

Little is known of the exact origins of the Unique Art Manufacturing Company. Located in Newark, New Jersey, the firm was in business as early as 1916, the period in which it introduced its Merry Juggler and Charlie Chaplin toys. Unique was still operating as late as 1952.

GI Joe Jouncing Jeep, 7" l, tin, windup,
   orig box, 1940s 321.00
GI Joe and His K–9 Pups, 9" h, litho tin,
   windup, carrying pups in dog cages,
   orig box 300.00
Hee–Haw, 10" l, litho tin, windup,
   farmer driving wagon loaded with
   milk cans, mule, orig box, c1930 .. 375.00
Kiddy Cyclist, 9" h, litho tin, windup,

boy on tricycle, jointed legs, ringing
bell, orig box 303.00
Lincoln Tunnel, 24" l, litho tin, windup,
cars and buses, orig box 418.00
Rodeo Joe Crazy Car, tin, windup 200.00

UNKNOWN MAKERS

Germany, Tumbling Clown, 4" h litho
tin clown, tumbles down 13" h tin
slotted tower, prewar 138.00
Japan
  Airport Limousine, friction, siren . . .   75.00
  Baby Cadillac, friction 95.00
  Broadway Trolley, moving driver,
    headlight, clanging sound, orig box   165.00
  Crazy Clown, crazy car windup 95.00
  Duck Carriage, 5" l, celluloid,
    windup, mother duck pulling car-
    riage, two ducklings inside, spin-
    ning umbrella, orig box 94.00
  Electric Tractor, Kiss, tin driver, orig
    box 145.00
  Fire Truck, 9" l, litho tin, friction, lad-
    der, five firemen figures, 1960s . .   80.00
  Ford Station Wagon, 8" l, tin, friction,
    orig box, 1956 . . . .   202.00
  G–Men Motorcycle and Sidecar, 3½"
    l, litho tin, friction, c1945 . . . .   185.00
  Grand Prix Racing Car, friction, driver   145.00
  Happy Plane, 7" l, litho tin, friction,
    cartoon face, diecut moving eyes
    and wings, #711, 1960s 45.00
  Marine Plane, friction, dark green,
    red, white, and blue, marked "Ma-
    rine" and "Made in Japan," 1960s   18.00
  Mustang, racing car, flip over 120.00
  Police Car, 6" l, litho tin, friction, orig
    box, pop–up policeman, shooting
    sounds, 1960s 75.00
  Tractor Trailer, friction, ten wheels .   65.00
  USAF Plane, 9" l, litho tin, friction,
    red, white, and yellow,
    marked "US Air Force FC–453,
    Convair," and "Made in Japan,"
    1960s 20.00
  Walking Turtle, 4½" l, litho tin,
    windup, orig box, 1960s 23.00
  Western Auto Hauler and Trailer, 12",
    tin, friction, rubber tires, rear doors
    open, orig box, 1950s 95.00
  Yellow Taxi Cab, 5" l, litho tin, fric-
    tion, yellow, 1960s 28.00
Korea, boy on tricycle, 4½" l, 5" h,
  windup, litho tin cycle, soft vinyl figure, spinning bell, pennant, balloon,
  marked "Made in Korea," orig box,
  1970s 60.00
Spain, El Vagabundo, 7" h, plastic,
  windup, Charlie Chaplin, carrying
  two suitcases, twirling cane, bounc-
  ing hat, orig box 150.00

West Germany
  Mystery Car, 4" l, litho tin car and
    garage, windup, orig box 155.00
  Trans Canada Air Lines, 11" wing-
    span, litho tin, trigger activated,
    Maple Leaf Viscount logo, spinning
    propellers, retractable landing gear,
    orig box, 1950s 205.00

WOLVERINE

The Wolverine Supply & Mfg Co was founded
in 1903 and incorporated by Benjamin F. Bain
in 1906. The first type of toys they produced were
lithographed tin sand toys. They began to make
girls' housekeeping toys and action games by the
1920s. Production of toys continued and expanded in 1959 to include children's appliances,
know as "Rite–Hite." The name was changed to
Wolverine Toy Company in 1962. The company
was originally located in Pittsburgh, PA, but relocated to Booneville, AK in 1970 after being
acquired by Spang and Company.

Adding Machine, metal, red, 4 column
  ladder 15.00
Cookstove/Refrigerator, Snow White,
  metal 55.00
Express Bus 300.00
Farm Wagon, 10" l, plastic, windup,
  horse pulls wagon, orig box 100.00
Iron, red handle 10.00
Ironing Board, 8 x 27", 21" h, tin, white,
  Snow White and Seven Dwarfs top .   125.00
Kitchen Range, litho burners, deep fry,
  oven 30.00
Loop the Loop, 19" l, 4" w, tin, windup,
  2¼" l car, orig box, #30 . . . .   303.00
Luxury Liner, tin, windup, MIB 165.00
Merry Masons, automatic sand toy, 16"
  h, litho tin, building shape, three litho
  tin masons, orig box, 1950s 115.00
Mustang 3000, white, 1950s 85.00
Shooting Gallery, tin 30.00
SS Wolverine Oceanliner, orig box . . .   250.00
Stove, Snow White 20.00
Washboard 10.00
Wringer Washer, 9", crack in lid 85.00

WYANDOTTE

All Metal Products Company, located in
Wyandotte, Michigan, has been in operation
since the early 1920s. The company, better
known as Wyandotte Toys, originally produced
wood and steel toy weapons. In 1935 it introduced an innovative line of streamlined wheeled
vehicles. The firm ceased operations in 1956.

Ambulance 110.00
Automatic Repeater, #40, 7" l, tin, pop
  gun, orig box 35.00

Car, 13" l, steel, wooden wheels, red and brown, convertible tin hard top, trunk opens, 1940s 70.00

Chicken, tin, wood eggs 80.00

Fire Engine Truck, 12" l, pressed steel and tin, wood tires, two metal ladders, marked "Engine Co No 4," 1939 194.00

Haulaway Truck, 8½" l, litho tin, yellow, red, and black, orig box, 1950s 40.00

Medical Corps Truck, 12" l, pressed steel, wood tires, c1939 .... 138.00

Official AAA Service Car, 12" l, pressed steel and tin, wood tires, crank hoist, 1939 .... 176.00

Pickway Pasture Truck 65.00

Pistol, 8½" l, litho tin, red and blue, star, #5 .... 45.00

Racer, 5", white tires 90.00

Red Ranger Ride Em Cowboy, #515, 6½" l, litho tin, windup, orig box . 160.00

Spur Set, western, mint on orig card .. 22.00

Target Set, 14 x 23", litho tin, duck hunting illus, three bull's eyes, 21" long rifle, six suction cup darts, orig box, 1950s 70.00

Trailer, semi, stainless steel 195.00

Truck

Highway Freight, 16" l, pressed steel, red trailer, blue and yellow cab, early 1950s 24.00

Railway Express Agency, 6" l, pressed steel and tin, "Wyandotte Toys for Girls and Boys," 1940s 80.00

United Super Mainliner DC–4, 13" wing span, pressed steel, decals, four propellers, wood tires, c1939 .... 300.00

TRAINS, TOY

Collecting Hints: Prices do fluctuate. Prices from mail order houses and stores generally are higher than those found at train swap meets. A large train swap meet is held in York, Pennsylvania each year. Condition is critical. Items in fair condition (scratched, chipped, dented, rusted or warped) and below generally have little value to the collector.

Restoration is accepted, provided it is done accurately. It does enhance the price one or two grades. Spare parts are actively traded and sold among collectors to assist in restoration efforts.

Exterior condition often is more important than operating condition. If you require a piece to operate, you should test it before you buy it.

Toy trains is a very specialized field. Collectors tend to have their own meets. A wealth of literature is available, but only from specialized book, railroad or toy train dealers. Novice collectors should read extensively before beginning to buy.

History: Railroading was an important part of many boys' childhoods, largely because of the romance associated with the railroad and the emphasis on toy trains. Almost everyone had a train layout; basements, back rooms, or attics allowed the layout to remain up year–round.

The first toy trains were cast iron and tin; the wind–up motor added movement. The golden age of toy trains was 1920–1955 when electric powered units were available, and Ives, American Flyer and Lionel were household names. Construction of the rolling stock was of high quality. The advent of plastic in the late 1950s lessened this quality considerably.

Toy trains are designated by a model scale or gauge. The most popular are HO, N, O, and S. Narrow gauge was a response to the modern capacity to miniaturize. Its popularity has lessened in the last few years.

References: Paul V. Ambrose, *Greenberg's Guide to Lionel Trains, 1945–1969, Volume III, Sets*, Greenberg Publishing, 1990; Susan and Al Bagdade, *Collector's Guide To American Toy Trains*, Wallace–Homestead, 1990; John O. Bradshaw, *Greenberg's Guide To Kusan Trains*, Greenberg Publishing Co, 1987; Richard Friz, *The Official Indentification and Price Guide To Toy Trains*, House of Collectibles, 1990; Bruce Greenberg (edited by Frank Reichenbach), *Greenberg's Guide To Ives Trains, 1903–1932, Volume I* Greenberg Publishing, 1991; Bruce Greenberg, (edited by Christian F. Rohlfing), *Greenberg's Guide To Lionel Trains: 1901–1942, Volume 1* (1988), *Volume 2* (1988), Greenberg Publishing Co.; Bruce Greenberg (edited by Paul V. Ambrose), *Greenberg's Guide To Lionel Trains:1945–1969, Volume 1* (1991), *Volume 2* (1988), Greenberg Publishing Co.; John Hubbard, *The Story of Williams Electric Trains*, Greenberg Publishing Co., 1987; Steven H. Kimball, *Greenberg's Guide To American Flyer Prewar O Gauge*, Greenberg Publishing Co., 1987; Roland La Voie, *Greenberg's Guide To Lionel Trains, 1970–1988*, Greenberg Publishing Co., 1989; Lionel Book Committee Train Collectors Association, *Lionel Trains: Standard of the World, 1900–1943*, Train Collectors Association, 1989; Dallas J. Mallerich III, *Greenberg's American Toy Trains From 1900 with Current Prices*, Greenberg Publishing, 1990; Dallas J. Mallerich, III, *Greenberg's Guide to Athearn Trains*, Greenberg Publishing Co., 1987; Eric J. Matzke, *Greenberg's Guide To Marx Trains*, Greenberg Publishing Co., 1989; Robert P. Monaghan, *Greenberg's Guide to Marklin OO/HO*, Greenberg Publishing Co., 1989; John R. Ottley, *Greenberg's Guide To LGB Trains*, Greenberg Publishing Co., 1989; James Patterson and Bruce C. Greenberg, *Greenberg's Guide To American Flyer S Gauge, Third Edition*, Greenberg Publishing Co., 1988; Vincent Rosa and George J. Horan, *Greenberg*

Guide To HO Trains, Greenberg Publishing Co., 1986; Alan R. Schuweiler, *Greenberg's Guide to American Flyer, Wide Gauge,* Greenberg Publishing Co., 1989.

Note: Greenberg Publishing Company (7543 Main Street, Sykesville, MD 21784) is the leading publisher of toy train literature. Anyone interested in the subject should write for their catalog and ask to be put on their mailing list.

Collectors' Clubs: Lionel Collector's Club, P.O. Box 11851, Lexington, KY 40578; The National Model Railroad Association, P.O. Box 2186, Indianapolis, IN 46206; The Toy Train Operating Society, Inc., 25 West Walnut Street, Suite 305, Pasadena, CA 91103; The Train Collector's Association, P.O. Box 248, Strasburg, PA 17579.

Note: All prices given are for items in very good condition, meaning that the piece shows some signs of use but all parts are present and damage from use is minor.

AMERICAN FLYER N GAUGE

Locomotive
1093, 7", two tone green	155.00
3198, black, brass trim	225.00

Rolling stock
1106, log car, 6½"	12.00
1114, caboose, 6½"	15.00
3102, automobile car	18.00
3141, pullman, brass trim	15.00

Set
Major Leaguer 1329, locomotive and tender 3193, tank car 3018, sand car 3016, automobile car 3015, caboose 3017	400.00
The Explorer 1333, locomotive 3110, baggage car 1204, pullman 1203, observation 1209	275.00
Vanguard 1312, locomotive 3100, pullman 3141, observation 3142, 88" track	200.00

AMERICAN FLYER S GAUGE

Accessories
Bridge, trestle, 750, 1946–56	12.50
Cartridge, smoke, 25, 1947–56	3.00
Crossing gate, 592, 1949–50	12.00
Flasher signal, 23764, 1969–64	4.50
Tunnel, 249, 1947–56, orig box	5.50

Engines, Diesel, Electric, and Steam
Diesel and Electric
290, electric	80.00
360A, diesel, tender	125.00
21234, Chesapeake and Ohio, GP–7, 1961–62	110.00
21573, New Hampshire diesel, GE Electric	250.00
21918/21918–1, Seaboard, Baldwin, 1958	175.00

Motorized Unit, 741, handcar and shed	50.00

Steam Locomotive
320, 4–6–4, Hudson, 1946–47	60.00
332, 4–8–4, 1946–49	100.00
343, 0–8–0, 1953–54	80.00
21130, 4–6–4, 62–63, 1959–60	110.00

Rolling stock
Box car
639, light yellow	25.00
923, Illinois Central	10.00
994, Union Pacific	25.00
24052, United Fruit Growers Express	8.00

Caboose
630	4.50
806	12.00
24634	12.00

Flat Car
627, American Flyer Lines	8.00
928, New Haven	6.50
969, rocket launcher	18.00
24556, Rock Island	20.00

Gondola
631, T&P, green	12.00
24120, T&P	15.00

Hopper and Dump Car
640, Wabash, black	30.00
24219, Western Maryland	20.00
9200, B & O, Fundimensions Production	10.00

Passenger Car
502, American Flyer Lines, Vista Dome	70.00
649, circus coach	30.00
732, operating baggage car, unpainted red plastic shell, 1951–54	18.00
953, baggage and club car, 1953–56	32.50
24739, Niagara Falls	165.00
24868, American Flyer Lines, observation	40.00

Tank Car
625G, Gulf	8.00
958, Mobilgas, 1957	10.00
9101, Union, 1980	12.00

IVES

Acessories
Bridge, arch base, two sections, 21" l	275.00
Passenger station, 113, 1906–28	200.00
Scenery, 80, pastoral, six 20 x 15" sections	250.00
Semaphore, double arm, 107D, 1908–30	80.00
Tunnel, 105, mountain style, 11" l	120.00

Locomotive
5, Steam, 0–4–0, mechanical, 1911–28	180.00

10, Electric, standard gauge, 1931–32 .... **260.00**

20, Steam, 4–4–0, mechanical, 1908–14 .... **175.00**

258, Steam, 2–4–0, O gauge, 1931–32 .... **255.00**

1760, Steam, 4–4–2, standard gauge, 1931–32 .... **700.00**

Passenger Car

50, baggage car, O gauge, 1901–30 **75.00**

186, observation car, standard gauge, 1922–30 .... **65.00**

339, pullman, standard gauge, 1931–32 .... **95.00**

1812, observation, O gauge, 1931–32 .... **120.00**

Rolling stock

65, stock car, O gauge, 1908–30 ... **35.00**

70, caboose, O gauge, 1929–30 ... **4.00**

123, lumber car, O gauge, 1911–30 **75.00**

190, tank car, standard gauge, 1921–30 .... **130.00**

559, lumber car, O gauge, 1930 ... **40.00**

1677, gondola, O gauge, 1931–32 . **50.00**

1774, box car, standard gauge, 1931–32 .... **225.00**

1775, tank car, standard gauge, 1931–32 .... **65.00**

Lionel, engine #8, pullman #377, observation #378, $285.00.

LIONEL, O GAUGE

Accessories

Beacon, 394, swivel action, blue ... **5.00**

Billboard, 310, "B. P." **4.00**

Bridge, single span, 270, standard gauge **150.00**

Coal loader, 97, scoop and drawer, shoot action **150.00**

Diner, 442, aluminum style, simulated windows **350.00**

Left hand switch, 5021 .... **15.00**

Log loader, 364, crane and hook ... **90.00**

Oil derrick, 455, movable arms **110.00**

Station, 122, chimney lighted, benches, dome **160.00**

Engines, Diesel, Electric and Steam

Diesel and Electric

153, Electric, 0–4–0, 1917–27 ... **50.00**

204, Santa Fe, Alco AA units, 1957 **60.00**

706, Electric, 0–4–0, 1913–1916 **240.00**

1700E, Diesel, 1935–37 .... **110.00**

2023, Erie, Alco AA units, 1952–54 .... **115.00**

2344, New York Central, F–3, 1950–52 .... **160.00**

3927, Lionel Lines, 1956–60 .... **60.00**

Handcar, 1100, Mickey Mouse, 1935–37 .... **600.00**

Steam Locomotive

203, 0–6–0, 1940–42 .... **325.00**

233, 0–6–0, 1940–42 .... **800.00**

665, 4–6–4, 1954–59 .... **75.00**

Rolling stock

Box car

514, Union Pacific **75.00**

1514, Baby Ruth **30.00**

2954, 1940–42 .... **145.00**

3366, circus car, 1959–62 ...... **65.00**

3428, United States Mail, 1959 .. **20.00**

6014, Campbell Soup, 1969 ..... **28.00**

6454, Erie, 1949–53 .... **16.00**

6464–735, New Haven, 1969 ... **15.00**

Caboose

657 .... **12.00**

801, 1915–26 .... **15.00**

1007, Lionel Lines, 1948–52, SP Die 3 .... **1.50**

2357, silver and blue **18.00**

4457, Pennsylvania, 1946–47, N5 **40.00**

6417–50, Lehigh Valley, 1954, N5C, gray **32.00**

6517–75, Erie, 1966, bay window **200.00**

Flat car

811, 1926–40 .... **40.00**

831, 1927–34 .... **28.00**

2461, transformer car, 1947–48 .. **20.00**

3364, log dump, 1965–69 ...... **15.00**

3519, satellite car, 1961–64 ..... **18.00**

6361, flat, timber, 1960–61, 1964–69 .... **20.00**

6413, Mercury Project, 1962–63 . **18.00**

6819, flat, helicopter, 1959–60 .. **25.00**

Gondola

812, 1926–41 .... **35.00**

2812, 1938–42 .... **30.00**

3444, Erie, 1957–59 .... **30.00**

4452, Pennsylvania, 1946–48 ... **48.00**

6462, NYC, red **4.50**

Hopper and Dump Car

816, 1927–42 .... **55.00**

2816, 1935–42 .... **48.00**

3456, N&W, 951–55	20.00

Passenger Car
530, observation, 1926–32	16.00
604, observation, 1920–25	20.00
605, pullman, 1925–32	65.00
607, pullman, 1926–27	30.00
637, coach, 1936–39	55.00
783, coach, 1935–41	240.00
1687, observation	145.00
1813, baggage	18.00
2400, Maplewood, green and gray	25.00
2442, brown, gray trim	35.00
2445, Elizabeth, pullman, 1955– 56	35.00
2522, President Harrison, 1962–66	60.00
2533, Silver Cloud, pullman, 1952–60	45.00
2615, baggage, 1928–42	175.00
2631, observation, 1938–42	25.00

Tank Car
815, 1926–42	48.00
1515, 1933–37	25.00
2555, Sunoco, 1946–48	30.00
2955, 1940–42	165.00
6463, rocket fuel, 1962–63	12.00
6465, Lionel Lines, 1958–59	5.00

N GAUGE

Bachmann
Locomotive
EMF GP40 diesel, Union Pacific .	15.00
GE U36B diesel, Seaboard Coast Line, Bicentennial	18.00
4–4–0, steam, Central Pacific	25.00

Rolling stock
Hopper, 5523, Reading	2.25
Passenger coach, Pennsylvania, lighted	4.00
Reefer, 5181, Gerber's	1.50

Con–Cor
Locomotive
Alco PA–PB diesel, Pennsylvania, powered	35.00
4–6–4, J3A Hudson, Union Pacific	50.00

Rolling stock
Box car, wood, New York Central, 1021F	4.00
Caboose, bay window, Illinois Central, 1251N	4.00
Flat car, US Steel, 1201E	4.50
Passenger cars, smooth sides	6.50
Tank car, Cities Services, 1601A .	5.00

Revell/Rapido
Locomotive
EMD FP9 Diesel, Santa Fe, set . . .	18.00
Steam, medium, Baltimore and Ohio, yellow lettering	60.00

Rolling stock
Hopper, Boston and Maine, 2543	7.75
Tank car, Sinclair, 0484R	6.50

TRIVETS

Collecting Hints: A vast majority of the trivets found in today's marketplace were once part of an iron set. The triangular shape of a trivet is a clue to this use.

Trivets can be collected by shape, material, maker, or design. A new collector might focus on trivets which are not cast iron, wrought iron, or brass. There were pottery trivets, although not much has been written about them.

A trivet that does not show signs of wear should be suspect. Trivets were meant to be used. Although decorative, the ornamental function always was secondary to the utilitarian function.

History: A trivet is a three-legged stand used to support hot vessels, either in an open fireplace, workroom, or on a table top. The trivet gained its greatest popularity in the late 19th century when it was used as a base for irons.

Cast iron trivets provide some of the finest examples of the ornate iron products of American industry. The decorative motifs are endless. Many groups commissioned souvenir trivets as mementos of outings or conventions.

By the mid-20th century the trivet was more decorative than functional. Its location moved from the table to the wall. A fancified trivet became a popular American souvenir item.

REPRODUCTION ALERT. In the 1960s reproduction wrought iron and cast iron trivets from Europe and Japan flooded the market. Many were aged to resemble the early models. Collectors and dealers are having a hard time telling early models from these modern fakes.

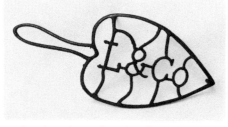

Cast iron, heart, loop handle, "L & Co" in center, tripod feet, 8⅛" l, $50.00.

Brass, cast
Cathedral, #4	40.00
Fan, 8½", curved lattice design	10.00
Heart, 8", scrolls	55.00
Horseshoe, "Take Simmons Liver Regulator in Time"	35.00
Masonic, 8"	45.00
Shield shape 6¾", leafy foliage, English registry mark	15.00

7¼", scrolled **15.00**
Tree and horse **30.00**
Star and clover, 9¼", sheet brass,
  turned feet **70.00**
Cast Iron
  Bless our house **15.00**
  Broom, painted black, 8" **12.00**
  Cat's head, 8¾", well detailed **140.00**
  Eagle
    GAR, flag **75.00**
    Heart in laurel wreath, 8¾" **35.00**
    Round, heart, laurel leaves on outer
      edge **35.00**
  Fan shape, 9", foliage scroll design . **20.00**
  Flower, five petal, ring handle **48.00**
  Fox and geese track **50.00**
  Horseshoe
    Ancient Order of Foresters, flag .. **45.00**
    Bust of General Grant in center .. **60.00**
    Eagle, clasped hands, "Good
      Luck," gold paint, 6½" **28.00**
    God bless our home, 1889 ...... **45.00**
    Good Luck, cupid with garlands . **40.00**
    Sailor's house blessing **35.00**
  House, girl and dog in lacy frame-
    work, large **45.00**
  Howell, W H Co, Geneva, IL **15.00**
  Jenny Lind, 10½ " I **20.00**
  Pinwheel and urn, 11" I **25.00**
  Spade shape, handled, shield, can-
    non, crossed swords **65.00**
  Star, sunrise **25.00**
  Sun with face, nickel plated, scroll
    work, marked "Muster, Geschutz,"
    12" I **20.00**
  Swastika **30.00**
Wrought Iron
  Cross with crown **20.00**
  Heart, 2 x 5½", 3 feet **65.00**
  Round, three arrow shaped prongs,
    6½ x 9" **50.00**
  Spider web **25.00**

TYPEWRITERS

Collecting Hints: Patent dates found on frames
and parts are not accurate indicators of the age
of a machine, as these only indicate the date of
the mechanical innovation's patent. A machine
with an 1890s patent date may have been made
as long as twenty–five or more years later. The
serial number is a far more useful tool in dating
a machine. However, there are many different
manufacturers numbering systems that are unknown, extremely confusing, or illogical.

In quite a number of cases, the only way to
date a particular machine may be through the
use of old advertisements and catalogs. These
types of references can also reveal particular
models, colors, and unusual features produced.
Most manual typewriters produced after 1920

have little value. Electro–mechanical (or electric)
typewriters manufactured before 1933 may,
however, be of great rarity and value. As with all
other collectibles, there may be a particularly
interesting and rare machine made later than this
that will be desirable.

The domestic typewriter collectors are a small
but steadily growing group. There is a well established and active international typewriter collecting community, especially in Europe where
mechanical objects and typewriters are highly
sought after. Domestic collectors have generally
swapped and traded among themselves, thus
keeping prices reduced. This seems to be changing with the increased attention and interest generated by the international collectors.

History: The first commercially produced typewriter in America was the Sholes & Glidden
Typewriter, manufactured by E Remington &
Sons, in 1874. This typewriter produced a row
of tiny, uneven capital letters. In 1876, Remington exhibited an example of the Sholes & Glidden at the United States Centennial Exposition in
Philadelphia. For twenty–five cents people
watched souvenir messages being typed, letters
which are highly collectible today. Mark Twain
was one of the first to purchase one of these
typewriters. Although his review of it was rather
mixed, his book *Life on the Mississippi* is thought
to have been the first typewritten manuscript.

In 1878 Remington produced the Perfected
Type Writer #2, later named the "Standard Remington Typewriter #2." This machine was far
more reliable and useful than its predecessor.
Both of these typewriters typed on paper wound
on a platen suspended over a circular typebasket.
To view the typing performed, the carriage had
to be lifted away from the basket. This was
known as a blind writer, and was the most common machine style for the next thirty years.

Like so many other manufacturers of the time,
five major typewriter companies joined together
in 1893 to form the Union Typewriter Company,
in essence a trust formed to limit competition
and fix prices. Members of this trust produced
thick, squat, blind writing office machines exclusively, with little impetus for innovation. Two
companies formed in competition to the Union
Typewriter trust, with machines based on the
visible writing principle; the Underwood Typewriter Co. in 1895, and the LC Smith & Brothers
Typewriter Co in 1903. These companies would
become the powerhouses of the typewriter manufacturers for the next thirty years.

The first electric machines made in America
appeared, and quickly disappeared just after the
turn of the century. The famous Blickensderfer
Electric and rather unknown Cahill Electric typewriter are the two earliest examples. The first very
successful electric typewriter was the IBM Model
01, introduced in the early 1930s.

Early typewriters generally have a glossy black finish, sometimes decorated with colored pinstripes or, less frequently, highly detailed painted designs and inlays. This was the general trend until the 1920s, when various bright colors were used, generally on portable machines. Many examples even show a woodgrain finish. Black typewriters with a "two–tone" finish of gloss and "crackle" panels were exclusively produced during the 1930s. Starting in the 1940s typewriters and other office equipment began to be produced with "designer" colors to match office interiors.

The newest development in typewriting technology, the electronic typewriters, are light, have very few moving parts, and many more features than possible with mechanical typewriters. With the growth in personal computers and related printers, typewriters are fast becoming an obsolescent office fixture.

References: Michael H Adler, *The Writing Machine,* George Allen & Unwin Ltd, 1973; Wilfred A Beeching, *Century of Typewriters,* William Heinemann, 1974; Richard N Current, *The Typewriter and the Men Who Made It,* University of Illinois Press, 1954; Darryl Matter, *Simplex Typewriters from the Early Twentieth Century,* Green Gate Books, 1984; Dan R Post, *Collectors Guide to Antique Typewriters,* Post–Era Books, 1981.

Periodicals: *Historische Burowelt* (w/translations), IFHB, Postfach 50 11 68, D–5000 Koln–50, Germany; *Borsen Speigal* (yearly catalog of past auction results), published by IFHB; *The Typewriter Times* 1216 Garden St, Hoboken, NJ 07030; *The Typewriter Exchange,* 2125 Mt Vernon St, Philadelphia, PA 19130; *EtCetera,* 11433 Rochester Ave #303, Los Angeles, CA 90025.

Collectors Clubs: IFHB Internationales Forum Historische Burowelt, address above; Early Typewriter Collectors Association, 11433 Rochester Ave #303, Los Angeles, CA 90025.

Museums: National Office Equipment Historical Museum, Kansas City, MO; Onandaga Historical Association, Syracuse, NY; Milwaukee Public Museum, Milwaukee, WI; Henry Ford Museum, Dearborn, MI; National Museum of American History, Div of Industry/Mechanisms (Smithsonian), Washington, DC.

Note: All prices given are for items in very good condition working order. Complete. Case is nice, but not necessary. Shows little or no corrosion.

Advisor: Todd Holmes

Adler	125.00
American/Globe	425.00
Barlock No 7–14	225.00
Bennett	325.00
Bing	130.00
Blickensderfer No 5–9	200.00

Boston	17,000.00
Caligraph	600.00
Chicago	800.00
Columbia No 2	3,400.00
Corona Folding	60.00
Demountable	80.00
Densmore No 2–5	600.00
Emerson No 3	700.00
Fox	
No 2–4	350.00
No 23–24	140.00
Franklin No 7–10	700.00
Hall	750.00
Hammond	
Multiplex	225.00
No 1	1,200.00
No 2–12	275.00
Harris Visible No 4	90.00
Junior	350.00
Lambert	800.00
LC Smith No 2–8	25.00
Merritt	1,000.00
Mignon No 4	150.00
Molle No 3	275.00
National No 2–5	100.00
New American No 5	1,600.00
Noiseless	175.00
Odell No 2–4	1,000.00
Oliver	
No 2	200.00
No 3–11	100.00
Pittsburgh Visible No 11–12	800.00
Postal	750.00
Rem–Sho	250.00
Remington	
No 2	700.00
No 4	2,800.00
No 6	100.00
No 7	100.00
No 10–12	50.00
Royal	
No 1	75.00
No 5	25.00
No 10	25.00
Sholes & Glidden	4,000.00–12,000.00

Underwood, Standard #5, $25.00.

Simplex	**25.00–200.00**
Smith Premier	
No 1	650.00
No 2–10	50.00
Standard Folding	250.00
Sun No 3	250.00
Underwood	
No 5	25.00
Portable	25.00
Varityper	150.00
Wellington	150.00
Williams No 2–6	600.00
Woodstock No 5	25.00
World	700.00
Yost No 4–10	300.00

Books, 1982; Harvey Duke, *The Official Identification and Price Guide To Pottery and Porcelain, Seventh Edition,* House of Collectibles, 1989; Betty Newbound, *The Gunshot Guide To Values of American Made China & Pottery,* Book 2, privately printed, 1983.

Periodicals: *The Daze,* P.O. Box 57, Otisville, MI 48463; *The New Glaze,* P.O. Box 4782, Birmingham, AL 35206.

Calico Fruits, casserole, cov, $24.00.

UNIVERSAL POTTERY

Collecting Hints: Not all Universal pottery carried the Universal name as part of the backstamp. Wares marked "Harmony House," "Sweet William/Sears Roebuck and Co.," and "Wheelock, Peoria" are part of the Universal production. Wheelock was a department store in Peoria, Illinois, that controlled the Cattail pattern on the Old Holland shape.

Like many pottery companies Universal had many shapes or styles of blanks, the most popular being Camwood, Old Holland, and Laurella. The same decal might be found on several different shapes.

The Cattail pattern had many accessory pieces. The 1940 and 1941 Sears catalogs listed an oval wastebasket, breakfast set, kitchen scale, linens, and bread box. Calico Fruits is another pattern with accessory pieces.

The Calico Fruits decal has not held up well over time. Collectors may have to settle for less than perfect pieces.

History: Universal Potteries of Cambridge, Ohio, was organized in 1934 by The Oxford Pottery Company. It purchased the Atlas–Globe plant properties. The Atlas–Globe operation was a merger of the Atlas China Company (formerly Crescent China Co. in 1921, Tritt in 1912 and Bradshaw in 1902) and the Globe China Company.

Even after the purchase, Universal retained the Oxford ware, made in Oxford, Ohio, as part of their dinnerware line. Another Oxford plant was used to manufacture tiles. The plant at Niles, Ohio, was dismantled.

The most popular lines of Universal were "Ballerina" and "Ballerina Mist." The company developed a detergent–resistant decal known as permacel, a key element in keeping a pattern bright. Production continued until 1960, when all plants were closed.

References: Jo Cunningham, *The Collector's Encyclopedia of American Dinnerware,* Collector

Ballerina		
Coaster		3.50
Coffeepot, wine		20.00
Chop plate, 12" d		5.00
Creamer		5.00
Cup and saucer		
Burgundy		8.00
Dark green		3.00
Gray		3.00
Egg cup		10.00
Gravy boat, gray		6.50
Plate		
6" d		
Chartreuse		1.75
Dark green		1.50
Gray		1.50
Maroon		1.50
9" d, dinner		
Dark green		3.00
Gray		3.00
10" d, dinner, dark green		4.00
Platter, 11½" l, lug handle		
Green		5.50
Maroon		5.00
Salt and pepper shakers, pr, burgundy		8.00
Saucer		
Chartreuse		1.00
Green		1.00
Yellow		1.25
Stack set, cov, 3 pcs		35.00
Sugar, cov		8.50
Tidbit tray, two tiers, green		6.00
Tumbler		10.00
Calico Fruits		
Batter jug		24.00
Cookie jar, cov		25.00
Creamer		4.00
Cup		6.50

Custard cup	5.00
Plate, 10″ d, dinner	7.50
Salt and pepper shakers, pr	12.00
Saucer	2.00
Spice set, glass, tray	20.00
Camwood, utility tray, peach, 13½″ d .	12.00

Cattail

Batter pitcher, metal top	80.00
Bowl	
5″ d	4.00
5¼″ d	2.75
6″ d, tab handle	9.00
7½″ d, cov	15.00
8½″ d	8.00
8¾″ d	12.00
Butter dish, cov	35.00
Casserole, cov, 9½″ d	22.00
Coffee percolator, electric	135.00
Creamer	8.00
Cup and saucer	9.00
Custard cup	8.50
Gravy boat	20.00
Ice tub, glass	80.00
Kitchen scale	18.00
Pie baker	20.00
Pie server	22.00
Plate	
6″ d	1.00
7″ d, luncheon	5.00
9½″ d, dinner	5.00
10″ d, grill	12.00
Platter	
11″ sq	11.00
11½″ l, oval	11.00
13½″ l, oval	12.00
Salad bowl, 9¾″ d	15.00
Salad serving set, fork and spoon ...	20.00
Soup, flat, 7¾″ d	10.00
Spoon	10.00
Sugar, cov	10.00
Syrup, metal top	65.00
Teapot	22.00
Vegetable bowl, oval, 10″ d	18.00

Circus

Salt and pepper shakers, pr	16.00
Teapot, red	15.00
Water jug, large	15.00

Iris

Bowl, 9″ d	10.00
Casserole, cov	15.00
Pie baker	12.00
Plate, 10″ d, dinner	6.50
Platter, 11″ d	10.00
Soup bowl, tab handle	5.00
Stack set, cov, 4 pcs	24.00
Tray, 11½″ d	10.00

Woodvine

Creamer	4.50
Cup	5.00
Gravy boat	8.50
Jar, cov, 6″ h	10.00

Plate

6″ d, bread and butter	2.50
7″ w, salad, sq	2.75
9″ d, dinner	3.50
Relish	7.50
Saucer	1.75
Utility bowl, cov, 6″ d	15.00

VALENTINES

Collecting Hints: Valentine collectors tend to focus on cards made before 1930, with special emphasis on the nineteenth century. Cards made before 1800 are known, but most are in the hands of museums.

At present collectors tend to specialize in one type of card, e.g., transportation theme cards, lacey, honeycomb, etc. Comic sheets, Art Nouveau, and Art Deco cards are gaining in popularity. Valentine collectors now face heavy competition from other theme collectors who want valentines as supplements to their collections.

Condition of the card is more important than age in most cases. Collectors like clean cards in very good repair.

Early German mechanical cards open and close from the middle; later examples and reproductions pull down. Early mechanicals used more delicate pastel shades. Bright red is found on later cards.

Keep cards out of the light to prevent fading and brittleness. Store cards in layers in a drawer with acid free paper between them.

History: Early cards were handmade, often containing both handwritten verses and hand drawn pictures. Many cards also were hand colored and contained cutwork.

Mass production of machine made cards featuring chromolithography began after 1840. In 1847 Esther Howland of Worcester, Massachusetts, established a company to make valentines which were hand decorated with paper lace and other materials imported from England. They had a small "H" stamped in red in the top left corner. Howland's company eventually became the New England Valentine Company [N.E.V. Co.].

George C. Whitney and his brother founded a company after the Civil War which dominated the market from the 1870s through the first decades of the twentieth century. They bought out several competitors, one of which was the New England Valentine Company.

Lace paper was invented in 1834. The 1835 to 1860 period is known as the "golden age" of lacey cards.

Embossed paper was used in England after 1800. Embossed lithographs and woodcuts developed between 1825–40, with early examples being hand colored.

References: Ruth Webb Lee, *A History of Valentines, Fifth Edition,* Lee Publications, 1952; National Valentine Collectors Association, *Bulletins;* Frank Staff, *The Valentine And Its Origins,* out of print.

Collectors' Club: National Valentine Collectors Association, Box 1404, Santa Ana, CA 92702.

Diecut, folding, three dimensional, 3⅞ x 6⅞", $7.50.

Animated, child
  1915, artist sgd **10.00**
  1923, 6" h **4.00**
Art Deco
  Folder
    Child's, Whitney, 3 x 5" **3.00**
    Fancy, orig lined envelope **14.00**
  Standup, flapper, 8" **8.00**
Art Nouveau
  Booklet, fancy, emb, cupids, vines, 5 x 7" **8.00**
  Diecuts, boxed, emb, pretty girls, flowers **12.00**
  Folder, fancy, cutwork, butterfly, cherubs **10.00**
  Standup, layered
    5 x 8", parchment **8.00**
    10 x 14", silk inserts **18.00**
  Standup, pasteboard, easel back, 4 x 6" **6.00**
Comic
  McLoughlin
    4 x 6", 1898 .... **6.00**
    8 x 12", sheet, sgd "CJH" **15.00**
    8 x 14", sheet, sgd "H" **10.00**
    Unknown, sheet, 8 x 10", 1925 .... **5.00**
Heart Shape
  Clapsaddle design, 6 x 9" **10.00**
  Diecut, F. Brundage, 3 x 3" **8.00**
  Folder
    McLoughlin, cupids, 1915 .... **4.00**

Whitney, children, 5 x 5", 1925 .. **3.00**
Honeycomb, pull out to open
  Beistle
    1926, red, 6" h **5.00**
    1927, light red, 10" h **8.00**
  German
    5 x 6", umbrella **25.00**
    7 x 12", blue and white scale **35.00**
Lacy
  Handwritten, poem on front, emb lace, 5 x 7", 1855 .... **30.00**
  McLoughlin, three dimensional folder, lace and ribbons, 5 x 8", 1885 .... **10.00**
  N.E.V. Co, folder, lace attached, 3 x 5", 1875 .... **20.00**
Mechanical, pull down
  American
    Automobile, 8 x 12", 1923 ...... **35.00**
    Cupids and flowers, 5 x 8", 1925 . **10.00**
    Seaplane, 8 x 12", 1930 .... **35.00**
  German, pre-WWI
    Coronation Coach, 8 x 10" **30.00**
    Ship, 8 x 10" **45.00**
  German, small children, 3 x 5", 1915 **7.50**
Post card, Victorian, silk fringe
  Prang
    3 x 5" **7.50**
    5 x 7" **12.00**
  Tuck, R
    3 x 5" **4.50**
    5 x 7" **8.00**
Unknown, folder
  2 x 4", cameo style, lace front, c1850 **8.00**
  5 x 8", fancy, pasted–on cupids and flowers, 1930 .... **2.50**
Whitney
  Folder, lace front, 3 x 4", 1865 .... **10.00**
  Three dimensional folder
    7 x 10", 1895 .... **15.00**
    8 x 10", applied ribbon and lace, 1915 .... **12.00**

VENDING MACHINES

Collecting Hints: Since individual manufacturers offered such a wide range of models, some collectors choose to specialize in a particular brand of machine. Variations are important. Certain accessories, porcelain finish, colors or special mechanical features on an otherwise common machine can add much to its value.

Original paint adds value. But numerous machines, especially peanut vendors with salt damaged paint, have been repainted. Most vendors were in service for ten to twenty years or more. Repainting normally was done by the operator as part of the repair and maintenance of his route. Repaints, recent or otherwise, if nicely done, do not necessarily lessen the value of a desirable machine. Original paint should be retained if at all possible.

Decals add much to the appearance of a vendor and often are the only means of identifying it. Original decals, again, are the most desirable. Reproductions of many popular styles have been made and are a viable alternative if originals are not available.

Some reproduction parts also are available. In some cases, entire machines have been reproduced using new glass and castings. Using one or two new parts as a means of restoring an otherwise incomplete machine is generally accepted by collectors.

Collecting vending machines is a relatively new hobby. It has increased in popularity with other advertising collectibles. New machines constantly are being discovered, thus maintaining the fascination for the collector.

History: Most of us still remember the penny gumball or peanut machine of our childhood. Many still survive on location after thirty years or more of service, due in part to the strength and simplicity of their construction.

The years 1910 to 1940 were the heyday of the most collectible style of vendor, the globe type peanut or gumball machine. Machine manufacturers invested a great deal of money throughout this period in the form of advertising and research. Many new designs were patented.

The simple rugged designs proved the most popular with the operator who had an established route of vendors as a means of making a living. Many operators made their fortunes "a penny at a time," especially during the Depression when dollars were hard to come by. Fifty years later, the same vendor that originally cost four to fifteen dollars commands a much higher price.

In addition to the globe-style variety of vendor is the cabinet-style machine. These usually incorporate a clockwork mechanism and occasionally mechanical figurines to deliver the merchandise. The earliest examples of these were produced in the 1890s.

References: Nic Costa, *Automatic Pleasures: The History of the Coin Machine*, Kevin Frances Publishing, Ltd., 1988; Bill Enes, *Silent Salesmen: An Encyclopedia of Collectible Gum, Candy & Nut Machines*, published by author, 1987; Roger Pribbenow and Jimm Lehmann, *Gumball Guide*, privately printed.

Periodical: *Coin Op Newsletter*, 909 26th Street, N. W., Washington, DC, 20037.

Acorn, gumball, 5¢, box shape, Oak
  Mfg Co acorn symbol, c1950 ...... **50.00**
Adlee E–Z, gumball, slips inside for cash
  awards, cast iron, sq ftd base **325.00**

Ajax 5¢ Nut, commonly known as Challenger, aluminum, 1947, $175.00.

Advance, matchbook, 1¢, glass dome,
  cast iron base, ornate feet, 1915 ... **400.00**
Ajax Hot Nut, triple globe heated nut
  vendor, aluminum, light up marquee **180.00**
Appleton, gumball, solid brass, nickel
  plated top, c1920 .... **200.00**
Bluebird, gumball or peanut, polished
  aluminum, globe decals **175.00**
Chicago, peanut, nickel plated, cylinder
  globe with round bulge at center,
  c1900 ....**2,000.00**
Columbus
  Model A, hourglass shaped base,
    round globe, circled star logo,
    painted cast iron **150.00**
  Model 21, peanut, 1¢, oct globe and
    base **175.00**
  Model 34, gumball, green porcelain
    or painted finish, cast iron, oct
    globe, 1930s **275.00**
  Model V, marble and gumball, cylinder globe, tin body, cast iron and
    aluminum mechanism, 1930s **500.00**
Diamond, matchbook, window in upper left corner, allowed merchant to
  set quantity, c1920 .... **365.00**
Doremus, cigar, slanted top, c1907 ...**1,400.00**
Double Nugget, polished aluminum
  double vendor, heavy glass globes,
  1930s **100.00**
Empire, Art Deco cabinet, polished aluminum, Empire state building and
  name emb on front, 1930s **80.00**
Ford, gumball, 1¢, chrome **45.00**
Grandbois, gumball, aluminum, cylindrical body, marked on bottom,
  1930s **125.00**

Griswold, peanut, 1¢, painted, cast iron, unusual six legged base, brass tray at front catches peanuts, early 1910s **600.00**

Hawkeye, gumball, six sided, cast aluminum base, c1931 .... **120.00**

HiLo, cast iron, faucet handle on front, tapered cylinder globe, 1910–1920s **500.00**

Leebold, polished aluminum, Victorian style dec, round globe, 1920s **1,000.00**

Magna Vendor, polished aluminum, geometric styling, fourteen sided faceted globe, 1¢ or 5¢ mechanisms .. **150.00**

Master Model 77, Fantail, large front mechanism, fan shaped **400.00**

Mutoscope, Old Mill, 1¢, disperses one to four products randomly, unusual graphics, 1928 .... **700.00**

Northwestern 31 Merchandiser, porcelain and painted finishes, tapered sq base, round knob at front, 1931 .... **100.00**

Penny King, gumball, name on bottom, 1930s **100.00**

Postage Vendor, cast iron base and top, beveled glass displays mechanism, c1910 .... **300.00**

Premiere, gumball and personality card vendor, c1950 .... **60.00**

Regal, candy, straight line modular base, 5¢, c1935 .... **70.00**

Selmor, nickel plated or painted finishes, round cast iron base, pull lever style mechanism, round base, 1930s **120.00**

Simpson, cast iron, similar to Columbus Model A, round base, three feet, "S" marking on door, 1920s **400.00**

Simpson Junior, miniature version of Simpson, 1920s **500.00**

Tom Thumb, gumball, miniature size, c1920 .... **100.00**

Victor, sq base and globes, turn handles at front, 1930–40s **70.00**

Yu Chu, Jar Top vendor, refills sold complete with new globe, 1930s **150.00**

Zeno, stick gum, clockwork mechanism, 1¢, 1890s **300.00**

VERNON KILNS

Collecting Hints: Vernon Kilns used 48 different marks during its period of operation. Collect examples which are in very good condition and concentrate on the specialty items rather than dinnerware.

History: During the Depression, many small potteries flourished in southern California. One of these, Poxon China, was founded in Vernon, California, in 1912. This pottery was sold to Faye G. Bennison in 1931. It was renamed Vernon Kilns and also was known as Vernon Potteries,

Ltd. Under Bennison's direction, the company became a leader in the pottery industry.

The high quality and versatility of its wares made it very popular. Besides a varied dinnerware line, Vernon Kilns also produced Walt Disney figurines, advertising, political, and fraternal items. One popular line was historical and commemorative plates, which included several plate series, featuring scenes from England, California missions, and the West.

Vernon Kilns survived the Depression, fires, earthquakes, and wars. However, it could not compete with the influx of imports. In January, 1958, the factory was closed. Metlox Potteries of Manhattan Beach, California, bought the trade name and molds along with the remaining stock.

Reference: Maxine Nelson, *Versatile Vernon Kilns, An Illustrated Value Guide, Book II,* Collector Books, 1983.

Newsletter: Vernon View, P. O. Box 945, Scottsdale, AZ 85252.

COMMEMORATIVE PLATES

Alexandria, LA, brown and white **10.00**
Arkansas, map, blue and white **10.00**
Carlsbad Cavern, brown and white ... **10.00**
MacArthur, maroon **20.00**
Marineland, FL, blue and white **10.00**
New Mexico, map, blue and white ... **10.00**
New York, multicolored **15.00**
North Carolina, multicolored **15.00**
Presidents, 1942 .... **20.00**
Tennessee, multicolored **15.00**
Texas, blue and white **10.00**

Salt and pepper shakers, Organdie pattern, yellow and green stripes, white ground, $16.00.

DINNERWARE

Barkwood
    Cup **3.00**
    Egg cup **5.00**
    Gravy **6.00**
    Pitcher, 6" h **7.00**
Blueberry Hill, set, 44 pcs **85.00**

Brown Eyed Susan
Cereal bowl 4.00
Chop plate 12.00
Cup and saucer 5.00
Fruit bowl 3.00
Pitcher, 5", bulbous 7.50
Plate
   6¼" d 3.00
   7½" d 4.00
   9¾" d 5.00
Platter, 12" 10.00
Salt and pepper shakers, pr 15.00
Sugar, cov 10.00
Dreamtime
Chowder Bowl, 6" d 2.00
Plate, 6" 2.00
Early California
Coffee carafe, brown 24.00
Cup and saucer, light turquoise 3.00
Platter, 12", orange 15.00
Salt and pepper shakers, pr, yellow . 15.00
Saucer, turquoise 2.00
Set, service for 8, turquoise, 44 pcs . 125.00
Vegetable bowl, orange, 8½" 8.00
Gingham
Chop plate 12.00
Chowder bowl 5.00
Egg cup 15.00
Pitcher, pint 17.00
Plate, 6" d 2.00
Salt shaker 4.00
Teapot 24.00
Tumbler, 5½" h 12.00
Homespun
Coaster, 3⅞" d 8.00
Creamer 5.00
Cup 5.00
Demitasse cup 7.00
Pitcher, 8½" 18.00
Plate, 6" 2.00
Salt shaker 8.00
Saucer 1.00
Sugar, cov 12.00
Lollipop, coffeepot 15.00
Monterey
Chowder bowl 5.00
Cup 12.00
Pitcher, 2 qt 25.00
Plate
   7" d 3.00
   10" d 4.00
Salt and pepper shakers, pr 12.00
Saucer 3.50
Serving bowl, 9" 12.00
Sugar, cov 10.00
Organdie
Bowl
   5½" d 8.00
   8¾" d 13.50
Casserole, cov, individual 12.00
Chop plate 22.00
Chowder bowl, 6" d 12.00

Creamer 6.00
Cup and saucer 5.00
Gravy 18.00
Plate
   6" d 2.00
   7" d 3.00
   9½" d 12.00
Salt and pepper shakers, pr 16.00
Sugar, cov 7.00
Raffia
Chop plate, 12¾" 15.00
Cup and saucer 4.00
Pitcher, 12" h 25.00
Syrup pitcher 30.00
Tam O'Shanter
Chop plate, 13" d 22.00
Plate
   9½" d 4.50
   10" d 12.00
Vegetable, divided 12.00
Tickled Pink
Butter Dish, cov 12.50
Creamer 4.00
Cup and Saucer 4.50
Fruit bowl, 5¾" d 2.00
Plate
   7" d 3.00
   10" d 4.50
Platter
   10" l 8.00
   11" l 10.00
   13¼" l 12.00
Salad set, large bowl, six small bowls 15.00
Salt and pepper shakers, pr 6.00
Sugar, cov 6.00
Vegetable 4.00

VETERINARY COLLECTIBLES

Collecting Hints: Individuals collect veterinary items for a variety of reasons. Many prefer to collect items which pertain to the pet which is currently in residence within their home or which was a devoted companion during childhood. Veterinarians often decorate their offices with a variety of antique veterinary items.

History: Iowa State established the first veterinary college in the United States in 1879. By 1900 many additional veterinary colleges were founded. Veterinary research advanced. Pharmaceutical companies began developing medical products strictly for veterinary use.

Following World War II, there was an acute shortage of veterinarians. The period from 1945–1984 is the "golden age" of veterinary education.

Interest in veterinary products ranges from the farm to the city. 4–H projects introduce farm youngsters to the proper use of veterinary products. Studies have shown that individuals with pets are less likely to suffer from stress. Recently, cats surpassed dogs as the most common form of household pet. Specialty cat and dog catalogs are part of the mail order business. Individuals in limited accommodations often choose fish or birds as pets. Of course, there are always those individuals who focus on the exotic.

References: PEW National Veterinary Education Program, *Future Directions for Veterinary Medicine*, Institute of Policy Sciences and Public Affairs, Duke University, 1988; Jack J. Stockton, *A Century of Service, Veterinary in Indiana, 1884–1984*, Purdue University.

Advisor: Patricia McDaniel.

Bird
  Hartz Mountain Products Corp
    Canary Charm, bell–shaped seed biscuit with wheel, yellow, brown, and white cardboard box, one charm, 2⅞ x 1⅞ x 1¾", full **7.00**
    E–Z Kleen Cage Mat, pink, yellow, purple, and cream cellophane pkg, 9½ x 15", 12 sheets, 1933 **10.00**
  House of Huston, Inc, Finer Dinner Bird Seeds for your Canary, yellow, blue, red, green, and cream cardboard box, canary on front, 7 x 3⅞ x 1⅜", 12 oz, full **7.00**
  RT French Company, French's Canary Exercise Ball, red, yellow, and black box, bird on front, 1½ x 1½ x 1½" **7.00**
  William Cooper & Nephews, Inc, Pulvex Bird Powder, red, yellow, and black cardboard can, 2⅞ x 1⅝" .. **6.00**
Cat, House of Huston, Inc, Kitty Care, pinks, brown, white, and black cardboard box, kitty on front, 5¼ x 1⅞", full **7.50**
Cow
  Brown Co, Nibrock Kowtowls, disposable towel for cleansing cow's udder and teats, sample pkg, shades of brown, cow on front, 13¼ x 5¾" envelope **8.50**
  Dairy Association Co, Inc, Kow–Kare, iron tonic stimulant, tan, white, and brown label, 4¾ x 4½", 1¼ lb full can **10.00**
  Globe Laboratories, Inc, Globe Cal–O–Dex, sterile solution milk fever treatment, red, yellow, and blue, cows on label border, 7¾ x 2¾", 16 fl oz, full bottle **10.00**
  Hess & Clark, Division of Richardson–Merrell, Inc, Pol Dehorner, yellow, white, black, and red card-

board carton, 3⅜ x 1¾", full 1 fl oz bottle **7.00**
Dog
  Adams Supply Co, Adams No–No, expels tape worm, yellow and black, hunting dog on front, 2½ x 1⅝ x 1", 15 tablets **8.50**
  Dr LD LeGear Medicine Co, Dr LeGear's Kennel Disinfectant, red, cream, and black cardboard box, 3 dogs on front, 8¾ x 2¾ x 1½", full 6 oz bottle **12.00**
  House of Huston, Sunday Shower, The Quick Dog Cleaner, red, white, and blue label, Boston bulldog on back, 7 x 2¾", full 1 pt bottle **12.00**
  Polk Miller Products Corp
    Sergeant's Dog Care Book, multicolored booklet, puppies on cov, 7¾ x 5", 42 pgs **10.00**
    Sergeant's Eye Wash, red, black, yellow, and white label, 4⅝ x 1⅛ x 1¼", full 4 oz bottle **9.00**
    Sergeant's Laxative Tablets, yellow, black, red, and white cardboard box, hound on front, 2¾ x 2 x1½", 20 tablets **6.50**
  Spratt's Patent Limited, Spratt's Flea and Insect Powder, white, red, and black tin, St Bernard on front, 4⅜ x 1¾ x⅞", 1 oz **15.00**
  Triangle Eng Prod Co, U–Turn Stake, animal repellent, tan, cream, and black cardboard box, running dog on front, 14¼ x 3½ x 2⅜", 12 stakes **16.00**
  Unknown Manufacturer, Morton's Oven–Toasted Vitamized Kibbies, contains dextrose, red, white, and blue, puppy on front, 9⅛ x 6⅞", empty 5 lb tin **23.00**
  Wilke Laboratories, Inc, Car Sickness Capsules, yellow, white, red, and black cardboard box, dog on front, 3¾ x 2 x 1", 20 capsules **7.00**
Fish
  Metaframe Corp, Metaframe Soft Spun Glass Wool, blue, yellow, red, and white cardboard box, 5½ x 4 x 1½", 23 grams, full **4.50**
  RT French Company, French's Fish Food, blue, 2¼ x 1¾ x 1¼", 1½ oz tin, full **4.00**
  Wil–Nes Corp
    Wil–Nes 5 Disposable Aqua–Vac Filter Bags, blue, white, and yellow cardboard box, 5⅛ x 3 x½" **8.00**
    Wil–Nes Sodium Bicarbonate, reduces acidity, blue, yellow, and white cardboard box, 3¾ x 1¾ x 1¾", 4 oz **5.00**

Hog

Dr Hess & Clark, Inc, Dr Hess Hog Special, tonic and mineral supplement, red, yellow, black, and white cardboard box, 10½ x 6 x 4¼", 10 lbs, full **10.00**

Dr LD LeGear Medicine Co, Dr LeGear's Hog Worm Powder, black, red, cream, and yellow box, Dr LeGear's picture on front, "The Roundworm's Journey Thru The Pig" illus, supplied by USDA Farmers Bulletin No 1787, 8½ x 5¾ x 3", 3 lbs 2 oz **16.00**

Dr Salsbury's Laboratories, Dr Salsbury's Hog Oil, roundworm expulsion, maroon, cream, and black cardboard box, 5⅞ x 2½ x 2½", half pt bottle, full **7.25**

Tobacco States Chemical Co, Inc, Tobacco States 5% Ronnel Granular Insecticide, controls hog lice, red, blue, yellow, and black cardboard cylinder, 9 x 3", 12 oz, full **7.00**

Vernost Products Co, VerNost Improved Hog Powder, roundworm remover, double dose treatment, orange, black, and blue cardboard container, 3½ x 2¾", 5 oz, full . . **6.00**

Horse

Bickmore Co, Bickmore Powder, treats superficial wounds, yellow and black tin, horse on front, 4½ x 2½ x 1¼", 3 oz **15.00**

Dr AC Daniels Inc, Dr A.C. Daniel's C.C. & F. Drops, respiratory disturbances fever reducer, blue and white cardboard box, Dr Daniel's picture on front, 5 x 2 x 1¼", 2 oz bottle, full **15.00**

Dr David Roberts Veterinary Co, Dr David Roberts' Physic Balls, cream and black cardboard box, Dr Roberts' picture on front, 4 x 1¼ x 1¼", two physic balls **8.50**

Dr LD LeGear Medicine Co, Dr LeGear's Gall Salve, red and black tin, Dr LeGear's picture on tin, 2½ x 2½", 2 oz, full **9.00**

HW Naylor Co, Dr Naylor's Linite, hoof rot, canker, and thrush treatment, tan, red, and brown cardboard box, 6¾ x 3 x 2½", 12 oz bottle, full **7.50**

Miscellaneous

Chemical Products Co, Burfiend's Famous Black Capsules for Dogs, Puppies, Cats, and Kittens, tapeworm and roundworm treatment, red, tan, and black cardboard pkg, 2½ x 2½ x⅞", 12 capsules, full . . **6.50**

Dr LeGear, Inc

Dr LeGear's Screw Worm Bomb, temporary repellent for wounds caused by shearing, dehorning, docking, and wire cuts, red, black, and yellow aerosol can, 6 x 2⅝", 10 oz, full **8.00**

Pep,R Up,R Vitamin Mineral Supplement for All Pets, blue, red, yellow, and white can, 4¼ x 2¾", full **8.00**

ER Squibb & Sons, Squibb Veterinary Vionate Feed Supplement, brown and tan container, 3⅞ x 2⅝ x 2⅝", 8 oz, full **9.50**

Johnson & Johnson Filter Products Division, Johnson & Johnson Animal Antiseptic Ointment, antibacterial, aqua, tan, and cream tube, 7⅐ x 1¾", full **6.75**

Parke, Davis, & Co, Nema Worm Capsules, brown and tan cardboard box, 2¼ x 2⅜ x⅝", 12 capsules, full **5.75**

Sergeant's Dry Cleaner and Deodorant for Dogs and Cats, red, yellow, white, and black can, dog on front, 4⅞ x 2½", 5 oz, full **9.00**

Poultry

Dr LD LeGear Medicine Co, Dr LeGear's Poultry Inhalant, concentrated, respiratory inflammation expectorant, red, yellow, and black cardboard box, roosters and Dr LeGear on front, 5¾ x 2¼ x 1⅛", 4 fl oz bottle **8.25**

Geo H Lee Co, Lee's Flock Wormer, roundworm and pinworm controller, yellow, blue, and black can, 4⅝ x 2½", 8 oz, full **8.50**

Mayer's Hatchery, Mayer's Laymore, tonic, gray–green cardboard box, 5¼ x 1⅜ x⅜", full **8.00**

Puritan Products Co, Poultry PEP, white diarrhea, cholera, and roup prevention aid, yellow and black cardboard box, 4⅜ x 2⅜ x 2⅜", 125 tablets **8.00**

Walker Remedy Co, Walko Tablets, drinking water antiseptic, yellow and black cardboard box, chicken on front, 5⅜ x 3¼ x 2", 2000 tablets **8.25**

Rabbit, Sudbury Laboratory, Rabbit Chaperone, foliage protector, glass bottle, yellow, pink and cream label, 6 x 2¼", 12 oz **9.00**

Sheep

Coopers & Nephews, Cooper's Sheep Drench, stomach and tape worm remover, bottle, yellow, red, and

black label, 6 x 2⅜ x 1½", 8 oz,
full **5.00**
Globe Laboratories, Globe Phen–
Ovine Sheep and Goat Drench,
stomach and nodular worm elimi-
nator, clear bottle, red, yellow, and
blue label, pictures of sheep, 8 x
3¼", 1 qt, full **8.00**
Veterinary Instruments
Eisele & Co, ECO Veterinary Dose Syringe, dark green cardboard box,
one 6½" syringe **11.00**
Ideal Instrument & Mfg Co
Ideal Stainless Hypodermic
Needle, 3" l **1.50**
Ideal Vaco Syringe Filler, blue–gray
cardboard box, one 6" syringe,
rubber tubing **8.50**

VIEW-MASTER PRODUCTS

Collecting Hints: Condition is the key in determining price. In most cases because of relative
newness of this collecting category and quantities
of material made, viewers and reels in mint or
near new condition may still be found.

Original packaging is sought by collectors.
Many viewers and reels were removed from
boxes and envelopes and became subject to
damage and excessive wear.

History: The first View–Master viewers and reels
were made available in 1939. Invented by William Gruber, View–Master products were manufactured and sold by Sawyer's, Inc., of Portland,
Oregon. The sudden growth of View–Master was
cut short by World War II. Shortages of film,
plastic, and paper would have crippled the operation and possibly ended the existence of
View–Master had not the Army and Navy recognized the visual training potential of this product. Between 1942 and the war's end, about
100,000 viewers and 5 to 6 million reels were
ordered by the military.

After the war, public demand for View–Master
products soared. Production barely satisfied the
needs of the original 1,000 dealer network. 1946
saw the introduction of the Model C viewer
which was practically indestructible, thus making it the most common viewer found by collectors today.

In October 1966, General Aniline & Film Corporation (GAF) bought Sawyer's and revamped
the View–Master line. GAF introduced new 2–
D projectors and 3–D Talking View–Master.

In late 1980 GAF sold the View–Master portion
of their company to a limited partnership headed
by businessman Arnold Thaler. Further acquisition resulted in the purchase of Ideal Toys. Today

the 3–D viewers and reels are manufactured by
View– Master Ideal, Inc.

Reference: Roger T. Nazeley *View–Master Single
Reels, Volume I,* published by author, 1987; John
Waldsmith, *Stereo Views: An Illustrated History
And Price Guide,* Wallace–Homestead, 1991.

Collectors' Club: Many View–Master collectors
are members of the National Stereoscopic Association, Box 14801, Columbus, OH 43214.

Advisor: John S. Waldsmith.

VIEWER

Model B, black bakelite, streamlined,
flip–front, 1944–48 . . . .   **28.00**
Model C, black bakelite, insert in top,
light attachment, batteries, no corro-
sion, 1946–56 . . . .   **23.00**
Model D, focuses, orig box **85.00**
Model F, lighted, dark brown plastic,
pressure bar on top **18.00**
Model H, lighted, round bottom, GAF
logo on front, 1967–81 . . . .   **13.00**
Modern Viewers **1.50**

PROJECTOR

S–1, metal, brown, single lens, carrying
case **48.00**
Sawyer's, plastic, single lens **10.00**
Stereomatic 500, 3–D, two lens, carry-
ing case **250.00**

CAMERA

Personal 3–D, custom film cutter **175.00**
Mark II, film cutter, made in Europe . .   **200.00**

REEL, SINGLE

Early hand–lettered, white reel, blue
and white envelopes
16, Bryce Canyon, National Park, UT   **10.00**
58, Golden Gate Exposition, Flowers
and Landscaping **14.00**
62, Hawaiian Hula Dancers **3.00**
86, World's Fair, New York, Sculp-
ture, 1939 . . . .   **15.00**
92, Oregon Caves National Monu-
ment **2.00**
101, Rocky Mountain National Park,
CO **2.00**
129, Yellowstone National Park, Gey-
sers and Pools **4.00**
137, Washington DC **3.00**
145, Sanctuary of Our Sorrowful
Mother, Portland, OR **10.00**
152, Water Falls along Columbia
Highway **5.00**
167, Marine Studios, St Augustine . .   **5.00**

181, Colonial Williamsburg, VA **10.00**
189, Mission San Juan Capistrano . .   **2.00**
203, The Black Hills, SD **2.00**
236, The Million Dollar Highway . .   **4.00**
253, Carlsbad Caverns National Park   **4.00**
267, Cranmore Mt Skimobile Tram-
   way, White Mountains **8.00**
284, Death Valley National Monu-
   ment **5.00**
295, St Louis Zoological Park **3.00**
339, Mammoth Cave National Park .   **6.00**
348, Gettysburg National Military
   Monument, PA, II **10.00**
501, Mexico City and Vicinity **3.00**
510, Lake Patzcuaro and Paricutin
   Volcano **6.50**
515, Typical Scenes in Mexico **4.00**
623, Ruins of Pachacamac, near
   Lima, Peru **21.00**
667, La Plata, Argentina **4.00**
Standard white reels, printed titles, blue
and white envelopes
14, Reno, "Biggest Little City in the
   World" **8.00**
43, Grand Teton National Park III,
   WY **5.00**
57, Golden Gate Exposition, Build-
   ings **15.00**
72, Island of Kuai, HI **6.00**
94, Storytown, USA, Lake George,
   NY **10.00**
110, Mt Rainier National Park, Wild
   Flowers **4.00**
158, Rockefeller Center, Empire State
   Building, New York City, 1948 . . .   **1.00**
175, Navajo Indians, NM and AZ . .   **2.00**
192, Cave of the Mounds, Blue
   Mounds **10.00**
236, The Million Dollar Highway . .   **1.50**
269, Old Covered Bridges, New Eng-
   land **8.50**
299, Hot Springs National Park, AR   **1.00**
313, Victoria, BC and Butchart's Gar-
   dens **6.00**
363, Ross Allen's Reptile Institute,
   Seminole Indian Village, Silver
   Springs **20.00**
401, Girl Scouts Serve Their Country   **35.00**
530, Panama City, Panama, 1946 . .   **3.00**
585, Port of Spain and Saddle Road,
   Trinidad **2.50**
675, Carnival, Rio de Janiero, Brazil   **4.00**
702, A Day at the Circus II, Ringling
   Bros and Barnum & Bailey **2.00**
747, Television Stars III **20.00**
951, Gene Autry in "The Kidnap-
   ping" **5.00**
1075, Scarborough, Yorkshire, Eng-
   land **15.00**
1513, Berchtesgaden Country I, Ger-
   many **7.50**
1920, Tulip Time, Holland **18.00**

3005, Table Mountain and Cableway,
   Union of South Africa **8.00**
4012, Region of Haifa, Israel, booklet   **1.00**
5025, Canberra, Capital of Australia   **10.00**
9047, Gettysburg National Military
   Park, PA **3.00**
B–3731, Robin Hood Meets Friar
   Tuck, 1956 . . . .   **10.00**
DR–27, Highlights from Fairy Tales,
   green ink, demonstration reel,
   came with viewer **5.00**
FT–7, The Three Little Pigs, booklet   **1.50**
FT–10, Sleeping Beauty, booklet . . .   **5.00**
FT–27, Rudolph the Red–Nosed Rein-
   deer and Uncle Bigby the Blue–
   Nosed Reindeer **8.00**
H–500, "King of the Cowboys" Roy
   Rogers and Trigger **4.00**
MG–1, Miss Muffet to Jack and Jill,
   booklet **1.50**
SAM–4, Sam in Darkest Africa **4.00**
SP–88, New York World's Fair I **20.00**
SP–285, Death Valley National Mon-
   ument II **10.00**
SP–9001, Skyline Caverns, Front
   Royal, VA **1.00**
SP–9051, Martha's Vineyard Island,
   MA **4.00**

3–REEL PACKETS

Values are for complete near new packets. In
most cases the 3–reel packets came with story
booklets. Sawyer issues (SAW) 1953–1966, GAF
issues (GAF) 1967–1981, and View–Master International (VMI) 1981–1982.

Aircraft Carrier in Action at Sea, 760 A,
   B, and C, SAW **45.00**
Arabian Nights, FT–50 A, B, and C,
   SAW **11.00**
Bobby the Bunny, 830 A, B, and C, SAW   **9.00**
Boy Scout Jamboree, 8th World, 435 A,
   B, and C, SAW **40.00**
Christmas Story, XM– 1, 2, and 3, SAW   **4.00**
Cowboy Stars, 950, 955, and 960, SAW   **10.00**
Fairy Tales III, FT–7, 8, and 9, SAW . .   **10.00**
Goofy, Traveling Cameraman, 844 A, B,
   and C, SAW **7.00**
20,000 Leagues under the Sea, 974 A,
   B, and C, SAW **3.00**
A–033, Upper Canada Village and Fort
   Henry, SAW **7.00**
A–193, Sea World, San Diego, CA,
   Packet No 2, SAW **10.00**
A–331, Colorado Ski Country, GAF . . .   **6.00**
A–372, Grand Canyon River Expedi-
   tion, GAF **4.00**
A–452, Gay 90's Melody Museum, St
   Louis, MO, SAW **30.00**
A–647, New York City at Night, GAF .   **5.00**
A–856, The Old South, GAF **8.00**

A–895, Santa's Land Park and Zoo, SAW **6.00**
B–095, In Darkest Africa, SAW **20.00**
B–311, Carlo Collodi's Pinocchio, SAW **3.00**
B–342, Walt Disney's Robin Hood, GAF **4.00**
B–501, Walt Disney Productions Presents The Love Bug, GAF, 1968 .... **3.00**
B–570, Beverly Hillbillies, SAW **25.00**
B–597, Emergency, GAF **8.00**
B–795, Old–Time Cars, GAF **10.00**
H–13, Smithsonian Air and Space Museum, SAW **6.00**
H–19, Disney World, Tomorrowland, VMI **4.00**
J–11, MASH, GAF **10.00**
J–32, Thailand, GAF **6.00**
J–79, US Spaceport, Kennedy Space Center, FL, VMI **4.00**
K–57, Star Trek, The Motion Picture, GAF, 1979 .... **4.00**
L–1, Can't Stop the Music, GAF, 1980 **7.00**

WATCH FOBS

Collecting Hints: The most popular fobs are those relating to old machinery, either farm, construction or industrial. Advertising fobs are the next most popular group.

The back of a fob is helpful in identifying a genuine fob from a reproduction or restrike. Genuine fobs frequently have advertising or a union trademark on the back. Some genuine fobs do have blank backs; but a blank back should be a warning to be cautious.

History: A watch fob is a useful and decorative item attached to a man's pocket watch by a strap. It assists him in removing the watch from his pocket. Fobs became popular during the last quarter of the 19th century. Companies such as The Greenduck Co. in Chicago, Schwabb in Milwaukee, and Metal Arts in Rochester produced fobs for companies who wished to advertise their products or to commemorate an event, individual, or group.

Most fobs are made of metal and are struck from a steel die. Enamel fobs are scarce and sought after by collectors. If a fob was popular, a company would order restrikes. As a result, some fobs were issued for a period of twenty-five years or more. Watch fobs still are used today in promoting heavy industrial equipment.

Reference: John M. Kaduck, *Collecting Watch Fobs*, Wallace-Homestead, 1973.

Collectors' Club: International Watch Fob Association, Inc., 6613 Elmer Drive, Toledo, OH 43615.

REPRODUCTION ALERT

Allis–Chalmers, tractor **75.00**

Lorain, Thew Shovel Co, Lorain, Ohio, plated brass, $25.00.

Altman–Taylor **90.00**
American Lumber Co, Pittsburgh, Indian head **35.00**
Armour Meats **40.00**
Arrowhead, saddle, Texas souvenir ... **35.00**
Atlantic City, city seal, 1854 .... **20.00**
Atlantic Fleet, Panama Canal, 1913 ... **125.00**
Avery Tractor Co **85.00**
Baseball bat and glove, sterling silver, 1920s **75.00**
Bucking bronc rider **75.00**
Buffalo Bill–Pawnee Bill, bullet hole .. **145.00**
Bull Durham **75.00**
Case Eagle **45.00**
Champlin Oils, enamel, red, white, and blue **75.00**
Cincinnati Horseshoe Company **85.00**
Compass **65.00**
Covered wagon and team **47.50**
Defender of Freedom, 1¼ x 1½" silvered brass, eagle and patriotic shield, inscribed "War Declared April 6/First US Troops Landed In France June 26, 1917" **20.00**
De Laval Separator, 1¾" l, oval, silvered brass, blue, white, pink, and cherry red porcelain accents, back inscribed "De Laval Cream Separators/World's Standard/Over 2,500,000 In Use," early 1900s **85.00**
Diamond Edge **32.00**
Elk, stamp case, sgd "Marathon" **30.00**
Fireman **35.00**
Flint Wagon Works **40.00**
Ford Tractor, orig box, 1965 .... **30.00**
Galion Tandem Rollers, Galion, OH, 1950s **12.00**
Grand Island Horse and Mule Co, 1916 **50.00**
Highway Equipment, Attleboro, MA .. **7.50**
Horseshoe and horse, gold filled, chain **110.00**

Hutchinson, KS, sunflower, button and
  ribbon **48.00**
Hunter, trader, trapper, Columbus, OH **75.00**
Indian Motorcycles, 1¼ x 2″, brass,
  bronze–like finish, diecut arrowhead,
  Indian logo head center, early 1900s **75.00**
Jewelry type, intaglio dec, yellow gold
  setting
    Black onyx **65.00**
    Carnelian, sq, Roman soldier bust .. **65.00**
John Deere, mother–of–pearl **125.00**
Kansas Livestock Co, horse and shoe . **45.00**
Kellogg's Toasted Corn Flakes **75.00**
Keystone Lumber, elephant **40.00**
Kress Corp, Brimfield, IL, cement truck **10.00**
Leaders For A Change/Jan 20, 1977/Our
  36th President/Carter, white metal,
  brass finish, Carter and American
  flags **12.00**
Mack Trucks, bulldog **35.00**
MacLarens Imperial Cheese, multicol-
  ored enamel **75.00**
Masonic, yellow gold **40.00**
Mayflower, calf skin, German **12.50**
Nash Hardware, Panther Cutlery &
  Tools, Ft Worth **75.00**
National Park Gun Club, sterling silver,
  1908 .... **145.00**
New Mexico, 1908 Territorial Fair **37.50**
Novary Pure Foods, silvered brass **12.00**
Paul Revere Life Insurance Co **15.00**
Peace Bridge, Toronto, 1930 .... **12.00**
Plymouth Division, military meet, best
  regimental parade, Nov 1918 ...... **25.00**
Poll Parrot Shoes **65.00**
Race Horse **37.50**
Red Man Tobacco **30.00**
Rock Island RR **35.00**
Roosevelt and Fairbanks, 1¾″ sq, brass,
  bronze color finish, diecut elephant **85.00**
Saddle, JH Haney, Omaha **135.00**
Sam Houston, 1½″ white metal, raised
  portrait, reverse "Compliments of F W
  Heitmann Co/Hardware/Houston,
  TX," early 1900s **40.00**
Smith Oil and Gas Separator, diecut .. **75.00**
Stirrup, brass **22.00**
Shawmut Rubbers, Boston, celluloid .. **25.00**
Texas Electric Service, enamel, red,
  white, and blue, 1926 logo **75.00**
Traveler's Protective Ass'n, diecut, state
  of IL shape, small enclosed compass,
  1917 .... **25.00**
US Horseshoe Company **75.00**
Vandium–Alloys Steel Co Red Cut Co-
  balt High Speed Steel, brass, red devil
  on machinery **64.00**
Waltham Grinding Wheel Co, three
  grinding wheels **50.00**
Wards Tip Top Bread **50.00**
Western Live Stock Insurance Co, sterling silver **15.00**

Winchester **125.00**
Woman's Liberty Bell/Justice–Equality–
  1915–Pennsylvania, brass, inscription on reverse **50.00**

WELLER POTTERY

Collecting Hints: Because of the availability of large numbers of pieces in Weller's commercial ware, prices are stable and unlikely to rise rapidly. Forest, Glendale, and Woodcraft are the popular patterns in the middle price range. The Novelty Line is most popular in the lower priced items.

Novice collectors are advised to look to figurals as a starting point. There are over fifty variations of frogs in the figural area. Many other animal shapes also are available.

Pieces in the middle range tend to be marked with an impressed "Weller" in block letters or a half circle ink stamp with the words "Weller Pottery." Late pieces are marked with a script "Weller" or "Weller Pottery." Many new collectors see this dated mark and incorrectly think the piece is old.

There are well over a hundred Weller patterns. New collectors should visit other collectors, talk with dealers, and look at a large range of pieces to determine which patterns they like and want to collect. It is pattern, not shape or type, by which most collections are organized.

History: In 1872 Samuel A. Weller opened a small factory in Fultonham, near Zanesville, Ohio, to produce utilitarian stoneware, such as milk pans and sewer tile. In 1882 he moved his facilities to Zanesville. In 1890 Weller built a new plant in the Putnam section of Zanesville along the tracks of the Cincinnati and Muskingum Railway. Additions followed in 1892 and 1894.

In 1894 Weller entered into an agreement with William A. Long to purchase the Lohnuda Faience Company, which had developed an art pottery line under the guidance of Laura A. Fry, formerly of Rookwood. Long left in 1895 but Weller continued to produce Lonhuda under a new name, Louwelsa. This shaded brown pottery with hand decoration under glaze was produced in over 500 different shapes. Replacing Long as art director was Charles Babcock Upjohn. He, along with Jacques Sicard, Frederick Hurten Rhead and Gazo Fudji, developed Weller's art pottery lines.

At the end of World War I, many prestige lines were discontinued and Weller concentrated on commercial wares. Rudolph Lorber joined the staff and designed lines such as Roma, Forest and Knifewood. In 1920 Weller purchased the plant of the Zanesville Art Pottery. Weller claimed to be the largest pottery in the country.

Art pottery enjoyed a revival when the Hudson Line was introduced in the early 1920s. The 1930s saw Coopertone and Graystone Garden ware added. However, the Depression forced the closing of a Putnam plant and one on Marietta Street in Zanesville. After World War II inexpensive Japanese imports took over Weller's market. In 1947 Essex Wire Company of Detroit bought the controlling stock. Early in 1948 operations ceased.

Reference: Sharon and Bob Huxford, *The Collectors Encyclopedia of Weller Pottery*, Collector Books, 1979, 1989 value update; Ann Gilbert McDonald, *All About Weller: A History and Collectors Guide To Weller Pottery, Zanesville, OH*, Antique Publications, 1989.

Collectors' Club: American Art Pottery Association, 9825 Upton Circle, Bloomington, MN 55431.

Note: For pieces in the middle and upper price range see *Warman's Antiques And Their Prices.*

Basket
    Cameo, blue, 7½" 25.00
    Roba, brown to tan 45.00
    Wild Rose, peach, 6" 31.00
Bowl
    Bonito, underplate 110.00
    Cornish 35.00
    Pierre, 8", round, seafoam 20.00
    Square, 8" 65.00
    Squirrel, glossy 82.00
Candlesticks, Glendale, pr 150.00
Console Bowl, 7 x 16", handled, orig
    liner, roses, leaves, stems 195.00
Console Set, Blossom, bowl and two
    candlesticks 50.00
Creamer and Sugar, Pierre, seafoam .. 35.00
Ewer
    Cameo, blue, 10" 30.00
    Floretta, 12½" 260.00
    Louwelsa, iris 200.00
Figure, Muskota, fishing boy 215.00
Flower Frog, Cameo 50.00
Ginger Jar
    Golden Glow, pr 125.00
    Greora 175.00
Hanging Basket
    Creamware, reticulated pattern, 11½" 45.00
    Forest, 10", chains 225.00
    Scenic Green, chains 95.00
Jardiniere, Turada, 8½" h 125.00
Jug, currants, 6½" 160.00
Lamp Base
    Dickensware I, oil lamp 125.00
    LaSa 425.00
    Pelican, multicolor 195.00
    Turada 550.00
Mug
    Child's 29.00

Dickensware
    Dolphin handle and band, scraffito
      ducks 250.00
    Stag Deer, green 450.00
Pitcher, Louwelsa, artist sgd, 14", #750 600.00
Planter, Woodcraft, log, 5 x 11" 50.00
Plate, 9½", dinner, Zona 20.00
Teapot, pumpkin, 6 " 75.00

Vase, Cornish, apricot ground, 3¼" h, 4¹⁵⁄₁₆" w handle to handle, $25.00.

Vase
    Blossom, 9" 39.00
    Blossomtime, green, double bud, 6½" 36.00
    Bronzeware, 10½" 200.00
    Cameo, blue, 7" 20.00
    Darsie, pale blue, 5½" 32.00
    Delsa 58.00
    Florenzo, 5½" 90.00
    Floretta, tri–cornered, grape clusters,
      6½" 125.00
    Forest, 4½" 90.00
    Hudson
      7", sgd Pillsbury 350.00
      8", yellow roses, dark blue to pink,
        light green, and dark green, sgd
        HP 450.00
      13", Timberlake 475.00
    LaSa, 11¼" 325.00
    Louwelsa
      4½" h, pansies, green to brown,
        artist sgd 150.00
      5½" h, buttercups, squat, artist sgd 155.00
      6" h, pansies, brown, 3 handled,
        ftd 195.00
    Manhattan, 6½" 40.00
    Patricia, white 60.00
    Roma, 8" 50.00
    Sabrinian, 9½" 140.00
    Sicard, 6" 650.00
    Silvertone 130.00
    Wild Rose, double bud, 6" 30.00
    Woodcraft, double bud 45.00
Wall Pocket
    Glendale 215.00
    Owl 160.00
    Squirrel 120.00
    Wood Rose 75.00

Woodcraft, squirrel **120.00**
Woodland, azaleas **135.00**
Window Box, Wood Rose **85.00**

WESTERN AMERICANA

Collecting Hints: Western Americana is a relatively new field. The initial emphasis has been on books, prints, and paper products. The barbed wire craze of the early 1970s drew attention to three dimensional objects.

Texas material is the most sought after. All collectors tend to focus on the 19th century, rather than modern material. Within the last decade, Indian materials have moved into the level of sophisticated antique collecting.

Collectors should pick a theme or subject. The military west, exploration accounts and maps, and early photography are a few of the more popular focuses. The collecting field now has progressed to the point where there are over a half dozen dealers specializing solely in western materials.

History: From the Great Plains to the Golden West, the American west was viewed as the land of opportunity by settlers from the mid-19th century to the early 20th century. Key events caused cataclysmic changes—the 1848 Gold Rush, the opening of the Transcontinental railroad, the silver strikes in Nevada, the Indian massacres, and the Oklahoma land rush. By 1890 the west of the cowboy and cattle was dead; Indians had been relocated onto reservations.

The romance did not die. Novels, movies and television, whether through the Ponderosa or Southfork, keep the romance of the west alive. Oil may have replaced cattle, but the legend remains.

References: Robert T. Clifton, *Barbs, Prongs, Points, Prickers & Stickers: A Complete and Illustrated Catalogue of Antique Barb Wire*, University of Oklahoma Press, 1970.

Museum: Gene Autry Western Heritage Museum, Los Angeles, CA.

Branding iron, wood handle, $45.00.

Advertising
Salt and Pepper Shakers, pr, Rod's
Steak House, Williams, Arizona .. **35.00**
Trade Card, 9½ x 5", Never Rip Non-
pariel, blue jeans, San Francisco
dry goods store, c1890 .... **8.50**
Belt Buckle, lady's, small, bull head .. **35.00**
Bill Hanger, Austex Mexican Foods
Products **37.50**
Book
Apache Gold And Yanqui Silver, Frank
J Dobie, New York, 1939, 384 pgs,
illus by Tom Lea **25.00**
2—Gun Montana, Better Little Book,
1939 .... **9.00**
The Overland Trail, Jay Monaghan,
Indianapolis, 1947, 432 pgs,
plates, maps, 1st ed **40.00**
*The War In Kansas, A Rough Trip To
The Border*, Douglas G Brewerton,
New York, 1856, 400 pgs, hard
cover **75.00**
Bookends, horse, iron, pr **45.00**
Bootjack
Metal, Superior Foundry, Cleveland . **42.50**
Wood, Lee Rivers **42.50**
Bottle, blob top, Deadwood, SD **150.00**
Bowl, Monterray Ware **8.00**
Brand Book, Montana, 1935 .... **45.00**
Brand Certificate, Montana, 1917 .... **12.00**
Cabinet Card, 5 x 8", Hop Pickers, Puy-
allup, WA, group with rakes and other
equipment standing in front of their
crops and horses **12.00**
Catalog
J Johnston, guns, rifles, 1879 ...... **20.00**
Numismatic Co of Texas, 1931, 208
pgs **12.00**
Check
Gould and Curry Silver Mining Com-
pany, Virginia City, NV, 8 x 3", Nov
1876, IRS stamp and Nevada State
Revenue stamp **25.00**
Wells Fargo, 7¾ x 3", San Francisco,
1972, ornate **65.00**
Chuck—A—Luck, Nickie Dice **90.00**
Clicker, 4½", litho metal, full color,
cowboy and spurs illus **6.00**
Cowboy Cuffs, leather **40.00**
Cup, cow horn, 1916, San Antonio, TX **78.00**
Document
Reward Notice, hand written, Jan 25,
1886, by Gov Blasdel of Nevada . **350.00**
Timetable, Nevada Pony Express,
1960 Centennial Re—Run, offset
litho, 22 x 14", framed **75.00**
Glass
Buffalo hunter's, shooter's, metal
case, set **125.00**
Figural, cactus, green, emb "Carls-
bad, New Mexico," handmade ... **7.50**
1936 Texas Centennial **38.00**

Leg Covers, bronc riding, leather, pr .. **21.00**
Letterhead, Montana, longhorn steer, 1911 .... **15.00**
Magazine Article, *TV Guide*, Paladin, May 10, 1958, cov with full color photo of Richard Boone **10.00**
Magazine Cover, *Harper's Weekly*, Jan 1849, Elk Hunting in The Bandlands of the Upper Missouri, W M Cary, artist, 11 x 16" **20.00**
Map
  Cherokee Nation, Indian Territory, Dept of Interior, Commission to the Five Civilized Tribes, 1900, issued folded, 37 x 27" **75.00**
  Nevada Pony Express Map, 1860–1960, published by the Nevada Pony Express Centennial Committee, chromolithograph, 23 x 17", framed **250.00**
  Texas, Mitchell, 1860, 12 x 15" **45.00**
Matchbook, Silver Spur Bar, Rawlings, WY **6.00**
Matchsafe, cowboy roping buffalo **75.00**
Medal
  Chicago Fat Stock Show, horns, 1886 **85.00**
  Ohio Horseshoer's Ribbon, 1917 ... **57.50**
Mug, wagon scene **40.00**
Photo
  Northern Pacific, cattle drive at Bones Bros ranch, Montana **15.00**
  Rancher on horse, mountain scene . **15.00**
  Will Rogers, 8 x 10" **6.00**
  William S Hart **8.50**
Pin
  Enameled, rope circled horse rider, 1920s **32.50**
  Sterling Silver, horse, Richardo **37.50**
Pinback Button
  Enid, Oklahoma Stock Show, 1909 . **45.00**
  Wilson Brothers Jewelers, black, white, brown, and red, Indian riding unicycle **7.50**
Pipe Holder, bronze, double, cowboy riding horse **75.00**
Pocket Watch Chain, Silver Gents, horses slide **157.00**
Poster
  14 x 36", Outlaws Of Texas, 1950 Monogram Pictures, Whip Wilson and Andy Clyde, minor creasing . **15.00**
  27 x 41"
    Along The Rio Grande, 1941 RKO Radio Film, Tim Holt **50.00**
    Heroes Of The Alamo, red, white, and blue, 1937 Sunset Productions, Bruce Warren and Rex Lease, marked Continental Litho Corp, Cleveland **40.00**
  30 x 40", Rodeo Parade In The Montana Wyoming Dude Ranch Country, Edward P Brewer, c1935,

Northern Pacific Railway adv, full color litho, Indian chief leading parade of cowboys **275.00**
Pouch, canvas, 101 Ranch & Wild West Show **250.00**
Program
  1940, Silver Jubilee of Old Trail Driver's Assn of Texas **35.00**
  1975, Pendleton round–up **9.50**
Radio Premium Kit, "Wild West Rodeo," General Electric, 15 x 16", red, white, and blue envelope, punchout sheets, 1952 .... **25.00**
Ribbon
  Fredonia Texas Rodeo, bucking horse, 1929 .... **42.50**
  Salt Lake City Cattlemen's Convention, 1901 .... **85.00**
  St Joseph, MO Livestock Show, 1899, buffalo fob **95.00**
  Texas Cowboy Reunion, Stamford, 1938, attached fob **75.00**
Saddle Ring, SS **35.00**
Saucer, branding marks, Wallace **20.00**
Scale, buffalo hide **95.00**
Scarf Slide
  Leather, studs **9.00**
  Steer head **10.00**
  Saddle **18.00**
Schedule, Whitlock rope selling, framed **28.00**
Shooting Glasses, buffalo hunter's, metal case **125.00**
Sign
  Nevada Brewery Steam Beer, glass, gold rim, white letters, green ground, emb metal frame, 13 x 25" **2,200.00**
  Wells Fargo & Co Express, metal, blue and white, 15 x 10" **900.00**
Spoon, Cheyenne, WY, bucking horse, SS **22.00**
Spurs
  Drop Shank
    1⅝" rowels **85.00**
    1¾" rowels, chasing **127.50**
  Regulation officer's **40.00**
  Straight Shank, 1" rowels **67.50**
Steak Platter, enamelware, wagon, branding marks, pr **100.00**
Tablecloth, Colorado, Western figs and branding marks **35.00**
Tie Bar, Life Time Gate Mineral Wells, TX **32.50**
Tintype, Jessie James, framed **200.00**
Toy
  Cap Gun
    Fanner 50, 10½" black enameled white metal, brown simulated wood grain plastic grips, Mattel, c1960 .... **50.00**
    Pony Boy **6.00**
    Rodeo, 7", silvered metal, white plastic grips, inscription and red

star on each side, marked "Hubley," orig 1¼ x 3¼ x 7" box ... **40.00**
Cowboy outfit, Pony Boy, single holster, MIB **95.00**
Cowgirl outfit, Lasso 'em Bille, Keystone Bros, San Francisco, MIB .. **150.00**
Cuffs, boy's, leather, Lasso 'em Bille, MIB **85.00**
Guitar, 14" l, plastic, black, multicolored decals, four metal strings, pick, and crank handle, plays tune "Red River Valley," marked "Mattel," c1960 .... **15.00**
Pistol
Daisy BB Air, target special, holster, #177 .... **45.00**
Deputy Pistol, 10½", cap gun, white metal pistol, 2" red and silver plastic "Hubley Deputy" star badge, orig 4½ x 11 x 2" box .. **45.00**
Rifle
Buffalo Rifle, Hubley **85.00**
Frontier Rifle, Hubley **65.00**
Wanted Dead or Alive, Pony Boy **15.00**
Winchester, licensed by Winchester, Mattel **85.00**
Rifle Target, Daisy Air Rifle Target, 4½ x 5" pad, red and white targets, black and white ad for Daisy rifles and shot, late 19302 .... **8.00**
Spurs and Straps, Rangeland, MIB .. **65.00**

Whiskey Bottle, Lionstone, Wild West series, Woodhawk, 1969, $65.00.

Watch Fob
Grand Island Horse & Mule Co, Nebraska, 1916 .... **45.00**
Kansas Livestock Co, horse and shoe **45.00**
New Mexico Territorial Fair, 1908 .. **37.50**
Nobby Harness Co, Fort Worth, TX . **75.00**
Saddle, copper **95.00**

WESTMORELAND GLASS COMPANY

Collecting Hints: The collector should become familiar with the many lines of tableware produced. English Hobnail made from the 1920s to 1960s is popular. Colonial designs were reproduced frequently, and accessories with dolphin pedestals are distinctive.

The trademark, an interwined "W" and "G", was imprinted on glass since 1949. After January, 1983, the full name "Westmoreland" is on all glass. Early molds were reintroduced. Numbered, signed, dated "Limited Editions" were offered.

History: The Westmoreland Glass Company was founded in October, 1899, at Grapeville, Pennsylvania. From the beginning, Westmoreland made handcrafted high quality glassware. In early years the company processed mustard, baking powder, and condiments to fill its containers. During World War I candy-filled glass novelties were popular.

Although Westmoreland is famous for its milk glass, large amounts of other glass were produced. During the 1920s, Westmoreland made reproductions and decorated wares. Color and tableware appeared in the 1930s; but, as with other companies, 1935 saw the return to mainly crystal productions. In the 1940s to 1960s, black, ruby, and amber colors were made.

In May 1982 the factory closed. Reorganization brought a reopening in July, 1982. The Grapeville plant closed again in 1984.

Reference: Hazel Marie Weatherman, *Colored Glassware of the Depression Era, Book 2*, Glassbooks, Inc., 1982.

Collectors' Club: National Westmoreland Glass Collectors Club, 333 Main Street, Irwin, PA 15642.

Animal Dish, cov
Cat, vaseline **200.00**
Duck on nest, blue milk glass **185.00**
Hen on nest
Milk glass, red trim, 3½" **15.00**
Variegated yellow **45.00**
Lamb, picket fence base, blue milk glass **75.00**
Lovebirds on nest, black **50.00**
Robin on nest, blue **40.00**
Rooster on nest, ruby carnival **50.00**
Appetizer Set, Paneled Grape, milk glass, 3 pcs **40.00**
Ashtray, English Hobnail, 5¼" sq, milk glass **22.50**
Basket, Swirl and Ball, amber, 5" **18.50**
Bell, ruby, small **8.00**

Bowl

Lotus, amber, frosted, 9½" d 28.00
Old Quilt, milk glass, 9" d, ftd 40.00
Paneled Grape, milk glass, cupped,
  8" d 30.00
Butter Dish, cov, quarter pound
Old Quilt, milk glass 22.50
Paneled Grape, milk glass 28.00
Cake Salver, Paneled Grape, milk glass,
  skirted 60.00
Candlesticks, pr
English Hobnail, crystal, 4" 15.00
Lace Edge, milk glass 35.00
Lotus, amber, frosted, twisted, 9½" h   30.00
Paneled Grape, milk glass 25.00

Candy Dish, Bramble, milk glass, sgd in lid, 1955, 5¾" h, $10.00.

Candy Dish, cov
Beaded Grape, milk glass, ftd
  5½" sq 25.00
  7" sq 22.50
Old Quilt, milk glass 25.00
Swirl and Ball, amber 35.00
Wanger, milk glass, half pound, ftd .   30.00
Celery, Old Quilt, milk glass, 6½" l . . .   25.00
Champagne, English Hobnail, crystal,
  round base 6.30
Cheese Dish, milk glass, round
Old Quilt 40.00
Paneled Grape, 7" 55.00
Chocolate Box, Della Robia, round, ftd,
  8" 70.00
Cocktail
English Hobnail
  Amber 15.00
  Crystal
    Round base 7.50
    Square base 6.75
Rooster, milk glass 10.00
Thousand Eye, ruby and marigold
  flashing 15.00
Compote
English Hobnail, crystal, sq base, 6"
  d 15.00
Paneled Grape, milk glass, 9" d 60.00

Console Set
Frosted Green, 12½" pedestal bowl,
  pr #1060 candlesticks 115.00
Pink, 14" d bowl, cut design and flow-
  ers, pr #1060 candlesticks 115.00
Cordial, English Hobnail, crystal, round
  base 12.50
Creamer
Beaded Grape, milk glass 15.00
English Hobnail, crystal, ftd 12.50
Creamer and Sugar, pr
Della Robia 40.00
Old Quilt, milk glass, individual size   20.00
Paneled Grape, milk glass
  Individual size 18.00
  Large size 20.00
Cruet
English Hobnail, crystal, orig stopper   25.00
Old Quilt, milk glass 22.00
Paneled Grape, milk glass 18.00
Cup and Saucer
Paneled Grape, milk glass 12.50
Princess Feather, crystal 22.00
Epergne, Paneled Grape, milk glass, 12"
  bowl, 2 pcs 125.00
Figure
Lovebirds, blue 40.00
Owl, blue 30.00
Flower Pot, Paneled Grape, milk glass,
  4" 20.00
Goblet
English Hobnail, crystal, round base   12.50
Old Quilt, milk glass 15.00
Paneled Grape, milk glass 17.50
Gravy Boat, underplate, Paneled Grape,
  milk glass 60.00
Hat, English Hobnail, milk glass, 2½" .   10.00
Honey Jar, 5" h, ftd, Beaded Grape, milk
  glass, gold trim 40.00
Ice Tub, crystal, rocker 7.00
Iced Tea Tumbler, Paneled Grape, milk
  glass 20.00
Ivy Ball, English Hobnail, milk glass,
  6¾" 35.00
Jardiniere, Paneled Grape, milk glass,
  ftd, 6½" h 28.00
Liquor Set, decanter, five wine glasses,
  Paneled Grape, milk glass 110.00
Marmalade, English Hobnail, crystal,
  chrome lid 16.50
Mayonnaise Set, Paneled Grape, milk
  glass, 3 pcs 35.00
Mustard, English Hobnail, milk glass, 3
  pcs 25.00
Nappy, Blackberries, milk glass 10.00
Nut Dish, English Hobnail, crystal, in-
  dividual size, set of 3 . . . .   20.00
Pansy Basket, crystal, flashed red 17.00
Parfait, English Hobnail, crystal 8.00
Pickle, Old Quilt, milk glass 30.00
Pitcher
Old Quilt, milk glass 45.00

Paneled Grape, milk glass
Pint	38.00
Quart	40.00
Planter, Paneled Grape, 5 x 9" | 32.50
Plate
Blackberries, milk glass, beaded edge, 7½" d	12.00
English Hobnail, crystal, 8½" d	6.00
Lace Edge, black, 8½" d	18.50
Lotus, amber, frosted, 13½"	22.00
Paneled Grape, milk glass, 8"	18.00
Punch Cup, Paneled Grape, milk glass	12.00
Punch Set, Pineapple and Grape, milk
glass, red hooks, 15 pcs | 400.00
Salt and Pepper Shakers, pr
Old Quilt, milk glass	15.00
Paneled Grape, milk glass	20.00
Server, English Hobnail, crystal, center
metal handle, 10½" | 15.00
Sherbet
English Hobnail, crystal, round base	5.50
Paneled Grape, milk glass, ftd	20.00
Princess Feather, crystal, 3½"	18.00
Thousand Eye, crystal	12.00
Sugar, cov, English Hobnail, crystal | 10.00
Tumbler
English Hobnail, crystal, round base, flared, 4¾"	9.00
Old Quilt, milk glass, 11 oz	16.00
Vase
Old Quilt, milk glass, fan	17.50
Paneled Grape, milk glass
9½"	27.50
11½", flared sides	47.50
12", straight sides	97.50
Roses and Bows, milk glass, 6" h, ftd, belled	28.00
Wine
English Hobnail, crystal, round base	11.00
Thousand Eye, ruby and marigold flashing	18.50

WHISKEY BOTTLES, COLLECTORS' SPECIAL EDITIONS

Collecting Hints: Beginning collectors are advised to focus on bottles of a single manufacturer or collect around a central theme, e.g., birds, trains, western, etc. Make certain to buy bottles whose finish is very good (almost no sign of wear), with no chips, and with the original labels intact.

A major collection still can be built for a modest investment, although some bottles now command over $1,000, such as the Beam Red Coat Fox. Don't overlook miniatures if you are on a restricted budget.

Finally, it is common practice to find bottles empty. In many states it is against the law to sell liquor without a license; hence, collectors tend to focus on the empty bottle.

History: The Jim Beam Distillery began the practice of issuing novelty (collectors' special edition) bottles for the 1953 Christmas trade. By the late 1960s over one hundred other distillers and wine manufacturers followed suit.

The Jim Beam Distillery remains the most prolific of the bottle issuers. Lionstone, McCormick and Ski Country are the other principal suppliers today. One dealer, Jon–Sol, Inc., has distributed his own line of collector bottles.

The "Golden Age" of the special edition bottle was the early 1970s. Interest waned in the late 1970s and early 80s as the market was saturated by companies trying to join the craze. Prices fell from record highs. Many manufacturers dropped special edition bottle production altogether.

A number of serious collectors, clubs, and dealers have brought stability to the market. Realizing that instant antiques cannot be created by demand alone, they have begun to study and classify their bottles. H. F. Montague deserves special recognition for his classification work. Most importantly, collectors have focused on those special edition bottles which show quality of workmanship and design and which have true limited editions.

References: Ralph and Terry Kovel, *The Kovels' Bottle Price List, Eighth Edition,* Crown Publishers, Inc., 1987; H. F. Montague, *Montague's Modern Bottle Identification and Price Guide, Third Edition,* H. F. Montague Enterprises, Inc., 1984.

Collectors' Clubs: International Association of Jim Beam Bottle & Specialties Clubs, 5120 Belmont Road, Suite D, Downers Grove, IL 60515; Michter's National Collectors Society, P.O. Box 481, Schaefferstown, PA 17088.

Museum: American Outpost, James B. Beam Distillery, Clermont, KY.

JIM BEAM

Beam Clubs and Conventions
Akron–Rubber Capital, 1973	22.50
Blue Hen Club, 1982	25.00
Convention
First, Denver, 1971	15.00
Third, Detroit, 1973	25.00
Fourth, Lancaster, 1974	100.00
Ninth, Houston, Cowboy, antique, 1979	150.00
Eleventh, Las Vegas, Dealer Fox, 1981	35.00
Twelfth, New Orleans, 1982, King Rex	35.00
Evergreen Club, 1974	15.00

Jim Beam, Antique Trader, Regal China, 1968, $10.00.

Fox
Red coats, 1973	2,000.00
Uncle Sam, 1971	12.00
White, 1969	45.00
Monterey Club, 1977	15.00
Twin Bridge Club, 1971	55.00

Beam on Wheels
Cable Car, 1968	5.00
Ernie's Flower Car, 1976	35.00
Fire Truck, Mack, 1982	70.00
Ford, Model A, 1928 Roadster	35.00
Jewel Tea Van, 1976	90.00

Train
Baggage Car	50.00
Dining Car	55.00
Passenger Car	55.00

Casino Series
| Barney's Slot Machine, 1978 | 27.50 |
| Golden Gate, 1970 | 15.00 |

Harold's Club
Covered Wagon, 1969, green	5.00
Nevada Silver, 1964	150.00
VIP, 1968	60.00
VIP, 1977	35.00
Horseshoe Club, Reno, 1968	8.00

Centennial Series, First Issued, 1960
Alaska Purchase, 1966	8.00
Anitoch, 1967, arrow	7.00
Civil War, North, 1961	25.00
Civil War, South, 1961	50.00
Colorado Springs, 1972	5.00
Key West, 1972	6.00
Reidsville, 1973	7.00
St. Louis Arch, 1966	18.00
Washington Bicentennial, 1976	15.00

Clubs and Organizations
Ahepa, 1972	5.00
Blue Goose, 1971	5.00
C. P. O. Open Mess, 1974	10.00
Ducks Unlimited, #1, 1974	40.00
Fleet Reserves 1974	5.00

Marine Corps, 1975	40.00
Shriner	
Indiana, 1970	6.00
Rajah Temple, 1977	20.00
Telephone, #1, Wall, 1975	65.00
VFW, 1971	10.00

Customer Specialties
Armanetti
Bacchus, 1970	8.00
Fun Shopper, 1971	7.00
First National Bank, Chicago, 1964	3,000.00
Hyatt House, Chicago, 1971	15.00
Poulan Chain Saw, 1979	25.00
Travel Lodge, 1972	8.00

Zimmerman
Blue Beauty, 1969	14.00
Eldorado, brown	14.00
Vase, 1972, green	15.00

Executive Series, First Issue, 1955
1957, Royal DiMonte	75.00
1959, Tavern Scene	70.00
1963, Royal Rose	50.00
1969, Sovereign	12.00
1982, Executive	30.00

Glass Series, First Issue, 1952
| Cannon, 1970, no chain | 7.00 |
| Cocktail Shaker, 1953 | 6.00 |

Crystal, Pressed
| 1969, Opaline | 6.00 |
| 1972, Marbelized | 5.00 |

Crystal, Sunburst
Amaretto, 1974	4.00
Poor Man's White Speckled Beauty, 1975	20.00
Crystal, Tea Blue, 1973	5.50
Ducks & Geese, 1955	6.50

Pin Bottle
Gold Top, Amber	20.00
White Top	9.00
Rockwell, Norman, series of Post covers, each	4.00
Spey Royal, 1976	5.00

Foreign Countries
Australia
| Kangaroo, 1978 | 15.00 |
| Sydney Opera, 1978 | 20.00 |

Germany
Germany, 1970	5.00
Weisbaden, 1973	6.00
New Zealand, Kiwi Bird, 1974	8.00

People Series
Buffalo Bill, 1971	7.00
Emmett Kelly, 1973, Kansas autograph	65.00
Indian Chief, 1980	17.50
Mortimer Snerd, 1976	30.00
Sea Captain & Mate, 1980	15.00

Political Series
Football, 1972
| Donkey | 7.00 |
| Elephant | 7.00 |

Superman, 1980

Donkey	12.50
Elephant	12.50

Regal China Series

A–C Spark Plug, 1977	10.00
Bellringer #2, Afore Ye Go, 1970	12.00
Franklin Mint, 1970	8.00
Jug, 1982, 1.75 liters	25.00
London Bridge, 1971	6.00
Ohio State Fair, 1972	7.50
Seattle World's Fair, 1962	15.00
Truth or Consequences, 1974	10.00

Sport Series

Bing Crosby National Pro–Am

33rd, 1974	27.50
37th, 1978	25.00
Bob Hope Desert Classic, 15th, 1974, case	12.50
Football Hall of Fame, 1972	8.00

Hawaiian Open

1972, Pineapple	6.00
1975, Outrigger	11.00
Kentucky Derby, 95th, 1969, pink roses	7.50
Louisville Downs, 1978	8.50

Mint 400

4th, 1971	8.00
8th, 1975	12.00
Red Mile Race, 1975	8.00
U.S. Open, 1972	15.00

State Series

Alaska, Star, 1958–64–65	60.00
Florida, Shell, 1968, pearl	4.50
Kansas, 1960	59.00
Michigan, 1972	8.50
New Jersey, 1963, blue	65.00
Ohio, 1966	12.00
South Dakota, Mt. Rushmore, 1969	6.00
West Virginia, 1963	225.00

Trophy Series, First Issue, 1957

Bird

Cardinal, male, 1968	40.00
Goose, Blue, 1979	10.00
Dog, St. Bernard, 1979	40.00

Fish

Bass, smallmouth, 1973	10.00
Muskie, 1971	16.00
Sturgeon, 1980	24.00
Horse Series, rearing, 1967–68	15.00
Rabbit, 1971	12.00

EZRA BROOKS

Animal Series

Bear, 1968	6.00
Charolais, 1972	12.00
Elephant, Big Bertha, 1970	7.50
Elk, 1972	20.00
Leopard, Snow, 1980	40.00
Penguin, 1973	10.00

Automotive/Transportation Series

Corvette, 1962, Mako Shark, 1979	25.00

Ezra Brooks, American Legion National Convention, Miami Beach, Heritage China, 1974, $15.00.

Farthington Bike, 1972	9.00
Motorcycle, 1971	12.00
Pontiac Indy Pace Car, 1980	30.00
Stagecoach, Overland Express, 1969	10.00
Train, Casey Jones #1, 1980	45.00

Bird Series

Duck, Canadian Loon, 1979	32.50
Owl, Old Ez #1, 1977	60.00
Phoenix Bird, 1971	20.00
Turkey, white, 1971	20.00

Fish Series

Maine Lobster, 1970	25.00
Trout & Fly, 1970	10.00

Heritage China Series

Cannon, Antique, 1969	8.00
C B Convoy, 1976	8.00
EZ Jug #2, 1980, 1.75 liters	25.00
Telephone, 1971	12.00
Truckin an Vannin, 1976	14.00

Institutional Series

American Legion

1973, Hawaii	15.00
1982, Chicago	75.00
Bucket of Blood, 1970	7.00
Club #4, Old Ez Owl, miniature, 1980	18.00
Drum & Bugle, Conquistadors, 1971	9.00
F.O.E., 1980	30.00
Foremost, Astronaut, 1970, gallon	55.00
Indian, Ceremonial, 1970	20.00

Kachina

#1, Morning Singer, 1971	165.00
#3, Antelope, 1974	50.00
#7, Mud Head, 1978	40.00
Political, 1972, Donkey or Elephant	12.00
Shrine, Fez, 1976	9.00
Tonopah, 1972	15.00
Walgreen Drugs, 1973	25.00

People Series

Court Jester, 1971	9.00
Dakota Cowboy, 1975	40.00
Dakota Cowgirl, 1976	30.00

Groucho Marx, 1977	40.00
Mr. Merchant, 1970	10.00
Senator, 1971	12.00
West Virginia Mountain Man, 1970	90.00

Sport Series

Auburn War Eagle, 1982	35.00
Bareknuckle Fighter, 1971	9.00
Casey at Bat, 1973	15.00
Gator #1, passing, 1972	15.00
Greater Greensboro Open, 1977	35.00
Jayhawk–ansas, 1969	10.00
Ski Boot, 1972	10.00
Vermont Skier, 1972	14.00

Cabin Still, Quail, 1968, $8.00.

CABIN STILL

Anniversary, 1960	10.00
Deer Browsing, 1967	7.00
Gold Coaster, 1955	18.00
Hillbilly, fishing, quart	90.00
Mallard, 1966	10.00

CYRUS NOBLE

Animal Series

Bear & Cub, 1978, miniature	15.00
Buffalo Cow & Calf, 1977, Second Edition	80.00
Moose & Calf, First Edition	100.00
Mountain Lion & Cubs, 1979, miniature	15.00

Mine Series

Assayer, 1972	175.00
Blacksmith, 1974	50.00
Landlady, 1977	30.00
Mine, 1979, miniature	20.00
Whiskey Drummer, 1975	40.00

Miscellaneous

Dancers, South of the Border, 1978	35.00
Delta Saloon Suicide Table, 1971, miniatures, 4 units	300.00

Cyrus Noble, Assayer, miniature, Haas Brothers, 1974, $20.00.

Sea Animal

Harp Seal, 1979	50.00
Penquin Family, 1980, miniature	18.00
Seal Family, 1978	40.00

J. W. DANT

American Legion, 1969	6.00
Boeing 747	10.00
Ft. Sill, 1969	10.00
Stove, Pot Belly, 1966	8.00

DOUBLE SPRINGS

Bicentennial Series, Washington Monument

California	45.00
Iowa	50.00
Washington, DC	12.00

Car Series

Cale Yarborough, 1974	25.00
Ford, Model T, 1970	40.00
Rolls Royce, 1971	40.00

Miscellaneous

Milwaukee Buck, 1971	12.00
Water Tower	15.00

FAMOUS FIRSTS

Airplane Series

Lockheed C–130 Hercules, 1979	50.00
Spirit of St. Louis, 1969, large	100.00
Winnie Mae, 1972, miniature, 1972	30.00

Animal Series

Butterfly, miniatures, series of 4, each	15.00
Panda, baby, 1980	50.00
Tiger, Circus, 1980	25.00

Car–Transportation Series

Bugatti Royale, 1974	200.00
Cable Car, miniature, 1973	20.00

Corvette 1963 Stingray, 1977, white **45.00**
Duesenberg, 1980 . . . . **225.00**
Marmon Wasp #32, type 1, 1968 . . **70.00**
Porsche Targa, 1979 . . . . **50.00**
Yacht America "13," 1970 . . . . **35.00**
Miscellaneous
Coffee Mill, 1971, orange or blue . . **50.00**
Hurdy Gurdy, miniature, 1979 . . . . . **14.00**
Roulette Wheel, miniature, 1980 . . . **20.00**
Swiss Chalet, 1974 . . . . **35.00**

Grenadier, Kings African Rifles, Feb 1971, $50.00.

GRENADIER

American Revolution Series
Baylor's 3rd Continental, 1969 . . . . . **30.00**
Second Maryland, 1969 . . . . **35.00**
Third New York, 1970 . . . . **20.00**
Bicentennial Series, 1976, 10ths, 13
types, each **20.00**
British Army Series
Fusileer Guards, Scots, Officer, 1971 **20.00**
Guard Regiment, 3rd, Officer, 1971 **20.00**
Civil War Series
Captain, Union, 1970 . . . . **20.00**
General Robert E. Lee, 1976, ½ gal . **120.00**
Miscellaneous
Arabian, 1978 . . . . **30.00**
Fire Chief, 1973 . . . . **85.00**
Moose Lodge, 1970 . . . . **14.00**
San Fernando Electric Mfg Co, 1976 **60.00**
Napoleonic Series
Eugene, 1970 . . . . **20.00**
Murat, 1970 . . . . **20.00**

HOFFMAN

Band Series, Street Swingers #1, 1978,
miniature music, six types, each . . . **15.00**
Bird Series
Blue Jays, 1979, pr **35.00**
Dove, Closed Wing, 1979, ½ pint . . **25.00**

Hoffman, Band Series, fiddler with music, 1978, $15.00.

Eagle, 1977, music **45.00**
Love Birds, 1979, ½ pint **20.00**
Cheerleader
Dallas, 1979, nude, ½ pint **150.00**
Rams, 1980, miniature **20.00**
Children of the World Series, 1979,
miniature, music, six types, each . . . **30.00**
Horse Series, 1979, miniature, six types,
each **12.00**
Mr. Lucky Series, music
Cobbler, 1973 . . . . **25.00**
Dentist, 1980 . . . . **35.00**
Mr. Lucky, 1973 . . . . **40.00**
Policeman, 1975 . . . . **25.00**
Rodeo Series, 1978, six types, each . . **35.00**
Rodeo Belt Buckle Series, 1979, six
types, each **25.00**
School Series
Kentucky Wildcats, basketball **30.00**
Nevada Wolfpack **40.00**
Tennessee Volunteers **27.50**
Wildlife Series
Bear & Cub, 1978 . . . . **38.00**
Falcon & Rabbit, 1978, miniature . . **10.00**
Panda, 1976 . . . . **50.00**
Wildlife bottles were designed by Lucas
Miguer (LM), Bill Ohrman (BO), and
Jack Richardson (JR)
Bear, 1978, BO **40.00**
Fighting Rams, set, 1977, JR **250.00**
Stranger This Is My Land, 1979, LM **425.00**

JAPANESE FIRMS

House of Koshu
Boy on Barrel, 7 oz **5.00**
Geisha
Cherry Blossom, 1969 . . . . **25.00**
Violet, 1969 . . . . **30.00**
Mask, Noh, 1961 . . . . **35.00**
Sake God, 1969, colored **10.00**
Kamotsuru
God #1, Daikoku (God of Wealth),
1965 . . . . **17.50**

Golden House, 1969 .... 20.00
Kikukawa
  Eisenhower, 1970 .... 15.00
  Lincoln, 1970 .... 15.00
  Washington, 1970 .... 17.50

KONTINENTAL

Dock Worker, 1978 .... 25.00
Homesteader, 1978 .... 30.00
Medicine Man, 1977 .... 40.00
Saddle Maker, 1977, miniature 15.00
Stephen Foster, 1975 .... 25.00

LEWIS AND CLARK

General Custer, 1974 .... 70.00
Major Reno, 1975 .... 42.50
Sitting Bull, 1976 .... 115.00
State Series, miniatures, each 10.00
Troll Family
  Daughter Troll, 1979 .... 25.00
  Mr. Troll, 1979 .... 20.00

Lionstone, Indian Chief, 1973, $35.00.

LIONSTONE

Bicentennial Series
  Betsy Ross, 1975 .... 25.00
  Valley Forge, 1975 .... 22.50
Bird Series
  Blue Bird, Eastern, 1972 .... 20.00
  Capistrano Swallow, 1972, gold bell . 25.00
  Meadowlark, 1969 .... 22.50
  Woodpecker, 1975 .... 35.00
Car–Transportation Series
  Johnnie Lightning #2, 1973, silver . 55.00
  Turbo Car STP, 1972, red 25.00
Clown Series
  #2, Sad Sam, 1978 .... 40.00
  #6, Lampy, 1979 .... 35.00
European Workers Series, 1974, six
  types, each 25.00

Firefighter Series
  Fireman #1, 1972, yellow hat 125.00
  Fireman #4, 1978, emblem 30.00
Old West Series
  Bar Scene, nude, 1970 .... 600.00
  Bath, 1976 .... 60.00
  Cowboy, 1969 .... 10.00
  Highway Robber, 1969 .... 12.50
  Indian Squawman, 1969 .... 25.00
  Lucky Buck, 1975, miniature 12.00
  Molly Brown, 1973 .... 25.00
  Sheepherder, 1969 .... 50.00
  Telegrapher, 1969 .... 18.50
Oriental Workers Series, 1974, six
  types, each 32.50
Sports Series
  Basketball Players, 1974 .... 20.00
  Hunter, 1980 .... 45.00

LUXARDO

Apple, figural 15.00
Cellini 32.50
Coffee Carafe 20.00
Duck, green 30.00
Gondola 7.50
Owl, onyx 35.00
Pheasant, black 125.00
Puppy, base 25.00
Squirrel 30.00
Venus 20.00
Zodiac 22.50

McCormick, passenger car, 1970, $75.00.

McCORMICK

Bicentennial Series
  Betsy Ross 25.00
  John Hancock, miniature 20.00
  Paul Revere 45.00
Bird Series
  Eagle, 1983, white 140.00
  Wood Duck, 1980 .... 30.00
Bull Series
  Brahma, 1973 .... 40.00
  Hereford, 1972 .... 45.00
Elvis Series, #3, 1980, black 50.00
  Aloha, 1981 .... 80.00
  Bust, 1978 .... 25.00
  Gold, 1979 .... 225.00

Silver, 1980 .... 110.00
Entertainment Series
  Jimmie Durante, 1981 .... 50.00
  Tom T. Hall, 1980 .... 25.00
Football Mascot
  Georgia Bulldogs, black helmet, red
    jersey 15.00
  Iowa Cyclones, 1974 .... 42.50
  Michigan Wolverines, 1974 .... 20.00
  New Mexico Lobo 30.00
  SMU Mustangs, 1972 .... 20.00
Great American Series
  Stephen Austin, 1977 .... 20.00
  William Clark, 1978 .... 22.50
  Henry Ford, 1977, miniature 12.00
  Charles Lindbergh, 1977 .... 30.00
  Mark Twain, 1978, miniature 15.00
Miscellaneous
  Airplane–Spirit of St. Louis, 1969 ... 125.00
  Clock, Queen Anne, 1970 .... 25.00
  Globe, Angelica, 1971 .... 25.00
  Lobsterman, 1979 .... 30.00
  Mikado, 1980 .... 200.00
  Paul Bunyan, 1979 .... 25.00
  Thelma Lu 35.00
  Yacht America, 1970 .... 35.00
Pirate Series, 1972, miniature, twelve
  types
    #1 to #9, each 8.00
    #10 to #12, each 17.50
Train Series, Engine, Jupiter, 1969 .... 25.00

Michters, Atlantic City, GVI China, $25.00.

MICHTER'S

Barn, Daniel Boone Homestead, 1977   45.00
Canal Boat, Union Canal, 1977 ...... 50.00
Conestoga Wagon, 1976 .... 200.00
Halloween Witch, 1979 .... 50.00
Jug, 1957, adv, pint 20.00

Pennsylvania Dutch Hex, 1977 ...... 15.00
Volunteer Fireman, 1979 .... 85.00

Garnier, German Shepherd, Creme de Menthe, 1972, $15.00.

MISCELLANEOUS

Aesthetic Specialties, Inc
  Bing Crosby National Pro–Am, 39th,
    1979 .... 30.00
  Cadillac, 1903, gold, white trim,
    1980 .... 1,500.00
  Model T, Telephone Truck, 1980 ... 45.00
  Oldsmobile, 1910, black, 1980 .... 65.00
  World's Greatest Golfer, 1979 ..... 40.00
Anniversary
  Atlanta, GA, 1972 .... 15.00
  Happy Birthday, 1974, blue 20.00
  Ohio Presidents, 1972 .... 18.00
Beneagle
  Burns Cottage, miniature, green 6.00
  Eagle, 1969, golden 35.00
  Pheasant, miniature 5.00
Bischoff
  Bell House 27.50
  Cat, black 12.00
  Fish, ashtray 10.00
  Pirate 15.00
Collector's Art
  Charolais Bull, 1974 .... 30.00
  Goldfinch, miniature 15.00
  Irish Setter, miniature 15.00
  Meadowlark, miniature 25.00
  Rabbit, miniature 25.00
  Texas Longhorn, 1974 .... 32.50
Dallas Cheerleader, miniature 80.00
George Dickel
  Jug 8.00
  Powder Horn, gal 150.00
Dugs Nevada Brothels, miniature
  #2, Shamrock Ranch 40.00
  #6, Fran's Ranch 20.00
  #10, Barbara's My Place 20.00

Eagle Rare
Eagle #4, 1982 .... 50.00
Nature Series #1, 1983 .... 65.00
Garnier (France)
Alladins Lamp 18.00
Coffeepot 15.00
Ford, 1913 .... 30.00
Maharajah 32.50
Violin 10.00
Gemini, miniature
David, 1980 .... 10.00
Okinawain, pr 18.00
I. W. Harper
Croquet Players 20.00
Guitar 10.00
Harper Man, 1955, white 45.00
Inca Pisco, miniature
#1, black 5.00
#7, black 10.00
#10, gold 15.00
Jon–Sol, Inc, miniature
Blue Jay 10.00
Warner Bros, set #2 .... 25.00
Mike Wayne
Christmas Tree, 1979, green 50.00
Mercedes Benz 450SL, 1980 .... 35.00
Norman Rockwell Series, 1978, each 20.00
OBR
Hockey Players Series, 1971, each . 15.00
Transportation Series
Balloon, 1969 .... 15.00
Titanic, 1970 .... 40.00
Old Bardstown
Bulldog, 1980, 1.75 liter 200.00
Foster Brooks, 1978 .... 35.00
Kentucky Colonel, #1, 1978 ...... 25.00
Wildcat #1, 1978 .... 70.00
Old Crow
Bugatti Royale, 1974 .... 250.00
Chess Series
Pawn, each 20.00
Rug 100.00
Pancho Villa
Pancho Villa & Fierro 35.00
Pancho Villa on Horse, 1976, minia-
ture 15.00
Potters
Clydesdale, 1978 .... 50.00
Eskimo Dog Sled, 1977 .... 175.00
Gold Panner 40.00
Totem Pole, 1971, miniature 10.00
Raintree, miniature
Clown #2, 1976, tramp 40.00
Clown #4, 1977, hunter 25.00
Jim Stranger Originals, Owl, 1981 .... 45.00

OLD COMMONWEALTH

Apothecary Series
Alabama University, 1980 .... 27.50
Thomas Jefferson/University of Vir-
ginia, 1979 .... 20.00

Coal Miner, #1, 1975 .... 90.00
Fireman, Modern, Series
#2, Nozzleman, 1983, miniature .. 25.00
#4, Fallen Comrade, 1983 .... 65.00
#5, Harmony, 1984 .... 65.00
Miscellaneous
Cottontail Rabbit, 1981 .... 30.00
Golden Retriever, 1979 .... 25.00
Indian Chief Illini, University of Illi-
nois, 1979 .... 60.00
Lumberjack, Oldtime, 1979 .... 20.00

OLD FITZGERALD

America's Cup, 1970 .... 25.00
Blarney (Irish Toast), 1970 .... 14.00
Classic, 1972 .... 6.00
Executive, 1960 .... 7.00
Geese, 1970 .... 6.00
Huntingdon, WV, 1971 .... 22.50
Irish Patriots, 1971 .... 17.50
Ohio State, 1970 .... 20.00
Ram Bighorn, 1971 .... 5.00
Rip Van Winkle, 1971, blue 35.00
Triangle Bond, 1977 .... 4.00

Old Mr. Boston, Amvet, Royal Halburton China, $15.00.

OLD MR. BOSTON

Assayrian Convention, 1975 .... 15.00
Black Hills Motor Classic, 1976 ...... 25.00
Dan Patch, 1970 .... 10.00
Fire Engine, 1974 .... 35.00
Greensboro Open, 1978 .... 30.00
Lincoln on Horseback, 1972 .... 10.00
Nebraska #1, gold, 1970 .... 15.00
Ships Lantern, 1974 .... 15.00
Town Crier, 1976 .... 16.00

PACESETTER

Camaro Z28, 1982, gold, edition limited to 500 .... **125.00**
Corvette
    1975, red **40.00**
    1980, silver **75.00**
Olsonite Eagle #8, 1974 .... **32.00**
Tractor Series, #1, Big Green Machine, 1982, John Deere name **175.00**
Vokovich #2, 1974, Sugarripe **50.00**

SKI COUNTRY

Christmas Series
    Ebenezer Scrooge, 1979 .... **40.00**
    Mrs. Cratchit, 1978 .... **42.00**
Circus Series
    Circus Wagon, 1977, giraffe **30.00**
    Elephant on Drum, 1973, miniature **35.00**
    Jenny Lind, yellow **75.00**
    Ringmaster, 1975 .... **25.00**
Customer Specialties
    Burro—Colorado School of Mines, 1973 .... **50.00**
    Oregon Cave Man, 1974 .... **17.00**
    Skier, 1975, gold plated **100.00**
Domestic Animal Series
    Bassett, 1978, miniature **20.00**
    Labrador Dog, 1977, mallard **100.00**
Indian Series
    Arizona Eagle Dancer, 1979 .... **200.00**
    Dancers of Southwest Series, miniature **25.00**
    End of Trail, 1976, miniature **65.00**
    Warrior #1, 1975, hatchet **110.00**
Waterfowl Series
    Duck
        King Eider, 1977 .... **45.00**
        Pintail, 1979, ½ gal **175.00**
        Widgeon, 1979 .... **32.50**
    Pelican, 1976, brown **40.00**
    Swan, Australian, 1974, black **30.00**
Wildlife Series
    Bear, 1974, brown **25.00**
    Coyote Family, 1977 .... **45.00**
    Eagle, Majestic, 1972 .... **300.00**
    Elk, 1979 .... **80.00**
    Fox Family, 1979 .... **50.00**
    Hawk, Red Shoulder, 1972 .... **65.00**
    Kangaroo, 1974 .... **25.00**
    Owl
        Baby Snow, miniature **40.00**
        Northern Snowy, 1972 .... **100.00**
    Peace Dove, 1973 .... **100.00**
    Sheep, Dall, 1980 .... **90.00**
    Skunk Family, 1978 .... **40.00**

WILD TURKEY

Series #1
    #1, Male, 1972 .... **300.00**

Wild Turkey, No. 5, The Spirit of 76, $25.00.

#4, With Poult, 1974 .... **80.00**
#6, Striding, 1976 .... **20.00**
#8, Strutting, 1978 .... **40.00**
Lore Series
    #1, 1979 .... **50.00**
    #3, 1981 .... **45.00**

WHISKEY PITCHERS (PUB JUGS)

Collecting Hints: Whiskey pitcher or pub jug collectors do specialize. Some concentrate on pitchers with a certain type of liquor—bourbon, scotch, rum, etc. Others deal only with figural pitchers or in pitchers associated with only one brand of liquor.

Collect pitchers that have in them the "mandatory," the statement on the proof of the liquor and its origin. Federal law requires this of all distillery-originated advertising in the United States. Pitchers without the mandatory may not be distillery-authorized.

Don't neglect foreign pub jugs. Many of these are made by fine potteries such as Royal Doulton, Royal Norfolk, Burleigh Ware, and Euroceramics. Pitchers by the Wade pottery are the most sought after by collectors.

The interest in pub jugs has fallen from the highpoint of the craze in the early 1970s. The market is stable and consists primarily of serious collectors.

History: Whiskey pitchers, more correctly pub jugs, are water pitchers with liquor advertising on them and are issued by distilleries around the world. The pub jug originated in England before the advent of modern plumbing. The pub owner kept a pitcher of water handy for the "Scotch

and water" drinkers. An enterprising liquor salesman took notice of this and suggested to his firm
that they provide a jug with their own name on
it. The pub jugs were given by distillers to pub
owners who promised to display them.

The early pub jugs were made of earthenware.
Glass, porcelain, and pewter examples followed.
Distilleries competed with each other to make
their jugs the most attractive. Patrons quickly
began asking for the pub jugs as gifts, especially
the figural and more colorful ones.

By the mid-1960s the whiskey pitcher craze
hit the United States. American interest stimu-
lated the market. Britain is still the leader in pub
jugs, but Italy, France, Japan, and the United
States are not far behind. Almost every distiller
has issued a pub jug with its name on it at one
time or another. Some distillers issue a new form,
color or letter pattern each year.

The typical pub jug is five to six inches in
height and one of the basic colors. Older pitchers
were black, brown, blue, green, or white. Today
yellow, orange, and red pitchers occur. Promotional distribution of whiskey pitchers is uneven
in the United States since local and state laws
differ. Records on production levels of pub jugs
are unknown. Collectors estimate that over 2,000
different types have been produced.

Periodical: *The Pub Jug* was issued in 1979 and
1980. It is no longer in print; issues are sought
by collectors.

Canadian Club, $8.50.

Ballantine, figural, Scotch Knight head	20.00
Bell's 12 Year Old Scotch on one side, 8 Year Old Scotch on other side, Hublein, bell shape, light tan ground ...	10.00
Buchanan's Black & White, checkerboard trim	15.00
Canadian Windsor, figural, guard	20.00
Crawfords, white, black and gold	12.00
Dewars, white, red and black letters ..	10.00
Dickel, whiskey barrel	12.00
Famous Grouse, bulbous, gold trim, black letters, marked "McCoy Pottery"	7.50
G & W Seven Star	12.00

Lionstone, figural, lion	20.00
Marie Brizard, blue, marked "Made in France"	10.00
Murphy's green, replica of label on front, Irish	12.50
Nicholson's Lamplighter Distilled English Dry Gin, gray ground	12.00
Old Granddad	
Square, medallion	12.75
Wash pitcher shape, white with gold trim, orange and brown letters ...	7.50
Old Weller Original 107 Proof Bourbon, barrel shape, 5½ x 8½", 24K gold trim, black letters	14.00
100 Pipers	14.00
Seagrams	
Gin, The Perfect Martini Gin, decal, blue top, green bottom	8.00
V.O. Canadian, blue, gold letters and trim	13.50
Hiram Walker's Ten High, A True Bourbon, gray ground, black, gold, red and blue letters	17.50
The White Horse Cellar Dry Scotch, glass, mug shape	7.50
Wild Turkey, turkey decal	17.50
Wolfschmidt Genuine Vodka, Seagrams, label on white ground	10.00

WINE BOTTLES

Collecting Hints: Having the wine in the bottle
does not add significantly to the value. The original labels are nice, but, again, add little to the
bottle's value. Decoration, whether in relief or
painted, is the key element. All coloration must
be present to make the bottle collectible.

Interest in wine bottles has fallen during the
last several years as collectors have withdrawn
from this area. Most selling now takes place at
collectors' clubs and through specialized publications and dealers.

History: Figural wine bottles were developed in
the 1960s to help entice buyers to try foreign
wines, especially those imported from Italy. The
bulk of the bottles are pressed glass or ceramic
figurals. Several examples are covered in leather
or have a wicker basket around them.

The majority of the bottles are collected for
decorative purposes with concentration on shape
and color.

References: H. F. Montague, *Montague's Modern Bottle Identification And Price Guide, 2nd
Edition,* privately printed, 1980.

Note: Bottles for wine and wine derivatives are
included in this list. Liquor bottles are found
under "Whiskey Bottles, Special Collector's Editions."

Green, embossed monkey, 13¼" h, $9.50.

Angus Bull	22.00
Arch of Triumph, 1968	10.00
Bacchus	15.00
Buddah	8.00
Burgundia Coca, emb	60.00
Cannon, Imperial, 1969	22.00
Cask, Monastery, 1968	15.00

Chess

Bishop, 1968	8.00
Castle, 1968	8.00
King, 16"	10.00
Pawn, 16"	10.00
Dog, long neck	8.50
Donkey, 11¾", ceramic, glazed	18.00
Eagle, bald, 1970	25.00
Elephant, sitting in chair	8.00
Giraffe and baby, 1970	28.00
Harlequin, 1968	10.00
Kangaroo, leather cov, 1966	25.00
Leaning Tower, 1967	10.00
Locomotive, 13"	15.00
Mirror, Florentine	10.00
Napa Valley S F Wine Co, sealed, 1883–94	32.00
Paul Masson Rare Dry Sherry, heart shape, amber	25.00
Pipe, alpine, 1968	8.00
Pistol, green glass, 1964	8.00

Pitcher

Egyptian, 1969	12.00
Michaelangelo	10.00
Roman, 1966	15.00
Policeman, 1950s	22.00
Ponte Vecchio	14.00
Queen, seated, 1950s	22.00
Rabbit, carrot, 1969	20.00
Saki, blue and gold, six sided	30.00
Soldier, 12½"	15.00
Totem Pole	12.00
Turkey, leather cov, 1966	22.00
Urn, Florentine, 1966	15.00

WOODENWARE

Collecting Hints: Preserve the patina of your wood pieces. Don't clean and restore a wood implement to look new; the age and wear from use is what adds character and charm to the piece. Be aware that wood containers, especially buckets, may dry out, shrink and fall apart. Occasional use will prevent this problem.

History: Wood implements played an important role in the early American household and on the farmstead. Wood was used to make a wealth of utilitarian household objects from boxes to washboards, and was the principal element in most early American tools, except for cutting surfaces. Wood objects were valued and well taken care of by their owners. They were meant to last and did!

Wood survived as a key element in implements until the late 19th century. Cast and die-cast metals took over many of the household functions; aluminum and plastic absorbed the rest. Today wood survives on the farm but primarily as tool handles.

Reference: Mary Earle Gould, *Early American Wooden Ware*, Charles E. Tuttle, 1962.

Note: This category serves as a catchall for wood objects which do not fit into other categories in this book.

Apple Butter Stirrer, 34" l	12.00
Ballot Box, walnut, key, c1860	48.00
Barrel, "Briggs"	14.00

Bowl

6", round	50.00
13", maple	40.00
8½", maple, marked "Munising"	15.00
10½", maple	18.00
13", maple	25.00

Box

6", Shaker, round, finger construction, copper tacks, natural finish	75.00
8" d, bentwood, reddish finish	200.00

Bucket

6 x 6 x 7½", wire hoops, wire bail handle	22.00
9 1 /2 x 12 x 10", lid, metal hoops	50.00
Butter Carrier, 11½", round, old red paint, wire bail, c1850	225.00
Butter Mold, small, flower pattern, plunger type	18.00
Butter Paddle, 9¾", stylized bird head handle	45.00

Butter Print, 1 pc, turned handles, carved

Leaf, 4"	25.00
Pineapple, 4¾"	85.00
Sheaf, 4¼"	55.00
Swan, 3¾" d, swan	125.00
Tulip, 3⅜"	175.00

Sugar Bucket, C S Hershey, painted, 9" h, 9½" d, $50.00.

Chalice, 4½", turned, dark finish	10.00
Cheese Box, 15", round	30.00
Cheese Press, 36" h, blue	170.00
Compote, 6½ x 9" d, poplar, turned, red paint	25.00
Container, 19" h, stave constructed, laced wood bands	100.00
Cookie Board, carved, design on both sides	
4 x 7", urn of fruit	25.00
18½ x 4¼", twelve primitive animals and people, six on each side	225.00
26½ x 4⅝", animals, birds, cat, etc	225.00
Crumber, hand carved, painted yellow and red blossom branches, Japanese characters carved into matching tray, "Made in Japan"	10.00
Cutting Board, elephant shape, cherry	85.00
Display Box, 8 x 12", dovetailed, 6 compartments	15.00
Dough Bowl, 9"	12.00
Dough Box, 16 x 26", 9" h, pine, paneled lid, repainted	160.00
Dumbbell, hand weights, 11" l, turned, pr	15.00
Dustpan, pine, gray and blue, lollipop extended handle, tapered lip, c1840	130.00
Fabric Stamp, 6", carved	18.00
Figure, New England Fisherman, blue shirt, black boots, scarf, beard, c1890	95.00
Flour Sifter, brushes and screen, marked "J. H. Day & Co"	120.00
Food Mold, 3½ x 8½", cut turtle design, handle	50.00
Footstool, 6½ x 11¾", splayed legs, removed finish	25.00
Herb Drying Tray, wire nail construction	45.00
Horse Shoeing Box, 14¾ x 20", pine, blacksmith, primitive, iron legs	55.00
Inkwell, 2¾ x 4½", turned, glass insert and cork stopper, brown graining, gold stencil detail, orig red wool bot-	

tom label, marked "S. Silliman & Co, Chester, CT"	85.00
Jar, 8¼", birch bark, matching pine lid, orig red paint, bird and flowers, handmade, 1827	125.00
Keg, rum, stave construction, metal bands	80.00
Knife, cut out hole in handle	15.00
Knife Box, 9½ x 13½", hardwood, turned handle, refinished	55.00
Ladle, 15" l, treen, maple	30.00
Lectern, 32½" h, country, quarter sawed oak, old finish, 19th C	25.00
Lemon Squeezer	35.00
Measure, bentwood	
5⅞" d, Shaker, turned handle, brown paint	35.00
9¼ x 13½", wood handles, no finish	100.00
Nail Sorter, eight section	20.00
Needle Case, 12", treen, umbrella shape, black and natural, brass trim	40.00
Noggin	
6½" h	60.00
8½", primitive	70.00
Nutcracker, 10", Prussian soldier	18.00
Pail, 7 x 14", stave construction, wire bands, bail and wood handle	20.00
Pantry Box, 6", cov	40.00
Plate, 8", oil painted pear, peach, and leaves	39.00
Potato masher, leather strap	15.00
Pudding Stick, hewn handle, shaped blade	12.00
Raisin Seeder, plunger handle, wire grid, Everett	48.00
Rope Bed Tightener	25.00
Salt Box, hanging, 6¾ x 9 x 6¼", walnut, dovetailed, hanger hole in crest	125.00
Seed Box, 25 x 8", stave construction, int. divider	130.00
Shoe Sole Pattern, 11", marked "9AAA MA Whinney Last Co, Brockton, Mass"	15.00
Soap Mold, 2½ x 10", 3 part, 2 blocks and a scalloped circle	25.00
Spatula, 10¼"	10.00
Spice Box, round, 8 inner spice containers	150.00
Tote Box, pine, divided	60.00
Towel Rack, 24½ x 32¼", pine, turned, worn finish	75.00
Treen Box, 8½", poplar	135.00
Trencher, 9 x 9½", oval, turned detail	145.00
Urn, 6", cov, treen, walnut, acorn finial	20.00

WORLD WAR I COLLECTIBLES

Collecting Hints: Most veterans of World War I have died, so nostalgia does not play as large a part in this collecting area as it does for World War II. Also, America's involvement was much more limited both in time and personnel. Equipment was not as sophisticated and patches to differentiate units were not used until the end of the war.

Reenactment groups have been organized; several mock encounters have been staged on the European battlefields.

Try to obtain as much information as you can about the source of the material you buy. Many uniform and equipment pieces were prewar models and some forms lasted into the peace time army. Purists want equipment that was "over there."

History: The assassination of Archduke Ferdinand of Austria in 1914 set in motion a series of internal conflicts within Europe that eventually led to full-scale war. After initial German successes, the war evolved into a series of trench engagements. In 1917 America entered the war. After a series of military defeats, Germany and its allies surrendered on November 11, 1918.

Periodicals: *Military Collectors News,* P. O. Box 702073, Tulsa, OK 74170.

Collectors' Club: American Society of Military Insignia Collectors, 1331 Bradley Avenue, Hummelstown, PA 17036; Association of American Military Uniform Collectors, 446 Berkshire Road, Elyria, OH 44035.

See: Newspapers (Headline Editions), Posters, Sheet Music, Dimestore Soldiers, etc.

Document, US Army Discharge, photograph, Warren Bennethum, 1919, reverse painting on glass flag, framed, 16⅛ x 20⅛", $65.00.

Battle Map, Boston Sunday Advertiser, Jan, 1918, color	12.00
Belt Buckle, Prussian, leather, gray, crown and motto	70.00
Book, *The Plattsburger,* souvenir Plattsburg Training Camp, NY, Mutt and Jeff comic art, 8½ x 12", hard cov, 240 pgs	75.00

Button, pinback	
⅞", Western Electric Soldier's Comfort Club, black and white	8.00
13/16", Women's Service, War Savings, black and white	8.00
1", Bond Seller Buffalo Public Schools, 1919	10.00
1¼", World Peace, flags	8.00
1¾", Welcome Home Soldiers Of York County, PA	20.00
Magazine Cover, The Literary Digest, March 30, 1918, US Army Supplies in France	25.00
Helmet	
Army	50.00
English, shallow skull, edged, fairly wide brim, khaki	15.00
Pilot, marked "322 Pursuit," sgd	275.00
Lighter, brass, soldier peeking through peephole at nude	35.00
Mother's Pin, SS	4.00
Mug, china, white, full color decal, white dove sitting on top of world, flags, inscribed "Peace, Nov 11, 1918", marked "Grimwald's Stoke–on–Trent, England"	20.00
Pillow Cover, 24 x 24" picture, Wilson, Statue of Liberty, eagle	25.00
Post Card	
Chicago Daily News, battle photo	3.00
Diecut, 10½ x 3", "Soldier's Dispatch"	22.00
Poster	
11 x 20", "Some Backing! The Empire State Needs Soldiers–Join The New York State Guard!" James Montgomery Flagg	195.00
14 x 21", "Can Vegetables, Fruit, And The Kaiser, Too," John Paul Verrees, humorous image of unhappy Kaiser in jar of "Kaiser Brand Unsweetened" vegetables	150.00
27 x 41", "I Want You For The US Navy," Howard Chandler Christy, pretty blonde in Navy jacket	500.00
28 x 41", "Help Uncle Sam Stamp Out The Kaiser–Buy US Government Bonds," Harry S Bressler, huge foot about to step on tiny, terrified Kaiser, bright yellow background	185.00
Ribbon, 8½ x 2½", silk, Memorial To Our Heroes Who Made the Supreme Sacrifice in the European War April 1917–November 11, 1918–Victory Day–America First	28.00
Spinner, The Kiss For Victory, soldier in uniform, issued by Dallas, TX jeweler, silvered brass	20.00
Stud, ⅞", Liberty Army, WSS, red, white, blue, and brown	18.00
Tablet, writing paper, glossy paper cov,	

eagle and flag illus, marked "Victory,"
8 x 10" **6.00**
Uniform
   Blouse, Army enlisted man's issue,
    89th Division patch, bronze US on
    right collar, Signal Corps on left
    side, single overseas chevron **45.00**
   Fatigue Pants, white, blue stripes ... **100.00**
   Overcoat, Army, officer's, Melton,
    black trefoil braid on lower sleeves,
    double breasted, five bone buttons **35.00**
   Tunic, US Army, officer's light weight,
    division patch **38.00**
Watch Fob, USA soldier and sailor, brass **20.00**
Window Card, Navy, "Man from this
   Home Now Serving His Country" .. **18.00**

WORLD WAR II COLLECTIBLES

Collecting Hints: World War II material still is
plentiful. Collectors should specialize either in
actual military equipment or material issued for
children and adults on the home front. Many
collectors narrow the topic further by focusing
on one form, e.g., manuals, patches, sheet music, toys, etc.

   Uniforms and cloth material should be stored
and cleaned carefully. Remember that World War
II items are now forty-five or more years old;
cloth may not hold up in a modern washing
machine.

   The more personal information about an object
you can obtain the better. Whenever possible
identify the military unit and theater of operation.
Collectors tend to favor materials related to the
United States. The principal foreign collectible is
Nazi items.

History: Although America's formal involvement
in World War II lasted from 1941 to 1945, World
War II collectors focus on the 1936 to 1948 period. The early dates cover America's response
to the German military activities in Europe and
Japan's invasion of Korea and China. The later
period covers the time of American military occupation in Europe and Japan.

   Besides equipping and supplying American
Armed Forces abroad, the U. S. government and
industry produced a wealth of material to prepare
America for possible invasion and to bolster
American morale. Any collectible field active
during World War II should be checked for related material.

Periodicals: *Military Collectors News,* P. O. Box
702073, Tulsa, OK 74170.

Collectors' Clubs: American Society of Military
Insignia Collectors, 1331 Bradley Avenue, Hummelstown, PA 17036; Association of American

Military Uniform Collectors, 446 Berkshire Road,
Elyria, OH 44035.

Advisor: Dick Bitterman.

See: Bubble Gum Cards, Cracker Jack, Newspapers (Headline Editions), Posters, Sheet Music,
Dimestore Soldiers, Toys, etc.

**Badge, Defense Worker ID, Shuron Op-
tical Co Inc, 2" d, $5.00.**

Arm Band
   Civilian Defense Air Raid Warden, 4"
    w, white, 3½" blue circle, red and
    white diagonal stripes within a tri-
    angle **12.00**
Beanie, felt, multicolored, "Remember
   Pearl Harbor–Keep Em Flying" **28.00**
Book, *World War II in Headlines and
   Pictures,* Philadelphia, "Evening Bul-
   letin," 10½ x 14", softbound, 1956 . **32.00**
Bottle Stopper, 4½", three dimensional
   head, marked with maker's name,
   "Achatit," and "Made In Germany"
    Hitler **195.00**
    Roosevelt **75.00**
    Stalin, Josef **100.00**
    Truman, President **70.00**
Cap, AAF Officer's "50–Mission," crash
   cap, small gilded eagle, front and
   back straps, soft bill, gabardine,
   marked "Flighter by Bancroft, O.D." **120.00**
Card Game, "Navy Aircraft Squadron
   Insignia," 4 x 5 x 1" box **28.00**
Coca Cola String Tag Sign, sgd
   Mitchell bomber attacking **35.00**
   P–30 fighter attacking **35.00**
   P–40 fighter attacking **35.00**
Drinking Glass, silk screen design, 4⅝"
   h, 2⅝" d, "Remember Pearl Harbor–
   Dec. 7, 1941," multicolored **30.00**
Envelope, Iwo Jima flag, raising, 8/29/
   45, artist G F Hadley **20.00**
Factory I D Badge, Mullins Mfg Co,
   Salem, OH, #1630, worker shown as
   5'7" tall **12.00**
Flight Jacket, GI, US Navy, artwork on

back, picture of Hellcat Aircraft, printing "Launch Officer USS Detrof Bay CVE–80," orig spec label in lining **1,800.00**

Gas Mask, Japanese, head straps, attached canister **70.00**

Letter Opener, brass, rifle diecut, "Compliments of Dreifus & Co" **25.00**

Manual

Bureau of Aeronautics, Navy Department, Washington, D C, June 1943, *Recognition Pictorial Manual,* contains silhouettes and technical information on Allied and Axis aircraft, 6 x 10", 80 pgs, black and white **70.00**

German pilot's aircraft recognition manual, pocket size, shows British, German and Italian aircraft silhouettes and specifications, 1941 .... **50.00**

Map, silk, AAF rayon escape map, Holland, Belgium, France, and Germany, 1944, orig carrying case, mint **35.00**

Model Airplane, spitfire, Royal Australia Air Force markings, orig decals, pilot sitting in cockpit **95.00**

Navy ID Ships, scale 1:500, manufactured by Framburg & Co, "Teacher Size," dated 1944, British ships, wood case, sixteen ships **750.00**

Patch

Bombardier Wings, embroidered silver gray on tan cotton **12.00**

Pilot's Wings, leather, AAF, emb, standard design, flying jacket attachment type **25.00**

Pencil holder, 3½", plastic, red, white, and blue, "Victory," back lumber yard adv **10.00**

Pincushion, 5" l, solid plaster, molded as rat, long curled tail, turning head of Hitler and head of Emperor Hirohito, olive drab, 1942 patent pending **75.00**

Post Card

Boeing Flying Fortress, one of series of 10, details about plane on back **6.50**

Curtiss Hawk P–40, one of series of 10, details about plane on back .. **6.50**

Seabees, dated June 15, 1943 ...... **7.00**

Poster

Back 'Em Up–Buy Extra Bonds, artist Boris Chaliapin, fold lines, 1944, 28 x 20" **40.00**

Bits of Careless Talk Are Pieced Together By The Enemy–Convoy Sales For England Tonight, artist Steve Dohanos, a hand with a Nazi finger ring putting a puzzle together, fold lines, 1943, 28 x 20" **95.00**

Fill It! Help Harvest War Crops, artist sgd Dohanos, full color, 22 x 28" **45.00**

Gasoline Powers The Attack–Don't

Waste A Drop, artist sgd Pursell, 18 x 24" **95.00**

I'll Carry Mine Too! Trucks & Tires Will Last Till Victory, full color, housewife carrying home groceries, fold marks, 22 x 28" **55.00**

Next–Japan–6th War Loan, artist sgd Bingham, GI looking at the island of Japan, fold lines, 1944, 28 x 20" **45.00**

United We Win, artist Liberman, photo of war workers building airplane, 1942, 40 x 28" **65.00**

Sheet Music, Song of the Seabees, full color, Robbins Music Corp, $5.00.

Sheet Music

Comin' in on a Wing and a Prayer, Robbins Music Corp, cov features Eddie Contor **6.00**

G I Jive, Johnny Mercer, published by Capitol Songs, Inc, G I jiving cov, Holley (artist) **5.00**

He's 1–A in the Army, Redd Evans, published by Valiant Music Co, blue and white cov **5.00**

The Army Corps, Robert Crawford, published by Carl Fischer, red, white, and blue cov **6.00**

The Caissons Go Rolling Along, Calumet Pub Co, US Army song **7.00**

When The Kaiser Does The Goose Step To A Good Old American Flag, 10½ x 13½", 1917, 4 pgs .. **20.00**

Silverware, knife, fork, and spoon, marked with RAF insignia, dated 1938, sgd "Lewis Rose & Co Ltd Silverplate" **35.00**

Tank, miniature, copper colored metal, 3" l, green felt bottom **20.00**

Toy Airplane, Hubley

P–38, 12¾" wing span, 9" l body, silver color, red pilot cockpit and undercarriage, twin fuselage **30.00**

P–40, die cast, 8¼" wing span, 7¾" l

body, yellow wings, orange balance and propeller, rubber wheels **35.00**
Wall Plaque, "Victory–Liberty," "God Bless Those In Our Service," 9", red, white, blue, and gold, octagonal cardboard, 1943 . . . . **12.00**
Window Banner, "Welcome Home," 8 x 12", red, white, and blue, cloth brown eagle, gold fringe **15.00**

WORLD'S FAIRS AND EXPOSITIONS

Collecting Hints: Familiarize yourself with the main buildings and features of the early World's Fairs and Expositions. Many of the choicest china and textiles pictured an identified building, assuming the buyer was aware of the significance. Many exposition buildings remained standing long after the fair was over, and souvenirs proliferated. Prices almost always are higher in the city or area where an exposition was held.

There have been hundreds of local fairs, state fairs, etc., in the last hundred years. These events generally produced items of little value except to local collectors.

History: The Great Exhibition of 1851 in London marked the beginning of the World's Fair and Exposition movement. The fairs generally feature exhibitions from nations around the world displaying the best of their industrial and scientific achievements.

Many important technological advances have been introduced at world's fairs. Examples include the airplane, telephone, and electric light. The ice cream cone, hot dog, and iced tea were products of vendors at fairs. Art movements often were closely connected to fairs with the Paris Exhibition of 1900 generally considered to have assembled the best of the works of the Art Nouveau artists.

References: *American Art, New York World's Fair, 1939,* Apollo Books, 1987; Carl Abbott, *The Great Extravaganza: Portland and the Lewis and Clark Exposition,* Oregon Historical Society, 1981; S. Applebaum, *The New York World's Fair 1939–40,* Dover Pub., 1977; Patricia F. Carpenter and Paul Totah, *The San Francisco Fair, Treasure Island, 1939–40,* Scottwall Associates, 1989; Richard Friz, *World's Fair Memorabilia,* Collector Books, 1989; Kurt Krueger, *Meet Me In St. Louis—The Exonumia of the 1904 World's Fair,* Krause Publications, 1979; Howard Rossen and John Kaduck, *Columbia World's Fair Collectibles,* Wallace–Homestead, 1976, revised price list 1982.

Periodical: *World's Fair,* P. O. Box 339, Corte Madera, CA 94925.

Collectors' Club: World's Fair Collectors' Society, Inc., P. O. Box 20806, Sarasota, FL 33583.

1876, PHILADELPHIA, Centennial Exposition
Booklet, *Centennial Book,* 2½ x 3", 16 pgs, issued Orange Judd Company **15.00**
Inkwell, glass, Memorial Hall **100.00**
Ticket, admission **20.00**
Trade Card, Rockhill & Wilson Tailors, exhibition building **20.00**

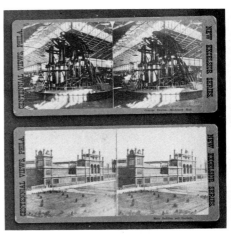

Philadelphia Centennial, stereoscopic card, New Excelsior series, top: Corliss Engine, Machinery Hall; bottom: Main Building and Grounds, orange ground, each $10.00.

1893, CHICAGO, The Columbian Exposition
Bell, etched glass, frosted handle . . . **65.00**
Book **28.00**
Fan, hand, large **50.00**
Glass, 3½", clear, frosted white inscription "World's Fair Agricultural Building" and building illus **10.00**
Matchsafe, Columbus head **125.00**
Medal, brass, two piece, "Wisconsin–Columbian Exposition 1893" . **20.00**
Medallion, 1½", brass, emb **16.00**
Paperweight
    Administration Bldg **50.00**
    Liberty Bell, fused glass, "Made at World's Fair by Libbey Glass Co" **82.00**
Prints, 15¾ x 11½", architecture, color, "Book of Builders," 1894, set of twelve **100.00**
Puzzle, egg shape, silvered brass, Christopher Columbus portrait on one end, inscribed 1492–1892 . . . **56.00**
Spoon, Fisheries building in bowl,

4¼" silvered brass handle with Christopher Columbus portrait and 1492–1893 dates 16.00

Ticket, admission, Manhattan Day, NY, Oct 21, 1893 .... 38.00

Trade Card, Traveler's Insurance Co, color 22.00

1898, OMAHA, Trans–Mississippi Exposition

Handkerchief, embroidered 6.50

Souvenir cup, ruby flashed 58.00

1901, BUFFALO, Pan American Exposition

Letter Opener, buffalo 30.00

Stickpin, frying pan shape, emb buffalo head 36.00

Whiskey Glass, etched, "Pan American Exposition 1901," orig round box 60.00

1904, ST LOUIS, Louisiana Purchase Exposition

Card, 3 x 5", tin, litho, full color aerial panorama illus, company text and logo on reverse, issued by American Can Company 45.00

Corset, orig box 30.00

Matchsafe, plated, relief scenes 55.00

Shaker, ruby flashed, two in one, inside glass bladder holds pepper, salt on outside 99.00

Spooner, custard, enamel flowers ... 65.00

Tray, 3¼ x 5", tin, litho, issued by American Can Company 50.00

1915, SAN FRANCISCO, Panama–Pacific International Exposition

Pin, 2¼", 1915 Pan–Pac Closing Day, brass hanger bar with attached silk ribbon 35.00

Watch Fob, leather, black, holds diecut brass poinsettia 75.00

New York World's Fair, 1964-1965, plate, 10¼" d, Unisphere center, six medallions, blue and white, back stamp "Crown, copyright 1961, 1963, N.Y.W.F. Unisphere, Presented by United States Steel," $35.00.

1926, PHILADELPHIA, Sesquicentennial Exposition

Pin, blue Liberty Bell, "Crane's Ice Cream Served Everywhere—Keep Cool During The Fair" adv 12.50

Pinback Button, 1¼", multi design .. 25.00

Ring, metal, silvered, diecut Liberty Bell underneath seated eagle, patriotic motifs, inscribed "1776 Sesquicentennial 1926" 35.00

1933, CHICAGO, Century of Progress

Booklet

Firestone, 32 pgs 5.00

Ford At The Fair, 5¼ x 8", 24 pgs, issued by Ford Motor Co 25.00

Pullman's Diamond Jubilee 5.00

Card Set, building and exhibit ext. views, self–mailer design packet folder with snap fastener, set of 20 cards, unused 18.00

Cigarette Case, 2½ x 3½ x 2", wood, black, hinged brass lid with symbol in center, unfinished int. 28.50

Compact, chrome, emb, COP 12.00

Glass, 5½", clear, black and red inscriptions, silvered illus of Fort Dearborn building 22.00

Hotpad, set of 3, emb silver foil covering, orig clear cellophane wrap attached with purple ribbon, orig box 32.00

Key, 8½", metal, "Key to Chicago World's Fair 1933" 20.00

Master Salt Dip 19.00

Paperweight, metal, painted gold, Fort Dearborn exhibit shape, inscribed "1833 Fort Dearborn Chicago 1933," orig box 30.00

Pillow Cover, 20½", leather tan, stitched fringe border, hand colored scenes, W A L Co, 1934 copyright 75.00

Plate, 7½", china, white, blue illus of Carillon Tower and buildings, "Chicago 1934" title, stamped "Pickard" 25.00

Playing Cards, "54 Different Views", COP 14.00

Poster, 13 x 19½", globe image, color, "World's Brightest Spot," COP 27.00

Ring, man's, sterling silver, COP ... 20.00

Tray, bronzed, round, 4½" d, twelve relief buildings and fountain, box . 22.00

View Cards, sixteen cards, full color, linen–textured paper, orig mailing envelope, unused 15.00

Watch Fob, 1833–1933 .... 25.00

1939, NEW YORK, New York World's Fair

Ashtray, metal, white, diving figure, raised Trylon and Perisphere, inscription 50.00

Bag, suitcase shape, contains pictures to color **175.00**

Bank

Glass, Esso on one side, logo on other side **85.00**

Wood, 5" h, horseshoe shape, orange and blue tinted Trylon and Perisphere, brown inscription and horseshoe markings, pull—out drawer **50.00**

Banner, felt, 26½ x 8½", "World of Tomorrow 1939" **15.00**

Book

Official Guide Book, 5 x 8", Expositions Publications Inc, 256 pgs **45.00**

Official Souvenir Book, 10 x 14", sprial bound, orange and blue cov with Trylon and Perisphere illus **50.00**

Bookend, pr, figural, Trylon and Perisphere, marble, licensed for Italian exhibit **125.00**

Booklet, Futurama, 7 x 8¼", 20 pgs, General Motors Building **25.00**

Bottle, 9", milk glass **30.00**

Bracelet

Brass, seven scenic charms **15.00**

Expansion, hammered pattern design, orange and blue fair insignia symbol **25.00**

Card Table **125.00**

Chocolate Tin, 4½ x 6½ x 3", colorful, building illus **75.00**

Compact

Enamel, Deco, color, fair scene .. **33.00**

Plastic, red, marbleized, tricolor brass fair image inset, "1939 World's Fair New York" **45.00**

Cup, 3" h, china, yellow, Trylon and Perisphere imprinted around side . **24.50**

Folder, opens to 10 x 14¼", map illus on one side, photos reverse, titled "Highways and Horizons," General Motors **18.00**

Glass, 4½", clear, colorful design, inscribed "Twentieth Century Transportation" and "Exhibits Of Railroads And Railroad Equipment Display—The Transportation Bldg" **38.00**

Letter Opener **15.00**

Movie Viewer, three film rolls, orig box **100.00**

Nappy, 6", multicolor, handled **20.00**

Nut Bowls, Mr Peanut, four small, one large, set **45.00**

Pencil, 10½", mechanical, eagle, MIB **41.00**

Purse, child's, plastic, white and red, Trylon and Perisphere **55.00**

Puzzle, Trylon and Perisphere; orange trylon, five blue pcs form per-

isphere, includes instruction sheet, orig box **48.00**

Salt and Pepper Shakers, pr, plastic, Trylon and Perisphere

Cream color, black base, pr **20.00**

Orange, dark blue tear shape base, gold inscription **35.00**

Scarf, 19 x 20½", printed design, dark blue, light blue, lime green, red, and white **30.00**

Snowdome, Trylon and Perisphere .. **95.00**

Souvenir Book

Billy Rose's Aquacade, Weissmuller **30.00**

Touraide, 9 x 12", spiral bound, 48 pgs, information and maps, includes typed letter from company, issued by Conoco **26.00**

Spoon

Agriculture **20.00**

Trylon and Perisphere on handle, "New York World's Fair" and stars in bowl, 6" **23.00**

Tapestry, 21½ x 40½", woven, Trylon, Perisphere, and Lagoon, sky background, rust colored fringe .. **110.00**

Tray, 12", metal, silvered, engraved illus, "World's Fair New York 1939" inscription, Made in England on bottom **52.50**

1962, SEATTLE, Century 21 Exposition

Lighter, space **12.00**

Shoehorn, 5½" l, metal, gold gilt, crown design on handle **18.00**

Sugar and Creamer, miniature **20.00**

Tray, 11" d, tin, litho, full color illus of Space Needle **18.00**

1964, NEW YORK, New York World's Fair

Bank, metal, litho, dime register, full color design, orig retail card **15.00**

Book, Official Souvenir Book, 7 x 10", 24 pgs **20.00**

Booklet, Progressland, Disney exhibit **18.00**

Bookmark, 2¼ x 5¾", woven, silvery white, Unisphere illus, Alkahn Silk Label Co, orig clear cellophane packet **22.00**

Camera, Kodak World's Fair Flash Camera, plastic and metal, black and gray, foil sticker with Unisphere on front lens, black fabric strap **25.00**

Game, World's Fair Game, Milton Bradley, vinyl plastic playing sheet, orig box **25.00**

Glass, 4¼", clear, orange and white Unisphere illus **12.00**

Magazine, Newsweek, Jan 13, 1964, 5 pg article with six black and white photos **12.00**

Pencil Sharpner, plastic, Unisphere
shape, blue, orig box 15.00
Pennant, 27", felt, dark blue, day–glo
orange and white design and letter-
ing 18.00
Pin, diecut, Unisphere shape, red and
blue enamel accents, brass finish,
orig retail card 12.50
Poster, Progressland, Disney exhibit   40.00
Salt and Pepper Shaker, pr, glazed ceramic, Unisphere illus, plastic stop-
per on bottom 25.00
Stein, 6", raised scene of Unisphere,
tan and black striping around top
and bottom 25.00
Tile, 6" sq, ceramic, full color Unis-
phere, Statue of Liberty, and skyline
illus, gold accented border, copyright sticker and hanging loop on
back 18.00
Tray
GM Futurama, glass, orig box 20.00
Unisphere, circular 25.00
1967, MONTREAL, Montreal Expo
Cup, 3", china, white, full color aerial
illus, Montreal background, bottom
marked "Royal Darwood/Expo 67/
Bone China/England" 18.00
Lapel Pin, brass, repeated motif
around edge, threaded post fastener
on back 10.00
Stickpin, ½", brass, diecut, dark red
enamel, maple leaf shape 8.00
Tab, 1½", tin, litho, blue and white,
US Pavilion, compliments of Avis
car rental on reverse 5.00
1976, PHILADELPHIA, Bicentennial,
pin, brass, flag, red, white, and blue
enamel, 76 design, orig sponsor card   8.00
1982, KNOXVILLE, World's Fair
Cap, sailor type, black and red inscription on brim 5.00
Glass, 5½", clear, tapered, illus and
"Energy Turns The World" theme,
McDonald's and Coca–Cola Co
trademarks 8.00
Pennant, 25", felt, red scene and en-
ergy symbol, white background . .   6.00
Plate, oval, clipper ships, Galerie Bar-
bizon limited edition 15.00
Visor, terrycloth, white, clear dark
blue plastic visor, white inscription   4.00

WRIGHT, RUSSEL

Collecting Hints: Russel Wright worked for many
different companies in addition to creating material under his own label, American Way.
Wright's contracts with firms often called for the
redesign of pieces which did not produce or sell

well. As a result, several lines have the same
item in more than one shape.

Wright was totally involved in design. Most
collectors focus on his dinnerware; however, he
also designed glassware, plastic items, textiles,
furniture, and metal objects. Bleached and
blonde furniture were part of his contributions.
His early work in spun aluminum often is overlooked as is his later work in plastic for the Northern Industrial Chemical Company.

History: Russel Wright was an American industrial engineer with a design passion for domestic
efficiency through simple lines. His streamlined
influence is found in all aspects of living. Wright
and his wife, Mary Small Einstein, wrote *A Guide
To Easier Living* to explain the concepts.

Russel Wright was born in 1904 in Lebanon,
Ohio. His first jobs included set designer and
stage manager under the direction of Norman
Bel Geddes. He later used this theatrical flair for
his industrial designs, stressing simple clean
lines. Some of his earliest designs were executed
in polished spun aluminum. These pieces, designed in the mid-1930s, included trays, vases,
teapots, and other items. Wright received awards
from the Museum of Modern Art in 1950 and
1953. His designs garnered many other awards.

Among the companies for which Russel Wright
did design work are Chase Brass and Copper,
General Electric, Imperial Glass, National Silver
Co., Shenango, and Steubenville Pottery Company. In 1983 a major exhibition of Wright's
designs was held at the Hudson River Museum
in Yonkers, New York, and at the Smithsonian's
Renwick Gallery in Washington, D.C.

Reference: Ann Kerr, *The Collector's Encyclopedia of Russel Wright Designs*, Collector Books,
1990.

AMERICAN MODERN

Made by the Steubenville Pottery Company,
1939–59. Initially this pattern was issued in Sea-
foam Blue, Coral, Chartreuse Curry, Granite
Gray, White, and Bean Brown, also issued in
Black Chutney, Cedar Green, Cantaloupe, and
Glacier Blue. The Ideal Toy Co made a set of
miniature dishes, which was distributed by Sears,
Roebuck.

Baker, 8" oval, Bean Brown **15.00**
Butter, cov, Granite Gray **150.00**
Casserole, cov, stick handle
Cantaloupe **110.00**
Coral **30.00**
Seafoam Blue **42.00**
Celery, Chartreuse Curry **20.00**
Child's plate, Coral **95.00**
Chop Plate, Granite Gray **18.00**
Coffee Pot, Chartreuse Curry **120.00**

Creamer
   Chartreuse Curry **7.00**
   Seafoam Blue **8.00**
Cup and Saucer
   Black Chutney **6.50**
   Cedar Green **6.00**
   Chartreuse Curry **6.00**
   Seafoam Blue **6.00**
Demitasse Cup and Saucer, Coral **9.00**
Fruit Bowl, Chartreuse Curry **5.00**
Gravy
   Coral **13.00**
   Granite Gray **13.00**
Hostess Plate
   Coral **40.00**
   Granite Gray **40.00**
Mug
   Black Chutney **40.00**
   Chartreuse Curry **35.00**
   Granite Gray **40.00**
Pickle, Granite Gray **10.00**

Pitcher, American Modern, Granite Gray, 10¾" h, $45.00.

Pitcher, water
   Bean Brown **150.00**
   Chartreuse Curry **35.00**
Plate
   6" d, Cedar Green **3.00**
   10" d
      Chartreuse Curry **5.00**
      Coral **8.00**
Salad Bowl
   Chartreuse Curry **38.00**
   Coral **30.00**
Salt and Pepper Shakers, pr, Granite
   Gray **8.00**
Sugar, cov
   Chartreuse Curry **7.00**
   Seafoam Blue **7.50**
Vegetable, oval
   Chartreuse Curry, cov **28.00**
   Granite Gray **14.00**

IROQUOIS

Made by the Iroquois China Co and Garrison Products, 1946–60s. Initially it was issued in Ice Blue, Forest Green, Avocado Yellow, Lemon Yellow, Nutmeg Brown, and Sugar White. Also issued in Lettuce Green, Charcoal, Ripe Apricot, Pink Sherbet, Parsley Green, Cantaloupe, Oyster Gray, Aqua, Brick Red, and Grayed–Blue. A patterned line was offered in 1959.

Bowl
   5" d, Avocado Yellow **5.00**
   5½" d, Avocado Yellow **4.00**
Creamer, stacking
   Avocado Yellow **7.00**
   Ice Blue **7.00**
Cup and Saucer
   Avocado Yellow **6.00**
   Cantaloupe **6.00**
   Nutmeg Brown **6.50**
   Pink Sherbet **8.00**
   Sugar White **6.50**
Plate
   6" d
      Avocado Yellow **3.00**
      Nutmeg Brown **3.00**
   7½" d
      Lemon Yellow **4.00**
      Sugar White **4.00**
   9" d
      Avocado Yellow **5.00**
      Sugar White **5.00**
   9¼" d, Ice Blue **5.50**
   10" d, Avocado Yellow **5.00**
Platter
   12½" l, Ice Blue **14.00**
   14" l, Avocado Yellow **17.00**
Vegetable Bowl, cov, divided, 10" l, Avocado Yellow **25.00**

INDEX